# FORAGING AND FARMING

# TITLES OF RELATED INTEREST

# FORAGING AND FARMING

## The evolution of plant exploitation

Edited by

David R. Harris
Gordon C. Hillman

*Institute of Archaeology, University College London*

London
UNWIN HYMAN
Boston    Sydney    Wellington

Published by the Academic Division of
**Unwin Hyman Ltd**
15/17 Broadwick Street, London W1V 1FP, UK

Unwin Hyman Inc.,
8 Winchester Place, Winchester, Mass. 01890, USA

Allen & Unwin (Australia) Ltd,
8 Napier Street, North Sydney, NSW 2060, Australia

Allen & Unwin (New Zealand) Ltd in association with the
Port Nicholson Press Ltd,
60 Cambridge Terrace, Wellington, New Zealand

First published in 1989

---

**British Library Cataloguing in Publication Data**

Foraging and farming. – (One world archaeology).
1. Plants. Use to 1987 by man
I. Harris, David R.   II. Hillman, Gordon C.   III. Series
831'.09

ISBN 0-04-445025-7
ISBN 0-04-445235-7 Pbk

---

**Library of Congress Cataloging in Publication Data**

Foraging and farming: the evolution of plant exploitation/edited
by David R. Harris and Gordon C. Hillman.
   p.   cm. – (One world archaeology)
Results of a symposium held at the World Archaeological
Congress, held in Southampton, England, in Sept. 1986.
Includes bibliographies and index.
ISBN 0-04-445025-7 (alk. paper).
ISBN 0-04-445235-7 (pbk.: alk. paper)
1. Agriculture, Prehistoric – Congresses.
2. Hunting and gathering societies – Congresses.
3. Plant remains (Archaeology) – Congresses.
4. Man, Prehistoric – Food – Congresses.
I. Harris, David R. (David Russell)   II. Hillman, Gordon C.
III. World Archaeological Congress (1986: Southampton, England)
IV. Series.
GN799.A4F67 1989
630'.93 – dc19          88-28751 CIP

---

Typeset in 10 on 11 point Bembo by
Computape (Pickering) Ltd, Pickering, North Yorkshire
and printed in Great Britain at the University Printing House, Oxford

# List of contributors

*An Zhimin*, Institute of Archaeology, Chinese Academy of Social Sciences, Beijing, China.

*Ofer Bar-Yosef*, Institute of Archaeology, Hebrew University, Jerusalem, Israel.

*Duccio Bonavia*, Laboratorio de Prehistoria, Departamento de Biología, Universidad Peruana Cayetano Heredia, Lima, Peru.

*Susan Bulmer*, New Zealand Historic Places Trust, Auckland, New Zealand.

*Ann Butler*, Department of Human Environment, Institute of Archaeology, University College London, UK.

*Scott Cane*, Anutech Pty Ltd, Australian National University, Canberra, Australia.

*T. T. Chang*, International Rice Research Institute, Manila, Philippines.

*A. K. Chase*, School of Australian Environmental Studies, Griffith University, Nathan, Queensland, Australia.

*V. E. Chikwendu*, Department of Archaeology, University of Nigeria, Nsukka, Nigeria.

*Susan M. Colledge*, Department of Human Environment, Institute of Archaeology, University College London, UK.

*Lorenzo Costantini*, Istituto Italiano per il Medio ed Estremo Oriente, Rome, Italy.

*Michael R. Dove*, Winrock International Institute for Agricultural Development, Islamabad, Pakistan.

*John Evans*, Department of Physical Sciences, North East London Polytechnic, London, UK.

*James P. Gallagher*, Mississippi Valley Archaeology Center, University of Wisconsin-La Crosse, Wisconsin, USA.

*Jack Golson*, Department of Prehistory, Research School of Pacific Studies, Australian National University, Canberra, Australia.

*Alexander Grobman*, Grobman Genotecnica S.A., Lima, Peru.

*Les Groube*, Department of Anthropology and Sociology, University of Papua New Guinea, Port Moresby, Papua New Guinea.

*Sylvia J. Hallam*, Centre for Prehistory, University of Western Australia, Nedlands, Western Australia.

*Jack R. Harlan*, Crop Evolution Laboratory, Agronomy Department, University of Illinois, Urbana, Illinois, USA.

*David R. Harris*, Department of Human Environment, Institute of Archaeology, University College London, UK.

*J. G. Hawkes*, Department of Biological Sciences, University of Birmingham, UK.

*Charles B. Heiser, Jr.*, Department of Biology, Indiana University, Bloomington, Indiana, USA.

*Charles Higham*, Department of Anthropology, University of Otago, Dunedin, New Zealand.

*H. Edward Hill*, Department of Human Environment, Institute of Archaeology, University College London, UK.

*Gordon C. Hillman*, Department of Human Environment, Institute of Archaeology, University College London, UK.

*Timothy Johns*, School of Dietetics and Human Nutrition, Macdonald College of McGill University, Ste. Anne de Bellevue, P.Q., Canada.

*Rhys Jones*, Department of Prehistory, Research School of Pacific Studies, Australian National University, Canberra, Australia.

*M. D. Kajale*, Department of Archaeology, Deccan College, Pune, India.

*Mordechai E. Kislev*, Department of Life Sciences, Bar-Ilan University, Ramat-Gan, Israel.

*Gideon Ladizinsky*, School of Agriculture, The Hebrew University, Jerusalem, Israel.

*Bernard Maloney*, Department of Geography, The Queen's University of Belfast, Northern Ireland, UK.

*T. L. Markey*, Department of Germanic Languages and Literatures, University of Michigan, Ann Arbor, Michigan, USA.

*Betty Meehan*, Division of Anthropology, Australian Museum, Sydney, Australia.

*A. M. T. Moore*, Department of Anthropology, Yale University, New Haven, Connecticut, USA.

*C. E. A. Okezie*, Department of Botany, University of Nigeria, Nsukka, Nigeria.

*Deborah M. Pearsall*, Department of Anthropology, University of Missouri, Columbia, USA.

*Barbara Pickersgill*, Department of Agricultural Botany, University of Reading, UK.

*Dolores R. Piperno*, Smithsonian Tropical Research Institute, Balboa, Republic of Panama.

*Kosum Pyramarn*, Department of Botany, Chulalongkorn University, Bangkok, Thailand.

*David Rindos*, Department of Natural Science, Michigan State University, East Lansing, Michigan, USA.

*Mario Sanoja*, Sección de Arquelogía, Facultad de Ciencias Económicas y Sociales, Universidad Central de Venezuela, Caracas, Venezuela.

*Florence C. Shipek*, Department of History, University of Wisconsin-Parkside, Wisconsin, USA.

*M. A. Smith*, Museums and Art Galleries of the Northern Territory, Alice Springs, Australia.

*Ann B. Stahl*, Department of Anthropology, State University of New York, Binghamton, New York, USA.

*Patty Jo Watson*, Department of Anthropology, Washington University, St. Louis, Missouri, USA.

*Joyce C. White*, University Museum, University of Pennsylvania, Philadelphia, USA.

*Garrison Wilkes*, Department of Biology, University of Massachusetts, Boston, USA.

*Zoya V. Yanushevich*, Institute of Botany, Moldavian SSR Academy of Sciences, Kishinev, USSR.

*D. E. Yen*, Department of Prehistory, Research School of Pacific Studies, Australian National University, Canberra, Australia.

*Daniel Zohary*, Department of Genetics, The Hebrew University, Jerusalem, Israel.

# Foreword

This book is one of a major series of more than 20 volumes resulting from the World Archaeological Congress held in Southampton, England, in September 1986. The series reflects the enormous academic impact of the Congress, which was attended by 850 people from more than 70 countries, and attracted many additional contributions from others who were unable to attend in person.

The *One World Archaeology* series is the result of a determined and highly successful attempt to bring together for the first time not only archaeologists and anthropologists from many different parts of the world, as well as academics from a host of contingent disciplines, but also non-academics from a wide range of cultural backgrounds, who could lend their own expertise to the discussions at the Congress. Many of the latter, accustomed to being treated as the 'subjects' of archaeological and anthropological observation, had never before been admitted as equal participants in the discussion of their own (cultural) past or present, with their own particularly vital contribution to make towards global, cross-cultural understanding.

The Congress therefore really addressed world archaeology in its widest sense. Central to a world archaeological approach is the investigation not only of how people lived in the past but also of how, and why, changes took place resulting in the forms of society and culture which exist today. Contrary to popular belief, and the archaeology of some 20 years ago, world archaeology is much more than the mere recording of specific historical events, embracing as it does the study of social and cultural change in its entirety. All the books in the *One World Archaeology* series are the result of meetings and discussions which took place within a context that encouraged a feeling of self-criticism and humility in the participants about their own interpretations and concepts of the past. Many participants experienced a new self-awareness, as well as a degree of awe about past and present human endeavours, all of which is reflected in this unique series.

The Congress was organized around major themes. Several of these themes were based on the discussion of full-length papers which had been circulated some months previously to all who had indicated a special interest in them. Other sessions, including some dealing with areas of specialization defined by period or geographical region, were based on oral addresses, or a combination of precirculated papers and lectures. In all cases, the entire sessions were recorded on cassette, and all contributors were presented with the recordings of the discussion of their papers. A major part of the thinking behind the Congress was that a meeting of many hundreds of participants that did not leave behind a published record of its academic discussions would be little more than an exercise in tourism.

Thus, from the very beginning of the detailed planning for the World Archaeological Congress, in 1982, the intention was to produce post-Congress books containing a selection only of the contributions, revised in the light of discussions during the sessions themselves as well as during subsequent consultations with the academic editors appointed for each book. From the outset, contributors to the Congress knew that if their papers were selected for publication, they would have only a few months to revise them according to editorial specifications, and that they would become authors in an important academic volume scheduled to appear within a reasonable period following the Southampton meeting.

The publication of the series reflects the intense planning which took place before the Congress. Not only were all contributors aware of the subsequent production schedules, but also session organizers were already planning their books before and during the Congress. The editors were entitled to commission additional chapters for their books when they felt that there were significant gaps in the coverage of a topic during the Congress, or where discussion at the Congress indicated a need for additional contributions.

The origin of this book was a two-day symposium at the Congress on the theme of 'Recent Advances in the Understanding of Plant Domestication and Early Agriculture', which was organized under four major headings. The first, on 'Plant Gathering and Manipulation by Non-Agricultural (Hunter–Gatherer) Peoples and the Plant Component in their Diet' lasted for more than half a day, and was itself subdivided into two sessions, on 'Ethnobiological and Archaeological Perspectives', and on 'Defining, Observing and Explaining Domestication'. The rest of the first day was focused on 'Plant Domestication and Early Agriculture in Western Eurasia', discussion being split between 'Early Plant Exploitation and Cultivation in Southwest Asia' and 'The Beginnings of Agriculture in Europe'. The first part of the second day's meeting considered 'Plant Domestication and Early Agriculture in the Indo-Pacific Region', divided into 'Mainland South and East Asia' and 'Island Southeast Asia and the Pacific', with the second part of the day being devoted to discussion of the Americas, by focusing successively on 'Domestication and Diffusion of Seed Crops', 'Domestication of Tuberous Crops' and 'Emergence and Intensification of Agriculture', and concluding in the evening with a lively discussion of general themes arising from the symposium as a whole.

The original choice of the overall theme derived from the conviction that it was again timely to consider the processes of plant domestication by human beings, most particularly from as wide a world-view as possible. Very early on it became evident that to do so in a meaningful way – given that studies of plant domestication, and particularly archaeobotanical studies, have multiplied rapidly in recent years – would mean separating the discussions of plants and animals, despite the traditional inclusion of crops *and* livestock in the 'Neolithic Revolution'. The exploitation and domestication of animals is in fact considered in another book in the *One World Archaeology* series, *The walking larder* (edited by J. Clutton-Brock).

The organization of the symposium on plant domestication and early agriculture kept, perhaps more closely than any other thematic discussion, to the original intention behind the (expensive and time-consuming) circulation of pre-Congress full-length papers to all potential participants in the symposium. This aim was achieved, and all discussion was therefore based on the expectation that papers had been read and digested before the meeting. As a consequence, no papers were read out by authors and the 18 hours of meeting were devoted to intense discussion and debate. Such a mode of conference organization is difficult to achieve but, when it does occur, the results are not only enormously worthwhile but they achieve a level of informed interchange unique to such a format. A successful meeting of this kind not only relies very heavily on the prior preparation of those chairing sessions, and on the quality of previously chosen section discussants, but it also converts writers into active participants.

The main themes explored and exemplified in *Foraging and farming* are outlined in the editorial Introduction (pp. 1–8). My aim in what follows is to examine a few of the points that have struck me personally as being of particular note or fascination.

*Foraging and farming*, quite apart from many other virtues, successfully reflects much of the excitement and cohesion of the symposium itself (and see Harris 1987). Many of the individual chapters have been cross-referenced by the editors and refer to other contributions in the volume, and the result is a uniquely coherent approach to the fascinating and complex problems with which the book is concerned. Much of the excitement with the subject which the book conveys derives from the realization that this area of archaeological enquiry has become even more interdisciplinary than before, and that new approaches to the material and processes under consideration have not only shattered some long-held assumptions but have important implications for our overall understanding of human social and cultural developments.

Examples of new discoveries abound in this book, but one of the most dramatic must be the realization that agriculture was already practised in the Waghi Valley in the Papua New Guinea Highlands some 9000 years ago, and that by at least 6000 years ago swamps in the valley were being drained in order to cultivate root crops such as taro. A world perspective, as demonstrated in *Foraging and farming*, removes attention from the traditional European preoccupation with attempting to discover where and when an assumed 'original' discovery of plant cultivation and domestication first took place. Instead attention shifts to attempts to understand the social and environmental circumstances which must have led to the independent adoption of plant cultivation and domestication at different times in different parts of the world. At about the same time that agriculture was being practised on the hillsides of the Waghi Valley, plants were being cultivated in the Andean Highlands of Peru. Such early dates for cultivation and agriculture in different parts of the world draw attention to the ecological skills and manipulative attainments of hunter–gatherer societies: a theme that is very fully explored and discussed in this book. Refreshingly, *Foraging and farming* does not accept the popular myth of today that all hunter–gatherer societies have lived in a utopia of easy self-sufficiency (for example, in the Panamanian tropical forests).

Not surprisingly, *Foraging and farming* has to contend with problems of definition. It sets forth many arguments in favour of modifying existing usages. These are not merely semantic arguments, of little real value. They are necessary attempts to match our vocabulary to the complexities, and new understandings, of the practices which were, until recently, often lumped together under the undifferentiated (partly chronological and partly developmental) term 'Neolithic'. That this term hid a diversity of human, plant, and animal behaviour was already clear in 1968 when, with Geoffrey Dimbleby, I edited a book with somewhat similar aims to this one (Ucko & Dimbleby 1969), but – however seminal that book may have been at the time – it is now evident that to classify a culture as 'Neolithic' only has useful meaning when developed agriculture and a sedentary way of life have become well established. An appreciation of the potential complexity of developed agriculture is gained from some of the contributions to *Foraging and farming*, for example, in the discussion of Maori gardens and of early agriculture in the American Midwest. However, even prior to the adoption of sedentary life, human societies already manipulated and used plants in a great variety of different ways.

Discussion of such variety leads inevitably to fundamental questions regarding the relative influences of natural and social selection, in a Neo-Darwinian (or sociobiological) sense, and of the vagaries of human choice in creating variety and development. Both views are advanced in this book and both raise important questions about the adequacy of current anthropological and archaeological models which attempt to explain innovation and change in human societies (see *What's new?*, edited by S. Van der Leeuw & R. Torrence). Whichever approach is favoured, there is no doubt that the complex process of plant domestication receives new scrutiny in this book. It is the combination of redefinition and reanalysis of existing assumptions that makes the book so evidently a threshold to further theoretical advances in the discipline. Conceptualizing plant domestication in processual terms, rather than as a historic 'event', creates its own new insights. One of the most striking is the realization that the fact that Australian Aborigines did not adopt agriculture (in the strict sense) does not in any way imply a lack of understanding of, or a capacity to modify, the ecology of the plants around them. Indeed, the hunting and gathering Australian Aborigines 'domestic-ated' the environment, *including plants, not* by practising agriculture but by developing a complex system of mental categorizations which gave them control over their plants (and animals). In this sense, as is emphasized in *Foraging and farming*, the actual domestication of plants is a relatively late form of manipulation of the environment and not one which is necessarily always adaptively advantageous in the long term (see *Pleistocene perspective*, edited by A. M. ApSimon & S. Joyce). This conclusion can be seen to be true in different ways; for example, it may be easier to *ritually* control food sources (and to explain failure in this way) by carrying out appropriate ceremony, rather than to be subject (as is the farmer) to unpredictable fluctuations of climate and changes in soil fertility; or to harvest wild plants when it is more energetically cost-effective than to grow them.

Many of the contributions appear, at first sight, to be determinedly scientific, both in methodology and in interpretation. Indeed, many of the new developments in the study of plant exploitation and domestication derive from the application of rigorous techniques of archaeological investigation and interpretive analysis. Advances in the subject depend as much on the secure identification of plant remains – often below the species level – as on accurate dating and the correct characterization of cultural contexts. Nevertheless, *Foraging and farming* also exemplifies how social and cultural factors can never, and *should* never, be entirely divorced from the formulation of hypotheses and the strict application of scientific techniques. For example, even after the most exhaustive analyses the 'scientific' conclusion that a paste is toxic may, or may not, be the essential factor relevant to explaining its use in a society which may in fact choose to associate it with the *spiritually*-induced actions of vomiting and hiccuping. Such dilemmas of interpretive emphasis – conventionally thought of as respectively etic and emic – remain tantalizingly in the wings of explanation. Now, however, the indigenous ideologies of the societies which took up 'agriculture', or chose to 'reject' such 'innovations', are recognized as essential ingredients of the data base from which interpretations must derive. Can it have been factors such as culture-specific and presumably subjective judgements about the pleasant taste of some wheats as opposed to others, which may have led humans to species-specific exploitation and the neglect of additional or alternative grasses? Is it possible that the cultural and symbolic role of certain non-edible gourds in demonstrating age, seniority, and status (Ucko 1969) through the wearing of specially trained gourds as penis sheaths was the kind of influence which may have preceded the explicitly economic exploitation of these plants?

Consideration of such cultural matters represents a striking departure from other scientifically-oriented books. For these reasons, perhaps *Foraging and farming* foreshadows a book, in another twenty years' time, which will be more sophisticated in its treatment of concepts such as social or biological 'selection' and social and cultural 'stability' or 'complexity', and which will be even more concerned with ethnoclassification than is the present volume. For the first time in the history of the subject this volume is really able to approach the previously untrodden, and immensely difficult, path of investigation and explication which must attempt to assess the relative importance of the inward-looking 'emic' attempts to understand and classify, as opposed to the comparative 'etic' systems of classification which are based on assumptions about 'development' and 'evolution'. Despite its explicitly evolutionary subtitle, this book brings much nearer the moment when conventional archaeological assumptions about what social and cultural messages can legitimately be assumed to be incorporated in the so-called 'continuity' of religious belief or 'continuity' of art styles (see *The meanings of things*, edited by I. Hodder, and *Animals into art*, edited by H. Morphy) will receive new challenges from the direct bioarchaeological evidence of plant (and animal) exploitation. Already, in this book, the glimpses into the complexities of emic explanatory systems and ethnoclassification show that, in the future, our analytical terminologies will have to be further refined to cover all aspects of the harnessing of plants to human social endeavour. Plant processing, for example, is an immensely complex affair associated with many different social practices which explanatory models based on assumptions of economic maximization appear unable to accommodate. It is becoming more and more evident that plants may have been manipulated for many reasons, varying, for example, from the provision of fodder for stock (Southwest Asian legumes), to attempts to better understand the ancestors (maize). It is also clear that humans may not always have been the primary or sole agents of change. In the case of Andean maize, for example, it is argued that birds may have been the first to spread the wild plants, with humans only coming in on the act subsequently.

*Foraging and farming* will long remain in the forefront of attempts to bring the evolutionary/ecological and the cultural into a satisfactory intellectual relationship. It demonstrates forcibly that complexity is not confined to the biology and ecology of the plants themselves, but is at least equally evident, and significant, in the social conditions which affect the cultural classification not only of the plants but also of matters of 'taste' and eating behaviour.

The nature, and almost certainly the degree, of involvement of people with particular crops and, therefore, whether or not they were essential components in the migrations of peoples from one area to another, appear to be intricately linked with social choices and conventions, such as the perceived palatability of particular plants, or their perceived suitability for technological processes such as dyeing. Whether or not such cultural attitudes are corollaries of actual usage, or should be seen as *post hoc* rationalizations of existing practice, remains one of the most intriguing questions implicitly posed in several chapters. Only when further consideration has been given to these questions will we be able to do more than note the very elaborate systems which different societies employ to classify the plants in their environment. Only in the future will we be able to assess the implications, for any economic agricultural activity, of some societies employing quite gross classifications of plants, while in others the cultivator is said to know (and be able to name) each plant in his field.

This book, as already suggested, moves onto the offensive in its re-evaluation of the role of hunter–gatherer societies in the manipulation of plants. This is perhaps the single most important shift in emphasis since the publication in 1969 of *The domestication and exploitation of plants and animals*. At that time it was still commonly assumed that once the advantages of agriculture had been realized about 7000 years ago somewhere in the Near East, it was somehow inevitable that all hunter–gatherer societies within the region (and beyond) would move over to an agriculturally based economy.

The prevailing model of the 1960s was based on the concept of an essentially static and receptive group of human beings, whatever their particular form of social organization. Here, in contrast, the model is a far from passive one which assumes an active role in the future activities of any group of foragers, both in their relationships to the plant resources in the environment and in their choice of how subgroups exploit those resources under varying conditions. Thus *Foraging and farming* raises many new questions about the nature of social dynamics.

It is a measure of the success of this book that almost all the conventional interpretations of the 1970s and 1980s are subjected to renewed scrutiny in its pages. Gone are the convenient assumptions so often made in the past about the presumed almost automatic effects of population and other pressures on resources. No longer can it be simply assumed that the main crop plants in Papua New Guinea must have derived from Asia. 'Static modelling' of agricultural communities, assuming them to be quite distinct from hunting-foraging ones, now appears unsatisfactory; and it is clearly revealed in several examples that the interrelations of either of the above economically-defined social groups with pastoralists may have had the most profound results, both on the plant-ecological and the social options available to the cultures concerned. Reanalysis of the available information about particular plant species, and of the archaeological evidence from particular regions, also highlights the possibility of, for example, new interpretations of the number and nature of dispersals (of people and plants?) from Africa into India (see *Food, metals and towns in African history*, edited by T. Shaw *et al.*), possible diffusion routes in and around China, and the absence of any evidence for irrigation practices associated with the earliest Chinese agriculture.

Each chapter of this book reveals new information, or new results from the reanalysis of material evidence, within new frameworks of interpretation. This is part of the novelty and value of the whole volume. Within the Americas, for example, genetic studies suggest diffusionary influences within Middle and South America that are contrary to those previously deduced from more traditional archaeological evidence. Many of the complexities of analysis and interpretation based on the investigation of plant-genetic variability are especially well exemplified by the studies of maize. It is salutory to be reminded that the complexities and uncertainties of the evidence still do not allow us to determine the routes and times of the spread of the sweet potato from South America across the Pacific. It is even more important to realize that many of our interpretations of agricultural development can be transformed by the approach and preconceptions of the investigation – 20 years ago the possibility of indigenous plant domestication in the Eastern Woodlands of North America was barely conceived, and the region was regarded as one of the backwaters of world prehistory, whereas the picture now revealed is one of early and intensive cultural (including agricultural) activity. Equally, there can be little doubt that much still remains to be learned about the origins and development of New Guinea agriculture – current analyses and interpretations necessarily have to be carried out in a sort of vacuum because we do not know the nature of the explanatory parameters which should be applied to the evidence.

The 'Neolithic Revolution' in the Near East has often been regarded as a classic example of a simple invention, followed by adoption and subsequent wide diffusion. In the 1960s interest and emphasis switched to the multiple origins of plant domestications in numerous parts of the world. This book strongly maintains the latter emphasis with, for example, fascinating reviews of the evidence for the independent beginnings of maize cultivation in and around the Andes, but it also reconsiders the evidence for the classic Near Eastern pattern of plant domestication. In this latter case, at least, it still appears likely that the domestication of plants was a relatively rare occurrence rather than a frequent event which would have been often rejected by those who could have taken advantage of the innovation (see *What's new?*, edited by S. Van der Leeuw & R. Torrence). Such an interpretation must, nowadays, be considered in the context of evidence that the human societies of the time were exercising considerable choice in the wild plant, meat, and fish foods which they chose to exploit or reject. Such re-evaluations are fundamental to this book.

It is perhaps not surprising to learn that, since 1968, an array of new techniques has been brought to bear on archaeobotanical studies, illuminating, for example, by the application of scanning-electron and phase-contrast light microscopy, such questions as the identity of tropical American starches. It is not only the application of scientific techniques which is impressive in this book but also, and surprisingly, the fact that in some contexts, such as in Indonesia, it is the record of indigenous ritual and myth which provides the best evidence for past agricultural activities. The challenges for future research remain immense, and are clearly brought to the fore in many chapters. As the evidence of plant exploitation becomes better known in all its complexities in many different parts of the world, and from many different periods of the past, so such understanding often challenges the models of social change which have frequently been applied to the more traditional archaeological data. An example of this is the processing of the *zamia* plant in Venezuela to convert it into flour. The processes involved – including pulping, allowing the plant to rot, and then cooking it – resemble those adopted widely for the treatment and preparation of manioc. This evidence is bound to rekindle interest in the mechanisms of cultural innovation, and the role that transference of techniques from one context to another may have played in such innovative developments. In some cases, the implications of the evidence presented will take many years to assimilate into new explanatory models. One such example comes from Southeast Asia where, on present evidence, it appears that the significant changes in the social system which led to the development of chiefdoms and ranking took place as a result of sedentism but without any observable changes in agricultural practice or the selection of different foods. It is exactly such details of practice and preference which challenge the conventional linkage of social development, as revealed by the archaeological data of architecture or

funerary customs, with assumed changes in the economic, and technological, basis of the society concerned.

This Southeast Asian case exemplifies a much wider switch in interpretive
orientation which is to be found in several of the chapters of *Foraging and
farming*, and which is likely to dominate debate for many years to come. If
there are no necessary correlations between major imposed shifts in the
economic or technological basis of a society and changes to a different mode
of livelihood or form of social organization, then attention is again focused
on the *internal* societal conditions which may have caused the human beings
constituting a particular society to move, for example, from a mobile
hunter–gatherer to a pastoral transhumant or sedentary way of life (or to
some combination of these or other available options). However, such a
focus on the internal dynamics of a society inevitably leads to a consideration
of the external socio-economic conditions within which such internal choices
will have been made, for no human society exists in complete isolation.
*Foraging and farming* invites us to re-examine current assumptions about the
nature of the external influences on societies, and the factors which may
condition the viewpoints of the people involved in such interactions (see
*Centre and periphery*, edited by T. C. Champion). Most important of all,
perhaps, is the conclusion that the very nature of the concept of 'societal
consensus' will have to be re-examined and refined, both in relation to
studies of the dynamics of cultural innovation and to those undertaken in the
framework of Neo-Darwinian evolutionism.

In an unexpected way we have come almost full circle, to the realization
that improved understanding of the evolution of plant exploitation requires
detailed knowledge of the indigenous views, and possibly even the classificatory systems, of the members of the societies who undertook such
exploitation. This book contains numerous examples of the ways that such
emic views may coincide with biological explanations and biologically
effective ways of manipulating and reproducing plants. Thus it is tempting
to imagine that the Andean example of cultural selectivity operating at the
level of taste and tradition in the mixture of particular clays with particular
tubers on a scale of culinary preferences – which in turn affects the choice of
which tubers should be exploited (rather than their relative toxicity) – may
have much wider implications for interpretations which attempt to link
ethnobotanical and archaeobotanical evidence with socio-cultural developments.

It is indicative of the quite exceptional nature of this book that such a
variety of critical problems and methodological issues should be raised
within the pages of one cohesive volume. In addition, the diversity and the
world-wide coverage of its examples is without parallel. Novelty is thus to
be found on almost every page, best exemplified perhaps in the account of
current experiments in the domestication of West African yams, experiments which not only cast light on how yams may have been domesticated
in the past, but which also link the past to the future, through the possibilities
that such experiments may offer to the undernourished, and often starving,

people of (at least) tropical Africa. In 1968 I wrote (Ucko & Dimbleby 1969, p. xx) that 'Domestication did not, of course, happen only once but has recurred time and time again in different parts of the world and at different times. Domestication as a process still continues.' *Foraging and farming* is an eloquent testament, 20 years later, both to the new approaches and to the new techniques which are now being applied to the study of the domestication by human beings of their environment. As such, this book is, and will remain for a long time, an exceptionally broad-ranging and thought-provoking account of a unique human endeavour.

P. J. Ucko
*Southampton*

# References

Harris, D. 1987. In *Academic freedom and apartheid: the story of the World Archaeological Congress*, P. J. Ucko, 159–61. London: Duckworth.

Ucko, P. J. 1969, Penis sheaths: a comparative study. *Proceedings of the Royal Anthropological Institute*, 27–67.

Ucko, P. J. & G. W. Dimbleby (eds) 1969. *The domestication and exploitation of plants and animals*. London: Duckworth.

# Contents

# Preface

In today's world plants provide the 'daily bread' of over five billion human beings. With very few exceptions, human societies have relied more heavily on plant than on animal foods for their sustenance, and the history of human intervention in the plant world no doubt reaches back uninterruptedly to our earliest hominid ancestors. During the many millennia of interaction between people and plants, humans have learnt to exploit plants in diverse ways for myriad purposes, especially for food. In so doing they have developed ingenious methods of processing plant parts that would otherwise remain inedible, and have thus extended the range of species which could be exploited.

Looking back over the thousands of years of interaction between people and plants, we can recognize thresholds when new methods of exploitation came to be applied, and the often symbiotic relationships established between plants and people underwent major changes. Among such thresholds we can include the earliest use of pounding stones to macerate fibrous stems, roots, and tubers, and to crack nuts; the controlled burning of vegetation to enhance the yields of edible plant products (or, indirectly, of game animals); the elaboration of methods of harvesting and storing seeds; cooking by boiling plant foods in pottery, shell, or wooden vessels; fermentation; the detoxification of bitter and poisonous roots, tubers, and seeds by leaching; and, of course, cultivation. All these technical innovations could be, and no doubt were, applied to wild plants, but at some time in the evolution of the increasingly close relationship between people and plants, human control over the reproductive systems of particular species became so direct that those plants lost their ability to survive in the wild without human assistance. Thus domestication (in the orthodox sense) came about, and, in combination with cultivation, led to agriculture (see Chapter 1).

There has long been a tendency to regard 'the origins of agriculture' as an overwhelmingly important 'stage' or 'event' in the development of human society. In terms of its consequences for humankind it undoubtedly was; but we prefer to see it as part – though certainly a very significant part – of the long-term evolution of plant exploitation. Our aim in this book is therefore to bring together the results of recent research on plant domestication and early agriculture within an evolutionary framework which emphasizes the continuities as well as the thresholds in the intensifying relationship over time of people to plants.

The origins of the book go back to 1983 when one of us (DRH) first became involved in helping Peter Ucko to plan the academic content of what was to become, in 1986, the World Archaeological Congress held at Southampton. It was soon agreed that the broad international forum of the

Congress would provide a unique opportunity to organize a symposium on plant domestication and early agriculture viewed from a world-wide perspective. It had been apparent for some time that a re-examination of that long-debated topic was overdue, because so much new evidence had become available since it was last reviewed at an international conference. So, we agreed to take on the task of organizing the symposium, and, if it proved academically successful, of publishing the result. Thus began a five-year commitment to what became a gargantuan, often daunting, but always exciting task which led eventually to the appearance of this book.

From the first, we took the view that the symposium would depend for its success on the participation of a core of botanists and archaeologists who had made major contributions to the subject. We also hoped to attract many less established scholars who had new research results to report. Among those who were on our original list of 'invitees', and who did in fact participate in the symposium at Southampton, were Jack Golson, Jack Harlan, Jack Hawkes, Charles Heiser, Timothy Johns, Rhys Jones, Mukund Kajale, Barbara Pickersgill, David Rindos, Garrison Wilkes, and Daniel Zohary. Many other archaeologists, botanists, and anthropologists also contributed papers to the symposium and participated in the discussion; and we were fortunate in being able to persuade several scholars who did not come to Southampton, but who we knew could make very valuable contributions to the eventual book, to set aside time to write chapters specifically for it: Ofer Bar-Yosef and Mordechai Kislev, Lorenzo Costantini, Gideon Ladizinsky, Florence Shipek, Patty Jo Watson, Joyce White, and Douglas Yen. Five contributors to the book were prevented by lack of funds and other reasons from attending the symposium in Southampton although they had written papers for pre-Congress circulation: Te-Tzu Chang, Michael Dove, Charles Higham, Kosum Pyramarn, and Zoya Yanushevich; three – Alexander Grobman, Bernard Maloney, and Betty Meehan – became co-authors of papers which were initially presented at Southampton; and one – Les Groube – made a spontaneous verbal contribution to the symposium which formed the basis of what became his chapter in the book. We are also pleased to be able to include a second chapter by Jack Harlan – on the tropical African cereals – which is an edited version of a recording of the seminar he gave at the Congress in the session on 'The Neolithic of Africa'.

Although it was never our intention to try to include in the symposium contributions dealing with all the main geographical regions of the world, we did, because the Congress proved to be a uniquely international gathering, benefit from the active participation of representatives from an extraordinarily wide range of national and cultural backgrounds. This has, in turn, enlarged the geographical and chronological scope of the book, which now includes data from most regions of the world where research relevant to the evolution of plant exploitation is being carried out. We had hoped, in fact, to include four further contributions which would have helped to fill what may now be perceived as 'gaps' in the scope of the book – dealing with early agriculture in India, Pakistan, Northeast Asia, and Southeast Europe –

but unfortunately this proved impossible to achieve before the final publication deadline.

We look back on the symposium itself as in some ways the most improbable and yet productive academic meeting we have ever experienced. From the start we insisted that the two days allotted to it would be devoted only to discussion, based on the unedited papers that had already been circulated to all registered participants. All but the last-minute papers were included in the pre-Congress publication entitled 'Recent Advances in the Understanding of Plant Domestication and Early Agriculture' which provided the substantive background to the symposium. In the event, everyone's natural inclination to at least summarize their paper was diverted into a collective commitment to vigorous discussion. This was due in no small measure to the enthusiasm with which all those whom we had asked to join us in the task of 'creative chairmanship' and to act as discussants at the end of each session, took up their successive tasks: Peter Bellwood, Noel Broadbent, Athol Chase, Ian Glover, Jack Golson, Jack Harlan, Jack Hawkes, Charles Heiser, Rhys Jones, and Barbara Pickersgill. We thank them all again most warmly for contributing so much to the success of the symposium, and thereby to the eventual appearance of this book. At the end of the symposium we were elated *and* exhausted, but very satisfied that so many botanical, archaeological, and anthropological colleagues from all the inhabited continents had met, mixed convivially, and sustained two days of intensive academic debate at a frontier of knowledge.

So, by September 1986, this book, conceived in 1983, had attained embryonic form. Since then it has undergone an 18-month period of gestation during which all the contributors have uncomplainingly accepted the unavoidable delays and sometimes radical revisions involved in the editorial process. We thank them all, and Peter Ucko, for joining – and bearing – with us in the travail that preceded its birth, an event which would never have happened had we not had the unfailing help of two successive, efficient, and unflappable departmental secretaries: Sally Davis and Heather Binney. If this book awakens – and enlarges – interest among people of many nations in the obscure history of how humankind made the fateful transition from foraging to farming, the effort of all involved in producing it will be well rewarded.

David R. Harris
Gordon C. Hillman
*Institute of Archaeology*
*University College London*
*1 April 1988*

## Radiocarbon dates

Throughout the text, bp, bc and ad refer to uncalibrated radiocarbon dates. BC and AD are used to indicate calibrated radiocarbon dates and calendric dates.

## Note

The final date for revision by authors of their contributions to this book was 30 June 1988.

# Introduction

DAVID R. HARRIS and GORDON C. HILLMAN

Twenty years have passed since the first major international seminar to be held on plant and animal domestication took place at the Institute of Archaeology in London. That remarkable meeting led to the publication of *The domestication and exploitation of plants and animals* (Ucko & Dimbleby 1969), a seminal volume which both reviewed the then state of knowledge of the subject and anticipated many of the research topics which were to be actively pursued by anthropologists, archaeologists, biologists, and other scholars in the next two decades. Although what Flannery referred to in 1973 (p. 271) as 'the bandwaggon of agricultural-origins research' now commands proportionately less attention in archaeology than it did in the 1960s, much new evidence on domestication and early agriculture has been recovered since then, not only in such relatively well-studied regions as Southwest Asia and Mesoamerica but also in many other parts of the world. At the same time there has been, since 1969, a major new development in the subject, focusing on the investigation of hunter–gatherer subsistence, as a topic in its own right and for its relevance to understanding 'the origins of agriculture'. Several new scientific techniques for probing the prehistory of human subsistence have also become available, particularly new bioarchaeological methods of recovering, identifying, and analysing plant and animal remains from archaeological sites, and, most recently, the revolutionary technique of radiocarbon dating by accelerator mass spectrometry (Gowlett & Hedges 1986, Harris 1987) which allows extremely small (<5 mg) samples, such as individual seeds, to be dated directly.

As the subject broadens in its geographical, thematic, and technical scope there is a danger of it becoming so diffuse – with individual researchers scattered across the globe preoccupied with their own particular projects – that the world-wide comparative perspective (which was achieved at the seminar in 1968) is lost, and the wider significance of new evidence is not realized. The aim of this book, therefore, after an interval of two decades, is to re-examine the theme of domestication and early agriculture on a global scale, to make new evidence generally available, and to assess our present understanding of how humans came to make the fundamental shift from dependence on wild foods to dependence on domesticated plants and animals, a dependence which today sustains almost the entire human population.

In 1969 it was possible within the confines of one – admittedly large – volume to encompass plant *and* animal domestication, although even then several important areas of study, for example animal domestication in the Americas, were not represented. To do so now would be impracticable, however methodologically desirable, because of the great growth in knowledge of both plant and animal domestication. We therefore make no apology for limiting the theme of this book to plant exploitation – and at the same time allowing animals a mention whenever they are integral to the topic of a chapter (e.g. in the contributions of An, Golson, Groube, Higham & Maloney, Kajale, Ladizinsky, Markey, Moore, and Pearsall). We also take the view that, overall, the emergence of agriculture is more closely linked to the pre-agrarian exploitation and domestication of plants than of animals, notwithstanding the fact that in certain regions of the world, notably Southwest Asia and the Central Andes, plants and herd animals may have interacted synergistically under human exploitation in the evolution of local agricultural systems. Cultivated and domesticated crop plants are, after all, in a very literal sense the essential biotic elements of production in all systems of agriculture (apart from the people themselves), the only possible exception being the marginally 'agricultural' system of nomadic pastoralism.

The cardinal theme of this book, then, is the evolution of plant exploitation from 'foraging' to 'farming', which subsumes within it such ill-defined but crucial concepts as food procurement, food production, cultivation, domestication, and, of course, agriculture. The connotations and interconnections of these terms are examined in the first chapter, which serves in some ways as an extended introduction to the general theme of the book: that of interaction between people and plants as a continuum, and also a gradient of increasing intensity, through time. We thus regard human exploitation of plant resources as a global evolutionary process which, in different regions at varying times in the past, incorporated the beginnings of cultivation and crop domestication. This approach reduces but does not deny the conceptual dichotomy between 'hunter–gatherers' and 'agriculturalists' by treating the development of all techniques of plant exploitation as an integral part of the evolutionary ecology of Homo sapiens.

One of our main objectives in organizing the international symposium out of which this book has grown, was to bring together biologists who have made major contributions to the study of plant domestication and archaeologists whose research has focused explicitly on the beginnings and early development of agriculture. We did not set out to achieve world-wide geographical or comprehensive chronological coverage, although in the end we have been able to include contributions dealing with a very wide range of regions and time periods. Most contributors report newly discovered evidence in their chapters, and in some cases they have also discussed new applications of scientific techniques (e.g. Pearsall's and Piperno's discussions of phytolith analysis, Pickersgill's of isozyme analysis, Butler's of anatomical micromorphology, and Hill's & Evans' of infra-red spectroscopy applied to the analysis of organic residues in pottery). These demonstrations of the relevance of such techniques add a further valuable dimension to the book, but we should emphasize that it has not been part of our purpose comprehensively to review the range of new techniques that are beginning to be applied to the study of past plant exploitation. That is a fast-developing field which deserves a book to itself.

Our aim throughout this volume is to treat the prehistory and history of plant exploitation as a continuous evolutionary process. The division of the book into separate parts on agrarian, and non- and pre-agrarian, plant exploitation may appear to contradict this aim, but we believe the contents of the individual chapters belie that objection. In fact, in some cases our decision to include a particular contribution in one part rather than another borders on the arbitrary. Although an implicitly chronological arrangement – from pre- and non-agrarian subsistence through cultivation and domestic- ation to agriculture – could have been adopted (indeed, that was our original intention), we finally decided that the book should start with four theoretical contributions which discuss, from different perspectives, the concepts we use and the processes we examine when studying the evolution of plant exploitation.

The four chapters in the first part introduce two other distinctive aspects of the book: the diversity of intellectual perspectives and scholarly skills which are represented in it, and the major contribution made to it by data on 'hunter–gatherer' subsistence, especially from recent studies in Australia (see particularly the chapters by Cane, Chase, Hallam, Jones & Meehan, Smith, and Yen). In terms of their academic affiliation, the contributors to the book range from the biological sciences to archaeology, anthropology, history, and linguistics. Biological and archaeological-ethnographic studies predo- minate, but social–anthropological, historical, and linguistic data also consti- tute an important part of several chapters (e.g. those by Chase, Dove, Hallam, Harlan, Markey, and Shipek).

Within the primarily biological contributions, evidence and insights from a wide range of specialisms are presented. All the biological contributors share an ecological and evolutionary approach, within which they bring their particular skills to bear on the subject, e.g. Grobman's, Hawkes', Heiser's, Pickersgill's, and Wilkes' discussion of the taxonomic, genetic, and cytological evidence for the domestication and diffusion of maize and other crops of the American tropics; Chikwendu's & Okezie's experimental study of yam domestication; Johns', and Hill's & Evans', biochemical approaches to, respectively, Andean root and tuber crops, and Pacific Island crops; Butler's application of anatomical micromorphology to the Southwest Asian grain legumes; Maloney's palynological investigation of the local environ- ment of a key archaeological site in Thailand; Stahl's discussion of the dietary implications of plant-food processing; and the ecological–genetic reviews of the domestication of the major grain crops of Southwest Asia by Zohary, Kislev, and Ladizinsky, of the tropical African cereals by Harlan, and of rice by Chang.

The specifically archaeobotanical contributions are a distinctive feature of the book, in that they focus on the analysis and interpretation of assemblages of plant remains recovered from particular archaeological sites. Like the other biological contributors, the authors of these chapters approach their data from an ecological–evolutionary perspective. Some of them are concerned with single pre-(or non-)agrarian sites (Costantini, Hillman, Hillman et al., Kajale, Pyramarn), others with regionally defined clusters of sites which either encompass the domestication process itself and/or early post-domestication agriculture (Pearsall, Piperno, Watson, Yanushevich).

Another group of contributors approaches the subject from a more exclusively archaeological point of view by focusing attention on lithic and ceramic artefacts used in processing plant foods and for other subsistence-related activities (Cane, Groube, Sanoja, Smith); on regional subsistence-settlement patterns and chronological sequences (An, Bar-Yosef, Bonavia, Higham, Moore, Sanjoa); and on field and stratigraphic evidence for agricultural (and 'horticultural': cf. Harris in Ch. 1) systems (Bulmer, Gallagher, Golson); though these authors, too, share the ecological orientation which characterizes the entire book (and which is made particularly explicit in the three chapters written jointly by archaeologists and botanists: Bar-Yosef & Kislev, Bonavia & Grobman, Higham & Maloney).

Finally, we emphasize again the central importance of ethnographic, or what we might more aptly call 'ethnoecological', data in the book as a whole. It forms an important part of most of the biological and archaeological contributions, and it is an essential ingredient in many of those that are concerned with agrarian, as well as with all those that focus on non- and pre-agrarian, plant exploitation (perhaps most conspicuously in the chapters by Cane, Dove, Hallam, Harlan (Ch. 5), Jones & Meehan, Shipek, White, and Yen).

Our decision to divide the book into five parts – a largely theoretical first one followed by two parts each on non- and pre-agrarian, and agrarian, plant exploitation – has already been referred to, but it does require some further justification of the individual parts and of the sequence of chapters within them. In Chapter 1, discussion of the concepts of cultivation, domestication, and agriculture provides a unifying framework for the more specialized and 'factual' contributions which follow. In Chapters 1–4, a clear distinction emerges between the use of the term domestication to denote (crop) plants that have been genetically and/or phenotypically modified by human intervention in their reproductive systems (the orthodox connotation), and the enlargement of the term to embrace the concept of the domesticated environment. This latter connotation is developed here on a magisterial scale by Yen, on a more local scale by Chase who, with Hynes (1982), introduced the neologism 'domiculture', and it is also implicit in Rindos' division (1984 and here) of the concept into 'incidental', 'specialized', and 'agricultural' domestication.

Having explored the conceptual framework of the subject as well as initiating discussion of the processes involved in plant domestication, we then introduce in the second part (Chs 5–11) an array of ethnographic data on plant exploitation by 'hunter–gatherers' which demonstrates the diversity and complexity of the techniques used, many of which are shown closely to resemble agronomic practices of agriculturalists (cf., in the first part, Yen's use of the phrase 'the agronomy of hunter–gatherers', and Harris' inclusion of such activities as sowing, transplanting, tilling, irrigation, and drainage in pre-domestication wild plant-food production). The ethnographic data in the second part relate mainly to the non-agricultural exploitation of wild grasses and other seed-yielding plants, and such tuber-bearing taxa as yams, examples being drawn from Africa, Asia, Australia, and North America. It ends with a comprehensive discussion by Stahl of plant-food processing techniques and their nutritional implications.

In the third part (Chs 12–19) we turn to the archaeological evidence of pre-agrarian plant exploitation, and present the results of eight recent archaeobotanical studies which range geographically from Mediterranean Europe and North Africa through Southwest, South, and Southeast Asia to New Guinea, Australia, and South America. Collectively, these chapters represent a major contribution to the investigation of pre-agrarian plant use, diet, and seasonality, and the authors of three of them (Costantini, Groube, and Pearsall) also develop locally applicable models for transitions from 'hunter–gatherer' to 'agricultural' or 'horticultural' subsistence.

In the fourth and fifth parts (Chs 20–45) we cross the threshold of crop domestication (in the orthodox sense of the term) and present a wide range of evidence on the evolution of crops and of agriculture. The diversity of contributions to these sections of the book is so great that their separation into two parts, and the sequence of the chapters within each part, is somewhat arbitrary. But we believe that the division we have adopted between, on the one hand, the domestication and diffusion of crops and crop assemblages (fourth part, Chs 20–32), and, on the other hand, the evolution of agricultural systems (fifth part, Chs 33–45), is both logical and useful, although we readily admit that not all the contributions to the fifth part are concerned with agricultural *systems* as such. In arranging the individual chapters in the fourth and fifth parts we have adopted a sequence that, as far as possible, groups together contributions relating to similar crops, geographical regions, and continents.

A book as large and diverse as this one defies editorial distillation of a comprehensive series of general conclusions. Instead we end this Introduction with brief comments on three aspects of our subject that appear to us to have general relevance to future investigations. The first is the question of how we should attempt to identify the areas of earliest cultivation and domestication of particular crops. The conventional ('Vavilovian') approach has been to assume that the present-day distributions of the (known or assumed) progenitors, or the nearest modern relatives and/or the 'primitive' varieties, of the crops under investigation are likely to represent the 'homelands' of those crops (Harris in press). This assumption has often been challenged on the grounds that it ignores the possibility of climatically induced or other environmental changes having so altered the distribution of plant communities, in the interval since the crops were first cultivated and domesticated, that the present-day distribution patterns cannot be used as a guide to the areas where the progenitors were first taken into cultivation. How much weight should be given to this criticism will depend on how precisely the 'homeland' is being defined, and how much is securely known about environmental change – or lack of it – in the area. All we wish to do is to stress the importance of developing new and more refined methods of reconstructing past distribution patterns of the relevant plant communities, not only by means of pollen analysis but also by developing and applying the less proven techniques of phytolith and wood-charcoal analysis. This approach to vegetation change needs also to be combined with detailed ecological studies of the plant communities in which the progenitors, or their nearest modern relatives, occur today, so that the habitats in which the progenitors formerly occurred can be characterized. The principal value of studying the distribution patterns of present-day plant communities therefore lies in what they can tell us about the habitat preferences of the progenitors, and not in what we may uncertainly infer about where those communities occurred in the past.

Our second concluding comment relates to the long-debated question of how particular taxa came to be selected (whether deliberately or not) as cultigens. This is a complex question, which invites contrasted types of 'explanation', such as 'co-evolution' versus 'cultural preference'. Our present purpose is only to point to the potential value of detailed comparative studies of the basic morphological and ecological characteristics of groups of closely related plants in a given type of habitat to identify potential cultigens according to stated criteria of selection. Kislev's comparison (Ch. 40) of 23 species of large-seeded grasses that grow in the Jordan Valley well illustrates the value of this approach, which could profitably be applied to many groups of plants from which the selection of cultigens may appear to have been relatively arbitrary.

Our third conclusion relates directly to one of the central themes of the book, namely the process of domestication. Here we use the term in its orthodox sense, already referred to, to mean human intervention in the reproductive system of the plant, resulting in genetic and/or phenotypic modification. We suggest that three distinct, though not mutually exclusive, pathways to the state of domestication are represented in this book.

(a)  The first pathway selects for very rapid genotypic change involving the loss of the ability of the plant to survive in the wild. This pathway is represented by Ladizinsky's discussion (Ch. 23) of the (according to his model, pre-cultivation) domestication of the Southwest Asian grain legumes, in which he postulates the mechanisms involved *and* estimates the possible rate of the domestication process. It is also represented by Zohary's discussion (Ch. 22) of the (post-cultivation) domestication of the Southwest Asian cereals and pulses, although he does not attempt to specify the mechanisms involved nor speculate about the rates of domestication. Investigation of domestication rates is potentially most important for our understanding of the beginnings of agriculture, and can be approached experimentally, as work by Hillman and Davies (in press) has recently shown.

(b) The second pathway to domestication selects for gradual genotypic change, and again involves (eventual) loss of the ability of the plant to survive in the wild. It is a process of slow incremental 'ennoblement' dependent on sustained 'anthro-selection' (to use Wilkes' term) which has often continued to the present in areas of 'primitive' agriculture. This pathway is exemplified by Wilkes' discussion of the evolution of maize (Ch. 28).

(c) The third pathway contrasts with the other two in not apparently involving any directional genotypic change between the wild progenitor and the domesticated form. Although the changes in the appearance of plants may be dramatic, they involve only 'plastic' phenotypic changes occurring within the limits of phenotypic plasticity determined by the unaltered genotype. Such changes can be very rapid and they are reversible, in the short term at least. This pathway is exemplified by Chikwendu's and Okezie's experimental domestication of West African yams (*Dioscorea rotundata*) (Ch. 21), and it may have occurred quite widely among root and tuber crops.

As already stated, we do not suggest that these three pathways are mutually exclusive – indeed, most plant domestication is likely to have combined genotypic changes with conspicuous (but still partially reversible) plastic changes in the phenotype, as Heiser's discussion of the *Cucurbita* squashes (Ch. 30) and Hawkes' of the potato (Ch. 31) imply – but the three pathways do appear to represent distinctly different routes from wild progenitor to cultigen, and study of them is therefore fundamental to understanding the evolution of plant exploitation.

It is that understanding which we hope this book will advance, not by debating hypothetical 'explanations' of the *origins* of agriculture but by focusing on the *processes* and *effects* – biological, ecological, demographic, economic, and social – of the exploitation of plants by people. We offer the book as a conspectus of much of what is presently known about *how* humans have harvested, planted, processed, and altered plants over the millennia, and in so doing have 'domesticated' themselves.

## References

Flannery, K. V. 1973. The origins of agriculture. *Annual Reviews of Anthropology* **2**, 271–310.

Gowlett, J. A. J. & R. E. M. Hedges (eds) 1986. *Archaeological results from accelerator dating*. Oxford: Oxford University Committee for Archaeology, Monograph 11.

Harris, D. R. 1987. The impact on archaeology of radiocarbon dating by accelerator mass spectrometry. *Philosophical Transactions of the Royal Society of London Series* **A 323**, 23–43.

Harris, D. R. in press. Vavilov's concept of centres of origin of cultivated plants: its genesis and its influence on the study of agricultural origins. *Botanical Journal of the Linnean Society*.

Hillman, G. C. & M. S. Davies in press. Domestication rates in wild-type einkorn wheat under primitive cultivation. *Botanical Journal of the Linnean Society*.

Hynes, R. A. & A. K. Chase 1982. Plants, sites and domiculture: Aboriginal influence upon plant communities in Cape York Peninsula. *Archaeology in Oceania* **17**, 38–50.

Rindos, D. 1984. *The origins of agriculture: an evolutionary perspective*. New York: Academic Press.

Ucko, P. J. & G. W. Dimbleby (eds) 1969. *The domestication and exploitation of plants and animals*. London: Duckworth.

# THE EVOLUTION OF PLANT EXPLOITATION: CONCEPTS AND PROCESSES

# 1 An evolutionary continuum of people–plant interaction

DAVID R. HARRIS

## Introduction

Philosophical speculation about how plants and animals were domesticated and about how agriculture arose can be traced in the Western intellectual tradition at least back to Classical times – for example in Lucretius' discussion of animal domestication (Glacken 1967, pp. 139–40) – but substantive enquiry into the beginnings of agriculture and the history of domesticated plants and animals is little more than a century old. Indeed, field and laboratory investigations designed specifically to throw light on the emergence of agriculture, conducted by archaeologists and biologists, have been underway for little more than four decades. During that brief period an impressive array of bioarchaeological evidence has been recovered from early agrarian sites in many tropical and temperate regions of the world, and ethnographic and historical research has made a major contribution to the interpretation of that evidence. But the exciting and often controversial debates that have accompanied attempts to understand 'the origins of agriculture' have often been bedevilled by confusion over the meanings attributed to such terms as agriculture, cultivation, domestication, and food production.

To point this out is not to engage in semantic quibbling, because the meanings attributed to such general concepts can and do directly affect research design and the interpretation of evidence. The purpose of this chapter is therefore to present – against the background of a review of earlier uses of such concepts – a classificatory model which arranges them along a continuum of people–plant interaction. It is hoped that this will help to clarify our thinking about the processes involved in the emergence of agriculture, and also that it will provide a useful prelude to the other contributions to this part of the book. The concept of a continuum of interaction, developed in this chapter, need not of course be restricted to *plants* and people; it could productively be extended to animal–people interaction. Its limitation here to plants is a function of the overall theme of the book, and in part also a reflection of the primacy of plants in the structure and function of agricultural systems (agroecosystems), whether or not they incorporate domesticated animals.

The intellectual assumptions that underlie the model presented here are ecological and evolutionary: ecological in that the analytical target is *interaction* between people and plants, evolutionary in that the *results* of the processes involved in domestication and the emergence of agriculture – i.e. the crops, domestic animals, and agricultural practices that we seek to trace in the archaeological record – are assumed to be the products of selection working on both biological and cultural variation. It is therefore evolutionary in a Darwinian sense (cf. Rindos Ch. 2, this volume), but not in the progressive sense of the cultural-evolutionary school of mid-twentieth century American anthropology exemplified by Sahlins & Service (1960). Before discussing the model itself (in the last section of this chapter), it is therefore necessary to emphasize that it is not unidirectional, and it certainly does not imply that, given sufficient 'time', human societies would inevitably progress from one level of interaction with plants (or animals) to the next. The levels of interaction specified in the model (Fig. 1.1) are not to be regarded as pre-ordained steps on a ladder of increasingly 'advanced' stages of general societal development; nor is it implied that transitions from one level to another, e.g. from cultivation to domestication, are necessarily irreversible. However, the model *is* progressive in one specific sense, in that the proposed continuum is presented as a gradient of increasing input of human energy per unit area of exploited land (Fig. 1.1). This and other aspects of the model are examined more fully below, but first it needs to be set against the background of the ecological and evolutionary paradigm that has strongly influenced recent approaches to understanding the emergence of agriculture.

## Ecological and evolutionary approaches to understanding the emergence of agriculture

It was during the 1960s that models were first proposed in explicitly ecological and evolutionary terms to attempt to explain the transition from hunting and gathering (dependence on wild foods) to agriculture (dependence on domesticated plants and animals). The gradualistic view of that transition which was adopted by such ecologically minded students of the subject as Binford (1968), Flannery (1968, 1969), Harris (1969), and Higgs & Jarman (1969) can be traced at least as far back as Darwin's characteristically cogent description (1868, p. 309) of 'the first step[s] in cultivation'; but it only came to be widely accepted during the last twenty years. The contributions of these authors to the ecological-evolutionary paradigm need little rehearsal here, but it is worth signalling some of the changes in terminology which they introduced.

The new, more explicitly ecological orientation of the 1960s, which stressed the continuities rather than the contrasts between hunting and gathering and agriculture, was in part a reaction to the then prevalent view, derived from Gordon Childe's seminal concept of the 'Neolithic Revolution', of the transition to agriculture as a relatively abrupt event induced by a climatic shift to greater aridity in Southwest Asia in the early Holocene. Childe contrasted the Neolithic 'food-producers' with the 'food-gatherers' of earlier times, but he did not distinguish conceptually between agriculture, cultivation, and domestication, although he used all three terms in his accounts of the Neolithic Revolution (Childe 1936, 1942).

The use of the term 'food production', as synonymous with agriculture, was further promulgated by Braidwood (eg. 1952, 1960), and has continued to the present. In the 1960s, particularly in two highly influential papers by Binford (1968) and Flannery (1968), it came to be contrasted with the term 'food procurement' which was applied to the food-gathering and food-collecting activities of hunter–gatherers. This tended, at one level of analysis, to reinforce the long-established dichotomy between hunter–gatherers and agriculturalists, but because both Binford and Flannery were exploring the transition to agriculture in systemic terms by postulating positive and negative interactions of particular environmental and behavioural variables, their papers also had the effect of emphasizing continuities that linked hunter–gatherer 'food procurement' to agricultural 'food production'.

A diminished emphasis on the dichotomy between hunter–gatherer and agriculturalist – or forager and farmer – within a systemic framework of analysis, was also implicit in my ecological approach to the study of the beginnings of agriculture in the tropics (Harris 1969, 1972, 1973). In particular, I proposed a distinction between the 'manipulation' of biotic resources which could lead to sufficiently sustained intervention in the breeding systems of wild plants and animals that 'domestication' resulted; and the 'transformation' of natural into artificial ecosystems which accompanied the later establishment of fully developed agricultural economies. Manipulation and transformation were thus envisaged as two phases on a gradient or continuum of ecological change induced by human modification of natural ecosystems, which led, in the remote past, from hunting and gathering through domestication to agriculture. I did not at that time, however, make any finer distinctions in terms of such variables as gathering, tending, planting, sowing, tilling, etc., nor did I distinguish conceptually between cultivation and agriculture.

It was during the 1960s that Eric Higgs and his associates at the University of Cambridge also sought to broaden the study of 'agricultural origins'. They redefined the objective as the study of prehistoric economies, regardless of whether such economies were predominantly of hunter–gatherer or agricultural type. Higgs argued that the archaeological record should be interpreted in terms of biological and economic principles, and ethnographic analogies, and he selected the term 'husbandry', in preference to domestication, to denote the whole spectrum of human intervention in and control over the biology and behaviour of animals and plants – intervention which, he postulated, reached back into Palaeolithic times (Higgs 1972).

By the mid 1970s these ecological and evolutionary approaches had brought about a transformation in how the study of early agriculture was perceived: it was no longer viewed in isolation but in the broader context of prehistoric 'subsistence systems' or 'palaeoeconomies', and the formerly rigid dichotomy between hunter–gatherers and agriculturalists had become blurred. Since then, the attention of ecologically oriented students of prehistoric subsistence has begun to focus more precisely on the diversity and interconnections of the activities through which people have, in the past, exploited both 'wild' and 'domestic' plants and animals.

Theoretical contributions to this recent phase in the development of the ecological–evolutionary paradigm were made during the 1980s by Rindos (1980, 1984), Hynes & Chase (1982), Jarman *et al.* (1982), and Ford (1985). Their contributions relate directly but differently to the model proposed in this chapter, and they are, accordingly, briefly reviewed as a prelude to presentation of the model.

The third and final volume of the *Papers in economic prehistory*, in which Higgs and his colleagues reported the results of their research on early agriculture in Europe and Southwest Asia, appeared in 1982 after his death. In it, Jarman *et al.* looked back over the development of the Higgs' 'school' of palaeoeconomy and offered their revised formulation of its theoretical basis and methodology. They reaffirmed Higgs' distinction between domestication, in the strict sense of morphological change in plants and animals resulting from their selective breeding by humans, and the much broader concept of husbandry. They then went on to elaborate the distinction by proposing more complex classifications of both 'man–animal' and 'man–plant' relationships, as follows: for animals, six categories (random predation, controlled predation, herd following, loose herding, close herding, factory farming); and for plants, five categories (casual gathering, systematic gathering, limited cultivation, developed cultivation, intensive cultivation); stressing, however, that such classifications did not represent 'an economic ladder of progress, with one stage inevitably developing towards, and eventually into, the next' (Jarman *et al.* 1982, pp. 51–4). As we are concerned in this chapter with plants, it is also worth pointing out that they strongly endorsed Helbaek's original distinction (1960) between plant cultivation and plant domestication – a distinction which first introduced into the study of early agriculture the concept of 'pre-domestication cultivation' that has since been used effectively by Hillman (1975) and others.

A more comprehensively biological and ecological-evolutionary approach to 'the origins of agriculture' has been developed recently by Rindos (1980, 1984). In the context of this chapter, his major contribution has been to embed the concept of domestication within that of 'co-evolution', defined as 'an evolutionary process in which the establishment of a symbiotic relationship between organisms, increasing the fitness of all involved, brings about changes in the traits of the organisms' (Rindos 1984, p. 99). This approach – by which domestication is regarded as but one type of biologically defined symbiotic relationship – was originally introduced into the study of prehistoric domestication (of animals) by Zeuner (1963, pp. 36–64), and Rindos has extended and elaborated it, specifically in relation to plants and agricultural systems. In so doing, he has proposed a new three-fold classification of 'the domestication relationship' consisting of 'three conceptually distinct aspects mediated by different types of human behaviour and occurring in distinct environments', i.e. 'incidental domestication' which is 'the result of human dispersal and protection of wild plants in the general environment'; 'specialized domestication' which is 'mediated by the environmental impact of humans, especially in the local areas in which they reside'; and 'agricultural domestication' which is the 'culmination of the other two processes, involves the further evolution of plants in response to the conditions existing with the agroecology' and 'is roughly equivalent to what has simply been termed *domestication* in the literature of agricultural origins' (Rindos 1984, p. xiv–xv). The classification is explicitly evolutionary, but, like Jarman *et al.* in respect of their classifications, Rindos denies that his scheme represents 'stages' in the development of all agricultural systems. He emphasizes that the three types of human–plant relationship are not mutually exclusive; indeed, that the boundaries between them are inevitably artificial because the three categories are 'components of an integrated, natural process' (Rindos 1984, p. 53).

Rindos' full discussion of his taxonomy of plant domestication (1984, pp. 152–66) represents the most comprehensive attempt (since Zeuner's for animal domestication) to broaden and systematize the ecological-evolutionary concepts which can be applied to the study of past (and present) people–plant interactions. In its comprehensiveness his taxonomy encompasses at a high level of generality the two other recent theoretical contributions already referred to – Hynes & Chase (1982) and Ford (1985) – although they differ from Rindos in some important respects. Hynes & Chase (1982) coined the term 'domiculture' to describe the interaction of people and biotic resources in local 'hearth-centred' environments or 'domuses'. They developed their ideas in the context of Australian Aboriginal attitudes towards, and uses of, plants, but the concept of domiculture has more general application. In ecological terms, it is equivalent to Rindos' category of incidental domestication (and in part also to that of specialized domestication), although Chase in Chapter 3 of this book objects to that equation, arguing that to see hunter–gatherers as 'incidental' domesticators is to beg the central issue – which, in his view, is the primacy of human sociality in initiating, articulating, and maintaining the production and distribution of resources. According to Chase, domiculture is the result of intentional human action focused on culturally recognized plants (and animals), and is not, as is Rindos' incidental domestication, a more general biological phenomenon which people share with other domesticatory organisms. However, with that important qualification, Hynes' and Chase's concept of domiculture does closely resemble – and could be said to fit as a subsidiary concept, restricted to human actions, within – Rindos' categories of incidental and specialized domestication. So, too, does the concept of 'agronomy' among Australian hunter–gatherers which Yen develops in Chapter 4 of this book.

In the Preface to his 1985 publication on *Prehistoric food production in North America*, Ford remarks that inclusion of the term husbandry in the original title of the seminar, held in 1980, on which the book is based – 'The origins of plant husbandry in North America' – was rejected on two grounds: that it implied 'a skewed division of labor in favor of men', and because it 'customarily is applied to the management of animals' (which as domestic-ates – except for the dog and the turkey – were absent in prehistoric North America); so, 'following the lead of Braidwood in the Near East' the term food production was adopted instead (Ford 1985, p. xii). This anecdote neatly illustrates the conceptual difficulties that have troubled students of prehistoric subsistence, and it raises echoes not only of Braidwood, but of Childe before him and of Higgs after him. Ford himself, in his introductory contribution to the book, outlines his own classification of the 'stages and methods of plant food production', (Ford 1985, pp. 2–7). He proposes two major successive stages: 'foraging' and 'food production', and divides the latter into two successive sub-stages: 'cultivation' and 'domestication'. Three main methods of food production are recognized as succeeding one another: 'incipient agriculture', 'gardening', and 'field agriculture', and several types of human behaviour toward plants, viewed as a continuum of types of interaction, are added to the classification, namely 'tending', 'tilling', 'transplanting', 'sowing', and 'plant breeding'. This sequence of behaviours or 'cultural activities' leads from the least biologically disruptive to complete domestication, when plants become completely dependent on humans for their continued existence; and the types of interaction are regarded as cumulative over time.

Ford's scheme is a more comprehensive and detailed categorization of plant-food production than the other classifications discussed, and it does help to clarify the complex interactions between people and plants that are involved. However, although it is viewed by Ford as a continuum, it is not explicitly based on any stated variable(s), such as energy input or population density; although it is, by implication, related to time, to the degree of human disruption of plant biology and ecology, and, more implicitly still, to increas-ing cultural complexity and size of human populations. It resembles in some ways the model of people–plant interaction presented in the next section – although when constructing early versions of that model some years ago I was unaware of Ford's scheme – and the two classifications certainly share the twin aims of attempting to clarify the concepts we use when investigating the prehistory of plant exploitation, and of specifying more precisely the relation-ships of those concepts along a continuum of people–plant interaction.

## The model: an evolutionary continuum of people–plant interaction

As has been stated in the introduction to this chapter, the model summarized in Figure 1.1 is based on ecological and evolutionary assumptions, but it is

| Plant-exploitative activity | Ecological effects (selected examples) | Food-yielding system | Socio economic trends | Time |
|---|---|---|---|---|
| Burning vegetation | Reduction of competition; accelerated re-cycling of mineral nutrients; stimulation of asexual reproduction; selection for annual or ephemeral habit; synchronization of fruiting | WILD PLANT-FOOD PROCUREMENT (Foraging) | Increasing sedentism (settlement size, density, and duration of occupation) | |
| Gathering/collecting | Casual dispersal of propagules | | Increasing population density (local, regional, and continental) | |
| Protective tending | Reduction of competition; local soil disturbance | | Increasing social complexity (ranking → stratification → state formation) | |
| Replacement planting/sowing | Maintenance of plant population in the wild | WILD PLANT-FOOD PRODUCTION with minimal tillage | | |
| Transplanting/sowing | Dispersal of propagules to new habitats | | | |
| Weeding | Reduction of competition; soil modification | | | |
| Harvesting | Selection for dispersal mechanisms: positive and negative | | | |
| Storage | Selection and redistribution of propagules | | | |
| Drainage/irrigation | Enhancement of productivity; soil modification | CULTIVATION with systematic tillage | | |
| Land clearance | Transformation of vegetation composition and structure | | | |
| Systematic soil tillage | Modification of soil texture, structure, and fertility | AGRICULTURE (Farming) | | |
| Propagation of genotypic and phenotypic variants: DOMESTICATION → | Propagation of genotypic and phenotypic variants: DOMESTICATION | Evolutionary differentiation of agricultural systems | | |
| Cultivation of domesticated crops (cultivars) | Establishment of agroecosystems | | | |

PLANT-FOOD PRODUCTION

Increasing input of human energy per unit area of exploited land

(I, II, III — energy thresholds)

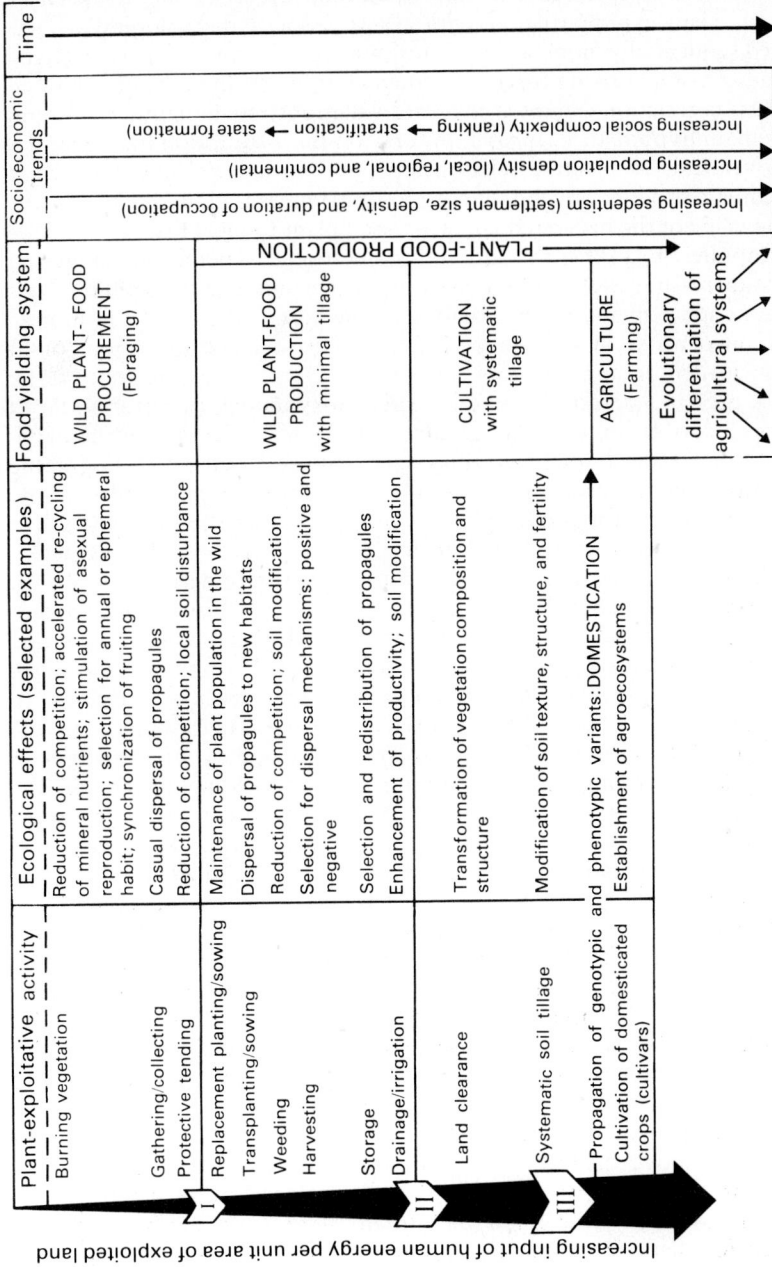

**Figure 1.1** Schematic diagram of an evolutionary continuum of people–plant interaction (the Roman numerals indicate postulated energy thresholds).

not unidirectional and deterministic. It does not address the question of *why* some past human societies shifted from primary dependence on wild plant foods to primary dependence on cultivated crops. It seeks only to specify a series of plant-exploitative activities and associated ecological effects arranged sequentially along a continuum which is, however, also conceived as a gradient of increasing input of human energy per unit area of exploited land. This correlation cannot at present be demonstrated quantitatively and must remain hypothetical. It rests, in turn, on the assumption that there has been, over time, a positive relationship between energy input into food procurement/production and energy output measured in terms of the calorific value of the harvested and processed plant foods. However, I make no attempt here to answer the underlying question of whether the suggested trend of increasing energy input and output per unit area of exploited land was a function – in any given situation in the past – of increases in human population density, in sedentary settlement, in social stratification, or in other socio-demographic factors, in varying systemic combinations. The aim is to present a descriptive not an explanatory model, except in so far as the posited correlation with energy input can be regarded as 'explanatory'.

In Figure 1.1 the human activities specified are based on ethnographic observations and historical accounts of interactions between people and the plants they exploit for food, and it is presumed that these activities had prehistoric antecedents which, to varying degrees, may be archaeologically traceable. Although the activities, from burning vegetation to the cultivation of domesticated crops and the differentiation of agricultural systems are presented as sequential, it is not implied that they succeeded *and replaced* one another over time, except in the very general sense of comparative import- ance on a world scale. To put it another way, all the specified activities are still practised today in agricultural, and, to a reduced extent, in non-agricul- tural contexts (environments), but as agriculture progressively replaced gathering (and hunting) as the predominant food-yielding system, so the relative importance of those activities by which wild plant foods were exploited declined. Activities such as planting and sowing, harvesting and storage, irrigation and drainage, land clearance and tillage, which are assumed to pre-date agriculture (as here defined), were, of course, incorpo- rated into evolving systems of cultivation and eventually became highly elaborated, integral components of agricultural production. Likewise, the burning of vegetation was incorporated as an essential technique into certain agricultural systems, notably shifting or swidden cultivation, and the protective tending of 'naturally' occurring useful plants anticipated the weeding of intentionally planted or sown crops. Even the gathering of edible parts of 'wild' plants has persisted as a minor, but sometimes dietarily significant, activity in developed agroecosystems.

Given the above qualifications, Figure 1.1 is intended to represent a gradient as well as a continuum of progressively closer people–plant interaction. Along it, the input of human energy per unit area of land exploited for plant foods increases, and so too does the modification of 'natural' ecosystems, and their replacement by agroecosystems, which results from that energy input. The gradient of interaction extends from the (relatively) spatially diffuse activity of burning vegetation, through the more localized gathering, collecting, and protective tending of wild plant products, to the planting, sowing, weeding, harvesting, and storing of (undomesticated) crops, with associated irrigation and drainage, land clearance, and tillage, eventually to crop domestication: this latter condition having come about (according to the orthodox criterion of domestication accepted here) when the reproductive system of the plant population has been so altered by sustained human intervention that the domesticated forms – genetically and/or phenotypically selected – have become dependent upon human assistance for their survival. Figure 1.1 makes a distinction between cultivation, as a method of plant-food production which incorporates land clearance and systematic tillage but which can be (and in the past widely was) applied to undomesticated crops, and agriculture, which term is restricted to the cultivation of domesticated crops. I readily acknowledge that the distinction between undomesticated and domesticated crops is not absolute, if for no other reason than that the genetic/phenotypic selection processes leading to domestication are cumulative, but the distinction between cultivation and agriculture proposed here is at least clear, and it has the added merit of making redundant the vague (and by implication deterministic) category of 'incipient agriculture'.

It will be apparent that I have not introduced the term 'horticulture' into the model. It could have been equated with agriculture or regarded as a distinctive type of agricultural system in order to distinguish between small-scale garden cultivation or *gartenbau* and larger scale field cultivation or *ackerbau*. But, although that is a valid and useful distinction to make when discussing the evolution of agricultural systems, it raises at least two definitional difficulties. The first arises from the fact that in some of the literature on agricultural systems and their evolution, particularly much of that which relates to Melanesia and the Pacific Islands, the term horticulture or 'gardening' has come to be used as a synonym for agriculture (e.g. Groube Ch. 17, this volume; Jones & Meehan Ch. 7, this volume) rather than as a means of distinguishing between 'field' and 'garden' cultivation.

The second difficulty is more problematic and arises from the distinctive ecology of 'house' or 'door-yard' gardens to which Anderson first (1952, pp. 136–42) and Kimber later (1966, 1973, 1978) drew particular attention. Investigation by Kimber of present-day 'traditional' gardens in Puerto Rico and elsewhere revealed that nearly 50 per cent of the plant species present in them were adventitious wild and weedy taxa rather than domesticated crops, although almost all the taxa were perceived by the owners of the gardens as making useful contributions to the household economy. This situation contrasts strongly with the ratio of wild and weedy taxa to domesticated crops that tends to characterize field cultivation, even in situations where within-field mixed cropping rather than within-field monoculture is the norm. House gardens characteristically combine the cultivation of domesticated crops with a significant component of wild plant-food production, and indeed, as I have previously suggested (Harris 1973, pp. 398–401), they probably functioned in the past as important arenas for plant domestication. Therefore, if the term horticulture *is* to be used to denote small-scale garden cultivation involving the exploitation of almost as many 'wild' as domesticated species, than it should not be equated with agriculture but instead regarded as a distinctive type of agroecosystem.

It is not necessary in this discussion to exemplify from ethnographic and historical sources all the plant-exploitative activities listed in Figure 1.1. Many of the contributions to this book do so in considerable detail, particularly in Chapters 5–19, e.g. the replacement planting of yams and the incidental 'tillage' of yam grounds in Australia referred to by Hallam, Jones & Meehan, and Yen; the transplanting of acorns in southern California mentioned by Shipek; and the sowing, harvesting, and processing of wild-grass seeds in southern California, North Africa, and Australia described, respectively, by Shipek, Harlan, and, for Australia, by Cane, Jones & Meehan, Smith, and Yen (see also Allen 1974). There are fewer references in this book to the burning of vegetation to enhance the yields of plant foods and to make their gathering easier (but see Yen for a summary discussion of Australian Aboriginal use of fire to promote the productivity of cycads, grasses, and tuberous plants), and still fewer to non-agricultural contexts in which irrigation and drainage were applied to the exploitation of wild plants to regularize and increase harvests – probably the best-known example of which is the relatively large-scale irrigation of grasses and tuberous plants (such as *Cyperus esculentus*, cf. Hillman Ch. 13, this volume, pp. 226–7) which was practised in historical times (and perhaps earlier) by the Paiute Indians of Owen's Valley in eastern California (summarized in Harris 1984).

It has already been suggested that the sequence of plant-exploitative activities in Figure 1.1 represents a gradient of increasing input of human energy per unit area of exploited land. It can now be further suggested that, qualitatively at least, we can envisage thresholds along the gradient which represent stepped increases in energy input, at which points markedly more effort is invested in selected areas of exploitation, and human intervention in the ecology and reproductive biology of particular plants intensifies. Three such thresholds are postulated in Figure 1.1. The first is between the spatially diffuse and low-energy activities of burning, gathering, and protective tending, and it can be said to separate the food-yielding system of 'wild plant-food procurement' or 'foraging' from 'wild-food production'. The second is between the more spatially focused, labour-demanding, and ecologically interventionist activities that range from planting and sowing to irrigation and drainage, and the still more energy-intensive activities of land clearance and systematic tillage.

The second threshold separates 'wild plant-food production' from 'cultivation'. This is seen as a crucial threshold because, once land clearance and tillage is practised regularly on more than a very small scale, the energy-input demands of the system increase substantially. The biblical injunction

**Figure 1.2** The beginning of agriculture, according to Larry Gonick (© Larry Gonick, all rights reserved, reproduced with his permission).

(Genesis 3:17–19) is indeed true, that 'In the sweat of thy face shalt thou eat bread', or, as Rousseau (1755) ironically described the beginning of agriculture when 'vast forests were changed into smiling fields which had to be watered with the sweat of men'. Larry Gonick (1978) makes the same point (Fig. 1.2) visually but equally emphatically! The separation of cultivation from wild plant-food production by the second energy threshold may appear somewhat arbitrary, in that transplanting, weeding, and drainage and irrigation all involve some degree of soil disturbance, but, in the context of wild plant-food production, such disturbance amounts to no more than minimal tillage, and does not undermine the contention that systematic clearing of the land and tilling of the soil (presumably initially by digging stick or hoe rather than by plough) require much greater investment of energy.

We can, then, define cultivation as a combination of systematic land clearance and tillage with the planting or sowing (as well, of course, as harvesting, etc.) of undomesticated crops. Its inception marks an important point on the evolutionary continuum of people–plant interaction, but it does not necessarily lead to domestication. Crop domestication (in the narrow orthodox sense), or at least the adoption from elsewhere of already domesticated crops, is, however, a necessary component of agriculture. And, in so far as the cultivation of domesticates, if successfully developed and maintained, required that additional effort be devoted to such activities as soil preparation, the maintenance of soil fertility, weeding, seed selection and storage, and the exclusion of potential predators attracted by the enlarged food-storage organs of domesticated plants, then the division between cultivation and agriculture can be said to constitute a third energy threshold on the continuum.

Although only three energy thresholds are postulated in Figure 1.1, we could of course define further thresholds *within* the general category of agriculture which would separate different agricultural systems – such as horticulture, swidden cultivation, floodwater farming, irrigation agriculture, mixed grain-livestock farming, etc. – along the gradient of increasing energy input: an elaboration of the model which is, however, not attempted here.

In characterizing the interaction continuum as a gradient of increasing input of human energy, and postulating thresholds along it, I here disregard the question of how that input was provided, e.g. by a larger population and/or by changes in the sexual or age-related division of labour and/or by changes in the seasonal scheduling of activities. These are important but subsidiary aspects of the present model, which deliberately adopts as an organizing principle the key variable of increasing input of energy per unit of exploited land. Nor do I explore possible correlations between the energy gradient and such socio-demographic trends as increasing sedentism, increasing population density, and increasing social complexity: all aspects of what has recently come to be referred to by some authors as the process of 'intensification' (cf. Lourandos 1983; Yen Ch. 4, this volume). It is sufficient here just to portray them in Figure 1.1 as assumptive correlations only. The variable of time is treated similarly in Figure 1.1, because any attempt to attach a scale in millennia to the continuum requires more knowledge than we presently have of the chronology of plant exploitation. Such a calibration might, however, usefully be attempted for those few regions of the world, such as parts of Southwest Asia, Europe, Middle and North America, where we are beginning to assemble a chronological overview of the evolution of plant exploitation.

The last aspect of the model which calls for comment here is the question of its utility – or lack of it. As stated at the start, my main aim is to help clarify the general terminology we use in thinking and writing about the emergence of agriculture. It is hoped that the model has at least logical validity and some theoretical value, but, if it is to prove useful in investigating the actual history and prehistory of plant exploitation in particular geographical regions, more comprehensive means than we have at present will have to be devised to trace in the archaeological record the range of plant-exploitative activities that make up the continuum. At present, relatively few of those activities are open to direct archaeobotanical or palaeoenvironmental investigation.

Palynology, and the less advanced technique of the stratigraphic analysis of charcoal frequencies, can provide some information on land clearance and fire history. Phytolith analysis, too, is proving a promising technique for the investigation of vegetation change and crop history. The most important set of techniques, however, are those that are applied to the study of macroscopic plant remains preserved by charring, mineralization, water-logging, and desiccation. Thus far they have been applied principally to the investigation of domesticated seed crops, particularly the staple cereals of modern agriculture, maize, wheat, barley, and rice; much less so to pulses (but see Butler Ch. 24, this volume) and other non-cereal seed crops, and hardly at all to root and tuber crops. New chemical and anatomical-micromorphological techniques are now being developed which may open new avenues to the identification of the remains of roots and tubers (Hill & Evans Ch. 26, this volume; Hather 1988) and there is also growing interest among archaeobotanists in the investigation of pre-agrarian plant exploitation (see the contributions to this book by Costantini, Hillman, Hillman *et al.*, Pearsall, Piperno, and Pyramarn).

Field archaeology can sometimes provide direct evidence of irrigation (e.g. Oates & Oates 1976) and of drainage systems in swamp environments (e.g. Golson Ch. 44, this volume), and it is beginning also to reveal the capacity of some prehistoric agriculturalists for large-scale landscape modi-fication by mound and terrace construction, etc. (e.g. Gallagher Ch. 36, Bulmer Ch. 45, this volume). But in the absence of surviving traces of such features in the landscape, it is extremely difficult to demonstrate whether such activities as irrigation, drainage, and tillage were practised. A new experimental approach to the question of tillage is currently being devel-oped by Unger-Hamilton (in press) who has combined harvesting experi-ments on a range of Southwest Asian wild grasses and other herbaceous plants with microwear studies of flint sickle blades. It appears that striations on the blades may be attributable specifically to the harvesting of plants growing on tilled as opposed to untilled soils. If this is confirmed by more comprehensive experiments, the technique could provide us for the first time with a direct method of determining, at least in parts of Southwest Asia, how long ago soil tillage was practised and thus of tracing the begin-nings of cultivation (as here defined).

There are therefore a variety of methods, some well established and others highly experimental, for investigating several of the activities that make up the continuum of people–plant interaction outlined here. In presenting it, I emphasize that it is highly schematic and tentative, but I also hope that it may help to clarify our thinking and assist future enquiry into the theme of this book: the evolution of plant exploitation from foraging to farming.

# References

Allen, H. 1974. The Bagundji of the Darling Basin: cereal gatherers in an uncertain environment. *World Archaeology* **5**, 309–22.

Anderson, E. 1952. *Plants, man and life*. Berkeley: University of California Press.

Binford, L. R. 1968. Post-Pleistocene adaptations. In *New perspectives in archeology*, S. R. Binford & L. R. Binford (eds), 313–41. Chicago: Aldine.

Braidwood, R. J. 1952. From cave to village. *Scientific American* **187**, 62–6.

Braidwood, R. J. 1960. The agricultural revolution. *Scientific American* **203**, 130–48.

Bulmer, S. 1989. Gardens in the south: diversity and change in prehistoric Maaori agriculture. In *Foraging and farming: the evolution of plant exploitation*, D. R. Harris & G. C. Hillman (eds), ch. 45. London: Unwin Hyman.

Butler, A. 1989. Cryptic anatomical characters as evidence of early cultivation in the grain legumes (pulses). In *Foraging and farming: the evolution of plant exploitation*, D. R. Harris & G. C. Hillman (eds), ch. 24. London: Unwin Hyman.

Cane, S. 1989. Australian Aboriginal seed grinding and its archaeological record: a case study from the Western Desert. In *Foraging and farming: the evolution of plant exploitation*, D. R. Harris & G. C. Hillman (eds), ch. 6. London: Unwin Hyman.

Chase, A. K. 1989. Domestication and domiculture in northern Australia: a social perspective. In *Foraging and farming: the evolution of plant exploitation*, D. R. Harris & G. C. Hillman (eds), ch. 3. London: Unwin Hyman.

Childe, V. G. 1936. *Man makes himself*. London: Watts.

Childe, V. G. 1942. *What happened in history*. Harmondsworth: Penguin Books.

Costantini, L. 1989. Plant exploitation at Grotta dell'Uzzo, Sicily: new evidence for the transition from Mesolithic to Neolithic subsistence in southern Europe. In *Foraging and farming: the evolution of plant exploitation*, D. R. Harris & G. C. Hillman (eds), ch. 12. London: Unwin Hyman.

Darwin, C. 1868. *The variation of animals and plants under domestication*. Vol. I. London: John Murray.

Flannery, K. V. 1968. Archeological systems theory and early Mesoamerica. In *Anthropological archeology in the Americas*, B. J. Meggers (ed.), 67–87. Washington, DC: Anthropological Society of Washington.

Flannery, K. V. 1969. Origins and ecological effects of early domestication in Iran and the Near East. In *The domestication and exploitation of plants and animals*, P. J. Ucko & G. W. Dimbleby (eds), 73–100. London: Duckworth.

Ford, R. I. 1985. The processes of plant food production in prehistoric North America. In *Prehistoric food production in North America*, R. I. Ford (ed.), 1–18. Anthropological Paper No. 75, Museum of Anthropology, University of Michigan, Ann Arbor.

Gallagher, J. P. 1989. Agricultural intensification and ridged-field cultivation in the prehistoric upper Midwest of North America. In *Foraging and farming: the evolution of plant exploitation*, D. R. Harris & G. C. Hillman (eds), ch. 36. London: Unwin Hyman.

Glacken, C. J. 1967. *Traces on the Rhodian shore: nature and culture in western thought from ancient times to the end of the eighteenth century*. Berkeley: University of California Press.

Golson, J. 1989. The origins and development of New Guinea agriculture. In *Foraging and farming: the evolution of plant exploitation*, D. R. Harris & G. C. Hillman (eds), ch. 44. London: Unwin Hyman.

Gonick, L. 1978. *The cartoon history of the universe*. San Francisco: Rip Off Press.

Groube, L. 1989. The taming of the rain forests: a model for Late Pleistocene forest exploitation in New Guinea. In *Foraging and farming: the evolution of plant exploitation*, D. R. Harris & G. C. Hillman (eds), ch. 17. London: Unwin Hyman.

Hallam, S. J. 1989. Plant usage and management in Southwest Australian Aboriginal societies. In *Foraging and farming: the evolution of plant exploitation*, D. R. Harris & G. C. Hillman (eds), ch. 8. London: Unwin Hyman.

Harlan, J. R. 1989. Wild grass-seed harvesting in the Sahara and Sub-Sahara of Africa. In *Foraging and farming: the evolution of plant exploitation*, D. R. Harris & G. C. Hillman (eds), ch. 5. London: Unwin Hyman.

Harris, D. R. 1969. Agricultural systems, ecosystems and the origins of agriculture. In *The domestication and exploitation of plants and animals*, P. J. Ucko & G. W. Dimbleby (eds), 3–15. London: Duckworth.

Harris, D. R. 1972. The origins of agriculture in the tropics. *American Scientist* **60**, 180–93.

Harris, D. R. 1973. The prehistory of tropical agriculture: an ethnoecological model. In *The explanation of culture change: models in prehistory*, C. Renfrew (ed.), 391–417. London: Duckworth.

Harris, D. R. 1984. Ethnohistorical evidence for the exploitation of wild grasses and forbs: its scope and archaeological implications. In *Plants and ancient man: studies in palaeoethnobotany*, W. van Zeist & W. A. Casparie (eds), 63–9. Rotterdam: Balkema.

Hather, J. G. 1988. *The morphological and anatomical interpretation and identification of charred vegetative parenchymatous plant remains*. Unpublished Ph.D. dissertation, Department of Human Environment, Institute of Archaeology, University College London, University of London.

Helbaek, H. 1960. The palaeoethnobotany of the Near East and Europe. In *Prehistoric investigations in Iraqi Kurdistan*, R. J. Braidwood & B. Howe (eds), 99–118. Chicago: Chicago University Press Studies in Ancient Oriental Civilization 31.

Higgs, E. S. (ed.) 1972. *Papers in economic prehistory*. Cambridge: Cambridge University Press.

Higgs, E. S. & M. R. Jarman 1969. The origins of agriculture: a reconsideration. *Antiquity* **43**, 31–41.

Hill, H. E. & J. Evans. 1989. Crops of the Pacific: new evidence from chemical analysis of organic residues in pottery. In *Foraging and farming: the evolution of plant exploitation*, D. R. Harris & G. C. Hillman (eds), ch. 26, London: Unwin Hyman.

Hillman, G. C. 1975. The plant remains from Tell Abu Hureyra: a preliminary report. In A. M. T. Moore The excavation of Tell Abu Hureyra in Syria: a preliminary report. *Proceedings of the Prehistoric Society* **41**, 70–3.

Hillman, G. C. 1989. Late Palaeolithic plant foods from Wadi Kubbaniya, Upper Egypt: dietary diversity, infant weaning, and seasonality in a riverine environment. In *Foraging and farming: the evolution of plant exploitation*, D. R. Harris & G. C. Hillman (eds), ch. 13 London: Unwin Hyman.

Hillman, G. C., S. M. Colledge & D. R. Harris. 1989. Plant-food economy during the Epipalaeolithic period at Tell Abu Hureyra, Syria: dietary diversity, seasonality, and modes of exploitation. In *Foraging and farming: the evolution of plant exploitation*, D. R. Harris & G. C. Hillman (eds), ch. 14. London: Unwin Hyman.

Hynes, R. A. & A. K. Chase 1982. Plants, sites and domiculture: Aboriginal influence upon plant communities in Cape York Peninsula. *Archaeology in Oceania* **17**, 38–50.

Jarman, M. R., G. N. Bailey & H. N. Jarman 1982. *Early European agriculture: its foundations and development*. Cambridge: Cambridge University Press.

Jones, R. & B. Meehan. 1989. Plant foods of the Gidjingali: ethnographic and archaeological perspectives from northern Australia on tuber and seed exploitation. In *Foraging and farming: the evolution of plant exploitation*, D. R. Harris & G. C. Hillman (eds), ch. 7. London: Unwin Hyman.

Kimber, C. T. 1966. Dooryard gardens of Martinique. *Yearbook of the Association of Pacific Coast Geographers* **28**, 97–118.

Kimber, C. T. 1973. Spatial patterning in the dooryard gardens of Puerto Rico. *Geographical Review* **63**, 6–26.

Kimber, C. T. 1978. A folk content for plant domestication: or the dooryard garden revisited. *Anthropological Journal of Canada* **16**, 2–11.

Lourandos, H. 1983. Intensification: a late Pleistocene–Holocene archaeological sequence from southwestern Victoria. *Archaeology in Oceania* **18**, 81–94.

Oates, D. & J. Oates 1976. Early irrigation agriculture in Mesopotamia. In *Problems in economic and social archaeology*, G. de G. Sieveking, I. H. Longworth & K. E. Wilson (eds), 109–35. London: Duckworth.

Pearsall, D. M. 1989. Adaptation of prehistoric hunter–gatherers to the high Andes: the changing role of plant resources. In *Foraging and farming: the evolution of plant exploitation*, D. R. Harris & G. C. Hillman (eds), ch. 19. London: Unwin Hyman.

Piperno, D. R. 1989. Non-affluent foragers: resource availability, seasonal shortages, and the emergence of agriculture in Panamanian tropical forests. In *Foraging and farming: the evolution of plant exploitation*, D. R. Harris & G. C. Hillman (eds), ch. 34. London: Unwin Hyman.

Pyramarn, K. 1989. New evidence on plant exploitation and environment during the Hoabinhian (Late Stone Age) from Ban Kao Caves, Thailand. In *Foraging and farming: the evolution of plant exploitation*, D. R. Harris & G. C. Hillman (eds), ch. 16. London: Unwin Hyman.

Rindos, D. 1980. Symbiosis, instability, and the origins and spread of agriculture: a new model. *Current Anthropology* **21**, 751–72.

Rindos, D. 1984. *The origins of agriculture: an evolutionary perspective*. New York: Academic Press.

Rousseau, J.-J. 1755 (1964). *Discours sur l'origine et les fondements de l'inégalité parmi les hommes*. Amsterdam: Michel Rey. (English translation (1964) by R. D. & J. R. Masters. In *Jean-Jacques Rousseau. The first and second discourses*, R. D. Masters (ed.). New York: St Martin's Press.)

Sahlins, M. D. & E. R. Service (eds) 1960. *Evolution and culture*. Ann Arbor: University of Michigan Press.

Shipek, F. C. 1989. An example of intensive plant husbandry: the Kumeyaay of southern California. In *Foraging and farming: the evolution of plant exploitation*, D. R. Harris & G. C. Hillman (eds), ch. 10. London: Unwin Hyman.

Smith, M. A. 1989. Seed gathering in inland Australia: current evidence on the antiquity of the ethnohistorical pattern of exploitation. In *Foraging and farming: the evolution of plant exploitation*, D. R. Harris & G. C. Hillman (eds), ch. 18. London: Unwin Hyman.

Unger-Hamilton, R. Epipalaeolithic Palestine and the beginnings of plant cultivation – the evidence from harvesting experiments and microwear studies. *Current Anthropology*, in press.

Yen, D. E. 1989. The domestication of environment. In *Foraging and farming: the evolution of plant exploitation*, D. R. Harris & G. C. Hillman (eds), ch. 4. London: Unwin Hyman.

Zeuner, F. E. 1963. *A history of domesticated animals*. London: Hutchinson.

# 2 *Darwinism and its role in the explanation of domestication*

DAVID RINDOS

**Dedicated to the memory of
Michael E. Whalen**

'he was a scholar, and a ripe and good one'

Henry VIII

## Introduction

Anthropology has long been pre-eminently a discipline unto itself. It has separated itself from its sister social sciences by acceptance of the rather sublime observation that humans are, at least in some sense, animals, mammals, and primates. Divorce from the biological sciences has been uncontested and amicable. Anthropology has been able to provide the grounds for the divorce by providing expert testimony on how humans are totally unlike the rest of creation. And, in providing itself with the justification of its own existence, it has provided the rest of biology with defences for continued belief in the fundamental difference between our own species and the rest of the animal kingdom. In a rather rare instance of interdisciplinary co-operation, anthropology has been able to provide biology with all the reasons necessary to maintain an unquestioned and unquestioning acceptance of the incommensurability of one species with all others. One might expect a critical mind to note the self-serving nature of the argument and question it on those grounds if no other.

The fundamental and underlying rationale for compartmentalizing the study of human behaviour in a separate discipline may best be understood by appreciating the role given to a specific type of 'cultural' process in the explanation of human behaviour. Humans, it is held, are cultural animals. Human culture, however, is seen as the means by which humans *consciously and intentionally* adapt to a multitude of environments. Here, intentional adaptation effectively removes humankind from the materialistic and mechanistic processes that govern other natural processes. My purpose in this chapter is to attack this central belief. In it I defend the idea that cultural processes are natural; that cultural change is best understood by means of a natural process. Darwinian evolution provides the theoretical backdrop for the approach that I advance, in place of intentional cultural adaptation and adjustment; change in subsistence patterning provides the context for the discussion.

My intent here is to shed some light on a central problem in human cultural change – the evolution of agricultural systems – by looking at human culture and cultural change in a different way. I do not criticize in this chapter earlier models for cultural evolution, whether in general or specifically in terms of agricultural origins (see Rindos 1984, 1985, 1986). Instead, I focus upon agricultural change using a specific Darwinian model – the 'cultural-selectionist' view of culture.

Cultural selectionism is based upon three interrelated postulates.

(a)   The human capacity for culture (and the innate morphologies and psychological processes thereby implied) has evolved by means of natural selection. Humans are not cultural because they choose to be cultural; instead the capacity for culture may only be explained in terms of the enhanced fitness that it induced in those hominids who had a greater capacity for cultural behaviours.

(b)   The same processes which originally brought about the genetic capacity for culture in humans, continued, and indeed continues, to act upon the specifics of cultural acts, beliefs, and structures. Here, natural selection is the ordering force in non-genetically transmitted cultural phenomena. It is important to note that cultural selectionism, in contradistinction to sociobiology, holds that, while human culture taken as a whole is genetically permitted, *none* of the differences existing between human cultures may be explained on the basis of genetic differences between members of those cultures. Instead, these differ-ences arise as the result of differing selective pressures experienced by various human cultures during their history.

(c)   In contrast to the 'evolutionism' of Spencer, White, and Sahlins & Service, cultural selectionism posits a strictly Darwinian model for cultural function and change. Here the most significant statement of cultural selectionism is that no inherent direction underlies cultural evolution and that, instead, all change is the result of selection acting upon the undirected variant cultural forms existing at earlier points in time.

## The Darwinian perspective on plant domestication and agricultural evolution

Darwinists hold that evolutionary change results from the natural selection of heritable variation. Ernst Mayr has repeatedly pointed out (e.g. 1942, 1969, 1982, pp. 519–20) that Darwinian evolutionary change is based upon a two-step process: (1) the production of undirected variation, and (2) its sorting by means of the differential success and failure of various forms over time. In this, Darwinism, unlike any other evolutionary theory, places major emphasis upon the *undirected nature of the processes generating variation* in heritable traits. Yet, in saying this, it is essential to stress that the Darwinian concept of undirected variation does not hold to the absurd claim that variation is generated 'randomly' in the mathematical sense of that term, i.e. that the process is totally stochastic and unbounded. Clearly, no human will exhibit variation in wing structure or photosynthetic pathways. Instead, variation at any moment in time will always be bounded in very important ways by the nature of the organism itself, i.e. by its evolved history.

An example stressing the historicity of Darwinism may be seen in the process underlying the earliest beginnings of plant domestication. As I have pointed out (1984), a simple relationship exists between humans and the plants on which they feed. Over long periods of time, human feeding behaviour will alter the local flora in such a manner as to place certain morphological traits of members of a plant species at a competitive advantage over others. This competitive advantage arises in terms of how effective a particular morphology is in attracting human consumers as dispersal agents for the plant. The further evolution of the plant species, therefore, will be altered by the feeding and dispersal behaviour of humans (cf. Chase Ch. 3, Harris Ch. 1, this volume). Yet this evolution, in any specific case, takes place in the context of two interdependent historical processes – that of the plant genome, including mutation and recombination, and that of the learned subsistence behaviour of the humans. A subsistence pattern that lacks a particular behaviour, for example the processing of tubers for starch, will place limits upon the development of specific domestication events quite as effectively as the non-appearance of an 'appropriate' genetic event within the plant. Hence, we must recognize that speaking of the general evolutionary pressures within the development of agricultural systems may only sensitize us to the types of symbioses that might have occurred; it cannot replace the careful study of the particulars that have occurred in any specific system (as exemplified by many contributions to this volume, e.g. by Chikwendu & Okezie, Johns, Ladizinsky, Pearsall, and Zohary).

The possible direction of evolution will also be affected by the peculiarities of the specific transmission system that codes for variation. The nature of the coding system is of major importance when we discuss any evolutionary process. For example, the effects of recombination during evolutionary change must be explained with a sensitivity to the fact that different organisms may have radically different types of recombination options open to them. Prokaryotes (bacteria and their allies) may exchange variable amounts of genetic information during 'mating', while eukaryotes ('higher' organisms) are generally forced by the existence of true sexuality and meiosis to contribute equal amounts of information to individuals of the next generation. In the same manner, information that is coded and transmitted genetically will have different evolutionary potentialities and limitations than information affecting the organism's behaviour that is transmitted directly from one phenotype to another (i.e. 'culturally' in the broadest sense of that term). Hence, we may see that while variation does not exist independently of organisms, organisms do not exist independently of their evolutionary history. This is true both in terms of the types of traits that may vary and also in terms of the inheritance systems that transmit traits, and their variant forms, between organisms over time. Yet, when we wish to explain changes in traits existing in biological entities, an understanding of the evolved peculiarities of organisms is literally the object of our inquiry. Therefore, we will expect that our understanding of evolution must be informed by the peculiarities of the specific inheritance systems of the organisms we are studying.

In this context, the properties of the cultural transmission system that governs variable human behaviours must be taken into account when we seek to understand the origin and evolution of cultural traits. Here, much useful work has already been done by Cavalli-Sforza & Feldman (1981) and Boyd & Richerson (1985). Cultural change may profitably be analogized with genetic evolution (Campbell 1965, 1976). For example, innovations appear in populations, and spread if favoured or are abandoned if not, by processes showing striking similarities to natural selection and random drift. Nevertheless, we must recognize that these sorts of general descriptions are only a heuristic model and that the explanation of specific cultural changes must take into account the specifics of the system being considered. Secondly, and of greater importance, we must stress that transmission processes should not be confused with evolutionary ones. Transmission mechanisms may indeed place biases upon the possible direction of evolution (Boyd & Richerson 1985), but the changes that *have* occurred in cultural evolution 'are hardly made intelligible by the transmission modes, but rather by examining the interaction between demography, environment, technology, and organizational variables' (Marks *et al.* 1983, p. 15).

## Plant domestication and prehistoric agriculture in the American Bottom

For an example of this type of interactive analysis, we may consider work that has been done on domestication and the origins and further development of agricultural systems in an area of the central United States known as the American Bottom (Rindos & Johannessen 1988 and cf. Watson Ch. 35, this volume). Following a long period of 'incidental domestication' (Rindos 1984, pp. 154–8) of several species of nut-bearing trees, a complex of starchy and oily seeded native plants began to grow in importance in this region during the Middle Woodland period (c. 150 BC–AD 300). The contribution of this complex of seed plants to the diet increased, in both absolute and relative terms, until the latest phases of the Mississippian period (AD 1000–1500). At about AD 800, maize begins to appear in the archaeobotanical record from the region, with the evidence indicating a widespread and remarkably abrupt adoption of this imported plant. Yet, the fact that the starchy seed complex remains abundant in the record, despite the introduction of maize, indicates that this new crop was not grown *instead of* the existing plant complex, but *in addition to* plants that had been part of an evolved agricultural system with humans for as much as 1000 years. Furthermore, the speed at which maize appears in the record is remarkable. Seeds and cobs, often in very substantial quantities, have been recovered from 50 per cent to 90 per cent of the features analysed at sites of the Emergent Mississippian period (AD 800–1000). In the sites dated to the immediately previous phase, maize is virtually unknown, having been recovered in minute quantities from only 2 per cent of the features analysed. The data clearly indicate that the appearance of maize in the record marks the introduction of a new crop rather than the appearance of agriculture itself.

The most parsimonious explanation for the rapid rise of maize in importance in the area holds that while maize had been present for a very long time in the region, it was represented by soft-seeded varieties that were grown for their immature cobs. The Mississippian maize horizon represents not the introduction of the species itself into the area, but rather the appearance of a new variety having hard seeds that were used in the mature form. In the context of this discussion, it is important to note that the diffusion of this new, hard-seeded variety of maize into the region could not have been successful unless humans were already practising the necessary agricultural behaviours. Hence, the spread of the new crop was not in any sense a 'random' event based upon any inherent qualities of the maize plant, but was preconditioned by the existence of an already functioning indigenous agricultural system.

As has been stressed, the Darwinian view of cultural change does not claim that the variant forms upon which selection was to act over time had to be generated in a totally 'random' manner. We need not claim that specific human characteristics such as decision-making, experimentation, or cultural bias must be excluded from consideration in understanding the genesis of the original variant behaviours that were to form the foundations for the evolution of new cultural traits. We need only claim that these processes *in and of themselves* were insufficient to generate the evolved systems.

Adopting a Darwinian perspective involves a reorientation of our thought processes. Rather than concentrating upon the *origin* of the particular variant trait that was to form the basis for future developments, we stress the *effect* the possession of this trait, in its incipient form, was to have upon humans and their cultures. Here our attention is directed to the fact that all cultural behaviours have some influence, no matter how small, upon human survival and reproductive success. This will be true even if changes in these behaviours are completely independent of any change in gene frequencies in the populations under consideration. Put in other terms, cultural behaviours may affect human demography. Hence, the concept of 'pure' or 'demographic' Darwinian fitness is wholly applicable to the effects of cultural traits upon human populations.

Let us return to the introduction of maize into the American Bottom. We have already noted that it was introduced into a cultural and agricultural system that had been in operation for at least a millennium. Nevertheless, following its adoption, major changes may be seen in the archaeological record. These include increases in population, nucleation, social complexity, and centralization. We have argued (Rindos & Johannessen 1988) that some of these changes were precipitated by the introduction of the storable form of maize which, by means of its higher yield potential, permitted increases in populations in the region. Of greater importance, however, is the possibility that the qualities of the varieties of maize that came into use may have had major effects upon the reliability and predictability of the agricultural system itself, and hence upon the social structuring of the region.

As population increased as a function of the higher average yield obtainable from maize, so did the need for farm land. Increased farm land could be obtained only by clearing the native forests. Our evidence indicates that this occurred, at least in part, by clearance of the incidentally domesticated 'nut groves' that had arisen over many centuries in regions of human habitation. A major change occurs in the charcoal record when maize appears as a major component of the diet. Before the introduction of maize, most firewood was from soft-wooded genera such as *Populus* (poplars) and *Salix* (willows). The burning of hard-wooded genera such as *Carya* (hickory) and *Juglans* (walnut) appears to become common only after maize becomes abundant, with charcoal from these species appearing for the first time in the archaeological record in large quantities.

We should note that, all other things being equal, the hard woods make a better source of fuel for both cooking and heating than do the soft woods. Yet despite this, soft-wooded genera were utilized preferentially throughout the pre-maize periods. We assume that the nut trees were originally valued more for their mast crops than as a superior source of firewood. We might also note that culinary change involving a new need to cook the maize as a gruel cannot be invoked to explain this change in patterns of wood utilization. Braun (1983) has tied changes in ceramic technology during pre-maize periods to the demands placed upon the vessels in response to the increasing use of cooked starchy and oily seeds in the diet. Hence, we cannot explain the change in wood utilization as a response to new cooking requirements. We might also note, in passing, that acceptance and integration of the new variety of maize into the diet might also have been facilitated by a pre-existing procedure for the preparation of the dried, starchy seeds.

It follows that the most logical explanation for the change in charcoal would be population pressure. The growing need for land on which to grow maize to support a burgeoning population probably brought about the destruction of what had previously been an important dietary resource – the mast crops harvested from nut trees. We should not lose sight of the fact that this destruction of resources probably represents the loss of a valuable oil and protein supplement in a region that lacked both domesticated animals (save the dog which was little consumed) and domesticated sources of plant and animal fats.

Much data indicates that while maize is higher yielding in the region than the native complex of starchy seed crops, this increased yield is probably accompanied by a radical increase in the variability of that yield, i.e. even though average yield obtainable from maize cultivation increases dramatically, the year-to-year variance on yield increases even more. It must be stressed that any change in absolute yield is 'progress' only at the moment of its first occurrence; over relatively short periods of time increases in yield will literally be eaten up by the increased populations they generate. Yet, as population increases, the negative effects of increased variability on yield become increasingly severe: one cannot consume during times of scarcity the no longer existing surplus that had been generated during times of abundance.

The most obvious way to deal with the interacting factors of increasing population, increasing potential yield, and increased variance in that yield would be an attempt to buffer the system by increased association and trade within and between regions. Then, if a crop is bad in one locality, maize could be imported from other localities during the crisis period. This is a type of activity that requires no foresight, merely a response to a specific condition of immediate reduced food availability. Furthermore, over time such arrangements could grow and have consequences that were totally unforseeable at the moment that the exchange systems were initially established. Thus, the increased centralization and integration characteristic of Mississippian culture may be traced to attempts to deal with the new variability in yield characteristic of a maize-based agricultural system.

## The evolution of agricultural systems

There is no doubt that agriculture, and changes in agricultural systems, may have major effects upon local demography and these, in turn, may affect social systems in radical ways. However, it is significant that differential fitness, the 'currency' of evolutionary change, requires that more than one state may be observed in the population of concern. If all individuals have exactly the same set of traits, evolutionary change is, by definition, impossible, because no differential fitness associated with specific traits can exist when only one set of traits exists. Cultural processes may be of major importance in determining which traits are acceptable to members of a culture. Therefore, a Darwinian view of cultural evolution does not restrict itself solely to the demographic aspects of cultural behaviours, but must also look inside the system and consider the impact of variable, culturally defined behaviours upon the further evolution of the system. I have dealt elsewhere with this distinction between the 'demographic' and 'symbolic' aspects of cultural-transmission systems under the rubric of cultural selection of the first and second types ($CS_1$ and $CS_2$: Rindos 1985).

Redirection of our thoughts to a Darwinian perspective requires a reinterpretation of most of our preconceptions regarding cultural practices and beliefs. We have generally seen the meaning of human innovations solely in terms of their *causal* role in cultural evolution. I claim that these innovations are better viewed as events that *facilitate* evolution. The distinction is of major importance. And again, I will draw upon a genetic analogy. Provine (1983) has recently reviewed some aspects of the development of Sewall Wright's genetic theorizing, and he provides a useful account of the changing interpretations given to Wright's theory of genetic drift. He notes that when Wright first proposed genetic drift in the late 1920s and early 1930s it was widely adopted to explain what appeared to be 'adaptively neutral' differences between species. However, with the development of the 'New Synthesis' in the 1940s and 1950s, it was discovered that many of these traits, in fact, were of adaptive significance. Given this change in intellectual atmosphere, Provine notes that Wright

> could now emphasize the view his shifting balance theory had incorporated from the very beginning – that random drift served the important function of providing novel genetic interaction systems upon which natural selection could act to yield more rapid progress of adaptive evolution than could occur under mass selection alone (Provine 1983, p. 65).

Hence, the significance of random genetic drift is not that it *causes* evolution, but that it *facilitates* evolution. Likewise, cultural processes such as innovation or discovery are processes that *permit*, but do not directly cause, cultural change. In the case under consideration here, the true reason for cultural change may be detected only in the social and demographic consequences of agriculturally induced changes in environment and behaviour.

As should be apparent with a little reflection, the manifold variations produced in any cultural setting can explain nothing in and of themselves. If we were to claim that a given change in subsistence patterning resulted solely from a change in a cultural pattern, we have, in fact, explained nothing. We have merely recast the problem in new terms. Instead of wondering why the subsistence pattern changed we must now query why the culture changed. We cannot use the evolved capacity of humans within a cultural setting to respond to the environment as explanation for the specific cultural changes that have occurred within a given historical setting. To explain the specific we cannot merely invoke the general; instead, we should seek insights by investigating directly the system itself that is of interest.

Consider another example from the American Bottom. As already noted, it is likely that the 'introduction' of maize around AD 800 into the region actually marked the appearance of new varieties of flinty, early maturing maize which were stored as dry grain. Previously, it is likely that maize was grown for its immature ears which were stored in a processed form. Here, culinary and storage techniques and traditions interacted to affect the growth potential of the agricultural system. If a crop is stored in a processed form, the seed needed to plant the next year's crop must be estimated and left unharvested until it is mature. In a year with a particularly good crop, much food could be preserved and this could serve as a buffer against unpredictable reductions in other resources. Of course, the same can be done if the crop is stored as a dry grain. However, the potential growth rates of these two systems would not be the same.

Consider years of abundance: the stored crop is not consumed in its totality. If the stored crop were in a processed form, some might even end up going to waste. But if the stored crop were a dry grain, an alternative exists – planting of some of the left-over grain, increasing the area under cultivation by a slight amount. In this manner, potential mean productivity could rise as the result of a succession of favourable years. Storage of a crop in its reproductive form may increase the potential rate of growth of the system. However, this same identity of 'food' and 'seed' would have negative effects during bad seasons. Under conditions of moderate stress, some of the seed grain for the next season's planting could be consumed. Here, the farmer is willing to take a gamble that next year's crop will be sufficiently good that it is worth risking consuming some portion of the seed in the face of present needs. Of course, this is a risky tactic, in that it reduces the long-term stability of the system. And it is important to note that such a reduction in stability is far less likely to occur when the crop is stored in a processed form: a cultural and culinary marker sets the processed, 'edible' food apart from the 'seed'. In the most extreme form, the edible part of the plant is totally differentiated from the reproductive part both culturally and biologically (for example, manioc and many other tropical tubers). Here the much discussed stability of tropical systems of root-crop cultivation (cf. Hawkes Ch. 31, this volume) may be seen, in part, as a function of cultural classification systems concerning what is edible.

## Fitness and relative, limited adaptation

The distinction between culture seen as explanation and culture seen as the result of natural, evolutionary processes is neither trivial nor purely defi-nitional. Instead, adopting the Darwinian perspective completely changes the manner in which we approach the historical, ethnographic, and archaeo-logical records. It is not an easy point of view to adopt. Much of the aversion to treating cultural processes as natural arises from a cultural bias (Rindos 1985), and is largely centred upon the issue of the potency of human intentionality in explaining cultural change (Rindos 1984). Translated into evolutionary terms, the common-sense view of cultural change holds that *the variations are generated as specific responses to adaptive needs* – i.e. *that the variations arising in cultural systems are directional, and therefore the variations themselves, not selection, order evolutionary processes in human culture.*

This observation is of great importance for the understanding of cultural processes, in that it completely eliminates any need to presume an adaptive function for all cultural traits. Traits, of course, may be adaptive but this is a result of the fact that they gave a relative advantage to the individuals with these traits. Here we analyse cultural traits in exactly the same terms used for the evolution of adaptations within any species. But we must also be willing to go beyond this analysis. Cultural traits may spread not because they are adapative to some need but because they indirectly increase the relative fertility (fitness in the pure Darwinian sense) of individuals within a cultural setting. If, for example, religious affiliation is strongly transmitted from one generation to the next, then we can expect that over time (and all other things being equal) the proportion of individuals within any group belonging to 'procreative' religions such as Islam, Roman Catholicism, Orthodox Judaism, and Mormonism will rise. It is absurd to call any such change in the proportions of individuals belonging to these sects a result of an 'adaptation' by its members to any environmental 'need' or, put in other terms, that a positive correlation between relative fitness and environmental adaptation must always exist.

In a previous discussion of the spread of agricultural systems (Rindos 1984), I maintained that fitness and 'adaptiveness' may even show a negative correlation. The relative fitness induced in a culture by means of its agricultural behaviour is seen as being simply the result of a higher realized rate of population growth – agricultural behaviours increase the carrying capacity of the local environment for humans and, hence, the proportion of individuals per unit area who will have agricultural modes of subsistence will inevitably be larger than the proportion of individuals with most other subsistence strategies. It is important to realize that this will hold true even if agricultural behaviours bring with them a decrease in robustness, a decline in life expectancy, an increase in morbidity and mortality, or a higher infant mortality rate (accompanied, of course, by an even higher fertility rate). While all of these factors may easily be judged as indicators of decreased adaptation, the higher growth rate of agriculture will nevertheless favour it over other forms of human subsistence.

A very striking example of how fitness and adaptiveness may become decoupled may be seen by considering the relative fitness of competing agricultural traditions. Begin with the assumption that agricultural behaviours bring with them a decrease in overall 'adaptiveness' of human populations (as measured by the types of parameters mentioned above). Consider two competing agricultural populations, one of which has a more adaptive agricultural tradition than the other, measured in terms of variables such as stability in average yield. It is easily demonstrated (Rindos 1984, pp. 254–85), that, on the average, decreased stability in productivity will increase the probability that a given agricultural tradition will spread. Here, instability in agricultural production serves as a driving force in spreading a particular agricultural tradition by literally driving out individuals to colonize new regions. Occasional episodes of lowered productivity, induced not by the environment but rather by the plants and techniques of the agricultural system itself, will cause the spread of that tradition to occur at a rate greater than that of other, more adaptive and stable, agricultural traditions. Hence, not only is agriculture more fit while being less adaptive, but a positive selection for instability in production will tend to increase the maladaptiveness of agricultural systems over time.

A recent volume, edited by Cohen & Armelagos (1984), presents abundant evidence which indicates that the archaeological record is largely in accord with predictions that may be drawn from the co-evolutionary model for the origins and spread of agriculture. Under the co-evolutionary model, it would be predicted that major population stress would originate with highly developed agricultural systems (the phase of 'agricultural domestication' described in Rindos 1984, pp. 164–72 and his discussion of population pressure (ibid., pp. 205–17). It would be further intensified as agricultural systems developed and spread by means of the positive selection for optimally unstable systems during diffusion episodes.

These predictions stand in stark contrast to those of the two other contemporary schools modelling the origins of agriculture. The first school represents the mainstream of anthropological and archaeological theory. Despite great differences in approach by specific authors, it is unified by an adaptationistic, cultural-ecological perspective. An equilibrium-based analysis of cultural function and change is one of the major assumptions underlying work done by members of this school. I include here such authors as Flannery (1965, 1968, 1973), Binford (1968), Harris (1969, 1972, 1977), Bray (1976, 1977), Reed (1977), and Wright (1977). As Roosevelt (1984, p. 569) points out, an equilibrium-centred view of cultural change has clear implications in terms of stress on humans that might be found in the archaeological record: 'the equilibrium theory predicts that physiological stress should occur only rarely and that cultural adaptation should increasingly buffer people from stress'. Under this mode, the transition to sedentism would be expected to be accompanied by a 'decrease in mortality'. Cultural ecology, with its emphasis upon adaptation and homeostasis, sees cultural change as motivated by human adaptation; *increased adaptiveness* should therefore result from realized cultural changes.

The other contemporary school of thought concerning agricultural origins applies a population–pressure model. This is best exemplified in the work of Cohen (1977), although others such as Smith (1972), Spooner (1972), Grigg (1976), and Abernathy (1979) have advanced similar views. The theory (which I will not criticize here on theoretical grounds) holds that cultural change is the result of human adaptations to their own increasing numbers. Population pressures generated by the slow increase of human populations forces new adaptations to be adopted if humans are simply to 'stay in the same place'; cultural change is the result of the need to *maintain adaptiveness*. Here the predictions for the archaeological record would be 'that physiological stress should be recurrent and persistent, with particularly severe stress possibly occurring during incipient agriculture' (Roosevelt 1984, p. 569).

In Roosevelt's review (1984) of the archaeological indicators of skeletal stress, she was able to make the following generalizations:

Although there is a relative lack of evidence for the Paleolithic stage, enough skeletons have been studied that it seems clear that seasonal and periodic stress regularly affected most prehistoric hunting–gathering populations . . . What also seems clear is that severe and chronic stress . . . is not characteristic of these populations. There is no evidence of frequent, severe malnutrition, so the diet must have been adequate . . .

Stress, however, does not seem to have become common and widespread until after the development of high degrees of sedentism, population density and reliance on intensive agriculture. At this stage in all regions the incidence of physiological stress increases greatly, and average mortality rates increase appreciably . . . Stature in many populations appears to have been considerably lower than would be expected if genetically-determined height maxima had been reached, which suggests that the growth arrests documented by pathologies were causing stunting . . .

It seems that a large proportion of most sedentary populations under intensive agriculture underwent chronic and life-threatening malnutrition and disease, especially during infancy and childhood. The causes of the nutritional stress are likely to have been the poverty of the staple crops in most nutrients except calories, periodic famines caused by the instability of the agricultural system, and chronic lack of food due to both population growth and economic expropriation by elites (Roosevelt 1984, pp. 572–73).

As Roosevelt notes in summary, '[t]he origin of agriculture, then, cannot accurately be attributed to the existence of unusually high levels of [population] pressure at the time.' Furthermore, the increased stress occurring with the appearance of developed agricultural systems contradicts the expectations of the cultural ecologists, whereas the general pattern and the specific timing of the appearance of indicators of greatly heightened stress is completely congruent with the predictions of the co-evolutionary model.

## Natural selection and cultural change

The issue of *undirected* variation is critical to the development of a scientific understanding of human cultural evolution. Viewing variation as undirected brings about a change in the way in which we set about attempting to explain cultural evolution. Here, the spread of behaviour throughout a society, or the spread of a particular type of behaviour (rather than another) throughout the species, is the result of the fitness induced by that behaviour (and, again, I am using 'fitness' in a broad sense that includes both demographic and symbolic aspects and goes beyond simple genetic contribution to future generations). Rather than seeing change as a consequence of the adoption of a particular form of behaviour, emphasis is placed upon the historical *con-sequences* of a particular variant form of behaviour for the humans exhibiting that behaviour.

The critical issue in this context is whether natural selection is the process responsible for the changes that have occurred over time in human subsistence patterns. The centrality of natural selection in Darwinism arises from its ability to bring about evolution. From the Darwinian perspective, undirected variation is important for its role in fuelling the engine of evolutionary change by generating new forms which may then be subject to selection. Indeed, we may claim confidently that without a true concept of undirected variation, natural selection is not only unnecessary but is actually impossible. Natural selection, within Darwinian theory, is the only directional force in evolution. If variation is less than undirected, then natural selection cannot be seen as a *creative* force in evolution and must perforce maintain its simple, pre-Darwinian role of removing those variant forms that accidentally deviate from the true type of the species (see discussion in Rindos 1984). Only if we see variation as being produced randomly with respect to selective pressures, may we claim that the directionality that may be observed in evolution over time is the result of natural selection.

# References

Abernathy, V. 1979. *Population pressure and cultural adjustment*. New York: Human Science Press.

Binford, L. R. 1968. Post-Pleistocene adaptations. In *New perspectives in archeology*, S. R. Binford & L. R. Binford (eds), 313–41. Chicago: Aldine.

Boyd, R. & J. Richerson 1985. *Culture and the evolutionary process*. Chicago: University of Chicago Press.

Braun, D. 1983. Pots as tools. In *Archaeological hammers and theories*, J. A. Moore & A. S. Keene (eds), 107–34. New York: Academic Press.

Bray, W. 1976. From predation to production: the nature of agricultural evolution in Mexico and Peru. In *Problems in economic and social archaeology*, G. de G. Seveking, T. H. Longworth & K. E. Wilson (eds), 73–95. London: Duckworth.

Bray, W. 1977. From foraging to farming in early Mexico. In *Hunters, gatherers and first farmers beyond Europe*, J. V. S. Megaw (ed.), 225–50. Leicester: Leicester University Press.

Campbell, D. T. 1965. Variation and selective retention in sociocultural evolution. In *Social change in underdeveloped areas: a reinterpretation of evolutionary theory*, R. W. Mack, G. Blanksten & H. R. Barringer (eds), 19–48. Cambridge: Schenkman.

Campbell, D. T. 1976. Comment on Richards' 'natural selection model for conceptual evolution'. *Philosophy of Science* **44**, 502–7.

Cavalli-Sforza, L. L. & M. W. Feldman 1981. *Cultural transmission and evolution: a quantitative approach*. Princeton NJ: Princeton University Press.

Chase, A. K. 1989. Domestication and domiculture in northern Australia: a social perspective. In *Foraging and farming: the evolution of plant exploitation*, D. R. Harris & G. C. Hillman (eds), ch. 3. London: Unwin Hyman.

Chikwendu, V. E. & C. E. A. Okezie. 1989. Factors responsible for the ennoblement of the African yams: inferences from experiments in yam domestication.

In *Foraging and farming: the evolution of plant exploitation*, D. R. Harris & G. C. Hillman (eds), ch. 21. London: Unwin Hyman.

Cohen, M. N. 1977. *The food crisis in prehistory: overpopulation and the origins of agriculture*. New Haven: Yale University Press.

Cohen, M. N. & G. J. Armelagos (eds) 1984. *Paleopathology at the origins of agriculture*. Orlando: Academic Press.

Flannery, K. V. 1965. The ecology of early food production in Mesopotamia. *Science* **147**, 1247–56.

Flannery, K. V. 1968. Archeological systems theory and early Mesoamerica. In *Anthropological archeology in the Americas*, B. J. Meggers (ed.), 67–87. Washington DC: Anthropological Society of Washington.

Flannery, K. V. 1973. The origins of agriculture. *Annual Review of Anthropology* **2**, 271–310.

Grigg, D. B. 1976. Population pressure and agricultural change. *Progressive Geography* **8**, 135–76.

Harris, D. R. 1969. Agricultural systems, ecosystems and the origins of agriculture. In *The domestication and exploitation of plants and animals*, P. J. Ucko & G. W. Dimbleby (eds), 3–15. London: Duckworth.

Harris, D. R. 1972. The origins of agriculture in the tropics. *American Scientist* **60**, 180–93.

Harris, D. R. 1977. Alternative pathways toward agriculture. In *Origins of agriculture*, C. A. Reed (ed.), 179–243. The Hague: Mouton.

Harris, D. R. 1989. An evolutionary continuum of people–plant interaction. In *Foraging and farming: the evolution of plant exploitation*, D. R. Harris & G. C. Hillman (eds), ch. 1. London: Unwin Hyman.

Hawkes, J. G. 1989. The domestication of roots and tubers in the American tropics. In *Foraging and farming: the evolution of plant exploitation*, D. R. Harris & G. C. Hillman (eds), ch. 31. London: Unwin Hyman.

Johns, T. 1989. A chemical-ecological model of root and tuber domestication in the Andes. In *Foraging and farming: the evolution of plant exploitation*, D. R. Harris & G. C. Hillman (eds), ch. 32. London: Unwin Hyman.

Ladizinsky, G. 1989. Origin and domestication of the Southwest Asian grain legumes. In *Foraging and farming: the evolution of plant exploitation*, D. R. Harris & G. C. Hillman (eds), ch. 23. London: Unwin Hyman.

Marks, J., E. Staski & M. B. Schiffer 1983. Cultural evolution: a return to the basics. *Nature* **302**, 15–16.

Mayr, E. 1942. *Systematics and the origin of species*. New York: Columbia University Press.

Mayr, E. 1969. *Principles of systematic zoology*. New York: McGraw-Hill.

Mayr, E. 1982. *The growth of biological thought*. Cambridge, Mass.: Harvard University Press.

Pearsall, D. M. 1989. Adaptation of prehistoric hunter–gatherers to the high Andes: the changing role of plant resources. In *Foraging and farming: the evolution of plant exploitation*, D. R. Harris & G. C. Hillman (eds), ch. 19. London: Unwin Hyman.

Piperno, D. R. 1989. Non-affluent foragers: resource availability, seasonal shortages, and the emergence of agriculture in Panamanian tropical forests. In *Foraging and farming: the evolution of plant exploitation*, D. R. Harris & G. C. Hillman (eds), ch. 34. London: Unwin Hyman.

Provine, W. 1983. The development of Wright's theory of evolution: systematics, adaptation and drift. In *Dimensions of Darwinism: themes and counterthemes in twentieth-century evolutionary theory*, M. Grene (ed.), 43–70. Cambridge: Cambridge University Press.

Reed, C. A. 1977. Origins of agriculture: discussion and some conclusions. In *Origins of agriculture*, C. A. Reed (ed.), 879–953. The Hague: Mouton.

Rindos, D. 1984. *The origins of agriculture: an evolutionary perspective*. New York: Academic Press.

Rindos, D. 1985. Darwinian selection, symbolic variation and the evolution of culture. *Current Anthropology* **26**, 65–88.

Rindos, D. 1986. The evolution of the cultural capacity: structuralism, sociobiology and cultural selectionism. *Current Anthropology* **27**, 315–32.

Rindos, D. & S. Johannessen. 1988. Agriculture and cultural change in the American Bottom. In *Cahokia and its hinterlands*, T. E. Emerson & R. B. Lewis (eds). Kent, Ohio: Kent State University Press.

Roosevelt, A. C. 1984. Population, health, and the evolution of subsistence: conclusions from the conference. In *Paleopathology at the origins of agriculture*, M. N. Cohen & G. A. Armelagos (eds), 559–83. Orlando: Academic Press.

Smith, P. E. L. 1972. Changes in population pressure in archaeological explanation. *World Archaeology* **4**, 5–18.

Spooner, B. (ed.) 1972. *Population growth: anthropological implications*. Cambridge, Mass.: MIT Press.

Watson, P. J. 1989. Early plant cultivation in the Eastern Woodlands of North America. In *Foraging and farming: the evolution of plant exploitation*, D. R. Harris & G. C. Hillman (eds), ch. 35. London: Unwin Hyman.

Wright, H. E., Jr. 1977. Environmental change and the origin of agriculture in the Old and New Worlds. In *Origins of agriculture*, C. A. Reed (ed.), 281–318. The Hague: Mouton.

Zohary, D. 1989. Domestication of the Southwest Asian Neolithic crop assemblage of cereals, pulses, and flax: the evidence from the living plants. In *Foraging and farming: the evolution of plant exploitation*, D. R. Harris & G. C. Hillman (eds), ch. 22. London: Unwin Hyman.

# 3 Domestication and domiculture in northern Australia: a social perspective

A. K. CHASE

The concept of domestication has recently been extended by some authors from its orthodox biological definition (cf. Harris Ch. 1, this volume) to embrace wider aspects of the relationships that exist between people and plants. Hynes & Chase (1982) was an attempt to apply such an approach. In it we discussed Australian Aboriginal influence upon plant communities in the Cape York Peninsula of northern Queensland. The main aim of that paper was to query an over-simplistic application of the concept of domestication to the Australian Aboriginal case, and in doing so, to elaborate upon the quite complex relationships that existed between plants and Aboriginal people, with particular reference to a coastal site in the peninsula. These complexities ranged from the way plants are classified, valued, and related to the social world, to the ways they were used by individuals and groups in the seasonal cycle. We emphasized that Australian hunter–gatherers cannot be considered ecologically passive in a supposedly 'natural' landscape simply because they did not engage in a pattern of behaviour usually subsumed under the concept of agriculture. Neither, we argued, can plant-community modification by long-term hunter–gatherer occupation and use be presumed to be the result of 'accidental' or 'unconscious' action. We proposed that the human–plant interaction process has three ecologically related dimensions:

(a) The cultural and social 'stance' of the human groups toward their particular domain, as expressed in the rules of the society concerning use of plants and other parts of the habitat at particular times. We can refer to this as the rationalization of action (Giddens 1979, p. 215).
(b) The range of actual plant-exploitation practices as they affect different plant communities at particular times, and the means by which these practices are maintained by a society.
(c) The dynamic processes involved in changing the morphology, distribution, and genetics of certain species, and, through interaction, changing aspects of the exploiting society.

Summarizing these, we may consider human–plant relationships as time-and-space specific, and involving human social action in a complex environment: an economic process which involves more than plants in the production system. The point which forms the central contention of this chapter is the essentially *social* nature of human economy; interrelationships among humans are likely to be of a higher order of importance in maintaining social continuity than the relations of particular individuals or groups to any resource base in the environment.

To return briefly to the 1982 paper; at that time we were concerned with disentangling domestication, as an analytical construct, from that of agriculture. Furthermore, we were anxious to free discussion from the still prevalent notions of 'progress' and 'development' which unfortunately remain attached to this area of discourse. We drew attention to certain behaviours which complicate any simplistic division between hunter–gatherers on the one hand and domesticators/agriculturalists on the other. Examples given included replacement planting, the planting of yams in new island environments, the husbanding of fruit trees, etc. (cf. Harris Ch. 1, Yen Ch. 4, this volume). All such behaviours, we argued, need to be viewed against a backdrop of small-group local organization, long-term coastal occupation, and a complex Aboriginal science of speciation, plant behaviour, and extractive technologies. We suggested that the process of plant (and other) resource exploitation needed to be viewed from the perspective of localized social groups intersecting spatially and temporally with particular environments. This intersection results in a series of hearth-based areas of exploitation (domuses), each carrying with it a package of resource locations, restrictions upon open-ended exploitation (religious prohibitions, strategic planning for delayed harvesting, etc.), and localized technologies to fit particular domuses. We suggested the term *domiculture* for these localized packages of interaction between people and resources.

## The domain of plants and people

After that paper was published, David Rindos produced his major work on the origins of agriculture (Rindos 1984) addressing the use of the terms agriculture and domestication as analytical constructs. While I find much to disagree with in his Darwinian perspective on the evolution of agriculture (1984, & Ch. 2, this volume), and with his use of the somewhat nebulous notion of culture traits, he has dealt firmly with the problem of unshackling domestication from the conventional role ascribed to it as the necessary prime-mover and precursor of agriculture (cf. Harris Ch. 1, this volume). But, at the same time, he perpetuated the myth that Australian hunter–gatherer systems of resource exploitation are 'simple' (Rindos 1984, p. 162). One can well ask in what terms such simplicity exists. In the cultural views of the society? In the technologies of exploitation employed? In the social organization of groups appropriating resources from the environment, and in the patterns of distribution resulting from the organized use of human labour? The point here is that categorizing hunter–gatherer beliefs and/or actions as simple – or, indeed, seeing hunter–gatherers as 'incidental' domesticators (Rindos 1984, pp. 154–8) – begs the central issue. This issue is the importance of human sociality in the production and distribution process. When we talk of economic processes – as surely we must when we discuss plant and other natural-resource use – we are dealing essentially with processes which are socially initiated, articulated, and maintained. Furthermore these are processes which are used to perpetuate social goals over and above simple biological survival of the individual actors in a given environment.

This is, of course, a matter well recognized by economists and anthropologists of many theoretical hues and which has been most productively explored by analysts who have taken Marxist ideas as their inspiration (e.g. Sahlins 1972, Friedman 1975, Godelier 1977, Ingold 1980, Meillassoux 1981). Terms such as modes and means of production, despite some overuse, do have the advantage of recognizing the importance of social processes in the interaction of human groups with their environments in resource exploitation. In this chapter my purpose is to approach the issue of domestication and agriculture from the social and cultural side of the coin, rather than from that of the natural world of plants and animals, and in order to do so it is necessary to introduce some social theory.

Giddens has produced a large and complex synthesis of ideas in his general theory of society and social change (Giddens 1979, 1984). I shall do inadequate justice to his work by summarizing some of the ideas which I see as having relevance to those issues of social change which are ultimately involved in any discussion of the origins of agriculture. His basic thesis is that any analysis of societies and of what they do should involve the concept of social actors as knowledgeable agents who rationalize their actions in routine daily life as members of social groups. Social action takes place at particular contextual intersections of time and space. Social change involves both of these dimensions. In this sense, according to Giddens, historical and geographical concepts (and, I would add, human ecological ones as well) are synthetically involved in social analysis – perhaps best expressed through the concept of regionalization (Giddens 1984).

Importantly, although humans must be seen as knowledgeable agents in routinized activities (which keep reproducing the social collectivity) there can be unintended consequences of action which can lead to transformational change; a 'traditional' society is small and isolated, with tradition dominating as the normative base for the rules of routinized daily life. Such societies are 'cold' in that they exhibit strong closure in respect of traditional rules of behaviour, action in time and space, and future reproduction of social structure (rules and resources drawn upon in daily life to sustain the systemic patterning of social relations across time and space). Tradition, as it were, underwrites the continuity of practices, which in turn reflexively organize the future structure (Giddens 1979, p. 220). In such societies deroutinization of practices, as Giddens refers to it – and we must assume this happens in a shift to agricultural practices – is not an easy matter.

Traditions can be replaced without shifting routines of action, even where major natural events may rapidly alter the environment, or where the society comes in contact with other tradition-oriented societies with radically different practices. What is needed for major transformations, according to Giddens, is the emergence of radically divergent interpretations of the normative base. This can allow rapid shifts in the rule system which governs daily routines of social interaction and resource exploitation. In small communities organized on traditional rules this can happen quite quickly, as in the case of rapid interpenetration and domination by quite different societies, or perhaps at a slower rate when a destabilized normative base allows certain individuals to influence others and to establish new routines of actions with new structures to validate them.

A framework of this kind affords some insight into why continuities of hunter–gatherer modes of social organization and production in northern Australia remained in place despite considerable contact with Macassans in the Arnhem-Land area (Jones & Bowler 1980) and despite regular inter-actions with subsistence agriculturalists at the northern tip of Cape York (Harris 1977, Moore 1978). Here, presumably, knowledge of others who operated under different rules (jural frameworks which govern daily lives) and carried out different routines was not sufficient to challenge extant traditions and, thus, existing rules of sociality and economic production in a hunter–gatherer regime: a theme to which we return later.

At this point we can usefully introduce the notion of *domain* as a central element in the relation between social groups and their habitats. In Austra-lian anthropology the term is most closely associated with W. E. H. Stanner (1965) who maintained that any consideration of Aboriginal–environment interaction must account for territorial dimensions beyond those of the primary patrilineal *estate* or 'heartland' to which each individual was affili-ated by birth or adoption, and over which an individual, together with his or her fellow estate-group members, possessed major potential authority in terms of action. Stanner maintained that the regular seasonal round of economic activity included a *range* of terrain which might or might not include the estate, depending on the regional resource bases. Conceptually, the estate, in conjunction with the range, formed an area of authorized rights of access and usufruct in varying degrees, and this was legitimated through social links of kinship and descent creating a political legitimacy of action in the affairs of people and land. This geographical area of legitimized use he called the domain.

Putting the unlikely bedfellows Stanner and Giddens together, we may state that the routinized actions of small hunter–gatherer groups operate both spatially and temporally within a geographically defined domain which includes, in the relations of production, particular patterns of inter-actions with other regional groups. In the forces of production there are particular exploitative interactions with particular natural environments. Reflexively, in Gidden's terms, these interactions draw upon local traditional authority from the past and, at the same time, they create the interaction windows for the future. Unintended consequences of routine activity (e.g. domesticatory effects on plants and animals, modification of the landscape, etc.) result in amplitude variations to the hunter–gatherer trajectory of interaction, but no major directional variation. This takes account of the localization and differentiation of Aboriginal cultural and social systems in time and space within the Australian continent (with all its environmental variation) and the continent-wide retention of a non-agricultural hunter–gatherer mode of subsistence (cf. Yen Ch. 4, this volume).

There is another way in which the concept of domain is useful in considerations of domestication: by its application to what Giddens calls 'practical consciousness', as it applies to the Aboriginal knowledge domain of plants (and animals). Leaving aside matters of logical classification of the natural environment, what this should mean for ethnobotanists is the organized knowledge about plants in a particular society in terms of their authorized manipulative potential in the resource base, as applicable to particular times and places, and in particular social contexts. My contention here is that this type of information is critical for issues of domestication, and far more revealing than the lists of plant names, and statements about potential use, and seasonal availability, which commonly form the body of ethnobotanical information. The research I am suggesting calls for particularly fine-grained ethnographic recording, with great attention paid to rule variation in time, space, and social contexts within a domain. Thus, for example, a particular plant may only be approachable in resource terms at quite specific times, or at quite specific locations, or at a combination of both. For example, plants which are used in ceremony for food or artefact material may have one set of rules for exploitation in pre-ceremonial periods, and another during ceremony. Categories of people who can take the plants will change accordingly, as will those who can consume them.

At the plant-community level, certain geographical areas fall under specific prohibitions for varying periods and for varying categories of people. Particular plants or communities may be owned by specific individuals or groups, and their exploitation subject to restrictions of time (as for example the yam scrubs discussed in Hynes & Chase 1982). This suggested level of recording raises ethnobotanical data from a static perception of time, space, and social interaction to a dynamic perception of these three important variables. I am not aware of such detailed study having been carried out on the Australian continent, and the complex nature of such a task is no doubt daunting. But until these dynamic complexities are recognized we are unlikely to understand the domesticatory processes which bind together knowledge, action, and environment in the ecological process. What happens to plants in a genetic sense is the *result* of such processes.

Domains then, as both knowledge (or 'practical consciousness') and territories of potential exploitation, are eminently social in their conception. This social dimension has often been neglected in Australian archaeology in discussions of resource exploitation, as Thomas (1981) has so tellingly observed, and as Friedman (1974), Ingold (1980), and Hodder (1982) have emphasized in other contexts. We may note Thomas's major point that 'social relations do not simply mediate subsistence practices. The explanation of subsistence modes has a necessary social component, if it is to be adequate' (Thomas 1981, p. 172.). And from Ingold: 'To dismiss such [social] events as "noise" is to deem irrelevant the whole course of social evolution or to appeal to a time scale of palaeontological rather than prehistoric dimensions' (Ingold 1980, p. 93). Since Thomas's critique, some Australian archaeologists have begun to address issues of social change by associating the intensification of production through time with increasing complexity of social factors in interpreting archaeological sites (e.g. Lourandos 1983, Murray & White 1985).

Having elaborated on the centrality of social phenomena in human–environment interaction, I turn now to the particular issue of domestication (especially with regard to Australian hunter–gatherers) as a concept conventionally used to analyse those interactions.

## Domestication and domicultural action

Rindos, working from the other end of the human–environment spectrum, has described domestication as a 'coevolutionary process in which any given taxon diverges from an original gene pool and establishes a symbiotic protection and dispersal relationship with the animal feeding upon it' (Rindos 1984, p. 143). It therefore cannot 'be held to be an exclusively human-mediated phenomenon' (Rindos 1984, p. 127). It follows that I see this approach as severely limiting interpretive discussion about domestication and/or agriculture as a human process. Rather than domestication being a co-evolutionary process of taxon divergence, I perceive it to be a human social and cultural process relating to the structured knowledge by which individuals and groups agree upon a certain interpretation of the natural realm of plants and animals and carry out their routine daily actions on the basis of this interpretation. It is evident that Rindos and I disagree upon the extent of domestication of species in a human habitat. For Rindos, all plant (and animal) species must have undergone genetic modification either directly or indirectly through human (and other organism) interference in the habitat. I wish to restrict the definition firstly to human interference, and secondly to those species which are culturally recognized and known about, and which are thus seen emically as part of the manipulable environment, even if they are not linguistically separated as part of an indigenous taxonomy. In this way, I do not see the concept of domestication applying to microflora and microfauna beyond the realm of social knowledge. It also follows that I do not hesitate to apply the term to entities which are not within the domain of Western science. I have no difficulty in accepting certain spiritual entities in the landscape as domesticated, for the purpose of understanding human action. In the Cape York Peninsula such entities and forces lose their domesticatory qualities when humans are removed from the landscape, and interaction ceases. It is only then that the entire landscape in all its empirical and non-empirical diversity is considered by Aboriginal people to have 'come wild' and, thus, to have become potentially dangerous for humans who have lost the practical knowledge for 'correct' (i.e. authorized) interaction. Accordingly, when groups return to their countries after a long absence resulting from their removal to settlements, they are very cautious in their actions until they feel the necessary human signature has again been imposed upon the land (Hynes & Chase 1982).

The major (though not exclusive) routines of action are economic ones, and it is for this reason that I find it useful to conceive of the interaction of hunter–gatherers with their physical domains as operating around a specific point in time and space which I refer to as a *domus* or hearth base. Group location at a domus involves both general and specific 'practical consciousnesses'. At the general level, actors at a domus have recourse to a background knowledge about the general behaviour of species, their potential usefulness, the extractive technology to be applied, ecological relationships with other species (often in the form of cross-domain referencing: for instance, when a certain plant species flowers, a particular fish species swarms in rivers for egg-laying), and so on. This background knowledge is the source of most information published as ethnobotanical data. Thus in the Cape York Peninsula the plant species *Manilkara kauki* and *Eugenia carrisoides* are known to inhabit littoral dunes in conjunction with other species, are recognized as having edible fruit, and are known to fruit in the late dry season immediately before the monsoonal period. It is, however, the *specific* interpretive knowledge as it relates to particular domuses which controls the actual routines carried out by people in time and space, and which thus actually affects the populations of plants and animals. I refer to these actual routines in the environment as domicultural actions. By domiculture I mean, in the ordinary dictionary meaning of the term, the 'household economy', and in terms of production (ignoring for the moment the distributive networks and storage processes) the knowledge and activity bundles which relate temporally to a specific habitat.

Australian hunter–gatherers are probably best known for certain categories of restrictive knowledge about their domains: their structures of religious beliefs which restrain and create particular routine actions, both at the general level (species prohibition for certain social categories through totemic relationships; certain ordained uses for ritual of otherwise 'unused' species) and at the specific level (permanent or temporary restrictions or ordinations at quite specific sites for certain people). Examples of the former in the Cape York Peninsula are the restrictions upon eating certain plants or animals through their affiliation to certain 'dreamings', and the consumption of others (e.g. dugong) only in certain ritual contexts, and then only by adult males of a certain ritual status. Examples of the latter include the total prohibition of use upon plants and animals at certain sites where dreaming ancestors came to rest, and the graded restriction of use for various social categories (age, sex, mourning relatives, etc.) at specific locations, and for various sizes of species. Domicultural knowledge is then both specific and general, but domicultural action is always interpretively specific within the landscape. The geographical or territorial domain then, *contra* Stanner and his intellectual predecessor Donald Thomson (1939), cannot be understood as an undifferentiated area whose productive potential is limited only by seasonality. All in all, for Australian (and other) hunter–gatherers the domus site occupied at a particular time is the one which traditional knowledge authorizes for spiritual safety of routine action, even if this increases budgetary costs in time and energy for the production process.

Lourandos (1983) has speculated that the growth of such complex religious beliefs and action (in the form of ceremonial interaction) may have dramatically increased in the late Holocene period, and that this social evolution could have resulted in the intensification of use of certain domuses which can be observed in the Australian archaeological record. Why such changes in beliefs and social restructuring might have occurred at this time is another issue which does not immediately bear upon the general theme of this chapter (but cf. Yen Ch. 4, this volume). Such intensification in time–space relations with the habitat could well have unintended consequences for the population dynamics of species in terms of gene pools and niche regeneration around domuses. We can conceive of this process as one of the intensification of cultural and social filters in the economic process, as well as the intensification of environmental filters to plant regeneration (cf. Hynes & Chase 1982, Fig. 8). If Lourandos' interpretation is correct, it may well be that once such elaboration takes place, the options for major transformations (for example, the adoption of agriculture) are severely curtailed through integrative closure in systemic and structural aspects of the society, in those areas where knowledge of such alien cultural practices existed. At a certain time in the Australian past, the cultural filters perhaps became just too dense and too finely articulated for major interpenetrations to take place.

The point here is that domicultural events and outcomes, for plant species in particular, are not just so much background 'noise' either in plant evolution or in social process. They are significant and continuous events which, until the European era in Australia (and in some cases after), were remoulding both people and plants. They were, in all probability, even creating initial plant communities on emerging shorelines (Hynes & Chase 1982). Domuses, then, represent particular intersection points in the processual affairs of people and natural species. Domestication is one facet of the people–plant equation, primarily a cultural phenomenon expressed in attitudes towards the natural environment, influencing routine economic activities and natural processes among species. This is the obverse side of the interaction coin from that presented by Rindos, for whom the biological rather than the social processes are the focus of detailed analysis. It is this theoretical perspective that allows him to speak of co-evolution, to use predator–prey concepts, and to adopt and adapt models from evolutionary ecology.

The social-anthropological approach developed here emphasizes human collective *action* in a dynamic sense. Rindos, as I understand his position, is concerned with human *behaviour* as one of a general series of organism behaviours within the natural environment, with particular attention paid to changes within the biotic environment in terms of human biological success. It is in this sense that he can argue for an understanding of domestication and agriculture (and, by implication, any other regularized human behaviour impinging on the environment) in terms of a Darwinian model of natural selection. Thus, cultural and social phenomena are largely given in behavioural terms, exhibiting little 'error' in transmission across generations, and, where error does occur, it is explicable by recourse to a 'mechanism' (Rindos 1984, p. 254). Agriculture, in behaviourist terms, is defined as 'environmental manipulations within the context of the human coevolutionary relationship with plants' (Rindos 1984, p. 100), and agricultural *systems* we assume are regularized patterns of manipulation; although what the explanation of regularity in behaviours or 'traits' (itself a behaviourist term) in human systems is, is unclear. I suggest that Rindos can explain nothing about either regularized or changing patterns of economic behaviour among humans unless he is prepared to go into some detail about the causes of such regularity or change in social phenomena. I know of no adequate way this can be achieved without at least recognizing some of the concepts social scientists use for explaining such patterns. The normative base for human action is well recognized, and while both norms and practices change through time, these changes take place primarily not through factors of the natural environment but through culturally authorized human interpretations of both social and natural environments in the ongoing social life of people. There is no real evidence that changes in routinized action (e.g. a shift to agricultural practices) are directed any more towards establishing a 'natural' balance of relationships with the natural resource base than they are towards establishing any new 'natural' balance with the social resource base in terms of more complex institutions and greater populations.

Finally, in this examination of Rindos' position, we can note his statement that his definition places the emphasis in the most useful place: the interaction of society, domesticated plants, and their environment (Rindos 1984, p. 257). This is disputable. While domesticated plants and their environments receive detailed analytical treatment in his book, the same cannot be said for 'society', if we take this term to mean more than a collectivity of organisms. My conclusion is that his theorizing may well be useful if domestication and agriculture are defined entirely in terms of effects upon plants. But it fails to take account of the cultural and social phenomena involved in the interaction process.

# Aboriginal Australia, domestication, and agriculture

The Australian continent and offshore islands, with very few exceptions (e.g. Kangaroo Island, South Australia, which was uninhabited), were entirely occupied by hunter–gatherers at the time of European intrusion. By 'occupation' I mean that the whole area was divided socially into recognizable territorial units and was used economically within those units on some regular basis, although not necessarily annually. Systems of rights – often quite complex – pervaded and sustained this pattern of occupation. A continuous mosaic of territorial units extended from tropical and highly seasonal coastal areas of immense environmental diversity in the far north at 11°S latitude, across arid grasslands and deserts, warm-temperate forests and riverine plains, into subalpine highlands and cool-temperate lowlands to the far south at 43°S latitude. It is reasonable to assume that such an occupational pattern has been imposed by Aboriginal social processes for at least 20 000 years, even if particular territorial patterns have changed, and even though considerable biological and geomorphological changes have taken place. Despite the presence, and exploitation, in northern Australia of plants used in horticulture elsewhere in southeastern Asia (Jones & Bowler 1980, Jones & Meehan Ch. 7, Yen Ch. 4, this volume) and also of grasses which represent potential cereal crops (Allen 1974, Cane Ch. 6, Smith Ch. 18, this volume), all Aboriginal groups pursued in their routine economic activity a hunter–gatherer mode of subsistence. Nowhere did they develop a tradition of clearing land in order to create a special environment as a system which humans could manipulate for production in ways other than hunting and gathering. Agriculture implies a radically different perception of the environment and its legitimate human occupants, and it authorizes a radically different manipulation of plants and their habitats (cf. Harris Ch. 1, this volume). I have suggested earlier that with the development of highly complex and deeply integrated religious beliefs and practices, societies such as those in Aboriginal Australia may have passed a critical threshold of receptivity to major alteration which would be required for acceptance of agricultural practices from neighbours or visitors.

Domus-based activities involve rational planning for the future in terms of both people and material resources, and this planning is done within a charter of acceptability. Individuals or small groups may, on occasions, have carried out innovative actions with plants, such as occasional transplantation (Harris 1977, Hynes & Chase 1982). For all we know, they may have attempted to create gardens in imitation of alien systems which had entered the realm of Aboriginal knowledge in the north. It is not unlikely that, within the last 10 000 years, individuals independently experimented with plant regeneration in ways we label as agriculture. But, as we know from the history of ideas in our own society, there is a large barrier between the creation of new ideas and practices at this level, and their public acceptability as a new authority for routine action. The adoption from outside the continent of large outrigger canoes, Melanesian-type drums, ceremonial gear, and even whole ceremonies is evidence that the Aboriginal social systems in northern Queensland were not totally impervious to penetration from outside (Thomson 1933, 1934, Chase 1980). But these examples of adoption do not challenge what I referred to earlier as the hunter–gatherer stance in social and cultural terms towards their natural resource base, because they are incorporated within the belief-action structure of economic strategy. It is interesting that even today, in Aboriginal societies where social integration is emically perceived as exhibiting unbroken continuity with the pre-European period and where it is exhibited through fine-grained interpretations of the landscape in terms of sites, territories, and spiritually authorized human action, agricultural practices are still not accepted, even though other European technologies and artefacts have been adopted.

At the Lockhart River mission (which later became a government settlement) on the east coast of the Cape York Peninsula, societies were forcibly confined to the settlement and great efforts were made to 'raise' the inhabitants to a Melanesian-type village agricultural life (Chase 1980). Taro, cassava (manioc), and other exotic food crops were introduced and grown under European direction. More recently, government managers there have consistently attempted to create a self-sufficient garden system, and the environs of the township are scarred with overgrown and failed plots. A few pawpaw, banana, and mango trees grow around the houses, and the occasional houseplot has a small self-regenerating sweet-potato patch. But these are food crops which require no maintenance, which are now seen as 'natural' to the European-induced environment of the settlement, and whose productivity is desultory, even negligible. It is also significant that those inhabitants who make some attempt at gardening are people of Torres Strait or Melanesian origins and people of mixed origins, who have no authoritative connection with the region. They are often 'outsiders' in the social sense, those whose immediate forebears reached the settlement during its wild frontier phase when coastal luggering, sporadic mining, and government clearances of the new frontier disrupted many groups.

For the Umpila, Kuuku Ya'u, and other Aboriginal peoples of this immediate area, agricultural practices are a wasteful and illegitimate activity in the landscape – 'It is not our way; it is alright for other people. We get our food from the bush'. What they mean here is that, despite their present reliance on store foods and beef, bush plant and animal foods from their own country have a priority and an authorization in cuisine which is part of their claim for traditional legitimacy in their homelands. Despite enormous pressures by a government of European derivation to assimilate them into a European perspective of society, economy, and religion, there is a stubborn resistance to such shifts in beliefs, a recalcitrance which in Queensland is often categorized by administrators as the Aboriginal 'problem'. This recalcitrance is expressed by camping in the bush away from the settlement whenever possible, despite, on occasions, active intervention to prevent it by the administrators. When the people camp out, their routine activities are those of hunter–gatherers, and they take pride in their skills in appropriating bush foods from these new domuses. To explain such beliefs and actions in what is, after all, part of the reality of modern Aboriginal life in a European-dominated continent, recourse must be taken to social, rather than to natural-selection processes. The people's present-day routine bush activities as hunter–gatherers leave material evidence in the landscape, and this, together with settlement remains, will no doubt be investigated by future archaeologists. But if archaeologists are to explain the material evidence in settlement and bush, they will need to understand the modern social processes that are taking place. Only this will provide an adequate explanatory interpretation of both hunting–gathering and agricultural activities at this location, and the domesticatory outcomes of these upon the plant and animal species of the region.

# References

Allen, H. 1974. The Bagundji of the Darling Basin: cereal gatherers in an uncertain environment. *World Archaeology* **5**, 309–22.

Cane, S. 1989. Australian Aboriginal seed grinding and its archaeological record: a case study from the Western Desert. In *Foraging and farming: the evolution of plant exploitation*, D. R. Harris & G. C. Hillman (eds), ch. 6. London: Unwin Hyman.

Chase, A. K. 1980. *Which way now? Tradition, continuity and change in a north Queensland Aboriginal community.* Unpublished PhD thesis, Department of Anthropology, University of Queensland.

Friedman, J. 1974. Marxism, structuralism and vulgar materialism. *Man(ns)* **9**, 444–64.

Friedman, J. 1975. Tribes, states and transformations. In *Marxist analyses in social anthropology*, M. Bloch (ed.), 161–202. London: Malaby.

Giddens, A. 1979. *Central problems in social theory.* London: Macmillan.

Giddens, A. 1984. *The constitution of society.* Cambridge: Polity Press.

Godelier, M. 1977. *Perspectives in marxist anthropology.* Cambridge: Cambridge University Press.

Harris, D. R. 1977. Subsistence strategies across Torres Strait. In *Sunda and Sahul: prehistoric studies in Southeast Asia, Melanesia and Australia*, J. Allen, G. Golson & R. Jones (eds), 421–63. London: Academic Press.

Harris, D. R. 1989. An evolutionary continuum of people–plant interaction. In *Foraging and farming: the evolution of plant exploitation*, D. R. Harris & G. C. Hillman (eds), ch. 1. London: Unwin Hyman.

Hodder, I. 1982. Theoretical archaeology: a reactionary view. In *Symbolic and structural archaeology*, I. Hodder (ed.), 1–16. Cambridge: Cambridge University Press.

Hynes, R. A. & A. K. Chase 1982. Plants, sites and domiculture: Aboriginal influence upon plant communities in Cape York Peninsula. *Archaeology in Oceania* **17**, 38–50.

Ingold, T. 1980. *Hunters, pastoralists and ranchers.* Cambridge: Cambridge University Press.

Jones R. & J. Bowler 1980. Struggle for the savanna: northern Australia in ecological and prehistoric perspective. In *Northern Australia: options and implications*, R. Jones (ed.), 3–31. Canberra: Research School of Pacific Studies, The Australian National University.

Jones, R. & B. Meehan 1989. Plant foods of the Gidjingali: ethnographic and archaeological perspectives from northern Australia on tuber and seed exploitation. In *Foraging and farming: the evolution of plant exploitation*, D. R. Harris & G. C. Hillman (eds), ch. 7. London: Unwin Hyman.

Lourandos, H. 1983. Intensification: a late Pleistocene–Holocene archaeological sequence from southwestern Victoria. *Archaeology in Oceania* **18**, 81–94.

Meillassoux, C. 1981. *Maidens, meal and money*. Cambridge: Cambridge University Press.

Moore, D. R. 1978. *Islanders and Aborigines at Cape York*. Canberra: Australian Institute of Aboriginal Studies.

Murray, T. & J. P. White (eds) 1985. Trends towards social complexity in Australia and Papua New Guinea (i & ii). *Archaeology in Oceania* **20**, 41–104.

Rindos, D. 1984. *The origins of agriculture: an evolutionary perspective*. London: Academic Press.

Rindos, D. 1989. Darwinism and its role in the explanation of domestication. In *Foraging and farming: the evolution of plant exploitation*, D. R. Harris & G. C. Hillman (eds), ch. 2. London: Unwin Hyman.

Sahlins, M. 1972. *Stone age economics*. Chicago & New York: Aldine-Atherton.

Smith, M. A. 1989. Seed gathering in inland Australia: current evidence on the antiquity of the ethnohistorical pattern of exploitation. In *Foraging and farming: the evolution of plant exploitation*, D. R. Harris & G. C. Hillman (eds), ch. 18. London: Unwin Hyman.

Stanner, W. E. H. 1965. Aboriginal territorial organisation: estate, range, domain and regime. *Oceania* **36**, 1–25.

Thomas, N. 1981. Social theory, ecology, and epistemology: theoretical issues in Australian prehistory. *Mankind* **13**, 165–80.

Thomson, D. F. 1933. The hero cult, initiation and totemism on Cape York. *Journal of the Royal Anthropological Institute* **63**, 453–537.

Thomson, D. F. 1934. The dugong hunters of Cape York. *Journal of the Royal Anthropological Institute* **64**, 237–62.

Thomson, D. F. 1939. The seasonal factor in human culture: illustrated from the life of a contemporary nomadic group. *Proceedings of the Prehistoric Society* **5**, 209–21.

Yen, D. E. 1989. The domestication of environment. In *Foraging and farming: the evolution of plant exploitation*, D. R. Harris & G. C. Hillman (eds), ch. 4. London: Unwin Hyman.

# 4 *The domestication of environment*

## D. E. YEN

The concept of the evolution of agriculture from hunting and gathering through domestication is seldom questioned; it implies that the hunter–gatherer societies found during the European age of discovery were relicts of an earlier stage in human social development or on a slower track of the evolutionary process, and therefore describable as backward and primitive. As a major inspiration for later theories of social evolution, Charles Darwin, in his account of the voyage of the *Beagle*, exemplified some differentials among contemporary Pacific peoples on an implied scale of social development and degree of environmental control. The food-gathering tribes of Tierra del Fuego, with their 'perfect equality among the individuals' and what we might term a Melanesian big-man form of leadership, were used as a basis of comparison with the Tahitian agriculturalists (questionably ascribed the supplementary *wild* resources of sugar cane, yam, and aroids which we know to be among the major traditional cultigens of the Society Islands) governed by 'hereditary kings'. The New Zealand Maori, described in more wretched terms, 'although benefited by being compelled to turn their attention to agriculture, were republicans in the most absolute sense'. The ethnocentricism of these 19th-century evaluations of Darwin (1845, p. 219) reflects not only the imperial primacy of the time and the association of richness of resources that mirror environmental control, but also European criteria of progress in terms of happiness, hygiene, and receptivity to Christianity. Notwithstanding, these statements, together with the subsequent development of the theory of natural selection and Darwin's embrace of the Spencerian concept of human history as 'the necessary acquirement of each mental power and capacity by gradation' (1859, p. 462), were to influence thought on the transformation of forager to agriculturalist as a cultural phenomenon, and as cultural evolution.

Although not all anthropologists accept the evolution of culture as other than analogy, there is a tendency to assent to the biological configuration as a convenient form of developmental sequence from simple to complex. An example is the search for evidence of proto-agriculture among current hunter–gatherers to reflect the evolutionary steps in the prehistory of agriculture. It is a case of seek and find; for it is impossible not to educe agricultural parallels among people who do not plant or herd, but who do dig for roots, harvest fruit and seed, butcher animals and fish. Perhaps we have taken too far the processual rebuttals of hunter–gatherer and horticulturist as dichotomy and the 'revolutionary' domestication of plant and animal as event (cf. Harris Ch. 1, this volume). While it is true that domestication was a process, in that all domesticates in any given region did not arise at one time, it would be implausible to suggest that the first domestications did not alter the subsistence modes of their domesticators. The disruptive selection of the simply inherited non–shattering character in cereal-grain species from wild and predominantly shattering populations, as one manifestation of ethnoscientific knowledge, was to set off the adaptive processes which resulted in the increasingly complex technologies of field agriculture. The genetic effects of selection were to continue, in response to changing environments and social requirements, as themselves the dynamic and 'unnatural' directions for selection. If one may be permitted a literary indulgence, most historical events may be described as non–events, for the declarations of war, the day the revolution began, the invention of machinery marking the beginning of of industrialization, are all products of prior social process. The role of domestication in the hunter-to-horticulture transformation may be seen in this directorial light. This may all seem to be in the realm of semantic quibble; for on this interpretation domestication is inevitable, in the past for agriculturalists, and for non-agriculturalists either in the future or as recognizably formative elements of the ethnographic present. It is on the second 'inevitability' that I wish to focus this discussion.

The Australian Aborigine has been widely regarded as representing the hunter–gatherer estate on which, in world terms, agriculture was built. Aboriginal subsistence systems in their regional variations show, in the ethnographic present, no sign of having adopted agriculture, despite Australia's proximity to New Guinea (and their existence as a single land mass until some 8000 years ago), despite the protohistoric contacts with Macassan trepang fishers, and despite a 200-year familiarity with European farming. Thus Harlan (1975), discussing the rise of domestication in the context of his innovative and stimulating theory for multiple agricultural origins (Harlan 1971), reviews the foraging groups remaining in the world and recognizes the Australian as the most reliable source of data on pre-agricultural man.

Lourandos (1980, 1983) is the foremost Australian archaeologist to deny a static state in Aboriginal subsistence by stressing the accumulation of evidence for 'intensification' in the Holocene. He attributes such phenomena to the motor force of increasing social complexity, and, invoking Bronson's exposition (1975), among others, of the hunting-to-horticulture transformation as continuum, places the 'intensified' level of Aboriginal hunter–gatherer technology on that scale. Gamble (1986), in an interesting comparison of the Eurasian Mesolithic and the 4000–5000-year-old small-tool tradition in Australia, argues against change in the social relations of Aboriginal production; he suggests that the perceived instances of intensification cited by Lourandos and other researchers should be examined in an 'ecological framework and as variation within hunter–gatherer strategies'. The prehistoric restructuring of this framework in Europe is admissible though 'archaeologically difficult to detect' (Gamble 1986, p. 40), but in Australia the restructuring was historic, with the advent of Captain Cook. If these passages have been read correctly, what was missing was domestication, which, if it had occurred in Australian prehistory, and had Cook's arrival been delayed to allow time for agricultural development according to Gamble's hypothetical reconstruction (1986, p. 39), earlier social restructuring could have been deduced from the same subsistence evidence that he presently rejects. He is then, in effect, denying any substantial indication in the archaeological or ethnographic records for domestication in Australia, and in this respect parallels the contention of this chapter, that Aboriginal subsistence may not have been on the 'obligatory' track of transformation to agriculture.

In putting this case, I recapitulate in summary, with some additions, the familiar 'agronomic' resemblances of Australian hunter–gathering and the social adjustments to production viewed by some to be developmental, evolutionary trends. I hope to illustrate the commonality between the systemic structures of subsistence of the Aborigines and those of their agricultural neighbours in New Guinea (the northern part of ancient Sahuland). There is really only one discriminatory feature: the domestication of the genetic components – the species – so that it is the 'domestication of the environment' that is shared between hunter–gatherer and agricultural subsistence production.

## The agronomy of Australian hunter–gatherers

The cyclic methods of foraging by hunter–gatherers, regulated in time and space, are usually conditioned by the distribution and seasonal production of important species within the peoples' group domains. The Australian Aborigine is no exception, whether of the tropical monsoonal north (Meehan 1982) or of the arid desert at the continent's centre (Meggitt 1962). This constant bespeaks of traditional environmental knowledge, the basic ethnobiology on which are formed these characteristically 'broad-spectrum' subsistence systems. The Aborigines are more than 'professional botanists' (Harlan 1975, p. 24). This expression has to be extended to zoology, in the Aborigines' understanding of the life cycles, reproductive behaviour, and feeding habits of faunal quarry, whether hibernating or aestivating species of marsupials or reptiles, edible larvae or moths, or the seasonal fish resources of coast or stream. The manipulation of the environmental settings of the exploited species have parallels with those of agriculturalists, particularly the shifting cultivators or swiddeners of Southeast Asia and the Pacific.

Jones (1969) has dubbed the Aboriginal practice of burning 'fire-stick farming' because it is a controlled renewal of resources dictated by season, and by the constraints of social territory. As with swidden agriculture, in which fire is used for clearing prior to planting, burning is circumscribed, and the biotic consequences are generally recognized in terms of the disposal of exhausted plant growth and its conversion to nutrients for successive vegetation recovery, or as a device to improve hunting. The use of cycad seeds for food after detoxification has been reported from the tropical north (Harris 1977a, pp. 426–9, Meehan 1982, pp. 31–2, 38–9), Western Australia (Crawford 1984), and Queensland (Beaton 1982). In the latter case, the use of fire in *Macrozamia* stands has been attributed a specific agronomic objective because it results in an evening of productivity with the equalizing of flowering and fruiting within populations which naturally vary in this character. In his account of desert practices, Kimber (1983) emphasized the relatively small size of such purposely lit fires, contrasting them with burns exceeding 100 km$^2$, which are rare and normally the product or supplementary effect of lightning strikes. As a practice that was applied to subsistence throughout Australia, including in the wetlands of the temperate southeast (Gott 1982), Aboriginal firing over a significant period of the continent's 40 000-year prehistory could have been a powerful selective force on its vegetation. Using pollen and charcoal evidence, Clark (1983) states that climate was the more important determining factor for floral distribution, but allows that Aboriginal burning must have had an environmental effect on the early Holocene sequence in which the spread of *Casuarina* into grassland and shrubland was followed by its displacement by the more fire-resistant eucalypts.

The development of grass-seed gathering on the scale observed in the penetration of the Australian hinterland by European explorers (summarized by H. Allen 1974, and see Cane Ch. 6, this volume) was dependent on the use of fire (Latz & Griffin 1978). Its success in favouring desirable species called forth technical innovations to deal with the products of bulk harvest: storage techniques and processing tools for the conversion of grain to food (Smith 1986 and Ch. 18, this volume). Gregory's observations (1886) of the *Panicum* harvest outline the harvesting procedures which, in themselves, suggest that seed could be incidentally dispersed to increase the size and density of natural stands, resulting in an aggregative crop-like effect for subsequent exploitation. Smith's interpretation of the development of large-scale grass-seed gathering in Australia's arid and semi-arid zones as response to environmental stress in the late Holocene and human population densities that 'were already nearing the carrying capacity of the region', intimates earlier, lower-intensity exploitation by smaller populations. However, the recent find of a Pleistocene site in the MacDonnell Ranges, earlier by 12 000 years than any other site discovered in the region, reflects to its discoverer (Smith 1987) an Aboriginal penetration of the desert 'independent of the development of distinctive seedgrinding technology'. Among the surprising plant resources of the Australian desert (Latz 1982), the earlier staple foods could have been the less technologically demanding tuberous plants. The comprehensive review of Aboriginal firing practices by Latz (1982, p. 137) indicates the flexibility of the fire-stick as a tool whose use was ultimately dependent on the complexities of ethnogeological knowledge. Undoubtedly, if grass seed as staple food had its forerunner in *Ipomoea* tubers (see later), it was not only changes in exploitative toolage that had to be effected, but also firing regimes that directed plant and plant–animal relationships. Perhaps this is an example of a mimicry of the long postulated tuber-to-seed succession among agriculturalists reflected in prehistoric hunter–gatherers!

The closest parallel to planting practice in Aboriginal gathering pertains to the *Dioscorea* yam in subtropical and tropical Australia. Observations of replanting, described in detail for Arnhem Land by Jones (1975) and Jones & Meehan (Ch. 7, this volume), for the eastern Cape York Peninsula by Harris (1977a, pp. 433–7), and deduced on historical evidence for Western Australia (Hallam Ch. 8, this volume), entail a rather casual replacement of the stem-attached top of the tuber at harvest, and are identical both to the informal procedures of the Tasaday foragers of the Philippines (Yen 1976a), and to the supplementary activities of agriculturalists in the collection of wild resources in northwestern Thailand and Papua New Guinea (Yen 1977 and field notes). Of the five species of *Dioscorea* identified in the recent revision of the genus in Australia by Telford (1986), there are three of importance as Aboriginal food sources. *D. bulbifera* (found on only a few Pacific Islands as a cultigen but, generally, as a feral, and emergency only, tuber food there and in Southeast Asia) is a resource distributed throughout the tropical north of Australia from northern Western Australia to southern coastal Queensland. There are two endemic species, *D. transversa*, with the same distribution as *D. bulbifera* but extending southeast into New South Wales, and *D. hastifolia*, restricted to coastal southern Western Australia. On largely ethnographical grounds, Jones & Meehan (Ch. 7, this volume) suggest that their Arnhem Land evidence on *Dioscorea*, as well as on a range of species of other genera represented in Melanesia and Southeast Asia as cultigens, may exemplify horticultural bridges to agricultural development. Hallam (1986 and Ch. 8, this volume) makes a similar suggestion from archaeological and historical sources, with the striking observation that *D. hastifolia* has adapted from its natural habitat of granitic and basaltic soils in open forest, woodland, and shrub communites (Telford 1986) to the alluvial plains in Western Australia. The naturalization of a dominant crop in traditional Pacific Island systems, the greater yam *D. alata*, into the gathering systems of the northern Australians may indicate a receptivity to desirable species and a resistance to agricultural production.

In northern Australia there are three tuber-bearing species of *Ipomoea* of considerable importance in traditional Aboriginal subsistence. *I. gracilis* grows in the tropical estuarine and savanna areas, whereas the woody perennial shrub species *I. costata* has a wide distribution from near the coast of northern Western Australia across the central sand sheets to the western border of southern Queensland. Among the species of the genus recently named by Johnson (1986) is *I. polpha*, an annual whose above-ground parts die each winter. It is distributed disjunctively, with one small population in the central desert north of Alice Springs, and two populations in western Queensland. Although they are taxonomically inseparable some variability between populations is indicated in the reported poisonous quality of the foliage to stock in the Queensland representatives. Field observations of Aboriginal harvesting of the two desert species indicate the same informal 'replanting' that is reported for *Dioscorea*. Latz (pers. comm.) opines that the rarer desert species may have soil requirements, as yet unspecified, which restrict its distribution. However, there are differences in adventitious, vegetative reproduction in the two species, both of which are notably fecund in true seed development. *I polpha* sets its tubers rather closer to the plant crown than *I. costata*, i.e. the underground tuber-bearing rhizomes are much shorter. In harvests of the latter species by informants, the ends of rhizomatous growths were not reached, although old tubers along their length were seen to produce vegetative growths, as Latz (1982) has reported. An additional reproductive capacity of this species is its production of above-ground stolons of prodigious length (up to some 20 m), with the potential for clonal replication at nodal joints. Significant are our observations of the preference of modern Aborigines, while demonstrating the harvesting of the 'bush potato' in the vicinity of Barrow Creek, for disturbed areas such as the edges of bulldozed roads and railway survey lines. Such choices probably reflect ethnobotanical knowledge from an earlier time and may, indeed, indicate the incidental 'tillage', not only from root harvesting but also from the quest for underground vertebrate and invertebrate fauna, that could stimulate the spread of plants such as *I. costata*. Harlan's reference (1975, p. 50) to 'yam' harvests and the digging up of the Australian landscape, and to the similarity of intensive gathering and cultivation, may not be far off the prehistorical mark. Certainly the illustration of still-exploited stands of *I. costata* in Cane's (1984) study of the Western Desert demonstrates a field- or garden-stand effect very similar to that described repeatedly for *Dioscorea* in 19th-century records of Australian exploration.

Although horticultural experiments at the Arid Zone Research Institute (Latz, pers. comm.), the Queensland Herbarium (Johnson, pers. comm.), and in our own cytological work have shown that the naturally hard seed of the desert species is easily germinated, seedlings are not often recognized in the field and must occur after infrequent heavy rain. Sexual reproduction in *I. costata* thus performs a secondary function in the foraging context of the Aborigines as part of the desert's seed bank, with its greater potential for the expression of genetic variability generally held in suspension. This is paralleled by the sweet potato, the related American *I. batatas*, in the agricultural Pacific Islands (Yen 1974) where, occasionally, seedling varieties arise by accident.

Among the most important members of the desert flora are the drug plants: two of the genus *Nicotiana*, and the related *Duboisia hopwoodii*. The latter may have been the most valued in traditional times, because the processed leaf and stem, known as *pituri*, was recorded by early eyewitnesses as a principal item of trade networks that were virtually transcontinental (Mulvaney 1976). The manufacturing centre for this trade was in the Mulligan–Georgina Rivers region of southwestern Queensland, and Watson

(1983) explains that the *pituri* grown in this region was sought for its high nicotine content, and because, unlike the species in other parts of the desert, the content of the associated poisonous d–nor–nicotine was minimal. Because natural populations of *Duboisia* are normally scattered and low in stand density, Watson (1983) suggests that the use of fire and incidental cultivation may have produced the stands necessary to sustain the Queensland centre of *pituri* trade. These agronomic factors may well have contributed to the earlier distribution of the species. Its history, however, has to be considered with the wattle species *Acacia ligulata* whose wood provides the ash favoured for consumption with *pituri* because it releases the drug component. The modern distribution of both species is roughly the same, extending from the central desert to the northwestern and central-southern coasts of the continent, but during the Pleistocene phase of aridity (according to the reconstruction of Buckley 1982) the two were separate: *Acacia ligulata* in the central and central-western sand dunes and *Duboisia hopwoodii* restricted to the northwestern and southwestern coasts and mesic zones of the continent. The necessary confluence of these species must have occurred in more recent times, and although it may have been the result of purely natural migration, it could well have been consonant with Holocene human settlement, or at least with the time of significant population increase in the interior.

In these examples, attaching an agronomic label to the subsistence methods of the Australian Aborigine may be justified: the shifting cultivator of the Pacific and Southeast Asia uses fire in clearing; replanting after the 'bandicooting' method of progressively harvesting root crops; minimal tillage. The combination of these techniques, when used by the forager, results in aggregative effects that can simulate the fields or gardens of the agriculturalist. They may together comprise a factor in plant distribution, a part of Anderson's (1952) 'dumpheap' effect in respect of domestication, which was derived from Darwin and which Hynes & Chase (1982) seem to have translated as Australian 'domiculture', although without the implication of an evolutionary agricultural succession.

In drawing such parallels, however, it must be acknowledged that of the 'agronomic methods' employed by gatherers, only fire is clearly used (in part) for the same purposes as it is by agriculturalists. The remainder, which we might stretch to include weeding, are inadvertent for the most part, incidental to harvesting actions, as indeed are the aggregative effects which mimic fields. To the example of the harvesting of tubers and the other methods of acquiring subterranean foods from which 'fields' may result, we should add grass-seed exploitation. It is clear from the historical accounts summarized by Allen (1974), that the aggregating effect of harvesting with techniques which result in 'hay-cocks' of straw on grassland landscapes is a source of seed-spread after the operations of threshing and winnowing. The reported magnitude of such harvesting has suggested storage of grain as a further agricultural parallel, which as yet lacks firm archaeological attestation. The repeated firing of such tracts tends to replicate the well-known (e.g. Robbins 1963), often monospecific, grassland formation in New Guinea, which has resulted from agricultural clearance of earlier forests. The contrast, of course, lies in the utilization of grassland, for there is no record of grass-seed consumption in New Guinea, and grasslands pose greater difficulty than forests to the agriculturalist preparing the ground for crop production.

In summary, it is worth re-stating that the element of plant domestication is absent from the Australian hunting–gathering systems, but that domestication of the environment in which those plants grow is not. The 'inadvertency' of environmental manipulation by the hunter–gatherers contrasts with the agriculturalists' deliberate modification of the environment to fit the genetically controlled physiological needs of cultigens – one of the most obvious examples being water provision and control for *Colocasia* in Oceania. However, before these statements are developed further, we need to make a further comparison, which takes into account the inclusive view of environment expressed in the classic definitions of Conklin (1963) in which social factors are regarded as an integral part of any consideration of environmental modification by agriculturalists. Indeed, here we extend that view to encompass all production – hunter–gatherer, agricultural, and industrial – in human society.

## Social adjustments to foraging

Two major social influences on subsistence systems, which are often connected, are trade (or exchange) and the intensification of production. The effect of trade in its simplest form is towards the equalization of unevenly distributed resources, and its elaboration tends to add value to those resources, which was not apparent initially in their respective places of provenance. The production of manufactured goods may still reflect the redistributional function of trade at more complex levels, but the values of congress, which includes ceremonial and marriage exchange, assume the greater social importance. It should be noted that the simplest form of exchange has not been recorded ethnographically, at least in the Pacific, except under crisis conditions. Such an example occurred in 1972 in the eastern Solomon Islands where, in the wake of a disastrous cyclone that seriously curtailed food supplies on Santa Ana Island, trading partners on nearby and unaffected San Cristobal Island, who traditionally exchanged canoes, shell ornaments, and marriage partners, sustained a supply of tubers, coconuts, and other food for Santa Ana before government aid could be organized. Direct reciprocity was suspended.

In the preceding discussion of Australian Aboriginal 'agronomy' the trading aspects of economies were mentioned. There is no evidence for food exchanges, such as tubers for grain, or wetland for dryland products, but in reference to the continent-wide scale of trade networks Mulvaney (1976, p. 80) states that:

it was possible for a man who brought pituri from the Mulligan River and ochre from Parachilna to own a Cloncurry axe, a Boulia boomerang and wear shell pendants from Carpentaria and Kimberley.

If trade, apart from in its simplest form, implies intensification and often specialization of production beyond subsistence on the part of trading partners, then the available Australian evidence suggests that such developments occurred in prehistory. The parallel with the New Guinea agriculturalists is demonstrable through the synthesis by Hughes (1977) of traditional trade networks and the products of exchange within them. There are a considerable number of New Guinea case studies which illustrate the intensification characteristics of trade or exchange, and we need only cite the well-known work of Rappaport (1967) among the Tsembaga Maring, wherein the provision of pigs for inter-group ceremonial exchange entails a cyclic agronomic intensification. The importance (and accompanying stress) of social production beyond subsistence is patent in such environmental adjustments. In Australia there is no possibility of carrying out such detailed studies with virtually unacculturated peoples, but the existence of exchange cycles in prehistory has been postulated, for example by Beaton (1982) who has interpreted the remains of large quantities of cycad seeds found in Queensland sites dated to some 4000 years ago as indicative of the ceremonial requirements of traditional 'communions' of related and often distant groups of the region.

Allen (1976, 1977) in his studies of the coastal trading systems of the Papuan Gulf unequivocally identifies their subsistence bases, whereby subsistence products such as sago, wallabies, and fish underly the pottery and shell products by which such systems are often characterized. Redistribution of food resources not held in common among partners, the role of valuables and the specialization of production, and middlemen established on small islets and promontories, are all represented in this absorbing analysis; and it is interesting that the cyclic rise and fall of the systems is interpreted by McIntyre & Allen (unpublished) as centred on the entrepreneur, whose accumulated wealth could not compensate for the lack of a subsistence base in an otherwise socially unsupported status. Although we cannot apply this to the Australian Aboriginal trade network, and particularly not its dynamism through time, Mulvaney's discrimination of production and distribution centres (markets?) suggests possible intermediaries in trade that transcend group boundaries.

In terms of intensification and technological progression in agriculture, Brookfield with Hart (1971) has comprehensively reviewed the Melanesian settings. Unlike Polynesia, archaeologists in Melanesia have not been able to use production as an indicator of the rise of complex societies and hereditary chiefdoms, although all the relevant agricultural techniques are present. As we have noted, there is a trend in current Australian archaeology to seek social complexity through evidence for the intensification of production and the development of sedentism, both debated and both construable as being on the arrested road to agriculture. Yoffee (1985) and Gamble (1986) have both warned against this interpretive trend in terms of the nature of the evidence, its construction, and, indeed, the identification of complexity. There does seem to be evidence for possible intensification in the examples of *pituri*, grass-seed exploitation, the near-horticulture of tuber acquisition, and especially Lourandos'/evidence (1980) for large-scale water control for the entrapment of eels and other fish in inland Victoria; as well as the broader manifestations of increasingly intensive occupation in the Holocene, suggested by Lourandos' (1983) archaeological analysis of coastal and inland sites in Victoria. Whether these phenomena are the consequences of changing social forms, or the imprints of population increase without significant change in the production system (cf. technological modification), or just assumptive correlation, is a matter for debate (e.g. Beaton 1983, Lourandos 1984) and one that is not restricted to the Australian prehistorical scene.

However, without disengaging the issue of social complexity completely from the intensification of production, it may be profitable to view Australian prehistory from a wider perspective. Archaeologically there is a minimum of 40 millennia of prehistory, and the most persuasive model of colonization of the continent has been that advanced by Bowdler (1977) which emphasizes the primacy of coastal settlement, at a time of lower-than-present sea-levels, and the penetration of inland waterways. At the other extreme of the time-scale is the end-point of endogenous Aboriginal development, the near-fatal advent of the European, when the continent, on cultural and linguistic criteria (Tindale 1974), was already divided into tribal, group, and subgroup regions. Without translating Tindale's tribal boundaries into the stricter lineal political boundaries of modern conception, it is clear that a pattern of territoriality came into being, breachable by treaty or trespass. This 'event' climaxed the colonization of the continent which, unless we view it as exploration for its own adventurous sake, radiated inland from the favourable coasts and riverine environments to the less hospitable hinterlands. Such a scenario of human adaptation was played out against a backdrop of an environment changing from Pleistocene to more favourable Holocene climatic conditions, and, as botanical research (exemplified above) indicates, changing resources. In the earlier phases of colonization, the resource areas must have seemed spatially limitless, and their exploitations would have been determined more by the quantity and concentration, variety and seasonal behaviour, of useful biota than by social dictates. Indeed, one may interpret the Bowdler model of settlement in formative social terms, beginning with the isolation of early colonizing groups and continuing with succeeding separate penetrations of the continent (although the efforts to maintain social ties may well be a partial illusion of the modern cultural and linguistic record). The contention is, then, that in the Holocene the whole of Australia had been settled, giving rise to its territorialization.

This speculative excursion into Aboriginal history (cf. Birdsell 1977) has the implications of population growth which have already been discussed in the Australian archaeological literature, and is designed to convey the amplitude of subsistence that had to be its accompaniment: the early wide-ranging nature of systems, the later obligatory recognition of territory through the relative concentration that social boundaries impose on hunting–gathering systems, and their peaceful breaching through trade and exchange alliances. There are, however, geographical differentials of population densities that correlate with resource supply: one such example is Lourandos' archaeological work in Victoria, which tends to confirm the high population and considerable subgroup identification indicated by Tindale's mapping; another is Harris' (1978) ethnohistorical analysis of population distribution in the Queensland rainforest, which does likewise. In what its prefator claims to be the first monograph on intertribal relationships among peoples of 'lower stages of civilization', Wheeler (1910) stressed the division of Australia into tribally defined Aboriginal territory with subgroup subdivision, alliances, and the periodic congress of confederations. Intermarriage and initiation were ceremonial occasions, and the bartering of specialized items of manufacture, such as arms, implements, and *pituri* by certain tribes were noted. Trade seems to have been centred on valuables, and although there are no accounts of direct food exchanges, the necessity of concentrated food production at centres of trade has been inferred, e.g. by Watson (1983). Indeed, most of the scattered archaeological and ethnohistorical evidence for intensification of production is usually discussed as possibly indicating the development of ceremonial forms, as well as in the more secular terms of demographic change through time. It may be that trading of less valuable subsistence items was carried out at less conspicuous local levels, or at earlier stages in the development of trade.

Viewed overall, the presumed progressive subdivision of Australia through time certainly implies regionally differential population growth. It has, in terms of subsistence, the inescapable implication of intensification – the narrowing of the radii of potential hunting–gathering cycles – and it reflects the surprisingly bountiful natural resources available over much of the continent, as well as the ability of the original Australians to cope by means of the varying forms of 'agronomic' intensification that were necessary through the shrinkage of environmental domains by social attrition. In applying the evolutionary model of Harris (1977b) for transitions to food production (agriculture), the end-point of development of Aboriginal systems most resembles System C (p. 191), in which population pressure is related to reduction in residential mobility, as well as to its relief by cultural regulation. Williams (1985) has already pointed out the difficulties attendant in the archaeological calculation of populations in one of the favourable environments of Australia, Victoria, so that the attribution by Harris of stress as the major motivation for change may be difficult to demonstrate in the context of the advent or invention of the small-tool tradition in the Holocene. If Gamble (1986) means that 'restructuring' is synonymous with agriculture among the Aborigines, it has not happened yet; but the prehistoric restructuring process implied by the onset of territorial division was a major adaptive change whose effects appear to have been imprinted archaeologically in the Holocene.

## The domestication of environment

The feature of territoriality completes the portrait of structural parallels between hunter–gatherer and agricultural systems. Although finer grained analyses can accentuate differences, it is in the purposive actions that are associated with, and sustained in, the domestication process that the major conceptual distinction lies. Biota must undergo selection in hunter–gatherer contexts, but this process is incidental to the domestication of the environment as a whole: it is more akin to natural selection in which man's role is largely inadvertent. Thus, in the *pituri* example, the Mulligan–Georgina region that produced a high nicotine and low toxin product was the centre of production for the virtually transcontinental trade as an environmental specialization. From what is known, no diffusion of this desirable form of the species of *Duboisia* was effected to other arid and semi-arid regions to which the same species is adapted but whose variable populations contain highly toxic as well as low-nicotine bearing plants. Neither is there any sign of domestication – in the sense of direct selection within the species – in any part of its range, unless, indeed, the Mulligan–Georgina populations are the remains of a long-forgotten and isolated instance. Dobzhansky (1962, p. 11) has described the difference between natural and artificial selection as antonymous, and Maynard Smith (1975, p. 149) has characterized the latter under laboratory conditions of evolutionary experiment in terms of its high relative rate of effected change. Domestication as artificial selection has this characteristic, but its objectives are not necessarily in the same direction, with the same natural survival value. Indeed, without the constant provision of the complementary ecological requirements of the genotype, domestic species may not survive natural competition. Thus, in many respects, the effect of the hunter–gatherer domestication of environment may be likened to a form of group selection, in which the plant targets are aggregated as interbreeding units, compared with the individual selection practised by the agriculturalist, which establishes closer control over the plants' breeding systems and can result in the varietal differentiation of species into physiological types, e.g. wet and dry adaptations in rice and *Colocasia* taro.

None of this constitutes a denial of the derivation of agriculture from hunting–gathering roots; rather it questions that contemporary (ethnographic) hunter–gatherers are the backward relics of a single evolutionary line which most accounts of agricultural development seem to suggest. On the basis of the broad parallels we have drawn here, on an admittedly small number of exemplars, what we have seen ethnographically are not pristine hunter–gatherers, but groups who, in achieving qualitatively distinctive cultural end-points, have followed different pathways of subsistence-system development from common beginnings. This brings to mind modern descriptions of hunter–gatherers to which epithets such as transitional or proto-agricultural have been applied. Among these are such Pacific-rim peoples as the Semang of Malaysia described by Rambo (1985), and the Agta of the Philippines studied by Griffin (1984) and Griffin & Estioko-Griffin (1985), who practise elements of agriculture with seeming reluctance and to degrees proportionate to the proximity of farming neighbours (Estioko-Griffin & Griffin 1981, Headland 1985). Rambo (1985) agrees with Hutterer (1983) that Southeast Asian examples of such adaptations, despite the lack of archaeological evidence, date long into the past. The Agta, however, provide a rare instance of horticultural technique in the planting of *Miscanthus* at camp sites (Estioko-Griffin & Griffin 1981, p. 61), which could indicate an earlier agricultural tradition (a notion not entertained by Griffin in personal communication). Whatever the case, Griffin's recent description (in press) of planting among more distal groups of Agta demonstrates an uncertain integration into Philippine agriculture of largely American adventives such as maize, manioc, and sweet potato, indicating comparatively recent diffusion. Indeed, such studies of contemporary 'transitional' groups may offer ethnoarchaeological explanations of the process of diffusion of agriculture rather than its invention. The acceleration of such diffusion may be initially through trade between agriculturalists and foragers, then territorial incursions by the former into uncultivated tracts. Peterson & Peterson (1977), in earlier ethnographic and archaeological studies among Agta groups, have suggested that forager–agriculturalist trading is an indication of earlier, intra-forager exchanges, as ancient as agriculture in the region. Their interpretation was that such exchange systems could have delayed the intensification of subsistence systems through the partial adoption of agriculture to yield the present-day mixed mode of subsistence. This implies an effective means of resource sharing in the past.

The stress of external pressures on land among hunter–gatherers has been magnified with the modern value of land and its natural resources such as timber and minerals, and with the political oppression of minorities, which have rendered helpless most traditional ways of adjustment. Even though Agta and Semang groups have taken on agriculture in spasmodic fashion, they have maintained trade with, and provided labour for, agricultural neighbours who, through a chain of rural centres and provincial towns, provide a supply of goods that goes beyond the exchange of unevenly distributed resources for the hunter–gatherer to participation, at the absolute margin, in the economies of metropolitan capitals. A variant is the Mlabrai people, or Phi Tong Luang, of central northern Thailand, known since the early 1920s, and now being studied by Pookajorn (1985) as mobile foragers virtually hemmed in by cultivators with whom they have traditionally traded for agricultural produce, and whom they have recently provided with labour.

Lévi-Strauss (1963, p. 112) referred to the difficulties of accepting modern hunter–gatherers as representative of static pasts, being concerned with possible 'pseudo-archaism', compared with the 'real archaism' of a few groups such as the Fuegians. Apart from the environmental determinism that the latter may imply, pseudo-archaism meant that others could represent the remains of earlier, more complex societies. If such complexity may be equated with food production and therefore earlier agriculture, then Levi-Strauss' later claim (1976, p. 325) that such history 'is and will remain unknown' may be subject to modification through archaeological investigations. The recent journalistic exposure of the embattled Tasaday as a hoax ignored the earlier evidence (Molony with Tuan 1976, Yen 1976b) on lexical grounds that the group could have derived from agricultural Manobo antecedents, and Crawford & Yoshizaki (1987) have stronger and more direct evidence from archaeology that the Ainu of northern Japan – the prototypic sedentary hunter–gatherers – had within their subsistence system in the 9th century AD at least a strong element of agriculture based on an early East Asian crop assemblage. The latter case suggests an historical diffusion of agriculture that could not be sustained on the social substrate (from implied earlier hunter–gatherer status) until the modern reintroduction of agriculture by the Japanese, this time with the integrational factors of resettlement and indeed assimilation into the intrusive society. Some parallels, albeit asynchronous, may be drawn between the Ainu example and the Agta, wherein the coexistence of foragers with agriculturalists may allow for 'experimental' diffusion of agricultural methods and materials which only under external social pressure transforms the mode of production. The studies of the contemporary Agta by Estioko-Griffin & Griffin (1981, p. 61) indicate a recent sequence of contact with Paranan agricultural neighbours, largely by spasmodic trade, the maintenance of the hunter–gathering mode of production as advantageous over planting (with the exception of *Miscanthus* for spear shafts), followed by pressure on land by the Paranan resulting in a decline in hunting by the Agta, their adoption of part-time farming, and increased intercourse with the Paranan agriculturalists. It might be conjectured that if political support for increasing pressure on land were withdrawn, there could be a reversal of the sequence as a function of the Agta resistance to agriculture which has been documented since Spanish times in the Philippines (Headland 1985).

The environmental dictate of isolation may have been the significant factor in galvanizing resistance to the diffusion of agriculture to Australia. Harris (1977a) clearly charts the potential passage through the Cape York region from New Guinea. The nature of acceptance may be indicated by the appearance of two of the most important root crops of the Pacific Islands in the plant gathering rosters of the Aborigines of northern Australia, the greater yam and *Colocasia* taro. Cytological studies on taro (Coates *et al.* in press) indicate that the Australian representatives have chromosome numbers and karyotype identical with New Guinea wild types and cultivars, and may thus signify either that the natural range of taro extends to northern Australia or that it became naturalized there in Aboriginally modified habitats. In these examples of the greater yam and, perhaps, taro in Australia, diffusion has taken the form of the feralization of formerly cultivated species into environments already 'domesticated' by long-term hunter–gatherers, 'domicultural' in the terms of Hynes & Chase (1982) and Chase (Ch. 3), but who never underwent the agricultural transformation.

The foragers of Australia, who date back at least 40 000 years, continued a much older tradition, but primary colonization meant restarting the process of adaptation and the acquisition of new sets of ethnoscientific knowledge in the vast, varied environment empty of established competitive human groups, a process which, with endogenous cultural development and population increase, eventually led to the relative complexity and variability of Aboriginal lifeways. On the wider hunter–gatherer canvas, the conservatism that we have observed indicates that the structural change of societies which fitted some to adapt their ethnobiological concepts to cultivation was not equally shared. Thus at *c.* 10 000 years ago this was manifest in the branching of the continuing developmental line of hunting–gathering into horticulture in which the domestication of the environment was channelled, by the genetic dictates of species, and artificial selection replaced the more incidental selection integral to human foraging that some writers have equated with animal feeding habits. Artificial selection, the control of breeding systems, and the provision of edaphic media for cultivation, firstly enacted on a wide range of genera, resulted in a narrowing of the subsistence base, but also conferred an ability to extend the radius of distribution of the reduced species spectrum. A factor in cultigen survival was probably the early diffusion from domestication 'centres', the influence of locational differences on the directions of selection, and cultural differentials on selection intensities.

## Summary and conclusion

Figure 4.1 attempts to represent diagrammatically the world transformation of hunting–gathering through agricultural systems of increasing complexity to modern global agriculture; the sins of simplification and idealization (among others) should be acknowledged here. Also, against precepts of scientific presentation, it may be seen that the departures of the subsistence agricultural line (II) from the continuing development of the integral foraging line (I) are succeeded by regional state formation and the class specialized agricultural systems of line III, which have not been discussed in the preceding text. The divergences of line II to line III are partially extracted from Wright's recent synthesis (1986) of the evolution of civilizations, and form a bridge to line IV: the development of modern international primary production and the control by political economies. We have considered the latter as the ultimate source of pressure on the land of the remaining subsistence agriculturalists and hunter–gatherers of today. These realignments accentuate the socio-political influences on, and decreasing regionalism of, economic systems as the successive descendants of subsistence systems, and thus point to the importance of social factors in the earlier

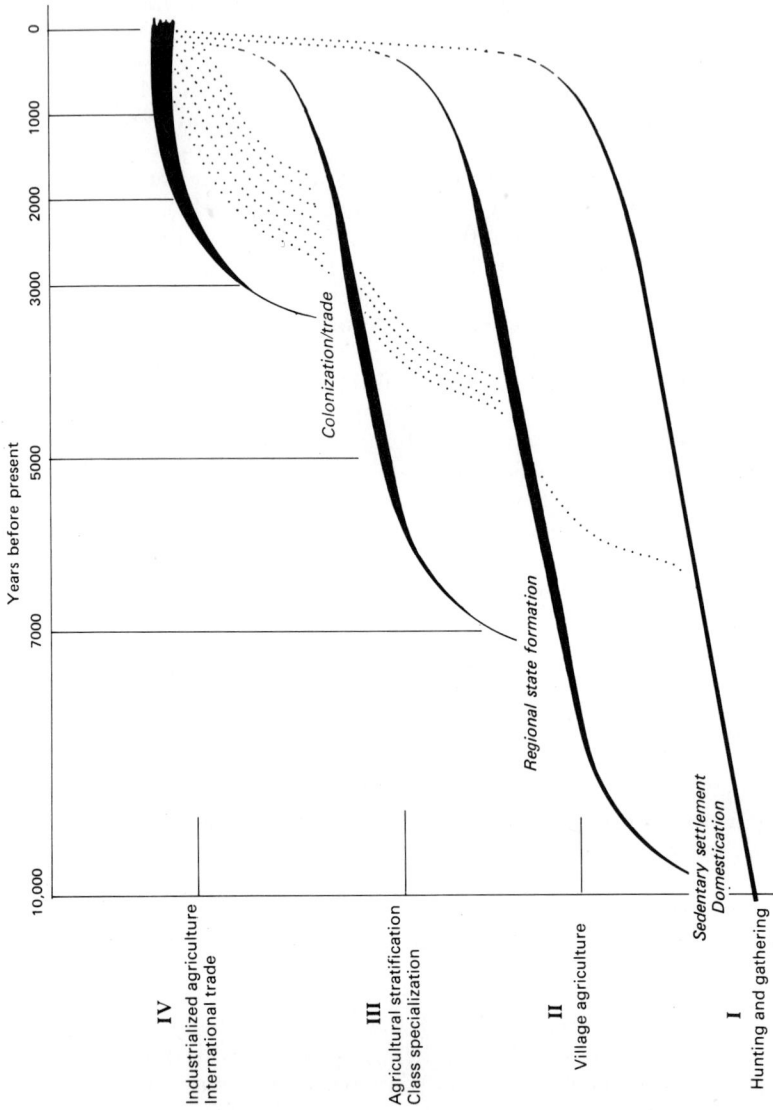

**Figure 4.1** The 'domestication of environment' as transformation from hunting–gathering (I) through agricultural forms of increasing complexity (II–IV). The inclination of the parallel lines of the systems through time represents the internal development of social and technological elaborations that affect environment, while the varying thickness of the lines indicates uneven amplitudes of such development. Diffusion between systems is portrayed by dotted lines which, in the 17th century and the beginnings of global colonization, signalled the end to come of independence of subsistence systems I and II. Domestication, regional state formation, and colonization as single lines should be recognized as gross simplifications of history.

transformation from gathering through genetic domestication and increasing sedentism. The figure conveys that the initial branching produced two parallel forms of production that were to develop independently, even though some diffusion occurred between them. The technological development of agriculture through intensive methods of cultivation is seen as a narrowing of species range associated with the provision of genetically dictated edaphic environments. Intensification of foraging is more directly a function of social development, since it lacks the artificial selection that changes natural biota and effects their transport into unnatural but modifiable environments.

The conversion of village to state agriculture is the loss of importance of subsistence identity, or its restructuring with specialization of crops becoming more pronounced as supra-subsistence surpluses take on deeper economic meaning. Indeed, the diagram could be simplified if the European age of discovery and the full development of global trade are regarded as extensions of the transformation of regional states. Whatever view is taken, the long-posited evolutionary line of increasing social complexity on a world scale produced expanding economies in which the subsistence character of early agricultural and hunter–gatherer modes of production was lost, or relegated to relative insignificance. The point remains, however, that well into the eras of regional states, all three modes of production existed virtually side by side, although we cannot maintain that the subsistence peoples did not suffer from pressures on their land, whether it was used agriculturally or as a result of their being crowded into smaller foraging ranges. Such trends are incorporated into the diffusion connections portrayed between the developmental lines. AD 1500 represents the beginnings of circumglobal trade, the most powerful of diffusive forces with its implications of conquest and colonization, which eventually has left no group of subsistence peoples untouched – whether in terms of commodities (including land) sought, or as recipients of material and spiritual benefits of 'civilization'. At the final extension of the diagram is portrayed history of the not too distant future when subsistence production as integral systems will no longer exist.

The domestication of the environment by the hunter–gatherer had a long developmental history which, only near its end, branched, through plant and animal domestication, to a more focused, yet more mobile, environmental ennoblement dictated by the physiological requirements of the favoured biota. The transformation of subsistence to the more highly institutionalized agriculture, while not causative, fuelled the emergence of political states and the world economy, which sometimes seems not too great an advance in environmental domestication. Within the span of human cultural development, and assuming it has a future, the 10 000 years of subsistence agriculture was a temporal episode in the domestication of the world environment, and domestication, in the normally used genetic sense, a moment.

## Acknowledgements

This chapter arose from separate discussions with Bion Griffin, David Harris, Gordon Hillman, Karl Hutterer, Matthew Spriggs, Henry Wright; these acknowledgements do not imply approval of the result. Eric Komori and Winifred Mumford developed the diagram from a confused design by the writer.

## References

Allen, H. 1974. The Bagundji of the Darling Basin: cereal gatherers in an uncertain environment. *World Archaeology* **5**, 309–22.

Allen, J. 1976. Fishing for wallabies: trade as mechanism for social interaction, integration and elaboration on the central Papuan coast. In *The evolution of social systems*, J. Friedman & M. J. Rowlands (eds), 419–55. London: Duckworth.

Allen, J. 1977. Sea traffic, trade and expanding horizons. In *Sunda and Sahul: prehistoric studies in Southeast Asia, Melanesia and Australia*, J. Allen, J. Golson & R. Jones (eds), 387–417. New York: Academic Press.

Anderson, E. 1952. *Plants, man and life*. Berkeley: University of California Press (1967 reprint).

Beaton, J. M. 1982. Fire and water: Aspects of Aboriginal management of cycads. *Archaeology in Oceania* **17**, 51–8.

Beaton, J. M. 1983. Does intensification account for changes in the Australian Holocene archaeological record: *Archaeology in Oceania* **18**, 94–7.

Birdsell, J. B. 1977. The recalibration of a paradigm for the first peopling of Greater Australia. In *Sunda and Sahul: prehistoric studies in Southeast Asia, Melanesia and Australia*, J. Allen, J. Golson & R. Jones (eds), 113–67. New York: Academic Press.

Bowdler, S. 1977. The coastal colonization of Australia. In *Sunda and Sahul: prehistoric studies in Southeast Asia, Melanesia and Australia*, J. Allen, J. Golson & R. Jones (eds), 205–46. New York: Academic Press.

Bronson, B. 1975. The earliest farming: demography as cause and consequence. In *Population, ecology and social evolution*, S. Polgar (ed.), 53–78. Chicago: Aldine.

Brookfield, H. C. with D. Hart 1971. *Melanesia: a geographical interpretation of an island world*. London: Methuen.

Buckley, R. 1982. Central Australian sand-ridge flora 18,000 years ago: Phytogeographic evidence. In *Evolution of the flora and fauna of arid Australia*, W. R. Barker & P. J. M. Greenslade (eds), 107–17. Frewville (S. Australia): Peacock Publications.

Cane, S. 1984. *Desert camps: A case study of stone artifacts and Aboriginal behaviour in the Western Desert*. Unpublished PhD thesis, The Australian National University, Canberra.

Cane, S. 1989. Australian Aboriginal seed grinding and its archaeological record: a case study from the Western Desert. In *Foraging and farming: the evolution of plant exploitation*, D. R. Harris & G. C. Hillman (eds), ch. 6. London: Unwin Hyman.

Chase, A. 1989. Domestication and domiculture in northern Australia: a social perspective. In *Foraging and farming: the evolution of plant exploitation*, D. R. Harris & G. C. Hillman (eds), ch. 3. London: Unwin Hyman.

Clark, R. 1983. Pollen and charcoal evidence for the effects of Aboriginal burning on the vegetation of Australia. *Archaeology in Oceania* **18**, 32–7.

Coates, D. J., D. E. Yen & P. M. Gaffey in press. Chromosome variation in taro, *Colocasia esculenta*: implications for origin in the Pacific. *Cytologia*.

Conklin, H. C. 1963. *The study of shifting cultivation.* Washington, DC: Union Panamericana.

Crawford, G. W. & M. Yoshizaki 1987. Ainu ancestors and prehistoric Asian agriculture. *Journal of Archaeological Science* **14**, 201–13.

Crawford, I. M. 1984. *Aboriginal traditional plant resources in the Kalumburu area: aspects in ethno-economics.* Perth: Records of the Western Australian Museum, Supplement No. 15.

Darwin, C. 1845. *Journal of researches into geology and natural history of the various countries visited during the voyage of H.M.S.* Beagle *round the world.* (1906 edn). London: Dent.

Darwin, C. 1859. *The origin of species.* (1928 edn). London: Dent.

Dobzhansky, Th. 1962. *Mankind evolving.* New Haven: Yale University Press.

Estioko-Griffin, A. & P. B. Griffin 1981. The beginnings of cultivation among the Agta hunter–gatherers in northeast Luzon. In *Adaptive strategies and change in Philippine swidden-based societies,* J. Olofson (ed.), 55–72. Laguna (Philippines): Forest Research Institute.

Gamble, C. 1986. The mesolithic sandwich: ecological approaches and the archaeological record of the early postglacial. In *Hunters in transition: Mesolithic societies of temperate Eurasia and their transition to farming,* M. Zvelebil (ed.), 33–42. Cambridge: Cambridge University Press.

Gott, B. 1982. The ecology of root use by the Aborigines of southern Australia. *Archaeology in Oceania* **17**, 59–67.

Gregory, H. C. 1886. Memoranda on the Aborigines of Australia. *Journal of the Anthropological Institute* **16**, 131–3.

Griffin, P. B. 1984. Forager resource and land use in the humid tropics: the Agta of northeastern Luzon. In *Past and present in hunter gatherer studies,* C. Schrire (ed.), 95–121. New York: Academic Press.

Griffin, P. B. in press. Hunting, farming and sedentism in a rain forest foraging society. In *Farmers as hunters – on implications of sedentism,* S. Kent (ed.). Cambridge: Cambridge University Press.

Griffin, P. B. & A. Estioko-Griffin (eds) 1985. *The Agta of northeastern Luzon.* Cebu City: San Carlos Publications.

Hallam, S. J. 1986. Yams, alluvium and 'villages' on the western coastal plain. In *Archaeology at ANZAAS, Canberra,* G. K. Ward (ed.), 116–32. Canberra: Canberra Archaeological Society.

Hallam, S. J. 1989. Plant usage and management in Southwest Australian societies. In *Foraging and farming: the evolution of plant exploitation,* D. R. Harris & G. C. Hillman (eds), ch. 8. London: Unwin Hyman.

Harlan, J. R. 1971. Agricultural origins: centers and noncenters. *Science* **174**, 468–74.

Harlan, J. R. 1975. *Crops and man.* Madison: American Society for Agronomy.

Harris, D. R. 1977a. Subsistence strategies across Torres Strait. In *Sunda and Sahul: prehistoric studies in Southeast Asia, Melanesia and Australia,* J. Allen, J. Golson & R. Jones (eds), 421–63. New York: Academic Press.

Harris, D. R. 1977b. Alternative pathways toward agriculture. In *Origins of agriculture,* C. A. Reed (ed.), 179–243. The Hague: Mouton.

Harris, D. R. 1978. Adaptation to a tropical rainforest environment: Aboriginal subsistence in northeastern Queensland. In *Human behaviour and adaptation,* N. Blurton-Jones and V. Reynolds (eds), 113–34. London: Taylor & Francis.

Harris, D. R. 1989. An evolutionary continuum of people–plant interaction. In

*Foraging and farming: the evolution of plant exploitation*, D. R. Harris & G. C. Hillman (eds), ch. 1. London: Unwin Hyman.

Headland, T. N. 1985. Imposed values and rejection among Casiguran Agta. In *The Agta of northeastern Luzon*, P. B. Griffin & A. Estioko-Griffin (eds). Cebu City: San Carlos Publications.

Hughes, I. 1977. *New Guinea Stone Age trade*. Terra Australis **3**. Canberra: Department of Prehistory, Research School of Pacific Studies, Australian National University.

Hutterer, K. 1983. The natural and cultural history of Southeast Asian agriculture: ecological and evolutionary considerations. *Anthropos* **78**, 169–212.

Hynes, R. A. & A. K. Chase 1982. Plants, sites and domiculture: Aboriginal influence on plant communities in Cape York Peninsula. *Archaeology in Oceania* **17**, 38–50.

Johnson, R. W. 1986. Four new species of *Ipomoea* L. (Convolvulaceae) from Australia. *Austrobaileya* **2**, 217–23.

Jones, R. 1969. Firestick farming. *Australian Natural History* **16**, 224–8.

Jones, R. 1975. The Neolithic Palaeolithic and the hunting gardeners: man and land in the Antipodes. In *Quaternary studies*, R. P. Suggate & M. M. Cresswell (eds), 21–34. Wellington: Royal Society of New Zealand.

Jones, R. & B. Meehan. 1989. Plant foods of the Gidjingali: ethnographic and archaeological perspectives from northern Australia on tuber and seed exploitation. In *Foraging and farming: the evolution of plant exploitation*, D. R. Harris & G. C. Hillman (eds), ch. 7. London: Unwin Hyman.

Kimber, R. 1983. Black lightning: Aborigines and fire in central Australia and the western desert. *Archaeology in Oceania* **18**, 38–44.

Latz, P. K. 1982. *Bushfires and bushtucker: Aborigines and plants in central Australia*. Unpublished MA thesis, University of New England, Australia.

Latz, P. K. & G. F. Griffin 1978. Changes in Aboriginal land management in relation to fire and to food plants in central Australia. In *The nutrition of Aborigines in relation to the ecosystem of central Australia*, B. S. Hetzel & H. J. Frith (eds), 77–85. Melbourne: CSIRO.

Levi-Strauss, C. 1963. The concept of archaism in anthropology. In *Structural anthropology*, Vol. I, 101–19. New York: Basic Books. Published first in French 1952.

Levi-Strauss, C. 1976. Race and history. In *Structural anthropology*, Vol. II, 323–62. New York: Basic Books. Published first in French 1952.

Lourandos, H. 1980. Change or stability? Hydraulics, hunter–gatherers and population in temperate Australia. *World Archaeology* **11**, 245–64.

Lourandos, H. 1983. Intensification: a late Pleistocene–Holocene archaeological sequence from southwestern Victoria. *Archaeology in Oceania* **18**, 81–94.

Lourandos, H. 1984. Changing perspectives in Australian prehistory: a reply to Beaton. *Archaeology in Oceania* **19**, 29–33.

McIntyre, M. & J. Allen. Unpublished. Trading for subsistence: the case from the southern Massim. Paper delivered to XV Pacific Science Congress, Dunedin, New Zealand, 1983.

Maynard Smith, J. 1975. *The theory of evolution*, 3rd edn. Harmondsworth: Penguin.

Meehan, B. 1982. *Shell bed to shell midden*. Canberra: Australian Institute of Aboriginal Studies.

Meggitt, M. 1962. *Desert people*. Sydney: Angus & Robertson.

Molony, C. with D. Tuan 1976. Further studies on the Tasaday language: texts and vocabulary. In *Further studies on the Tasaday*, D. E. Yen & J. Nance (eds), 13–96. Makati Panamin Foundation Research Series No. 2.

Mulvaney, D. J. 1976. 'The chain of connection': the material evidence. In *Tribes and boundaries in Australia*, N. Peterson (ed.), 72–94. Canberra: Australian Institute of Aboriginal Studies.

Peterson, J. T. and W. Peterson 1977. Implications of contemporary and prehistoric exchange systems. In *Sunda and Sahul: prehistoric studies in Southeast Asia, Melanesia and Australia*, J. Allen, J. Golson & R. Jones (eds), 533–64. New York: Academic Press.

Pookajorn, S. 1985. Ethnoarchaeology with the Phi Tong Luang (Mlabrai): forest hunters of northern Thailand. *World Archaeology* **17**, 206–21.

Rambo, A. T. 1985. *Primitive polluters: Semang impact on the Malaysian tropical forest ecosystem*. Ann Arbor: Museum of Anthropology Papers 76.

Rappaport, R. A. 1967. *Pigs for the ancestors: ritual in the ecology of a New Guinea people*. New Haven: Yale University Press.

Robbins, R. G. 1963. Correlations of plant patterns and population migration into Australian New Guinea highlands. In *Plants and the migrations of Pacific peoples*, J. Barrau (ed.), 45–59. Honolulu: Bishop Museum Press.

Smith, M. A. 1986. The antiquity of seed grinding in central Australia. *Archaeology in Oceania* **21**, 29–39.

Smith, M. A. 1987. Pleistocene occupation in arid Central Australia. *Nature* **328**, 710–11.

Smith, M. A. 1989. Seed gathering in inland Australia: current evidence on the antiquity of the ethnohistorical pattern of exploitation. In *Foraging and farming: the evolution of plant exploitation*, D. R. Harris & G. C. Hillman (eds), ch. 18. London: Unwin Hyman.

Telford, I. R. H. 1986. Dioscoreaceae. In *Flora of Australia*, Vol. 46, 196–202. Canberra: Australian Government Publishing Service.

Tindale, N. B. 1974. *Aboriginal tribes of Australia*. Berkeley: University of California Press.

Watson, P. 1983. *This precious foliage*. Sydney: Oceania Monographs 26.

Wheeler, G. C. 1910. *The tribe, and intertribal relations in Australia*. London: Murray.

Wright, H. E. 1986. The evolution of civilizations. In *American archaeology past and future*, D. J. Meltzer, D. D. Fowler & J. A. Sabloff (eds), 323–65. Washington DC: Society for American Archaeology and Smithsonian Institution Press.

Williams, E. 1985. Estimations of prehistoric populations of archaeological sites in southwestern Victoria: some problems. *Archaeology in Oceania* **20**, 73–80.

Yen, D. E. 1974. *The sweet potato and Oceania*. Honolulu: Bishop Museum Bulletin 236.

Yen, D. E. 1976a. The ethnobotany of the Tasaday: III. Notes on the subsistence system. In *Further studies on the Tasaday*, D. E. Yen & J. Nance (eds), 159–83. Makati: Panamin Foundation Research Series No. 2.

Yen, D. E. 1976b. The ethnobotany of the Tasaday: II. Plant names of the Tasaday, Manobo Blit and Kemato Tboli. In *Further studies on the Tasaday*, D. E. Yen & J. Nance (eds), 137–58. Makati: Panamin Foundation Research Series No. 2.

Yen, D. E. 1977. Hoabinhian horticulture? The evidence and the questions from northwest Thailand. In *Sunda and Sahul: prehistoric studies in Southeast Asia, Melanesia and Australia*, J. Allen, J. Golson & R. Jones (eds), 567–99. New York: Academic Press.

Yen, D. E. & J. Nance (eds) 1976. *Further studies on the Tasaday*. Makati: Panamin Foundation Research Series No. 2.

Yoffee, N. 1985. Perspectives on 'trends towards social complexity in prehistoric Australia and Papua New Guinea'. *Archaeology in Oceania* **20**, 41–9.

# PLANT EXPLOITATION IN NON-AGRARIAN CONTEXTS: THE ETHNOGRAPHIC WITNESS

# 5 Wild-grass seed harvesting in the Sahara and Sub-Sahara of Africa

JACK R. HARLAN

## Introduction

Over 60 species of grasses have been harvested for their grains in Africa. Most of these are famine or scarcity foods or are harvested casually and opportunistically. Several species, however, have provided food on a massive scale and have been staples for a number of tribes. These include: *Aristida pungens*, a staple of the northern Tuareg; *Panicum turgidum*, basic in central Sahara; *Cenchrus biflorus*, a major food of the Sahel; *krebs*, a complex of a dozen or more species including *Panicum laetum*, several species of *Eragrostis*, *Dactyloctenium*, *Brachiaria*, etc., providing staples from Bornu to Kordofan; *Oryza barthii*, widely harvested from swamps in the savanna, but a staple from Bornu to Kordofan; *Paspalum scrobiculatum*, a companion weed–crop of rice in the forest zone of West Africa; and *Echinochloa stagnina*, a sugar crop as well as a grain crop in the central Niger delta and around Lake Chad.

Methods of harvest include: beating into a container, rubbing with the hands into a basket, cutting with a knife or sickle and threshing with a stick; using a swinging basket or calabash; sweeping or raking off the sand; tying up clumps with string before harvest. The grains are consumed in many forms: pounded and eaten raw; as dilute flour or *semoula* in a drink; gruel; porridge; flat bread; pastry; couscous; and beer. Bran may be removed in the mortar and used separately.

Some of these practices may have started in the Palaeolithic, and they all have relevance to the processes of plant domestication and the beginnings of agriculture.

Some of us who have studied plant domestication in Africa have noted that the continent appears to be a vast laboratory for the study of crop evolution (Harlan *et al.* 1976, p. 5). The progenitors of African crops are usually obvious, and the abundance of intermediate states and conditions makes the pathways of crop evolution easy to follow. This is not the case in the Americas, for example, where we have not identified with any assurance the progenitors of some domesticated *Cucurbita* and *Capsicum* species and where the origins of maize, sweet potato, tobacco, peanut, bottle gourd and the A genome of cotton are still under debate (cf. Heiser Ch. 30, Pickersgill Ch. 27, Wilkes Ch. 28, this volume). In Eurasia, we have yet to locate the B genome of wheat in a diploid species or the progenitors of fava bean, pigeon pea, the bottle gourd, and a few others (cf. Ladizinsky Ch. 23, Zohary Ch. 22, this volume). The story in Africa seems to be simpler and the evidence more clear-cut.

Not only are intermediate states between wild and domesticated races still present, but ancient practices that may have had their origins in the Palaeolithic may persist into historical times when ethnographic observations could be recorded. A suite of these practices concerned with the harvesting of wild-grass grains for food is the focus of this chapter. Harvesting seeds from natural or induced stands does not necessarily result in domestication. The seeds of many species have been harvested for millennia without the evolution of domesticated races, but harvesting and developing some degree of dependence on a plant does establish the kind of intimate relationship between plants and people out of which plant domestication may proceed. Regularly scheduled harvests are probably a precondition for domestication, whether it takes place or not. The wild-grass harvests of Africa are, therefore, pertinent subjects for examination in the context of the evolution of plant exploitation in general and the emergence of cereal agriculture in particular.

## Grass-seed productivity

There seems to be a widespread misconception about wild-grain harvests to the effect that these are desperation or last-resort practices to avert starvation, and that yields are feeble and unpredictable. There are instances when this is so, but natural stands of wild grasses can give very respectable yields of high-quality food, and in some circumstances may be more dependable than cultivated crops. I have had some personal experience of these matters. For over 25 years, I directed research on seed production of several wild species, mostly native North American grasses. Yields of 500–800 kg/ha were not uncommon and 1 ton/ha could occasionally be obtained. This is in the range obtained by many subsistence farmers growing domesticated cereals. Gallais (1984), for example, gives the typical yield of rice grown in the bend of the Niger as 6–700 kg/ha. Good yields with perennial species could not be sustained year after year even with fertilizers and irrigation; seed production of perennial grasses tends to be cyclic (Harlan et al. 1956). Annual species tend to yield more and be more dependable. The annual habit requires reseeding each year, and natural selection has favoured the partitioning of more metabolic effort into the reproduction phase of the life cycle than in perennial species, where annual reproduction is unnecessary.

My often-cited experiment with wild einkorn wheat in Turkey yielded almost 1 kg of pure-grain equivalent per hour of work, and the grains were far more nutritious than domesticated wheat (Harlan 1967). Zohary (1969) performed a somewhat similar experiment with wild emmer in Israel and calculated the yield at 500–800 kg/ha. This is as much or more than farmers in England obtained from domesticated wheat in the Middle Ages (Titow 1972). Chevalier (1932) described an African wild-grass harvest (see below) and stated that one adult could easily gather 10 kg in a morning's effort. There is no evidence that he actually weighed the harvest and the grains still had the hulls attached. Removal of the hull in *Panicum* would reduce the yield by about 20 per cent. But, making allowance for over-estimation and processing, the figure of 1–2 kg/h could surely be achieved and the effort would be highly rewarding. Indeed Evans (1975, p. 329) calculated that my wild wheat harvest returned 40–50 kcal of energy for every kcal expended on my part, and this is far more efficient in terms of the ratio of consumable output energy to energy expended in harvesting than any form of agriculture so far studied. (However, see Cane Ch. 6 for a discussion of the high-energy costs of processing wild-grass seed once it is harvested.)

On another occasion, I used a Mexican wooden paddle for a beater and a plastic wastebasket for a receiving container and harvested a stand of tall fescue (*Festuca arundinacea* Schreb.). Six 15-minute trials averaged a little over 1 kg per quarter hour or 4.5 kg/h, if I worked hard and continuously. A real gatherer would probably work at a more leisurely pace, but it was necessary to fill the time interval with work in order to get a measurement. Decortication of the grain would reduce the yield of pure-grain equivalent by about 30 per cent, or in round figures 3 kg/h net yield.

I also conducted a harvest of teosinte or 'wild' maize (*Zea mays* ssp. *mexicana* (Schrader) Iltis) in Michoacan (unpublished). In five 30-minute trials, the average yield was 485 g cleaned, filled fruit-cases per hour. This is a much lower production in terms of grain equivalents than the others, but if one were to consume 150 g/day, a short 3.5-hour gatherer's day would accumulate more than a 10-day supply. This is still worth the effort, even though teosinte is not nearly as productive as many other grasses in terms of pure-grain yield.

Hunter–gatherers have developed an appreciation for wild-grass grains the world over. They certainly would not overlook so rich a source of nutritious plant food, and especially one so easily harvested and stored for future use. Ethnographic data indicate that people have exploited this resource on a large scale on every continent, often harvesting different species of the same genera (Harlan 1975, pp. 15–18).

For Africa, Jardin (1967) lists about 60 species harvested in the wild. The exact number cannot be determined because of synonymy, and because few of the observers were botanists and reference specimens were seldom obtained. The number is conservative, and more species could be added. However, most of the species are, in fact, famine foods collected in times of scarcity or harvested casually as opportunity presents. I am not much concerned with these here, but concentrate instead on those harvested regularly on such a scale that they may be considered staples for some tribes. Wild-grass seeds are still harvested in Africa, but cultures have been so

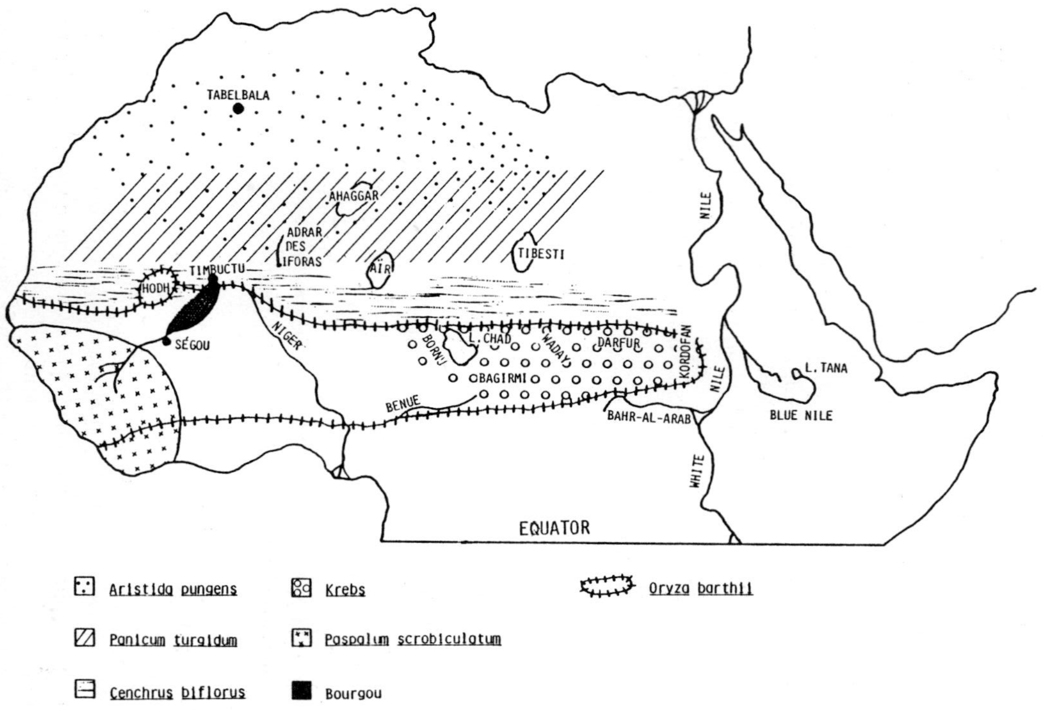

**Figure 5.1** Map of northern and central Africa indicating major areas of wild-grass grain harvests.

distorted and transformed in recent decades that a better picture of traditional diets and customs can be obtained from 19th- and early 20th-century observations than from contemporary studies. These suggest at least three distinct ecological zones of major wild-grain exploitation.

## The desert zone

*Aristida pungens Desf.* Drinn *(Arabic);* tessiya *(Tabelbala);* tullult, touloult *(Tuareg)*

This is a relatively tall (to 1.5 m) tufted perennial grass with a plume-like inflorescence and black grains when ripe which bear the triple awns characteristic of the genus. In this species all three branches of the awn are plumose. It grows in abundance in wadi beds and low areas that catch runoff from occasional rains. Duveyrier (1864) in his study of the northern Tuareg said it was the most common and widespread of the grasses and the most useful to the Tuareg, providing pasturage for their livestock and food for the people: 'this grain is often the people's only food' (p. 204). It was then harvested in such quantities that it sold in the markets for one-third the price of barley. Gast (1968), in his beautifully illustrated study of the people of Ahaggar, commented that *touloult* was still harvested, but it had been 60–80 years since wild grains were really important in the diet. With the rise of living standards and purchasing power, the Tuareg have become less dependent on desert foods and more dependent on the market place.

Nicolaisen (1963) commented that the grass was found in certain parts of Ahaggar but was much more common to the north. He did not list it as a food resource for the Aïr. Champault (1969), however, wrote that it is still a significant item of food in Tabelbala oasis in the northwestern Sahara. The primary area of harvest would, therefore, appear to be from Ahaggar northward and westward (Fig. 5.1).

The great abundance of the grass, at least in former times, was commented upon frequently by Cortier (1908). He used the Arabic '*drinn*' and such descriptive phrases as: 'The luxuriant tussocks of "drinn" in seed . . .' (p. 133); '. . . drinn in huge tussocks . . .' (p. 136); and even more poetically: 'The hillocks of sand and the whole plain are studded with huge tussocks of "drinn", their black seeds on the end of the long stems swaying and sweeping over the ground' (p. 129). He noted that grazing could be banned in certain areas for 2–3 months until the seed was ripe and could be harvested (p. 354). Nicolaisen (1963, p. 179) indicated such bans are still practised even though wild-grain harvests are not as important as they used to be.

According to Nicolaisen (1963) harvest is usually effected by cutting off the inflorescences with a sickle and placing them in a piece of cotton cloth to dry. They are then threshed by beating with a stick, winnowed in the wind and stored in a skin bag (p. 176). Chapelle (1958, p. 193) stated that the swinging-basket technique (described below) was sometimes used.

The wild cereals are consumed in several ways. They may be pounded in a mortar and eaten raw (*tébik*), or more commonly ground into flour. Porridge is made by pouring flour into boiling water and cooking until a thick paste is obtained which is eaten with butter and/or sour milk. A thick dough may also be baked in ashes or on hot sand with a small twig fire or ashes and coals over the top. Chevalier (1932) noted that *drinn* may be made into couscous as well. All of these techniques are well illustrated by Gast (1968). A beer is also made among not-too-strict Muslims. The nomads often use Neolithic grinding tools they find in the desert rather than carrying grindstones from camp to camp. They know where they can be found and use them year after year as they make their rounds.

## Panicum turgidum *Forssk.* Mrokba, merkba *(Arabic);* afezu, afeso *(Tamacheg, Tuareg)*

This is a common grass throughout the Sahara and across the desert lands to Pakistan. Its grains are harvested more or less throughout its range. It is a deep-rooted, drought-resistant perennial that spreads by long, slender stolons forming a loose mat which is very useful for erosion control. The internodes are unusually long and hard; buds grow from the nodes and, under repeated pruning by goats or other grazing animals, large knots are formed. The leaves are highly palatable but the stolons are fibrous and often used by desert people to weave mats or cordage. According to Gast (1968), in the days before poor people could afford cloth, the dead might be buried wrapped in a mat of *P. turgidum*, and a few seeds of *drinn* thrown on the corpse at the ceremony. The custom reflects the importance of both grasses to the desert people.

The inflorescences are appressed panicles rising sparsely from the mat of vegetation. The grains are rather large for a wild grass, and they are free-threshing from the glumes although they remain covered with a tough lemma and palea. Nicolaisen (1963) noted that this grass was extremely common in the lower valleys of Ahaggar. 'Seeds are collected in receptacles (e.g. *ahaga*, Fig. 213) by beating the ears of the grass with a stick. The seeds are not suitable for bread, but are esteemed for porridge and *tébik*, that is seeds pounded in the mortar and eaten without further preparation. Ashes of the grass contain soda and are often mixed with tobacco for chewing' (p. 175). The receptacle in his Figure 213 consists of a circular hoop of wood with a piece of camel-hide laced to it to form a fairly deep bowl. In the Aïr, collecting is carried out by rubbing the ears between the hands so that the seeds fall into a plaited bowl (p. 180).

This is another of the grasses protected from grazing until after the seed is harvested (Gast 1968, Nicolaisen 1963). The practice was also recorded for Adrar des Iforas, although it was enforced less stringently there than in Ahaggar because somewhat greater rainfall made it less necessary (Cortier 1908). In Ahaggar, according to Gast (1968), the prohibition issued by the local chief states that if camels are found grazing in a prohibited valley he will slaughter one of them, and if goats are found he will slaughter 5–10.

Cenchrus biflorus *Roxb.* Kram-kram *(a term in wide usage);* karéngia *(Tuareg of Aïr);* wujjeg, uzak *(Tuareg)*

This is an annual sandbur that has put thorns in the flesh of innumerable people for millennia. Grains are enclosed in a fascicle with many sharp thorns that adhere to the fur of animals and the clothing of people, and that penetrate flesh with ease. Removal of burs often leaves small slivers in the flesh which fester and may cause infection. It is extremely abundant in the southern Sahara and adjacent Sahel. The species often builds massive, nearly pure, stands on sandy soils and stabilized dunes. In Sudan I have seen essentially pure stands of several square kilometers in extent producing enormous amounts of burs. These heads of burs shatter readily at maturity, and, once the burs fall to the sand, they often adhere to each other and form masses that roll in the wind.

Burs are allowed to fall to the ground where they are swept into piles with a bunch of straw (Nicolaisen 1963, p. 180) or raked up with a giant wooden 'comb' with a handle (Chevalier 1932, p. 140). If some of the burs have not fallen, the plants may be beaten with a stick. Assembly is relatively easy and production considerable. The burs are put in a mortar for pounding and the large grains separated by winnowing.

Barth (1857), travelling south across the desert from Tripoli, did not encounter the *kram-kram* until the Aïr (Vol. I, p. 313). After much complaint about its 'troublesome nature' and 'constant inconvenience', he had to admit: 'But, it is not a useless plant, for besides being the most nourishing food for cattle, it furnishes even man with a rather slight but by no means tasteless food. Many of the Tawarek, from Bornu as far as Timbuctu, subsist more or less upon the seeds . . .'. Later he observed, near Agades, activities of the Tagama tribe (Vol. I, p. 409): 'Their slaves were busy collecting and pounding the seeds of karéngia, or uzak, which constitutes a great part of their food'. Much later at Gógó on the Niger he provisioned himself and his horses with *Cenchrus* grain, there being no other available (Vol. I, p. 482).

Barth was decidedly prejudiced against the food value of wild-grass seeds, but chemical analyses do not support him. Busson (1965) reports 21 per cent protein and 9.3 per cent fat in grains of *Cenchrus biflorus.* It is, in fact, one of the most nutritious of cereals and much esteemed by those who use it. The flour is more versatile than some of the others derived from wild grasses and can even be used for pastries (Chevalier 1932, p. 140).

All three of the desert staples may be collected by robbing the nests of harvester ants. I have done the same when collecting samples of buffalo grass *(Buchloë dactyloides* (Nutt.) Engelm.) in the southern Great Plains, USA, and can testify that substantial quantities can be recovered in this way.

Another feature of the desert grass-seed economy should be pointed out. There was, even as late as 1968, a considerable trade in the grains (Gast 1968). The nomads are mobile and caravans still roam the desert with loads of produce, bringing grains from surplus areas to deficit areas. Gast found that the Tuareg of Ahaggar often consumed wild-grass grains that did not occur locally but were brought in from other regions. One may suppose that such long-distance trade was more extensive in times past.

## Savanna

Here, we encounter a complex of grass species either not identified or, worse, misidentified by observers. In many cases the harvest was probably a mixture of species growing together and maturing seed at about the same time. They are given the collective term of *kreb* or *kasha* over a considerable region focused on the area south of Lake Chad and ranging from Bornu in Nigeria to Darfur in Sudan. Some quotations may explain the situation.

> I observed a woman collecting the seeds of an edible *Poa*, called 'kréb' or 'kashá', of which there are several species, by swinging a sort of basket through the rich meadow-ground. These species of grasses afford a great deal of food to the inhabitants of Bornu, Bagirmi, and Waday, but more especially to the Arab settlers in these countries, or the Shiwa; in Bornu, at least, I have never seen the black natives make use of this kind of food, while in Bagirmi it seems to constitute a sort of luxury, even with the wealthier classes. The reader will see in the course of my narrative that in Mas-eña I lived principally on this kind of *Poa*. It makes a light, palatable dish, but requires a great deal of butter. (Barth 1857, Vol. II, p. 247.)

Mas-eña was the capital of Bagirmi, and Barth was stranded there for 105 days. The epithet *Poa* is certainly incorrect, but the fact that he elsewhere compared it to *Poa (Eragrostis) abyssinica* suggests that much of his *kreb* was *Eragrostis* spp. and could even have been *E. pilosa* Beauv., the presumed progenitor of cultivated teff (*E. tef* Trott.). Barth was not a grass taxonomist, and we do not know the identity of the grasses collected, but the *kreb*, together with wild rice, was his main food for the duration of his stay in Bagirmi (Vol. 2, p. 559).

A similar but more detailed observation was made by Chevalier (1932), which I translate as follows:

> We were able to observe this harvest in September 1903 among the Krédas or Goranes of the Bahr-el-Ghazal (effluent of the Chad). They collect the grains in the morning with the dew on the grass with a basket woven of Doum (palm) called Sompo. The gleaner of krebs crosses the grassy meadow with great strides striking his basket against the tops of the grass whose ripe grains are easily detached. The jolt makes them fall into the basket whose lid shuts immediately like a valve and prevents them from coming out. An adult workman can collect some 10 kg of krebs in a morning. They then spread them on mats in the sun until

competely dry, then the women winnow and pound as much as they
need. Most of the Gramineae used this way south of Chad are
Panicums. They could not all be identified. I have published a list. The
best kreb is the Dofrai (*Edi* or Eri in Kréda). It is a *Panicum*. They exploit
at least ten species. To these should be added wild rice and Kramkram.
(Chevalier 1932, pp. 138–9.)

Busson (1965) shows a photograph (Fig. 192, p. 475) of two women
using the swinging-basket technique on a stand of *Panicum laetum* Kunth.
near Loga, Niger. This is probably the *Panicum* that Chevalier could not
identify because it is the species harvested most abundantly in the region and
often occurs in nearly pure stands in extensive prairies. Gast (1968) indicated
that *P. laetum* was harvested on such a scale that it even reached Ahaggar by
caravan trade. Dalziel (1937) commented: 'One of the best of the small wild
cereals, often seen in markets and an important food in scarcity; used by the
people in cakes, porridge, etc., and appreciated by Europeans. It sometimes
forms extensive meadows and is collected by a sweeping movement with a
calabash or a small finely woven, handled tray called *akaimi* in Hausa.'
(p. 535.)
     Several species of *Eragrostis* are important in the *kreb* complex. These
include: *E. cilianensis* Lutati, *E. ciliaris* R.B., *E. gangetica* Steud., *E. pilosa*
Beauv., and *E. tremula* Hochst. (Dalziel 1937). Other commonly harvested
wild grasses include *Brachiaria deflexa* C. E. Hubbard, with a domesticated
race in Futa Djalon, Guinea, *Dactyloctenium aegyptium* Beauv., several species
of *Digitaria*, *Latipes senegalensis* Kunth, and others (Dalziel 1937, Schnell
1957). Tothill (1948) noted that the *Dactyloctenium* went by the name of *koreb*
or *kreb* in Darfur where it was still harvested at that time. Heuglin (1869)
witnessed harvesting of steppe grasses in eastern Kordofan in 1862, and
specified: '*Triachyrum (Setaria) cordofanus, Eragrostis tremula, E. pilosa* and
*Panicum*-Arten' (p. 34).
     These are not necessarily famine foods. Nachtigal (1881) became very
familiar with varieties of *krebs* as he travelled through the region from Bornu
to Darfur, and commented: 'The varieties of *kreb*, among which the *kashâ
ngorogo* or *nagaia* is well known and popular in Bornu, provide such a rich,
nutritious, easily digested, and tasty dish that they are often used when there
is no condition of distress' (p. 656). He noticed harvests on a number of
occasions and remarked on the popularity of these wild cereals as food. *Kreb*
was an item of extensive trade among tribes and abundant in the markets.
Denham (p. 317 in Denham *et al.* 1826) noted the wild-grass harvests in
Bornu, but said the grain was a luxury.
     Most of the people who harvested wild-grass grains in Bornu and Bagirmi
were also farmers growing sorghum, pearl millet, cowpea, and other crops,
but in Waday there were great empty tracts devoid of villages but which
were seasonally occupied by nomads with their flocks who harvested wild
grasses (Nachtigal 1971, Vol. 4, p. 40).
     The published ethnographic observations are incomplete. Few and

passing comments are made about harvesting wild sorghum (*Sorghum bicolor* (L.) Moench) but there are massive stands of it in Sudan and westward to Bornu. Harvesting takes place today and it must have been much more common in the past. Weed sorghums are troublesome in Sudan and Ethiopia especially, and I know from visiting with the local people that grains of the weed races are harvested, especially for beer.

## Swamp lands

### Oryza barthii *A. Chev.* and O. longistaminata *A. Chev. et Roehr*

The first of the two species is an annual and progenitor of the African domesticated rice. Its natural habitat is in shallow waterholes and playa lakes that stand in water during the rains and dry up in the dry season. The second is perennial and requires more permanent water. As a perennial, it is a relatively shy seeder, but may still be harvested in sufficient quantities to appear in the markets (personal observation). The annual plant seeds abundantly and is harvested on a considerable scale even today. In former times it was a staple for a number of tribes.

In the 19th century, rice was not cultivated in Bornu or Bagirmi but was harvested wild on a massive scale. Travellers commented on the sacks of it in warehouses, camel-loads of it being transported, and on the fact that the local rice in the markets was wild and not cultivated (Barth 1857 Vol. II, p. 559, Rohlfs 1872, p. 3, Dalziel 1937, p. 532). Nachtigal (1881, p. 219) commented of the great market at Kuka, Bornu, that 'Wheat and barley cost at that time twice as much as *dukhn* (pearl millet) and *durra*, and even rice was dearer, though it requires no kind of sowing or cultivation, and only the labor of collecting the seed grains.' Rohlfs (1872, p. 3) noted, south of Kuka near Lake Chad:

> In this region, which consists entirely of swamps, we found a good deal of wild rice, which the people were engaged in collecting and which is the main component of their diet. It is natural that it should be so. They do not need to plant it or cultivate it: each year it appears in the rainy season of its own accord and all they need do is to cut it down.

The eastern limit of the wild–rice harvests appears to have been in southern Sudan south of the Bahr-al-Arab, judging from Schweinfurth's (1874) rather petulant remark:

> . . . as to the culture of rice, nothing throughout the whole of Nubia was known about it . . .; in the whole district south of the Gazelle the wild rice of Senegal grows quite freely, and this I always found of a better quality than the best kinds of Damietta. During the rains the wild rice (*Oryza punctata*) environs many a pool with its garland of reddish

ears, and seems to thrive exceedingly, but it never occurs to the sluggish natives to gather the produce that is lost in the water; and it is only because the Baggara and some of the inhabitants of Darfoor had saved some quantity, that I contrived to get my small supply. (Vol. 1, pp. 247–8.)

Heuglin (1869) noted wild rice harvests in Kordofan sufficient for export to other regions. He wrote (p. 48): 'The grains are somewhat smaller than those of Indian rice, the colour not such a clear white, the husks reddish and the taste less subtle.' All of which is true. I learned from visiting the people of Kordofan and Darfur that wild rice was still harvested in 1968 but was not esteemed as much as imported Asian rice. It was only for those who had nothing better. Nachtigal (1971) remarked that wild rice was abundant in the Dar-Ziyud region (Waday) but not highly regarded as food (Vol. IV, p. 204). The limit of harvest on the eastern side of its range seems to have been determined by food preference and prejudice rather than by availability.

If negative evidence is valid, the southern limit of both wild rice and *kreb* harvests was in southernmost Bagirmi and Bornu. Brunache (1894), coming up from Brazzaville to about 8°N on the Chari and thence westward to the junction of the Benue and the Niger, did not mention wild-grass harvests, although he regularly reported on crops seen and provisions obtained. This may have been due to time of year and lack of trading routes, however.

To the west, wild rice was harvested wherever it occurred all the way to the Atlantic, and on a scale sufficient to ensure that it still reaches the markets. Barth's comment concerning wild rice in the Hodh is worthy of notice: '. . . wild rice is procured from the numerous swamps formed in the rainy season as is also the case in the whole of El Hodh' (Barth 1857, Vol. III, p. 703). The Hodh is a great depression in Mauritania that some centuries ago was studded with villages. It is nearly empty now, but Munson (1976) was able to present archaeological data indicating that at least some of the people harvested wild-grass seeds on a large scale, mostly *Cenchrus*, but also *Panicum laetum* and *Brachiaria deflexa*. About AD 1000, pearl millet (*Pennisetum typhoides* (Burm f.) Stapf & Hubbard syn. *P. americanum* (L.) K. Schum.) began to be grown and the wild harvests declined. The final abandonment may have been due to military action rather than desertification.

Oka & Morishima (pers. comm.) witnessed wild-rice harvesting near Lake Chad. Not only was the swinging-basket technique used (Fig. 5.2), but in some fields the wild rice was tied in small bundles before the seed was ripe to minimize pre-harvest losses due to shattering (Fig. 5.3). This technique was extensively used by North American Indians near the Great Lakes to help with the *Zizania* wild-rice harvests and it was also practised in South America on *Rhynchoryza* and in India on wild rice, *Oryza sativa* L. (Harlan 1975, pp. 15–17). I have not seen previous reference to the practice in Africa.

Explorers of the 19th century who were botanical enough to apply Latin names, usually used the epithet *Oryza punctata* Kotschy for wild rice. In most

**Figure 5.2**   Wild–rice harvest using swinging-basket technique near village of Tom Mareffing, Bagirmi region of Chad, near Lake Chad. (Photo courtesy of Dr Hiroko Morishima, National Institute of Genetics, Misima, Japan.)

cases this is incorrect, because it was not then known that there are several species of wild rice in Africa. The wild rice which grows in such abundance that it was harvested by the ton and transported by the camel–load is *O. barthii* A. Chev., but it was not named until 1911 (Clayton 1972). Kotchy's specimen was named in 1854 and was the only name available for an African wild rice for the rest of the century. The true *O. punctata* is a much smaller plant and easily distinguished from *O. barthii*. It occasionally occurs in sufficient abundance to be worth harvesting, but is better suited to shady pools in the forest than to the open waterholes of the savanna where *O. barthii* occurs in such enormous quantities. They do occur together, however, and I found on checking my field notes that I had collected both species at a waterhole south of El Obeid in Kordofan in 1968. Apparently,

**Figure 5.3** Wild rice tied in clumps before harvest to reduce pre-harvest loss due to shattering, near village of Tom Mareffing, Chad. (Photo courtesy of Dr Morishima.)

Kotschy obtained a specimen of one species, but not of the other. Schweinfurth (1926) tried to straighten the matter out in 1926. Appropriately, the type specimen of O. *barthii* came from Massena in Bagirmi where Barth subsisted mostly on wild rice and *kreb*.

## Paspalum scrobiculatum *L. var.* commersonii *Stapf*

The grass is widespread in subtropical and tropical parts of the Old World and widely naturalized in the New World. It is well suited to clay soils where water stands in the rains, and in disturbed areas along paths, roadways, ditchbanks, and the like. It is a common weed of rice fields in West Africa. The seeds are relatively large and can be used as most other cereals are used. Dalziel (1937, p. 536) wrote of it:

A wild grass with edible grain, not cultivated in West Africa, but often collected in scarcity and ground on stones like millet. In N. Nigeria it is recognized as unwholesome, the Hausa name probably indicating digestive disturbance due to having to depend on it. Experience with cultivated forms of P. *scrobriculatum* in India is similar.

In Sierra Leone it is common in rice fields, and is harvested with hill rice and mixed with it for food; the best crop is said to be from dry land rather than swamp.

As a weed in rice fields, it often prospers when the rice does poorly. Harvested with the rice, it helps to make up for poor rice yields, but the people perceive problems of toxicity and do not like to eat too much of it (Portères 1976, p. 431).

## Avena abyssinica *Hochst.*

The tetraploid Ethiopian oat (*Avena abyssinica* Hochst.) is another weed-crop in Africa. It is regularly harvested with the main crop of emmer or barley and no effort is made to remove it from either the field or the harvested material. Some farmers maintain that malt containing some admixture of oats makes a better beer than pure emmer or barley malt.

## Bourgou *grasses*

These are grasses of seasonally flooded swamps, especially in the central delta of the Niger and shores of Lake Chad. The dominant grass is usually *Echinochloa stagnina* P. Beauv., which may occur in massive, nearly pure stands. Common admixtures are *E. pyramidalis*, Hitch. and Chase, *E. colona* Link., and *Oryza longistaminata*. Chevalier (1900, p. 652) stated: 'Of all the wild plants around Timbouctou, *Bourgou* is undoubtedly of the greatest value to the people of the region.' It was an enormously important resource for the Peul (Fulani), because, as the floodwaters receded, the fodder became available for their livestock (Gallais 1984). This was the best fodder of the year, and those tribes with cattle could fatten them in order to carry them through the dry season when weight losses were often drastic. In early colonial times, mounted troops were headquartered at Ségou because of the abundance of this grass.

Grains are harvested when ripe and consumed as other cereals, but more importantly, *E. stagnina* is a sugar plant. The first notice to the Western world was published by Caillié (1830). I have translated the passage as follows:

> I saw in the surrounding swamps many negroes busy at harvesting a large grass that only grows in swampy areas; they call this plant *Koudou*; they dry it in the sun, then burn the leaves off with a light flame; they keep only the stems; of these they make large bundles which they carry on their heads to their homes; I also saw several donkeys loaded with it. I asked my companions what usage they made of this grass; they told me that after the women wash and dry it, they will reduce it to powder as fine as possible; having reduced it, they put it in a large earthen jar specially made with little holes in the bottom; they pour hot water over it; the water carries out all the juice of the plant; this juice is very sugary; the water takes on a rather clear violet colour. This drink is highly esteemed by the natives who taste it with pleasure; but it has the effect of a purgative for people not used to it and it almost always retains a slight

smoky flavour which makes it disagreeable to drink. The Mohamedans permit its use without question; the Moors also drink it but always mix it with sour milk. (Caillié 1830, Vol. 2, pp. 270–1.)

Chevalier reported in 1900 that the leaves of *bourgou* were used to calk canoes; the ash from burned leaves was used to make soap; the ash was also used as a mordant with indigo dye; stems were used for matting and thatching, the seed for food, the sugar for confections and pastries, and a company was looking into the possibility of using alcohol derived from it to fuel shipping on the middle Niger. A Captain M. A. de Bat estimated the area of *bourgou* of the bend of the Niger at 250 000 hectares (Chevalier 1900). Much of that area is now under cultivated rice.

## Discussion

The problem now is to relate the ethnographic data to plant domestication. The African cereal domesticates (which I discuss more fully in Ch. 20) are, more or less in scale of production, as follows: (1) sorghum, one of the world's major cereals; (2) pearl millet, very important in the drier zones of the tropics and subtropics, especially in Africa and South Asia; in USA a forage plant, not a cereal; (3) finger millet (*Eleusine coracana* Gaertner), mostly East Africa and India; the rest are largely confined to Africa; (4) African rice, which once sustained millions in West Africa but is now largely replaced by Asian rice; (5) teff, the crop sown on a greater area than any other in Ethiopia, but somewhat below barley in total yield and of minor value elsewhere; (6) *fonio* (*Digitaria exilis* Stapf), widespread in West Africa, sometimes called 'hungry rice', but grown more as a delicacy or chief's food than to relieve starvation; makes the best couscous; (7) black *fonio* (*D. iburua* Stapf), very restricted in area, although important in some localities; (8) Guinea millet (*Brachiaria deflexa*), perhaps the most restricted of all cultivated plants and grown only in Futa Djalon. The Ethiopian oat is considered to have about the same status as *Paspalum scrobiculatum*, even though it has semi-shattering and non-shattering races.

Of the wild-grass staples, none from the desert zone was domesticated. Pearl millet was very probably domesticated in the Sahara or its margins, but we have no evidence of recent usage of its wild races. Of the wild grasses of the savanna, *Brachiaria deflexa*, *Digitaria exilis*, *D. iburua*, *Eragrostis pilosa*, and *Sorghum bicolor* evolved domesticated forms, but although harvested to some extent, none seems to have been a staple in the last century. Of the swamp plants, rice was harvested in the wild on a grand scale only where it was *not* cultivated.

The inverse relationship seems to be consistent. Once a plant is domestic-ated, there is less need to harvest it in the wild. Conversely, if it can be harvested in abundance in the wild, there is no need to invest effort in growing it. There is a complementarity here resembling the crop and weed-crop systems: one prospers as the other fails. There is also a population complementarity: the denser the population the more the people depend on domesticated plants, and the sparser the population the more they depend on wild harvests (cf. Harris Ch. 1, Fig. 1.1). Finally, there is an environmental complementarity: the more favourable environments favour cultivation of crops and the less favourable encourage the preservation of wild harvests. These relationships may probably be generalized around the world. There may be nothing new here, but observations tend to confirm a theoretical pattern.

It is not surprising that the desert grasses were not domesticated. Harvesting may be the first step in domestication of a seed crop, but the process does not proceed until the material harvested is planted. Planting in the desert without irrigation is too risky to be worthwhile (Harlan 1981).

The area of most interest, here, is the *kreb* zone of central Africa. This is a remarkable subsistence system that seems to have escaped the notice of anthropologists in general. The region is rather well defined by early travellers (see Fig. 5.1). Barth's comment to the effect that the blacks of Bornu did not make use of it is curious. They certainly have used it more recently, but the statement could imply some intrusion into the *kreb* zone by arabicized tribes to the north.

Are these wild harvests a stage in incipient agriculture? Was the system once more widespread? Were the several African cereals selected (consciously or unconsciously) from a complex of this sort? Do we have here a living record of a pathway from hunting and gathering to farming? Or, is it a system that persisted because it was less hard work than farming? If it is a model of incipience, we would do well to study what is left of it very carefully and then see if we can detect such a system in the archaeological record elsewhere. Munson's data (1976) suggest that wild-grain harvesting can be detected, archaeologically, even from a small sample of grain impressions in pottery. His sequence does not suggest the evolution of agriculture, but rather the conversion of an economy from wild harvest to farming following the introduction of already domesticated pearl millet. (See Hillman *et al.* Ch. 14, this volume, and Pearsall Ch. 19, this volume for examples of direct archaeological evidence of wild-grain exploitation, and both Cane Ch. 6, and Smith Ch. 18, this volume for examples of indirect evidence from artefacts.) African archaeology has not really addressed this problem. We do not even have a very good geographical focus. The bend of the Niger is supposed by a number of scholars to be a centre of agricultural innovation, but McIntosh & McIntosh (1981) were unable to find early sites in the region. The nature of the plant evidence that we need to look for is clear enough, but the time and place remain obscure. Some focused archaeological research is urgently needed.

Wild-grass seed exploitation was probably practised in the Late Palaeolithic. Grinding stones have been found in some abundance on ancient floodplains of the Nile in Upper Egypt dating to about 16 000 bc (Wendorf & Schild 1976). However, specific 'seed-grinder' typologies have not been defined for northern Africa as they have for Australia by both Cane and Smith (in Chs 6 and 18, this volume), and Stahl's review (Ch. 11, this volume) indicates that grinders can be used to process a broad spectrum of plant foods. Certainly, at Wadi Kubbaniya in Upper Egypt, at 16 000 bc, the evidence indicates that at least some of the stones were being used to grind *Cyperus* tubers and other 'root' foods, including, perhaps, rhizomes of the reed *Phragmites* (Hillman *et al.* in press; Hillman Ch. 13, this volume). But these authors note that it is highly probable that the occupants were also gathering the grain of wild grasses such as *Panicum repens* and *Paspalidium germinatum* which would have become available when the annual Nile flood receded.

The climate of Upper Egypt was hyperarid at the time and any vegetation outside the Nile Valley was probably very different from that at the present. During the 7th and 6th millennia bc, 'pluvial' conditions permitted a general occupation of what is now the Sahara. Playa lakes formed which expanded during the rainy season and shrank during the dry season. People settled in camps or villages along the shores of these lakes. They fished and hunted hippopotamuses; they exploited upland game such as gazelle, antelope, giraffe, etc. and tended flocks and herds of domestic animals (Krzyzaniak & Kabusiewicz 1984). Grinding stones were used in abundance. We do not know if they were gathering wild grain or actually cultivating cereals by some sort of *décrue* agriculture (Harlan & Pasquereau 1969). We have suggested elsewhere that this would have been a logical time and place to learn the arts of *décrue* and that possibly pearl millet was domesticated in the process (Harlan *et al.* 1976, Brunken *et al.* 1977). In any case, the abundance of grinding tools stretching back at least into the Late Palaeolithic is perhaps suggestive of a very long tradition of wild-grain exploitation in northern Africa (assuming the grinders were not used primarily for processing tubers). However, until more excavators of early sites focus their efforts on the recovery of the direct evidence, namely remains of the food plants themselves, proof will remain elusive.

# References

Barth, H. 1857. *Travels and discoveries in north and central Africa.* 3 Vols. New York: Harper & Bros.

Brunache, P. 1894. *Le centre de l'Afrique: autour du Tchad.* Paris: Félix Alcan.

Brunken, J. N., J. M. J. de Wet & J. R. Harlan 1977. The morphology and domestication of pearl millet. *Economic Botany* **31**, 163–74.

Busson, F. 1965. *Plantes alimentaires de l'ouest Africain.* Marseille: L'Imprimerie Leconte.

Caillié, René, 1830. *Journal d'un voyage à Temboctou et à Jenné dans l'Afrique centrale, précédé d'observations faites chez les Maures Braknas, les Nalous et d'autres peuples; pendant les années 1824, 1825, 1826, 1827, 1828.* 3 vols. Paris: Imprimerie Royale.

Cane, S. 1989. Australian Aboriginal seed grinding and its archaeological record: a case study from the Western Desert. In *Foraging and farming: the evolution of plant exploitation*, D. R. Harris & G. C. Hillman (eds), ch. 6. London: Unwin Hyman.

Champault, F. D. 1969. *Une oasis du Sahara nord-occidental, Tabelbala*. Paris: Editions CNRS.

Chapelle, J. 1958. *Nomades noirs du Sahara*. Paris: Plon.

Chevalier, Aug. 1900. Une nouvelle plante à sucre de l'Afrique française centrale (*Panicum Burgu*. Aug. Chev.). *Comptes Rendus de l'Association pour l'Avancement des Sciences*, 1900 (29th Session), 642–56.

Chevalier, Aug. 1932. *Ressources végétales du Sahara et de ses confins nord et sud*. Paris: Musée d'Histoire Naturelle.

Clayton, W. D. 1972. Gramineae. In *Flora of West Tropical Africa*, F. N. Hepper (ed.), Vol. 3, Part 2, 349–512. London: Royal Botanic Gardens, Kew.

Cortier, M. 1908. *D'une rive à l'autre du Sahara*. Paris: Émile Larose.

Dalziel, J. M. 1937. *The useful plants of West Tropical Africa*. London: Crown Agents for the Colonies.

Denham, D., H. Clapperton & W. Oudney 1826. *Narrative of travels and discoveries in northern and central Africa in the years 1822, 1823 and 1824*. London: John Murray.

Duveyrier, H. 1864. *Les Touareg du Nord*. Paris: Challamel Ainé, Libraire-Editeur. Reprint Liechtenstein: Kraus.

Evans, L. T. 1975. The physiological basis of crop yield. In *Crop physiology: some case histories*, L. T. Evans (ed.), 327–55. Cambridge: Cambridge University Press.

Gallais, J. 1984. *Hommes du Sahel*. Paris: Flammarion.

Gast, M. 1968. *Alimentation des populations de l'Ahaggar, étude ethnographique*. Mémoires du Centre de Recherches Anthropologiques Préhistoriques et Ethnographiques (Conseil de la Recherche Scientifique en Algérie) VIII. Alger: Publs CRAPE.

Harlan, J. R. 1967. A wild wheat harvest in Turkey. *Archaeology* **20**, 197–201.

Harlan, J. R. 1975. *Crops and man*. Madison: American Society for Agronomy.

Harlan, J. R. 1981. Ecological settings for the emergence of agriculture. In *Pests, pathogens and vegetation*, J. M. Thresh (ed.), 3–21. London: Pitman Books.

Harlan, J. R. 1989. The tropical African cereals. In *Foraging and farming: the evolution of plant exploitation*, D. R. Harris & G. C. Hillman (eds), ch. 20. London: Unwin Hyman.

Harlan, J. R. & J. Pasquereau 1969. Décrue agriculture in Mali. *Economic Botany* **23**, 70–4.

Harlan, J. R., R. M. Ahring & W. R. Kneebone 1956. *Grass seed production under irrigation in Oklahoma*. Okla. Agric. Expt. Sta. Bull. No. B-481, Stillwater.

Harlan, J. R., J. M. J. de Wet & A. Stemler 1976. Plant domestication and indigenous African agriculture. In *Origins of African plant domestication*, J. R. Harlan, J. M. J. de Wet & A. B. L. Stemler (eds), 3–19. The Hague: Mouton.

Harris, D. R. 1989. An evolutionary continuum of people–plant interaction. In *Foraging and farming: the evolution of plant exploitation*, D. R. Harris & G. C. Hillman (eds), ch. 1. London: Unwin Hyman.

Heiser, C. B. 1989. Domestication of Cucurbitaceae. *Cucurbita* and *Lagenaria*. In *Foraging and farming: the evolution of plant exploitation*, D. R. Harris & G. C. Hillman (eds), ch. 30. London: Unwin Hyman.

Heuglin, M. Th. 1869. *Reise in das Gebiet des weissen Nil und seiner westlichen Zuflüsse in den Jahren 1862–1864*. Leipzig: C. F. Winter 'sche Verlagshandlung.

Hillman, G. C. 1989. Late Palaeolithic plant foods from Wadi Kubbaniya, Upper Egypt: dietary diversity, infant weaning, and seasonality in a riverine environment. In *Foraging and farming: the evolution of plant exploitation*, D. R. Harris & G. C. Hillman (eds), ch. 13. London: Unwin Hyman.

Hillman, G. C., S. M. Colledge & D. R. Harris 1989. Plant-food economy during the Epipalaeolithic period at Tell Abu Hureyra, Syria: dietary diversity, seasonality, and modes of exploitation. In *Foraging and farming: the evolution of plant exploitation*, D. R. Harris & G. C. Hillman (eds), ch. 14. London: Unwin Hyman.

Hillman, G. C., E. Madeyska & J. G. Hather in press. Wild plant foods and diet at Late Palaeolithic Kubbaniya: evidence from charred remains. In *The prehistory of Wadi Kubbaniya*. Vol. 2: *Palaeoeconomy, environment and stratigraphy*, F. Wendorf, R. Schild & A. Close (eds). Dallas: Southern Methodist University Press.

Jardin, C. 1967. *List of foods used in Africa*. Rome: FAO.

Krzyzaniak, L. & M. Kobusiewicz (eds) 1984. *Origin and early development of food-producing cultures in north-eastern Africa*. Poznan: Polish Academy of Sciences, Poznan Branch.

Ladizinsky, G. 1989. Origin and domestication of Southwest Asian grain legumes. In *Foraging and farming: the evolution of plant exploitation*, D. R. Harris & G. C. Hillman (eds), ch. 23. London: Unwin Hyman.

McIntosh, S. K. & R. J. McIntosh 1981. West African prehistory. *American Scientist* **69**, 602–13.

Munson, P. J. 1976. Archaeological data on the origins of cultivation in southwestern Sahara and their implications for West Africa. In *Origins of African plant domestication*, J. R. Harlan, J. M. J. de Wet & A. B. L. Stemler (eds), 187–209. The Hague: Mouton.

Nachtigal, G. 1881. *Sahara und Sudan*. Vol. II: *Kawar, Bornu, Kanem, Borku, Ennedi*. Berlin: Paul Parey.

Nachtigal, G. 1971. *Sahara and Sudan* (A. G. B. Fisher & H. J. Fisher trans.), 4 vols. Berkeley: University of California Press.

Nicolaisen, J. 1963. *Ecology and culture of the pastoral Tuareg*. Copenhagen: Copenhagen National Museum.

Pearsall, D. M. 1989. Adaptation of prehistoric hunter–gatherers to the high Andes: the changing role of plant resources. In *Foraging and farming: the evolution of plant exploitation*, D. R. Harris & G. C. Hillman (eds), ch. 19. London: Unwin Hyman.

Pickersgill, B. 1989. Cytological and genetical evidence on the domestication and diffusion of crops within the Americas. In *Foraging and farming: the evolution of plant exploitation*, D. R. Harris & G. C. Hillman (eds), ch. 27. London: Unwin Hyman.

Portères. R. 1976. African cereals: *Eleusine*, fonio, black fonio, teff, *Brachiaria*, *Paspalum*, *Pennisetum*, and African rice. In *Origins of African plant domestication*, J. R. Harlan, J. M. J. de Wet & A. B. L. Stemler (eds), 409–52. The Hague: Mouton.

Rohlfs, G. 1872. Gerhard Rohlfs' Reise durch Nord-Afrika vom Mittelländischen Meere bis zum Busen von Guinea 1865 bis 1867. 2. Hälfte: von Kuka nach Lagos (Bornu, Bautschi, Saria, Nupe, Yoruba). Ergänzungsheft No. 34 zu Petermann's 'Geographischen Mitteilungen'. Gotha: Justus Perthes.

Schnell, R. 1957. *Plantes alimentaires et vie agricole de l'Afrique noire; essai de phytogéographie alimentaire*. Paris: Editions Larose.

Schweinfurth, G. 1874. *The heart of Africa* (E. E. Frewer trans.), 2 Vols. New York: Harper & Bros.

Schweinfurth, G. 1926. Über wild gesammelte Arten von Reis in Afrika. *Berichte der Deutschen Botanischen Gesellschaft* **44**, 165–7.

Smith, M. A. 1989. Seed gathering in inland Australia: current evidence from seed-grinders on the antiquity of the ethnohistorical pattern of exploitation. In *Foraging and farming: the evolution of plant exploitation*, D. R. Harris & G. C. Hillman (eds), ch. 18. London: Unwin Hyman.

Stahl, A. 1989. Plant-food processing: implications for dietary quality. In *Foraging and farming: the evolution of plant exploitation*, D. R. Harris & G. C. Hillman (eds), ch. 11. London: Unwin Hyman.

Titow, J. Z. 1972. *Winchester yields: a study in medieval agricultural productivity*. Cambridge: Cambridge University Press.

Tothill, J. D. 1948. *Agriculture in the Sudan*. London: Oxford University Press.

Wendorf, F. & R. Schild 1976. The use of ground grain during the late Paleolithic of the lower Nile Valley, Egypt. In *Origins of African plant domestication*. J. R. Harlan, J. M. J. de Wet & A. B. L. Stemler (eds), 269–88. The Hague: Mouton.

Wilkes, G. 1989. Maize: domestication, racial evolution, and spread. In *Foraging and farming: the evolution of plant exploitation*, D. R. Harris & G. C. Hillman (eds), ch. 28. London: Unwin Hyman.

Zohary, D. 1969. The progenitors of wheat and barley in relation to domestication and agricultural dispersal in the Old World. In *The domestication and exploitation of plants and animals*, P. J. Ucko & G. W. Dimbleby (eds), 47–66. London: Duckworth.

Zohary, D. 1989. Domestication of the Southwest Asian Neolithic crop assemblage of cereals, pulses, and flax: the evidence from the living plants. In *Foraging and farming: the evolution of plant exploitation*, D. R. Harris & G. C. Hillman (eds), ch. 22. London: Unwin Hyman.

# 6 Australian Aboriginal seed grinding and its archaeological record: a case study from the Western Desert

SCOTT CANE

## Introduction

The data relating to Aboriginal seed-grinding activities presented in this chapter were collected in the Great Sandy Desert in northwestern Australia (Fig. 6.1a & b). This country was occupied by Pintubi- and Kukatja-speaking Aborigines until as recently as the 1950s and 1960s, when Aboriginal families left their homelands to live on missions, cattle stations, and government settlements.

This chapter presents original data and describes:

(a)  the distribution, use, and importance of seeds;
(b)  the technology used to process seeds; and
(c)  the extent and nature of the probable correlation between the archaeological record and the relative importance of seeds to Aboriginal people who lived in the region.

In this area Aboriginal people collected food from 70 plant species of which 42 (60 per cent) produced edible seeds. These included 15 species of grass, three species of sedge, 11 species of acacia, four species of eucalypts, three succulents, two herbs, and four other miscellaneous shrubs (Table 6.1).

The research was conducted over an 18-month period spread between 1982 and 1985. During this time Aboriginal people returned to their country and reconstructed much of their traditional way of life. Old campsites were reoccupied, traditional resources were gathered, and detailed memories of Aboriginal economies, social, and religious life were relived. As part of this neo-traditional experience, a rare opportunity presented itself to document traditional methods of seed processing. This opportunity was seized and the seed-processing methods of these desert hunter–gatherers were recorded on tape, film, and paper. In many instances this documentation took place at the

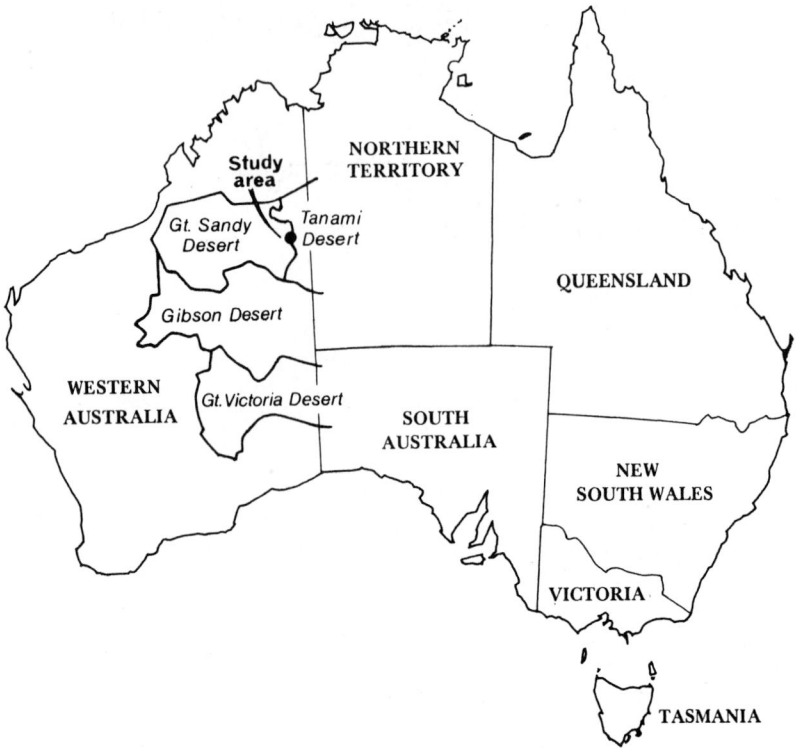

**Figure 6.1a**   Location of study area

same camp locations using the same resources and seed-grinding implements left at sites abandoned by the Aborigines 20–30 years previously.

## Distribution

Among the sedges and grasses found in the region, the most important are *Fimbristylis oxystachya* (a sedge) and *Panicum australiense* (a grass of the millet group). These species are often found growing together scattered on sandplains and adjacent to water bodies throughout the region. They are also found concentrated in several large areas on the sand plains. Both species respond quickly to fire. *Panicum cymbiforme* is probably the most common of the remaining species and occurs in abundance around the lunettes of waterholes and claypans.

The variety and abundance of edible grasses found in the hills and on the laterite plains is quite limited. The most common is *Eragrostis tenellula*, which also occurs in small quantities everywhere else in the region.

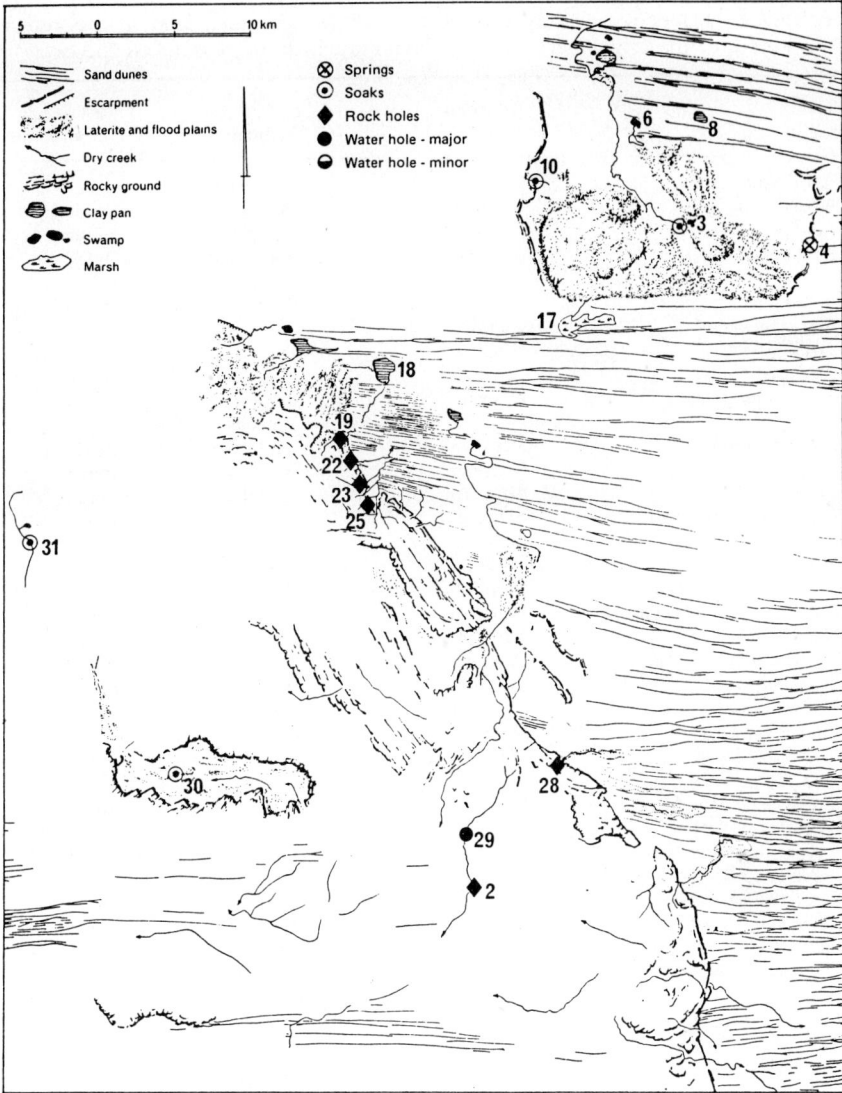

**Figure 6.1b** Location of the sites mentioned in the text.

**Table 6.1** Plants of the study area yielding edible seeds: their relative importance in recent Aboriginal diet, and the habitats in which they commonly occur.

| Scientific name | Aboriginal name | Habitat | Relative importance |
|---|---|---|---|
| *Acacia acradenia* | Wildbud | sandplains | minor |
| *Acacia adsurgens* | Nganamarra | sandplains | moderate |
| *Acacia ancistrocarpa* | Wadayurru | sandplains | moderate |
| *Acadia aneura* | Mandja | flood, laterite plains | moderate |
| *Acacia coriacea* | Gunandru | deep sandplains | major |
| *Acacia holosericea* | Gilgidi | adjacent water | major |
| *Acacia ligulata* | Wadarrga | sandplains | moderate |
| *Acacia monticola* | Birrbin | sandplains | moderate |
| *Acacia stipuligera* | Djibrin | deep sand, dune flanks | major |
| *Acacia tenuissima* | Minvinggurra | sandplains | moderate |
| *Acacia tumida* | Girriling | sandplains | minor |
| *Acacia tumida* | Nadurrdi | sandplains | major |
| *Brachiaria miliiformis* | Balgurrba | adjacent water | minor |
| *Bulbostylis barbata* | Lyillyil | adjacent water | minor |
| *Capparis loranthifolia* | Yidaringgi | flood plains | minor |
| *Chenopodium inflatum* | Garndubungba | clayey sand | minor |
| *Chenopodium rhadinostachyum* | Galbarri | clayey sand | major |
| *Cyperus iria* | Yanmid | adjacent water | moderate |
| *Dactyloctenium radulans* | Burrandjarri | adjacent water | moderate |
| *Daspalidium rarium* | Yulumburru | rocky ground | minor |
| *Diplachine fusca* | Miarr Miarr | floodplains | minor |
| *Echinochloa colonum* | Dudjurnba | adjacent water | moderate |
| *Eragrostis eriopoda* | Wangganyu | sandplains; near water | moderate |
| *Eragrostis laniflora* | Burrindjurru | deep sand | minor |
| *Eragrostis tenellula* | Marradjurralba | various | moderate |
| *Eucalyptus camaldulensis* | Yabulin | creeks | minor |
| *Eucalyptus microtheca* | Dindjil | adjacent water | moderate |
| *Eucalyptus odontocarpa* | Warilyu | deep sand | moderate |
| *Eucalyptus pachyphylla* | Djibuburru | deep sand | moderate |
| *Fimbristylis oxystachya* | Lugarra | sandplains | major |
| *Hedyotis pterospora* | Yurrundju yurrundju | sandplains | minor |
| *Panicum australiense* | Yidagadji | sandplains | major |
| *Panicum cymbiforme* | Gumbulyu | deep sand | major |
| *Panicum decompositum* | Willinggiri | floodplains | minor |
| *Portulaca filifolia* | Bulyulari | sand ground | moderate |
| *Portulaca oleracea* | Wayali | sand ground | moderate |
| *Scirpus dissachanthus* | Gunamarradju | adjacent water | moderate |
| *Sida* 'sp. A' (unnamed) | Dadji dadji | sand dunes | minor |
| *Stylobasium spathulatum* | Nirdu | sandplains | major |
| *Tecticornia verrucosa* | Mangil | clay pans | minor |
| *Triodia basedowii* | Nyanmi | sandplains | minor |
| *Triodia longiceps* | Lanu lanu | rocky ground | minor |
| *Triodia pungens* | Djinal | sandplains | minor |

The majority of acacias with edible seeds grow abundantly on the sandplains, although some of the major edible acacias are confined to deep sand (*Acacia coriacea*), along the flanks of dunes (*A. stipuligera*), and around water bodies (*A. holosericea*). At present, acacias are so widely distributed that it could reasonably be assumed that their seeds would have been of major importance in the past. In pre-European contact times, however, the high fire frequency appears to have reduced their numbers dramatically. The local Aborigines said they frequently burnt the landscape within the study area and explained that it was once 'real desert' whereas now it had turned into 'jungle'. This is supported by the accounts of explorers travelling through the general area, who recorded very large areas of burnt ground and numerous smokes from fires (see Warburon 1875, Carnegie 1898, Kimber 1983). From these accounts and my own observations of the effect of the fires on the present landscape, it is apparent that acacias were not as widely distributed in the past as their present distribution would suggest.

Unlike acacias, the pre-contact distribution of eucalypts may have been similar to that seen in the region today. Only four species of eucalypt were harvested for seeds (Table 6.1) and these grew either in restricted areas around water bodies or as mallees on the sandplains. Some of them have now reached a considerable size, and their large knotted roots provide evidence of a relatively stable distribution in the recent past.

Three succulents were eaten by Aborigines in the past (Table 6.1). Two of these (*Portulaca filifolia* and *P. oleracea*) occur in small but frequently encountered concentrations around water bodies as well as on floodplains and on patches of sandy ground in the hills.

Two herbaceous chenopods (*Chenopodium rhadinostachyum* and *C. inflatum*) were also utilized throughout the region and grow on saline patches of clayey sand. These are quite abundant throughout the sandplains and to a lesser extent on the floodplains.

The seeds of four miscellaneous shrubs were eaten. Two of these species (*Sida* 'species A' and *Stylobasium spathulatum*) respond well to fires and formerly grew widely on the sandplains and dunes. The seeds of a wild orange (*Capparis loranthifolia*) were also eaten, but the distribution of this species was restricted.

## Seasonal availability

The seasonal availability of edible seeds depended on the relative amount of water in the soil and varied according to the distribution and quantity of the annual rainfall. In the desert region the quantity and timing of rainfall varied considerably. Consequently, there was no specific time of year at which any particular species could be harvested. Instead, there was a sequence of several, traditionally defined, seasons through which particular seeds might be expected to ripen.

Beginning with the wet season (January), the first edible seeds available were those of the wild orange (*Capparis loranthifolia*). However, its distribution was limited and it was therefore of no great importance at that time of year. As soon as the weather became 'a little bit dry' following rain, three species of spinifex (*Triodia* spp.) came into seed (Table 6.1). Spinifex seeds were not highly ranked by the Aborigines but filled a gap at a time of year when vegetable foods were unpleasantly scarce. These seed foods were closely followed by the early succulents (*Portulaca* spp.) and then, from May to September, during the winter and spring, virtually all the grass seeds ripened.

It was mentioned above that the most important grass and sedge were *Panicum australiense* and *Fimbristylis oxystachya*, respectively. These two plants responded quickly to fire, grew in several dense concentrations, and produced an abundance of seeds. These seeds could be either gathered directly from the plant or collected from the ground after they had fallen. The seeds were also collected by ants, which ate the attached fatty nodules (the eliaosome, see Berg 1975, O'Connell *et al.* 1983) and left the seeds piled around the entrance of their nests. These last two characteristics extended into September the season over which the seeds of this grass and sedge could be harvested.

From about September some of the miscellaneous seed plants ripened (*Stylobasium* sp., *Tecticornia* sp.) as well as the acacias and eucalypts. Acacia and eucalyptus seeds were often stored for consumption during the hot season (see below), and I was told that the seeds from some acacias (*A. holosericea, A. stipuligera, A. coriacea,* and possibly *A. tumida*) were kept for use into the wet season as well. Food supplies during the wet season were otherwise relatively poor.

Seed storage was a very important aspect of the economic strategy in this part of arid Australia. Without it, survival during the last few months of each year would have been very difficult. Even with the benefit of seed storage, supplies of vegetable food within the vicinity of the major waterholes often ran out. When this occurred the local Aborigines had to rely heavily on meat from stray catches of game and lizards.

Seed storage was previously unrecorded in the Western Desert, but it was clearly an important aspect of the economy in other arid regions of Australia (Newland 1923, p. 13, Horne & Aiston 1924, p. 33, Tindale 1972, p. 250, 1977, p. 346). Dried *Solanum* fruits represent the only example of plant storage previously documented for the Western Desert (Carnegie 1898, p. 230, Sweeney 1947, p. 290, Gould 1969, p. 261, Thomson 1975, p. 24).

## Seed processing

Seed processing was a time consuming and arduous task. The time spent processing seeds varied a little depending on the amount of litter admixed with the seeds, the freshness with which the women approached each stage in the procedure, and the number of women helping. Nevertheless, seed preparation was clearly the most strenuous aspect of traditional subsistence activities. (For further comment on the relatively low energy input required for gathering seed foods compared with their processing see Smith, Ch. 18, this volume.)

In order to get some idea of the techniques and technology required to process seeds, we worked with a group of the Aboriginal women and prepared five seed cakes from several different plant species. These studies are detailed in Cane (1984) and described briefly below.

## Grass and sedge seeds

### COLLECTION AND DEHUSKING

Seed collection was relatively easy and it was possible to collect roughly 1000 g of seeds in about half an hour. Most grass and sedge seeds were stripped straight from the plant into a wooden dish. Some of the seeds (particularly from *Fimbristylis oxystachya* and *Panicum australiense*) could also be collected from the ground or from ants' nests (see above). Once collected, the outer husks of most seeds were removed by rubbing handfuls of seed between the heel of one hand and the palm of the other. As this was done the seeds were dropped on to wooden dishes so that the wind could blow some of the unwanted vegetable matter away (see also Tindale 1974, p. 99, and O'Connell *et al.* 1983 for different techniques).

### CLEANING BY 'YANDYING'

When seeds had been dehusked they were placed into a large softwood dish for the process of separating them from contaminating sticks, sand, and stones by 'yandying', i.e. a special form of agitation within the dish which serves in place of both the winnowing and sieving of western Eurasian grain processing. The women I worked with were very efficient at separating seeds and, at their best, could separate about 1.5 kg of rubbish from 500 kg of seeds in about 40 minutes. I should point out, however, that this time varied according to the kind of litter mixed up with the seeds collected. Each class of material had to be yandied out separately and this often necessitated between three and five different yandying operations (Fig. 6.2).

Seeds collected from the ground took greater effort to clean. To do this a large quantity of seeds was first placed in a softwood dish (*luandja*). The dish was then held firmly in both hands and rocked, with an upwards flick, backwards and forwards repeatedly. When the seeds began to separate, the dish was tilted slightly and balanced between the last three fingers and the ball of the thumb of the lower hand. The rocking motion was continued with the other hand, and the ball of the thumb on the lower hand was used to jar the lower end of the dish and spill the clean seeds on to another dish (*wirra*) where they were collected for grinding.

### GRINDING

After the seeds had been cleaned they were either ground directly or soaked for several hours beforehand. Seeds were only soaked to soften them, and

**Figure 6.2** Cleaning gathered seeds by 'yandying' with a wooden dish. This operation separates the seeds from sand, chaff, and any other detritus, and replaces both the winnowing and the sieving of Eurasian grain-cleaning traditions.

this was not done if the Aborigines were hungry. Seed grinding was the most arduous part of the seed-preparation process and took about 50 per cent of the total time required to make the few seed cakes we made. I recorded an average time of about one hour to grind approximately 200 g of seeds.

When the women were ready to start grinding they set the grinding slab into the ground and placed a wooden dish under the lip of the slab. A small quantity of seeds was placed on the grinding slab and a steady trickle of water was dribbled on to the seeds to facilitate grinding and to help the flow of seeds down the grinding groove and on to the wooden dish (Fig. 6.3).

When the seeds were ground, the paste (*luganba*) was either eaten raw or several small dampers were baked in a camp fire. In the latter case, the raw paste was placed in a shallow depression dug into the hot ashes. A small fire of spinifex or dry twigs was then lit over the paste to dry the crust of the damper. When dry, it was covered with hot ashes and baked for 10–20 mins.

**Figure 6.3**  The wet-grinding of gathered seeds after they have been cleaned by 'yandying'.

We prepared four dampers from different grass and sedge seeds. The details of these operations are documented in Cane (1984) and the nutritional analysis of the dampers produced is documented in Table 6.2. Briefly, the preparation time for each meal involved a handling time of about five hours per kilogram of damper and gave a return of about 350 kcal/h.

## Acacia seeds

### COLLECTION AND STORAGE

Acacia seeds were relatively easy to collect but were more difficult to process than grass or sedge seeds. I did not observe this technique but was told that the seeds were collected by stripping pod-laden branches straight from trees just prior to ripening or when they had ripened. The branches were piled into heaps on hard, flat surfaces of (subterranean) termites' nests and beaten with sticks. This dislodged the seeds which were then scraped up, free of

**Table 6.2**  Nutritional analysis of some bush foods discussed in this chapter.

| Latin names | Aboriginal names | Moisture (g/100 g) | Protein (g/100 g) | Fat (g/100 g) | Ash (g/100 g) | Carbohydrate (g/100 g) | Minerals (mg/100 g) Ca | K | Na | kcal per 100 g |
|---|---|---|---|---|---|---|---|---|---|---|
| *Seeds* | | | | | | | | | | |
| *Panicum australiense* and *Fimbristylis oxystachya* } mixed (cooked damper) | Yidagadji Lugarra | 53.30 | 5.28 | 1.83 | 11.16 | 28.43 | 12.01 | 91.52 | 34.89 | 158.57 |
| *Chenopodium rhadinostachyum* (cooked damper) (raw seed) | Galbarri | 3.67 51.09 | 12.32 14.30 | 6.29 1.31 | 11.30 11.86 | 66.42 21.44 | 21.23 127.39 | 172.02 282.38 | 50.37 39.84 | 373.86 161.69 |
| *Panicum australiense* (cooked damper) (raw seed) | Yidayadji | — 25.71 | 15.37 13.32 | — 1.83 | — 21.84 | — 37.30 | — 25.15 | — 175.41 | — 45.58 | 365.01 241.76 |
| *Fimbristylis oxystachya* (cooked damper) (raw seed) | Lugarra | — 32.60 | 13.82 7.10 | 4.78 11.96 | 9.80 22.57 | — 25.77 | — 16.90 | 50.73 182.70 | 22.55 43.96 | 380.99 244.70 |
| *Panicum cymbiforme* (cooked damper) (raw seed) | Gumbulyu | 6.54 47.54 | 10.72 8.47 | 19.03 4.33 | 22.93 7.51 | 40.78 32.25 | 10.97 25.25 | 78.96 216.98 | 12.06 54.81 | 404.57 196.01 |
| *Styloblasium spathulatum* (raw nut) | Nirdu | 10.88 | 0.31 | 0.11 | 1.51 | 87.19 | 321.00 | 290.43 | 55.79 | 300.04 |

sand, from the termites' nest without much difficulty. The same technique
was used when the Aborigines wanted to store the seeds, but in this case the
piles of seed pods and branches were covered with spinifex. This protected
them from birds and reptiles until the Aborigines returned.

GRINDING

Acacia seeds were usually ground before they were eaten, but three species
(*A. holosericea*, *A. tumida* and *A. coricea*) did not need to be processed in this
way. These species could simply be roasted in hot ashes and eaten directly.
O'Connell *et al.* (1983, p. 92) recorded that the return for acacias cooked in
this way was as high as 4000–5000 kcal/h but they pointed out that the
period over which they could be collected and eaten was short.

I did not observe the processing technique used to render seeds of other
acacia species edible, although the Aborigines told me how this was done.
Apparently the acacia seeds were first soaked in water and squashed up. This
produced a milky liquid which could be drunk. The remaining squashy
mixture was spread on to the surface of a flat termites' nest and dried in the
hot sun. When this was dry it was collected and roasted in hot sand. This
roasted mixture was then yandied to get rid of any contaminating sand.
When cleaned, the mixture was ground up and re-yandied in order to
separate the edible seed cotyledons from the inedible, black seed-cases
contained within the mixture. The clean seed cotyledons were then re-
ground with water for consumption. The ground watery paste was eaten
raw and never cooked.

It appears from information supplied by Aborigines that several species of
acacia seeds utilized in this region were of a third type and were toxic:

'That the different one, he got no law. We can't cooking damper;
nothing. No. He can burn you, finish you. You'll drop.'

The Aborigines described the raw paste from such toxic acacia seeds as
*kurrunpa*, a spirit responsible for involuntary actions such as vomiting and
hiccups (Hansen 1977, p. 35). The Aborigines identified *A. tenuissima* as
specifically toxic, and referred to *A. holosericea*, *A. tumida*, and *A. coriacea* as
generally in the same context. With the exception of this account, there is
no other reference to the use of toxic acacia seeds in arid Australia.
Ethnobotanists who have worked with acacias have not recorded anything
about the chemical basis of their toxicity (Latz pers. comm.).

Clearly this is an area of desert subsistence that requires more research.
Toxic plants other than seeds were treated and consumed elsewhere in
Australia (Beaton 1977, Jones & Meehan Ch. 7, this volume), and the
Tonga people of Zambia also apparently utilized the toxic seeds of *Acacia
albida* (Lee 1979, p. 181). The Western Desert example may be another
instance in which processing techniques have been developed to overcome the toxic properties of an abundant and potentially valuable
resource.

## Seeds of chenopods

Preparing seed cakes from the two herbs (*Chenopodium inflatum* and *C. rhadi-nostachyum*) utilized in the region was also relatively complicated. In these instances the Aborigines had to remove the aromatic flavour of the plant and the herbaceous material (the persistent perianth and thin ovary walls) sur-rounding the seeds before they could be consumed. This was achieved by rubbing the seeds with spinifex ash until the seeds started to separate from their herbaceous cover. The seeds were then cleaned by yandying and soaked several times until the water in which they were washed tasted clean.

We prepared one seed cake from *C. rhadinostachyum* and undertook a nut-rient analysis. The handling rate worked out at 5.3 hours per kilogram and the energy value of the damper converted to a return of 300 kcal/h.

## Eucalypt seeds

The seed from *Eucalyptus* spp. were collected and stored in the same way as the acacias. With the exception of the red mallee (*E. pachyphylla*), eucalyptus seeds were processed in the same way as grass seeds. They simply required cleaning of contaminants, grinding with water, and baking in the fire. The red mallee apparently had quite large seeds which could be roasted in hot ashes and eaten directly.

## Seeds of succulents

Seeds from two of the three succulent herbs (*Portulaca oleracea* and *P. filifolia*) were also easy to process. These were in fact the softest and the easiest to grind of all the seeds collected in the region. Another succulent (*Tecticornia verrucosa*) grew on saline claypans and its edible seeds had to be soaked in water before it was ground.

## Seeds of shrubs

Edible seeds of shrubs were processed in the same way as grass seeds with the exception of the seeds from *Stylobasium* shrubs. *S. spathulatum* produced an abundance of seemingly impervious seeds and these were roasted in hot ashes or sand until their hard seed-coat cracked. The highly nutritious kernel was then removed and eaten (Table 6.2). These seeds usually ripened in about August but were left to fall to the ground and were collected later, during the hot season.

## Dietary importance of seed foods

Seeds were clearly an important part of traditional diet in the study area but were a difficult resource to process. The processing times recorded in Cane

(1984) convert to handling rates of between three and six hours for each kilogram of damper processed from various seeds. This translates into an energy return of between 246 kcal/h and 810 kcal/h. The average is a handling time of five hours to produce 1 kg of food and a return of only 340 kcal/h. This handling time is twice that recorded in a poorly quantified description by Brokensha (1975, p. 25), but accords with O'Connell's estimate for mulga seeds (O'Connell & Hawkes 1981).

My figures suggest that a woman would have to work for six hours just to feed herself, i.e. to produce 2000 kcal of food (Meehan 1977, p. 518), and indicate that seeds could not have been as dominant an aspect of the traditional diet as is generally believed. If, for example, grasses were 'staple' foods and had to constitute between 30 per cent and 50 per cent of the traditional diet, as suggested by Gould (1969, 1980), then one woman would have to work for between 10 and 15 hours a day simply to provide an average family of five people (see Cane 1984) with less than half their daily calorific requirement. These figures might be slightly exaggerated given that the women I worked with were relatively unfit and out of practice, but nevertheless they give some idea of the effort involved in processing seeds.

The ethnographic data suggest that, unless large supplies of relatively easily processed grass or sedge seeds were available, seeds would generally have been used only as a supplement to other dietary staples and would probably have provided no more than c. 20 per cent of the daily diet. The Aborigines explained that they would always prefer to get large game, lizards, tubers, and various fruits in preference to grass seeds. This is not surprising given the effort involved in processing seeds compared to the return from, for example, tubers and fruits: native *Ipomoea* tubers could be gathered at an average rate of 1700 kcal/h and *Solanum* fruits at a rate of over 9000 kcal/h with minimal energy or time expended on processing (Cane 1984). This explains why seeds, unlike many other traditional resources, are so unimportant in the contemporary Aboriginal economy, a phenomenon similarly accounted for in detail by O'Connell & Hawkes (1981, 1984) in terms of optimal foraging theory. It may also account for why the people appear (from artefact analysis, see below) to have been unprepared to walk more than a relatively short distance to gather seed foods.

The unique value of seeds in the past appears to have been, first, that they could be stored and, secondly, that some could always be found somewhere in the landscape (unlike many other food items which were available only seasonally and could fail to ripen in abundance in any given year). This made seeds of fundamental importance in traditional diet. Seeds were most abundant and of greatest economic importance during the coldest seasons (May–September), and became quite scarce during the hot and wet seasons (November–March). Grass and sedge seeds were particularly important during large ceremonies when other local resources were exploited to their limits. They were also important at sites where the proximity and abundance of grass and sedge seeds compared to other food supplies made them a viable resource.

With regard to the relative importance of individual species of seeds, it was apparent that, with the exception of the three species of spinifex, the grass and sedge seeds were the most desirable. Among the grasses and sedges, *Panicum australiense*, *P. cymbiforme*, and *Fimbristylis oxystachya* appear to have been the most important. Most of the other grass and sedge seeds were of moderate importance and were used as supplements to the diet at various camps. The edible seeds of shrubs, acacias, eucalypts, spinifex, and the succulent *Tecticornia verrucosa* were generally at the bottom of the list of preferences, although their relative importance in the daily diet increased during the hot season when everything else was in short supply.

## Seed-grinding implements

Women in this region used two types of seed-grinding implements. These included a grinding slab (*yipiyanu*) and a handstone (*djungari*). They were the only stone tools used by women and were used specifically for the purpose of grinding seeds (Hamilton 1980, p. 8). Each married woman had her own set of grinding tools and these were kept at the respective base camps throughout her country (Horne & Aiston 1924, Davidson & McCarthy 1957, Hamilton 1980).

Seed-grinding slabs were generally made from a naturally occurring piece of flat sandstone with the margins trimmed to the desired shape [*yadungugalbung*, *yabungu* (grinding surface); *galbung* (broken rock)]. A great deal of work was required to make a good seed-grinding dish and this must have resulted in amorphous flakes and broken chunks of sandstone being deposited on archaeological sites. The vast majority of sandstone flakes recorded in this project were thought by present-day Aborigines to provide evidence of manufacturing and repairing grindstones.

When used, a grinding slab was tilted slightly away from the sitting position of the woman. A pile of seeds was taken from a wooden dish next to the woman and placed on the raised end of the grinding slab. A steady trickle of water was then run from a second wooden dish, on to the seeds while they were being ground. Another wooden dish was placed under the low end of the slab to catch the wet stream of ground seeds which flowed down the groove and over the end of the grinding slab.

Seeds were crushed and ground using a handstone made from water-rolled pebbles (Basedow 1904, p. 26, Peterson 1968, p. 567, Gould *et al.* 1971) or a hammer dressed from suitable blocks of stone. A rounded or domed handstone was best suited to the technique used to grind seeds. This involved pushing the handstone away from the body with a downward rocking motion and then drawing it back lightly over the grinding slab. In this process the grinding force was applied vertically, then horizontally through the handstone from the wrists and heels of both hands. With continual use this motion produced a long, narrow grinding groove, which became deeper near the centre of the groove, and extended from one edge of the slab for about 20 cm. This kind of groove is characteristic of wet-seed grinding (see Tindale 1977).

The older the grinding tools became, the more wear they began to display. Handstones became progressively smaller and, as a result, the groove on the grinding slab changed from a broad, flat groove to a narrow, deep groove. The deeper the groove became, the more uncomfortable it was to use, as the base of the woman's hands began to rub on the outer surface of the groove. A grinding groove probably wore down in this way quite quickly. When a grinding groove reached this stage it was either discarded or the high parts of the slab were hammer-dressed down (*yungiranu*), such that they no longer touched the woman's hands. Alternatively, a new groove could be started adjacent to the old groove or on the underside of the grinding slab.

A grinding stone also became more difficult to use because of asymmetrical deepening of the groove near its centre. This interrupted the flow of seeds along the groove to the wooden dish and consequently required extra work to clear. As the groove deepened it also lengthened and this also caused the woman extra effort. To overcome this, the length and angle of the groove were reduced by continually flaking away the mouth or edge of the grinding groove.

Eventually the groove became too small for all but the softest seeds and a new groove would have to be started. This process of groove reduction left in the archaeological record flakes of sandstone with diagnostic convex ground edges.

Assuming, on the other hand, that a grinding slab reached old age and was not broken in transportation, in domestic arguments, or at the death of a woman, or when being maintained, it would change from a flat block of ground sandstone to a highly distinctive grinding slab, displaying between one and four grinding grooves, with hammer-dressing around the periphery of the deepest grooves and length reduction of at least one groove. Grinding slabs that reached this level of maturity were usually light enough to be transported but were often quite unstable. To make transportation easier and to stabilize them, they were occasionally hammer-dressed, and unnecessary grooves were detached.

When finally discarded, grinding slabs were often used to crush reptile vertebrae or to break the ends of long bones. They were also used as heat retainers (*gardang*) to cook termites and, less frequently, to cook kangaroos (by placing the stone inside the visceral cavity), and also to grind ochre for non-sacred decoration.

Handstones were also commonly used as impromptu hammers to crush bone or, even more frequently, to flake stone tools. Handstones were not designed for this and were only used when better materials were not immediately available. Generally, however, separate eating camps were set up at respective waterholes and suitable bone-crushing stones were selected and kept near the cooking area. Men usually preferred water-rolled quartzite pebbles for the task of manufacturing stone tools because they were harder and because this avoided the risk of breaking good handstones and incurring the anger of the women of the group. Nevertheless, handstones invariably display percussion damage resulting from these additional functions.

As a result of both grinding and hammering, a discarded handstone eventually reduced to about 7 cm × 5 cm, became pecked and ground on several surfaces, and displayed percussion damage on its peripheral margins.

## Archaeological evidence for the use of seeds

Following the process of reduction, breakage, and discard, fragments of seed-grinding implements entered the archaeological record, thus becoming part of larger assemblages of stone artefacts, with their potential for revealing past patterns of behaviour. (For a discussion of the *antiquity* of such assemblages in arid zone Australia, see Smith Ch. 18, this volume). Seed-grinding artefacts are directly related to the production of food from seeds, so it is reasonable to postulate that the proportions of seed-grinding artefacts used, reduced, broken, and discarded at a site will be related closely to the quantity of seeds consumed. On this basis, then, one would expect to find, for example, a greater proportion of seed-grinding artefacts at sites where seeds were a more important resource, and conversely, a low proportion of seed-grinding artefacts where seeds were processed less frequently.

In conclusion, therefore, it is worth using the ethnographic data summarized above to test the reliability of such interpretation based on remains of grinding stones in the archaeological record. This can be done by simply examining whether there is any correlation between the abundance of these artefacts on sites used by Aborigines in the recent past and their own account of the relative importance of seeds in their diet at times when they were occupying these same sites.

In the area investigated, the accounts of the Aborigines indicated that the relative importance of seeds in the economy of each site varied. Several factors appears to have influenced this, the most notable being the time of year when camps were occupied, the availability of each type of seed in the local vegetation, and the availability of alternative food resources which were easier to gather or process.

Seeds were important in the Aboriginal economy at sites which were close to large areas of grasses or sedges productive of edible seed and which were occupied during the late winter and spring (when such seeds were most abundant). Examples of this type included Sites 2, 18, 19, and 29 in the study area (Fig. 6.1b). At these sites I would estimate from the accounts of Aborigines that seeds contributed about 30–40 per cent of the food consumed.

At the other end of the scale were sites at which seeds were not an important resource. These sites were occupied in the late dry season and wet season, when most supplies of seed had run out and before new supplies of seeds had fully ripened. At these sites, seeds were of minor importance in the economy and did not contribute more than about 5 per cent of the food

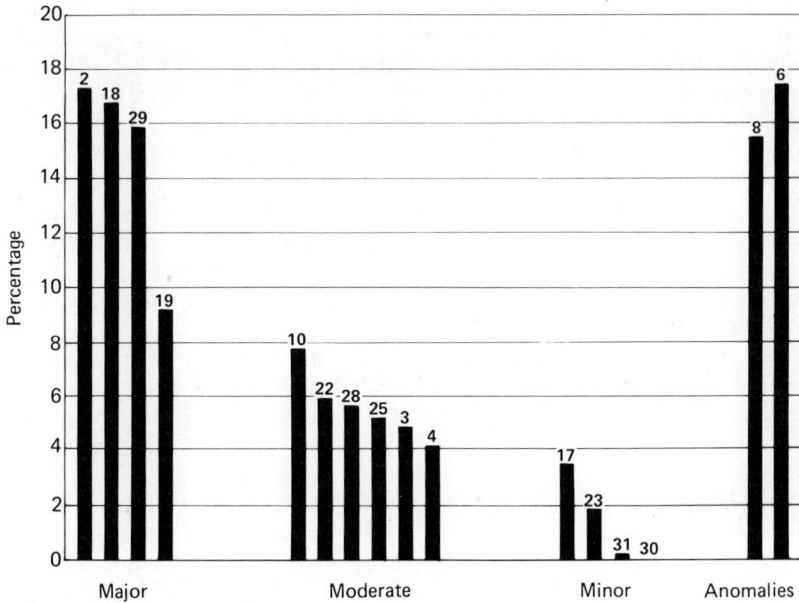

**Figure 6.4** Diagram showing the degree of correlation between (i) the importance of seed foods in recent Aboriginal diet at a range of recently occupied sites (horizontal axis), and (ii) the relative abundance of seed-grinding artefacts at the same site (vertical axis). The importance of seed foods was determined from the oral account of Aborigines who occupied the sites. The relative abundance of seed-grinding artefacts was measured as a percentage of the total number of all classes of artefact identified from that same site.

eaten. In the study area, examples included Sites 17, 23, 30, and 31 (Fig. 6.1b).

There was also a group of sites at which seeds made a moderate contribution to the diet. At these sites seeds were an integral part of the diet, but their contribution was supplementary, somewhere in the vicinity of 20 per cent. The sites were not adjacent to large expanses of grass or sedge seeds, and were occupied during winter and spring in locations where good supplies of reptiles, game, tubers, and fruits were available. Examples here included Sites 3, 4, 6, 8, 10, 22, 25, and 28 (Fig. 6.1b).

Figure 6.4 provides a diagrammatic summary of the proportion of seed-grinding artefacts at each of these sites compared with the relative importance of seeds in each economy. From this it is apparent that a relationship exists between the relative abundance of the seed-grinding artefacts found and the relative importance of seeds in the diets reported for the same sites. At the sites where seed foods were most important (and most extensively processed), seed-grinding artefacts constituted between 9.2 per cent and 17.2 per cent of all the artefacts found at the sites. The obverse is true at Sites 17, 23, and 31: here the ethnographic evidence suggests that seeds were a relatively unimportant resource, and here the percentage of seed-grinding artefacts ranged from 0 per cent to 3.6 per cent of the assemblage of artefacts at each of the camp sites concerned. A statistical comparison of the difference between the percentage of seed-grinding artefacts at sites in these groups reveals a difference significant at a very high level of confidence ($P$ varies between 0.01 and 0.001).

Between both these extremes are sites at which seeds made a moderate contribution to the diet. These sites are less easy to define statistically but, nevertheless, the proportion of seed-grinding artefacts recorded falls between the ranges observed in the two groups of sites cited above, namely 4.2–7.8 per cent.

This clearly demonstrates that there is a basic correlation between the archaeological record and this aspect of Aboriginal subsistence behaviour. It indicates that at least one attribute of an archaeological assemblage (i.e. seed-grinding artefacts) is a relatively reliable indicator of dietary balance and subsistence activity.

The only major anomalies in the distribution of seed-grinding artefacts in this study were the unexpectedly high proportions of these artefacts at two sites (6 and 8). To the best of my knowledge, seeds were not of major economic importance at these sites, and yet the proportion of seed-grinding artefacts was as high (17.6 per cent and 15.6 per cent respectively) as at other sites where seeds were a substantial resource.

I have no convincing explanation for the high proportion of seed-grinding artefacts at Site 8. It is possible that my reconstruction of economic activities at this site was inaccurate and seeds were more important than I thought (possibly *Panicum cymbiforme* growing on a lunette on the western margin of this site). It is also possible that the sample of artefacts taken at this site was too small to be representative. The most likely factor contributing to the proportion of grindstone fragments at Site 6 is the location of a small sandstone rise next to the site. Sandstone from here was sometimes used to make seed-grinding artefacts. This is indicated archaeologically both by a high proportion of sandstone flakes and by fragments of ground sandstone at that site. The high manufacture of seed-grinding artefacts at Site 6 probably reflects, therefore, the manufacture of seed-grinding implements rather than their use for preparing great quantities of seed foods for on-the-spot consumption. Another factor may also contribute to the unexpectedly high proportion of grindstone fragments at the site. Site 6 was an important ceremonial site and contained the highest proportions of ochre in the region. It seems likely, therefore, that the relatively high proportion of grindstone fragments may also be the result of their use in the preparation of ochre for ceremonial purposes.

There is a strong correlation between the geographical availability of edible seeds and the proportions of seed-grinding artefacts at archaeological sites in the region. This relationship is represented in Figure 6.5, and it can be seen that the proportion of seed-grinding artefacts decreases quite sharply as

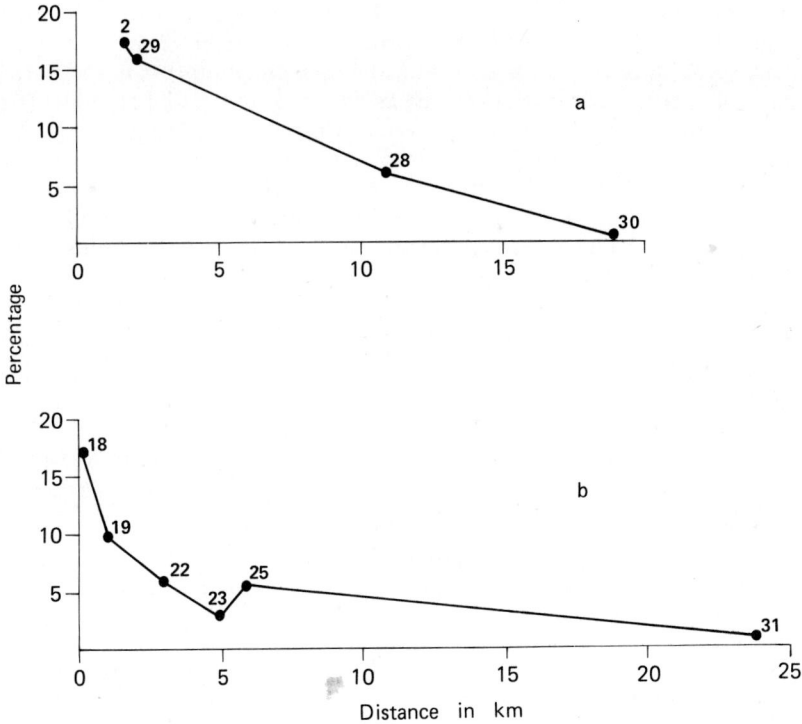

**Figure 6.5** Graphs showing decrease in the proportion of seed-grinding artefacts with increased distance between the sites and major concentrations of grass seeds. Separate graphs are plotted for sites in two different areas. The numbers on the lines of the graphs represent individual sites and correspond to the site numbers in Figure 6.1b.

the distance between sites, and the major concentration of grass seeds, increases. Specifically, the proportion of grindstones decreases from 17.2 per cent at Site 2, which is adjacent to a concentration of grass seeds, to 5.8 per cent at Site 28, which is only 10 km away. The same pattern is more evident at sites near another concentration of grass seeds. Here the proportion of grindstones drops from 16.8 per cent at Site 18, which is next to this concentration, to approximately 5 per cent at Sites 22 and 25 which are 5 km away.

The magnitude of this decline in both cases is very significant statistically ($P < 0.001$) and suggests that grass seeds were only a major resource at sites adjacent to the major concentrations of grass seeds. It also indicates that the foraging radius over which people were prepared to collect seeds was small, in this case less than 5 km. The proportional distribution of grindstones is therefore consistent with the ethnographic evidence indicating that seed processing was a time-consuming and arduous task, and that the effort required for processing made it unprofitable to travel great distances to collect seeds. It is also consistent with the interpretation that in the normal course of events seeds were not used as an important resource unless large quantities of easily gathered seeds were readily available at sites.

In summary, the Aboriginal oral testimony reveals considerable variation between sites in the importance of seed foods in diet, and, with rare exceptions, this pattern is closely reflected in the relative abundance of remains of seed grinders recovered from the same sites. This result suggests that the relative abundance of grindstones may have some potential for predicting the relative importance of seed foods in much earlier diets in this region, assuming some measure of technological continuity over time.

## References

Basedow, H. 1904. Anthropological notes made on the South Australian Government N.W. prospecting expedition 1903. *Royal Society of South Australia, Transactions* **28**, 12–51.

Beaton, J. 1977. *Dangerous harvest*. Unpublished PhD thesis, Department of Prehistory, Australian National University, Canberra.

Berg, R. Y. 1975. Myrmecochorous plants in Australia and their dispersal by ants. *Australian Journal of Botany* **23**, 475–508.

Brokensha, P. 1975. *The Pitjandjara and their crafts*. Sydney: Aboriginal Arts Board.

Cane, S. B. 1984. *Desert camps: a case study of stone tools and Aboriginal behaviour in the Western Desert*. PhD thesis, Department of Prehistory, Australian National University, Canberra.

Carnegie, D. W. 1898. *Spinifex and sand*. London: Pearson.

Davidson, D. S. & F. D. McCarthy 1957. The distribution and chronology of some important types of stone implements in W.A. *Anthropos* **52**, 390–458.

Gould, R. A. 1969. Subsistence behaviour among the Western Desert Aborigines of Australia. *Oceania* **39**, 253–74.

Gould, R. A. 1980. *Living archaeology*. Cambridge: Cambridge University Press.

Gould, R. A., D. A. Koster & A. H. L. Sontz 1971. The lithic assemblages of Western Desert Aborigines. *American Antiquity* **36**, 149–69.

Hamilton, A. 1980. Dual social systems: technology, labour and women's secret rites in the eastern desert of Australia. *Oceania* **51**, 4–77.

Hansen, L. E. 1977. *Pintubi/Luritja dictionary*. Alice Springs: Summer Institute of Linguistics.

Horne, G. & G. Aiston 1924. *Savage life in Central Australia*. London: Macmillan.

Jones, R. & B. Meehan. 1989. Plant foods of the Gidjingali: ethnographic and archaeological perspectives from northern Australia on tuber and seed exploitation. In *Foraging and farming: the evolution of plant exploitation*, D. R. Harris & G. C. Hillman (eds), ch. 7. London: Unwin Hyman.

Kimber, R. 1983. Black lightning: Aborigines and fire in Central Australia and the Western Desert. *Archaeology in Oceania* **18**, 38–44.

Lee, R. B. 1979. *The Kung San*. London: Cambridge University Press.

Meehan, B. 1977. Man does not live by calories alone: the role of shellfish in a coastal cuisine. In *Sunda and Sahul: prehistoric studies in Southeast Asia, Melanesia and Australia*, J. Allen, J. Golson & R. Jones (eds), 493–531. London: Academic Press.

Newland, S. 1923. Annual address of the President. *Proceedings of the Royal Geographic Society of Australasia: South Australian Branch* **22**, 1–64.

O'Connell, J. F. & K. Hawkes 1981. Alyawara plant use and optimal foraging theory. In *Hunter–gatherer foraging strategies: ethnographic and archaeological analyses*, B. Winterhalder & E. Smith (eds), 99–125. Chicago: University of Chicago Press.

O'Connell, J. F. & K. Hawkes 1984. Food choice and foraging sites among the Alyawara. *Journal of Anthropological Research* **4**, 504–35.

O'Connell, J. F., P. K. Latz & P. Barnett 1983. Traditional and modern plant use among the Alyawara of Central Australia. *Economic Botany* **37**, 80–109.

Peterson, N. 1968. The pestle and mortar: an ethnographic analogy for archaeology in Arnhem Land. *Mankind* **6**, 567–70.

Smith, M. A. 1989. Seed gathering in inland Australia: current evidence on the antiquity of the ethnohistorical pattern of exploitation. In *Foraging and farming: the evolution of plant exploitation*, D. R. Harris & G. C. Hillman (eds), ch. 18. London: Unwin Hyman.

Sweeney, G. 1947. Food supplies of a desert tribe. *Oceania* **17**, 289–99.

Thomson, D. F. 1975. *Bindubi country*. Melbourne: Nelson.

Tindale, N. B. 1972. The Pitjandjara. In *Hunters and gatherers today*, M. G. Bicchieri (ed.), 217–68. New York: Holt, Rinehart & Winston.

Tindale, N. B. 1974. *Aboriginal tribes of Australia*. Canberra: Australian National University Press.

Tindale, N. B. 1977. Adaptive significance of the Panara or grass seed culture of Australia. In *Stone tools as cultural markers*, R. V. S. Wright (ed.), 345–9. Canberra: Australian Institute of Aboriginal Studies.

Warburton, P. E. 1875. *Journey of the Western Australian*. London: Sampson and Low.

# 7 Plant foods of the Gidjingali: ethnographic and archaeological perspectives from northern Australia on tuber and seed exploitation

RHYS JONES & BETTY MEEHAN

The coast of Arnhemland in northern Australia lies about 12° south of the Equator within the tropical monsoonal climatic zone characterized by an alternating wet and dry season. One group of Aborigines, the Gidjingali, live on the floodplains of a large coastal river, the Blyth (Fig. 7.1), where they exploit riverine wetlands, the coastline, the river edge, and also the eucalypt forests growing on the low hills of laterite behind. Until the mid 1950s, they subsisted entirely through hunting and gathering for their food, and much of this activity is carried out at the present day (Jones 1980, Meehan 1982). We carried out a systematic study of their subsistence economy over a continuous period of 12 months in 1972–73, backed by extensive re-visits in 1974, 1978, 1979, and 1986.

## The ethnographic present

Several plants important in horticultural systems of New Guinea or Southeast Asia, such as *Dioscorea*, *Colocasia*, *Ipomoea*, and *Oryza* spp., formed part of Gidjingali diet prior to their contact with Europeans. However, in this Australian hunter–gatherer system, some of these plants were of no great importance.

### Gidjingali plant foods past and present

Carbohydrate foods utilized by the Gidjingali in pre-contact times can be ranked using three categories:

(a)  staples;
(b)  those which were important either during a particular season of the year, or in a particular location; and

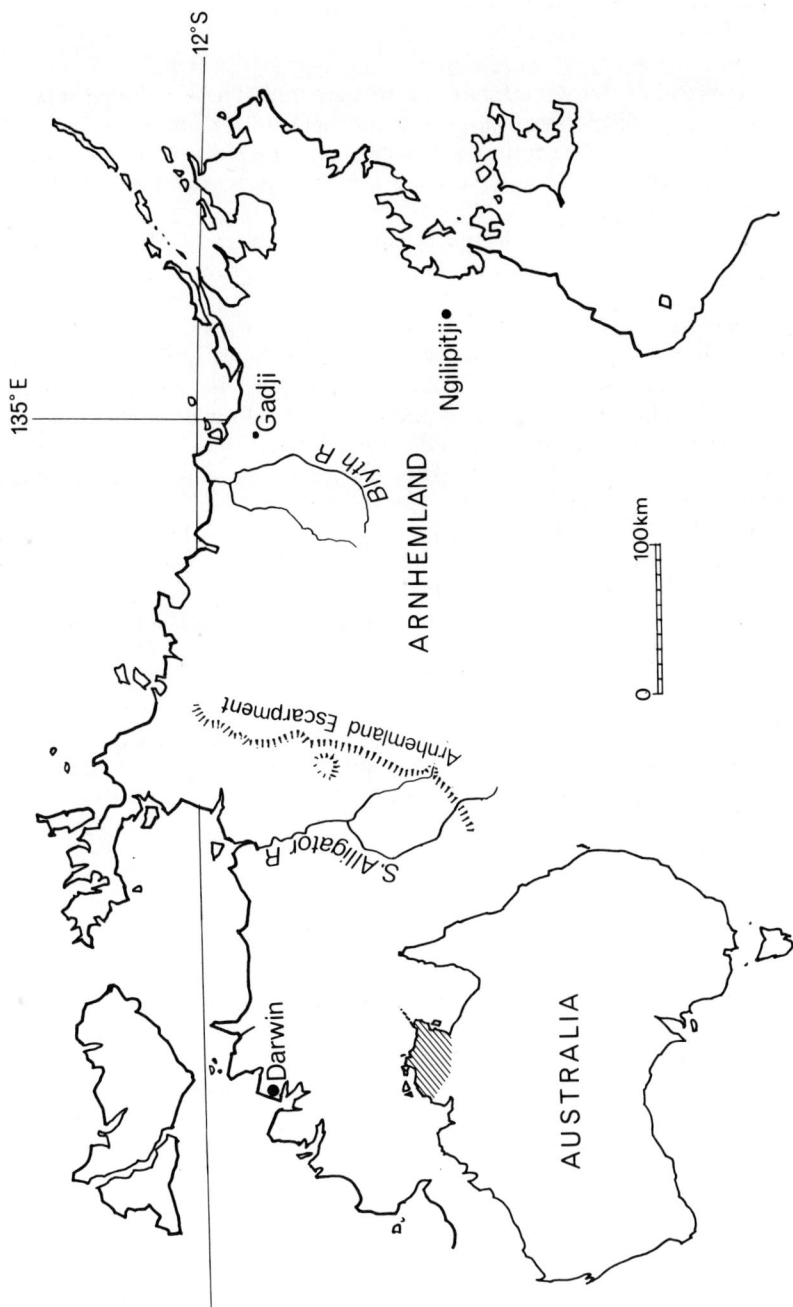

**Figure 7.1** Arnhemland, northern Australia: location of places mentioned in the text.

(c)    those which were used only as famine relief, or as an occasional supplement to the main diet.

Four genera of carbohydrate staples were gathered. These included at least three taxa of waterlilly (*Nymphaea* spp.); two species of *Dioscorea* – the long yam *D. transversa*, and the round or 'cheeky' type *D. bulbifera*; the so-called Chinese water chestnut or spike rush, *Eleocharis dulcis*; and the nut of the cycad tree (*Cycas* spp.).

Significant plant foods collected during a particular season or from a special location included nuts from *Pandanus spiralis*, pith from the trunk of the palm *Livistonia humilis*, and tubers of Polynesian arrowroot (*Tacca leontopetaloides*), *Ipomoea* spp., and *Vigna vexillata*.

Carbohydrate plant foods used only occasionally included rhizomes of the sedge *Cyperus* sp. which can be found growing in the wettest parts of swamps, and is thus available during the driest part of the year; rhizomes of the water plant *Triglochin procera*; seeds of wild rice (*Oryza meridionalis* syn. *O. rufipogon*); trunk pith from the palm *Corypha elata*; and in inland areas with flowing fresh water *Colocasia esculenta*.

In addition to these carbohydrate foods a wide variety of tree fruits were eaten, the most important coming from species of *Terminalia*, *Canarium*, *Syzygium*, *Persoonia*, *Ficus*, *Morinda*, *Planchonia*, *Vitex*, and *Sterculia*. Most of these genera are also found in New Guinea and, indeed, in island Southeast Asia.

## POISONOUS, BITTER, AND SWEET

To understand the way in which the Gidjingali classify the edible qualities of plants, some knowledge of their language is necessary. The Gidjingali language makes use of four noun classes which are indicated by the use of prefixes:

*an* – objects of male gender;
*djin* – objects of female gender;
*gun* – mostly objects of inanimate or inorganic class,
        e.g. rocks, water;
*man* – objects of the organic class, mostly plants (and some
        Macassan trade items).

Three Gidjingali adjectives refer to the taste, including poisonous and unpalatable qualities, of plants. A plant can be described as *man-bala* meaning that it is 'sweet' and also edible. The same suffix, *bala*, can also be used to indicate a quiet or 'good' man, as in *an-bala*. Another category, *man-baitjarra* refers to plants which are considered to have a 'fierce' or bitter taste. These plants are not poisonous but are unpalatable, and they usually have to undergo a process of leaching and/or cooking to render them edible. The same suffix with the *gun* prefix, is the word for seawater as opposed to *gun-bala*, freshwater. In the human domain a man called *an-baitjarra* is a fierce and potentially dangerous man but one capable of being calmed or tamed by human actions. The third category is *man-erra*, which refers to plants which are poisonous. Thus the fruit borne by the *Strychnos lucida* tree is referred to as *man-erra*, i.e. 'poison'. A piece of rotting meat might be referred to as *an-erra* indicating that the flesh should not be eaten. A man can also be called *an-erra*, meaning that he is 'no-good' or evil – and probably cannot be redeemed by human intervention.

THE CONTEMPORARY SITUATION

The Gidjingali today, having access to social security payments like other Australian citizens, and in some cases wages, possess some wealth with which to buy as much flour, sugar, and other carbohydrate foods as they desire. Most camps contain drums of flour and cartons of sugar. Despite this assurance of basic carbohydrate needs, indigenous vegetable foods continue to be gathered regularly. This is done mostly by the women. They do it, they say, because they like the taste of bush foods and because they enjoy moving around the country foraging. Considerable prestige accrues to women who produce large quantities of well-prepared foods such as *Cycas* bread and long yams.

It is of interest to note that of the carbohydrate foods used by the Gidjingali before the arrival of Europeans, those that have dropped out tend to be *man-baitjarra*, those that are bitter or 'cheeky' and have to be treated before they are pleasant to eat. The notable exception is *Cycas* bread which continues to be manufactured for large ceremonies. Its maintenance as a food may well have as much to do with its religious connotations as it does with dietary satisfaction.

*Procurement and processing of yam tubers and cycad nuts*

*Dioscorea* spp. yams are found beneath the shade of vine-thicket trees. Usually they are collected by women who seek out the yam tendrils twined around trees and then follow them down to the surface of the ground. In digging out the long yam, *D. transversa*, women use a stick and their hands to remove soil, creating a cylindrical hole. This begins about 10 cm away from the spot where the tendril enters the ground, and proceeds obliquely downwards so as to meet with the top of the tuber about 5–10 cm beneath ground surface. This is followed down and the tuber is removed by snapping it off near the top. The part still attached to the vine is left intact in the soil. The women say they do this because plants left in this condition will grow again the following year. The yam holes are not filled in but, due to rapid processes of leaf mould formation and movement of soil, they are quickly refilled, often by mulch. Gatherers tend to go to the same areas year after year to collect yams and it is a predictable activity, women usually managing to find productive areas and to meet their declared targets.

Several important carbohydrate foods are treated in order to remove toxins or bitter qualities (Meehan & Jones 1977, Beck 1985). After gathering round or 'cheeky' yams (*D. bulbifera*), they are cooked in earth ovens for about 20 minutes and then grated with the shell of a land snail (*Xanthomelon* sp.). A circular hole cut in the outer whorl of these shells makes an efficient grater. The shell is held in one hand against a vertical digging stick which is embedded in the ground. The yam is held in the other hand and moved up and down rapidly against the sharp edge of the hole in the snail shell. The grated yam passes through the open mouth of the shell into a receptacle. It is rinsed several times in fresh water and then left to soak overnight. Next morning it receives a final rinse before being eaten.

The nuts of *Cycas media* require lengthy and careful treatment. In their raw state they are extremely poisonous, containing neurotoxins which affect the central nervous system. Cattle eating them exhibit what is called the 'Zamia staggers' and Sir Joseph Banks became violently ill after experimentally eating them, having seen discarded nut shells on Aboriginal campsites in Queensland. The plant also contains the insidious carcinogenic substance cycasin, which is used in cancer research (Beck *et al.* in press). The Gidjingali people make a 'bread' from *Cycas* nuts which they call *ngatjo*, the same term which they use for European bread. *Ngatjo* was a staple food usually during the middle to late dry season and is specifically associated with important ceremonial occasions such as the performance of Kunapipi, when hundreds of people congregate for several months.

Following collection from the cycad groves, the nuts were dehusked by women who used a hardwood baton on a wooden or stone anvil. During this process they were careful not to put their fingers to their lips or to allow children to lick any of the nuts or artefacts associated with the dehusking. After the nuts had been dried for a couple of days they were crushed using stone mortars and pestles. The resulting paste was placed into open-weave bags and immersed in large pits containing fresh water which had been excavated beforehand by the men. The bags were left in the water for five or six days during which time they fermented, causing a thick, foul-smelling foam to form on the surface of the water. The soaked nuts were ground once again, then wrapped in paperbark and secured with thin strips of pandanus leaf, each bundle measuring about 30–40 cm long and 10–12 cm wide, and weighing about 10 kg. The loaves were placed in an earth oven with heated ant-bed lumps, lined with green leaves, and then sealed with sand. The cooking continued for about five hours. Before being opened, a hot fire was ignited on top of the oven, often using dry pandanus nuts as fuel. The *Cycas* bread in its wrapping could be kept for several months before being eaten. The Gidjingali said that this process changed the cycad from being *mun-erra* to *mun-bala*, and it was the only example of a food rendered edible from a poisonous state. Other plants which were given special treatment were merely unpalatable (Beck 1985). Old cycad nuts which had been leached by the rains of a full wet season also lost their poisonous qualities and these were sometimes collected and eaten with minimum preparation (Beck *et al.* 1988).

## The seasonal pattern of exploitation

Seasonal exploitation of plant foods was a feature of Gidjingali subsistence (cf. Jones 1980). In the late wet season when the rains were easing, but the swamps still full, a major source of carbohydrate consisted of the waterlilies (*Nymphaea* spp.). The stalks were eaten fresh like celery, the tiny black seeds from the flowers were ground and formed into small unleavened cakes which were cooked in the ashes before being eaten, and corms about the size of a golf ball were retrieved from the mud lining the swamps, then cooked in an earth oven before being consumed.

During the early dry season, the collecting focus shifted to yams (*Dioscorea* spp.), when the tubers were large and the tendrils still green for easy location. This May–June period was often referred to in Aboriginal English as 'yam time', when vegetable foods were available in greatest abundance. As the season progressed and the widespread but shallow water bodies gradually shrank to the deeper swamps, people moved their wet-season home bases on the coastal dunes to the edges of these wetlands, where men hunted geese while women waded into the swamps to dig out the corms of the spike rush (*Eleocharis dulcis*). About August, in the late dry season, when the mud became hard, it was difficult to dig out the corms, even though at this time they were extremely sweet.

Attention then focused on the cycad nuts, which, although laborious to prepare, tended to occur in extensive stands as the understorey of open eucalypt forest and thus could provide enough food to support large gatherings of people. The end of the dry season was a period of stress for the Gidjingali. Cycads were important if sufficient fresh water for their leaching was available. Other less favoured foods, such as the roots of *Cyperus* sp. and *Vigna* sp., were also collected. A short season of storms usually heralded the arrival of the wet season. The rains brought by these storms stimulated the regrowth of yams, and the Aborigines could again find them for a short time just prior to the major rains. Some important tree fruits appeared at this time also.

## Rates of production

Skilled women were able to obtain about 2–3 kg of long yam (*D. transversa*) in about one hour of hard work. When the time taken to travel to the yam patches, to search the area, to chat about the quality and quantity of the yams, and to transport the haul to a 'dinner-time' camp for cooking is taken into account, the rate of production was of the order of 2000–2500 kcal per woman hour. Similar rates of production were obtained for the collection of the corms of the spike rush. Very little preparation is necessary for these two foods once they have been gathered.

In contrast, considerable work had to be done to obtain the edible nuts from the large, woody, composite fruits of *Pandanus spiralis* which had to be chopped transversely with an axe and the small nuts removed with the aid of a spike-like implement especially manufactured for the job (Meehan *et al.* 1979). The nuts taste similar to the Mediterranean pine nut, and they are oily and rich in energy, containing some 6000–7000 kcal per kg. However, comparing the work done with food gained, the rate of production is again of the order of 2000 kcal per person per hour. With *Cycas*, the collection and preparation of this food extended over a week or so, with each woman being responsible for her own yield, but with closely related groups working together for the crushing of nuts and other preparatory tasks. A good worker was able to prepare some 40–50 kg of bread in a single baking session – this weight representing the result of a week of intermittent effort. With careful documentation, we estimated that, once again, women were producing about 2000 kcal per hour. Thus, in theory, a woman would be able to feed herself on the result of about one or one and a half hours of gathering the various carbohydrate foods described above. In practice, most women provided food for their hearth group, including children, spouses, and other relatives, and thus worked considerably longer each day.

## Plant foods in the total diet

The Gidjingali procured a range of animal flesh, including fish, reptiles, wallabies, birds, and shellfish, totalling some 130 species (Meehan 1982). Nowadays flesh foods contribute some 50 per cent of the total calorific intake. About two-thirds of the remainder is provided by European flour and sugar. Despite this, the gathering of traditional carbohydrate foods is still an important occupation, taking place almost every day.

In an attempt to assess the contribution of vegetable foods to the 'pre-European' diet, the production rates discussed above and demographic factors have been examined. In our opinion, if women had worked harder, had fewer surviving children to support, and were to endure a somewhat harsher nutritional regime at least seasonally, they would have been able to contribute approximately 50 per cent of the total calorific intake from the plant foods that they collect today. The older Gidjingali people themselves confirm that such a 50:50 ratio of animal to vegetable food reflected the nature of their pre-European diet: that vegetable food (*balidjar*) and animal food (*an-gala*) contributed roughly equal parts to the total diet (Meehan 1982, p. 150, Meehan & Jones 1986).

## Horticulturally significant plants of minor importance to the Gidjingali

### TARO

*Colocasia esculenta*, or taro, is an important staple crop in a number of horticultural systems in Melanesia, Southeast Asia, and the Indian sub-continent. It is of only minor dietary importance in Gidjingali and other Arnhemland economies. The first sample which we saw collected was on the banks of an inland freshwater stream near Gadji (Fig. 7.1), a camping place of the Djinang community in 1972–73. Our companions named it *djamandar*, said it was edible, but gave no indication that this was any different from a dozen other edible tuberous plants of minor importance in their diet. The sample was identified by Clive Dunlop at the Herbarium in Darwin as *C. esculenta*. Although subsequent research has shown that this plant had been recorded before in Australia – notably by Sir Joseph Banks – ours was the first modern identification of *Colocasia* in Arnhemland. Because we considered the possibility that this plant might have been introduced into Australia by Chinese immigrants during the last century, or even by Macassan visitors from Sulawesi prior to that, a special effort was made to collect more specimens. In 1979 a growing plant was sent to us in Canberra by Peter Cooke, and it has since been successfully propagated in the Australian National Botanic Gardens. Cytological analysis indicated that this specimen contained 28 chromosomes, thus being diploid and similar to other specimens which Yen and others had identified from the interior of New Guinea and parts of the Solomon Island chain. It was different from the 42-chromosome triploid plant, the common domesticated variety found in Southeast Asia and India today.

In 1981, on an expedition with N. White and N. Scarlett to the remote stone quarry, Ngilipitji (Fig. 7.1), in the interior of northeastern Arnhemland, one of us (R.J.) was shown by the Ritharrngu people there a large patch of *C. esculenta* growing on the edge of a freshwater stream. Since then about a dozen other locations have been found both by ourselves, and by White and Scarlett in inland locations of central and eastern Arnhemland and in the east Kimberley region (Scarlett 1986).

The Gidjingali referred to *Colocasia* as a plant of the 'stone country'. They said that its 'feet' (*rrapra midjerre*) stood in flowing fresh water. These were the parts of the plant which were cooked and eaten. The uncooked corms, they said, had a 'hot' taste (probably due to oxalates). To remove this hot taste, the corms had to be cooked for 20–30 minutes in the ashes of a fire. For the Gidjingali, the plant was part of the natural order in their land. They saw nothing strange or exotic about it. It had a moiety affiliation and was one of the totems associated with a particular clan. Recent introductions to their landscape such as some modern weeds, or the buffalo, lack the full set of these classificatory ascriptions. Even the dingo, which reached Australia some 4000 years ago, is perceived in Aboriginal mythology as a 'recent' intrusive element, and is not fully absorbed into the classificatory system. This cultural evidence, combined with botanical enquiries, suggests that taro is indigenous to the Australian continent or, at least, has been here for a very long time.

RICE

Rice (*Oryza* spp.) is a key plant in the agricultural systems of Southeast Asia, but it is insignificant in the foraging economy of Gidjingali and other Arnhemland groups. Wild rice (*O. meridionalis*) can be found in many wetland areas, such as in swales between fossil dunes. The grain heads used to be collected into a wooden container, then winnowed so that the husks were blown away. The resulting grains were ground into a paste, using a stone pestle and mortar, and baked as small cakes in hot ashes. The Gidjingali were convinced that this wild rice (*bortjal*) was the same as the cultivated rice (*birraitja*, a word of Malay origin) brought in by Macassan traders at the beginning of this century and by Japanese pearlers in the period immediately preceding the Second World War. Although the process of preparing this food was demonstrated to us by the older people, we did not observe this activity being carried out as part of normal food-gathering activities during our fieldwork.

IPOMOEA

This genus is one of the largest and most widely distributed plant groups in the world, probably originating in Gondwanaland. Although Australia hosts few species, a disproportionately high number of these produce edible tubers. In northern Australia at least four such edible species are found in sheltered vine thickets or in woodlands, i.e. *I. abrupta*, *I. diversifolia*, *I. gracilis* and *I. graminea* (Russell-Smith 1985, pp. 255–6). The Gidjingali regarded them as an inland food source. They referred to *Ipomoea* as *binya binya*, or in English as 'bush potato' or 'sweet potato'. *I. batatas* the true sweet potato or *kumara* is nowadays grown in European and Tongan gardens on some of the settlements in Arnhemland and is sometimes on sale in the settlement shop. While *binya binya* was highly prized when some of it was collected, no systematic utilization of it occurred. It played a minor role in the economy of the Gidjingali and adjacent coastal Aboriginal groups (see Yen Ch 4, this volume for further discussion of *Ipomoea* exploitation in northern Australia).

*Foraging, domestication, and horticulture*

Golson (1971) has pointed out that many of the plants utilized by the Aborigines of northern Australia occurred also in New Guinea and on the islands and mainland of Southeast Asia. Several of them are important staples within the horticultural systems functioning in those areas. None of these plants has been domesticated in Arnhemland, but they continue to be collected as part of foraging activities. In the case of the long yam (*D. transversa*) there appears to be some degree of symbiosis between foragers and plants, in the sense that the activities of the collectors help to create favourable conditions for the propagation and growth of the plant. The disturbance of wetland clay floors to dig out the corms of *E. dulcis* seems to aerate the soils, which may be advantageous to the growth of this plant. Several tree-fruit species are incidentally distributed by people dropping seeds in suitable locations, especially midden-enriched soils on sand dunes, associated with their own abandoned camping sites (Jones 1975). This passive relationship between plant propagation and human behaviour is well recognized by the Gidjingali people. However, at no time during our observations did we note any systematic attempts to nurture or to domesticate these plants, despite the fact that most of the Aborigines we knew had lived for many years on government and missionary settlements where gardens had been established. What Chase (Ch. 3, this volume) for Cape York calls 'domiculture', and Yen (Ch. 4, this volume) refers to as Australian hunter–gatherer 'agronomy', was, in Arnhemland, very much an implicit or incidental process. The Gidjingali had a deep sense of 'curation' of the country and of its spiritual essence; indeed this was one of the mainsprings of their world view. Despite this, in an ecological sense, they saw themselves as hunters. Gardening or farming in an explicit interventionist sense was the way of life of other people – Balanda (Whites) or Mankatjarra (Macassans).

## Archaeological evidence

Archaeological excavations in the rockshelter site of Anbangbang in Kakadu National Park, situated in an outlier west of the Arnhemland Escarpment (Fig. 7.1), revealed that its uppermost deposits contained excellently pre-served plant material to a degree unexcelled in tropical Australia (Jones & Johnson 1985). In a preliminary analysis of this material, Clarke (1985) was able to identify the remains of plants used both for the manufacture of artefacts such as spear barbs, fire-sticks, and string, and also as food. Prominent amongst the latter were *Triglochin* sp. rhizomes; rootlets of waterlily (*Nymphaea* spp.); woody fragments of *Pandanus*; and several fruits, identified from their seeds, such as *Terminalia*, *Canarium*, and *Syzygium*. The deposits containing these plant remains dated back to some 800–1200 years ago (Jones & Johnson 1985, p. 52) and suggested that the prehistoric occupants were systematically exploiting the freshwater wetlands situated at the foot of the slope in front of the cave as well as the rain-forest grove on the cliff behind. This exploitation probably took place some time during the wet season and also at the beginning of the dry.

Phytoliths were searched for in deposits, both from the rockshelter sites on the edges of the escarpment outliers and from the extensive open occupation sites bordering the major wetlands of the South Alligator River, 20 km to the west (Fig. 7.1 and Fujiwara *et al.* 1985). Phytoliths of Gramineae were common in the open sites, and remains of rice (*Oryza* sp.) and *Phragmites* were identified. The latter was used in spear-shaft manufac-ture. The open sites were probably occupied during the full dry season when the corms of *Eleocharis* from the deeper swamps were the chief staple, supplemented by such plants as rice. Significantly, no rice phytoliths were found at Anbangbang, the mostly wet-season site situated away from areas where rice occurred naturally but where other types of plant remains occurred in abundance. Geomorphological work in the Kakadu region has shown that as the sea rose to its present level in early Holocene times, it flooded the mouths of the Pleistocene river valleys. About 6000 years ago mangrove forests began to grow in these drowned valleys, some 70 km inland from the present coastline (Hope *et al.* 1985). This zone of mangroves eventually migrated in a seaward direction with the prograding shoreline, behind which tended to be a complex of hypersaline mud flats of low productivity which soon filled the floors of the river valleys. Further formation of coastal-parallel sand dunes and river's edge levees allowed the ponding of freshwater swamps and lagoons, which had extremely high natural productivity levels of plant growth. On the southern edge of the South Alligator coastal plain adjacent to the open sites which we investigated, it seems that the main swamps did not form until about 2000 years ago (Hope *et al.* 1985, p. 237). The increased level of natural production in the region was paralleled by an increased density of occupation, not only on the wetland-edge sites themselves, but also in related outlier rockshelters which provided refuge from the wet-season rains.

Systematic archaeological research carried out by ourselves on the Blyth River plains, the heartland of the Gidjingali territory, has failed to reveal a single site older than about 1500 years. The oldest sites are large earth-and-shell mounds adjacent to relict fluvial systems, some situated several kilometres from the present coast. This rich landscape, too, may be a recent geomorphological feature.

Swamp plants such as spike rush, rice, and waterlilies would all have increased in abundance following the formation of the late Holocene wetlands. Yams are also particularly common on geomorphologically recent units, such as fossil sand dunes. Thus, in terms of carbohydrate foods, the productivity of Gidjingali (and Kakadu) land is greater now than it was a few thousand years ago before the full formation of the riverine plains. The population density of the Gidjingali nowadays is 30–50 times greater than that of the people living in forested areas of the Arnhemland hinterland (Jones 1985, pp. 291–2). Population densities in the South Alligator River area would have been similar before European buffalo shooters and cattlemen entered the area in the last century (Keen 1980). Increases in the natural productivity of these river-mouth plains allowed much greater population densities and degrees of residential sedentism than was the case generally across the tropical savannas of northern Australia. Despite these environmental and social processes, the presence of suitable horticultural plants within the environment, and an intimate knowledge of plant manipulation, processing, and cooking, there is no sign of a horticultural system having been established by the hunting and gathering Aborigines of Arnhemland.

## Regional implications

Research over the past 15 years in the highlands of Papua New Guinea by Golson and his co-workers, has shown the existence there of large-scale integrated drainage ditches in the floors of inter-montane swamps some 2000 m above sea level. At the site of Kuk in the Wahgi Valley the oldest evidence indicative of horticultural activity dates to 9000 years ago (Golson 1977 & Ch. 44, this volume), and is associated with a major phase of forest clearance and alluviation in the valley floors (Hope 1982, Hope *et al.* 1983). These events heralded the development of horticultural systems in this region. Before this, at such high altitudes, late glacial conditions would have inhibited the use of the relevant horticultural plants, except possibly *Pandanus*. It is probable that experimental phases of horticulture prior to this had been carried out at lower altitudes, perhaps along the lowland swamp edges of New Guinea. Groube has recently discussed large waisted bifacial stone tools, probably hafted, which were recovered from the Huon terrace sequence, Papua New Guinea, and dated to some 40 000 years ago (Groube *et al.* 1986 and Groube Ch. 17, this volume). He suggests that they may have been used to ring-bark trees in order to open out the rain-forest canopy and so promote the natural growth of favoured food plants such as yams and sugar cane. Waisted, ground axe-heads of dolerite have also been found in 24 000-year-old levels in the Alligator Rivers region (Schrire 1982).

These archaeological data make the issue of the status of *Colocasia* on the 'Greater Australian' or 'Sahuland' continent a matter of crucial importance. If this plant was not endemic there, it would need to have been adapted as an exotic plant to New Guinea well prior to 9000 years ago. The alternative explanation, which has already been mentioned, is that *Colocasia* was an endemic element in the flora of the continent. If this was so, then experimentation with it could have taken place within the northern part of the Australian–New Guinea landmass in terminal Pleistocene times.

It may be that some of the ways in which contemporary Aborigines of northern Australia exploit their plant foods can shed light on incipient processes of domestication of the same or closely allied species – perhaps in terminal Pleistocene or early Holocene times both in New Guinea and Southeast Asia. However, the thrust of the histories of the two regions – Australia and the Asian–Melanesian world of the horticulturalists – has been quite different during this period.

While it may sometimes be fruitful to look to contemporary hunter–gatherer economic systems as a source of ideas by which to model pre-agrarian ones, there is also the danger of falling into the 'progressionist' trap. This posits modern hunting and gathering as a 'fossil' version of an earlier or antecedent stage in some process that culminated in farming; that there was a tendency for one to lead into the other, that hunting societies would have become farming ones had not certain restricting circumstances such as climatic severity or geographical isolation been operating.

The ethnographic and archaeological evidence from northern Australia suggests that the hunting and gathering system in the region, indeed on the entire continent, was one of immense stability. It had been maintained throughout the major climatic and environmental changes of the past 15 000 years, and also despite seasonal or intermittent contact across Torres Strait and on the coast of Arnhemland with horticultural peoples to the north, during the past several centuries at the very least. Analysis of such systems should concentrate on the structural reasons for this stability. There would be need to consider the integration of the entire range of species exploited, animal as well as plant; the natural rates of production in the various trophic levels of the environment; and the patterns of varibility through time, both seasonally and in terms of rare but perhaps ecologically decisive catastrophies such as droughts or cyclones. Social parameters would include population-density levels, social organization, rates of work and the division of labour, and the degree of social intensification and of hierarchical structures, etc. (cf. Chase Ch. 3, this volume).

It has been pointed out by one of us (Jones 1980) that, when the first drainage ditches were being dug at the Kuk site in the New Guinea highlands, Australia and New Guinea were still part of the same landmass, being connected by a narrow isthmus where Torres Strait is now situated; and that shortly before that, northern Australia extended northward in a flat plain to join the very foot of the New Guinea cordillera (Jones 1980, Fig. 6). It is possible that the first experimental cultivation of such plants as *Colocasia* and possibly yams, bananas, sugar cane, and *Pandanus*, took place at this time when New Guinea and Australia were part of the same landmass. The southern boundary of this experimental horticultural province may have been on what is now Australia. Later, with the post-glacial rise of sea-level, the experimental zone was covered with sea water, thus forming a barrier between the area of rich soils and constant rainfall of New Guinea, and the savanna environment of northern Australia which is characterized by poor soils and distinct dry and rainy seasons. Rice, freely available on the plains of Arnhemland, played no significant role in the prehistory of the region. In contrast, in ecologically comparable areas north of the Equator, on the newly formed deltaic and estuarine shores of 'Sundaland' in what is today southern China, Indo-China, and Thailand, rice cultivation transformed the economies of the peoples of the region in mid-Holocene times (Fujiwara 1979, Higham & Maloney Ch. 42, this volume). Similarly, *Colocasia*, with its feet in the running freshwater streams of remote interior Arnhemland, probably illustrates the type of condition from which experimentation developed into the full-scale horticultural systems of New Guinea.

Finally, there is the crucial importance of that most difficult of all cultural aspects to investigate in the past, namely the ideology of a society. For the Gidjingali, their religious system was the key to their world view which linked them to the land, predicated their economic and social relations, and acted as a mnemonic for their understanding of the past. Above all, it acted as a reinforcer of traditional values and as a sanction against innovation or disturbance to the natural or social order. Key religious rites usually involved the depiction of totemic and cryptic designs – on the body in ceremonies, on hollow-log coffins of the dead, and on sheets of bark and the walls of rockshelters. In the vast corpus of the rock art of western Arnhemland there is a fundamental unity to its style, some elements of which most probably date back to Late Pleistocene times (Chaloupka 1985). In Cape York, complex geometric designs identical to some contemporary totemic motifs have been found engraved on a rockshelter panel and covered with deposits radiocarbon dated to 14 000 years bp. (Rosenfeld *et al.* 1981). The Australian system was one of great stability – these were the successful hunters. As a model for the type of economic or social systems that historically led to the earliest practices of systematic horticulture in New Guinea or Southeast Asia, we may need to think of societies quite different from these – perhaps systems of inherent instability, of less bounded organization of resources, and of conceptual categories of what could and what could not be done to the natural world.

## Acknowledgements

Some ideas in this chapter were formulated during discussions with Neville White, Neville Scarlett, Jack Golson, and Doug Yen. An earlier version was presented at a workshop on Australian food plants organized by Yen at the Australian National University in Canberra on 4 July 1986.

We also thank Clyde Dunlop of the Herbarium in Darwin for initial botanical identifications. Our greatest thanks, however, go to our hosts among the Gidjingali, in particular Frank Gurrmanamana and his wife Nancy Bandiyama. The manuscript was typed by Pamela Maljkovic and the figure was drawn by Winifred Mumford.

## References

Beck, W. 1985. *Technology, toxicity and subsistence: a study of Australian Aboriginal plant food processing.* Unpublished PhD thesis, La Trobe University, Melbourne.

Beck, W., R. Fullager & N. White 1988. Archaeology from ethnography: the Aboriginal use of cycad as an example. In *Archaeology from ethnography: an Australian perspective*, B. Meehan & R. Jones (eds), 137–47. Canberra: Department of Prehistory, Research School of Pacific Studies, Australian National University.

Chaloupka, G. 1985. Chronological sequence of Arnhemland plateau art. In *Archaeological research in Kakadu National Park*, R. Jones (ed.), 269–80. Canberra: Australian National Park and Wildlife Service.

Chase, A. K. 1989. Domestication and domiculture in northern Australia: a social perspective. In *Foraging and farming: the evolution of plant exploitation*, D. R. Harris & G. C. Hillman (eds), ch. 3. London: Unwin Hyman.

Clarke, A. 1985. A preliminary archaeobotanical analysis of the Anbangbang I site. In *Archaeological research in Kakadu National Park*, R. Jones (ed.), 77–96. Canberra: Australian National Park and Wildlife Service.

Fujiwara, H. 1979. Fundamental studies in plant opal analysis (3): estimation of the yield of rice in ancient paddy fields through quantitative analysis of plant opal. *Archaeology and Natural Sciences* (in Japanese) **12**, 29–42.

Fujiwara, H., R. Jones & S. Brockwell 1985. Plant opals (phytoliths) in Kakadu archaeological sites. In *Archaeological research in Kakadu National Park*, R. Jones (ed.), 155–64. Canberra: Australian National Park and Wildlife Service.

Golson, J. 1971. Australian Aboriginal food plants: some ecological and culture-historical implications. In *Aboriginal man and environment in Australia*, D. J. Mulvaney & J. Golson (eds), 196–238. Canberra: Australian National University Press.

Golson, J. 1977. No room at the top: agricultural intensification in the New Guinea Highlands. In *Sunda and Sahul: prehistoric studies in Southeast Asia, Melanesia and Australia,* J. Allen, J. Golson & R. Jones (eds), 601–38. London: Academic Press.

Golson, J. 1989. The origins and development of New Guinea agriculture. In *Foraging and farming: the evolution of plant exploitation,* D. R. Harris & G. C. Hillman (eds), ch. 44. London: Unwin Hyman.

Groube, L. 1989. The taming of the rain forests: a model for Late Pleistocene forest exploitation in New Guinea. In *Foraging and farming: the evolution of plant exploitation,* D. R. Harris & G. C. Hillman (eds), ch. 17. London: Unwin Hyman.

Groube, L., J. Chappell, J. Muke & D. Price 1986. A 40 000 year old occupation site at Huon Peninsula, Papua New Guinea. *Nature* **324,** 453–5.

Higham, C. & B. Maloney. 1989. Coastal adaptation, sedentism, and domestication: a model for socioeconomic intensification in prehistoric Southeast Asia. In *Foraging and farming: the evolution of plant exploitation,* D. R. Harris & G. C. Hillman (eds), ch. 42. London: Unwin Hyman.

Hope, G. 1982. Pollen from archaeological sites: a comparison of swamp and open archaeological site pollen spectra at Kosipe Mission, Papua New Guinea. In *Archaeometry: an Australasian perspective,* W. Ambrose (ed.), 211–19. Canberra: Department of Prehistory, Research School of Pacific Studies, Australian National University.

Hope, G., J. Golson & J. Allen 1983. Palaeoecology and prehistory in New Guinea. *Journal of Human Evolution* **12,** 37–60.

Hope, G., P. J. Hughes & J. Russell-Smith 1985. Geomorphological fieldwork and the evolution of the landscape of Kakadu National Park. In *Archaeological research in Kakadu National Park,* R. Jones (ed.), 229–40. Canberra: Australian National Park and Wildlife Service.

Jones, R. 1975. The Neolithic Palaeolithic and the hunting gardeners: man and land in the Antipodes. In *Quaternary studies,* R. P. Suggate & M. M. Creswell (eds), 21–34. Wellington: Royal Society of New Zealand.

Jones, R. 1980. Hunters in the Australian coastal savanna. In *Human ecology in savanna environments,* D. R. Harris (ed.), 107–46. London: Academic Press.

Jones, R. (ed.) 1985. *Archaeological research in Kakadu National Park.* Canberra: Australian National Park and Wildlife Service.

Jones, R. & I. Johnson 1985. Rockshelter excavations: Nourlangie and Mt Brockman massifs. In *Archaeological research in Kakadu National Park,* R. Jones (ed.), 39–76. Canberra: Australian National Park and Wildlife Service.

Keen, I. 1980. The Alligator Rivers Aborigines: retrospect and prospect. In *Northern Australia: options and implications,* R. Jones (ed.), 171–86. Canberra: Research School of Pacific Studies, Australian National University.

Meehan, B. 1982. *Shell bed to shell midden.* Canberra: Australian Institute of Aboriginal Studies.

Meehan, B. & R. Jones 1977. Preliminary comments on the preparation of *Cycas media* by the Gidjingali of coastal Arnhemland. Appendix to *Dangerous harvest: investigations in the late prehistoric occupation of upland south-east central Queensland,* by J. N. Beaton, 1–7. Unpublished PhD thesis, Australian National University, Canberra.

Meehan, B. & R. Jones 1986. Hunter–gatherer diet: an archaeological perspective and ethnographic method. In *Proceedings of the XIII International Congress of Nutrition,* T. G. Taylor & N. K. Jenkins (eds), 951–5. London: John Libby.

Meehan, B., P. Gaffey & R. Jones 1979. Fire to steel: Aboriginal exploitation of *Pandanus* and some wider implications. In *Readings in material culture,* P. Lauer (ed.),

73–96. Occasional papers in anthropology No. 9, Anthropology Museum, University of Queensland.

Rosenfeld, A., D. Horton & J. Winter 1981. *Early Man in north Queensland: art and archaeology in the Laura area. Terra Australis* **6**. Canberra: Department of Prehistory, Research School of Pacific Studies, Australian National University.

Russell-Smith, J. 1985. Studies in the jungle: people, fire and monsoon forest. In *Archaeological research in Kakadu National Park*, R. Jones (ed.), 241–67. Canberra: Australian National Park and Wildlife Service.

Scarlett, N. 1986. *Papers of the east Kimberley research project*. Canberra: Centre for Research in Environmental Studies, Australian National University.

Schrire, C. 1982. *The Alligator Rivers: prehistory and ecology in western Arnhemland. Terra Australis* **7**. Canberra: Department of Prehistory, Research School of Pacific Studies, Australian National University.

Yen, D. E. 1989. The domestication of environment. In *Foraging and farming: the evolution of plant exploitation*, D. R. Harris & G. C. Hillman (eds), ch. 4. London: Unwin Hyman.

# 8 *Plant usage and management in Southwest Australian Aboriginal societies*

SYLVIA J. HALLAM

## Introduction

To understand the origins of farming we need to examine ecological, ethnographic, historical, and archaeological data relating to peoples who are conventionally regarded as hunter–gatherers or, as we can more appropriately describe them, forager–hunters, for 'woman the gatherer' has been too long eclipsed by 'man the hunter'. The balance has been recently somewhat redressed, as the hunting interpretation of material in some archaeological sites has been called in question (Balme *et al.* 1978, Binford 1983), and as more sites with preserved plant material have been sought out for investigation (Beaton 1982, Smith 1982, Dillehay 1984, Clarke 1985, and Chs 12–19 in this book).

The important role of plant staples in non-agricultural subsistence systems has also been increasingly emphasized in recent ethnographic studies, e.g. by Murty (1985) and Nagar (1985) in peninsular India; and, in Australia, those by McCarthy & McArthur (1960) and Meehan in Arnhem Land (Meehan 1977, 1982, Jones & Meehan, Ch. 7, this volume), by Harris (1977) in the Cape York Peninsula, by Gould, O'Connell, and Cane in the Western and Central Desert (Gould 1977, 1980, O'Connell & Hawkes 1981, Cane Ch. 6, this volume), by Dix & Lofgren (1974) in the Murchison, by Vinnicombe (1987, pp. 34, 42) in the Pilbara, and by Crawford (1984) and Smith & Kalotas (1985) in the Kimberleys.

Such ethnographic evidence relates mainly to tropical and desert environments. In temperate Australia, where the impact of European colonization was greater, historical evidence can assume a major role. Although predominantly male observers have tended to write more about spectacular male activities, such as kangaroo drives, historical evidence of plant exploitation is none the less impressive (e.g. Golson 1971, Allen 1974, Meagher 1974, Tindale 1977, Meagher & Ride 1979, Gott 1982, see also Bates 1985, pp. 260–3).

The capacity of historical evidence to throw light on Australian Aboriginal practices of plant use and management is particularly well illustrated in southwestern Australia where, from the coastal plain, there is evidence for a great variety of phenomena associated with plant exploitation. These include evidence of intensive use of clearly defined areas where plants with subterranean storage organs were harvested; well-defined usage rights; seasonal scheduling of plant exploitation; harvesting and husbanding prac- tices which encourage maintenance and proliferation (of, for example, reed rhizomes or *Dioscorea* tubers); investment of labour in resource improve- ment and management; burning to open up access to localized resource patches; associated fixed facilities (path networks, wells, and groups of substantial dwellings); semi-sedentism; processing equipment (e.g. grind- stones) and technologies (pulverizing, addition of alkaline ash, roasting of cakes, etc.); and evidence of ancient, large-scale geomorphological effects (Hallam 1986).

## Types of evidence

This chapter focuses particularly, but not exclusively, on Aboriginal use of the yam *Dioscorea hastifolia* on riverine alluvium down the west coast. Many different types of evidence illuminate this usage:

(a)  field evidence of the 'humps and hollows' of locally known 'warran diggings';
(b)  the botanical evidence of *Dioscorea* plants in these and other localities, examined in association with Dixon (Pate & Dixon 1982);
(c)  historical sources, published and unpublished, for Aboriginal land-use during European exploration and settlement, e.g. Dutch reference to 'land under cultivation' in 1658 (Major 1859, p. 62, Heeres 1899). Grey and others – from the botanist Drummond (Landor 1847, p. 368) in the 1840s to Sara Meagher (1974, p. 267) in the 1960s – sketch the distri- bution of yam usage. Journals of the 1830s clarify the schedule of harvesting and processing yams and other plant resources in relation to seasonal activities, including the aggregation and dispersal of Aborigi- nal groups; and maps of the 1840s show several precise locations for yam-diggings emphasizing the highly localized nature of the distri- bution. Indeed, the distribution of these types of evidence shows that yam patches were nearly all on riverine alluvium.
(d)  Archaeological surface survey of a sample transect across the Swan coastal plain has shown that, at all periods, the alluvial terraces of the Swan River and its tributaries carried a relatively high density of archaeological sites, with more large sites than the rest of the coastal plain. Several known yam-digging localities, particularly those adja- cent to other staples, e.g. reed rhizomes (*Typha* sp.) and zamia seeds (*Macrozamia* sp.), supported large occupation complexes spanning long time periods (e.g. Gingin, Walyunga).
(e)  Archaeological excavations have demonstrated the longevity of such occupation, e.g. back to 8000 bp at Walyunga, to 29 000 bp on the

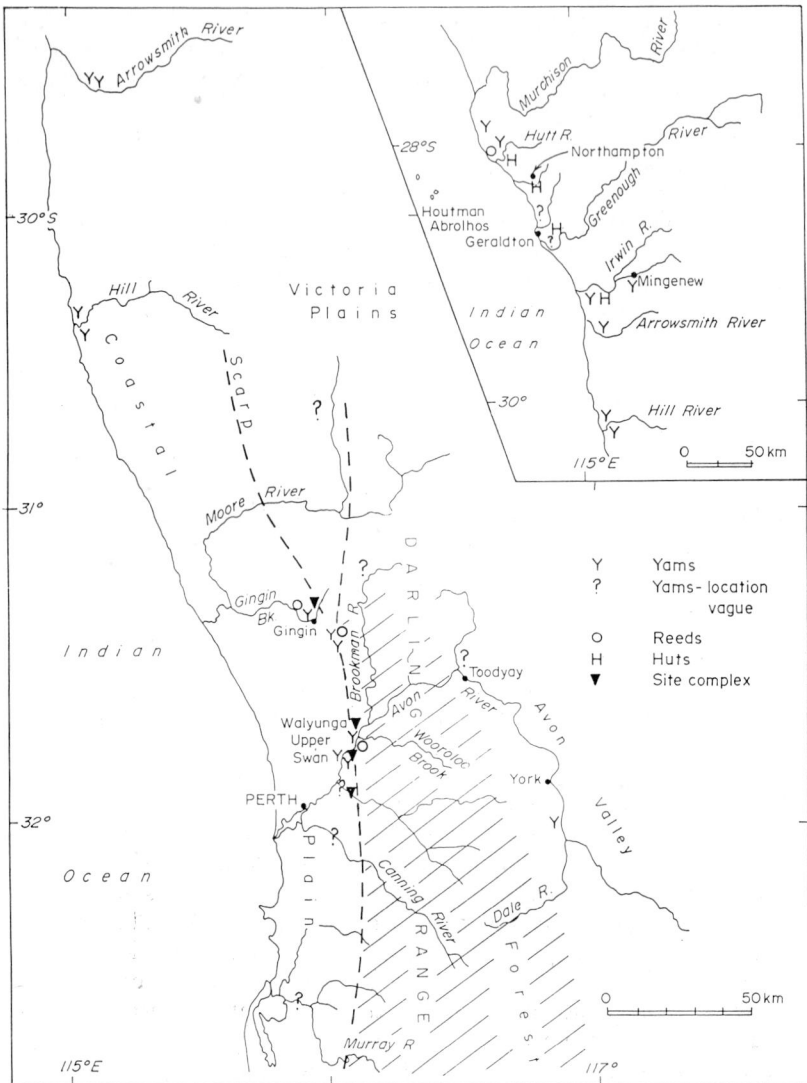

**Figure 8.1** Map showing Western Australian locations mentioned in the text.

Helena, and to 39 000 bp in the charcoal-rich alluvial deposits at Upper
Swan (see below).

(f)  Geomorphological investigations of the alluvium of the Greenough,
the Swan, and the Helena show substantial deposition around 40 000 to
20 000 bp, with charcoal throughout, suggesting human impact (see
below).

# Patch resources and sedentism

The use of fixed patch resources involved a considerable degree of sedentism. European explorers describe populations concentrated by, and focused
on, route centres which were also resource centres. From Pelsaart and
Volkerson in the 17th century to Backhouse and Clifton in the 19th, they
report 'fields' of yams and solid huts, on the fertile alluvium of the Hutt,
Greenough, Irwin, and Hill Rivers, often close to swamps providing reed
rhizomes, or to lagoons with fish and fowl (Hallam 1986). (Fig. 8.1 shows
the location of the yam grounds, settlements, etc. mentioned in this section.)

In May 1839 Sir George Grey, shipwrecked at the mouth of the Murchison
River on the central west coast of Australia (about 28°S), set off towards the
European settlement on the Swan River at 32°S. This coast lies at the limit of
the range of tropical storms from the north in summer or Mediterranean rain
from the south in winter, and has low and variable precipitation. North of
the Hutt River he encountered 'light fertile soil quite overrun with *warran*
plants . . . a species of *Dioscorea*, a sort of yam like the sweet potatoe' over an
extensive area five or six kilometres long by perhaps two kilometres wide,
approached by permanent paths, and serviced by deliberately constructed
deep soaks. Grey commented: 'It was now evident that we had entered the
most thickly populated district of Australia that I had yet observed, and
moreover one which must have been inhabited over a long series of years,
for more had here been done to secure a provision from the ground by hard
manual labour than I could have believed it in the power of uncivilised man
to accomplish' (Grey 1840, p. 124, 1841, Vol. 2, p. 11). Two miles farther
on, Grey's party came upon another equally fertile warran ground, and in the
next valley 'a chain of reedy fresh water swamps' with 'the *yun-tid* or flag, a
species of *Typha*', where 'native paths ran in from all quarters' (Grey 1841,
Vol. 2, pp. 12–13).

Thus yam tubers and reed rhizomes lay within a few kilometres of each
other, with fish and fowl in the nearby lagoon. Close by Grey passed 'two
native villages', with large huts 'very nicely plastered over the outside with
clay, and clods of turf, so that . . . they were evidently intended for fixed
places of residence . . . '. He concluded that 'these superior huts, well
marked roads, deeply sunk wells and extensive warran grounds, all spoke of
a large and comparatively speaking resident [i.e. sedentary] population'
(Grey 1841, Vol. 2, pp. 19–20). Extensive semi-cultivated areas near the
Hutt River represented a massive labour investment, involving repeated
frequenting over long periods of time.

'Warran' diggings were also reported from the next streams south, the
Oakagee and the Oakabella (Western Australian Museum Sites Department); from the Chapman River, near present Geraldton, with 'numerous
native paths', deep holes, and 'clay-plastered huts' (Hallam 1986); and from
the Greenough alluvial flats with 'a large assemblage of native huts, of the
same permanent character . . . two groups of those houses close together
. . . would have contained at least a hundred and fifty natives' (Grey 1841,

Vol. 2, p. 37). At the Irwin River 'a well-beaten native path' led to another 'warran ground, full of holes'; 'the whole [Arrowsmith] valley was an extensive warran ground', where Grey encountered Aboriginal women and children digging for roots, then cooking them by a pool in the sandy river bed (ibid. pp. 54–61). At the Hill River the Dutch had found 'land under cultivation' almost 200 years before Grey, although the area receives very little rain, summer or winter.

Around Gingin, on a tributary of the Moore River the humps and hollows of 'warran holes' remain visible, with yams growing along the adjacent road verge. On the slopes of the scarp bounding the coastal plain nearby are several extensive dense scatters of Aboriginal artefacts. The humps and hollows of 'warran diggings' are still visible in pasture at Lennard's Brook, just south of Gingin, and yams grow nearby. Here nearly 100 men, women, and children assembled to greet George Fletcher Moore in 1835 and invited his party to eat the processed pulp of zamia nuts, then entertained them with dances and songs. The land was so fertile that several Europeans took up grants there (Hallam 1986).

Forty kilometres farther south the Avon/Swan River lies within the Mediterranean belt of winter rains. By a permanent pool just within the hills the extensive campsite at Walyunga was occupied from before 8000 bp until after European contact (Pearce 1978). Reed rhizomes, yam tubers, and zamia nuts all grow around the living area. There is a group of extensive Aboriginal sites a few miles downstream where the Swan/Avon emerges westward from the hills. Maps of the 1840s show two patches of 'warran diggings' on the left-bank high terrace, and another patch a kilometre or so farther downstream on the right bank. Moore's diary refers to Aborigines frequent-ing this area in considerable numbers, harvesting reed rhizomes and yam tubers.

The documentary, cartographic, botanical, and archaeological evidence relating to the alluvium of these rivers, from the Hutt to the Swan (Hallam 1986), thus shows concentrations of yam-digging areas, often adjacent to water sources and to other resource concentrations: zamias; reed rhizomes; swamps, lakes, and lagoons with fish and fowl, frogs, turtles, and crustaceans, frequented by large game. Fixed facilities – path networks, wells, and large groups of substantial dwellings – concentrate around these resource foci. Northward, where the surrounding terrain is dry and infertile (and in the arid inland), it is probably true, as Drum-mond remarked, that 'The abundance of "Warrang" and paucity of animals may in some measure account for the greater concentration of these tribes'. He added 'In these parts the "Warrang" a kind of yam greatly abounds and grows to a large size. When roasted it is repre-sented as superior to the potato, sweet, pleasant and nourishing' (Hallam 1986). Even in the well-watered south, with more varied resources, the alluvium of the Moore and Swan Rivers supported distinct concentra-tions of settlement, frequented by big groups for long stretches of the year.

## Seasonal schedules of harvesting and occupance

Digging for yams extended through much of the year. In January 1838 a Quaker evangelist visited Moore: 'A considerable number of the Blacks were assembled on one farm . . . We examined some holes where the natives had been digging for roots of a *Dioscorea*, or Yam, for food. This plant climbs among bushes, in a strongish soil . . . and the Natives have a tradition, respecting its roots having been conferred upon them, in which there are traces of the deluge' (Backhouse 1843, pp. 538–40). The maximum usage of yams, however, fell not in midsummer (December–February) when the plants were dormant and the ground hard, but in March or April. 'The yam is sought chiefly at the commencement of the rains when it is ripe and when the earth is most easily dug; and it forms that principal article of food for the natives at that season' (Moore 1884, *Vocabulary*, p. 74). Moore's diaries show large aggregations of Aborigines near his house, close by the Upper Swan yam-diggings, in the autumn. In March 1833 he had 24 male visitors, implying that 60 or more people were encamped close by (Moore 1884, *Diary*, p. 169). In February 1834 Moore was remarking on 'numbers of natives' (*Diary*, p. 211). At the beginning of March he felt himself 'beset by natives', with a 'lot of natives, boys and girls' splashing merrily in the river while their elders made festive drinks by steeping redgum blossoms in water (*Diary*, pp. 212–18). In mid-March he still complained: 'I have the natives much more about me than usual', some baking their yam or reed flour into cakes (*Diary*, p. 215). By the end of May *Typha* had become the basic staple: 'Natives . . . are now busy digging the root of a broad sort of flag which grows in a swamp . . . '. A few days later: 'Got from the natives a piece of bread made of the root of the flag . . . . It tastes like a cake of oatmeal. They peel the root, roast and pound it, and bake it' (*Diary*, p. 220).

   Thus, during the wet winter months (May–August), when regenerating yam vines would be taking nutriment from last summer's dormant tubers and new tubers forming below the old head, alternative plant staples, such as reed rhizomes, enabled groups to remain in the same localities. Moore continued 'plagued by natives' through June and into July. By the autumn the Aborigines could harvest the new season's yam tubers before the ground hardened for the summer. At Upper Swan 'great numbers' were around again in October, 1834. East of the hills, in September 1842 Drummond and Gilbert were unable to obtain native guides, for around Toodyay they were gathered in great numbers to dig these tubers.

   Thus yam usage is predominant in spring and autumn, but possible throughout the dry summer period of dormancy. Other staples span the early winter, so that areas like Upper Swan could support large groups in all months except possibly August and December.

## Labour investment, husbandry, and usage rights

Digging yams was most laborious. 'It is generally considered the province of women to dig roots, [with] a long pointed stick . . . they dig with great rapidity. But the labour, in proportion to the amount obtained, is great . . . a considerable portion of the time of the women and children is therefore passed in this employment . . . ' (Grey 1841, Vol. 2, pp. 292–3; also Moore 1884, *Vocabulary*, p. 74). Phillip Chauncy, who in the 1840s mapped 'warran holes' on the Swan terraces, saw 'both men and women sinking loose sandy soil for an edible root called *warran* . . . which generally grows about the thickness of a man's thumb, and to the depth of four to six or eight feet. It is dangerous to travel on horseback through the country where it grows, on account of the frequency and depth of the holes' (Chauncy 1878, pp. 245–6). The scale of operation is made clear by both Grey and Chauncy.

Harvesting improves the growth of root staples, whether they are reed rhizomes or yam tubers, and leads to their greater abundance and spread (Gott 1982). Digging loosens and aerates the soil, and separates new tubers from old dead ones attached to the same head. A woman taking most of a tuber for food, will inevitably break it up and leave portions in the ground, probably dispersing remnants, and so increasing the number of plants and the extent of the tuber patch, or even carrying some of the 'setts' to another locality. In northern Australia (e.g. Jones 1975) diggers leave undisturbed the vine itself and the rhizomatous head below it, and take only the one or two tubers which sprout from that head. As in Chauncy's account, the holes are left open, and this enables the digger next year to crop new tubers from the same vine. Loose soil and litter, gradually filling the hole, provide a well-aerated substrate for further growth. Similar harvesting/cultivating techniques are used by horticulturalists (see below).

Labour investment led to proprietary rights. Families held harvesting and digging rights in their own particular patches. European observers usually interpreted this in terms of *men's* property rights. Thus Moore, on a journey northward in 1835, traced five individual land-holdings in 50 km along the foot of the Darling Scarp between Upper Swan and the Lennard's Brook/ Gingin area, each where a stream emerged from the scarp, providing water and a patch of fertile ground (Moore 1835). He lists the 'brothers' Mullewar and Cogat as land-holders on Lennard's Brook and a neighbouring stream. In 1836 Mullewar defended his family's usage rights at Upper Swan 40 km south, threatening William Shaw with his spear when Shaw tried to prevent the women and children from taking potato and turnip crops, which Shaw had planted there previously Aboriginal families had dug yams (Colonial Secretary's Office Records 49, 37, Battye Library, Perth). Probably Mullewar held rights at Lennard's Brook through his mother; while at Upper Swan he was defending his wife's holdings. Families tracing their descent through the female line formed the focus of sedentism in and around these cropping areas. Great families were focused in particular localities, e.g. the brothers Weban and Helia, plus their eight or nine wives, their daughters, and often their daughters' husbands, and some (the younger and unmarried) of their many sons, were associated with Upper Swan. From such foci young men like Mullewar could travel widely, or whole groups could gather for ceremonial and social occasions (Hallam & Tilbrook in prep.).

Usage rights, firing rights, and proprietary rights were closely linked, in practice and in Aboriginal vocabulary. The word *Kalla* carried the meaning of fire, and also of hearth and home (Hallam 1975, p. 43).

Firing of the countryside opened up access to some resources, which were carefully kept unburnt (e.g. yams), and encouraged the growth of others, e.g. zamias (Beaton 1982) and pasture grasses (Hallam 1975, 1985, Lewis 1985). Thus, Bunbury in 1836 described fires by which 'the country is kept comparatively free from underwood and other obstructions, having the character of an open forest through most parts of which one can ride freely; otherwise, in all probability, it would soon become impenetrably thick' (Bunbury in Hallam 1975, p. 47). Firing also improved pasture and concentrated game: 'The burnt ground . . . sends up in the rainy season a sweeter crop of grass which attracts the kangaroo' (Wollaston in Hallam 1975, p. 42); and was also used to drive game, both large and small. The Aboriginal vocabulary made distinctions between different stages and different overall effects of a variety of different usage and firing regimes: e.g. '*Kunkyl* – Young grass springing after the country has been burned' (Moore 1884, *Vocabulary*, p. 45) or '*Nappal* – Burned ground; ground over which fire has passed. Over this ground the natives prefer walking; it is free from all scrub and grass and their progress is not therefore obstructed' (ibid., p. 60).

Burning was carefully controlled. Fire was prevented from reaching resource patches which it would damage. Thus, on 1840s maps 'warran grounds' were shown surrounded by 'dogwood thickets', e.g. on the right-bank high terrace of the Swan River just west of Upper Swan church, and at two localities on the left-bank terrace, on the northern boundary of William Shaw's land, where Mullewar had defended his family's usage rights (Hallam 1975, pp. 14–58, 1986).

Aboriginal burning created a mosaic pattern of open country and dense bush, creating zones of easy movement and access on the coastal plain to the west and along the woodland margin east of a denser forest zone. Game abounded most in open, frequented zones (the scarp-foot alluvium, or wide valleys within the forest); and plant resources were best preserved in unburnt patches (as at Upper Swan), with access through open country around.

## Settlement patterns and archaeological survey

In parts of the eastern Australian coastal plains, localities rich in resources acted as foci of occupation for large numbers of people over long periods. In Victoria (Lourandos 1980) the foci were inland wetlands. Swamps with *Typha* as a plant staple, fish, fowl, and additional plant foods (daisy-yam, *Microseris*, rather than true yam, *Dioscorea*, Gott 1982) made possible semi-permanent populations; and trap and water-control systems for harvesting eels also focused groups on similar localities. Similarly, on the Swan coastal plain in historical times the fixed facilities were reed swamps and 'warran grounds'. 'Wetland' and alluvial areas were the real gathering points. River gaps in the scarp combined all these factors. Did similar patterns operate earlier?

To elucidate the imprint of such flexible but focused patterns of occupation, archaeological studies must be area-centred rather than site-centred. The Swan area survey has aimed to sample from the totality of artefact scatters generated over time by groups throughout their area of movement; to show which portions of that territory bore heavy and which bore light usage; which zones carried many large sites frequented by many people over long periods and which had few; how small sites were grouped or dispersed in relation to large; and what were the changes over time. Almost 600 sites have been located in a transect 30 km long and 15 km wide across the Swan coastal plain (Hallam 1975, 1977, 1986).

Usage patterns for different zones differ between phases, particularly the proportions of large to small sites. Of sites occupied at European contact about one-sixth were large, while on the alluvium the figure was nearer a quarter. Of sites occupied in the Late (immediately pre-contact) phase, about one-fifth had such quantities of materials, including grinders, as to indicate intensive frequenting, by large numbers of people, and/or for long spans of the year; just over one-third were of moderate extent and density, suggesting recurrent visits by smaller groups; nearly half (45 per cent) of sites had a few artefacts only, probably representing a single visit. The alluvial zone carried an unduly high proportion (33 per cent) of major sites, with only a quarter small. There was even greater concentration of usage on the alluvium earlier – both in the Early (pre-5000 bp) and in the Middle (5000 to 500 bp) phases around 45 per cent of sites on the alluvium were major, as against only 30 per cent overall. In each phase the density of large sites on the alluvium was at least double the average for the entire coastal plain, quadruple after European contact. The density of sites of all sizes exceeded the mean both on the alluvium and also around the swamps and lakes of the coastal sandplain, where more sites were small. There are 1.6 discovered sites of all ages per $km^2$ on the alluvium, as against 0.9 $km^{-2}$ for the entire coastal plain, a quarter of them large on the alluvium, but only one-sixth overall. The alluvial zone thus shows a higher usage than the rest of the coastal plain, and also a greater concentration of that usage.

Thus, the archaeological evidence confirms the ethnohistorical evidence of large groups focused on the resources of swamps, lakes, and alluvial floodplains (e.g. reed rhizomes) and alluvial terraces (e.g. yams), from before the advent of backed-tool assemblages about 5000 bp. How great is the antiquity of such patterns of usage and occupance?

# Antiquity and geomorphological impact

Localities which at European contact had available a wide range of resources, and a focal position, had these over a long time-span. The Walyunga site had been in use for more than 8000 years prior to contact (Pearce 1978); and at other major sites along the Darling Scarp, commanding coastal plain swamps and scarp-slope or scarp-foot yam-diggings, abundant surface material of similar typological variety suggests a similar span of continuous use (e.g. Gingin, Bullsbrook).

Schwede's investigations in the alluvium of the Helena gave dates around 28 000 and 29 000 bp for charcoal at depths of 2.2 and 1.2 m. Artefact density was highest in the top 50 cm, dated 4000 to 200 bp, penetrated by pits (Schwede 1983), possibly yam-diggings, which may have introduced the assemblage of small quartz artefacts (cf. Alexander 1969).

Charcoal associated with artefacts within the top metre of the northern high (20 m) terrace of the River Swan (2 km upstream from the 19th-century yam-diggings near Upper Swan church, and immediately across the river from the warran grounds along Shaw's boundary on the 20 m terrace opposite) dated from 35 100 to 39 500 bp, giving a statistical mean of 38 000 bp as a minimal age for the deposit (Pearce & Barbetti 1981). On both sides of the Swan at Upper Swan, pounding and grinding material forms a major component in the assemblages (Schwede pers. comm.), suggesting that plant processing was important throughout the 40 000 years' timespan of occupation of the Swan alluvium.

From the Greenough northward, a number of short streams have deposited, and later dissected, a thick and extensive 'Red Alluvium' on the coastal plain, backed here by a range of hills with unstable soils liable to landslides. Wyrwoll (1984) obtained a date of more than 37 000 bp from the upper levels of this 'Red Alluvium', which, like the Swan and Helena terraces, is rich in charcoal throughout. Does this massive deposition on the Greenough and Murchison rivers and associated streams correlate with initial human presence (Jones 1979, Bordes et al. 1983, Wyrwoll 1984) and, on the Swan, possibly with firing to obtain access to, and to improve and maintain, the plant and animal resources of the coastal plain? Partial devegetation on the inland plateau could be a factor in deposition (and later dissection) on the coastal plain. Colonists from the north, perhaps under conditions less arid than the present (Jones & Bowler 1980, Horton 1982), would have encountered familiar plant genera on the Hutt–Greenough–Irwin alluvium (cf. Golson 1971), and would gradually have opened up and penetrated the more densely vegetated coastal plain south to the Swan and beyond, with extensive geomorphological impact. Burning was also making a decisive impact during this early period on the rain forests of Queensland and on the tableland around Canberra (Singh et al. 1981, Singh & Geissler 1985). The new alluvial deposits provided soils ideally suitable for yam growth.

## Distribution and growth requirements of Australasian yams

*Dioscorea hastifolia* of the west coast is botanically akin to some of the culti-vated yams of Southeast Asia and the margins of the Indian and Pacific Oceans. The varieties of *Dioscorea bulbifera*, alternatively known as *D. sativa* (Golson 1971, pp. 217–18; Harris 1977, pp. 433–7, Jones & Meehan Ch. 7, Yen Ch. 4, this volume), common in Arnhem Land and Cape York, are members of the section *Opsophyton* which climb by twining to the left. They are common wild in both Asia and Africa, and cultivated forms spread into Oceania (Burkill 1958, Coursey 1967, 1972, 1976). *D. hastifolia*, on the other hand, belongs to the *Enantiophyllum* section of Dioscoreaceae, which twine to the right. *D. transversa*, the commonest yam of northern and eastern Aus-tralia, also belongs to this group; as does *D. alata*, which is not known wild, but whose many cultivated varieties spread from mainland Southeast Asia, throughout Indonesia, and into New Guinea, the Pacific, and Indian Oceans (Coursey 1967, Alexander & Coursey 1969). In the Pacific, *D. alata* yams were grown as far south as the north island of New Zealand, selected for a shorter growing season than in the tropics and for long storage (Leach 1984).

The yams are in origin tropical plants requiring water in the growing season, but their tubers represent an evolutionary adaptation to a prolonged dry season. The most widespread *Enantiophyllum* yams, *D. alata* and *D. rotunda*, need a seven- or eight-month growing period. But other related species such as *D. opposita* and *D. japonica* in China and Japan, like *D. hastifo-lia*, represent adaptations to areas with a shorter growing season and lower temperatures. *D. hastifolia* shows an interesting reversal of the tropical situ-ation, having its growing period in the winter and dormancy in the summer.

The tropical yams require nutrient-rich, well-aerated soils (Coursey 1967, Vasey n.d.), being planted usually in mounds or ridges, although they can be grown 'on the flat' where the soil is soft and deep, as in river alluvium. In New Guinea, long yams are planted in deep holes filled with loose topsoil (Vasey n.d.). They benefit from mulching or from being planted in areas rich in minerals from burning, and can be grown in successive years where an annual increment of alluvium restores fertility. *D. hastifolia* appears to share these ecological preferences. Cultivated *Enantiophyllum* yams may be harves-ted twice in the year – an early crop early in the growing season, extracted carefully leaving the head in place; and a main crop at the end of the wet or beginning of the dry (Coursey 1967, pp. 85–6). West coast harvesting shows two similar peaks. Like its cultivated relatives, *D. hastifolia* produces only a few yams from one head, but these are large.

Australian Aborigines on the central west coast were cropping a plant which shares many of the characteristics and requirements of its cultivated kin, using harvesting methods which provided the necessary aerated soil condition, in appropriately nutrient-rich localities. The soils which sup-ported the greatest concentrations are Late Pleistocene deposits, probably resulting from the extensive geomorphological impact of the first humans to reach the Australian continent.

## Conclusion

The south and central areas of the west coast of Australia provide a variety of types of evidence for the intensive use of fixed patch resources of plants with subterranean storage organs, particularly *Dioscorea hastifolia*. Taking together documentary, cartographic, botanical, and archaeological field survey and excavated evidence, plus geomorphological data, a consistent picture emerges of extensive but clearly defined plant-harvesting areas, at least one on the alluvium of each river from the Murchison to the Murray (Fig. 8.1). These resource patches, particularly where multiple staples were available in close proximity, were closely associated with other fixed facilities – path networks, wells, and in the central west coast large groups of substantial dwellings, implying semi-sedentism. This was made possible by a seasonal schedule which used these very substantial plant resources for a large part of the year, and allowed families to be based on particular localities for long periods, although the young men moved freely about these bases. Everywhere harvesting and husbanding of plant resources (both tubers for direct subsistence, and pasture to encourage game) implied substantial labour investment and concomitant proprietary and usage rights. Husbandry and management practices, including firing, encouraged the maintenance, improvement, and extension of tuber and pasture resources. Patterns of occupation on the coastal plain and its hinterland showed selective intensive usage of alluvial terraces (providing yams) and swamp areas (providing reed rhizomes). Plant processing equipment, both pounding/grinding equipment and axes, and their associated technologies, have a high antiquity in the west and in Australia as a whole. Geomorphological evidence attests to the large-scale landscape impact of these plant-husbanding populations and suggests a chronology of more than 40 000 years for the intensive use of plant resources in Australia.

## Acknowledgements

I wish to thank the Australian Research Grants Scheme for funding for many years the archaeological surveys which form the basis for this chapter; and also the Department of Anthropology and the Centre for Prehistory in the University of Western Australia for continuing support.

## References

Alexander, J. 1969. The domestication of yams: a multi-disciplinary problem. In *Science in archaeology*, D. Brothwell & E. Higgs (eds), 2nd edn, 229–34. London: Thames & Hudson.
Alexander, J. & D. G. Coursey 1969. The origins of yam cultivation. In *The domestication and exploitation of plants and animals*, P. J. Ucko & G. W. Dimbleby (eds), 405–25. London: Duckworth.
Allen, H. 1974. The Bagundji of the Darling Basin: cereal gatherers in an uncertain environment. *World Archaeology* **5**, 309–22.

Backhouse, J. 1843. *A narrative of a visit to the Australian colonies.* Facsimile edition 1967. New York: Johnson Reprint Co.

Balme, J., D. Merrilees & J. Porter 1978. Late Quaternary mammal remains, spanning about 30 000 years, from excavations in Devil's Lair, Western Australia. *Journal of the Royal Society of Western Australia* **61**, 33–65.

Bates, D. 1985. In *The native tribes of Western Australia*, I. White (ed.). Canberra: National Library of Australia.

Beaton, J. M. 1982. Fire and water: aspects of Aboriginal management of cycads. *Archaeology in Oceania* **17**, 51–8.

Binford, L. R. 1983. *In pursuit of the past.* London: Thames & Hudson.

Bordes, F., C. Dortch, C. Thibault, J-P. Raynal & P. Bindon 1983. Walga Rock and Billibilong Spring. *Australian Archaeology* **17**, 1–26.

Burkill, I. H. 1958. The organography and the evolution of the Dioscoreaceae, the family of the yams. *Journal of the Linnaean Society (Botany)* **56**, 319–412.

Cane, S. 1989. Australian Aboriginal seed grinding and its archaeological record: a case study from the Western Desert. In *Foraging and farming: the evolution of plant exploitation*, D. R. Harris & G. C. Hillman (eds), ch. 6. London: Unwin Hyman.

Chauncy, P. 1876. Notes and anecdotes of the Aborigines of Australia. In *The Aborigines of Victoria and other parts of Australia and Tasmania*, R. Brough Smythe. Appendix A, Vol. 2, 221–84. Melbourne: Government of Victoria, and London: Robertson.

Clarke, A. 1985. A preliminary archaeological analysis of the Anbangbang I Site. In *Archaeological research in Kakadu National Park*, R. Jones (ed.), 77–96. Canberra: Australian National Park and Wildlife Service.

Coursey, D. G. 1967. *Yams: an account of the nature, origins, cultivation and utilisation of the useful members of the Dioscoreaceae.* London: Longman.

Coursey, D. G. 1972. The civilisations of the yam: interrelationships of man and yams in Africa and the Indo-Pacific region. *Archaeology and Physical Anthropology in Oceania* **7**, 215–33.

Coursey, D. G. 1976. Yams, *Dioscorea* spp. (Dioscoreaceae). In *Evolution of Crop Plants*, N. W. Simmonds (ed.), 70–4. London: Longman.

Crawford, I. M. 1984. *Aboriginal traditional plant resources in the Kalumburu area: aspects in ethno-economics.* Perth: Records of the Western Australian Museum, Supplement No. 15.

Dillehay, T. D. 1984. Late ice-age settlement in southern Chile. *Scientific American* **251**, 100–9.

Dix, W. & M. E. Lofgren 1974. Kurumi: possible Aboriginal incipient agriculture associated with a stone arrangement. *Records of the Western Australian Museum* **3**, 73–7.

Golson, J. 1971. Australian Aboriginal food plants: some ecological and culture-historical implications. In *Aboriginal man and environment in Australia*, D. J. Mulvaney & J. Golson (eds), 196–238. Canberra: Australian National University Press.

Gott, B. 1982. The ecology of root use by the Aborigines of southern Australia. *Archaeology in Oceania* **17**, 59–67.

Gould, R. A. 1977. *Puntutjarpa rockshelter and the Australian desert culture.* New York: American Museum of Natural History.

Gould, R. A. 1980. *Living archaeology.* Cambridge: Cambridge University Press.

Grey, G. 1840. *Vocabulary of the dialects of south western Australia.* London: Boone.

Grey, G. 1841. *Journals of two expeditions of discovery in north-west and western Australia during the Years 1837, 38 and 39.* London: Boone. Facsimile edition 1964. Adelaide: Public Library of South Australia.

Hallam, S. J. 1975. *Fire and hearth: a study of Aboriginal usage and European usurpation in southwestern Australia*. Canberra: Australian Institute of Aboriginal Studies.

Hallam, S. J. 1977. Stone tools and topographic archaeology. In *Stone tools as cultural markers*, R. V. S. Wright (ed.), 166–77. Canberra: Australian Institute of Aboriginal Studies.

Hallam, S. J. 1979. Population and resource usage on the western littoral. *Memoirs of the Victorian Archaeological Survey. A collection of papers presented to ANZAAS 1977, Section 25A*, Vol. 2, 16–36.

Hallam, S. J. 1983. The peopling of the Australian continent. *Indian Ocean Newsletter* **4**, 11–15.

Hallam, S. J. 1985. The history of Aboriginal firing. In *Fire ecology and management in Western Australian ecosystems*, J. Ford (ed.), 7–20. Perth: Western Australian Institute of Technology.

Hallam, S. J. 1986. *Yams, alluvium and villages on the west coastal plain*. Paper delivered to the 54th ANZAAS Congress, Canberra, May 1984. Canberra: Australian Institute of Aboriginal Studies.

Hallam, S. J. & L. Tilbrook. *Dictionary of Western Australian Aboriginal biographies, 1829–1840*, in preparation.

Harris, D. R. 1977. Subsistence strategies across Torres Strait. In *Sunda and Sahul: prehistoric studies in Southeast Asia, Melanesia and Australia*, J. Allen, J. Golson & R. Jones (eds), 421–63. London: Academic Press.

Heeres, J. E. 1899. *The part borne by the Dutch in the discovery of Australia, 1706–1765*. London: Luzac; Leiden: E. J. Brill.

Horton, D. R. 1982. Water and woodland: the peopling of Australia. *Australian Institute of Aboriginal Studies Newsletter* **16**, 21–7.

Jones, R. 1975. The Neolithic Palaeolithic and the hunting gardeners: man and land in the Antipodes. In *Quaternary studies*, R. P. Suggate & M. M. Cresswell (eds), 21–34. Wellington: Royal Society of New Zealand.

Jones, R. 1979. The fifth continent: problems concerning the human colonisation of Australia. *Annual Review of Anthropology* **8**, 445–66.

Jones, R. & J. M. Bowler 1980. Struggle for the savannah: northern Australia in ecological and prehistoric perspective. In *Northern Australia: options and implications*, R. Jones (ed.), 3–31. Canberra: Research School of Pacific Studies, Australian National University.

Jones, R. & B. Meehan 1989. Plant foods of the Gidjingali: ethnographic and archaeological perspectives from northern Australia on tuber and seed exploitation. In *Foraging and farming: the evolution of plant exploitation*, D. R. Harris & G. C. Hillman (eds), ch. 7. London: Unwin Hyman.

Landor, E. W. 1847. *The bushman: or life in a new country*. Facsimile edition 1970. New York: Johnson Reprint Co.

Leach, H. 1984. *1000 years of gardening in New Zealand*. Wellington: A. H. & A. W. Reed.

Lewis, H. T. 1985. Burning the 'top end': kangaroos and cattle. In *Fire ecology and management in Western Australian ecosystems*, J. Ford (ed.), 21–31. Perth: Western Australian Institute of Technology.

Lourandos, H. 1980. Change or stability? Hydraulics, hunter–gatherers and population in temperate Australia. *World Archaeology* **11**, 245–64.

McCarthy, F. D. & M. McArthur 1960. The food quest and the time factor in Aboriginal economic life. In *Records of the American–Australian scientific expedition to Arnhem Land. Vol. 2: Anthropology and nutrition*, C. P. Mountford (ed.), 145–94. Melbourne: Melbourne University Press.

Major, R. H. 1859. *Early voyages to Terra Australis, now called Australia: a collection of documents and extracts from early manuscript maps . . . from the beginning of the sixteenth century to the time of Captain Cook.* London: Hakluyt Society. 1963 edn, Australian Heritage Press.

Meagher, S. J. 1974. The food resources of the Aborigines of the south-west of Western Australia. *Records of the Western Australian Museum* **3**, 14–65.

Meagher, S. J. & W. D. L. Ride 1979. Use of natural resources by the Aborigines of south-western Australia. In *Aborigines of the West: their past and their present*, R. M. & C. H. Berndt (eds), 66–80. Nedlands: University of Western Australia Press.

Meehan, B. 1977. Man does not live by calories alone. In *Sunda and Sahul: prehistoric studies in Southeast Asia, Melanesia and Australia*, J. Allen, J. Golson & R. Jones (eds), 493–531. London: Academic Press.

Meehan, B. 1982. *Shell bed to shell midden.* Canberra: Australian Institute of Aboriginal Studies.

Moore, G. F. 1835. *Perth Gazette* 25 May.

Moore, G. F. 1884. *Diary of ten years of an early settler in Western Australia*, [Diary]; and *A descriptive vocabulary of the language of the Aborigines*, [Vocabulary]; paginated separately. Facsimile edn, C. T. Stannage (ed.) 1978. Nedlands: University of Western Australia Press.

Murty, M. L. K. 1985. The uses of plant foods by some hunter–gatherer communities in Andrah Pradesh. In *Recent advances in Indo-Pacific prehistory*, V. N. Misra & P. Bellwood (eds), 329–36. New Delhi: Oxford & IBM Publishing.

Nagar, M. 1985. The use of wild plantfoods by Aboriginal communities in central India. In *Recent advances in Indo-Pacific prehistory*, V. N. Misra & P. Bellwood (eds), 337–42. New Delhi: Oxford & IBM Publishing.

O'Connell, J. & K. Hawkes 1981. Alyawara plant use and optimal foraging theory. In *Hunter–gatherer foraging strategies: ethnographic and archaeological analyses*, B. Winterhalder & E. A. Smith (eds), 99–125. Chicago: Chicago University Press.

Pate, J. S. & K. W. Dixon 1982. *Tuberous, cormous and bulbous plants.* Nedlands: University of Western Australia Press.

Pearce, R. H. 1978. Changes in artifact assemblages during the last 8000 years at Walyunga, Western Australia. *Journal of the Royal Society of Western Australia* **61**, 1–10.

Pearce, R. H. & M. Barbetti 1981. A 38,000 year old site at Upper Swan, Western Australia. *Archaeology in Oceania* **16**, 173–8.

Schwede, M. 1983. Super-trench – Phase two: a report of excavation results. In *Archaeology at ANZAAS 1983*, M. Smith (ed.), 53–62. Perth: Western Australian Museum.

Singh, G. & E. A. Geissler 1985. Late Caenozoic history of vegetation, fire, lake levels and climate at Lake George, New South Wales. *Philosophical Transactions of the Royal Society of London* **B311**, 379–447.

Singh, G., A. P. Kershaw & R. Clark 1981. Quaternary vegetation and fire history in Australia. In *Fire and the Australian biota*, A. M. Gill, R. A. Groves & I. R. Noble (eds), 23–54. Canberra: Australian Academy of Science.

Smith, M. 1982. Late Pleistocene zamia exploitation in southern Western Australia. *Archaeology in Oceania* **17**, 117–21.

Smith, M. & A. C. Kalotas 1985. Bardi plants: an annotated list of plants and their use by the Bardi Aborigines of Dampierland, in northwest Australia. *Records of the Western Australian Museum* **12**, 317–59.

Tindale, N. B. 1977. The adaptive significance of the Panara or grass-seed culture of

Australia. In *Stone tools as cultural markers*, R. V. S. Wright (ed.), 345–9. Canberra: Australian Institute of Aboriginal Studies.

Vasey, D. n.d. Agricultural systems in Papua New Guinea: adapting to the humid tropics. In *A time to plant and a time to uproot*, D. Denoon & C. Snowden (eds), 17–32. Port Moresby: Institute of Papua New Guinea Studies.

Vinnicombe, P. 1987. *Dampier archaeological project. Resource document, survey and salvage of Aboriginal sites, Burrup Peninsula, Western Australia*. Perth: Department of Aboriginal Sites, Western Australia Museum.

Wyrwoll, K. H. 1984. The sedimentology, stratigraphy and palaeoenvironmental significance of a Late Pleistocene alluvial fill: central coastal areas of Western Australia. *Catena* **11**, 201–18.

Yen, D. E. 1989. The domestication of environment. In *Foraging and farming: the evolution of plant exploitation*, D. R. Harris & G. C. Hillman (eds), ch. 4. London: Unwin Hyman.

# 9 *Ethnoecological observations on wild and cultivated rice and yams in northeastern Thailand*

JOYCE C. WHITE

Rice and yams are two of the most important crop plants of Southeast Asian agriculture. Their occurrence as wild and cultivated plants in northeastern Thailand was observed as part of an ethnoecological study of modern-day natural resources (with an emphasis on edible plants) conducted between October 1979 and May 1981 when the author lived in the village of Ban Chiang, the site of an early village community dating back to the fourth millennium bc (Higham & Kijngam 1979, White 1982a, 1982b, 1984 and, for a revised chronology for Ban Chiang, White 1986). The study grew out of a general interest in prehistoric plant exploitation in Southeast Asia, particularly issues surrounding the emergence of domestication, and one of its many aims was to attempt to identify in the Ban Chiang region 'wild' examples of plant species which botanists have considered to be originally domesticated in Southeast Asia.

Particular attention was directed towards documenting the presence of wild rice, because, at the time of the study, some form of rice was the only plant identified archaeologically at Ban Chiang (Yen 1982, Chang & Loresto 1984). Although not yet identified from archaeological contexts, yams were also a key focus of the study because they figure hypothetically in many discussions about the earliest agriculture of mainland Southeast Asia. Hundreds of other plants and resources were documented in the study, but this chapter addresses only three selected topics relating to rice and yams: (a) the presence of wild rice and yams in the Ban Chiang region today; (b) some ecological characteristics of rice and yam species, including differences in habitat preference; and (c) the seasonal availability of rice and yams and its impact on the scheduling of exploitation.

Information on the local plant resources was derived from extensive interviews with the villagers, in particular from one principal informant who was unusually knowledgeable about the local flora, and from on-foot surveys of the local area. Plant specimens were identified at the Royal Forest Herbarium in Bangkok.

The term 'wild', as used in this chapter, implies that a plant is considered a wild and not a cultivated variety by the local villagers. Such 'wild' plants are found in uncultivated areas, and they may, of course, be feral, i.e. a plant originally brought into the area as a cultivar which subsequently escaped and established itself in uncultivated habitats.

The ethnoecological study reported in this chapter was seen as an initial step towards identifying the local occurrence of wild relatives of eventual domesticates in an area that may have witnessed an early, if not necessarily an incipient, stage in the development of agriculture.

## Environmental setting

The landscape of the Ban Chiang region can be characterized as a gently undulating plateau. The climate is tropical but with distinct wet and dry seasons, each of about six months' duration. During the dry season, which lasts approximately from November through April, many of the smaller lakes and the upper reaches of watercourses dry up. The water table can drop several metres. The marked annual fluctuation of water resources represents the major environmental condition to which plants and animals must adapt. The response of much of the forest vegetation in northeastern Thailand to low water availability is deciduous behaviour. Most trees drop at least some of their leaves during the dry season.

The Royal Forestry Department describes the predominant forest type (Deciduous Dipterocarp Forest) as open, grassy, and often savanna-like (Royal Forestry Dept. 1962, p. 7). However, local inhabitants recognize a diverse set of plant communities which form a patchy mosaic across the landscape, determined to some extent by local variations in soil and drainage conditions. Furthermore, knowledgeable inhabitants not only consider plant and animal resources to have a patterned distribution relative to the overall system of plant communities, but are also able to estimate the possible presence of plant and other resources in the vicinity by observing the vegetation type of a locale.

Although not scientifically measured, the floristic diversity of the locally recognized plant communities is considerable; they range from highly diverse to nearly monospecific stands, although, compared with equatorial rain forests, seasonal tropical forests tend to exhibit lower species diversity. Ecological behaviours that affect the distribution of individual plants, such as seed-dispersal mechanisms, can promote relatively localized relationships among plant generations. As a result, plant resources are not necessarily widely and randomly dispersed, as has sometimes been suggested for the forests of Southeast Asia (e.g. Hutterer 1976, although see Hutterer 1983 for a revised view). In northeastern Thailand, at least, wild plant resources are, in some cases, densely clustered.

## Wild rice

Local inhabitants of the Ban Chiang area refer to wild rice as *khao nok* meaning 'bird rice'. It is easily recognizable from the awns which are

5–10 cm long and sometimes reddish in colour. The panicles are small and bear fewer and smaller seeds relative to the rice cultivated in the paddy fields. How the plants which local inhabitants refer to as *khao nok* relate to the taxonomy for wild and weedy varieties of rice discussed by Chang (1976 & Ch. 25, this volume) is not yet known. What villagers of the Ban Chiang area refer to as *khao nok* may be attributable by botanists to several different species of wild rice.

*Khao nok* grows along lake and stream edges, sometimes in dense stands. Such stands may not be truly monospecific, but competing species appear to occur at a low density. *Khao nok* can also be found in disturbed or man-made habitats, such as fallow paddies and roadside ditches. A key characteristic of these habitats relates to the local water regime. The areas where *khao nok* grows experience some, usually gradual, inundation during the wet season to depths of 50 cm or less, but during the dry season the land area dries out. Another way of describing the preferred habitat of *khao nok* is as the zone along lakes and rivers between the wet season high-water line and the dry season low-water line. According to informants, wild rice is sensitive to turbulence and does not grow along river edges on stretches that experience fast-moving floodwaters from heavy rains.

Towards the end of the rainy season the seeds of wild rice disperse onto the drying ground where they remain dormant until the rains come several months later, when they germinate. Thus the annual seeding habit of *khao nok* is closely synchronized with the seasonal fluctuation of water.

During October and November several patches of *khao nok* are observed to ripen at different times and even the seeds on the same panicle ripen on different days. Seeds usually disperse within a day or so of hardening, although quite often they even disperse before hardening. Within a day or two the seeds are either 'empty', filled with a milky substance, or already dispersed. Once dispersed, they are very difficult to collect from the tangle of leaves and stems on the ground. To achieve a maximum yield, ancient wild-rice collectors would therefore have had to be strategically poised at selected locales at the time of maximum yield.

## Comparisons between wild and cultivated rice

Traditional rice cultivation in the Ban Chiang region parallels the *khao nok* ecology in terms of life cycle and water regime. Shortly after the start of the rainy season rice seed is broadcast onto prepared seed beds which can be best described as planes of mud. After about one month's growth, seedlings are transplanted into prepared fields bounded by low dikes. In these paddies the water level gradually increases, commonly to depths of 10–20 cm. There is no large-scale irrigation in the Ban Chiang area, and little in northeastern Thailand as a whole. Farmers practise some small-scale water control, involving the channelling of water between fields and occasionally the lifting of water from streams. However, most of the water comes from rain falling

**Table 9.1** Common wild yams in the Ban Chiang area.

| Local name | Tentative binomial |
| --- | --- |
| *man hoerp* and *man luang* | *Dioscorea alata* |
| *man goy* | *Dioscorea hispida* |
| *man perm* | *Dioscorea esculenta* |
| *man nok* | *Dioscorea (?) glabra* |
| *man sang* | *Dioscorea* sp. |

directly into the paddies. This type of wet-rice cultivation is described as 'rainfed rice agriculture'. By the time that the rice has matured and is ready for harvest, the rains have virtually ceased and the fields have dried up.

The growth cycle and maturation process of both cultivated and wild rice in the Ban Chiang area, from germination to production of viable seed, are clearly keyed to the course of the rainy season. Both cultivated and wild rice grow in dense, nearly monospecific, stands on land that over the course of the year is dampened, becomes slowly inundated, and then dries up. In this context paddies may be considered as a close ecological analogy to the natural lake-edge environment.

## Wild yams

Only the most common of the edible wild yams (*man*) recognized by villagers in the Ban Chiang area are discussed here. Some of them have been tentatively identified by their Latin binomials (Table 9.1).

The five types of *man* listed in Table 9.1 are commonly eaten steamed as a snack food, and, in the appropriate season, can be found in the Ban Chiang morning market. Each is known to have a preferred habitat, differing in drainage, soil richness, and plant community.

*Man sang* produces a few relatively small ovoid tubers 2.5–7.5 cm in diameter. At one end of the drainage spectrum, this type (the species could not be identified) can be found along stream edges which overflow their banks for two or more days. It therefore occurs in riparian habitats near wild rice. The residents characterize this tuber by remarking that *man sang* can withstand flooding.

*Man nok* is found at the drier end of the drainage spectrum. Examples dug up by the author and her main co-worker were from well-drained soils, usually white sand, which supported an open dipterocarp forest of rather short stature. *Man nok* produces one long, thin tuber, usually less than a metre in length, but one example excavated (in about 10 min) was 80 cm long and weighed 200 g.

*Man hoerp* corresponds to the (domesticated) greater yam (*Dioscorea alata*). One large specimen which was over 2 m long and weighed 4 kg took about two and a half hours to dig out. Relative to the preferred habitat of *man nok*, *man hoerp* is found in well-drained but deeper and richer soils which support a taller, denser, and richer type of forest.

*Man goy* (*Dioscorea hispida*) produces a large, stumpy, knobbly tuber. A specimen weighing 1 kg was excavated in less than a minute. *Man goy* contains toxins which must be leached out before the tuber can be eaten. Its preferred habitat is similar to that of *man hoerp*, i.e. well-drained and rich soils which support a relatively diverse forest.

*Man perm* seems to be equivalent to the (domesticated) lesser yam (*Dioscorea esculenta*). It produces several ovoid tubers somewhat larger in size than *man sang*, about 7.5–10 cm in diameter. In the wild, most of the plants have sharp, thorny roots just under the soil surface and above the tubers (cf. the wild West African yams discussed in Ch. 21, this volume, by Chikwendu & Okezie). *Man perm* grows in relatively rich soil, like *man goy* and *man hoerp*, but the local people say that it prefers a different plant community.

The life cycles of all the wild yams are basically similar. Vines develop during the rainy season, using the nourishment available from the previous season's tubers. Thus, during the rainy season the previous season's tubers become shrivelled and fibrous, and are not considered edible. In the latter part of the rainy season – the precise time varying with the species – new tubers begin to form, and by the end of the season, between September and November, they are fully formed. During the dry season the vines die back, but viable tubers remain undergound until the next rainy season when the cycle is repeated. The timing of the growth of vines and tubers differs in each species and the differences appear to relate to the drainage conditions. For example, by the time *man nok* in the well-drained soils has produced a substantial tuber, perhaps in September, *man sang*, which is adapted to much wetter soils, may have begun to form its tubers.

## Comparisons between wild and cultivated yams

Several varieties of yams were observed under cultivation in the Ban Chiang area, most often in house gardens. A few examples were regarded by the gardeners as transplanted wild types and these are not discussed here. Some varieties, however, were considered to be strictly propagated types.

The leaf morphology (shape and size) of most of the cultivated yam varieties (at least three) seen by the author was similar to wild *man hoerp*. The tubers of these cultivated yams were comparable in weight to specimens of *man hoerp* but differed in their morphology. Instead of a long, thin tuber reaching 1–2 m below the soil surface, the cultivated varieties form a thick, shallow tuber. Directly under the soil surface *man khao kam*, a relatively common variety, forms a lumpy, bag-like tuber with a purplish skin. A type called *man ngoo*, which means bending or turning tuber, has an elongated tuber which extends vertically for 20–30 cm and then turns to extend horizontally for another 40–50 cm. *Man kha chang*, or elephant-leg yam, forms a tuber with a broad part just under the surface which tapers to a narrower part at greater depths.

Our observations suggest that the tubers of all the cultivated varieties form at much shallower depths (usually less than 50 cm) than do the very deep tubers of the wild *man hoerp*, and their excavation therefore takes only 10–30 min (maximum) as opposed to over two hours for a comparable 2–4 kg wild sample.

Both wild and garden yams are propagated in the same manner. After excavation of the tuber, the lower, more recently formed part is cut off for consumption. The upper part, which is older, reputedly less flavourful, and which includes secondary roots, is left attached to the vine. This upper part is then reinterred. The soft, loose soil created by digging up the yams is reputed to encourage large yams to grow in the following year.

The yam which seems to be most commonly eaten is *man goy*, the toxic wild yam (*Dioscorea hispida*). Although it is easily excavated, it takes considerable effort and expertise to prepare the tuber for consumption, a process which involves peeling, slicing, and leaching. There are several recipes for leaching. One requires soaking the slices for three nights in salted water, followed by 2–3 days in fresh water, which is changed daily. This variety is apparently preferred because it keeps for days, whereas the other non-toxic varieties are only edible for a day or two. The slices of the *man goy* tuber can also be dried and stored for several months.

## Conclusion

One of the major differences in exploiting wild rice and wild yams is in the importance of the timing of harvesting. In the case of wild rice this is critical because the ripe grains must be gathered during a relatively brief period of time, whereas yams can be harvested over a comparatively broad time-span. There is, presumably, some flexibility with regard to rice, in so far as different patches may ripen at slightly different times, but in the case of yam tubers the flexibility is much greater. For example *man goy* is often eaten before the end of the rainy season during August when water is easily obtained for the leaching process; and, in any case, viable tubers remain underground during the dry season and can be located over several months from the withered remnants of the vines. Their harvesting can therefore be spread over several months. It is important to note, therefore, that, although both rice and yams produce their starchy reserve at the end of the rainy season, the time of their harvesting (and consumption) do not necessarily conflict.

The field observations of rice and yams summarized in this chapter demonstrate how narrow is the dividing line between 'wild' and 'domestic' varieties, in terms both of their habitats and of the people's perceptions of them – a dividing line of which the prehistoric domesticators of these plants in Southeast Asia may initially have been unaware.

# References

Chang, T. T. 1976. The rice cultures. *Philosophical Transactions of the Royal Society, London* **B275**, 143–57.

Chang, T. T. 1989. Domestication and spread of the cultivated rices. In *Foraging and farming: the evolution of plant exploitation*, D. R. Harris & G. C. Hillman (eds), ch. 25. London: Unwin Hyman.

Chang, T. T. & E. Loresto 1984. The rice remains. In *Prehistoric investigations in northeastern Thailand*, Part ii, C. Higham & A. Kijngam (eds), 384–5. Oxford: BAR International Series 231.

Chikwendu, V. E. & C. E. A. Okezie. 1989. Factors responsible for the ennoblement of African yams: inferences from experiments in yam domestication. In *Foraging and farming: the evolution of plant exploitation*, D. R. Harris & G. C. Hillman (eds), ch. 21. London: Unwin Hyman.

Higham, C. & A. Kijngam 1979. Ban Chiang and northeast Thailand; the palaeoenvironment and economy. *Journal of Archaeological Science* **6**, 211–33.

Hutterer, K. L. 1976. An evolutionary approach to the Southeast Asian cultural sequence. *Current Anthropology* **17**, 221–42.

Hutterer, K. L. 1983. The natural and cultural history of Southeast Asian agriculture: ecological and evolutionary considerations. *Anthropos* **78**, 169–212.

Royal Forestry Department 1962. *Types of forests of Thailand*. Bangkok.

White, J. C. 1982a. Natural history investigations at Ban Chiang. *Expedition* **24**, 25–32.

White, J. C. 1982b. Prehistoric environment and subsistence in northeast Thailand. *South-east Asian Studies Newsletter* **9**, 1–3.

White, J. C. 1984. Ethnoecology at Ban Chiang and the emergence of plant domestication in Southeast Asia. In *Southeast Asian archaeology at the XV Pacific Science Congress*, D. Bayard (ed.), 26–35. University of Otago Studies in Prehistoric Anthropology, Vol. 16, Dunedin.

White, J. C. 1986. *A revision of the chronology of Ban Chiang and its implications for the prehistory of northeast Thailand*. PhD dissertation, Department of Anthropology, University of Pennsylvania. Ann Arbor: University Microfilms.

Yen, D. E. 1982. Ban Chiang pottery and rice: a discussion of the inclusions in the pottery matrix. *Expedition* **24**, 51–64.

# 10 An example of intensive plant husbandry: the Kumeyaay of southern California

FLORENCE C. SHIPEK

## Introduction

During the early stages of agriculture, as recognized on the basis of botanical evidence, tool complexes did not differ materially from those of hunting–gathering societies (Meighan *et al.* 1958, pp. 131–50, Alexander 1969, pp. 123–9, Higgs & Jarman 1972, pp. 9–10). It is thought that before the cultural selection of genetically variable plants had led to their domestication, the social and economic structure necessary for food production had developed, modifying the relationships of humans to plants and land, and of person to person within society (Jarman 1972, p. 15). Processes leading to food production are not well understood and many theories are being tested (Harris 1969, 1977, Jones 1971, Struever 1971, Yarnell 1971). Most recent is the search for evidence of the change in human activity in regions other than early agricultural centres of complex civilizations, and also the examination of plant use among hunter–gatherer societies (Harris 1984).

The definition of agriculture is crucial to a discussion of the transition. Harris (1969, pp. 6–7) defined agriculture as manipulation of the natural ecosystem by substituting domesticated species for wild species in appropriate ecological niches. However, the original process began by substituting desired wild food-plants for those which did not produce food. Higgs & Jarman (1972) suggested the term 'plant husbandry' to distinguish production activity from simply collecting what nature produced. That is, plant husbandry is manipulating an ecosystem by substituting species desired by humans for food, medicine, and technology for unused species. This definition modifies the Harris definition by omitting the word 'domesticated', that is, omitting reference to the selection of plant genetic variability and emphasizing other changes in human economic activity.

This chapter describes plant-husbandry practices of the Kumeyaay (also known as Diegueño-Kamia, or Tipai-Ipai) of southern California. This American Indian nation occupied the region extending from coastal southern

California almost to the Colorado River and for about 80 km both north and south of the Mexican–United States international boundary. When the Spanish entered coastal California in 1769, they did not observe such American plant domesticates as corn, beans, or squash, nor fields cleared for agriculture growing crops they recognized, and they therefore described Indians as gathering wild seeds and other foods. Only recently have ethnographic, ethnobotanical, and ecological studies been co-ordinated with ethnohistorical records (Bean & Lawton 1968, 1973, Bean 1972, Bean & Saubel 1972, Shipek 1968, 1969, 1972, 1977) to provide evidence that Kumeyaay, Cahuilla, Cupeño, and San Luiseño Indians used plant husbandry to modify the landscape. This system may provide a model for processes which led to the domestication of major food sources early in human history.

Sauer (1963, p. 47) hinted at the possibility of some form of agriculture in California when, in his discussion of the under-evaluation of Indian agriculture, he noted, 'some of our California grasslands and in particular the characteristic open park-like stands of ancient oaks in grassy country, which commanded the attention of early visitors . . . are not known to be climatically determined, but are significantly grouped about the more important sites of Indian habitation.'

Several researchers have presented evidence that southern California Indians planted the cultigens, corn, beans, and squash in selected locations having summer water (Gifford 1931, Treganza 1947, Bean & Lawton 1968, Bean 1972, Bean & Saubel 1972, Shipek 1972, 1977, 1979, Lawton 1974). Throughout California they used fire for environmental management to produce a succession of native plant foods on chaparral slopes (Bean & Lawton 1973, Lewis 1973, Shipek 1977). But it was not understood why they did not develop reliance upon the domesticates instead of upon native wild species; some thought that it was due to the natural richness of the acorn supply (Merriam 1905, Kroeber 1939, p. 46). However, evidence exists that the region was not naturally rich in plant foods; that the Kumeyaay planted oak trees; and that acorns did not dominate the California economy, a grain-yielding grass and various other plant foods being equally important.

To understand the Indian economy of southern California requires understanding of an environment which, though 'Mediterranean', varied tremendously from the coast through high mountains to desert and riverine desert, with each valley varying erratically from the next in rainfall and temperature, and from season to season, including the incidence of frequent droughts and floods (Wolcott 1929, Fritts 1965, Kenneally 1965, Shipek 1977, 1981). In this environment, reliance upon a set of crops with specific temperature and water requirements, such as corn, beans, and squash, would not allow the development of the large dense populations existing in 1769, varying from approximately 2.5 persons per square kilometre at the Mexican border to approximately 5 per square kilometre in the Los Angeles basin (White 1963, Bean 1972, pers. comm., Shipek 1977, 1981, 1986). Instead Indians developed a multiplicity of foods which responded to whatever weather conditions existed each season and each year, in each valley as well as regionally.

Ethnographic evidence indicates that southern California Indians, rather than reducing plant diversity by concentrating upon a few highly productive species, increased diversity and numbers by experimentally interplanting each food in every eco-niche, even experimenting with seeds traded from other regions. Thus, they developed a more stable food-supply in this erratic environment.

Papers and testimonies prepared for Mission Indian Land and Water Claims Cases (Shipek 1963, 1969, 1972, 1980) summarize southern California plant-husbandry and fire-management data and were based upon work with 17 Kumeyaay elders. To avoid contact with authorities, some elders had slipped back and forth into Mexico, maintaining Kumeyaay practices until recent decades. Two were alive in, and described events of, the 1860s, five were born in the 1870s, five in the 1880s, and five in the 1890s; all were raised and taught past practices by grandparents and great-grandparents. The original homes of the elders included coastal, foothill, and mountain valleys, and the New River, a Colorado River delta distributary in the desert, and they ranged from southern through northern Kumeyaay territory. All were descendants of leadership or shamanistic families, i.e. of tribal and band socio-political leaders, or of shamans specializing in plant knowledge. Two different processes of plant husbandry were described. The first is validated by Spanish and early American descriptions of the grassland environment (e.g. Smith & Teggart 1909, pp. 47–51, Bolton 1927, p. 129, Priestly 1937, pp. 5–10, Tibesar 1955, pp. 101–21). This chapter describes the process of grass production and harvest by which the Kumeyaay developed what must have been a semi-domesticated grain, now extinct. Secondly, it describes other Kumeyaay plant-husbandry practices, including the experimental mixed planting of species described by elders and observed in some archaeological contexts.

## Semi-domesticated grain

The ten oldest Kumeyaay described a grain-grass, about half the size of domesticated wheat, which was harvested by cutting off grain heads, by grasping several stalks to break them off, or by stripping grains from the stalk. Sparkman (1908, p. 196) obtained identical information on gathering from the San Luiseño, and Drucker (1937, pp. 5, 9, 1941, pp. 92, 98) recorded it for the southern and northern Kumeyaay. Drucker and I interviewed elders who had only gathered grain from small isolated valleys after losing control of large valleys to non-Indian cattlemen and sheep-herders. In contrast, in 1773, Father Palou, a Spanish missionary, observed the gathering process in large coastal valleys and described gathering cut grain-stalks into 'sheaves as is the custom to do with wheat' (Englehardt 1920, p. 51). This description preceded any grain harvest at San Diego Mission, thus the technique was aboriginal not Spanish.

After the grain harvest in June or July, the elders described burning fields and broadcasting seed over it. Broadcasting seed is a well-recorded aboriginal technique through the Southwest. In contrast, about 1770, the Spanish Jesuit, Miguel del Barco (1973, pp. 115–20), described the Spanish as having Indian converts plant wheat seed in holes made with a digging stick.

The Kumeyaay elders stated that the native grain sprouted after fall rains. If winter rain was scant, grain developed on short stalks, if plentiful, the stalk was tall. Spanish and Euro-American observers (e.g. Froebel 1859, pp. 539–48, Wolcott 1929, pp. 290–2, Griffin 1943, p. 48) corroborate this statement, describing the grain as similar to European wild oats but more prolific and nutritive to domestic animals. Broadcast over fields with the grain seed were the seeds of green leafy foods and other annuals which were ready for harvest at the same time or earlier than the grain. This produced an interplanted field not recognized by Europeans accustomed to plough-cleared monocultural fields containing wheat or vegetable row crops.

Gradually, as loss of Indian access to land caused abandonment of burning and broadcasting, European pasture grasses and weeds replaced the native grain-grass. By 1900, the native grain-grass survived in a few small isolated southern mountain valleys where Kumeyaay continued the aboriginal broadcasting practices. It disappeared entirely after the Indians were restricted to small reservations. Spanish and American settlers repeatedly commented negatively upon Indian burning, finally forbidding it early this century. They did not realize that to keep California open and grass-covered required annual burning. Chaparral gradually replaced grasses and various annual greens in most areas.

The disappearance of the grain-grass when no longer broadcast by Indians increases the probability that it was a semi-domesticate. Also, the harvesting method of cutting and gathering stalks into sheaves would be effective only for gathering seed from non-brittle, non-shattering inflorescences (Zohary 1969, p. 60). To maintain such a grain in the fields required resowing, as described by Kumeyaay elders. Finally, Europeans found this grain-grass highly nutritive to domestic animals, a contrast with east-coast grasses that Euro-American settlers found so non-nutritive that domestic animals starved; indeed, eastern settlers quickly replaced native grasses with European pasture grasses (Bidwell & Falconer 1925, p. 160). The greater nutritive value of the California grain-grass may add to the probability that it had undergone some genetic selection due to Kumeyaay harvesting and broadcasting techniques.

## Other plant-husbandry practices

Kumeyaay elders described how food and medicinal plants used to be planted experimentally in a great variety of eco-niches, from coastal sandbars and moist cool coastal marshes, valleys, and mesas; through foothills to high mountain crests, desert mountains, and valleys; and down across the partly below sea-level desert to the floodplain and distributaries of the Colorado River. They described being taught by grandparents to grub, or hand clear, small plots for experimental plantings. Experimental planting in diverse eco-niches accords with Anderson's (1956, pp. 763–77) theory that extensive plant hybridization occurs only when a plant's customary niche is disturbed, allowing new forms to compete for space. Experimentally moving plant species, as the Kumeyaay described, causes niche disturbance. Anderson also pointed to extensive hybridization among oak and chaparral species in California as an illustration of man's effect upon nature, including the hybridization of species which did not naturally grow in one region. Southern California oaks (*Quercus* spp.) exhibit such hybridization, and botanists have identified as hybrids the acorns gathered by elderly Kumeyaay from six different oak groves.

In addition to hybridization, other evidence indicates that Indians planted oak groves. A northern Kumeyaay story describes how they formerly lived near the ocean but moved to the mountains on discovering that the oaks they planted grew better at higher elevations. One elderly Kumeyaay reported that women gave sprouted acorns to the *Kwaipai*, or village chief, who selected the planting area. This matches Kumeyaay ownership data that some oak groves were family-owned, some band-owned, and some open to any tribal member. Elders stated that wild areas were always open to any member, but that planted areas belonged to those who planted and cared for them. Some early Euro-American settlers reported old oak groves resembling orchards with trees in straight lines.

The Kumeyaay, like the Cahuilla (Bean & Saubel 1972, pp. 148–9) increased the number of locations at which native desert palms (*Washingtonia filifera*) grew, including planting them in one particular coastal valley, Jamul. The Kumeyaay also planted mesquite seed (*Prosopis* sp.) in coastal sites and increased its locations and numbers in the desert. They planted the wild plum tree (*Prunus* sp.) at many locations, and ground plum seeds to flavour acorn flour. After any grove was well established, they flash burned it yearly to maintain peak fruit or nut production, to prune dead wood, and to destroy insects and parasites, such as dodder (*Cuscuta* sp.) and mistletoe (*Phoradendron* sp.). One archaeologist (Shackley 1980) recently noted that throughout a large mountain region many medicinal and food plants exist only near Kumeyaay village sites, which matches ethnographic descriptions of the planting of desired species near villages.

Pine trees producing edible nuts were planted in mountain locations with sufficient rainfall or moisture. Like wild oaks, wild pine groves were open to all Kumeyaay, but other groves belonged to specific bands or families. The rare coastal Torrey Pine (*Pinus torreyana*), which depends on fire to open its closed cone and release the large seeds, belonged to one band, known as *Istaguay* (trees are there), and was guarded by that band. They burned the grove regularly and planted seeds to enlarge it, but they apparently did not trade viable seed. It was the only plant food not found in multiple locations, which accords with its very restricted distribution as an endemic species.

Many shrubs, such as manzanita (*Arctostaphylos* sp.) and ceanothus (*Ceanothus* sp.), provided food and were planted in numerous eco-niches, including steep slopes, as were wild grapes (*Vitis* sp.) and various berries. Seeds of agave (*Agave* sp.) and yucca (*Yucca* sp.), plants which provided both food and fibre, were saved and tried in many locations. The seed was planted immediately before burning a slope, and germination was induced by the heat of the fire. These plants, like trees, did not provide immediate food but needed several years to mature to usable size, providing more evidence for long-term plant husbandry by southern California Indians.

According to all elders, all varieties of sage (*Artemesia* sp., *Salvia* sp.) used for food and medicine were planted in many locations. The elders knew that sage required protection from the regular burning accorded other plants, because frequent burning destroyed it. The Kumeyaay burned sage only at rare intervals, particularly very old plants, or those infested with parasites. In contrast, to maintain peak food production, stands of agave, yucca, ceanothus, and manzanita were burned once every 5–10 years to destroy insect or dodder infestations.

The Kumeyaay planted vegetative cuttings of many species of cacti and other succulents near villages and in other favourable locations. These desert plants were spread to the coast, and early southern California archaeologists (Farmer pers. comm.) located archaeological sites by looking for thickets of prickly pear (*Opuntia* sp.). Spanish reports describe some Kumeyaay villages as surrounded by a 'fortress' of *Opuntia* (Tibesar 1955, p. 121), and White (1963, pp. 129–30) recorded such fortresses around some San Luiseño villages.

Interplanted among shrubs, in tree groves, and in grain-grass 'fields' were a variety of annuals such as amaranths, compositae, curcurbits, and others which responded to different yearly rainfall conditions and to various burning patterns – from annual to five- or ten-year sequences. When rain, temperature, and burning patterns coincided, the seeds sprouted; otherwise they remained dormant until the correct conditions occurred. To protect river and stream banks from erosion, the Kumeyaay planted riparian forests of willow (*Salix* sp.), sumac (*Rhus* sp.), and elderberry (*Sambucus* sp.), all medicinal plants. Valleys, low slopes, and mesas were generally sown with grain-grass and other annuals, and burned yearly. Indians managed basketry grasses and arrow-reed resources in riparian areas by burning them every 3–5 years. Occasionally they burned riparian forests to prune and clear them of insects and parasites. Steeper slopes of interplanted shrubs, perennials, herbs, and annuals were burned on a five- , ten- , fifteen- , or twenty-year sequence depending upon the plants desired. Grain-grass, annual, and some perennial seeds were broadcast immediately after any burn. If fall rains came as expected, the annuals and grain-grass provided fresh greens by early spring and grain by early summer. Chaparral shrubs provided greens, fruits, or seeds several years. Regular burning of chaparral also improved browse for deer, thus doing double duty by providing food for meat animals. Elders described dividing and transplanting root and bulb plants (also recorded by Luomala 1978) to increase them and move them to additional locations, often interplanting them with seeds and vegetative cuttings.

A specific example illustrating the long-term planning involved in inter-planted slopes is that, during an observed twenty-year period, in only one year did heavy mid-September rainfall occur after a spring drought. An unrecorded fleshy plant sprouted on one reservation on the slope above each house. The elders said, 'Oh, we forgot this one' and described grinding the seed as food. Indians occupied this location only after 1911 when moved there by the government. The plant sprouted only on the slope above each house, and was too large to blow or move uphill except by deliberate human agency. Its unexpected appearance revealed maintenance of knowledge about a food rarely available, but supplying emergency food when staples failed. To maintain this source of food, an Indian plant specialist had brought seed to the site when the isolated mountain group was first restricted to the reservation.

Although this chapter has concentrated upon a few major food plants, medicinal and technological plants were also increased by planting seeds, vegetative cuttings, and by transplanting young plants. Among the elders interviewed were several healing specialists who knew exactly which medicinal plants could be transplanted, which increased by vegetative cuttings, and which needed seed. As we explored regions to which they had not had access for years, they asked for and received permission to take seed, vegetative cuttings, root divisions, bulbs, or young plants as appropriate. Among the plants described, but not found, was the domesticated devil's claw (*Proboscidea parviflora*) (Nabhan et al. 1981) which had been traded from Arizona to use as the black decorative element on baskets. All mentioned that they used to grow tobacco for trade to the Colorado River (Luomala 1978), as well as for their own use.

The Kumeyaay elders stated that special knowledge was needed to successfully transplant some species, such as mesquite and jojoba (*Simmondsia* sp.), but that they no longer had that knowledge. However, Stoffle & Dobyns (1983, pp. 58–64), in ethnobotanical research with Southern Paiutes in Nevada, Utah, and northern Arizona (also in the past called hunter–gatherers), discovered that some elders knew how to transplant mesquite. They said that orientation to the sun must be marked and retained in the new location for the tree to grow. Botanists have only recently learned that some plants have magnetic orientation which must be retained for transplantation. Paiutes, like Kumeyaay, planted, transplanted, and used vegetative cuttings to increase supplies of native food plants (Stoffle & Dobyns 1983). Among Paiutes, as among the Kumeyaay, this complex ecological knowledge was learned through long-term experimentation combined with means to maintain accumulating knowledge.

## Maintenance of complex knowledge

This chapter has described some of the complex knowledge of plant biology and ecology which the Kumeyaay acquired by experimentation and which they maintained over time. It would require a book to describe the climatic and botanical knowledge, as well as the understanding of animals, birds, fish, and shellfish, which was organized, maintained, and used to manage and sustain the dense tribal populations of southern California. For example, many people kept quail and doves in cages for their eggs; and the village chief kept breeding pairs of rabbits in a deep hole to provide the village with a steady meat supply.

The stratified socio-political hierarchy of specialists necessary to develop, maintain, and manage this knowledge, and the degree of authority with which the different tribes were controlled, has been described in detail elsewhere (Boscana 1933, Rudkin 1956, White 1963, Bean 1972, Shipek 1977, 1982) and will only be outlined here to relate the socio-political religious system to the plant-husbandry system. Each band of the southern California tribes had a council of shamans or specialists, with each specialist responsible for developing and maintaining knowledge about one particular species or type of food, plant, animal, or seafood, or about the weather and the seasonal movements of the sun. Each specialist chose and trained a successor for his office, passing on the detailed biological and ecological knowledge from generation to generation. Each specialist had the time to experiment and observe conditions throughout the tribal territory because village members paid for his services by bringing him part of each day's plant or animal harvest. Council members reported the condition of their specialty to the chief, *Kwaipai* (Kumeyaay), *noot* (San Luiseño), or *net* (Cahuilla), who made the decision concerning immediate actions to be taken: to burn an area; to broadcast seed; to move to the mountains, coast, or desert; to harvest food; or to prepare for a ceremony, war, peace, or trade expedition. Specialists combined all action with rituals validated by religious belief. The only persons knowing the reason for any particular action were the hierarchical council. Depending upon the tribe, the people of the band obeyed unquestioningly, or followed because these men were competent leaders.

## Conclusion

The Kumeyaay, like other southern California tribes, and like Basin-Plateau tribes such as Paiute, maintained a plant-husbandry system which, under less erratic climatic conditions, might eventually have led to the domestication of one, or possibly several, species of plants. The most important staple was the now extinct grain-grass. Kumeyaay harvesting techniques, cutting stalks and gathering them into sheaves, were similar to those used in Europe for wheat. The difference may have been the use of fire to clear land of stubble, and the interplanting of grain with other annuals while broadcasting seed. This process could have been similar to the techniques and processes which elsewhere led to the domestication of wheat and other grains. But in this erratic climate, increasing the diversity of plant foods sustained a larger population than was possible with reliance upon any one, or even several, staples.

The disappearance of the grain-grass when Indians no longer burned and broadcast it over the fields, combined with its nutritive quality for domestic animals, implies that it may have been semi-domesticated; and the large seed size suggests that, over time, Indian specialists responsible for broadcasting seed may have selected for larger grain.

The socio-political hierarchy, whose positions were validated by religion and ritual, had developed and controlled the knowledge necessary to manage the plant–husbandry system. As populations grew to the size observed by the Spanish, the need for specialists increased. Perhaps, in a less unpredictable environment, the elaborate hierarchical system of management might have developed into a priestly class, controlling a stratified state society, if further intensification of plant husbandry and domestication had created a larger and more assured food supply which could support increased population and the concentration of settlement in urban centres.

# References

Alexander, J. 1969. The indirect evidence for domestication. In *The domestication and exploitation of plants and animals*, P. J. Ucko & G. W. Dimbleby (eds), 123–9. Chicago and New York: Aldine-Atherton.

Anderson, E. 1956. Man as a maker of new plants and new plant communities. In *Man's role in changing the face of the Earth*, W. L. Thomas (ed.), 763–77. Chicago: University of Chicago Press.

Barco, M. del 1973. *Historia Natural y Cronica de la Antigua California*. Edicion estudio preliminar, notas y apendices: Miguel Leon-Portilla. Mexico City: Universidad Nacional Autonoma de Mexico, Instituto de Investigaciones Historicas Mexico.

Bean, L. J. 1972. *Mukat's people: the Cahuilla Indians of southern California*. Berkeley and Los Angeles: University of California Press.

Bean, L. J. & H. W. Lawton 1968. A preliminary reconstruction of aboriginal agricultural technology. *The Indian Historian* 1, 18–24.

Bean, L. J. & H. W. Lawton 1973. Some explanations for the rise of cultural complexity in native California with comments on proto-agriculture and agri-culture. In *Patterns of Indian burning in California ecology and ethnohistory*, H. T. Lewis (ed.), v–xi. Menlo Park: Ballena Press.

Bean, L. J. & K. S. Saubel 1972. *Temalpakh: Cahuilla Indian knowledge and usage of plants*. Morongo Indian Reservation, Banning, Calif.: Malki Museum Press.

Bidwell, P. W. & J. D. Falconer 1925. *History of agriculture in northern United States 1620–1860*. Washington, DC: Carnegie Institute.

Bolton, H. E. 1927. *Fray Juan Crespi, missionary explorer on the Pacific Coast 1769–1774*. Berkeley: University of California Press.

Boscana, Fr. G. 1933. Chinigchinich. In *Chinigchinich, a revised and annotated version of Alfred Robinson's translation of Father Geronimo Boscana's historical account of the beliefs, usages, customs, and extravagancies of the Indians of the Mission of San Juan Capistrano called the Acagchemen tribe*, P. T. Hanna (ed.). Santa Ana: Fine Arts Press.

Drucker, P. 1937. Culture element distributions. V: Southern California. *Anthropological Records* 1, 1–52. Berkeley and Los Angeles: University of California Press.

Drucker, P. 1941. Culture element distributions. XVIII: Yuman Piman. *Anthropological Records* 6, 91–230. Berkeley and Los Angeles: University of California Press.

Englehardt, Fr. Z. OFM 1920. *The missions and missionaries of California, new series: local history: San Diego Mission.* San Francisco: James H. Barry.

Fritts, H. C. 1965. Tree ring evidence for climatic changes in western North America. *Monthly Weather Review* **93**, 421–43.

Froebel, J. 1859. *Seven years travel in Central America, Mexico, and the far west of the United States.* London: Richard Bentley.

Gifford, E. W. 1931. The Kamia of Imperial Valley. *Bureau of American Ethnology Bulletin 97.* Washington, DC: Smithsonian Institution.

Griffin, J. S. 1943. *A doctor comes to California: the diary of John W. Griffin, M.D. 1846–1877,* G. W. Ames (ed.). San Francisco: California Historical Society.

Harris, D. R. 1969. Agricultural systems, ecosystems and the origins of agriculture. In *The domestication and exploitation of plants and animals,* P. J. Ucko & G. W. Dimbleby (eds), 3–15. Chicago and New York: Aldine-Atherton.

Harris, D. R. 1977. Alternative pathways toward agriculture. In *Origins of agriculture,* C. A. Reed (ed.), 179–243. The Hague: Mouton.

Harris, D. R. 1984. Ethnohistorical evidence for the exploitation of wild grasses and forbs: its scope and archaeological implications. In *Plants and ancient man: studies in palaeoethnobotany,* W. van Zeist & W. A. Casparie (eds), 63–9. Rotterdam: Balkema.

Higgs, E. S. & M. R. Jarman 1972. The origins of animal and plant husbandry. In *Papers in economic prehistory,* E. S. Higgs (ed.), 3–13. Cambridge: Cambridge University Press.

Jarman, H. N. 1972. The origins of wheat and barley cultivation. In *Papers in economic prehistory,* E. S. Higgs (ed.), 15–26. Cambridge: Cambridge University Press.

Jones, V. H. 1971. Review of 'The grain amaranths: a survey of their history and classification' by Jonathan Deininger Sauer. In *Prehistoric agriculture,* S. Struever (ed.), 544–9. Garden City, New York: American Museum of Natural History.

Kenneally, F. OFM 1965. *The writings of Fermin Francisco de Lasuen,* Vol. I. Washington, DC: Academy of American Franciscan History.

Kroeber, A. L. 1939. Cultural and natural areas of native North America. *University of California Publications in American Archaeology and Ethnology* **38**. Berkeley and Los Angeles.

Lawton, H. 1974. Agricultural motifs in southern California Indian mythology. *The Journal of California Anthropology* **1**, 55–79.

Lewis H. T. 1973. *Patterns of Indian burning in California: ecology and ethnohistory.* Menlo Park: Ballena Press.

Luomala, K. 1978. Tipai and Ipai. In *Handbook of North American Indians.* Vol. 8: *California,* R. F. Heizer (ed.), 592–609. Washington, DC: Smithsonian Institution.

Meighan, C., D. M. Pendergast, B. K. Swartz, Jr. & M. D. Wissler 1958. Ecological interpretations in archaeology: Part II. *American Antiquity* **24**, 131–50.

Merriam, C. H. 1905. The Indian population of California. *American Anthropologist (n.s.)* **7**, 594–606.

Nabhan, G., A. Whiting, H. Dobyns, R. Hevley & R. Euler 1981. Devil's claw domestication: evidence from Southwestern Indian fields. *Journal of Ethnobiology* **1**, 135–64.

Priestly, H. I. 1937. *A historical, political and natural description of California 1775 by Pedro Fages.* Berkeley and Los Angeles: University of California Press.

Rudkin, C. (trans. and ed.) 1956. *Observations on California 1772–1790 by Father Luis Sales O.P.* Los Angeles: Dawson's Book Shop.

Sauer, C. O. 1963. *Land and life: a selection from the writings of Carl Ortwin Sauer,* John Leighly (ed.). Berkeley and Los Angeles: University of California Press.

Shackley, M. S. 1980. Late prehistoric settlement patterns and biotic communities in Cuyamaca Rancho State Park, San Diego County, Calif. *Pacific Coast Archaeological Society Quartery* **16**, (3).

Shipek, F. C. 1963. *Kumeyaay (Diegueño-Kamia) land use and agriculture.* Report to Attorneys, Docket 80, Mission Indian land clams case.

Shipek, F. C. 1968. *The autobiography of Delfina Cuero.* Los Angeles: Dawson's Book Shop.

Shipek, F. C. 1969. *Preliminary affidavit in the case of Rincon Band of Mission Indians, La Jolla Band of Mission Indians vs. Escondido Mutual Water Co. No. 69–217–K.* United States District Court: Southern District of California.

Shipek, F. C. 1972. *Prepared direct testimony of Florence C. Shipek, Anthropologist.* Exhibit B–50, B–51 and B–52, Federal Power Commission Project No. 176, San Diego County, California.

Shipek, F. C. 1977. *A strategy for change: the Luiseño of Southern California.* Unpublished PhD dissertation, Department of Anthropology, University of Hawaii, Honolulu.

Shipek, F. C. 1979. *Kumeyaay farming and other aspects of land use.* APS/SDG&E Interconnection Project Environmental Impact Statement, Chapter 5. San Diego: Wirth Associates.

Shipek, F. C. 1980. *Prepared direct testimony Part 2. History of agriculture and irrigation for the La Jolla, Pala, Pauma, Rincon, and San Pascual Indians of southern California.* Submitted to US Court of Claims for San Luis Rey Reservation Water Case, Docket 80A.

Shipek, F. C. 1981. A native American response to drought as seen in the San Diego Mission Records, 1769–1799. *Ethnohistory* **28**, 295–312.

Shipek, F. C. 1982. Kumeyaay socio-political structure. *Journal of California and Great Basin Anthropology* **4**, 296–302.

Shipek, F. C. 1986. The impact of Europeans upon Kumeyaay culture. In *The impact of European exploration and settlement on local native Americans*, 5–25. San Diego Cabrillo Historical Association.

Smith, D. E. & F. J. Teggart (eds and trans.) 1909. *Diary of Gaspar de Portola during the California expedition of 1769–1770.* Publications of the Academy of Pacific Coast History, No. 3.

Sparkman, P. S. 1908. The culture of the Luiseño Indians. *University of California Publications in American Archaeology and Ethnology* **8**, 187–234. Berkeley and Los Angeles.

Stoffle, R. W. & H. F. Dobyns 1983. *Nüvagantü: Nevada Indians comment on the Intermountain Power Project.* Bureau of Land Management Cultural Resource Series Monograph No. 7, Reno, Nevada.

Struever, S. 1971. Implications of vegetal remains from an Illinois Hopewell Site. In *Prehistoric agriculture*, S. Struever (ed.), 383–90. Garden City, New York: American Museum of Natural History.

Tibesar, A. 1955. *Writings of Junipero Serra*, 4 vols. Washington, DC: Academy of American Franciscan History.

Treganza, A. E. 1947. Possibilities of an aboriginal practice of agriculture among the Southern Diegueño. *American Antiquity* **XII**, 169–73.

White, R. C. 1963. Luiseño social organization. *University of California Publications in American Archaeology and Ethnology* **48**, 91–194. Berkeley and Los Angeles: University of California.

Wolcott, M. T. 1929. *Pioneer notes from the diaries of Judge Benjamin Hayes.* Los Angeles: Privately printed.

Yarnell, R. A. 1971. Early woodland plant remains and the question of cultivation. In *Prehistoric agriculture*, S. Struever (ed.), 550–6. Garden City, New York: American Museum of Natural History.

Zohary, D. 1969. The progenitors of wheat and barley in relation to domestication and agricultural dispersal in the Old World. In *The domestication and exploitation of plants and animals*, P. J. Ucko & G. W. Dimbleby (eds), 47–66. Chicago and New York: Aldine-Atherton.

# 11 *Plant-food processing: implications for dietary quality*

ANN B. STAHL

## Introduction

Studies that focus on the evolution of plant exploitation often describe the range of plant foods used by past populations and may identify associated technologies. Despite a long-standing interest in studying the exploitation of plant foods, archaeologists know remarkably little about the advent of different plant-processing techniques, and even less about the ways that processing affects the nutritional quality of foods. We frequently ask why societies changed their patterns of plant-food exploitation, but seldom turn our attention to why new processing technologies are adopted. Changes in processing are most often discussed in contexts of changing patterns of resource exploitation, betraying a linkage in our minds between a specific resource and a given technology. Those who have attempted to integrate a consideration of processing into their analyses of subsistence change view processing as an energy expenditure contributing to the 'cost' of resource exploitation (e.g. Glassow 1978, Green 1980, Christenson 1980, Earle 1980, pp. 5–6). Such studies treat processing costs as fixed in relation to a resource, and view processing as a source of nutrient loss (e.g. Reidhead 1980, p. 156, Keene 1985). A resource can, however, be processed in numerous ways resulting in different nutritional 'payoffs'. Moreover, processing can result in nutrient gains as well as losses. Thus, prehistoric populations could have affected the nutritional value of foods by processing them in different ways. By extension, plant-food processing provides a potential avenue for intensification of subsistence that is independent of resource change.

The purpose of this chapter is to explore the dynamics between processing and the nutritive value of plant foods, and to demonstrate the importance of considering processing as an independent variable in our attempts to model the subsistence decisions made by prehistoric populations.

### Overview of plant-food processing

Plant foods may be processed in a variety of ways toward a number of ends. In some instances processing is necessary to remove tissue enclosing the desired plant part (e.g. seed husks/exocarp). Removal of secondary compounds ('toxins'; Rhoades & Cates 1976) may involve several processing techniques. Preservation or preparation for storage may be another goal of processing. Finally, although I do not deal with the issue here, we also must consider the degree to which people engage in processing purely for culinary enhancement.

A given processing sequence (e.g. detoxification) may involve serial application of several distinct techniques, each of which affects the nutritional quality of the finished product. These sequences must be broken down into their component parts in order to understand changes wrought by processing. Thus, for heuristic purposes, individual techniques are considered separately in the sections that follow. Once the nutritional impact of these techniques is established, they can be considered as components of larger processing sequences, enabling a better understanding of their combined impact on nutritive value.

## Techniques of plant-food processing

Techniques of plant-food processing that may have nutritional impact include the following: grinding/pounding/grating; soaking/leaching; drying; heat treatment; and fermentation. The changes wrought by these processes may be physical (e.g. reduction in particle size), or chemical (as in the case of fermentation). Generally speaking, physical changes act to make nutrients more available to the digestive enzymes or to remove less digestible constituents (e.g. fibre). Chemical changes alter the form of nutrients, as in fermentation where complex carbohydrates (e.g. starch) are reduced to simpler sugars.

### Grinding/pounding/grating

Although involving a range of equipment and applied to a variety of plant foods, grinding, pounding, and grating are directed toward a restricted range of goals:

(a)  the separation of desirable from undesirable (e.g. fibrous) elements;
(b)  changing the physical form of a food; or
(c)  a step toward detoxification.

The nutritional impact of each of these will be considered separately.

Grinding, pounding, or grating that are directed toward separating fibrous from non-fibrous elements can serve to concentrate more readily digested starchy reserves if combined with a process of winnowing or sieving. Most of us are familiar with processes involved in threshing, de-husking, winnowing, and sifting of seed crops (e.g. Harlan 1967, Hillman 1981b, 1984a, b, 1985) or with grinding their grains (e.g. Doebley

1984). However, it is perhaps less well recognized that tuberous crops may also be subject to a similar process of pounding and sieving directed toward the removal of fibre (e.g. O'Connell *et al.* 1983, Etejere & Bhat 1985). Dietary fibre is resistant to hydrolysis by human pancreatic enzymes (but see Southgate 1973 and Spiller & Amen 1975 for a discussion of its digestion by gut microflora and potential nutritional implications). It can also affect the digestibility of other nutrients as well. Fibre may further act as a complexing agent, reducing bio-availability of minerals (Camire & Clydesdale 1981, Lee & Garcia-Lopez 1985), and can protect starch from enzymatic attack (Jenkins *et al.* 1980). *In vitro* and *in vivo* studies document reduced digestibility of protein in the presence of increasing levels of dietary fibre (Gagne & Acton 1983). Fibre also results in lowered activity of the pancreatic enzymes amylase and chymotrypsin (Dunaif & Schneeman 1981).

The attribute of fibre that has received most attention in the literature is its ability to affect transit time, or the time that it takes food residues to pass through the gastrointestinal (GI) tract (see Cummings *et al.* 1976). The effect on transit time varies depending upon the source of fibre (van Soest *et al.* 1978). Certain forms of dietary fibre, such as pectin, common in fruits and vegetables (van Soest *et al.* 1978), serve to slow the passage of residues through the small intestine by increasing their viscosity. Others like hemicellulose and lignin which are common in bran serve to reduce transit time (Payler *et al.* 1975, Spiller & Amen 1975, Jenkins *et al.* 1978). Transit time, in turn, affects the rate and degree of absorption of nutrients in the small intestine. A very rapid transit time, induced by high levels of structural carbohydrates (e.g. cellulose or hemicellulose), may result in nutrients passing through the GI tract unabsorbed (Southgate 1973, p. 135). Thus, although the recommendation for people ingesting the extremely processed low-fibre diets characteristic of industrialized societies is to increase levels of dietary fibre as a means of reducing transit time and softening stools, people ingesting already high-fibre diets may well strive for the opposite effect. By removing excess fibre, transit time is slowed, nutrients such as starch are concentrated (Cummings 1973, Oke 1967), and digestibility of minerals and protein improved. It should be noted that fibre need not necessarily be removed by processing prior to consumption. Vincent (1985, pp. 137–8) notes that the Hadza expectorate the pith of a tuber after mastication. Flannery (1968) has interpreted 'quids' from maguey (*Agave* sp.) in archaeological context as a product of similar behaviour.

Grinding, pounding, and grating serve to reduce the size of food particles, which in turn affects digestion. Clinical studies have shown a consistent relationship between the physical form of food and rate of digestion (Thorne *et al.* 1983). *In vitro* and *in vivo* studies conducted with ground vs. unground cooked rice have demonstrated a significant increase in the rate of hydrolysis of the former as compared to the latter (O'Dea *et al.* 1980, 1981), results that were confirmed in a study of legumes (Wong & O'Dea 1983). The increased digestibility of ground forms is attributed to an increase in surface area that allows greater exposure of starch to digestive enzymes (O'Dea *et al.* 1980,

p. 763). Particle size also affects the rate at which ingested food leaves the stomach, smaller particles entering the small intestine at a more rapid rate than larger ones, thus reducing the time from ingestion to absorption (Holt *et al.* 1982, Torsdottir *et al.* 1984). Finally, milling or grinding of high-fibre foods, such as bran, mitigates its accelerating effect on transit time (Payler *et al.* 1975).

Reduction of particle size also increases the efficiency of detoxification procedures such as leaching (see below) by increasing the surface area exposed to solution (e.g. Driver 1953, Spier 1978, Wilson & Towne 1978).

Milling of grains can result in loss of nutrients if the nutrient-rich aleurone layer and embryo are removed, as occurs in the production of polished rice or in the grinding of corn (Bressani *et al.* 1958, Oke 1967). The importance of processing losses must, however, be viewed within the context of the total diet (Bender 1966, p. 285). A loss of vitamin $B_1$ due to milling of grain might be unimportant where other sources of thiamine are available; however, it can be critical for groups with an otherwise marginal intake, and result in deficiency diseases such as beriberi.

Minerals found in grinding stones may contribute to increased mineral content of foods (Greenhouse 1981); however, it is unclear to what extent these minerals (e.g. iron and calcium) are available for absorption (see Hallberg *et al.* 1983).

Only in the case of manioc does grating appear to be a technique of detoxification. Grating or pounding ruptures cells, bringing cyanogenic glycosides into contact with the extracellular enzymes that hydrolyse the toxin (hydrogen cyanide). Exposure to air is then sufficient to volatilize the toxin (DeBoer 1975, p. 420, Lancaster *et al.* 1982, p. 16).

Archaeological evidence of grinding/pounding/grating may take the form of equipment, by-products, or residues. A range of equipment may be used, the archaeological visibility of which is highly variable (see Kraybill 1977 for a thorough review). Whether one pounds, grinds, or grates is dependent on a variety of factors, including: the moisture content of the plant food in question; whether the operation precedes or succeeds cooking; the availability of raw materials such as stone or wood; and, that elusive variable, cultural preference. Stone equipment is generally associated with grinding and may take various forms (see Kraybill 1977). Stone grinding equipment may be used to process dry fruits such as achenes, grains (domestic or wild; e.g. Doebley 1984), or nuts (e.g. Driver 1953, see Alexander 1969 for more examples). Although stone grinding equipment is often linked to relatively sedentary populations, stone mortars may be left at a site and re-used on periodic visits, as was the case with bedrock mortars in California, or in Australia where stone mortars and pestles are buried between visits (Levitt 1981, p. 49). Grinding equipment may be used to process non-food items such as pigments; however, chemical studies, although in their infancy, may help to sort out the kinds of materials processed with grinding equipment, and even distinguish between grinding of tubers and seeds (e.g. Hillman *et al.* in press, Hillman, Ch. 13 this volume). Significant reliance on stone-ground foods may be witnessed in patterns of tooth wear resulting from ingestion of rock 'flour' (Molnar 1972, Greenhouse 1981).

A milling device that might leave distinctive archaeological traces is used by the Alyawara in Australia (O'Connell *et al.* 1983, p. 89). Used to dehusk seeds, the mill consists of a hole 45 cm deep and 45 cm in diameter into which a mixture of grain and pebbles is poured. A tree-trunk rotated in the hole serves to separate the grains from their glumes.

Wooden mortars or bowls are commonly used in the processing of moist foods (e.g. tubers: Yen 1975, Marshall 1976, p. 107, Whitten 1976, p. 84, Etejere & Bhat 1985). They are also used to process leafy foods (Dirar 1984), leguminous seeds (Campbell-Platt 1980), and for dehusking grains (Harlan 1967, Hillman 1981b, 1984b, pp. 129–30). Preservation of wooden processing equipment is unlikely under most preservational regimes, especially in areas of the tropics where it is commonly used.

Grating equipment is said to find archaeological expression in areas of South America where quantities of small flakes or microblades are thought to be analogues of the teeth set into boards used for grating manioc (Lathrap 1970, p. 52). Less durable materials and unspecialized implements were also used (e.g. thorns, bone splinters, prickly palm roots, coarse-grained rock; Lathrap 1970, Lancaster *et al.* 1982, DeBoer 1975). Chips used in contemporary grater boards exhibit distinctive forms and wear patterns that should assist in recognition of analogues in archaeological contexts (DeBoer 1975, p. 430).

Equipment for the chopping and pounding of sago preparatory to starch extraction (see below) is associated ethnographically with adze-like implements that exhibit distinctive forms of use-wear and should facilitate their identification in archaeological contexts (Crosby 1976).

Less attention has been paid to the residues of pounding/grinding/grating than to the equipment used. Exceptions are Hillman (1981b, 1984a, b, 1985) and Jones (1984) who have made substantial contributions toward defining the composition of residues created by different types of grain processing as a basis for identifying the forms of processing method applied in antiquity. Hillman has marshalled ethnographic information from Turkey as an aid to interpreting archaeobotanical remains in relation to site context and agrarian practice (e.g. Hillman 1973, 1981a), and Jones has now done the same in Greece (e.g. Jones *et al.* 1986). Palaeofaeces may also provide clues to whether foods were ground or pounded prior to consumption, and in rare instances where gut contents are preserved it is again possible to distinguish the processing techniques applied to the foods concerned (Hillman 1986).

*Soaking/leaching*

Soaking/leaching is a component of several processing strategies and may serve to:

(a)    soften or hydrate plant tissue;

(b)   aid detoxification;
(c)   precipitate starch from plant foods; or
(d)   contribute to fermentation, the nutritional effect of which is considered
      in a separate section below.

Legumes are commonly soaked during the course of processing. One goal of soaking is to hydrate or soften the seed coat, thereby facilitating its removal. This has important implications for the digestibility of legumes. Tannins, which are phenolic compounds that combine with protein, starch, and digestive enzymes to form insoluble complexes (Swain 1979), are often found concentrated in the seed coats of legumes (e.g. Deshpande *et al.* 1982). Tannic acid binds legume starch at room temperature and may reduce its digestibility by up to 17 per cent (Deshpande & Salunkhe 1982). Dehulling reduces the tannin level and results in greater availability of the starch and protein fractions during digestion (Deshpande *et al.* 1982). Removal of the seed coat in cowpeas (*Vigna unguiculata*), which are a staple in many parts of West Africa, results in increased digestibility (Akpapunam & Markakis 1981) and a reduction in the level of some oligosaccharides, the poorly digested carbohydrates that can cause flatulence and diarrhoea (Onigbinde & Akinyele 1983) (see also Cane, Ch. 6, this volume on the removal of the seed coats of certain *Acacia* species in Australia).

Soaking/leaching is a common means of ridding foods of digestibility-reducing compounds, such as tannins and other 'toxic' compounds (e.g. cyanogenic glycosides). Well-known examples include the native Californians who employed leaching or soaking as a means of removing tannins from acorn meats (*Quercus* spp.; Driver 1953). Soaking is used as a means of detoxifying nut products in Australia as well (Lawrence 1968, Levitt 1981, Jones & Meehan, Ch. 7, this volume). In the South Pacific, soaking was employed to remove tannins from the mangrove species *Bruguiera eriopetala* (Barrau 1959, see also Harris 1977, pp. 432–3) and to rid the fruits of *Corynocarpus laevigatus* of glycosides (Yen 1959). Domesticated plants which are soaked as an aid to detoxification include cassava or manioc (Lancaster *et al.* 1982, Etejere & Bhat 1985), potatoes (Werge 1979), and legumes (Khokhar and Chauhan 1986a). In light of the digestibility-reducing properties of tannins, it is clear that their reduction through soaking can significantly improve nutritive value. Soaking of sorghum, in which tannins are concentrated in the pericarp, resulted in the removal of 31 per cent of these polyphenols in 24 hours (Chavan *et al.* 1979). Aw & Swanson (1985), however, have noted negative results of soaking on tannin concentration. Soaking of black beans for 18 hours resulted in a higher retention of tannins and reduced digestibility. This was thought to be the result of tannins diffusing from the seed coat into the cotyledons.

Soaking in alkali or salt solutions can facilitate detoxification of foodstuffs (e.g. Chavan *et al.* 1979). Soaking legumes in a salt solution led to a greater reduction in anti-nutritional factors compared to soaking in tap water (Khokhar & Chauhan 1986b). Acorns were processed in lye solution in northeastern North America, a process also reported to facilitate removal of tannins (Driver 1953).

Soaking with additives of this sort may also enhance the nutritive value of a food. Lime or wood ash added to the water in which maize is cooked and soaked during preparation of *masa* and *tortillas* serves to improve the availability of amino acids and niacin (Bressani & Scrimshaw 1958, Bressani *et al.* 1958, Katz *et al.* 1974). Katz *et al.* (1974, p. 773) suggest that the development of alkaline processing techniques was critical to the adoption of maize as a staple food.

Soaking may lead to losses of soluble nutrients through leaching, and minerals and vitamins (especially C and those of the B complex) are particularly susceptible (Bender 1966, Akpapunam & Markakis 1981). Variables that affect the degree of nutrient loss are the time and temperature of soaking, the volume of solution, and food particle size. Greater volumes of water at a higher temperature will leach more nutrients from more finely comminuted foods than will soaking of whole plant parts in cool water (Bender 1966). The pH of a solution is also a factor: negligible vitamin losses are reported for solutions of distilled water, compared with losses of 36 per cent for well water (Bender 1966, p. 264). Driver (1953, p. 57) noted that the use of warm water in leaching acorn meal reduced the tannin levels more rapidly, but also removed desirable fats. Nutrient gains have been noted to occur during soaking, and presumably result from the absorption of minerals such as calcium and sodium from the water (Akpapunam & Markakis 1981). Again, the relative importance of these gains and losses can be determined only in the broader context of the dietary regimen as a whole. Losses of vitamins and minerals may be far outweighed by gains made through detoxification which allows increased ingestion of a carbohydrate-rich food, such as tubers or nuts. Soaking also serves to reduce cooking time, an important consideration at high elevations or in areas where fuel availability is a problem (e.g. Khokhar & Chauhan 1986b).

Starch extraction is a common goal of soaking and is reported for a variety of plants including the following: sago (*Metroxylon* spp.; Barrau 1959, Yen 1975); maize (Oke 1967); potatoes (Werge 1979); and cassava (Etejere & Bhat 1985). Exposure to water is generally preceded by pounding or grating. The pulverized mass is then added to water and filtered to separate indigestible fibrous constituents from the non-fibrous carbohydrate fraction, such as the starch. The latter, suspended in solution, is allowed to precipitate out, after which it may be dried.

Again, the literature on the dietary implications of fibre are relevant in understanding the potential benefits of starch extraction. Removal of fibre serves to slow the movement of residues through the digestive tract, allowing greater opportunity for the absorption of nutrients. One would therefore predict improved utilization of the starch when extracted from its fibrous matrix. The act of concentrating this high-energy foodstuff may be particularly important when a large proportion of the diet is composed of high-fibre foods such as tubers.

Recognizable material correlates of soaking/leaching are restricted to specialized vessels, or features such as pits. Leaching pits are constructed by some native Californian groups (Driver 1953, Wilson & Towne 1978). Preferentially located in sandy areas in proximity to water, these features would prove difficult to locate archaeologically. Moreover, pits were not used by all California groups. The Monache constructed raised platforms on which the acorn meal was spread for leaching (Spier 1978, p. 428). Other groups used tightly woven baskets (Elsasser 1978, pp. 636–7) which would preserve only under exceptional conditions. Neither would the troughs used in extracting starch from sago (Barrau 1959) be expected to preserve. Unspecialized ceramic vessels are used in other parts of the world for precipitation of starch. Preparation of *dawadawa*, a fermented (see below) product of the African locust bean (*Parkia* spp.), involves soaking and sieving, and is associated with the use of distinctive earthenware 'colanders' (Campbell-Platt 1980). These occur commonly on archaeological sites and have, on occasion, been used to infer *dawadawa* processing.

## Fermentation

Fermentation involves chemical reduction of complex organic substances such as starch into simpler substances. Fermentation is used to enhance the flavour of foodstuffs, facilitate their preservation, detoxify them (e.g. Sturtevant 1969, p. 190) or to produce beverages.

Fermentation as a means of preserving foods is applied to a range of plant foodstuffs. Traditional fermented plant foods are found in the following regions: the Pacific, e.g. breadfruit (Cox 1980), maize (Yen 1959); Africa, e.g. millets and sorghum (Au & Fields 1981), legumes (Achinewhu 1983, Campbell-Platt 1980), maize (Oke 1967), teff (Stewart & Getachew 1962, Gashe 1985), cassava (Etejere & Bhat 1985); South America, e.g. maize, potatoes (Rick & Anderson 1959), rice (Van Veen & Steinkraus 1970), cassava (Lancaster *et al.* 1982); Asia, e.g. soybeans (Smith *et al.* 1964, Wang *et al.* 1968), vegetables (Orillo *et al.* 1969); and Europe, e.g. vegetables (Pederson & Albury 1969). Fermented beverages are also found throughout the world and are made from an array of starchy foods, including grains and tubers (e.g. Ekundayo 1969, Whitten 1976, p. 84), and tree saps (Okafor 1975a, b). The nutritional contribution of these fermented beverages must not be underestimated; in some instances they are a primary source of calories (e.g. Whitten 1976, p. 84).

The nutritional impact of fermentation is well investigated. Digestibility of legumes (Achinewhu 1983) and grains (Kazanas & Fields 1981) is improved (see also Wang & Hesseltine 1981) as a result of the reduction of starches to more soluble sugars (Kazanas & Fields 1981). Degradation of fibre may also contribute to improved digestibility (Van Veen & Steinkraus 1970). Improved availability of amino acids has been consistently reported for a variety of foods (Murata *et al.* 1967, Wang *et al.* 1968, Hamad & Fields 1979, Tongnual & Fields 1979, Zamora & Fields 1979, Au & Fields 1981,

Kazanas & Fields 1981, Tongnual *et al.* 1981, Umoh & Fields 1981, Nanson & Fields 1982, 1984, Achinewhu 1983, Neuman *et al.* 1984, see also Wang & Hesseltine 1981 for general comments). These changes are not so much in the direction of increasing the total nitrogen content of a food; rather, fermentation serves to degrade the existing proteins into more readily utilized amino acids. Especially significant may be the increase in the availability of certain limiting amino acids (e.g. lysine, methionine, tryptophan) which are freed by proteolytic enzymes from microflora during fermentation (Wang *et al.* 1968, Hamad & Fields 1979, Tongnual & Fields 1979, Au & Fields 1981, Kazanas & Fields 1981, Tongnual *et al.* 1981, Umoh & Fields 1981, Nanson & Fields 1984). People may, in fact, perceive of fermented foods as meat substitutes (Dirar 1984).

Fermentation has a variable impact on vitamin composition. Vitamins affected by the fermentative process are those of the B complex, especially thiamine ($B_1$), riboflavin ($B_2$), and niacin ($B_5$). Consistent, significant increases in the riboflavin content of fermented foods are reported (Murata *et al.* 1967, Ekundayo 1969, Tongnual & Fields 1979, Zamora & Fields 1979, Campbell-Platt 1980, Kazanas & Fields 1981, Wang & Hesseltine 1981, Lancaster *et al.* 1982). Whereas increases in niacin and thiamine are reported for some foods (Ekundayo 1969, Kazanas & Fields 1981, Wang & Hesseltine 1981), decreases have been documented in other studies (Murata *et al.* 1967, Tongnual & Fields 1979, Campbell-Platt 1980). The improvements in B-complex vitamins, especially thiamine and riboflavin, may be of special importance in areas where rice is a dietary staple (Van Veen & Steinkraus 1970).

Fermentation may contribute to detoxification (e.g. Sturtevant 1969). Zamora & Fields (1979) reported a reduction in the level of trypsin inhibitors (anti-enzymes that inhibit the ability of digestive enzymes to degrade protein; Rackis & Gumbmann 1981) in fermented legumes, and the elimination of oligosaccharides (see above). Levels of phytate, which forms insoluble complexes with minerals, protein, and starch (Yoon *et al.* 1983, Thompson & Yoon 1984), were significantly decreased by fermentation (Lopez *et al.* 1983, Sutardi & Buckle 1985); however, tannins must be removed from a substrate prior to fermentation as they inhibit the activity of bacteria and yeast (Watson 1975).

Fermented foods may be stored for long periods, even under tropical conditions. Preservation is related in part to the formation of acids which serve to lower the pH and inhibit the growth of bacteria (Wang & Hesseltine 1981, Fleming *et al.* 1983). *Masi*, a Pacific foodstuff made by semi-anaerobic fermentation of breadfruit, taro, or manioc (Cox 1980, Kirch & Yen 1982, pp. 43–4), was an important stored foodstuff that would last several seasons or longer. Concealed in pits, *masi* provided an insurance against crop failure due to vagaries of weather or invading marauders (Cox 1980). Fermented manioc may be stored in underground pits for up to two years (Lancaster *et al.* 1982, p. 24). Fermented maize will keep indefinitely if kept submerged in water (Rick & Anderson 1949, Yen 1959). The acid character of fermented cereal products also serves to inhibit spoilage (Stewart & Getachew 1962, Wang & Hesseltine 1981). Other fermented products store less well and are consumed within a short time of production; here fermentation may be viewed as enhancing palatability and nutritive value (Van Veen & Steinkraus 1970, Wang & Hesseltine 1981, p. 81).

A final factor that must be weighed is the reduced time needed to prepare fermented foods. *Tempeh*, a fermented soybean product of Indonesia, can be prepared by a ten-minute boil, compared with the six hours required to cook raw soybeans. Fermented rice used in the Ecuadorian Sierra requires less cooking time, an important consideration at high elevations (Van Veen & Steinkraus 1970).

Archaeological visibility of processing by fermentation will be dependent on the use of specialized structures or vessels or else the application of chemical analyses. Underground pits are a feature of *masi* production (Yen 1975, Cox 1980). Similar pits associated with archaeological sites in western Polynesia dated to the past two millennia are interpreted as *masi* pits (Kirch & Yen 1982, p. 353). Production of *dawadawa* in West Africa may involve underground burial (Campbell-Platt 1980), as may fermentation of cassava in areas of the Amazon basin (Lancaster *et al.* 1982). Small underground chambers carved in bedrock in parts of the Yucatan peninsula are interpreted as fermentation chambers used in the production of alcoholic beverages (Dahlin & Litzinger 1986). Fermentation may also be carried out in ceramic vessels (e.g. Stewart & Getachew 1962), and it is reported that older vessels are superior to new vessels (Dirar 1984, p. 346). Proper fermentation is assured only if vessels are *not* subject to thorough cleaning (Stewart & Getachew 1962). In some instances (Dirar 1984) jugs used for fermentation may be buried in the ground. Although specialized vessel forms may not accompany fermentation, it is possible that fermentation may leave distinct chemical residues. The acid environment combined with the tendency to clean the vessels less thoroughly might result in a distinctive chemical signature on containers used in fermentation which would be identifiable through analyses of the sort applied by Hill & Evans (Ch. 26, this volume). Equally, however, fermentation can be conducted without pits or specialized vessels. Maize is placed in sacks and submerged in running water or irrigation ditches in New Zealand (Yen 1959) and in the Andes (Rick & Anderson 1949).

A case in which we might expect fermentation to be accompanied by distinctive vessel forms is in beverage production. *Chicha* brewing in Central and South America involves the use of large-capacity storage jars (Rick & Anderson 1949, Whitten 1976, p. 84), and Lathrap (1970, p. 55) has suggested that archaeological vessels with large rim diameters (40 cm and greater) were probably involved in the production of fermented beverages. In Ghana, production of *pito*, or sorghum beer, involves large vessels in the initial stages of production, after which the *pito* is poured into small pots (*c.* 1 litre) with constricted necks. The distinct size and shape of these pots combined with a lack of evidence of charring on pot bases might suggest beverage production.

As a final point, malted grain, which can represent a preliminary step in the production of fermented beverages (e.g. Rick & Anderson 1949, Ekundayo 1969), may be identified in archaeobotanical remains (Hillman 1982). Malting is not always associated with beverage production, however. Lawrence (1968, p. 208) notes the use of sprouted seeds of the mangrove species *Candelia* which are consumed after baking or steaming. Sprouting increases the availability of amino acids, especially lysine, in wheat, rice, barley, and oats (Hamad & Fields 1979). Germination may lead to a breakdown in toxins as they are transformed into growth substances for the germinating plant (e.g. Khokhar & Chauhan 1986b); however, in at least one instance (sorghum), germination led to a 13-fold increase in the amount of cyanogens (Panasiuk & Bills 1984).

## Heat treatment

Heat treatment as a food-processing technique is universally applied amongst extant peoples and its application to food preparation has significantly expanded the hominid food niche (e.g. Stahl 1984, Clark & Harris 1985). Foods may be cooked by exposure to dry heat (roasting, parching), moist heat (boiling, steaming, simmering), or hot oil (frying). Each of these has a set of nutritional implications. Heat treatment may also be employed for purposes other than straight cooking: to dry foods for storage; to facilitate removal of grains from hulls; to chemically alter the structure of foods, thereby enhancing digestibility; to eliminate or reduce the impact of certain 'toxins' or digestibility-reducing compounds; and to enhance the culinary quality of a foodstuff.

Cooking improves the digestibility of some nutrients (e.g. starch). Although the digestibility of raw starch varies from plant food to plant food (Booher *et al.* 1951), cooking serves to make starch more available to the digestive enzymes (French 1973, Jenkins *et al.* 1982, Thorne *et al.* 1983). Heat treatment splits starch granules and increases their availability to amylase, the digestive enzyme responsible for starch hydrolysis (Collings *et al.* 1981). *In vivo* studies showed elevated serum glucose responses (e.g. increased digestibility) to cooked as compared to raw corn starch (Collings *et al.* 1981), while an *in vitro* study of the composition of raw versus baked sweet potatoes documented higher proportions of readily digested reducing sugars in the baked product (Losh *et al.* 1981).

Moist heat appears to enhance digestibility to a greater extent than does dry heat. Cooking of starchy foods in the presence of a large volume of water permits swelling of the starch granules, increasing their solubility in the digestive tract (Osman 1975). Improved digestibility of legumes has been reported for moist as compared to dry heat treatment (Sathe *et al.* 1982), although one must question the degree to which this improvement should be linked to detoxification (see below). Whereas binding of metals with fibrous constituents was lessened in the presence of moist as compared to dry heat (Camire & Clydesdale 1981), prolonged dry heat (12 h) served to liberate starch from fibre better than did moist heat, and it enhanced digestibility of legumes (Jenkins *et al.* 1982).

Enhancement of nutritive value has been linked to roasting foods directly in a hearth. Contact with wood ash may supplement foods with particular nutrients, as is documented for hidden-ash bread, where iron and calcium content were elevated (Greenhouse 1981, see also Driver 1953, p. 57).

Cooking is often linked with nutrient loss (e.g. Keene 1985, p. 170). Nutrients particularly liable to loss are vitamins and minerals (Bender 1966). The water-soluble vitamins (e.g. B complex and C) may leach from foods in significant quantities in cooking water. Loss varies with food form (e.g. particle size), water temperature, duration of cooking, and pH of water (Bender 1966, p. 264). Peeling of tuberous foodstuffs prior to cooking elevates the loss of vitamin C (Gomez 1982), minerals (Mondy & Ponnampalam 1983), and amino acids (Talley *et al.* 1983). In the case of water-soluble vitamins, losses are reduced when cooked via dry heat (Gomez 1982). Baking at high temperatures (over 100° C) can lead to loss of amino acids through combination with carbohydrates, making them metabolically unavailable (Maillard reaction; Bender 1966, Osner & Johnson 1968). Again, the importance of these losses must be gauged in the context of a total diet, and are probably important only in instances where intake of a given nutrient is marginal (Bender 1966).

Heat treatment serves to mitigate the impact of many toxins and digestibility-reducing substances (e.g. proteinase inhibitors, cholinesterase inhibitors, cyanogenic glycosides, lectins, lathyrogens, etc.; see Stahl 1984 for a review). Temperature has been demonstrated to alter the effectiveness of detoxification procedures (Coffey *et al.* 1985). Moist heat is more effective in inactivating lectins and proteinase inhibitors (Sitren *et al.* 1985) and in reducing levels of phytic acid (Clydesdale & Camire 1983, Thorne *et al.* 1983, p. 483). Boiling serves to reduce the level of oligosaccharides in legumes which cause flatulence (Onigbinde & Akinyele 1983). Other toxins or digestibility-reducing substances are, however, heat stable (e.g. some lectins and proteinase inhibitors, psoralens; see Huang *et al.* 1981, Ivie *et al.* 1981, Stahl 1984).

Archaeological correlates of cooking may include features (e.g. hearths, ovens), utensils, or residues. Cooking with dry heat (or partial steaming) can be accomplished in pit or earth ovens (Yen 1959, 1975), Heat is supplied by pre-heated rocks, or the oven itself may be pre-heated with an *in-situ* fire. Earth ovens may have archaeological visibility (Binford *et al.* 1970, Kirch & Yen 1982, pp. 119–20). Above-ground ovens may be constructed from rocks and sod (Barrau 1959, Brush *et al.* 1981, Hyndman 1984). Kilns are durable forms of ovens (see Hillman 1982 for a discussion of kilns and interpretation of their function). The role of such durable features in food preparation may be more easily reconstructed than in the case of open hearths. Roasting of foodstuffs (e.g. tubers, breads) in the ashes of open hearths is a common cooking technique amongst hunter–gatherers (e.g. Lawrence 1968, Marshall 1976, pp. 107–23, Levitt 1981, p. 50, Yen &

Gutierrez 1976) and amongst plant cultivators (e.g. Yen 1975, Lancaster *et al.* 1982, p. 22). In my experience in West Africa, roasting of tubers is restricted to the preparation of 'quick' meals on farmsteads, whereas preparation of 'proper' meals involves cooking with containers (e.g. boiling). For Southwest Asia Hillman (1985) reports a similar 'snack' role for roasted grain products such as the Turkish *kavurmaç* and *firig*. Lancaster *et al.* (1982, p. 22) report that in South America roasting is a means of cooking in situations where utensils are lacking, e.g. on journeys. There is a tendency to think of boiling and cooking with moist heat as associated with ceramics, but we must keep in mind instances in which this was accomplished without the use of pottery. Bamboo is used as a cooking vessel in Southeast Asia, and can be used to prepare a variety of wild or domesticated foods, including rice (Yen & Gutierrez 1976, Pookajorn 1985). Stone boiling in basketry vessels was commonly practised by native Californians (e.g. Elsasser 1978).

Where ceramics were used, cooking vessels may give clues to the kinds of foods prepared or the manner in which they were cooked. Vessel forms may be functionally specific (e.g. Harcum 1921). The presence of griddles, or flat ceramic trays used to cook bread-like foods (*tortillas*, manioc bread, *injera*, etc.; DeBoer 1975, Gashe 1985), while not necessarily providing a clue to the plant food involved (e.g. Sturtevant 1969, p. 193, DeBoer 1975), does give an indication of the form of preparation and method of cooking. Residues from cooking pots can help to elucidate the kinds of foods cooked and their method of preparation, as illustrated by recent application of isotopic analysis to the study of residues (Hastorf & DeNiro 1985) and by similar applications of gas chromatography, high-performance liquid chromatography and infra-red spectroscopy (Evans & Biek 1976, Hill 1984, Hill *et al.* 1985; also Hill & Evans Ch. 26, this volume).

Plant remains, when viewed in the context of a sequence of processing and expected by-products, may also inform on cooking techniques. Hillman (1981a), for example, makes a case for grain roasting at the British Late Iron Age site of Pembrey, based on the abundance of charred 'prime' unmalted grains that occur free of chaff and weed seeds in numerous site contexts. Its widespread occurrence argues against accidental burning of a grain hoard and strengthens Hillman's interpretation of grain roasting for direct consumption. Finally, application of electron spin resonance spectroscopy can identify the maximum temperature to which cereal grains or remains of farinaceous foods have been subjected to within 30° C (Hillman *et al.* 1983, 1985) and so provide clues to the form of cooking which had been applied (Hillman 1986, Robins *et al.* 1986).

## Summary

Although processing of plant foods can result in losses of nutrients through milling, soaking, and, especially, heat treatment, substantial gains in nutritive value may also occur. Reduction of particle size can enhance digestibility and improve the effectiveness of subsequent detoxification. Removal of fibre enhances the availability of digestible carbohydrates, amino acids, and minerals. Fermentation can enhance digestibility, allow greater access to nutrients (e.g. amino acids), and add to the vitamin content of foods, in addition to allowing storage. Heat treatment makes the digestible carbohydrates more available and can contribute to detoxification. Detoxification, which may involve one or a number of processing techniques, enhances nutrient availability and may allow ingestion of greater quantities of a given foodstuff. While for generalists the diverse composition of their diet cushions them from the negative effects of any given toxin or digestibility-reducing substance (see Stahl 1984, pp. 153–4), specialists who focus on a limited range of resources are in greater jeopardy of suffering their effects.

## Plant-food processing and subsistence change

One of the few theoretical approaches that has explicitly considered the contribution of plant-food processing to subsistence is optimal foraging theory. Too often, however, these studies treat processing as a constant input relative to a given resource and as a source of nutrient loss (e.g. Reidhead 1980, p. 156, Keene 1985, pp. 170–1). This caricature of the dietary implications of processing over-simplifies the dynamics that exist between processing and food quality, and prevents us from looking at processing as a potential avenue for intensification. One can process the same plant food in a variety of ways, resulting in very different nutritive values. Unprocessed tubers may be high in toxins or digestibility-reducing substances; nevertheless, we can find examples of people utilizing them raw in small quantities. Hunter–gatherers who ingest substantial quantities of underground storage organs often prepare them by simple roasting (e.g. Lawrence 1968, pp. 120, 205–6), which may serve to partially detoxify them and enhance their nutritive value. As an element of a varied diet, the high-fibre content of tubers and effect of residual toxins might be offset by the contribution of meat or other plant foods. We might predict, however, that greater specialization on such high-fibre resources in which toxins are frequently localized (Stahl 1984, p. 156) would be accompanied by more elaborate processing techniques aimed at reducing the level or impact of fibre and 'toxins'. In the parlance of optimal foraging theory, the increased input of effort would be offset by the enhanced availability of nutrients. It has further been suggested that seasonal patterns of accumulation of fibre in tuber food such as *Cyperus rotundus* would have prompted cyclical adjustments of this energy balance by varying the amount of processing required (Hillman *et al.* in press).

Although quantitative data are lacking, it is instructive to consider examples of extant hunter–gatherers. Lawrence (1968) provides a compilation of species used by the aboriginal inhabitants of Australia with notes on methods of preparation. In most instances foods derived from 'rootstocks' are baked or roasted. An interesting exception is provided by *Dioscorea sativa* var. *rotunda* as used on the east coast of Cape York (Lawrence 1968, p. 205). Lawrence lists this as a main article of food from February to May. It is prepared by baking, mashing, repeated rinsing, and straining. It is tempting to view this increased involvement in processing as linked to the heavy seasonal reliance on this tuber. Similarly, Driver (1953, p. 57) has noted variation in the degree to which acorns were processed that corresponds to the degree of reliance on acorn as a staple food. In all areas where they were a staple, acorns were pulverized before leaching. Outside this area nuts were leached whole and subsequently boiled or roasted. This is presumably less effective in removing tannins. An analysis of nutrient value would very likely show the highly processed form to have a higher nutrient value due to greater availability of carbohydrates resulting from a reduction in particle size and removal of tannins.

Groups who are heavily dependent on underground storage organs often expend considerable energy in processing (pounding, sieving, starch extraction, or fermentation). Removal or degradation of fibre appears to be one goal (e.g. Lancaster *et al.* 1982, Etejere & Bhat 1985). As described above, improved utilization of nutrients accrues from a reduction of fibre in foods. It may be postulated, therefore, that the increased availability of nutrients in processed versions of otherwise fibrous foods offsets the costs of processing, and, further, that increased extraction of nutrients becomes more critical with increased specialization on these high-fibre resources. Even with the significant processing efforts common amongst African populations, levels of dietary fibre remain high, and the mean transit time is extremely rapid (33–36 hours, Payler *et al.* 1975, as compared to 2.3 days for subjects in a British study, Cummings *et al.* 1976, p. 214). Although fibre is not the only factor affecting transit time (Cummings *et al.* 1976, pp. 216–17), its importance has been clearly demonstrated.

What I hope I have demonstrated is the importance of viewing plant processing as a dynamic factor contributing to the nutritive value of a given food. Elaboration of processing can provide an avenue for intensification of subsistence pursuits that is quite apart from the adoption of agricultural technology. Yen (1975, p. 153) suggests that developments in New Guinea took agrarian pathways precisely because they lacked elaborate techniques of plant-food processing. Conversely, the application of elaborate food-processing technologies to a wide range of wild species by both hunter–gatherers and plant cultivators may well represent intensification of subsistence efforts that took other than agrarian directions. Although, as always, the archaeological record may be frustratingly incomplete as regards techniques of processing, gaining an understanding of the importance of a variable often helps us to frame new questions and to look for evidence that we might otherwise have thought unimportant. More innovative ways of looking at the material at our disposal are exemplified by some of the recent work directed toward, for example: defining the residues of processing amongst archaeobotanical materials (Hillman 1981b, 1984a, b, 1985); the study of organic residues on processing equipment (e.g. Hastorf & DeNiro

1985 and Hill & Evans, Ch. 26 this volume); and more sophisticated analyses of palaeofaeces and gut contents for evidence of food processing and cooking methods (Hillman 1986, Robins *et al.* 1986).

A review of the significant impact that processing can have on the nutritional quality of plant foods indicates that prehistoric populations may have manipulated their diets not only by changing patterns of resource exploitation, but also through modifying the technology of food processing. Thus, we must renew our efforts to understand the development of processing technology in our attempts to model changing patterns of plant exploitation.

## Acknowledgements

Thanks are extended to David Harris who encouraged me to research and write this chapter, and to Gordon Hillman who provided me with a number of useful references. The comments of Anthony R. Leeds, Department of Food and Nutritional Sciences, Kings College, London, are gratefully acknowledged. Peter Stahl's comments on the original manuscript have led to clarification of a number of points and his help is also gratefully acknowledged.

## Postscript on sources

Information on the nutritional impact of processing techniques is culled from the nutritional literature. Much of the literature cited stems from clinical studies of the ways in which dietary fibre (plant material resistant to the digestive enzymes of the human gastrointestinal tract, i.e. cellulose, hemicellulose, lignin, etc.; see Cummings 1973), carbohydrate source, and food form affect the rate at which the products of digestion enter the bloodstream (postprandial glycemic response; e.g. Jenkins *et al.* 1980, 1981). The goal of these studies is to define optimal diets for controlling diseases such as diabetes, and preventing diverticular disorders, colonic cancer, haemorrhoids, and other so-called diseases of affluence (O'Dea *et al.* 1980, p. 760). The comparative rarity of such disorders in non-Western societies has led many specialists to postulate a link with highly processed foods (see Cummings 1973, Van Soest *et al.* 1978 for a review). Gastric disorders increase in areas of the Third World where dependence has shifted to Western style foods (O'Dea *et al.* 1981), prompting some nutritionists to investigate the impact of traditional forms of processing on nutrition and health. There is thus a wealth of literature on how processing affects the way in which food is digested and its resultant nutritive value. I have only sampled this vast literature; however, I hope that I have demonstrated its applicability to our understanding of prehistoric subsistence adaptations.

## References

Achinewhu, S. C. 1983. Protein quality of African oil bean seed (*Pentaclethra machrophylla*). *Journal of Food Science* **48**, 1374–5.

Akpapunam, M. A. & P. Markakis 1981. Physiochemical and nutritional aspects of cowpea flour. *Journal of Food Science* **46**, 972–3.

Alexander, J. 1969. The indirect evidence for domestication. In *the domestication and exploitation of plants and animals*, P. J. Ucko & G. W. Dimbleby (eds), 123–9. London: Duckworth.

Au, P. M. & M. L. Fields 1981. Nutritive quality of fermented sorghum. *Journal of Food Science* **46**, 652–4.

Aw, T-L. & B. G. Swanson 1985. Influence of tannin on *Phaseolus vulgaris* protein digestibility and quality. *Journal of Food Science* **50**, 67–71.

Barrau, J. 1959. The sago palms and other food plants of marsh dwellers in the South Pacific Islands. *Economic Botany* **13**, 151–62.

Bender, A. E. 1966. Nutritional effects of food processing. *Journal of Food Technology* **1**, 261–89.

Binford, L. R., S. R. Binford, R. Whallon & M. A. Hardin 1970. *Archaeology at Hatchery West*. Society for American Archaeology, Memoir 24.

Booher, L. E., I. Behan & E. McMeans 1951. Biologic utilizations of unmodified and modified food starches. *Journal of Nutrition* **45**, 75–95.

Bressani, R. & N. S. Scrimshaw 1958. Effect of lime treatment on the *in vitro* availability of essential amino acids and solubility of protein fractions in corn. *Journal of Agricultural and Food Chemistry* **6**, 774–8.

Bressani, R., R. Paz, Y. Paz & N. S. Scrimshaw 1958. Chemical changes in corn during preparation of tortillas. *Journal of Agricultural and Food Chemistry* **6**, 770–4.

Brush, S. B., H. J. Carney & Z. Huamán 1981. Dynamics of Andean potato agriculture. *Economic Botany* **35**, 70–88.

Camire, A. L. & F. M. Clydesdale 1981. Effect of pH and heat treatment on the binding of calcium, magnesium, zinc, and iron to wheat bran and fractions of dietary fiber. *Journal of Food Science* **46**, 548–51.

Campbell-Platt, G. 1980. African locust bean (*Parkia* species) and its West African fermented food product, Dawadawa. *Ecology of Food and Nutrition* **9**, 123–32.

Cane, S. 1989. Australian Aboriginal seed grinding and its archaeological record: a case study from the Western Desert. In *Foraging and farming: the evolution of plant exploitation*, D. R. Harris & G. C. Hillman (eds), ch. 6. London: Unwin Hyman.

Chavan, J. K., S. S. Kadam, C. P. Ghonsikar & D. K. Salunkhe 1979. Removal of tannins and improvements of *in vitro* protein digestibility of sorghum seeds by soaking in alkali. *Journal of Food Science* **44**, 1319–24.

Christenson, A. L. 1980. Change in the human food niche in response to population growth. In *Modeling change in prehistoric subsistence economies*, T. K. Earle & A. L. Christenson (eds), 31–72. New York: Academic Press.

Clark, J. D. & J. W. K. Harris 1985. Fire and its roles in early hominid lifeways. *The African Archaeological Review* **3**, 3–27.

Clydesdale, F. M. & A. L. Camire 1983. Effect of pH and heat on the binding of iron, calcium, magnesium, and zinc and the loss of phytic acid in soy flour. *Journal of Food Science* **48**, 1272–4.

Coffey, D. G., M. A. Uebersax, G. L. Hosfield & J. R. Brunner 1985. Evaluation of the hemagglutinating activity of low-temperature cooked kidney beans. *Journal of Food Science* **50**, 78–81.

Collings, P., C. Williams & I. MacDonald 1981. Effects of cooking on serum glucose and insulin responses to starch. *British Medical Journal* **282**, 1032.

Cox, P. A. 1980. Two Samoan technologies for breadfruit and banana preservation. *Economic Botany* **34**, 181–5.

Crosby, E. 1976. Sago in Melanesia. *Archaeology and Physical Anthropology in Oceania* **11**, 138–55.

Cummings, J. H. 1973. Dietary fibre. *Gut* **14**, 69–81.

Cummings, J. H., D. J. A. Jenkins & H. S. Wiggins 1976. Measurement of the mean transit time of dietary residue through the human gut. *Gut* **17**, 210–18.

Dahlin, B. H. & W. J. Litzinger 1986. Old bottle, new wine: the function of chultuns in the Maya lowlands. *American Antiquity* **51**, 721–36.

DeBoer, W. R. 1975. The archaeological evidence for manioc cultivation: a cautionary note. *American Antiquity* **40**, 419–33.

Deshpande, S. S. & D. K. Salunkhe 1982. Interactions of tannic acid and catechin with legume starches. *Journal of Food Science* **47**, 2080–1.

Deshpande, S. S., S. K. Sathe, D. K. Salunkhe & D. P. Cornforth 1982. Effects of dehulling on phytic acid, polyphenols, and enzyme inhibitors of dry beans (*Phaseolus vulgaris* L.). *Journal of Food Science* **47**, 1846–50.

Dirar, H. A. 1984. Kawal, meat substitute from fermented *Cassia obtusifolia* leaves. *Economic Botany* **38**, 342–9.

Doebley, J. F. 1984. 'Seeds' of wild grasses: a major food of Southwestern Indians. *Economic Botany* **38**, 52–64.

Driver, H. E. 1953. The acorn in North American Indian diet. *Proceedings of the Indiana Academy of Science* **62**, 56–62.

Dunaif, G. & B. O. Schneeman 1981. The effect of dietary fiber on human pancreatic enzyme activity *in vitro*. *American Journal of Clinical Nutrition* **34**, 1034–5.

Earle, T. K. 1980. A model of subsistence change. In *Modeling change in prehistoric subsistence economies*, T. K. Earle & A. L. Christenson (eds), 1–29. New York: Academic Press.

Ekundayo, J. A. 1969. The production of pito, a Nigerian fermented beverage. *Journal of Food Science* **4**, 217–25.

Elsasser, A. B. 1978. Basketry. In *Handbook of North American Indians*. Vol. 8: *California*, R. F. Heizer (ed.), 626–41. Washington, DC: Smithsonian Institution.

Etejere, E. O. & R. B. Bhat 1985. Traditional preparation and uses of cassava in Nigeria. *Economic Botany* **39**, 157–64.

Evans, J. & L. Biek 1976. Overcooked food residues on potsherds. *Proceedings of Archaeometry Symposium*. Edinburgh: National Museum of Antiquities in Scotland.

Flannery, K. V. 1968. Archeological systems theory and early Mesoamerica. In *Anthropological archeology in the Americas*, B. J. Meggers (ed.), 67–87. Washington DC: Anthropological Society of Washington.

Fleming, H. P., R. F. McFeeters, R. L. Thompson & D. C. Sanders 1983. Storage stability of vegetables fermented with pH control. *Journal of Food Science* **48**, 975–81.

French, D. 1973. Chemical and physical properties of starch. *Journal of Animal Science* **37**, 1048–61.

Gagne, C. M. & J. C. Acton 1983. Fiber constituents and fibrous food residue effects on the *in vitro* enzymatic digestion of protein. *Journal of Food Science* **48**, 734–8.

Gashe, B. A. 1985. Involvement of lactic acid bacteria in the fermentation of tef (*Eragrostis tef*), an Ethiopian fermented food. *Journal of Food Science* **50**, 800–1.

Glassow, M. A. 1978. The concept of carrying capacity in the study of culture process. In *Advances in archaeological method and theory*, Vol. 1, M. B. Schiffer (ed.), 31–48. New York: Academic Press.

Gomez, M. I. 1982. Sources of Vitamin C in the Kenya diet and their stability to cooking and processing. *Ecology of Food and Nutrition* **12**, 179–84.

Green, S. W. 1980. Toward a general model of agricultural systems. In *Advances in archaeological method and theory*, Vol. 3, M. B. Schiffer (ed.), 311–55. New York: Academic Press.

Greenhouse, R. 1981. Preparation effects on iron and calcium in traditional Pima foods. *Ecology of Food and Nutrition* **10**, 221–5.

Hallberg, L., E. Björn-Rasmussen, L. Rossander, R. Suwanik, R. Pleehachinda & M. Tuntawiroon 1983. Iron absorption from some Asian meals containing contamination iron. *American Journal of Clinical Nutrition* **37**, 272–7.

Hamad, A. M. & M. L. Fields 1979. Evaluation of the protein quality and available lysine of germinated and fermented cereals. *Journal of Food Science* **44**, 456–9.

Harcum, C. G. 1921. Roman cooking utensils in the Royal Ontario Museum of Archaeology. *Journal of the Archaeological Institute of America* **25**, 37–54.

Harlan, J. R. 1967. A wild wheat harvest in Turkey. *Archaeology* **20**, 197–201.

Harris, D. R. 1977. Subsistence strategies across Torres Strait. In *Sunda and Sahul: prehistoric studies in Southeast Asia, Melanesia and Australia*, J. Allen, J. Golson & R. Jones (eds), 421–63. New York: Academic Press.

Hastorf, C. A. & M. J. DeNiro 1985. Reconstruction of prehistoric plant production and cooking practices by a new isotopic method. *Nature* **315**, 489–91.

Hill, H. E. 1984. Chemical analysis of pottery residues. *Bulletin of Experimental Firing Group* **2**, 86–9.

Hill, H. E. & J. Evans 1989. Crops of the Pacific: new evidence from chemical analysis of organic residues in pottery. In *Foraging and farming: the evolution of plant exploitation*, D. R. Harris & G. C. Hillman (eds), ch. 26. London: Unwin Hyman.

Hill, H. E., J. Evans & M. Card 1985. Organic residues on 3000 year old potsherds from Natunku, Fiji. *New Zealand Journal of Archaeology* **7**, 125–8.

Hillman, G. C. 1973. Crop husbandry and food production: modern models for the interpretation of plant remains. *Anatolian Studies* **23**, 241–4.

Hillman, G. C. 1981a. Possible evidence of grain-roasting at Iron Age Pembrey. Appendix to G. Williams' 'Survey and excavation on Pembrey Mountain.' *The Carmarthenshire Antiquary* 1981, 25–30.

Hillman, G. C. 1981b. Reconstructing crop husbandry practices from charred remains of crops. In *Farming Practice in British Prehistory*, R. Mercer (ed.), 123–62. Edinburgh: Edinburgh University Press.

Hillman, G. C. 1982. Evidence for spelt malting at Catsgore. In *Excavations at Catsgore 1970–1973*, R. Leech (ed.), 137–41. Bristol: Western Archaeological Trust.

Hillman, G. C. 1984a. Interpretation of archaeological plant remains: the application of ethnographic models from Turkey. In *Plants and ancient man: studies in palaeoethnobotany*, W. van Zeist & W. A. Casparie (eds), 1–41. Rotterdam: Balkema.

Hillman, G. C. 1984b. Traditional husbandry and processing of archaic cereals in recent times: the operations, products and equipment which might feature in Sumerian texts. Part 1: the glume wheats. *Bulletin on Sumerian Agriculture* **1**, 114–52.

Hillman, G. C. 1985. Traditional husbandry and processing of archaic cereals in recent times: the operations, products and equipment which might feature in Sumerian texts. Part 2: the free-threshing cereals. *Bulletin on Sumerian Agriculture* **2**, 1–32.

Hillman, G. C. 1986. Plant foods in ancient diet: the archaeological role of palaeo-faeces in general and Lindow Man's gut contents in particular. In *Lindow Man: the body in the bog*, I. M. Stead, J. B. Bourke & D. Brothwell (eds), 99–115. London: British Museum.

Hillman, G. C. 1989. Late Palaeolithic plant foods from Wadi Kubbaniya, Upper Egypt: dietary diversity, infant weaning, and seasonality in a riverine environment. In *Foraging and farming: the evolution of plant exploitation*, D. R. Harris & G. C. Hillman (eds), ch. 13. London: Unwin Hyman.

Hillman, G. C., E. Madeyska & J. G. Hather in press. Wild plant foods and diet at late Palaeolithic Wadi Kubbaniya, Egypt: evidence from charred remains. In *The prehistory of Wadi Kubbaniya*. Vol. 2: *Palaeoeconomy, environment and stratigraphy*, F. Wendorf, R. Schild & A. Close (eds). Dallas: Southern Methodist University Press.

Hillman, G. C., G. V. Robins, D. Oduwole, K. D. Sales & D. A. C. McNell 1983. Determination of thermal histories of archaeological cereal grains with Electron Spin Resonance spectroscopy. *Science* 222, 1235–6.

Hillman, G. C., G. V. Robins, D. Oduwole, K. D. Sales & D. A. S. McNell 1985. The use of Electron Spin Resonance spectroscopy to determine the thermal histories of cereal grains. *Journal of Archaeological Science* 12, 49–58.

Holt, S., J. Reid, T. V. Taylor, P. Tothill & R. C. Heading 1982. Gastric emptying of solids in man. *Gut* 23, 292–6.

Huang, D. Y., B. G. Swanson & C. A. Ryan 1981. Stability of proteinase inhibitors in potato tubers during cooking. *Journal of Food Science* 46, 287–90.

Hyndman, D. C. 1984. Ethnobotany of Wopkaimin *Pandanus*: significant Papua New Guinea plant resource. *Economic Botany* 38, 287–303.

Ivie, G. W., D. L. Holt & M. C. Ivey 1981. Natural toxicants in human foods: psoralens in raw and cooked parsnip root. *Science* 213, 909–10.

Jenkins, D. J. A., T. M. S. Wolever, R. H. Taylor, H. Ghafari, A. L. Jenkins, H. Barker & M. J. A. Jenkins 1980. Rate of digestion of foods and postprandial glycaemia in normal and diabetic subjects. *British Medical Journal* 281, 14–17.

Jenkins, D. J. A., T. M. S. Wolever, A. R. Leeds, M. A. Gassull, P. Haisman, J. Dilawari, D. V. Goff, G. L. Metz & K. G. M. M. Alberti 1978. Dietary fibres, fibre analogues, and glucose tolerance: importance of viscosity. *British Medical Journal* 1978 Vol. 1, 1392–4.

Jenkins, D. J. A., M. J. Thorne, K. Camelon, A. Jenkins, A. V. Rao, R. H. Taylor, L. U. Thompson, J. Kalmusky, R. Reichert & T. Francis 1982. Effect of processing on digestibility and the blood glucose response: a study of lentils. *American Journal of Clinical Nutrition* 36, 1093–101.

Jenkins, D. J. A., D. M. Thomas, M. S. Molever, R. H. Taylor, H. Barker, H. Fielden, J. M. Baldwin, A. C. Bowling, H. C. Newman, A. L. Jenkins & D. V. Goff 1981. Glycemic index of foods: a physiological basis for carbohydrate exchange. *American Journal of Clinical Nutrition* 34, 362–6.

Jones, C. E. R. in press. Archaeochemistry: fact or fancy. *The prehistory of Wadi Kubbaniya*, Vol. 2: *Palaeoeconomy, environment and stratigraphy*, F. Wendorf, R. Schild & A. E. Close (eds). Dallas: Southern Methodist University Press.

Jones, G. E. M. 1984. Interpretation of archaeological plant remains: ethnographic models from Greece. In *Plants and ancient man: studies in palaeoethnobotany*, W. van Zeist & W. C. Casparie (eds), 43–61. Rotterdam: Balkema.

Jones, G. E. M., K. Wardle, P. Halstead & D. Wardle 1986. Crop storage at Assiros. *Scientific American* 254, 96–103.

Jones, R. & B. Meehan 1989. Plant foods of the Gidjingali: ethnographic and archaeological perspectives from northern Australia on tuber and seed exploitation. In *Foraging and farming: the evolution of plant exploitation*, D. R. Harris & G. C. Hillman (eds), ch. 7. London: Unwin Hyman.

Katz, S. H., M. L. Hediger & L. A. Valleroy 1974. Traditional maize processing techniques in the New World. *Science* 184, 765–73.

Kazanas, N. & M. L. Fields 1981. Nutritional improvement of sorghum by fermentation. *Journal of Food Science* **46**, 819–21.

Keene, A. S. 1985. Nutrition and economy: models for the study of prehistoric diet. In *The analysis of prehistoric diets*, R. I. Gilbert, Jr. & J. H. Mielke (eds), 155–90. New York: Academic Press.

Khokhar, S. & B. M. Chauhan 1986a. Antinutritional factors in moth bean (*Vigna aconitifolia*): varietal differences and effects of methods of domestic processing and cooking. *Journal of Food Science* **51**, 591–4.

Khokhar, S. & B. M. Chauhan 1986b. Effect of domestic processing and cooking on *in vitro* protein digestibility of moth bean. *Journal of Food Science* **51**, 1083–4.

Kirch, P. V. & D. E. Yen 1982. *Tikopia. The prehistory and ecology of a Polynesian outlier*. Bernice P. Bishop Museum Bulletin 238.

Kraybill, N. 1977. Preagricultural tools for the preparation of foods in the Old World. In *Origins of agriculture*, C. A. Reed (ed.), 485–521. The Hague: Mouton.

Lancaster, P. A., J. S. Ingram, M. Y. Lim & D. G. Coursey 1982. Traditional cassava-based foods: survey of processing techniques. *Economic Botany* **36**, 12–45.

Lathrap, D. W. 1970. *The upper Amazon*. London: Thames & Hudson.

Lawrence, R. 1968. *Aboriginal habitat and economy*. Occasional paper 6. Dept. of Geography. Canberra: Australian National University.

Lee, K. & J. S. Garcia-Lopez 1985. Iron, zinc, copper and magnesium binding by cooked pinto bean (*Phaseolus vulgaris*) neutral and acid detergent fiber. *Journal of Food Science* **50**, 651–3, 673.

Levitt, D. 1981. *Plants and people: Aboriginal uses of plants on Groote Eylandt*. Canberra: Australian Institute of Aboriginal Studies.

Lopez, Y., D. T. Gordon & M. L. Fields 1983. Release of phosphorous from phytate by natural lactic acid fermentation. *Journal of Food Science* **48**, 953–4, 985.

Losh, J. M., J. A. Phillips, J. M. Axelson & R. S. Schulman 1981. Sweet potato quality after baking. *Journal of Food Science* **46**, 283–6.

Marshall, L. 1976. *The !Kung of Nyae Nyae*. Cambridge, Mass.: Harvard University Press.

Molnar, S. 1972. Tooth wear and culture: a survey of tooth functions among some prehistoric populations. *Current Anthropology* **13**, 511–26.

Mondy, N. I. & R. Ponnampalam 1983. Effect of baking and frying on nutritive value of potatoes: minerals. *Journal of Food Science* **48**, 1475–8.

Murata, K., H. Ikehata & T. Miyamoto 1967. Studies on the nutritional value of tempeh. *Journal of Food Science* **32**, 580–6.

Nanson, N. J. & M. L. Fields 1982. Effect of *Lactobacillus fermentum, Bacillus subtilis, Bacillus cereus, & Pseudomonas maltophilia* singly and in combination on the relative nutritive value of fermented corn meal. *Journal of Food Science* **47**, 1294–5.

Nanson, N. J. & M. L. Fields 1984. Influence of temperature of fermentation on the nutritive value of lactic acid fermented cornmeal. *Journal of Food Science* **49**, 958–9.

Neumann, P. E., C. E. Walker & H. L. Wang 1984. Fermentation of corn gluten meal with *Aspergillus oryzae & Rhizopus oligosporus*. *Journal of Food Science* **49**, 1200–1.

O'Connell, J. F., P. K. Latz & P. Barnett 1983. Traditional and modern plant use among the Alyawara of Central Australia. *Economic Botany* **37**, 80–109.

O'Dea, K., P. J. Nestel & L. Antonoff 1980. Physical factors influencing postprandial glucose and insulin responses to starch. *American Journal of Clinical Nutrition* **33**, 760–5.

O'Dea, K., P. Snow & P. Nestel 1981. Rate of starch hydrolysis *in vitro* as a predictor of metabolic responses to complex carbohydrate *in vivo*. *American Journal of Clinical Nutrition* **34**, 1991–3.

Okafor, N. 1975a. Microbiology of Nigerian palm wine with particular reference to bacteria. *Journal of Applied Bacteriology* **38**, 81–8.

Okafor, N. 1975b. Preliminary microbiological studies on the preservation of palm wine. *Journal of Applied Bacteriology* **38**, 1–7.

Oke, O. L. 1967. Chemical studies on the Nigerian foodstuff 'ogi'. *Food Technology* **21**, 98–100.

Onigbinde, A. O. & I. O. Akinyele 1983. Oligosaccharide content of 20 varieties of cowpeas in Nigeria. *Journal of Food Science* **48**, 1250–1, 1254.

Orillo, C. A., E. C. Sison, M. Luis & C. S. Pederson 1969. Fermentation of Philippine vegetable blends. *Applied Microbiology* **17**, 10–13.

Osman, E. M. 1975. Interaction of starch with other components of food systems. *Food Technology* **29**, 30–5.

Osner, R. C. & R. M. Johnson 1968. Nutritional changes in proteins during heat processing. *Journal of Food Science* **3**, 81–6.

Panasiuk, O. & D. D. Bills 1984. Cyanide content of sorghum sprouts. *Journal of Food Science* **49**, 791–3.

Payler, D. K., E. W. Pomare, K. W. Heaton & R. F. Harvey 1975. The effect of wheat bran on intestinal transit. *Gut* **16**, 209–13.

Pederson, C. S. & M. N. Albury 1969. *The sauerkraut fermentation*. New York State Agriculture Expt. Station Bulletin 824.

Pookajorn, S. 1985. Ethnoarchaeology with the Phi Tong Luang (Mlabrai): forest hunters of northern Thailand. *World Archaeology* **17**, 206–21.

Rackis, J. J. & M. R. Gumbmann 1981. Protease inhibitors: physiological properties and nutritional significance. In *Antinutrients and natural toxicants in foods*, R. L. Ory (ed.), 203–37. Westport, Conn: Food and Nutrition Press.

Reidhead, V. A. 1980. The economics of subsistence change: a test of an optimization model. In *Modeling change in prehistoric economies*, T. K. Earle & A. L. Christenson (eds), 141–86. New York: Academic Press.

Rhoades, D. F. & R. G. Cates 1976. Toward a general theory of plant antiherbivore chemistry. In *Biochemical interaction between plants and insects*, J. W. Wallace and R. L. Mansell (eds), 168–213. New York: Plenum.

Rick, C. M. & E. Anderson 1949. On some uses of maize in the Sierra of Ancash. *Annals of the Missouri Botanical Gardens* **36**, 405–12.

Robins, D., K. Sales, D. Oduwde, T. Holden & G. Hillman 1986. Postscript: last minute results from ESR spectroscopy concerning the cooking of Lindow Man's last meal. In *Lindow Man: the body in the bog*, I. M. Stead, J. B. Bourke & D. Brothwell (eds), 140–2. London: British Museum.

Sathe, S. K., V. Iyer & D. K. Salunkhe 1982. Functional properties of the Great Northern bean (*Phaseolus vulgaris* L.) proteins, amino acid composition, *in vitro* digestibility and application to cookies. *Journal of Food Science* **47**, 8–11, 15.

Sitren, H. S., E. M. Ahmed & D. E. George 1985. *In vivo* and *in vitro* assessment of antinutritional factors in peanut and soy. *Journal of Food Science* **50**, 418–23.

Smith, A. K., J. J. Rackis, C. W. Hesseltine, M. Smith, D. J. Robbins & A. N. Booth 1964. Tempeh: nutritive value in relation to processing. *Cereal Chemistry* **41**, 173–81.

Southgate, D. A. T. 1973. Fibre and the other available carbohydrates and their effects on the energy value of the diet. *Proceedings of the Nutrition Society* **32**, 131–6.

Spier, R. F. G. 1978. Monache. In *Handbook of North American Indians*. Vol. 8: *California*, R. F. Heizer (ed.), 426–36. Washington, DC: Smithsonian Institution.

Spiller, G. & R. Amen 1975. Dietary fiber in human nutrition. In *Critical reviews in food science and nutrition*. Vol. 7, T. E. Furia (ed.), 39–70. Cleveland, Ohio: CRC Press.

Stahl, A. B. 1984. Hominid dietary selection before fire. *Current Anthropology* **25**, 151–68.

Stewart, R. B. & A. Getachew 1962. Investigation of the nature of injera. *Economic Botany* **16**, 127–30.

Sturtevant, W. C. 1969. History and ethnography of some West Indian starches. In *The domestication and exploitation of plants and animals*, P. J. Ucko & G. W. Dimbleby (eds), 177–99. London: Duckworth.

Sutardi & K. A. Buckle 1985. Reduction in phytic acid levels in soybeans during tempeh production, storage and frying. *Journal of Food Science* **50**, 260–3.

Swain, T. 1979. Tannins and lignins. In *Herbivores; their interaction with secondary plant metabolites*, G. A. Rosenthal & D. H. Janzen (eds), 657–82. New York: Academic Press.

Talley, E. A., R. B. Toma & P. H. Orr 1983. Composition of raw and cooked potato peel and flesh: amino acid content. *Journal of Food Science* **48**, 1360–1, 1363.

Thompson, L. U. & J. H. Yoon 1984. Starch digestibility as affected by polyphenols and phytic acid. *Journal of Food Science* **49**, 1228–9.

Thorne, M. J., L. U. Thompson & D. J. A. Jenkins 1983. Factors affecting starch digestibility and the glycemic response with special reference to legumes. *American Journal of Clinical Nutrition* **38**, 481–8.

Tongnual, P. & M. L. Fields 1979. Fermentation and relative nutritive value of rice meal and chips. *Journal of Food Science* **44**, 1784–5.

Tongnual, P., N. J. Nanson & M. L. Fields 1981. Effect of proteolytic bacteria in the natural fermentation of corn to increase its nutritive value. *Journal of Food Science* **46**, 100–4.

Torsdottir, I., M. Alpstein, D. Andersson, R. J. M. Brummer & H. Andersson 1984. Effect of different starchy foods in composite meals on gastric emptying rate and glucose metabolism. 1. Comparisons between potatoes, rice and white beans. *Human Nutrition: Clinical Nutrition* **38C**, 329–38.

Umoh, V. & M. Fields 1981. Fermentation of corn for Nigerian agidi. *Journal of Food Science* **46**, 903–5.

Van Soest, P. J., J. B. Robertson, D. A. Roe, J. Rivers, B. A. Lewis & L. R. Hackler 1978. *The role of dietary fiber in human nutrition*. Proceedings, Cornell Nutrition Conference, 5–12.

Van Veen, A. G. & K. H. Steinkraus 1970. Nutritive value and wholesomeness of fermented foods. *Journal of Agricultural and Food Chemistry* **18**, 576–8.

Vincent, A. S. 1985. Plant foods in savanna environments: a preliminary report of tubers eaten by the Hadza of northern Tanzania. *World Archaeology* **17**, 131–48.

Wang, H. L. & C. W. Hesseltine 1981. Use of microbial cultures: legumes and cereal products. *Food Technology* **35**, 79–83.

Wang, H. L., D. I. Ruttle & C. W. Hesseltine 1968. Protein quality of wheat and soybeans after *Rhizopus oligosporous* fermentation. *Journal of Nutrition* **96**, 109–14.

Watson, T. G. 1975. Inhibition of microbial fermentation by sorghum grain and malt. *Journal of Applied Bacteriology* **38**, 133–42.

Werge, R. W. 1979. Potato processing in the central highlands of Peru. *Ecology of Food and Nutrition* **7**, 229–34.

Whitten, N. E., Jr. 1976. *Sacha Runa. Ethnicity and adaptation of Ecuadorian jungle Quichua*. Urbana: University of Illinois Press.

Wilson, N. L. & A. H. Towne 1978. Nisenan. In *Handbook of North American Indians*. Vol. 8: *California*, R. F. Heizer (ed.), 387–97. Washington, DC: Smithsonian Institution.

Wong, S. & K. O'Dea 1983. Importance of physical form rather than viscosity in determining the rate of starch hydrolysis in legumes. *American Journal of Clinical Nutrition* **37**, 66–70.

Yen, D. E. 1959. The use of maize by the New Zealand Maoris. *Economic Botany* **13**, 319–27.

Yen, D. E. 1975. Indigenous food processing in Oceania. In *Gastronomy. The anthropology of food and food habits*, M. L. Arnott (ed.), 147–68. The Hague: Mouton.

Yen, D. E. & H. G. Gutierrez 1976. The ethnobotany of the Tasaday: 1. The useful plants. In *Further studies on the Tasaday*, D. E. Yen & J. Nance (eds), 97–136. Rizal, Philippines: Panamanian Foundation.

Yoon, J. H., L. U. Thompson & D. J. A. Jenkins 1983. The effect of phytic acid on *in vitro* rate of starch digestibility and blood glucose response. *American Journal of Clinical Nutrition* **38**, 835–42.

Zamora, A. & M. L. Fields 1979. Nutritive quality of fermented cowpeas (*Vigna sinesis*) and chickpeas (*Cicer arietinum*). *Journal of Food Science* **44**, 234–6.

# PLANT EXPLOITATION IN PRE-AGRARIAN CONTEXTS: THE ARCHAEOLOGICAL EVIDENCE

# 12 *Plant exploitation at Grotta dell'Uzzo, Sicily: new evidence for the transition from Mesolithic to Neolithic subsistence in southern Europe*

LORENZO COSTANTINI

The excavation of Grotta dell'Uzzo represents a significant contribution to our understanding of the evolutionary processes affecting human societies during the transition from the Mesolithic to the Neolithic in Sicily and in southern Italy in general. The cave's stratigraphic sequence offers a clear record of the resource environment and the chronology of the transition from subsistence based on the hunting of large mammals and the gathering of wild fruit to an economy based on food production.

## Site location and environment

Grotta dell'Uzzo is a large natural cave, 45 m high, 50 m wide, and 50 m deep, 65 m above present sea-level on the eastern coast of the San Vito lo Capo promontary, overlooking the Gulf of Castellamare (38° 6′ 55″ N, 12° 48′ 17″ E) in northwestern Sicily. It looks out over a wide bay whose shelving coast affords an easy approach to the site from the sea, whereas access from the land is particularly difficult. This partial geographical isolation led Vaufrey (1928), who discovered the site in 1928, to doubt its importance as a Mesolithic station and to abandon his study of the deposit almost immediately, although it must then still have been well preserved.

Despite the area's partial isolation, it offers the resources of a number of contrasting ecosystems lying close at hand: the sea itself, the coastal communities of the San Vito lo Capo promontory, and the slopes leading up to the peak of Monte Speziale, 913 m above sea-level. There are springs of fresh water, too, not just above the shore line but even a short way out under the waves (Cassinis 1967).

The isolation of the cave is thus more apparent than real. Indeed, the territory still supports olives, vines, and almonds representing remnants of crops which, together with cereals, were the main agricultural output of a small neighbouring settlement until the 1930s. The area was also used by flocks of sheep and goats which came down from the slopes of Monte Speziale in the winter and found shelter in the huge cave.

## The cave deposits and their chronology

Unfortunately, the modern occupation of the cave by flocks led to the destruction of the uppermost archaeological levels, which were removed with the dung to fertilize the fields. This was the state of affairs in 1975, when the systematic excavation of the cave was begun by the Soprintendenza Archeologica di Palermo in collaboration with the Istituto Italiano di Paleontologia Umana and, from 1979, with the Soprintendenza Speciale al Museo Preistorico ed Etnografico, L. Pigorini (Segre & Piperno 1975, Piperno & Tusa 1976, Piperno et al. 1980b).

The archaeologists have detected more-or-less continuous use of the site from the 9th millennium bc until the end of the Middle Neolithic, and the sequence therefore provides important evidence relating to the transition from the Mesolithic to the Neolithic. Subsequent occupation into the Bronze Age is attested by unstratified material found in various parts of the cave. The chronology is based on eight radiocarbon dates (Meulengracht et al. 1981, Piperno 1985). The oldest of these dates is 10 070 ± 90 bp (P–2736) and marks the beginning of the Mesolithic occupation, while the most recent date is 6750 ± 70 bp (P–2733) and relates to spits 7, 8, and 9 in Trench F, in the talus outside the cave. This latest phase of occupation is characterized by impressed ware and pre- Stentinello pottery, typical of the end of the Middle Neolithic.

Within this date range, from the 9th to the 5th millennium bc, three distinct occupation phases may be distinguished, each characterized by its own cultural assemblage and covering the period from the Mesolithic (8330 ± 80 bp; P–2735) to the Early Neolithic (7910 ± 70 bp; P–2734) (Piperno et al. 1980b, Piperno 1985).

## Recovery of plant remains

The archaeobotanical work began at the same time as the excavation and has continued in parallel, thanks to the continued and dedicated assistance of the archaeologists, this despite problems with the water supply for flotation recovery of the plant remains in the early years. There were no springs sufficiently close to the site, so sea water was often used to flush the soil samples. This practice was soon abandoned, however, because charred remains were damaged by subsequent crystallization of the dissolved salts.

In eight excavation seasons, more than 20 different areas have been sounded both inside the cave and in the thicker deposits outside, but whereas wood charcoal is present in all the trenches, charred seeds and fruits have been found in only eight of them.

## Plant-food economy during the Mesolithic

Archaeobotanical data from the Mesolithic levels are sparse, with vegetal remains scattered about trenches C, D, E, and Q in only small quantities. By contrast, the Early and Middle Neolithic deposits have yielded significant quantities of cereal and legume seeds, mostly concentrated in Trenches F and W.

The lowest Mesolithic layers, dated to around 8500 bc, yielded remains of fruits of the strawberry tree *Arbutus unedo* which, in the strata immediately above, were associated with legume seeds (*Lathyrus* or *Pisum* sp.) – presumably gathered from wild stands (see Fig. 12.1). This association of legumes and arboreal fruits continues throughout the Mesolithic to the Early Neolithic. Later in the Mesolithic, *Arbutus* and the legumes are joined by an oak (*Quercus* sp.) represented by acorn cotyledons, and by the wild grape (*Vitis silvestris*), remains of which have been found in levels dating from the middle of the 8th millennium bc. At the close of the Mesolithic and, more particularly, during the transition from Mesolithic to Early Neolithic, the first olive remains appear.

The existence of wild olive in the natural landscape from even the earliest occupation of Grotta dell'Uzzo is confirmed by the results of analyses of wood charcoal from the Mesolithic levels: these revealed the presence of *Quercus* cf. *ilex*, *Olea* sp. and *Phyllirea* sp. These three evergreen species represent, more than any others, the archetypical elements of the Mediterranean *macchia* in which, today, the holm oak is generally associated with olive, lentiscus, carob, lime, heather (*Erica* spp.) and the strawberry tree. The *macchia* and associated woodlands also provide an ideal refuge for many animal species.

The animal remains from the Mesolithic deposits confirm that the landscape was dominated primarily by *macchia* and woodlands in which boar and deer were the dominant animal species. In a presumably broad spectrum of mammalian species, these two creatures apparently represented the preferred and/or most accessible prey for the Mesolithic hunters of the Grotta dell'Uzzo, just as they did in many other areas of central southern Europe (Jarman 1972).

It was therefore in a xerophyll, *macchia*-dominated environment that wild fruit and legumes were gathered for inclusion in the diet of Mesolithic Uzzo. However, the high incidence of caries, noted in six individuals from the Mesolithic burials at Uzzo, is unlikely to be due to a great quantity of sweet fruits in the diet (Borgognini, Tarli & Repetto 1985), because this would surely have been reflected in the archaeobotanical record. Certainly, foraging

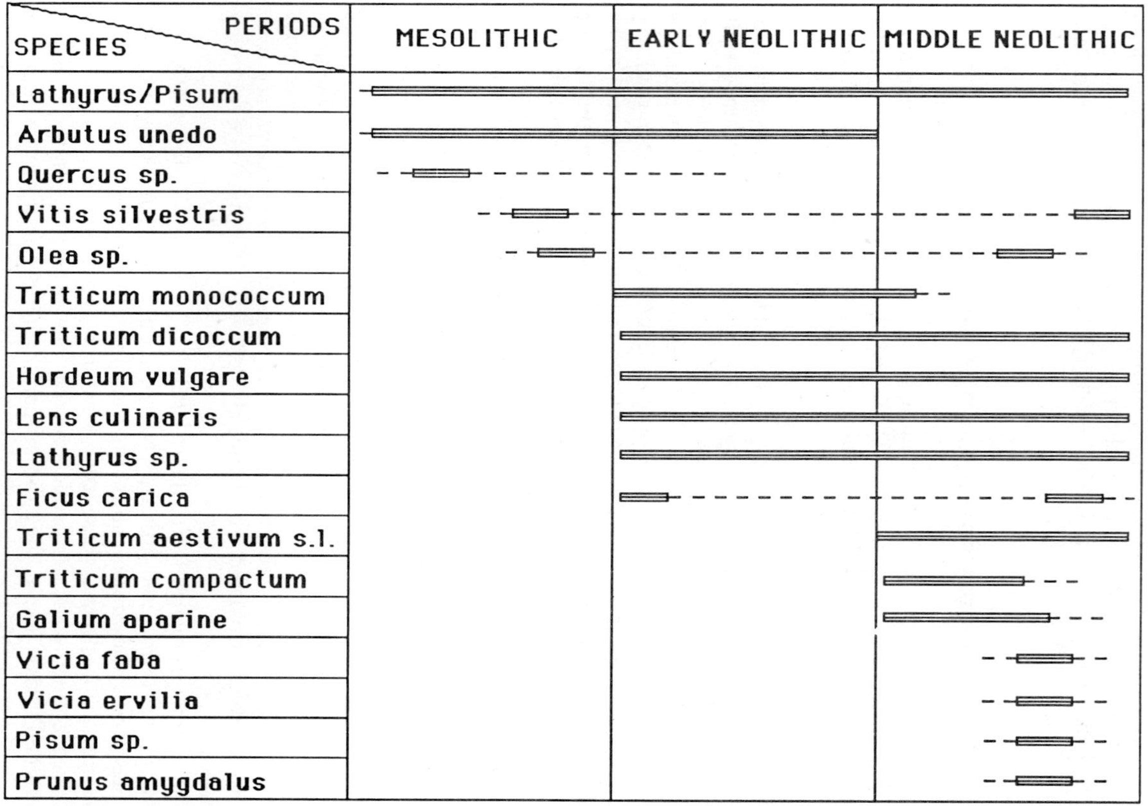

**Figure 12.1**  Chronological sequence of the charred remains of plants identified from Grotta dell'Uzzo, Sicily.

was not limited to the sweet but somewhat astringent fruit of the strawberry tree. On the contrary, wild-grape pips, wild-olive stones and charred legumes indicate a much broader-spectrum pattern of plant foods throughout the Mesolithic.

Although Sicily's geology has given rise to the formation of numerous caves occupied from the Palaeolithic era onwards (Tusa 1983, 1987), the only record of plant macro-remains from pre-Mesolithic occupations is provided by the Grotta di San Teodoro near Messina. Hearth charcoal from the Upper Palaeolithic levels at this site indicates a vegetation dominated by deciduous oaks, maples, and roses of a typical mesophytic fascies (Lona 1949). This apparently represents a continuation of the warm, wet Quaternary flora shown in the Palermo Travertines and on the eastern volcanic slopes of Etna (Pampaloni 1904, Beguinot 1929a, b). Such associations contrast starkly with the evergreen *macchia* indicated by the remains of wood charcoal from the Mesolithic levels at Uzzo cave. One must, therefore, assume that the local vegetation altered between the Upper Palaeolithic and the Mesolithic as a result of progressive desiccation which forced the mesophytic species to retreat to ever greater altitudes, with a corresponding extension of xerophyll flora.

This apparent change in the plant-resource base (and presumably also in diet) between the Late Palaeolithic at Grotta di San Teodoro and the Mesolithic at Grotta dell'Uzzo stands in stark contrast to the record from Franchthi Cave in southern Greece which, with its plant remains recovered from an unbroken sequence of Late Palaeolithic and Mesolithic occupations, is perhaps the only European site with archaeobotanical evidence to match that from Grotta dell'Uzzo. At Franchthi Cave, the Mesolithic occupants continued to gather the same fruits as those consumed at the same cave earlier during the Upper Palaeolithic (Hansen 1978, Hansen & Renfrew 1978). The Franchthi Cave data demonstrate a particularly well articulated subsistence strategy which included the collection of fruitlets of a terebinth tree (*Pistacia* sp.), almonds (*Prunus amygdalus*), fruits of a wild pear (*Pyrus amygdaliformis*), and a precocious interest in wild barley (*Hordeum spontaneum*) and wild legumes (*Vicia* sp., *Lens* sp., and *Pisum*). The substantial differences between food types at Franchthi and Uzzo in terms of the species and numbers of individuals exploited clearly cannot be ascribed either to differential excavation techniques or to advances in current research strategies (Tusa 1985), and so they probably represent differences in the local ecosystems and vegetal resources upon which the survival of the human communities depended.

## Emergence of Neolithic subsistence

At Uzzo the shift from Mesolithic to Early Neolithic was a gradual process and far from traumatic, albeit marked by major additions to the economy. It has, in fact, been possible to identify a transition phase (Piperno 1985,

Costantini *et al.* 1987) characterized by a marked interest in a diverse range of marine resources, including large cetaceans, and with conspicuous continuation of the exploitation of other animal species already found throughout the Mesolithic levels below.

The record of plant foods gathered from the wild during the Neolithic shows no great change, except for the appearance of fruit stones of the wild olive and fig. However, one must remember that the discovery of *Olea* charcoal in the Mesolithic levels probably demonstrates its availability in the local *macchia* from the Upper Palaeolithic onwards, so the delay in the appearance of its fruit stones until the Neolithic may be no more than the result of chance.

The earliest sign that a substantial economic change was already underway came from the sediments in spit 13 in Trench F, representing an aceramic occupation phase dated to 7910 ± 70 bp (P–2734). The evidence consisted of a single grain of domestic einkorn wheat (*Triticum monococcum*), which at first raised some doubts about the feasibility of being able to infer cultivation in northwestern Sicily at such an early date from a single cereal grain (Costantini 1981). However, the subsequent investigation of Trench W permitted the collection of further charred fruits, legumes, and cereal grains to add to those from Trench F, thus establishing a clear stratigraphical continuum of finds of domesticates of far greater significance than the solitary grain of *T. monococcum*.

In Trench W, charred seeds appear from spits 15 and 14 upwards and include einkorn wheat *T. monococcum*, emmer wheat *T. dicoccum*, an indeterminate wheat *Tritcum* sp., a vetchling *Lathyrus* sp., domestic lentil *Lens culinaris*, and an unripe fig. Barley (*Hordeum* sp., *Hordeum vulgare*) is present in the immediately overlying levels and completes the list of the earliest imported and cultivated species (see Fig. 12.1). These spits relate stratigraphically to spits 12 and 11 in Trench F which, at first sight, seemed simply to reflect a continuation of the gathering of wild fruits and legumes of the Mesolithic, making the explanation of the one grain of *T. monococcum* somewhat troublesome. (Spit 13 of Trench F, from which the grain came, lies below spits 11 and 12.) However, the new evidence from Trench W shows that a new form of food production, based on the cultivation of cereals and legumes, was being introduced from 6000 bc.

It is interesting to note the close chronological concordance between the appearance of cultivated plants at the Grotta dell'Uzzo (P–2734: 7910 ± 70 bp) and at Franchthi Cave (P–2095: 7981 ± 105 bp). Thus at both sites, the first cultivated plants appear around 6000 bc. At Franchthi Cave, it was *Triticum dicoccum* which appeared first, whereas at Uzzo it was *Triticum monococcum* which had that privilege. Thus, the new economy at Franchthi was based on *T. dicoccum*, *H. vulgare*, and *Lens culinaris*, whereas at Uzzo it was based on *T. monococcum*, *T. dicoccum*, *H. vulgare*, and *Lens culinaris*.

At the same time (in spits 13 and 12 in Trench F, Piperno *et al.* 1980a), the earliest domesticated animals – *Bos taurus*, *Ovis/Capra*, and *Sus domesticus* appeared together with the first plant cultivars, and they seemingly came to play an ever more important role in the diet, although wild species were also still hunted.

A second change, perhaps of less importance in terms of absolute innovation but just as significant for the further development of the agricultural economy, took place around 4800 bc ($6750 \pm 70$ bp, P–2733). This seems to have been the time of the introduction of the naked hexaploid wheats: bread wheat (*Triticum aestivum*) and club wheat (*Triticum aestivo-compactum*), and of three new species of domesticated legume: horse bean (*Vicia faba*), bitter vetch (*Vicia ervilia*), and pea (*Pisum* sp.), all of which were added to the range of cultivars which had been grown since the early Neolithic. *T. dicoccum* continued to dominate the cereal remains, while *T. monococcum* tended to lose importance with the appearance of the hexaploid wheats. Barley remained a fairly constant component (see Fig. 12.1).

At the same time, figs (*Ficus carica*) and almond (*Prunus amygdalus*) became more abundant, whereas no traces of the fruits of *Arbutus unedo* have been found. The presence of *Vitis* and *Olea* poses, once again, the problem of inferring their cultivation merely from evidence for the consumption of their fruit. Remains of these two plants (primarily in the form of wood charcoal) have been identified from deposits dating back to the Upper Palaeolithic, but they permit us only to demonstrate their presence without shedding much light on the question of the beginnings of their propagation. Such records nevertheless usefully contribute to the general picture of the emergence of the local landscape from the Upper Palaeolithic onwards. An analogous presence of olive and vine, again associated with *T. monococcum*, *T. dicoccum*, barley, and lentils, has been noted at the Torre Canne site, near Fasano in Puglia, preserved in daub from a hut dated to $6900 \pm 80$ bp (GIF–6725) (Coppola & Costantini 1987).

Further comparison can be made with Middle Neolithic sites in southern Italy. These indicate that, in the early 5th millennium bc, the agricultural economy was dominated by various cereals (einkorn, emmer, and barley) and legumes (bean, vetch, and lentil) in recurrent associations producing a spatial and chronological framework similar to that found at the Grotta dell'Uzzo. Thus, to Torre Canne may be added the sites of Rendina (Follieri 1982), Masseria Candelaro, Masseria Santa Tecchia, Masseria Valente, and Masseria Fontanarosa (Sargent 1983), Fontanelle and Le Macchie (Coppola & Constantini 1987), Ripatetta (Constantini & Tozzi 1987), and Torre Sabea (Castelleti *et al.* 1987). By contrast, at Franchthi Cave in Greece, a different situation obtained in which the only new species which appears to have been added to those grown in the Late Neolithic was, oddly enough, *Triticum monococcum*.

Important differences between the Neolithic sites in Italy are beginning to emerge, however, especially in the cereals. In particular, the adoption of free-threshing (naked) wheats seems to have been a determining factor of some considerable economic importance. The earliest evidence for free-threshing wheats outside the Near East comes from the Rendina site in the mid Ofanto Valley, where they have been found in contexts related to the first occupation phase dated to 7110 bp (Follieri 1982), which immediately pre-dates spits 9 and 8 in Trenches F and W at Uzzo.

There is a general lack of weed seeds in the archaeobotanical record of Neolithic sites. This is to be interpreted more as a result of the prehistoric techniques of harvesting and processing (as well as perhaps our own data-recovery systems) than as indicating a real absence of weeds in the crop. At Grotta dell'Uzzo, one of the commonest of the weed species, *Galium* sp. (cleavers), first appears at the same time as the free-threshing wheats. This may reflect a major change in harvesting methods, such as shifting from cutting the ears separately from the straw to cutting both together (by reaping low on the straw). Such a change could have resulted in many more of the *Galium* fruitlets being harvested with the grain. Any such systematic changes in husbandry practice clearly merit further investigation.

## Conclusions

In summary, therefore, the plant remains reveal that, between the 7th and 5th millennia bc, the people who frequented the Grotta dell'Uzzo underwent changes in subsistence which transformed them from foragers to crop-cultivators (Fig. 12.1). The introduction of cereals and legumes inevitably changed dietary habits and influenced the social and economic conditions of populations who had hitherto depended on the diverse array of natural resources offered by three distinct local ecosystems. This transformation would not have been a passively accepted phenomenon but a dynamic process which will eventually have included conscious improvement of cultivation, harvesting, and crop-processing techniques, as well as the selection of the crop varieties most productive under local conditions.

## References

Beguinot, A. 1929a. Cenni sulle filliti dei travertini quaternari del palermitano. *Bollettino della Societa di Scienze Naturali ed Economiche di Palermo* **9**, 4–8.

Beguinot, A. 1929b. Illustrazione delle filliti quaternarie dei travertini palermitani conservate al Museo di Geologia della Regia Universita di Palermo. *Archivio Botanico per la Sistematica, Fitogeografia e Genetica* **5–6**, 143–73.

Borgognini Tarli, S. & E. Repetto 1985. Dietary patterns in the Mesolithic samples from Uzzo and Molara Caves (Sicily): the evidence of teeth. *Journal of Human Evolution* **14**, 241–54.

Cassinis, R. 1967. Ricerca sugli afflussi di acqua dolce lungo le coste siciliane mediante misure di salinita in mare. *La ricerca scientifica* **37**, 267–80.

Castelletti, L., L. Costantini & C. Tozzi 1987. Considerazioni sull'economia e l'ambiente durante il neolitico in Italia. In *Atti della XXVI Riunione dell' Istituto Italiano di Preistoria e Protoistoria (1985)*, 37–55. Firenze: Stamperia Editoriale Parenti.

Coppola, D. & L. Costantini 1987. Le Néolithique ancien littoral et la diffusion des céréales dans les Pouilles durant le VIᵉ millénaire: les sites de Fontanelle, Torre Canne et Le Macchie. In *Premières communautés paysannes en Méditerranée occidentale*, 249–55. Paris: CNRS.

Costantini, L. 1981. Semi e carboni del mesolitico e neolitico della Grotta dell'Uzzo, Trapani. *Quaternaria* **23**, 233–47.

Costantini, L. & C. Tozzi 1987. Un gisement a céramique imprimée dans le subappenin de la Daunia (Lucera, Foggia): le village de Ripa Tetta. Economie et culture matérielle. In *Premières communautés paysannes en Méditerranée occidentale*, 387–94. Paris: CNRS.

Costantini, L., M. Piperno & S. Tusa 1987. La néolithisation de la Sicile occidentale d'après les résultats des fouilles à la grotte de l'Uzzo (Trapani). In *Premières communautés paysannes en Méditerranée occidentale*, 397–405. Paris: CNRS.

Follieri, M. 1982. Le piu antiche testimonianze dell'agricoltura neolitica in Italia meridionale. *Origini* **77**, 337–44.

Jarman, M. R. 1972. European deer economies and the advent of the Neolithic. In *Papers in economic prehistory*, E. S. Higgs (ed.), 125–46. Cambridge: Cambridge University Press.

Hansen, J. M. 1978. The earliest seed remains from Greece: Palaeolithic through Neolithic at Franchthi Cave. *Berichte der deutschen botanischen Gesellschaft* **91**, 39–46.

Hansen, J. M. & J. M. Renfrew 1978. Palaeolithic–Neolithic seed remains at Franchthi Cave, Greece. *Nature* **271**, 349–52.

Lona, F. 1949. I carboni dei focolari paleolitici della Grotta di S. Teodoro (Messina). *Rivista di Scienze Preistoriche* **4**, 187–93.

Meulengracht, A., P. McGovern & B. Lawn 1981. University of Pennsylvania Radiocarbon Dates XXI. *Radiocarbon* **23**, 227–40.

Pampaloni, L. 1904. Notizie sopra alcune piante fossili dei tufi della costa orientale dell'Etna. *Nuovo Giornale Botanico* **11**, 566–70.

Piperno, M. 1985. Some C¹⁴ dates for the palaeoeconomic evidence from the Holocene levels of Uzzo Cave, Sicily. In *Papers in Italian archaeology IV, Part ii, Prehistory*, C. Malone & S. Stoddart (eds), 83–6. Oxford: British Archaeological Reports, International Series 244.

Piperno, M. & S. Tusa 1976. Relazione preliminare sulla seconda campagna di scavi alla Grotta dell'Uzzo. *Sicilia Archeologica* **31**, 39–42.

Piperno, M. S. Scali & A. Tagliacozzo 1980a. Mesolitico e Neolitico alla Grotta dell'Uzzo (Trapani). Primi dati per un'interpretazione paleoeconomica. *Quaternaria* **22**, 275–300.

Piperno, M., S. Tusa & I. Valente. 1980b. Campagne di scavo 1977 e 1978 alla Grotta dell'Uzzo (Trapani). Relazione preliminare e datazione dei livelli mesolitici e neolitici. *Sicilia Archeologica* **42**, 49–64.

Sargent, A. 1983. Neolithic plant remains from the Tavoliere of Apulia. In *Studi del neolitico del Tavoliere della Puglia*, S. M. Cassano & A. Manfredini (eds), 250–2. Oxford: British Archaeological Reports, International Series 160.

Segre, E. & M. Piperno 1975. Scavi alla Grotta dell'Uzzo. Relazione preliminare. *Sicilia Archeologica* **27**, 11–16.

Tusa, S. 1983. *La Sicilia nella preistoria*. Palermo: Sellerio Editore.

Tusa, S. 1985. The beginning of farming communities in Sicily: the evidence of Uzzo Cave. In *Papers in Italian Archaeology IV, Part ii, Prehistory*, C. Malone & S. Stoddart (eds), 61–82. Oxford: British Archaeological Reports, International Series 244.

Tusa, S. 1987. Il Neolitico della Sicilia. In *Atti della XXVI Riunione Scientifica dell'*
    *Istituto Italiano di Preistoria e Protoistoria*, 361–80. Firenze: Stamperia Editoriale
    Parenti.
Vaufrey, R. 1928. Le Paléolithique Italien. *Archives de l'Institut de Paléontologie*
    *Humaine* **3**, 1–196.

# 13 *Late Palaeolithic plant foods from Wadi Kubbaniya in Upper Egypt: dietary diversity, infant weaning, and seasonality in a riverine environment*

## GORDON C. HILLMAN

This chapter concerns remains of wild-plant foods and human palaeofaeces from a series of Late Palaeolithic sites in Wadi Kubbaniya, to the west of the Nile Valley in Upper Egypt. The remains date from 16 000 to 15 000 bc, and provide the earliest substantive information on the plant component of hunter–gatherer subsistence so far recovered in the Old World. Full details of the remains examined to date are published elsewhere (Hillman *et al.* in press), and the present chapter offers merely a summary discussion of some of the major finds, methods, and conclusions.

## Source and nature of the remains

### Sites and location

Wadi Kubbaniya joins the Nile about 12 km north of Aswan and is one of the three major palaeo-drainage systems from the southwestern desert. Today, no water flows – except once or twice a century when there is heavy rain (Wendorf & Schild 1986) – and there is practically no plant life outside the narrow green strip of the Nile Valley. (For a field botanist, working in this plant-free Saharan environment is a strangely liberating experience!) At the time the sites were occupied, the region was hyper-arid, with even less surviving outside the valley than today. The Nile was also less incised than now, and at high water in late summer it flooded the wadi for several kilometres.

Most of the Late Palaeolithic sites in Wadi Kubbaniya are located in a large area of fossil dunes and interfingering silt-deposits about 3 km from the wadi mouth. The dunes would have been flooded briefly in late summer, but, thereafter, the dune sites offered a commanding position overlooking the swampy floodplain with fish-rich pools trapped behind the dunes (Wendorf *et al.* 1980, in press). The sites are characterized by backed bladelets, heavy grinding stones (some of them in the form of shallow mortars), high concentrations of fish bones and charcoal, together with bones of birds and mammals. A Middle Palaeolithic burial was also found in the wadi, with two occupations of this earlier period nearby (Wendorf *et al.* 1986). It is noteworthy that, after many years of archaeological survey in this part of. Egypt, Wendorf & Schild have found no other substantial Late Palaeolithic sites (Wendorf *et al.* 1986, in press). That the only sites of this period should be found in Wadi Kubbaniya is thought to reflect the richness of the floodplain resources which were probably unique in this part of the Nile Valley.

Sixteen of the sites were excavated (and numerous pits dug to study sediments) under the direction of Fred Wendorf of the Southern Methodist University, Dallas, and Romauld Schild of the Institute for the History of Material Culture, Polish Academy of Sciences, with additional support from the Geological Survey of Egypt (Wendorf *et al.* 1980, 1986, in press).

## Sources of plant remains

Just four of the sites produced remains of food plants and/or faeces. In all cases the remains were preserved by charring. (The only items preserved by desiccation were some recent intrusives.) All four of these productive sites were located on the tops of the dunes overlooking the floodplain. Each of the sites was re-occupied many times, and plant or faecal remains were recovered from a large proportion of the re-occupation levels at all four sites. However, the plant remains were confined to just small areas of these production levels, and the overall bulk of food-plant remains finally recovered was quite small, especially when compared with somewhat later sites such as Abu Hureyra (see Hillman *et al.* Ch. 14, this volume). Nevertheless, viewed as a single assemblage, the fact that the remains derive from so many successive occupations clearly improves their chances of being representative of certain aspects of local diet and subsistence during the Late Palaeolithic period.

## The plant remains in general

We have so far isolated 25 different types of seeds, fruits, and soft vegetable tissues, of which 13 are now identified to varying degrees (Table 13.1 summarizes both the ubiquity of each taxon across the four sites, and its absolute abundance in each unit of deposit). All 13 of the identified types are edible and grow wild in the Nile Valley today. Ethnohistorical records further reveal that each of the identified plants (or their close relatives) have served as food amongst hunter–gatherers in recent times. Dominating the loose (non-faecal) remains from three of the sites are charred fragments of parenchymatous tissues (soft vegetable matter), mostly from tubers of the wild nut-grass *Cyperus rotundus* – a type of sedge – (see Fig. 13.1), but including a tuber fragment of club-rush (*Scirpus* sp. of the *S. tuberosus* or *S. maritimus* type), and a rhizome fragment of a dictyostelous fern. Up to five other types of parenchymatous tissue remain indeterminate. Other food species include the fruit of the dóm palm (*Hyphaene thebica*), nutlets ('seeds') of the club-rush (*Scirpus* – of apparently the same type that produced the tuber remains), tiny seeds of what appear to be three different species of the chamomile tribe (Compositae, tribe Anthemidae), a schizocarpous fruit charred while it was still immature – probably a *Tribulus* sp. (the fruits are edible if roasted while green and soft), a fragment of thick fruit-skin of the caper type (cf. *Capparis* sp.), and the immature receptacle of a flower-bud of a seemingly extinct genus of waterlily (fam. Nymphaceae). The club-rush and the three types of chamomile seed were in the remains of faeces (see Fig. 13.2). Fragments of seven other types of seed and fruit remain totally indeterminate.

Plants such as the wild nut-grass (*Cyperus rotundus*), the club-rush (*Scirpus*), and the waterlily are typical of wet places. Heavy use of such foods clearly accords with the probable abundance of swamp species in this arid-zone riverine environment during the Late Pleistocene. It also parallels the evidence from the same sites for regular exploitation of fish (Gautier *et al.* 1980, Gautier & van Neer, in press). In terms of the major classes of food, then, the evidence fits the expected pattern of hunter–gatherer subsistence in riverine and lacustrine ecosystems in general – namely, heavy use of root foods and fish (cf. Harris 1976).

Even with the work still unfinished, it is clear that, for sites of this period, the plant food remains are exceptional:

(a)  First, they represent the most diverse assemblage of food-plant remains so far recovered from an Old World Palaeolithic site. That even 13 different types of plant food (with an additional 12 or more still indeterminate) should be represented in so small a quantity of remains recovered with coarse sieves – especially in an assemblage preserved via the vagaries of charring – suggests that a relatively broad-spectrum subsistence was probably already established in the Nile Valley by the beginning of the Late Palaeolithic.

(b)  Secondly, the remains included charred fragments of human faeces – almost certainly from infants, the earliest of their kind so far published. They provide not only direct evidence of what foods were consumed and, perhaps, how they were processed and cooked (cf. Robins *et al.* 1986), but also offer clues to the role of plant foods in the weaning of Palaeolithic infants.

(c)  Thirdly, the remains are dominated by charred fragments of soft vegetable foods. Remains of such low 'archaeological visibility' are rarely recorded from habitation sites other than dry caves, and certainly

**Table 13.1** Charred remains of food plants identified from four sites at Wadi Kubbaniya: numbers of productive contexts at each site. The table presents site totals only, and amalgamates the results from different layers within each site.

*The first number* entered in any column represents the number of independent contexts and/or levels from which the species or tissue-type was identified.

*The numbers in round brackets* represent the total no. of items identified from the site as a whole or, in the case of tuber fragments of Cyperus, the no. of whole tuber equivalents★ (see Hillman *et al.* in press).

*The numbers in square brackets* represent the volume of fragments of rhizomes or other tissues where the numbers of items would have little meaning. (*Note:* the plant remains were concentrated in small areas of about two-thirds of the layers.)

| Site code | E–81–6 | E–78–3 | E–81–1 | E–78–4 |
|---|---|---|---|---|
| Layers sampled | (all one layer) | (layers 18–24) | (layers 1–8) | (layers a–h) |
| Radiocarbon dates from *Cyperus* and *Scirpus* tubers (yrs bp) | ca. 19 000 | 18 000–17 600 | 18 000–17 200 | 17 800–17 300 |
| Total numbers of units (layers and squares) sampled for plant remains | 6 units | 27 units | 10 units | 78 units |
| Average volume dry-sieved for plant remains from each unit | 2.2 m³ | 5.1 m³ | 7.5 m³ | 1.9 m³ |
| Total volume dry-sieved for plant remains at each site | 13 m³ | 137 m³ | 75 m³ (+100 m³ of levels 1–16 which were unproductive) | 130 m³ |

I. CHARRED REMAINS OF VEGETATIVE TISSUES AND ORGANS

| | E–81–6 | E–78–3 | E–81–1 | E–78–4 |
|---|---|---|---|---|
| *Cyperus rotundus* (wild nut-grass) {whole tubers | — | 4 (7) | 3 (8) | 12 (14) |
| tuber fragments | — | 28 (43)★ | 10 (73)★ | 24 (31)★ |
| either *C. rotundus* or *Scirpus marit.*, tuber fragments | — | 3 (6)★ | 3 (5)★ | 3 (4)★ |
| *Scirpus maritimus/tuberosus* type {whole tubers | — | — | 1 (4 cm³) | — |
| tuber fragments | — | 1 (1)? | — | — |
| Pteridophyte (fern), dictyostelous rhizome fragments | — | — | 1 (2 cm³) | — |
| type A | — | — | 1 [5 mm³] | — |
| type B | — | — | 2 [8 mm³] | — |
| indeterminate parenchyma fragments {type C | — | 2 [3 mm³] | — | — |
| type D | — | 1 [5 mm³] | — | — |
| type E | — | — | — | 1 [3 mm³] |
| indeterminate monocot. stem fragment (in coprolites) | — | — | 2 [···] | 1 [6 mm³] |
| indeterminate monocot. leaf fragments (in coprolites) | — | — | 2 [···] | — |

## II. CHARRED REMAINS OF FRUITS AND SEEDS

| | 1 [4 mm³] | | 3 [8 mm³] |
|---|---|---|---|
| *Hyphaene thebica* (the dóm palm), fruit mesocarp fragments | — | — | — |
| *Scirpus maritimus/tuberosus* (club-rush), nutlets | — | 1 (4+) in coprolite | — |
| *Compositae* – tribe Athemidae (chamomile tribe), achenes | — | — | — |
| embedded within coprolites { achene type 'a' | — | 1 (3+) | — |
| achene type 'b' | — | 1 (28+) | — |
| achene type 'c' | — | 1 (12+) | — |
| *Nymphaceae* (waterlily family), immature bud receptacles | — | — | 1 (1) |
| Schizocarpous fruit (*Tribulus* type), green and immature when charred | 1? (1?) | 1 (1) | — |
| *Balanites* type, cotyledon fragment | 1? (1?) | — | — |
| Liliaceae type 'a', resembling an *Asparagus* seed, but compressed-ovoid and with strongly curved embryo (3 mm φ) | 2 (2) | — | — |
| Liliaceae type 'b', seed (ovoid >3 mm φ, embryo ± straight) | 1 (1) | — | — |
| cf. *Umbelliferae* type (aniseed family), kernel of mericarp   type 'a' | 1 (1) | 1 (1) | — |
| type 'b' | — | — | — |
| type 'c' | 1 (1) | — | — |
| type 'd' | 1 (1) | 1 (1) | — |
| type 'e' | 1 (1) | — | — |
| indeterminate seed/fruit | 1 (1) | — | — |
| indeterminate fruit-skin fragment (*Capparis* type) | 1 (1) | — | — |

## III. CHARRED REMAINS OF COPROLITES

The different types of coprolite of human origin are tabulated in detail in Hillman *et al.* (in press), and are here amalgamated in three broad categories: ××× = abundant; ×× = occasional; × = rare.

| | 1 [4 mm³] | | 3 [8 mm³] |
|---|---|---|---|
| cf. human faeces of extremely fine texture (from infants?) | ×× | ×× | ××× |
| cf. human faeces of slightly coarser texture (from children?) | × | ××× | × |
| cf. avian faecal segments, resembling those of the *Anserinae* and *Anatinae* (water-fowl) | ××× | ××× | ××× |

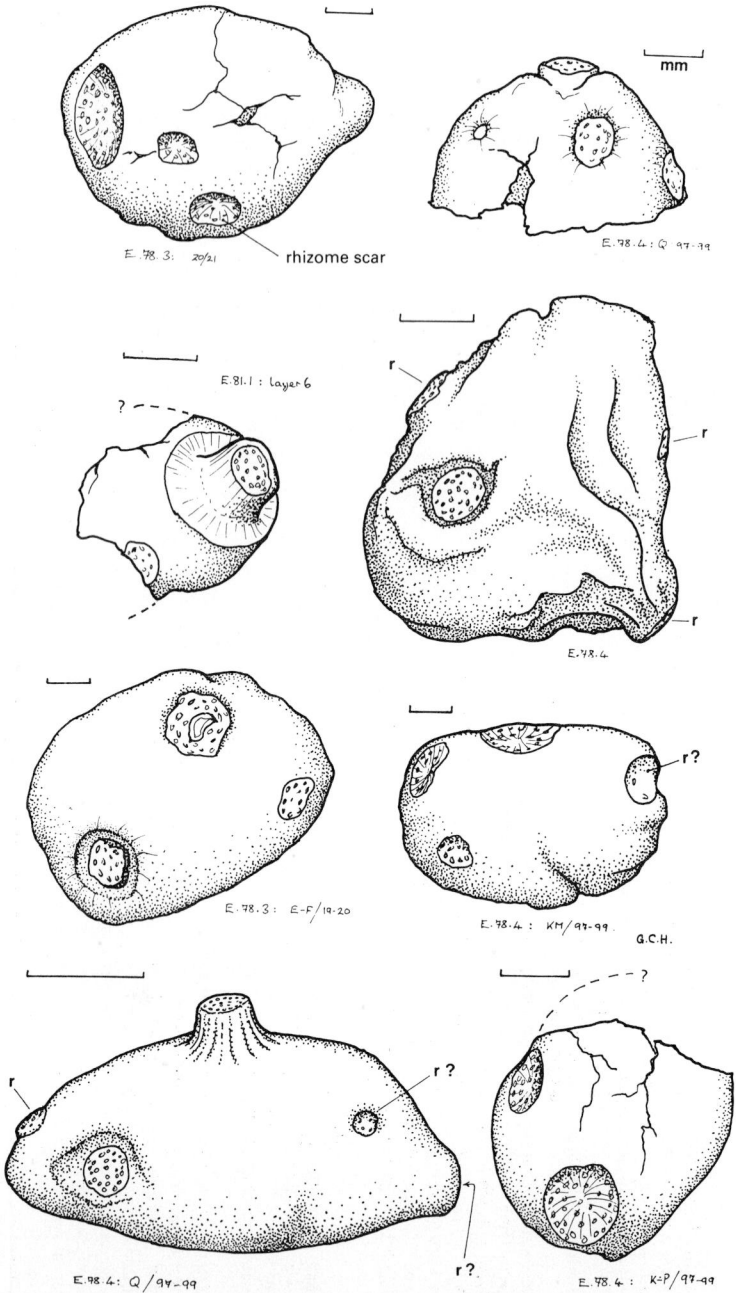

**Figure 13.1**  Charred remains of stem tubers of the wild nut-grass (*Cyperus rotundus*) – a type of sedge – from sites E–78–3, E–78–4, and E–81–1. This type of wild tuber was probably a major source of carbohydrate at Wadi Kubbaniya, and its remains abound on all three of these sites, although absent from site E–81–6. The tubers drawn here are unusually intact but are smaller than the apparent original size of the majority which survived in fragmented form. (Drawing: G. Hillman; from Hillman *et al.* in press.)

never before from a site of this antiquity. As such they add an additional dimension to our understanding of the possible role of starch-rich vegetable foods in pre-agrarian diet in the Old World.

That such an exceptional assemblage of charred remains of food plants and faeces was recovered from this particular group of Palaeolithic sites is probably attributable to two factors: (a) the unwavering commitment of the excavators to recovering plant remains; and (b) the remarkable preservation of charred material as a result of its burial by sand immediately after each round of deposition. At other early sites where equivalent factors have not operated, therefore, the significance (in terms of subsistence reconstruction) of the apparent absence of such remains is questionable.

## Radiocarbon dates

The Tuscon (Arizona) Laboratory obtained accelerator (AMS) radiocarbon dates from 11 different charred specimens of tubers of *Cyperus rotundus* (the most abundant of the food remains) and from one charred fragment of *Scirpus* tuber. Each specimen derived from a different excavation level. The spectrum of dates (all uncalibrated) were as follows: from site E–78–3: 18 000–17 870 bp; from site E–81–1: 17 990–17 210 bp; and from site E–84–4: 17 810–17 300 bp, all with errors ranging from ±150 to ±280 years (Donahue *et al.* in press, Wendorf *et al.* in press). The dates accord closely with those based on wood charcoals from the same levels.

## Earlier claims of 'Palaeolithic cultivation' at Wadi Kubbaniya

At an earlier stage of the Wadi Kubbaniya Project, identifications of domesticated crops by other workers had led to suggestions that the Late Palaeolithic occupants of Kubbaniya were already practising crop husbandry (Wendorf & Schild 1979, Wendorf *et al.* 1979, el Hadidi 1980, Stemler & Falk 1980, Stemler 1984, Wendorf & Schild 1980, 1984). The identifications included domesticated six-rowed barley, chick peas, and lentils, and the Southwest Asian affinities of the assemblage were further reinforced by the presence of remains of wild-type enkorn wheat – a common weed of Near Eastern crops.

Subsequent study has allowed this putative evidence for Palaeolithic domestication to be dismissed at two levels. First, the cereal remains and lentil were found to be uncharred and therefore incapable of surviving the regular inundations which continued until about 3000 bc; they were clearly recent intrusives (Hillman unpublished report 1982, Hillman *et al.* 1983). This was subsequently confirmed by radiocarbon accelerator (AMS) dates on some of the barley grains (Wendorf: addendum to Wendorf & Schild 1984, Wendorf *et al.* 1984, Harris 1986, 1987). Secondly, what earlier workers had thought to be chick peas proved to be wild-plant foods of types still available today along the banks of the Nile. (These last specimens were all genuinely charred and of Late Palaeolithic date.)

Claims of pre-Neolithic cultivation at Wadi Kubbaniya can therefore be dismissed, as can equivalent suggestions for Epipalaeolithic Abu Hureyra, 'Ain Mallaha, El Wad (Nahal Oren), and Rakafet (Harris 1986, 1987, Legge 1986, Hillman *et al.* Ch. 14, this volume). The earliest unequivocal evidence of the large-scale cultivation of major food plants in the western half of the Old World therefore comes, as hitherto, from the finds of fully domesticated crops in Pre-Pottery Neolithic occupations of Levantine sites such as Netiv Hagdud and Gilgal (Kislev *et al.* in press, Bar-Yosef & Kislev Ch. 40, this volume), Jericho (Hopf 1983), and Tell Aswad (van Zeist & Bakker-Heeres 1982).

## Recovery of the plant remains

Recovery of the plant remains posed a problem for the excavators. The charred remains were not only fragile with age but also totally dry. They consequently disintegrated on contact with water as soon as flotation recovery was attempted (Wendorf pers. comm.). Disintegration was presumably due to surface-tension effects as well as to absorption of water by caramelized carbohydrates: charred remains from archaeological sites are seldom, if ever, truly carbonized (Slocum *et al.* 1978, as cited by Keepax 1988, Hubbard in press). (The reason flotation recovery has encountered no such problems on sites in Southwest Asia is that the charred remains in that area are invariably damp on excavation.) The excavators at Wadi Kubbaniya were therefore forced to devise a system of large-scale dry-sieving. However, the size of sand and gravel granules dominating the deposits obliged them to use coarse-meshed sieves (2 mm$^2$). Nevertheless, test samples from every deposit were also sieved with much finer meshes (and then hand-sorted), though no small seeds were recovered (Wendorf pers. comm.). The fact that small seeds of *Scirpus* and a chamomile were found in charred fragments of human faeces therefore suggests that any specimens of these (or other) small seeds which formed part of the Kubbaniyan diet but were preserved loose (outside faeces) either failed to survive the intervening 17–19 000 years in identifiable form, or were lost during the coarse sieving.

Altogether, the excavators meticulously dry-sieved a staggering total of 455 m$^3$ of occupation deposits (see details in Table 13.1). Despite this, the earliest levels produced no recognizable remains of plant foods: e.g. the entirety of site E–81–6 and 100 m3 sieved from the earliest occupations at site E–78–3 were unproductive. Furthermore, in even the productive levels, charred food remains were generally concentrated in small areas around camp fires.

## The problems of identifying fragments of soft vegetable foods

We were fortunate that some specimens of 'root' foods had survived almost intact (Fig. 13.1) and could therefore be identified from relatively accessible features such as the distribution of scars left by lateral buds or rhizomes, and the development of terminal buds. On this basis, it was concluded that almost all the more intact specimens derived from the wild nut-grass *Cyperus rotundus*.

Most of the large number of fragments of charred parenchymatous tissue had a texture and colour closely similar to that of the interior of the identifiable *Cyperus* tubers. However, their secure identification clearly required the use of anatomical or histological criteria, and here we faced a problem: plant anatomists had scarcely studied parenchymatous tissues of these types. A new project was therefore initiated to screen such tissues from a wide range of modern specimens of edible roots, tubers, rhizomes, and corms (charred, dried, and fresh) in the hope of isolating new diagnostic criteria for identifying ancient remains of each type (see Hather 1988). It was Hather's eventual application of some of his new histological criteria which finally allowed him to: (a) confirm the identity of the more intact tubers of *C. rotundus*; (b) identify most of the small fragments as deriving from the same (or a closely related) species; (c) identify a hitherto indeterminate tuber as a *Scirpus* species of the *S. maritimus* or *tuberosus* type; and (d) identify a further indeterminate item as a rhizome fragment of a dictyostelous fern (see Hillman *et al.* in press). (The criteria applied in identifying fragments of dóm palm fruit, and remains of other fruiting structures are also outlined in the same report.)

## Were 'foods' such as nut-grass tubers really gathered for human consumption?

This was the first and most urgent question considered in interpreting the remains of edible plants, especially in respect of the superficially unappetizing tubers of *Cyperus rotundus* which might be thought to have become charred through growing in the soil beneath where camp fires were lit.

It was finally concluded that all the food plants so far identified must have been brought into the occupation areas by humans, and probably exposed to fire as part of their preparation as food, for the following reasons.

(a)   Food plants such as *Cyperus* could not have grown on the dune-tops where the fires were lit (see below).
(b)   The stratigraphy below the excavated hearths shows that the fires were lit on flat surfaces and not in hollows dug down towards the level where *Cyperus* tubers might mistakenly be argued to have grown: burned material had accumulated on top of the fire bed, rather than being dug from below it.
(c)   The finds of tubers consistently occurred together with finds of other foods, regardless of fluctuations in the relative abundance of wood charcoal and bone remains: wherever one plant food was preserved, other food species were also likely to be present.

**Type A**

A clear perianth scar
(= 'disc')

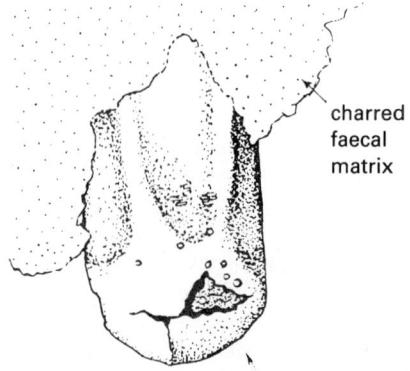

charred
faecal
matrix

0.1 mm

the absence of any perianth
scars suggests that this is
the proximal end of the seed

This apparently pointed cypsela-base
is merely the product of a fracture.
(All of them had originally been
parallel-sided.)

**Type B**

faecal
matrix

transversely
elongated cells

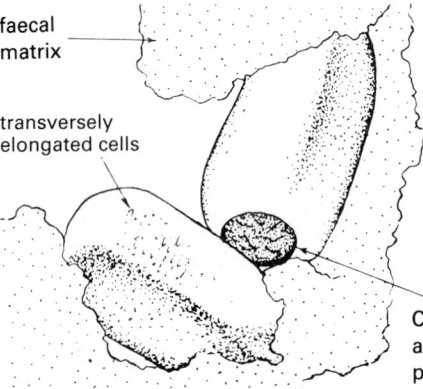

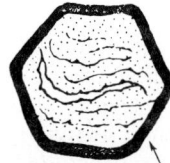

T.S. of fractured seed revealing
hints of folding of cotyledons.

Circular area lacking pericarp/testa
and presumably coinciding with the
perianth scar

(d)   All the species identified have served as hunter–gatherer foods in recent times, and their exploitation as food in the Late Palaeolithic offers the simplest explanation for their presence in these occupation deposits.

(e)   Fragments of tissue superficially resembling *Cyperus* parenchyma have been observed in fragments of human faeces, although proper identification awaits chemical analysis.

Each of these aspects is discussed in greater detail in Hillman *et al.* in press.

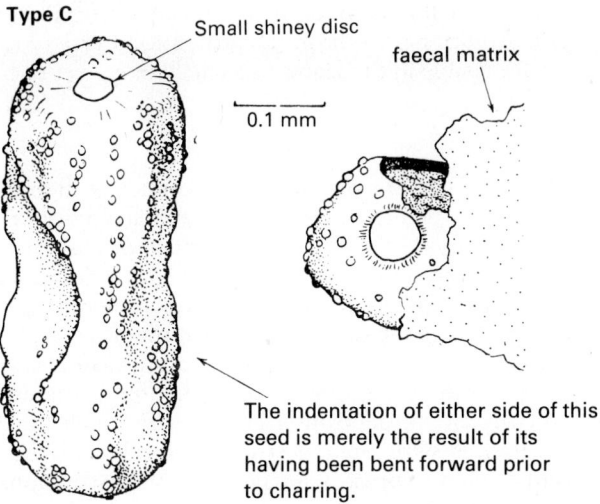

**Figure 13.2**  Drawings of some of the charred 'seeds' (cypselas) of three different types (species?) of the chamomile tribe (Anthemidae) found embedded within fragments of human faeces from site E–81–1. As usual in seeds of this family found in human faeces, their outermost layer appears to have been digested away. This complicates their identification. Three types could be recognized, though they might theoretically all derive from a single species: the Anthemidae often produce capitulums (heads) containing two or more seed types. Type A: these seeds were conspicuously larger than the others; their discs (perianth scars) were large, but less than half the width of the 'seeds'. Type B: these seeds were short and squat with a disc diameter at least half that of the width of the seed; 5–6-sided: this was the most common type. Type C: these seeds were more elongated and had small discs; they were mostly 6-sided. These two specimens of type 'c' were from separate faecal fragments, and were each accompanied by many other seeds of like form. (Drawings: G. Hillman; from Hillman *et al.* in press.)

## Dietary diversity and 'missing foods'

### Diversity in the charred remains

Even at this stage of the work, it is already clear that, for a site of this antiquity, the Kubbaniya remains include a diverse array of food plants. So far, 13 different types have been identified (to varying degrees) in the loose plant remains and in the charred remains of human faeces (Table 13.1). (Remains of six other types of parenchymatous tissue and seven other types of seed and fruit are still unidentified.) The identified types include small food-seeds/fruits (providing starch, oil, protein, and fibre), sedge tubers (providing starch and lots of fibre), arboreal fruit (in this case, providing sugars and fibre), and flower buds (providing protein and oil from the copious pollen). Additional to the 13 identified food types are leafy foods whose remains are visible in the faeces but which have yet to be identified.

## 'Missing foods'

Any realistic assessment of the original extent of dietary diversity at the site must take account of possible gaps in the archaeological record. Plant remains inevitably provide an incomplete picture of past diet, and this is especially true when preservation is by charring, as foods eaten raw or cooked by boiling are unlikely to come into contact with fire, and even of the foods which do, many fail to survive in identifiable form; (cf. discussion of this topic in Hillman 1981, pp. 138–40, also Hillman *et al.* Ch. 14, this volume). The problem is compounded on hunter–gatherer sites where preservation subsequent to deposition is generally much poorer than on, say, agrarian tell sites with their destruction levels and their protective layers of decomposed mud brick. Clearly, then, reconstructions of past diet which fail to take explicit account of these gaps in the record are potentially misleading.

In attempting to identify the additional plant species that could have been exploited, we used a combination of ecological models of the plant resources available in the site catchment at the time it was occupied, and ethnographic models of patterns of preference amongst recent hunter–gatherers. However, for the reasoning to be scientifically repeatable, it was clear that both the models and their mode of application must be explicitly defined.

### ECOLOGICAL MODELS

Ecological models used in reconstructing past availability of food resources in the Kubbaniya area included the following:

(a)   Pollen-based reconstructions. These indicate (i) hyper-aridity in North Africa at 16 000 bc, (ii) probable absence of plant life outside the Nile Valley, and (iii) tentatively suggest only minor north–south shifts in vegetation zones within the Valley itself – at least in its upper reaches (see, for example, Butzer 1959, van Zinderen Bakker & Coetzee 1972, Livingstone 1980).

(b)   Models of the extent and duration of ancient flooding regimes in the Nile Valley and their probable effect on local vegetation, especially studies in Wadi Kubbaniya itself (see, for example, Butzer & Hansen 1968, Butzer 1980, Schild & Wendorf 1980 and in press, Hassan 1984, Hill in press).

(c)   Detailed ecological models of intra-zonal composition of the recent local valley flora – both before and after the construction of the Aswan dams (see El Hadidi & Springuel 1978, in press a & b), though with due reference to possible differences between the precise composition of ancient vegetation formations and those of the present day (cf. Davis 1986).

(d)    Autecological studies of each of the principal food-producing species indicated in (a), (b) and (c) above, especially studies of their productivity in seasonally flooded environments in the arid zone – both in North Africa and elsewhere.

(e)    Calcified fossils of trees and shrubs on the dune-tops and the culm-bases of cane thickets (cf. *Saccharum*) on the skirts of the dunes. (Although these fossils might post-date the dune occupations, they nevertheless provide clues to the sort of vegetation the Wadi supported under the old flooding regime.)

On the basis of these ecological data, it was concluded that the Kubbaniyans would probably have had access to a range of wild-plant foods additional to the species so far identified in the charred remains. The additional foods would have included

(i)    the rhizomes of food plants such as catstail (*Typha* spp.), bulrushes (*Schoenoplectus* spp.), common reed (*Phragmites*), several *Cyperus* spp., including the papyrus reed (*C. papyrus*), waterlilies, and a bistort (*Polygonum senegalense*);

(ii)   grain of grasses of the millet group such as *Paspalidium germinatum* and *Panicum repens*, nutlets of *Polygonum senegalense*, seeds of waterlilies (Nymphaceae) and nutlets of many local members of the sedge family, including species of *Cyperus*, *Scirpus*, *Schoenoplectus*, *Holoschoenus*, *Fimbristylis*, and *Eleocharis*;

(iii)  edible pollen (e.g. from catstail).

The floodplain would almost certainly have supported sizeable stands of several of these swamp species, and, collectively, they could have yielded considerable quantities of not only the edible 'roots', but also 'seed' foods (see details of *Cyperus* yields, below).

The ecological models also indicate that trees and shrubs growing either round the edge of the floodplain or down in the main valley would have included species with edible seeds or fruits, such as *Acacia nilotica*, the jujube *Zizyphus spina-Christae*, and possibly even the wild ancestor of the date palm (all these in addition to the dóm palm (*Hyphaene thebica*) which is represented in the remains). Finally, the models suggest that a number of desert or dry-wadi species would have survived at the periphery of the flood zone. Many of these plants produce edible seeds, though the quantities would probably have been small.

ETHNOGRAPHIC MODELS

Having decided which plant foods would probably have been available, we can next turn to ethnographic models of plant-food preferences amongst recent arid-zone hunter–gatherers who had access to a similar spectrum of riverine or lacustrine resources. The rationale here is that, if a range of culturally and geographically distinct hunter–gatherers – all with access to a similar spectrum of plant foods – are recorded to have consistently preferred the same types of food, then this provides a useful basis for modelling patterns of preference amongst hunter–gatherers occupying similar environments in the past. Fortunately for the present study, arid-zone riverine floras in many parts of the world share many of the same genera, and we were able to trace a number of relevant ethnohistorical studies (these are all referenced in Hillman *et al.* in press). It should be noted, however, that, in applying these models, it has been assumed that perceptions of plant-food edibility in the Palaeolithic were similar to those of recent hunter–gatherers (see below).

The first 'common denominator' apparent in the ethnographic models is a general preference for 'root' foods over 'seed' foods (see, in particular, Woodburn 1968, Gott 1982, Latz 1982, O'Connell *et al.* 1983, Cane Ch. 6, this volume, Jones & Meehan Ch. 7, this volume). Cane (Ch. 6) notes that this preference reflects the greater energy expenditure required to process seed foods. It certainly seems to make good sense of the domination of the Kubbaniyan remains by charred 'root' foods, although the possible loss of small seeds prior to (or during excavation) precludes any firm conclusions on this point.

Ethnographic records of recent hunter–gatherers further suggest that, amongst those 'root' foods indicated by our ecological models, certain types were consistently favoured as staples almost wherever they were available, notably the rhizomes of catstail, waterlilies, and, to a lesser degree, bulrush; also papyrus rush amongst some farming groups. (The records show that the two 'root' foods already identified in the remains – club-rush and nut-grass – were also highly esteemed among recent groups.)

The ethnographic records further reveal that, of the 'missing' seed foods indicated in the ecological model, four were consistently favoured as staples (especially when 'root' foods were not available): these were acacia seeds (cf. Cane Ch. 6, this volume), seeds of waterlilies, grains of grasses in the millett group (cf. Harlan, Ch. 5, this volume, Cane Ch. 6, this volume), and nutlets of several of the sedges (in addition to the club-rush nutlets already represented in the remains). They also reveal heavy use of pollen, especially from catstail, though also in the form of waterlily buds roasted and eaten whole (a practice possibly represented in the remains by the charred receptacle of a waterlily bud).

## APPLICATION OF AN ETHNOECOLOGICAL MODEL

Applied to Palaeolithic Kubbaniya, a combined ethnoecological model suggests that it is unlikely that the tubers of nut-grass (*Cyperus rotundus*) and club-rush (*Scirpus maritimus/tuberosus*) were the only 'root' foods eaten. Rhizomes of *Typha* spp., *Cyperus papyrus*, Nymphaceae, and *Schoenoplectus* spp. are equally likely to have served as carbohydrate staples. Their absence from the remains identified so far quite possibly reflects the fact that any charred remains of fragments of such spongey rhizomes discarded on the fires would be morphologically unrecognizable – if they survived at all.

As for additional seed foods likely to have served as staples (or as heavily used supplementary foods), the most obvious candidates are seeds of *Acacia nilotica*, seeds of Nymphaceae, grains of *Panicum repens* and *Paspalidium germinatum*, and nutlets of a range of Cyperaceae. Several other seed foods are likely to have made minor contributions to the local diet, as would many types of green leaves and perhaps some pollen – all these in addition to the foods already represented in the remains.

If, therefore, the Kubbaniyans were as aware of the potential of plant foods as were recent hunter–gatherers (see below), then the rich resources offered by the Kubbaniya floodplain would have allowed a remarkable level of dietary diversity. With a number of seed types and soft vegetable tissues from the remains still to be identified, and with the faecal remains yet to be fully analysed, there is every hope of identifying other foods and thus of further testing the ethnoecological model of missing foods outlined above.

## Comparisons with species diversity at other hunter–gatherer sites

In the Old World, plant-food remains have been recovered from relatively few pre-agrarian sites. Reports on three of these rare assemblages (all of them Mesolithic and later than Wadi Kubbaniya) appear in this volume. Of these, Beli-Lena produced four food species (Kajale Ch. 15, this volume); Ban Kao yielded six species – if possible intrusives are excluded (Pyramarn Ch. 16, this volume); and Abu Hureyra 157 (Hillman *et al*. Ch. 14, this volume). Clearly, Abu Hureyra stands apart, although Wadi Hammeh (an Epipalaeolithic site in Jordan) shows signs of soon joining the same league (Colledge 1988). With 38 species, the terminal Epipalaeolithic occupation at Tell Mureybit in Syria (dated to 8300–8200 bc; Cauvin 1986) probably also belongs to the Abu Hureyra type (van Zeist & Bakker-Heeres 1986).

However, comparison with Abu Hureyra, Wadi Hammeh, and Mureybit is probably misleading, as the diversity of their food-plant remains appears to reflect what Hillman & Vaughan (forthcoming) describe as the 'lawn-mower' system of seed-gathering. This system can be applied in certain Southwest Asian habitats, such as glades in arid-zone forest and moist hollows in steppe, where: all the plants in certain patches of the mosaic yield edible seeds, are herbaceous, grow at high density, produce their seed in a single vegetation layer (i.e. at more-or-less the same height), and ripen their seeds at roughly the same time. In plant communities of this type, it is possible to harvest the entire carpet of vegetation, dry it, and thresh out the seeds. (In grass-dominated stands, burning the harvest can also be used to separate the seeds from the straw and chaff; Hillman *et al*. in press.) In harvesting experiments applied to such vegetation in Syria and Jordan, Hillman & Vaughan have found that a remarkably broad spectrum of edible types of seed can be gathered from a single square metre of sward. It therefore requires the archaeological preservation of seed from only a few such harvesting episodes in different habitats to generate an impressive list of edible seed species.

The Nile Valley in Upper Egypt supports no plant communities of such extreme diversity, and comparisons with the spectrum of foods found in the charred remains from Abu Hureyra are therefore misleading.

## Comparisons with the dietary diversity of recent hunter–gatherers

Assuming that recent hunter–gatherer parallels are relevant at all (and it would be surprising if they were not), more instructive comparisons can be made with the range of species exploited by recent hunter–gatherers in arid-zone Africa (with no species-rich swards of the Southwest Asian type), but who are nonetheless regarded as having had diverse diets; e.g. the Dobe !Kung, the ≠Kade San, and the eastern Hadza. While the total number of plant foods exploited in the course of a full year by these three groups was 100, 79, and 'a large number' respectively, the vast bulk of the plant food was provided by just 23, 13 and 10 species (Woodburn 1968, p. 51, Tanaka 1976, Yellen & Lee 1976, p. 38). Against this background, the 13 plant foods so far identified from Kubbaniya can perhaps be regarded as reflecting some degree of dietary diversity, especially in view of the vagaries of preservation by charring, the losses likely from coarse sieving, the inevitable sparseness of very early remains, and the fact that we can expect more foods to be identified as work progresses.

## The antiquity of broad-spectrum diets

Even without any 'missing foods', the plant and animal remains from 18 000 bp Kubbaniya provide some of the earliest direct evidence of broad-spectrum subsistence so far recovered. (For the latest account of the bone remains of fish, birds, and mammals, see Gautier et al. 1980, Gautier & van Neer in press). The early date of this assemblage will come as no surprise to most in the field, but is earlier than predicted in some of the literature.

### THE TRADITIONAL VIEW

Binford & Binford (1966) emphasized what they interpreted as a funda- mental shift in subsistence strategies at some point during the Upper Palaeolithic. The ensuing phase termed 'the late pre-agricultural period' (by Washburn & Lancaster 1968) was, they suggested, characterized by increas- ing use of fish, shellfish, bows, hunting dogs, and the start of heavy dependence on plant foods, which they generally described as 'seeds'. 'Grinding and boiling of otherwise inedible seeds and nuts' together with 'the use of products of river and sea' were seen by Washburn & Lancaster

(1968), amongst others, as 'the final adaptation' preceding the adoption of agriculture.

In this traditional scenario, the most worrying feature is not so much the late date proposed for a shift to broad-spectrum subsistence, but the criteria used in its identification, namely the rarity on earlier sites of (a) grinding stones, and (b) remains of plant foods (Kraybill 1977, Eaton & Konner 1986). On many (if not most) sites, neither criterion is acceptable.

(a)  For most plant foods, grinding stones can be substituted by wooden mortars which are unlikely to survive on the majority of sites. Indeed, since wooden mortars are apparently less trouble to make (even with bone or stone tools: Chris Bergman, pers. comm.), one might suppose that wooden mortars would be the preferred option whenever the appropriate trees are available (Aboriginal peoples of Australia pose a puzzling exception in this regard: Cane & Smith pers. comms). Certainly, for the !Kung San, Lee (1979, p. 153) observes that wooden mortars (and nut-cracking stones) featured in the preparation of every meal. We may therefore conclude that the absence of stone grinders is not proof of a predominantly carnivorous diet.

In some parts of the world, grinding stones have, in any case, now been recovered from sites pre-dating the 'terminal Pleistocene', and several examples are presented in this volume (see Cane Ch. 6, Groube Ch. 17, and Smith Ch. 18, this volume).

(b)  The apparent absence of the remains of plant foods is equally inadmissable as evidence of their minimal role in human diet. The factors involved in the preservation and recovery of the Kubbaniya remains (see above) have not necessarily existed at other early excavations, and the claimed absence of plant-food remains on such sites offers little more than an index of poor preservation, or of questionable standards of archaeological recovery.

MORE RECENT ARGUMENTS

Stahl (1984) notes that dietary diversity would have conferred powerful selective (evolutionary) advantages, especially on hominids dependent on plant foods eaten without cooking. But while this could have favoured the early emergence of broad-spectrum diets, the inclusion of large quantities of the more energy-rich foods, such as roots and seeds (as opposed to mere leaves and fruits), required the use of fire and pounders/grinders (Stahl 1984). This suggests that the bulk consumption of raw grain by hominids (as in phase 1 of Jolly's 'seed-eater' model: 1970, p. 20–1) would not have been feasible, but it nevertheless underlines the possibilty of large-scale seed-eating (and, more importantly, root-eating) from the point at which fire was first used to cook plant foods and, in the case of some of the root foods, sticks used for digging them up (Stahl 1984; also Mann 1972, Coursey 1973, Peters

& O'Brien 1981, Hallam, Ch. 8, this volume). In fact, many 'root' foods can be gathered without digging sticks: the underwater rhizomes of most reeds and rushes need only to be cut or torn free from the parent plant and entangled vegetation, and nut-grass tubers can be 'grubbed-up' with the bare hands if the mud is damp (Hillman *et al.* in press).

Current evidence therefore favours the possibility of a very early establishment of broad-spectrum diets, and thereby (a) validates (in part, at least) the use of information on plant-food exploitation by recent hunter–gatherers in modelling for 'missing foods' at Kubbaniya (as above), and (b) reinforces the probability that the Kubbaniyans, with their unusually resource-rich floodplain, enjoyed a very diverse diet.

## Wild nut-grass (*Cyperus rotundus*) as a possible staple source of carbohydrate

A series of ecological and ethnographic models was applied above in examining which plant foods (additional to those represented in the remains) would have been available to (and probably favoured by) the Kubbaniyan hunter–gatherers. When applied to the food species actually identified in the remains, these same models indicate that wild nut-grass and club-rush could also have served as staples. The bitter tubers of wild nut-grass might appear an unlikely staple food, so it is appropriate to summarize some of the evidence. Two questions will be considered: (a) do the tubers contain the necessary nutrients; and (b) could enough of them have grown on the floodplain to make a significant contribution to diet?

(a)    First, do nut-grass tubers provide the necessary nutrients? Nutrient analyses of samples from different Egyptian and Indonesian populations of modern tubers were organized as part of the project, and revealed that they are rich in available carbohydrate (25–30 per cent of fresh weight), have a very high fibre content ($\geqslant$12 per cent, even when peeled), and are very poor in both protein (c. 2.5 per cent) and fat (c. 1.6 per cent). However, the small amount of protein is relatively rich in the essential amino acid, lysine (Bulman 1985, Hillman *et al.* in press). The carbohydrate content compares well with sweet potato (22 per cent), cassava (31 per cent), and cocoyam (21 per cent) (World Health Organization 1973, Tan *et al.* 1985). The high fibre content would have posed no problem if all the more mature (fibrous) tubers were ground and sifted prior to consumption (cf. Stahl 1984, Ch. 11, this volume). However, the mature tubers also contain toxins (Apperbekova 1967, Singh & Singh 1980, Kinchi *et al.* 1983, Bulman 1985). These could have been eliminated by drying, pounding, and then leaching the tubers, though some modern groups eat them after more perfunctory processing. Geophagy, too, could theoretically have played a role in detoxification (see Johns 1986 a & b, Ch. 32, this volume) (the processing of nut-grass tubers is discussed in detail in Hillman *et al.* in press).

(b)   Secondly, would the tubers have been available in sufficient quantities? Springuel's studies of recent vegetation around Kubbaniya Island (El Hadidi & Springuel 1978, in press a & b) suggest that 'sedge formations' dominated by nut-grass would then have grown below the *Saccharum* zone, starting a short distance out from the dunes and ending above the reed zone. Relative to the present-day river-terrace systems, the silts of the floodplain would have formed a very gentle slope, with the nut-grass formations occupying a very broad swathe of vegetation – certainly much broader than that on the present-day first terrace of the main valley. Around the floodplain as a whole, therefore, there would almost certainly have been a hectare or more of sward dominated by wild nut-grass available for tuber exploitation as soon as each summer's flood started to recede.

Measurements of tuber yield were made in 13 populations of wild nut-grass occupying a range of habitats on what Springuel's model terms the 'first terrace', 'first slope', 'ridge', and 'second terrace' of Kubbaniya Island towards the west side of the River Nile. In permanently wet niches at the water's edge, each square metre of nut-grass sward produced an astounding 21 200 tubers with a total fresh weight of 3.3 kg (for photographs, see Hillman *et al.* in press). The yield was lower in drier areas, although tuber quality was better. Average figures from a transect from waterlogged to relatively dry habitats in areas where nut-grass was abundant were roughly 500 tubers/m$^2$, with a total fresh weight of *c.* 260 g. Despite obvious differences between modern and ancient conditions, it seems clear that nut-grass tubers from the Kubbaniya floodplain could, even on their own, probably have met the annual calorie requirements of a large band of gatherers.

The modern nutritional and ecological data thus suggest that wild nut-grass could well have fulfilled the role of a carbohydrate staple, along with some of the 'missing foods' considered above.

(c)   This possibility is further supported by records of the use of *Cyperus rotundus* and some of its close relatives as staples amongst recent hunter–gatherers (see, for example, Cane Ch. 6, this volume, Jones & Meehan Ch. 7, this volume) and as a famine food amongst recent farming groups (the ethnographic records are explored in detail in Hillman *et al.* in press).

Tanaka (1976, p. 115) notes that 'the presence of some staple plant-food base is generally a necessary requirement for people whose subsistence depends on gathering, whether this plant base comprises one species like the mongongo nut of the Dobe !Kung, the acorn of the California Indian, or the two (or more) species observed amongst the ≠Kade San.' At Palaeolithic Kubbaniya, nut-grass was probably just one of several carbohydrate staples, which included not only the club-rush tubers and sugary dóm palm fruits identified in the remains, but also the rhizomes of swamp plants such as catstail (*Typha*), and the seeds of acacia.

## Wild-tuber management? The possibility of 'incidental propagation'

The response of wild nut-grass to disturbance suggests that intensive harvesting could have led to a form of management falling somewhere between Harris's 'protective tending' and 'replacement planting', together, perhaps, with elements of his 'systematic soil tillage' as well (see Harris Ch. 1, this volume, Fig. 1.1).

Nut-grass is stimulated into more active tuber-production by soil disturbance, such as results from digging up the wild tubers. In modern fields where *Cyperus rotundus* is established as a weed, cultivation merely makes the infestation worse (Holm *et al* 1981). Equivalent effects have been observed in other wild 'root' foods. For the wild *Dioscorea* yams, Hallam (1977, 1983, Ch. 8, this volume) notes that the mere process of harvesting yams with digging sticks leads to their increased abundance and spread. Jones and Meehan (Ch. 7, this volume) note the same phenomenon in both yam tubers and *Eleocharis* corms exploited by the Gidjingale. Gott (1982, p. 65) has observed a range of similar responses in several other 'root' foods used by southeastern Australian Aborigines, including catstail rhizomes, and the root tubers of wild orchids, a *Triglochin*, and a salsify (*Microseris*).

In nut-grass, however, regular disturbance from harvesting may have yielded additional advantages not found in most of the other 'root' foods. In most *Dioscorea* yams, for example, the stored nutrients of the previous year's tubers are re-absorbed early in the next growing season and translocated into the newly forming tuber(s). In nut-grass, by contrast, the old tubers are retained and become ever more woody and inedible; the soil eventually becomes choked with old tubers, so the plant as a whole becomes ever less productive of succulent new tubers fit for human consumption. Annual harvesting of nut-grass tubers would largely have prevented this build-up of old, woody tubers, and would thus have been even more effective in stimulating rapid production of young palatable tubers than is the regular harvesting of wild yams.

Wild nut-grass would also have responded well to disturbance on account of the remarkable rate at which it produces new tubers once competition is removed (such as when harvesting clears an area of tubers, leaving just a few to grow on). In greenhouse plantings of isolated tubers of *Cyperus rotundus*, Nambiyor (as cited in CSIR 1950, p. 424) found that '146 tubers and basal "bulbs" are produced from a single tuber in just 3½ months'. Heavy annual harvesting of the wild swards of nut-grass would thus, of itself, have guaranteed an equally heavy harvest of succulent freshly formed tubers in each ensuing year.

It would certainly not have escaped the notice of foragers regularly exploiting the same stands of nut-grass that tuber quality was best in those areas which had been harvested the previous year. And with their intimate knowledge of plant behaviour, most foragers would doubtless have under-stood the reason why (as presumably did the Paiute Indians in exploiting *c. esculentus* tubers, see Harris, Ch. 1, this volume, p. 20). It is therefore possible that the tuber-harvesters of Palaeolithic Kubbaniya had already evolved a system of exploitation which included not only Harris's 'replacement planting' (probably by default, as it's pointless trying to dig up every last tuber), but also specialized elements of 'land clearance' and/or 'systematic soil tillage' as well (see Harris Ch. 1, this volume, Fig. 1.1).

However, in the absence of the relevant stress factors, such a system of 'incidental propagation' would not have led inexorably to any overriding dependence on food production in place of foraging, any more than it has in equivalent circumstances amongst the recent wild-yam foragers of south-western Australia (Hallam Ch. 8, this volume). There would have been no obvious justification for accepting the extra energy input (and, maybe, some loss of mobility) that such a shift to obligate cultivation would have imposed.

## Role of the Kubbaniya grinders

One of the notable features of the dune sites at Wadi Kubbaniya is the large numbers of grinding stones and mortars (Banks 1980, Wendorf & Schild 1980, Roubet, in press a & b). Of the plant foods identified from Kubbaniya (and the various 'missing foods' considered above), those most in need of grinding are the tubers of wild nut-grass and club-rush: mature nut-grass tubers are both fibrous and toxic and so require grinding prior to sifting and leaching; club-rush tubers are just rich in coarse fibre which again needs breaking up (cf. Stahl Ch. 11, this volume).

To resolve the matter, C. E. R. Jones (in press) analysed organic residues surviving on or in the working surfaces of three of the grinding stones, using the powerful analytical systems of laser dissorbtion time-of-flight spec-trometry (=laser microprobe mass analysis or LAMMA) and pyrolysis mass spectrometry (PYMS). In comparing PYMS spectra from the working and non-working surfaces of one of the stones (the best buried of the three), he concluded that the working surfaces were characterized by traces of 'cellulo-sics' (e.g. cellulose or starch) with almost no protein (on the two other stones, the organic traces were too slight, even for PYMS).

This result would fit tissues from much of the plant kingdom. There are, however, relatively few plants with protein-poor tissues on which a Palaeo-lithic population of hunter–gatherers living in the Nile Valley would have reason to expend time and energy in grinding/pounding. Of the most obvious candidates for large-scale grinding cited above (viz. the tubers of nut-grass and club-rush), both have the necessary low protein content, and may have been amongst the plant foods ground on this particular stone 18 000 years ago. The near absence of protein on the stone surface further suggests that no seed foods were ground on it.

## Faecal remains and evidence of infant weaning in the Palaeolithic

Charred remains of faeces were recovered from several deposits. Most were from infants, but a few appear to derive from older children or adults. I currently know of no other published report of charred faeces from early sites, and it is therefore appropriate to offer full details of the basis of their identification as infant faeces. Also outlined is evidence for the role of finely ground plant mush in the weaning of Palaeolithic infants.

### Identification

In the course of sorting the charred remains, we isolated a number of small (2–3 mm$^3$) fragments of material which, while black and charred on the outside, paled within to a coffee-brown colour. On the basis of internal texture they fell into two classes: those of bland, clay-like material and those of coarser material.

SMOOTH-TEXTURED FRAGMENTS

The presence of finely ground particles of vegetable matter embedded within the bland, clay-like matrix suggested that we might be dealing with either:

(a)    some sort of finely ground plant mush which had splashed into the fire during food preparation;
(b)    vomit derived from fine-ground food; or
(c)    faeces of some animal which had ingested fine-ground food.

The third possibility was supported by the presence, on the presumed original outer surface of one fragment, of what appeared to be the 'moulding' or imprint left by the internal surface of the donor's colon. This conclusion is to be tested by analysing the remains for residues of coprosterols (as in the tests applied by Knights *et al.* 1983).

The archaeological context (a camp site) argues for the donor having been either a dog or a human, while the conformation and fine texture argue for a specifically human origin. Indeed, the extremely fine-ground texture of most of the specimens further suggests that they are the faeces of infants who were being weaned onto some sort of fine mush. (Much of the smooth matrix around the 'mush' fragments is probably the usual bacterial sludge.) The infant hypothesis finds additional support in the context of the finds: infants are likely to have spent much of their time in camp and to have voided their faeces on-the-spot whenever the need overtook them, so that their faecal donations stood a reasonable chance of being scuffed onto the fires and thus preserved by charring. Certainly, amongst the !Kung, children under ten seldom left the camp except when being carried as babies on gathering forays (Draper 1976, pp. 201 & 205). The case is further supported by Jones and Meehan's detailed observations of patterns of adult and infant faecal deposition amongst the Gidjingale (see Jones & Meehan Ch. 7, this volume). They found that, while adult (or dog) faeces are unlikely to find their way onto domestic hearths, there is a constant input of infant faeces onto the fires at all base camps (Jones, pers. comm.). Similar observations have been made amongst other hunter–gatherers such as the Onge of the Andaman Islands (Zarine Cooper pers. comm.), and the Carib Tirigos and Ge-speaking Kayapos of the Amazon Basin (Frank Black pers. comm.).

Further support for the infant origin of the (otherwise) fine-textured faecal remains comes from the quantity of sand present throughout the charred matrices of several fragments. An infant crawling on sand will ingest the occasional handful, but this is seldom true of adults. Unlike clay-rich earths, sand is unlikely to have been deliberately incorporated into food to buffer toxicity in the manner reported by Johns (1986 and Ch. 32, this volume), although whether the bland texture of the Kubbaniya faeces owes anything to clay eating is another matter. Either way, the analysis of coprosterols and other compounds to be undertaken will not only determine whether they are, indeed, faeces, but also, hopefully, verify their human origin, provide an estimate of the ages of the donors, and detect any practice of geophagy, all this in addition to identifying the food constituents (preliminary analyses of similar charred faecal fragments from Abu Hureyra [cf. Hillman *et al*. Ch. 14, this volume] are already producing promising results; Wales & Evans 1987).

The specimens would appear to have been wet when they hit the fire: while the outer surface is black and charred, the interior is merely coffee-brown and crumbly. This greatly enhances the possibilities of chemical analyses (Hillman *et al*. in press).

COARSER-TEXTURED FRAGMENTS

The second class of apparent human faeces are fragments of much coarser composition, although the food nevertheless appears to have been partially ground before consumption (cf. Hillman 1986, p. 103). The context would again argue for an infant origin, although these specimens might be from children who had already been weaned onto solids.

It has been possible to roughly classify the larger fragments of food present in these specimens, by microscopic examination. Particles of several different types of parenchymatous tissue predominate; although there are also many finely comminuted fragments of leaf or stem epidermis, and masses of short segments of seemingly well-ground vascular strands. The last two classes may ultimately be identifiable from their histology. Some items could be immediately identified more precisely: in a few faecal fragments there were large numbers of seeds of a member of the chamomile tribe (Compositae, tribe Anthemidae; Fig. 13.2), and in one fragment, several broken seeds of the club-rush (*Scirpus* cf. *tuberosus/maritimus*). It is of particular interest that the seeds of club-rush are considerably more charred than was the faecal matrix, suggesting that they had been roasted (perhaps rather over-zealously) prior to ingestion.

*Evidence for Palaeolithic infants being weaned on plant mush*

The recovery of apparent infant faeces containing finely ground plant mush from 19th millennium bp Kubbaniya undermines the proposition of Binford (1968) and Hassan (1981, p. 227) that such foods were first used in this role in the terminal Pleistocene as part of a process leading directly to agriculture. Their model proposed that, once the potential of fine-ground plant mush for weaning infants was discovered, it allowed them to be weaned earlier, thus leading to shorter periods of lactational amenorrhoea, closer spacing of births, increased population, stress on carrying capacity of the land, and the consequent adoption of agriculture. Our evidence from Kubbaniya suggests that soft, mushable foods were both available and used for the weaning of infants at least nine millennia before their advent is proposed in the Binford model.

Of the plant-foods available to the Kubbaniyans, ethnographic parallels suggest that it was probably the 'root' foods that provided the bulk of the mush: even amongst farming groups, foods such as papyrus rhizomes were recognized as being particularly nourishing for children (Herodotus: *Lib.* II, 1.92). That chemical evidence showed a grinding stone to have been used on vegetable tissues low in protein may prove significant here, although further analyses of additional grinding stones are needed.

## Seasonality

The principal components of seasonality examined in this study were:

(i)    the seasons of availability of plant-food resources, (this, in turn, was considered in terms of seasonal patterns of plant growth, cycles of accessibility of the relevant vegetation formations, and palatability cycles of the relevant food organs);
(ii)   probable seasons of food gathering; and
(iii)  possible seasons of site occupation.

Palatability cycles were included under 'seasons of availability' because, once foods such as catstail rhizomes become fibrous and unpalatable in late summer, they are effectively unavailable as food.

Seasons of availability and gathering – (i) and (ii) above – were examined in respect of each of the food plants identified in the charred remains, and also in respect of those 'missing foods' (see above) likely to have served as carbohydrate staples but not identified in the remains so far. In this exercise, the same ecological and ethnographic models were used as in identifying possible 'missing foods' (see pp. 218–21). Figure 13.3 summarizes the conclusions reached in respect of both classes. The possible seasons of site occupation were assessed in respect of two contrasting scenarios: in the first, the Kubbaniyans were assumed to have stored no plant foods; in the second scenario, it was assumed they did.

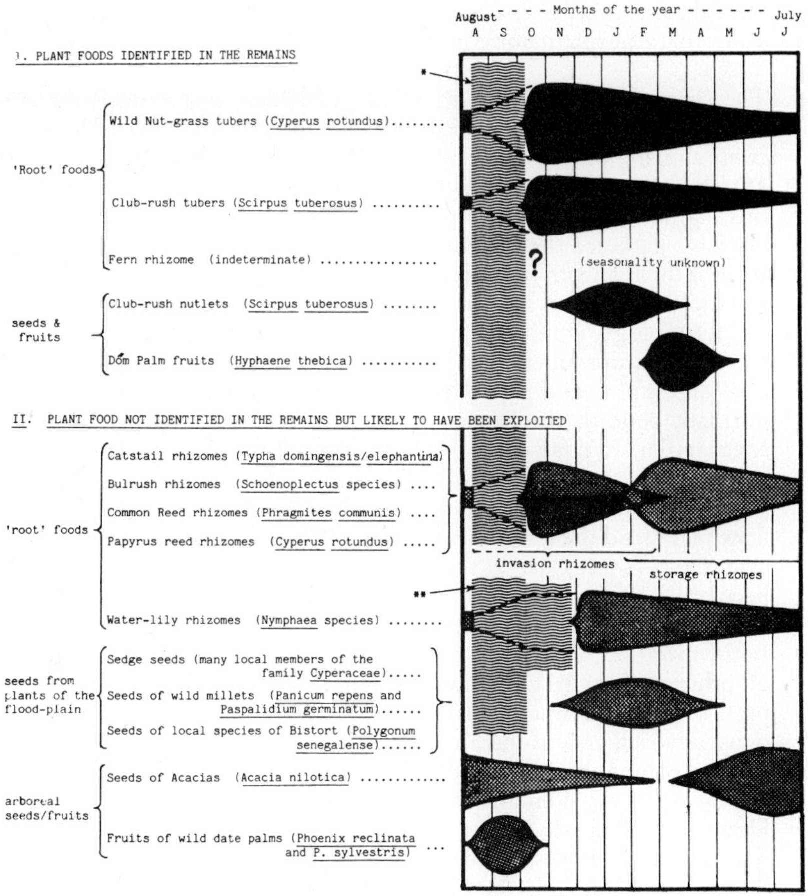

Months of the year
August - - - - - - - - - July
A  S  O  N  D  J  F  M  A  M  J  J

**1. PLANT FOODS IDENTIFIED IN THE REMAINS**

'Root' foods
- Wild Nut-grass tubers (Cyperus rotundus)........
- Club-rush tubers (Scirpus tuberosus) ..........
- Fern rhizome (indeterminate) .................

seeds & fruits
- Club-rush nutlets (Scirpus tuberosus) ........
- Dóm Palm fruits (Hyphaene thebica) ...........

? (seasonality unknown)

**II. PLANT FOOD NOT IDENTIFIED IN THE REMAINS BUT LIKELY TO HAVE BEEN EXPLOITED**

'root' foods
- Catstail rhizomes (Typha domingensis/elephantina)
- Bulrush rhizomes (Schoenoplectus species) ....
- Common Reed rhizomes (Phragmites communis) ....
- Papyrus reed rhizomes (Cyperus rotundus) .....
- Water-lily rhizomes (Nymphaea species) ........

invasion rhizomes    storage rhizomes

seeds from plants of the flood-plain
- Sedge seeds (many local members of the family Cyperaceae).....
- Seeds of wild millets (Panicum repens and Paspalidium germinatum)......
- Seeds of local species of Bistort (Polygonum senegalense)......

arboreal seeds/fruits
- Seeds of Acacias (Acacia nilotica) .............
- Fruits of wild date palms (Phoenix reclinata and P. sylvestris) ...

**Figure 13.3** Possible seasons of exploitation of major plant foods at Late Palaeolithic Wadi Kubbaniya – assuming no storage of food. The diagram is based on (a) ecological models of seasonal patterns of growth and availability of present-day populations of the same species growing under local conditions, and (b) ethnographic models of the response of recent hunter–gatherers to seasonal variations in the palatability of each food. No account could be taken of either possible periods of absence of the local populations from their Kubbaniyan sites, or possible storage of these plant foods (all the foods are storable to some degree, and, if the Kubbaniyans stored them in large quantities, their consumption could have continued for much longer than indicated in this diagram, if not throughout the year).★ The wave-patterned vertical band represents the time (c. two months) when floodwaters probably covered the upper floodplain.★★ This band is broader beside the entry for waterlilies as these probably grew in the lower parts of the floodplain and would therefore have been covered by water for a longer period, i.e. they were inaccessible for longer (from Hillman et al. in press).

Each of these aspects is discussed in detail in Hillman *et al.* (in press), and only a summary of the major conclusions is offered here, as follows.

(a)   The charred remains of plant foods so far identified from Kubbaniya indicate that at least some of the population were in occupation – either continuously or intermittently – between October and February/March at the very least; had they left any earlier, they would have missed the start of the dóm palm (*Hyphaene*) fruiting season and could not have gathered the fruits represented in the remains (see Fig. 13.3).

(b)   Even if the Kubbaniyans practised no food storage and were limited to just those food plants so far identified in the charred remains, their grinding technology would almost certainly have enabled them to render even the mature tubers of wild nut-grass and club-rush both palatable and digestible, and so allowed late-season exploitation of tubers dormant beneath the hardening mud of the floodplain (cf. Jones & Meehan Ch. 7, this volume). Occupation of the wadi could then have extended throughout the year – barring the 6–8 weeks of August and September when the floods were at their height and the foods of the floodplain (and the dune sites themselves) became inaccessible. Indeed, even the 6–8-week gap at the height of the floods could possibly have been bridged locally by the fish and large mammals which are also represented in the remains (Gautier *et al.* 1980, Gautier & van Neer in press).

(c)   In the more likely event that the Kubbaniyans also exploited a number of other potential staples which almost certainly grew locally (see pp. 218–21), and practised food storage, year-round occupation of this unusually rich area of the Nile Valley should have posed no problem – barring competition from other bands (for which there is no archaeological evidence; Wendorf & Close, pers. comm.).

(d)   However, the feasibility of year-round occupation is no proof of its practice. Nevertheless, during this hyper-arid period, they could not have survived outside the Nile valley system, and, as the Kubbaniya floodplain probably offered the richest resources of this part of the Nile Valley, it is difficult to suggest anywhere better that they could go. On the other hand, the availability of staple foods is clearly not the only factor determining patterns of mobility and sedentism, and seasonal shifts to other parts of the valley during late spring and high summer cannot be excluded.

## Conclusions

The results of our initial analyses of the plant remains from four of the dune-top sites at Kubbaniya, tentatively indicate:

(a)   a level of dietary diversity that was probably as broad as that of recent hunter–gatherers in arid-zone Africa;

(b)   the pre-eminent role of 'root' foods;
(c)   the use of fine-ground plant mush to wean Palaeolithic infants; and
(d)   the theoretical feasibility (in terms of plant-food availability) of year-round occupation of the wadi.

However, much more work remains to be done, especially on the application of chemical criteria for identifying the diverse array of parenchymatous food particles within the charred fragments of human faeces. There is every prospect that the next few years of laboratory work will add significantly to our knowledge of the diet and systems of plant exploitation of these early Nilotic peoples.

## Acknowledgements

Grateful thanks go to Chris Parker of the Weed Research Organization (now closed down by the Thatcher (British) Government as one of their 'invisible' cuts in Third World aid) for kindly providing additional bulk samples of *Cyperus rotundus* for nutrient analysis.

## References

Apperbekova, B. A. 1967. Isolation of substances from air-dried powdered root of *Cyperus rotundus*. *Farmatsiya* **16**, 36–41.

Banks, K. M. 1980. The grinding implements of Wadi Kubbaniya. In *Loaves and fishes. The prehistory of Wadi Kubbaniya*, F. Wendorf, R. Schild & A. Close (eds), 239–44. Dallas: Southern Methodist University, Department of Anthropology.

Bar-Yosef, O. & M. E. Kislev. 1989. Early farming communities in the Jordan Valley. In *Foraging and farming: the evolution of plant exploitation*, D. R. Harris & G. C. Hillman (eds), ch. 40. London: Unwin Hyman.

Binford, L. R. 1968. Methodological considerations in the archaeological use of ethnographic data. In *Man the hunter*, R. B. Lee & I. DeVore (eds), 268–73. Chicago: Aldine.

Binford, L. R. & S. R. Binford 1966. The predatory revolution: a consideration of the evidence for a new subsistence level. *American Anthropologist* **68**, 508–12.

Bulman, J. C. 1985. *A nutritional evaluation of the tuber of the plant* Cyperus rotundus. Unpublished MSc dissertation, Department of Nutrition and Food Science, King's College, University of London.

Butzer, K. W. 1959. Environment and human ecology in Egypt during Predynastic and early Dynastic times. *Bulletin de la Société de Géographie d'Egypte* **32**, 43–87.

Butzer, K. W. 1980. Pleistocene history of the Nile Valley in Egypt and Lower Nubia. In *The Sahara and the Nile*, M. A. J. Williams & H. Faure (eds), 248–76, Rotterdam: Balkema.

Butzer, K. W. & C. L. Hansen 1968. *Desert and river in Nubia*. Madison: University of Wisconsin Press.

Cane, S. 1989. Australian Aboriginal seed grinding and its archaeological record: a case study from the Western Desert. In *Foraging and farming: the evolution of plant exploitation*, D. R. Harris & G. C. Hillman (eds), ch. 6. London: Unwin Hyman.

Cauvin, J. 1985. Chronologie relatif et absolue dans le Néolitique du Levant Nord et d'Anatolie entre 10 000 et 8000 bp. In *Chronologie relatif et chronologie absolue dans le Proche Orient*, Lyon: CRNS, Maison de l'Orient Mediterranéen (Colloque international du CNRS, Lyon, Nov. 1986).

Colledge, S. M. 1988. In T. F. Potts, S. M. Colledge & Q. C. Edwards, Preliminary report on a sixth season of excavation by the University of Sydney at Pella in Jordan (1983/84). *Annual of the Department of Antiquities of Jordan* 29, 181–210 (and plates on pp. 329–40).

Coursey, D. G. 1973. Hominid evolution and hypogeous plant foods. *Man* 8, 634–5.

CSIR (Council of Scientific and Industrial Research) 1948–    . *The wealth of India: a dictionary of Indian raw materials and industrial products*. New Delhi: CSIR.

Davis, M. B. 1986. Climatic instability, time lags and community disequilibrium. In *Community ecology*, J. Diamond & T. J. Case (eds), 269–84. New York: Harper & Row.

Draper, P. 1976. Social and economic constraints on child life among the !Kung. In *Kalahari hunter–gatherers. Studies of the !Kung San and their neighbors*, R. B. Lee & I. DeVore (eds), 200–17. Cambridge, Mass.: Harvard University Press.

Donahue, D. J., A. J. T. Jull, T. W. Linick & T. Zahel. In press. AMS radiocarbon measurements on materials from Wadi Kubbaniya. In *The prehistory of Wadi Kubbaniya*. Vol. 2: *Palaeoeconomy, environment and stratigraphy*, F. Wendorf, R. Schild & A. Close (eds). Dallas: Southern Methodist University Press.

Eaton, S. B. & M. Konner 1985. Palaeolithic nutrition: a consideration of its nature and implications. *New England Journal of Medicine* 312, 283–89.

El Hadidi, N. 1980. Plant remains from Late Palaeolithic sites in Wadi Kubbaniya. In *Loaves and fishes. The prehistory of Wadi Kubbaniya*, F. Wendorf, R. Schild & A. Close (eds), 295–8. Dallas: Southern Methodist University, Department of Anthropology.

El Hadidi, N. & I. Springuel 1978. Plant life in Nubia (Egypt). I. Introduction: plant communities of the Nile islands at Aswan. *Taeckholmia* 9, 103–9.

El Hadidi, N. & I. Springuel. In press a. The natural vegetation of the Nile Region at Wadi Kubbaniya, North of Aswan (Egypt). In *The prehistory of Wadi Kubbaniya*. Vol. 2: *Palaeoeconomy, environment and stratigraphy*, F. Wendorf, R. Schild & A. E. Close (eds). Dallas: Southern Methodist University Press.

El Hadidi, N. & I. Springuel. In press b. Plant life in Nubia (Egypt). II. Floristic features of the natural vegetation of the island of the first cataract at Aswan, Egypt. *Taeckholmia*, in press.

Gautier, A. & W. van Neer. In press. Animal remains from the Late Palaeolithic sequence at Wadi Kubbaniya. In *The prehistory of Wadi Kubbaniya*. Vol. 2: *Palaeoeconomy, environment and stratigraphy*, F. Wendorf, R. Schild & A. Close (eds). Dallas: Southern Methodist University Press.

Gautier, A., P. Ballmann & W. van Neer 1980. Molluscs, fish, birds and mammals from the Late Palaeolithic in Wadi Kubbaniya. In *Loaves and fishes. The prehistory of Wadi Kubbaniya*, F. Wendorf, R. Schild & A. Close (eds), 281–93. Dallas: Southern Methodist University, Department of Anthropology.

Gott, B. 1982. The ecology of root use by the Aborigines of southern Australia. *Archaeology in Oceania* 17, 59–67.

Groube, L. 1989. The taming of the rain forests: a model for Late Pleistocene forest exploitation in New Guinea. In *Foraging and farming: the evolution of plant exploitation*, D. R. Harris & G. C. Hillman (eds), ch. 17. London: Unwin Hyman.

Hallam, S. J. 1977. The relevance of Old World archaeology to the first entrance of man into new worlds: colonisation seen from the antipodes. *Quaternary Research* 8, 128–34.

Hallam, S. J. 1983. The peopling of the Australian continent. *Indian Ocean Newsletter* **4**, 11–15.

Hallam, S. J. 1989. Plant usage and management in Southwest Australian Aboriginal societies. In *Foraging and farming: the evolution of plant exploitation*, D. R. Harris & G. C. Hillman (eds), ch. 8. London: Unwin Hyman.

Harlan, J. R. 1989. Wild grass-seed harvesting in the Sahara and Sub-Sahara of Africa. In *Foraging and farming: the evolution of plant exploitation*, D. R. Harris & G. C. Hillman (eds), ch. 5. London: Unwin Hyman.

Harris, D. R. 1976. Traditional systems of plant food production and the origins of agriculture in West Africa. In *Origins of African plant domestication*, J. R. Harlan, J. M. J. de Wet & A. B. L. Stemler (eds), 311–56. The Hague: Mouton.

Harris, D. R. 1986. Plant and animal domestication and the origins of agriculture: the contribution of radiocarbon accelerator dating. In *Archaeological results from accelerator dating*, J. A. J. Gowlett & R. E. M. Hedges (eds), 5–12. Oxford: Oxford Committee for Archaeology, Monograph no. 11.

Harris, D. R. 1987. The impact on archaeology of radiocarbon dating by accelerator mass spectrometry. *Philosophical Transactions of the Royal Society London*, **A323**, 23–43.

Harris, D. R. 1989. An evolutionary continuum of people-plant interaction. In *Foraging and farming: the evolution of plant exploitation*, D. R. Harris & G. C. Hillman (eds), ch. 1. London: Unwin Hyman.

Hassan, F. 1981. *Demographic archaeology*. New York: Academic Press.

Hassan, F. 1984. Environment and subsistence in Predynastic Egypt. In *From hunters to farmers: the causes and consequences of food production in Africa*, J. D. Clark & S. A. Brandt (eds), 57–64. Berkeley: University of California Press.

Hather, J. G. 1988. *The morphological and anatomical identification and interpretation of charred vegetative parenchymatous plant remains*. Unpublished PhD dissertation, Department of Human Environment, Institute of Archaeology, University College London.

Hill, C. L. In press. Petrography of Quaternary sediments in the Nile Valley of Upper Egypt. In *The Prehistory of Wadi Kubbaniya*. Vol. 2: *Palaeoeconomy, environment and stratigraphy*, F. Wendorf, R. Schild and A. E. Close (eds). Dallas: Southern Methodist University Press.

Hillman, G. C. 1981. Crop husbandry practices from charred remains of crops. In *Farming practice in British prehistory*, R. Mercer (ed.), 123–62. Edinburgh: Edinburgh University Press.

Hillman, G. C. 1986. Plant foods in ancient diet: the archaeological role of palaeo-faeces in general, and Lindow Man's gut contents in particular. In *Lindow Man: the body in the bog*, I. Stead, J. Bourke & D. R. Brothwell (eds), 99–115, 198–202. London: British Museum Publications.

Hillman, G. C. and M. D. Vaughan. Forthcoming. The lawn-mower hypothesis: an explanation for extreme species diversity in food-seed assemblages from arid zone archaeological sites.

Hillman, G. C., G. V. Robins, D. Oduwole, K. D. Sales & D. A. C. McNeil. 1983. Determination of thermal histories of archaeological cereal grains with electron spin resonance spectroscopy. *Science* **222**, 1235–6.

Hillman, G. C., S. M. Colledge & D. R. Harris 1989. Plant-food economy during the Epipalaeolithic period at Tell Abu Hureyra, Syria: dietary diversity, seasonality, and modes of exploitation. In *Foraging and farming: the evolution of plant exploitation*, D. R. Harris & G. C. Hillman (eds), ch. 13. London: Unwin Hyman.

Hillman, G. C., E. Madeyska & J. G. Hather. In press. Wild plant foods and diet at

Late Palaeolithic Wadi Kubbaniya: the evidence from charred remains. In *The prehistory of Wadi Kubbaniya*. Vol. 2: *Palaeoeconomy, environment and stratigraphy*, F. Wendorf, R. Schild & A. Close (eds). Dallas: Southern Methodist University Press.

Holm, L. G., D. L. Plucknett, J. V. Pancho & J. P. Herberger 1981. *The world's worst weeds: distribution and biology*. Honolulu: University of Hawaii Press (for East-West Food Institute).

Hopf, M. 1983. Jericho plant remains. In *Excavations at Jericho*, Vol. 5, K. M. Kenyon & T. A. Holland (eds), 576–621. London: British School of Archaeology at Jerusalem.

Hubbard, R. N. L. B. in press. A practical guide to field environmental archaeology. *Institute of Archaeology Bulletin, Occasional Papers*.

Johns, T. A. 1986a. Detoxification function of geophagy and domestication of the potato. *Journal of Chemical Ecology* **12**, 635–46.

Johns, T. A. 1986b. Chemical selection in Andean domesticated tubers as a model for the acquisition of empirical plant knowledge. In *Plants used in indigenous medicine and diet: bio-behavioral approaches*, N. L. Etkin (ed.), 266–88. South Salem, N.Y.: Redgrave.

Johns, T. A. 1989. A chemical–ecological model of root and tuber domestication in the Andes. In *Foraging and farming: the evolution of plant exploitation*, D. R. Harris & G. C. Hillman (eds), ch. 32. London: Unwin Hyman.

Jolly, C. T. 1970. The seed eaters: a new model of hominid differentiation based on baboon analogies. *Man* **5**, 5–26.

Jones, C. E. R. In press. Archaeochemistry: fact or fancy? In *The prehistory of Wadi Kubbaniya*. Vol. 2: *Palaeoeconomy, environment and stratigraphy*, F. Wendorf, R. Schild & A. Close (eds). Dallas: Southern Methodist University Press.

Jones, R. & B. Meehan. 1989. Plant foods of the Gidjingale: ethnographic and archaeological perspectives from northern Australia on tuber and seed exploitation. In *Foraging and farming: the evolution of plant exploitation*, D. R. Harris & G. C. Hillman (eds), ch. 7. London: Unwin Hyman.

Kajale, M. 1989. Mesolithic exploitation of wild plants in Sri Lanka: archaeobotanical study at the cave site of Beli-Lena. In *Foraging and farming: the evolution of plant exploitation*, D. R. Harris & G. C. Hillman (eds), ch. 15. London: Unwin Hyman.

Keepox, C. A. 1988. *Charcoal analysis, with particular reference to archaeological sites in Britain*. Unpublished PhD dissertation, Department of Human Environment, Institute of Archaeology, University College London.

Kinchi et al. 1983. Prostoglandin inhibiting substances in *Cyperus rotundus*. *Chemical Abstracts* **99**, 21845.

Kislev, M. E., O. Bar-Yosef & A. Gopher. In press. Domesticated and wild barley from early Neolithic Netiv Hagdud. *Israel Journal of Botany* **35**.

Knights, B. A., C. A. Dickson, J. H. Dickson & D. J. Breeze 1983. Evidence concerning Roman military diet at Bearsden, Scotland, in the 2nd century AD. *Journal of Archaeological Science* **10**, 139–52.

Kraybill, N. 1977. Preagricultural tools for the preparation of foods in the Old World. In *Origins of agriculture*, C. A. Reed (ed.), 485–521. The Hague: Mouton.

Latz, P. K. 1982. *Bushfires and bushtucker: Aborigines and plants in central Australia*. Unpublished MA dissertation, University of New England, Australia.

Lee, R. B. 1979. *The !Kung San. Men, women and work in a foraging society*. Cambridge: Cambridge University Press.

Lee, R. B. & I. DeVore 1968. Problems in the study of hunters and gatherers. In *Man the hunter*, R. B. Lee & I. DeVore (eds), 3–12. Chicago: Aldine.

Legge, A. J. 1986. Seeds of discontent: accelerator dates on charred plant remains from the Kebaran and Natufian cultures. In *Archaeological results from accelerator dating*, J. A. J. Gowlett & R. E. M. Hedges (eds), 13–21. Oxford: Oxford Committee for Archaeology, Monograph 11.

Livingstone, D. A. 1980. Environmental changes in the Nile headwaters. In *The Sahara and the Nile*, M. A. J. Williams & H. Faure (eds), 335–55. Rotterdam: Balkema.

Mann, A. 1972. Hominid and cultural origins. *Man* **7**, 379–86.

O'Connell, J. F., P. K. Latz & P. Barnett 1983. Traditional and modern plant use among the Alyawara of central Australia. *Economic Botany* **37**, 80–109.

Peters, C. R. & E. M. O'Brien 1981. The early hominid food niche: insights from the analysis of plant exploitation by *Homo*, *Pan* and *Papio* in eastern and southern Africa. *Current Anthropology* **22**, 127–40.

Pyramarn, K. 1989. New evidence on plant exploitation and environment during the Hoabinhian (Late Stone Age) from Ban Kao Caves, Thailand. In *Foraging and farming: the evolution of plant exploitation*, D. R. Harris & G. C. Hillman (eds), ch. 16. London: Unwin Hyman.

Robins, G. V., K. D. Sales, D. Oduwole, T. Holden & G. C. Hillman. 1986. Postscript: last minute results from ESR spectroscopy concerning the cooking of Lindow Man's last meal. In *Lindow Man: the body in the bog*, I. Stead, J. Bourke & D. R. Brothwell (eds), 140–2. London: British Museum Publications.

Roubet, C. in press. The grinding-stones of site E–78–3, Wadi Kubbaniya. In *The prehistory of Wadi Kubbaniya*. Vol. 3: *Late Palaeolithic archaeology*, F. Wendorf, R. Schild & A. Close (eds). Dallas: Southern Methodist University Press.

Roubert, C. in press. Report on site E–82–1: a workshop for the manufacture of grinding-stones at Wadi Kubbaniya. In *The Prehistory of Wadi Kubbaniya*. Vol. 3: *Late Palaeolithic archaeology*, F. Wendorf, R. Schild & A. E. Close (eds). Dallas: Southern Methodist University Press.

Schild, R. & F. Wendorf 1980. The Late Pleistocene lithostratigraphy and environment of Wadi Kubbaniya. In *Loaves and fishes. The prehistory of Wadi Kubbaniya*, F. Wendorf, R. Schild & A. E. Close (eds), 11–47. Dallas, Southern Methodist University, Department of Anthropology.

Schild, R. & F. Wendorf in press. The Late Pleistocene Nile in Wadi Kubbaniya. In *The prehistory of Wadi Kubbaniya*. Vol. 2: *Palaeoeconomy, environment and stratigraphy*, F. Wendorf, R. Schild & A. Close (eds), Dallas: Southern Methodist University Press.

Singh, P. N. & S. B. Singh 1980. A new saponin from mature tubers of *Cyperus rotundus*. Phytochemistry **19**, 2056.

Slocum, D. H., E. A. McGinnes & F. C. Bell 1978. Charcoal yield, shrinkage and density changes during carbonization of oak and hickory weeds. *Wood Science* **11**, 42–47.

Smith, M. A. 1989. Seed gathering in inland Australia: current evidence on the antiquity of the ethnohistorical pattern of exploitation. In *Foraging and farming: the evolution of plant exploitation*, D. R. Harris & G. C. Hillman (eds), ch. 18. London: Unwin Hyman.

Stahl, A. B. 1984. Hominid dietary selection before fire. *Current Anthropology* **25**, 151–68.

Stahl, A. B. 1989. Plant-food processing: implications for dietary quality. In *Foraging and farming: the evolution of plant exploitation*, D. R. Harris & G. C. Hillman (eds), ch. 11. London: Unwin Hyman.

Stemler, A. B. L. & R. H. Falk 1980. A scanning electron microscope study of cereal grains from Wadi Kubbaniya. In *Loaves and fishes. The prehistory of Wadi Kubbaniya*, F. Wendorf, R. Schild & A. Close (eds), 299–306. Dallas: Southern Methodist University, Department of Anthropology.

Stemler, A. B. 1984. The transition from food collecting to food production in Northern Africa. In *From hunters to farmers: the causes and consequences of food production in Africa*, J. D. Clark & S. A. Brandt (eds), 127–31. Berkeley: University of California Press.

Tan, J. P., R. W. Wenlock & D. H. Buss 1985. *Immigrant foods*. London: HMSO.

Tanaka, J. 1976. Subsistence ecology of central Kalahari San. In *Kalahari hunter–gatherers. Studies of the !Kung San and their neighbors*, R. B. Lee & I. DeVore (eds), 98–119. Cambridge, Mass.: Harvard University Press.

van Zeist, W. & J. A. H. Bakker-Heeres 1982. Archaeobotanical studies in the Levant. 1: Neolithic sites in the Damascus basin: Aswad, Goraife, Ramad. *Palaeohistoria* **24**, 165–256.

van Zeist, W. & J. A. A. Bakker-Heeres 1986. Archaeobotanical studies in the Levant. 3: Late Palaeolithic Mureybit. *Palaeohistoria* **26**, 171–99.

van Zinderen Bakker, E. M. & J. A. Coetzee 1972. A re-appraisal of Late Quaternary climatic evidence from tropical Africa. *Palaeoecology of Africa*, **7**, 151–81.

Wales, S. & J. Evans 1987. New possibilities of obtaining archaeological information from coprolites and similar remains. Paper presented to the Science and Archaeology Conference, University of Glasgow, September 1987.

Washburn, S. L. & C. S. Lancaster 1968. The evolution of hunting. In *Man the hunter*, R. B. Lee & I. DeVore (eds), 293–303. Chicago: Aldine.

Wendorf, F. & R. Schild 1979. Some implications of Late Palaeolithic cereal exploitation at Wadi Kubbaniya (Upper Egypt). In *Origin and early development of food-producing cultures in north-eastern Africa*. L. Krzyżaniak & M. Kobusiewicz (eds), 117–27. Poznań: Polska Akademia Nank-Oddział w Poznaniu.

Wendorf, F. & R. Schild 1980. Summary and conclusions. In *Loaves and fishes. The prehistory of Wadi Kubbaniya*, F. Wendorf, R. Schild & A. Close (eds), 259–79. Dallas: Southern Methodist University, Department of Anthropology.

Wendorf, F. & R. Schild 1984. The emergence of food production in the Egyptian Sahara. In *From hunters to farmers: the causes and consequences of food production in Africa*, J. D. Clark & S. Brandt (eds), 93–101. Berkeley: University of California Press.

Wendorf, F. & R. Schild 1986. Introduction. In *The prehistory of Wadi Kubbaniya. Vol. 1: The Wadi Kubbaniya skeleton: a Late Palaeolithic burial from southern Egypt*, F. Wendorf, R. Schild & A. Close (eds), 1–5. Dallas: Southern Methodist University Press.

Wendorf, F., R. Schild, A. E. Close, D. J. Donahue, A. J. T. Jull, T. H. Zabel, H. Więckowska, M. Kobusiewicz, B. Issawi & N. El Hadidi 1984. New radiocarbon dates on the cereals from Wadi Kubbaniya. *Science* **225**, 645–6.

Wendorf, F., R. Schild, N. El Hadidi, A. E. Close, M. Kobusiewicz, H. Więckowska, B. Isscawi & H. Haas 1979. The use of barley in the Egyptian Late Palaeolithic. *Science* **205**, 1341–7.

Wendorf, F., R. Schild & A. Close (eds) 1980. *Loaves and fishes. The prehistory of Wadi Kubbaniya*. Dallas: Southern Methodist University, Department of Anthropology.

Wendorf, F., R. Schild & A. E. Close (eds) 1986. *The prehistory of Wadi Kubbaniya. Vol. 1: The Wadi Kubbaniya skeleton: a Late Palaeolithic burial from southern Egypt*. Dallas: Southern Methodist University.

Wendorf, F., R. Schild & A. Close (eds) in press. *The prehistory of Wadi Kubbaniya. Vol. 2: Palaeoeconomy, environment and stratigraphy*. Dallas: Southern Methodist University Press.

Wendorf, F., R. Schild, A. E. Close, G. C. Hillman, A. Gautier, W. van Neer, D. J. Donahue, A. J. T. Jull & T. W. Linick 1988. New radiocarbon dates and Late Palaeolithic diet at Wadi Kubbaniya, Egypt. *Antiquity* **62**, 279–83.

Woodburn, J. 1968. An introduction to Hadza ecology. In *Man the hunter*, R. B. Lee & I. DeVore (eds), 49–55. Chicago: Aldine.

World Health Organisation (WHO) 1973. Technical report series no. 532.

Yellen, J. E. & R. B. Lee 1976. The Dobe/Du/da environment. Background to a hunting and gathering way of life. In *Kalahari hunter–gatherers. Studies of the !Kung San and their neighbors*, R. B. Lee & I. DeVore (eds), 28–46. Cambridge, Mass.: Harvard University Press.

# 14 *Plant-food economy during the Epipalaeolithic period at Tell Abu Hureyra, Syria: dietary diversity, seasonality, and modes of exploitation*

GORDON C. HILLMAN,
SUSAN M. COLLEDGE and
DAVID R. HARRIS

## Introduction

During the past two decades many theoretical discussions of prehistoric subsistence in Southwest Asia have been published. Some of these consider the region in the context of general models of the emergence of agriculture (e.g. Binford 1968, Cohen 1977, Harris 1977), whereas others focus on the region itself (e.g. Flannery 1969, Hassan 1977, Legge 1977, Reed 1977, Redman 1978, Moore 1985). These theoretical statements have reinforced the prevailing assumption that Southwest Asia was a major centre of early agriculture, and some of the models have helped to specify more precisely the processes involved in the transition from hunter–gatherer to agrarian economies. However, they have tended to be propounded at too high a level of generality to be readily tested against the existing archaeological record, which is itself too exiguous to yield decisive evidence of the transition to agriculture in the region.

Most of the Southwest Asian sites that were initially interpreted as the settlements of 'incipient agriculturalists' have subsequently proved either to represent relatively late stages in the emergence of crop husbandry, e.g. the Aceramic (pre-pottery) Neolithic levels at Jarmo and Can Hasan III, or to have yielded insufficient plant remains for any detailed analyses to be undertaken of patterns of subsistence and seasons of occupation, e.g. the Aceramic Neolithic levels at Ali Kosh, Beidha, Çayönü, Hacılar, and Jericho, and such Epipalaeolithic sites[1] as 'Ain Mallaha, Wadi Fellah (Nahal Oren), and Rakafet.

It is in this context that the site of Tell Abu Hureyra takes on particular significance. Occupation deposits at the site span the period during which the transition to agriculture is thought to have occurred, and the assemblage of plant and animal remains (together with that from Can Hasan III, French *et al.* 1972) is one of the first recovered in Southwest Asia that is sufficiently abundant and diverse to support well-founded inferences about the nature of the early subsistence economy.

## The site and its setting

Tell Abu Hureyra is a large mound site, half a kilometre in diameter, located at the edge of the Euphrates Valley in northern Syria at the junction between two contrasted ecosystems. On one side, stretching away to the south and west, is the arid *Artemisia*–Chenopodiaceae steppe. On the other side is the lush Euphrates Valley once covered by dense riverine forest but, by the early 1970s, dominated by irrigated cotton, *Tamarix* scrub, and *Phragmites* backswamp. The site was excavated during 1972 and 1973 by Moore (1975, 1979), but today, the tell lies drowned beneath the waters of the huge artificial Lake Assad.

The site was occupied during the Epipalaeolithic and the ensuing Neolithic. Conventional and accelerator radiocarbon dates obtained from bone and charred seeds range from *c.* 9200 bc to *c.* 6000 bc – uncalibrated[2] – (Harris 1986, 1987, Legge & Rowley-Conwy 1986, Moore *et al.* 1986). Moore's application of large-scale flotation recovery yielded exceptionally large, diverse assemblages of charred remains of plants; each of the 712 floated samples contained, on average, more than 500 identifiable seeds from over 70 different taxa (Hillman 1975). Many of the Epipalaeolithic samples also included charred remains of faeces, most of which appear to have originated from human infants (cf. Hillman *et al.* in press, Hillman Ch. 13, this volume). Animal bones were recovered in equally impressive quantities by dry sieving (Legge 1975, Legge & Rowley-Conwy 1986, 1987).

These bioarchaeological data from Abu Hureyra have been used to address a range of specific questions concerning pre- (and early-) agricultural modes of exploitation, dietary diversity, and seasons of occupation (see Moore *et al.* forthcoming). In this chapter, however, we focus on the pre-Neolithic plant-food economy and attempt to answer three main questions: (*a*) whether the Epipalaeolithic occupants of the site were already cultivating some of their main food plants; (*b*) how diverse was the range of plant foods exploited; and (*c*) during which season(s) was the site occupied during the Epipalaeolithic?

## Were the Epipalaeolithic populations already cultivating major food plants?

The possibility of pre-Neolithic, pre-domestication cultivation at both Abu Hureyra and at the slightly later occupation at Tell Mureybit (30 km to the north) has long been a source of controversy (van Zeist & Casparie 1968,

Hillman 1975, Cauvin 1977, 1978, 1986, Moore 1979, van Zeist & Bakker-Heeres 1984).

Subsequent to this Epipalaeolithic occupation, the Aceramic Neolithic occupants of Abu Hureyra cultivated a number of fully domesticated cereals, including emmer wheat *Triticum dicoccum*, einkorn wheat *T. monococcum*, 6-rowed hulled barley *Hordeum sativum* Jessen var. *hexastichum* (L.) Korn., and what appears to be domestic rye *Secale cereale* ssp. *cereale* (Hillman 1975). Charred remains of these crops have been identified from even the earliest of these Neolithic levels.

From the Epipalaeolithic levels, however, all the cereal remains were of wild species (as were all the other food plants), and included wild-type einkorn wheat *Triticum boeoticum* and what appears to be a wild form of annual rye *Secale cereale* ssp. *vavilovii* (Zohary & Hopf 1988). When first taken into cultivation, such crops would have retained the most obvious of their wild-type characteristics for an indefinite period – so long as certain harvesting and plot-rotation systems of cultivation were applied (see Hillman & Davies in press). Of itself, therefore, the presence of wild-type cereals offers no proof of the mode of subsistence.

From the start of the archaeobotanical work in 1972, therefore, priority was given to investigating the possibility that the wild-type cereals found in the Epipalaeolithic levels were already under cultivation as a case of 'pre-domestication agriculture'. This, together with two other possibilities, was discussed by Hillman (1975), and evidence from patterns of site distribution which appeared to favour the hypothesis of Epipalaeolithic cultivation was thereafter discussed by Moore (1979). In further testing this hypothesis, we have explored four different lines of evidence, as follows:

(a) Evidence from the histology of grain remains of the wild-type cereals themselves. Regrettably this approach proved unworkable.
(b) Evidence from the association of wild einkorn and wild annual rye with a second species of rye (*Secale montanum*) which is perennial and uncultivable. This line of evidence suggested that the cereals were gathered from wild stands and were not under cultivation.
(c) Evidence from weed floras. This again strongly suggested that the cereals were gathered from the wild.
(d) Indications from the proximity of stands of wild einkorn to Abu Hureyra. This approach proved inconclusive.

*(a) Evidence from the histology of remains of the wild-type cereals*

This line of investigation proved unworkable in the Abu Hureyra remains and produced no conclusions.

THE RATIONALE

Even though macro-morphological features such as rachis fragility and grain size or shape may often have remained unaltered during early cultivation, it is theoretically possible that certain histological characteristics in one or more layers of the grain pericarp and testa automatically underwent much more rapid changes. In the pulses, for example, it is possible that selection against dormancy during the earliest phases of cultivation may have induced changes (at the population level) not only in the presence of germination inhibitors but also, perhaps, in the structure of certain layers of the seed testa visible under the scanning electron microscope (SEM) (for detailed discussion, see Butler Ch. 24, this volume). It was therefore hoped that any such changes might survive in ancient remains, and that their first appearance in the archaeobotanical record might provide reliable clues to when the plants concerned were first taken into cultivation. It was further hoped that such criteria might be found not only in the seed coat of pulses, but also in one or more of the outer layers of cereal grains.

These hopes were reinforced by two sets of observations. In certain races of cereals, such as rye, differences between the dormancy behaviour of the two grains of any one spikelet have been linked with differences in bran colour, while in certain pulses dormancy differences have been found to be linked with differences in both testa colour and testa structure (Butler Ch. 24, this volume). These observations raised the possibility that dormancy-related colour differences in the bran of cereals such as rye might also be associated with differences in the bran cell-structure of the sort described by Körber-Grohne (1981) and Körber-Grohne & Peining (1980), and that these differences that might be observable under SEM in grains preserved by charring.

TESTING THE HYPOTHESIS

Extensive SEM examination (by S.M.C.) of the 'transverse cell' layer of grain testas from a range of modern populations of wild einkorn and wild rye growing in primary habitats or as weeds of cultivated cereals, failed to reveal any systematic differences in cell patterns or cell structure that could be attributed to differences in exposure to the selective pressures of agriculture. Indeed, the observed differences between such ecological groups in respect of any one histological criterion were matched by not only the differences between populations of any one 'ecotype' but also by variation between different groups of cells from the same central section of any one grain (Colledge, forthcoming). It was, in any case, quickly realized that the poor state of preservation of the transverse cell layers of the charred ancient grains of wild einkorn and wild rye, while sometimes allowing identification at the generic level, precluded all possibility of observing these more subtle differences. It was, in any case, often impossible to tell whether the smaller fragments of charred grain originated from the histologically more reliable central part of the parent grain.

(b)    *Evidence from the association of wild einkorn and cf. wild annual rye with a second species of wild rye,* Secale montanum, *which is perennial and uncultivable*

This line of evidence suggests that the wild-type cereals were gathered from wild stands and that they were not under cultivation.

THE MAJOR PLANT GROUPS AND PROBABLE SOURCE HABITATS (BASED ON MODERN ANALOGUES) → FRUIT TREES OF FOREST

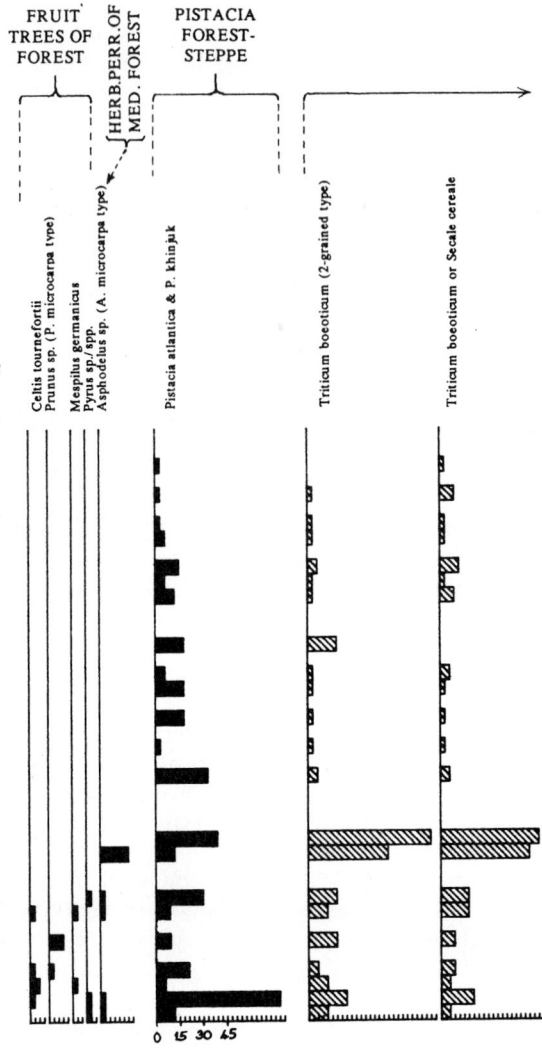

[HERB.PERR.OF MED. FOREST]

PISTACIA FOREST-STEPPE

Column labels (histograms):
- Celtis tournefortii / Prunus sp. (P. microcarpa type)
- Mespilus germanicus
- Pyrus sp./spp.
- Asphodelus sp. (A. microcarpa type)
- Pistacia atlantica & P. khinjik
- Triticum boeoticum (2-grained type)
- Triticum boeoticum or Secale cereale

| Phase no. | Trench & layer codes | Excavators deposit classification | Buckets of deposit floated | Vol. of charred remains recovered | Nos. of items identified |
|---|---|---|---|---|---|
| 1 | E-400 | occupation debris } | 174 | 192 ml | 186 |
| | E-402 | ·· | 104 | 154 ml | 368 |
| | E-405 | ·· | 90 | 133 ml | 488 |
| | E-411 | ·· | 104 | 192 ml | 273 |
| | E-412 | ·· | 210 | 176 ml | 490 |
| | E-420 | ··/floor | 60 | 112 ml | 293 |
| | E-418 | ··/· | 312 | 245 ml | 343 |
| | E-419 | ··/· | 180 | 304 ml | 390 |
| 2 | E-427 | hearth | 3 | 42 ml | 244 |
| | E-425 | occ.debris | 132 | 560 ml | 189 |
| | E-426 | ·· | 324 | 168 ml | 317 |
| | E-430 | ·· | 144 | 424 ml | 540 |
| | E-438 | ·· | 198 | 224 ml | 274 |
| | E-449 | ·· | 126 | 472 ml | 612 |
| | E-454 | firepit | 36 | 240 ml | 13 |
| | E-455 | occ.debris | 60 | 360 ml | 1280 |
| | E-457 | ·· | 18 | 144 ml | 1650 |
| 1 | E-467 | ··at pit top | 156 | 512 ml | 740 |
| | E-468 | ····· | 93 | 136 ml | 873 |
| | E-473 | ·· of 3 pits | 6 | 11 ml | 53 |
| | E-474 | ·· of 2 pits | 36 | 152 ml | 705 |
| | E-469 | occupation | 222 | 528 ml | 810 |
| | E-470 | debris of pit | 210 | 222 ml | 967 |
| | E-471 | complex no.2 | 30 | 98 ml | 256 |

0  15  30  45

**Figure 14.1**  Frequencies of charred seeds and fruits from Epipalaeolithic levels at Tell Abu Hureyra, Syria. Frequencies are expressed as numbers of items per 100 litres of excavated deposit. Most taxa which were present as single occurrences have been excluded, and many species are combined. (In some cases where the scores from several different taxa have been combined in one histogram [with solid shading], the histograms for the component taxa are also drawn, but are distinguished by their stipple shading.) In almost all cases, the seeds and fruits are edible, and the only plausible explanation for their presence on-site in charred form is that they had been gathered as food.

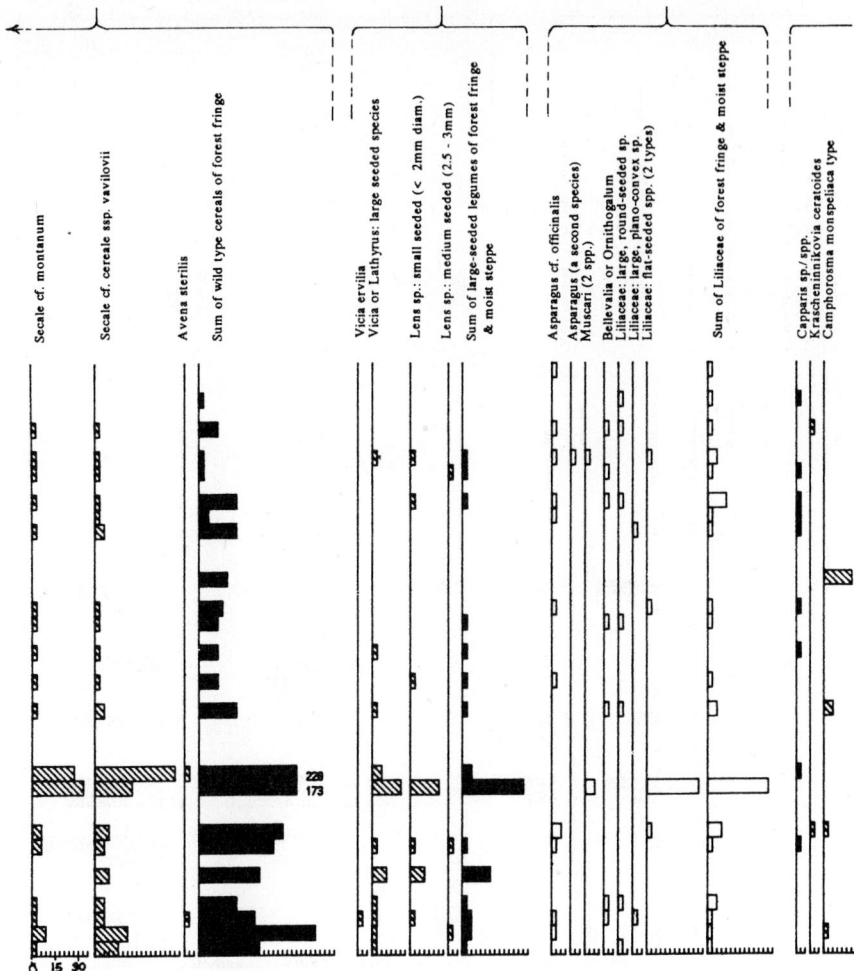

WILD CEREALS TODAY TYPICAL OF
OPEN OAK FOREST AND ECOTONE
BETWEEN OAK FOREST & STEPPE

EDIBLE WILD
LEGUMES OF
SAME ZONES

LILIACEAE - PROBABLY
OF FOREST FRINGE
THROUGH TO MOIST STEPPE

Secale cf. montanum

Secale cf. cereale ssp. vavilovii

Avena sterilis

Sum of wild type cereals of forest fringe

Vicia ervilia
Vicia or Lathyrus: large seeded species

Lens sp.: small seeded (< 2mm diam.)

Lens sp.: medium seeded (2.5 - 3mm)

Sum of large-seeded legumes of forest fringe & moist steppe

Asparagus cf. officinalis

Asparagus (a second species)

Muscari (2 spp.)

Bellevalia or Ornithogalum
Liliaceae: large, round-seeded sp.
Liliaceae: large, plano-convex sp.
Liliaceae: flat-seeded spp. (2 types)

Sum of Liliaceae of forest fringe & moist steppe

Capparis sp./spp.
Krascheninnikovia ceratoides
Camphorosma monspeliaca type

228
173

0  15  90

Scale (on horizontal axis) = nos. of charred seeds or fruits per 200 litres of deposit.

■ = edible (or potentially edible) seeds and fruits.

▨ = {edible seeds or fruits whose histogram has also contributed to a solid-shaded summary histogram for the group as a whole.

□ = inedible seeds or fruits possibly used medicinally, as dyes, for thatching, or for bedding.

Accelerator (AMS) C14 dates on charred grains of wild einkorn and charred bones of *Bos* and gazelle range from 11,090 bp in the basal Mesolithic levels to 10,250 bp in the upper Meso. levels.

EDIBLE-SEEDED SHRUBLETS OF
STEPPE AND DESERT (mainly
winter-flg.Chenopodiaceae)

PERENNIAL TUSSOCK-GRASSES
OF STEPPE & FOREST FRINGE
(ALL EDIBLE-GRAINED)

Kochia prostrata type
Salsola - sect. Arbuscula type
Noaea mucronata or Salsola sp. (not Arbuscula)
Hammada or Salsola sect. Salsola type
Anabasis or Noaea type
Aellenia autrani
Suaeda (non-fruticosa) or small Salsola
Chenopodiaceae - tribe Champhorosmae indet. (cf. Chenolea arabica)
Sum of shrubby Chenopodiaceae of steppe
Salvia sp. (S. cryptantha type)
Other labiates (Thymbra, Phlomis, etc.)
Sum of shrubs of steppe

Stipa parviflora type

Stipa holoserices, S. hohenackeriana & S. barbata types

Stipa gigantea type
Sum of all Stipa spp.

108
233

152
359

260
599

106

130

0  15  30  45

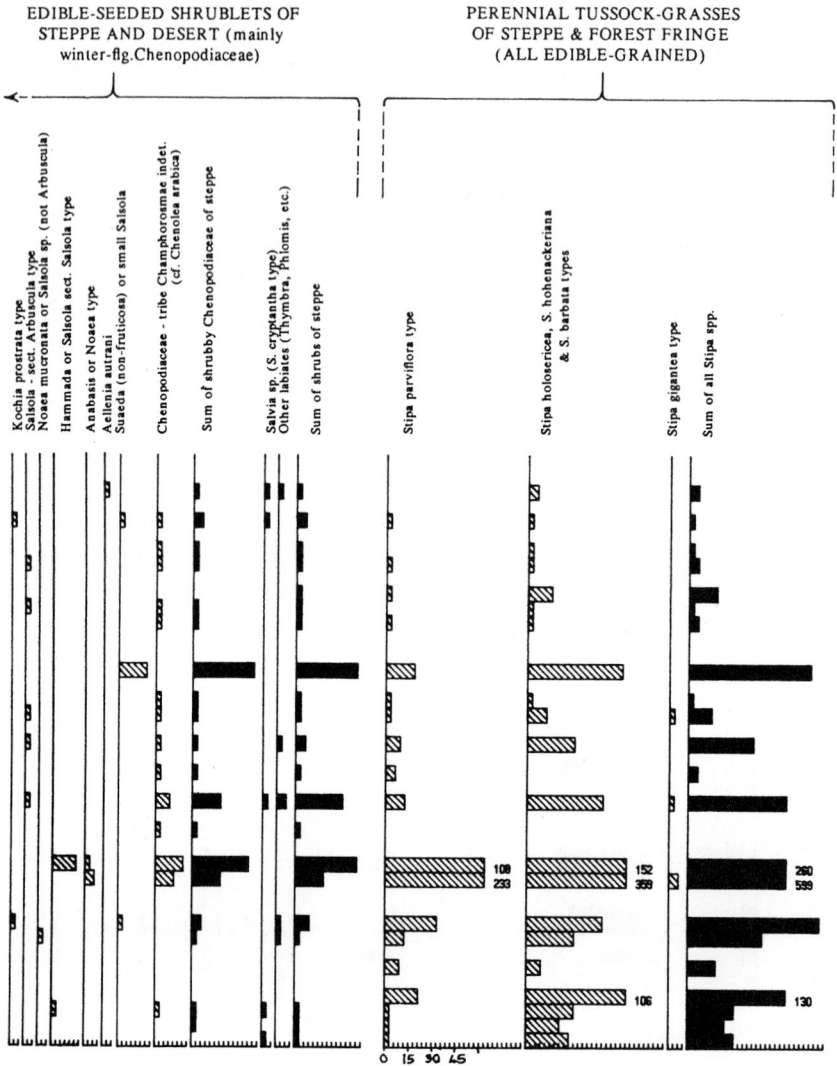

Scale (on horizontal axis) = nos. of charred seeds or fruits per 200 litres of deposit.

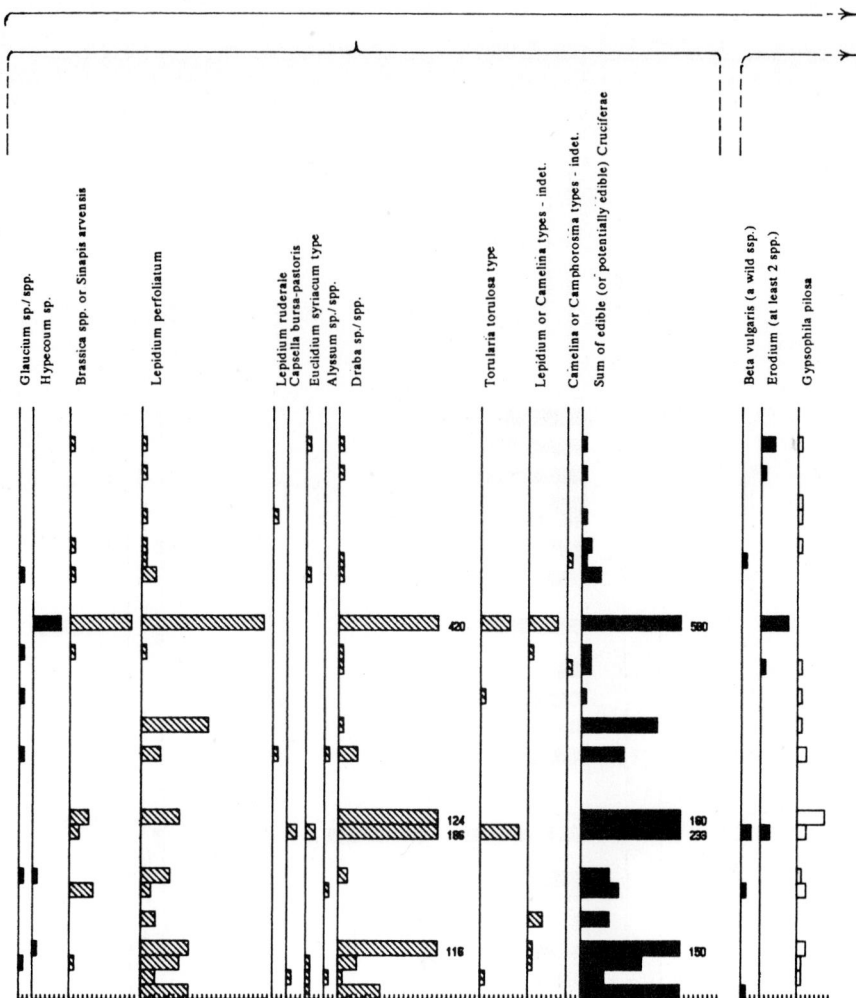

HERBACEOUS PLANTS (MAINLY ANNUALS) OF STEPPE & OPEN FOREST
(many are today typical of steppe, but others have broader spectrum affinities)

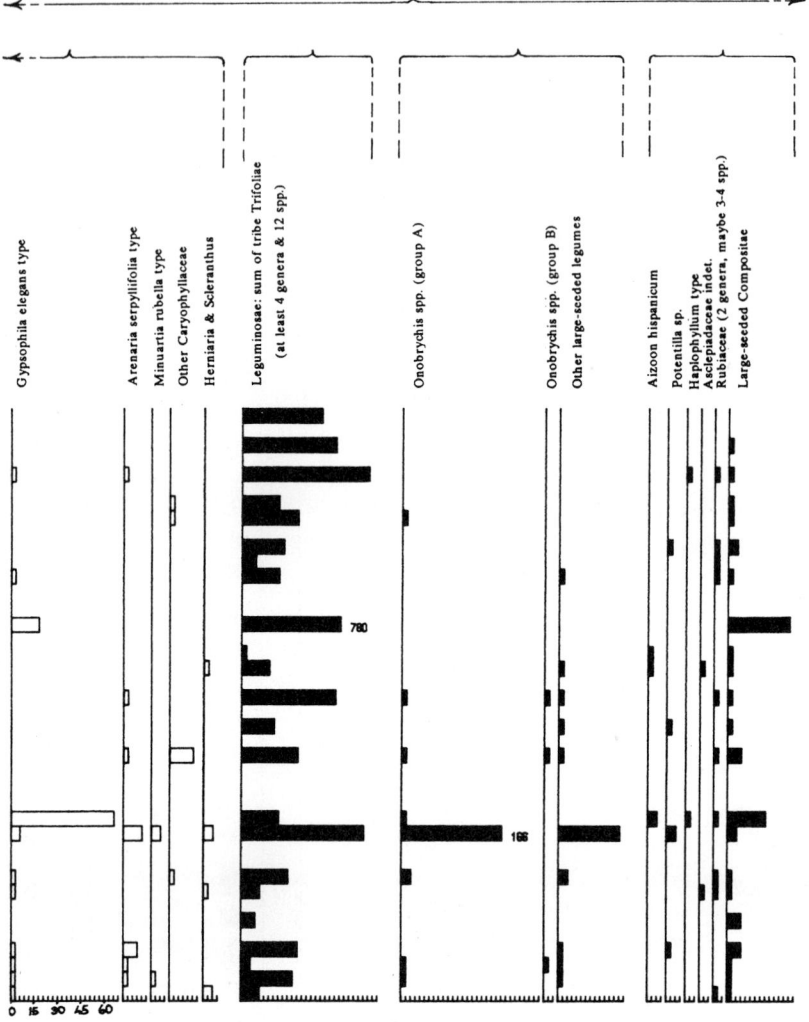

Scale (on horizontal axis) = nos. of charred seeds or fruits per 200 litres of deposit.

BORAGINACEAE OF STEPPE (AND FOREST FRINGE) WITH
SILICIFIED NUTLETS WHICH SURVIVE WITHOUT CHARRING
AND ARE RELATIVELY OVER-REPRESENTED

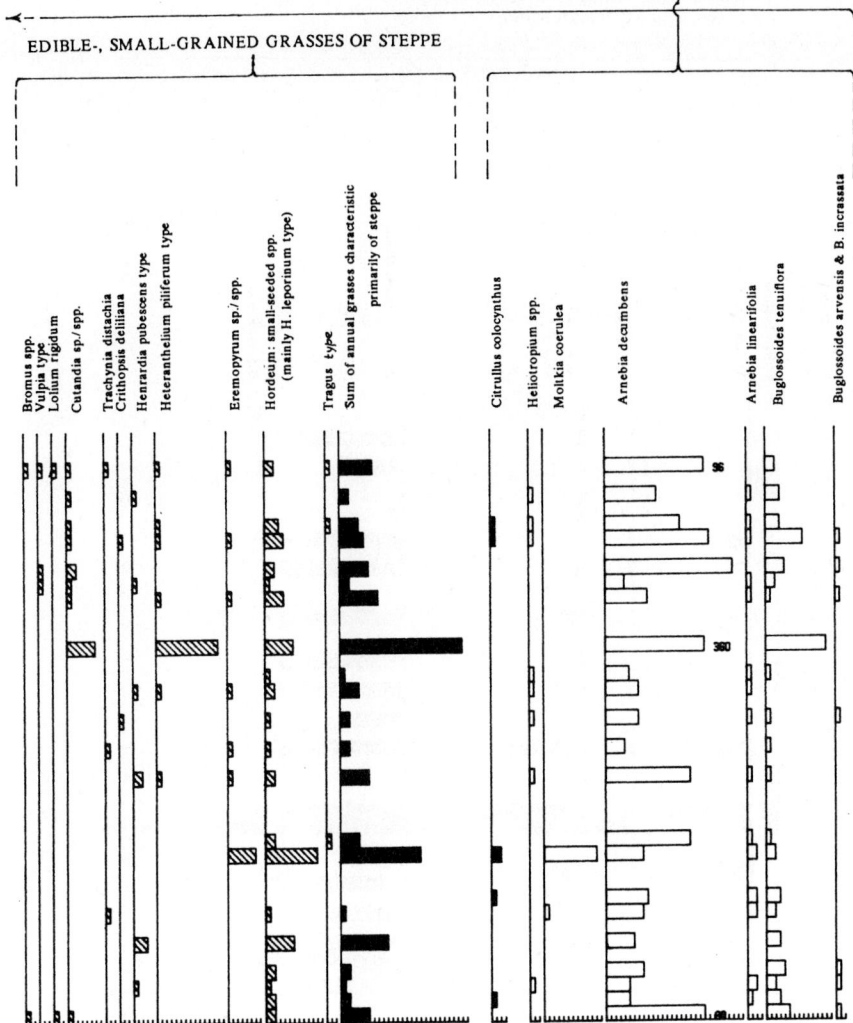

EDIBLE-, SMALL-GRAINED GRASSES OF STEPPE

Bromus spp.
Vulpia type
Lolium rigidum
Cutandia sp./spp.
Trachynia distachia
Crithopsis delileana
Henrardia pubescens type
Heteranthelium piliferum type
Eremopyrum sp./spp.
Hordeum: small-seeded spp. (mainly H. leporinum type)
Tragus type
Sum of annual grasses characteristic primarily of steppe

Citrullus colocynthus
Heliotropium spp.
Moltkia coerulea
Arnebia decumbens
Arnebia linearifolia
Buglossoides tenuiflora
Buglossoides arvensis & B. incrassata

EDIBLE PLANTS OF WADIS,
WADI-BANKS, VALLEYS AND
N-ENRICHED RUDERAL HABS.

**Scale** (on horizontal axis) = nos. of charred seeds or fruits per 200 litres of deposit.

PLANTS TYPICAL OF EUPHRATES VALLEY-BOTTOM
- ALL WITH EDIBLE SEEDS

BEDDING &
THATCHING
PLANTS

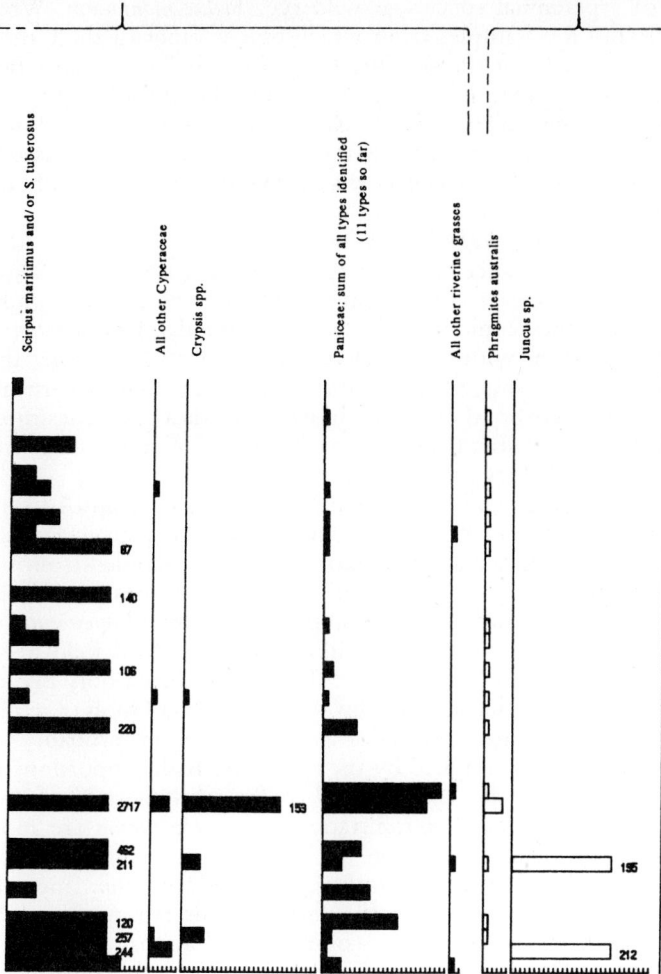

(i)   Our identifications indicated that the remains of *T. boeoticum* and what appears to be wild annual rye *Secale cereale* ssp. *vavilovii* (both potentially cultivable annuals) were consistently accompanied by remains of a perennial species of wild rye, *Secale montanum*. While there were too few samples from which one or other of these three cereals were absent for the significance of their apparent association to be properly tested, it can be seen from Figure 14.1 that the variations in abundance of *S. montanum* appear to follow closely those of wild einkorn and the other wild rye. This apparent association suggests that *S. montanum* was harvested together with the other two cereals.

(ii)  As a tufted perennial, *S. montanum* is not tolerant of tillage or other forms of soil disturbance. Zohary (pers. comm.) notes that 'small patches of *S. montanum* could maintain themselves in areas under cultivation, but they could not penetrate crop stands'. If *S. montanum* really was harvested with the other two wild cereals, therefore, this intolerance of tillage suggests that the associated annuals – einkorn and cf. annual rye – were not themselves under cultivation but were simply harvested from wild stands (however, the effects of cultivation with digging sticks in this regard remain uncertain).

(iii) It is unlikely that the relatively small number of grains identified as *S. montanum* derived from stray weeds which happened to survive tillage in fields of cultivated wild-type einkorn. This is concluded from the fact that its grains are probably substantially under-represented in the charred remains: in studies of over 50 populations of *S. montanum* in present-day southeastern Turkey, Hillman (unpublished field notes 1969–76) found that, on most plants, the ears produced only one or two fertile grains. In the stands from which the Abu Hureyra grains were harvested, therefore, plants of *S. montanum* were probably far more abundant than is implied by the relatively small proportions of charred cereal grains they contributed to the total assemblage (see Fig. 14.1) and such dense concentrations of *S. montanum* are most unlikely to occur under cultivation.

(iv)  The suggestion that all three cereals were harvested from the same wild stands is further reinforced by the fact that, in recent times, *S. montanum* has been a conspicuous component of almost all of those primary stands of wild einkorn studied by one of the authors in eastern Turkey. Indeed, in harvesting-experiments in natural stands of wild einkorn in primary habitats, large numbers of spikelets of *S. montanum* (most of them sterile) were consistently and unavoidably gathered together with the spikelets of wild einkorn.

(v)   It could perhaps be argued that the grains of *S. montanum* were gathered separately from wild stands while the einkorn came from cultivated fields. However, the low grain yield from most ears of *S. montanum* is likely to have made this an unacceptably energy-expensive strategy, if, indeed, the *S. montanum* at Epipalaeolithic Abu Hureyra yielded as little grain as do present-day populations of *S. montanum* in southeastern Turkey.

This second line of evidence therefore appears to suggest that the wild-type einkorn and the *cf.* wild-type annual rye were probably gathered from wild stands rather than cultivated.

## (c)    Evidence from weed floras

This line of evidence again suggests that the wild-type cereals were gathered from wild stands and were not under cultivation.

RATIONALE

Plants such as *Adonis dentata*, *A. aestivalis*, *Papaver* spp., some *Glaucium* spp., *Hypecoum* spp., *Brassica* spp., some *Lepidium* and *Camelina* spp., many of the *Trifoliae* and *Vicieae*, *Heliotropium* spp., *Arnebia* and *Buglossoides* spp., *Muscari* and *Bellevallia* spp., *Vulpia* spp., small-seeded *Hordeum* species, *Setaria glauca*, *Echinochloa colonum*, and *E. crus-galli* are conventionally regarded as typical segetals or ruderals, i.e. weeds of arable fields and other areas of disturbance. If it is correct to assume that such species are rare outside agriculture and that they become abundant only under cultivation, then an abundance of their seed remains in association with grain or chaff remains of cultivable wild-type cereals might suggest that the cereals were under cultivation.

Such an association characterized the Abu Hureyra assemblage: most Epipalaeolithic samples proved to contain large numbers of seeds of ostensibly segetal species associated with grain remains of wild-type einkorn. However, before concluding that this association of cereals and 'weeds' proved that the cereals were under cultivation, it was first necessary to test the conventional view that an abundance of these 'weedy' taxa is uniquely indicative of cultivation and that such species are relatively rare in any 'natural' (primary) habitats of the Near East.

FIELD STUDIES TO TEST THE ASSUMPTION THAT 'WEEDY' SPECIES ARE RARE OUTSIDE SEGETAL AND RUDERAL HABITATS

Fieldwork undertaken with this broad objective in the 1970s (by G.C.H.) initially appeared to confirm the accepted view of the primarily segetal/ ruderal status of many of the better known 'weedy' species. The fieldwork was carried out in Syria and Turkey, and included many different areas of steppe and forest–steppe which had been either very lightly grazed, heavily grazed, recently cultivated for the first time, or exposed to many years of cultivation. These field studies suggested that, in general, the diversity and density of the segetal flora increased rapidly during the first years of steppe cultivation and then levelled off.

However, further floristic surveys were undertaken by us in the central Syrian steppe in the spring of 1983, following the wettest winter in the living memory of local Bedouin. Many of the 'weedy' annuals and ephemerals had germinated in great profusion, producing, in many locations, continuous carpets of colour. Particularly prominent were *Adonis dentata*, *A. microcarpa*, *A. aestivalis*, *Papaver* spp., *Roemeria hybrida*, *Hypecoum* spp., *Diplotaxis harra*, *Malva aegyptia*, several *Erodium* spp., many members of the *Trifoliae*, *Vicia* spp., *Arnebia decumbens*, *A. linearifolia*, *Buglossoides tenuiflora*, *B. arvensis*, *Koelpinnia linearifolia*, *Muscari* spp., *Ornithogalum* spp., *Vulpia myuros*, *Crithopsis delileana*, *Eremopyrum* spp., *Heteranthelium piliferum*, *Hordeum leporinum*, *Anisantha rubens*, *A. fascicularis*, *A. tectorum*, *A. madritensis*, *Bromus danthoniae*, and *B. japonicus*. Such species are normally present as relatively minor components of the steppe flora, and achieve higher frequencies only in damp depressions and areas of natural disturbance, such as moderately mobile mountain screes. In 1983, however, almost *all* those areas of uncultivated steppe which were not exposed to very heavy grazing from domestic sheep and goats were found to support populations of these same 'weed' species at densities comparable to those of weed-infested arable fields.

The implication of this result for the archaeobotany of steppe sites is clear. Conspicuous abundance of seeds of supposedly 'segetal' species in association with remains of wild-type cereals or pulses does *not* necessarily indicate that the cereals or pulses were under cultivation; such 'weed' seeds could equally have derived from natural steppe.

REMAINS OF 'WEED' FLORAS FROM EPIPALAEOLITHIC ABU HUREYRA

The charred 'weed' seeds identified in these early levels include the following: *Hypecoum* sp. or spp., *Brassica* sp./ *Sinapis arvensis*, *Lepidium ruderale*, *L. perfoliatum*, *Draba* sp. or spp., cf. *Camelina* sp., *Arenaria serpyllifolia*, *Gypsophila pilosa*, *G. elegans*, *Atriplex tatarica*, several species of *Trifolium*, *Trigonella*, *Medicago* and *Melilotus*, *Onobrychis*, (2 or more possible weedy species), *Rumex* spp., *Heliotropium* spp., *Arnebia decumbens*, *A. linearifolia*, *Buglossoides tenuifolia*, *Hordeum leporinum*, *Eremopyrum* spp., *Heteranthelium piliferum* and *Crithopsis delineana*.

On the basis of our fieldwork (above), the seeds of such plants could have arrived on site (and ended up on household fires) by one of two routes: (a) from weeds growing in crops of wild-type cereals and brought in with the harvested crop, and (b) seeds of wild plants of the steppe gathered as food, medicines, dyes, or hallucinogens. The question to be resolved, therefore, was: which of these alternatives is supported by the archaeological evidence? We used two lines of evidence.

First, we compared the Neolithic and Epipalaeolithic 'weed' species for their edibility. The fully domesticated crops of the Neolithic levels were clearly under cultivation, and it is inevitable that many weed seeds would have arrived in the settlement along with the harvested grain. Appropriately, the weed seeds of the Neolithic involved the usual mixture of toxic and non-toxic types. By contrast, in the Epipalaeolithic levels, all the most toxic 'weed' species were missing. Instead, all the 'weed' seeds from these levels were either (a) edible species such as *Atriplex*, *Aizoon*, and several grasses; (b) species such as small-seeded legumes, and several Cruciferae such as *Lepidium* spp., which are readily detoxified; or (c) species which are traditionally valued as a source of dyes and medicines, such as *Arnebia* and *Buglossoides*. (All references to ethnographic parallels are excluded here but will be included in Moore *et al.* forthcoming.) This difference between Neolithic and Epipalaeolithic 'weed' floras suggests that the 'weed' species of the Epipalaeolithic were selected primarily for their edibility (or, in a few cases as dyes or medicines), i.e. that they were specifically gathered from the wild rather than arriving fortuitously with the crops.

Secondly, we compared the degree of correlation between the abundance of remains of 'weed' seeds and remains of cereal grain in both the Neolithic and Epipalaeolithic levels. In the Neolithic samples, the abundance of all the typical 'weed' seed species broadly parallels the abundance of crop remains. In the Epipalaeolithic samples, by contrast, the abundance of many of the most typical 'weed' species (e.g. *Arnebia decumbens*, *Buglossoides tenuifolia*, *Hordeum leporinum*, and the many Trifoliae types) follows the opposite pattern to the cereals, suggesting, once again, that they did not arrive as contaminants of cereal crops, but were gathered separately (see Fig. 14.1). (It is possible that the increase in apparent utilization of seeds of Trifoliae and Graminae represents an attempt to compensate for decreased availability of wild cereals due to increasing aridity during the Epipalaeolithic occupation).

Had the wild-type cereals of the Epipalaeolithic been under cultivation, we would expect the abundance of weed-seed remains to follow a pattern of changes in frequency similar to that in the ensuing Neolithic. Instead, the pattern of 'weed' seeds suggests that many of them were gathered separately from the wild cereals. Our field studies further indicate that most, if not all, of these 'weed' species would have grown in considerable abundance in the adjacent areas of steppe, as long as (a) the steppe was slightly damper than today (this is indicated by the pollen record; van Zeist & Bottema 1982), and (b) grazing pressure was less intense than today (this was certainly the case, cf. Legge & Rowley-Conwy 1987).

### (d)  Indications from the probable proximity to Abu Hureyra of wild stands of cereals during the Epipalaeolithic occupation

Because this line of evidence produced no firm conclusions, and in deference to space constraints, only a brief outline is offered here.

The basic rationale used in this fourth line of evidence is that, had wild einkorn (and what appears to be wild annual rye) grown naturally in dense stands close to the site, then the Epipalaeolithic population is unlikely to have bothered to cultivate it.

(i)   It is generally agreed that dense primary stands of wild einkorn are today confined to more open areas of the ecotone between *Quercus*–Rosaceae forest and steppe (see, for example Harlan & Zohary 1966,

Zohary & Hopf 1988, Zohary Ch. 22, this volume). (Wild annual rye occurs in the same general zone, although there are some problematic exceptions; Sencer 1974, Sencer & Hawkes 1985, Zohary pers. comm., Zohary & Hopf 1988.)

(ii)  The sparse pollen record suggests that, at 9000 bc, the ecotone between oak forest and steppe probably came no closer to Abu Hureyra than *c.* 150 km to the west (van Zeist & Bottema 1982). This view is tentatively reinforced by the apparent absence of oak wood-charcoal in a range of Epipalaeolithic samples examined specifically to this end (Alvin 1983, unpublished manuscript) and by the complete absence of acorn remains. On the other hand, the lowest Epipalaeolithic levels produced a few fruit remains of hackberry (*Celtis*) and three members of Rosaceae which are all characteristic of the oak-forest zone. (They are all absent from higher levels.) This may suggest that forest was not so far away as to pre-empt occasional exploitation of forest fruits – if only on the more distant hunting forays. However, this is not persuasive evidence for einkorn having been close enough for its systematic exploitation as a staple.

(iii)  Present-day field studies reveal the existence of stands of *Pistacia atlantica* woodland on isolated mountains in the Syrian steppe well beyond the limits of oak forest, though not within 50 km of Abu Hureyra (see e.g. Parbot 1957, and the final vegetation map in M. Zohary 1973). The presence of charred remains of *Pistacia* nutlets in all our Epipalaeolithic samples (see Fig. 14.1) further suggests that, at that time, *Pistacia* woodland of this sort was growing not far from Abu Hureyra. This raises a hitherto unresolved question: can (and could) wild einkorn grow in *Pistacia* woodland, and does the fact that the Epipalaeolithic Abu Hureyrans had access to *Pistacia* automatically imply that they had equally ready access to wild einkorn?

Detailed field surveys in 1983 and 1985 of all recorded areas of remnant *Pistacia* woodland in Syria revealed that, unlike wild barley, einkorn does not grow in these areas today. If it is assumed that this non-association was also true of the Near East at 9000 bc, then it is clear that our evidence from Abu Hureyra for local availability of *Pistacia* fruits offers no basis for assuming that wild einkorn also grew close enough to the settlement to pre-empt attempts at its cultivation.

However, it should be noted that it can be dangerous to rely on uniformitarian assumptions of plant-community structure – such as in this case where present patterns of non-association of wild einkorn with *Pistacia* woodland are suggested to have existed in similar form in the past. This caveat applies especially to periods of rapid climatic change and plant migration such as the Late Pleistocene (cf. Davis 1986).

(iv)  In line with this last cautionary comment, Hillman (in press) has argued that, with the increases in moisture at the end of the Pleistocene in the northern Levant and Antitaurus Mts, wild einkorn would have spread into areas of steppe well in advance of the spreading forest frontiers. In consequence, the absence of oak or Rosaceae charcoal (as indicators of nearby oak-forest fringe) cannot be used as evidence for the absence of einkorn. The einkorn may therefore have been closer to Abu Hureyra than charcoal and pollen data seem to imply when interpreted via modern models of wild-cereal ecology.

(v) In addition, Blumler (1984, forthcoming & pers. comm.) has argued convincingly on the basis of ecological studies in both California and Southwest Asia that, even without rapid climatic change, annuals such as wild einkorn could have extended into the steppe well beyond the limits of oak forest in many of those areas where oak-forest distribution is limited by its relative inability to compete 'on plains, deep soils, fine-textured soils, and where summer drought is severe' (Blumler pers. comm.). A perfect example of such conditions exists in the gently sloping terrain between Abu Hureyra and the edge of the forest zone c. 150 km to the west. This again suggests therefore that the absence of oak charcoal in the Hureyra remains cannot be used to exclude the possibility that einkorn grew in dense stands a short distance to the west. Indeed, although it is too dry for einkorn to survive there today, Blumler notes that 'it would probably not need a very great climatic change to bring the area within the einkorn belt' (pers. comm.).

(vi) It would, therefore, appear that the different models predicting the proximity of wild einkorn currently disagree. Certainly, they fail to resolve the question of whether dense stands of wild einkorn grew sufficiently close to Abu Hureyra to pre-empt attempts at its cultivation, although the Blumler model is persuasive.

### Summary of evidence for and against Epipalaeolithic cultivation of wild cereals

Viewed separately, the lines of evidence summarized in each of the sections a–d (above) remain inconclusive. Taken together, however, lines (b) and (c) strongly suggest that the wild-type cereals present in the Epipalaeolithic levels at Abu Hureyra were not cultivated.

Of the many food plants represented in the remains, these wild-type cereals would have been the most amenable to cultivation (cf. Bar-Yosef & Kislev Ch. 40, this volume). It is therefore probable, that, if the cereals were not cultivated, then no other food plants were cultivated either, and that all of them were gathered from wild stands. However, whether these stands of wild food plants were subject to any of the forms of 'pre-agricultural' intervention outlined by Harris Ch. 1, this volume) remains unclear.

It should be noted that, if this conclusion is correct, the work of Cane (Ch. 6, this volume) would suggest that the source of our seed foods (including the wild einkorn and what appears to be wild annual rye) must have been quite close; amongst recent Aboriginal peoples of northwestern Australia, Cane observed that the high-energy costs of processing small seed or grain foods (relative to 'root' foods) were such that the Aborigines were rarely prepared to travel more than 5 km to gather them (see, in particular, Cane's Fig. 6.5, this volume).

## How diverse was the range of plant foods exploited during the Epipalaeolithic?

Having considered the probable form of subsistence practised at Epipalaeolithic Abu Hureyra, it is now appropriate to examine the diversity of the wild plant-food component of their diet. We will first itemize the major food plants represented in the charred remains, and then consider whether they might have arrived on-site and become charred by routes *other* than by being gathered as food. Thirdly, we will consider what plant foods additional to those identified in the charred remains are likely to have been exploited by the Epipalaeolithic population.

### (a)   The gathered foods

The diversity of seed-food plants preserved in the remains is remarkable. The most abundant (though not necessarily the most heavily utilized) of the 157 seed-food plants represented in the charred remains were the following types:

(i)    Plants which are today characteristic of the ecotone between oak–Rosaceae forest, forest–steppe, and damp steppe: *Triticum boeoticum*, *Secale* cf. *cereale* (ssp. *vavilovii*), *S. montanum*, *Lepidium perfoliatum*, *Draba* spp., *Pistacia atlantica* and/or *P. kinjuk*, *Stipa* cf. *holosericea* (syn. *S. lagascae*), and some members of the Trifoliae.

(ii)   From either the same zones or from more arid steppe: *Stipa* cf. *barbata*, *S.* cf. *parviflora*, *Hordeum glaucum/leporinum*, and several members of the Trifoliae.

(iii)  From the valley bottom: *Polygonum corrigioloides*, *Scirpus maritimus/tuberosus*, riverine grasses such as *Crypsis* and the ten panicoids including species of *Setaria* and *Echinochloa*. It is of particular interest that all these plants, except *Scirpus maritimus/tuberosus*, would have been unable to grow abundantly either in riverine forest or in back-swamp. Their relative abundance in the Epipalaeolithic levels at Abu Hureyra may imply a degree of forest clearance, which is independently suggested by the wood-charcoal evidence for the burning of *Salix*, *Populus*, *Acer*, and *Tamarix*.

In most of these groups we see varying degrees of decline in their frequency during the Epipalaeolithic, although the Trifoliae and steppic Gramineae exhibit the opposite trend (Fig. 14.1). The decline in the apparent use of foods such as the wild cereals and the perennial *Stipa* species may be attributable to advancing desiccation during the terminal Epipalaeolithic. On this basis, the synchronous increase in the use of steppe Trifoliae and smaller-seeded Gramineae may represent an attempt to balance these losses rather than any general broadening of the subsistence spectrum. The record from bone remains provides no basis for attributing these segetal changes to systematic shifts in grazing pressure from wild herbivores such as gazelle or onager.

## (b)  Were all the edible seed types identified in Epipalaeolithic levels really used as food?

Ethnobotanical studies indicate that the majority of the seed and fruit species identified in the charred remains from Epipalaeolithic levels are edible, if only after detoxification (cf. Stahl Ch. 11, this volume). Those that are not edible have well established traditional uses as medicines, dyes, or furnishing materials. However, this does not automatically prove that all of the seeds and fruits arrived on the site as gathered foods, medicines, etc. It was, therefore, necessary to explore other possible modes of arrival and use.

First, the seeds (especially those of woody plants such as *Hammada*, *Capparis*, and *Pistacia*) could theoretically have been on plants gathered as fuel. However, this seems unlikely as all the wood charcoal identified so far (including charcoal from small twigs) comes from just four riverine trees and shrubs: *Salix*, *Populus*, *Acer*, and *Tamarix*.

Secondly, seeds could have arrived with animal dung (Bottema 1984, Hillman 1984, Miller 1984). Again, this is improbable in most cases as (a) none of the characteristic remains of burned dung were found in our samples, and (b) all the bone remains identified from Epipalaeolithic levels by Legge & Rowley-Conwy (1987, and in Moore *et al.* forthcoming) were from wild species (mainly gazelle), and dispersed gazelle pellets from kilometres away on the steppe are unlikely to have been collected for burning when there was plenty of wood available in the local riverine forest.

Thirdly, seeds could have arrived with plants gathered as bedding, thatching, or for basketry. In fact, the only food seeds in this category are the very rare nutlets of *Schoenoplectus*. Nutlets of its close relative, *Scirpus maritimus*, were also found (in large numbers), but the sharp, three-angled stems of this plant are unsuitable for bedding and rather brittle and uneven for basketry.

Fourthly, it is possible that some of the seeds were blown into the settlement by the wind. Certainly, it is possible to observe this process in action in villages in the area today, especially during the periods of Hamsin winds from the south. However, it is difficult to see how this would lead to more than very occasional seeds getting onto domestic fires and being preserved by charring.

It therefore appears that, for most of the 157 edible seed species identified so far, the simplest explanation for their arrival on-site and for their becoming charred on domestic fires, is that they were gathered as food, flavourings, medicines, or dyes and then (in the case of food species) exposed to fire as part of the processing required to make them palatable, digestible, and/or to eliminate toxins (see Stahl 1984 and Ch. 11, this volume).

This is not to say that each was gathered separately. Indeed, in harvesting modern einkorn grain from wild stands, it was found that 23 other ± edible species (seven of them grasses) were inadvertently gathered with the einkorn (Hillman, unpublished field notes, 1970–72). Indeed, in view of the nutritional advantages of dietary diversity (Stahl 1984), hunter–gatherers may well have specifically adapted their harvesting methods to maximize the spectrum of edible seeds included (Hillman & Vaughan forthcoming, and Hillman Ch. 13, this volume).

### (c)   Food plants not represented in the charred remains but quite likely to have been exploited as food

SOFT VEGETABLE FOODS

Reports of identifications of charred food remains seldom include foods based on leaves, flowers, shoots, or tissues from organs such as tubers, rhizomes, corms, and bulbs. This results from the fact that

(i)    during their preparation as food, they generally require to be brought into direct contact with fire less often than seed foods;
(ii)   most of them are poorly (if ever) preserved by charring;
(iii)  their charred residues rarely survive in archaeological deposits in recognizable form, and, because they bear little resemblance to ancient food, they are commonly overlooked during coarse sorting of the flots; and
(iv)   even if charred residues are successfully isolated, it is difficult to identify them to genus (Hather 1988, Hillman et al. in press, Hillman Ch. 13, this volume).

At a site such as Abu Hureyra, located at the boundary of steppe and riverine forest, a wealth of soft vegetable foods would have been available to the Epipalaeolithic population. Apart from the leafy foods, these plants would have included rich sources of starch or insulin such as the tubers of *Scorzonera* spp. and *Bieberstenia*, and, from the river valley, the tubers of *Cyperus rotundus*, the corms of *Butomus* and *Alisma* spp., and the young rhizomes of *Scirpus tuberosus*, *Schoenoplectus* spp., *Typha* spp., and *Phragmites communis*. Some of these 'root' foods were certainly being used in Upper Egypt by 18 000 bp. (Hillman et al. in press, Hillman Ch. 13, this volume), and, given the preference for 'root' foods over seed foods amongst many recent hunter–gatherers (cf. Cane Ch. 6, this volume), it is not unlikely that several root foods were at least as heavily exploited as the seeds.

MISSING SEED FOODS

Even with seed-based foods, the only types likely to be regularly preserved by charring are those that need to be roasted or parched to make them more palatable or digestible, to detoxify them, or to make them easier to grind. It is probable, therefore, that the 150 edible species of seed identified in Epipalaeolithic levels at Abu Hureyra represent only part of the full spectrum of seeds and fruits actually eaten.

In summary, the charred remains of the food plants identified in the Epipalaeolithic levels indicate exploitation of a diverse array of seed-based foods, but it is probable that this represents only one segment of the spectrum of plant foods actually exploited. The work of Legge and Rowley-Conwy (1987, and in Moore et al. forthcoming) has revealed that the Epipalaeolithic population also consumed gazelle, onager, wild cattle, wild sheep and goat, hares, and the occasional pig, fish, and bird. Overall, therefore, their diet was remarkably diverse, especially when compared with the seemingly narrow spectrum of foods exploited during the ensuing Neolithic (c. eight types of plant food) and, indeed, by most populations of the present day.

## At what seasons was the site occupied during the Epipalaeolithic?

The components of seasonality considered in interpreting the Abu Hureyra remains were: seasons of plant-food availability, probable seasons of gathering, and the possible seasons of site occupation (the rationale is discussed in detail in Hillman et al. in press, and outlined in Hillman, Ch. 13, this volume).

### Seasons of availability of wild seed-foods

The principal periods of fruiting observed in present-day Syria for some of the species identified in the Epipalaeolithic deposits are indicated in Table 14.1. They suggest that these wild resources would have been available from April through to January (or even March), with no obvious gaps. This 9–11 month period of overlapping availability is only marginally reduced if we omit all but the most abundantly represented species. However, this block of time represents the seasons when the foods would have been *available*, not the seasons when they were gathered or consumed.

### Seasons of exploitation

Most of the individual major food species are available for two months or more (Table 14.1). This allows a large measure of scheduling based on preferences for particular resources (cf. Jones & Meehan Ch. 7, this volume). It is therefore impossible to identify the precise points at which each species

**Table 14.1** Seasons of fruit/seed production of the principal taxa identified in Epipalaeolithic levels at Abu Hureyra – as recorded in the present-day steppe and Euphrates Valley of central Syria.

| Month code | Taxon or group (these refer only to those species represented in the remains) |
|---|---|
| 4–6 | wild cereals |
| | wild pulses |
| | Liliaceae |
| | Papaveraceae (steppe species) |
| | Caryophyllaceae |
| | Leguminosae – Trifoliae |
| | *Chenopodium* species |
| 5–6 | *Erodium* species |
| | Caryophyllaceae of wadi fans |
| 5–7 (–9) | Boraginaceae (steppe species only) |
| 6–7 | *Zygophyllum* |
| | *Haplophyllum* |
| | Asclepiadaceae (steppe species only) |
| 5–8 | *Beta maritima* (steppe forms only) |
| | perennial *Stipa* species |
| | *Salvia* and other perennial Labiatae |
| 6–11 | fruits of trees/shrubs of *Quercus brantii* zone |
| | *Pistacia* species |
| | *Capparis spinosa/ovata* |
| | *Glychyrrhiza* species |
| 6–11 | *Polygonum corrigioloides* |
| 8–10 | *Prosopis stephaniana* |
| | *Aellenia autrani* |
| 7–11 | *Scirpus maritimus* |
| (6–) 8–11 (–12) | riverine Gramineae |
| 9–1 | *Noaea mucronata* |
| | *Hammada* (most species) |
| | some of the smaller-seeded *Salsola* species |
| | *Krascheninnikovia ceratoides* |
| (10–) 11–3 (–5) | *Suaeda fruticosa* |

was gathered from the wild. What is clear, however, is that the Epipalaeolithic population must have been active in the area during at least one period between May and July, and at least one other period sometime between August and November: this is the bare minimum for them to have harvested the full range of food seeds preserved in the remains. Results from the study of animal bones further extend the first block: the mass kills of migratory gazelle are likely to have occurred in March or April (Legge & Rowley-Conwy 1987).

Nevertheless, concentration of harvesting into two narrow periods was unlikely for the following reasons:

(a)   The fruits/seeds of several of the species mature over an extended period, so repeated visits would have been necessary to harvest any one area efficiently.

(b)   To gather the same total amount from harvests concentrated into shorter periods would correspondingly have required increased travel to more remote areas, and this would have increased energy expenditure per unit of energy return – compared with more extended periods of harvesting confined to one locality.

(c)   Harvests concentrated into short 'bursts' would also have necessitated increased storage of the products (with the ever attendant risks of spoilage and predation) and greater expenditure of energy on the construction of these storage facilities.

It therefore seems more probable that the wild foods represented in the Epipalaeolithic remains were gathered over a period of several months sometime between April and December but including a minimum of two blocks: one extending from spring into early summer; the other in the autumn.

## Seasons of occupation

In view of the fact that dry seeds and many 'root' foods can be stored for later consumption, the seasons of seed gathering indicated above do not necessarily represent periods of occupation at the site. However, no storage facilities were detected during the excavation of Epipalaeolithic Abu Hureyra in the form of either pits or mud-brick structures of the sort found in pre- or early-agrarian occupations at Ganj Dareh level D (Smith 1971). On the other hand, the Neolithic levels at Abu Hureyra have yielded fragments of bitumen with basketry impressions, and bitumen-, clay- or plaster-lined baskets could perhaps have provided storage facilities in the Epipalaeolithic also.

The minimum of two periods of exploitation (spring to early summer, and autumn) can also be assumed to represent the minimum period of site occupation, as it is very probable that some, at least, of the resources which ended up in the Abu Hureyra remains were gathered and hunted from Hureyra itself. (Bulky plant foods are unlikely to have been regularly carried to Hureyra from other occupation sites.) In exploring the possibility of site occupation in the remaining blocks of time theoretically available between periods of local resource exploitation, it is necessary to decide where else they could go, and for what. At Abu Hureyra we are left with two such unaccounted-for blocks: (a) early winter through to spring, and (b) high summer.

(a)   Winter is a bleak period on the steppe, and not much better on the mountains which flank it. There would have been no important resources available elsewhere that would not also have been available near Hureyra, and there would seem little point in leaving the Euphrates Valley which would have offered not only a reliable water supply, but also a range of additional 'root' foods from swamp plants, e.g. the rhizomes of catstail (*Typha*), common reed (*Phragmites*) and bulrush (*Schoenoplectus*) which, in this area, are at their most palatable during the winter months (Hillman *et al.* in press, Hillman Ch. 13, this volume).

(b)    That the summer period was also spent close to the river valley, and presumably at Abu Hureyra with its advantaged position next to the Wadi Hibna, is suggested by the general lack of water out in the steppe during those seasons.

Apart from the Euphrates itself, seepage from Wadi Hibna (the largest side-stream in this part of the valley) would, even in high summer, have maintained the growth of a range of food plants, just as it did in recent times. (The mouth of the wadi is almost certain to have been cleared of trees as it was so close to a site.

Another reason for spending the summer at Abu Hureyra would have been to enjoy the tubers of club-rush (*Scirpus maritimus/tuberosus*) and wild nut-grass (actually a sedge – *Cyperus rotundus*), both of which would be at their prime at this point (Hillman *et al.* in press). Although these and other 'root' foods are missing from the remains, the local availability of at least one of them (*Scirpus maritimus/tuberosus*) is evidenced by charred remains of its nutlets – apparently gathered as food.

Year-round occupation at Abu Hureyra is therefore very probable.

## Conclusion

At the beginning of this paper we posed three main questions: (a) did the Epipalaeolithic occupants of Abu Hureyra cultivate their main food plants, in particular the wild-type cereals? (b) How diverse was the range of plant foods exploited? (c) During which season(s) was the site occupied, in particular was it occupied year-round?

Although the results reported here must be regarded as preliminary, we can summarize our present answers to the three questions as follows:

(a)    There is no conclusive evidence to support the hypothesis that the wild-type cereals recovered from the Epipalaeolithic levels at Abu Hureyra were cultivated; instead it is probable that they were harvested from wild stands which might have been quite close to the site. As the wild-type cereals were the most readily cultivable of the identified wild foods, it seems unlikely that any other major food plant was cultivated.

(b)    In addition to the wild cereals, a remarkably broad spectrum of other wild plants was exploited for food and other domestic purposes during the Epipalaeolithic: some 150 species of edible seeds and fruits have been identified in the charred plant remains of this period. Despite this remarkable record of dietary diversity, it is probable that a number of major foods are missing from the remains, particularly 'root' foods from the valley bottom. Leafy foods may also have played an important (though archaeologically unattested) role in human diet (cf. evidence of leaf eating at Palaeolithic Kubbaniya in Hillman Ch. 13, this volume).

(c) Even during the Epipalaeolithic, the site was occupied for much of the year, and possibly year-round.

Our overall conclusion is, therefore, that sedentary life probably preceded agriculture at Abu Hureyra; that the cultivation of cereals did not pre-date the Neolithic; that the pre-agrarian subsistence economy involved exploitation of a very broad spectrum of wild-plant foods; that, at this particular site, the transition to an economy which was at least partly agrarian took place relatively rapidly, within the time-span of a few centuries (between *c.* 8000 and 7000 bc); and that this transition involved the introduction of crops from elsewhere rather than local plant domestications.

## Postscript

While the general conclusions reached in this chapter are relatively secure, it must be stressed that certain categories of the botanical data used are strictly provisional. At least another decade of work is required to research the criteria tentatively used in identifying the seeds of the many members of the tribe Trifoliae and family Cruciferae which can today be found in steppe and forest fringes. Similarly, a vast amount of work remains to be done on the ecological limits of many members of the Gramineae, Cruciferae, and Trifoliae which are represented in the charred remains.

## Acknowledgements

The laboratory and field research undertaken between 1981 and 1984 was supported by a three-year grant from the British Science and Engineering Research Council which we gratefully acknowledge. The field and laboratory studies undertaken by Hillman between 1972 and 1976 were funded by (a) scholarships from the Johannes-Güttenborg University in Mainz (Germany) and the University of Reading Faculty of Agriculture, and (b) a research fellowship from the British Institute of Archaeology at Ankara. We are also indebted to many other organizations and individuals in Britain, Syria, and elsewhere. We wish particularly to acknowledge the detailed comments on this chapter kindly provided by Mark Blumler of the University of California at Berkeley, Richard Hubbard of North-East London Polytechnic, and Mordechai Kislev of Bar Ilan University.

## Notes

1   In this chapter the term Epipalaeolithic is regarded as equivalent to the Late Natufian period in the Levant, which, at Abu Hureyra, extends from $11\,090 \pm 150$ bp (OxA-468) to $10\,600 \pm 200$ bp (OxA-170) – uncalibrated. The term Mesolithic is not conventionally applied to Southwest Asian sites, but it could be regarded as equivalent to the Epipalaeolithic.
2   The calibrated (calendric) date would be *c.* 2000 years earlier.

## References

Bar-Yosef, O. & M. Kislev 1989. Early farming communities in the Jordan Valley. In *Foraging and farming: the evolution of plant exploitation*, D. R. Harris & G. C. Hillman (eds), ch. 40. London: Unwin Hyman.

Binford, L. R. 1968. Post-Pleistocene adaptations. In *New perspectives in archeology*, S. R. Binford & L. R. Binford (eds), 313–41. Chicago: Aldine.

Blumler, M. A. 1984. *Climate and the annual habit.* Unpublished MA thesis, Department of Geography, University of California.

Blumler, M. A. in press. The two Mediterranean climates. (Place of publication undecided.)

Bottema, S. 1984. The composition of some modern charred seed assemblages. In *Plants and ancient man: studies in palaeoethnobotany*, W. van Zeist & W. A. Casparie (eds), 207–12. Rotterdam: Balkema.

Butler, A. 1989. Cryptic anatomical characters as evidence of early cultivation in the grain legumes (pulses). In *Foraging and farming: the evolution of plant exploitation*, D. R. Harris & G. C. Hillman (eds), ch. 24. London: Unwin Hyman

Cane, S. 1989. Australian Aboriginal seed grinding and its archaeological record: a case study from the Western Desert. In *Foraging and farming: the evolution of plant exploitation*, D. R. Harris & G. C. Hillman (eds), ch. 6. London: Unwin Hyman.

Cauvin, J. 1977. Les fouilles de Mureybet (1971–1974) et leur signification pour les origines de la sédentarisation au Proche-Orient. *Annual of the American Schools of Oriental Research* **44**, 19–48.

Cauvin, J. 1978. *Les premiers villages de Syrie-Palestine du IXème au VIIème millénaire avant JC.* Lyons: Maison de l'Orient.

Cohen, M. N. 1977. *The food crisis in prehistory.* New Haven: Yale University Press.

Colledge, S. M. in press. *Scanning-electron microscope studies of the pericarp layers of wild wheats and ryes. Methods and problems.* Paper presented to the conference 'Scanning-electron microscopy in Archaeology', London, April 1986.

Davis, M. B. 1986. Climatic instability, time lags, and community disequilibrium. In *Community ecology*, J. Diamond & T. T. Case (eds), 269–84. New York: Harper & Row.

Flannery, K. V. 1969. Origins and ecological effects of early domestication in Iran and the Near East. In *The domestication and exploitation of plants and animals*, P. J. Ucko & G. W. Dimbleby (eds), 73–100. London: Duckworth.

French, D. H., G. C. Hillman, S. Payne & R. J. Payne 1972. Excavations at Can Hasan III, 1969–1970. In *Papers in economic prehistory*, E. S. Higgs (ed.), 181–90. Cambridge: Cambridge University Press.

Harlan, J. R. & D. Zohary 1966. Distribution of wild wheats and barley. *Science* **153**, 1074–80.

Harris, D. R. 1977. Alternative pathways toward agriculture. In *Origins of agriculture*, C. A. Reed (ed.), 179–243. The Hague: Mouton.

Harris, D. R. 1986. Plant and animal domestication and the origins of agriculture: the contribution of radiocarbon accelerator dating. In *Archaeological results from accelerator dating*, J. A. J. Gowlett & R. E. M. Hedges (eds), 5–12. Oxford: Oxford University Committee for Archaeology, Monograph 11.

Harris, D. R. 1987. The impact on archaeology of radiocarbon dating by accelerator mass spectrometry. *Philosophical Transctions of the Royal Society London*, **A323**, 23–43.

Hather, J. G. 1988. *The morphological and anatomical identification and interpretation of charred vegetative parenchymatous plant remains*. PhD dissertation, Department of Human Environment, Institute of Archaeology, University College London.

Hassan, F. A. 1977. The dynamics of agricultural origins in Palestine: a theoretical model. In *Origins of agriculture*, C. A. Reed (ed.), 589–609. The Hague: Mouton.

Hillman, G. C. 1975. The plant remains from Tell Abu Hureyra: a preliminary report. In The excavation of Tell Abu Hureyra in Syria: a preliminary report, A. M. T. Moore. *Proceedings of the Prehistoric Society* **41**, 70–3.

Hillman, G. C. in press. The adoption of cereal cultivation in S. W. Asian steppe: a model. In *Plant exploitation in prehistory: data and techniques*, P. Anderson-Gerfaud (ed.). Lyon: CNRS, Maison de l'Orient Méditerranéen.

Hillman, G. C. 1989. Late Palaeolithic plant foods from Wadi Kubbaniya in Upper Egypt: dietary diversity, infant weaning, and seasonality in a riverine environment. In *Foraging and farming: the evolution of plant exploitation*, D. R. Harris & G. C. Hillman (eds), ch. 13. London: Unwin Hyman.

Hillman, G. C. & S. M. Davies in press. Domestication rates in wild-type einkorn wheat under primitive cultivation. *Botanical Journal of the Linnean Society*.

Hillman, G. C. & M. D. Vaughan in press. The lawn-mower hypothesis: an explanation for extreme species diversity in food-seed assemblages from arid zone archaeological sites.

Hillman, G. C., E. Madeyska & J. Hather in press. Wild plant foods and diet at Late Palaeolithic Wadi Kubbaniya: the evidence from charred remains. In *The prehistory of Wadi Kubbaniya*. Vol. 2: *Palaeoeconomy, environment and stratigraphy*, F. Wendorf, R. Schild & A. Close (eds). Dallas: Southern Methodist University Press.

Körber-Grohne, Ü. 1981. Distinguishing prehistoric grains of *Triticum* and *Secale* on the basis of their surface patterns using scanning electron spectroscopy. *Journal of Archaeological Science* **8**, 197–204.

Körber-Grohne, Ü. & U. Peining 1980. Microstructure of the surfaces of carbonised and non-carbonised grains of cereals as observed in scanning electron and light microscopes as an additional aid in determining prehistoric findings. *Flora (Jena)* **170**, 189–228.

Legge, A. J. 1975. The fauna of Tell Abu Hureyra: a preliminary report. In The excavation of Tell Abu Hureyra in Syria: a preliminary report, A. M. T. Moore. *Proceedings of the Prehistoric Society* **41**, 73–7.

Legge, A. J. 1977. The origins of agriculture in the Near East. In *Hunters, gatherers and first farmers beyond Europe*, J. V. S. Megaw (ed.), 51–67. Leicester: Leicester University Press.

Legge, A. J. & P. Rowley-Conwy 1986. New radiocarbon dates for early sheep at Tell Abu Hureyra, Syria. In *Archaeological results from accelerator dating*, J. A. J. Gowlett & R. E. M. Hodges (eds), 23–35. Oxford: Oxford University Committee for Archaeology, Monograph 11.

Legge, A. J. & P. Rowley-Conwy 1987. Gazelle killing in Stone Age Syria. *Scientific American* **255**, 88–95.

Miller, N. 1984. The interpretation of some carbonised cereal remains. *Bulletin on Sumerian Agriculture* **1**, 45–7.

Moore, A. M. T. 1975. The excavation of Tell Abu Hureyra in Syria: a preliminary report. *Proceedings of the Prehistoric Society* **41**, 50–77.

Moore, A. M. T. 1979. A pre-Neolithic farmers' village on the Euphrates. *Scientific American* **241**, 50–8.

Moore, A. M. T. 1985. The development of Neolithic societies in the Near East. *Advances in World Archaeology* **4**, 1–69.

Moore, A. M. T., J. A. J. Gowlett, R. E. M. Hedges, G. C. Hillman, A. J. Legge & P. Rowley-Conwy 1986. Radiocarbon accelerator (AMS) dates for the Epipalaeolithic settlement at Abu Hureyra, Syria. *Radiocarbon* **28**, 1068–76.

Moore, A. M. T., G. C. Hillman & A. J. Legge in press. *The Epipalaeolithic and Neolithic occupations at Abu Hureyra, Syria: the people, their economy, settlement, technology and environment.* New Haven, Conn.: Yale University Press.

Pabot, H. 1957. *Rapport au gouvernement de Syrie sur l'écologie végétale et ses applications.* Rome: UN/FAO Report No. 663.

Redman, C. L. 1978. *The rise of civilization: early farmers to urban society in the ancient Near East.* San Francisco: Freeman.

Reed, C. A. 1977. A model for the origin of agriculture in the Near East. In *Origins of agriculture*, C. A. Reed (ed.), 543–67. The Hague: Mouton.

Sencer, H. Â. 1975. *Study of variation in the genus Secale L. and on the origins of cultivated rye.* Unpublished Ph.D. dissertation in the Faculty of Science & Engineering, University of Birmingham, UK.

Sencer, H. Â. & J. G. Hawkes 1980. On the origin of cultivated rye. *Biological Journal of the Linnean Society (London)* **13**, 219–313.

Smith, P. E. L. 1971. Iran 9000–4000 BC. The Neolithic. *Expedition* **13**, 6–13.

Stahl, A. B. 1984. Hominid dietary selection before fire. *Current Anthropology* **25**, 151–68.

Stahl, A. B. 1989. Plant-food processing: implications for dietary quality. In *Foraging and farming: the evolution of plant exploitation*, D. R. Harris & G. C. Hillman (eds), ch. 11. London: Unwin Hyman.

van Zeist, W. & S. Bottema 1982. Vegetational history of the eastern Mediterranean and the Near East during the past 20,000 years. In *Palaeoclimates, palaeoenvironments and human communities in the eastern Mediterranean region in later prehistory*, (eds). British Archaeological Reports, International Series 133.

van Zeist, W. & W. A. Casparie 1968. Wild einkorn wheat and barley from Tell Mureybit in northern Syria. *Acta Botanica Neerlandica* **17**, 44–53.

van Zeist, W. & Bakker-Heeres 1984 (1986). Archaeobotanical studies in the Levant. 3: Late Palaeolithic Mureybit. *Palaeohistoria* **26**, 171–99.

Zohary, D. 1989. Domestication of the Southwest Asian Neolithic crop assemblage of cereals, pulses, and flax: the evidence from the living plants. In *Foraging and farming: the evolution of plant exploitation*, D. R. Harris & G. C. Hillman (eds), ch. 22. London: Unwin Hyman.

Zohary, D. & M. Hopf 1988. *Domestication of plants in the Old World. The origin and spread of cultivated plants in West Asia, Europe and the Nile Valley.* Oxford: Oxford University Press.

Zohary, M. 1973. *Geobotanic foundations of the Near East*, 2 vols. Stuttgart and Amsterdam: Springer.

# 15 *Mesolithic exploitation of wild plants in Sri Lanka: archaeobotanical study at the cave site of Beli-Lena*

M. D. KAJALE

## Introduction

The chapter outlines the results of preliminary examination of the archaeo-logical plant remains recovered by wet sieving during the 1983 excavations of the prehistoric site at Beli-Lena (Kitulgala). The site is located at the edge of the moist evergreen forest belt, about 38 km east of Colombo, capital of Sri Lanka (Figs. 15.1 & 15.2). Earlier seasons of excavations carried out by Deraniyagala had yielded abundant plant remains in the form of granular bodies which previous workers had regarded as unidentifiable (Deraniyagala pers. comm.). In 1982 I examined a sample of these supposedly domesticated 'grains', but none of the granular bodies showed evidence of a hilum scar, and it was therefore suggested to the excavator that the specimens could not possibly belong to any category of seed, let alone a domesticated cereal. Indeed, artificial (laboratory) carbonization of both dried and moistened grains of various millets such as finger millet (*Eleusine coracana* (L.) Gaertn.), pearl millet (*Pennisetum typhoides* (Burm. f.) Stapf. and Hubbard), Sumatran millet (*Panicum sumatrense* Roth ex. Roem. & Schult. syn. *P. milare* Lamk.), and Italian millet (*Setaria italica* Beauv.) was also undertaken in 1982, but none of these cereals exhibited anatomical characteristics or a rupturing pattern comparable to the specimens recovered from Beli-Lena. Thus, prior to attending the excavations in 1983, it was already apparent that the granular bodies recovered in earlier seasons did not represent a cereal cultigen.

During September 1983, another set of ancient plant assemblages was recovered by wet sieving from levels already radiocarbon dated to *c.* 10 500–8000 bc (Deraniyagala 1985). Morphological examinations of the specimens allowed their taxonomic affinities to be suggested, and, on this basis, a field survey was undertaken to collect fruits of living plants belonging to the families Moraceae, Burseraceae, and Musaceae. Simple carbonization experiments were undertaken in the field by heating the various seeds and fruits in the periphery of fires. Critical examination of

**Figure 15.1**   General view of the cave site at Beli-Lena (Kitulgala) located in the moist evergreen forest zone and with the River Kelaniya flowing close by the cave.

**Figure 15.2**   Inside Beli-Lena cave: excavation work in progress.

these modern carbonized materials in the field confirmed that the hitherto unidentifiable granular specimens from Beli-Lena Cave were probably formed by the rupturing of the prickly epicarp of the wild breadfruit, locally called '*waldil*' or '*bedidel*' (*Artocarpus* sp. of the *A. nobilis* Thw. type). The other seeds compared closely with those of wild bananas (*Musa* spp.,

**Figure 15.3**    Charred remains of fruits of the wild breadfruit type (*Artocarpus* sp. cf. *A. nobilis* Thw.). Granular bodies from the outer portion of the epicarp (outermost fruit coat), each with a minute perforation. The granules on the left (A) are still interconnected – just as they are in modern fruits of *A. nobilis*. In the larger granules on the right (B), the interconnections have broken (magnification: × 12.5).

of the *M. balbisiana* Colla type and probably also of the *M. acuminata* Colla type, locally termed '*attikehel*' and '*unel*' respectively), while the nut shells belonged to *Canarium* sp. of the *C. zeylanicum* Bl. type known locally as '*kekuna*'.

Thus the probable modern counterparts of the ancient specimens were tracked down in the field itself. Subsequent laboratory examination of ancient and modern (experimentally carbonized) specimens lent further support to the tentative diagnoses.

## Descriptions of the four types of plant-food remains from Beli-Lena

### *Wild breadfruit:* Artocarpus *sp. of the* A. nobilis *Thw. type*

Several granular bodies bore fracture marks which seem to represent the position of interconnections, and each granule shows a slightly raised upper area with a perforation (Figs. 15.3 & 15.4). A few pieces of interconnected granules could also be observed (specimens labelled 'A' in Figs. 15.3 & 15.4). Granules of precisely this form can be seen on the outermost fruit coat of modern wild breadfruits, where they protrude slightly above the general surface and form a roughly rhomboidal pattern. A few seeds of *Artocarpus* type were found with traces of seed coat (testa) still attached and with an indication of a hilum scar (Fig. 15.5). However, their poor state of preservation precluded further analysis. A few pieces of what was probably burnt fibrous mesocarp (in fact, modified perianth) were also detected (Fig. 15.6).

**Figure 15.4** This shows the reverse side of the same granules photographed in Figure 15.3

## Wild bananas: Musa *spp. of the* M. balbisiana *Colla and* M. acuminata *Colla types*

A few seeds with a globose to sub-globose outline, minute warts, and prominent hilum scar were isolated (Fig. 15.7). They compare with *Musa balbisiana* Colla, locally called '*attikehel*'. A few seeds with a more irregular and angular outline and with a depressed central portion were also observed (Figs. 15.8 & 15.9). These are tentatively identified as *Musa* sp. of the *M. acuminata* Colla type.

**Figure 15.5** Charred seed of *A. nobilis* type with poorly preserved testa (magnification: × 8).

**Figure 15.6** Small fragment of the charred remains of woody sub-dermal tissues of a fruit of the *A. nobilis* type (magnification: × 8).

There were also two fragments of seed coat with the outline of a roundish hilum scar (left-hand item in Fig. 15.10). These compare with the hilum scar region of seeds of *Musa balbisiana* Colla. When modern seeds of this species were artificially carbonized, it was observed in a few cases that the seed coat adjacent to the hilum scar becomes detached precisely as in these ancient seed-coat fragments found in the Beli-Lena assemblage.

### Canarium *sp. of the* C. zeylanicum *Bl. type*

The plant remains included a number of nut shells. A few of them were spindle shaped, with a triangular outline and slightly pointed at the apex.

**Figure 15.7** The charred remains of two seeds of wild banana of the *Musa balbisiana* type showing the globose to sub-globose form typical of this species (magnification: × 17.5).

**Figure 15.8**    The charred remains of a wild-banana seed of the *Musa acuminata* type showing the angular form and central depression typical of this species (magnification: × 8).

**Figure 15.9**    The charred remains of another wild-banana seed of the *Musa acuminata* type showing more clearly the characteristic central depression (magnification: × 11).

Some shells also showed faint vertical striations on the outer surface (Fig. 15.11), while the inner surface showed an impression indicating the area where the kernel probably existed (Fig. 15.12). Most of the pieces were in fragmented form, as if purposely broken to remove the kernel.

**Figure 15.10**  Two charred fragments of detached testa (seed coat) from seeds of a wild banana (*Musa* sp.). The fragment on the left is from the area of the hilum scar, while that on the right is from elsewhere on the seed surface (magnification: × 15).

## Role of these wild-plant foods in local subsistence

At present the local inhabitants of jungle habitats exploit the wild breadfruit for its seeds, which are eaten either roasted or boiled. The fleshy, fibrous mesocarp surrounding the seeds is also edible. In the case of wild bananas, the seeds are inedible but the parenchymatous tissue surrounding the seeds is sub-sweet and edible, and is also consumed by animals such as monkeys, fruit-bats, and squirrels. *Canarium zeylanicum* Bl. is a wild tree producing nuts whose kernels are rich in fatty substances and are still eaten today.

**Figure 15.11**  Outer surface of a charred nut-shell fragment of *Canarium zeylanicum* Bl., showing the characteristic faint striations (magnification: × 6.6).

**Figure 15.12**   Inner portion of the nut-shell fragments of *Canarium zeylanicum* Bl., showing the depression occupied by the edible kernel (magnification: × 6.6).

From the evidence unearthed at Beli-Lena, it appears that all four of these plant foods were available in the area and exploited by local Mesolithic foragers. It is, however, interesting to note that, barring occasional seed fragments of the wild breadfruit, it is the inedible portions that have been preserved. They were apparently thrown onto the fires by the cave occupants after they had consumed the edible portions, there to be charred and thereby preserved as archaeological remains. In all probability, it was a case of foraging without any purposeful management or domestication of the plants.

The evidence for exclusively wild animals at Beli-Leni is perhaps significant in this context. The bone assemblage included remains of wild animals such as elephant (young), gaur, wild water-buffalo, sloth bear, wild pig, sambar, spotted deer, muntjac, chevrotain, hare, giant squirrel, flying squirrel, pangolin, civet cat, land monitor-lizard, soft-shelled terrapin, tout tortoise, mahsier, small fish (e.g. *Pruntius titeya*), freshwater crabs and molluscs, terrestrial and arboreal molluscs – notably of the genus *Acavus* (Deraniyagala 1985). The general picture is thus of non-specialized, broad-spectrum hunting. There appears to be a general tendency for the smaller vertebrates, such as porcupine, to be more frequently represented than the bigger forms, such as bovids. This probably reflects the greater ease of hunting smaller animals compared with more formidable ones such as the gaur. The bone remains also indicate that the heavier carcasses were butchered at the kill sites, thus implying that they were not herded or otherwise managed by prehistoric man (Deraniyagala 1985). By contrast, the plant remains were represented by only four species. However, the

**Table 15.1** Radiocarbon dates of charred plant remains from Mesolithic deposits at Beli-Lena.

| Excavators' sample no. | Depth (cm) | BSIP no. | Age of sample based on the Libby half-life of 5570 ± 30 years |
|---|---|---|---|
| 10G/2 | 10 | BS–287 | 10 200 ± 170 bp |
| 10G/3 | 10 | BS–288 | 10 200 ± 170 bp |
| 10G/4 | 6.5 | BS–289 | 10 010 ± 160 bp |
| 10G/5 | 8 | BS–290 | 11 550 ± 180 bp |
| 10G/6 | 20 | BS–291 | 11 570 ± 210 bp |
| 10G/7 | 18 | BS–292 | 11 520 ± 220 bp |
| 10G/8 | 8 | BS–293 | 12 240 ± 160 bp |
| 10G/10 | 10 | BS–294 | 11 570 ± 390 bp |

preservation of plant-food remains generally relies on their being charred, and most plant foods are unlikely to leave identifiable traces. Thus, the three distinct classes of wild-plant food preserved at Beli-Lena can perhaps also be regarded as indicating a broad-based exploitation of natural resources. They certainly provide no evidence of any purposeful selection leading towards cultivation and domestication.

## Chronology of the remains

Radiocarbon dating of the archaeological deposits was carried out by S. Rajgopalan of the Birabal Sahani Institute of Palaeobotany, Lucknow, and the dates listed in Table 15.1 have been communicated to me by Deraniyagala.

The dates provide a more-or-less consistent and reliable chronology for the ancient plant assemblage under study. A few plant remains also occur in levels below those radiocarbon dated, thus providing evidence for pre-Mesolithic (terminal Pleistocene) plant exploitation. However, these very early plant remains have yet to be studied.

## Previous records of the same plant foods

To the best of my knowledge, there is no record of plant remains from such an early Mesolithic site anywhere in the Indian subcontinent or in Sri Lanka, except, perhaps, from Bata-domba Lena near Kuruvita (Deraniyagala pers. comm.)

The specimens of wild breadfruit and wild banana also represent their first recorded occurrence from any archaeological context. Although there have been reports of fossil leaf impressions from Tertiary beds from various parts of tropical America, referred to as *Musophyllum* and which were taken as evidence of the pre-Colombian presence of *Musa* in that continent, they are, by general consent, now treated as *Heliconia* (Simmonds 1962). Simmonds, however, reports an occurrence of fossil banana from the early Tertiary of central India (R. N. Lakhanpal, pers. comm. to Simmonds).

*Canarium* nut-shells have been reported from several Southeast Asian countries, and useful surveys of archaeological plant-remains have been made by Yen (1977) and Glover (1985). Evidence for *Canarium* comes from the following sites:

(a)  Spirit Cave, Banyan Valley Cave, and Tham Pa Chan Cave, all in northwestern Thailand;
(b)  Sulawesi in Indonesia; and
(c)  Middle Bronze-Age levels dated to *c.* 3228 ± 100 bp in Vietnam.

## Phytogeographical and taxonomic affinities

### Wild breadfruit

According to Jarrett (1959) the wild breadfruit (*Artocarpus nobilis* Thw.) is today endemic to Sri Lanka, growing as an evergreen component of the forests, and extending up to 650 m in the wetter parts of the island. The recent revision of the Sri Lankan flora by Dasanayake and Fosberg (1981) confirmed this view and notes that this fine tree not only holds an anomalous taxonomic position in the subgenus *Artocarpus*, but also, despite being so common in Sri Lanka, has never been found in southern India. The present discovery of plant remains resembling *Artocarpus nobilis* Thw. is particularly significant since it now represents the westerly limit of palaeogeographical distribution of one of the probable relatives of cultivated breadfruit. Cultivated breadfruit (*Artocarpus communis* Fosb., syn. *Artocarpus altilis* (Park.) Fosb.) is a staple food-plant in several Pacific islands. According to Barrau (1977), the wild progenitor of the cultivated breadfruit has not been identified, but it probably belonged to the series Incisifolii from the eastern borders of Indonesia, western Micronesia, and New Guinea. The other two domesticates, jack fruit (*Artocarpus heterophyllus* Lamk., syn. *Artocarpus integra* (Thunb.) Merr.) and champadek (*Artocarpus integer* (Thunb.) Merr.) are closely related but belong to a different series, the Cauliflorii (Barrau 1977). They have a more westerly distribution than the breadfruit and grow mainly in Southeast Asia and Indonesia. Although evidence is lacking, Barrau considers that introgression from local wild species has probably played a part in the evolution of these cultigens, all three of which are outbreeders. *Artocarpus mariannensis* of western Micronesia is taxonomically similar to breadfuit and some authors have implicated *Artocarpus* in its evolution.

## Wild bananas

As with the remains of wild breadfruit, the finds of seeds of the *Musa acuminata* type provide a westerly extension of the proposed centre of origin of the cultivated derivatives.

According to Cheeseman (1948), all the wild progenitors of the cultivated edible bananas of the section Eumusa fall into two species, *Musa balbisiana* Colla and *Musa acuminata* Colla. *Musa balbisiana* includes not only wild forms but numerous cultivated varieties. However, Cheeseman places the cultivated varieties derivable exclusively from *Musa acuminata* in the species *Musa paradisiaca* L. and the cultivated varieties combining both *acuminata* and *balbisiana* genes in *Musa sapientum* L.

According to Chandraratna (1951) both *Musa acuminata* and *Musa balbisiana* have a wide distribution. The range of *M. acuminata* includes Malaysia, Burma, Assam (northeastern India), Siam, Indo-China, and the Philippines, while *M. balbisiana* extends over Ceylon, India, Java, Malaysia, Burma, and Siam. Within Ceylon, *M. balbisiana* grows widely from sea-level up to 900 m, and the Pali chronicle *Mahavamsa*, written in the 5th century AD, cites its occurrence there under the name 'ettikehel'. It was known to Trimmen (1898) who placed it under *Musa paradisiaca* L. and suggested that this one wild species may have been the ancestor of the numerous seedless forms now in cultivation and distinguished from each other by differences in the shape and colour of the fruits.

Another wild-banana species bearing the local name of 'unel' has been tentatively identified by Chandraratna as a form of *Musa acuminata* Colla. It occurs locally along with *Musa balbisiana* in the foothills of the Kiripangala range in Uda-bullathagama korali. Chandraratna (1951) notes that, in the system of shifting cultivation that prevails in Kiripangala, seedlings of both 'ettikehel' and 'unel' are common weeds after a burn. As naturally occurring hybrids cannot effectively compete with the parent species in the undisturbed forest environment, the occurrence of these weed seedlings is of interest: burnt land would long have provided hybrid seedlings with a niche in which they could survive and evolve. Much of the variation exhibited by Sri Lankan races of cultivated bananas could possibly have resulted from introgressive hybridization between 'ettikehel' and 'unel' under these conditions (Chandraratna & Nayanakkara 1951).

*Musa acuminata* exhibits considerable variation, and has been split into five subspecies on the basis of cytogenetic and phytogeographical studies. All forms included within the subspecies are interfertile and the whole assemblage forms a panmictic unit (CSIRO 1962). According to Cheeseman (1948) both seeded (wild) and seedless (cultivated) forms of *Musa acuminata* occur as normal diploid plants. Triploid edible forms are thought to have arisen first through outcrossing of cultivated, parthenocarpic diploids with wild (diploid) forms of *Musa acuminata* and *Musa balbisiana*, followed by human selection; and secondly through polyploidy and hybridization both within and between *Musa acuminata* and *Musa balbisiana*, thus resulting in two genetically distinct types of triploids.

   Similar views have been reiterated by Simmonds (1977) who suggests that the seedless ('edible') state first evolved in *Musa acuminata*. The species is very variable, and taxonomic evidence indicates that the primary centre of diversity was the Malay Peninsula, together, perhaps, with immediately adjacent territories. The present discovery of seeds comparable to those of *Musa acuminata* thus provides a westerly extension of the palaeogeographical limits of the proposed primary centre of origin of this wild ancestor of an important crop of the present day.

## Conclusion

Against the chronological and palaeogeographical background of the discovery of wild breadfruit and wild bananas, and with the possibility of further finds in the future, there is reason to hope that we may ultimately be able to trace the major stages of cultivation, domestication, and diffusion of the important cultigens which they spawned. Even as they stand, however, identifications of charred remains of four of the wild-plant foods exploited by the Mesolithic occupants of Beli-Lena add a new dimension to our perception of the diversity of pre-agrarian diet in this area at the Pleistocene–Holocene transition.

## Acknowledgements

The author is grateful to Dr Siran Deraniyagala and M. Roland Silva for entrusting to him the archaeobotanical investigations and for general help at the cave site of Beli-Lena (Kitulgala). Thanks are due to Professor S. B. Deo and Professor M. K. Dhavalikar for providing laboratory facilities. Grateful thanks are also due to the authorities of the University Grants Commission, New Delhi, for support for this short-term project during 1984–86. The author is grateful to Prof. P. J. Ucko of the World Archaeological Congress, Southampton, and the Indian National Science Academy, New Delhi, for each providing one-way travel support which enabled him to participate in the Congress. Sincere thanks are due to Prof. D. R. Harris and Gordon Hillman for helpful criticism and encouragement.

## References

Barrau, J. 1977. Breadfruit and relatives. In *Evolution of crop plants*, N. W. Simmonds (ed.), 201–2. London: Longman.
Chandraratna, M. F. 1951. The origin of cultivated races of banana. *The Indian Journal of Genetics and Plant Breeding* **11**, 29–33.
Chandraratna, M. F. & K. D. S. S. Nayanakkara 1951. Cultivated varieties of banana in Ceylon. *Tropical Agriculture* **107**, 70–91.

Cheeseman, E. E. 1948. Classification of bananas III a- *Musa balbisiana* Colla; b- *Musa acuminata* Colla. *Kew Bulletin* **1**, 11–28.

CSIR = (Council for Scientific and Industrial Research) 1962. *The wealth of India – raw materials*, Vol. 6: L–M, 449–451. New Delhi: Council for Scientific and Industrial Research.

Dasanayake, M. D. & F. R. Fosberg 1981. *A revised handbook to the flora of Ceylon*, Vol. 3. New Delhi: Oxford and IBH.

Deraniyagala, S. 1985. The prehistory of Sri Lanka: an outline. In *Festschrift James Rutnam*, A. R. B. Amarsinghe and S. J. Sumansekera (eds), 14–21. Colombo: UNESCO.

Glover, I. 1985. Some problems relating to the domestication of rice in Asia. In *Recent advances in Indo-Pacific prehistory*, V. N. Misra & P. Bellwood (eds), 257–79. Bombay: Oxford and IBH.

Jarrett, F. M. 1959. Studies on *Artocarpus* and allied genera. III: A revision of subgenus *Artocarpus*. *Journal of Arnold Arboretum* **60**, 327–68.

Simmonds, N. W. 1962. *The evolution of bananas*. London: Longman.

Simmonds, N. W. 1977. Bananas. In *Evolution of crop plants*, N. W. Simmonds (ed.), 211–15. London: Longman.

Trimmen, H. 1898. *A handbook to the flora of Ceylon. Part IV*. London: Dulau.

Yen, D. 1977. Hoabinhian horticulture? The evidence and the questions from northwest Thailand. In *Sunda and Sahul: prehistoric studies in Southeast Asia, Melanesia and Australia*, J. Allen, J. Golson & R. Jones (eds), 567–99. London: Academic Press.

# 16 New evidence on plant exploitation and environment during the Hoabinhian (Late Stone Age) from Ban Kao Caves, Thailand

KOSUM PYRAMARN

## Introduction

It is nearly 20 years since the first publication of Late Pleistocene and early Holocene plant remains from Spirit Cave in northwestern Thailand (Gorman 1969, 1973, Yen 1977) drew the attention of archaeologists to the possibility of testing Sauer's (1952) hypothesis proposing Southeast Asia as an early centre of plant domestication. In the intervening period, few other Hoabinhian (Late Stone Age) sites have been excavated (or at least published), and the Hoabinhian Research Project of Silpakorn University, Bangkok, led by Surin Pookajorn, represents an important step forward in our understanding of this crucial episode in Southeast Asian prehistory. The Project's excavations near Ban Kao in central Thailand have now produced remains of possible food plants associated with Hoabinhian habitation debris from three cave sites. Although the assemblage is small, it is highly significant in view of the dearth of direct evidence for pre-agrarian plant exploitation in this region.

All 28 items of remains of possible food or medicinal plants recovered from the three sites were seeds or fruits, and came from levels dated to between 11 000 and 2500 bp. Associated with the seed remains were tools of Hoabinhian type, bone remains, and, in the later levels, potsherds. The plant remains indicate that the local vegetation was of a type characteristic of the dry monsoon forest zone and include species which have served as food or medicines in recent times.

### The sites and their excavation

Kanchanaburi Province is in the west-central part of Thailand at latitude 14° 0′ 15″ N. and longitude 99° 19′ E. In 1977 and 1979, Surin Pookajorn undertook excavations in Kanchanaburi Province in order to further investi-gate local evidence of the Hoabinhian Culture previously known in the area from Sai Yok Cave (van Heekeren & Knuth 1967). Three sites were excavated: Khao Talu and Ment Caves in 1977 and Heap Cave in 1979. All three caves are located near Ban Kao village at the top of limestone hills which rise to a height of about 120 m above sea-level. The hills lie between Khao Kaeo and Khao Pathawi at a distance of about 4.5 km to the north of the River Kwai. All three sites contained human habitation debris extending from the surface to 120 cm depth and dating from 11 000 to 2500 bp. The sediment samples were of reddish brown colour and rich in ferric oxide and carbonates (Pookajorn 1977, 1979a & b).

## Preservation and abundance of the plant remains

Unfortunately, very few remains of seeds or other parts of higher plants were found in the excavated deposits. This is probably the result of rapid decomposition after deposition, and poor conditions for the survival of charred remains. Of the seed remains which survived, most are preserved by calcification and many are in poor fragmentary condition. In the 1977 excavations, four trenches at Khao Talu Cave yielded plant remains, but at Ment Cave only a single specimen was found, at a depth of 110–120 cm (Table 16.1). In 1979, excavation in Heap Cave resulted in the recovery of a total of just 25 specimens from a total of 16 layers. The plant remains were recovered by dry sieving followed by hand-sorting.

In most excavation layers, occasional plant remains were recovered at random intervals from the surface layers down to a depth of 70 cm. They were absent between 70 and 100 cm, but were present again at depths between 100 and 120 cm. The significance of this pattern remains uncertain. Besides seed remains, there were associated flint tools of Hoabinhian type, bones, and potsherds (Pookajorn 1979a, b). The seed and other plant remains from Khao Talu and Ment Caves were previously studied in 1980 by the late Professor Kasin Suwatabundhu, but the work was unfinished at his death.

## The plant types identified and their possible prehistoric uses

All the plant specimens identified from the three cave sites are itemized in Table 16.1, and typical examples appear in Figures 16.1–16.5.

### Licuala spinosa *Wurmb.*

Fruit shells and seeds of this palm (Fig. 16.1) were the most common class of plant remains so far identified from the three sites and all were preserved by calcification. This palm is commonly found in monsoon forests, rain forests, teak forests, and adjacent to sandy beaches. It grows well in dry lands as well as on limestone, but not in muddy areas. It is distributed widely

**Table 16.1** Numbers of fragments of food plants identified from excavations of Khao Talu Cave, and Heap Cave near Ban Kao Village, Kanchanaburi Province, Thailand, in 1977 and 1979. Cultural Level I corresponds to Early Hoabinhian, Level II to Late Hoabinhian, and Level III to Late Stone Age and Early Metal Age. The specimens from Heap Cave derived from different parts of the cave and from a range of different depths, but the results are here combined for each of the three cultural levels.

| | Khao Talu Cave | Ment Cave | Heap Cave | | |
|---|---|---|---|---|---|
| Cultural levels | II | I | I | II | III |
| Range of the $^{14}$C dates obtained from the levels concerned (all bp) | 4215 | 8400 | 8400–5200 | 4320–4215 | 3200–2150 |
| Seeds preserved by charring or calcification (and probably genuinely ancient) | | | | | |
| *Licuala spinosa* (a fan palm): fruit shells & seeds | | 1 (calc.) | 1 (calc.) | 8 (calc.) | 19 (calc.) |
| An indeterminate palm: fruit shells | | | | 4 (calc.) | 1 (calc.) |
| *Eugenia cumini* (the black plum): fruit stone | | | | 1 (calc.) | |
| *Croton tiglium* (croton oil plant): seeds | | | | | 1 (calc.) |
| *Phaseolus lathyroides* (a bean): seeds | cf. 1 (charred) | | | | |
| Seeds preserved without charring or calcification (and probably recent intrusives) | | | | | |
| *Phaseolus adenanthera* (another legume): seeds | | | | cf. 1 | cf. 2 |
| *Crotalaria bracteata* (another legume): seeds | | | cf. 4 | 1 | |
| *Cirtullus lanatus* (a melon): seeds | | | | | cf. 1 |
| *Benincasa hispida* (another cucurbit): seeds | | | ?1 | | |
| Rutaceae (indet.): seeds | | | ?2 | | |

**Figure 16.1**  Fruits of the palm *Licuala spinosa* Wurmb. Items labelled 'a' are ancient specimens preserved by calcification. Items labelled 'm' are modern specimens for comparison.

throughout the central, western, and peninsular parts of Thailand, Malaysia, and Java. It grows to about 5 m high with a stout stem, and has large fan-like orbicular leaves. Its fruits are drupaceous, small (6–8 mm diameter), and sub-globose with a persistent perianth. Mature fruits have a rather woody pericarp of reticulate appearance caused by secondary thickening of surface layers.

*Licuala* leaves were probably used as sleeping mats by the ancient peoples living in the caves, just as more recent hunter–gatherers spread large leaves on the ground on which to sleep out of doors. A typical example comes from the Mlabri, hunter–gatherers of the forests of North Thailand who are regarded by Pookajorn (1984) as the cultural descendants of Hoabinhian society. The Mlabri used to build temporary shelters out of locally available bamboo or wood and roofed with banana, palm, or rattan leaves, and these same large leaves were also spread on the ground as sleeping mats. Even among agrarian peoples, palm leaves are commonly used as roofing material.

The fruits of *Licuala* are also utilized today for medicinal purposes, for example by Thai village doctors. In phytochemical screening of Thai medicinal plants, Boonyaratavaj *et al.* (1983) reported the fruits of *Licuala* spp. to contain an alkaloid, flavanoid, and leucoanthocyanin. However, whether the fruits were gathered for their medicinal properties, or even detoxified and used as food, must remain uncertain.

**Figure 16.2** Calcified remains of the fruit case of an indeterminate species of palm. The photographs show inner and outer surfaces.

## Indeterminate palm type

Two calcified specimens from Heap Cave, chamber 2, trench 1, and Heap Cave, chamber 3, trench 1 also resembled some form of palm fruit (Fig. 16.2). The half-broken specimens are of oval shape, 18–20 mm long, with a single conspicuous straight ridge running down the external surface from the top, with a woody outer layer up to 2 mm thick, and with a crescentic hollow inner side. There was a distinct concave furrow around the base which could be the scar of what had been a persistent perianth. These distinctive features are similar to those of certain edible one-seeded palms, for instance coconut and betel-nut palm, having a woody endocarp and a crescentic cotyledon. Modern reference specimens of palm seeds of equivalent type are not currently available and the specimens could not be identified further.

## Eugenia type

Calcified specimens resembling the black plum *Eugenia cumini* Druce were recovered from deposits at depths of 50–60 cm in Heap Cave II, and one of the ancient specimens is illustrated in Figure 16.3 alongside modern specimens of both wild and domestic forms. Today, *Eugenia cumini* has many uses: not only are the fruits edible, but the bark from stem and roots provides a traditional Thai herbal medicine, as do the ripe fruits and seeds.

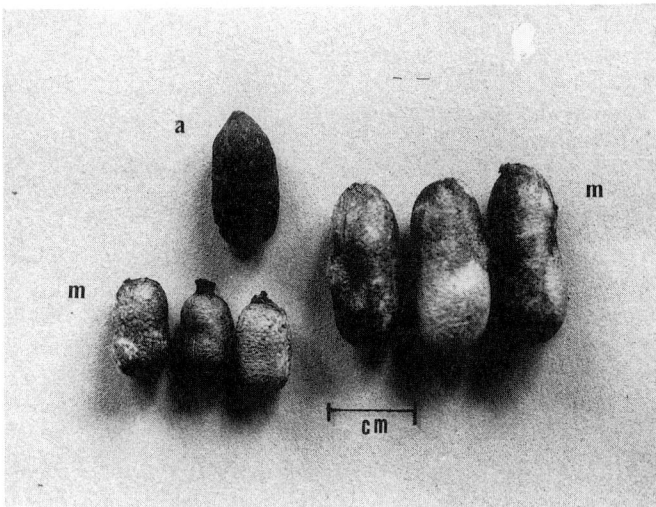

**Figure 16.3** One of the calcified seeds of *Eugenia* type. The item at the top left labelled 'a' is the ancient specimen. The others (labelled 'm') are modern; the small specimens are of the wild type, while the larger ones are of the domestic type.

## Croton

Calcified remains of seeds resembling those of the croton oil plant (*Croton tiglium* Linn.) were recovered from shallow deposits in Heap Cave III. Today, oil extracted from *Croton* seeds is prescribed as a strong purgative by traditional village doctors. The recovery of such seeds in occupation debris suggests that the cave occupants knew the value of such seeds, either as a medicine, or, if they could be readily detoxified, perhaps as a food.

## Seeds of legumes

A number of seed remains found in Heap Cave deposits ranging in depth from 0 to 60 cm bear close resemblance to the seeds of *Crotalaria bracteata* Roxb. ex DC. (Niyomdtham 1978). This herbaceous legume is common in Kanchanaburi Province and grows well on dry land with lateritic soils of the sort found today in the vicinity of the sites. Other leguminous seeds found in Heap Cave were of *Phaseolus adenanthera* G. M. F. Mey. One seed of *P. lathyroides* Linn. was also found in Khao Talu Cave. Apparently both the *Crotalaria* and *Phaseolus* seeds are edible (T. Johns pers. comm.). However, of these leguminous seeds, all but the seed of *P. lathyroides* were preserved without being charred or calcified, and they differed from modern seeds of the same species only in the altered colour of their testas. It is unlikely that seeds and fruits lacking siliceous pericarps, testas, or endocarps would survive in this climatic zone in aerobic deposits such as these without having been charred or mineralized. In view, therefore, of the universal problem of vertical intrusion into deep aerobic deposits by modern seeds (and some-times charred seeds from more recent deposits as well), it is probable that only the *P. lathyroides* is genuinely ancient and that the other legumes are recent intrusives.

## Seeds of cucurbits

Seeds of a water melon (*Citrullus* cf. *lanatus*) were recovered from shallow deposits of Cultural Level III in Heap Cave and those of a gourd (*Benincasa hispida*) from two deposits dated to 9980 bp and 9530 bp in Cultural Level I of the same site. Not only are the fruits of many cucurbits edible, but so are their seeds which are rich in starch, protein, and calcium, and both fruits and seeds may have been eaten. Like the legumes, however, the seed testas of cucurbits are not naturally silicified, and the seed remains were here preserved without having been either charred or calcified. Although cucurbit seeds are heavily lignified and can survive longer than most other plant debris, it is unlikely that the excavated specimens could have survived several millennia in these deposits in this form. They are therefore probably modern intrusives.

## Rutaceae *type*

A seed specimen from Heap Cave (from a layer at a depth of 60–70 cm) was of a distinctive shape with a straight ridge running upwards from the base. Although the shape and size of the sample were rather similar to seeds of the Rutaceae (the rue and citrus family), the present lack of a sufficiently wide range of reference specimens of modern equivalents has so far precluded a more specific identification. Many members of the Rutaceae, such as the orange, lemon, and pummelo, have edible fleshy fruits and their wild ancestors are native to this area. It is not impossible, therefore, that this specimen from Heap Cave derives from the edible fruit of a wild species of this type. However, its preservation without charring or calcification suggests that it may be yet another modern intrusive.

## 'Rice'

Pookajorn (1984) refers a specimen resembling a charred grain of rice to Cultural Level III of Khao Talu Cave dated to about $2800 \pm 300$ bp and belonging to the Late Neolithic to Early Metal Age. However, although this charred specimen has the same thickness as grains of present-day cultivated rice (*Oryza sativa*) and the same length as wild rice (*O. rufipogon*), closer examination of the specimen showed that it lacked the distinctive micromorphology of rice and it is probably a charred piece of woody twig.

## Conclusions

If the specimens of dubious antiquity are excluded, we are left with five types of seed or fruit: the *Licuala* palm; a second, unidentified type of palm seed; the black plum (*Eugenia*); a wild bean *Phaseolus lathyroides*; and the *Croton* oil plant. Of these five, the seeds of *Licuala* were by far the most abundant. From the presence of remains of the four positively identified types it can be concluded that the local vegetation of the Hoabinhian period resembled modern dry-monsoon forest, with large-leaved palms as probably one of the more conspicuous components.

From ecological studies of modern dry-monsoon forests, and from ethnographic studies among recent hunter–gatherers, it is known that such vegetation would have offered a rich resource environment for pre-agrarian subsistence. However, of the wide range of plant foods which is likely to have been used by the Hoabinhian inhabitants of these three caves, little survives. This may result from their dietary staples having consisted primarily of 'root' foods. Such foods are inherently unlikely to have been preserved by charring or mineralization and are almost never identified from pre-agrarian sites in the Old World (for a rare exception see Hillman Ch. 13, this volume). Certainly, heavy dependence on 'root' foods has characterized the diets of most tropical hunter–gatherers studied in recent times.

It may nevertheless be significant that, of the five types of plant remains preserved by calcification or charring in these Hoabinhian deposits, two are known food plants and two are used in present-day traditional medicine. Furthermore, the sophistication of historical hunter–gatherer technology in removing or neutralizing toxins from potential foodstuffs is such that we cannot altogether exclude the possibility that seeds of *Licuala*, *Croton*, and the second type of palm were also used as food (see, for example, Stahl Ch. 11, this volume and Jones' & Meehan's account of the detoxification of cycad seeds in Ch. 7, this volume). This possibility clearly deserves further investigation.

It should be noted that the plant types identified from these three caves at Ban Kao are entirely different from those identified from Spirit Cave in northwestern Thailand. This probably reflects the fact that the vegetation (and wild food resources) of northwestern Thailand is (and perhaps was) very different. It also underlines the fact that bioarchaeologists have barely begun to define the nature and range of 'typical' Hoabinhian subsistence.

## Acknowledgements

I wish to thank the curators of the Bangkok Herbarium, Ministry of Agriculture (BKK) and of the Forest Herbarium, Royal Forestry Department (BKF) for kindly providing access to herbarium specimens. Also my appreciation to Dr Chawalit Niyomdtham of the Royal Forestry Department for his valuable advice on *Crotalaria* seeds. But above all my gratitude to Mr Surin Pookajorn, the leader of the Hoabinhian research project, Silpakorn University, for allowing me to participate in this project.

## References

Boonyaratavaj, S. *et al.* 1983. Phytochemical screening tests in Thai medicinal plants III: *Journal of Science Report Bangkok* **8**, 93–109.

Gorman, C. F. 1969. Hoabinhian: a pebble-tool complex with early plant associations in Southeast Asia. *Science* **163**, 671–3.

Gorman, C. F. 1973. Excavations at Spirit Cave, North Thailand: some interim interpretations. *Asian Perspectives* **13**, 79–107.

Hillman, G. C. 1989. Late Palaeolithic plant foods from Wadi Kubbaniya in Upper Egypt: dietary diversity, infant weaning, and seasonality in a riverine environment. In *Foraging and farming: the evolution of plant exploitation*, D. R. Harris & G. C. Hillman (eds), ch. 13. London: Unwin Hyman.

Jones, R. & B. Meehan 1989. Plant foods of the Gidjingali: ethnographic and archaeological perspectives from northern Australia on tuber and seed exploitation. In *Foraging and farming: the evolution of plant exploitation*, D. R. Harris & G. C. Hillman (eds), ch. 7. London: Unwin Hyman.

Niyomdtham, C. 1978. A revision of the genus *Crotalaria* Linn. (Papilionaceae) in Thailand. *Thai Forestry Bulletin* **11**, 105–81.

Pookajorn, S. 1977. *Preliminary report of excavations at Khao Talu, Ment, and Petch Kuha Caves in 1977*, Vol. 1, no. 1. Silpakorn University Press (in Thai).

Pookajorn, S. 1979a. *The results of scientific analysis of excavations at Khao Talu, Ment, and Petch Kuha Caves in 1977*, Vol. 1, no. 2. Silpakorn University Press (in Thai).

Pookajorn, S. 1979b. *Preliminary report of excavation at Heap Cave in 1979*, Vol. 2, no. 1. Silpakorn University Press (in Thai).

Pookajorn, S. 1984. The Hoabinhian of mainland Southeast Asia, new data from the recent Thai excavation in the Ban Kao area. Thammasat University Press.

Sauer, C. O. 1952. *Agricultural origins and dispersals*. New York: American Geographical Society.

Stahl, A. B. 1989. Plant-food processing: implications for dietary quality. In *Foraging and farming: the evolution of plant exploitation*, D. R. Harris & G. C. Hillman (eds), ch. 11. London: Unwin Hyman.

van Heekeren, H. R. & E. Knuth 1967. *Archaeological excavations in Thailand*, Vol. I: *Sai Yok*. Copenhagen: Munksgaard.

Yen, D. E. 1977. Hoabinhian horticulture? The evidence and the questions from northwest Thailand. In *Sunda and Sahul: prehistoric studies in Southeast Asia, Melanesia and Australia*, J. Allen, J. Golson & R. Jones (eds), pp. 567–99. London: Academic Press.

# 17 The taming of the rain forests: a model for Late Pleistocene forest exploitation in New Guinea

LES GROUBE

In what must surely be among Pleistocene man's greatest achievements, the large island continent of Sahuland (New Guinea, Australia, and Tasmania) was colonized from Southeast Asia over 40 000 years ago (Groube *et al.* 1986). Even when sea-levels were at a low of − 90 m below present levels, about 52 000 years ago (Chappell 1983), open ocean distances of over 100 km had to be negotiated. How this remarkable and precocious maritime adventure was actually achieved, whether by raft, canoe, or on natural floating vegetation, may never be known. What is clear is that in crossing this ocean barrier man became only the third placental mammal (after the ubiquitous rats and bats) to invade Sahuland. There humans found a continent which had already been invaded by many floristic elements from their tropical humid-forest homeland, at least along its northern boundaries.

## Human colonization of the Late Pleistocene forest environment

Botanical investigations (Paijmans 1976, Flenley 1979, pp. 77–81) have clearly demonstrated that the lower altitude and coastal vegetation of northern Sahuland (now New Guinea) belongs firmly with the rich Malesian flora of Southeast Asia, although it contains many ancient botanical elements inherited from the breakup of Gondwanaland over 100 million years ago. Higher altitudes are dominated by remnants of the Gondwanaland flora, the cooler climate having offered an ideal refuge for many plants. Added to this rich floristic mix were other elements – also derived ultimately from the breakup of Gondwanaland but routed via India, a Gondwanaland remnant – which reinvaded northern Sahuland as it moved northward close to southern Asia. As is apparent from Balgooy (1976, Fig. 1.2), the end product of this complex floristic inheritance is that mainland New Guinea contains a more diverse range of genera than any island group farther west in the Malesian heartland.

This complex floristic history of northern Sahuland played an important role in human colonization. There seems little reason to doubt that the first human penetration, coming as it did from tropical forested southern Asia, was by people already physically and culturally adapted to humid-forest conditions. Macfarlane's remarkable demonstration, from tests on Australian Aborigines and Europeans in arid central Australia, that the Europeans were better physiologically adapted to aridity than were the Aborigines, whose sweat-gland characteristics showed an obvious inheritance from humid, forested conditions (Macfarlane 1976), has many implications for archaeology. One of the most important of these is that models derived from the more arid areas of Australia may be misleading. The overpowering authority of the ethnography of the Australian Aborigines, largely based on the study of surviving groups in the more arid areas of the continent, from which archaeologists have built the concept of the classic hunter–gatherer, represents not so much a relic of formerly more widespread lifestyles as a complex adaptation, within Australia itself, to non-tropical forest environments. Such adaptation was not required in the humid forests of northern Sahuland which, to the initial colonists, must have been familiar. Along the coast also, environmental conditions must have been almost identical to those in their southern Asian homeland, with similar varieties of shellfish, lagoonal, and mangrove resources available.

In the Late Pleistocene the coastal forests of Sahuland must have, at various times, reached full maturity. Climatic shifts during the Pleistocene, fluctuating cloud cover, and associated temperature changes would have ensured that the vegetation was not uniformly mature. Mid- and lower-altitude forests, less susceptible to climatic fluctuations, would have been relatively stable, although local adjustments to landslips, volcanic eruptions, naturally occurring forest fires, and cyclones would have accentuated the mosaic pattern of regeneration of forest stands. Only in the frequently altering alluvial river systems, however, would there have been extensive tracts of immature, regenerating vegetation. In the coastal areas many of the genera of trees and shrubs – although often represented by different species – would have been familiar to the new colonists, but at higher altitudes the increasingly dominant ancient Gondwanaland taxa would have been unfamiliar.

Coming from comparable tropical humid forests, it must be assumed that the new migrants were already familiar with appropriate methods of preparation of many of the food plants which contained toxins or inedible tissues. Many varieties of forest yams (*Dioscorea* spp.), the giant swamp taro (*Cyrtosperma* sp.), the bush taro (*Alocasia* sp.), trees with edible pith such as cycads (*Cycas* spp.) and sago (*Metroxylon* sp.), as well as many nut trees would have offered immediately available food resources. Initial survival in the tropical forests of northern Sahuland should have had few problems for migrants from the Malesian forests; exploration and experiment would have soon discovered adequate substitutes for missing elements familiar in their former homeland. How many of the rich Malesian-forest food plants were already present in the forests of northern Sahuland before the arrival of man will probably never be known, but it is abundantly clear from the botanical evidence now available that it can no longer be assumed that the cultivated food plants common to both Southeast Asia and Sahuland were transported to New Guinea from the northwest (Yen 1982, Golson Ch. 44, this volume). Each plant taxon exploited in both New Guinea and Asia must be examined separately to establish whether it was part of the original New Guinea flora or whether it was introduced by man. This is a task of such magnitude that it seems pointless to speculate, although on present evidence it seems probable that two of the staple root crops – yam (*Dioscorea alata* and *D. esculenta*) and taro (*Colocasia esculenta*) – were imported into Sahuland at some time during prehistory. For most of the other important food plants of Sahuland, judgement as to their original provenance must be suspended until current research is completed (Yen 1982). What is abundantly clear is that the assumption of a decade ago, that man brought in the bulk of his food plants from Asia, can no longer be sustained; indeed, some important foods plants present in Southeast Asia (e.g. *Pandanus* sp.) may have been transferred in the opposite direction.

Although details of the native plant resources in northern Sahuland available to the initial colonists are as yet unclear, there is less debate about animal resources. The absence of the familiar placental mammals of Asia must have surprised the new colonists, although there is no reason to think that the marsupial fauna of Sahuland was any less abundant than the placental fauna of Asia, particularly during initial colonization. Hunting strategies developed in the Southeast Asian homeland may have had to be adapted to the new species, but it seems unlikely that this would have required any major changes in the techniques of food procurement. Along the coast the abundance of shellfish, turtles, dugong, and lagoonal fish would have provided a ready source of protein.

Thus, for people already adapted to the humid forests of southern Asia, the coastal forests of northern Sahuland would have presented few difficulties. Expansion southward into the non-tropical areas and away from the familiar rain forests would, however, have required considerable cultural adaptation. Similarly, the colonization of the interior high-altitude forests of the north (the Highlands of New Guinea), which contained many unfamiliar species of plants, would have presented problems of adaptation. Despite this, the mid- and upper-montane forests appear to have been penetrated remarkably early, as the evidence reviewed below suggests.

## Evidence for Late Pleistocene forest exploitation

Evidence for some sort of human interference with the forests of New Guinea well before the end of the Pleistocene is now compelling. Following White's discovery of distinctive stone axes (then called 'waisted blades') at Kosipe in the central Papuan Highlands (White *et al.* 1970) dating to 26 000 bp, Hope (1982) recovered from the adjoining swamp evidence of forest disturbance and charcoal in pollen cores dating to 30 000 bp. White's tentative suggestion (op. cit. p. 168) that the 'waisted blades' might be associated with exploitation of the rich stands of *Pandanus* in the nearby swamp is made more plausible by this palynological evidence. Comparable evidence of forest alteration in the Late Pleistocene from other Highlands areas has been reviewed by Hope *et al.* 1983, and from this it is clear that man was exploiting the mid- and upper-montane forests of Papua New Guinea up to and above the treeline at a very early date. Provocative, but still unproven, evidence of the deliberate splitting of timber in mid-montane forests at Yonki, in the Eastern Highlands of Papua New Guinea firmly dated to 40 000 bp (Haberle pers. comm.) is the latest and most direct evidence we have for forest exploitation during the Pleistocene (unless some sort of natural splitting process can be established for the long 'planks' found). Thus, we now know that man had successfully penetrated, and was already modifying, the inland forests of Papua New Guinea during the Late Pleistocene, testimony to the successful adaptation of rain-forest dwellers to colder montane forests. Relatively large tools suitable for forest clearance or manipulation (the 'waisted blades') are plausibly associated with this penetration of the interior.

Direct evidence of interference with coastal forests is not yet available. The vast changes to coastal drainage systems, the inundation of the coastline, the infilling of former river valleys, and the formation of vast alluvial deltas as the sea-level rose during the last 20 000 years has irretrievably removed the crucial evidence. Existing coastal swamps are of Holocene age (most of them late Holocene), formed after the coastal drainage patterns stabilized about 6000 years ago. Basal muds from the Waigani swamp (near Port Moresby) have yielded late Holocene dates (Osborne & Polunin pers. comm.). The distortion of our record of the past by this massive removal of all coastal sites cannot be remedied easily. The reasonable assumption that, preceding the well-documented human penetration of the highlands (unaffected by the rising sea-levels), is an earlier period of successful coastal exploitation must remain unproven, except where geological circumstances have allowed the survival of relict Pleistocene coasts.

Such circumstances, fortunately, occur on the Huon Peninsula in Morobe Province in northern Papua New Guinea, where coastal uplift, achieving a remarkable maximum rate of nearly 3 m per 1000 years, has thrust Pleistocene coastlines upwards, above the rising sea-levels of the Pleistocene amelioration (Chappell 1974, Groube 1986). Unfortunately, the fractured and porous relict coral-reef formations along this coastline have not favoured swamp development. No suitable sites for pollen investigation have yet been located. In addition, coralline soils yield poor pollen records, although the presence of many blanketing horizons of volcanic ash along various section of the uplifted coral reefs offers some consolation. Somewhere along the 80 km or so of uplifted coast there may be a site with the right sedimentary or soil environment for the preservation of pollen.

The indirect evidence of coatal forest exploitation on the Huon Peninsula

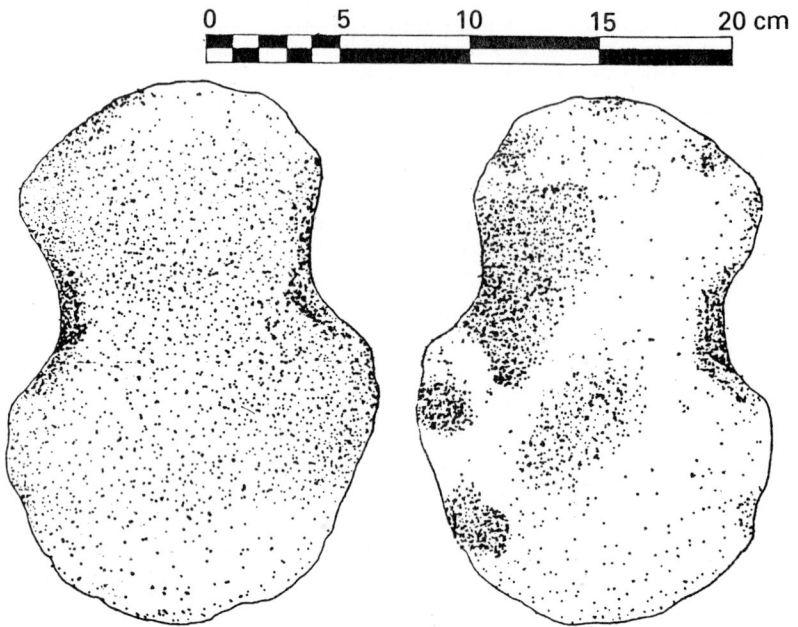

**Figure 17.1**   Waisted axe from the Huon Peninsula, Papua New Guinea.

is, however, excellent. Large waisted 'axes', very similar to, although larger than, those found at Kosipe, have been recovered from numerous streams at altitudes between 100 and 200 m above present sea-level, associated with a firmly dated coral-reef development (Reef IVa, Chappell 1974). This date has been directly confirmed by the discovery of waisted axes sealed beneath volcanic ashes dating to *c.* 40 000 bp (Groube *et al.* 1986).

These large, unifacial stone tools (Fig. 17.1), made by a rare spallation technique and furnished with opposed notches (or waisting), have been described elsewhere (Muke 1984, Groube 1986 & forthcoming). Here we are concerned with their possible function as 'pioneering forest-clearance tools' (Groube 1986, p. 175). The reasons for considering these axes in this role are argued fully elsewhere (Groube forthcoming) and are only summarized here:

(a)   The size and weight of the majority of the tools (average weight 1.9 kg, largest 2.64 kg) (Fig. 17.1), combined with the fact that they were almost certainly hafted (several have clear wear-marks from an encircling lashing around the waist, and one is distinctively grooved around both sides), suggests a task requiring a heavy energy input.

(b)   The material they are invariably made from – coarse-grained but tough andesite – does not maintain a sharp edge; it 'rounds-off' almost at first impact. Incision cutting with these tools is unlikely, but their sheer weight assures penetration even with the relatively blunt cutting edge.

(c)     A large number of broken waisted axes has been recovered, together with about 60 complete examples. The broken ones are invariably fractured across the waist, parallel to the cutting edge, suggesting that during their working life they often hit hard material, the percussion being transmitted through the coarse-grained material to the point of greatest weakness and the centre of the leverage, the waisting.

(d)     The presence of large damage scars on some of the axes is also consistent with a heavy work-load and hard material.

These characteristics are consistent with a suite of functions associated with forest clearance: ring barking, branch trimming, root clearance, and, perhaps, in association with fire, the felling of smaller trees. Their weak edge-characteristics rule out the working of hardwoods, although combined with the use of fire these blunt but heavy tools could be employed in a wide range of tasks. They would be suitable also for some forms of more direct food procurement; e.g. in most stages of sago production, for splitting cycad trunks, or for thinning *Pandanus* stands to promote ripening of the fruit.

One possible function of these axes, as mattocks or hoes, for which their weight characteristics might be an advantage, has been seriously examined. Despite the fact that there is a well-recorded use of almost identical tools (hafted mattock-style) for weeding and gardening from Botel Tobago, a small island south of Taiwan (Leach 1938, Groube 1986, p. 169), and the fact that similar tools are invariably called hoes in Northeast Asia (ibid.), the absence of the 'polishing' which is characteristic of wear on stone tools used in tillage, and the lack in the area where they have been found of soils stiff enough to justify such heavy mattocks or hoes, has led to rejection of this possibility. Nevertheless, in stiff soils and for very large earth-working tasks, these waisted axes, hafted adze- or mattock-style, would be a useful tool. Hardwood digging sticks, however, are equally useful for this purpose.

If the axes were used for forest clearing or trimming, as their size and shape recommends, they are a lithic witness to forest interference on the coast of Sahuland, earlier than any palynological evidence presently available from the Highlands.

That the incursions into the forests of Pleistocene New Guinea suggested by the lithic evidence may have been more than casual foraging is hinted at by the presence on the surface of Tephra 3 at the Jo's Creek site at Bobongara, Huon Peninsula (Groube *et al.* 1986), dating to 40 000 years ago, of two parallel, flat-bottomed, shallow 'ditches'. Examination of these features is still underway and they may yet prove to be illusory. More certain is the evidence from Cole's pioneering survey in the Eastern Highlands where at one site (NFX) the remains of a post belonging to a probable house and hearth complex was dated to *c.* 18 000 bp (Watson & Cole 1978, pp. 35–40, 130, 194–5). This is surely one of the earliest recorded houses in the world.

It is evident from numerous rockshelter excavations carried out during the past two decades that the forests of northern Sahuland were yielding a harvest for hunters during the Pleistocene (White 1972, Bulmer 1975, Gillieson & Mountain 1983). What effect these hunting parties had upon the vegetation, and whether fire (as in Australia) was used as a principal weapon in hunting, is unknown. Actual vegetal remains (such as the woody fruits of *Pandanus*) have been found in some rockshelters (Christensen 1975, Mangi 1984), but the fluctuating Pleistocene climate, with associated shifts of the treeline and of resources, makes interpretation of these remains very difficult. Hunting strategies alone could well have had sufficient impact upon the vegetation to account for the Pleistocene pollen records of forest interference as early as 30 000 years ago. It is only the less ambiguous evidence from the immediately post-Pleistocene site of Kuk in the Western Highlands of Papua New Guinea (Golson 1977 & Ch. 44, this volume), where swamp manipulation for food production appears to have started by 9000 years ago, which allows us to be certain that we are not dealing with hunting activities. That this manipulation began at Kuk almost as soon as the climate was warm enough after the end of the Pleistocene suggests that it may have been practised at lower altitudes during the Pleistocene.

The evidence of forest interference in the Late Pleistocene, culminating in the impressive Holocene exploitation of the Kuk swamp, suggests that the forest dwellers of northern Sahuland had developed strategies of survival in the forest which involved alteration of the existing vegetation. The principal tools used in this process appear to have been fire and/or waisted axes; but whether this strategy enhanced hunting success (by creating grassland) or promoted vegetal resources, or both, is unknown. What is certain is that the forest dwellers of northern Sahuland were not passive in their environment but actively altered it.

## Interpretation of Late Pleistocene forest exploitation

As has already been argued, the evidence of interference with the Pleistocene forests of northern Sahuland could be explained as the accumulated result of casual hunting and foraging activities over the 30 000–40 000 years of Pleistocene occupation. This assumes of course – except when fires are accidental – some significant advantage in clearance and/or thinning of the forests for hunting. Expanding the areas of open land and grassy vegetation would enhance opportunities for hunting terrestrial marsupials, such as wallabies, but only at the expense of arboreal and forest species. Over the long time-span of man's presence in the forests of northern Sahuland, the accumulated effect of accidental forest firings, particularly in regions with marked dry seasons such as the Eastern Highlands or the southeastern rain-shadow area, could have been considerable. The vegetation in the Port Moresby area, where there is a long dry-season, is distinctively Australian in character (Paijmans 1976, pp. 53 & 76–9), yet many botanists consider that the dominance in Australia of the fire-tolerant eucalypts (common in the landscape around Port Moresby) is partially, at least, a result of a long history of human firing of vegetation (Singh *et al.* 1981).

Outside the sensitive rain-shadow areas, the systematic removal of rain forest is a formidable task which would never have been undertaken without necessity. Hunting strategies alone seem insufficient to account for the widespread evidence of forest interference in the Pleistocene, but manipulation of the forests to enhance and improve stocks of existing plant foods offers a more plausible explanation of the scale of the inferred interference. Although the plant resources of the northern Sahuland forests were rich, particularly during initial settlement, most of the useful and productive food plants grow only in particular habitats: in ecotonal areas, between naturally occurring stands of different maturity (the boundaries of landslips for example), on river, swamp, or cliff edges, in the ecotones between the different altitudinal zones, and in all 'disturbed' areas. A study of Powell's pioneering survey of plants utilized in Papua New Guinea shows the dominance of plants requiring both sunlight and shade (Powell 1976). Few of the food plants of the northern Sahuland forest can tolerate the perpetual dimness of the mature rain forest; all require sunlight but also some shade. Their ideal habitat is an area of variable canopy height, with some sunlight and some shade, the typical environment of mixed or disturbed forest, most frequently found on the edges of clearing, i.e. the classic forest fringe (e.g. Sorenson 1976).

Thus, the first task of the forest dweller in northern Sahuland seeking to improve food resources would be to increase the area of 'disturbance' by opening up the canopy to sunlight and encouraging the plants sought for food. Restricted natural stands of food plants such as aerial yams, local bananas, swamp taro, and such tree crops as sago and *Pandanus*, could be promoted by judicious trimming, canopy-thinning, and ring-barking, and perhaps, with the aid of fire, some minor felling.

This strategy is close to that observed in certain parts of Papua New Guinea today, even where gardening (horticulture) is well established. Sago production in the Western Province, for example, seldom requires the planting of trees: merely maintenance of existing natural stands by clearing encroaching trees, keeping swamp channels clear, and promoting new shoots by felling mature trees (Rhoads 1980, Wijaszek & Poraituk 1981). It is a form of forest management which stretches the meaning of the word 'agriculture'. To call the sago palm itself a 'domesticate', when it appears to be unaltered from the wild plant, is another terminological problem. A more neutral term such as 'intensification' covers this case quite well, but fails to identify that the focus of the effort is not the food plant but its environment. In the case of sago, as with many other forest plants in Papua New Guinea, the plant itself remains unmolested but its surrounding environment is 'improved', 'manipulated' or, more exactly, 'managed'. Thus, with the sago palm, although not itself a domesticate in the strict sense of the word, production is 'improved' through the 'domestication' of its surrounding environment (cf. Yen Ch. 4, this volume). This terminological juggling indicates the difficulty of fitting the model of forest management proposed here into the standard jargon: hence the title of this chapter; the 'taming' of the forests. The 'Taming of the Shrew' is distinctly different from the 'Domestication of the Shrew' (mammologists forgive) and this distinction of being controlled but still wild, or subdued but not altered, which is implicit in the meaning of 'tamed', is important when considering subsistence in the rain forests of New Guinea.

Sago is not the only plant handled in this manipulative manner. *Pandanus*, an important seasonal food crop in the Highlands, is planted and maintained at lower altitudes but seldom planted at higher altitudes in its natural habitat. Here natural stands of this valuable tree are jealously maintained, either by groups or individuals (Barth 1975, p. 41, Sorenson 1976, p. 53). On seasonal visits, the surrounding vegetation is cleared and the ideal conditions for the maintenance of good crops are sought. *Pandanus*, however, is not a rain-forest plant, although it can, under certain environmental conditions, form a dense and dominant ground cover (Paijmans 1976, p. 43). The giant swamp-taro, which must have been present at river and swamp margins at the time of man's first arrival, is an ideal plant for intensification via 'taming' of the environment. Some clearing of the river margins where it occurs, to increase sunlight and the potential area for its expansion, together with continual maintenance of the stand, could elevate this forest plant to a reliable staple. The same could be argued, perhaps, for some coastal varieties of the bush taro, which, with suitable processing, may have been used in the past. Local bananas, yams, and particularly the nutritious green vegetables aibica (*Abelmoschus* (syn. *Hibiscus*) *manihot*), rungia (*Rungia klossii*), and winged bean (*Psophocarpus tetragonolobus*) would all prosper with an expansion of cleared areas.

The effectiveness of this 'minimal' manipulation strategy in rain forests was evident around the Tabubil area only six years ago. With the establishment of the new town of Tabubil by the Ok Tedi Mining Consortium, many Mountain Ok people moved down from their villages to work for the company. Although they had well-developed gardens in their own high-altitude villages they employed a minimal clearance and felling strategy (Barth 1975). In the heavy rainfall area of Tabubil the Mountain Ok people had explored the forests surrounding the town and had exposed all the natural stands of food plants (taro, bananas, etc.). Connected by faint trails running in all directions through the dense, dripping rain forests around Tabubil, there were flourishing stands of taro and bananas in barely discernible clearings with only minimal openings in the canopy. These stands were a valuable supplement to the canteen food, allowing many of the Mountain Ok to bring their families down to the township. Whether they were long-established stands, or ones opportunistically established after the development of the town, is not known, but with a minimal alteration to the forest they became a controlled food resource (presumably 'owned' by individuals or groups).

This strategy of minimal manipulation to enhance the growth of existing forest food plants is, I suspect, an extremely ancient, if not universal, method of food-extraction in rain forests. It is analogous to the 'fire-stick' farming of Australian Aborigines (Jones 1969, 1975) involving minimum manipulation by means of fire to maintain resources.

In forested regions with a lower rainfall than Tabubil, or with a distinct dry season, this strategy of minimal clearing would eventually result in the development of extensive cleared areas through burning and the expansion of grassland. Plant manipulation would thus be restricted to the forest fringes, the ideal habitat for the majority of food plants in the forests of Sahuland. Such grasslands also may have had hunting advantages. Thus, even with this minimum strategy of canopy thinning and the promotion of existing natural stands, there would probably be a slow increase in grasslands at the expense of forest in certain climatic areas brought about by burning, particularly if fire were being used to hunt terrestrial marsupials such as wallabies.

## From forest foraging to gardening: an evolutionary model

With this concept of minimal forest exploitation strategies it is possible to envisage an entirely different (forest) route to the development of horticulture in northern Sahuland, independent of transitions to horticulture or agriculture elsewhere. The stages in this hypothetical transformation from forest foraging to gardening are given below.

1   *Forest foraging/hunting*. This would be the period of initial exploration of the new forest resources, both plant and animal. As the new colonists almost certainly brought with them traditional skills from the humid forests of southern Asia, this would be rapidly transformed into:
2   *Food-plant promotion*. The selection of desirable plants and their promotion through minimal clearance and/or expansion of the forest fringes. This strategy is one of environmental manipulation not food-plant manipulation. Gradually, as group territories stabilized, this system of plant promotion would become one of:
3   *Forest management*, with permanent or semi-permanent promoted stands (as with sago today). This stage could have been highly productive and, depending on rainfall, extremely stable. In very wet forested regions, where the effect of burning would be minimal, this strategy could persist with little change for thousands of years, as it may well have done for many sago-growing areas. In regions with a dry season, where the forest was susceptible to long-term modification, the forest-fringe areas, where more of the food plants grew, would have slowly shrunk. Perhaps it was this sort of pressure or as discussed below, competition from pigs, that caused the management of scattered natural stands to be transformed into the management of:
4   *Forest gardens*. In the terms of this model of forest exploitation, a garden is

merely a concentration or aggregation of the scattered natural stands. It is only at this stage that the plants are themselves manipulated, being transferred from their natural habitat to the garden. It is then that sustained selection can begin, through close control of the plant's reproductive system, and true domestication can be said to occur (cf. Harris Ch. 1, this volume).

Why should this last stage become necessary? In the drier seasonal areas suitable natural stands may have become so rare as forest boundaries shrank that a strategy of concentration of resources was necessary. Intergroup competition for natural forest resources, also, may have played a role. More important, perhaps, was competition for these same food-plant resources from another alien placental mammal, the Asian pig.

From the absence of the pig in prehistoric Australia, it is apparent that this ground-foraging animal could not have been introduced much before the breakup of Sahuland by rising sea-levels between 9000 and 7000 years ago. There seems little doubt that the pig was well established in Papua New Guinea by 5000 years ago, and two sites suggest the presence of the pig as early as 10 000 years ago (Bulmer 1966, Golson 1982, pp. 125–30, White with O'Connell 1982, pp. 187–9).

The pig, both domesticated and feral, was a direct threat to many of the native food plants of the forests of northern Sahuland, which up to the time of its introduction were – in terms of large placental mammals – the exclusive domain of man. With the establishment of the pig we see the final stage in the local development of horticulture which is:

5   *Fenced or ditched gardens.* It is possible that this final development was quite late in most of New Guinea. As taro, because of its toxins, is not foraged by pigs, their impact upon gardens would have been of nuisance rather than threat value. After the introduction of the sweet potato (*Ipomoea batatas*), for which pigs have a particular relish, protection for gardens would have become essential.

This evolutionary model, which envisages the slow emergence of forest horticulture from foraging through forest management, satisfactorily accounts for the presence of large stone tools. It is apparent that for stage 2, food-plant promotion requiring minor clearing, canopy-thinning, ring-barking, etc., the waisted axes as known from the Huon Peninsula and Kosipe are ideal. Thus it can be argued that by at least 40 000 years ago the forest dwellers of northern Sahuland were already effectively manipulating their environment for food production, just as their brothers to the south were, with the aid of fire, manipulating the varied environments of southern Sahuland.

# References

Balgooy, M. M. J. van 1976. Phytogeography. In *New Guinea vegetation*, K. Paijmans (ed.), 1–22. Canberra: CSIRO, Australian National University Press.

Barth, F. 1975. *Ritual and knowledge among the Baktaman of New Guinea*. New Haven, Conn.: Yale University Press.

Bulmer, S. 1966. Pig bone from two archaeological sites in the New Guinea Highlands. *Journal of the Polynesian Society* **75**, 504–5.

Bulmer, S. 1975. Settlement and economy in prehistoric Papua New Guinea: a review of the archaeological evidence. *Journal de la Société des Océanistes* **31**, 7–75.

Chappell, J. M. A. 1974. Geology of coral terraces, Huon Peninsula, New Guinea: a study of Quaternary tectonic movements and sea-level changes. *Bulletin of the Geological Society of America* **85**, 553–70.

Chappell, J. M. A. 1983. A revised sea-level record for the last 300 000 years from Papua New Guinea. *Search* **14**, 99–101.

Christensen, O. 1975. Hunters and horticulturalists: a preliminary report on the 1972–4 excavations in the Manam valley, Papua New Guinea. *Mankind* **10** 71–5.

Flenley, J. 1979. *The equatorial rainforest: a geological history*. London and Boston: Butterworths.

Gillieson, D. & M-J. Mountain 1983. Environmental history of Nombe rockshelter, Papua New Guinea Highlands. *Archaeology in Oceania* **18**, 45–53.

Golson, J. 1977. No room at the top: agricultural intensification in the New Guinea Highlands. In *Sunda and Sahul: prehistoric studies in Southeast Asia, Melonesia and Australia*, J. Allen, J. Golson & R. Jones (eds), 601–38. London: Academic Press.

Golson, J. 1982. The Ipomoean revolution revisited. Society and the sweet potato in the Upper Waghi Valley. In *Inequality in New Guinea Highland societies*, A. Strathern (ed.), 109–36. Cambridge: Cambridge University Press.

Golson, J. 1989. The origins and development of New Guinea agriculture. In *Foraging and farming: the evolution of plant exploitation*, D. R. Harris & G. C. Hillman (eds), ch. 44. London: Unwin Hyman.

Groube, L. 1986. Waisted axes of Asia, Melanesia and Australia. In *Archaeology at ANZAAS, 1984*, G. K. Ward (ed.), 168–77. Canberra: Canberra Archaeological Society.

Groube, L. in press. A new Pleistocene stone tool assemblage: implications for the settlement of Sahuland. *Antiquity*.

Groube, L., J. Chappell, J. Muke & D. Price 1986. A 40 000 year-old human occupation site at Huon Peninsula, Papua New Guinea. *Nature* **324**, 453–5.

Harris, D. R. 1989. An evolutionary continuum of people–plant interaction. In *Foraging and farming: the evolution of plant exploitation*, D. R. Harris & G. C. Hillman (eds), ch. 1. London: Unwin Hyman.

Hope, G. 1982. Pollen from archaeological sites: a comparison of swamp and open archaeological site pollen spectra at Kosipe Mission, Papua New Guinea. In *Archaeometry: an Australian perspective*, W. Ambrose & P. Duerden (eds), 211–19. Canberra: Department of Prehistory, Research School of Pacific Studies, Australian National University.

Hope, G., J. Golson & J. Allen 1983. Palaeoecology and prehistory in New Guinea. *Journal of Human Evolution* **12**, 337–60.

Jones, R. 1969. Firestick farming. *Australian Natural History* **16**, 224–8.

Jones, R. 1975. The Neolithic Palaeolithic and the hunting gardeners: man and land in the Antipodes. In *Quaternary studies*, R. P. Suggate & M. M. Cresswell (eds), 21–34. Wellington: Royal Society of New Zealand.

Leach, E. 1938. Stone implements from Botel Tobago Island. *Man* **38**, 161–3.

Macfarlane, W. 1976. Aboriginal palaeophysiology. In *The Origin of the Australians*,

R. L. Kirk & A. G. Thomas (eds), 181–94. Canberra: Australian Institute of Aboriginal Studies.

Mangi, J. 1984. *Prehistory of the Manam rockshelter, Western Highlands, Papua New Guinea.* Unpublished B.Litt. thesis, Department of Prehistory, Research School of Pacific Studies, Australian National University, Canberra.

Muke, J. 1984. *The Huon discoveries.* Unpublished B.Litt thesis, Department of Prehistory, Research School of Pacific Studies, Australian National University, Canberra.

Paijmans, K. (ed.) 1976. *New Guinea vegetation.* Canberra: CSIRO, Australian National University Press.

Powell, J. M. 1976. Ethnobotany. In *New Guinea vegetation*, J. Paijmans (ed.), 106–83. Canberra: CSIRO, Australian National University Press.

Rhoads, J. W. 1980. *Through a glass darkly: present and past of Papuan sago palm users.* Unpublished PhD dissertation, Department of Prehistory, Research School of Pacific Studies, Australian National University, Canberra.

Singh, G., A. P. Kershaw & R. Clarke 1981. Quaternary vegetation and fire history in Australia. In *Fire and the Australian biota*, A. M. Gill, R. H. Groves & I. R. Noble (eds), 23–54. Canberra: Australian Academy of Sciences.

Sorenson, E. R. 1976. *The edge of the forest.* Washington, DC: Smithsonian Institution Press.

Watson, V. D. & J. D. Cole 1978. *Prehistory of the Eastern Highlands of New Guinea.* Canberra: Australian National University Press.

White, J. P. 1972. *Ol tumbuna: archaeological excavations in the eastern central highlands, Papua New Guinea. Terra Australis* 2. Canberra: Department of Prehistory, Research School of Pacific Studies, Australian National University.

White, J. P. with J. F. O'Connell 1982. *A prehistory of Australia, New Guinea and Sahul.* Sydney: Academic Press.

White, J. P., K. A. W. Crook & B. P. Buxton 1970. Kosipe: a Late Pleistocene site in the Papuan Highlands. *Proceedings of the Prehistoric Society* 36, 152–70.

Wijaszek, S. & S. P. Poraituk 1981. *Sago subsistence of the Purari River delta.* Port Moresby: Office of Environment and Conservation, Department of Minerals and Energy, Papua New Guinea Government.

Yen, D. E. 1982. The history of cultivated plants. In *Melanesia: beyond diversity.* Vol. 1, R. May & H. Nelson (eds), 281–95. Canberra: Research School of Pacific Studies, Australian National University.

Yen, D. E. 1989. The domestication of environment. In *Foraging and farming: the evolution of plant exploitation*, D. R. Harris & G. C. Hillman (eds), ch. 4. London: Unwin Hyman.

# 18 Seed gathering in inland Australia: current evidence from seed-grinders on the antiquity of the ethnohistorical pattern of exploitation

M. A. SMITH

There is now an impressive body of information about the systematic exploitation of wild seeds for food in the arid interior of the Australian continent (e.g. Allen 1972, 1974, Tindale 1972, 1977, Brokensha 1975, O'Connell & Hawkes 1981, Latz 1982, O'Connell *et al.* 1983, Cane 1984, Ch. 6, this volume, Kimber 1984). The harvesting and processing of grain by foragers in Australia invites comparison with late pre-agrarian groups, such as the Natufian in the Levant, which are known only through archaeological research (cf. Bar-Yosef & Kislev Ch. 40, Hillman *et al.* Ch. 41, and Moore Ch. 39, all in this volume). The Australian ethnography therefore has often been seen as contributing to a broader understanding of the ways in which prehistoric foragers may have exploited the useful plant species in their environment, and as providing some clues as to the processes underlying the beginnings of cereal-based agricultural systems elsewhere (e.g. Harris 1984). The value of such comparisons would be greatly enhanced if seed-gathering economies in inland Australia were themselves better understood in terms of their history and development. This chapter contributes to that objective by summarizing what is currently known of the antiquity of this pattern of plant use in inland Australia.

## Recognizing the use of seed foods in the archaeological record

It is first necessary to consider the ways in which seed exploitation might be detected in the archaeological record. There are two complementary lines of inquiry: (a) the direct recovery of the remains of plant foods, and (b) the identification of seed-grinding implements. The former has not been systematically applied in Australia, but both McBryde (1976, p. 65, 1977, p. 237) and Hayden (1979, pp. 137–8) have experimented with flotation techniques and have successfully recovered crushed seeds from archaeological deposits: these were of *Eragrostis* and *Sporobolus* in the former case and of *Aristida* in the latter case. Bowdery (1984) has also experimented with the recovery of phytoliths from archaeological contexts.

A major difficulty with this line of inquiry is that, for the results to be generally useful, seeds or phytoliths need to come from a recognized feature – such as a hearth, a storage or husking pit, the surface of a grindstone, or from within human coprolites – where their taphonomic history and probable role is unambiguous. This is particularly important in the Australian context where the plant species have not been genetically altered by the pattern of exploitation, and where useful seed-food species are also commonly occurring plants that often continue to grow on or near archaeological sites today.

The second line of inquiry is to identify in archaeological sequences seed-grinding implements of types which, in recent times, have been used specifically. This approach has been widely employed by archaeologists (e.g. Tindale 1959, Allen 1972, McBryde 1974) but generally without the benefit of any detailed study of the form of ethnographically known seed-grinders. In my own research I sought to rectify this by examining the morphology and usewear of such seed-grinding implements, and then comparing these with grindstones in archaeological assemblages (Smith 1985, 1986).

Although specialized or 'dedicated' seed-grinding implements are distinctive (cf. O'Connell 1977, pp. 274–7, Tindale 1977, pp. 346–7, Cane 1984, pp. 138–44, Smith 1985), problems of identification do arise because most archaeological specimens are fragments of larger implements and not all have retained sufficient features to be positively identified as part of a seed-grinder. The identification of organic residues or phytolith polish on artefacts suspected of having been used to process seeds would clearly be an advantage here. Certainly, it should theoretically be possible to distinguish microscopically (especially by SEM) between traces of ground seeds and microscopic fragments from the processing of, say, root foods (for examples of the use of such criteria in identifying seed remains, see Butler Ch. 24 and Piperno Ch. 34, this volume). Grass and sedge seeds, with their phytolith-laden husks, are especially likely to leave identifiable traces. However, there remains the formidable problem of distinguishing these ancient traces from modern contaminants; the deposits are, after all, full of phytoliths and other organic debris, both ancient and modern. In analysing organic traces from the surfaces of grinding stones and mortars from the 18 000 bp site of Wadi Kubbaniya in Egypt, both problems were addressed by chemical analysis: Jones (as cited by Hillman *et al.* in press, and Hillman Ch. 13, this volume) applied the technique of pyrolysis mass spectrometry

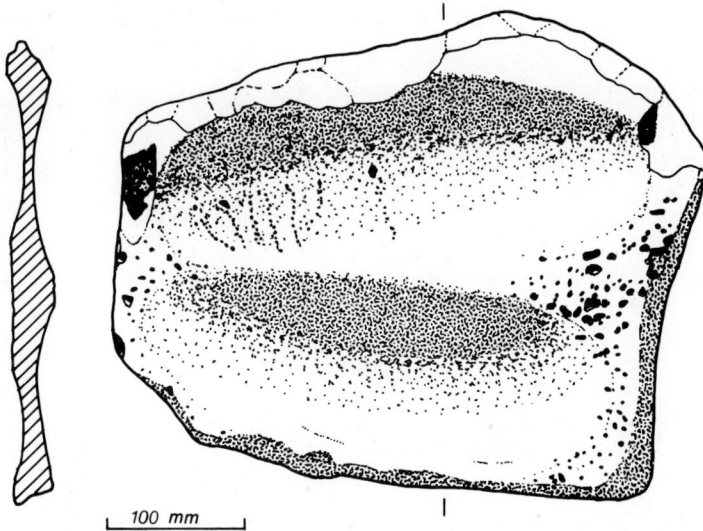

**Figure 18.1**   A millstone from Central Australia.

to the analysis of not only the working surfaces of the stones, but also the other surfaces as controls, and he was able to demonstrate:

(a)   that the ground foods had been rich in 'cellulosics' but extremely poor in protein, so were probably 'root' foods rather than seed foods; and

(b)   that the traces were unique to the working surfaces and were therefore unlikely to derive from organics in the source deposits.

However, these new techniques have yet to be applied outside Britain.

There are several types of seed-grinding implement, each with a different function (see Smith 1985 for details). At present the most important of these types for tracing the use of seed foods are millstones and mullers (see Figs 18.1 & 18.2, and cf. Tindale 1977, p. 346). These form a pair of grindstones used together for the wet milling of seeds. In excavated assemblages, fragments of millstones which retain either sections of the ground groove, the rim, or the median keel between grooves are easily identifiable. Indeed, mullers are often recovered as substantially intact specimens (Fig. 18.3). (The pattern of correlation between the abundance of remains of grinders and the degree of dependence on seed foods is discussed in the ethnographic context by Cane in Ch. 6, this volume, who also discusses modes of grinder use and wear.) Other types of seed-grinding implement, such as mortars and pestles which were used in the preliminary preparation of certain hard varieties of seed, have only rarely been found in archaeological contexts. The few examples that have been recovered fall within the chronological distribution established for millstones and mullers.

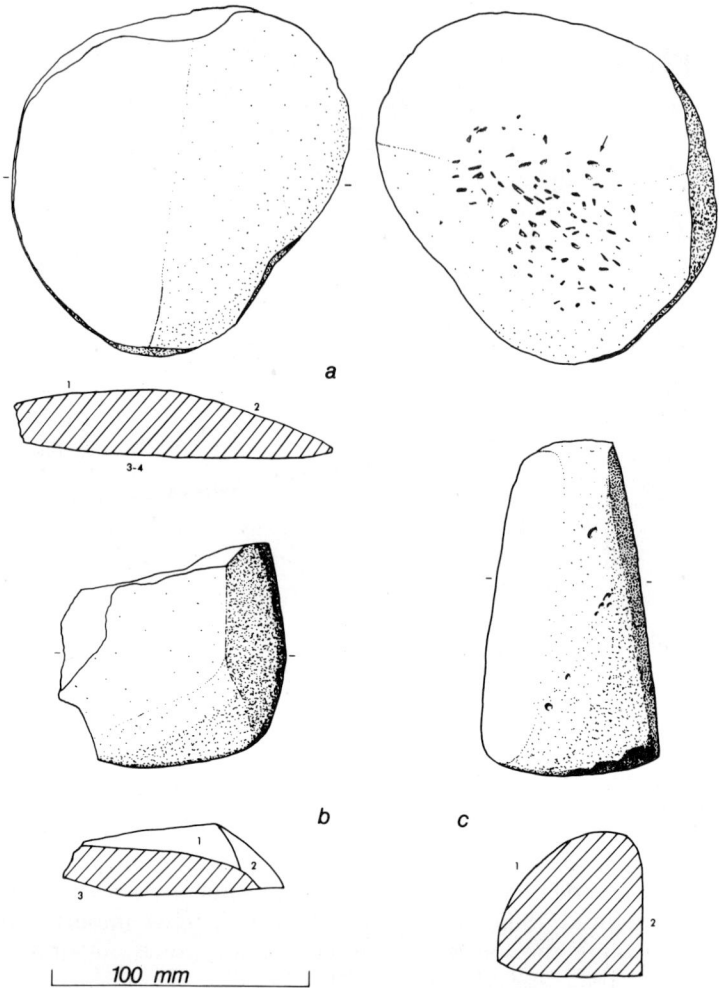

**Figure 18.2**   Examples of mullers from Central Australia.

## The chronological distribution of seed-grinding implements

Until recently it was thought that seed exploitation dated back to 12 000–15 000 bp on the eastern fringes of the arid zone (Allen 1972, 1974) and to about 10 000 bp in the central part of the continent (Gould 1977), thus coinciding with the first evidence for human occupation of the latter area (Bowdler 1977, O'Connell & Hawkes 1981). However, a re-assessment of the evidence suggests that the ethnohistorically observed patterns of plant

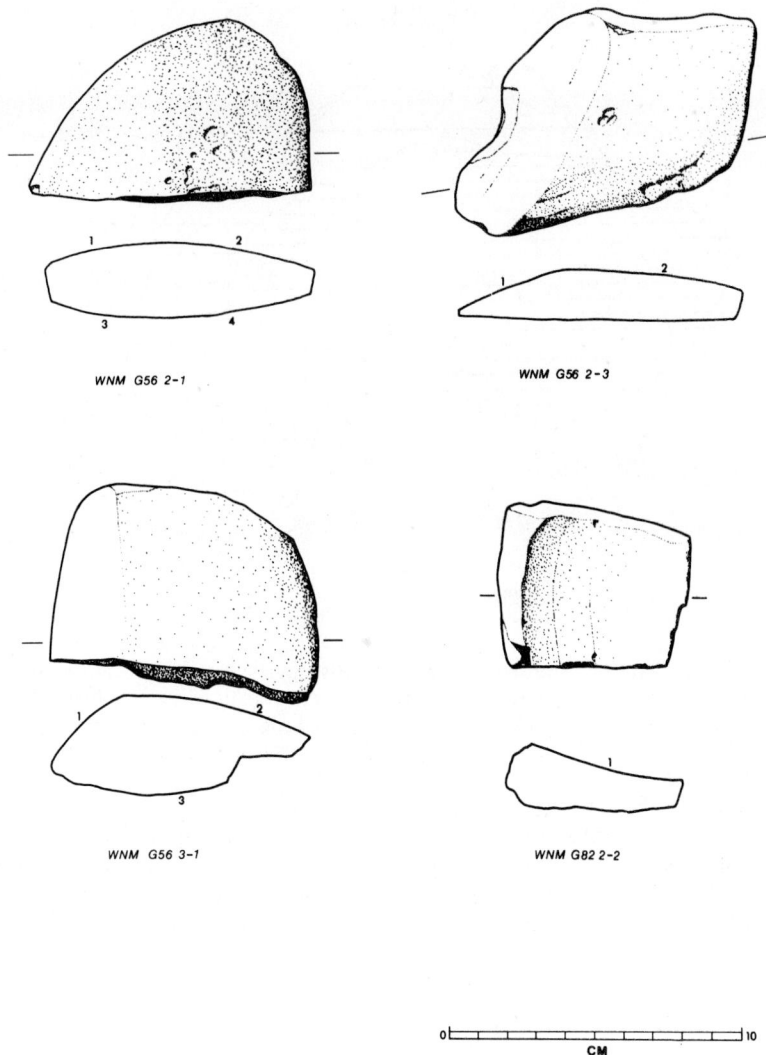

WNM G56 2-1

WNM G56 2-3

WNM G56 3-1

WNM G82 2-2

**Figure 18.3** Examples of mullers (top and lower left) and a rim fragment of a millstone excavated from Wanmara, in Central Australia and dated to within the past 1300 years.

use cannot be extrapolated to the terminal Pleistocene (Allen 1983, in press, Smith 1985). For instance, a recent study of the key artefacts (Smith 1985) has shown that there are no grounds for interpreting the Pleistocene grindstones from the Darling Basin in northern Australia as specialized seed-grinding implements. At present the evidence indicates that the

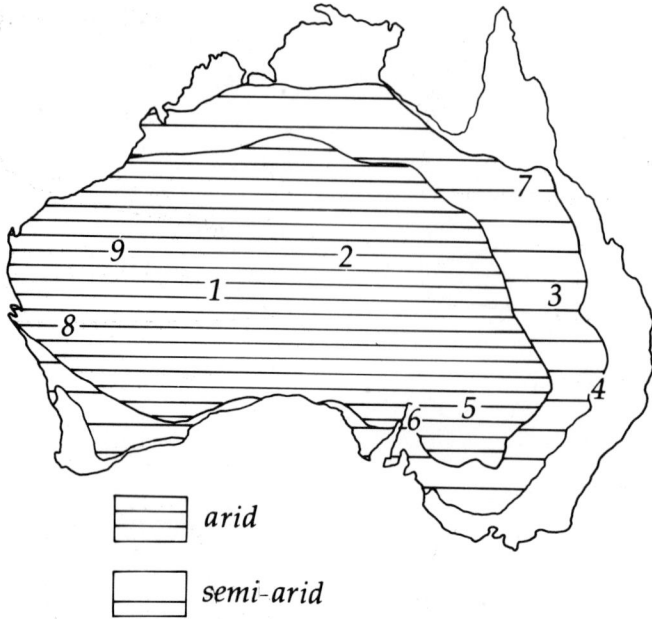

**Figure 18.4**   The arid and semi-arid zones showing the location of sites mentioned in the text. (1) Puntutjarpa, (2) the Central Australian sites, (3) Native Well, (4) Graman, (5) Burkes Cave, (6) Hawker Lagoon, (7) Quippenburra Cave (8) Walga Rock and Billibilong Spring (9) Newman Rockshelter and Ethel Gorge.

exploitation of seeds at levels of intensity comparable to the ethnohistorical pattern is a late Holocene phenomenon. It is a development that may have taken place as early as 3000–4000 bp, but is most clearly demonstrated for the past 2000 years. Information on the chronological distribution of seed-grinding implements is summarized below. The locations of the sites discussed in the text are shown in Figure 18.4.

## The Central Australian ranges

The appearance of seed-grinding implements in archaeological sites in the Central Australian ranges coincides with a substantial increase in occupation in the region beginning about 500–1400 bp. More than 60 specimens of seed-grinding implements – mostly fragments – have been recovered from archaeological excavations at 16 sites in the region. Although one specimen is from a level pre-dating the changes in site use (a rim fragment of a millstone from Intirtekwerle rockshelter) none of the seed-grinding implements is from a stratigraphic context earlier than about 1400 bp.

From Puntutjarpa rockshelter on the southwestern margin of the ranges, there are five seed grinders from levels above the upper rockfall (Smith 1986).

Although there are major difficulties in interpreting the chronology of the deposits, none of the seed grinders is likely to date to much before 500–1000 bp.

In general, the nature of the changes in site use, in particular the small size of assemblages in levels preceding the change, makes it difficult to establish whether seed-grinding implements are present in the region between 3000 bp and 1400 bp.

### Other parts of the arid zone

Other sites in the arid zone reveal a similar picture. At Burkes Cave in western New South Wales, grindstones and seed-grinding implements are restricted to levels younger than 1850 ± 240 bp (Allen 1972, pp. 138–218). Seed-grinding implements were not recovered in excavations at Walga Rock (Bordes *et al.* 1983), Newman rockshelter (Maynard 1980), Ethel Gorge rockshelter (Brown 1987), or Hawker Lagoon (Lampert & Hughes 1987, Lampert pers. comm.), although at some of these sites seed-grinding implements lay on the surface of the deposits.

### The eastern part of the semi-arid zone

For earlier evidence of seed-grinding implements we need to look at several sites located on the eastern margin of the semi-arid zone. From Native Well 1 (Morwood 1981, Smith 1986, p. 35) there is part of a millstone from levels estimated to date to about 3000 bp. This specimen is bracketed by radiocarbon dates of 1270 ± 70 (ANU 2002) and 4320 ± 90 bp (ANU 2003). From Graman site B1 there is a millstone, and from site B4 a muller (McBryde 1974, 1977), but at both sites the stones derive from levels estimated to postdate 3000 bp. New finds from an excavation at Quippenburra Cave in the northeastern section of the semi-arid zone (Morwood pers. comm.) may also add several specimens to the number of dated seed-grinding implements which predate 2000 bp, although full details are not yet available.

Taken at face value, evidence from these three regions suggests a time-lag between the first appearance of seed-grinding implements on the margins of the semi-arid zone and their subsequent appearance in the arid core of the continent. However, in my view, the available information is simply too tenuous to sustain such an interpretation at present. Nevertheless, a real time difference would be consistent with the view that the semi-arid zone in the eastern part of the continent is a climatically sensitive region where human populations are likely to have experienced greater environmental fluctuations than in the arid core (Bowler 1976, pp. 74–5).

## Economic and technological precursors

An understanding of the historical processes leading to the development of the ethnohistorical pattern of plant use is still severely limited by the paucity of dated archaeological sequences from the arid zone and by the lack of detail in those that are available. However it seems likely that, when compared with the Late Pleistocene situation, the ethnohistorical pattern of seed exploitation represents more a shift in emphasis than a new pattern of plant use. For example, certain relatively highly favoured seed foods presumably fulfilled a role in Pleistocene subsistence throughout Australia similar to the role played by the seeds of *Cycas* spp., *Oryza* spp., and *Nymphaea* spp. in recent subsistence in the monsoonal north of the continent (cf. Jones & Meehan Ch. 7, this volume), namely as a small part of an economy focused primarily on other types of resources. From this perspective the importance of seed foods within the past 2000–4000 years marks an intensification of use of a particular class of resources rather than an innovation.

Similar observations can be made of the implements used to process seeds. Amorphous or expedient grindstones form a small component of Pleistocene assemblages throughout the continent (e.g. Jones & Johnson 1985, p. 218, Smith 1985). The specialized seed-grinding implements that are characteristic of the arid interior are an elaboration of this generalized grindstone technology rather than a major technical innovation. The development of seed-grinding implements out of the rather nondescript, abraded implements present in Pleistocene and early Holocene assemblages cannot yet be traced. However, because many of the distinctive features of late Holocene seed-grinders are a result of repetitive use rather than design, there may not be much of an evolutionary sequence to recover.

## Initial colonization of the arid zone

The technical ability to exploit seeds has been seen as an integral part of the first human movements into the arid zone. Golson (1971, p. 209) suggested that ancient patterns of plant exploitation would have channelled early human settlement into northern and eastern Australia. Subsequent expansion into the arid zone would have necessitated a new pattern of plant use, in particular a greater reliance on seeds rather than roots and tubers and upon Australian rather than Indo-Malaysian plant genera. Bowdler (1977, pp. 229–30) and O'Connell & Hawkes (1981, p. 115) argued that this expansion was delayed until about 10 000–12 000 bp when the technical ability to process seeds was developed by groups living on the fringes of the arid zone. However, the discovery of Pleistocene occupation in Central Australia (Smith 1987), together with a revised late Holocene date for specialized seed-grinding implements, has now broken the hypothesized link between the first appearance of seed-grinding technology and colonization of the arid zone. The recent archaeological work in Central Australia serves to show that not only the peripheral parts of the arid zone but also the arid core were occupied by human groups by 20 000 bp.

## Explanations for an intensification of seed use

Explanations for the development of a more intensive pattern of seed use in the Australian context during the late Holocene include those that view it as a response to (a) new resource opportunities, (b) increased production pressure, or (c) resource stress. These explanations can be weighed against accounts of the role of seed foods in the contemporary and ethnohistorical systems of land use (Cane 1984, Ch. 6, this volume, O'Connell 1977, O'Connell & Hawkes 1981, O'Connell *et al*. 1983, Smith 1986). However, it is too early to risk being doctrinaire about the factors leading to more intensive use of seeds by Australian foragers in the late Holocene. The extent of basic archaeological work in the Australian arid zone is not sufficient to be confident that even the chronological framework summarized here will withstand the test of further excavation or the recovery of larger assemblages of grindstones (or the remains of plant foods) from dated contexts.

### New resource opportunities

An early suggestion by Tindale (1959, pp. 49–50, cf. Cane 1984, pp. 85–6) was that seed exploitation began as a response to new resource opportunities provided by a post-Pleistocene increase in grassland. This scenario can be discounted on two grounds, irrespective of the issue of whether or not a significant increase in grassland coincides with the first appearance of seed-grinding implements. First, it does not account for the extensive use of seeds from other sources such as trees, shrubs, and succulents. For instance, plant species such as *Acacia aneura* and *Portulaca oleracea* were at least as important in Central Australia in recent times as were grasses such as *Eragrostis eriopoda* or *Panicum decompositum*. Secondly, an increase in grassland would not necessarily make seeds a more attractive proposition unless it was also accompanied by an increase in the costs of procuring other, more desirable, bush foods. An increase in the abundance of grasses would not significantly reduce the labour costs associated with exploiting seed foods because it is the processing time, rather than the collecting time, that makes seeds so energetically costly. For example, estimates of the processing time required to produce a kilogram of flour from various grass or acacia seeds range from two to four hours (Brokensha 1975, p. 25, O'Connell & Hawkes 1981, pp. 124–5, O'Connell *et al*. 1983, pp. 90–2, Cane 1984, pp. 76–86, Ch. 6, this volume), and it is worth noting that collecting time makes up less than 10–15 per cent of the total handling time. In addition to the labour costs of processing seeds there is also the cost of acquiring suitable stone for seed-grinding implements. In parts of the arid zone this was considerable, and these costs are likely to have been similar in the past.

### Increased production pressure

Lourandos (1985) suggests that the ethnohistorical pattern of seed exploitation is yet another manifestation of a widespread phase of economic expansion that began about 3000–4000 bp. This expansion is attributed to a continuous interplay between an increasing demand for production for ceremonies, economic intensification, and population growth. Certainly, the appearance of seed-grinding implements is paralleled by the appearance elsewhere in the continent of other labour-intensive production techniques, for example the leaching of cycad seeds in central Queensland (Beaton 1982) and the construction of a system of channels for swamp management in Victoria (Lourandos 1980). However, all these developments took place around 3000–4000 bp, and there is little evidence in the archaeological record to support the idea of continuing pressure for increases in economic production. Furthermore, this period coincided with a climatic shift to a marginally drier climate, suggesting that all these developments could reflect economic adjustments to environmentally induced changes in the resource base.

*Resource stress*

Allen (1972, pp. 228–44, 338–51) interpreted the appearance of grindstones in the Darling Basin at 12 000–15 000 bp as reflecting an economic change towards the exploitation of seeds which was itself a response to the final phase of drying of the formerly extensive Willandra Lakes system. Although these interpetations have changed somewhat since Allen first formulated them, the idea of seed exploitation as a solution to the problem of maintaining the status quo in the face of resource stress is consistent with what we know of the role of seeds in ethnohistorical patterns of resource exploitation. Thus, in recent times, seeds were an important but not dominant element in a very diversified pattern of subsistence, and they were principally important for the greater logistic flexibility that they made possible. It is not difficult, therefore, to see the ethnohistorical pattern emerging as a response to resource stress caused by enforced reductions in the mobility or foraging range of Aboriginal groups. The latter could arise from any sustained reduction in the permanent or seasonal distribution of reliable watering points, or from population growth and competition for territory. The scenario I have proposed elsewhere (Smith 1986) is that population growth in the arid zone, under the favourable environmental conditions of the early to mid-Holocene, resulted in demographic packing and effectively limited future opportunities for any longer-term redistri-bution of population (cf. Yen, Ch. 4, this volume). The difficulties sub-sequently imposed by a gradually diminishing resource base about 3000–4000 bp would therefore have had to have been resolved locally (without any migration), and this would have provided strong incentives to exploit labour-intensive bushfoods such as seeds.

It is therefore increased resource stress which offers the most plausible explanation for the expanding role of seed foods in the Late Holocene, as reflected in the appearance of abundant remains of seed-grinding implements in the archaeological record of inland Australia.

# Acknowledgements

I wish to thank various people and institutions who permitted access to archaeo-logical collections and assisted me to locate the relevant specimens – C. E. Dortch and Milada Zlatnik, I. McBryde, R. J. Lampert and S. Florek, M. Quinell and N. Richardson, M. J. Morwood, the Northern Territory Museum, the Western Australian Museum, the Queensland Museum, and the Australian Museum. I have especially benefited from discussions with M. J. Morwood, R. J. Lampert, and A. Ross. The research summarized here was carried out under the auspices of the Museums and Art Galleries board of the Northern Territory while I was an external research scholar in the Department of Archaeology and Palaeoanthropo-logy, University of New England. This version was substantially written while I enjoyed a Visiting Fellowship in the Department of Prehistory, Research School of Pacific Studies, at the Australian National University. Figures 18.1, 18.2 and 18.4 are reproduced with the permission of Oceania Publications, University of Sydney.

# References

Allen, H. R. 1972. *Where the crow flies backwards: man and land in the Darling Basin*. Unpublished PhD thesis, Department of Prehistory, Australian National University.

Allen, H. R. 1974. The Bagundji of the Darling Basin: cereal gatherers in an uncertain environment. *World Archaeology* **5**, 309–22.

Allen, H. R. 1983. 19th century faunal change in western NSW and NW Victoria. *Working Papers in Anthropology, Archaeology, Linguistics and Maori Studies*, no. 64. Department of Anthropology, University of Auckland.

Allen, H. R. Environmental history in southwestern New South Wales, northwestern Victoria during the late Pleistocene. *The late Palaeolithic global record*, in press.

Bar-Yosef, D. & M. E. Kislev. 1989. Early farming communities of the Jordan Valley. In *Foraging and farming: the evolution of plant exploitation*, D. R. Harris & G. C. Hillman (eds), ch. 40. London: Unwin Hyman.

Beaton, J. M. 1982. Fire and water: aspects of Australian Aboriginal management of cycads. *Archaeology in Oceania* **17**, 51–8.

Bordes, F., C. Dortch, C. Thibault, J-P Raynal & P. Bindon 1983. Walga rock and Billibilong spring: two archaeological sequences from the Murchison basin, Western Australia. *Australian Archaeology* **17**, 1–26.

Bowdery, D. 1984. *Phytoliths: a multitude of shapes*. Unpublished BA (Hons) thesis, Department of Prehistory and Anthropology, Australian National University.

Bowdler, S. 1977. The coastal colonisation of Australia. In *Sunda and Sahul: prehistoric studies in Southeast Asia. Melanesia and Australia*, J. Allen, J. Golson & R. Jones (eds), 205–46. London: Academic Press.

Bowler, J. M. 1976. Recent developments in reconstructing late Quaternary environments in Australia. In *The origin of the Australians*, R. L. Kirk & A. G. Thorne (eds), 55–77. Canberra: Australian Institute of Aboriginal Studies.

Brokensha, P. 1975. *The Pitjandjara and their crafts*. Sydney: Aboriginal Arts Board.

Brown, S. 1987. Towards a prehistory of the Hamersley Plateau, north west Australia. *Occasional Papers in Prehistory*, no. 6. Department of Prehistory, Australian National University, Canberra.

Butler, A. 1989. Cryptic anatomical characters as evidence of early cultivation in the grain legumes (pulses). In *Foraging and farming: the evolution of plant exploitation*, D. R. Harris & G. C. Hillman (eds), ch. 24. London: Unwin Hyman.

Cane, S. B. 1984. *Desert Camps: a case study of stone artefacts and Aboriginal behaviour in the Western Desert*. Unpublished PhD thesis, Department of Prehistory, Australian National University, Canberra.

Cane, S. B. 1989. Australian Aboriginal seed grinding and its archaeological record: a case study from the Western Desert. In *Foraging and farming: the evolution of plant exploitation*, D. R. Harris & G. C. Hillman (eds), ch. 6. London: Unwin Hyman.

Golson, J. 1971. Australian Aboriginal food plants: some ecological and culture-historical implications. In *Aboriginal man and environment in Australia*, D. J. Mulvaney & J. Golson (eds), 196–238. Canberra: Australian National University Press.

Gould, R. A. 1977. Puntutjarpa rockshelter and the Australian Desert Culture. *Anthropological Papers of the American Museum of Natural History* **54**, 1–187.

Harris, D. R. 1984. Ethnohistorical evidence for the exploitation of wild grasses and forbs: its scope and archaeological implications. In *Plants and ancient man: studies in palaeoethnobotany* W. van Zeist & W. A. Casparie (eds), 63–9. Rotterdam: Balkema.

Hayden, B. 1979. *Palaeolithic reflections: lithic technology and ethnographic excavation among Australian Aborigines*. Canberra: Australian Institute of Aboriginal Studies.

Hillman, G. C. 1989. Late Palaeolithic plant foods from Wadi Kubbaniya in Upper Egypt: dietary diversity, infant weaning, and seasonality in a riverine environment. In *Foraging and farming: the evolution of plant exploitation*, D. R. Harris & G. C. Hillman (eds), ch. 13. London: Unwin Hyman.

Hillman, G. C., S. M. Colledge & D. R. Harris 1989. Plant-food economy during the Epipalaeolithic period at Tell Abu Hureyra, Syria: dietary diversity, seasonality, and modes of exploitation. In *Foraging and farming: the evolution of plant exploitation*, D. R. Harris & G. C. Hillman (eds), ch. 14. London: Unwin Hyman.

Hillman, G. C., E. Madeyska & J. G. Hather in press. Wild plant foods and diet at Late Palaeolithic Kubbaniya: evidence from charred remains. In *The prehistory of Wadi Kubbaniya*. Vol. 2: *Palaeoeconomy, environment and stratigraphy*, F. Wendorf, R. Schild & A. Close (eds). Dallas: Southern Methodist University Press.

Jones, C. E. R. in press. Archaeochemistry: fact or fancy? In *The prehistory of Wadi Kubbaniya*. Vol. 2: *Palaeoeconomy, environment and stratigraphy*, F. Wendorf, R. Schild & A. Close (eds). Dallas: Southern Methodist University Press.

Jones, R. & I. Johnson 1985. Deaf Adder gorge: Lindner site, Nauwalabila 1. In *Archaeological research in Kakadu National Park*, R. Jones (ed.), 165–228. Canberra: Australian National Parks and Wildlife Service.

Kimber, R. G. 1984. Resource use and management in central Australia. *Australian Aboriginal Studies* **2**, 12–23.

Lampert, R. J. & P. J. Hughes 1987. The Flinders ranges: a Pleistocene outpost in the arid zone. *Records of the South Australian Museum* **20**, 29–34.

Latz, P. K. 1982. *Bushfires and bushtucker: Aborigines and plants in Central Australia*. Unpublished MA thesis, Department of Prehistory and Archaeology, University of New England. Armidale.

Lourandos, H. 1980. Change or stability? Hydraulics, hunter-gatherers and population in temperate Australia. *World Archaeology* **11**, 245–64.

Lourandos, H. 1985. Intensification in Australian prehistory. In *Prehistoric hunter-gatherers: the emergence of cultural complexity*, T. D. Price & J. A. Brown (eds), 385–423. New York: Academic Press.

McBryde, I. 1974. *Aboriginal prehistory in New England: an archaeological survey of north-eastern New South Wales*. Sydney: Sydney University Press.

McBryde, I. 1976. Subsistence patterns in New England prehistory. *University of Queensland Occasional Papers in Anthropology* **6**, 48–68.

McBryde, I. 1977. Determinants of assemblage variation in New England pre-history. In *Stone tools as cultural markers: change, evolution and complexity*, R. V. S. Wright (ed.), 225–50. Canberra: Australian Institute of Aboriginal Studies.

Maynard, L. 1980. A Pleistocene date from an occupation deposit in the Pilbara region, Western Australia. *Australian Archaeology* **10**, 3–8.

Moore, A. M. T. 1989. The transition from foraging to farming in Southwest Asia: present problems and future directions. In *Foraging and farming: the evolution of plant exploitation*, D. R. Harris & G. C. Hillman (eds), ch. 39. London: Unwin Hyman.

Morwood, M. J. 1981. Archaeology of the central Queensland highlands. *Archaeology in Oceania* **16**, 1–52.

O'Connell, J. F. 1977. Aspects of variation in central Australian lithic assemblages. In *Stone tools as cultural markers: change, evolution and complexity*, R. V. S. Wright (ed.), 267–81. Canberra: Australian Institute of Aboriginal Studies.

O'Connell, J. F. & K. Hawkes, 1981. Alyawara plant use and optimal foraging theory. In *Hunter–gatherer foraging strategies: ethnographic and archaeological analyses*, B. Winterhalder & E. Smith (eds), 99–125. Chicago: University of Chicago Press.

O'Connell, J. F., P. K. Latz & P. Barnett 1983. Traditional and modern plant use among the Alyawara of Central Australia. *Economic Botany* **37**, 80–109.

Piperno, D. R. 1989. Non-affluent foragers: resource availability, seasonal short-ages, and the emergence of agriculture in Panamanian tropical forests. In *Foraging and farming: the evolution of plant exploitation*, D. R. Harris & G. C. Hillman (eds), ch. 34. London: Unwin Hyman.

Smith, M. A. 1985. A morphological comparison of Central Australian seedgrinding implements and Australian Pleistocene-age grindstones. *The Beagle: Occasional Papers of the Northern Territory Museum of Arts and Sciences* **2**, 23–38.

Smith, M. A. 1986. The antiquity of seedgrinding in arid Australia. *Archaeology in Oceania* **21**, 29–39.

Smith, M. A. 1987. Pleistocene occupation in arid Central Australia. *Nature* **328**, 710–11.

Tindale, N. B. 1959. The ecology of primitive man in Australia. In *Biogeography and ecology in Australia*, A. L. Keast, R. L. Crocker & C. S. Christian (eds), 36–51. The Hague: W. Junk.

Tindale, N. B. 1972. The Pitjandjara. In *Hunters and gatherers today*, M. G. Bicchieri (ed.), 217–68. New York: Holt, Rinehart & Winston.

Tindale, N. B. 1977. Adaptive significance of the Panara or grass seed culture of Australia. In *Stone tools as cultural markers: change, evolution and complexity*, R. V. S. Wright (ed.), 340–9. Canberra: Australian Institute of Aboriginal Studies.

Yen, D. E. 1989. The domestication of environment. In *Foraging and farming: the evolution of plant exploitation*, D. R. Harris & G. C. Hillman (eds), ch. 4. London: Unwin Hyman.

# 19 *Adaptation of prehistoric hunter–gatherers to the high Andes: the changing role of plant resources*

DEBORAH M. PEARSALL

## Introduction

This chapter examines adaptation of prehistoric hunter–gatherers to the high Andes of Peru, utilizing archaeobotanical data for Panaulauca Cave. The primary focus is on the role of wild-plant resources in hunter–gatherer adaptations to this zone, and the sources of data are the charred remains of various small-seed taxa, and root remains identified as *Lepidium* sp.

Examining patterns of plant use through time at Panaulauca reveals changes in two taxa which can be ascribed to the process of domestication. Incipient cultivation of local weedy plants is linked to the process of domestication of camelids (llama, alpaca), and a model for co-evolution of a component of the Andean herding and agricultural system is proposed.

Panaulauca Cave is a limestone rockshelter located at 4150 m elevation on the land of SAIS Atocsayco, Department of Junin, Peru. Excavations were directed by John W. Rick of Stanford University (Rick 1984). Panaulauca is located in the high–altitude grassland, or *puna*, zone of the Lake Junin region. The Junin *puna* is a cold, rigorous environment, but one in which there are many native plant and animal resources available to human populations (Pearsall 1980, Pearsall & Moore in press). All food plants recovered in the Panaulauca deposits (Table 19.1), with the exception of maize (*Zea mays*), are available in quantity within 5 km of the site. Among locally available plant resources are numerous taxa of succulent roots and tubers, cactus fruits, herbs providing small seeds and greens, and small-seeded grasses such as *Festuca* spp. and *Calamagrostis* spp. Among animal resources of the zone are waterfowl and other bird life, the rabbit-like viscacha, wild camelids (vicuña, guanaco), and both while–tailed and huemal deer (Rick 1980).

Sparsely occupied today by herders, in prehistory the *puna* was an inviting habitat for hunting–gathering populations. Rick (1980) has proposed that sedentary bands of camelid hunters occupied rockshelters year-round throughout the Junin *puna*. Plant resources are available to human beings and

**Table 19.1** Sources of seeds in the Panaulauca deposit.

| | |
|---|---|
| Seeds used as food<br>  *Festuca*<br>  Gramineae (large)★<br>  *Chenopodium*<br>  *Amaranthus*<br>  *Portulaca*<br>  *Trifolium*<br>  *Lupinus*<br>  Leguminosae<br>  *Polygonum*<br>  *Zea mays*<br><br>Seeds brought in with non-food items<br>  *Festuca*<br>  Gramineae (large)<br>  *Scirpus*<br>  *Relbunium*<br>  *Galium*<br>  Compositae<br>  *Plantago*<br>  Labiatae<br><br>Seeds in mat<br>(a) Chupacancha observations:<br>  Gramineae (small)<br>  Gramineae (medium)<br>  *Relbunium*<br>  Cyperaceae<br>  Gramineae (large)<br>(b) Comparative mat observations:<br>  Gramineae (large)<br>  Gramineae (small)<br>  *Luzula*<br>  Umbelliferae, ridged<br>  Cyperaceae<br>  Compositae | Seeds brought in with food items<br>  *Scirpus*<br>  *Lepidium*<br>  *Opuntia floccosa*<br>  *Echinocactus*<br>  *Solanum*<br><br>Seeds present in dung<br>(a) Chupacancha observations:<br>  Cyperaceae<br>  *Sisyrinchium*<br>  *Relbunium*<br>  *Calandrinia*<br>  Gramineae (large)<br>  Gramineae (medium)<br>(b) Panaulauca observations:<br>  *Calandrinia*<br>  Caryphyllaceae<br>  *Opuntia floccosa*<br>  Gramineae (small)<br>(c) Comparative vicuna observations:<br>  *Sisyrinchium*<br>  *Relbunium*<br>  Gramineae (small)<br>  Gramineae (large)<br>  *Lupinus*<br>  *Calandrinia* |

★Numerous grass seeds were observed in flotation, and in comparative mat and dung samples, which were difficult to identify to genus because of the great diversity of grasses in the *puna* zone. These are, for convenience, divided into small (*c.* 0.5 mm), medium (0.2–1.0 mm), and large (>1.0 mm) types.

camelids throughout the year. In most months moisture is adequate for plant growth. Many plants initiate new vegetative growth, flower, and fruit during the rainy season (November–March), while others flower and fruit during the drier months (April–October). Still others have been observed in flower and/or fruit during both seasons.

In the Panaulauca rockshelter, deposits reach a depth of 4.2 m, in 41 stratigraphic levels, 22 of which have been fully excavated. The uppermost intact level (level 7) is dated to ad 1200 and the lowermost fully excavated level (level 22) is dated just prior to 3000 bc. The pre-ceramic–ceramic transition occurs in level 16 (1600 bc). Initial occupation of Panaulauca is dated to 7700 bc. Most data discussed here come from levels 7–22, which fall into the last five phases of site occupation (Phases 4–8) (Rick 1984).

## The charred plant remains

Only charred archaeobotanical materials are preserved at Panaulauca. Flotation samples were taken from all levels in all units. Materials as small as 0.5 mm were recovered. The materials recovered included wood charcoal, whole tap roots, and other large fragments. The abundance of charred seeds and root remains is presented here by percentage presence. This is calculated by determining in what percentage of units (i.e. 1 × 1 m squares) on a given level each taxon occurred.

To discuss the role of plants as food resources, it is necessary to understand probable sources of recovered macroremains, so that remains of food plants may be distinguished from those brought to a site for other purposes (Pearsall in press a). This is especially relevant for small seeds, which can be deposited in a site in a variety of ways. For example, burning of camelid dung as fuel was probably an important source of some seeds in the Panaulauca deposits. By using ethnographic sources and examining dung and sod samples, seed types can be divided by probable source (Table 19.1). Patterns of occurrence through time of seeds used as food, seeds brought in with food items, and edible roots are considered below.

*Small-seed remains*

Data on occurrence of seeds from food plants are presented for five completely excavated floors: level 11, level 16 ceramic, level 16 pre-ceramic, level 18, and level 21 (Table 19.2). All materials come from one depositional context: cave-mouth midden.

Several interesting patterns of change in the relative abundance of plant foods are evident from Phase 4 to Phase 7. Occurrence of *Opuntia* and *Echinocactus* cactus fruits declines through time, while use of *Chenopodium* seeds increases, especially from level 16 ceramic onwards. *Festuca* and seeds of other Gramineae rank higher by presence in the earlier levels (level 21, 18), declining thereafter. This pattern is particularly true of *Festuca*, which falls below 25 per cent presence by level 11. Leguminosae and *Trifolium* usually occupy middle rankings in the presence table, along with *Scirpus*. *Portulaca*, *Polygonum*, *Amaranthus*, *Solanum*, and *Lupinus* are consistently ranked low.

Occurrence of *Chenopodium* is of particular interest because two species in this genus, *Chenopodium quinoa* (quinoa) and *C. pallidicaule* (cañihua), were ultimately domesticated. Because of seedling competition, larger seeds,

**Table 19.2**  Uncorrected presence rankings of foods recovered on five Panaulauca floors.

| % | Level 11 | Level 16C | Level 16P | Level 18 | Level 21 |
|---|---|---|---|---|---|
| 100 | | *Chenopodium*<br>*Opuntia* | *Opuntia* | *Opuntia* | |
| 90 | | *Leguminosae* | | | *Opuntia* |
| 80 | *Opuntia* | | *Leguminosae*<br>*Gramineae* | *Festuca*<br>*Gramineae* | *Gramineae* |
| 70 | *Chenopodium* | *Gramineae* | | | |
| 60 | *Gramineae*<br>*Leguminosae* | *Festuca* | *Chenopodium* | *Leguminosae* | |
| 50 | *Lepidium* (R) | *Lepidium* (R)<br>*Trifolium*<br>*Scirpus* | *Festuca* | | *Festuca* |
| 40 | | | *Lepidium* (R) | | *Leguminosae* |
| 30 | | | | *Trifolium* | *Trifolium*<br>*Echinocactus* |
| 25 | *Scirpus* | | *Trifolium* | | *Lepidium* (R) |
| <25 | *Festuca*<br>*Trifolium*<br>*Portulaca*<br>*Polygonum* | *Portulaca*<br>*Amaranthus*<br>*Lupinus*<br>*Solanum*<br>*Echinocactus* | *Scirpus*<br>*Portulaca*<br>*Echinocactus*<br>*Lepidium*<br>*Solanum* (R) | *Scirpus*<br>*Amaranthus*<br>*Echinocactus*<br>*Chenopodium*<br>*Solanum*<br>*Lepidium* (R) | *Scirpus*<br>*Chenopodium* |

All remains are seeds, except when designated (R): root/tuber. One kernel of *Zea mays* occurs in Level 7. No other remains of maize occur.

better able to store more energy for the emerging plant, are selected for automatically in the early stages of domestication (Harlan 1975). It can be argued therefore that increasing seed size over time is one indication of the process of domestication of a seed crop.

To determine whether *Chenopodium* seed size increased over time at Panaulauca, all seeds with an intact diameter from all samples were measured for largest diameter. Charred seeds do not make the best population for studying size changes. Of the 1153 *Chenopodium* seeds measured, 32 per cent were judged to be somewhat reduced in diameter due to the absence of the seed coat. The size curve generated by these data may be depressed accordingly. Mean largest diameter, standard deviation, and standard error were calculated for each level (Fig. 19.1).

Student's *t*-tests calculated on seed-diameter means for adjacent levels showed that significant changes (0.05 level) in diameter occurred between levels 14 and 14B, levels 15 and 16 ceramic, and levels 20 and 21 (Pearsall in press b). By examining standard error for each mean it is possible to observe the following:

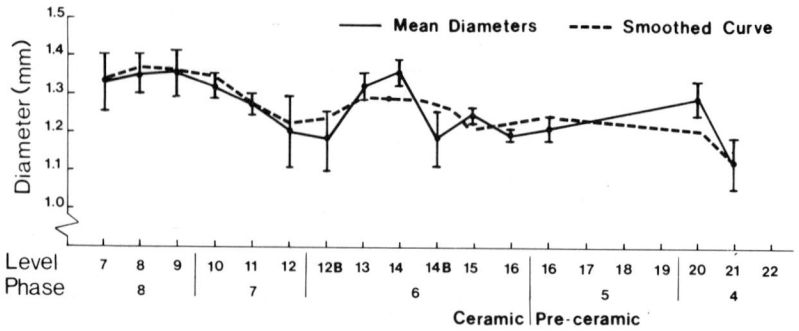

**Figure 19.1**   Mean diameters of *Chenopodium* seeds.

(a)   that mean seed diameters in the upper four levels (7–10) overlap in standard error;

(b)   that smaller mean diameters of seeds in levels 11, 12, and 12B overlap with each other in standard error, but overlap little with the upper four levels;

(c)   that mean seed diameters in levels 13 and 14 return to the range of the uppermost levels; and

(d)   that several significant changes in mean diameters occur in the lower levels (14B–21), which include reversals of seed-size change.

If the curve of mean diameters is smoothed by running averages an overall trend of increasing diameters over the length of the curve becomes more evident. There is, in fact, no overlap in standard error of mean seed diameters for level 21 and upper ceramic levels (7–10).

Largest mean *Chenopodium* diameters at Panaulauca fall short of means for modern cultivated *quinoa* (i.e. 2.0 mm in Simmonds 1965; 2.21 mm in Pearsall 1980). Some seeds recovered from Panaulauca do overlap the range of cultivated *quinoa*, however, especially in the upper levels, where mean diameters rise to 1.33–1.35 mm, and a small number of seeds of diameter 1.8 mm and larger occur. Seed shape tends to be rounded, with only smaller seeds being elliptical (tear-drop shaped). In most levels there is a bimodel distribution of seed diameters, with a cluster at 1.2–1.4 mm, and another at 0.8–0.9 mm (Pearsall in press b). Two 'kinds' of *Chenopodium* may thus be present. These could represent (a) a wild/weedy species and a primitive cultivar, (b) two cultivated species or varieties, or (c) two wild, collected species. Data support the presence of at least one primitive cultivar.

## *Lepidium* root remains

A total of 267 whole charred tap roots were recovered from Panaulauca. Most were recovered from the latest intact excavation level (7) through level 16, the ceramic–pre-ceramic transition.

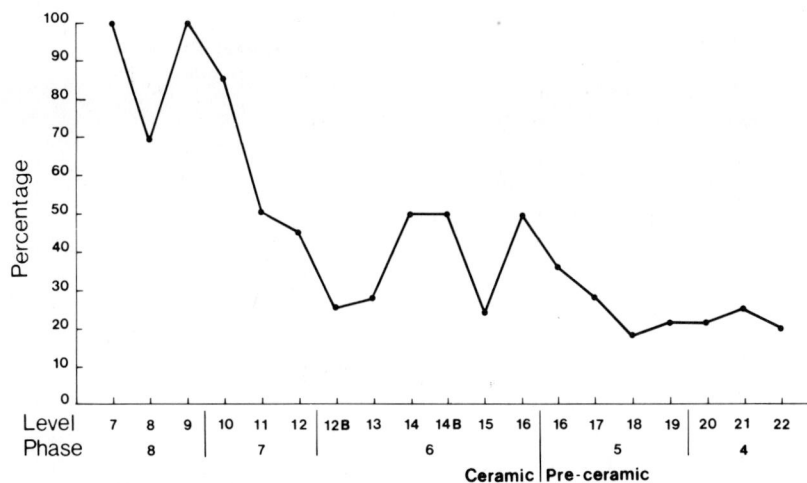

**Figure 19.2**   Percentage presence of *Lepidium* roots.

The shape of these roots, the form of the leaf-attachment scars, and the nature of the internal tissue indicate that they are small tap roots, many of which show secondary thickening of the root cortex. This gives a bulbous or turnip-shaped appearance to many specimens. Other examples are more cylindrical in shape, and appear to be of more indeterminate growth. Larger bulbous specimens are very similar to small examples of the cultivated root crop, *maca* (*Lepidium meyenii*). *Maca* is a very cold-tolerant crop, and has been observed under cultivation as high as 4400 m (Timothy Johns pers. comm. and Ch. 32, this volume). Old field-ridges for the cultivation of this crop and cold-tolerant 'bitter' potatoes, are still visible in areas of the Junin *puna*.

Because many archaeological root specimens are smaller in diameter than modern *maca* (size range of archaeological specimens: 3.2–21.5 mm; modern *maca*: 10.7–45.4 mm; wild *Lepidium*: average 6.37 mm), and show much more variation in shape, a detailed study of the roots was undertaken to test preliminary identification as *Lepidium* (Pearsall in press b). Using the scanning electron microscope, the internal microanatomy of the roots was studied, and compared to known comparative specimens. These included modern *maca*, wild *Lepidium*, and roots of a variety of plants collected near Panaulauca. When root shape, leaf attachment, and internal microanatomy are all taken into account, identification as small *Lepidum meyenii* is confirmed.

Figure 19.2 is a graphic representation of the percentage presence of *Lepidium* roots in Panaulauca deposits. There are three distinct phases in a pattern of overall increasing presence through time. From level 22 to level 18, presence remains at 30 per cent or less. Levels 16 pre-ceramic through 14 show a rise in presence to 50 per cent, with a drop in level 15 breaking up this

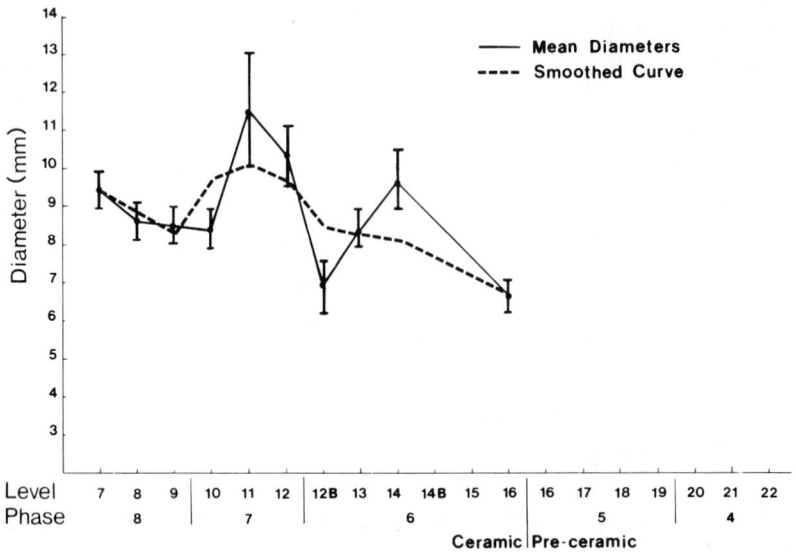

**Figure 19.3**    Mean diameters of *Lepidium* roots.

plateau. This period is followed by low occurrence of root remains in levels 12B and 13. Occurrence then rises gradually to 100 per cent presence by level 9.

What evidence is there as to whether these *Lepidium* roots were gathered wild or grown under cultivation? Because modern cultivated *maca* is larger in mean diameter than wild *Lepidium*, an increase in size of archaeological roots through time would be one indication of the process of domestication. Figure 19.3 shows mean root diameters of measurable remains for each excavation level. Student's *t*-tests indicate that changes between levels 10 and 11, levels 12 and 12B, and levels 14 and 16 ceramic are significant at the 0.05 level (Pearsall in press b). Although there is evidence for an increase in root diameter between early Phase 6 and mid–Phase 7, this trend is reversed later (refer to smoothed curve). There is no clear trend towards more determinate root form later in time.

Panaulauca *Lepidium* root specimens are not identical in size or shape to wild *Lepidium*, nor are they identical to modern cultivated *maca*. Panaulauca data capture an intermediate stage in the developmental history of this crop. Increased root size and more consistent determinate root shape perhaps developed late in prehistory, during the Incaic horizon or in the Colonial period, or may have occurred elsewhere in the Andes.

## The role of plant resources in adaptation to the *puna*

Analysis of small seeds and root remains from upper strata (3000 bc to ad 1200) of Panaulauca Cave has revealed both change and continuity in the utilization of plant resources. What role did plants play in the successful adaptation of human populations to the *puna*? This question will be addressed from two viewpoints: the overall role of plants in diet and the importance of plant foods in allowing year-round occupation on the *puna*.

It is difficult to discuss the nutritional contribution of plant foods in diet using archaeobotanical data. There is no way of knowing if Table 19.1 is a complete list of vegetable foods used by Panaulauca's inhabitants. To avoid undue speculation, however, the following discussion focuses only on those nutrients which known vegetable foods brought to the diet, and on how the changes in plant use, detailed above, may have affected nutrition.

Food-composition data are lacking for many of the taxa under discussion. Leon (1964) states the *Lepidium meyenii* roots are rich in starches and sugars. Dried *maca*, which can be easily stored for long periods, is probably similar to *chuño* (dried potatoes) in calories (327 kcal 100 g$^{-1}$ edible portion) and carbohydrate (79.2 g 100 g$^{-1}$ edible portion) (Wu Leung & Flores 1961). *Polygonum erectum*, a North American knotweed, is considered a starchy seed by ethnobiologists (Asch & Asch 1980, Johannessen 1984). Seeds of *Trifolium*, *Lupinus*, and other Leguminosae can be considered sources of vegetable protein, as well as food energy. *Lupinus* seeds, for example, contain 407 kcal calories, 44.7 g of protein, and 28.2 g carbohydrates per 100 g edible portion; they are also high in phosphorus (Wu Leung & Flores 1961). It is likely that *Festuca* and other wild-grass seeds are similar to domestic grasses, such as maize, in their food composition, i.e. good sources of calories and carbohydrates, but lower in protein than legumes. Wild 'cool-season' grasses such as *Festuca* are considered by Bohrer (1975) to be sources of abundant calories.

Human beings have two major dietary requirements: to supply the body with energy to sustain its functioning, and to replenish protein and mineral components (Wing & Brown 1979). Meat is an excellent source of balanced protein, fat, and vitamins and minerals, as well as serving as a source of food energy. Given abundant evidence for the use of camelids, deer, and a variety of small animals at Panaulauca (Moore 1984), it is unlikely that more than occasional input of protein from vegetable sources was required.

Plant taxa occupying higher presence rankings (Table 19.2) in Phases 4 and 5, *Opuntia* and Gramineae or *Festuca*, provided predominantly vitamins and calories, respectively, to the diet. *Opuntia* fruits are a source of vitamins A and C (Wu Leung & Flores 1961). Grass seeds are a source of carbohydrates. It is likely that additional carbohydrates were provided by wild root or tuber resources not preserved directly in the deposits (e.g. *Solanum*, *Scirpus*, and the like).

Beginning in level 16 pre-ceramic, and continuing in Phases 6 and 7, *Chenopodium* seeds replace grass seeds as an important source of food energy. *Chenopodium* is also a good source of calcium, phosphorus, and iron (Wu Leung & Flores 1961). *Lepidium* roots also take on an increasingly important role in the plant-food component of diet in these later phases. In addition to calories provided by *Lepidium* roots, the stems and leaves would have been good sources of vitamins A and C. This is also the case of *Trifolium* and *Portulaca* greens (Wu Leung & Flores 1961, Watt & Merrill 1975, FAO 1982).

In summary, the variety and relative abundance of plant foods in the diet of Panaulauca inhabitants varied over the four phases studied (Phases 4–7), but the nutritional contribution of plant foods to the diet remained stable. Starchy seeds provided a constant source of food energy, with an increasing contribution from root and tuber foods in later phases. Vegetable protein was available throughout the sequence, as were sources of vitamins A and C.

It is also difficult to assess the relative importance of plant and animal foods in the diet. It is not possible to compare quantities of seeds, roots, and bones directly. One direct method of determining the relative importance of these differing food sources is through analysis of trace elements in human bone. Final results of strontium and calcium analyses of two burials from level 21 (late Phase 4) are not yet available, but preliminary results suggest that diet at this point in time was heavily oriented towards meat (Barbara Bocek, pers. comm.).

Information on seasonal availability of plant and animal resources on the *puna* is scant. Available data on the flowering and fruiting of food plants suggest that plant resources were available for human use throughout the year (Pearsall & Moore in press). The following collecting strategy is proposed for optimizing plant use, and providing foods important for supplementing and adding variety to a meat-dominated diet:

(a)   In the early rainy season succulent roots and tubers are collected in rock-outcrop areas, where a number of taxa not available elsewhere may be found in concentration.

(b)   As the rainy season progresses, perennial rosettes and annual herbs put out new growth, providing pot herbs and early seeds. These are available throughout the zone, but especially on rock outcrops and grassland areas dominated by *Festuca* spp.

(c)   Herbs (*Portulaca, Amaranthus, Chenopodium,* and *Lepidium*) are collected from disturbed areas.

(d)   Mature fruits of *Opuntia floccosa* and *Echinocactus* are gathered from rock outcrops and rocky slopes.

(e)   Collecting trips are made to lakes near the cave for *Scirpus* roots and moist-area herbs, such as *Polygonum*.

(f)   In the early dry season, mature grass seeds are collected and processed for storage. The same strategy is followed for *Chenopodium*, other plants of disturbed areas, and wild legumes.

(g)   As the dry season progresses, tubers and roots maturing in that season are harvested. These can be collected most easily in disturbed habitats and rock-outcrop areas.

# Domestication of weedy plants and camelids: a model for co-evolution of Andean herding and agriculture

Cultivation of high-altitude crops and herding of llamas and alpacas is the traditional subsistence system of the region above 3000 m in much of Peru. Cultivars of this region include potatoes (*Solanum* section *tuberosum*), *oca* (*Oxalis tuberosa*), *mashua* (*Tropaeolum tuberosum*), *ullucu* (*Ullucus tuberosus*), *maca* (*Lepidium meyenii*), *quinoa* (*Chenopodium quinoa*), *cañihua* (*C. pallidicaule*), *tarhui* (*Lupinus mutabilis*), and *achis* (*Amaranthus caudatus*). Cultivation of cold-resistant potatoes and *maca* takes place today above 4000 m in Junin. *Oca* and *ullucu* have also been observed under cultivation in the high *puna* (Bird 1970; see also Hawkes Ch. 31 & Johns Ch. 32, this volume for discussion of the root and tuber crops of the high Andes).

In modelling how this system may have evolved, one is hindered by lack of knowledge of the wild ancestors of many of the species involved. Only the potato has been extensively studied, and even for this crop, relatively little is known about its wild ancestors (cf. Hawkes Ch. 31, this volume).

If crops of the high-altitude agricultural system were brought under domestication at multiple times and places in the Andes, the possibility of local domestication exists for Junin. It is likely that many crops in this system were domesticated by peoples living in the 3000–4000 m zone, the primary range of tuber and 'pseudocereal' cultivation today. The higher *puna* is viewed primarily as an area for pasturing herd animals.

The focus on camelids in the *puna* zone suggests that any manipulation of plants which occurred there would have been linked to animal manipulation. A logical linkage exists between herd animals and the creation of disturbed habitats favourable to certain plant species. The notion that disturbed habitats can play a role in the origin of domesticated plants was postulated by Anderson (1952). Areas disturbed by the corraling of camelids would provide fertile habitats for the development of new plant varieties. A model combining manipulation of camelids with harvesting plants in disturbed areas is presented below. The sequence of changes in camelid populations follows Wheeler Pires-Ferreira *et al.* (1976) and Wing (1977):

(a)   Following a long period of hunting camelids, including the guanaco-like ancestor of the llama and alpaca, manipulation of wild populations leads to the tending of semi-domesticated forms. Tending includes the use of corrals, and leads to the creation of manure-rich, disturbed habitats which favour the growth of weedy plants, including *Lepidium* spp. and *Chenopodium* spp. The rich soil of corral areas supports vigorous plants, and provides a favourable habitat for new forms.

(b)   The increase in disturbed habitats, and of the plants associated with them, leads to an increase in gathering of useful weedy taxa. Both seeds and roots are more easily harvested in quantity from corral areas than from along paths or in naturally disturbed areas. Gathering roots such as *Lepidium* regularly from the same areas results in an increase in harvesting of shorter, rounder roots. Perennial root crops which are harvested annually tend to produce shorter, thicker roots than plants allowed to grow for multiple seasons. There would also be a tendency to harvest more roots with determinant growth, because, if plants are abundant, deeply rooted specimens might be avoided.

(c)  Following increased use of the seeds, greens, and edible roots of weedy plants, such plants are encouraged by sowing seeds in abandoned corral areas. Once a cycle of sowing–harvesting–sowing is established, genetic change in plant populations accelerates. The process of unconscious selection for increased seed or root size, uniform maturation, and the other hallmarks of the early stages of domestication (Harlan 1975) becomes established.

(d)  With establishment of the regular sowing of hardy weedy plants, abandoned corrals or casually disturbed areas provide an insufficient area for cultivation. Garden plots, and later more extensive field areas, replace the planting areas created by camelid disturbance. The relationship between animals and plants continues, however, with the use of manure to fertilize fields, and the pasturing of animals on fallow fields.

(e)  Once cultivation of endemic local plants is established, new plants can be easily placed under trial cultivation and added to the system. These might include other *puna* plants, or tubers and seed plants domesticated in Andean valleys and introduced to the *puna*.

If this model is correct, wholly or in part, the timing of changes in the occurrence and size of *Lepidium* and *Chenopodium* which are attributed to domestication should correspond to changes in the manipulation of camelid populations at Panaulauca.

Occurrence of *Lepidium* roots is quite low until late Phase 5 or early Phase 6 (Fig. 19.2). Levels remain moderate for most of Phase 6, and show an overall increase thereafter. Abundance in Phases 7 and 8 is especially apparent when measures are compared to late Phase 5 and early Phase 6 levels. However, periodic declines in abundance also occur. Occurrence data for *Chenopodium* are similar. *Chenopodium* occurs sporadically until level 16 pre-ceramic, the end of Phase 5 (Table 19.2). From that point, until near the end of Phase 7, abundance is high. Both taxa show a change in occurrence at roughly the same time: late Phase 5, about 1900 bc, or early Phase 6, the pre-ceramic–ceramic transition, about 1600 bc. *Chenopodium* occurrence appears more stable than that of *Lepidium*, which peaks in abundance somewhat later.

When size data on *Lepidium* roots (Fig. 19.3) and *Chenopodium* seeds (Fig. 19.1) are examined, neither taxon exhibits a unidirectional trend of size change, although both show an overall increase in size from their appearance to the end of the Panaulauca sequence. Mean diameter of *Lepidium* roots increases during Phase 6 and into the middle of Phase 7. Highest mean root diameter is reached in level 11. From late Phase 7 through early Phase 8, mean diameter declines to levels observed in late Phase 6. Mean diameter rises again in Phase 8, but by the end of the sequence has not risen to the diameter observed in level 11. Changes in mean diameter of *Chenopodium* seeds show a somewhat different pattern. Mean diameter actually declines from the first appearance of quantities of *Chenopodium* seeds, in level 16 pre-ceramic, until level 15. Size then increases through the middle of Phase 6. Late Phase 6 and early Phase 7 is another period of declining mean diameters, similar to the decline observed early in Phase 6. During most of Phase 7, and into Phase 8, however, the pattern is one of increasing diameter.

If *Lepidium* and *Chenopodium* occurrence and size data are interpreted in the light of the proposed model, the sequence and timing of events can be summarized as follows:

(a)    Changes in *Chenopodium* occurrence begin the sequence. Heavy use of *Chenopodium* seeds begins late in Phase 5, while use of *Lepidium* roots is just beginning to increase. This indicates that disturbed habitats favourable to *Chenopodium* growth are present, at least from level 16 pre-ceramic. Whether seeds were gathered from wild plants growing in corral areas or were being harvested from cultivars planted in old corrals is difficult to assess. Seeds up to 2.0 mm in diameter, the average size for modern *quinoa*, occur, but mean diameter still falls in the range of wild *Chenopodium*. The most conservative interpretation would be that these early concentrations represent seeds gathered from concentrated weed growth. It is also possible, however, that cultivation began with *Chenopodium*.

(b)    After the first appearance of any concentration of *Lepidium* roots, root diameter begins to increase slowly, reaching a plateau late in Phase 6. The earlier roots are only slightly larger than wild *Lepidium*. By the end of Phase 6, the mean has risen significantly. This stage may represent the transition from collection to the beginning of cultivation, with unconscious selection operating to increase root size.

(c)    Beginning in the middle of Phase 6, increasing mean seed size in *Chenopodium* marks more clearly the early stages of cultivation of this taxon. The plateau reached at this time corresponds somewhat with the plateau in *Lepidium* diameter.

(d)    The period from late Phase 6 to the middle of Phase 7 is characterized by accelerated selection for increased root size in *Lepidium*, and a reversal for *Chenopodium*. For *Lepidium*, this may represent the transition from casual to more systematic cultivation, perhaps including use of dung fertilizer and preparation of garden areas. The decline in mean diameter for *Chenopodium* is difficult to explain, because conditions favourable to cultivation (at least of roots) were apparently present. If *Chenopodium* was moved out of a corral or garden setting into open-field cultivation before *Lepidium*, the decline may represent the stress of this change.

(e)    The pattern for late Phase 7 and Phase 8 is essentially the reverse of the previous period: mean *Lepidium* root diameters decline in late Phase 7 and early Phase 8, while mean diameter of *Chenopodium* increases to a new plateau. This may represent the stabilization of cultivation of *Chenopodium*. The decline in *Lepidium* size may have resulted from loss of developed seed stocks or stress of a shift to more extensive field cultivation at this time.

(f)   Whatever the cause of the decline in *Lepidium* root size observed in late Phase 7 and early Phase 8, this trend is subsequently reversed. However, neither *Lepidium* nor *Chenopodium* reaches the mean diameters of modern cultivars before the end of the Panaulauca sequence.

In summary, both *Lepidium* roots and *Chenopodium* seeds show slow change in mean diameters after their first appearance in any quantity between 1900 bc and 1600 bc. Phase 6 (1620–1024 bc) is a transitional phase in the history of use of these plants, a period of change from the use of wild or tended plants to incipient cultivation. Phase 7 (1024–333 bc) is a period of accelerated change, with a peak in *Lepidium* mean diameter, and size increase in *Chenopodium*. Changes in the two taxa are not synchronous, however, with *Chenopodium* 'leading' changes. Finally, in Phase 8 (333 bc–ad 1195), *Chenopodium* seems to have reached a plateau in terms of seed-size development while *Lepidium* continues to undergo change.

If the model of co-evolution of animal and plant domestication proposed here is valid, then herding of semi-domesticated camelids, with a concomitant increase in disturbed habitats, should be underway by late Phase 5, or just after 2000 bc. Timing of this stage is later than has been proposed by Wing (1977) and Wheeler Pires-Ferreira *et al.* (1976): 4000–2500 bc for the herding of semi-domesticates, with domesticated forms by 2500 bc or slightly after. However, faunal data from Panaulauca, under analysis by Moore (1984; final report in preparation), support the timing suggested by the botanical data. The first good evidence for domesticated forms occurs in level 16 ceramic, or after 1600 bc. A date of just after 2000 bc for the beginning of corraling and the manipulation of wild populations fits well with the faunal data.

## Conclusions

The availability of complete data only from the strata dated after 3000 bc has both limited and focused the analysis presented here. This limitation arises from the lack of detailed information on the first 5000 years of occupation at Panaulauca. Test-pit samples do suggest, however, that a relatively unchanging pattern of use of wild-plant foods, similar to that observed for level 21, characterizes earlier occupations (Pearsall in press b). This pattern is similar to that observed at Pachamachay Cave (Pearsall 1980). Plant foods were probably a minor component of diet during the pre-ceramic compared with hunted camelids and deer, but they did provide valuable seasonal supplements and variety. These *puna* sites provide examples of subsistence systems focused on hunting, where this activity, rather than plant collecting, structured settlement and the round of yearly activities. Data show just as clearly, however, that 'man did not live by camelids alone', and that charred remains of food plants are abundant if the archaeologist makes the effort to recover them.

## Acknowledgements

I thank John W. Rick for the opportunity to analyse plant remains from Panaulauca Cave. Research was supported by a grant to Rick from the National Science Foundation, and funds from the University of Missouri Research Council. Figures were drawn by Thomas Holland. Laboratory facilities and staff support were provided by the American Archaeology Division, Michael J. O'Brien, Director.

## References

Anderson, E. 1952. *Plants, man, and life*. Berkeley: University of California Press.
Asch, N. B. & D. L. Asch 1980. The Dickson Camp and Pond sites: Middle Woodland archaeobotany in Illinois. In *Dickson Camp and Pond: two Early Havana traditions in the Central Illinois Valley*, A. Cantwell (ed.), 152–60. Illinois State Museum, Reports of Investigations, no. 36, Dickson Mounds Museum Anthropological Studies.
Bird, R. McK. 1970. *Maize and its cultural and natural environment in the Sierra of Huanuco, Peru*. Unpublished PhD Dissertation, University of California, Berkeley. Ann Arbor, Michigan: University Microfilm.
Bohrer, V. L. 1975. The prehistoric and historic role of the cool-season grasses in the Southwest. *Economic Botany* **29**, 199–207.
FAO 1982. *Food composition tables for the Near East*. FAO Food and Nutrition Paper 26. Rome: FAO.
Harlan, J. R. 1975. *Crops and man*. Madison, Wisconsin: American Society of Agronomy.
Hawkes, J. G. 1989. The domestication of roots and tubers in the American tropics. In *Foraging and farming: the evolution of plant exploitation*, D. R. Harris & G. C. Hillman (eds), ch. 31. London: Unwin Hyman.
Johannessen, S. 1984. Paleoethnobotany. In *American Bottom archaeology*, C. J. Bareis & J. W. Porter (eds), 197–214. Urbana, Illinois: University of Illinois Press.
Johns, T. 1989. A chemical–ecological model of root and tuber domestication in the Andes. In *Foraging and farming: the evolution of plant exploitation*, D. R. Harris & G. C. Hillman (eds), ch. 32. London: Unwin Hyman.
Leon, J. 1964. *Plantas alimenticias Andinas*. Instituto Interamericano de Ciencias Agricolas Zona Andina. Boletin Tecnico No. 6.
Moore, K. 1984. Animal procurement and use in prehistoric highland Peru. Paper presented at the 49th Annual Meeting of the Society for American Archaeology, Portland, Oregon.
Pearsall, D. M. 1980. Pachamachay ethnobotanical report: plant utilization at a hunting base camp. In *Prehistoric hunters of the high Andes*, J. W. Rick (ed.), 191–231. New York: Academic Press.
Pearsall, D. M. in press a. Interpreting the meaning of macroremain abundance: the

impact of source and context. In *Current paleoethnobotany: analytical methods and cultural interpretations of archaeological plant remains*, C. Hastorf & V. Popper (eds). Chicago: University of Chicago Press.

Pearsall, D. M. in press b. Floral background and data. In *Hunting and herding in the high altitude tropics: the early prehistory of the Central Peruvian Andes*, J. W. Rick (ed.).

Pearsall, D. M. & K. Moore in press. Prehistoric economy and subsistence. In *Hunting and herding in the high altitude tropics: the early prehistory of the Central Peruvian Andes*, J. W. Rick (ed.).

Rick, J. W. 1980. *Prehistoric hunters of the high Andes*. New York: Academic Press.

Rick, J. W. 1984. Structure and style at an early base camp in Junin, Peru. Paper presented at the 49th Annual Meeting of the Society for American Archaeology, Portland, Oregon.

Simmonds, N. W. 1965. The grain Chenopods of the tropical American highlands. *Economic Botany* **19**, 223–35.

Watt, B. K. & A. L. Merrill 1975. *Handbook of the nutritional contents of food*. New York: Dover.

Wheeler Pires-Ferreira, J., E. Pires-Ferreira & P. Kaulicke 1976. Preceramic animal utilization in the Central Peruvian Andes. *Science* **194**, 483–90.

Wing, E. S. 1977. Animal domestication in the Andes. In *Origins of agriculture*, C. A. Reed (ed.), 837–59. The Hague: Mouton.

Wing, E. S. & A. B. Brown 1979. *Paleonutrition*. New York: Academic Press.

Wu Leung, Woot-Tsuen & M. Flores 1961. *Food composition tables for use in Latin America*. Bethesda, Md.: National Institutes of Health.

# AGRARIAN PLANT EXPLOITATION:
# THE DOMESTICATION AND DIFFUSION OF CROPS AND CROP ASSEMBLAGES

# 20 *The tropical African cereals*

JACK R. HARLAN

In this chapter the domestication, probable areas of origin, and agronomic and cultural contexts of the African cereal crops is reviewed.[*] There is as yet relatively little direct archaeological evidence on the antiquity of African cereals, and here only passing reference is made to such archaeological data as are available. Particular attention is paid to sorghum because of its importance in world, as well as in African, agriculture, and brief comments are offered on a further seven cereals indigenous to Africa.

## Sorghum

Sorghum (*Sorghum bicolor*) is one of the great cereals of the world. From our studies at the Crop Evolution Laboratory in Illinois, we can say that its history in Africa is now rather clear, although the same can not be said of its history in East Asia which needs to be studied much more thoroughly. Extensive fieldwork over many years, combined with the growing of varieties under controlled conditions in nurseries, and thorough examination of herbarium collections, led us to classify the varieties of sorghum into five major races and ten two-by-two combinations (Harlan & de Wet 1972, Harlan & Stemler 1976) which turned out correlate remarkably well with the language map of Africa.

(a)   The most primitive race, the one that looks most like the wild progenitor, we call the *bicolor* race. It is found just about everywhere sorghum is grown, so it is not much help in identifying the area or areas of origin of domestic sorghum. It has a very loose, open panicle, very like wild sorghum. Its spikelets and grains are larger and do not shatter as well as the wild types, and there are fewer branches, so it is definitely a cultivated, domesticated race, although morphologically rather similar to wild sorghum.

(b)   The *guinea* race is primarily a West African race. It has special modifications for growing in high-rainfall conditions, i.e. rainfall that

[*] Editors' note: this chapter is based on a recording of an informal seminar given by Professor Harlan at the World Archaeological Congress in September 1986. It is therefore not fully referenced. He kindly agreed to its inclusion in this volume, and we have incorporated in it information that arose during the discussion at the seminar.

is high for sorghum, which is a dry-land crop: the glumes open up, the stalk twists so that it will dry out after rain, and the seed is very hard. It is a sorghum primarily of the Niger-Congo language family, but, because of its adaptation to high rainfall, we find a sprinkling of it in the highlands of East Africa and southward along the mountain ranges where rainfall is high. It reached India, where it is also found in areas of high rainfall, but basically it is a West African race.

(c)    The *caudatum* race belongs to the area of the Chari-Nile language group. It is quite distinctive: its grain is flat on one side and convex on the other. It is found primarily from Lake Chad to the Ethiopian border, and filtering out from there.

(d)    The *kafir* race is a Bantu sorghum which belongs to southern Africa.

(e)    The fifth race is *durra* and it is also quite distinctive. It is a highly derived sorghum, with very dense compact heads and other morphological characteristics which make it easy to identify. In Africa it is grown mainly by Islamic peoples along the edge of the Sahara, and its main centre of cultivation is India.

This curious distribution of the races of sorghum has suggested to us the following history. The first race to be domesticated was *bicolor*, the primitive one, and it was spread widely, as it still is today. From the *bicolor* race people in West Africa began to develop their own local adaptations of the *guinea* races, peoples in southern Africa developed the *kafirs*, and people in the area from Chad to eastern Sudan and Uganda developed the *caudatums*. The *bicolor* race at some time reached India, where the *durras* were developed, and we think it came back to Africa, probably in Islamic times. This history of sorghum makes sense in terms of biology, ecology, history, and human linguistic and cultural diversity.

Where did sorghum domestication start? To try to discover this, we have examined the wild races, of which there are several. One of them is the *arundinaceum* race, a West African race adapted to the tropical forest zone. Cultivated sorghum does not do very well in the forest zone; it is grown, but the rainfall is too high and for that reason we discount any great contribution to domesticated sorghum from the *arundinaceum* race. The *virgatum* race is a very small sorghum, which is basically a grass of the Nile floodplain which grows along the river and beside irrigation ditches. The race known as *aethiopicum* is of uncertain status. We have never seen it growing in what appear to be natural stands. It just occurs here and there, and we suspect that it is really a secondary derivative of cultivated sorghum by hybridization with wild forms. This leaves the *verticilliflorum* race as the primary candidate for the role of progenitor of the domesticated sorghums. It is extremely abundant in the eastern half of Africa, from Sudan right down to southern Africa, but not in western Africa. In the area of greatest abundance, in Sudan for instance, or parts of Chad, you can drive for a hundred kilometres through tall-grass savanna, a marvellous formation extending as far as you can see, with spiny acacia dotted through it here and there, unploughed, uncultivated, not even grazed very much. This is clearly a primary habitat, and there is a lot of it left. The chief dominant of this grassland is the *verticilliflorum* race of sorghum, present in enormous quantities. It is a very productive plant which can grow 4 m high, with many panicles and lots of seed; if you want to get the seed you have to harvest it over a week or so, but it has enormous productivity in its native state.

Our hybridization studies have shown the *verticilliflorum* race to be fully fertile with cultivated sorghums. They both have ten chromosomes, the chromosomes pair in the hybrids, and the hybrids are fertile. There may be some secondary introgression, particularly in West Africa, and the *arundi-naceum* race may have introgressed into cultivated sorghums to help provide adaptation to high rainfall. So, on grounds of distribution, ecology, and morphology we think that the primary location of domestication was in the northeastern quadrant of Africa, probably the Sudan–Chad area, where the *bicolor* race was developed and from where it spread through Africa and on to India.

The next question is when did this occur, what time range is involved? But here we come against the deficiencies of the archaeological record. The earliest dates for domesticated sorghum we appear to have are from India, which in effect puts a minimum age on its domestication. It seems to have reached India by around 2000 bc, so it has to be older than that in Africa. There are, as yet unconfirmed, reports of sorghum from the Khartoum area dated to the 6th millennium bc, and in southern Africa dates in the 3rd millennium bc were initially claimed for sorghum from the cave site of Shongweni in Natal. However, they were obtained from charcoal in the same layer as the sorghum grains, which were later radiocarbon dated independently and proved to be much more recent.

I do not see any cogency in the argument that the domestication of sorghum in Africa was late because of the absence of stone tools for harvesting it. There is nothing inefficient about using a beating basket (cf. Harlan Ch. 5, this volume). The glossed-edge trapezoids from the Nigerian site of Iwo Eleru, probably hafted in a sickle-like implement and making their appearance about 1500 bc, are not suitable for cutting sorghum stalks; they are much more likely to have been used for cutting grasses or reeds for basket making. Indeed, I doubt whether we shall ever be able to detect the domestication of sorghum from a change in the tool-kit; the tools that one would use for wild sorghum would be essentially the same as those used for cultivated sorghum.

There are also uncertainties about when and how sorghum reached India. There are reports of pottery impressions of sorghum grains from Arabia dating to about 2500 bc, and there is now evidence in the form of potsherds with Harappan script on them, found on the Arabian coast, for direct connections with Harappan civilization, indicating some sort of intercourse between Arabia and the northwestern coast of the Indian sub-continent by 2000 bc. The whole system of circum-Arabian Sea contact apparently developed quite early and facilitated the movement of material in both directions. However, I doubt whether sorghum reached India directly across the Arabian Sea; one might think that transmission by coastal shipping was more likely at that time. Finds of sorghum recently reported from highland Yemen and dated to about 2000 bc tend to reinforce that supposition. If we had some dated sorghum from Pakistan we might find it to be older there than in India. I do not visualize just a single introduction to India; rather that there were contacts over a long period of time through coastal trade. We know that by Roman times, or a little earlier, direct maritime trade was conducted between East Africa and southern India. So I would think of an ebb and flow of material between the two continents. The fact that *bicolor* was the first sorghum to reach India does not help us very much with dating the time at which the other sorghums were selected and developed. If the Indian archaeological materials were good enough to identify as to race, it could be very helpful, but, as far as I know, the early sorghums found in India are all *bicolors*.

Despite its primitive characteristics, the *bicolor* race of sorghum has persisted together with all the specialized varieties because it is used for special purposes. The sweet sorghums are of that race and the broomcorns also. People like sweet sorghum, and we find in a typical village in the sorghum belt of Africa that there will be several local varieties grown, and also a few small patches of *bicolor* because the people like to chew it like sugar-cane. Sorghums are high in tannin, some much more so than others. There is selection both for and against tannin content. People tend to prefer high-tannin varieties for beer making, and then there is no need to use hops or some other substitute for hops, so beer sorghums tend to have a high tannin content. Also, some sorghums with a high tannin content are selected because they deter birds from feeding on the grain. I have not studied the distribution of the dye sorghums in detail, but I believe that the dyes which were used in, say, making 'Moroccan' leather came from the central part of the sub-Saharan zone – northern Nigeria and Niger – and that they were selected for an abundance of red pigment; I think these are mostly *bicolors*.

The selection pressures on sorghum in Africa are tremendous. At harvest time the first thing the cultivator does is to go through the field and harvest heads for next year's seed stock. He may have a mixed field of various kinds of sorghum and he will only select what is to be planted next year. So the selection pressure is very strong for what the cultivator wants, and his wants may be very varied and to us unexpected, for example the ease of pounding grain in the morning. In parts of Mali where they grow both the soft-seeded and the very hard-seeded sorghums, women do not like to pound the hard-seeded variety because it is hard work; but they still grow it because it has high insect-resistance in storage, and so it is saved for the latter part of the season and they eat up the soft sorghums first.

Among the distinctively African techniques of cultivating sorghum two particularly deserve mention: *décrue* and transplanting. *Décrue* is practised primarily along the Niger and Senegal floodplains (Harlan & Pasquereau 1969). When the floodwaters recede in the early dry season, seeds are planted in the mud and the crop is grown on stored moisture, without rain or irrigation. *Décrue* is a complex system of cultivation. Along the great bend of the Niger – the so-called 'inland delta' – the water spreads very slowly and recedes very slowly. Therefore, the closer you are to the river the deeper is the water, the farther from the river the shallower the water; a situation that requires different cultivars for each location. Cultivars are selected for short flooding and long flooding, and there are even very special *décrue* varieties grown down near the river which are harvested by canoe – and sorghum is a dry-land plant!

Transplanting after the rains is another distinctive technique used where the moisture supply is marginal. It is a sort of modified *décrue* in that there are vast areas in the savanna which stand in water during the rains – too much water to grow a crop. After the land dries up the people burn off the grass and sow the crop on residual moisture, but they have to do it quickly. Therefore, they have already started seedlings in a seed bed which are then transplanted as rice is transplanted in Asia. They uproot the seedlings and plant them in a deep hole dug with a special digging stick, add a little water, and the crop then grows entirely on the moisture remaining in the soil from the wet season.

These two distinctively African techniques of cultivation are applied not only to sorghum but also to pearl millet, and varieties are selected for these special purposes. The same cultivator may have *décrue* varieties and non-*décrue* varieties depending on his land resources. He will adapt his planting from year to year, to adjust to high and low floods, by switching between sorghum varieties and even from sorghum to pearl millet. The cultivators select very intensively for what they want, and they get it. Selection for the non-shattering inflorescence of domesticated sorghum was almost certainly a conscious process, because sorghum is handled plant by plant, and the cultivator knows every plant in his field. In Ethiopia, for example, a crook-neck variety has been selected because it is easier to hang in the roof over the fire, which keeps the insects out and makes good conditions for the storage of seed stock.

The introduction of maize has in some places caused the cultivation of sorghum to decline or disappear. In most of West Africa, maize has not really become a field crop; it is a garden crop, grown in small patches, although recently it has been more widely cultivated where soils are poor and exhausted, as on the Jos Plateau. In parts of East Africa, on the other hand, and in southern Africa, it has become the staple cereal. It fits a niche in which it will grow better with a little more rainfall than sorghum, and I think it is a niche that was not very well filled before maize became available.

## Pearl millet

From the world point of view the next most important African cereal is pearl millet (*Pennisetum typhoides*, previously *P. americanum*). The history of pearl millet is different from that of sorghum. The wild forms occur deep in the Sahara and do not extend very far out from the desert into the Sahel. It is the most drought-resistant of all the hot-season millets/cereals. We suspect it was domesticated in the Sahara, and later moved into the Sahel where it is most common now. It is grown well beyond the Sahel in sub-Saharan Africa because people like it; they generally prefer it to sorghum. It is a very palatable cereal with one of the best nutritional profiles. It has been enormously modified from the wild form. Wild pearl millet has a head no more than 10 cm long, whereas cultivated races have inflorescences up to 2 m long. The changes in the morphology of the inflorescence, and in the size and colours of the grain are astonishing. The colours of the cultivated grain range from brick-red to grey to black, the commonest being grey, which is why it is called pearl millet. These changes are of the same order of magnitude as, or perhaps even greater than, the huge changes that distinguish domesticated maize from the (postulated) form of ancestral wild maize.

The distribution of the cultivated, wild, and hybrid forms of pearl millet is somewhat puzzling. In Senegal, large hybrid swarms occur between the wild and the cultivated, and between the cultivated and the weed forms, called *shibra* in that area: very complex populations with all kinds of wild, weedy, and cultivated forms all mixed up in the same area. Then there is a geographical gap, eastward as far as Djebel Marra and Sudan. I do not know why the gap should be there; perhaps we have not looked hard enough. But in the Djebel Marra area large swarms of wild/weed/cultivated mix-ups again occur. The weed form apparently did not get to India, but domesticated pearl millet did. It is a very important crop in the dry zones of India, where it is the most drought-resistant of the cereals, and it is grown particularly in Rajasthan and around the margins of the Thar desert. It probably reached India a little later than sorghum. It is also grown in southern Africa around the margins of the Kalahari desert.

## Finger millet

Wild forms of finger millet (*Eleusine coracana*) occur in the highlands of eastern Africa, in Uganda, Ethiopia, and Kenya. Again, there are wild, weedy, and cultivated forms, including some primitive cultivated races. Finger millet was introduced to India where it evolved typically Indian races, both in the hill country in the north and in the southern hills. Today, it is used primarily for beer in Africa. I think at one time it must have been an important food crop, but was subsequently largely replaced by other cereals. The grain is not palatable, but it makes good beer. Finger millet probably reached India around the same time as sorghum and pearl millet. I do not know of any possible wild ancestors of finger millet, or of pearl millet, in southern Arabia. There is virtually no archaeological record of finger millet, but Phillipson excavated definitely domesticated remains of it from a site in

Ethiopia which was dated to about the end of the 3rd millennium bc. However, the remains were not charred, and, particularly as it is an isolated find at present, I am inclined to reserve judgement on the validity of the dating for the time being.

## African rice

To the rice-eating peoples of West Africa, African rice (*Oryza glaberrima*) is enormously important, although declining in recent times and being replaced by Asian rice (cf. Chang Ch. 25, this volume). The progenitor of African rice is quite clear: it is an annual grass of the savanna zone, adapted to water holes that fill up during the rains and dry out in the dry season. There is a perennial rice related to the wild annual, but it requires more moisture, is a shy seeder, and morphologically would not be a presumed progenitor of African rice. Again, we have the wild, weedy, and cultivated forms; in fact the cultivated form can be weedy. One of the more serious problems in growing Asian rice is weedy African rice in the fields.

A distinctive West African culture has developed based on rice: to rice-eating people no meal is a meal without rice. A whole oral literature, and many religious and cultural practices, have grown up based on rice cultivation. There are also specialized indigenous tools for levelling land, digging ditches, conducting water, and so on. It is a complete and elaborate rice-cultivation complex, ranging from very simple techniques, such as just throwing the seed into a pond during the rains and then harvesting the crop later, to terrace cultivation with transplanting.

## Teff

Teff (*Eragrostis tef*) is seeded on more hectares than any other crop in Ethiopia, although total production is less than barley. Teff has an exceedingly small seed, the smallest of all cereals. It is a greater yielder, and makes an excellent, nutritious bread, the preferred bread in Ehtiopia. It is curious that in the case of teff we do not have hybrid swarms in the area of native production. The presumptive wild progenitor is *Eragrostis pylosa*, which belongs to the *kreb* complex of harvested wild grasses (see Harlan Ch. 5, this volume). Presumably it somehow sorted out of the *kreb* complex and was taken to Ethiopia where the domesticated form was really created.

## *Digitaria* spp.

There are two species of digitaria: *Digitaria exilis* and *D. iburua*. *D. exilis*, or *fonio*, is also sometimes called 'hungry rice' which is a misnomer. There have been two other species of *Digitaria* domesticated, one in India and one in

Europe. In fact, *D. sanguinalis* was harvested in Europe until recently. The important characteristic of *fonio* is its quality: it is highly palatable, grown for feast days and the like, even as chief's food. It does not yield very well, but it persists in cultivation, I think, because of its palatability. It makes the best couscous, better than wheat. The other digitaria in Africa, *D. iburua*, is grown in very restricted locations. It does not have the quality of *D. exilis* and remains restricted two very small regions in West Africa.

## *Brachiaria deflexa*

As a cultigen, *Brachiaria deflexa* is grown only in Fouta Djallon, in Guinea. It is the most restricted of all cultivated cereals in the world. It has quite large-seeded cultivars and rather well-developed domesticated forms, and although the wild form is quite widespread, the domesticated race occurs only in Fouta Djallon.

## Abyssinian oat

The Abyssinian oat (*Avena abyssinica*) is a tetraploid, whereas the more widely cultivated green oat is a hexaploid. The tetraploid developed from a weed, which probably travelled with wheat, barley, lentils, and chickpeas when they were introduced to the highlands of Ethiopia. However, I have never seen it deliberately grown in a field. It is a weed in emmer wheat and barley fields, and the cultivators do not try to weed it out of the field, nor do they try to separate it on the threshing floor. They just plant the seed mixture, and so there are non-shattering types, semi-shattering types, and shattering types. It makes a good weed and the cultivators do not object to it. Some say that the malt is a little better if you have some oats in it, it makes a better beer. If this is a domesticate, it is a domestication by default rather than by design. Another cereal that has a somewhat similar status to Abyssinian oat is *Paspalum scrobiculatum*, a weed of rice fields in West Africa. This, however, is a real weed, not a positively tolerated one like the Abyssinian oat. It causes digestive problems, and there are some toxins that can come in with fungus infection. But, if the rice crop does badly, the weed may do well and the people may then get a bigger total harvest.

## Conclusion

In this brief outline, I have tried to summarize what is currently known from a botanical and agronomic point of view about the origins and early history of Africa's cereal crops. It demonstrates very clearly the dearth of archaeobotanical evidence from the continent. Indeed, it is unfortunately true that little has been added to our knowledge of the prehistory of even the most important cereals – sorghum and pearl millet – since the publication over a decade ago of *Origins of African plant domestication* (Harlan *et al.* 1976). Until greater efforts are made at archaeological sites in tropical Africa to recover direct evidence in the form of charred and other remains of the cereals themselves we shall not advance our understanding of the 'when' and 'where' of their original cultivation and domestication. The task is formidable, but the archaeobotanical techniques are now available with which to tackle it.

# References

Chang, T. T. 1989. Domestication and spread of the cultivated rices. In *Foraging and farming: the evolution of plant exploitation*, D. R. Harris & G. C. Hillman (eds), ch. 25. London: Unwin Hyman.

Harlan, J. R. 1989. Wild-grass seed harvesting in the Sahara and Sub-Sahara of Africa. In *Foraging and farming: the evolution of plant exploitation*, D. R. Harris & G. C. Hillman (eds), ch. 5. London: Unwin Hyman.

Harlan, J. R., J. M. J. de Wet & A. B. L. Stemler (eds) 1976. *Origins of African plant domestication*. The Hague: Mouton.

Harlan, J. R. & J. M. J. de Wet 1972. A simplified classification of cultivated sorghum. *Crop Science* **12**, 172–6.

Harlan, J. R. & J. Pasquereau 1969. Décrue agriculture in Mali. *Economic Botany* **23**, 70–4.

Harlan, J. R. & A. B. L. Stemler 1976. The races of sorghum in Africa. In *Origins of African plant domestication*, J. R. Harlan, J. M. J. de Wet & A. B. L. Stemler (eds), 465–78. The Hague: Mouton.

# 21 Factors responsible for the ennoblement of African yams: inferences from experiments in yam domestication

## V. E. CHIKWENDU and C. E. A. OKEZIE

Investigation of the beginnings of agriculture in tropical West Africa has been severely hampered by the absence of direct archaeological evidence of the tuberous plants, particularly yams of the genus *Dioscorea*, which remain the staple food of nearly half the human population of the region. Yam tubers have a low chance of archaeological preservation, especially in the generally acidic red soils (latosols), and under the hot and humid climatic conditions, of the tropical forest zone of West Africa. Progress in understanding the origins and development of yam cultivation in the region is therefore dependent on finding alternative sources of information, e.g. botanical and entomological evidence, as was pointed out long ago by Alexander (1969, 1971) and by Alexander & Coursey (1969). The central aim of the research reported here is to show how such evidence can contribute to our understanding of the process of yam domestication.

## Objectives

The assumption underlying our research is that if we are to understand how yams came to be domesticated in prehistoric times we need to simulate the process of early yam domestication. Speculation and guesswork will thus be minimized. Igboland (southeastern Nigeria) is an appropriate setting for the investigation because there is an abundance of wild yam species in the local forests. Our research programme (Chikwendu & Okezie 1983) is designed to test some of the assumptions and hypotheses concerning the origins of yam domestication in the region, and it has the following objectives:

(a) to establish the relationship between the wild and ennobled species of West African yams;
(b) to collect pedological and entomological data which may help archaeologists establish the presence or absence of yam remains in excavations;

(c)  to unravel what happened to the wild yam before it underwent domestication and assumed the present-day characteristics of cultivated yams (i.e. to isolate the factors responsible for the ennoblement of the wild yams);

(d)  to correct some of the misleading assumptions that have been made about how and why the African yams were domesticated; and

(e)  to find out how long it took our ancestors to bring about the biological changes observed in present-day domesticated yams.

Our overall objective is to develop new approaches to the archaeological investigation of yam domestication, but it may also prove possible to induce changes experimentally in the wild specimens under study by manipulating some of the factors responsible for the ennoblement of yams in prehistoric times.

## Research methods

### Sample collection

The first step is to survey areas of forest during the rainy season (March–October) to locate patches of wild yams. Between December and March the yams needed for the experiment are harvested and stored in a barn until the next rains. The most difficult aspect of the work is digging up the wild yams. Apart from tangles of forest roots, the yams themselves radiate roots with long, sharp thorns from head to tail. Initially we tried to dig them as we dig the ennobled forms, but we found that we could not. We therefore resorted to trenching round the yam patch using digging sticks, root cutters, sharp machettes, shovels and spades, wheelbarrows, etc. Even with all these implements it took us several days to uproot a single yam tuber. Figure 21.1a shows how large the wild tubers can grow; indeed some are double or treble this size. After harvesting, the tubers are taken to the laboratory where they are washed and weighed.

Our experience of wild-yam harvesting leads us to doubt the claim that the stone picks of the Sangoan Stone Age were used to 'grub' up yam tubers. It is clear that the stone pick would be ineffective for digging up wild-yam tubers. Apart from the hostile thorns of the wild yam, the maze of root tangles wedging in the tuber cannot be slashed with any stone tool that was known during the Sangoan period (Chikwendu 1979). We must therefore revise the interpretation of the pick as a tool for grubbing up yams.

### Identification

Identification of the species of yam being harvested is undertaken by the botanist of the survey and harvest teams. Coursey's (1967) identification key can usually be applied successfully, but there are so many varieties of wild yam that it is sometimes difficult to attribute particular ones to any known

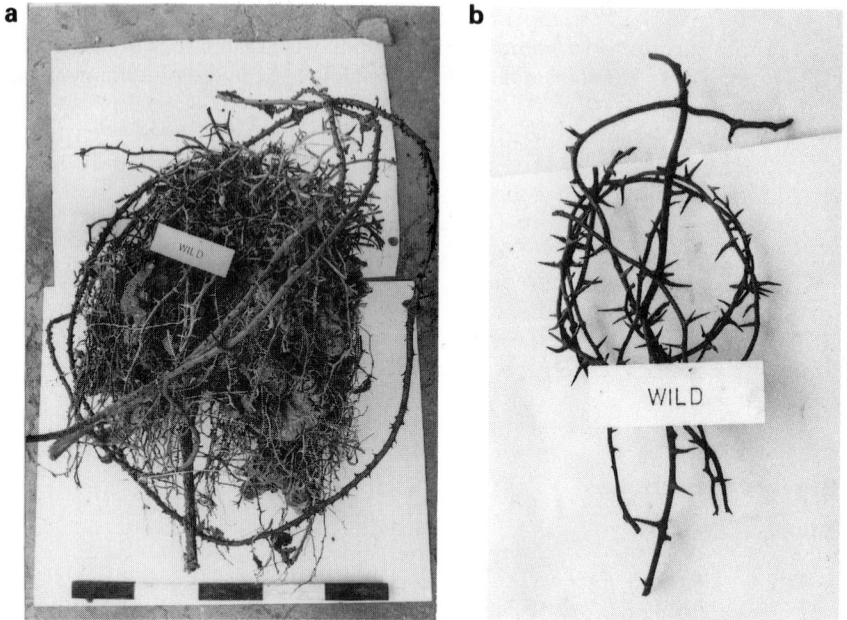

**Figure 21.1** (a) Wild-yam tuber (*Dioscorea rotundata*) harvested from the Agbamere Forest near Nsukka showing (i) roots radiating from the crown to the tail of the tuber, (ii) the length of the vine without any branches or leaves, and (iii) the thorns on roots and stem (5 cm-interval scale); (b) typical roots and thorns of the wild yam (*Dioscorea rotundata*).

species. The most common species in the wild are *Dioscorea rotundata, D. praehensilis, D. cayenensis, D. dumetorum* and *D. bulbifera*. A few of our specimens are yet to be identified to species level.

## Choice of experimental sites

We were very careful in choosing the experimental site. We avoided farmland saturated with chemical fertilizer because it might cause sudden changes or even radical mutations in the experimental specimens. Instead, we chose an open space (west of the Archaeology Department) which had not been used for any agricultural purpose within living memory.

## Controls

In order to identify the critical factors responsible for the domestication of wild yams we had to build some controls into the experiment, as follows.

EXPOSURE TO SUNSHINE

Some specimens are planted in the open to benefit from maximum solar radiation, while others are planted in their shady forest habitat.

TILLING, TENDING AND WEEDING

Some are planted in carefully prepared mounds while others are planted directly in the hard lateritic soil. Some are staked and supported, others are not, and, similarly, some are weeded and others not.

CUTTING INTO SETTS

The large wild tubers are usually cut into setts before planting. A careful record is kept of the morphological changes manifested in the stands derived from the head, mid-section, and tail of the yam tuber.

TIMING AND SOWING

Specimens are sown at the beginning, in the middle, and toward the end of the rainy season, and the differential effects on tuber growth are monitored.

TIMING THE HARVESTING

Some are 'milked' early, by August, to enhance the formation of secondary tubers, as is done with domesticated yams. Others are harvested in the middle of the harmattan season, in December–January. A few are not harvested at all. The effects of these three treatments are monitored and the results recorded.

INTERCROPPING

This control is to be applied in a future planting season, and is designed to monitor the changes (if any) which result from interaction between the experimental yams and other crops, e.g. *Zea mays*, *Capsicum* spp., *Lycopersicon esculentum*, *Telfaria occidentalis*, etc. To minimize wind and insect pollination, the two sections of intercrop and monocrop experiments have to be separately sited. The direction of wind during the rainy season must also be taken into consideration. By close monitoring we shall be able, after some years, to establish whether intercropping has any noticeable effect on the domestication of the wild yam.

APPLICATION OF FARMYARD MANURE

Competition for nutrients in the forest habitat of wild yams is severe and this is thought to be implicated in the development of such features as long, sharp thorns, stout shoots adorned with as many as 50 or more cataphylls before the appearance of true branches and leaves, highly toxic tubers, and a fantastic maze of thorny roots covering the entire body of the tuber from head to tail (Figs 21.1a & b). All these features are believed to be adaptive features which enhance the ability of the wild yam to compete favourably for nutrients in its forest habitat, e.g. the long, stout stem is capable of reaching out for sunlight irrespective of the height of the canopy of the forest. An additional set of treatments are therefore to be introduced into the experiment, designed to test whether the application of farmyard manure (of the type found in refuse dumps in the villages) helps reduce the wild characteristics of the experimental specimens.

Further treatments will be incorporated, as and when needed, and we hope that the experiment can be continued for several more years in order to achieve conclusive results.

## Data collected

The experiment is at present providing cytological, biochemical, and entomological – as well as agronomic – data, and, if further funding is obtained, it will be extended to cover other types of data. In this section the types of data collected so far are listed and briefly discussed.

### Fibrosity and starch content

In the pure wild forms, the tubers contain fibrous material from head to tail. We have devised a method of counting the strands of fibre in an 8 cm$^3$ cube of yam, taken from the tail end of the tuber. The cuboid sample is taken from the core part of the tail and then squashed. The strands of fibre are usually visible for morphological observation and counting. Continued experimental cultivation leads to a reduction in the number of fibre strands. Specimens which have undergone experimental cultivation for over seven years have shown remarkable reduction in the fibre content and a massive increase in the starch content.

### Chromosome counts

Chromosome counts have been taken from the root-tip samples, but recently it has been suggested to us that we can take samples from the flowers. Fortunately, some varieties of wild yam flower profusely immediately they are cultivated experimentally. In time, we intend to compare our chromosome data with those known for domesticated yams. The comparison may enable us to address more authoritatively the general question of whether domestication induces polyploidy in some cultivars.

### Raphide content

We intend to continue observing the raphide content in wild-yam tubers, in the experimental specimens, and in domesticated *D. rotundata*. Preliminary work indicates that raphide content increases with increase in starch content.

## Protein assay

Specialists usually lump together many varieties of white, roundish yam under the species name of *D. rotundata*. We have observed such definite differences in the flowering, fruiting, and seeding of these varieties to hypothesize that they do not belong to a single species. Electrophoretic analyses of the protein contents will enable us to establish filial relationship in the domesticated varieties of the yam. It will also enable us to observe similarities or differences between the wild forms, the experimental specimens, and the domesticated varieties of this yam.

## Diosgenic content

Measurement of the amount of the steroid diosgenin in different types of yam will be made to establish the relationship of this characteristic to the stages of experimental domestication. The diosgenic content of various other species and varieties of yam will also be recorded.

## Entomological and molluscan data

Recording of entomological data is an integral part of the experiment and some interesting observations have already been made. Yam leaves are eaten by several insects, e.g. the smelling grasshopper (*Zonocerus variagatus*), and also by garden snails: *Limicolaria* spp. Yam beetles (*Heteroligus meles* and *H. appius*) attack the tubers of the experimental specimens which have shown marked changes towards ennoblement. The entomological data we are gathering may prove to be particularly informative for tropical archaeology. Some of these insects possess hard mouths, thoracic cages, legs, and elytra which can survive in archaeological deposits long after yam tubers have completely decayed. The presence of the remains of one species may not be sufficiently indicative to infer past yam cultivation, but if the remains of several yam-predating species are found together, then the inference is much more secure.

## Morphological and ecological changes observed

In this section we summarize the changes which have been observed after eight years of sustained research, the experiment having been started in 1977.

## Tubers and roots

(a)   There is a highly significant reduction both in the number and length of the thorns borne on the tubers. Control experiments in which uniform weights of setts from wild tubers were grown on farmland and in the

a

EXPERIMENTAL SPECIMEN

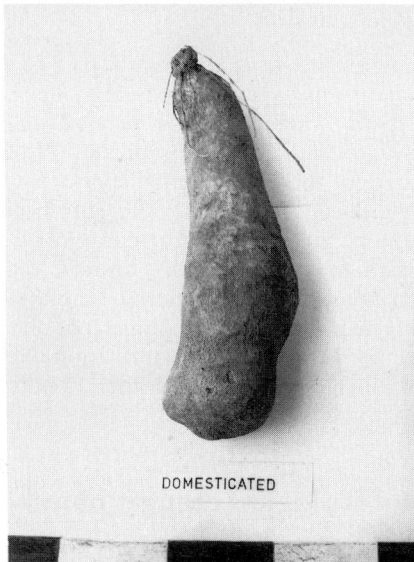

b

DOMESTICATED

**Figure 21.2** (a) Tuber from wild *Dioscorea rotundata* which has undergone five years of continuous experimental domestication. Compared with the tuber shown in Figure 21.1a, this shows (i) migration of the thorns to the crown of the tuber, (ii) a slim, smooth-bodied tuber, (iii) a reduction in the length of roots and thorns, and (iv) a beetle bite-mark in the middle of the tuber (5 cm-interval scale). (b) Tuber of domesticated *Dioscorea rotundata* with roots (some of which have been cut off by the harvester) restricted to the crown, as in the experimental specimen shown in (a) (5 cm-interval scale).

forest showed that more thorns were found on tubers produced in the forest than on tubers from the farmland (Figs 21.1a & b, 21.2a).

(b)   The fibrosity of the wild tubers is reduced and there is a corresponding increase in starch content. Cytological studies using light microscopy showed a greater concentration of starch grains per unit area of cells examined in the experimentally grown wild tubers.

(c)   The enormous size of the wild tubers and the thickness of the stems is reduced under experimental domestication. The varied and convoluted shape of the wild tubers tends to change with domestication, leading to the formation of more uniform, smaller tubers. In many of the specimens, there is the tendency for the tubers to become more rotund. Branching of tubers is reduced and the rhizomatous bulbous head of the tuber tends to decrease in size (Figs 21.1a, 21.2a & b).

(d)   Roots which radiate from all parts of the tuber in the wild form tend to become restricted to the head of the tubers in the experimental specimens, and they also become shorter, thinner, and less thorny (Fig. 21.2a).

## Vines, branches, leaves, flowers, fruits, and seeds

(a)   The great heights attained by the vines of the wild forms in the forest (up to 100 m) are much reduced in the experimental specimens (Figs 21.3a & b).

(b)   The number of cataphylls produced in the wild, before the appearance of true branches and leaves, is drastically reduced and comes to approximate the number in domesticated yams (Figs 21.3a & b).

(c)   The foliage of the experimental yams comes to resemble that of domesticated yams.

(d)   Profuse flowering, fruiting, and seeding has been observed in some of the experimental specimens. In fact, flowering was more profuse in the experimental plants grown from wild tubers than from the domesticated yam tubers (Figs 21.4a & b). Our experience is that domesticated forms do not flower profusely in the environs of Nsukka, although in some parts of southeastern Nigeria flowering can be profuse, resulting in a high incidence of fruiting and seeding. We have difficulty in adducing reasons for the profuse flowering of wild types growing around Nsukka, but it may be connected with the lack of interference in the forest environment where the wild yams grow, as opposed to the constant fragmentation of the tubers into setts when the domesticated forms are propagated vegetatively in the normal way. In fact, it has been suggested that the yam plant has tended to lose its capacity to flower as a result of long periods of continuous vegetative propagation (Onwueme 1978). Thus, in so far as domestication has involved the prolonged vegetative propagation of yams, it may well have led to decreased flowering in the dom-esticated forms.

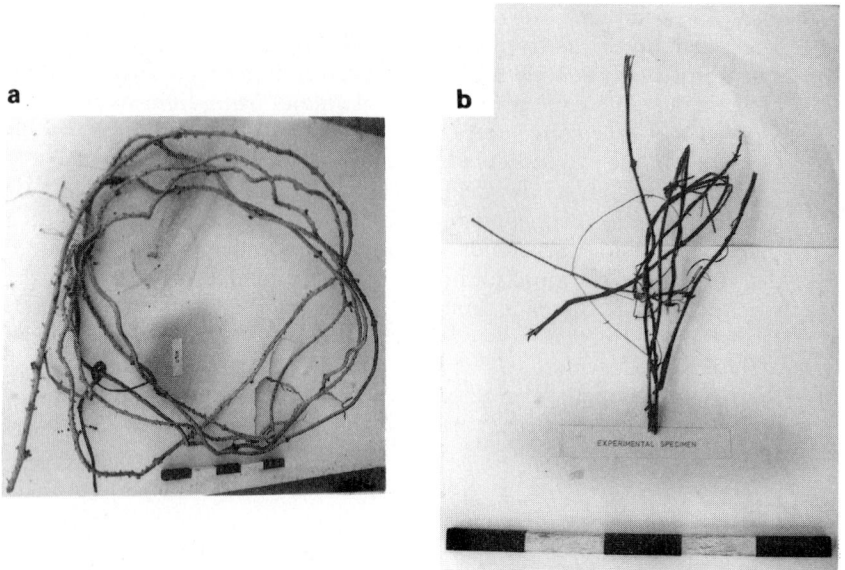

**Figure 21.3** (a) Vine of wild *Dioscorea rotundata* nearly 30 m in length, with a thick stem, no true branches or leaves, and many cataphylls (5 cm-interval scale); (b) Vine of five-year experimental *Dioscorea rotundata* showing reduced length and thickness compared with the wild form, and closely resembling the vines of domesticated yams (5 cm-interval scale).

(e)    The fruits and seeds of some of the experimental yams are facsimiles of the fruits and seeds of domesticated *Dioscorea rotundata*, with potentially a pair of winged seeds in each of the three loculi of each fruit. We have observed a higher seeding capacity in the experimental plants which originated from wild species than in domesticated *D. rotundata* (var. Obiaoturugo) plants. From the latter we were able to recover only one or two seeds per fruit, while from experimental wild plants we recovered two or three seeds per fruit in the 1982, 1983, 1984, and 1985 planting seasons. The greater seeding capacity of the experimental wild plants may be connected with the lower frequency of vegetative propagation to which they have been exposed compared with the domesticated plants (Figs 21.5a & b).

(f)    The embryos of the seeds from the experimental plants raised from tubers obtained in the wild are structurally similar to those obtained from domesticated *D. rotundata* seeds. The embryos are usually globular when freshly harvested and continue to grow in length and breadth through the dormancy period in the manner reported by Okezie (1981) for domesticated *D. rotundata* embryos. However, while in the domesticated types the embryo develops for at least 3–4 months in the seed

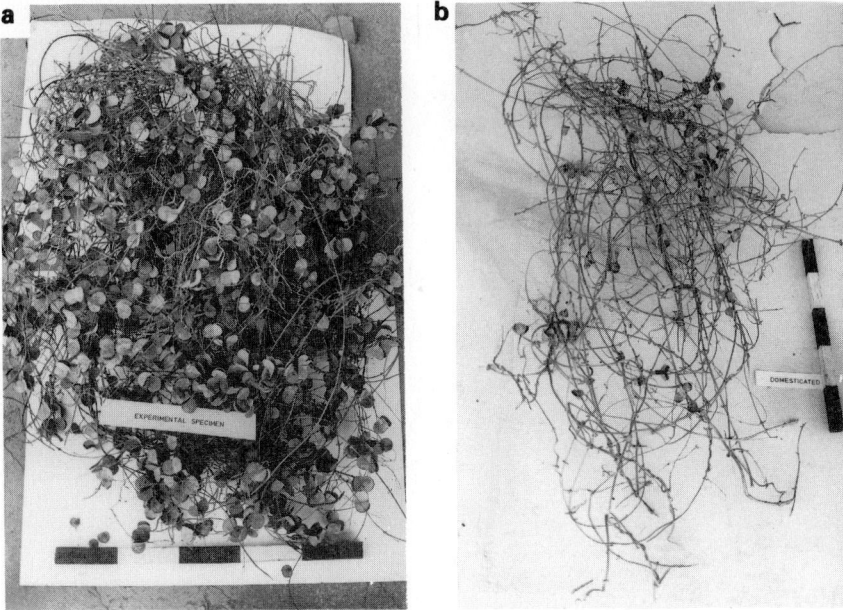

**Figure 21.4** (a) Profuse fruiting in experimentally cultivated wild *Dioscorea rotundata*. There are normally two seeds in each loculus and three loculi to each fruit (5 cm-interval scale). (b) Vine and fruits of domesticated *Dioscorea rotundata*. Most of the fruits have fallen off this specimen, but they are, in any case, not as numerous as those of the experimental specimen shown in (a) (5 cm-interval scale).

and attains a length of about 1115 μm and a breadth of about 822 μm before seed germination can take place, in the wild forms seed germination can occur as little as one month after seed harvest when the embryos are about 800 μm in length and about 680 μm in breadth. This clearly demonstrates a shorter period of seed dormancy in the wild than in the domesticated form. This dormancy period has tended to increase with time with continuous vegetative propagation using setts originally derived from wild tubers.

(g)  The same insect pests which attack the domesticated yams (Jerath 1965) also visit the experimental ones, e.g. the grasshopper *Zonocerus variagatus* which attacks the tender vines and leaves, and the beetles and crickets which attack the tubers. Snails (*Limicolaria* spp.) also attack the vines and leaves. In addition, we have noticed some thrips (*Larothrips dentipes*) around the shoots, especially among flowering populations, in late July and early August. Pitkin (1973) collected these thrips from pistillate yam flowers and they were observed carrying pollen grains

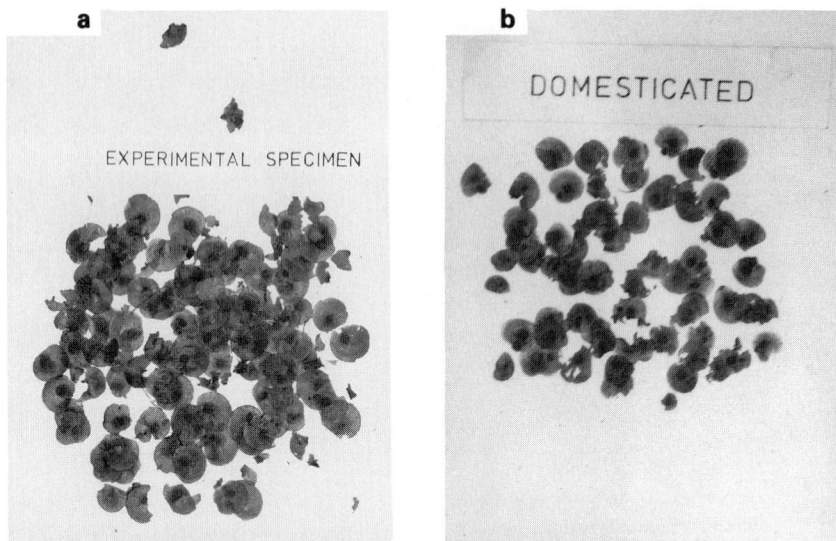

**Figure 21.5** (a) Seeds of five-year experimental *Dioscorea rotundata* equipped with wings for seed dispersal; (b) seeds of domesticated *Discorea rotundata*.

from staminate to pistillate flowers. They were therefore thought to be involved in the pollination of the female flowers. Our observation of thrips in late July and early August, when flowering was profuse, may implicate them in the pollination process of our experimental plants. This, however, needs further investigation.

## Factors responsible for the observed changes

The following factors, among others yet to be clearly understood, appear to be responsible for the changes observed in the experimental yam plants.

### *Exposure to sunshine*

The experimental plants need not grow to great heights in search of sunshine, unlike the wild forest forms. This has led to reduction in height (length of stem) and in the number of cataphylls before the appearance of true branches and leaves (Figs 21.3a & b).

### *Cutting the tubers into setts before planting*

This factor drastically reduces the vigour shown by the stout shoots observed in the wholly wild species which measure 2.5–3 cm in thickness and up to 100 m in length. Cutting the experimental tubers into setts tends to reduce stem thickness and length which, together with the foliage, come to resemble the stems and leaves of the domesticated forms.

## Tillage and mound heaping

In its forest habitat, the wild yam radiates thorny roots from all parts of the tuber: an adaptive defensive mechanism which also enables the plant to compete for nutrients in the forest soil. Some of the tubers are set as deep as 2–3 m below the soil surface to avoid predators. The heaping up of a mound of soil in which the yam is planted reduces the need for deep burial of the tubers. It also makes the protective maze of thorns unnecessary, allowing the development of a smoother, less convoluted tuber in the experimental specimens (Fig. 21.2b).

## Tending and weeding

Tending helps to expose as many leaves as possible to sunshine, and weeding reduces the severe competition which the wild yams experience in the forest. These factors reinforce the effects of tillage.

## Increased dormancy

In most of the wild yams the period of dormancy does not exceed one month, whereas in the domesticated species dormancy reaches 2–4 months. We have induced dormancy in some of the experimental specimens by clipping off the shoots until the normal planting season begins. A latent dormancy of two months has been demonstrated in the experimental specimens.

## Conclusion

As our project continues we hope to improve understanding of the factors responsible for the ennoblement of the wild yams until we can reproduce, in a short time-period, the transformation of the wild forms into edible yams, in imitation of their prehistoric domestication. In a region where hunger is a major health hazard, this project may bring relief to millions of yam-eaters in West Africa, as well as elsewhere in the tropics, if we succeed in shortening and cheapening the process of turning wild yams into edible varieties. Thus, new varieties of yam, with a better balance of nutrients and higher yields per plant, may result from this project.

Archaeologically, our investigation is charting a new direction for tropical archaeology which is especially valuable in view of the paucity of direct archaeological evidence for early food production in West Africa and, indeed, throughout the humid tropics (Harris 1972, 1976). The successful completion of this project will demonstrate to archaeologists a new approach to the investigation of prehistoric agriculture in the tropics, in which the domestication of yams and other tuberous crops played such an important part. More generally, it will encourage archaeologists to re-evaluate the weight accorded to different types of evidence for early agriculture and show that experimental data of the type generated by this project are a valid form of 'archaeobotanical' evidence.

The project will also help correct some of the earlier assumptions made by scholars with regard to early yam domestication. We particularly emphasize the need to reassess the functional efficacy of the 'Sangoan' tool-kit for grubbing up wild yams. We consider that wooden implements sharpened to points and edges would have been more effective for digging up wild yams than the Sangoan pick. The 'head stump' hypothesis which has been adduced by many writers trying to explain the beginnings of yam domestication also needs revision. Our investigation has shown that the experimental yam stands which grow from the tail section of the tuber lose their wild characteristics more rapidly than those grown from the head end. The 'head stump' stands usually manifest more wild characteristics than the stands derived from the middle or tail section of the tuber. It seems probable that the 'tail stumps' left behind by the impatient or careless harvester may have attracted man's attention to the yam's potential for vegetative propagation. This empirical observation may, indeed, have led to the domestication of the yam.

Finally, the project demonstrates the value of, and reaffirms the need for, an interdisciplinary approach to the solution of archaeological problems. Insistence on orthodox archaeological methods of investigation will never provide answers to the many unanswered questions about the way of life of prehistoric peoples in general and about the origins and development of food production in particular.

## References

Alexander, J. 1969. The indirect evidence for domestication. In *The domestication and exploitation of plants and animals*, P. J. Ucko & G. W. Dimbleby (eds), 123–9. London: Duckworth.

Alexander, J. 1971. The domestication of yams: a multi-disciplinary problem. In *Science in archaeology*, E. S. Higgs & D. Brothwell (eds), 2nd edn, 229–34. London: Thames & Hudson.

Alexander, J. & D. G. Coursey 1969. The origins of yam cultivation. In *The domestication and exploitation of plants and animals*, P. J. Ucko & G. W. Dimbleby (eds), 405–25. London: Duckworth.

Chikwendu, V. E. 1979. The occurrence of waisted stones axes in eastern Nigeria. *Nyame Akuma* **5**, 44–8.

Chikwendu, V. E. & C. E. A. Okezie 1983. Wild yam domestication experiment – preliminary statement. Paper read at the Pan African Congress, Jos, Nigeria.

Coursey, D. G. 1967. *Yams*. London: Longman.

Harris, D. R. 1972. The origins of agriculture in the tropics. *American Scientist* **60**, 180–93.

Harris, D. R. 1976. Traditional systems of plant food production and the origins of agriculture in West Africa. In *Origins of African plant domestication*, J. R. Harlan, J. M. J. de Wet & A. B. L. Stemler (eds), 311–56. The Hague: Mouton.

Jerath, M. L. 1965. *Yam pests and their known parasites and predators in Nigeria*. Nigerian Department of Agricultural Research, Memo 83.

Okezie, C. E. A. 1981. *Morphogenetic and growth analysis studies on the white Guinea yam (*Dioscorea rotundata *Poir.) raised from seed*. PhD thesis, University of Nigeria, Nsukka, Nigeria.

Onwueme, I. C. 1978. *The tropical tuber crops: yams, cassava, sweet potatoes, and cocoyams*. Chichester: John Wiley & Sons.

Pitkin, B. R. 1973. *Larothrips dentipes* (Thysanoptera, thripidae), a new genus and species of thrips from yam flowers in Nigeria. *Bulletin of Entomological Research* **62**, 425–8.

# 22 Domestication of the Southwest Asian Neolithic crop assemblage of cereals, pulses, and flax: the evidence from the living plants

DANIEL ZOHARY

## Introduction

Expertly identified and radiocarbon-dated plant remains are now available from hundreds of Neolithic and Bronze-Age sites in Southwest Asia and Europe. The volume of this archaeobotanical documentation and its recent rapid growth becomes apparent when one examines the proceedings of the workshops of European palaeoethnobotanists which took place in 1971, 1975, 1978, 1981, and 1984 (e.g. van Zeist & Casparie 1984), the annual reviews by Schultze-Motel (1968–1985), Maria Hopf's *Festschrift* (Körber-Grohne 1979), and such recent reviews as van Zeist (1980) and Zohary & Hopf (1988).

This rich documentation demonstrates the following facts.

(a)   Three cereal crops: emmer wheat *Triticum turgidum* subsp. *dicoccum*, barley *Hordeum vulgare*, and einkorn wheat *Triticum monococcum* (in this order of importance) were the principal founder crops of Neolithic agriculture in this part of the world. Definite signs of their cultivation first appear in Southwest Asia (the Near East) in the 8th and 7th millennia bc.

(b)   The domestication of these cereals went hand in hand with the introduction into cultivation of five companion plants: pea *Pisum sativum*, lentil *Lens culinaris*, chickpea *Cicer arietinum*, bitter vetch *Vicia ervilia*, and flax *Linum usitatissimum*, all of which were very probably domesticated simultaneously with wheat and barley, or taken into cultivation just a short time later.

(c)   The subsequent expansion of Neolithic agriculture to Europe, central Asia, and the Nile Valley was based on this same crop assemblage. The same crops that started food production in the Near Eastern 'nuclear area' also initiated agriculture in these vast territories.

(d)   The evidence for the early domestication of additional crops is much less convincing, although a recent find (Kislev 1985) hints that the broad bean, *Vicia faba*, might also belong to the early Neolithic Near Eastern crop assemblage.

This chapter does not aim to review the archaeological finds. Instead, it evaluates a complementary source of evidence, namely the living plants. More specifically, it focuses on the wild progenitors of the Neolithic crop assemblage in order to help answer the following questions:

(a)   Where and how were these plants domesticated?
(b)   Under which ecological conditions could early cultivation succeed?
(c)   How does the information obtained from the living plants correlate with the evidence retrieved from the archaeological excavations?

## Identification of the wild progenitors

A prerequisite for a sound assessment is the knowledge that the crops and their wild relatives are botanically satisfactorily explored and the wild progenitors reliably identified, preferably with the aid of genetic tests. With the exception of the problematic broad bean (for which the wild progenitor is still undetermined, see Zohary 1977), all members of the Neolithic crop assemblage now satisfy that prerequisite. In recent years their wild relatives were subjected to intensive studies. For most of them, genetic tests have clarified the affinities within each crop complex, and convincingly identified the wild plants from which the cultivars could have evolved. For these founder crops, therefore, the search for ancestry is more-or-less completed. It is highly unlikely that new wild types involved in the origin of these cultivated plants will be discovered in the future. The information assembled on the wild progenitors of the eight founder crops can be summarized as follows:

### Barley and einkorn wheat

In these two crops the identification of the wild progenitors is straight-forward. In each cereal a wild stock occurs which is fully interfertile with the cultivars and shows chromosomal identity with them. The geographical distribution and the ecological ranges of the wild types are also well delineated. In fact, only a few basic additions or corrections have to be made to Harlan and Zohary's (1966) and Zohary's (1969) surveys of these progenitors. The most important ones are: (a) the recent discovery of wild barley, *Hordeum spontaneum*, in the western Himalayan Mountains (Wit-combe 1978) and Tibet (Shao 1981), and (b) the realization that wild einkorn, *Triticum boeoticum*, thrives in primary habitats not only in western and southeastern Turkey but also in central Anatolia. A characteristic feature of

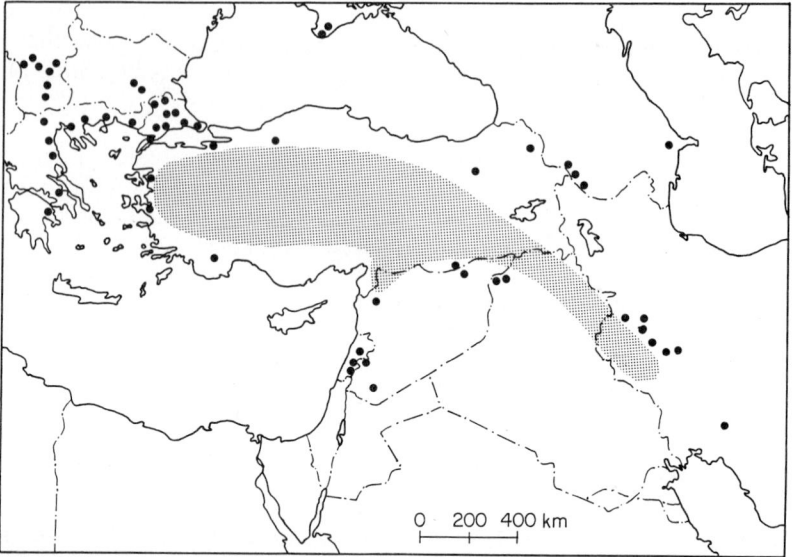

**Figure 22.1** Distribution of wild einkorn wheat, *Triticum boeoticum*. The area in which this wild wheat is massively spread is shaded. Dots outside this distribution centre represent more isolated stands, mostly of weedy forms. (Based on Harlan & Zohary 1966.)

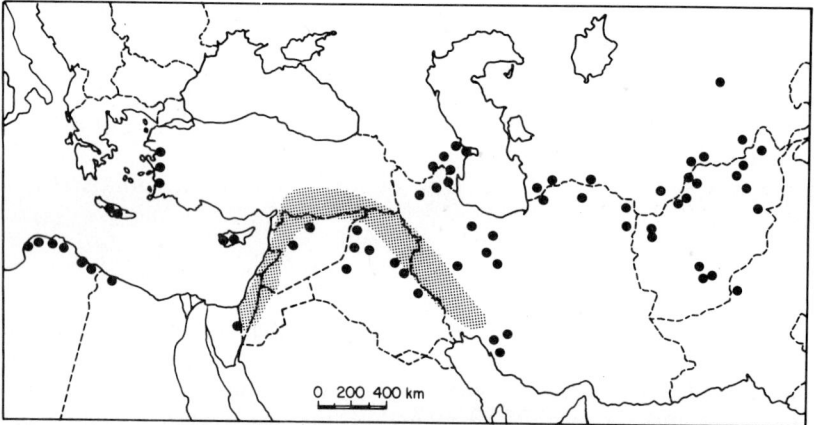

**Figure 22.2** Distribution of wild barley, *Hordeum spontaneum*. The area in which wild barley is massively spread is shaded. Dots outside this distribution centre represent more isolated populations, usually of weedy forms. Towards the east, these populations extend beyond the boundaries of this map into Ladakh and Tibet. (Based on Harlan & Zohary 1966.)

both crops is the build-up of 'wild–weed–cultivated' complexes: in addition to wild forms growing in primary niches, one encounters weedy forms which infest cultivation and colonize the margins of tilled ground, roadsides, and similar secondary habitats. Compared to the genuinely wild plants, which are centred in the Near East (Figs 22.1 & 22.2), the weeds occupy wider territories.

## Emmer wheat

The situation in this cereal is more complex. Here we are faced with two wild 'sibling species' which are morphologically indistinguishable but genetically well isolated from one another. One wild type, *Triticum dicoccoides*, is chromosomally identical and fully interfertile with all the tetraploid cultivated wheats which are today grouped under *T. turgidum* (genome constitution: AABB). It is therefore identified as the wild progenitor of cultivated emmer, *T. turgidum* subsp. *dicoccum*, and also of the more advanced free-threshing *durum*-type derivatives. The second wild type, *T. araraticum* (genome constitution: AAGG), is totally intersterile with *T. turgidum* cultivars, and played no part in their origin. It is linked to *T. timopheevi* (genome constitution: AAGG), a rare cereal crop endemic to the Georgian Soviet Socialist Republic, and very likely a local and recent episode in wheat domestication.

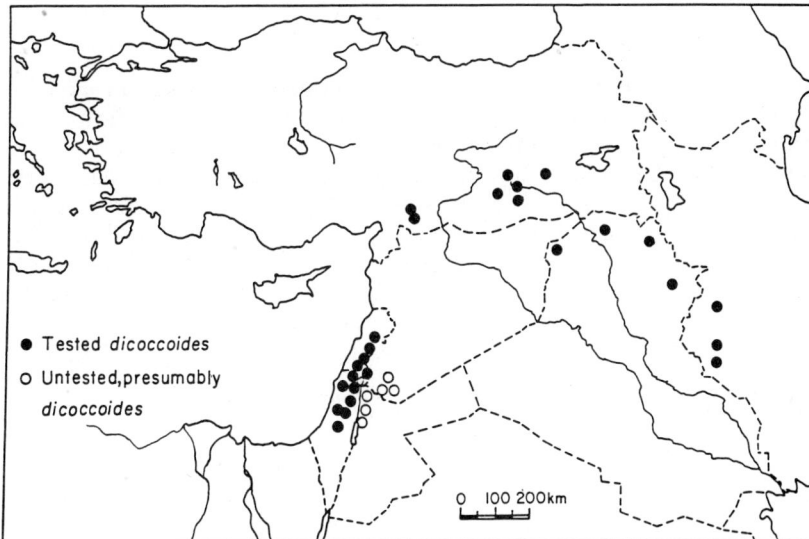

**Figure 22.3** Distribution of wild emmer wheat, *Triticum dicoccoides* (genome constitution AABB): sites of plants tested cytogenetically (compiled from Rao & Smith 1968, Dagan & Zohary 1970, Tanaka & Ishii 1973, and unpublished data of D. Zohary).

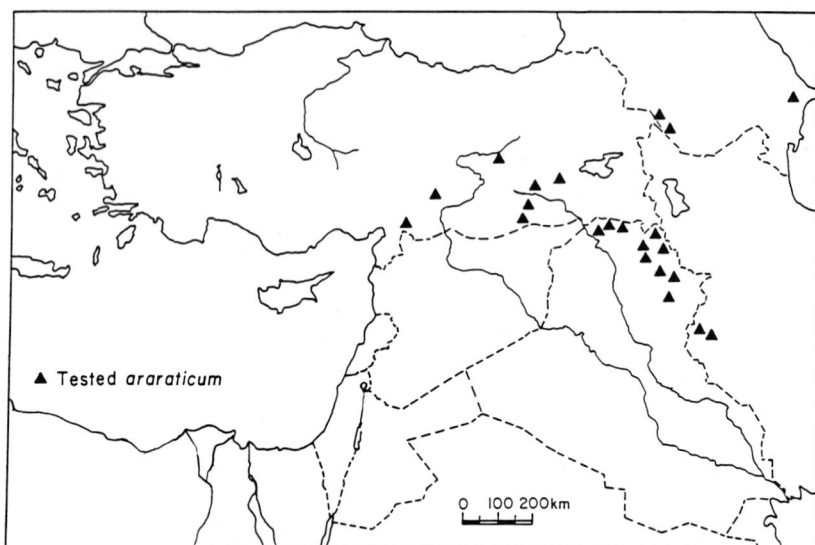

**Figure 22.4**  Distribution of wild Timopheev's wheat, *Triticum araraticum* (genome constitution AAGG): sites of plants tested cytogenetically (compiled from Rao & Smith 1968, Dagan & Zohary 1970, Tanaka & Ishii 1973, and unpublished data of D. Zohary).

It is practically impossible to distinguish between *dicoccoides* and *araraticum* wheats morphologically, either in herbarium collections or during field excursions. For these reasons, taxonomists (e.g. Bor 1968) lumped them together and Harlan and Zohary (1966) had to survey them collectively. Since then, numerous seed samples of tetraploid wild wheats have been collected in the Near East and cytogenetically tested to establish their genomic constitution. The results have already clarified the distribution areas of the two sibling species. These two wild wheats overlap considerably in their distribution, and occasionally they even grow side by side. Yet *dicoccoides* (AABB) is confined to the Near Eastern 'arc' (Fig. 22.3), while *araraticum* (AAGG) has a more northeasterly distribution. It is spread over eastern Turkey, northern Iraq, western Iran, and Soviet Transcaspia (Fig. 22.4).

In summary, the available cytogenetic evidence makes it possible to delimit the present-day distribution area of the wild ancestor of cultivated tetraploid AABB wheats. One can also compare it with the areas of wild einkorn and wild barley. While the latter have only their centre of distribution in the Near East and extend (mainly as weeds) far beyond this region, wild emmer is a strict endemic. It is confined to the Near Eastern arc. As previously stressed (Harlan & Zohary 1966, Zohary 1969), *T. diccoccoides*

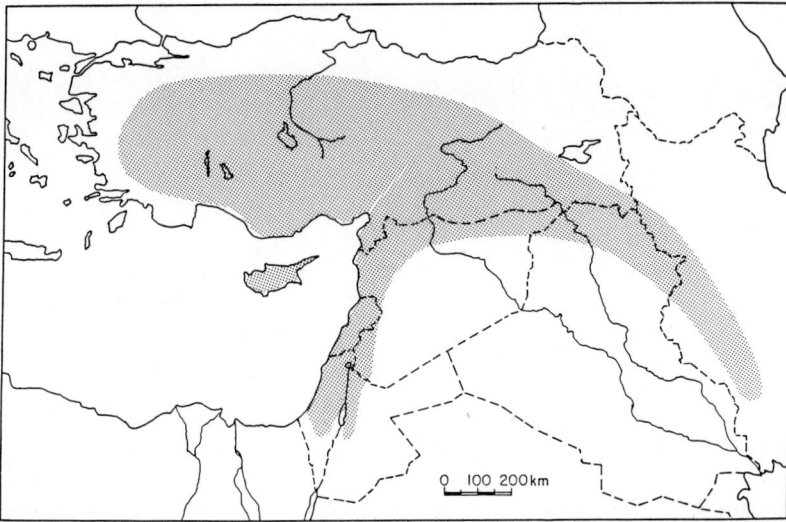

**Figure 22.5**   Distribution of wild *humile* peas (based on Zohary & Hopf 1973).

also differs from the two other progenitors in its habitat preferences. Weedy races did not develop in this wild grass; it grows almost entirely in primary niches.

## Pea

The cultivated pea, *Pisum sativum*, is closely related to a variable aggregate of wild and weedy peas which roughly fall into two morphological – and ecological – groups: (a) a tall '*maquis* type' traditionally named *P. elatius*, and (b) a shorter 'steppe type' traditionally called *P. humile* (= *P. syriacum*). The distribution and ecological preferences of these wild peas were surveyed by Zohary and Hopf (1973). No major additions have been made since then. *Elatius* peas are pan-Mediterranean in their distribution and grow as annual climbers in *maquis* formations. *Humile* peas are restricted to the Near East (Fig. 22.5). They thrive in steppe-like habitats and also invade cultivated fields. Of the two wild types, *P. humile* resembles more closely the cultivated crop. It is also a characteristic annual constituent of the oak-dominated park-forest formation in the Near Eastern arc, i.e. the same zone that also harbours the wild progenitors of emmer what, einkorn wheat, and barley.

Cytogenetic tests (Ben Ze'ev & Zohary 1973) have revealed that both *humile* and *elatius* peas are closely related to the cultivated pea and are fully, or almost fully, interfertile with it. The tests also showed that the wild peas contain two chromosome arrangements. *Elatius* forms tested so far differed from the *sativum* cultivars by a single reciprocal translocation. The same

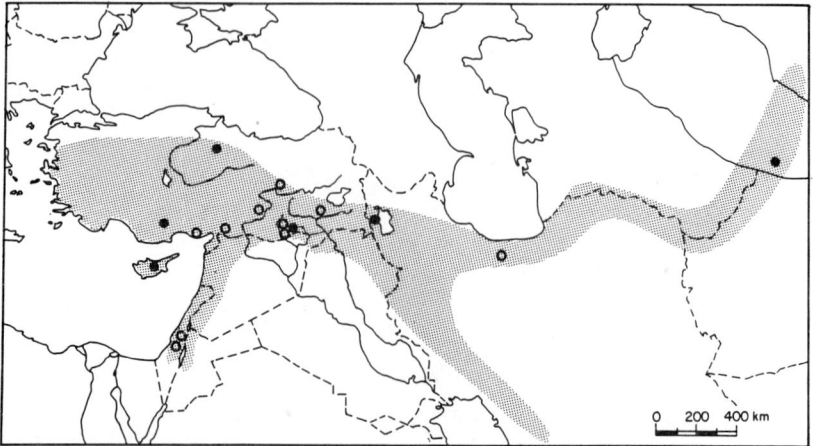

**Figure 22.6**  Distribution area of wild lentil, *Lens orientalis* (shaded). Black dots represent the locations of accessions known to contain the 'standard' chromosome complement, while open circles represent accessions with other chromosome types. (Based on Barulina 1930, Zohary & Hopf 1973, Ladizinsky *et al.* 1984.)

interchange is present in *humile* peas in southern and central Israel. In contrast, wild *humile* peas collected on the Golan Heights and in Turkey were found to contain chromosomes identical to those present in the *sativum* cultivars. The cytogenetic tests therefore indicate that both *elatius* and *humile* peas represent the *general* wild stock from which the cultivated crop developed, while those *humile* forms with chromosomes identical to those of *sativum* cultivars constitute the *direct* source for pea domestication.

## Lentil

The wild stock from which cultivated lentil, *Lens culinaris*, could have been derived is well identified (Zohary & Hopf 1973). The cultivated forms show close affinities with *L. orientalis*, an annual wild lentil distributed over the Near East and reaching into central Asia (Fig. 22.6). Cytogenic tests recently performed in the genus *Lens* (Ladizinsky *et al.* 1984) confirmed the close affinities between *L. culinaris* and *L. orientalis*. They also revealed that while *culinaris* cultivars were uniform as to their chromosome structure, *orientalis* collections were not. The latter showed several structural races which differed from one another by one or two reciprocal transloctions. Significantly, one of the chromosome arrangements found in the chromosomally polymorphic *L. orientalis* turned out to be identical with the 'standard' karyotype of the cultivated pulse. Therefore, this *orientalis* chromosome race should be regarded as the direct source from which cultivated lentil originated. The samples tested so far do not permit an exact delimination of the geographical distribution of the various chromosome races in *L. orientalis*. However, the 'standard' chromosome arrangement is relatively widely distributed. It was detected in Turkey, Cyprus, Iran, and central Asia (Fig. 22.6).

## Chickpea

The wild ancestry of the cultivated chickpea, *Cicer arietinum*, was clarified only 12 years ago (Ladizinsky & Adler 1976a, 1976b). The wild progenitor of this crop turned out to be a new species, *Cicer reticulatum*, discovered in southeastern Turkey. This wild chickpea was found to be interfertile with the cultivated pulse and it also showed full chromosomal homology with it. Other wild *Cicer* species turned out to be reproductively isolated from the crop and had to be excluded from the candidacy for its wild ancestry.

Although *C. reticulatum* was discovered only a few years ago, its distribution and ecological specificities seem to be well established. It is an element of the oak-dominated park–forest vegetation zone of the Near Eastern arc. It is today endemic to the middle segment of the crescent (Fig. 22.7). Future finds may extend the known distribution area of this wild progenitor, but probably not by very much. [See Zohary's Postscript to this chapter, p. 371. Eds.]

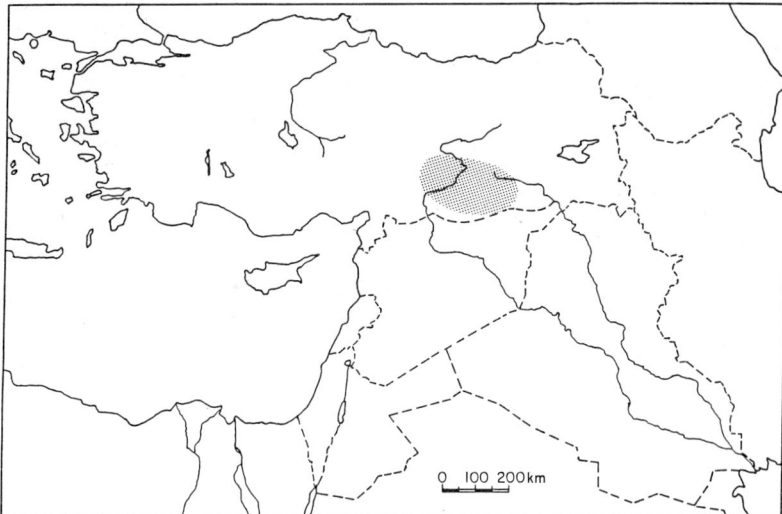

**Figure 22.7** Distribution area of wild chickpea, *Cicer reticulatum* (based on Ladizinsky & Adler 1976b).

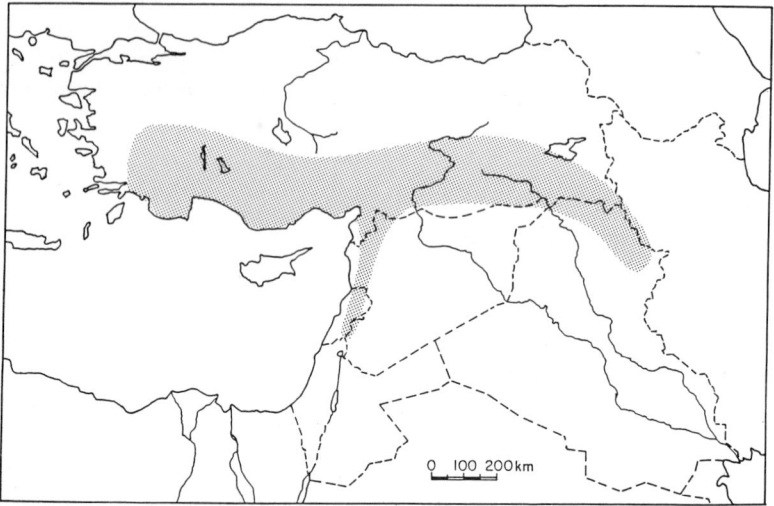

**Figure 22.8**   Distribution area of wild bitter vetch, *Vicia ervilia* (based on Zohary & Hopf 1973, Townsend 1974, Ladizinsky & van Oss 1984).

## Bitter vetch

Cultivated bitter vetch, *Vicia ervilia*, is closely related to an aggregate of wild and weedy forms which closely resemble the crop morphologically (Zohary & Hopf 1973). Weedy forms and feral types are quite common in the Near East. They infest grain cultivation and also occur at the margins of cultivated ground. Truly wild forms – growing in primary habitats – are somewhat smaller than the cultivated and weedy forms and more restricted in their distribution (Fig. 22.8). They are definitely known from southern Anatolia, northern Iraq, and Mt. Hermon (Zohary & Hopf 1973, Townsend 1974, Ladizinsky & van Oss 1984) where they usually grow on gravelly slopes, at 1000–1800 m altitude, sometimes together with wild lentil, *L. orientalis*. Very probably, wild bitter vetch is also native to the Anti-Lebanon mountain range.

## Flax

Wild *Linum bienne* (= *L. augustifolium*) is the recognized wild progenitor of cultivated flax *L. usitatissimum*. These two flaxes show close morphological resemblance. They also intercross readily and are fully interfertile (Gill & Yermanos 1967). Among the wild progenitors of the Neolithic crop plants, wild flax shows the widest distribution. It is spread over the Atlantic coast of Europe, the Mediterranean basin, the Near East, northern Iran, and Caucasia (Fig. 22.9). *Linum bienne* grows mainly in wet places, such as springs,

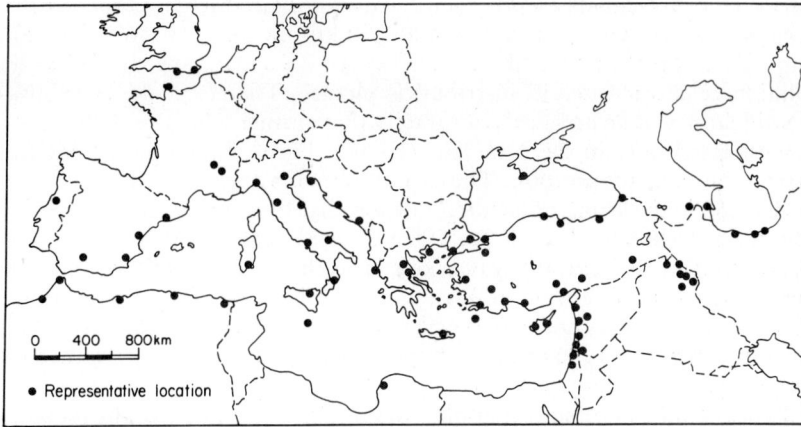

**Figure 22.9** Distribution of wild flax, *Linum bienne* (based on data recorded in floras covering various European and Near Eastern countries, and a survey of the herbarium specimens at the Royal Botanic Gardens, Kew, England).

seepage areas, marshy lands, and moist clay soils. In such habitats wild flax thrives also in the Near Eastern arc.

## Distribution areas and the place of domestication

Palynological data (van Zeist & Bottema 1982) suggest that by 10000–9000 bc the vegetation formations in which the wild progenitors thrive today (open oak forests, forest steppes, and steppes with scattered stands of trees) already occupied the western part of the Near Eastern arc and may possibly have started to establish themselves also in the Zagros Mountains. By 6000 bc the vegetation belts that characterize the Near East had already achieved their present-day gross distribution. Because domestication is a relatively recent development, it can be assumed that the distribution of the wild progenitors (weeds excluded) has not undergone drastic changes since the beginning of agriculture, at least in the western half of the arc. Delineation of the present-day distribution of the progenitor thus marks (more or less) the territory in which the crop could potentially have been domesticated: the narrower the distribution, the more precise the placement.

In the 1950s and 1960s archaeologists were recommended to take account of the distribution of wild progenitors (Helbaek 1959, Harlan & Zohary 1966) as a potent means of predicting where the earliest agricultural sites could be expected to occur. Now that substantial archaeological documentation is available from Europe and Southwest Asia, it is worthwhile to check again how the evidence from the two disciplines fits. Wild emmer, *T. dicoccoides* (genome constitution AABB), is an ideal indicator for such an assessment. Present–day wild emmer grows only in the Near East, where it occupies a narrow belt some 100–200 km wide and 1600 km long (Fig. 22.3). Furthermore, it did not evolve secondary weedy forms that could have complicated its distribution picture. Therefore, the distribution of wild emmer indicates fairly accurately that emmer wheat could have been domesticated only in the Near Eastern arc. The archaeological finds fully corroborate this supposition. The earliest remains of cultivated emmer were discovered in the string of farming villages that first appears in this very belt (for review see van Zeist 1976, 1980; Zohary & Hopf 1988, pp. 35–41). Because cultivated emmer was a key crop in the expansion of Neolithic agriculture to Europe, central Asia, and the Nile Valley, the distribution of *T. dicoccoides* delimits not only the place of origin of this cereal. It also marks the area where the type of agriculture which spread to Europe and central Asia could have originated.

The same line of reasoning applies to two other members of the Neolithic crop assemblage, namely chickpea and bitter vetch. The wild progenitor of the first crop is a strict endemic confined to southeastern Turkey (Fig. 22.7). This pins down the domestication of chickpea to a small territory indeed. Wild forms of bitter vetch are restricted to the Near Eastern arc and the Anatolian plateau (Fig. 22.8). Thus this crop, too, has to have been taken into cultivation in the Near East. For both pulses, the available archaeological evidence (van Zeist 1980, Zohary & Hopf 1988, pp. 101, 104) fully supports these suppositions.

The distribution areas of the wild ancestors of the other five crops are much wider, and were probably of similar breadth also by a short time after the start of the Holocene. They therefore carry much less weight. Yet it is encouraging to find that the information on the present-day distribution of these wild plants fully accords with the archaeological documentation. The wild progenitors of barley, einkorn wheat, pea, lentil, and flax all abound in the same geographical belt in which the earliest archaeological evidence of their cultivation has been retrieved. With the possible exception of wild flax, the Near East is also the centre of their distribution. Here they attain maximum density and occupy the widest ecological range.

Finally, chromosome polymorphism in pea and lentil also helps to delimit the areas of origin of these crops. At present, only preliminary information is available on the exact distribution of the various translocation races in the two wild pulses. But in each, working out the detailed geographical distribution of the 'standard' chromosome type, i.e. the karyotype that also characterizes the cultivated varieties, could indicate more precisely where domestication may have taken place. Yet it is noteworthy that the available tests already show that, in both pulses, wild types with the 'standard' chromosome arrangement grow in the Near East. Thus, this chromosomal evidence is also in full agreement with the available archaeological finds.

## Preadaptation for cultivation

Various projects aimed at the screening of disease resistance in local *Triticum dicoccoides* and *Hordeum spontaneum* populations were carried out in Israel in the past ten years. They involved growing large numbers of plants under field conditions, both in the Mediterranean belt (rain-fed cultivation) and in the drier areas (with supporting irrigation). In addition to the detection of useful genes, these experiments showed that wild emmer and wild barley can easily be taken into cultivation. The large seeds tolerate coverage by variable amounts of soil, and germinate quickly to produce vigorous seedlings. Stands and yields of both wild cereals approach quite closely to those produced by the local land races of wheat and barley grown under the same conditions. This demonstrates that it would have been easy to start wild emmer or wild barley cultivation both in the rain-fed belt or – with the help of irrigation – in the drier and warmer places below or beyond the oak-dominated park-forest belt. In the latter, an initial irrigation (in September–October) and one or two subsequent ones produce remarkable stands.

## Patterns of domestication: solitary versus multiple events

A problem yet to be solved is how the Near Eastern Neolithic founder crops were domesticated. In other words, was each of these plants taken into cultivation many times and in several locations (the multiple events model) or, alternatively, did domestication consist of solitary or very rare events. The cytogenetic information available from several wild progenitors seems to support the latter proposition.

The first indication comes from wild tetraploid wheats. As already noted, two genetically distinct but morphologically inseparable sibling species occupy sympatrically the northern and eastern segments of the Near Eastern arc (compare Fig. 22.3 with Fig. 22.4). Both are rather common plants in these areas, yet only the *dicoccoides* AABB genomes are present in the thousands of hulled and naked tetraploid land races of the Old World. AAGG *araraticum* derivatives are absent. The only exception is local *T. timopheevi* in Georgia which is most likely not an old relic but a more recent, secondary domesticate.

Wild pea and wild lentil provide additional indications. As already stressed, two translocation races occur in wild *Pisum humile* in the Near East while almost all cultivated varieties of pea are chromosomally uniform and conform with only one of the wild chromosome arrangements. The situation in wild lentil, *Lens orientalis*, is even more clear-cut. The wild stock of this legume contains several translocation races (Ladizinsky *et al.* 1984). In contrast, the cultivated lentil is chromosomally uniform and again conforms to only one of the *orientalis* chromosomal races.

All these cytological observations are compatible with a model of solitary domestication events. They are hard to explain on the basis of multiple, repetitive domestications.

Additional support for this conclusion is provided by those mutations that would have been strongly advantaged (selected for) soon after the wild progenitors were brought into cultivation. The best studied are those causing the breakdown of the wild mode of seed dispersal. In most of the Neolithic founder crops (except barley) this change (from brittle ears or dehiscent pods in the wild progenitors to non-brittle ears or non-dehiscent pods in the cultivated derivatives) was brought about by mutation in a single major gene. Furthermore, as far as we know, the same gene locus determines the change in the various cultivars (only in barley are two genes, $bt_1$ and $bt_2$, involved). The evidence for the last statement comes from intervarietal crosses. Breeders have already performed crosses between numerous culti- vars in each crop. Except for barley, none of these has been reported to result in brittle or dehiscent first degeneration ($F_1$) hybrids. Such results (for geneticists they constitute tests for allelism) indicate that within each crop the *same* gene determines the change, at least in all tested cultivars.

Mutations at single loci are compatible both with the model of solitary domestication and with the proposition of multiple events. After all, mutation in any given locus is bound to occur repeatedly, thus setting the stage for either a single domestication event or for repetitive, independent trials. But what is missing in the crops that founded Neolithic agriculture are frequent cases of parallel evolution. In other words, within each of these crops we lack mutations in several independent major genes which (a) each cause more or less the same change, and (b) are each restricted to a limited group of the full spectrum of cultivars. Patterns of parallel evolution are common when similar selection pressures operate in separate populations of the same species. In these Near Eastern crops, the almost total absence of such examples of parallel evolution in key traits, such as the loss of the wild mode of seed dispersal, again favours the proposition of single or very few domestication events in each crop.

Finally, one should note that Pinkas *et al.* (1985) recently reported on allozyme variation in *Lens culinaris* and *L. orientalis*. They interpreted the results they obtained as indicating multiple domestications in lentil. However, it is difficult to accept this interpretation, for the following reasons:

(a)   The *L. orientalis* samples tested frequently exhibited considerable intra-population allozyme polymorphism, this in spite of the fact that populations of this wild lentil are usually small and scattered. There- fore, even if lentil domestication happened in a single geographical location, the initial material taken into cultivation could have been variable.

(b)   Nine polymorphic gene loci were detected in *L. orientalis*; only six in *L. culinaris*. In other words, three out of the nine polymorphic loci found in the wild progenitor are monomorphic in the cultivars. At these three loci, eight alleles were detected in *L. orientalis*, but only three in *L. culinaris*. This is a substantial drop; the more so because, in these analyses, *L. culinaris* was sampled more extensively than *L. orientalis*.

To conclude, in terms of monophyletic vs. polyphyletic origin, the allozyme data obtained by Pinkas *et al.* (1985) can be argued both ways, and they do not prove or disprove either model. In contrast, chromosome polymorphism or parallel evolution patterns seem to be much more critical indicators, and these seem to favour a monophyletic origin for each of the crops concerned.

## Postscript

Dr C. R. Sperling, US Dept. of Agriculture, Beltsville MD, informs me that in 1987 he collected *Cicer reticulatum* west of Hakkâri, in the southeastern corner of Turkey. This find extends (eastward) the known distribution of wild chickpea (Fig. 22.7) by some 200 km.

## Appendix: note on botanical names of crop plants

According to the rule of botanical nomenclature, once the wild progenitor of a cultivated plant is soundly identified it should not be considered as an independent species but ranked as the *wild race* (subspecies) of the crop. The reason for this is that the wild-type and the cultivated derivatives are usually interconnected genetically. As

**Table 22.1**  Southwest Asian crop-plant nomenclature.

| Common name | Modern taxonomic ranking | Traditional botanical name |
|---|---|---|
| Wild emer | *Triticum turgidum* subsp. *dicocccoides* | *Triticum dicoccoides* |
| Wild einkorn | *Triticum monococcum* subsp. *boeoticum* | *Tricium boeoticum* |
| Wild barley | *Hordeum vulgare* subsp. *spontaneum* | *Hordeum spontaneum* |
| Wild lentil | *Lens culinaris* subsp. *orientalis* | *Lens orientalis* |
| Wild pea | *Pisum sativum* subsp. *humile* (= *P. sativum* var. *pumilio*) | *Pisum humile* |
| Wild chickpea | *Cicer arietinum* subsp. *reticulatum* | *Cicer reticulatum* |
| Wild bitter vetch | *Vicia ervilia* – wild type | Never named as an independent species |
| Wild flax | *Linum usitatissimum* subsp. *bienne* | *Linum bienne* |

the progenitors of the eight Near Eastern founder crops are now satisfactorily identified (both by morphological comparisons and by genetic tests), this rule should now be applied. Indeed, crop-plant evolutionists and taxonomists have already placed each wild plant, together with its cultivated derivatives, in a single biological species. Such a collective species is sometimes also referred to as the 'crop complex'. But traditions die hard. Most archaeobotanists and crop-plant evolutionists still refer to the wild progenitors by their traditional binomials. Thus, to avoid confusion, the traditional names are used in this chapter. With an eye to the future, however, the revised names of the wild progenitors are listed in Table 22.1.

# References

Barulina, H. I. 1930. Lentils in the USSR and other countries. *Bulletin of Applied Botany, Genetics and Plant Breeding* (Leningrad) Supplement 40, 1–319.

Ben Ze'ev, N. & D. Zohary 1973. Species relationships in the genus *Pisum* L. *Israel Journal of Botany* **22**, 73–91.

Bor, N. L. 1968. *Triticum*. In *Flora of Iraq*, Vol. 9, C. C. Townsend, E. Guest & A. Al-Rawi (eds), 194–208. Baghdad: Ministry of Agriculture.

Dagan, J. & D. Zohary 1970. Wild tetraploid wheat from West Iran cytogenetically identical with Israeli *T. dicocccoides*. *Wheat Information Service* (Kyoto) **31**, 15–17.

Gill, K. S. & D. M. Yermanos 1967. Cytogenetic studies on the genus *Linum*. I. Hybrids among taxa with 15 as the haploid chromosome number. *Crop Science* **7**, 627–31.

Harlan, J. R. & D. Zohary 1966. Distribution of wild wheats and barley. *Science* **153**, 1074–80.

Helbaek, H. 1959. Domestication of food plants in the Old World. *Science* **130**, 365–72.

Kislev, M. E. 1985. Early Neolithic horsebean from Yiftah'el, Israel. *Science* **228**, 319–20.

Körber-Grohne, U. (ed.) 1979. *Festschrift Maria Hopf*. Bonn: Rheinland-Verlag (= *Archaeo-Physika*, Vol. 8).

Ladizinsky, G. & A. Adler 1976a. The origin of chickpea *Cicer arietinum* L. *Euphytica* **25**, 211–17.

Ladizinsky, G. & A. Adler 1976b. Genetic relationships among the annual species of *Cicer* L. *Theoretical and Applied Genetic* **48**, 196–203.

Ladizinsky, G. & H. van Oss 1984. Genetic relationships between wild and cultivated *Vicia ervilia*. *Botanical Journal of the Linnean Society* **89**, 97–100.

Ladizinsky, G., D. Braun, D. Goshen & F. J. Muehlbauer 1984. The biological species of the genus *Lens* L. *Botanical Gazette* **145**, 253–61.

Pinkas, R., D. Zamir & G. Ladizinsky 1985. Allozyme divergence and evolution in the genus *Lens*. *Plant Systematics and Evolution* **151**, 131–40.

Rao, P. S. & E. L. Smith 1968. Studies with Israeli and Turkish accessions of *Triticum turgidum* L. emend. var. *dicoccoides* Korn. Bowden. *Wheat Information Service* (Kyoto) **26**, 6–7.

Schultze-Motel, J. 1968–85. Literatur über archäologische Kulturpflanzenreste. For 1965–67: *Kulturpflanze* **16**, 215–30 (1968). For 1968: *Jahresschrift für mitteldeutsche Vorgeschichte* **55**, 55–63 (1971). For 1969: *Kulturpflanze* **19**, 265–82 (1972). For 1970–71: *Kulturpflanze* **20**, 191–207 (1972). For 1971–72: *Kulturpflanze* **21**, 61–76 (1973). For 1972–73: *Kulturpflanze* **22**, 61–76 (1974). For 1973–74: *Kulturpflanze* **23**, 189–205 (1975). For 1974–75: *Kulturpflanze* **24**, 159–78 (1976). For 1975–76:

*Kulturpflanze* **25**, 71–88 (1977). For 1976–77: *Kulturpflanze* **26**, 349–62 (1978). For 1977–78: *Kulturpflanze* **27**, 229–45 (1979). For 1978–79: *Kulturpflanze* **28**, 361–78 (1980). For 1979–80: *Kulturpflanze* **29**, 447–63 (1981). For 1980–81: *Kulturpflanze* **30**, 255–72 (1982). For 1981–82: *Kulturpflanze* **31**, 281–97 (1983). For 1982–83: *Kulturpflanze* **32**, 229–43 (1984). For 1983–84: *Kulturpflanze* **33**, 287–305 (1985).

Shao, Q. 1981. The evolution of cultivated barley. *Barley genetics IV*. Proceedings of the 4th Barley Genetics Symposium, Edinburgh, 22–5.

Tanaka, M. & H. Ishii 1973. *Cytogenetic evidence on the speciation of wild tetraploid wheats collected in Iraq, Turkey and Iran*. Proceedings of the 4th Wheat Genetics Symposium, University of Missouri, Columbia, 115–21.

Townsend, C. C. 1974. *Vicia ervilia*. In *Flora of Iraq*, Vol. 3, C. C. Townsend & E. Guest (eds), 526. Baghdad: Ministry of Agriculture.

van Zeist, W. 1976. On macroscopic traces of food plants in southwestern Asia (with some references to pollen data). *Philosophical Transactions of the Royal Society London: Biological Sciences* **275**, 27–41.

van Zeist, W. 1980. Aperçu sur la diffusion des végétaux cultivés dans la région Méditerranéen. In: *Colloque sur la mise en place, l'évolution et la caractérisation de la flore et la végétation circumméditerranéenn*, L. Emberger (ed.), 129–45. Monpellier: Special volume of *Naturalia Monspeliensia*.

van Zeist, W. & S. Bottema 1982. Vegetational history of the eastern Mediterranean and the Near East during the last 20,000 years. In: *Palaeoenvironments and human communities in the eastern Mediterranean regions in later prehistory*, J. L. Bintliff & W. van Zeist (eds), 277–321. British Archaeological Reports, International Series 133.

van Zeist, W. & W. A. Casparie (eds) 1984. *Plants and ancient man: studies in palaeoethnobotany*. Rotterdam: Balkema.

Witcombe, J. R. 1978. Two rowed and six rowed wild barley from the western Himalaya. *Euphytica* **24**, 431–4.

Zohary, D. 1969. The progenitors of wheat and barley in relation to domestication and agricultural dispersal in the Old World. In *The domestication and exploitation of plants and animals*, P. J. Ucko & G. W. Dimbleby (eds), 47–66. London: Duckworth.

Zohary, D. 1977. Comments on the origin of cultivated broad bean, *Vicia faba* L. *Israel Journal of Botany* **26**, 39–40.

Zohary, D. & M. Hopf 1973. Domestication of pulses in the Old World. *Science* **182**, 887–94.

Zohary, D. & M. Hopf 1988. *Domestication of plants in the Old World*. Oxford: Oxford University Press.

# 23 Origin and domestication of the Southwest Asian grain legumes

## GIDEON LADIZINSKY

In the past few years valuable information has been accumulated on the wild progenitors and other wild relatives of the edible and forage legumes of Southwest Asia. This information is essential for the understanding and reconstruction of the process of pulse domestication. In this chapter the botanical and cytogenetic information that is currently available is summarized and the probable patterns of pulse domestication are assessed.

## Food legumes

### Pea

Wild peas can be separated into three main forms: one which has a creamy-brownish flower, which is known as *Pisum fulvum*, and two which have violet-purple flowers, known as *P. elatius* and *P. humile* or *P. syriacum*, which, in taxonomic literature, are commonly referred to as *P. sativum* ssp. *elatius* and *P. sativum* ssp. *humile* respectively. (For further synonyms of pulse binomials, see Butler Ch. 24, this volume). These two species differ from one another mainly in their growth habit and ecological preferences. *P. elatius* grows mainly in the *maquis* and exhibits a marked climbing ability, while *P. humile* grows in herbaceous vegetation and climbs less freely. *P. fulvum* is common in the Mediterranean region of the Levant and to a lesser extent in southern Turkey (Fig. 23.1). *P. humile* is common in Turkey, particularly in the southeastern parts of the country (Fig. 23.1) where it grows with other wild legumes. It also forms small populations in the Levant, but there it is usually confined to man-made habitats. *P. elatius* has a sporadic distribution in the Mediterranean regions of the Levant and Turkey and, although rare, has also been reported in southern Europe (Fig. 23.1).

Hybrids between the cultivated peas *P. sativum* and either *P. elatius* or *P. humile* are easy to make, are vegetatively normal, and are usually fertile. On the other hand, the cultivated peas can be hybridized with *P. fulvum* only when the latter is the male parent. That *P. fulvum* is more distantly related to the cultivated peas is also suggested by the complete absence of *P. sativum*

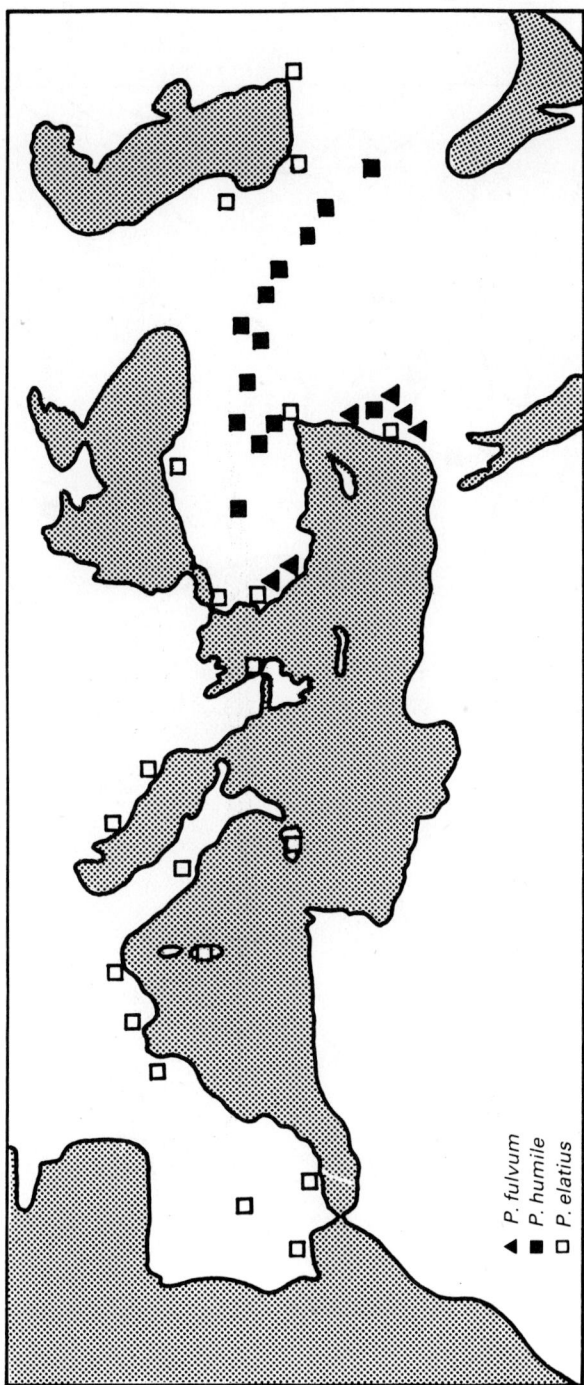

**Figure 23.1** Distribution of collections of wild peas.

▲ *P. fulvum*
■ *P. humile*
□ *P. elatius*

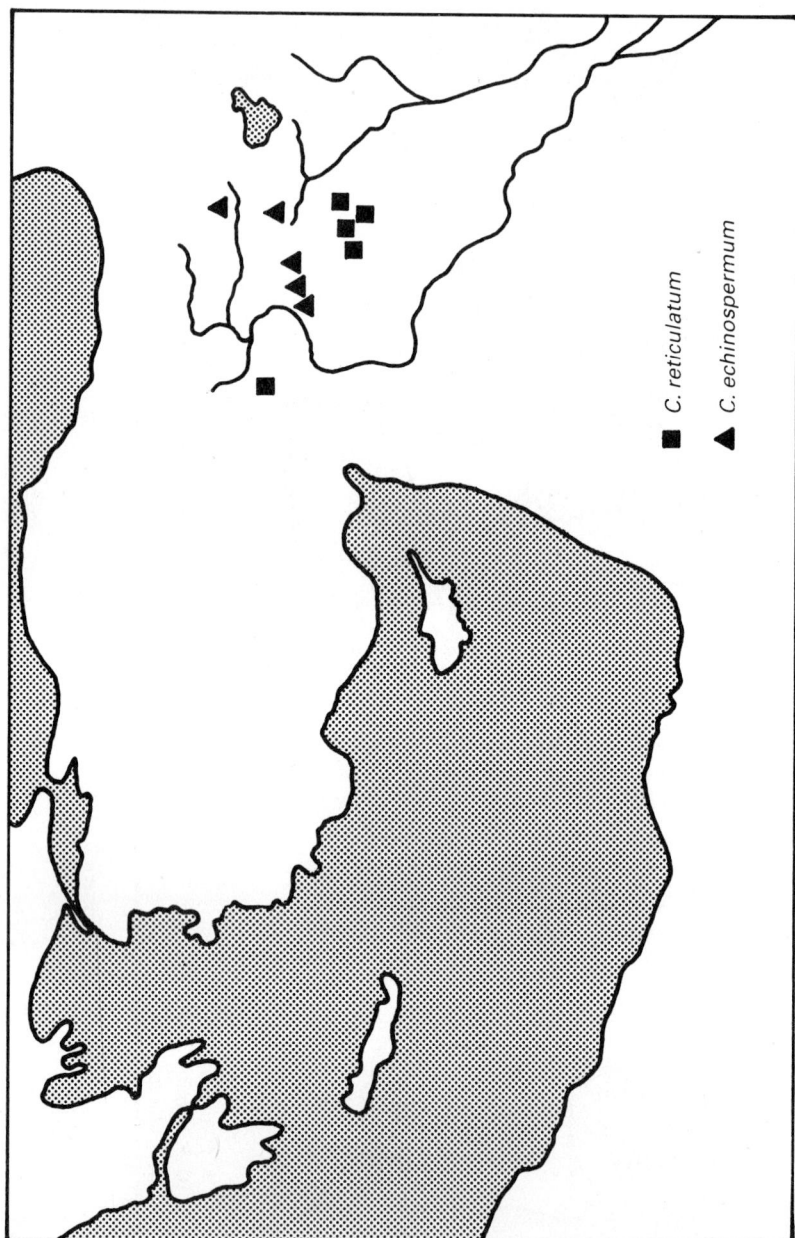

**Figure 23.2** Distribution of collections of those wild chickpeas that are cross-compatible with the cultivated species.

■ *C. reticulatum*

▲ *C. echinospermum*

types with creamy-brownish flowers. Thus, morphological and cytogenetical evidence indicates that the *P. elatius–P. humile* complex is the wild stock
from which the cultivated peas emerged. This ancestry is also suggested by
similarities in chromosome architecture between cultivated peas and populations of *P. elatius* and *P. humile* originating in Turkey (Ben Ze'ev & Zohary
1973).

## Chickpea

The genus *Cicer* contains more than 40 species, only nine of which are
annuals, the remainder being perennials. Only two of the annual wild
chickpeas are cross-compatible with the cultivated species, *C. arietinum*.
These two wild species are *C. reticulatum* and *C. echinospermum*. Of these, *C.
reticulatum* is easily hybridized with the cultivated chickpea and the $F_1$ and
segregating generations are fully fertile. These and other reasons have led us
to regard it as the wild progenitor (Ladizinsky & Adler 1976). The wild
species *C. echinospermum* is also cross-compatible with *C. arietinum*, but the
$F_1$ hybrids are almost totally sterile.

Both *C. reticulatum*, of which five populations are presently known, and
*C. echinospermum*, are restricted to southeastern Turkey (Fig. 23.2). *C.
reticulatum* grows on calcareous bedrock together with other wild legumes in
the Mardin area, and near Adiyaman it forms mixed stands with another
wild chickpea *C. pinnatifidum*. By contrast, *C. echinospermum* is restricted to
basaltic soils and occasionally forms mixed populations with another wild
species, *C. bijugum*. Both are quite common as weeds in legume and wheat
fields in the Siverek area of Urfa Province.

## Lentils

The genus *Lens* contains five taxonomic species: *L. nigricans*, *L. ervoides*, *L.
odemensis*, *L. orientalis*, and the cultivated *L. culinaris*. *Lens nigricans* is widely
distributed in the Mediterranean zone of southern Europe (Fig. 23.3); *L.
ervoides* occurs from Algeria to Turkey (Fig. 23.3); *L. odemensis* has so far
been collected from Israel and western Turkey and from Khios in the Aegean
(Fig. 23.4); and *L. orientalis* is found in Asia from Turkey to Uzbekistan
(Fig. 23.4). All the wild species of lentil are small plants. They usually form
tiny populations with a small number of individuals which are restricted to
poor stony habitats, although populations can be larger at higher altitudes.

The cultivated lentils, *L. culinaris*, are cross-compatible only with *L.
orientalis* and *L. odemensis*; upon hybridization with *L. nigricans* or *L. ervoides*
the embryos die about two weeks after fertilization (Ladizinsky *et al.* 1984).
Hybrids between *L. culinaris* and *L. odemensis* are vegetatively normal but
only partially fertile because of four chromosomal rearrangement differences
between the two species. Furthermore, *L. odemensis* has semi-hastate stipules
in contrast to the lanceolate stipules of *L. culinaris* and *L. orientalis*. These
differences leave *L. orientalis* as the wild progenitor of the cultivated lentils.

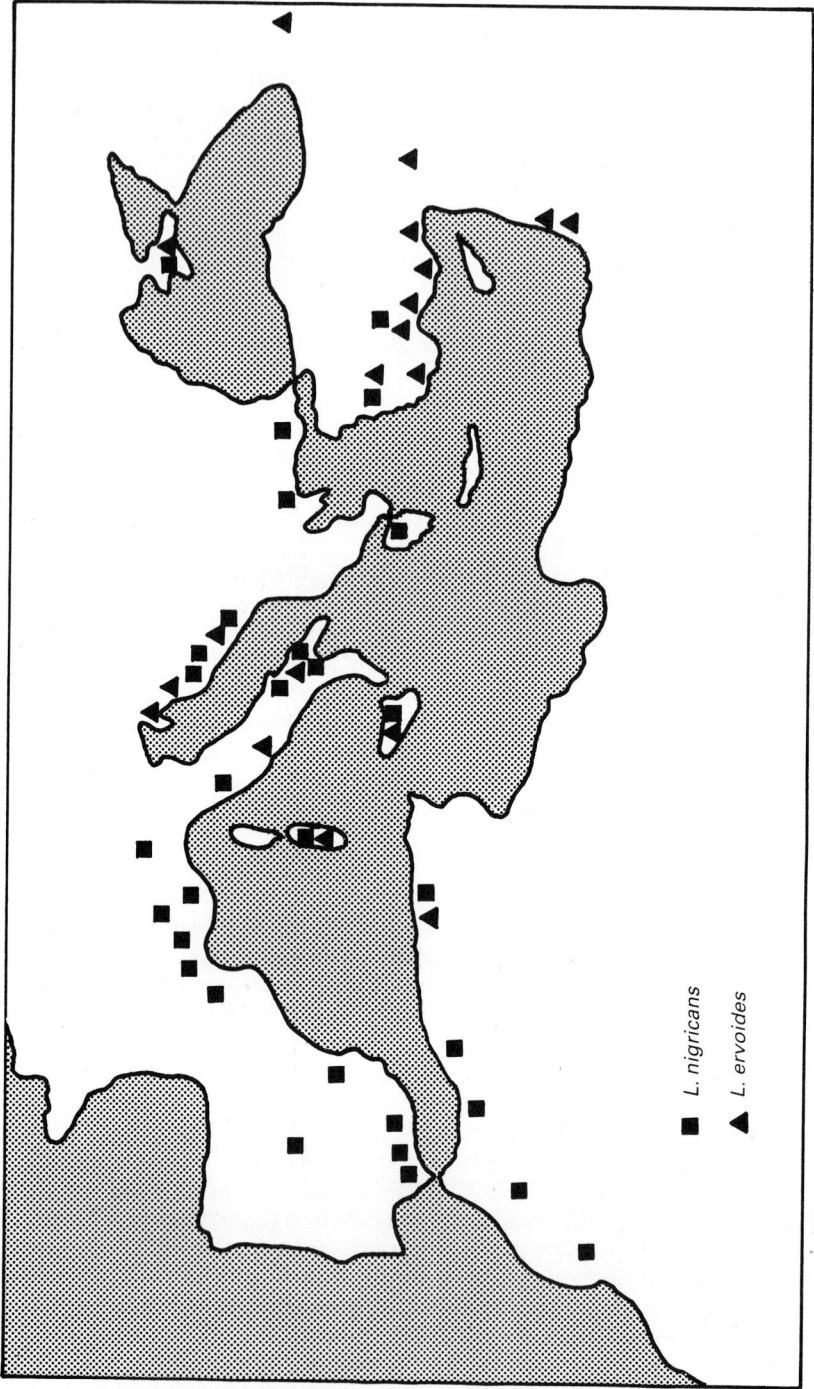

**Figure 23.3** Distribution of collections of wild lentil species that are not cross-incompatible with the cultivated lentil.

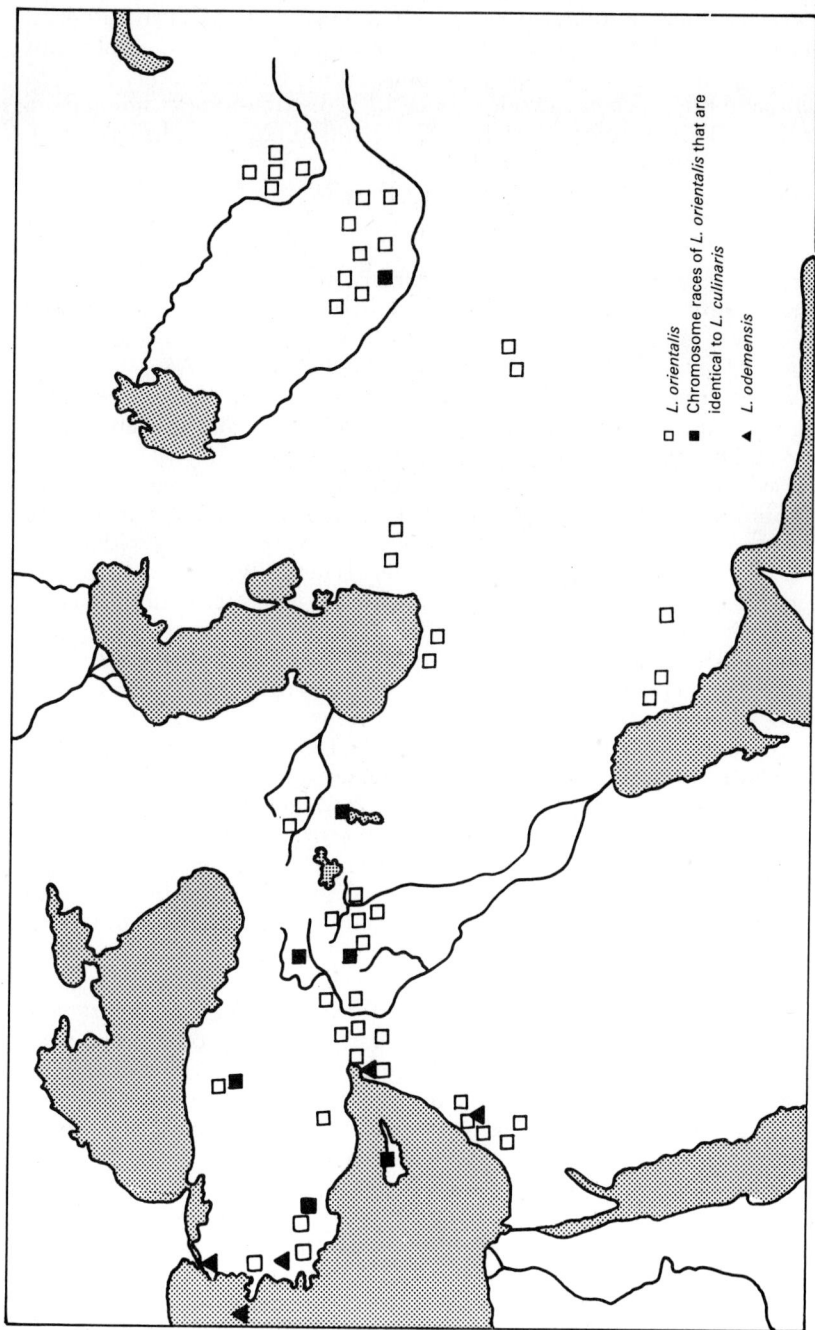

**Figure 23.4** Distribution of collections of wild lentils that are cross-compatible with the cultivated lentil.

However, in contrast to *L. culinaris* which is cytogenetically fairly uniform, *L. orientalis* exhibits considerable chromosomal variation. Only one cytogenetic stock of *L. orientalis* produces fully fertile hybrids with *L. culinaris*, and this stock has a wide geographical distribution extending from Cyprus and Turkey across Iran to Uzbekistan (Fig. 23.4) (Ladizinsky *et al.* 1984).

## Broad bean

It is not yet clear whether the broad or faba bean, *Vicia faba*, was domesticated in Southwest Asia. Most of the positively identified broad-bean seed remains from archaeological excavations are from southern and central Europe and date to the late Neolithic and the Bronze Age. Recently, however, faba-bean seeds dating from the 7th millennium bc were identified in large quantities from Yiftah'el in Israel (Kislev 1985) and as a single seed from Abu Hureyra in Syria (Hillman 1975).

The wild progenitor of the broad bean has not yet been identified. Taxonomically *V. faba*, together with seven wild species (most of them of the *V. narbonensis* group), belongs to the section *Faba*. But within this section, *V. faba* itself is morphologically, cytogenetically, and biochemically unique. All attempts to hybridize *V. faba* with any wild species of the section *Faba*, or with any other species of the genus *Vicia*, have been unsuccessful (Schafer 1973, Ladizinsky 1975). Thus the strong recommendation by Zohary & Hopf (1973) that the *V. narbonensis* group of species gave rise to the broad bean is unrealistic. Furthermore, the supposition by Zohary (1977) that this group is potentially karyotypically variable is similarly unfounded. All the chromosome counts made so far in material collected in Turkey have revealed a stable karyotype with $2n = 14$. At present, therefore, very little can be said on the origin, evolution, and domestication of this pulse.

For some crop plants, extinction has been claimed as the reason for unavailability of the wild ancestor. Recent evidence shows that the wild progenitors of the other cultivated legumes of Southwest Asia still exist, although they are confined to specific geographical areas or habitats. This seems likely to apply also to the broad bean. Some ideas regarding the putative ancestor of the broad bean may be obtained from the mating system of cultivated *V. faba* which is mainly allogamous, with some broad-bean lines even being self-incompatible. Assuming that the wild broad bean behaves (or behaved) the same way, one would expect it to have grown in relatively large populations like other annual cross-pollinated species. If the wild broad bean is native to, and still survives in, Southwest Asia it is difficult to understand how any such large populations have escaped the notice of the many experienced botanists who have traversed the region during the past century. It can, therefore, be assumed that the wild ancestor of the broad bean is either not indigenous to Southwest Asia, or that it grows solitarily as a self-pollinated species and has consequently been overlooked (Ladizinsky 1975).

## 'Forage' legumes

The common vetch, *Vicia sativa*, and the bitter vetch, *V. ervilia*, are today the two main forage crops of Southwest Asia and the Mediterranean basin. In historical times, they were used as human food only in cases of extreme famine. Both vetches have accompanied the better-known food legumes since the Neolithic, but whether they were grown as food grains or primarily for fodder is not clear.

The chromosome numbers of the cultivated common vetch are $2n = 10$ and $2n = 12$. These same numbers are also commonly found in the wild forms of *V. sativa*, together with types with the chromosome number $2n = 14$. Furthermore, karyotypic variation was recorded in each of the $2n$ types (Ladizinsky 1968, Hollings & Stace 1974). The available information on the ecological preferences of wild *V. sativa* indicates that the $2n = 10$ types prefer man-made habitats. The $2n = 12$ types grow mainly in primary habitats among other wild legumes in the Mediterranean vegetation zone, whereas types with $2n = 14$ are confined to stony and dry habitats, usually in steppe vegetation. *Vicia sativa* can therefore be considered an aggregate of wild, weedy, and cultivated forms. The wild forms of this aggregate have very wide geographical distribution in the Mediterranean climatic zone from the Iberian peninsula to central Asia. Hybrids between types with different chromosome numbers or karyotype are easily obtained and they are partially fertile (Ladizinsky & Tamkin 1978, Ladizinsky 1981).

In contrast to *V. sativa*, bitter vetch, *V. ervilia*, is highly uniform morphologically and cytologically. True wild *V. ervilia*, which is common in Turkey, particularly in the southeastern part of the country, has recently also been found on Mount Hermon in the Levant (Fig. 23.5). The wild form of *V. ervilia* grows together with other legumes such as wild pea, lentils, fenugreek, and *Lathyrus* sp. Hybrids between wild and cultivated bitter vetch are easily obtained and are fully fertile (Ladizinsky & van Oss 1984).

## The process of pulse domestication

Morphological, physiological, and genetical comparisons of legumes dom-esticated in Southwest Asia with their wild progenitors can provide sig-nificant clues to the process of domestication. Two main changes were apparently involved in the critical stages of pulse domestication and culti-vation. These changes involved the reduction of seed dormancy and the loss of pod dehiscence. The significance of these traits can be assessed in terms of their genetic control, and recent information of this kind in lentils has allowed a new model for pulse domestication to be proposed.

### Reduction of seed dormancy

Fresh seeds of most *L. culinaris* lines germinate instantly when adequate temperature and moisture conditions are provided. By contrast, fresh seeds

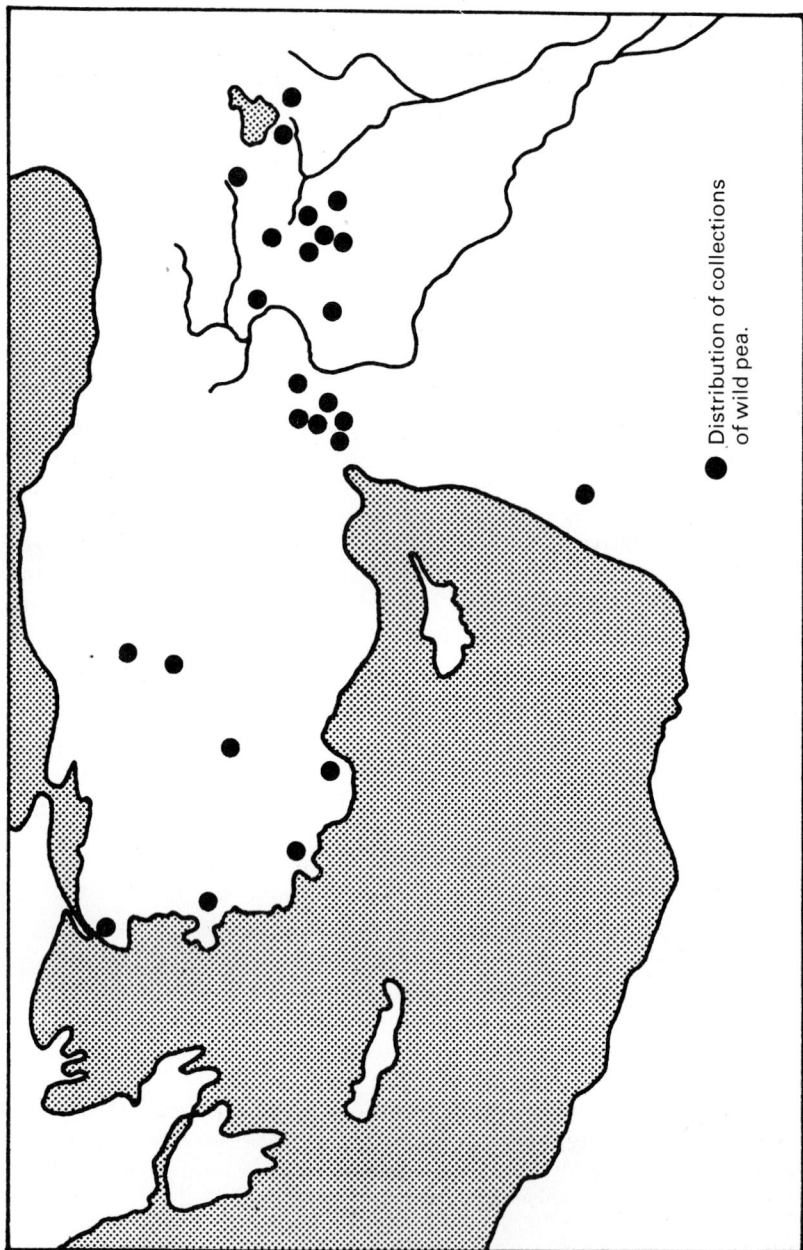

**Figure 23.5**  Distribution of collections of genuinely wild bitter vetch *Vicia ervilia*.

● Distribution of collections of wild pea.

of its wild ancestor *L. orientalis*, like those of other wild *Lens* species, do not germinate – due to the hardness of the seed coat. This dormancy remains effective even at the normal time of germination, both in the following and in the second season when about 10 per cent and 7 per cent of the dormant seeds germinate respectively. The difference in the germination pattern of the cultivated and wild lentils is governed by a single gene, and the cultivated type is dominant (Ladizinsky 1985).

Seed dormancy apparently offers strong selective advantage in wild lentils. First, it regulates germination time, thus avoiding extinction in the event of effective rains at the beginning of the winter being followed by a long period of drought. Secondly, it regulates population density. As already mentioned, *L. orientalis* grows in poor and stony habitats, and if all the seeds produced in one year were to germinate in the following year the population would become overcrowded and most of the plants would fail to reach maturity.

Plants of *L. orientalis* grow and produce flowers for as long as moisture is available in the soil. Occasionally, flowers and mature, or even dehiscent, pods can be found on the same plant. However, under natural conditions, each plant produces an average of about ten seeds per plant (Ladizinsky 1987). It is clear, therefore, that the collection of *L. orientalis* seeds in pre-agricultural times must have been a difficult and frustrating task. One hundred *L. orientalis* seeds weigh about 1 g; thus about 10 000 plants have to be collected to obtain 1 kg of clean seeds. The low seed set per plant and the open nature of wild stands indicate, therefore, that in pre-agricultural times lentils, and other pulses as well, are unlikely to have constituted a major portion of human diet. It can, therefore, be suggested that collection of wild lentils was not primarily for their seeds but for some other purpose, such as fodder. This may support Bohrer's (1972) contention that plant gathering by man in Southwest Asia in pre-agricultural times was undertaken mainly to provide captive animals with fodder.

Seed dormancy also poses problems for any attempt at increasing seed yields by means of cultivation. When 10 per cent of the sown seeds germinate, and each plant produces only ten seeds, the expected yield would be no greater than the amount of the sown seeds. A yield ratio of 1:1 would obviously have provided no incentive for further sowing (Ladizinsky 1987).

*Lens orientalis* would be more suitable for cultivation if it lost its seed dormancy either fully or partially before any attempts were made to sow it as a crop. The problem, however, is to explain how a type lacking seed dormancy could have become established in natural populations where it is negatively selected. In fact, gathering of wild lentils by man in pre-agricultural times could, indeed, have established genotypes lacking seed dormancy in the wild populations themselves, well before any attempt was made to cultivate them. Because of the sequential ripening of the legume pods on any one plant, even the heaviest gathering of wild seeds by foragers – most probably by uprooting the whole plant – is likely to have missed a few seeds of the lowest, earliest maturing pods which would have dehisced and ejected their seeds before or during the harvest. Such heavy annual gathering would have affected the wild population in two ways:

(a)    it would have selected strongly for types with quick germination (because there were so few seeds left to replace the parent plants);
(b)    it would have prevented any overcrowding that would otherwise have occurred with the loss of dormancy.

Given such a situation, it is possible to estimate the rate of such changes. Theoretically, when (a) the mutation rate of the seed dormancy gene is $10^{-4}$, (b) all the *L. orientalis* plants in a given population are collected annually by man, and (c) each plant sheds two seeds of the early maturing pods, then this would have allowed the type lacking seed dormancy to dominate the wild population after seven years of massive gathering (Ladizinsky 1987). Thus, when people eventually started sowing some of the wild seeds which they had collected, the seeds from populations with high proportions of dormancy-free type would form denser stands, produce higher yields, and thus provide the seed stock for future sowings.

It has been suggested that the harvesting of wild cereals in pre-agricultural times had a negligible effect on the genetic structure of the wild populations (Harlan *et al.* 1973). In pulses, however, intensive gathering of seed from wild populations would apparently have caused a genetic shift which would have allowed the type lacking seed dormancy (a prerequisite for cultivation) to become established. This implies that pulse domestication started before cultivation.

### Change of seed dispersal under domestication

Change of seed-dispersal mechanisms was a major step in the evolution of seed crops, although it was apparently of greater significance in cereals than in pulses. Wild legumes are equipped with various mechanisms for seed dispersal which ensure reseeding. Mature dry pods of wild peas and lentils dehisce, with each of the pod's valves twisting in a way that shoots the seeds to distances of several metres. In wild chickpeas, by contrast, the mature pods remain on the plant for a relatively long time; they then fall and burst on the ground in a similar way to that of peas and lentils. By contrast, mature pods of cultivated pea, chickpea, and lentil usually remain intact. In the lentil pod, indehiscence is governed by a single gene (Ladizinsky 1979a) and this is apparently also the case in the pea. In chickpea, however, indehiscence is controlled by several genes (Ladizinsky 1979b).

The potential effect of the loss of the seed-dispersal mechanism under domestication is well exemplified in lentil. In Southwest Asia and elsewhere lentils are usually grown in small plots and harvested by uprooting plants and gathering them in small heaps while the pods are still yellowish and not quite dry. The plants are left to dry for several days before they are gathered into bigger heaps, and, in some cases, threshed on the spot. This practice ensures that seed loss is minimal and that selection for pods of indehiscent type does not occur. However, when lentil is grown several kilometres from the farmer's dwelling, the dry plants are loaded onto donkeys and mules and brought to a threshing ground near the village. Considerable seed loss can occur at this stage, and pods of indehiscent type might, therefore, be favourably selected.

Theoretically, when the mutation rate of the pod-indehiscent gene is $10^{-4}$ and seed loss is 50 per cent, the pod-indehiscent allele would dominate the population of the cultivated lentil after 18 years (Ladizinsky 1987). Variation in rates of yearly loss might speed up or slow down the establishment of pod indehiscence. However, when seed loss is reduced to 10 per cent, there is only a small chance that this allele will be established at all. Pod indehiscence is common in modern lentil varieties, but various degrees of pod shattering are typical of land races and endemic cultivated varieties, and this can be taken as additional evidence that pod indehiscence was not an essential factor in lentil domestication.

## Domestication of the vetches

The domestication of the common and bitter vetches, which are today forage legumes, was apparently similar to that of the food legumes. Seed dormancy is typical of the wild forms of these vetches and absent in their cultivated counterparts. However, pod indehiscence would probably have been even less critical in the vetches than in food legumes.

The method by which these forage legumes are harvested in Southwest Asia is identical to that of the major food legumes. In many areas, however, only a small portion of the yield is threshed to provide the seed stock for the following year, suggesting that seed yield in forage legumes is (and in some cases probably was) of secondary importance – for as long as they were used only as green fodder. In historical times, the seeds of the two vetches have been eaten by humans only in times of famine. This could explain why such seed characteristics as size, shape, and colour are much less variable in the vetches than in the food legumes.

Seeds of *V. ervilia* can easily be recognized in charred plant remains recovered archaeologically because of their angular shape. At several prehistoric sites *V. ervilia* seeds have proved to be more common than the seeds of the major food legumes (van Zeist 1972, Zohary & Hopf 1973). This might perhaps be taken as an indication that, at such sites, *V. ervilia* was used primarily as fodder. However, at other sites, the converse pattern has been observed.

## Geographical pattern of pulse domestication

It is evident that only limited quantities of seed can be collected from wild populations of lentil, pea, and chickpea. This, together with the problem of seed dormancy, makes it unlikely that pulse cultivation started outside the distributional range of their wild progenitors.

The wild progenitor of chickpea, *C. reticulatum*, is today restricted geographically to a small area in southeastern Turkey. Assuming an absence of major changes in the distribution of Southwest Asian vegetation since *c.* 8000 bc, chickpea domestication may have occurred in this area and the crop spread later from it. However, this is difficult to demonstrate at the moment because chickpea seeds are not commonly found in prehistoric sites. The earliest seeds of *C. arietinum* type so far recovered come from Abu Hureyra in Syria (Hillman 1975) and PPNA levels at Jericho (Hopf 1983), both of which are well outside the present distributional range of *C. reticulatum*.

Pea and bitter vetch may have had more diffuse origins because, today at least, their wild progenitors are much more widely distributed than chickpea. The wide distribution of the wild forms of the common vetch and of the standard chromosome race of *L. orientalis* suggest that the common vetch and lentil could theoretically have been domesticated independently in several different areas (but, for a contrary view, see Zohary Ch. 22, this volume). The probable diffuse origin of lentil is affirmed by two additional pieces of evidence. It was explained above that the cultivated lentils were derived from just one of the range of cytogenetic stocks of *L. orientalis*, and that this particular race has recently been identified from Cyprus and Turkey to Iran and Uzbekistan. The genetic diversity in cultivated and wild lentils was recently assessed by isozyme electrophoresis (Pinkas 1985, Pinkas *et al.* 1985). Of the 15 loci studied in the cultivated lentil, six were polymorphic. These six loci (together with a further three loci) were also polymorphic in *L. orientalis*, this despite the fact that intra-population diversity in *L. orientalis* was usually rather low. Also no single population of *L. orientalis* contained all the electrophoretic variants that have been detected in the cultivated lentil. Parallel variation among wild and cultivated populations in such traits that have no (or very little) selective advantage may suggest that diversity in the cultivated lentil has occurred as a result of mutation, gene flow from wild populations, or polyphyletic origin of the cultivated species. Diversity due to mutation is unlikely because it is restricted to only six loci in the cultivated lentil. Gene flow is also an inadequate explanation because lentils are a highly self-pollinated species, and wild and cultivated populations very rarely occur side by side. The diversity in enzymic genes in the cultivated lentils is thus best explained by a hypothesis of polyphyletic origin.

This view is also supported by the pattern of diversity in the wild progenitor *L. orientalis* (Pinkas 1985, Pinkas *et al.* 1985). One of the alleles of the gene *GOT*-2 in the cultivated lentil, for example, was found in only a single *L. orientalis* population in southeastern Turkey. This population also possessed the standard chromosome race. However, another population of this same chromosome race from central northern Turkey shares with the cultivated lentil an allele of the gene *LAP*-1 which is absent in all other populations of the same chromosome race and is rare in other races of *L. orientalis*. A polyphyletic origin is therefore clearly indicated.

# Broad-spectrum domestication of legumes

Seed remains in prehistoric sites indicate that humans utilized legumes at least as early as 11 000 years ago (Hillman *et al.*, Ch. 14, this volume). The size and shape of charred seeds from archaeological sites show that these characteristics have changed very little over several millennia. In pea, chickpea, and lentil, for example, it is almost impossible to distinguish between the seeds of cultivated forms, the seeds of their wild progenitors, and the seeds of the other related species. As a result, criteria such as size and shape often fail to provide a reliable basis for distinguishing wild and cultivated forms, and we are still uncertain whether humans experimented with a broad spectrum of wild species before finally selecting a few of the most successful ones, or whether human selection focused from the outset on just a narrow part of the wild range. If the former were the case, it is difficult to understand why *P. fulvum*, for example, was neglected because this wild pea has tasty pods and seeds, and, in the Levant at least, it is much more common that either *P. elatius* or *P. humile*.

Lentils, on the other hand, may provide an example of a genus in which more than one wild species gave rise to domestic derivatives. One of the wild lentils, *L. nigricans*, grows in two different ecological niches. The first comprises primary habitats in Turkey, along the Adriatic coast of Yugoslavia, in southern Italy, and in southern Spain, where wild lentils form relatively large populations. The second ecological niche consists of man-made habitats such as abandoned terraces and plantations, and archaeological ruins, in central Spain, southern France, Italy, and Greece, where the plant occurs as a weed, for example in terraced vineyards in the Italian and French Alps. In all these habitats *L. nigricans* populations are very small and confined to the disturbed areas. Interestingly, the seeds characteristic of these small populations are significantly larger than those found in the primary habitats (Ladizinsky *et al.* 1983).

It is clear that *L. nigricans* in man-made habitats cannot be considered a weedy form. Like other wild lentils, it lacks the aggressiveness of weedy forms and is always found in small populations. Perhaps a more likely explanation for the occurrence of *L. nigricans* in man-made habitats around the Mediterranean is that it originated from plants which escaped from cultivation and re-acquired seed dormancy and pod dehiscence. But such plants could not have originated from the present cultivated lentil because the two species are morphologically distinct and even cross-incompatible. However, they could have derived from cultivated *L. nigricans* domesticated in southern Europe independently of the domestication of *L. culinaris* farther east. At present, no cultivated *L. nigricans* has been recorded: the lentil which is today cultivated in southern Europe is a large-seeded type of *L. culinaris* which was first recorded in the 4th century AD (Renfrew 1973). The spread of this type into Europe would therefore appear to have been relatively recent, but, during this short time, it has almost entirely replaced the small-seeded lentils. It has been suggested that cultivated *L. nigricans* might still survive in southern Europe at high altitudes (Ladzinsky *et al.* 1983), and, interestingly enough, small populations of wild *L. nigricans* were found near Tende in the French Alps. In that village, brown small-seeded lentils were commonly grown together with barley on narrow terraces until World War II, but terrace cultivation has been abandoned for the past 40 years and the cultivated lentils of that region no longer exist.

The possibility that *L. nigricans* was once domesticated in southern Europe should be taken into account in any attempt to reconstruct the diffusion of lentils as a crop. One should not overlook the possibility that the small-seeded lentils unearthed in excavations of archaeological sites in central Europe are actually *L. nigricans* rather than *L. culinaris* introduced from Southwest Asia. The recent identification of lentil seeds from a cave site in southern France dated to 10 000 bp (Vaquer *et al.* 1986) clearly lends credence to this hypothesis (assuming the seeds from these heavily disturbed deposits were not intrusive from later, agrarian occupation levels). At this particular site, however, the seeds were presumably gathered from wild plants as part of a hunter–gatherer economy.

# References

Ben Ze'ev, N. & D. Zohary 1973. Species relationships in the genus *Pisum* L. *Israel Journal of Botany* **22**, 73–91.

Bohrer, V. L. 1972. On the relation of harvest methods to early agriculture in the Near East. *Economic Botany* **26**, 145–55.

Butler, A. 1989. Cryptic anatomical characters as evidence of early cultivation in the grain legumes (pulses). In *Foraging and farming: the evolution of plant exploitation*, D. R. Harris & G. C. Hillman (eds), ch. 24. London: Unwin Hyman.

Harlan, J. R., J. M. J. deWet & E. G. Price 1973. Comparative evolution of cereals. *Evolution* **27**, 311–225.

Hillman, G. C. 1975. The plant remains from Tell Abu Hureyra: a preliminary report. In The excavation of Tell Abu Hureyra in Syria: a preliminary report, A. M. T. Moore, *Proceedings of the Prehistoric Society* **41**, 70–3.

Hillman, G. C., S. M. Colledge & D. R. Harris 1989. Plant-food economy during the Epipalaeolithic period at Tell Abu Hureyra, Syria: dietary diversity, seasonality, and modes of exploitation. In *Foraging and farming: the evolution of plant exploitation*, D. R. Harris & G. C. Hillman (eds), ch. 14. London: Unwin Hyman.

Hollings, E. & C. A. Stace 1974. Karyotype variation and evolution in the *Vicia sativa* aggregate. *New Phytologist* **73**, 195–208.

Hopf, M. 1983. Jericho plant remains. In *Excavations at Jericho*, K. M. Kenyon & T. A. Holland, Appendix B, 576–621. London: British School of Archaeology at Jerusalem, through The British Academy.

Kislev, M. E. 1985. Early Neolithic horsebean from Yiftah'el Israel. *Science* **228**, 319–20.

Ladizinsky, G. 1968. Chromosome polymorphism in wild populations of *Vicia sativa* in Israel. *Caryologia* **31**, 233–41.

Ladizinsky, G. 1975. On the origin of the broad bean, *Vicia faba* L. *Israel Journal of Botany* **24**, 80–8.

Ladizinsky, G. 1979a. The genetics of several morphological traits in the lentils. *Journal of Heredity* **70**, 135–7.

Ladizinsky, G. 1979b. Seed dispersal in relation to the domestication of Middle East legumes. *Economic Botany* **33**, 284–9.

Ladizinsky, G. 1981. Consequences of hybridization in the *Vicia sativa* aggregate. *Heredity* **47**, 431–8.

Ladizinsky, G. 1985. The genetics of the hard seed coat in the genus *Lens*. *Euphytica* **34**, 539–43.

Ladizinsky, G. 1987. Pulse domestication before cultivation. *Economic Botany* **41**, 60–5.

Ladizinsky, G. & A. Adler 1976. The origin of chickpea *Cicer arietinum* L. *Euphytica* **25**, 211–17.

Ladizinsky, G. & H. van Oss 1984. Genetic relationships between wild and cultivated *Vicia ervilia*. *Botanical Journal of the Linnean Society, London* **89**, 97–100.

Ladizinsky, G. & R. Tamkin 1978. The cytogenetic structure of *Vicia sativa* aggregate. *Theoretical Applied Genetics* **53**, 33–42.

Ladizinsky, G., D. Braun & F. J. Muehlbauer 1983. Evidence for domestication of *Lens nigricans* in S. Europe. *Botanical Journal of the Linnean Society, London* **87**, 169–76.

Ladizinsky, G., D. Braun, D. Goshen & F. J. Muehlbauer 1984. The biological species of the genus *Lens*. *Botanical Gazette* **145**, 253–61.

Pinkas, R. 1985. *Allozyme divergence and evolution in the genus Lens*. MSc thesis submitted to the Hebrew University, Jerusalem. (In Hebrew.)

Pinkas, R., D. Zamir & G. Ladizinsky 1985. Allozyme divergence and evolution in the genus *Lens*. *Plant Systematics and Evolution* **151**, 131–40.

Renfrew, J. M. 1973. *Palaeoethnobotany*. New York: Columbia University Press.

Schafer, H. I. 1973. Die Taxonomie der *Vicia narbonesis* Gruppe. *Die Kulturpflanze* **21**, 211–72.

Vaquer, J., D. Geddes, M. Barbaza & J. Erroux 1986. Mesolithic plant exploitation at Balma Abeurador (France). *Oxford Journal of Archaeology* **5**, 1–18.

van Zeist, W. 1972. Paleobotanical results of the 1970 season at Cayonu, Turkey. *Helinium* **12**, 3–19.

Zohary, D. 1977. Comments on the origin of cultivated broad bean *Vicia faba* L. *Israel Journal of Botany* **26**, 39–40.

Zohary, D. 1989. Domestication of the Southwest Asian Neolithic crop assemblage of cereals, pulses, and flax: the evidence from the living plants. In *Foraging and farming: the evolution of plant exploitation*, D. R. Harris & G. C. Hillman (eds), ch. 22. London: Unwin Hyman.

Zohary, D. & M. Hopf 1973. Domestication of pulses in the Old World. *Science* **182**, 887–94.

# 24 *Cryptic anatomical characters as evidence of early cultivation in the grain legumes (pulses)*

ANN BUTLER

## Introduction

The earliest stages in the domestication of seed crops involved increasing human control over two important phases in the life cycle of the plant: seed dispersal and germination. The progenitors of the plant groups that played the most significant roles in agrarian development in the temperate Old World, the wild grasses and herbaceous legumes, typically shed their seed at maturity. A high proportion of this seed resists early germination, thereby facilitating an extension of potential plant growth over one or more growing seasons, and this enables the species to evade the effects of short-term unfavourable environmental conditions. Selective pressures imposed by annual cultivation favour the retention of the mature seed on the plant, which provides an increased yield at harvest; they also favour high rates of germination on first sowing due to loss of dormancy, when the species are required as seed-yielding (grain) crops.

In the ancient remains of seed crops, a loss of their natural means of seed dispersal is conventionally used as evidence of the beginnings of crop domestication, and, thence, of the beginnings of crop cultivation. However, loss of seed dormancy has not hitherto been used as a diagnostic criterion of cultivation or domestication. The purpose of this chapter is to assess the extent to which the loss of dormancy might be recognized in the anatomy of the seed coat, or testa, of the seeds of the pulses, and thus be used as an indicator of their initial cultivation (see also Hillman *et al*. Ch. 14, p. 243, this volume).

## Recognition of dehiscence in pulse crops

The morphological changes associated with the development of cultivated forms among the cereals have been described in charred material from archaeological sites in such publications as those of Helbaek, exemplified in his report on the plant remains from Hacilar (1970, pp. 189–244). Evidence indicating the loss of the brittle rachis which leads to retention of the mature spikelet on the plant is therefore well known.

Similar evidence for domestication in the legumes has been harder to find. The modification of seed-dispersal mechanisms in a number of legume species has been described by Ladizinsky (1979, Ch. 23, this volume). His studies of *Lens* have shown that a single mutation is responsible for the loss of dehiscency, thus allowing for a potentially rapid selection for populations with this trait. A similar pattern of change has been postulated for *Pisum* and *Lathyrus*, also genera from the tribe Vicieae. However, in the legumes, seed dispersal is effected by the dehiscence of the seed pod or legume. Loss of dehiscency can only be recognized in remains of the pods, which rarely survive in the archaeological record. Thus, recognition of a state of dehiscency is very difficult, if not impossible, as has been stated by Ladizinsky (1979).

In exceptional circumstances, where non-charred material has survived in archaeological deposits, the entire legume may be preserved. For example, the remains of dried pods of *Phaseolus vulgaris*, dating from about 5000 bc in two cave sites in Mexico, have been described, where preservation was sufficient to show that dehiscency had already been lost, the valves of the legume being untwisted, and showing the anatomical characteristic of reduction in the parchment layers (Kaplan 1965). Because even in Mesoamerica such finds are extremely rare, a more promising method of seeking evidence for earliest cultivation of legumes in the Old World is considered to be study of characters in the seed that are associated with loss of dormancy.

## Seed dormancy and the nature of the legume testa

A characteristic feature in the Leguminosae is the hard seed coat, which is associated with reduced permeability to water and restricted gaseous exchange by the seeds. The resultant dormancy is typical of the wild legume species. Thus in lentil, for example, the seeds of the wild *Lens orientalis* may remain dormant for several months after sowing, yet scarification of the testa causes germination to take place (Ladizinsky 1985). Similarly in pea, the seeds of wild species remain impermeable to water before rupture of the seed coat (Werker *et al.* 1979). Most wild legume populations show a variation in the proportion of hard-seededness, and thus, from the seeds of a single season, seedling emergence is prolonged over several months or even years (Roberts & Boddrell 1985).

In legume fodder crops, such as *Vicia sativa*, *Trifolium incarnatum*, and *Medicago sativa*, the presence of such a range of dormancy within each population can be advantageous (Donnelly 1970, Potts *et al.* 1978). Therefore hard-seededness is a characteristic that may be retained in this particular type of cultivar. However, in species cultivated for their seed, dormancy is lost.

Dormancy due to the presence of a hard seed coat is under both genetic and environmental control. Genetic studies have shown that the soft testa in *Lens culinaris* has arisen following mutation at only one or two loci; thus it may be deduced that the development of a non-dormant population could be a relatively short process (Ladizinsky 1985). In *Lupinus angustifolius* a single gene is known to govern seed-coat permeability, and in *Vicia sativa* two genes are responsible (Donnelly 1980). Although in the different genera of cultivated pulses the genetic mechanism may vary in the production of a similar end result, it appears that generally the loss of dormancy may arise comparatively abruptly under conditions of positive selection.

The anatomy of the leguminous seed has been described by Corner (1951) and Rolston (1978) among others. Investigations have been carried out in certain genera to discover which tissues or features in the seed coat might be responsible for impermeability. Although early work suggested that the cuticle was water-repellent, it has been demonstrated that this uniformly thin covering is permeable to water (Baciu-Michlaus 1970).

The main causes for the impermeability of the leguminous seed have been summarized by Rolston (1978) and by Werker (1980/81), who have stated that the external cell layer, the palisade cells, are important, but not solely responsible, for this characteristic. The palisade cells have thickened external periclinal walls, which in *Pisum* have been shown to contain suberin encrustations (Spurny 1973); yet not all hard-seeded legumes have seeds that react positively to histochemical tests for suberin. Ballard (1973) considers that while suberization provides the main barrier to the penetration of water, other factors situated deeper in the palisade layer are also of significance. Experiments involving the puncturing of the testa to varying depths have indicated that, in *Coronilla varia*, an impermeable layer exists towards or beneath the base of the palisade cells (McKee *et al.* 1977). In *Trifolium subterraneum*, staining with fluorescent aniline blue has revealed an impermeable callose deposition within the innermost layers of the testa, in the nucellar remnant tissue (Bhalla & Slattery 1984).

Few reports have been published giving anatomical evidence of hard-seededness. Most recent work on fresh seeds has been concerned with possible biochemical constituents of the testa that might confer impermeable properties upon it. Thus Werker *et al.* (1979) have suggested, following studies of the wild and cultivated species of *Pisum*, that in wild species oxidation of phenolic compounds with the formation of quinones, within either the palisade cells or the inner layer of hourglass cells, may produce a continuous impermeable layer during seed maturation, with concomitant darkening in colour of the testa, whereas in cultivars phenols are absent or found in very low concentrations, correlating with a light-coloured seed coat (Marbach & Mayer 1975).

A variety of mechanisms appears to be responsible for hard-seededness in the leguminous seed; these are complex and as yet are not fully understood.

**Table 24.1** Species of the tribe Vicieae known to have been cultivated (sources: Zhukovsky 1924, Davis 1970, Townsend & Guest 1974, Duke 1981, Aykroyd & Doughty 1982, Thulin 1983, Summerfield & Roberts 1985).

| | |
|---|---|
| *Lathyrus anuus* | grain legume crop |
| *Lathyrus aphaca* | fodder crop, India |
| *Lathyrus cicera* | grain legume crop |
| *Lathyrus clymenum* | grain legume crop, Greece |
| *Lathyrus gorgoni* | animal fodder |
| *Lathyrus hirsutus* | winter pasture, USA |
| *Lathyrus latifolius* | cultivar, Turkey, W. Europe |
| *Lathyrus ochrus* | grain crop, Greece and Turkey |
| *Lathyrus odoratus* | essential oil extract, horticulture |
| *Lathyrus pratensis* | pasture |
| *Lathyrus rotundifolius* | horticulture |
| *Lathyrus sativus* | grain legume crop |
| *Lathyrus sylvestris* | forage crop |
| *Lathyrus tingitanus* | cultivar, Mediterranean, Morocco |
| *Lathyrus tuberosus* | edible tubers, W. Asia |
| | |
| *Lens culinaris* | grain legume crop |
| *Lens nigricans* | grain legume crop |
| | |
| *Pisum sativum* ssp. *elatius* | fodder crop |
| *Pisum sativum* ssp. *sativum* var. *arvense* | fodder and grain crop |
| *Pisum sativum* ssp. *sativum* var. *sativum* | grain legume crop |
| | |
| *Vicia articulata* | grain legume crop, Turkey |
| *Vicia benghalensis* | poultry feed, green manure |
| *Vicia cracca* | cultivar, China and Japan |
| *Vicia ervilia* | grain legume crop |
| *Vicia faba* | grain legume crop |
| *Vicia graminea* | cultivar, S. America |
| *Vicia hirsuta* | fodder crop, India, USSR |
| *Vicia johannis* | grain legume crop, Turkey |
| *Vicia michauxii* | spring forage crop, Portugal |
| *Vicia narbonensis* | grain legume and forage crop |
| *Vicia pannonica* | grain legume crop, Turkey |
| *Vicia sativa* ssp. *nigra* | green manure |
| *Vicia sativa* ssp. *sativa* | fodder crop, Europe |
| *Vicia tenufolia* | forage crop, Iraq |
| *Vicia unijuga* | cultivar, E. Siberia, Japan |
| *Vicia villosa* | green manure, USA; pasture, Ethiopia |

**Table 24.2**  Species of the tribe Vicieae examined in the study of seedcoat anatomy.

---

*Lathyrus anuus* L.
*Lathyrus aphaca* L.
*Lathyrus cicera* L.
*Lathyrus clymenum* L.
*Lathyrus hirsutus* L.
*Lathyrus inconspicuus* L.
*Lathyrus laxiflorus* (Desf.) Kuntze
*Lathyrus niger* (L.) Bernh.
*Lathyrus nissolia* L.
*Lathyrus ochrus* L. DC.
*Lathyrus pratensis* L.
*Lathyrus sativus* L.
*Lathyrus sylvestris* L.
*Lathyrus tuberosus* L.

*Lens culinaris* Medikus
*Lens ervoides* (Brign.) Grande
*Lens nigricans* (M. Bieb.) Webb & Berth.
*Lens odemensis* Ladizinsky
*Lens orientalis* (Boiss.) Schmahl.

*Pisum sativum* L. subsp. *elatius* (M. Bieb.) Asch. & Graebner
*Pisum sativum* L. subsp. *sativum* var. *arvense* (L.) Poiret
*Pisum sativum* L. subsp. *sativum* var. *sativum*

*Vicia bithynica* (L.) L.
*Vicia cracca* L.
*Vicia ervilia* (L.) Wild.
*Vicia faba* L. subsp. *faba* var. *minor* Beck
*Vicia faba* L. subsp. *paucijuga* (Alef.) Murat.
*Vicia lutea* L.
*Vicia melanops* Sibth. & Smith
*Vicia narbonensis* L.
*Vicia noeana* Reuter ex Boiss.
*Vicia peregrina* L.
*Vicia sativa* L.
*Vicia sativa* L. subsp. *nigra* (L.) Ehrh.
*Vicia sepium* L.
*Vicia sylvatica* L.
*Vicia tetrasperma* (L.) Schreber
*Vicia villosa* Roth subsp. *varia* (Host) Corbiere

---

However, the results of such investigations as have been described above, may form the basis of an approach to further studies that might have application to charred remains from archaeological sites.

## The present study

*Lathyrus*, *Lens*, *Pisum*, and *Vicia*, the four major genera in the tribe Vicieae, have contributed many species to the pool of economic plants. Although 36 or so species are documented as having been cultivated, this number probably was exceeded in the distant past (Table 24.1).

In this chapter the results are discussed of some preliminary surveys of characters of the morphology and anatomy of the testa of seeds of wild and cultivated members of the Vicieae, in which emphasis has been placed upon aspects which may be related to hard- or soft-seededness, and therefore to dormancy.

### Material

Fresh seeds have been examined from wild taxa, and cultivars used as forage crops as well as grain crops, from the genera *Lathyrus*, *Lens*, *Pisum*, and *Vicia*, including, where possible, several populations of the same taxon (Table 24.2).

### Methods

External seed morphology has been examined under light microscopy at magnifications of less than ×50. For micromorphological and anatomical investigations, whole seeds, and seeds halved by pressure-fracture transversely across the hilum, have been mounted in the adhesive UHU on aluminium stubs, gold-coated to a depth of 30–40 nm in a Polaron E5000 sputter coater, and scanned in either a Philips PSEM 500 or a JEOL JSM 35, using voltages of 12–25 kV at magnifications of between ×12 and ×6400.

## Discussion of results

### Surface morphology of the testa

Traditionally the texture of the surface of the testa has been used as a character for the separation of some wild and cultivated taxa in the Vicieae, and this can be clearly demonstrated in the genus *Pisum*. Helbaek (1970) described the rough seed coats that distinguished the seeds of the wild pea found associated with Late Neolithic and Chalcolithic levels at Hacilar and contrasted these with the smooth-coated variety from Çatal Hüyük identified as the seeds of a cultivar (Figs 24.1 & 24.2). This topographic criterion has been considered by Zohary and Hopf (1973) to be 'perhaps the most reliable indication for domestication'.

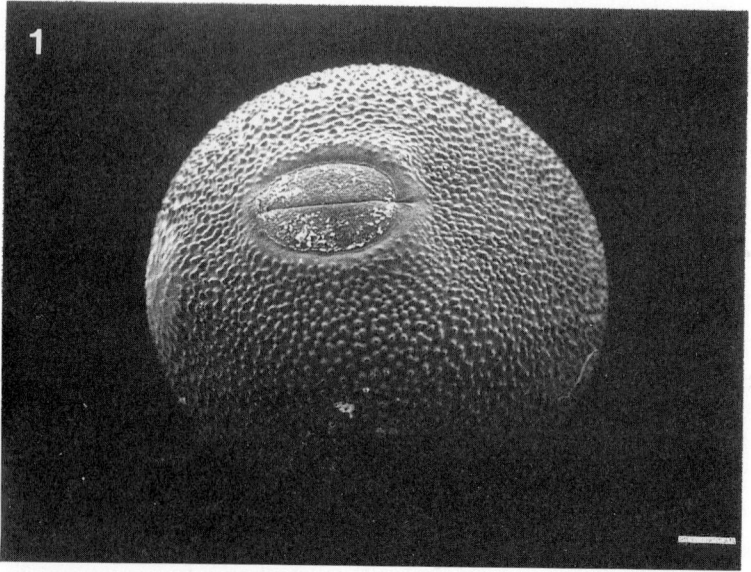

**Figure 24.1** *Pisum sativum* ssp. *elatius*, rough-coated seed; scale bar=300 μm.

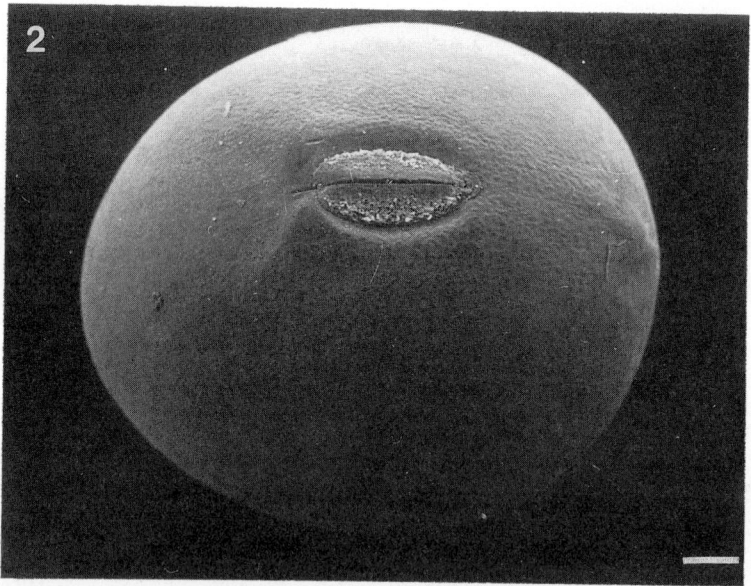

**Figure 24.2** *Pisum sativum* ssp. *sativum*, smooth-coated seed; scale bar=300 μm.

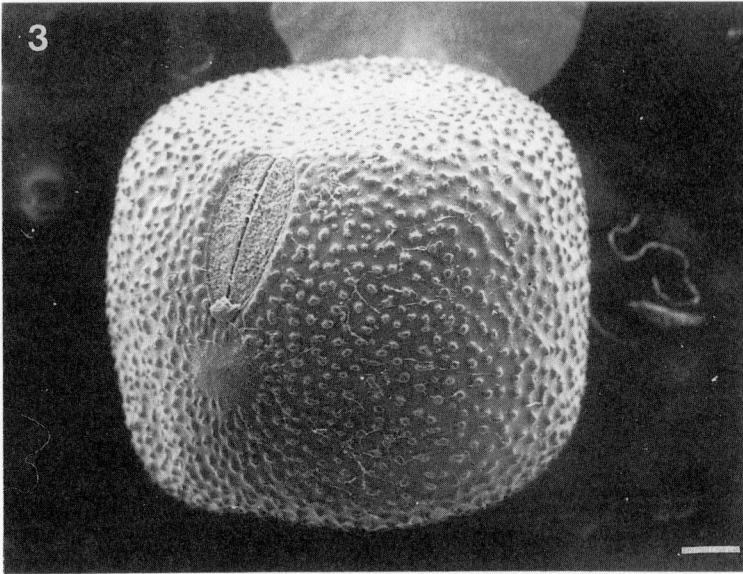

**Figure 24.3** *Lathyrus nissolia*, rough-coated seed; scale bar=300 μm.

Large-scale relief of the seed coat, which is readily visible under hand-lens magnifications, is a feature that is most commonly found among the Vicieae in the wild species of *Lathyrus*, such as *L. nissolia* (Fig. 24.3), and is more rare in *Vicia*. Examination of finer detail of surface morphology has been made possible by the high resolutions and greater magnifications of SEM, and has led to a number of reports in recent years describing the distinctive patterning on the testa of leguminous seeds, well illustrated by the work of Lersten and Gunn (1982).

In a study by SEM of the testa morphology of 30 species of the Vicieae (Butler in press) deposits have been described on the surface of the seed coat that seem to be associated particularly with cultivated taxa, such as *Lathyrus sativus*, *Lens culinaris*, *Vicia bithynica*, and *Pisum sativum* subsp. *sativum* (Fig. 24.4). It is suggested that these deposits derive from the parent legume, and may be the result of the mature seed remaining in prolonged contact with the inner surface of the pericarp of the ripe pod of an indehiscent species. Should this theory be verified, the presence of such extrinsic material upon the testa might be a useful indicator of indehiscency and thus of a cultivar. These deposits survive charring in experiments with modern specimens designed to simulate charred archaeological material. However, the deposits concerned are hard to distinguish from the generalized deposits of surface debris which commonly occur on material of archaeological origin and this might well limit their usefulness as a diagnostic criterion.

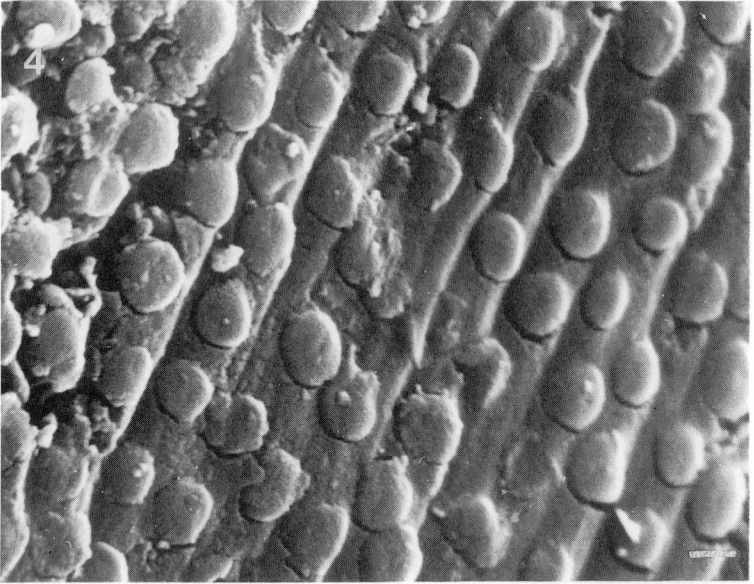

**Figure 24.4**    *Lens culinaris* testa with deposit; scale bar=2 μm.

The testas of many legume species exhibit finely papillose surfaces, due to the presence of projections from the external periclinal walls of the individual palisade cells. In lentil, these papillae are very long and acute in some of the wild taxa. *Lens odemensis* and some populations of *L. orientalis* show these features, in marked contrast with the very flat-walled palisade cells of the cultivar *L. culinaris* (Figs 24.5 & 24.6). A high relief in testa topography has been tentatively associated by Hadas (1982) with a reduction in permeability to water in chickpea, pea, and vetch seeds, by limiting the areas available for surface contact. However, further work is needed before the variation in seed-coat morphology in these legume genera can be associated clearly with differences in the physiology of germination: in *Lathyrus*, for example, there are a number of wild species, such as *L. aphaca*, *L. pratensis*, and *L. niger*, where a high level of hard-seededness is associated with a smooth seed coat.

Pits in the testa surface have been recorded by several authors in a number of leguminous species (Lersten 1981, Wolf *et al.* 1981, Yachlich *et al.* 1984). It has been suggested that these might be related to a differential uptake of water in certain zones in the testa (Riggio Bevilacqua *et al.* 1984). While this property might indeed be associated with the pits, investigations in the present study have indicated that, at least in the Vicieae, such features are unlikely to be intrinsic to the seed, but rather that they are the result of an outside agency, such as a pathogen (Butler 1986). Certainly, they appear to be of unstable occurrence even within single populations of a species and they are found in seeds of wild species as well as in cultivars.

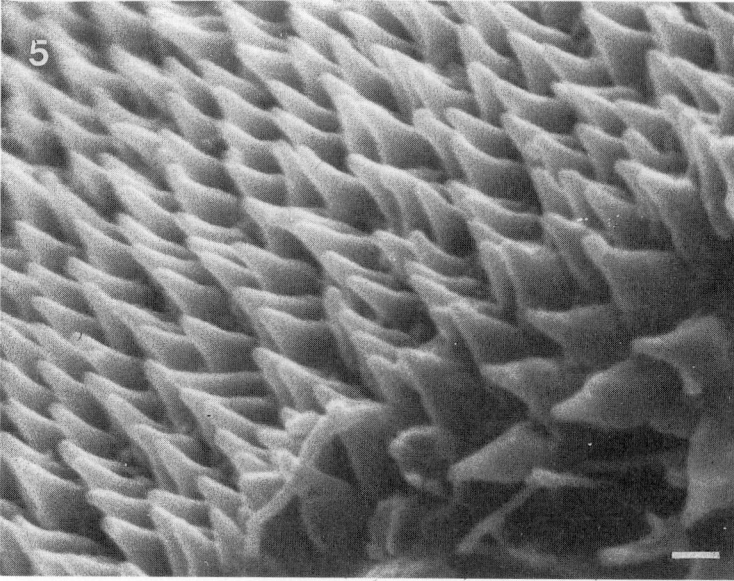

**Figure 24.5** *Lens odemensis*, acutely papillose testa; scale bar=2 μm.

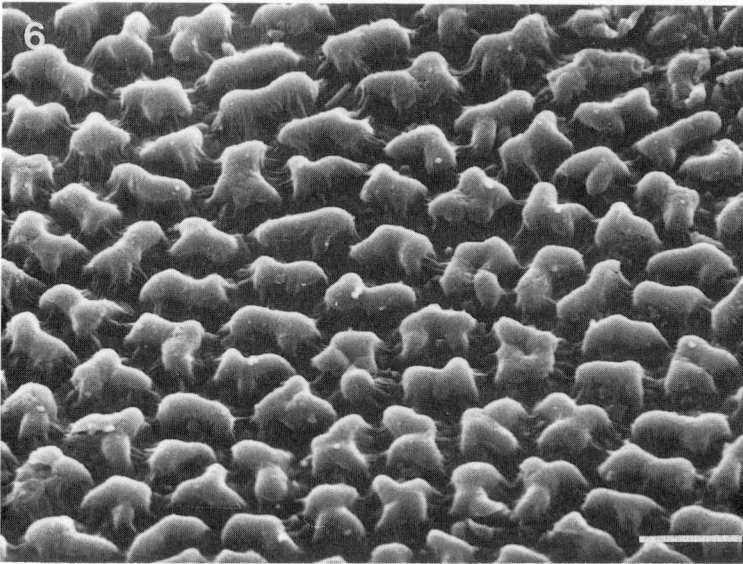

**Figure 24.6** *Lens culinaris*, testa with flat papillae; scale bar=10 μm.

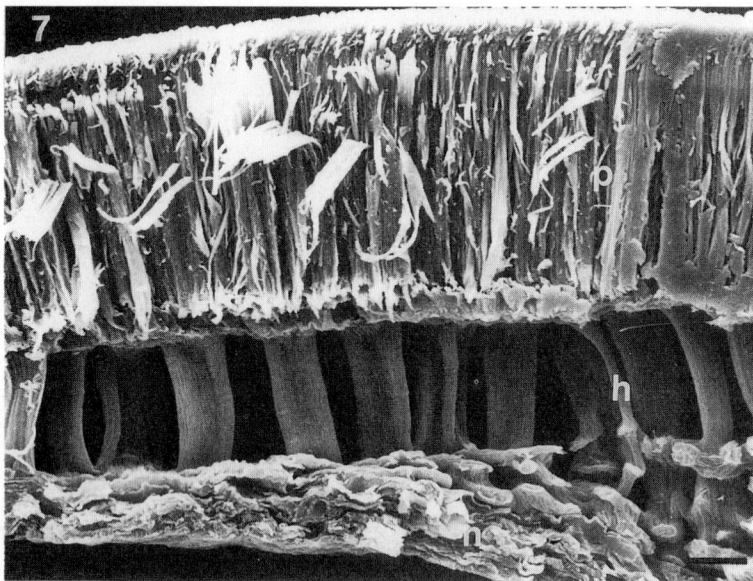

**Figure 24.7**  *Vicia villosa*, transection through testa adjacent to hilum; scale bar=20 μm; p=palisade cells; h=hourglass cells; n=nucellar remnant layer.

## Testa micromorphology

The thickness of the testa has been considered to contribute to the property of hard-seededness in legume species. Ojamo (1972) has reported a high correlation between seed-coat thickness and varietal differences in imbibition in *Vigna*, a genus from the tribe Phaseolae, closely related to the Vicieae. In the Vicieae, the testa consists of the two single-cell layers of palisade and hourglass cells, within which is a disorganized layer of nucellar remnants with some parenchyma (Fig. 24.7). In this study comparisons have been made between the dimensions of the testa components of wild and cultivated taxa. From electron micrographs taken under carefully standardized conditions, measurements have been made at three positions around the seed circumference, of the total testa depth, the height of the palisade cells, and the thickness of the nucellar remnant layer. Hourglass cells are known to vary in height with their proximity to the hilum (Lersten & Gunn 1982) and the hilar axis (Butler in press) and this dimension has been included indirectly and treated warily. From a preliminary analysis of the data from 31 species of *Lathyrus* and *Vicia* and the five species of *Lens*, no clear associations have emerged between the absolute thickness of any part of the testa and the state of wildness or domestication of the species that supplied the seeds. In *Pisum*, the pea, the seed coats of the wild subspecies *P. sativum* ssp. *elatius* were found to be markedly thicker than those of both

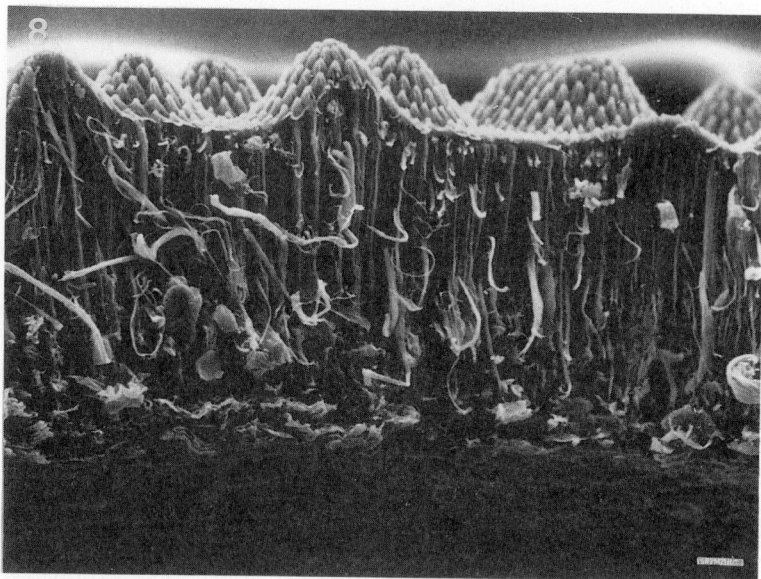

**Figure 24.8** *Pisum sativum* ssp. *elatius,* transection through thick testa; scale bar=30 μm.

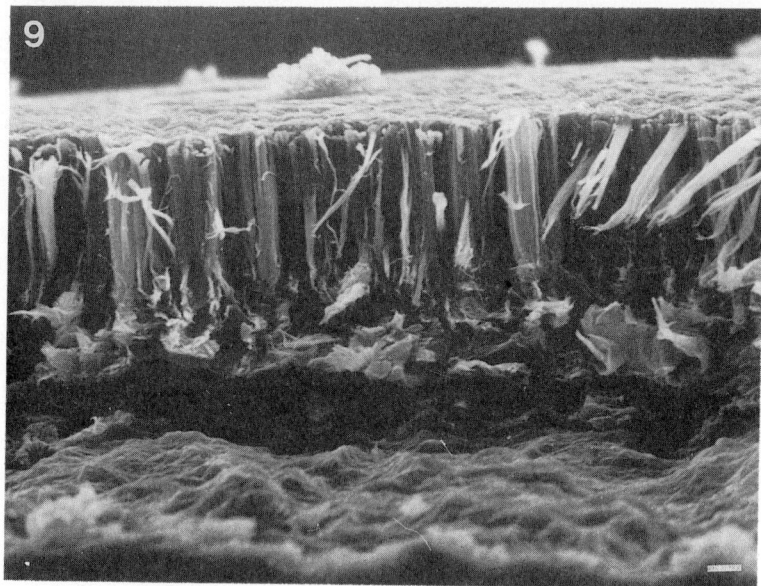

**Figure 24.9** *Pisum sativum* ssp. *sativum,* transection through thin testa; scale bar=10 μm.

cultivar varieties, *P. sativum* ssp. *sativum* var. *arvense* and *P. sativum* ssp. *sativum* var. *sativum* (Figs 24.8 & 24.9). This is in agreement with the findings of Werker *et al.* (1979) who also found significantly thinner seed coats in cultivated peas.

The seeds of members of the Vicieae show a wide range of morphology, and characters such as seed shape and size, although traditionally used to separate species, are known to be unreliable for purposes of identification (Gunn 1970). The gigantism of seeds found in many cultivars is not a feature of the earliest examples of cultivars from archaeological sites, and appears to be a later or more gradual modification from the wild form. Micromorphological observations of the testa made under the relatively high magnifications of up to ×6400 by SEM have also shown variations in detail, both between and within populations of a single species (Butler in press). In this study, with the exception of testa thickness in seeds of *Pisum*, no characters recorded in the seed coat of members of the Vicieae can be associated directly with presence or absence of hard–seededness.

## Hilar anatomy and phenolics

It appears that in the Vicieae the properties of the seed coat that confer impermeability or hard–seededness upon the seed may not be reflected by modifications in micromorphology. Taxonomists, faced with the problems of unravelling the relationships between members of this phenotypically plastic tribe, have increasingly turned to studies of the biochemistry. In this group of plants, chemotaxonomy has proved to be a useful method by which to classify the members. Harborne (1971) has described substances of systematic interest in the Leguminosae and mentioned the scattered appearance of quinones in this family. Quinones, as has been mentioned above, have been associated with the impermeable seed in wild species of *Pisum* (Werker *et al.* 1979).

Indirect evidence of the presence of phenolic compounds has been sought in the anatomy of the hilum. Beneath the hilar aperture in seeds of the Papilionaceae lies the tracheid bar, a derivative of the ovule vascular bundle (Lersten 1982) (Fig. 24.10). This is comprised of tracheoid elements that intercommunicate by means of perforations, similar to the pits seen in the elements in wood, all of which are bordered, but which show a range of ornamentation from smooth plain borders, through small warts, to elaborate vestures. The aetiology of the pit ornamentation in timbers has been explored by Scurfield (1972) who associates the formation of warts with polymerization of phenolic substances on the cell walls, as has also been suggested by Liese (1965). Ohtani *et al.* (1984) consider that warts and vestures have a common origin and similar nature, differing only in position or extent. By analogy with this work on pit structure in wood, it was decided to record the pit ornamentation in tracheoids of the seeds of the 93 taxa of the Vicieae, on the basis that the presence of highly developed pit ornamentation might be indicative of high levels of phenolics in the seed, and thus provide indirect evidence of dormancy.

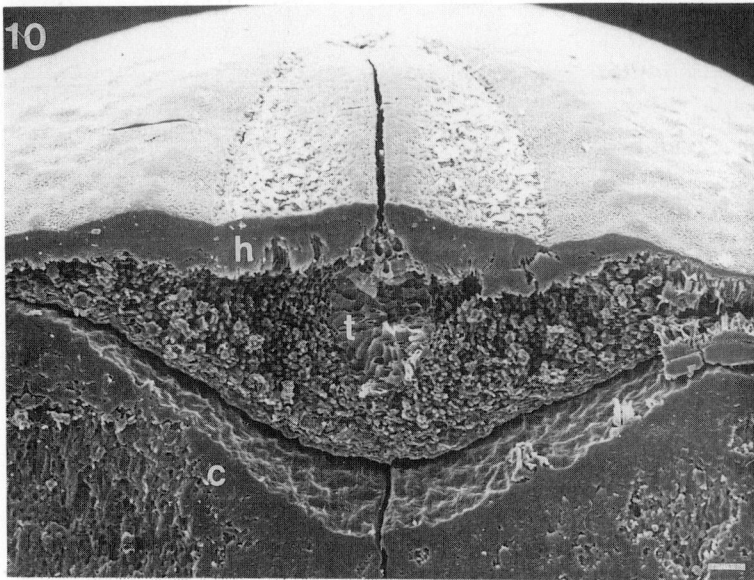

**Figure 24.10**  *Pisum sativum* ssp. *sativum*, vertical transection across hilum; scale
bar=10 μm; t=tracheid bar; h=hilum; c=cotyledon.

Tracheoid pits in the seeds of the Vicieae have been described by Lersten
and Gunn (1982) as typically regular and smooth-bordered. By contrast, in
this study, the pits were found to be of variable distribution, to show a wide
range of size and shape, both in the pits themselves and also in their
apertures, and to display ornamentation of the pit walls ranging from plain
borders to elaborate vestures; most commonly several types were seen not
only in the same species but even within the same seed specimen (Figs 24.11
& 24.12). A single species of *Lathyrus*, *L. annuus*, and some populations in all
species of *Lens* examined out of the 93 populations and 38 species studied,
had only smooth, plain-bordered pits.

The anatomy of tracheoid pits in these seeds has not yet been fully
explored. The significance of the presence or absence of pit ornamentation is
not yet understood. Currently, more detailed analysis of the data is in
progress. However, it is suggested that while direct evidence of dormancy
and therefore of 'wildness' of species in the Vicieae may be lacking in the seed
anatomy, some cryptic characters revealed under high magnification may
provide indirect biochemical information of value in the interpretation of
seeds from archaeological contexts, which might contribute to the recognition of very early stages of cultivation. Although this study has been carried
out on fresh seeds, the features described are all potentially discernible in
well-preserved charred archaeological material.

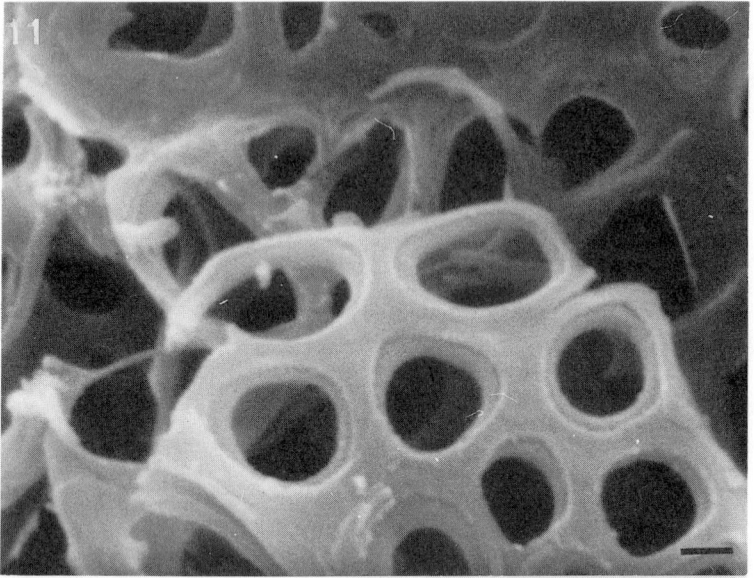

**Figure 24.11**  *Vicia ervilia*, tracheoid pits with plain borders; scale bar=1 μm.

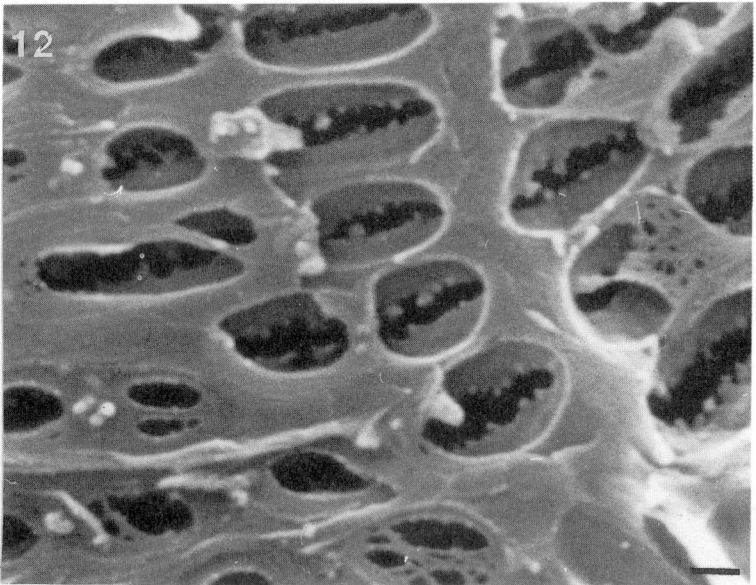

**Figure 24.12**  *Vicia ervilia*, tracheoid pits with vestures, same specimen as in Fig. 24.11; scale bar=1 μm.

# Acknowledgements

SEM facilities were kindly made available in the Biology Department, Imperial College, London and the Crystallography Department, Birkbeck College, London. The seed samples supplied by Dr Frank Bisby, Mr Gordon Hillman, Professor Gideon Ladizinsky, and the N. I. Vavilov All-Union Institute of Plant Industry, Leningrad, are gratefully acknowledged. I would like to thank Gordon Hillman for valuable discussion and advice. The work was funded by a grant from the British Science and Engineering Research Council.

# References

Aykroyd, W. R. & J. Doughty 1982. *Legumes in human nutrition*. Rome: FAO paper 20.

Baciu-Michlaus, D. 1970. Contribution to the study of hard seed and coat structure; properties of soybean. *Proceedings of the International Seed Testing Association* **35**, 599–617.

Ballard, L. A. T. 1973. Physical barriers to germination. *Seed Science and Technology* **I**, 285–303.

Bhalla, P. L. & H. D. Slattery 1984. Callose deposits make clover seeds impermeable to water. *Annals of Botany* **53**, 125–8.

Butler, A. 1986. Studies in the seedcoat of *Lathyrus*. In *Lathyrus and Lathyrism*, A. K. Kaul & D. Combes (eds), 25–38. New York: Third World Medical Research Foundation.

Butler, A. in press. *The Vicieae: problems in identification*. Proceedings of the 7th Symposium of International Work Group for Palaeoethnobotany, Cambridge 1986.

Corner, E. J. H. 1951. The leguminous seed. *Phytomorphology* **1**, 117–50.

Davis, P. H. 1970. *Flora of Turkey*, Vol. 3. Edinburgh: Edinburgh University Press.

Donnelly, E. D. 1970. Persistence of hard seed in *Vicia* lines derived from interspecific hybridisation. *Crop Science* **10**, 661–2.

Donnelly, E. D. 1980. Selecting lines of vetch that breed true for hard seed. *Crop Science* **20**, 259–60.

Duke, J. A. 1981. *Handbook of legumes of world economic importance*. New York: Plenum Press.

Gunn, C. R. 1970. A key and diagrams for the seeds of one hundred species of *Vicia* (Leguminosae). *Proceedings of the International Seed Testing Association* **35**, 773–90.

Hadas, A. 1982. Water uptake and germination of leguminous seeds in soils of changing metric and osmotic water potential. In *The physiology and biochemistry of seed development, dormancy and germination*, A. A. Khan (ed.), 507–27. Amsterdam: Elsevier.

Harborne, J. B. 1971. Terpenoid and other low molecular weight substances of systematic interest in the Leguminosae. In *Chemotaxonomy of the Leguminosae*, J. B. Harborne, D. Boulter & B. C. Turner (eds), 275–83. New York: Academic Press.

Helbaek, H. 1970. The plant husbandry of Hacilar. In *Excavations at Hacilar*, J. Mellaart (ed.), 189–244. Edinburgh: Edinburgh University Press.

Kaplan, L. 1965. Archaeology and domestication in American *Phaseolus* (bean). *Economic Botany* **19**, 358–68.

Ladizinsky, G. 1979. Seed dispersal in relation to the domestication of Middle East legumes. *Economic Botany* **33**, 284–9.

Ladizinsky, G. 1985. The genetics of the hard seed coat in the genus *Lens*. *Euphytica* **34**, 539–43.

Ladizinsky, G. 1989. Origin and domestication of Southwest Asian grain legumes. In *Foraging and farming: the evolution of plant exploitation*, D. R. Harris & G. C. Hillman (eds), ch. 23. London: Unwin Hyman.

Lersten, N. R. 1981. Testa topography in Leguminosae, subfamily Papilionoideae. *Proceedings of the Iowa Academy of Science* **88**, 180–91.

Lersten, N. R. 1982. Tracheid bar and vestured pits in legume seeds (Leguminosae: Papilionoideae). *American Journal of Botany* **69**, 98–107.

Lersten, N. R. & C. R. Gunn. 1982. *Testa characters in the tribe Vicieae, with notes about tribes Abreae, Cicerae and Trifolieae (Fabaceae)*. United States Department of Agriculture Technical Bulletin No. 1667.

Liese, W. 1965. The fine structure of bordered pits of softwoods. In *Cellular ultrastructure of woody plants*, W. A. Cote (ed.), 251–69. Syracuse: Syracuse University Press.

McKee, G. W., R. A. Peiffer & N. N. Mohsenin 1977. Seedcoat structure in *Coronilla varia* L. and its relation to hard seed. *Journal of Agronomy* **69**, 53–8.

Marbach, I. & A. M. Mayer 1975. Changes in catechol oxidase and permeability to water in seed coats of *Pisum elatius* during seed development and maturation. *Plant Physiology* **56**, 93–6.

Ohtani, J., B. A. Meylan & B. G. Butterfield 1984. Vestures or warts – proposed terminology. *IAWA Bulletin* (ns) **5**, 3–11.

Ojamo, O. A. 1972. Inheritance of seedcoat thickness in cowpeas. *Journal of Heredity* **63**, 147–9.

Potts, H. C., J. Duangpatra, W. G. Hairston & J. C. Delouche 1978. Some influences of hardseededness on soybean seed quality. *Crop Science* **18**, 221–4.

Riggio Bevilacqua, L., G. Roti-Michelozzi & G. Serrato 1984. Water entry in *Cercis siliquastrum* (Leguminosae) seeds. *Nordic Journal of Botany* **4**, 675–9.

Roberts, H. A. & J. E. Boddrell 1985. Seed survival and seasonal pattern of seedling emergence in some Leguminosae. *Annals of Applied Biology* **106**, 125–32.

Rolston, M. P. 1978. Water impermeable seed dormancy. *Botanical Review* **44**, 365–96.

Scurfield, G. 1972. Histochemistry of reaction wood cell walls in two species of *Eucalyptus* and in *Tristania conferta* R. Br. *Australian Journal of Botany* **20**, 9–26.

Spurný, M. 1973. The imbition process. In *Seed ecology*, W. Heydecker (ed.), 367–89. London: Butterworth.

Summerfield, R. J. & E. H. Roberts 1985. *Grain legume crops*. London: Collins.

Townsend, C. C. & E. Guest 1974, *Flora of Iraq*, Vol. 3. Baghdad: Ministry of Agriculture and Agrarian Reform of the Republic of Iraq.

Thulin, M. 1983. Leguminosae of Ethiopia. *Opera Botanica* **68**, 1–223.

Werker, E. 1980/81. Seed dormancy as explained by the anatomy of embryo envelopes. *Israel Journal of Botany* **29**, 22–44.

Werker, E., I. Marbach & A. M. Mayer 1979. Relation between the anatomy of the testa, water permeability and the presence of phenolics in the genus *Pisum*. *Annals of Botany* **43**, 765–71.

Wolf, W. J., F. L. Baker & R. L. Bernard 1981. Soybean seed-coat structural features: pits, deposits and cracks. *SEM* **III**, 531–44.

Yachlich, R. W., E. L. Vigil & W. P. Wergin 1984. Scanning electron microscopy of soybean seed coat. *SEM* **II**, 991–1000.

Zhukovsky, P. M. 1924. *Investigation of peasants' seed materials in E. Georgia.* Isvestia Tiflisskogo Gosudarstvennogo Politekhnicheskogo Instituta ii, Tiflis.

Zohary, D. & M. Hopf 1973. Domestication of pulses in the Old World. *Science* **182**, 887–94.

# 25 *Domestication and spread of the cultivated rices*

## T. T. CHANG

Rice vies with wheat in importance as a human food. Among the cereals, rice has the unique ability to tolerate continuous flooding and is often the sole crop for subsistence farmers in low-lying monsoonal regions. Its semi-aquatic plant structures transport air from the shoot to the root zone, enabling the micro-organisms associated with the rhizosphere to biologically fix nitrogen. As a result, subsistence farmers are able to reap some harvest without fertilization.

In view of the above features, it would be reasonable to assume that rice was one of the earliest plants to be cultivated or domesticated by food gatherers in both tropical and warm temperate regions where standing water or intermittent flooding prevailed during the growing season. This chapter discusses presently available evidence on the antiquity of rice, the process of cultivation and domestication, the diversification process following cultivation and domestication, and the proliferation of eco-cultural plant types following man-assisted dispersal to many parts of the world.

## Evolutionary pathway of the two rice cultigens

The genus *Oryza* consists of 20 wild species (both diploid and tetraploid forms) and two cultigens: the Asian *O. sativa* L. and the African *O. glaberrima* Steud.

The geographic distribution of the 22 species in the genus supports a hypothesis that the original home of *Oryza* was the Gondwana supercontinent which began to fracture in the early Cretaceous period. The main plates rafted apart to form South America, Australia, Antarctica, South and mainland Southeast Asia, Madagascar, and the major islands of Oceania (Chang 1976b, 1985).

A common pathway of evolution for the two cultigens has been suggested: a common progenitor originating in Gondwanaland → wild perennial species → wild annual species → annual cultivated species. Continuous intercrossing among the wild perennial, wild annual, and cultivated annual species has led to a great diversity of weed races, especially in the Asian Section Sativa Ghose. The Asian weed race is now predominantly infused with *O. sativa* genes in sites near cultivated fields (Chang 1976a, b). The coexistence of three or four types at a site has greatly impaired scientific analysis of natural populations. Typical specimens of the wild perennial and wild annual forms are now rarely found in nature and the ancestral species of the two cultigens should only be treated as conceptual taxa of the past (Chang 1976b, IBPGR–IRRI Rice Advisory Committee 1982). Indeed, it must be pointed out that the annual and perennial growth habits are not as precise as the terms indicate (Chang 1976c, Morishima *et al.* 1984).

Wild species that belong to the Section Sativa Ghose are also present in other Gondwana components: *O. glumaepatula* Steud. in Central and South America and *O. meridionalis* Ng in Australia. But in these areas there was no indigenous wetland agriculture to induce the formation of the annual cultigen (Chang 1987).

Most of the wild species of *Oryza* thrive under full sunlight, while a few species, such as *meyeriana*, *ridleyi*, and *granulata*, only tolerate partial sunlight and are found on the edges of forests. *O. officinalis* and *minuta* appear to be intermediate between the two groups.

The early forms of the Asian cultigen generally matured earlier than their wild progenitor. Thus, they flourished under drier and fluctuating climates during the Neothermal period (15 000 to 10 000 bp) and produced more seeds which enabled them to move farther northward than the perennial form. Increasing aridity on the northern border of the Himalayas and associated mountain ranges in mainland Southeast Asia also forced the early settlers in China to move into more humid areas toward the east and to the south. The movement of people and the dispersal of plants greatly accelerated the ecogenetic diversification process in rice (Chang 1976a, b).

## Beginning of rice cultivation

Rice grains were initially gathered and consumed by prehistoric people of the humid tropics and subtropics where the self-propagating plants grew on poorly drained sites. These people also hunted, fished, and gathered other edible plant parts as food. Soon they developed a liking for the easily cooked and tasty rice and searched for plants that bore larger panicles and heavier grains. The gathering-and-selection process was more essential to people who lived in environments with marked seasonal variations in temperature, rainfall, or both than to those who lived in areas of more equable climate (Chang 1976a).

In some parts of South Asia, such as the Jeypore Tract of Orissa State, India, and the Batticoloa district of Sri Lanka, the gathering of wild-growing rice panicles as food supplements can still be observed. In the Jeypore Tract the tribal women use a pan and, by a flicking movement of the hand, the highly shattering grains are thrown into a wicker basket held by the other hand. In other cases, a fish net is passed over the top of the plants to catch the grains which have rough awns. However, even in the tribal reserves of Jeypore, the wild rice has been infused with *sativa* genes

(IBPGR–IRRI Rice Advisory Committee 1982). For discussion of another example of present-day wild-rice exploitation, in Southeast Asia, see White (Ch. 9, this volume), and for reference to the collection of wild rice by foragers in northern Australia see Jones & Meehan (Ch. 7, this volume).

A new crop produced by naturally dropped seeds from the highly shattering panicles near homesteads could have triggered the idea of cultivating rice closer to the living quarters. This hypothesis suggests that cultivation began when men (or more likely women) purposefully dropped seeds on the soil in low-lying spots near their homesteads, kept out the weeds and animals, and manipulated the water supply. The cultivation sites were moved nearer to the homesteads as people found higher yields from plants grown in the enriched soil near the human settlements: a process which may have applied not only to rice but to many other cultivated plants as well (Engelbrecht 1916, quoted by Zeven 1973, Anderson 1952, Hawkes 1969, Chang 1976b).

The chronological sequence in growing rice in lowland (wetland) fields is assumed to have been from broadcasting to dibbling or row seeding, to transplanting, and the land-use sequence is from swidden agriculture (shifting cultivation) to unbunded permanent fields to bunded fields – first rainfed, later irrigated. It is further assumed that the progression is related to increasing human population density on the land (Chang 1987).

## Domestication versus cultivation

In the case of rice, I follow the terminology of Helbaek (1969) and Whyte (1974) that the domestication process proceeded from grain gathering to human cultivation to domestication. In tropical areas rice cultivation in early days could be sustained, without annual sowing, through the germination of seeds which fell onto the soil or growth from underground plant parts; whereas in temperate regions, such as central and northern China, rice became a true domesticate because seeding was an annual necessity. In the temperate regions the rice cultivars therefore depended entirely on human care for their perpetuation, although wild rice, probably of the O. sativa f. spontanea type, was reported in Chinese literature as far north as 38°N latitude (Chang 1983).

## Antiquity of rice cultivation in Asia

The chronology of rice cultivation in different parts of Asia is summarized in Table 25.1. The dates support the generally accepted thesis that the Asian cultigen evolved from an annual progenitor over a broad belt that extended from the southern foothills of the Himalayas, across Upper Burma, northern Thailand, and Laos, to north Vietnam, and southwest and south China (cf. Chang 1976b). The sites from which rice has been recovered and dated are,

**Table 25.1** Chronology of the oldest rice remains unearthed from different geographic regions of Asia.

| Site | Type of plant remains | Ecogeographic race | Estimated age | Reference |
|---|---|---|---|---|
| Koldihwa, Mahagara, U.P., India | rice grains embedded in earthern potsherds and husks in cowdung | *indica* | 6570–4530 bc | Sharma & Manda 1980[*] ex Sahara & Sato 1984 |
| Ban Chiang, Thailand | husk remains in potsherds | ? | 3500 bc | Yen 1982 |
| Ban Na Di, Thailand | milled rice kernels | ? | 1500–900 bc | Higham & Kijngam 1984 Chang & Loresto 1984 |
| Ulu Leang, S. Sulawesi, Indonesia | carbonized grains and glume fragments | ? | c. 4000 bc | Glover 1977 |
| Solana, N. Luzon, Phillippines | glume imprints on potsherds | ? | c. 3400 bp | R. Shutler, Jr. (pers. comm.) |
| Luo-jia-jiao, Zhejiang, China | carbonized grains and broken husks | *indica* and *sinica* (*keng*) | 7000 bp | Team of Luo-jia-jiao Site 1981 |
| Ho-mu-tu, Zhejiang, China | carbonized grains, husks, straw | *indica* | 5008 bc | Chekiang Provincial Cultural Commission & Chekiang Provincial Museum 1976· |
| Heng-ch'un, Taiwan, China | glume imprints on potsherds | *indica* | 3985 bp | Li 1983 |
| Chih-shan-yen, Taipei, Taiwan, China | carbonized grains and brown rice | *sinica* (*keng*) | 4095–3500 bp | Wang 1984 |
| Yang-shao, Honan, China | glume imprint on pottery | ? | c. 3200–2500 bc | Chang 1983 |
| Xom Trai Cave, northwest Vietnam | ? | *indica* and *sinica* | 6000–4000 bp | Dao 1985 |

[*] The age of rice cultivation at the Koldihwa site may be as recent as 1500 bc.

however, too few to provide critical information on the relative chronology of the beginnings of rice cultivation in different countries.

Within the above belt, the differentiation of the annual cultigen is thought to have taken place in different areas between 15 000 and 10 000 years ago. Similarly, the initial cultivation of rice could have evolved independently at different locations within or bordering the belt, especially the latter. However, contacts among the peoples of the different areas may have occurred much earlier than is traditionally believed (Chang 1976a, b, 1983).

## Ecogeographic diversification

The spread of the early forms of the cultigen into new environments generally occurred along a gradient of one or more of the following factors: latitude, altitude, water table or depth, edaphic, and biotic elements. In turn, these factors may be partitioned into (a) physical and chemical properties of the soil; (b) rainfall, temperature, and water regimes; (c) competition with other plants; (d) agronomic practices; and (e) the grower's needs and preferences; each of which may interact with each of the three main systems of cultivation: dryland, wetland, and deepwater (Chang 1976b, O'Toole & Chang 1979). Such interactions have led to a great proliferation in varietal diversity. In tropical and subtropical areas, where multiple cropping of rice was feasible, the crop season added another dimension to the diversification process. The resulting ecotypes are summarized in Figure 25.1 (Chang 1985).

A question frequently raised is which of the systems of cultivation is the most developed? Based on plant characters such as regeneration ability, tillering at the higher nodes, root system, grain dormancy, grain weight, grain pubescence, and photoperiodicity, as well as the evolution of the landscape, the dryland cultivars are the most advanced type, followed by the deepwater type and then the shallow-water wetland type (Chang 1976b). This indicates that upland rice cultivation is not the most ancient form of rice culture, as has been suggested on the basis of observations confined to hilly areas where local tribes retained many of their ethnic customs.

## Dispersal

The cultigens were dispersed primarily as seed (grain) – although the floating (very deep water) rices can be spread in floodwater by means of a separated tiller carrying some roots – whereas, in the wild relatives, the rhizomes and broken plant parts may have played a part in dispersal. The physical agents of dispersal were flowing water and mud, large animals, birds, and, most importantly, man. People moving from one place to another carried rice grain both as food and as a commodity for exchange (Chang 1983).

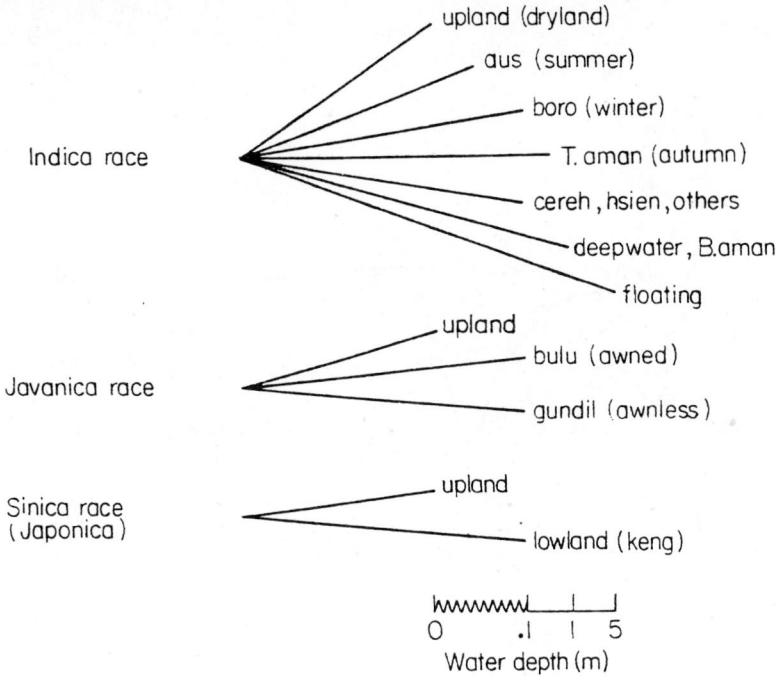

**Figure 25.1**  Grouping of Asian rice cultivars by ecogeographic race, hydrologic–edaphic–cultural regime and crop season. Cultivars grown in standing water belong to the lowland type (adapted from Chang 1985).

The proposed routes of dispersal of the three ecogeographic races of Asian rice (*indica*, *sinica*, and *javanica*) are shown in Figure 25.2 (Chang 1976a, b). More recent analyses have largely confirmed this pattern of spread (Naka-gahra *et al*. 1975, Chang 1985, Watabe 1985). The direction of dispersal from South Asia and mainland Southeast Asia to insular Southeast Asia is suggested by:

(a)  the relative paucity of the wild relatives of the cultigen in insular southeast Asia;
(b)  the shorter history of agriculture on the islands;
(c)  the abundance of root crops and relatively low population density on the islands until the last two millennia; and
(d)  the more advanced features of rice cultivars found in Indonesia, the Central Cordillera region of the Philippines, and the mountainous areas of Taiwan, as described below (see also Chang in press).

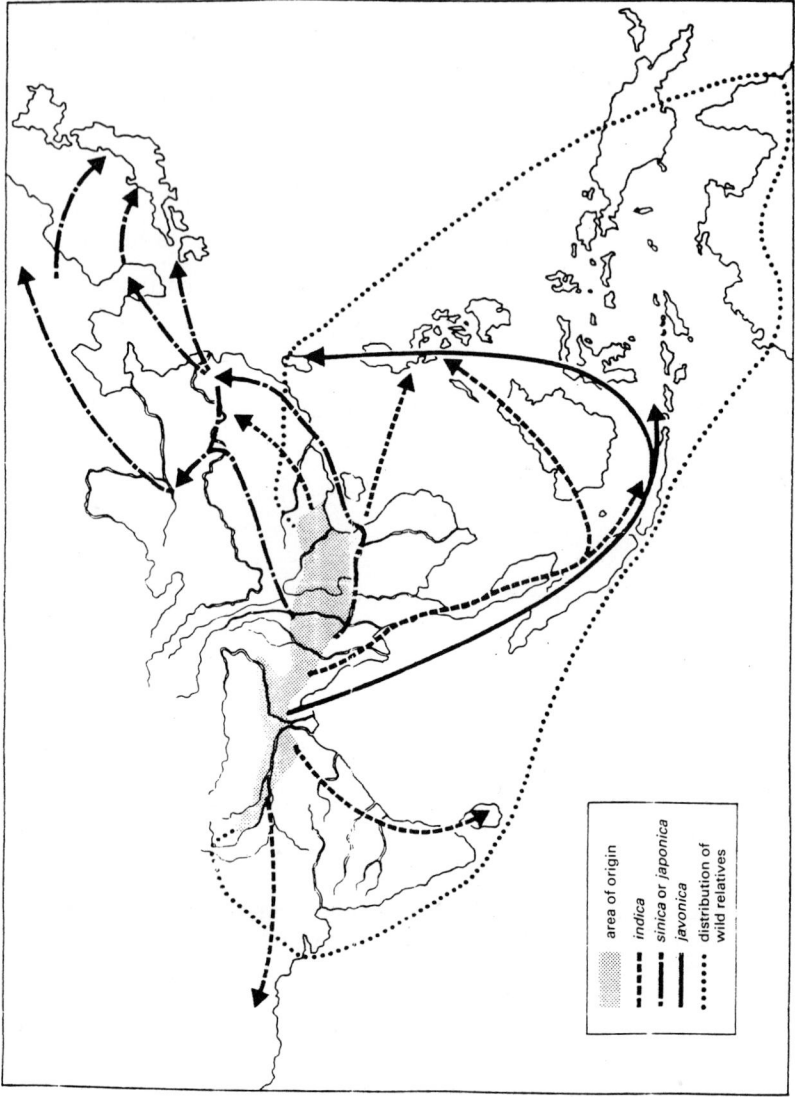

**Figure 25.2** Distribution of wild relatives and spread of ecogeographic races of *Oryza sativa* in Asia and southwestern Oceania (adapted from Chang 1976a).

Our recent studies of three ecotypes – the *bulu* varieties of Indonesia or the *javanica* race, the dryland (hill) rices of mainland Southeast Asia, and the *aus* type (summer, intermediate between wetland and dryland types) of the Bengal Bay area – have shown that the three groups are closely related, especially the *bulu* and the hill rices. These two groups share a number of common characteristics: tall plant stature; low tillering ability; large, bold and heavy grains; intermediate amylose content of the endosperm; and long and thick roots (Chang in press). The above characteristics also represent an advanced state of evolutionary changes. The hill rices are undoubtedly the most advanced ecotype of the semi-aquatic species (Chang 1976b).

## Contrasts between the Asian and African cultigens

The African cultigen (*O. glaberrima*) probably has a shorter history of cultivation than its Asian counterpart, dating back to about 1500 bc in West Africa (Portères 1956). The African cultivars have less diversity in many morphological and ecological features than the Asian cultivars largely due to more restricted human migrations and crop dispersals having taken place in Africa than in Asia. The contrast in these factors affecting ecogeographic diversification in Asia and West Africa is shown in Table 25.2. *O. glaberrima* has more primitive features than *O. sativa* (Chang 1985).

**Table 25.2** Contrast in ecogeographic diversification between *Oryza sativa* and *O. glaberrima*.

| Factor | Asia | West Africa |
|---|---|---|
| Latitudinal spread | 10°S–53°N | 5°N–17°N |
| Topography | hilly | flat |
| Population density | high | low |
| Movement of people | extensive | restricted |
| Iron tools | many | none or few |
| Draft animals | water buffalo and oxen | little used |

## Areas for future endeavour

In spite of a number of significant advances in archaeological and ethnobotanical findings during the past decade, and the multidisciplinary syntheses attempted by the author (Chang 1976a, b, 1985, 1987), the history and spread of the Asian rices is still obscured by many unresolved questions. These relate particularly to the following gaps in current knowledge.

(a)   Archaeological excavations remain insufficient in number and in geographic coverage (Table 25.1). This is particularly true of India, both mainland and insular Southeast Asia, and south and southwest China.

(b)    Information on the prehistory of the people of Southeast Asia and their kinship to the Chinese people is still meagre and divergent (see the proceedings of the 1985 Conference on Prehistory held at Peñablanca, Cagayan Valley of the Philippines by the Indo-Pacific Prehistory Association).

(c)    Many biologists have based their inferences concerning the evolution and spread of rice on specimens which have been subject to human dispersal or disturbance in rather recent times. Gaps in the biosystematics of the genus *Oryza* remain to be filled, and studies based on electrophoretic analyses have not been critically assessed in relation to ecological factors and the grain quality of the materials being sampled (Chang 1985, in press).

# References

Anderson, E. 1952. *Plants, man and life.* Berkeley: University of California Press.

Chang, T. T. 1976a. The rice cultures. *Philosophical Transactions of the Royal Society of London* **B275**, 143–57.

Chang, T. T. 1976b. The origin, evolution, cultivation, dissemination, and diversification of Asian and African rices. *Euphytica* **25**, 425–41.

Chang, T. T. 1976c. *Manual on genetic conservation of rice germplasm for evaluation and utilization.* Los Banos, Philippines: International Rice Research Institute.

Chang, T. T. 1983. The origins and early cultures of the cereal grains and food legumes. In *The origins of Chinese civilization*, D. N. Keightley (ed.), 65–94. Berkeley: University of California Press.

Chang, T. T. 1985. Crop history and genetic conservation: rice – a case study. *Iowa State Journal of Research* **59**, 425–55.

Chang, T. T. 1987. The impact of rice on human civilization and population expansion. *Interdisciplinary Science Reviews* **12**, 63–9.

Chang, T. T. in press. The ethnobotany of rice in insular Southeast Asia. *Asian Perspectives.*

Chang, T. T. & G. C. Loresto 1984. The rice remains. In *Prehistoric investigations in northeastern Thailand*, part ii, C. Higham & A. Kijngam (eds), 384–5, 390. Oxford: British Archaeological Reports, International Series 231.

Chekiang Provincial Cultural Commission and Chekiang Provincial Museum 1976. Ho-mu-tu discovery of important primitive society, an important site (in Chinese). *Wen Wu* **8**, 6–13.

Dao, T. T. 1985. Types of rice cultivation and its related civilization in Vietnam. *East Asian Cultural Studies* **24**, 41–56.

Glover, I. C. 1977. The Late Stone Age in eastern Indonesia. *World Archaeology* **9**, 42–61.

Hawkes, J. G. 1969. The ecological background of plant domestication. In *The domestication and exploitation of plants and animals*, P. J. Ucko & G. W. Dimbleby (eds), 17–29. London: Duckworth.

Helbaek, H. 1969. Plant collecting, dry-farming and irrigation agriculture in prehistoric Deh Luran. In *Prehistory and human ecology of the Deh Luran Plain,*

F. Hole, K. V. Flannery & J. A. Neely (eds), 384–426. Ann Arbor: University of Michigan.

Higham,. C. & A. Kijngam 1984. The excavation of Ban Na Di, Bang Muang Phruk and Non Kao Noi. In *Prehistoric investigations in northeastern Thailand*, part i, C. Higham & A. Kijngam (eds), 22–56. Oxford: British Archaeological Reports, International Series 231.

IBPGR–IRRI Rice Advisory Committee 1982. Conservation of the wild rices of tropical Asia. *Plant Genetic Resources Newsletter* **49**, 13–18.

Jones, R. & B. Meehan 1989. Plant foods of the Gidjingali: ethnographic and archaeological perspectives from northern Australia on tuber and seed exploitation. In *Foraging and farming: the evolution of plant exploitation*, D. R. Harris & G. C. Hillman (eds), ch. 7. London: Unwin Hyman.

Li, K. C. 1983. Problems raised by the K'en-Ting excavation of 1977. *Bulletin of the Department of Archaeology and Anthropology, National Taiwan University* **43**, 86–116, pl. I–IX.

Morishima, H., Y. Sano & H. I. Oka 1984. Differentiation of perennial and annual types due to habitat conditions in the wild rice *Oryza perennis*. *Plant Sytematics and Evolution* **144**, 119–35.

Nakagahra, M., T. Akihama & K. Hayashi 1975. Genetic variation and geographic cline of esterase isozymes in native rice varieties. *Japanese Journal of Genetics* **50**, 373–82.

O'Toole, J. C. & T. T. Chang 1979. Drought resistance in cereals – Rice: a case study. In *Stress physiology in crop plants*, H. Mussell & R. Staples (eds), 374–405. New York: Wiley.

Portères, R. 1956. Taxonomie agrobotanique des riz cultivés O. *sativa* Linne et O. *glaberrima* Steudel. *Journal d'Agriculture Tropicale et de Botanique Appliquée* **3**, 341–84, 541–80, 627–700, 821–56.

Sahara, M. & T. Sato 1984. The earliest rice culture of India (in Japanese). *Archaeology Journal* (Japan) **228**, 31–4.

Sharma, G. R. & D. Manda 1980. Excavations at Mahagara 1977–78 (A Neolithic settlement in the Belan Valley). *Archaeology of the Vindhyas and the Ganga Valley 6*. Department of Ancient History, Culture and Archaeology, University of Allahabad, India. (Original not seen.)

Team of Luo-jia-jiao Site 1981. Excavation at Luo-jia-jiao site in Tong-Xiang County of Zhejiang (in Chinese). *Bulletin of the Zhejiang Provincial Archaeological Institute* 1981, 1–44, pl. I–XVI.

Watabe, T. 1985. Origin and dispersal of rice in Asia. *East Asian Cultural Studies* **24**, 33–9.

Wang, S. C. 1984. *The Neolithic site of Chih-shan-yen* (in Chinese with English summary). Taipei, Taiwan: Literature Commission of Taipei City.

White, J. C. 1989. Ethnoecological observations on wild and cultivated rice and yams in northeastern Thailand. In *Foraging and farming: the evolution of plant exploitation*, D. R. Harris & G. C. Hillman (eds), ch. 9. London: Unwin Hyman.

Whyte, R. O. 1974. An environmental interpretation of the origin of Asian cereals. *Indian Journal of Genetics* **34A**, 1–11.

Yen, D. E. 1982. Ban Chiang pottery and rice. *Expedition* **24**, 51–64.

Zeven, A. C. 1973. Dr. Th. H. Engelbrecht's view on the origin of cultivated plants. *Euphytica* **22**, 279–86.

# 26 Crops of the Pacific: new evidence from the chemical analysis of organic residues in pottery

H. EDWARD HILL and JOHN EVANS

It has long been assumed that the cultivated plants of the Pacific Islands were introduced into Melanesia, Micronesia, and Polynesia, largely from South-east Asia, in prehistoric times. European accounts of the islands, from the 17th century onwards, often record the presence of particular cultigens on individual islands and island groups, and the oral traditions of the Pacific Islanders themselves add to the information available on crop history. But, to trace the introduction and spread of crops in the Pacific in early times, archaeobotanical evidence is needed. Unfortunately, this is unusually difficult to obtain in the Pacific because most of the cultigens are vegetatively propagated crops, such as taro (*Colocasia esculenta*), yams (*Dioscorea* spp.), and sweet potato (*Ipomoea batatas*), which normally reproduce asexually. Consequently, the archaeobotanist cannot expect to trace the prehistoric presence of Pacific cultigens through the recovery of charred seeds or even by pollen analysis, although some inferences can be drawn from the types of food-preparation tools which are sometimes discovered during excavation of archaeological sites in the islands.

If progress is to be made in tracing the spread of Pacific cultigens, new methods need to be devised to obtain direct evidence of prehistoric plant use. One such method, with which we are currently experimenting, is described in this chapter, and some preliminary results are presented. The method involves the chemical analysis of organic residues recoverable from excavated pieces of pottery.

## Chemical analysis of organic residues

The application of chemical analysis to the identification of plant-food residues in potsherds has recently offered new hope of recovering direct evidence of the chronology and routes of migration of plants southward and eastward into the Pacific (Hill 1984).

It was first demonstrated over a decade ago that the analysis of organic residues found on (or trapped within) the ceramic matrices of potsherds can yield information on vessel usage (Evans & Biek 1976). The procedure developed is as follows. Obvious residues are first scraped from the potsherd and the scrapings examined under the scanning electron microscope, (a) for any recognizable tissues, especially plant tissues, as these are more likely to survive in histologically identifiable form, and (b) for any signs of layering. Any inner surface of a pot which is less than perfectly smooth will tend not to have been cleaned thoroughly, and it is common to find overcooked or charred layers on top of previously unremoved thin layers of food from earlier cooking episodes.

The crude residues can then be examined by infra-red spectroscopy (IR); a small portion of the sample is crushed with potassium bromide (KBr), and pressed into a disk for examination in a twin-beam IR spectrometer. (By using a KBr disk as a reference in the twin second beam, any impurities in the KBr disk are cancelled out.) Chemical discontinuities caused by the presence of organic material on the sample disk will appear as frequency peaks corresponding to the chemical components present. If this initial test demonstrates the presence of any organic compounds, more sophisticated analyses are performed on the same material.

The sample is crushed and passed through a 100 μm-mesh sieve. The fine material is then extracted in a soxhlet apparatus with the solvents heptane, chloroform, propanol, and water. This group of solvents not only extracts specific groups of material, in each case, but is suitable for subsequent analysis by high performance liquid chromatography (HPLC). Heptane extracts are particularly useful for identifying non-polar lipids, triglycerides, and waxes; chloroform extracts for tree resins, drying oils, and wood tars; propanol for phospholipids, sugars, amino acids, and proteins; and water for polar lipids, salts, sugars, and other carbohydrates. Samples of the heptane extracts can then be analysed by HPLC without further treatment. However, further information can be obtained by hydrolising the extracts and converting any fatty acids obtained into naphthacyl esters – again for examination by HPLC. A proportion of the extracts can also be hydrolised to convert any fatty acids into methyl esters for examination by gas/liquid chromatography (GLC). As for the chloroform and propanol extracts, these can also be analysed by IR, GLC, HPLC, and ultraviolet spectroscopy (UV) for a range of component compounds including carbohydrates, and, by electrophoresis, for proteins. All water extracts are tested for a range of inorganic ions such as chlorides, carbonates, and phosphates. (The presence of significant concentrations of phosphates would suggest that the pot had contained food which involved meat or meat products.) Emission spectroscopy can also be used to identify any elements additional to those typical of soils and archaeological deposits generally.

The principal problems which we have encountered in this type of study are (a) incompleteness of extraction, (b) ascertainment of the degree of exchange of organic substances between the sherd and the surrounding soil (which is likely to have been rich in modern organic debris and micro-flora), (c) the shortage of data on the nature of the decomposition processes involved when food residues are buried for long periods, and (d) identification of the various compounds extracted from the organic residues.

The first of these problems, completeness of extraction, has been overcome by using the wide range of solvents described above, starting with a non-polar solvent such as heptane. In this way, extraction appears to be practically complete. The second problem of organic exchange with the archaeological deposit appears to be less serious than at first feared. In a study by Allan (1984) of medieval potsherds from Exeter, the samples proved to contain no detectable organic material, thus suggesting that there was only minimal contamination from organic substances in the surrounding archaeological deposits. Nevertheless, absorbtion of organic compounds from the archaeological deposits remains a possibility, and, in this type of study, analyses of soil samples are a desirable adjunct to analyses of the sherds (Morgan et al. 1984). Sampling environments and local vegetation should clearly also be noted.

Experience has indicated that the third problem of decomposition post-deposition is again less serious than was first supposed. In the case of charred residues it appears that the very act of charring (a) 'sterilizes' the material through the exposure to high temperatures, and (b) produces a protective, superficial layer of heavily charred material beneath which the plant tissues are often only slightly degraded by heat and are protected from reinvasion by microflora which would otherwise affect their decomposition. All the deeper tissues therefore remain relatively unchanged until sampled for analysis. Similarly, when organic materials penetrate the ceramic matrix, they are again protected by the microscopic pores of the pot, becoming sealed either by bacterial mucilages (from decomposition at the surface) or by other processes that show little penetration.

The fourth problem (that of identifying – at the chemical level – the components of each extract) is somewhat complex, but recent advances in instrumentation – especially in chromatography – have simplified the task (Condanin et al. 1976). The remaining difficulty concerns the small quantities of many of the extracted components. With samples of tens or hundreds of mg full analysis is feasible, but with samples of 10 mg or less, full analysis becomes impractical without special precautions, although it is possible to carry it out (thus pre-empting the necessity of sub-sampling), and thus complete at least the preliminary analysis.

The aim of the present project has been to develop an analytical method which is reasonably sensitive, easy to apply, and relatively cheap. The equipment should also prove to be more readily available than that required for more sophisticated forms of analysis. The result, we hope, is a methodology accessible to, and usable by, the archaeologist.

# Identification of Pacific food plants from the chemical–spectra 'characterization'

For the major Pacific cultigens under study, there are no published 'standards' defining their composition in terms of spectra (frequency distributions) from IR, HPLC, GLC, and UV analyses. In consequence, much of the first two years of this study has been devoted to analysing samples of modern specimens of the appropriate plants – wherever possible in both cooked and raw state. We have now produced standards for the following six major Pacific cultigens: banana, rice, sago, sweet potato, taro, and yam. These analyses have proved particularly successful at the comparatively crude first stage of their examination by IR (Hill *et al.* 1985). Some 42 plant samples were analysed in order to establish the extent of the components of variation within each species in (and potential information content of) spectra from this relatively simple first stage of chemical analysis. These ranged from fresh market samples, stored fresh samples, dried samples, and some dried and powdered samples, and included eight banana, eight rice, six sago, six sweet potato, eight taro, and seven yam specimens.

It was clear that all the plants would contain many compounds in common, and that there would be some duplication of spectrum frequencies. In order to establish an objective and valid 'fingerprint' for any plant, we therefore logged all peaks within the spectra from every sample with a view to identifying peaks which are either unique for any one plant, or else consistent and strongly developed for a particular plant.

Early on in our investigations, chloroform and propanol extracts appeared to be providing no additional information on wavelength peaks, at least for the particular plants we were studying. Once this was recognized, the heptane extracts were preferred for the full sequence of 42 plant samples, and were examined in detail.

For the cultigens studied, we were able to identify certain peaks which seemed to characterize each plant, and these were listed as a basis for identifying residues of the same plant food in archaeological samples (Table 26.1). On this basis, IR appears to offer some potential. On its own, however, it provides an insufficient basis for fully secure identifications of plant residues and requires independent chemo–taxonomic criteria generated from different forms of chromatographic analysis, such as thin–layer chromatography (TLC), HPLC, and GLC. Spectra from 'standards' and archaeological specimens respectively are matched by simple visual inspection via the use of transparent 'overlays' of each of the standard spectra.

## Analysis of archaeological samples

All the archaeological samples considered here have come from the site of Rungruw in the southern part of Yap Island in the Caroline Islands of Micronesia (Intoh & Leach 1985). The stratigraphy of the site was observed

**Table 26.1** Infra-red frequencies of the principal peaks from IR spectroscopic analysis of heptane extractions from (a) samples of modern plant foods, (b) samples of residues from pottery from the Micronesian site of Rungruw. (The frequencies do not represent a continuous scale, but merely those points at which the peaks occur, see Figs 26.1 & 26.2.) It can be seen that there are a number of peaks in the archaeological spectra which coincide precisely with these in the 'standards'.

| Wavenumber cm$^{-1}$: | 1750 | 1700 | 1660 | 1600 | 1510 | 1280 | 1260 | 1235 | 1110 | 1100 | 1020 | 970 | 900 |
|---|---|---|---|---|---|---|---|---|---|---|---|---|---|
| (a) Banana | | | | | / | / | / | | | | / | | |
| Sweet potato | | | | | | | | | | | | | |
| Rice | / | / | | | | | | | | | | | |
| Sago | | / | / | | | | | / | / | | | | |
| Taro | | | / | / | / | | | / | | / | | | |
| Yam | | | | | | | | | | | | / | / |
| (b) YP83–2262 | | | | | | | | | | | | | |
| YP83–2540 | | | | / | | | / | / | | | / | | |
| YP83–2618 | | | | / | | | / | / | | / | / | | |
| YP83–2673 | / | / | / | / | | / | | | | | | | |

NB   / denotes presence.

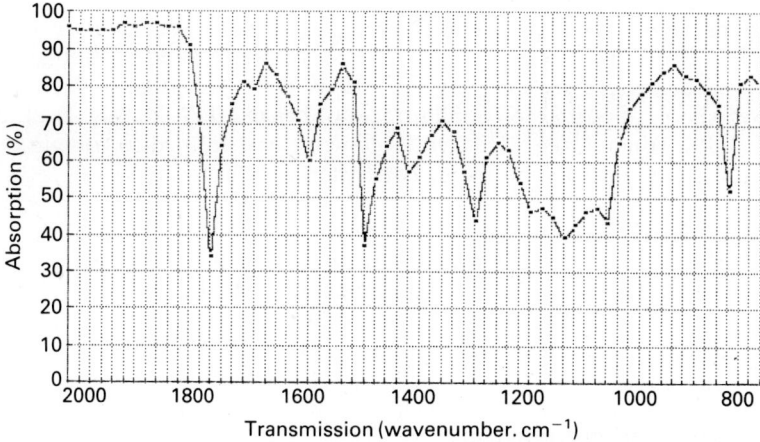

**Figure 26.1** Typical spectrum from infra-red spectroscopic analysis of a modern sample of banana.

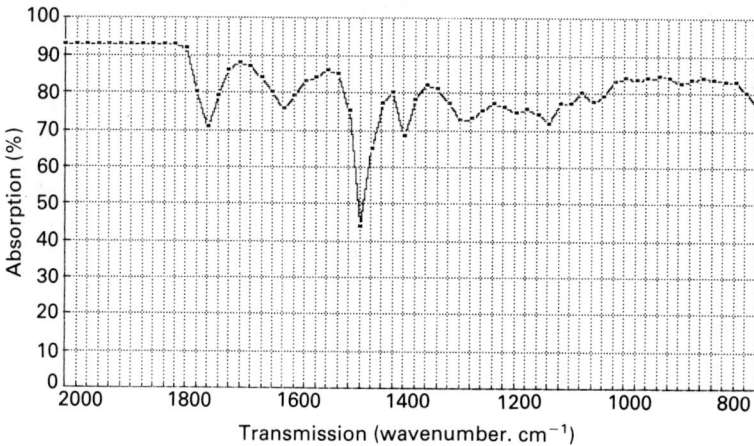

**Figure 26.2** Spectrum from infra-red spectroscopic analysis of a typical sample (YP83–2262) of a surface residue from pottery from the site of Rungruw on the Micronesian island of Yap.

from two test pits, and all 17 archaeological samples came from two squares between the test pits.

All the samples from the Rungruw site were extracted with heptane as outlined above. Their IR spectra were then compared with the 'standard' spectra from each of the six plants studied so far (Figs 26.1 & 26.2). Any peaks of matching IR transmission frequency were listed for each sherd (Table 26.1). All IR spectra with good matches were then compared with the transparencies of 'standard' spectra from the modern plant foods by means of the transparent overlays, not merely to confirm the coincidence of the relevant diagnostic peak positions (transmission frequency) but also to compare the pattern produced by the relative peak strengths.

Two sherds appeared to contain traces of banana (Figs 26.1 & 26.2), one appeared to contain rice traces, and a fourth sherd seemed to contain both taro and sweet potato. The sherds concerned were as follows:

YP83–2262   Calcareous sherd   Rungruw site, 2150 bp – banana
YP83–2540   Plain ware         Rungruw site,   550 bp – banana
YP83–2618   Plain ware         Rungruw site, 1900 bp – taro,
                                   sweet potato
YP83–2673   Calcareous sherd   Rungruw site, 2150 bp – rice

## Summary and conclusions

Although these results are very preliminary, they suggest that:

(a)   surface residues on ancient potsherd do, in many cases, contain organic residues;
(b)   these residues appear to have suffered little obvious denaturation since their deposition;
(c)   contamination by organics from the archaeological matrix is minimal if the specimens are sampled with due care;
(d)   IR peaks obtained from neptane extractions are sufficiently clear and strongly developed to allow comparison with the diagnostic peaks of 'standard' spectra from IR analyses of modern plant foods (both in respect of the transmission of the peaks (i.e. their position) and their strength); and thus
(e)   IR peaks allow tentative identifications of at least some of the foodstuffs formerly present in the pots concerned.

Further work, with a greater number of archaeological samples, is now in hand. Also, the validity of these preliminary identifications will be tested by means of full analyses using HPLC, GLC, and TLC applied to both reference plants and sherds. In view of the apparent presence of traces of sweet potato on a sherd dated as early as 50 ad, a full investigation is clearly justified.

Despite the success of these preliminary analyses, it must be stressed that IR analysis in itself is relatively insensitive, and confirmation is required by further analyses by TLC, GLC, and HPLC. If the results are confirmed, then IR can confidently be used as the basis for rapid screening of even very small samples and for the selection of those worth subjecting to other, more complex, forms of analysis which offer the prospect of even closer resolution of sample identity.

Further archaeological samples from the Santa Cruz and Reef Islands groups and from Ambon Island in Indonesia are now under analysis, and it is hoped that these further analyses will contribute more to our understanding of the prehistory of Pacific food plants.

While more elaborate analytical systems can doubtless yield similar information, for routine analyses they are beyond the limits of most archaeological budgets. The simpler techniques outlined in this chapter clearly offer a means of meeting the rapidly growing need for routine analysis of organic residues from potsherds found on archaeological sites.

## Acknowledgements

We are pleased to acknowledge with grateful thanks the supply of the following study materials. *Modern plant samples*: G. Sieveking (British Museum), F. Leach (University of Otago), B. Matthews (Australian National University), G. E. Wickens & J. Keesing (Royal Botanic Gardens, Kew), I. Glover (Institute of Archaeology, London). *Archaeological samples*: F. Leach (University of Otago).

## References

Allan, J. A. 1984. Medieval and post-medieval finds from Exeter 1971–1980. *Exeter Archaeological Reports* **3**, 37–9.

Condanin, J., F. Formenti, M. O. Metais, M. Michel & P. Blond 1976. The application of gas chromatography to the tracing of oil in ancient amphorae. *Archaeometry* **18**, 195–201.

Evans, J. & L. Biek 1976. *Overcooked food residues on potsherds. Proceedings of Archaeometry Symposium*, Edinburgh: National Museum of Antiquities of Scotland.

Hill, H. E. 1984. Chemical analysis of pottery residues. *Bulletin of the Experimental Firing Group* **2**, 86–9.

Hill, H. E., J. Evans & M. Card 1985. Organic residues on 3000 year old potsherds from Natunuku, Fiji. *New Zealand Journal of Archaeology* **7**, 125–8.

Intoh, M. & F. Leach 1985. *Archaeological investigations in the Yap Islands, Micronesia.* Oxford: British Archaeological Reports, International Series **277**.

Morgan, E. D., L. Titus, R. J. Small & C. Edwards 1984. Gas chromatographic analysis of fatty material from a Thule midden. *Archaeometry* **26**, 43–8.

# 27 Cytological and genetical evidence on the domestication and diffusion of crops within the Americas

## BARBARA PICKERSGILL

A roster of crops grown in the Americas before 1492 shows superficially striking similarities between the two principal centres of cultural development in the New World: Mesoamerica and the Andean area. In both, maize, beans, and squash were the main agricultural staples, with amaranths and chenopods as additional grain crops. Root crops such as manioc and sweet potato, and fruits such as pineapple and avocado, were also present in both areas by the time of European contact.

More critical scrutiny of the crop lists shows that, in a surprising number of genera, the same crop was represented by different species in Middle and South America (Heiser 1965). This is true of cotton, chile peppers, *Chenopodium*, *Amaranthus*, *Canavalia* beans, and four of the five domesticated species of *Cucurbita*, while common beans and lima beans were represented by different infraspecific variants. Maize certainly spread from one area to the other, but potatoes, which are also ecologically adaptable and culturally readily acceptable, did not.

Proponents of diffusion and proponents of independent invention of agriculture in the Americas have therefore both used botanical evidence to support their respective positions. The sorts of questions which require critical evaluation can be summarized as follows (see Pickersgill 1972 for further discussion):

(a)  When a given species (e.g. *Zea mays*) is found in both Middle and South America, does this indicate spread by man, or independent domestications from a widespread wild ancestor?

(b)  When a given crop (e.g. cotton) is represented by distinct species in Middle and South America, has speciation occurred after a single domestication and spread by man, or have there been independent domestications in each area from wild ancestors which already belonged to distinct species?

(c)  What is the role of companion weeds which share the same gene pool as the crop (e.g. the crop/weed pairs of chenopods in Mexico and the Andes)? Is the weed to be regarded as the probable progenitor of its corresponding domesticate, or are the companion weeds escapees derived from their respective domesticates?

Archaeobotanical evidence, although theoretically crucial in resolving questions of diffusion versus independent invention, has so far proved of limited value. The archaeobotanical record in the Americas is still so incomplete that additional excavations are liable to change the picture dramatically. Supposedly ancient specimens of New World crop plants may also be controversial as regards their age or identification. Finally, the archaeobotanical record may not include the plant parts necessary for critical identification to species.

Since we last reviewed the origins and spread of crops in the Americas (Pickersgill & Heiser 1977), little new archaeobotanical evidence has been found which is relevant to domestication versus diffusion. However, there has been new work on genetical and/or chromosomal differentiation in living representatives of some of these crops. To illustrate the potential of these new lines of evidence, some selected case studies will be reviewed. First, though, it is necessary to set the question of diffusion versus independent domestication in its phytogeographical context.

## Phytogeographical background

Data from plate tectonics indicate that North America (including Middle America) and South America are derived from fragmentation of different supercontinents. They have thus been essentially separate since the Jurassic (i.e. before the origin of flowering plants), until their present, comparatively recent, connection developed during the Pliocene. North and South America would thus be expected to have basically different floras, offering different bases for the exploitation and later domestication of useful plants. It may, therefore, seem unlikely that wild representatives of at least seven genera should be not only present in both continents but also domesticated independently in each.

However, over geological time, plants have a surprising capacity for natural long-distance dispersal. Gentry (1982) has recently reviewed plant migration between the two American continents, concentrating on genera which are not used by man and not found in man-disturbed habitats. The evidence which he summarizes demonstrates that extant genera and even species have had opportunities to move between Middle and South America, and that sufficient wild taxa have migrated in both directions for there to be no *a priori* need to invoke human intervention when an economically useful genus or species is found in both areas. It is not easy to determine whether disjunctions in range between Middle and South America are so ancient that man is unlikely to be implicated, or so recent that he is a prime suspect.

However, some indications may come from differentiation, or lack of differentiation, in modern representatives of the disjunct taxa.

## Nature and causes of differentiation in disjunct populations

A new disjunct population may be founded by individuals representing only a small part of the variation in the progenitor population (founder effect), or the variation introduced by the original immigrants may be reduced by random events in the initially small new population (genetic drift), or selective pressures may be different in the new environment, favouring a different complex of adaptive characters. Any or all of these factors may lead to morphological differences between the original and the disjunct populations, which are then often treated by taxonomists as distinct, though closely related, species.

Less visible parts of the plant, such as the chromosomes, may be similarly affected. Heterochromatin appears as dark knobs or bands on the chromosomes when appropriate staining methods are used. Its amount and position has proved useful in assessing relationships between races of maize from different geographical areas (see below). Larger-scale changes may also occur. Segments may be interchanged between non-homologous chromosomes, or may become inverted relative to their original arrangement. Such changes are usually comparatively rare, and may then prove to be useful evolutionary markers, as in *Capsicum* (see below).

When two populations, or two species, differ by a major chromosomal change, the hybrid between them is usually partially sterile. This form of hybrid sterility arises very rapidly because it represents a single, simple change. On the other hand, gradual accumulation of small differences between populations which have been isolated for a long time may also result in hybrid sterility. In deciding whether plants belong to different species, more weight is given to the second type of sterility than the first. Hybrid sterility cannot be used on its own to argue that similar crops in Middle and South America represents distinct species. However, if something is known about the causes, then hybrid sterility may be a useful ancillary source of information about relationships.

Recently, it has been found that enzymes which catalyse the same reaction, and which appear to be products of the same gene, may differ in their molecular structure. Again, these differences may occur within or between species. Different molecular forms of the same enzyme are known as isozymes. Isozyme studies are proving a powerful tool for investigating various evolutionary problems, and therefore figure largely in the case studies which follow. These have been selected to illustrate different histories of migration, domestication, and genetic differentiation in the crops of Middle and South America.

# Tomato

The red- and orange-fruited species of tomato form a closely related group within the genus *Lycopersicon*, consisting of the domesticated tomato (*L. esculentum* var. *esculentum*), the cherry tomato (*L. esculentum* var. *cerasiforme*), the currant tomato (*L. pimpinellifolium*), and a Galapagos endemic which does not concern us here. Apart from the cherry tomato, which has become a pantropical weed, wild species of *Lycopersicon* are all confined to north-western South America.

Many years ago, Jenkins (1948) concluded that the tomato was domestic-ated in Mexico, from the cherry tomato, after the latter had spread north as a weed (i.e. after the spread of agriculture). However, the domesticated tomato is also closely related to, and forms fertile hybrids with, the currant tomato. It could therefore be argued that the tomato was domesticated in northwestern South America, from *L. pimpinellifolium*, with the cherry tomato representing either an intermediate stage in domestication or an escape derived from the crop.

Isozymes of these species have been studied by Rick & Fobes (1975). The most variable species is *L. pimpinellifolium*, which contains all the isozyme alleles present in weedy and domesticated *L. esculentum*, as well as some unique alleles. Despite the striking morphological variation in fruits of Mexican domesticated tomatoes, both the domesticated tomato and the cherry tomato are isozymically remarkably uniform throughout their range, except in Ecuador and Peru. Here, where *L. esculentum* overlaps the range of *L. pimpinellifolium*, both the domesticated tomato and the cherry tomato carry many variant isozymes which are present also in the currant tomato.

Unfortunately, two interpretations of these data are possible. One is that *L. esculentum* was domesticated from *L. pimpinellifolium*, as described above, and initially contained many of the isozymes present in its progenitor. Speciation occurred subsequent to domestication, as first ecological and later geographical isolation permitted morphological divergence between the wild progenitor and its domesticated derivative. The second possibility is that the same variant isozymes are present in the currant tomato, the cherry tomato, and the domesticated tomato in Ecuador and Peru because these three interfertile taxa hybridize and exchange genes wherever they occur together. In that case, *L. esculentum* presumably diverged from *L. pimpinelli-folium* without the intervention of man, and the domesticated tomato is derived from conspecific weedy forms represented by the cherry tomato.

Rick & Fobes (1975) consider the second hypothesis more likely. It is not contradicted by the limited archaeological evidence. There are still no early archaeological records of tomatoes in Mexico, even though the seeds are almost inevitably ingested when the fruits are eaten, pass intact through the human digestive tract, and are easily recognized by their hairy seed coats. Tomato seeds would therefore be expected in coprolites from the Tehuacan valley and other sites if the fruits were being consumed. Until recently, there were no archaeological records of tomato in the Andean region either. Now,

however, Engel (1976) has reported 'alder or tomato seeds' in pre-agricultural and early agricultural sites in Peru. They are recorded as part of the diet,
but unfortunately do not seem to have been critically identified by a botanist.
It seems very unlikely that anyone would eat alder seeds (and also hard to
imagine alder seeds being confused with tomato), whereas both cherry and
currant tomatoes occur in coastal and highland regions of Peru. The absence
of tomatoes from later sites remains surprising.

*Lycopersicon* is thus a genus native to the Andean region which probably
remained confined to South America until after the advent of agriculture.
One of the edible-fruited species, *L. esculentum*, then spread north, perhaps as
a crop, but more likely as a tolerated weed, in the disturbed habitats
associated with agriculture. Founder effect and genetic drift during this
northward migration led to a loss of diversity in isozyme characters.
Historical, linguistic, and ethnobotanical data suggest that the tomato was
domesticated in Mexico, as a late addition to the list of cultivated plants;
spread back to South America even later; and re-acquired in South America
some of the genetic diversity lost on its northward migration.


## Maize

The genus *Zea* now includes domesticated maize and its closest known wild
relatives, the annual and perennial teosintes. Like *Lycopersicon*, *Zea* has a
limited natural range (Mexico, Guatemala, and Honduras). Unlike *Lycopersicon*, the crop seems to have been domesticated within the area of the wild
species, early in the agricultural history of the Americas. Like the domesticated tomato, domesticated maize was then spread by man from one
continent to the other. It reached the Andean highlands before 1000 bc and
became common on the coast after 850 bc (Bird 1984).

However, evidence continues to accumulate that Andean maize differs in a
number of respects from Middle American maize. Goodman & Bird (1977)
carried out a multivariate morphological analysis of 219 Latin American
races of maize. They found that Mexican and South American races
generally fell into different groups, and concluded that this supported the
view that they had developed largely independently.

Like Mexican tomatoes, Andean maize is extremely diverse in characters
subject to direct human selection. Popcorns, giant-kernelled flour corns,
sweet corns with many-rowed ears, and purple-grained corns for making
*chica* are all found in the Andes. However, again like tomato, these
morphologically diverse races are extremely uniform in at least one trait
which is not subject to direct human selection, and which betrays the narrow
genetic base of the domesticated complex. Andean maize is virtually without
heterochromatic knobs on its chromosomes (Kato-Y. 1984). The ancient
indigenous races of maize in Mexico also have low knob numbers (Wellhausen et al. 1952) and could therefore be progenitors of the Andean maize
complex. Mexican annual teosinte, often suggested as the wild ancestor of

domesticated maize, has predominantly intercalary knobs. Maize in general also has mainly intercalary knobs, but these occur at fewer positions on the maize chromosomes than on the teosinte chromosomes. Kato-Y (1984) interpreted this as indicating that maize was derived from Mexican annual teosinte and not vice versa. The restricted variation in knob position in maize would then be an example of either founder effect or genetic drift. However, it also seems possible that a primitively knobless maize could have acquired the characteristic knobs of teosinte through hybridization where the two grow together, in the same was that *Lycopersicon esculentum* acquired some of the isozyme alleles of *L. pimpinellifolium*.

Chromosomes are not the only bearers of genetic material: DNA is present also in the mitochondria and chloroplasts of plant cells. These organelles are inherited independently of the chromosomes, and variation in organelle DNA therefore provides an assessment of relationships independent of chromosomal studies. Weissinger *et al.* (1983) used two different restriction endonucleases to cleave into smaller segments the mitochondrial DNA from 93 Latin American races of maize. Digested DNA from each race was then separated by electrophoresis and the banding patterns on the gels compared. Almost all the Mesoamerican races, including three of the four ancient indigenous races of Mexico, were included in three of the 18 racial groups recognized, while maize of the Andean complex was contained in two further groups. Analyses of mitochondrial DNA therefore agreed with morphological studies and data on chromosome knobs in showing differences between Middle American and Andean maize, but the affinities between Mexican ancient indigenous and Andean maize apparent in the chromosome knob data did not show up in the mitochondrial DNA. This discrepancy may perhaps be resolved when more is known of the magnitude of the differences in mitochondrial DNA between Mesoamerican and Andean maize, and hence the number of mutational changes required to produce these differences.

At present, the evidence suggests that maize was domesticated in a single centre, in Middle America (cf. Wilkes Ch. 28, this volume, and, for a slightly different view, Bonavia & Grobman Ch. 29). However, data from morphology, chromosome knobs and mitochondrial DNA all indicate that maize underwent a considerable period of independent evolution in the Andean region after its initial introduction to South America. There seems to have been no subsequent extensive exchange or trade in maize between the two areas. South American races with Middle American affinities and Middle American races with South American affinities all seem to be relatively late introductions, emphasizing the essential independence of agricultural development in Middle and South America.

## Chile peppers

Chile peppers, the most widely used spice in the Americas at the time of European contact, represent several different species of *Capiscum*. Three entities can be clearly distinguished: *C. pubescens*, *C. baccatum*, and the *C. annuum-chinense-frutescens* complex. *C. pubescens* differs morphologically from the other domesticated peppers (except in fruit characters influenced by human selection), will not cross spontaneously with them, is separated from *C. baccatum* on the one hand, and the *C. chinense-frutescens* complex on the other hand, by at least one chromosomal interchange in each case (Pickersgill unpubl.), and carries different alleles at at least six genetic loci coding for various isozymes (McLeod *et al.* 1979). It is botanically quite inconceivable that *C. pubescens* could be directly derived from any of the other domesticates; it must have been independently domesticated from its own wild ancestor.

Similar arguments apply to *C. baccatum*, which is also morphologically, isozymically, and chromosomally distinct from the other domesticated peppers (Pickersgill *et al.* 1979; González de León 1986). *C. baccatum* and *C. pubescens* were both domesticated in the same general area (Bolivia and/or adjacent countries). Since they must each have been independently derived, from different wild ancestors, it becomes easier to accept the possibility of further independent domestications of chile peppers elsewhere in the Americas. There is, in fact, compelling evidence that there were at least two independent domestications within the *C. annuum-chinense-frutescens* complex. Domesticated *C. annuum* and domesticated *C. chinense* differ by one chromosomal interchange, which has a visible effect on the morphology of the mitotic chromosomes. Wild *C. annuum* can be divided into two different chromosome races, based on mitotic morphology: one race which is chromosomally identical to domesticated *C. annuum* and which is common in central and southern Mexico; and a second race whose mitotic chromosomes are similar to those of *C. chinense* and *C. frutescens* and which is more widespread, occurring from Colombia to the southern United States and the Antilles (Pickersgill 1971 and unpubl.). Studies on interspecific hybrids show that the chromosome race shared with domesticated *C. annuum* is further removed from the basic chromosome complement of *Capsicum*, and hence presumably evolved more recently, than the widespread chromosome race of wild *C. annuum*. In other words, a chromosomal interchange occurred before domestication in the complex of wild peppers ancestral to both domesticated *C. annuum* and domesticated *C. chinense*. Domesticated *C. annuum* developed from wild peppers belonging to the derived chromosome race, while *C. chinense* was domesticated from wild peppers belonging to the other chromosome race. The cytological uniformity of domesticated *C. annuum* is another example of founder effect, indicating its origin from a limited sample of wild peppers and enabling its place of origin to be pin-pointed more precisely, within the range of distribution of wild peppers of the appropriate chromosome race.

Morphological differences within the *C. annuum-chinense-frutescens* complex are relatively slight, and arguments based on hybrid sterility are confused by presence of the chromosomal interchange. One may therefore argue about whether wild forms in this complex should really be assigned to different species, and indeed about whether domesticated *C. annuum* and domesticated *C. chinense* are really conspecific. However, these taxonomic arguments should not be allowed to obscure, as Eshbaugh (1983) obscures, the overwhelming likelihood of at least two independent domestications of the chile peppers of this complex. Eshbaugh (1983) confuses the evolutionary lineages of the wild peppers with the chronologically later domestication of the cultivated peppers. Thus, I agree entirely with Eshbaugh that three distinct lines of evolution within *Capsicum* terminate respectively in *C. pubescens*, *C. baccatum*, and the *C. annuum-chinense-frutescens* complex. I disagree with Eshbaugh that this renders unlikely the suggestion that each domesticate arose from its own wild ancestors. I find his statement (p. 846) that the domesticated peppers had their centre of origin in south-central Bolivia, with subsequent migration and differentiation into the Andes and Amazonia, unfortunate, because it implies a single domestication for *all* the cultivated chile peppers; something which Eshbaugh himself rejects earlier in the same paper.

All the evidence favours independent domestication of *C. baccatum* and *C. pubescens* in southern tropical South America, *C. annuum* in Mexico, and *C. chinense* probably in Amazonia. The different domesticates then spread from their respective centres, so that today their distributions overlap, but each is still characteristic of a somewhat different region. I have recently reviewed evidence, or rather lack of evidence, for early spread of chile peppers between Middle and South America (Pickersgill 1984), and have suggested that the presence of similar domesticates, serving similar purposes, might act as a disincentive to exchange or diffusion of these particular crops between the regions concerned.

## Grain chenopods

Quinoa (*Chenopodium quinoa*) is still widely grown in the Andes at altitudes too high for maize. In Mexico, a closely related species, now treated as *C. berlandieri* ssp. *nuttalliae*, is today grown as a vegetable and grain crop (Wilson & Heiser 1979). In North America, another species of the same subsection of the genus, *C. bushianum*, is among the possible domesticates of the so-called Eastern Agricultural Complex which may have preceded the introduction of maize (Ford 1981, Watson Ch. 35, this volume).

Quinoa and the Middle American grain chenopod are both tetraploids, with four sets of chromosomes, and they have been considered by some (e.g. Simmonds 1976) to belong to the same species. It was then argued that the Mexican grain chenopod represented introduction or diffusion of an Andean domesticate in prehistoric times.

Wilson & Heiser (1979) have shown convincingly that this is not so. Convergent evolution in characters selected under domestication (massive terminal inflorescences, synchronous flowering, loss of dispersal mechanisms, pale grain) led earlier taxonomists to overlook differences in characters less likely to be affected by domestication. Moreover, hybrids between the two domesticates are extremely sterile, though the reasons for this sterility are not known.

Each domesticate has a companion weed, with which it crosses and produces fertile hybrids. The two weed forms cluster morphologically with their respective domesticates and, like the two domesticates, produce sterile hybrids when intercrossed. Wilson & Heiser (1979) therefore conclude that each weed/crop pair represents a separate species.

Weedy tetraploids related to this complex occur also in lowland Argentina, northeastern North America, and western North America. Diploids related to this group occur in western North America. Because tetraploids are, almost without exception, derived from diploids, the tetraploid complex as a whole probably originated in North America.

One consequence of the doubling of chromosome number associated with tetraploidy is duplication of the genes controlling enzyme production. Further evidence on the migrations and interrelationships of the tetraploid chenopods has come from study of isozymes of leucine aminopeptidase (LAP) (Wilson 1976, 1981; Wilson *et al.* 1983). Western North American tetraploids contain three alleles at the *Lap-1* locus and two alleles at *Lap-2*. Middle American weed and grain chenopods carry only one allele at each locus, *Lap-1M* and *Lap-2 (fast)* respectively. South American weed and grain chenopods likewise carry only one allele at each locus, this time *Lap-1M* and *Lap-2 (slow)*.

Because tetraploids carry duplicate genetic loci, they can survive even if one of these duplicated loci is inactivated. Mutants which inactivate isozyme loci are known as null alleles. The weedy tetraploid chenopods of lowland Argentina and eastern North America both carry null alleles at *Lap-2* and are assumed to be derived from tetraploid populations with two active loci.

These data eliminate, or at least render very unlikely, certain hypotheses on the origin of the two domesticates. The South American tetraploids did not originate in South America, because there are no closely related diploids in South America, but spread from the north. The lowland Argentinian weed is derived from, not ancestral to, the Andean crop/weed complex, and the eastern North American *C. bushianum* is similarly presumably derived from the *C. berlandieri* complex. The simplest exlanation of the isozyme data is that the western North American populations, with the greatest genetic diversity, are ancestral. Mexico was colonized by tetraploids which were fixed for *Lap-1M* (through accidents of founder effect or genetic drift) but carried both *Lap-2* alleles. As the Mexican crop/weed pair evolved from the ancestral complex, one *Lap-2* allele became fixed, and as South America was colonized, presumably by long-distance dispersal, the other *Lap-2* allele became fixed, in both cases through the further operation of founder effect and/or drift. Grain types were then independently domesticated in Middle and South America. Wilson & Heiser (1979) recognize that their data do not preclude a single domestication in Mexico, followed by spread of the domesticate by man to South America, where derived weedy types re-evolved and even spread beyond the limits of the crop, but this seems less likely.

Like the chile peppers, the grain chenopods illustrate the need for a sound taxonomic understanding before hypotheses are constructed about dispersals of crop plants. They also illustrate the ambiguities which often remain even after intensive study; ambiguities which will probably be resolved only by a more complete archaeobotanical record.

## Cotton

The American cottons include both wild lintless diploids and linted tetraploids. The tetraploids contain two sets of chromosomes homologous with those of the wild New World diploids and two sets homologous with those of the Old World diploid linted cottons. The archaeological record shows that tetraploid cotton was being used by man in coastal Peru by 2500 bc (Stephens & Moseley 1974) but the botanical data suggest that the tetraploids are much more ancient. The Middle and South American domesticated cottons belong to two distinct species, *Gossypium hirsutum* and *G. barbadense* respectively, and each has a conspecific wild or feral counterpart. An apparently relict tetraploid in northeastern Brazil, *G. mustelinum*, is also specifically distinct from *G. hirsutum* and *G. barbadense*. Tetraploids have, in addition, reached the Galapagos Islands and Hawaii. The status of all these 'wild' tetraploids has been questioned (see Pickersgill *et al.* 1975 for arguments on the wild versus feral status of *G. mustelinum*), but the consensus now seems to favour their being genuinely wild (Fryxell 1979).

No wild linted diploid has ever been found in the New World, and no New World wild diploid has even been found east of the Andes. We still do not know where or how the two progenitors of the tetraploids came into contact and hybridized, but this is now thought to involve trans-Atlantic spread of the Old World diploid. The origin of the tetraploids is an unlikely event which probably occurred once only. This is strongly supported by chromosomal studies which show that Middle American *G. hirsutum*, South American *G. barbadense*, Brazilian *G. mustelinum*, and Hawaiian *G. tomentosum* all carry an identical Old World genome (Hasenkampf & Menzel 1980). The more complex theories of Johnson (1975) and Parks *et al.* (1975) agree neither with one another nor with the cytological evidence. The data which these theories attempt to explain can be interpreted in other ways.

If it is accepted that the tetraploid cottons are of ancient origin, in which man is not implicated, and that they evolved into four distinct species through natural selection in geographically isolated populations, it follows that *G. barbadense* and *G. hirsutum* must have been independently domesticated in South and Middle America. Stephens & Moseley (1974) have identified a very early stage in domestication of *G. barbadense* in archaeological specimens from Peru, but a comparable sequence for *G. hirsutum* is lacking.

It has been suggested that each of these species could have been domesticated more than once. Stephens (1973) considers that Ecuadorian and
Amazonian types of G. *barbadense* were sufficiently distinct that they could
represent independent domestications. Similarly, the marie-galante cottons,
which differ morphologically and in their geographical distribution from
other types of G. *hirsutum*, may have been domesticated independently in
either Colombia (Stephens 1973) or northeastern Brazil (Harland 1970),
while other types of G. *hirsutum* were domesticated in Mexico (Smith &
Stephens 1971). In any event, the inter- and intraspecific differences between
cottons cultivated in different parts of the New World do not suggest much
active exchange or diffusion of this crop between these regions.

## Conclusions

Cytological and genetical studies of American crop plants and their wild
relatives lead to several general conclusions.

First, the data seldom lead to irrefutable conclusions, but can often be
interpreted in different ways. For example, it seems overwhelmingly likely
that the tetraploid species of *Chenopodium* sect. *Cellulata* (the grain chenopods and their wild relatives) spread from Middle to South America, and not
vice versa as some had previously suggested. However, man's role in this
spread remains ambiguous: unlikely but not impossible. Cytogenetical
studies only complement, not supplement, archaeobotanical studies.
However, they can help the archaeobotanist by focusing on particular
questions or particular areas that would repay archaeobotanical study.

Secondly, although there are plenty of examples of evolution of subspecies, varieties, or distinct racial groups under domestication (e.g. marie-
galante and Upland cottons within *Gossypium hirsutum*; kidney and Sea
Island cottons within G. *barbadense*), differentiation usually stops short of
speciation. The only convincing example of speciation under domestication
in an American crop plant is coca, where *Erythroxylum novogranatense*, which
is unknown in the wild, appears to have evolved from E. *coca* (Plowman
1984). There are, on the other hand, many examples of the independent
domestication of different species for similar purposes, e.g. *Gossypium
barbadense* and G. *hirsutum*, *Capsicum baccatum* and C. *pubescens*. In ambiguous
situations, such as the grain chenopods, the balance of probability favours
independent domestication, rather than speciation under domestication,
until proved otherwise.

Thirdly, there are relatively few examples of a fully domesticated crop
generating a derived weed. Examples that do exist usually involve hybridization between the crop and a sympatric wild species. In default of evidence
to the contrary, it seems more probable that the weed preceded the crop, for
example in the cases of the cherry tomato and the weedy chenopods.

Fourthly, botanists have become more willing to accept multiple domestications of the same species in different parts of its range. There is strong

evidence that this has occurred in the *Capsicum annuum-chinense-frutescens* complex, and Stephens (1973) suggested a similar phenomenon in both species of New World cultivated cotton. Kato-Y. (1984) concluded from chromosome knob patterns in maize and teosinte that maize had been domesticated in several centres in Mesoamerica. Domestication is thus no longer seen as a unique or particularly difficult event.

Fifthly, the fact that these regional patterns of differentiation persist to the present day indicates that there has been relatively little diffusion of crops between agricultural centres in the Americas. Not only the gross differences in the species lists of the crops of Middle and South America, but also the smaller-scale intraspecific differentiation within crops such as maize suggest considerable independence between the two areas.

Relatively few American crops have so far been subjected to the sorts of detailed studies carried out by Wilson *et al.* (1983) on the isozymes of *Chenopodium*, or reviewed by Kato-Y. (1984) for the chromosome knobs of maize. Techniques are now available to permit a reinvestigation of some American crop plants whose origins are unclear and whose archaeobotanical record is scanty, for example manioc and sweet potato. Views on the origins and diffusion of American crop plants have had in the past to adapt to and accommodate new evidence, and there is no reason to suppose that this process is at an end.

# References

Bird, R. McK. 1984. South American maize in Central America? In *Pre-Columbian plant migration. Papers of the Peabody Museum of Archaeology and Ethnology* 76, D. Stone (ed.), 39–65. Cambridge, Mass.: Harvard University Press.

Bonavia, D. & A. Grobman. 1989. Andean maize: its origins and domestication. In *Foraging and farming: the evolution of plant exploitation*, D. R. Harris & G. C. Hillman (eds), ch. 29. London: Unwin Hyman.

Engel, F. A. 1976. *An ancient world preserved: relics and records of prehistory in the Andes.* New York: Crown Publishers.

Eshbaugh, W. H. 1983. The genus *Capsicum* (Solanaceae) in Africa. *Bothalia* **14**, 845–8.

Ford, R. I. 1981. Gardening and farming before A.D. 1000: patterns of prehistoric cultivation north of Mexico. *Journal of Ethnobiology* **1**, 6–27.

Fryxell, P. A. 1979. *The natural history of the cotton tribe (Malvaceae, Tribe Gossypieae).* College Station: Texas A & M University Press.

Gentry, A. H. 1982. Neotropical floristic diversity: phytogeographical connections between Central and South America, Pleistocene climatic fluctuations, or an accident of the Andean orogeny? *Annals of the Missouri Botanical Garden* **69**, 557–93.

González de León, D. R. 1986. *Interspecific hybridization and the cytogenetic architecture of two species of chili pepper (Capsicum – Solanaceae).* Unpublished PhD Dissertation, Department of Agricultural Botany, University of Reading, England.

Goodman, M. M. & R. McK. Bird 1977. The races of maize IV: tentative grouping of 219 Latin American races. *Economic Botany* **31**, 204–21.

Harland, S. C. 1970. Gene pools in the New World tetraploid cottons. In *Genetic* resources in plants – their exploration and conservation, O. H. Frankel & E. Bennett (eds), 335–40. Oxford: Blackwell Scientific Publications, International Biological Programme.

Hasenkampf, C. A. & M. Y. Menzel 1980. Incipient genome differentiation in *Gossypium*. II. Comparison of 12 chromosomes in G. *hirsutum*, G. *mustelinum* and G. *tomentosum* using heterozygous translocations. *Genetics* **95**, 971–83.

Heiser, C. B., Jr. 1965. Cultivated plants and cultural diffusion in Nuclear America. *American Anthropologist* **67**, 930–49.

Jenkins, J. A. 1948. The origin of the cultivated tomato. *Economic Botany* **2**, 379–92.

Johnson, B. L. 1975. *Gossypium palmeri* and a polyphyletic origin of the New World cottons. *Bulletin of the Torrey Botanical Club* **102**, 340–9.

Kato-Y., T. A. 1984. Chromosome morphology and the origin of maize and its races. In M. K. Hecht, B. Wallace & G. T. Prance (eds), *Evolutionary Biology* **17**, 219–53. New York: Plenum Press.

McLeod, M. J., W. H. Eshbaugh & S. I. Guttman 1979. A preliminary biochemical systematic study of the genus *Capsicum* – Solanaceae. In *The biology and taxonomy of the Solanaceae*, J. G. Hawkes, R. N. Lester & A. D. Skelding (eds), 701–13. London: Academic Press.

Parks, C. R., W. L. Ezell, D. E. Williams & D. L. Dreyer 1975. The application of flavonoid distribution to taxonomic problems in the genus *Gossypium*. *Bulletin of the Torrey Botanical Club* **102**, 350–61.

Pickersgill, B. 1971. Relationships between weedy and cultivated forms in some species of chili peppers (genus *Capsicum*). *Evolution* **25**, 683–91.

Pickersgill, B. 1972. Cultivated plants as evidence for cultural contacts. *American Antiquity* **37**, 97–104.

Pickersgill, B. 1984. Migrations of chili peppers, *Capsicum* spp., in the Americas. In *Pre-Columbian plant migration. Papers of the Peabody Museum of Archaeology and Ethnology* 76, D. Stone (ed.), 105–23. Cambridge, Mass.: Harvard University Press.

Pickersgill, B. & C. B. Heiser, Jr. 1977. Origins and distribution of plants domesticated in the New World tropics. In *Origins of agriculture*, C. A. Reed (ed.), 808–35. The Hague: Mouton.

Pickersgill, B., S. C. H. Barrett & D. de Andrade-Lima 1975. Wild cotton in north-east Brazil. *Biotropica* **7**, 42–54.

Pickersgill, B., C. B. Heiser & J. McNeill 1979. Numerical taxonomic studies on variation and domestication in some species of *Capsicum*. In *The biology and taxonomy of the Solanaceae*, J. G. Hawkes, R. N. Lester & A. D. Skelding (eds), 679–700. London: Academic Press.

Plowman, T. 1984. The origin, evolution and diffusion of coca, *Erythroxylum* spp., in South and Central America. In *Pre-Columbian plant migration. Papers of the Peabody Museum of Archaeology and Ethnology* 76, D. Stone (ed.), 125–63. Cambridge, Mass.: Harvard University Press.

Rick, C. M. & J. F. Fobes 1975. Allozyme variation in the cultivated tomato and closely related species. *Bulletin of the Torrey Botanical Club* **102**, 376–84.

Simmonds, N. W. 1976. Quinoa and its relatives – *Chenopodium* spp. (Chenopodiaceae). In *Evolution of crop plants*, N. W. Simmonds (ed.), 29–30. London: Longman.

Smith, C. E., Jr. & S. G. Stephens 1971. Critical identification of Mexican archaeological cotton remains. *Economic Botany* **25**, 160–8.

Stephens, S. G. 1973. Geographical distribution of cultivated cottons relative to probable centres of domestication in the New World. In *Genes, enzymes and populations*, A. R. Srb (ed.), 239–54. New York: Plenum Publishing Corporation.

Stephens, S. G. & M. E. Moseley 1974. Early domesticated cottons from archaeological sites in central coastal Peru. *American Antiquity* **39**, 109–22.

Watson, P. J. 1989. Early plant cultivation in the Eastern Woodlands of North America. In *Foraging and farming: the evolution of plant exploitation*, D. R. Harris & G. C. Hillman (eds), ch. 35. London: Unwin Hyman.

Weissinger, A. K., D. H. Timothy, C. S. Levings, III, & M. M. Goodman 1983. Pattern of mitochondrial DNA variation in indigenous maize races of Latin America. *Genetics* **104**, 365–79.

Wellhausen, E. J., L. M. Roberts & E. Hernandez-Xolocotzi, in collaboration with P. C. Mangelsdorf 1952. *Races of maize in Mexico: their origin, characteristics and distribution*. Cambridge, Mass.: Bussey Institution of Harvard University.

Wilkes, G. 1989. Maize: domestication, racial evolution, and spread. In *Foraging and farming: the evolution of plant exploitation*, D. R. Harris & G. C. Hillman (eds), ch. 28. London: Unwin Hyman.

Wilson, H. D. 1976. Genetic control and distribution of leucine aminopeptidase in the cultivated chenopods (*Chenopodium*). *Biochemical Genetics* **14**, 913–19.

Wilson, H. D. 1981. Genetic variation among South American populations of tetraploid *Chenopodium* sect. *Chenopodium* subsect. *Cellulata*. *Systematic Botany* **6**, 380–98.

Wilson, H. D. & C. B. Heiser, Jr. 1979. The origin and evolutionary relationships of 'huauzontle' (*Chenopodium nuttalliae* Safford), domesticated chenopod of Mexico. *American Journal of Botany* **66**, 198–206.

Wilson, H. D., S. C. Barber & T. Walters 1983. Loss of duplicate gene expression in tetraploid *Chenopodium*. *Biochemical Systematics and Ecology* **11**, 7–13.

# 28   *Maize: domestication, racial evolution, and spread*

## GARRISON WILKES

Maize is a tropical American domesticate which has spread world-wide. It originated in the highlands of Mexico and now provides the third largest food-plant harvest in the world. It is one of a group of crops that originated in Mexico and includes: common bean, squash, chilli, tomato, avocado, cacao, papaya, guava, sapodilla, cotton and sisal fibres, and vanilla. These crops are the products of 8000 years of accumulated mutational events, which have been ecologically integrated and nutritionally balanced in a complex genetic system by very plant-sensitive indigenous peoples in the diverse and varied habitats of mountainous Mexico. Though all these plants are significant as food sources for humans around the world today, none is more important than maize. As a grass, maize is unique in bearing its male and female flowers in separate parts of the plant: the male flowers are borne terminally in the tassel and the female flowers in the ear, which occupies a lateral position halfway down the plant. The individual kernel, or fruit, of the maize plant is also unique in that the seed is not covered by floral bracts (glumes, lemmas, and paleas) as in all other grasses, except some of the domestic sorghums, but, instead is borne fully exposed on a massive stiff axis, the cob, and the entire structure is enclosed and protected by large modified leaf sheaths.

## The selection pressures of domestication

Domesticated plants represent the ultimate ethnobotanical relationship (cf. Harris Ch. 1, this volume). Without their assured food supply or other useful products, we would not be free to reach our human potential in such activities as the arts and learning, nor could we live at high densities in large metropolitan centres. Because of genetic changes brought about by artificial selection, these plants depend, in turn, on human care and protection, without which most would not be very productive and many would not survive at all. Humans and useful plants are thus locked into a relationship of mutual dependence.

There is no uniform evolutionary pattern followed in the origin of cultivated crops, and the transformation of wild plants into domesticated ones has involved a range of different routes. Some are ancient domesticates, while others have become domesticated only in this century (Harlan 1971, 1975). I emphasize this because maize, which has diverse endosperm types and lends itself to different cooking styles and uses, has a distinctive origin each time a landrace is formed. Heterosis between the unique gene systems found in distinct landraces accounts in part for the yield potential of this crop. Clearly, the evolution of maize has resulted more from a sequence of genetic changes over time than from the fixation of a particular trait. The changes from being a wild to a domesticated plant has been more a process than an event. Burkill called the process 'ennoblement' (Burkill 1953), and Ames referred to it as making plants 'into wards' (Ames 1939). Ironically, we know more about the changes in plant morphology which occur during the process than we do about the human-directed selection forces that powered it. This aspect of plant domestication, the ethnobotany of artificial selection, has thus been largely ignored: most analyses have equated domestication with the origin of a crop and have focused more on the crop's evolution than on the nature of those human activities likely to have generated the necessary selective pressures (for an exception to that generalization see Ladizinsky Ch. 23, this volume).

## Two rules in crop domestication

Over the millennia, cultivators have remained healthy and have had the energy to tend plants and maximize yields as long as they could derive from those plants a nutritionally balanced diet. This natural selection has promoted the cultivation of complementary protein plants such as maize (which is deficient in the amino acids lysine and methionine) and beans (which are deficient in tryptophan and cystine), or cooking styles that maximized the amount of digestible protein in the final product (refried beans, quick-fried vegetables). In this process maize has been adapted to a greater range of food-preparation styles than any other major cereal. The examples are sufficient to give meaning to the rule of the ethnobotany of food production which states that, *in indigenous agriculture in which crops are consumed and not sold, a reasonable level of nutritional adequacy has evolved and been maintained.*

A second rule of food production states that *in indigenous agriculture in which crops are consumed or sold a spiral of expanding carrying capacity develops.* The overall object of such agricultural systems is to replace a pre-existing, natural community with a cultivator-made community. If this potentially unstable spiral is to be maintained, it must be consistent with three aims: (a) to operate at maximal profit (labour/yield), (b) to minimize year-to-year instability in production, and (c) to operate so as to prevent long-term degradation of the production capacity of the agricultural system. Based upon the unspoken assumption of this 'common sense', cultivators make decisions that generate the artificial selection which has guided crop evolution.

The first point is self-evident: no subsistence peasant agriculture can be sustained for long that does not supply an adequate diet. Currently, many peasant agricultures do not sustain the cultivators, who are forced to seek seasonal off-land employment or cultivate cash crops such as coffee or opium poppies.

The second criterion of stability is exemplified in the following account as told by E. Hernandez-Xolocotzi, Professor of Agricultural Botany at the National School of Agriculture in Mexico (Hernandez-Xolocotzi 1970). In Tlaxcala, Mexico, he encountered an old Indian working in his cornfield and asked him what kind of corn he planted. The old man responded that he grew yellow corn, cream corn, and white corn. When asked which was the earliest maturing corn, he said that the yellow took five months, the cream six months, and the white seven months to mature. When asked which yielded the most, he informed Hernandez that the yellow corn gave a little, the cream more, and the white corn the most. Hernandez then asked him why he did not plant only the white since that was the most productive. The old man smiled and said, 'That is the question my son who works at the factory asks. Tell me Mr Agriculturalist, exactly how much and when will it rain next year?' Hernandez-Xolocotzi responded that he could not divine the future. With a knowing look, the old man said 'Exactly! Therefore, I plant all three, so if there is a little rain, I always have some yellow corn to eat. If there is more rain, I'll have enough to eat with the cream corn, and if it's a good year with plenty of rain, I will have white corn to sell.' He added drolly, 'Usually it isn't a good year.' This anecdotal account of biological stability nicely illustrates artificial selection in action (cf. Harlan's account of such selection acting of sorghum, Ch. 20, this volume). Because seeds with differing growth potentials were colour coded, the frequency of these potentials and water requirements could be maintained over the years. Had there been no selection, one of the genotypes would have predominated after a few years, or the three interfertile genotypes would have been homogenized into a single type of corn. This artificial selection for colour-coded growth potentials thus accomplishes not only the second, but also the third aim of agricultural systems, which is to prevent long-term degradation of production.

## Artificial selection ('anthro-selection') in traditional agriculture

Charles Darwin considered artificial selection to be human-assisted 'telescoped evolution' (Darwin 1868). He was right: recessive genes can be fixed in a population within one generation and dominant genes can be fixed with close inbreeding almost as quickly. As for terminology, the domestication process should perhaps be referred to as anthro-selection instead of artificial selection because it focuses much more on human activity than on the environment.

I am not aware of any ethnobotanical study that has tested genetically the effectiveness of folk agricultural-selection practices by means of progeny trials. It is, nevertheless, obvious from the racial diversity present in cultivated crops that these selection practices are effective. However, much of the literature contains nothing more than anecdotal notes about colour preferences for special occasions (e.g. blue corn), or bits of cloth tied around certain mature opium poppy capsules which presumably yielded more and were intended as the seed-source for the next year's crop.

An example is given by Anderson from his experience in measuring the racial variation of maize in Jalisco, Mexico. He would select 25 ears at random from the corn crib to establish a racial measurement for the field of a specific cultivator. Much to his displeasure, a specific cultivator kept bringing him selected, ideal ears. To please the fellow, Anderson measured these also but put a check by such measurements so he would know to ignore them in the final analysis (Anderson 1946, 1952). The story exemplifies a lost opportunity to make two important measurements: not only the variance of the field but also the ideal goal of the cultivator. By comparing the variance of the two, Anderson could have measured the effectiveness of this cultivator's selection over time.

In my own investigations, I have found a difference between the ears selected for seed and those fitting the harvest ideal (Wilkes 1979). I did some preliminary genetic analysis of the race Conejo from Guerrero, Mexico, but never went on to measure the effectiveness of the selection process. Obviously, I too have missed an opportunity and have not applied genetic analysis to the extent possible in exploring the effectiveness of traditional, indigenous selection practices.

In future, when both enthobotanical observations of cultivator practices and genetic progeny tests are made, we can expect truly new insights and models for seed-plant domestication (Heiser 1969, Harris 1972, Libby 1973). Maize is ideal for such studies.

## Selection pressures in the domestication of maize

In becoming domesticated, maize and other plants have crossed the threshold from being wild in the native vegetation under natural selection to being dependent on human care under anthro-selection. Wild maize was a highland plant with essentially a massive central spike with few to no branches in the tassel (the male inflorescence of stamens), and several small lateral ears, one at each of the upper nodes along the multiple tillers. Human selection has produced a plant with a single massive hand-full sized ear on a single stem and a many-branched tassel. At the same time the role of the lower glume in protecting the grain has decreased and the rachilla has been shortened and lost abscision so the ear does not shatter.

Because in all the maize relatives the silks (stigmas) usually become sexually receptive before the tassel starts producing pollen, there was an advantage for later maturing tillers that bore ears when the main tassel was shedding pollen. Selection pressures on wild maize in its highland habitat favoured effective outcrossing by wind-pollination, and resource allocation within the plant favoured prolific pollen production in a massive central spike. Wild populations of teosinte and *Tripsacum* spp. bear a high proportion of non-pollinated seed (often exceeding 50 per cent) and it is likely that the cob of wild maize was also only half-filled. There was therefore good reason for the prezygotic cost of mating to have been significantly male-based and to have exceeded the biomass investment in the female structure and subsequent seed (postzygotic cost) (Cruden & Lyon 1985). This biomass allocation between floral parts was reversed by anthro-selection with its focus on the female ear.

In wild maize, natural selection for the male function (polystichous central spike of the tassel) also maintained the polystichous (many ranked) female ear. The massive central male spike is still expressed in highland maize in both Mexico and Guatemala and to a lesser extent in the Andean zone. By contrast, in teosinte (the closest relative of maize), natural selection at lower elevations has favoured a prolonged period of flowering and a many-branched tassel made up of laterals and lacking a polystichous central spike. In teosinte, the female spikes are distichous (two rowed), and there are many branches per node. Hybridization with teosinte has moved genes governing those characteristics to maize and contributed to the branching of the modern maize tassel. In wild maize the female ear was polystichous but not massive, and the plant was highly tillered, with a weak root system which aided seed dispersal when the plant lodged or fell over.

In domestic maize, the ratio of pollen to ovules still exceeds 10 000 to 1, and only strong anthro-selection for a maize cob has increased investment in the female function. Cultivation of maize in dense stands has considerably decreased selection pressures on the male function through selection for single stems or decreased numbers of tillers. Domestication has thus reversed the sexual investment for maize.

This change in genetic architecture through anthro-selection can be viewed as part of the American complex of hoe cultivation. There were no large domesticated mammals suitable for pulling the plough, and seeds were not sown in ploughed fields by broadcasting, but in holes made in mounds with a pointed stick. Into each hole were placed seeds of maize, beans, and squash and the whole mound was smoothed over. The maize grew tall and upright, the bean twined around the maize stalk, and the squash with its large leaves formed a ground cover which decreased competition from weeds. Tomatoes and chillies were planted and tended individually. Even today Mexicans refer, not to their fields as places for cultivating crops, but to the maize or tomato plants themselves; their minds focus on the individual plants rather than the land under cultivation or the crop yield. There is a fusion in this thinking of the 'flower' (tangible) and the 'song' (concept or poetry of illusion), and, being forced to harvest one plant at a time, the cultivator approaches the plant on an almost personal (I/thou) level. This attitude has influenced the subconscious selection that has taken place in Mexico and Guatemala. Indigenous cultivators are not disturbed at having a diversity of crops, and they may grow segregating hybrid populations all in the same place. They do not view this situation as disorganization, because the individual plant is of greater concern to them than total uniformity in the field. This relationship between the cultivator and the plant is in part responsible for the tremendous genetic diversity found in Mexico. Subsequent hybridization between distinct taxa within this diversity, as well as the geographical isolation of populations by the mountainous terrain, has speeded the evolution of these crops. Today there is tremendous diversity in size, shape, plant colour, and taste in the landraces of maize. There are more than 50 recognized landraces of maize alone in Mexico and 15 in Guatemala (seven of those in Guatemala are also found in Mexico).

## Geographical centre for the origin of maize

Mexico and Peru are the centres of racial diversity for maize recognized by Vavilov (1926). They include the primary centre of genetic diversity (Mexico) and secondary centre (Andean zone) where the maize crop has undergone rapid evolution. Of the 50 races found in Mexico, seven have counterparts in Guatemala, six in Colombia, five in Peru, and two in Brazil. Clearly, Mexico has been a centre for landrace diffusion, although 27 of these landraces remain endemic to Mexico. Much the same pattern of endemism exists in Peru where 30 of the country's 48 races occur only within its borders. Based on over 2800 collections of maize made by the Vavilov Institute in the Americas, Mexico was recognized as the centre of greatest diversity (Kuleshov 1933). Like the Vavilov centres for other crops, Mexico was characterized by mountainous regions that bordered the tropics and has long been populated by agricultural people who were isolated by steep terrain, arid regions, or other natural barriers. Wellhausen et al. (1952) accounted for the racial diversity of Mexican maize in much the same way, citing the preservation of primitive races; the influx of exotic races from countries south of Mexico; hybridization with teosinte (the closest relative of maize); and the geography of Mexico, with its varied habitats and physical barriers to breeding which are conducive to rapid evolution.

Essentially the same conditions prevail in Peru, but because teosinte was native to Mexico and not found in Peru, Vavilov considered Mexico to be maize's area of origin (its primary centre). He also considered teosinte to be the progenitor of maize, an idea shared by Beadle (1972), Harlan and de Wet (1972), Galinat (1977, 1983, 1985), Iltis (1972, 1983), Doebley (1983), and Kato-Y. (1984), and he attached considerable significance to the fact that teosinte was fully fertile with maize and that hybrids occurring naturally between the two could be found in Mexico (Vavilov 1931).

Using evidence very different from that available to Vavilov, Harshberger (1893) had concluded years before that maize originated in Mexico and, more specifically, that it had once occurred as a wild plant in central Mexico at elevations above 1500 m in a semi-arid region with summer rains of approximately 35 cm. His conclusions were remarkable because, unknown to him, he had exactly described those areas of Mexico where the closest relative of maize, annual teosinte, occurs and had pin-pointed the sites where archaeological evidence of wild and early maize were to be found.

The naturally occurring teosinte populations are limited to the western escarpment of Mexico and Central America in a seasonally dry, subtropical zone 800–1800 m above sea-level which receives summer rains, and to the Central Plateau (1650–2000 m) also with summer rains. The teosinte population in the Valley of Mexico at Chalco (2250 m) is an anomaly. The vegetation is deciduous thorn scrub to oak woodland. The growing season (from June to October) begins with the summer rains and by August or September teosinte has reached the mid-flowering stage. The habitat preferences of *Tripsacum* spp. are very similar to those of teosinte but less restrictive.

## Archaeological evidence of maize from Tehuacan

Maize remains have been discovered at many archaeological sites, but many of these remains are comparatively recent and reveal little about the origin of maize. The oldest and most complete archaeological sequence of maize finds comes from Tehuacan, Puebla, in central Mexico. The Tehuacan sequence spans the evolution of maize from what is arguably a wild maize in early levels to modern races which are very similar, if not identical, to those currently being cultivated in fields in the same valley. Teosinte was not recovered in the Tehuacan material.

The earliest cobs (5000 bc) are characterized by uniformity of size and a bisexual condition, with the female, pistillate spikelets below the male staminate spike usually found only in the tassel-tip at the top of the ear. The cobs have relatively long protecting glumes that would have enclosed or partially enclosed each kernel. The seed was probably dispersed by disarticulation of the thin and fragile rachilla and not the rachis. These characteristics are all thought to be those of a wild plant and, indeed, are exactly the characteristics that maintain teosinte as a wild plant in Mexican maize fields, except that, in teosinte, it is the rachis which is brittle instead of the rachilla. It is not unusual to find teosinte standing erect six months after the plant died down and still retaining seed in its husk system. Wild maize could have done the same and when the plant finally fell in the violent wind storms that characterize the beginning of the rainy season, the well-dried ear would shatter and disperse its seed on impact. The seed would thus be shed at the very point in time at which there was rain to promote rapid germination, thus limiting the likelihood of predation by birds and rodents.

The remains of later cobs at Tehuacan are all larger and more varied. In all of its botanical characteristics except size, the earliest cultivated maize (3500–2300 bc) is virtually identical to the earliest wild material. The increase in size is attributed to improved growing conditions brought about by cultivation and irrigation. It appears from the cob specimens that an explosive period of variation must have occurred, starting about 1500 bc. Because of the sudden appearance of very hard rachis tissue and glumes in the cobs and because these characteristics also appear in the progeny of teosinte-× maize hybrids, the later cobs are thought to possess germplasm of teosinte. This variation still exists in Mexican maize fields where maize × teosinte hybrids occur. It is important to note that this introgression from teosinte only starts about 3500 years ago, half-way through the Tehuacan sequence.

The exact origin of the teosinte-introgressed maize at Tehuacan is unknown because teosinte has not been found among the plant remains. However, there is little doubt that variation in the maize cobs followed hybridization with teosinte. Over the mountains from Tehuacan, less than 150 km away at Mitla in neighbouring Oaxaca, a beautifully preserved series of specimens of teosinte, maize × teosinte hybrids, and teosinte-introgressed maize has been discovered which dates back to 0 ad. In northern Mexico in the mountains of western Tamaulipas, there was a comparable find of entire teosinte spikes and teosinte-introgressed maize cobs (the teosinte spikes must have been collected green to preserve the intact rachis tissue). From the evidence found at Tehuacan, it seems clear that the explosive evolution of maize in the archaeological sequence was brought about either by hybridization with teosinte or by hybridization with distinctly different races of maize possessing varying amounts of teosinte germplasm from previous introgressive hybridization with teosinte.

## The wild relatives of maize

Both annual teosinte ($2n = 20$) and maize ($2n = 20$) are wind-pollinated, tend to outcross, and are highly variable, interfertile species. Because the stalk, leaves, and tassel of the two taxa are quite similar, the casual observer can most reliably distinguish them by the pistillate fruit (ear). In teosinte the ear is distichous (two ranked), while in maize it is polystichous (many rowed). In teosinte the female spikelets are solitary whereas in maize they are paired. The seeds of teosinte are dispersed by the rachis breaking into single-seeded segments at maturity, and thence falling to the ground. In wild maize, by contrast, the seeds are thought to have been shed by disarticulation of the separate rachillas rather than the rachis itself, though this facility has been lost in domestic maize. This marked difference between maize and teosinte justifies their separation as distinct species. However, they are interfertile and the natural distribution of teosinte includes some of the best agricultural land in Mexico and Guatemala. It was inevitable, therefore, that, as maize cultivation spread from the highlands, the two taxa came into contact, with subsequent hybridization. In the progeny, the three differences between maize and teosinte segregate in Mendelian fashion.

There are six recognized races of annual teosinte *Zea mexicana* (Schrad)

Kuntze, four of which occur in Mexico (Nobogame, Central Plateau, Chalco, and Balsas) and two in Guatemala (Huehuetenango and Guatemala). The annual teosintes are classified either as six races (which I prefer) or as two subspecies of *Zea mays* L.: ssp. *mexicana*, which embraces the races Chalco, Central Plateau, and Nobogame, and ssp. *parviglumis* var. *parviglumis* (= the race Balsas), and ssp. *parviglumis* var. *huehuetenangenis* (= Huehuetenango), as well as the species *Zea luxurians* (= Guatemala) (Doebley 1983). My guess is that the annual teosinte recently rediscovered in Oaxaca after 140 years merits species status under the classification based on species and subspecies because of its distinctive tassel morphology, but I would prefer that it be considered a seventh race, Oaxaca, or part of the race Balsas. The perennial teosintes are of very limited distribution, being confined to the state of Jalisco, Mexico. These rhizome-producing teosintes are *Zea diploperennis* ($2n = 20$) and *Zea perennis* ($2n = 40$).

Because maize and teosinte are fully interfertile, any theory for the origin of maize by anthro-selection has to account also for the genetic isolation of the two taxa. Based on the free and open exchange of genes in fields where maize and teosinte now are grown together, I find it hard to envisage how maize was selected from teosinte in the past without genetic swamping taking place. The key to this problem might be the experimental discovery of the mechanism that promotes conservation of the distinct chromosome morphologies in teosinte–maize populations in areas where hybridization is known to occur (Kato-Y. 1984). But this problem has not been given the attention it merits, and future studies will perhaps reveal that maize–teosinte populations exhibit a unique pattern of abundant $F_1$ formation and low gene flow in the crop–weed complex (Pickersgill 1981).

Clearly, the simplest way to prevent gene exchange would be geographical isolation or else domestication of maize outside the natural range of teosinte. Unfortunately, there is no archaeological evidence of any transitional forms between teosinte and maize older than the oldest maize from Tehuacan. Galinat (1983) considers the discovery of such evidence improbable because the transition he has hypothesized is of very short duration: 'perhaps only 100 years for the intermediate forms of proto-maize'. The Galinat rapid-selection theory still has the problem of genetic isolation. To my mind it is a less complex theory if the three changes recognized by Beadle (1980) and Galinat (1983) took place before domestication, by natural selection and in geographical isolation (Wilkes 1967).

The genus *Tripsacum* has assumed increasing importance in research on the origin of maize ever since hybridization of maize with *Tripsacum* was first reported by Mangelsdorf and Reeves in 1931. All *Tripsacum* species are perennial rhizomaceous grasses, and unlike teosinte, are quite distinct in appearance from maize. Twelve of the 16 recognized *Tripsacum* species are native to Mexico and Guatemala; a thirteenth, *T. floridanum*, is native to the tip of Florida and Cuba; and the last three (plus other as yet undescribed species) are native to South America. The centre of variation for these grasses is the western escarpment of central Mexico. The area of highest species concentration (four species) is a 50-cm transect along the Chilpancingo Fault (Guerrero) at 1100 to 1250 m in a seasonally dry habitat that receives summer rains. The distribution of Balsas teosinte parallels that of three of these Guerrero species.

*Tripsacum* has evolved by polyploidy, unlike maize and annual teosinte, which have undergone introgressive hybridization at the diploid level. The diploid forms of *Tripsacum* ($2n = 36$) are all morphologically distinct and allopatric in their distribution. The polyploid forms cannot always be easily distinguished on either a morphological or geographical basis, and there is considerable evidence that they hybridize in the field.

Experimental results have established that exchanges can and do occur between maize and *Tripsacum* chromosomes, although the evidence indicates that recent evolution within the genus *Tripsacum* has occurred independently of evolution in maize. *T. dactyloides* ($2n = 72$) was the first *Tripsacum* that Mangelsdorf & Reeves (1931) successfully hybridized with maize. Since then, five other *Tripsacum* spp. have been hybridized with maize. Studies of the hybrids have indicated that certain segments of *Tripsacum* chromosomes can be substituted for corresponding segments in maize chromosomes and that the plants remain both viable and fertile. Galinat (1983) has mapped more than 50 homologous loci on the chromosomes of these two genera. The accumulated information on maize–*Tripsacum* hybrids and their derivatives indicates that the genetic architecture of maize ($2n = 20$) and *Tripsacum* ($2n = 36, 72$), while quite different, is more similar than their karyotypes would suggest.

## Theories of the origin of maize

The various theories for the origin of maize run the gamut from simple selection from teosinte (in which case maize would be a domesticated teosinte) to complex hybrid formation between now extinct grasses. All these theories fit one of the three evolutionary patterns: (a) direct evolution by domestication from a wild ancestor, whether teosinte, wild maize, or a 'wild grass'; (b) hybrid origin from two dissimilar parents; and (c) origin from a wild ancester with repeated hybridization from its closest wild relative, teosinte. Theories about the exact role of teosinte in the origin of maize vary depending on how the evidence is interpreted, but most investigators agree that any theory about the origin of maize must, at least, also account for teosinte.

That teosinte is the closest relative of maize is universally recognized, but there is no agreement about the exact relationship of the two. According to Beadle (1939, 1972), Galinat (1971, 1978), Harlan & de Wet (1972), and Iltis (1972, 1983), teosinte is the ancestor and wild form of maize, and differences in the structures that distinguish the two (polystichous versus distichous ears, paired versus solitary spikelets, naked versus covered grain) have come about through domestication. Mangelsdorf (1974) argued that teosinte is a mutant form of maize and that, contrary to the teosinte ancestor theory, 'corn was the ancestor not only of cultivated corn but also of teosinte'. In 1983 this position was modified such that maize is now considered to be an ancestor of annual teosinte and the perennial teosintes are thought to be more ancient wild plants (Mangelsdorf 1986).

These two explanations, that teosinte is the ancestor and wild maize is the ancestor, are diametrically opposed, but the evolutionary events and morphological changes assumed by both camps to have taken place are nearly identical. Galinat emphasized disruptive selections, Beadle selection under human guidance, Iltis the rational taxonomic imperative, and Mangelsdorf spatial isolation as the mechanisms that kept separate the evolution of these two genetically compatible grasses.

The ear is the part of the maize plant that has been changed most by domestication. An explanation of these changes to the ear would therefore provide at least a partial explanation of the origin of maize. The ear is now generally recognized as the female counterpart of the central spike in the tassel, as was suggested by Kellerman (1895), who pointed out the homology of these two floral structures. She also stated that the ear system came about by a shortening of the lateral branches until the terminal ear was enclosed in specialized leaves or a husk. Montgomery (1906) made these same observations about the relatives of maize and indicated that maize and teosinte may have had a common origin. In teosinte the ears developed from the homolog of the lateral branches of the tassel and in maize from the central spike. These ideas have recently been elaborated in a theory of catastrophic sexual transmutation for the origin of maize from teosinte (Iltis 1983). However, the evidence on which this theory is based can be interpreted quite differently. It could equally be, for example, that maize, with a single massive ear, and teosinte, having a fascicle of spikes, had developed separately along these parallel but distinct evolutionary lines. Similar views that the two plants had a common ancestor but evolved separately have been expressed by Weatherwax (1918, 1954) and Randolf (1955).

In reviewing the then current theories for the domestication of maize, Collins (1930) regarded direct selection from teosinte as improbable because teosinte, with its hard fruitcase, was unpromising as a wild food plant, let alone as a potential crop. Beadle (1939) thereafter showed that when heated, teosinte grains pop in much the same way as the common popcorns, and suggested that teosinte was once popped free of the enclosing fruitcase and consumed in that form. Subsequently, Beadle (1972) also experimentally ground the fruitcase and seed of teosinte to make small *tortillas*. Flannery has shown that about an hour of seed collecting in a naturally occurring wild stand of teosinte can meet a human's daily calorific and protein needs. Teosinte might thus have met hunter–gatherer nutritional and energy-expenditure requirements. (However, for the high-energy input likely to have been involved in cleaning and grinding seed foods of this sort ready for consumption, see Cane Ch. 6, this volume. On the other hand, if the Beadle system for popping the grains were sufficient to render the grains digestible (see Stahl Ch. 11, this volume) then the problem of energy-expensive grinding could well have been obviated.)

If the present distribution of wild teosinte populations on the Central Plateau and in the Valley of Mexico is the result of hybridization with cultivated maize, then the domestication of maize might very well have been spatially and genetically isolated from the large teosinte populations occurring at middle elevations between 1000 and 1500 m on the western escarpment. Only when the domestication of maize had begun, and native cultivators had started carrying the seed into new habitats, would the distribution of maize have been increased to then overlap with the natural distribution of teosinte.

The spatial isolation and narrow habitat preferences of early maize and wild teosinte would thus have been abruptly broken down, and the immediate effects of hybridization and concomitant introgression would thereafter have greatly increased the genetic potential of both species. During the reciprocal exchange of germplasm, maize became better adapted to the lower elevations and teosinte to the higher elevations. It was probably only after its hybridization with maize that teosinte spread farther north from the mid-elevations of west-central Mexico to invade the higher elevations of the Central Plateau. The teosinte-introgressed maize became partially adapted to the lowlands, and then seed of such populations was sown back in the highlands. The resultant hybridization of this teosinte-introgressed maize with pure maize (Nal-Tel/Chapalote) gave rise to the sudden appearance 3000 years ago of the very heterotic indurated cob, as observed in the Tehuacan archaeological sequence. As the area of maize cultivation increased, the size of the wild maize populations decreased until a situation developed resembling that of the small, isolated teosinte populations growing today on the margins of maize fields. Wild maize could have become extinct either by losing its ability to disperse seed (through introgression of tough-rachilla genes from the domestic crops) or by being completely absorbed genetically into cultivated maize.

## Continued hybridization with teosinte and the recent evolution of maize

The concept that teosinte is continuing to exchange genes with modern maize populations is not a recent discovery, but was reported by Harshberger (1893, 1896) for teosinte of the Central Plateau, by Lumholtz (1902) for teosinte of Southern Chihuahua, by Lopez & Parra (1908) for teosinte of the Valley of Mexico, and by Kempton & Popenoe (1937) for teosinte of northern Guatemala. At present, teosinte is known to hybridize with maize throughout the entire western escarpment of Mexico and Guatemala (Wilkes 1967).

The isolating mechanisms that prevent or limit genetic exchange between teosinte and maize in naturally occurring populations are primarily spatial and seasonal. The largest populations of teosinte are located in sparsely settled areas, and teosinte is isolated from the nearest maize field both by distance and by flowering time, which is about ten days later than in maize. In the Central Plateau and Valley of Mexico, however, teosinte occurs either in the maize fields or along the margins and is only partially isolated at flowering time.

Mexican maize fields contain among the most complex assemblages of maize germplasm in the Americas, and the extent of this variation within crops differs according to region, elevation, and rainfall. Mexican cultivators show a marked tolerance for wide variation within a single field, for the presence of 'unproductive' teosinte and other weeds, and for productive plants such as beans and squash being intercropped with the maize. They believe that a field with greater variation possesses greater potential than a more uniform one. Indeed, they actually follow practices that increase that diversity and even plant segregating hybrid seed. In both the Balsas and Huehuetenango areas, cultivators recognize that the dents, Conejo and Comiteco respectively, both outyield their parental segregates, and yet cultivators select ears from these extremes for seed. In both locations the cultivators' aim is to maintain yields (in the manner already described earlier in this chapter) and not in the uniform appearance of the field.

This process of selecting for diversity and the incorporation of heterotic germplasm from teosinte is postulated to be the same as that which started about 3500 years ago in Mexico, for which period there is archaeological evidence of explosive evolution. Introgression of teosinte is recognized in two-thirds of the races of maize being grown in Mexico today. The reflux of teosinte genes has been part of the spiral of expanding carrying-capacity that has made maize the predominant cereal of the Americas.

The 'dipping' of maize into teosinte on the Central Plateau, in Balsas, and in Huehuetenango is postulated to have contributed factors for straightening the rows and elongating the ear. At any one location, these two character-istics are expressed in only one form of the two extremes preferred for seed ears. This observation that distinct and opposite forms of maize manifest the greatest heterosis suggests that modern or incipient races of maize in Mexico originate in a manner similar to that of the world's most productive race: Corn Belt Dent (produced by the cross: eight-rowed Northern Flints × many-rowed Southern Dents).

## Maize: a human achievement in altering a plant

Modern maize is a genetically complex, highly heterozygous plant of which the wild form is extinct. It has been so altered in its basic biology that it is found only in cultivated fields. We often feel we can better understand something if we know where it came from or, in the case of living things, who their ancestors were. This explains much of the interest in the origin of maize. But after a full century of speculation and research, there is still no consensus on the matter. The ancestor of maize was either its closest relative, teosinte, or a wild maize, which was the half-ancestor of present-day races of both teosinte and maize. I favour the latter hypothesis.

Although the ancestor of maize is still not known with complete certainty, there is general agreement on many aspects of the crop's origin. Maize was domesticated in Mexico perhaps between 8000 and 10000 years ago, and there was possibly a secondary domestication in South America (cf. Bonavia & Grobman Ch. 29, Pickersgill Ch. 27, this volume). The habitat of wild maize was a highland region above 1800 m with seasonal rains of 50 cm. This postulated habitat was also the most populous region of Mesoamerica, with over five million indigenous inhabitants – the chief architects of maize – at the time of the Spanish Conquest.

# References

Ames, O. 1939. *Economic annuals and human cultures*. Cambridge, Mass.: Botanical Museum of Harvard University.

Anderson, E. G. 1946. Maize in Mexico – A preliminary survey. *Annals of the Missouri Botanic Garden* **33**, 147–247.

Anderson, E. G. 1952. *Plants, man and life*. Berkeley: University of California Press.

Ascherson, P. 1875. Veber *Euchlaena mexicana*. Schrad. *Bot. Vereins Prov. Brandenburgh* **17**, 76–80.

Beadle, G. W. 1939. Teosinte and the origin of maize. *Journal of Heredity* **30**, 245–7.

Beadle, G. W. 1972. The mystery of maize. *Field Museum of Natural History Bulletin* **43**, 2–11.

Beadle, G. W. 1980. The ancestry of corn. *Scientific American* **242**, 112–19.

Bonavia, D. & A. Grobman 1989. Andean maize: its origins and domestication. In *Foraging and farming: the evolution of plant exploitation*, D. R. Harris & G. C. Hillman (eds), ch. 29. London: Unwin Hyman.

Burkill, I. H. 1953. Habits of man and the origin of the cultivated plants of the Old World. *Proceedings of the Linnean Society* **164**, 12–42.

Cane, S. 1989. Australian Aboriginal seed grinding and its archaeological record: a case study from the Western Desert. In *Foraging and farming: the evolution of plant exploitation*, D. R. Harris & G. C. Hillman (eds), ch. 6. London: Unwin Hyman.

Collins, G. N. 1930. The phylogeny of maize. *Bulletin of the Torrey Botanical Club* **57**, 199–210.

Cruden, R. W. & D. L. Lyon 1985. Patterns of biomass allocation to male and female functions in plants with different mating systems. *Oecologia* **66**, 299–306.

Darwin, C. 1868. *The variation of animals and plants under domestication*. 2 Vols. London: John Murray.

Doebley, J. F. 1983. The maize × teosinte inflorescence: a numerical taxonomic study. *Annals of the Missouri Botanical Garden* **70**, 32–70.

Galinat, W. C. 1971. The origin of maize. *Annual Review of Genetics* **5**, 447–78.

Galinat, W. C. 1977. The origin of corn. In *Corn and corn improvement*, G. F. Sprague (ed.), 1–47. Madison: American Society of Agronomy.

Galinat, W. C. 1978. The inheritance of some traits essential to maize and teosinte. In *Maize breeding and genetics*, D. B. Walden (ed.), 99–111. New York: John Wiley.

Galinat, W. C. 1983. The origin of maize as shown by key morphological traits of its ancestor, teosinte. *Maydica* **28**, 121–38.

Galinat, W. C. 1985. Domestication and diffusion of maize. In *Prehistoric food production in North America*, R. Ford (ed.), 245–78. Anthropological Paper 75, Museum of Anthropology, University of Michigan, Ann Arbor.

Harlan, J. R. 1971. Agricultural origins: centers and noncenters. *Science* **174**, 468–74.

Harlan, J. R. 1975. *Crops and man*. Madison: American Society of Agronomy.

Harlan, J. R. 1989. The tropical African cereals. In *Foraging and farming: the evolution of plant exploitation*, D. R. Harris & G. C. Hillman (eds), ch. 20. London: Unwin Hyman.

Harlan, J. R. & J. M. J. de Wet 1972. Origin of maize: the tripartite hypothesis. *Euphytica* **21**, 271–9.

Harris, D. R. 1972. The origins of agriculture in the tropics. *American Scientist* **60**, 180–93.

Harris, D. R. 1989. An evolutionary continuum of people–plant interaction. In *Foraging and farming: the evolution of plant exploitation*, D. R. Harris & G. C. Hillman (eds), ch. 1. London: Unwin Hyman.

Harshberger, J. 1893. Maize, a botanical and economic study. *Contributions of the Botanical Laboratory at the University of Pennsylvania*, 1, 75–202.

Harshberger, J. 1896. Fertile crosses of teosinte and maize. *Garden and Forest* **9**, 522–3.

Heiser, C. B., Jr. 1969. Some considerations of early plant domestication. *Bioscience* **19**, 228–31.

Hernandez-Xolocotzi, E. 1970. *Exploracion Etnobotanica y su Metodologia*. Colegio de Postgraduados, Escuela Nacional de Agricultura, Chapingo, Mexico.

Iltis, H. 1972. The taxonomy of *Zea mays* L. (Gramineae). *Phytologia* **23**, 248–9.

Iltis, H. 1983. From teosinte to maize: the catastrophic sexual transmutation. *Science* **222**, 886–94.

Kato-Y., T. A. 1984. Chromosome morphology and the origin of maize and its races. In M. K. Hecht, B. Wallace & G. T. Prance (eds), *Evolutionary Biology* **17**, 219–53. New York: Plenum Press.

Kellerman, W. A. 1895. Primitive corn. *Meehan's Monthly* **5**, 44.

Kempton, J. H. & W. Popenoe 1937. Teosinte Guatemala: a report of an expedition to Guatemala, El Salvador, and Chiapas, Mexico. *Carnegie Institute Publication* **483**, 199–217.

Kuleshov, N. N. 1933. World's diversity of phenotypes of maize. *Agronomy Journal* **25**, 688–700.

Ladizinsky, G. 1989. Origin and domestication of the Southwest Asian grain legumes. In *Foraging and farming: the evolution of plant exploitation*, D. R. Harris & G. C. Hillman (eds), ch. 23. London: Unwin Hyman.

Libby, W. J. 1973. Domestication strategies for forest trees. *Canadian Journal of Forestry Research* **3**, 256–76.

Lopez y Parra, R. 1908. *El Teosinte*. Mexico.

Lumholtz, C. 1902. *Unknown Mexico*. New York: Charles Scribner.

Mangelsdorf, P. C. 1974. *Corn: its origin, evolution and improvement*. Cambridge, Mass.: Harvard University Press.

Mangelsdorf, P. C. 1983. The mystery of corn: new perspectives. *Proceedings of the American Philosophical Society* **127**, 215–47.

Mangelsdorf, P. C. 1986. The origin of corn. *Scientific American* **255**, 72–8.

Mangelsdorf, P. C. & R. G. Reeves 1931. Hybridization of maize, *Tripsacum* and *Euchlaena*. *Texas Agricultural Experimental Station Bulletin*.

Montgomery, E. G. 1906. What is an ear of corn? *Popular Science Monthly* **68**, 55–67.

Pickersgill, B. 1981. Biosystematics of crop–weed complexes. *Kulturpflanze* **29**, 377–88.

Pickersgill, B. 1989. Cytological and genetical evidence on the domestication and diffusion of crops within the Americas. In *Foraging and farming: the evolution of plant exploitation*, D. R. Harris & G. C. Hillman (eds), ch. 27. London: Unwin Hyman.

Randolph, L. F. 1955. Cytogenetic aspects of the origin and evolutionary history of corn. In *Corn and corn improvement*, G. F. Sprague (ed.). New York: Academic Press.

Stahl, A. B. 1989. Plant-food processing: implications for dietary quality. In *Foraging and farming: the evolution of plant exploitation*, D. R. Harris & G. C. Hillman (eds), ch. 11. London: Unwin Hyman.

Vavilov, N. I. 1926. Studies on the origin of cultivated plants (in Russian). *Bulletin of Applied Botany, Genetics and Plant Breeding* **16**, 1–248.

Vavilov, N. I. 1931. Mexico and Central America as the principal centre of origin of cultivated plants of the New World. *Bulletin of Applied Botany, Genetics and Plant Breeding* **26**, 135–99.

Weatherwax, P. 1918. The evolution of maize. *Bulletin of the Torrey Botanical Club* **45**, 309–42.

Weatherwax, P. 1954. *Indian corn in old America*. New York: MacMillan.

Wellhausen, E. J., L. M. Roberts & E. Hernandez-Xolocotzi, in collaboration with P. C. Mangelsdorf 1952. *Races of maize in Mexico*. Cambridge, Mass.: Bussey Institution of Harvard University.

Wilkes, H. G. 1967. *Teosinte: the closest relative of maize*. Cambridge, Mass.: Bussey Institution of Harvard University.

Wilkes, H. G. 1979. Mexico and Central America as a centre for the origin of agriculture and the evolution of maize. *Crop Improvement* (India) **6**, 1–18.

# 29 *Andean maize: its origins and domestication*

DUCCIO BONAVIA and
ALEXANDER GROBMAN

Diffusionism in the Americas, which goes back at least as far as the ideas of Spinden (1917), found in plant domestication one of the most fertile grounds for its tenets, and maize domestication became one of the most cherished arguments advanced in favour of the diffusionist position. In fact, up to very recent times, abundant archaeological evidence could be mustered that purported to show that the antiquity of this cultigen in Mesoamerica exceeded that of other finds of maize in other parts of the Americas. Furthermore, the reported existence of fossil maize pollen in Pleistocene strata in the Valley of Mexico reinforced the case for the existence of wild maize in that region as a precursor to domesticated maize. Everything seemed to indicate that maize diffused from the Mexican area to South America.

However, during the past 20 years, this scenario has changed due to the increase in archaeological research, especially the greater interest of archaeologists in ethnobotany, and the more sophisticated research techniques which are now being used. We believe that the suggestion of Grobman (Grobman *et al.* 1961) and Mangelsdorf (1974) of polyagrogenesis, which postulates the independent domestication of plants and the origin of agricultural systems for a given species in more than one centre, has become a viable alternative to the diffusionist hypothesis, and that new evidence increasingly supports it.

Although in this chapter we are concerned with maize, we believe that there is convincing evidence for polyagrogenesis having occurred in the evolution of several other species of cultivated plants in the Americas, such as chile peppers, cotton, several cucurbits, lima beans, amaranths, and common beans (see also Pickersgill Ch. 27 and Heiser Ch. 30, this volume).

## Archaeological history of maize in the Andean region

The first scientifically documented discovery of pre-ceramic maize in the Central Andean region was made in 1941–42 at Aspero by Willey & Corbett (1954). At that time the importance of the discovery was not fully grasped, because it was not until 1946, through the work of Bird at Huaca Prieta, that it began to be realized that the history of cultivated plants in the Andes was much older than had been thought. Nevertheless, in Towle's classical archaeobotanical study published in 1961, the Andean Pre-Ceramic period was typified as a 'pre-maize culture', in spite of the fact that Grobman *et al.* predicted – in the same year – a pre-ceramic age for Andean maize. Their study was based mainly on the present-day races of maize, supplemented by the archaeological data available at the time, and only the pre-ceramic maize from Los Gavilanes in Peru is mentioned in it (Grobman *et al.* 1961, p. 74).

Research on pre-ceramic maize in the Central Andean area was really opened up by Lanning in the 1950s, with his pioneering work in the central and north-central coastal areas of Peru where he was able to confirm the presence of maize in pre-ceramic strata. Kelley and Mangelsdorf stimulated Bonavia to initiate research along these lines (see Kelley & Bonavia 1963, Grobman *et al.* 1977), who since that time has co-operated with Grobman.

Between 1961 and 1977 Bonavia conducted systematic studies at the Los Gavilanes site, which allowed him to assemble the largest collection of pre-ceramic maize in the Central Andean area, and possibly in South America (Bonavia 1982). In 1961 Grobman had suggested to MacNeish the importance of exploring the caves of the Ayacucho region in Peru, a region at intermediate altitude similar in ecological context to Tamaulipas in Mexico. This resulted in the first highland research on ancient maize in Peru.

The finds of ancient maize can be divided into two categories: those based only on the archaeological data, and those which have also been studied botanically and published. We include in the first category the finds at Ancón, Culebras, and Las Aldas, and in the second group those at Aspero, Los Gavilanes, Guitarrero Cave, and Ayacucho. In this chapter we only outline the evidence; for detailed information see Bonavia (1982, pp. 346–86). In the summary that follows, in order to attain chronological consistency, we use the sequence proposed by Lanning (1967, p. 25) for the Pre-Ceramic Epoch.

At Ancón on the central coast of Peru, Lanning found two coprolites in layers of the Early Final Pre-Ceramic, one of which contained maize pollen (Patterson 1971 pers. comm.). At Culebras, a site on the north-central coast which he excavated, he found maize cobs in a Late Pre-Ceramic stratum (Lanning 1960, p. 40, 1967, p. 67, pers. comm., Bonavia 1982, p. 361). He also found maize remains at Las Aldas, near Culebras, in a context belonging to the Final Pre-Ceramic (Lanning 1960, p. 587, 1967, p. 67).

Aspero on the north-central coast is the first site of the second category, and here 49 maize cobs were found in the 1940s (Towle 1954, 1961, pp. 23, 108, 119 & 139, Willey & Corbett 1954, pp. 27–9 & 165). The discovery, however, was not understood because in those days the idea that maize cultivation, or even agriculture, might have preceded the appearance of ceramics was not accepted. Moseley & Willey (1973) re-studied the site, confirmed that it was pre-ceramic, and found another cob *in situ*. Feldman later excavated the same site extensively and he also found maize in a pre-ceramic context (Feldman 1977, p. 2, 1978, pp. 21–6, pers. comm.). He described 12 cobs, three of which were found in a stratigraphic situation which was clearly pre-ceramic (Feldman 1980, pp. 182–4). Grobman studied this material and confirmed that it belonged to the race Proto-Confite Morocho (1980, 1982, p. 176).

Los Gavilanes is the most important site for the investigation of maize on the north-central coast of Peru. It has been exhaustively studied and all its materials have been analysed and published (Kelley & Bonavia 1963, Grobman et al. 1977, Grobman & Bonavia 1978, Bonavia & Grobman 1978 & 1979, Bonavia 1982). Several pre-ceramic occupational epochs have been defined there. Maize belongs to those named Los Gavilanes 2 and 3. For Los Gavilanes 2 we have a radiocarbon date of 4140 ± 160 bp and another by thermoluminiscence analysis of 4800 ± 500 bp. For Los Gavilanes 3 there are four radiocarbon dates: 3750 ± 110, 3755 ± 155, 3595 ± 140, and 3250 ± 155 bp. At this site it was possible to identify and classify a large quantity of maize-plant parts. Grobman identified the racial types Proto-Confite Morocho, Confite Chavinense, and Proto-Kculli, as well as hybrids of these three races (Grobman 1982). A considerable quantity of human coprolites was also found at Los Gavilanes. They correspond in age to the maize remains and contained a high percentage of pollen grains and maize pericarps (Weir & Bonavia 1985).

The Guitarrero Cave in the Callejón de Huaylas of Peru has a complex stratigraphy which in some sectors was disturbed. The maize found in Complex III at the site was dated by Smith (1980) between 4000 and 2000 bc, but Lynch, who excavated the site, prefers to connect Complex III with the end of Complex II which dates to the 6th millennium bc (Lynch 1980, p. 306). Smith compared the maize remains with those of early Peruvian and Mexican maize. The relationship between his thin cobs and Confite Morocho suggests decreased cob condensation, and that tendency seems to have prevailed at the time of Complexes III and IV. He concluded that maize in the Callejón de Huaylas had a close relationship to the Peruvian and Colombian races of maize and that there is very little evidence of the direct introduction of Mesoamerican maize (Smith 1980, pp. 140–3). Grobman (1982, pp. 172–3), in an analysis of Smith's study, concluded that the distribution of the Complex III maize in terms of cob dimensions fits into the distribution of Confite Chavinense and its hybrids. Aikens (1981, p. 225) revised the work of Lynch and accepted that the earlier specimens of maize were indeed pre-ceramic. Vescelius (1981) questioned this conclusion. More recently, however, the chronology and absolute dating of the pre-ceramic levels of Guitarrero Cave have been confirmed by Lynch et al. (1985).

Only preliminary reports are available on the finds of maize at Ayacucho in which contradictions and data gaps are found. Initially, two pre-ceramic cobs were mentioned from the Chihua phase and these were assigned to Confite Morocho (correctly Proto-Confite Morocho), with dates between 2700 and 4300 bc (MacNeish 1969, p. 42, MacNeish et al. 1970, p. 38). Later

MacNeish *et al.* (1975, pp. 30, 32, 35) mention the same maize but attribute to it teosinte introgression, and consequently a Mesoamerican origin. Galinat (1972, pp. 107–8) demonstrated the existence for at least 4000 years in the Ayacucho area of the Confite Puneño and Confite Morocho races. He also indicated that the most ancient cobs belonged to a race he named Ayacucho. He later changed his mind (1977, p. 38) and assigned the maize from Ayacucho to the races Confite Morocho and Pollo (a Colombian race), and in a communication to Pickersgill & Heiser (1978, p. 137) relations between the Ayacucho race and the ancient Nal-Tel race of Mexico were indicated. Grobman re-examined the maize cobs at Galinat's laboratory in 1973 and was able to group all of them within the range of the two old Central Andean races, Proto-Confite Morocho and Confite Chavinense, thus conclusively discarding the so-called Ayacucho race (Grobman 1974, 1982, pp. 176–7).

Finally, we report the recent discovery by Uceda, in a pre-ceramic site called PV32–1 in the Casma valley on the north-central Peruvian coast, of a small maize cob among other botanical remains. The cob was classified by Grobman as a hybrid specimen between Confite Chavinense and Proto-Confite Morocho. This find is radiocarbon dated to 6070 ± 70 bp. At another site in the same area (PV32–2), with pre-ceramic characteristics, Uceda found leaves and stem fragments of maize plants. This site has been radiocarbon dated to 6050 ± 70 bp (pers. comm.).

Summarizing the available information, we conclude that in all the above-mentioned finds the maize specimens were basically related to Proto-Confite Morocho and Confite Chavinense, and to a lesser extent to Proto-Kculli, all three being postulated ancient races of maize from Peru. Accepting the finds at Casma, although they are still tentative, we find great consistency in the information available from both the highland and coastal regions of Peru. The coastal finds are in a time-band between the transition to Casma Pre-Ceramic IV/V, through epochs V and VI of Los Gavilanes, and Final Pre-Ceramic VI of all the other sites (Las Aldas, Culebras, Aspero, and Ancón). In the highlands, the Ayacucho maize specimens fall in the transition between Pre-Ceramic IV and V, and the Guitarrero Cave maize, if Lynch's interpretation is accepted, should belong to Pre-Ceramic IV, or, alternatively, following Smith, to the transition between Pre-Ceramic IV and V. In any event, this means that in terms of (uncalibrated) radiocarbon dating we see domesticated maize appearing in Peru about 4000 bc, or, if Lynch's interpretation of the Guiterrero Cave finds is accepted, as early as 6000 bc.

## Relationships between Mesoamerican and Andean maize

We accept Barghoorn's fossil pollen evidence which demonstrates the existence of a wild form of maize at the present location of Mexico City at 70 000–80 000 bp (Barghoorn *et al.* 1954, Mangelsdorf 1974, p. 181).[1]

Ancient maize from San Marcos Cave in the Tehuacán valley, Mexico, is pure maize. Both in Tehuacan and at Bat Cave in New Mexico, as well as in southern Mexico, teosinte appears in archaeological contexts at levels more recent than those of early maize (Mangelsdorf 1974).

During the 1970s Beadle and Galinat revived the hypothesis that maize was a direct descendant of teosinte. This theory was challenged by Mangelsdorf and others, whose argument was supported by the discovery of *Zea diploperennis*, a diploid perennial teosinte (Iltis *et al.* 1979) which appears to have a sympatric distribution with early maize. Annual teosinte may have originated from the hybridization of maize and perennial teosinte. The present-day races of teosinte, which exhibit chromosomal and morphological similarities, and genetic compatibility, with Mesoamerican maize, could thus have evolved through recurring back-crosses, and the infiltration of maize genes into teosinte. Thus, domesticated maize can again be postulated as having originated from wild maize, and Magoja *et al.* (1985) have now adduced further support, through cluster analysis of the biometrical characteristics of species of the genus *Zea*, for Mangelsdorf's original hypothesis that cultivated maize derived from wild maize.

The archaeologically recovered maize cobs from coastal pre-ceramic sites and the highland Peruvian caves which have been examined do not differ markedly from contemporary finds of maize in Mexico. Early Peruvian maize, as well as early Mexican maize, does not show evidence of teosinte introgression. Mexican maize from slightly later periods soon starts to show teosinte introgression. In Peru, however, maize does not exhibit introgression from teosinte, either in contemporary early periods or during the next three millennia.

From the very early periods (Los Gavilanes, Guitarrero Cave, Ayacucho) there is strong evidence of the simultaneous existence of three maize races (Proto-Confite Morocho, Confite Chavinense, and Proto-Kculli) in the Central Andean region. At least two of them are quite different in cob morphology, genetic systems of pigmentation, and condensation of cob and tassel, from the races of maize which existed at the same time in Mexico, which were no more than two, and most likely only one. The description given by Mangelsdorf of maize from the Coxcatlan Phase at Tehuacán, the earliest found in Mexico, is of only one type (race) which is remarkably uniform. This type could have given rise to the two primitive races of maize in Mexico: Chapalote and Nal-Tel. The cob characteristics of this single Mexican maize race are not very different from those of Proto-Confite Morocho, especially regarding row number (eight). Proto-Confite Morocho exhibits, however, longer cupules.

Without giving too many comparative details, the information presently available indicates the contemporaneous existence of one or two races of maize in Mexico and of three races of maize – well differentiated from the Mexican ones – in the Central Andean region by about 4000 bc. The very short time-lag between the oldest finds in the two regions, coupled with the low farming intensity at the oldest pre-ceramic coastal sites in Peru, argues against a diffusionist explanation for the great evolutionary advances and divergence of maize in the two regions by the early agricultural period. It is more reasonable to think in terms of independent maize evolution in both regions, based on wild-maize precursors for both groups, with a pre-existing base of genetic variability which gave rise to different domesticated races in the early agricultural periods. If Pira, an early maize race from Colombia, is accepted as a sixth race derived from wild maize, as postulated by Mangelsdorf (1974, p. 118), its morphological divergence of ear type from the races of the Central Andes makes even less plausible the hypothesis of diffusion of *domesticated maize* as an explanation of its early presence in South America and particularly in the Andean region.

The discovery of maize pollen in sediments of the Gatun Lake zone in Panama, dated to between 6200 and 7300 bp, provides proof of the existence of maize in an intermediate transitional area, which lacks evidence of agriculture in that early time-period. Bartlett and Barghoorn indicate that this early occurrence possibly derives from wild maize (Bartlett *et al.* 1969, Bartlett & Barghoorn 1973). It is worth pointing out that in the Gatun Lake sediments pollen of *Manihot esculenta*, *Ipomoea* sp., and Amaranthaceae was also found, the first of Amazonian origin, the second of South American origin, and the third very old in both Mexico and the Central Andes. It is possible that wild maize could have survived in the Gatun area in climates that in times past were less rainy than at present. In effect, Wijmstra and Van der Hammen (1966, cited by Bartlett & Barghoorn 1973), discovered palynological evidence of open savanna vegetation in Colombia between 4000 and 5000 years ago. Ths time interval between 7300 and 4000 bp in the central part of the Panama isthmus seems to have been more dry, allowing the growth of wild maize at the Gatun site, and present-day climatic conditions on the Pacific coast of Panama would allow the persistence of wild maize.

In recent years a new type of evidence based on phytolith analysis has been introduced. This method is still in an experimental phase and has some limitations. However, pollen and phytoliths of maize have been reported from the Los Ladrones Cave, in the Santa Maria Basin of Central Panama, in levels radiocarbon dated to 4910 bc; maize phytoliths were also recovered from another rockshelter (SE-179) radiocarbon dated to 5125 bc (Piperno Ch. 34, this volume). Although it is maintained that these phytoliths derive from domesticated maize, there is no conclusive proof for this assertion. It was initially indicated that 'the cross-shaped phytolith sizes and three-dimensional proportions in the archaeological samples do not now indicate the presence of such races as Nal-Tel, Chapalote, Tepecintle, Pisankalla and Cacahuacintle . . . It is likely, then, that this phytolith came from a race or races of maize that have not as yet been evaluated' (Piperno 1984, p. 375). However, we have since been informed by the author that this is only a working hypothesis and that there is no firm evidence one way or the other (pers. comm.). On the same occasion Piperno reported the identification of maize pollen from archaeological strata in the Calima valley, Colombia, radiocarbon dated to 5300 bp according to information communicated personally to her by Bray and Van der Hammen. In the case of Ecuador there is evidence, though scarce, of the existence of maize in the context of the Valdivia culture (3000 bc). Evidence claimed by Zevallos (Zevallos 1966–1971, Lathrap & Marcos 1975, Lathrap & Collier 1976, Zevallos *et al.* 1977) was refuted by Bonavia (1982, pp. 380–3) and Mangelsdorf (1977: MS published in Bonavia 1982, p. 383), and there now remains only the evidence of maize phytoliths published by Pearsall (1978), with an antiquity of 'at least' 2450 years.

From the phytolith and pollen evidence of maize obtained from Panama, Colombia, and Ecuador we can draw a single conclusion, which is that maize was present there in early epochs within the range of its antiquity in Mesoamerica and the Central Andean region. However, because at present it is impossible to associate this evidence with the racial complexes of maize, we do not rely on it for the present discussion.

For all the reasons already advanced, we propose the hypothesis that maize was diffused at a very early time by means other than man. Later on, man participated in and accelerated the diffusion process. The most probable means of pre-human diffusion of wild maize is by way of birds, as has happened with other grasses. As Mangelsdorf showed (1974, p. 180), wild maize inflorescences would have had male and female flowers in the same structure. The seeds were partially covered and protected by soft glumes. Additional protection was acquired later with the adaptation of leaves and shortened internodes of the floral branches to cover the ears as husks. Grobman (1982, Fig. 60) reconstructed an ideotype of the probable inflorescence of wild maize, based on the finds at Los Gavilanes. This type of inflorescence allows the shedding and dispersal of the seeds when a brittle rachilla that supports the seed on the cob is broken, or through violent separation by bird action. Small, flinty seeds, coloured red, brown, or purple (the latter is the case with the race Kculli), would be easily distinguished and eaten by birds. After a few hours in their digestive tracts, the seeds could be deposited in the droppings, at points quite distant from the original places of grain collection. One of the birds that might have been quite effective in spreading the seeds of wild maize is the dickcissel or 'rice bird' (*Spiza americana*), a migratory species that moves invariably every year from the northern hemisphere to the south and passes through Mesoamerica on its way to South America, eating and damaging rice, wheat, sorghum, and other crops. We have observed the dispersal effect of these birds on sorghum seeds in the northern coastal region of Peru, in the same way that we postulate for maize. This may explain the observed fact that the seed samples of very early maize in South America are all pop types with small kernels formed with a very dense protein matrix in the seed endosperm, and with acuminated or pointed shape, as a possible protection against birds.

This seed-dispersal mechanism, which has been documented by Pickersgill (1983) for other species, could explain the diffusion of maize in pre-agricultural periods which present evidence suggests took place. Wild maize could have been dispersed from Mesoamerica to South America and intermediate areas, in a fashion similar to and accepted for other species, and could later have been independently domesticated in Mesoamerica and the Central Andes. This hypothesis could also account for the greater variation in racial types of maize that subsequently evolved under domestication in the Central Andes as compared to Mesoamerica.

A north to south and a later south to north diffusion of maize within the Americas in the agricultural period has been postulated and accepted fairly widely. This process widened and enriched the variability of maize, and contributed through a larger genetic base and, through heterosis, to the increase in the size of ear, in the number and size of kernels, and in the number of ears per plant, as well as to the improved physiological functions of the plant which resulted in the improved yields gradually acquired by maize varieties in Mesoamerica and the Andes. It was not until maize agriculture was fairly well established that later diffusion from Mesoamerica started to contribute significantly to the characteristics mentioned above as components of maize yield in Peru (see Grobman *et al.* 1961, pp. 60–4 & Fig. 18).

The absence of chromosome knobs, except a small one on the long arm of maize chromosome 7, has effectively separated the so-called Andean chromosome types from the Mesoamerican types (McClintock 1959, Grobman *et al.* 1961, Blumenshein *et al.* 1981). From the most primitive to the most evolved of the pure Andean maize races, the Andean chromosome pattern remains constant. In Mexico, even the most primitive maize races possess abundant chromosome knobs (Kato-Y & McClintock 1981). Some localized races of maize in Mesoamerica still exhibit the Andean chromosome types, and this fact could be interpreted as indicating that all primitive maize was of this chromosomal type. This observation lends more credibility to the hypothesis of a very early, pre-agricultural beginning to the dispersal of wild maize from Mesoamerica to the Central Andes followed by independent domestication in both regions, and it certainly explains why teosinte introgression of morphological characters and chromosomal knobs into Mesoamerican maize does not appear in Central Andean maize until thousands of years later.

Present–day races of maize have lost their original characteristic of tunicate grains, which comes from genes *tu* (tunicate, recessive, chromosome 4), and *pn* (papirescent, recessive, chromosome 7). Either as a result of selection towards recessive forms, or by addition of the inhibitor gene of tunicate glumes (*Ti*, chromosome 6), present–day maize is uniformly free of the long tunicate type of glumes, this form of protection having been replaced by husks which are modified leaves that cover the whole ear. Nevertheless, semi-tunicate forms have been recovered from ancient archaeological contexts in the Andean region, and they continue to appear today in ears of maize, as their ancestral phenotypes, in low frequencies both in North and South America. This observation strongly suggests the initial presence of this trait in pre- and early agricultural times in both continents, and incidentally of its non-elimination in Mesoamerica before being transmitted to the maize of South America. If domestication had taken place in Mexico before the dispersal of wild maize, the frequencies of the tunicate phenotype would have been much lower in the maize that diffused south, and hence in the resulting populations of maize that would follow in successive generations. This did not occur. Frequencies of semi-tunicate and tunicate phenotypes are high in ancient archaeological contexts and even higher today in South American populations than they are in Mesoamerica. This added fact points again to the independent domestication of maize in both regions.

The differentiation of Andean and Mesoamerican maize types has been stressed by Goodman & Bird (1977), who have shown that Mexican and South American maize races form different groups, and have developed independently. The genetic investigations of Weissinger *et al.* (1983) with respect to maize DNA in Andean and Mesoamerican maize types, even though inconclusive as yet, also tend to confirm this regional pattern of diversity. We must, however, bear in mind that all these studies are done on present-day maize, so that what is being evaluated are differences at this time in the evolution of the maize species. Archaeological inferences based on this type of evidence must therefore be made very cautiously.

## Archaeological evidence of other crops in the Peruvian highland and coastal regions

It is important to reaffirm that a very early presence of domesticated maize, as is reported here, for the Central Andean region is not the exception but rather a confirmation of a general pattern of very early cultivation of a diverse complex of plants of high food and other utilitarian value. This pattern includes many cases of local plant domestication. Thus we find in the highlands in the Pre-Ceramic II period (9500–8000 bc) the presence of *Oxalis* spp., *Capsicum* cf. *chinense*, and probably *Ullucus tuberosus*. In the Pre-Ceramic II/III transition appear *Inga* sp., *Pouteria* cf. *lucuma* and *Phaseolus vulgaris*. In the Pre-Ceramic III period (8000–6000 bc) are found *Phaseolus lunatus* and *Cucurbita* sp. *Zea mays*, if Lynch's position is accepted, appears in the transitional phase between Pre-Ceramic III and IV, or according to Smith in Pre-Ceramic V (4200–2500 bc). In the Pre-Ceramic VI period (2500–1800/1500 bc) *Canna* sp. is found. At the coast, *Lagenaria siceraria* has been identified from the Pre-Ceramic IV period (6000–4200 bc) and in the Pre-Ceramic V period *Zea mays*, *Persea americana*, *Arachis hypogaea*, *Inga feuillei*, *Manihot esculenta*, *Psidium guajaba*, *Capsicum* sp., *Cucurbita ficifolia*, and *C. moschata*, *Pouteria lucuma*, *Gossypium barbadense*, and *Canna edulis*. And, finally, in the Pre-Ceramic VI period *Annona cherimolia*, *Canavalia* sp., *Pachyrrhizus tuberosus*, *Phaseolus lunatus* and *P. vulgaris*, *Capsicum baccatum* and *C. chinense*, *Ipomoea batatas*, *Solanum tuberosum* or *stenotomum*, *Ullucus tuberosus*, and *Oxalis tuberosa* are found (Martins-Farias 1976, Ugent *et al.* 1981, 1982, Bonavia 1982, 1984, Hawkes pers. comm.).

# Additional evidence of maize from Chile and Argentina

There is archaeological evidence of early maize in the northern areas of Chile and Argentina, but it is very limited and uncertain, and there are no botanical studies which provide exact data for comparative use. To our knowledge, evidence from Argentina is confined to maize found in the Huachichocana Cave in the Department of Tumbaya. Fernández Distel (1974, 1975) and Aguerre et al. (1975) reported the presence of maize remains in strata with radiocarbon dates of $9620 \pm 130$, $8679 \pm 550$, and $8930 \pm 3300$ bp. The information is, however, vague and the find has been questioned. There is no botanical report. But, in a recent publication, Fernández Distel (1985) insisted that maize is present in the most ancient layer of the cave, with an attributed antiquity of 7500–8000 years bp.

In Chile the existence of pre-ceramic maize was first reported by Bird (1943, 1960) from Arica, but there is no more recent information about the find. Maize has also been reported from a pre-ceramic site called Quiani, to which Rivera (1979) attributes ages of 6170 and 5630 bp, and states that the maize is a popcorn 'similar to modern Coroico'. This comment does not inspire confidence because present-day Coroico is a race from the lowlands of Bolivia and the Amazon Basin, is not a popcorn, and exhibits a characteristic interlocking of cupules in the ear. Pre-ceramic maize has also been reported from Tarapacá, but the authenticity of this find is in doubt. Nuñez and Moragas (1977–78) mention maize remains dated to 4480 bc, but this is based on the work of True et al. (1970) which cites a different date, i.e. 3500–4000 bp; and Rivera (1979) reports that the relevant stratigraphic layers date to 6830, 4780, and 4690 bp. Furthermore, there are no botanical reports on the maize finds themselves. Maize with an antiquity of 4700 years bp (Ampuero & Rivera 1971) was found at San Pedro Viejo in the Ovalle Department, which, according to Galinat, is related to the races Capio Chico Chileno, Negrito Chileno, and Curagua. Nuñez & Moragas (1977–78) reported on maize found at Tiliviche, inland from the coastal town of Pisagua, which was dated to between 5900 and 4850 bp and ascribed by Galinat to the Complex Piricinco-Coroico (this information was confirmed by Núñez Enriquez & Zlatar 1978). Rivera (1979) later claimed that these maize remains dated to 7850, 6950, and 6060 bp. Finally, Rivera (1979) reported pre-ceramic maize from the site of Camarones 14, which was similar to the maize of San Pedro Viejo and dated to 7420, 6650, and 6615 bp.

The potential importance of these discoveries lies in their antiquity, but in order to include this information in the scientific literature for comparative purposes it is necessary to undertake additional, especially botanical, research, or at least to publish the existing information in greater detail. In particular, as Grobman (1982) pointed out, it is very difficult to reconcile the chronology with the reported racial types which are claimed to be earlier here than in the Central Andean area.

## Conclusions

In conclusion, we argue that the question of the origin of maize as a species and its domestication should be clearly separated. There is no doubt that all the evidence points to a Mesoamerican origin of maize as a species, whether one accepts either that wild maize existed as such in nature, or that it originated from teosinte in the wild (cf. Wilkes Ch. 28, this volume). The latter concept has, however, given rise to the idea that maize originated from teosinte through *human selection*, and this has made many authors accept – *a priori* – a diffusionist interpretation of maize domestication.

On the basis of the present evidence, we visualize domesticated maize appearing at virtually the same time in Mesoamerica and the Central Andes. The dates we have for maize in the intermediate geographical region do not conflict with this view, but they throw little light on the problem of its domestication and diffusion. They demonstrate the early existence of maize, but we do not know whether it is wild or domestic.

The evidence as a whole shows clearly that Andean maize is different from Mesoamerican maize. As Pickersgill observes in Chapter 27 (this volume), morphological data, chromosome knobs, and mitochrondrial DNA all support this. It is therefore very difficult to sustain a diffusionist hypothesis for the origin of cultivated maize in the Central Andean region. Nor should maize be considered in isolation from other crops. Both in Mesoamerica and the Central Andes, a complex of domesticated plants appears very early, and in both areas it includes maize. In the light of present evidence the Central Andean complex appears to be the more ancient of the two. In the intermediate geographical region there is no evidence of an early complex of domesticated plants, although certain individual crops, such as manioc, may have been present at an early date.

When Pickersgill (1983, p. 290) discussed monotopic versus polytopic origins with reference to *Phaseolus vulgaris*, she wrote:

> 'There is little evidence of direct long distance contact between Peru and Mexico as early as this, and still less evidence that agriculture was practised before 4000 B.C. in all the intervening areas (a prerequisite for contact diffusion of the domesticate overland). On the other hand, the probable wild ancestor of domesticated *P. vulgaris* does not occur from highland Mexico to northern Argentina (Berglund-Brücher & Brücher 1976) so polytopic domestication seems a plausible explanation of the available data.'

We have no basis for thinking that this reasoning is not valid for maize. It is true that in the case of beans the wild ancestors are known over a large area, whereas wild maize is known only by its pollen, and according to Mangelsdorf as archaeological specimens, although some authors do not accept either of these categories of evidence. In South America wild maize has not been found, but this does not invalidate the reasoning that it did once exist and later disappeared, swamped out by domesticated maize or through other causes. The concept of multiple, independent domestications of cultivated plant species is becoming more widely accepted. We believe that the case for the independent domestication of maize is a strong one and that it should be added to the list of crop plants which appear to have been domesticated separately in South America and Mesoamerica.

## Note

1 Leonard Zeevaert of the Faculty of Engineering of the Universidad Nacional Autónoma de Mexico certified in a pers. comm. to E. Barghoorn (1973, copy with these authors) that the samples taken from the sample core were undisturbed and uncontaminated.

## References

Aguerre, A. M., A. A. Fernández Distel & C. A. Aschero 1975. Comentarios sobre nuevas fechas en la cronología precerámica de la Provincia de Jujuy. *Relaciones* **IX** (Nueva serie), 211–14.

Aikens, C. M. 1981. Review of Guitarrero Cave: *Early man in the Andes*, T. F. Lynch (ed.), XVIII, 328. Studies in Archaeology. New York: Academic Press. In *American Anthropologist* **83**, 224–6.

Ampuero Brito, G. & M. Rivera Diaz 1971. Secuencia arqueológica del alero rocoso de San Pedro Viejo-Pichasca (Ovalle, Chile). *Boletin del Museo Arqueológico de La Serena* **14**, 44–69.

Barghoorn, E. S., M. K. Wolfe & K. H. Clisby 1954. Fossil maize from the Valley of Mexico. *Botanical Museum Leaflets* **16**, 229–40.

Bartlett, A. & E. Barghoorn 1973. Phytogeographic history of the isthmus of Panama during the past 12,000 years (A history of vegetation, climate and sea level change). In *Vegetation and vegetational history of northern Latin America*, A. Graham (ed.), 203–99. New York: Elsevier.

Bartlett, A. S., E. S. Barghoorn & R. Berger 1969. Fossil maize from Panama. *Science* **165**, 389–90.

Bird, J. B. 1943. Excavations in northern Chile. *Anthropological Papers of the American Museum of Natural History* **38**, 171–318.

Bird, J. B. 1960. Preface to second edition. In *Andean culture history*, W. C. Bennet & J. B. Bird (eds), 1–6. New York: American Museum of Natural History.

Berglund-Brücher, O. & Brücher, H. 1976. The South American wild bean (*Phaseolus aborigineus* Burk.) as ancestor of the common bean. *Economic Botany* **30**, 257–72.

Blumenschein, A., B. McClintock & T. A. Kato-Y 1981. Chromosome constitution of races of maize in South America. In *Chromosome constitution of races of maize*, B. McClintock, T. A. Kato-Y & A. Blumenschein (eds), 125–63. Mexico: Colegio de Postgraduados.

Bonavia, D. 1982. *Los Gavilanes. Mar, desierto y oasis en la historia del hombre*. Lima: COFIDE-Instituto Arqueológica Alemán.

Bonavia, D. 1984. La importancia de los restos de papas y camotes de época precerámica hallados en el valle de Casma. *Journal de la Société des Américanistes* **LXX**, 7–20.

Bonavia, D. & A. Grobman 1978. El origen del maíz andino. In *Amerikanistische Studien*, R. Hartmann & U. Oberem (eds), 82–91. St. Agustin: Anthropos-Institut.

Bonavia, D. & A. Grobman 1979. Sistema de depósitos y almacenamiento durante el período precarámico en la costa del Perú. *Journal de la Société des Américanistes* **LXVI**, 21–43.

Feldman, R. A. 1977. *Preceramic corporate architecture from Aspero: evidence for the origins of the Andean state.* 76th Meeting of the American Anthropological Association, Houston.

Feldman, R. A. 1978. Informe preliminar sobre excavaciones en Aspero, Perú, y sus implicaciones teóricas. *Investigaciones Arqueológicas* **2**, 20–7.

Feldman, R. A. 1980. *Aspero, Peru: Architecture, subsistence economy and other artifacts of a preceramic maritime chiefdom.* Unpublished PhD Dissertation, Department of Anthropology, Harvard University, Cambridge, Massachusetts.

Fernández Distel, A. A. 1974. Excavaciones arqueológicas en la Cueva de Huachichocana, Dep. de Tumbaya, Prov. de Jujuy, Argentina. *Relaciones* **VIII**, 101–27.

Fernández Distel, A. A. 1975. Restos vegetales de etapas arcaicas en yacimientos del N.O. de la República Argentina (Pcia. de Jujuy). *Etnia* **22**, 11–24.

Fernández Distel, A. A. 1985. Huachichocana: informes específicos. Ficha técnica de la Cueva CH III. *Paleoetnológica* **IX**, 9–11.

Galinat, W. C. 1972. Common ancestry of the primitive races of maize indigenous to the Ayacucho area in Peru. *Maize Genetic Cooperation Newsletter* **46**, 107–8.

Galinat, W. C. 1977. The origin of corn. In *Corn and corn improvement*, G. F. Sprague (ed.), 1–47. Madison: American Society of Agronomy.

Goodman, M. M. & R. McK. Bird 1977. The races of maize IV: tentative grouping of 219 Latin American races. *Economic Botany* **31**, 204–21.

Grobman, A. 1974. Conceptos actuales sobre evolución del maíz. *Informativo del maíz* **3**.

Grobman, A. 1980. Informe sobre el maíz precerámico de Aspero enviado a R. Feldman. Unpublished typescript.

Grobman, A. 1982. Maíz (*Zea Mays*). In *Los Gavilanes. Mar, desierto y oasis en la historia del hombre*, D. Bonavia, 157–79. Lima: COFIDE-Instituto Arqueológico Alemán.

Grobman, A. & D. Bonavia 1978. Preceramic maize on the north-central coast of Peru. *Nature* **276**, 386–87.

Grobman, A., W. Salhuana, R. Sevilla & P. C. Mangelsdorf 1961. *Races of maize in Peru.* Washington: National Academy of Sciences.

Grobman, A., D. Bonavia, D. Kelley, P. C. Mangelsdorf & J. Cámara-Hernández 1977. Study of Pre-ceramic maize from Huarmey, north-central coast of Peru. *Botanical Museum Leaflets* **8**, 221–42.

Heiser, C. B., Jr. 1989. Domestication of Cucurbitaceae: *Cucurbita* and *Lagenaria*. In *Foraging and farming: the evolution of plant exploitation*, D. R. Harris & G. C. Hillman (eds), ch. 30. London: Unwin Hyman.

Iltis, H. H., J. F. Doebley, R. M. Guzmán & B. Pazy 1979. *Zea diploperennis* (Gramineae): a new teosinte from Mexico. *Science* **203**, 186–8.

Kato-Y, T. A. & B. McClintock 1981. The chromosome constitution of races of maize in north and middle America. In *Chromosome constitution of races of maize*, B. McClintock, T. A. Kato-Y & A. Blumenschein (eds), 9–124. Mexico: Colegio de Postgraduados.

Kelley, D. H. & D. Bonavia 1963. New evidence for preceramic maize on the coast of Peru. *Ñawpa Pacha* **1**, 39–41.

Lanning, E. P. 1960. *Chronological and cultural relationships of early pottery styles in Ancient Peru.* Unpublished PhD dissertation, Department of Anthropology, University of California, Berkeley.

Lanning, E. P. 1967. *Peru before the Incas.* Englewood Cliffs, NJ: Prentice-Hall.

Lathrap, D. W. & D. Collier 1976. *Ancient Ecuador. Culture, clay and creativity 3000–300 B.C./El Ecuador antiguo. Cultura, cerámica, creatividad 3000/300 A.C.* Chicago: Field Museum of Natural History.

Lathrap, D. W. & J. C. Marcos 1975. Informe preliminar sobre las excavaciones del sitio Real Alto por la Misión Antropológica de la Universidad de Illinois. *Revista de la Universidad Católica* **III**, 41–64.

Lynch, T. F. (ed.) 1980. *Guitarrero Cave. Early man in the Andes.* New York: Academic Press.

Lynch, T. F., R. Gillespie, J. A. J. Gowlett & R. E. M. Hedges 1985. Chronology of Guitarrero Cave, Peru. *Science* **229**, 864–7.

MacNeish, R. S. 1969. *First annual report of the Ayacucho Archaeological-Botanical Project.* Andover: Robert S. Peabody Foundation for Archaeology.

MacNeish, R. S., A. Nelken-Terner & A. Garcia-Cook 1970. *Second annual report of the Ayacucho Archaeological-Botanical Project.* Andover: Robert S. Peabody Foundation for Archaeology.

MacNeish, R. S., T. C. Patterson & D. L. Browman 1975. *The Central Peruvian prehistoric interaction sphere.* Andover: Robert S. Peabody Foundation for Archaeology.

McClintock, B. 1959. Chromosome constitution of some South American races of maize, *Carnegie Institute of Washington Yearbook* **58**, 454–6.

Magoja, J. L., I. C. Palacios, L. M. Bertoia & M. E. Streitenbger 1985. Evolution of *Zea. Maize Genetic Cooperation Newsletter* **50**, 61–7.

Mangelsdorf, P. C. 1974. *Corn. Its origin, evolution and improvement.* Cambridge, Mass.: The Belknap Press of Harvard University.

Martins-Farias, R. 1976. *New archaeological techniques for the study of ancient root crops in Peru.* Unpublished PhD Dissertation, Department of Plant Biology, University of Birmingham, Birmingham, England.

Moseley, M. E. & G. R. Willey 1973. Aspero, Peru: a reexamination of the site and its implications. *American Antiquity* **38**, 452–68.

Núñez, L. & W. C. Moragas 1977–78. Ocupación arcaica temprana en Tiliviche, Norte de Chile (I Región). *Boletin del Museo Arqueológico de La Serena* **16**, 53–76.

Núñez Henriquez, P. & V. Zlatar Montan 1978. Tiliviche IB y Aragón-1 (Estrato 5); dos comunidades precerámicas coexistentes en Pampa de Tamarugal, Pisagua Norte de Chile. In *Actas y trabajos, III Congreso Peruano 'El Hombre y la cultura andina',* Vol. II, R. Matos (ed.), 734–56. Lima.

Patterson, T. C. 1971. Central Peru: its population and economy (village developed in Central Peru long before the introduction of agriculture). *Archaeology* **24**, 316–21.

Persall, D. M. 1978. Phytolith analysis of archeological soils: evidence for maize cultivation in Formative Ecuador. *Science* **199**, 177–8.

Pearsall, D. M. 1989. Adaptation of prehistoric hunter–gatherers to the high Andes: the changing role of plant resources. In *Foraging and farming: the evolution of plant exploitation,* D. R. Harris & G. C. Hillman (eds), ch. 19. London: Unwin Hyman.

Pickersgill, B. 1983. Dispersal and distribution in crop plants. *Sonderband des naturwissenschaftlichen Vereins in Hamburg* **7**, 285–301.

Pickersgill, B. 1989. Cytological and genetical evidence on domestication and diffusion of crops within the Americas. In *Foraging and farming: the evolution of plant exploitation,* D. R. Harris & G. C. Hillman (eds), ch. 27. London: Unwin Hyman.

Pickersgill, B. & C. B. Heiser, Jr. 1978. Origins and distribution of plants domestic-ted in the New World tropics. In *Advances in Andean archaeology*, D. L. Browman (ed.), 133–65. Paris: Mouton.

Piperno, D. R. 1984. A comparison and differentiation of phytoliths from maize and wild grasses: use of morphological criteria. *American Antiquity* **49**, 361–83.

Piperno, D. R. 1989. Non-affluent foragers: resource availability, seasonal short-ages, and the emergence of agriculture in Panamanian tropical forests. In *Foraging and farming: the evolution of plant exploitation*, D. R. Harris & G. C. Hillman (eds), ch. 34. London: Unwin Hyman.

Rivera, M. A. 1979. La agriculturización del maíz en el Norte de Chile: actualización de problemas y metodología de investigación. In *Actas V Congreso Nacional de Arqueología Argentina*, 157–80. San Juan.

Smith, Jr., C. E. 1980. Ancient Peruvian highland maize. In *Guitarrero Cave. Early man in the Andes*, T. F. Lynch (ed.), 121–43. New York: Academic Press.

Spinden, H. J. 1917. The origin and distribution of agriculture in America. In *Proceedings of the 19th International Congress of Americanists*, 269–76. Washington, D.C.: Smithsonian Institution.

Towle, M. A. 1954. Plant remains. In *Early Ancon and Early Supe Cultures. Chavin Horizon sites of the central Peruvian coast*, G. R. Willey & G. M. Corbett (eds), 130–8. New York: Columbia University Press.

Towle, M. A. 1961. *The ethnobotany of Precolumbian Peru*. New York: Viking Fund Publications in Anthropology.

True, D. L., A. L. Núñez & H. P. Núñez 1970. Archaeological investigations in northern Chile: Project Tarapaca-Preceramic resources. *American Antiquity* **35**, 170–84.

Ugent, D., S. Pozorski & T. Pozorski 1981. Prehistoric remains of the sweet potato from the Casma valley of Peru. *Phytologia* **49**, 401–15.

Ugent, D., S. Pozorski & T. Pozorski 1982. Archaeological potato tuber remains from the Casma valley, Peru. *Economic Botany* **36**, 182–92.

Vescelius, G. S. 1981. Early and/or not-so-early man in Peru. The case of Guitarrero Cave Part 1. *The Quarterly Review of Archaeology* **2** (1), 11–15; **2** (2), 13, 19–20.

Weir, G. & D. Bonavia 1985. Coprolitos y dieta del Precerámica Tardio de la costa peruana. *Boletin del Instituto Francés de Estudios Andinos* **XIV**, 85–140.

Wilkes, G. 1989. Maize: domestication, racial evolution, and spread. In *Foraging and farming: the evolution of plant exploitation*, D. R. Harris & G. C. Hillman (eds), ch. 28. London: Unwin Hyman.

Weissinger, A. K., D. H. Timothy, C. S. Levings III & M. M. Goodman 1983. Patterns of mitochondrial DNA variation in indigenous maize races of Latin America. *Genetics* **104**, 365–79.

Willey, G. R. & J. M. Corbett 1954. *Early Ancon and Early Supe Cultures. Chavin Horizon sites of the central Peruvian coast*. New York: Columbia University Press.

Zevallos, M. C. 1966–71. *La agricultura en el Formativo Temprano del Ecuador (Cultura Valdivia)*. Guayaquil: Casa de la Cultura Ecuatoriana, Núcleo del Guayas.

Zevallos, M. C., W. C. Galinat, D. W. Lathrap, E. R. Leng, J. G. Marcos & K. M. Klumpp 1977. The San Pablo corn kernel and its friends. *Science* **196**, 385–9.

# 30 *Domestication of Cucurbitaceae:* Cucurbita *and* Lagenaria

CHARLES B. HEISER, Jr.

Several genera of the family Cucurbitaceae have furnished species that have been domesticated for food or other purposes in both the Old and New World. Species of two of these, *Cucurbita* and *Lagenaria*, are among the earliest to appear in the archaeological record in the Americas, and it is these that are discussed in this chapter. When investigating the beginnings of agriculture it is the earliest plants that are of greatest interest, although the older the domesticated plant is the more difficult it may be to determine its origin.

## The squashes: *Cucurbita* spp.

Five different species of *Cucurbita*, commonly known in English by such names as squash, marrow, and pumpkin, were domesticated in the Americas, four in Middle America and one in South America. Wild progenitors have now been proposed for all five species. *Cucurbita ficifolia*, a highland species and the only perennial among the domesticates, probably had its origin in Mexico but apparently had reached the Andes in pre-Conquest times. Whitaker (1980) has suggested that it may have been derived from *C. martinezii*, a wild species of southern Mexico. *Cucurbita maxima* is the only species that was clearly domesticated in South America and was confined there until the 16th century. Although in the past it was sometimes regarded as an escape from cultivation, *C. andreana* of Argentina and Uruguay is now accepted as its ancestor (Millan 1945, Whitaker 1980). *Cucurbita moschata* was cultivated from the southwestern United States to northern South America. It has been associated with *C. lundelliana* of southern Mexico which may be implicated in its origin (Whitaker 1980). *Cucurbita mixta*, which was grown in Mexico and the southwestern United States when the Spanish arrived, has recently been shown to be closely related to *C. sororia* of western and southern Mexico (Merrick 1984, Decker 1986). It is the fifth species, *C. pepo*, that has recently received the most attention.

The archaeological record reveals that *C. pepo* is the first species to have been domesticated, it having been recovered in the Valley of Oaxaca, Mexico at 10 750–9840 bp (Whitaker & Cutler 1971) and from the Ocampo Caves in Tamaulipas at 9000–7500 bp (Whitaker *et al.* 1957). Although Flannery (1973) has questioned whether the seeds from the earliest records represent domesticated plants, the seed pictured from Ocampo appears to be larger than that of wild pepo gourds. No measurements are given for the single seed found in the earliest level at Oaxaca, but more material is reported from the next level, dated to 9400–9200 bp. Although it is impossible to say exactly when *C. pepo* became domesticated, it certainly was quite early and it was one of the first plants to be domesticated in Mexico.

In the United States the earliest report of *C. pepo* comes from the Koster site in Illinois (Fig. 30.1) at 7000 bp (Conard *et al.* 1984). Only rind fragments were found, and although these are regarded as coming from 'cultivated' plants, they could represent a wild plant or weed. Pepo next appears at Phillips Spring, Missouri; the Tellico Reservoir, Tennessee; and in western Kentucky at around 4000 bp or slightly earlier. The material from Phillips Spring has been interpreted as an early domesticated form (Kay *et al.* 1980, King 1985).

Until very recently the only plant known that might be the progenitor of *C. pepo* is *C. texana*, the Texas gourd, of southeastern Texas. Although usually treated as a different species, it is quite clear from several lines of evidence that the Texas gourd belongs to the same species as *C. pepo* (Decker 1986, Heiser 1985a). Originally described as *Tristemon texana* in 1848, it was transferred to *Cucurbita* in 1857 by Gray who remarked that it might be a naturalized variety of *C. pepo* var. *ovifera*, the ornamental gourd, although he later pointed out that it might be a native plant (Gray 1850, 1857). It is sometimes very difficult to be certain whether a particular plant is a native, wild species or a naturalized escape from cultivation, although most botanists who have studied this plant since the time of Gray are inclined to consider it the former (Heiser 1985b). A recent study of allozyme variation (Decker 1986), while not conclusive, certainly does nothing to destroy the possibility that *C. texana* is a wild species. If it could be shown that Indians or European settlers cultivated *C. pepo* var. *ovifera* in central Texas before 1848 (although this in itself would not necessarily be decisive), there still might be some justification for regarding the Texas gourd as a naturalized plant. Spontaneous populations that had been identified as escapes from *C. pepo* are known from Alabama, Arkansas, Illinois, and perhaps Missouri, but a study of seeds and allozymes from some of these populations by Decker and Wilson (1986, Decker 1986) suggests that they might be remnants of *C. texana* that had been introgressed with *C. pepo*.

Thus it appears that *C. texana* once may have had a much more extensive distribution than it does today. Perhaps it reached Illinois during the Hypsithermal interval beginning about 8000 bp, at which time the climate of Illinois was warmer and drier (King 1981), and then its distribution became more restricted between 900 and 400 years ago when cooler temperatures began to prevail. The gourd from the Koster site, therefore, could have come

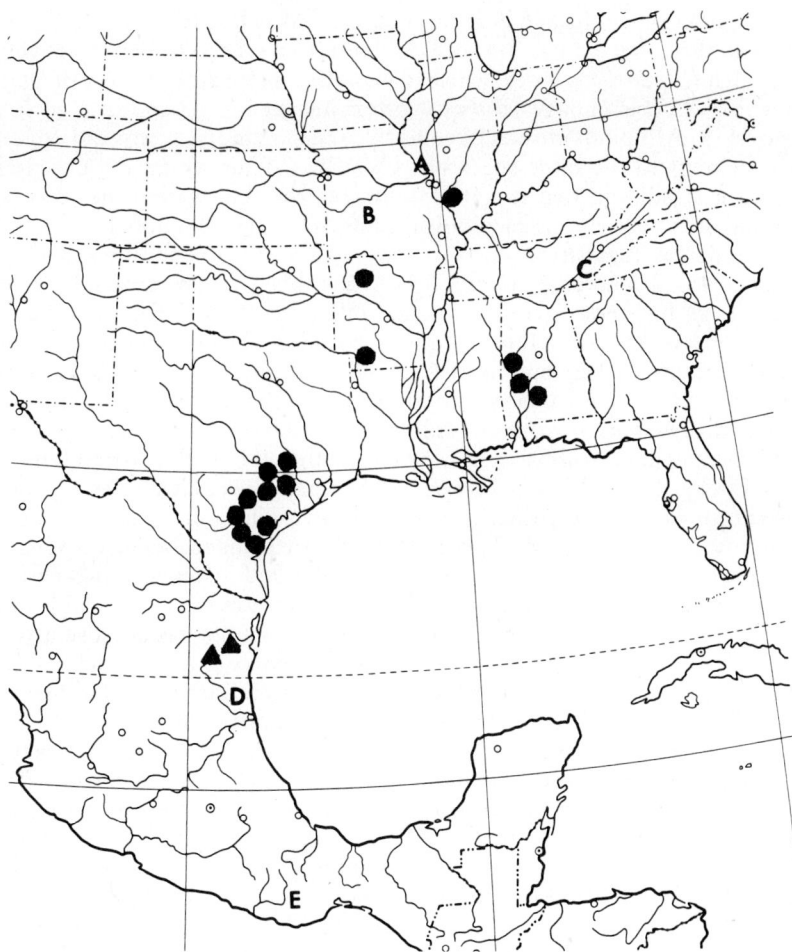

**Figure 30.1** Map showing some of the sites mentioned in connection with *Cucurbita pepo*: (A) Koster, Illinois; (B) Phillips Spring, Missouri; (C) Tellico Reservoir, Tennessee; ●, distribution of *C. texana* and plants approaching *C. texana*; ▲, distribution of *C. fraterna*; (D) Ocampo Caves, Tamaulipas; (E) Guila Naquitz, Oaxaca (from Goode Base Map Series, no. 202, University of Chicago, used with permission).

from naturally occurring plants in the area. In the paper presented by Heiser (1986) at the World Archaeological Congress, of which this is a revised version, the possibility that this gourd may also at one time have occurred in Mexico was mentioned. Such a gourd has now been reported by Andres *et al.* (1986), under the name of *C. fraterna*, from two localities in Tamaulipas, 400 km south of the range of *C. texana*. *Cucurbita fraterna* was described by

Bailey in 1943 and, although he thought there was a close relationship of it to *C. texana*, the roots, fruits, and seeds had not been seen. The new discovery reveals that *C. fraterna* is indeed close to *C. texana* in the morphology of all its characters. A preliminary study of allozymes tends to confirm such a relationship. Although crosses have not yet been made, it seems quite clear that it belongs to the same species as *C. texana*. Thus we have a potential progenitor (assuming that it is not an escape from cultivation) not too far from one of the earliest archaeological finds of *C. pepo* (Fig. 30.1).

Two separate domestications were proposed for *C. pepo* four decades ago (Carter 1945, Whitaker & Carter 1946) but this was not maintained by Whitaker in his more recent papers. The hypothesis of two separate domestications was revived by Heiser (1985a, b). The new information on the more extensive distribution of *C. texana* makes such a hypothesis more likely. Furthermore, it has been shown, based on the analysis of the enzyme systems, that two main groups of cultivars can be recognized in *C. pepo*, one of which could have originated in Mexico and the other in the eastern United States (Decker 1986). This, of course, could readily be explained by separate domestications, although other explanations involving a single origin cannot necessarily be ruled out. If *C. pepo* had two such independent origins, it might also explain why it was present in the United States so much earlier than the other domesticated Mexican food plants. On the other hand, one might also postulate that it appears early in the United States because it was the first domesticate among the food plants of Mexico. But, if so, why did it take so long for maize and other Mexican plants to reach the United States? Galinat (1985) has pointed out that maize was a short-day plant and that it took a long time for it to be acclimatized in the northern latitudes, but many other Mexican domesticates, including Mexican *C. pepo*, are also short-day plants. If *C. pepo* was independently domesticated in the eastern or central United States we do not face that problem, however. Thus, although a single domestication in Mexico cannot be ruled out, separate domestications in the United States and Mexico appear far more likely. The old idea that a domesticate had but a single origin can no longer be accepted for a number of other domesticated species (Heiser 1965, Mason 1984, Pickersgill Ch. 27, Bonavia & Grobman Ch. 29, this volume).

Why and how was the wild gourd domesticated? Because the wild gourds have little flesh and what little they have is extremely bitter, it is usually assumed that it was seeds that were first used by people for food. Today, seeds of *C. pepo*, considerably larger than gourd seeds, however, remain a fairly important source of food in Mexico. It has also been suggested that the pepo gourds served as containers and perhaps as rattles. I have found very little specifically on pepo gourds among the North American Indians. One difficulty is that when the word gourd alone is used one can not always be sure whether *C. pepo* or *Lagenaria* is meant, although often from the context one can be reasonably sure. One of the best discussions of gourds among the Indians is Speck's (1941), but even here in a few places it is difficult to interpret whether *C. pepo* or *Lagenaria* is the gourd being discussed.

Certainly, the larger size and thicker rind of *Lagenaria* make it far superior for use as containers and rattles, so it seems likely that if *C. pepo* was once used for these purposes, it was replaced by *Lagenaria* once people acquired the latter. Another possible explanation for the rarity (if indeed that is true) of pepo gourds among the Indians may be suggested. Once they had sweet-fleshed forms, i.e. squashes, perhaps some people realized that if they grew the gourds as well, it could result in some bitter tasting squash appearing the next year, for the two will readily intercross, produce fertile offspring, and bitterness will be dominant.

For *C. pepo* to have been used as a squash, mutations for loss of bitterness and increase of flesh would have had to occur. While weedy *C. pepo*, perhaps encouraged at times, could have served to supply seeds, containers, and rattles, I think we have to look to conscious human selection to account for the development of varieties with bitter-free flesh, and this would probably involve the deliberate planting of seeds. *Cucurbita pepo* bears separate 'male' and 'female' flowers on the same plant, is pollinated by bees, and is self-compatible so that selfing can take place. Selfing could have allowed a fairly rapid development of forms with bitter-free flesh. The plants – sumpweed (*Iva annua*), sunflower (*Helianthus annuus*), and chenopod (*Chenopodium bushianum*) – that followed *C. pepo* into domestication in the central and eastern United States (cf. Watson Ch. 35, this volume) have a very different floral biology. Although the sunflower is insect-pollinated, it is self-incompatible, and both the sumpweed and chenopod are wind-pollinated and the former is self-incompatible as well. Moreover, when planting began it is unlikely that seeds from single plants of these three plants were used, whereas seeds from a single fruit of *C. pepo* would likely have been used. Thus, the development of a domesticated *C. pepo* may have been accomplished fairly readily and this may, in part at least, account for its being one of the earliest domesticated plants.

## The bottle gourd: *Lagenaria siceraria*

The bottle gourd, *Lagenaria siceraria*, sometimes called calabash, and here-after simply referred to as gourd, leaves us with more unanswered questions than does *C. pepo*. It deserves discussion, however, if for no other reason than Lathrap's (1977) eloquence in associating it with the beginnings of agriculture in the Americas. Certainly, it occurs very early in the archaeo-logical record of the New World, both in Mexico – 9000 bp at Tamaulipas, 9400–9200 bp at Oaxaca, and 7500 bp at Tehuacan – and in Peru at 13 000 bp and 8000–7500 bp (Richardson 1972, King 1985). The earliest report is MacNeish's at Ayacucho, but Flannery (1973) believes that it may be intrusive there. For the United States it is reported from Missouri at 4300 bp and from Tennessee at 4400 bp (King 1985).

Now that the identification of material from Thailand dated at 8000 bp or earlier has been shown to be erroneous (Heiser 1979), there is no archaeological material from the Old World nearly as old as that from the Americas. Nevertheless, it is thought that the gourd is indigenous to Africa. The reason for this belief is that the other five species of the genus are African (Jeffrey 1980). The gourd is unlikely to have derived from any of these species, however. Truly wild forms of the gourd have yet to be documented, but it does commonly grow spontaneously in many places where it is usually thought to represent escapes from cultivation.

A morphological survey of gourds (Heiser 1973) revealed two major races or subspecies of *Lagenaria siceraria*, one from Asia and the other from Africa and the Americas. This accords well with the most recent hypothesis that the gourds of America came from Africa rather than from Asia. Whether the gourd arrived in the Americas by floating across the Atlantic or was carried there by man has long been a controversy (Richardson 1972, Heiser 1979). I favour the former. In fact, water may be the primary natural means of dispersal of gourds, and gourds could have been carried by rivers to the oceans where currents could have carried them to other continents. This, of course, could have happened to wild gourds so there is no need to call for a very early domestication of a gourd in Africa to account for the gourds in America more than 10 000 years ago.

Because indisputably wild gourds have not been found, we can only speculate as to the appearance of the wild form. From what is known of the other species of *Lagenaria*, we might suppose the wild gourd to have had relatively small, spherical fruits with bitter flesh and rather small seeds. On this basis we might also expect the wild gourd to have had rather thin rinds, but this may not necessarily be true for perhaps this species was originally selected for human use in preference to the other ones because it had thicker rinds.

We may assume that the wild species, not only in Africa but also in the Americas and perhaps in Asia as well, early became used as containers and rattles and the seeds may have been used for food, very much as in *C. pepo*. I have found only two references to the use of seeds for food in recent times, one from China and one from Africa. The seeds are reported to be bitter (Ford 1985) and to contain saponins (Watt & Breyer-Brandwijk 1962). My own sampling indicates otherwise. I have found seeds from a number of cultivars, including some with bitter flesh, to have a pleasant nut-like taste. There was some difficulty in removing the seed coat, but perhaps roasting would make it easier to remove. Ground seeds when placed in water and agitated do not form suds, a negative response for the presence of saponins.

Although there are reports of the young fruits of the bitter varieties being used for food, (Watt & Breyer-Brandwijk 1962), they probably were little used as such until bitter-free mutants were selected. Although gourds are usually regarded as a minor food source, their use for this purpose was quite widespread and they are still so used in some parts of the world, particularly in eastern Asia. The bitter-free gourds also had another advantage in that the dried gourd did not require special treatment before it could be used as a container for water and other liquids.

Great variation occurs in the size and shape of the gourd and in the thickness of the rind. This is hardly unexpected, for, as Darwin pointed out, a domesticated plant usually shows its greatest variation in that character for which people cultivate it. The variation in the seeds, particularly in Africa, however, is as great as that of the fruits. There does not seem to be any particular correlation between the seed characters and any characters of the fruit except size. The great seed variation is difficult to explain unless we assume that it results from deliberate selection for the seeds. This, of course, might have occurred if the seeds were an important food or if there was some ceremonial importance attached to them.

As the original wild gourd came to be used by people, we may suppose that the plant became a weed around human habitations. In fact, it may have already been pre-adapted to such habitats as a plant of naturally distributed sites along rivers. Thus, there would have been no need to cultivate the plants. Pickersgill (Pickersgill & Heiser 1977) was told by farmers in some parts of northeastern Brazil that they never sow gourds because sufficient plants for their needs volunteer spontaneously in disturbed habitats. The question may therefore be raised as to whether gourds among some people have come down to the present as weeds rather than as domesticated plants.

There is, of course, no doubt that the gourd exists as a domesticated plant today. As long as gourds remained weeds, people would probably have had to be content with limited variations in the size and shape of the fruits. If mutants occurred with larger fruits or unusual shapes, conscious selection would have been necessary for their development and maintenance. We can only speculate as to how this was accomplished, and, in fact, we have little knowledge of how different fruit types are maintained today in the tropics. It is also necessary to call upon artificial selection to explain the development of bitter-free gourds. Bitterness is controlled by a single dominant gene (Watt & Breyer-Brandwijk 1962), so it may have been relatively easy to stabilize the bitter-free characteristic. Like *C. pepo*, gourds can be self-pollinated, but we do not know the extent of inbreeding, nor do we know the pollinating insects in the tropics. We do know that among some people, the Polynesians for example (Best 1925, Handy & Handy 1972), in contrast to the earlier example from Brazil, great care was exercised with all aspects of gourd growing, including the planting of seeds. The question of when and where the gourd first became a domesticated plant cannot be answered. Quite aside from the fact that we cannot be sure of the nature of the wild gourd or the originally weedy gourd, the early archaeological records consist mostly of small rind fragments which tells us very little about the gourd.

Why the gourd became extinct as a wild plant, if indeed it has, also cannot be answered. If people started cultivation in the same area where the plants grow naturally, perhaps on river banks, its natural area may have been modified. Hybridization might occur between the newly domesticated gourd and the wild type. As a result the wild gourd would be contaminated with 'domesticated genes' so that it might lose its adaptation for a natural existence. It is difficult, however, to imagine these events happening unless the wild plant initially had a rather restricted range.

## Conclusion

The presence of the squash, *C. pepo*, and the gourd, *L. siceraria*, in the central and eastern United States earlier than any other domesticated plant has been used as evidence that agriculture in the United States came from Mexico and was not an indigenous independent development (Ford 1985 and cf. Watson Ch. 35, this volume). This is not necessarily true, for, as has been shown, the Texas gourd, which probably at one time had a more extensive distribution, qualifies as the likely ancestor of *C. pepo*. The bottle gourd, on the other hand, most likely had to come to the United States overland from Mexico, unless gourds floated up on the Gulf coast and then were carried inland by people. It does not necessarily follow, however, that it came as a domestic-ated plant, for it could have arrived as a weed that was subsequently domesticated. Even if the gourd was a Mexican domesticated plant, the people in the United States may have already domesticated *C. pepo* before it reached them.

Ford (1985) has asked why the bottle gourd did not come to the United States along with *C. pepo* when the two were known to be associated very early in the archaeological record of Mexico. If, as I suppose, the latter was domesticated independently in the United States from the Texas gourd, we have an answer.

## Acknowledgements

The author would like to thank Deena Decker, Michael Nee, and Hugh Wilson for providing him with unpublished material and calling his attention to some of the early literature.

## References

Andres, T., M. Nee, N. Weedon & J. Ward 1986. Rediscovery of *Cucurbita fraterna*, the alleged 'brother' to *C. texana*. *Abstracts of the 27th Annual Meeting of the Society for Economic Botany*, p. 9.

Bailey, L. H. 1943. Species of *Cucurbita*. *Gentes Herbarum* **7**, 267–322.

Best, E. 1925. *Maori agriculture*. New Zealand Dominion Museum Bulletin, no. 9.

Bonavia, D. & A. Grobman 1989. Andean maize: its origins and domestication. In *Foraging and farming: the evolution of plant exploitation*, D. R. Harris & G. C. Hillman (eds), ch. 29. London: Unwin Hyman.

Carter, G. F. 1945. *Plant geography and culture history in the American Southwest*. New York: Viking Fund Publications in Anthropology.

Conard, N., D. Asch, N. Asch, D. Elmore, H. Gove, M. Rubin, J. Brown, M. Wiant, K. Fransworth & T. Cook 1984. Accelerator radio-carbon dating of evidence for prehistoric horticulture in Illinois. *Nature* **308**, 443–6.

Decker, D. S. 1986. *A biosystematic study of* Cucurbita pepo. Unpublished Ph.D. dissertation, Department of Biology, Texas A & M University, College Station, Texas.

Decker, D. S. & H. D. Wilson 1986. Numerical analysis of seed morphology in *Cucurbita pepo*. *Systematic Botany* **11**, 595–607.

Flannery, K. V. 1973. The origins of agriculture. *Annual Reviews of Anthropology* **2**, 271–310.

Ford, R. I. 1985. Patterns of prehistoric food production in North America. In *Prehistoric food production in North America*, R. I. Ford (ed.), 341–64. Anthropological Paper No. 75, Museum of Anthropology, University of Michigan, Ann Arbor.

Galinat, W. C. 1985. Domestication and diffusion of maize. In *Prehistoric food production in North America*, R. I. Ford (ed.), 245–78. Anthropological Paper No. 75, Museum of Anthropology, University of Michigan, Ann Arbor.

Gray, A. 1857. Researches in the specific characters and the varieties of the genus *Cucurbita*. *American Journal of Science and Letters* **24**, 440–3.

Handy, E. S. C. & E. Handy 1972. *Native planters in old Hawaii: their life, lore and environment*. Bernice P. Bishop Museum Bulletin no. 233, Honolulu, Hawaii.

Heiser, C. B. 1965. Cultivated plants and cultural diffusion in nuclear America. *American Anthropologist* **67**, 930–49.

Heiser, C. B. 1973. Variation in the bottle gourd. In *Tropical forest ecosystems in Africa and South America*, B. J. Meggers, E. S. Ayensu & N. D. Duckworth III (eds), 121–8. Washington, D.C.: Smithsonian Institution Press.

Heiser, C. B. 1979. *The gourd book*. Norman: University of Oklahoma Press.

Heiser, C. B. 1985a. *Of plants and people*. Norman: University of Oklahoma Press.

Heiser, C. B. 1985b. Some botanical considerations of the early domesticated plants north of Mexico. In *Prehistoric food production in North America*, R. I. Ford (ed.), 57–72. Anthropological Paper No. 75, Museum of Anthropology, University of Michigan, Ann Arbor.

Heiser, C. B. 1986. Domestication of Cucurbitaceae: *Cucurbita* and *Lagenaria*. In *Recent advances in the understanding of plant domestication and early agriculture*, D. R. Harris & G. C. Hillman (eds). London: Allen and Unwin (mimeo).

Jeffrey, C. 1980. A review of the Cucurbitaceae. *Botanical Journal of the Linnean Society* **81**, 233–47.

Kay, M., F. King & C. Robinson 1980. Cucurbits from Phillips Spring: new evidence and interpretations. *American Antiquity* **45**, 806–22.

King, F. B. 1985. Early cultivated cucurbits in eastern North America. In *Prehistoric food production in North America*, R. I. Ford (ed.), 73–97. Anthropological Paper No. 75, Museum of Anthropology, University of Michigan, Ann Arbor.

King, J. E. 1981. Late Quaternary vegetational history of Illinois. *Ecological Monographs* **51**, 43–62.

Lathrap, D. W. 1977. Our father the cayman, our mother the gourd: Spinden revisited, or a unitary model for the emergence of agriculture in the New World. In *Origins of agriculture*, C. A. Reed (ed.), 713–51. The Hague: Mouton.

Mason, I. L. (ed.) 1984. *Evolution of domesticated animals*. London: Longman.

Merrick, L. C. 1984. Natural hybridization of wild *Cucurbita sororia* group and domesticated *C. mixta* in Mexico. *Abstracts of the 25th Annual Meeting of the Society for Economic Botany*, p. 9.

Millan, R. 1945. Variaciones del zapallito amargo cucurbita andreana y del origen de *Cucurbita maxima*. *Revista Argentina de Agronomia* **12**, 86–93.

Pickersgill, B. 1989. Cytological and genetical evidence on the domestication and diffusion of crops within the Americas. In *Foraging and farming: the evolution of plant exploitation*, D. R. Harris & G. C. Hillman (eds), ch. 27. London: Unwin Hyman.

Pickersgill, B. & C. Heiser 1977. Origin and distribution of plants domesticated in the New World tropics. In *Origins of agriculture*, C. A. Reed (ed.), 803–35. The Hague: Mouton.

Richardson, J. B. 1972. The pre-Columbian distribution of the bottle gourd (*Lagenaria siceraria*): a re-evaluation. *Economic Botany* **26**, 265–73.

Speck, F. G. 1941. *Gourds of the southeastern Indians*. Boston: New England Gourd Society.

Watson, P. J. 1989. Early plant cultivation in the Eastern Woodlands of North America. In *Foraging and farming: the evolution of plant exploitation*, D. R. Harris & G. C. Hillman (eds), ch. 35. London: Unwin Hyman.

Watt, J. M. & M. Breyer-Brandwijh 1962. *The medicinal and poisonous plants of southern and eastern Africa*. Edinburgh: Livingstone.

Whitaker, T. W. 1980. *Cucurbitaceas americanas utiles al hombre*. Buenos Aires: Comision de Investigaciones Cientificas.

Whitaker, T. W. & G. F. Carter 1946. Critical notes on the origin and domestication of the cultivated species of *Cucurbita*. *American Journal of Botany* **33**, 10–15.

Whitaker, T. W. & H. Cutler 1971. Prehistoric cucurbits from the Valley of Oaxaca. *Economic Botany* **25**, 123–7.

Whitaker, T. W., H. Cutler & R. MacNeish 1957. Cucurbit materials from the caves near Ocampo, Tamaulipas. *American Antiquity* **22**, 352–8.

# 31 *The domestication of roots and tubers in the American tropics*

## J. G. HAWKES

## Introduction

A study of the domestication of root and tuber crops, as with all other domesticates, demands not only detailed information on dated and accurately determined archaeological materials but also some idea of the palaeoclimatic and palaeoecological conditions under which they were first taken into cultivation. It also requires a solid basis of information about the present-day crop and its related wild species from taxonomic, phytogeographical, ecological, and cytogenetic standpoints. Finally, the results obtained from these studies need to be correlated and conclusions drawn from the various types of evidence obtained.

## Origins of root and tuber domestication

We know very little of the processes of domestication of roots and tubers, but we assume that they may have followed the generalized pattern for seed crops (Hawkes 1969). Wild species with weedy tendencies, it is assumed, began to colonize the open areas round dwellings, and were gathered as part of the normal plant-food procurement activities of hunter–gatherers. As the plants established themselves they grew better than in the wild because of the higher nitrogen levels round the caves or huts. This first stage led on naturally to the second stage where regular harvesting of roots and tubers took place at the end of the wet season and the onset of the dry season. Finally, and after perhaps a long time-lapse, the third phase of *planting* as well as harvesting took place, and fixed-plot or perhaps even swidden agriculture began to develop (Hawkes 1969, 1983). Once both planting and harvesting formed part of the seasonal operations, agriculture could be said to have begun, and the two early stages might well be described as 'incipient' or 'proto' agriculture. A stage of harvesting without planting has been described by Hawkes (1969, p. 24) and it is possible that examples of this stage still exist.

Harris (1969, 1972, 1973) has argued that tropical agriculture developed by means of ecosystem manipulation rather than by replacement, as happened in temperate regions. For the tropical forests he postulates a gradual replacement by man of species of little economic value by ones of greater value, while at the same time maintaining the general ecosystem structure. He suggests that this innovation may have taken place in marginal transition zones, or ecotones, between major ecosystems, such as forest or woodland margins bordering savannas, rivers, or coasts, as well as the transition zones between lowland and upland regions. In such ecotones the competition from the natural climax vegetation would not perhaps have been so intense and hence permanent settlements of hunter–gatherers would have been easier to establish and maintain.

Harris considers, furthermore, that root and tuber planting was first developed in tropical zones. He (and Sauer also, in 1952) rightly pointed out that the food-reserve systems of the wild ancestors of such plants must have developed in response to well-marked dry seasons of between 5 and 7½ months, because otherwise there would have been no reason for such food-reserve systems to have evolved. Seed cultures, he thought, would be better suited to areas with really long dry seasons.

We should therefore look for the origins of tropical root and tuber crops not in the rain forests, where continual humidity allows year-round vegetative growth, and there is no strong natural selection favouring the development of underground storage organs, but in the summer-green rain forests and woodlands with a well-marked dry season where the development of underground starchy food reserves helps the plant to survive the dry season and to regenerate quickly when the rain returns (Sauer 1952, p. 40).

No doubt such crops, once domesticated, would have been taken into the tropical rain forests at a later stage after the agricultural practices associated with them had become well understood. This implies that agriculture may have come later to the Amazon Basin than to the summer-green rain forests and thorn-scrub areas, where at least some of the lowland tropical root and tuber crops were originally domesticated. Figure 31.1 shows areas of 2.5–5 months' drought ($V_2$) all round the Amazon Basin, with even drier regions of 5–7.5 months or more ($V_{3-5}$) in northeastern Brazil and parts of northern Colombia and Venezuela, as well as in Central America and Mexico. In all these regions tropical root and tuber crops could have been domesticated.

## Climatic and phytogeographical crop groups

A particularly interesting aspect of root and tuber agriculture in the American tropics is the development of three climatically and phytogeographically distinct groups of crops (Table 31.1). The first occurs in the lowland tropics and comprises six distinct species or species groups. The second is to be found in the mid- to fairly high-altitude warmer valleys of the South American Andes and elsewhere. It comprises five distinct species or species groups. The third, which includes potatoes, is a group of high-Andean

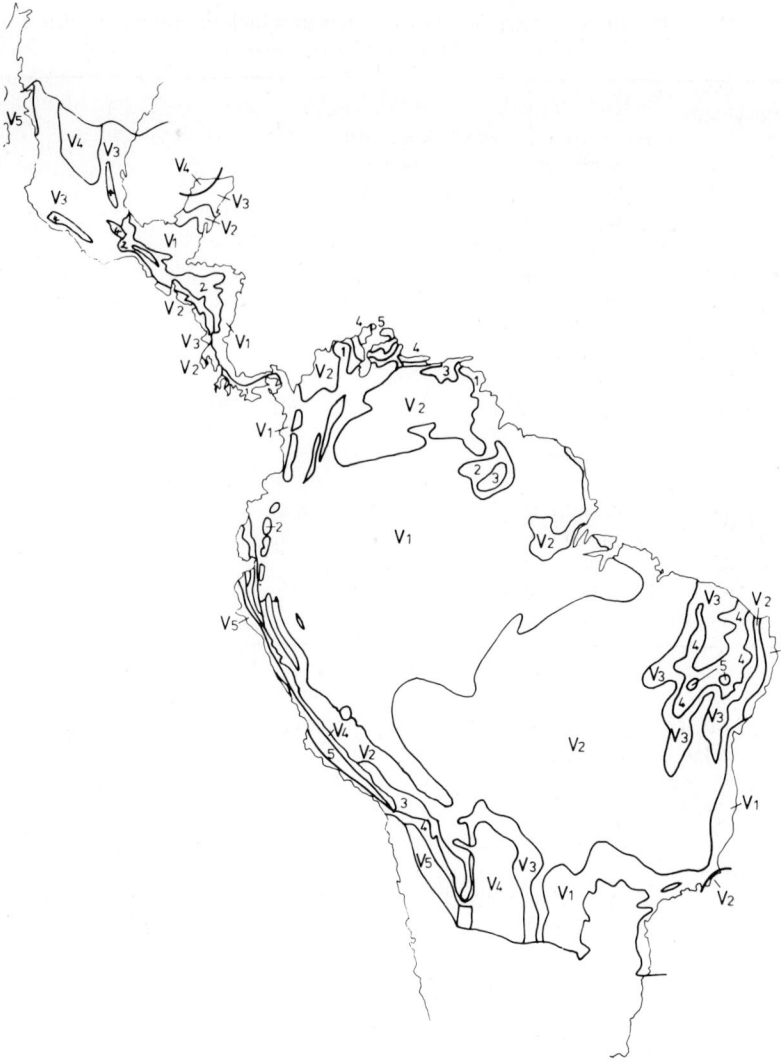

**Figure 31.1** Tropical season climates in Mexico, Central America, and South America (redrawn from Landsberg *et al.* 1965).

temperate to cool-temperate cold-resistant species. This group is ecologically unique, and without parallel elsewhere in the world. It contains five species or species groups. The ancestral wild forms of these plants can mostly still be found; they sustain a rather poor existence in the ecotones between high *páramo* forest and *puna* steppe, or colonize rocky areas with thin soils where no perennial grass or herb can survive.

**Table 31.1**   The three phytogeographical zones in which the root and tuber crops of the American tropics originated.

---

Tropical zone
   *Manihot esculenta*: manioc, cassava, *aypi, yuca*
   *Ipomoea batatas*: sweet potato, *batata, camote, kumara*
   *Dioscorea trifida*: Indian yam, *cush-cush, yampee*
   *Maranta arundinacea*: arrowroot, *ereu*
   *Xanthosoma sagittifolium*: coco-yam, *yautia, malanga, ocumo*
   *Calathea allouia*: topee tambu, *lerén, alluia, topinampur*
Warm temperate zone
   *Arracacia xanthorrhiza*: arracacha, *apio, yengo*
   *Canna edulis*: achira
   *Polymnia sonchifolia*: yacón, *llacón, aricoma*
   *Pachyrrhizus tuberosus*, *P. ahipa*, and *P. erosus*: yam bean, *ajipa, jícama, xíquima, catzotl*
   *Mirabilis expansa*: mauka
Cool temperate zone
   *Solanum tuberosum* and related species: potato, *papa*
   *Oxalis tuberosa*: oca, *cavi*
   *Ullucus tuberosus*: ulluco, *papa lisa*
   *Tropaeolum tuberosum*: añu, *isaña, mashua, cubio*
   *Lepidium meyenii*: maca

---

In total, then, we have 16 species or species groups, which, if we add to these related cultigens in the genera *Xanthosoma*, *Pachyrrhizus*, and *Solanum*, would be increased to over 25. This represents a greater range of root and tuber crops, in species and family diversity, as well as in the range of ecological adaptation which they encompass, than occurs anywhere else in the world.

The majority possess an underground stem, root tuber, or rhizome which is harvested for food and is the organ by which the plant propagates itself vegetatively. However, it should be pointed out that there are seven exceptions, as follows.

(a)   Two species, *Arracacia xanthorrhiza* and *Calathea allouia*, which possess a stem-like rootstock at, or just below, ground-level from which the plant is propagated, and root-storage tubers below this which are used for food but cannot serve as propagation organs.

(b)   *Manihot esculenta*, the root tubers of which are used for food but cannot be used for propagation. With this species, portions of the above-ground stem are used for propagation provided that they contain nodes from which buds and roots can grow.

(c)   *Lepidium meyenii* and three species of *Pachyrrhizus* (*P. ahipa*, *P. tuberosus*, and *P. erosus*). All these are propagated from true seeds and not (or perhaps only rarely) from the radish-like or turnip-like root/hypocotyl.

The method of propagation of *Mirabilis expansa*, although one might assume the plant to be seed propagated, is in fact by basal shoots or pieces of the succulent stems.

In these seven species a more sophisticated concept of propagation is needed on the part of the early cultivators than with the species where the part harvested for food is used also for propagation. It has been often remarked that root and tuber agriculture may have been older than seed agriculture, because the roots and tubers were harvested from and planted back into the earth, while seeds were harvested from near the top of the plant and sown in the soil. However, this hypothesis does not stand up to scrutiny, because, in certain ancient centres of agriculture (Southwest Asia, North China) there were no tuber crops at all. Nevertheless, the techniques of root and tuber planting applied to manioc and the other crops listed above may have been secondary, and derived from the earlier, less-sophisticated procedures of harvesting and eating or planting one and the same organ, as with the potato and the sweet potato. There is as yet insufficient evidence to prove or disprove this hypothesis, but it should certainly be borne in mind when more data become available.

## Individual crop origins

In this section the individual crops are discussed in the same sequence as is shown in Table 31.1. Detailed botanical and cytogenetical evidence on the relationship between the crops and their assumed wild prototypes cannot, however, be given here.

### Tropical crop species

#### *MANIHOT ESCULENTA*: CASSAVA, MANIOC, *AYPI, YUCA*

At the time of the discovery of America by Europeans, cassava was cultivated very widely in the lowland tropics of South America, Mesoamerica, and the Caribbean. The tuberous roots are an excellent source of starch though their protein content is very low.

All variants of cultivated cassava contain poisonous cyanogenic glycosides, but the so-called 'sweet' varieties which contain rather low amounts can be eaten after simple boiling; more complex methods are needed to extract the large quantities of glycosides from the 'bitter' varieties, but because they yield better than the sweet ones and their starch is of superior quality they are very widely grown. Where bitter varieties are grown, these form the major starch source, but in the areas of predominantly sweet varieties the major staple is maize. According to Harris (1973), it is likely that in recent years maize has spread farther into areas of cassava cultivation within the equatorial rain forests. There is a tendency for sweet varieties to be cultivated in the western Andes and in Central America and Mexico, with the bitter varieties concentrated east of the Andes in Venezuela, Brazil, and elsewhere. This led earlier authors to divide manioc into two distinct species, sweet and bitter, but the studies of Rogers and his co-workers have shown that such a distinction cannot be maintained (Rogers 1962, 1963, 1965, Rogers & Appan 1973, Rogers & Fleming 1973).

Although about 100 species of wild *Manihot* are now recognized not all of these may be close to the cultigen, *M. esculenta* (Rogers & Appan 1970). Concentrations of species are to be found in two dry areas, one on the Pacific coast of Mexico and Central America and the other in northeastern Brazil (Rogers 1963). This does not necessarily mean that the origin of cultivated manioc should be looked for in those areas. It is said by various authors that there is a concentration of diversity of the cultivated forms in each of those areas, but this may be due to hybridization with wild species rather than to antiquity of cultivation in the Vavilovian sense.

Work on cytogenetical relationships between wild and cultivated *Manihot* species has been undertaken by various workers, but very little of value from the point of view of the origin of the cultigen has resulted from this so far.

Archaeological data for *M. esculenta* are scattered and not all are authenticated. Thus, Smith (1980) speaks of fragments that 'may well be' manioc found in Guitarrero Cave in the northern Peruvian Andes which were possibly dated at about 2300 bp. This cave is at a rather high altitude for manioc so it is presumed that the materials came by exchange from an adjacent lower elevation. Engel (1970a) found 'possible' manioc at a high-altitude cave in Chilca Canyon, central Peru, claimed by him to be dated to *c.* 10 000 bp. However, both these records need exact verification. Remains of manioc reported from the Tehuacán Valley in central Mexico at *c.* 2900 bp must also be treated with caution (Callen 1967; Bray pers. comm.). The evidence of Martins-Farias (1976) for manioc dated at *c.* 4500 bp at Ancón-Chillón, central Peru, is definite, because it is based on careful microscopic analyses of the materials. Cohen (1978) mentions manioc from the same region at 2900 bp where, he states, 'along with achira (*Canna*) it appears to be the only crop of any dietary significance in the region'. Various other occurrences of manioc for the northern, central, and southern coasts of Peru are mentioned by Towle (1961) but undated. Remains from settlements on the northern Chilean coast reported by Rivera (1975) at ad 600 and by Muñoz Ovalle (1982) at 3700–3500 bp are also of interest. As Smith (1968) points out, manioc obviously did not originate on the Peruvian coast, and in general a more humid area would be indicated.

A number of workers including Lathrap (1970) cite the occurrence of clay griddles, assumed to have been used for baking cassava cakes made from bitter manioc, dated to *c.* 3000 bp in the floodplains of the major rivers of Colombia and Venezuela. He believes that manioc cultivation could have begun in the Amazon Basin (or more possibly along its margins) by 7000 to

9000 bp, but there is as yet no definite evidence for this (see also DeBoer 1975).

Ecological data, cited by various authors, point to the dry areas of northeastern Brazil, northern Brazil to Venezuela, or the dry Pacific coastlands of Mexico and Central America as the most likely areas of domestication. Rogers (1963) considers Mexico to be the most probable area. Renvoize (1971), basing her conclusions on the assumption that sweet and bitter maniocs might have had separate origins in Mexico and the interior of Venezuela respectively, decides on a dual origin. However, it is generally considered that the early cultivators may have started by domestic-ating sweet manioc and then little by little have devised methods for using bitter manioc (Rogers 1963). Unfortunately, we cannot tell whether the remains found archaeologically were sweet or bitter.

Thus at present, although an origin for manioc domestication in northern or northeastern South America seems most likely, the matter still cannot be resolved satisfactorily. If we knew the wild prototype of manioc, or were able to decide from which group of wild species it has evolved, we should perhaps be nearer to a solution of the problem. Rogers (1965) mentions several species, such as *M. aesculifolia*, *M. pringlei*, and *M. isoloba*, which could be considered as possible ancestors of the cultigen. These are from southern Mexico and Guatemala, and for this reason he thought that *M. esculenta* might have originated in that area. Perhaps he is right, but clearly much more taxonomic, biosystematic, and biochemical work, and more well authenticated archaeological finds, are needed before we can expect to resolve the problem of where and when manioc was domesticated.

## *IPOMOEA BATATAS*: SWEET POTATO, *BATATA, CAMOTE, KUMARA*

The sweet potato is generally assumed to have been domesticated some-where in tropical America, although it is now cultivated throughout the world in suitable tropical and subtropical regions. Its position as a possible ancient cultigen in Oceania is not discussed here.

The genus *Ipomoea* (family Convolvulaceae) is distributed in the Old and New Worlds, and even the section Batatas, which includes the sweet potato, although primarily American, possesses Old World representatives (Austin 1978). Unfortunately, the taxonomy of the section Batatas has not generally been agreed upon, though Austin's scheme seems to be acceptable. Simi-larly, the cytotaxonomic picture is confused. Although there is general agreement on the existence of a polypoid series, based on $x=15$, with diploids ($2n=30$), tetraploids ($2n=60$), and hexaploids ($2n=90$) (King & Bamford 1937), much of the work is difficult to interpret because some doubt attaches to the taxonomic identity of the material investigated. *I. batatas* is hexaploid ($2n=90$) and has been classed as an autohexaploid. Much cytological work has been carried out on *I. batatas* and its presumed ancestors, but until a clearer idea of the taxonomy develops, no definite conclusions on its ancestry can be drawn.

Sauer (1950) believed that the sweet potato was domesticated in northern

Venezuela or the Caribbean Islands, while Heiser (1979) cautiously agreed with Yen (1976) that it arose somewhere in South America. Austin (1973) considered that the few varieties and the unpopularity of the sweet potato in Mexico made that country an unlikely place of origin. The idea of a northern South American origin was also adhered to by O'Brien (1972). These views that place the origin of the sweet potato in northern South America co-ordinate satisfactorily with the hypothesis, already referred to, of tuber-crop origins in areas of long dry season.

How then do the archaeological data confirm or contradict this tentative conclusion? Linguistic evidence from the ancient Maya of Yucatán can be interpreted as indicating the use of sweet potato and manioc there before ad 900 to 1000 (Turner & Miksicek 1984), but this is too late a date to shed light on the origins of the sweet potato. O'Brien (1972) also quotes linguistic evidence from various sources, such as proto–Mixtec evidence at 1000 bc and proto–Maya at 2600 bc, but both these dates are much later than the earliest South American evidence.

Rosendahl & Yen (1971) mention sweet potato remains on Easter Island, dated to AD 1526, and in Hawaii at $295 \pm 90$ years bp. These finds in Polynesia are generally believed to be the result of diffusion of the crop from South America. Remains of sweet potatoes have been recovered from north Chilean coastal sites near Arica dated to about ad 600 (Rivera 1975) and at La Capilla in the same region dated to 3700–3500 bp (Muñoz Ovalle 1982).

Colombian material excavated by Correal & Pinto (1983) at Zipacón on the edge of the Sabana of Bogotá was radiocarbon dated to c. 3300 bp. It was carefully checked by cross-sections of the tubers compared with living materials. The interesting records published by Ugent et al. (1981) for a sweet potato tuber at a pre-ceramic site (Huaynuma) on the Peruvian coast near Casma (Ancash) show material dated at 4000 bp, and several tubers were found at another nearby site (Llama-Moxele) dated at 3800–3500 bp. These finds were identified by detailed examination of surface features and of starch grains by scanning electron microscopy. The material at the earlier site was associated with potatoes and *Canna*, and at the slightly later site with potatoes. At another site (Tortugas), dated to 3800–3500 bp, *Solanum* and yam beans were associated with eight sweet-potato tubers. Martins-Farias (1976) identified sweet potato tubers at Ancón-Chillón on the central Peruvian coast dated at 4500 bp, associated with potatoes and cassava. Occurrences there of sweet potato, associated with various other crops, were identified up to 3350 bp.

The oldest remains of sweet potato so far reported are from deposits at Tres Ventanas in the Chilca Canyon, claimed by Engel to date to $10\,080 \pm 170$ bp (Engel 1970a, b, 1984). They were identified by Yen, though he added (in Engel 1970a, p. 56) that he could not be positive that they were tubers of the cultivated species. The illustration in Engel (1984, Fig. 49) is not diagnostic, but because wild tuber-bearing species do not exist nowadays we could assume that these tubers were probably those of *Ipomoea batatas* (Yen 1976). It is clear that the tubers must have been brought up to the

Tres Ventanas site from lower elevations, though whether from the coast or from the eastern Andean slopes or valleys is impossible to tell.

From all these data one point of possible significance stands out clearly. This is, that no archaeological materials of sweet potatoes have been recovered from any of the ancient Mexican sites such as Tehuacán, Tamaulipas, and Nochixtlan (Mangelsdorf *et al.* 1964, Smith 1967, 1976), and there is only inferential evidence from Central America. This then tends to confirm the hypothesis of a South American origin.

Nevertheless, as with manioc, we are left in considerable doubt about the exact area of domestication of the sweet potato and the direction of diffusion of its cultivation. There are similar doubts as to its mode of evolution from wild prototypes, and exactly which wild species were involved. As usual, the early archaeological finds come from the coast of Peru and adjacent valleys, where aridity favours the preservation of organic remains, but where this crop could not have been first domesticated because no wild prototypes occur there. If the early Chilca Canyon materials of 10 000 bp are really authentic, we must look for an even earlier origin for the sweet potato in the semi-arid lowland tropics east of the Andes. Inspired guesses point to northern South America, but until the cytotaxonomic data are properly correlated and the early archaeological evidence re-confirmed, and greatly augmented, we shall remain as uncertain as ever.

## *DIOSCOREA TRIFIDA*: INDIAN YAM, *YAMPEE, CUSH-CUSH*

This is the only American species of yam (family Dioscoreaceae) to be domesticated, compared with the more numerous domesticated species in tropical Africa and tropical Asia. Coursey (1967, 1976, Alexander & Coursey 1969) pointed out that the American yams possess a base chromosome number of nine in contrast to the African/Asian number of ten, but in any case it seems clear that a separate domestication of *D. trifida* must be allowed. It is also possible that *D. convolvulacea* and the allied *Rajania cordata* may have been cultivated to some extent before the introduction of Asian and African species. A form of 'proto-culture' of *D. convolvulacea*, which is encouraged in orchards and cacao plantations, has been mentioned by León (1968) in Costa Rica, and *Rajania* is grown to a limited extent by two Carib communities in Dominica (Alexander & Coursey 1969) and was presumably domesticated there.

The distribution of cultivars of *D. trifida* suggests a domestication in the drier regions on the borders of Brazil and the Guianas, where many forms of this species are known. Thence it was probably taken by the Arawaks, who may have first domesticated it, through Trinidad along the island chain into Jamaica where only one or two forms are known. No archaeological finds of *D. trifida* have been reported, but a domestication date of before 5000 bp is suggested.

## *MARANTA ARUNDINACEA*: ARROWROOT, *EREU*

This is a perennial plant belonging to the family Marantaceae, with thickened rhizomes rich in starch, but needing thorough grinding or maceration to release the starch grains. It occurs as a wild plant in Brazil, northern South America, and perhaps Central America (Sturtevant 1969). Although it is widespread in cultivation now, we cannot be certain that it was ever cultivated in pre-Columbian times, though it was almost certainly used as an antidote for poisoned arrow wounds (Sturtevant 1969). Probably the presence of better and more readily available root crops such as manioc and sweet potato contributed to its neglect as a possible cultigen. No reports of archaeological finds of this plant appear in the literature.

## XANTHOSOMA SAGITTIFOLIUM: COCO-YAM, YAUTIA, MALANGA, OCUMO

The genus *Xanthosoma* (family Araceae) belongs to a group of aroid genera, the rest of which occur in Southeast Asia. *Xanthosoma* itself has been variously classified as one species, *X. sagittifolium*, or divided into three: *X. sagittifolium*, *X. violaceum*, and *X. atrovirens*. All are diploid with 26 somatic chromosomes, but great confusion exists concerning their taxonomy (Plucknett 1976). Indeed, León (1968) mentioned six species but thought that they might all be cultivars of a single one – a view shared by Plucknett.

The cultivated forms of *Xanthosoma* are distributed in the Antilles and South America, but apart from saying 'moist lowlands', Sauer (1950), in company with other authors, offers no detailed opinion as to their place of domestication. Towle (1961) mentions that Herrera and Weberbauer called the Peruvian forms '*uncucha*' and commented that the roots could be made into *chuño*. She also states that Constatin and Blois recovered two tubers from an archaeological site (location not designated). Turner & Miksicek (1984) mention that the ancient Maya of Yucután had *Xanthosoma* before ad 900–1000 (based on linguistic evidence) and they quote Mary Poll as saying that it was apparently found at Tikal. Plucknett (1976) hazards a guess that aroid crops might have been domesticated some 4000 to 7000 years ago, but there is no definite evidence for this. Clearly, much more botanical, cytological, and archaeobotanical research is needed in order to understand the origin of *Xanthosoma* as a crop.

## CALATHEA ALLOUIA: TOPEE TAMBU, LERÉN, ALLUIA, TOPINAMPUR

This tuber crop, belonging to the family Marantaceae, was well distributed in the north of South America and the Antilles when the Spaniards arrived (León 1968). Martin & Cabinallas (1976) state that it is native to Hispaniola, Puerto Rico, some of the lesser Antilles, and from the Guianas to Brazil, Venezuela, Colombia, Ecuador, and Peru. The tubers possess a crisp texture rather like water chestnut or bamboo shoots and range from 2–8 cm long and from 2–4 cm in diameter, propagation being from the rootstock, from which the edible tubers are produced. Only one variety is known and the plant does not set seed.

No tuber materials of this species have been reported from archaeological sites, and the present distribution does not give any clear indication of the original centre of origin, though an area in the drier parts of northern Brazil, Venezuela, and the Guianas is a possibility. Because there appears to be only one uniform variety, Vavilov's 'centre of diversity' technique cannot be applied. A study of the taxonomy and distribution of related wild species and the cytology of the whole group would be most valuable.

## Warm temperate crop species

### ARRACACIA XANTHORRIZA: ARRACACHA, APIO, YENGO

*Arracacha* is a little-known root crop of the temperate Andean valleys which grows at elevations of 1800–2500 m from Venezuela to northern Bolivia (León 1968). It belongs to the family Umbelliferae and produces a bunch of parsnip-like root tubers below the perennial rootstock (cf. *Calathea*). It has not penetrated into Central America or Mexico but has extended into the Caribbean, probably since the Spanish Conquest (Sauer 1950), and it is now of agricultural importance only in Colombia (Bukasov 1930, pp. 525–6, Hodge 1954). Many varieties are grown in Bolivia, in the Yungas of La Paz, and also in the Apurímac department of Peru (Cárdenas 1948).

An excellent account of this plant is given by Hodge (1954). Little is known of its origin and early history but wild forms are reported from various regions, though not on good authority. Hodge reports Constance (1949) as suggesting that the closest wild species to *A. xanthorrhiza* are *A. equatorialis* and *A. andina*, one or the other of which is native to the highlands from southern Ecuador to Bolivia.

The Colombian Chibcha and Pijao Indians are said to have been growing *arracacha* at the time of the Conquest, and Hodge (1954) claims that some of the Nazca pottery designs, formerly attributed to manioc, may in fact have been *arracacha*. These are illustrated by Yacovleff & Herrera (1934, Fig. 9, p. 270) and presumably date to about the beginning of the Christian era. Safford (1917), quoted by Hodge, states that *arracacha* is found in Peruvian Indian tombs, and this statement is also quoted by Towle (1961). Bukasov (1930), apart from mentioning its ancient origins and present-day import-ance in Colombia, does not refer to archaeological materials. Martins-Farias (1976) searched carefully for *arracacha* materials from the Ancón–Chillón sites but found nothing, even though comparisons were made between all the ancient tubers and modern voucher materials of *arracacha*.

Here, then, is another root crop worthy of investigation. The only tentative conclusions we can make as to its origins are that *arracacha* was domesticated somewhere in the northern Andes between Venezuela and Bolivia, at some point in pre-Columbian times.

### CANNA EDULIS: ACHIRA

*Achira* is a warm temperate crop belonging to the family Cannaceae and presumably at the time of the Conquest grown in or near the Andes up to altitudes of 2000 m or more, though its exact distribution is not known. Sauer (1950) considered it to be still fairly common as a market item in coastal Peru and in the temperate valleys to Jujuy and Salta in northern

Argentina. J. D. Sauer (1951) thought it might have been an older crop than maize in the Peruvian coastal river oases and said that it was still grown in the valleys, whereas Cárdenas (1948) spoke of it still existing in an almost wild state in the Bolivian *yungas*. According to Gade (1966) the most intensive present centre of cultivation is to be found in the upper Apurímac valley of southern Peru. Here the rhizome is larger than that of the wild species and can reach a length of 60 cm. The altitude of cultivation is from about 2350 to 2550 m, with about a seven months' dry season.

Archaeological materials have been identified here and there on the Peruvian coast. Towle (1961) mentions specimens recovered from Inca and Inca-associated levels at Pachacámac, near Lima, where Junius Bird was said to have found a rope made from twisted *Canna* leaves. Leaves and fragments of leafy rhizomes were also recovered by him at Huaca Prieta (north Peruvian coast; no date given, but presumably pre-ceramic, no later than 4100 bp). Towle also mentions materials that she recovered in the Nazca region (south Peruvian coast). Cohen (1978), discussing central Peruvian coastal materials, states that *achira* is the dominant food plant (along with cassava) from the Pre-Ceramic period 6. Although tubers are rare, skin and leaf bases identify the remains.

Gade (1966) asserts that no archaeological materials have been recovered from Central America, and Ugent *et al.* (1984) agree with this statement, adding that none is known either in Mexico or Colombia. This again reinforces the view that *achira* may well have been domesticated in Peru or Bolivia.

Ugent *et al.* (1984) made a careful study of materials from a late pre-ceramic site in the Casma valley, northern Peru, radiocarbon dated 4250–3750 bp. The material was studied by phase-contrast and scanning-electron microscopy of the starch grains as well as a macroscopic study of the tubers themselves, in each case compared with present-day voucher materials. Materials from Inca levels at Pachacámac were also identified as *achira*. The authors draw attention to ceramics of Nazca (AD 500) and Chimu (AD 1300–1480) style depicting this plant. Although they quote Moseley as describing *achira* from the Ancón–Chillón central Peruvian site dated to 4500–4300 bp, none of the material was identified as from this plant in the careful studies made by Martins-Farias (1976). Smith (1980b) records a possible *Canna* rhizome from the Guitarrero Cave (500 bc to ad 500).

Ugent *et al.* (1984) agree with several previous writers that *achira* is native to Peru and believe that its area and time of domestication was the north coast about 10 000 years ago, during a period of moister climate than the present. The wild *achira*, they think, would have grown naturally in bushy thickets in savanna areas near the coast and would have been taken into cultivation from such areas. While not entirely disagreeing with this hypothesis, I think we should exercise caution here because we know of other tuber crops from Peruvian coastal archaeological deposits, such as manioc, potatoes, sweet potatoes, oca (*Oxalis*), and *ulluco* (*Ullucus*), that were certainly not domesticated in the coastal region. However, one can certainly agree that domestication may well have taken place at least somewhere in the warm seasonally dry valleys of Peru or even possibly farther south in Bolivia and northern Argentina.

## POLYMNIA SONCHIFOLIA: LLACÓN, YACÓN, ARICOMA

This is a crop of very little importance now, though it might have been more widely grown in former times. Sauer (1950) states that its distribution ranges from Colombia to northwestern Argentina, and Cárdenas (1948, 1969) recorded seeing it in the La Paz and Cochabamba markets in Bolivia. He added that it was grown in the temperate valleys near these cities at altitudes from about 2000 to 2600 m. I myself have seen it in Cuzco in southern Peru. The tubers are sweet and juicy, 10–20 cm long and 6–8 cm in diameter, and are eaten raw (Sauer 1951, Cárdenas 1969). *Polymnia* is a relative of the sunflower in the family Compositae. No wild prototype or closely related wild species appears to be recorded in the literature.

Archaeological records are mentioned by Towle (1961) for the Peruvian coast, and Cohen (1978) states that Towle tentatively identified one specimen from the Colinos level, initial period, at the Ancón–Chillón Tank Site. However, destruction of the original starch content made it impossible to confirm this record.

Clearly, much more botanical and archaeological research is needed, though most authors, if they make any statements at all on the subject, hazard a reasonable guess that *Polymnia* was domesticated in the warm valleys of the high Andes, though not in the cool temperate regions.

## PACHYRRHIZUS SPP.: YAM BEAN, AJIPA, JÍCAMA, ETC.

There are generally agreed to be three species of cultivated *Pachyrrhizus* (family Leguminosae) that have been grown in the Americas from pre-Columbian times onwards (Cárdenas 1969, Smith 1976). These are as follows:

(a) *P. erosus*, which occurs wild in Mexico and northern Central America; this has been cultivated in Central America since before the Conquest and, like the other two species, possesses a thick juicy storage root. Propagation is by seeds in all three species, though there is some evidence of root propagation. *P. erosus* was taken to Asia, probably first by the Spaniards, and is widely grown, especially in Southeast Asia.

(b) *P. tuberosus*, which is native to the headwaters of the Amazon basin, 'where it is cultivated sporadically' (Cárdenas 1969).

(c) *P. ajipa* is native to high-altitude valleys in Bolivia and northwestern Argentina. In Bolivia, Cárdenas states that it is grown only in the *yungas* of La Paz at about 1800 m, but not in the *yungas* of Cochabamba. It is also cultivated in the Argentine province of Jujuy. In Bolivia the roots are always eaten raw. Sauer (1950) says it is almost unknown in modern Peru.

There are several references to yam beans from archaeological sites, both actual remains and ceramics, but there is uncertainty as to which species are represented. I am not aware of any archaeological records of yam beans in Mexico or Central America, and presumably *P. erosus* did not spread into South America. However, it has so far not been possible to distinguish with certainty in the recovered tuber remains from Peruvian sites between *P. tuberosus* and *P. ajipa*. Tropical and high-mountain representatives of other species are recovered in assemblages from the same archaeological deposits on the Peruvian coast (Martins-Farias 1976) so that the coastal location of such sites cannot be taken to indicate that the yam beans were necessarily grown there. Further critical examination of *Pachyrrhizus* specimens is needed to see whether they can be identified to species level.

Engel (1970a, 1984) records remains of '*Pachyrrhizus*, possibly *tuberosus*', claimed to date to $10\,080 \pm 170$ bp, from the high Tres Ventanas Cave in Chilca Canyon. These clearly must have been brought up from lower altitudes. Ugent *et al.* (1981) record yam bean with *Canna* and *Ipomoea* at the Tortugas coastal site in Peru near Casma (Ancash) dated at 3800–3500 bp. Grobman and Bonavia (1978) found *Pachyrrhizus* among maize remains at Los Gavilanes, Huarmey, (final pre-ceramic) dated at $3750 \pm 110$ bp. Towle (1961) mentioned a 'well-preserved tuber' of *P. ajipa* from the Paracas Necropolis (early horizon) remains, and quotes Yacovleff as recording *P. tuberosus* from a Paracas mummy bundle. Whole plants pictured on Paracas ceramics are assigned to *P. tuberosus* (Yacovleff & Herrera 1934), and Cohen (1978) has reported finds of *Pachyrrhizus* at Chuquitanta (La Gaviota phase) on the central Peruvian coast.

Clearly, all these records need to be re-checked as to species, but it seems that one or perhaps both of the South American yam beans, *P. tuberosus* and *P. erosus*, may have been brought into cultivation as long ago as 10 000 bp.

### MIRABILIS EXPANSA: MAUKA

This plant, belonging to the family Nyctaginaceae, was discovered by Rea in an enclosed valley of Bolivia to the north of La Paz in Camacho province (Rea & León 1965, Cárdenas 1969). It has swollen succulent lower stems and tuberous roots, and is cultivated at 2900 m above sea-level, but in a very restricted area. Other records come from Peru and Ecuador (Carlos Arbizu pers. comm.).

There are no published accounts of wild ancestral forms or archaeological remains, and it can only be supposed that the plant was brought into cultivation somewhere in the Andean valleys between Ecuador and Bolivia.

## Cool temperate crop species

### SOLANUM TUBEROSUM AND OTHER SPECIES: POTATO, PAPA

The potato has been recognized as a domesticated plant of the Americas since the 16th century, when it was first brought to Europe. The works of

Salaman (1949), Juzepczuk & Bukasov (1929) and Hawkes (1967, 1978) have, among those of many other workers, established its origin in western South America. Some controversy still exists, however, as to whether there was a single area of origin in the central Andes or whether there was also a second independent one in Chile.

The cultivated potatoes exist as a polyploid series of about seven species, ranging from diploid ($2n=2x=24$) to triploid ($3x=36$), tetraploid ($4x=48$), and pentaploid ($5x=60$). The region of potato cultivation at the time of the Conquest extended from Venezuela southward, along the Andean chain to northwestern Argentina, and again in the coastal belt from south-central to southern Chile. Potato cultivation in Central America and Mexico is generally agreed to have been post-Conquest.

Wild species related to the cultigens are very abundant in number, and extend from the southwestern states of the USA southward into Mexico and Central America, and thence southward along the Andes into Argentina and Chile, and out onto the plains of Paraguay, Uruguay, and southern Brazil. All these wild species possess tubers and most can hybridize with at least one of the cultigens.

The centre of species and varietal diversity of cultivated potatoes lies in the central Andes from central Peru to central Bolivia, and on Vavilov's hypothesis one might well place the origin of domestication in that area (Vavilov 1951). A careful study of the wild species most closely similar to the cultigens reveals that those in series Tuberosa could be candidates, and particularly the Bolivian S. leptophyes.

A study of diversity amongst the cultivated diploids (Tay 1979), revealed that the most 'primitive' wild-looking ones are to be found in S. stenotomum, at the southern end of its range in northern Bolivia. This area also coincides with the distribution area of S. leptophyes. It is thus tentatively postulated that the cultivated potato was first domesticated as a diploid species (S. stenotomum) in the highlands of northern Bolivia from the wild species S. leptophyes. As it spread northward into Peru, and particularly after the tetraploid S. tuberosum ssp. andigenum was formed, it is highly likely that it absorbed genetic diversity from other wild species through hybridization and introgression.

Archaeological data do not disprove this hypothesis. Towle (1961) mentioned probable potato records from Chiripa on the shores of Lake Titicaca, for c. 2500 bp, and Uhle obtained potatoes in the form of chuño at Pachacámac, dated approximately to ad 1000. Lynch (1980) mentions potato materials taken from the Ayacucho Cave, dated at 4500 bp, but Pickersgill (pers. comm.) considers that these records are doubtful. Nuñez Atencio (1982, p. 98) indicates that potatoes were present in coastal sites in northern Chile before ad 900 and after 400 bc.

Martins-Farias (1976) analysed Ancón–Chillón materials excavated by Moseley and co-workers. Phase-contrast light microscopy and scanning-electron microscopy (SEM) were used to identify starch grains, and the SEM studies revealed characteristic water-conducting vessel thickenings.

Potatoes, manioc, and sweet potatoes were established for 4500 bp, but potatoes were absent at higher levels, where sweet potatoes persisted, with manioc and other tuber crops from time to time. Martins-Farias (1976) also verified the Engel materials (Engel 1970a, 1984) from the Tres Ventanas site in the high Chilca Canyon, dated probably at 10 000 bp, the earliest record yet known for Andean tuber crops. This material was also re-verified by Ugent *et al.* (1982). Cohen (1978) also spoke of the potato material at Ancón–Chillón 'occurring sporadically through the sequence', but this does not completely agree with Martins-Farias' results.

Ugent *et al.* (1981) mention the presence of potato remains from Casma (Ancash) dated between 4000 and 3500 bp, in company with sweet potatoes, and in 1982 they described the remains in more detail, and confirmed the dating from the late Pre-Ceramic to the initial Ceramic period. Starch-grain analysis by phase-contrast and SEM techniques was carried out. Both Martins-Farias and Ugent *et al.* mention the effects of cooking; however, Martins-Farias provides evidence of boiling (presumably in gourds, because this was a pre-ceramic site), while Ugent *et al.* (1982) describe fire charring in certain samples.

All three of the studies quoted make a fairly definite statement that the materials analysed were of cultivated and not of wild tubers. The tubers were rather small, but there is not enough evidence to indicate whether they were from *S. stenotomum* or *S. tuberosum*. Nevertheless the archaeological results add weight to the botanical evidence, so that an origin of potato domestication in the high Andes of northern Bolivia some time before 10 000 bp appears likely.

### OXALIS TUBEROS: OCA, CAVI

Sauer (1950) considers that *oca* was probably the second most important root crop of the high Andes after the potato. It seems to have been cultivated from Venezuela to Chile, and had adapted itself in Chile to forming tubers in long days, just as the potato did.

Hodge (1951) also emphasizes the importance of *oca*, especially in southern Colombia and southern Peru, where he states that in some places it rivals the potato. *Oca* tubers when sun-dried are very sweet and are then known as *cavi*; *chuño* (=*caya*) is also made from *oca* at high altitudes, the bitter varieties being used for preference. The best crops are grown from about 2700 to 4200 m, and Hodge thinks that *oca* was first domesticated around the Lake Titicaca Basin.

Cárdenas (1948) records the cultivation of *oca* in the far south of Chile (Llanquihue) and speaks of a wild form, known as *kita*, with thin small white tubers. Gibbs *et al.* (1978) established a base chromosome number of $x=11$ and found near-pentaploids ($2n=58$) and hexaploids ($2n=66$). The latter number was also recorded by Cárdenas & Hawkes (1948).

Archaeological records of *Oxalis* are mentioned for the Guitarrero Cave (Ancash) by Smith (1980b) and Lynch (1980), some possibly wild, some cultivated, dating from about 10 500 bp to 7500 bp. Materials from

Ancón–Chillón, dated to 3750–3850 bp in the Initial Period, were recovered by Moseley (1975) and also analysed by Martins-Farias (1976) using the same methods as those for the potato.

There seems therefore to be good evidence for an ancient domestication of *Oxalis tuberosa*. Although it would be fairly safe to locate its domestication in the Central Andes of Peru and Bolivia it would be unwise at present to try to pin-point its area of origin more precisely.

*ULLUCUS TUBEROSUS: ULLUCO, PAPA LISA*

This again is a high Andean crop, cultivated from Colombia southward to northern Argentina. The tubers are very smooth-skinned (hence '*papa lisa*') and vary widely in colour according to variety. Consumption is mainly confined to the indigenous population. There is only one species, belonging to the family Basellaceae. It possesses rather fleshy leaves, a short creeping stem, and small greenish-yellow flowers.

Cárdenas (1948) mentions a 'wild *ulluco*' like the cultivated one but with tubers barely 1 cm in diameter and uniformly pale purple. These were at Unduavi, north of La Paz, Bolivia. I myself have seen wild plants in forest margins and in hedges in Cochabamba Department, Bolivia, and in Central Peru, near Huancayo. In both cases the tubers were small. Similarly, Brücher (1967) mentions a wild *ulluco* in the cloud-forest zone (as were the records of Cárdenas and of Hawkes, mentioned above), at 2800 to 3300 m altitude in northwestern Argentina (Jujuy province) and southern Bolivia. He calls it *Ullucus aborigineus* and mentions that it has long trailing stems to 2 m, and very small, bitter tubers 0.5–1 cm in diameter. The cultivated *ulluco*, by contrast, has 30-cm long stems and tubers 4–6 cm in diameter. It is rather unlikely that these wild forms are a distinct species, however. Brücher concludes that cultivation first took place in northern Argentina and Bolivia.

Archaeological materials described by Smith (1980b) from the Guitarrero Cave dating from *c.* 10 500 to 7500 bp may be *Ullucus* but this has not yet been verified. However, Martins-Farias (1976), using phase-contrast and SEM analysis of starch and SEM of vessel structure, made definite identifications of *ulluco* at Ancón–Chillón, radiocarbon dated to between *c.* 4000 and 3350 bp, at two distinct levels. These could not have been cultivated on the Peruvian coast, and, like potatoes and *oca*, must presumably have been obtained from the high mountains nearby. Engel (1970a, 1984) obtained what 'could be *ollucu*' from the Tres Ventanas Cave in the high Chilca Canyon, presumably from the 10 000 bp levels, but there is some uncertainty about the identification.

Thus, as with *Oxalis tuberosa*, we can state that *Ullucus tuberosus* was probably domesticated a long time ago, perhaps by or before 4000 bp, and was cultivated at high altitude, whence it was occasionally taken to the coast. The region from central Peru to northern Argentina, where wild forms have been found, seems to be indicated for its domestication.

498     DOMESTICATION OF AMERICAN ROOTS AND TUBERS

*TROPAEOLUM TUBEROSUM: AÑU, ISAÑA, MASHUA, CUBIO*

Belonging to the family Tropaeolaceae, this high–Andean cultigen is grown from Venezuela to northern Argentina. Johns (1981) states that it grows best at 2500–3700 m and, like *maca* (see below, & Johns Ch. 32, this volume), possesses glucosinolates which release mustard oils when the tissues are damaged.

Cárdenas (1948) reported seeing *añu* in its wild state, with long climbing stems in contrast to the rather short stems of the cultigen. Gibbs *et al.* (1978) spoke of both wild and cultivated forms being known in Ecuador, Peru, and Bolivia. Chromosome counts were partly aneuploid and partly 2$n$=52, from which they assumed that this plant was a tetraploid with a base number of 13.

Towle (1961) reports depictions of *añu* on Pacheco vessels dated at *c.* ad 1000, and these are also mentioned by Yacovleff and Herrera (1935). No archaeological remains of *añu* appear to have been reported.

As with the last two species we assume a domestication for *añu* in the high Andes, possibly in the region encompassing Ecuador to Bolivia.

*LEPIDIUM MEYENII: MACA*

Little is known about this crop (family Cruciferae). It is now confined to the high mountains of central Peru in Pasco and Junín Departments, though it was probably more widespread in Colonial and pre-Conquest days (León 1964). Cárdenas (1969) does not know if it has ever been grown in Bolivia. The food source is a root plus hypocotyl with cambial rings, developed as in radish, turnip, and other cruciferous root crops. It is adapted to very high altitudes, 3500–4000 m, and is grown in plots next to plots of frost-resistant potatoes (*Solanum juzepczukii?*). It is propagated by seed, produced in dehiscent pods, so that it would seem, on that criterion only, not to be domesticated (León 1964).

Johns (1981) draws attention to certain biochemical similarities between *maca* and *Tropaeolum* (*añu*) and suggests that there may have been conscious selection for these characters. Cárdenas (1969) mentions a record in a 1958 *Catalogue of the Flowering Plants of Bolivia* by R. Foster in which a wild subspecies *gelidum* of *Lepidium meyenii* is recorded as one of the components of the herbaceous (grass) sward of the *puna* zone. This has a woody rootstock. Because this is the ecological zone in which *maca* is cultivated, it may well have been simply derived there from the wild ancestral subspecies by selection for a non-woody fleshy rootstock and biennial habit (cf. Pearsall Ch. 19, Johns Ch. 32, this volume).

No archaeological remains of *maca* have been identified, but it was presumably domesticated in the high Peruvian Andes.

## Conclusions

From this survey of root and tuber crops it is very clear that much more work is needed on the detailed taxonomy of most of the cultigens and their wild relatives, linked to cytological and biochemical studies, particularly the lowland tropical taxa.

Further archaeological studies are needed in two ways. In the first place, a great deal of the older material needs to be re-studied by the scientific techniques used by Martins-Farias and Ugent. Verification of the age of these plant remains is also necessary, where enough material exists, and the new technique of radiocarbon dating by accelerator mass spectrometry, which allows exceedingly small samples to be dated (Harris 1987), now makes such verification much more feasible.

Secondly, more excavations are needed from sites in the seasonally arid borders of the Amazon Basin, particularly Venezuela and the Guianas, northeastern Brazil, and the southern, drier borders of the Amazon Basin. The seasonally arid medium-to-low-altitude valleys of the eastern Andes also require archaeological exploration.

In the long run, progress in our understanding of the origins of root and tuber cultivation in the American tropics will be made only if the already existing collaboration between archaeologists and botanists is maintained and strengthened.

## Acknowledgements

I would like to thank Professor David Harris and Mr Gordon Hillman for inviting me to participate in the Symposium which gave rise to this book. I am also grateful to Dr Susan Limbrey (Birmingham) for advice and discussions. My grateful thanks are due particularly to Dr Warwick Bray (Institute of Archaeology, University College London) for advice, references, and very valuable discussions. Some useful corrections were supplied by Professor Duccio Bonavia (Lima, Peru) to whom my thanks are also due.

## References

Alexander, J. & D. G. Coursey 1969. The origins of yam cultivation. In *The domestication and exploitation of plants and animals*, P. J. Ucko & G. W. Dimbleby (eds), 405–25. London: Duckworth.

Austin, D. F. 1973. The sweet potato allies: a taxonomic review. *Quarterly Journal of the Florida Academy of Sciences* (Suppl. 1), p. 7.

Austin, D. F. 1978. The *Ipomoea batatas* complex – I Taxonomy. *Bulletin of the Torrey Botanical Club* **105**, 114–29.

Brücher, H. 1967. *Ullucus aborigineus* n. sp., die Wildform einer andinen Kulturpflanze. *Berichte der Deutschen Botanischen Gesellschaft* **80**, 376–81.

Bukasov, S. M. 1930. *The cultivated plants of Mexico, Guatemala and Colombia*. Supplement 47 to the Bulletin of Applied Botany, Genetics and Plant Breeding. Institute of Plant Industry, Leningrad.

Callen, E. O. 1967. Analysis of the Tehuacán coprolites. In *The prehistory of the Tehuacán Valley: I. Environment and subsistence*, D. S. Byers (ed.), 261–89. Austin: University of Texas Press.

Cárdenas, M. 1948. Plantas alimenticias nativas de los Andes de Bolivia. I. Tubérculos, raices y otros productos similares. *Folia Universitaria, Cochabamba* **2**, 36–51.

Cárdenas, M. 1969. *Manual de plantas económicas de Bolivia*. Cochabamba, Bolivia: Imprenta Icthus.

Cárdenas, M. & J. G. Hawkes 1948. Número de cromósomas de algunas plantas nativas cultivadas por los indios en los Andes. *Revista de Agricultura* **5**, 30–2.

Cohen, M. N. 1978. Archaeological plant remains from the central coast of Peru. *Ñawpa Pacha* **16**, 23–50.

Constance, L. 1949. The South American species of Arracacia and some related genera. *Bulletin of the Torrey Botanical Club* **76**, 39–52.

Correal Urrego, G. & M. Pinto Nolla 1983. *Investigación arqueológica en el municipio de Zipacón, Cundinamarca*. Fundación de Investigaciones Arqueológicas Nacionales, Banco de la Republica, Bogotá, Colombia.

Coursey, D. G. 1967. *Yams*. London: Longman.

Coursey, D. G. 1976. Yams. *Dioscorea* spp. In *Evolution of crop plants*, N. W. Simmonds (ed.), 70–4. London: Longman.

DeBoer, W. R. 1975. The archaeological evidence for manioc cultivation: a cautionary note. *American Antiquity* **40**, 419–33.

Engel, F. 1970a. Exploration of the Chilca Canyon, Peru. *Current Anthropology* **11**, 55–8.

Engel, F. 1970b. Recolección y cultivo en los Andes precolombinos. *Anales Científicos UNA* **8**, 122–36.

Engel, F. 1984. Prehistoric Andean ecology. *Man, settlement and environment in the Andes. Chilca*. Department of Anthropology, Hunter College, City University of New York: Humanities Press.

Gade, D. W. 1966. Achira, the edible canna, its cultivation and use in the Peruvian Andes. *Economic Botany* **20**, 407–15.

Gibbs, P. E., D. Marshall & D. Brunton 1978. Studies on the cytology of *Oxalis tuberosa* and *Tropaeolum tuberosum*. *Notes from the Royal Botanic Garden, Edinburgh* **37**, 215–20.

Grobman, A. & D. Bonavia 1978. Pre-ceramic maize on the north-central coast of Peru. *Nature* **276**, 386–7.

Harris, D. R. 1969. Agricultural systems, ecosystems and the origins of agriculture. In *The domestication and exploitation of plants and animals*, P. J. Ucko & G. W. Dimbleby (eds), 3–15. London: Duckworth.

Harris, D. R. 1972. The origins of agriculture in the tropics. *American Scientist* **60**, 180–93.

Harris, D. R. 1973. The prehistory of tropical agriculture: an ethnoecological model. In *The explanation of culture change: models in prehistory*, C. Renfrew (ed.), 391–417. London: Duckworth.

Harris, D. R. 1987. The impact of archaeology on radiocarbon dating by accelerator mass spectrometry. *Philosophical Transactions of the Royal Society, London, Series A* **323**, 23–43.

Hawkes, J. G. 1967. The history of the potato. *Journal of the Royal Horticultural Society* **91**, 207–24, 249–62, 282–302, 364–5.

Hawkes, J. G. 1969. The ecological background of plant domestication. In *The domestication and exploitation of plants and animals*, P. J. Ucko & G. W. Dimbleby (eds), 17–19. London: Duckworth.

Hawkes, J. G. 1978. History of the potato. In *The potato crop: the scientific basis for improvement*, P. M. Harris (ed.), 1–14. London: Chapman & Hall.

Hawkes, J. G. 1983. *The diversity of crop plants*. Cambridge: Harvard University Press.

Heiser, C. B. 1979. Origin of some cultivated New World plants. *Annual Review of Ecology and Systematics* **10**, 309–26.

Hodge, W. H. 1951. Three native tuber foods of the high Andes. *Economic Botany* **5**, 185–201.

Hodge, W. H. 1954. The edible arracacha – a little-known root crop of the Andes. *Economic Botany* **8**, 195–221.

Johns, T. 1981. The añu and the maca. *Journal of Ethnobiology* **1**, 208–12.

Johns, T. 1989. A chemical–ecological model of root and tuber domestication in the Andes. In *Foraging and farming: the evolution of plant exploitation*, D. R. Harris & G. C. Hillman (eds), ch. 32. London: Unwin Hyman.

Juzepczuk, S. W. & S. M. Bukasov 1929. A contribution to the question of the origin of the potato. *Proceedings of the USSR Congress of Genetics, Plant and Animal Breeding* **3**, 593–611.

King, J. R. & R. Bamford 1937. The chromosome number in *Ipomoea* and related genera. *Journal of Heredity* **28**, 278–82.

Landsberg, H. E., H. Lippmann, KH.Paffen & C. Troll 1965. Seasonal climates of the earth. In *World maps of climatology*, E. Rodenwaldt & H. J. Jusatz (eds), 2nd edn. Berlin: Springer-Verlag.

Lathrap, D. W. 1970. *The Upper Amazon*. London: Thames & Hudson.

León, J. 1964. The 'Maca' (*Lepidium meyenii*). *Economic Botany* **18**, 122–7.

León, J. 1968. *Fundamentos botánicos de los cultivos tropicales*. Instituto Interamericano de Ciencias Agricolas de la O.E.A., San José, Costa Rica.

Lynch, T. F. 1980. *Guitarrero Cave: early man in the Andes*. New York: Academic Press.

Mangelsdorf, P. C., R. S. MacNeish & G. R. Willey 1964. Origins of agriculture in Middle America. In *Handbook of Middle American Indians*, R. Wauchope (ed.) *Natural environment and early cultures*, R. C. West (ed.), 427–45. Austin: University of Texas Press.

Martin, F. W. & E. Cabanillas 1976. Lerén (*Calathea allouia*), a little known tuberous root crop of the Caribbean. *Economic Botany* **30**, 249–56.

Martins-Farias, R. 1976. *New archaeological techniques for the study of ancient root crops in Peru*. Unpublished PhD Thesis, University of Birmingham, UK.

Moseley, M. E. 1975. *The maritime foundations of Andean civilization*. California: Cummings.

Munõz Ovalle, I. 1982. Las sociedades costeras en al litoral de Arica durante el periodo Arcaico Tardeo y sus vinculaciones con la costa Peruana. *Chungara* **9**, 124–51.

Nuñez Atencio, L. 1982. Temprana emergencia de sedentarismo en el desierto Chileno: proyecto Caserones. *Chungara* **9**, 80–122.

O'Brien, P. J. 1972. The sweet potato: its origin and dispersal. *American Anthropologist* **74**, 342–65.

Pearsall, D. M. 1989. Adaptation of prehistoric hunter–gatherers to the high Andes: the changing role of plant resources. In *Foraging and farming: the evolution of plant exploitation*, D. R. Harris & G. C. Hillman (eds), ch. 19. London: Unwin Hyman.

Plucknett, D. L. 1976. Edible aroids. In *Evolution of crop plants*, N. W. Simmonds (ed.), 10–12. London: Longman.

Rea, J. & J. León 1965. La Mauka (*Mirabilis expansa* Ruiz et Pavon), un aporte de la agricultura andina prehispanica de Bolivia. *Anales Científicos* **3**, 38–41.

Renvoize, B. S. 1971. The area of origin of *Manihot esculenta* as a crop plant – a review of the evidence. *Economic Botany* **25**, 352–60.

Rivera, Mario A. 1975. Una hipótesis, sobre movimientos poblacionales altiplánicos y transaltiplánicos a las costas del norte de Chile. *Chungara* **5**, 7–31.

Rogers, D. J. 1962. Origins and development of *Manihot esculenta* and allied species. *American Journal of Botany* **49**, 678.

Rogers, D. J. 1963. Studies of *Manihot esculenta* Crantz and related species. *Bulletin of the Torrey Botanical Club* **90**, 43–54.

Rogers, D. J. 1965. Some botanical and ethnological considerations of *Manihot esculenta*. *Economic Botany* **19**, 369–77.

Rogers, D. J. & S. G. Appan 1973 *Manihot, Manihotoides* (Euphorbiaceae). *Flora Neotropica*. Monograph 13. New York: Hafner.

Rogers, D. J. & H. S. Fleming 1973. A monograph of *Manihot esculenta* – with an explanation of the taximetric methods used. *Economic Botany* **27**, 1–113.

Rosendahl, P. & D. E. Yen 1971. Fossil sweet potato remains from Hawaii. *Journal of the Polynesian Society* **80**, 379–85.

Safford, W. E. 1917. *Food plants and textiles of ancient America*. Proceedings of the Second Pan-American Science Congress, Vol. I, 146–59.

Salaman, R. N. 1949. *The history and social influence of the potato* (new edn 1985). Cambridge: Cambridge University Press.

Sauer, C. O. 1950. Cultivated plants of South and Central America. *Handbook of the South American Indians*. Washington Government Printing Office. Bureau of American Ethnology Bulletin 143, Vol. 6, 487–543.

Sauer, C. O. 1952. *Agricultural origins and dispersals*. New York: The American Geographical Society.

Sauer, J. D. 1951. Crop plants of ancient Peru modelled in pottery. *Bulletin of the Missouri Botanical Garden* **39**, 187–94.

Smith, C. E., Jr. 1967. Plant remains. In *The prehistory of the Tehuacán Valley: I. Environment and subsistence*. D. S. Byers (ed.), 220–55. Austin: University of Texas Press.

Smith, C. E., Jr. 1968. The New World centers of origin of cultivated plants and the archaeological evidence. *Economic Botany* **22**, 253–68.

Smith, C. E., Jr. 1976. *Modern vegetation and ancient plant remains of the Nochixtlán Valley, Oaxaca*. Vanderbilt University Publications in Anthropology no. 16. Nashville, Tennessee.

Smith, C. E., Jr. 1980. Plant remains from Guitarrero Cave. In *Guitarrero Cave: early man in the Andes*, T. F. Lynch (ed.), 87–119. New York: Academic Press.

Sturtevant, W. C. 1969. History and ethnography of some West Indian starches. In *The domestication and exploitation of plants and animals*, P. J. Ucko & G. W. Dimbleby (eds), 177–99. London: Duckworth.

Tay, C. S. 1979. *Evolutionary studies on the cultivated diploid potatoes* Solanum stenotomum, S. gonicocalyx, *and* S. phureja. Unpublished PhD Thesis, University of Birmingham, UK.

Towle, M. A. 1961. *The ethnobotany of Pre-Columbian Peru*. Chicago: Aldine Publishing.

Turner, B. L. & C. H. Miksicek 1984. Economic plant species associated with prehistoric agriculture in the Maya lowlands. *Economic Botany* **38**, 179–93.

Ugent, D., S. Pozorski & T. Pozorski 1981. Prehistoric remains of the sweet potato from the Casma valley of Peru. *Phytologia* **49**, 401–15.

Ugent, D., S. Pozorski & T. Pozorski 1982. Archaeological potato tuber remains from the Casma valley of Peru. *Economic Botany* **36**, 82–192.

Ugent, D., S. Pozorski & T. Pozorski 1984. New evidence for ancient cultivation of *Canna edulis* in Peru. *Economic Botany* **38**, 417–32.

Vavilov, N. I. 1951. The origin, variation, immunity and breeding of cultivated plants. *Chronica Botanica* **13**, 1–366 (trans. K. Starr Chester).

Yacovleff, E. & F. L. Herrera 1934. El mundo vegetal de los antiguos Peruanos. *Revista del Museo Nacional, Lima* **3**, 243–322.

Yacovleff, E. & F. L. Herrera 1935. El mundo vegetal de los antiguos Peruanos. *Revista del Museo Nacional, Lima* **4**, 31–102.

Yen, D. E. 1976. Sweet potato *Ipomoea batatas*. In *Evolution of crop plants*, N. W. Simmonds (ed.), 42–5. London: Longman.

# 32 A chemical–ecological model of root and tuber domestication in the Andes

TIMOTHY JOHNS

Plant toxins restrict food selection by generalist herbivores including many species of non-human primates (Freeland & Janzen 1974, Wrangham & Waterman 1981). Although the food procurement of pre-Neolithic human foragers must have been subject to similar constraints, the cultivation of plants and the onset of agriculture made certain plant foods more available to humans. Selection for changes in secondary chemical constituents has been an essential aspect of the domestication of food plants (Rindos 1980, Stahl Ch. 11, this volume). However, it is problematic as to how the wild progenitors of staple cultigens with appreciable levels of plant defensive compounds would have been exploitable on more than a casual basis, and therefore subject to genetic manipulation. Technological and other cultural advances in conjunction with domestication were clearly important in overcoming toxicity in our crop plants. This chapter considers Andean root and tuber crops as a model for understanding chemically mediated inter-actions between humans and plants during the domestication process.

## Human chemical ecology

Awareness among biologists of the chemical basis for many interactions between organisms has increased over the past 20 years. Study of the chemical aspects of herbivory is part of the field of chemical ecology (Harborne 1982). Plants produce defensive compounds to limit predation by both insects and mammals. In turn animals have evolved physiological and behavioural mechanisms for avoiding the adverse effects of dietary toxins.

Investigations of primate feeding behaviour provide useful analogies for understanding human choice of plant chemicals. Research in primate chemi-cal ecology has concentrated on nutrient attainment (see Clutton-Brock 1977) and on secondary compounds as feeding deterrents (McKey et al. 1981, Wrangham & Waterman 1981). As omnivores faced with a changing food environment, apes and other higher primates including humans have highly evolved mechanisms for avoiding toxins. Learned responses to the physiological effects of food are essential for generalist foragers dealing with an unpredictable diet. Significantly, humans are particularly adept at forming conditioned taste aversions to ingested foods containing toxins (Bernstein 1978).

Determinants of feeding behaviour such as taste perception, physiological homeostasis, and learned preferences are shared by humans with other animal species. However, human interactions with the chemical environment are mediated as well by language communication and by technological manipulations of the natural environment. Human chemical ecology must address both biological and cultural concerns. Such a chemical–ecological model applied to the domestication process provides a new perspective on the origins of agriculture, as well as important insight into the evolution of the human diet. This chapter begins with an overview of the known secondary chemistry of Andean root and tuber crops. This is followed by a discussion of two specific research problems involving these crops. The first considers *Tropaeolum tuberosum* and *Lepidium meyenii*, and the second focuses on the potato. Data on the use of clays with bitter potatoes are used to make generalizations on the detoxification function of geophagy and its possible role in plant domestication. The concluding section includes a general discussion of principles governing human interactions with plant chemicals.

## Limiting the toxicity of crop plants

Cooking has been suggested as the major technological advance making plant foods more available to humans (Leopold & Ardrey 1972, Stahl 1984). Seed crops such as cereals and legumes which contain the proteinaceous haemaglutinins (lectins) and proteinase inhibitors, are unquestionably made edible with heating (Liener 1980). However, generally speaking, non–seed foods such as roots and tubers are characterized by non–protein secondary compounds, many of which are not destroyed by cooking. Harris (1977) emphasized the importance of examining toxicity in order to understand the process of cultural selection operating in root and tuber crops. The empirical record of chemical change in crop plants from around the world in comparison with their wild progenitors supports the idea that overcoming toxicity in roots and tubers was a crucial step in their domestication.

## Andean root and tuber crops

In the Andean centre of genetic diversity several root and tuber crops form a complex of common domestication history, cultivation, and use. Selection for changes in chemical composition appears to be a characteristic of these vegetatively propagated crops. Hawkes (Ch. 31, this volume) provides an overview of the biosystematics of the group. The following section summarizes the known chemical diversity found in some of those plants listed by Hawkes.

## Potato (*Solanum spp.* – Solanaceae)

Wild species of potato are generally high in potentially toxic glycoalkaloids (Gregory 1984) and reduction in glycoalkaloid content has been indicated as an essential step in the domestication process leading to *S. stenotomum* Juz. & Buk. (Simmonds 1976, Harborne 1982). The modern interactions of humans at high altitudes with glycoalkaloids in potatoes is discussed in detail below.

## Ulluco (*Ullucus tuberosus* Loz. – Basellaceae)

According to Brucher (1977) *ulluco* (*papa lisa*) produces tubers with less bitterness than its purported progenitor *U. aborigineus* Brucher. Bitterness in *ulluco* is probably due to saponins (Hegnauer 1964, Johns unpublished).

## Oca (*Oxalis tuberosa* Molina – Oxalidaceae)

Cultivators broadly classify *oca* as either for processing or for consumption, and unpalatable varieties are processed by leaching the tubers in running water for a period of weeks and freeze-drying them to produce a product called *caya* (Hodge 1951). More palatable tubers are eaten after little or no processing. Various observers (Hodge 1951) have attributed the recognized differences in *oca* to levels of oxalic acid, although a thorough evaluation of its secondary chemistry has not been undertaken. Oxalic acid is moderately soluble in water and would be removed in the *caya* process. *Oca* tubers are usually placed in the direct sun for several days before consumption to improve their edibility. However, it is unclear that oxalate would decompose with this treatment.

## Añu (*Tropaeolum tuberosum* R. & P. – Tropaeolaceae)

*Añu* (*mashua, isaño, cubio*) is characterized by glucosinolates which undergo enzymatic hydrolysis upon damage of the tissue to release the volatile isothiocyanates, or mustard oils. These are the compounds responsible for the distinctive taste and smell of cruciferous vegetables (MacLeod 1976).

The obligate cultigen, *T. tuberosum* subspecies *tuberosum*, releases only *p*-methoxybenzyl isothiocyanate, while the wild subspecies *silvestre* is characterized by benzyl, 2-propyl, and 2-butyl isothiocyanates (Johns & Towers 1981). Folk beliefs associating *añu* with *maca* (*Lepidium meyenii*), and the possible motivation for humans in selection for qualitative changes in glucosinolate chemistry, are discussed below.

*Añu* is believed to have a crop-protective effect toward other tuber crops in mixed plantings. Nematocidal and insecticidal properties of isothiocyanates may contribute to this quality (Johns *et al.* 1982). Secondary compounds in crops play an essential role in natural pest resistance, and cannot be eliminated without risking loss of yield.

## Yacón (*Polymnia sonchifolia* Poepp. & Endl. – Asteraceae)

*Yacón* is generally consumed raw. Its tubers contain inulin, a form of starch not digestible by humans. The genus *Polymnia* is characterized by sesquiterpene lactones (Seaman *et al.* 1980), although *P. sonchifolia* has not been investigated.

## Mauka (*Mirabilis expansa* R. & P. –Nyctaginaceae)

Hawkes (Ch. 31, this volume) mentions that astringency in *mauka* is eliminated by drying the roots in the sun. Flavonoids, saponins, and haemaglutinins have been reported from the genus *Mirabilis* (Hegnauer 1969, Hardman *et al.* 1983).

## Maca (*Lepidium meyenii* Walp. – Brassicaceae)

The edible root of *maca* is consumed as both food and medicine. It releases benzyl and *p*-methoxybenzyl isothiocyanates (Johns 1981). Chemical studies of wild forms of *L. meyenii* have not been undertaken.

## Biological and cultural aspects of chemical selection

A relationship between *maca* and *añu*, the two isothiocyanate-releasing Andean crops, provides an excellent example of the interrelations of biological and cultural factors in human interactions with secondary chemicals. Similarities in folk beliefs associating the two crops with effects on human reproduction are striking (Johns 1981, Johns 1986a). The association of two isothiocyanate-releasing 'root' crops with fertility suggests that secondary chemistry is in some way related to these folk beliefs. A negative effect of *T. tuberosum*, the *añu*, on male reproductive processes in rats (Johns *et al.* 1982) supports the belief of Andean peoples that the plant has an anti-aphrodisiac effect on males. Both *añu* and *maca* are regarded as having positive fertility effects on females. They are both characterized by aromatic isothiocyanates. At least in the perception of Andean peoples, there is a relationship between aromatic isothiocyanates and human reproduction. Although the use of isothiocyanates to affect human reproduction in general has a Western scientific basis, the specific emphasis on aromatic isothiocyanates seems culturally determined.

The significance of this association is emphasized by the replacement of the three non-aromatic constituents of wild *T. tuberosum* subsp. *silvestre* with *p*-methoxybenzyl isothiocyanate in cultivated subsp. *tuberosum*. Although conceivably this could occur without human intervention, in light of selection on tuber characteristics leading to the domestication of the *añu*, it seems likely that cultural selection for the particular chemistry of the cultigen has been important.

A basic male–female duality which underlies Andean social interaction and extends to interrelations with the natural world may influence the association made between *maca* and *añu*. This duality is particularly prevalent in plant taxonomy (Johns 1986a). *Maca* and *añu* are female in having a horizontal growth form and in growing close to the earth. The *añu* has as its antithesis the *oca*, a plant with an erect form which produces tubers similar to those of the *añu* but notably phallic in shape and in their role in Andean ritual and jest.

The relation between the biological characteristics and the cultural significance of these plants becomes somewhat circular; however, the experimental results supporting antireproductive activity in males are a logical starting point for drawing associations. Antiandrogenic activity adversely affecting libido or general well-being could lead to a conditioned taste aversion. The female benefiting designation could derive from the conceptually opposite effect on males and could be reinforced by its life form. A modern tonic use of *maca* may be purely a cultural artefact with no physiological basis. The *maca* could have been associated with the *añu* as an enhancer of female fertility only on the basis of taste and smell and because of the similarity in life form. Nonetheless, the empirical basis for some of the uses of these plants, and the associations made through taste and smell stand out as a driving force behind their medical uses and their domestication.

## Altiplano agriculturalists: limiting plant toxicity

Extension of cultivation into the frigid and arid areas of the altiplano of Peru and Bolivia represents a secondary phase of Andean agriculture that is primarily related to the ongoing domestication of the potato. Genes for frost and drought resistance have been acquired through introgressive hybridization involving wild species, in particular *S. acaule* Bitt. and *S. megistacrolobum* Bitt. The reintroduction of high levels of glycoalkaloids into potato cultigens through this hybridization, while a problem for Andean cultivators, provided an excellent model for studying the ongoing efforts of humans to limit the quantity of toxic phytochemicals during the domestication process.

Native seed crops make an important contribution to subsistence at high altitudes, to some degree supplanting non-potato tubers in dietary importance. However, these crops, too, contain potential toxins to which humans must be attentive, and they must be considered in any discussion of the chemical environment (Johns & Keen 1985). The edible chenopods, *quinoa* (*Chenopodium quinoa* Willd.) and *cañahua* (*C. canihua* Cook) contain saponins, and bitter forms must be processed to reduce toxicity. Varieties of *quinoa* with seeds selected for low levels of bitterness are known (Gade 1975). The edible lupine, *tarwi* (*Lupinus mutabilis* Sweet), contains high levels of quinolizidine alkaloids and is extensively leached before consumption. *Tarwi* varieties with low alkaloid levels have been produced by plant breeders (Williams 1984). Reduction in alkaloid levels, however, may result in decreased pest resistance. The dynamic between human selection for reduced levels of defensive chemicals and natural selection for high levels of these compounds is an important consideration related to the chemical ecology of domestication (see below).

## *Solanum×ajanhuiri* domestication complex

Selection by humans for changes in secondary chemistry presupposes that genetic diversity in chemical characters, upon which humans may exert selection pressure, exists in the plant populations. *Solanum×ajanhuiri* Juz. & Buk. is a diploid potato indigenous to the Lake Titicaca Basin in southern Peru and western Bolivia which, until its relationship to non-cultivated forms is understood, appears to have extremely restricted genetic diversity. Although only seven clones are known in cultivation, these are found sympatrically with both *S. megistacrolobum* and *S. stenotomum*, the wild and cultivated parents respectively of this hybrid species. Sympatric weed populations that infest altiplano fields are in fact conspecific with *S.×ajanhuiri* cultigens (Johns *et al.* 1987). Many weed *S.×ajanhuiri* clones produce tubers similar in size and appearance to the primitive *yari* clones of *S.×ajanhuiri*. *Yari* cultigens in turn are recognized by their Aymara cultivators as 'domesticated wild potatoes'. *Ajawiri* clones are likely backcrosses between *yari* and *S. stenotomum*. The hybrid swarm represented by wild, weed, and cultivated forms of *S.×ajanhuiri* provides an excellent example for studying the ongoing selection and domestication of new potato varieties. Members of the hybrid swarm which has wild (and high-glycoalkaloid containing) *S. megistacrolobum* as one parent and domesticated *S. stenotomum* as the other, might be expected to show a continuum of variation in glycoalkaloid levels, upon which humans apply selection pressure.

A chemotaxonomic study of the *S.×ajanhuiri* complex (Johns & Osman 1986, Osman *et al.* 1986) supported the close relationship of weeds and cultigens that was shown in a general phenetic study using numerical methods (Johns *et al.* 1987). Weeds and the primitive *yari* cultigens are unique in having level of total glycoalkaloids considerably lower than either *S. megistacrolobum* or the more advanced cultigens. The total glycoalkaloid contents of the components of this domestication complex, then, vary in a way contrary to the expected continuum, decreasing from *S. megistacrolobum* to weeds, to *yari*, to *ajawiri*, to *S. stenotomum*. Glycoalkaloid levels and the actual discontinuous pattern are summarized in Figure 32.1. The route to the domestication of *S.×ajanhuiri* from *S. megistacrolobum* must have brought about a reduction in levels of glycoalkaloids of some 15–20-fold. Within crop–weed–wild complexes (Small 1984) characteristics which show the greatest discontinuity are typically those that have been subject to directed human selection. In the *S.×ajanhuiri* complex glycoalkaloids are, then,

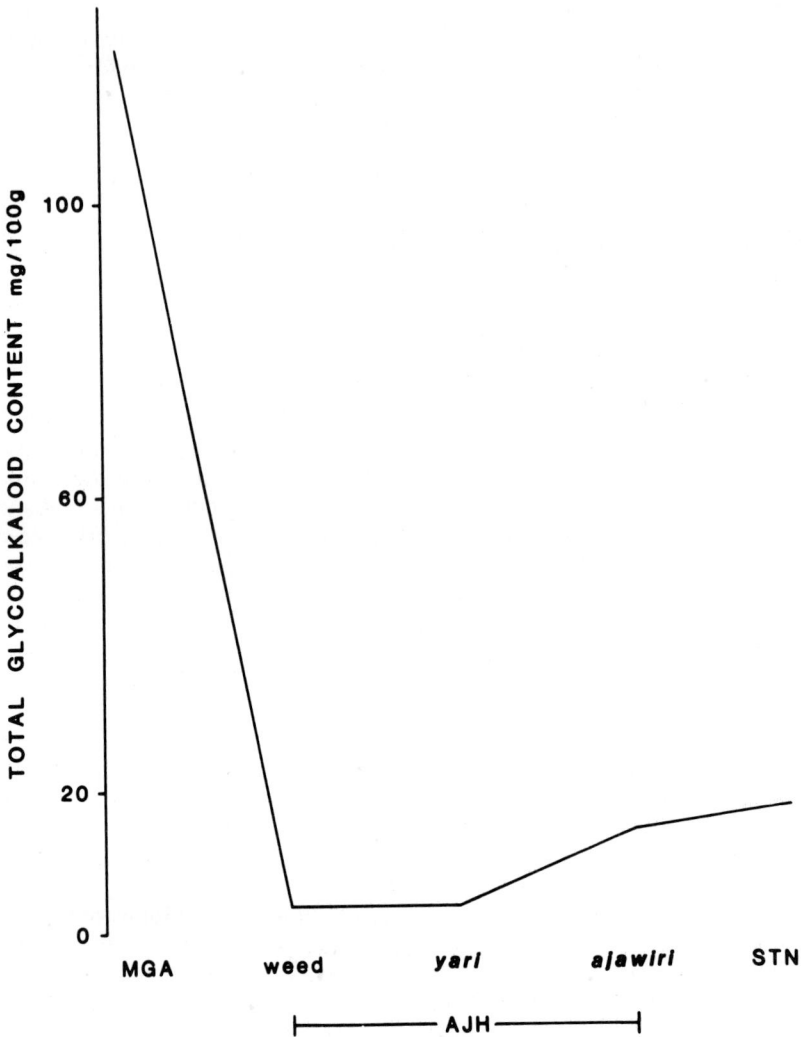

**Figure 32.1** Discontinuities in glycoalkaloid levels in the *Solanum×ajanhuiri* hybrid swarm. *Yari* and *ajawir* are cultivated clones, and weeds are sympatric non-cultivated populations of *S.×ajanhuiri* (AJH). Hybridization between wild *S. megistacrolobum* (MGA) with high levels of glycoalkaloids and the cultivated parent *S. stenotomum* (STN) was predicted to produce a range of intermediate total glycoalkaloid levels related to the phylogeny of the group, i.e. a line with a constant slope from MGA to STN.

among the tuber characteristics that show evidence of human selection in the domestication process.

## Taste perception and chemical selection

Human selection for reduced quantities of glycoalkaloids assumes a capacity to recognize differences in alkaloid levels between varieties. Evaluations of potato quality are likely to be made through taste, although more complex physiological mechanisms that provide feedback on glycoalkaloid content are conceivable. Solanine, the glycoalkaloid common in most potatoes, is considered to be toxic to humans in quantities about 20 mg/100g fresh weight (0.02 per cent) (Jadhav et al. 1981). Glycoalkaloids in potatoes in concentrations above 14 mg/100g are unpleasant to North Americans in taste sensitivity tests (Sinden et al. 1976).

To test the hypothesis that the Aymara have selected potato glycoalkaloid levels on the basis of taste, I carried out taste perception tests of glycoalkaloids in solution (Johns & Keen 1987). To address the capacity of the Aymara to gauge glycoalkaloid content in the domestication of S. ×ajanhuiri, whole potatoes of this and other species were presented to a taste panel and were subsequently analysed for glycoalkaloid content (Johns & Keen 1986). The Aymara are capable of evaluating potatoes on the basis of taste. However, judgements distinguishing most wild and cultivated tubers did not appear to be based, at least primarily, on glycoalkaloid content. Within the range of glycoalkaloid levels present in most potatoes used in this study (that is less than 20 mg/100g) some other factor, or combination of taste factors, determines flavour quality.

The Aymara potato taxonomy (Johns & Keen 1986b) makes only one distinction on the basis of taste. Potatoes are either *lug'i* or *ch'oke*, bitter or non-bitter. *Jank'o lug'i (S.×juzepczkii* Buk.) which contained 38 mg/100g is typical of the former category; all of the other cultivated potatoes used in the taste-panel test contained less than 20 mg/100g and were placed in the latter category. The participants' decision to reject *jank'o lug'i* was probably based on its high level of glycoalkaloids. This differentiation on the basis of glycoalkaloid content is consistent with data from the study on the perception of glycoalkaloids. Subjects determined no difference in strength at concentrations below 20 mg/100ml. However, as they perceived an increase in concentration up to 80 mg/100ml they also showed a significant and increasing rejection of these compounds. A breakpoint for glycoalkaloid preference by the Aymara occurs roughly between 20 and 38 mg/100g in whole tubers.

Potatoes are evaluated for glycoalkaloids alone only in terms of two character states – too high or acceptable. All of the cultigens included in Figure 32.1, therefore, have acceptable glycoalkaloid levels. The extremely low levels of glycoalkaloids in weed *S.×ajanhuiri* and *yari* appear to be strictly fortuitous. Genetic recombinants such as these, with almost no glycoalkaloid content, must have been selected at an early stage of the domestication process. The higher total glycoalkaloid levels of the more advanced *ajawiri* clones argues against a gradual reduction of glycoalkaloid content during cultivation by humans.

Three of the five clones of weed *S.×ajanhuiri* included in the taste-panel test were equally or more acceptable on the basis of taste than many of the clones currently grown by the Aymara. In view of the size achieved by some weed *S.×ajanhuiri* tubers (Johns & Keen 1986a), these hybrids between wild and cultivated potatoes seem likely candidates for cultivation. That more clones have not followed *yari* into domestication may relate more to other cultural and biological factors than to the genetic potential present in the wild populations. Undoubtedly *yari* was domesticated under similar circumstances to those seen in the field today. From ethnobotanical studies of *S.×ajanhuiri* cultivation by the Aymara of western Bolivia (Johns & Keen 1986a), I concluded that potato evolution continues today without direct human intervention. However, in years with serious crop failures in the past, weed forms of *S.×ajanhuiri* may have served as an important reservoir of seed potatoes. Thus, while humans are capable of making judgements on glycoalkaloid content and of selecting for non-toxic levels, the kind of selection decisions leading to domestication of favourable types takes place only under exceptional circumstances.

## A historical perspective on potato domestication

The toxic levels of glycoalkaloids in most wild potatoes (Gregory 1984) makes their exploitation by pre-agricultural hunter–gatherers as more than a casual resource rather unlikely. However, until humans became intimately associated with potato populations, domestication was equally unlikely. Total glycoalkaloid content varies widely between potato species and between populations of species. Genotypes of wild species with little or no glycoalkaloids are the exception but are not unknown. For example, many of the collections of *S. bulbocastanum* Dun. and *S. chacoense* Bitt. that have been studied contain no detectable glycoalkaloids, and levels of glycoalkaloids in *S.×bertaultii* Hawkes range from 10–600 mg/100g (S. L. Sinden pers. comm.). Tubers of *S. cardiophyllum* Lindl., which occurs as a weed in maize fields, are extensively exploited in north-central Mexico (Correll 1962) and are apparently non-bitter and non-toxic (Galindo Alonso pers. comm.). Perhaps early exploiters of wild potatoes could have successfully concentrated on types low in total glycoalkaloid content. However, it does not necessarily follow that the wild progenitors of the cultivated potato were low in glycoalkaloid content. Considering the widespread cultivation of potatoes in the Andes, the interfertility of cultivated and wild plants, and their tendency to hybridize, it is difficult to say which wild potatoes have not received genes through introgression from cultigens. Quite conceivably, low glycoalkaloid levels in certain modern wild species are secondarily derived, and do not reflect conditions at the onset of the domestication process.

## Detoxification techniques

Undoubtedly potatoes were an unpredictable and dangerous resource until some way was found to eliminate their potential toxicity. Various detoxification techniques have been applied to plant products around the world (Lancaster *et al.* 1982, Stahl Ch. 11, this volume). Detoxification of bitter potatoes by modern Andeans is most commonly carried out through elaborate and labour-intensive leaching and freeze-drying processes (Werge 1979, Mamani 1981).

Detoxification methods, such as those employed with potatoes, have undoubtedly been important in expanding the exploitation of otherwise poisonous wild and cultivated plant resources. However, such technological developments may not pre-date the initial stages in the development of agriculture. Sophisticated processing techniques are often species-specific and would only come about through an extended period in which humans were in intimate association with a food resource that is intrinsically poisonous. These technological developments offer little insight into the avoidance of toxicity by early hominid foragers with very limited or no processing technology.

## The detoxification function of geophagy

Present-day geophagous practices, associated with the consumption of wild potatoes and primitive potato cultigens in North and South America, suggest the possibility that this form of detoxification may have preceded and led up to their domestication (Johns 1985, Johns 1986b). Indians of the American Southwest and adjacent Mexico consume clays with the wild potato species, *S. jamesii* Torr. and *S. fendleri* Gray (Laufer 1930, Whiting 1939). The expressed reason for the consumption of specific clays is their effectiveness in eliminating bitterness, and in preventing stomach pains or vomiting that result from eating large quantities of these foods without clay. Similar reports of Andean native consumption of specific clays with potatoes date from the 16th-century chroniclers (Weiss 1953). Specific clays are still consumed with frost-resistant potato cultigens (*S. ×juzepczukii* and *S. ×curtilobum* Juz. et Buk.) by the inhabitants of the Central Andean altiplano, with the stated rationale of eliminating the bitter taste characteristic of these potatoes.

I have used binding assays to determine the adsorptive capacity *in vitro* of potato clays from North and South America for the glycoalkaloid tomatine (Johns 1986b). Adsorption studies over a range of conditions simulating gastrointestinal pH and ionic strength demonstrated the ability of these edible clays to bind tomatine and hence neutralize the bitterness, and eliminate the gastrointestinal irritation, associated with ingestion of glycoalkaloids in potatoes.

## Geophagy and domestication

The evolutionary nature of the clay–potato association provides insight into the general phenomenon of geophagy. Potato clays are used with a resource which is only modestly exploitable because of the presence of weak but quantitative toxins. The use of clays in this situation corresponds to geophagous practices of at least eight species of primates which include at least some leaves in their diet (Uehara 1982). Detoxification has been suggested as the adaptive function of geophagy by non-human primates (Hladik 1977) but has not been demonstrated experimentally. Thus geophagy appears to be a behaviour with pre-hominoid antecedents; and higher primates, including humans, have apparently maintained it as a mechanism for dealing with naturally occurring toxins. Clays are used by humans to detoxify tannins and quinones as well as alkaloids from specific plant foods around the world (Johns 1986b).

The clear demonstration of the detoxification function of geophagy in relation to the potato has important implications for domestication in general (Johns 1986b). Although wild potatoes frequently occur in abundance around sites of human occupation, in North America, at least, they were commonly consumed only during famine or periods of seasonal scarcity. Domestication was only likely once the plants could be exploited in sufficient quantity to make them worthy of an investment of time and energy. Geophagous practices associated with the gathering of potatoes from the wild, and with the cultivation of wild potatoes and primitive domesticates (in the Andes), directly link this detoxification phenomenon with stages in the process of human-directed evolution leading to plant domestication.

That the application of geophagy may be an important initial step in the domestication process, in general, is supported by reports of clay use to detoxify the most important African famine food, the wild yam *Dioscorea dumentorum* Pax. (Corkill 1948, Irvine 1952). Like the potato, *D. dumentorum* has cultivated forms that show selection for reduced levels of secondary compounds. Clays should be effective in neutralizing the saponins and alkaloids present in many *Dioscorea* species and could have enabled selection to take place. A chemical–ecological study of the domestication of yams in Africa and Asia is warranted (cf. Chikwendu & Okezie Ch. 21, this volume, for discussion of their experimental work on yam domestication in West Africa).

# An overview of chemical determinants of plant domestication

The role of plant secondary chemicals in determining the feeding preferences of generalist herbivores offers important analogies for understanding human dietary history and the domestication process. Undoubtedly, no plant chemical defences evolved specifically to deter humans. Rather their presence in crop plants is a response to threats from micro-organisms, insects, plants, and other organisms. Human selection for reduced plant toxicity during domestication, then, should be considered in a dynamic relationship with other ecological factors. The importance of natural forces in maintaining high levels of toxins in *añu* and *tarwi* are mentioned above. Particularly instructive in this regard is the case of the important Amazonian root crop, manioc (*Manihot esculenta* Crantz). Varieties with high levels of cyanogenic glycosides probably reflect selection by humans, probably unconsciously, to increase the resistance of the roots to pathogen attack and so to allow the production of larger roots (de Wet & Harlan 1975). Harris (1977) points out the important relationship between toxicity and storage in considering the domestication of manioc and yams.

Levels of secondary defences in plants show considerable variability resulting from physical stress such as drought and frost damage, and biotic stress such as herbivory (Rhoades 1985). Consequently, the diet of the Aymara, and other peoples dependent on foods containing marginally safe levels of phytochemicals, is unpredictable and potentially dangerous. Humans must be able to reliably perceive and recognize secondary compounds and to make behavioural and physiological adjustments in dealing with changes in toxin levels.

Interactions between humans and secondary chemicals have been discussed somewhat simplistically in this chapter in terms of the direct biological activities of particular compounds. However, among chemical ecologists there is an increasing awareness of the importance of multifold interactions among secondary toxins and nutrients in determining plant deterrence of predators (Berenbaum 1985). For example, two compounds may interact synergistically to produce an activity unattributable to either alone. Several types of plant toxins, such as proteinase inhibitors and phenolics, limit the availability of protein to animals (Pierpoint 1983). Phytochemicals may interact with other nutrients as well. Understanding of the complexity of human–phytochemical interactions will undoubtedly increase in the future.

Although support for selection by humans leading to chemical change in crop plants is found in the examples cited in this chapter, this phenomenon must also be considered in relation to other domestication factors. In relation to the potato it is arguable that selection has been primarily for increased tuber size rather than for reduced toxicity. Large tubers, even from the same plant, contain lower concentrations of glycoalkaloids than smaller tubers (Sinden *et al.* 1984). It is conceivable, then, that detoxification techniques such as geophagy facilitiated the domestication of potatoes while effectively eliminating the need for direct chemical selection. If selection for larger tubers coincidentally reduced toxicity, perhaps only then were detoxification techniques dispensed with. Nonetheless, as discussed above, discontinuities of glycoalkaloids in the *S.×ajanhuiri* complex clearly support the likelihood that direct selection against glycoalkaloids has taken place.

Human chemical ecology, as discussed in this chapter, encompasses cultural as well as biological aspects. For example, the Aymara language contains specialized terms to describe their taste taxonomy (Johns & Keen 1985) and their taxonomy for potatoes (Johns & Keen 1986b) which mediate their interactions with secondary compounds. As evidenced by the case of *añu* and *maca*, symbolism, historical belief, cognitive associations, and physiological effects together determine human interactions with phytochemicals. Taste preferences in humans are complicated by a high degree of ambiguity related to cultural norms and dietary experience.

This chapter has ignored the importance of the masticatory leaf *coca* (*Erythroxylon* spp.) in Andean culture and subsistence. Although *coca*'s adaptive significance remains an area of controversy, this plant must be integrated into any comprehensive considerations of Andean chemical ecology. Non-energy-providing staples such as *coca* are difficult to classify as either medicine or food. *Coca* is a stimulant, but also supplies a significant amount of vitamins and minerals (Duke *et al.* 1975). Traditional cultures often do not make distinctions between medicine and food; definitions of what is medicine or food, and what is not, are often culturally determined rather than biologically based. Among Andean tubers, *ulluco*, *añu*, *maca*, and *mauka* (Oblitas Poblete 1969) all have dual uses. From a chemical–ecological perspective, food, condiments, medicine, stimulants, and toxins can be viewed as parts of a continuum with a chemical basis, rather than as separate entities.

Harris (1977) suggested that some subsequently domesticated toxic tuberous plants may originally have been used for fish and arrow poisons. Specific food plants could have been first used as medicines as well. Others have suggested that poisonous and medicinal plants were among the first domesticates (Chang 1970). Certainly, human interaction with phytochemicals is a fundamental part of the domestication process. *Añu*, *maca*, potato, and *coca* are excellent examples of the interconnections of nutritional, pharmacological, physiological, cognitive, and cultural factors in directing the domestication process. A chemical–ecological model of domestication provides a new perspective on human interactions with plants. Further investigations of chemical change in cultivated plants from the Andes and elsewhere can offer new insights into this important aspect of human history, particularly because chemical ecology is capable of generating testable hypotheses concerning the domestication process.

# References

Berenbaum, M. 1985. Brementown revisited: interactions among allelochemicals in plants. In *Chemically mediated interactions between plants and other organisms. Recent advances in phytochemistry*, Vol. 19, G. A. Cooper-Driver, T. Swain & E. E. Conn (eds), 139–69. New York: Plenum.

Bernstein, I. L. 1978. Learned taste aversions in children receiving chemotherapy. *Science* **200**, 1302–3.

Brucher, H. 1977. *Tropische nutzpflanzen*. Berlin: Springer.

Chang, K.-C. 1970. The beginnings of agriculture in the Far East. *Antiquity* **44**, 175–85.

Chikwendu, V. E. & C. E. A. Okezie. 1989. Factors responsible for the ennoblement of the African yams: inferences from experiments in yam domestication. In *Foraging and farming: the evolution of plant exploitation*, D. R. Harris & G. C. Hillman (eds), ch. 21. London: Unwin Hyman.

Clutton-Brock, T. H. (ed.) 1977. *Primate ecology: studies of feeding and ranging behavior in lemurs, monkeys and apes*. London: Academic Press.

Corkill, N. L. 1948. The poisonous wild cluster yam, *Dioscorea dumetorum* Pax, as a famine food in the Anglo-Egyptian Sudan. *Annals of Tropical Medicine and Parasitology* **42**, 278–87.

Correll, D. S. 1962. *The potato and its wild relatives*. Renner, Tex.: Texas Research Foundation.

de Wet, J. M. J. & J. R. Harlan 1975. Weeds and domesticates: evolution in the man-made habitat. *Economic Botany* **29**, 99–107.

Duke, J. A., D. Aulik & T. Plowman 1975. Nutritional value of coca. *Botanical Museum Leaflets, Harvard Museum* **24**, 113–19.

Freeland, W. J. & D. H. Janzen 1974. Strategies in herbivory by mammals: the role of plant secondary compounds. *American Naturalist* **108**, 269–89.

Gade, D. W. 1975. *Plants, man and the land of the Villcanota Valley of Peru*. The Hague: Junk.

Gregory, P. 1984. Glycoalkaloid composition of potatoes: diversity and biological implications. *American Potato Journal* **61**, 115–22.

Harborne, J. B. 1982. *Introduction to ecological biochemistry*, 2nd edn. London: Academic Press.

Hardman, J. T., M. L. Beck & C. E. Owensby 1983. Range forb lectins. *Transfusion* **23**, 519–22.

Harris, D. R. 1977. Alternative pathways toward agriculture. In *Origins of Agriculture*, C. A. Reed (ed.), 179–243. The Hague: Mouton.

Hawkes, J. G. 1989. The domestication of roots and tubers in the American tropics. In *Foraging and farming: the evolution of plant exploitation*, D. R. Harris & G. C. Hillman (eds), ch. 31. London: Unwin Hyman.

Hegnauer, R. 1964. *Chemotaxonomie der Pflanzen*. Band III, Basel: Birkhauser.

Hegnauer, R. 1969. *Chemotaxonomie der Pflanzen*. Band V, Basel: Birkhauser.

Hladik, C. M. 1977. Chimpanzees of Gabon and Gombe: some comparative data on the diet. In *Primate Ecology*, T. H. Clutton-Brock (ed.), 481–501. London: Academic Press.

Hodge, W. H. 1951. Three native tuber foods of the Andes. *Economic Botany* **5**, 185–201.

Irvine, F. R. 1952. Supplementary and emergency food plants of West Africa. *Economic Botany* **36**, 84–99.

Jadhav, S.J., R. P. Sharma & D. K. Salunkhe 1981. Naturally occurring toxic alkaloids in food. *CRC Critical Reviews in Toxicology* **9**, 21–104.

Johns, T. 1981. The añu and the maca. *Journal of Ethnobiology* **1**, 208–12.

Johns, T. A. 1985. *Chemical ecology of the Aymara of western Bolivia: selection for glycoalkaloids in the Solanum ×Ajanhuiri domestication complex*. Unpublished PhD Dissertation, University of Michigan, Ann Arbor.

Johns, T. 1986a. Chemical selection in Andean domesticated tubers as a model for the acquisition of empirical plant knowledge. In *Plants used in indigenous medicine and diet: bio-behavioural approaches*, N. L. Etkin (ed.), 266–88. South Salem, NY: Redgrave.

Johns, T. 1986b. The detoxification function of geophagy and the domestication of the potato. *Journal of Chemical Ecology* **12**, 635–46.

Johns, T. & S. L. Keen 1985. Determinants of taste perception and taste classification among the Aymara of Bolivia. *Ecology of Food and Nutrition* **16**, 253–71.

Johns, T. & S. L. Keen 1986a. Ongoing evolution of the potato on the altiplano of western Bolivia. *Economic Botany* **40**, 409–24.

Johns, T. & S. L. Keen 1986b. Taste evaluation of potato glycoalkaloids by the Aymara: a case study in human chemical ecology. *Human Ecology*, **14**, 437–52.

Johns, T. & S. F. Osman 1986. Glycoalkaloids of *Solanum* Series *Megistacrolobum* and related potato cultigens. *Biochemical Systematics and Ecology*, **14**, 651–55.

Johns, T. & G. H. N. Towers 1981. Isothiocyanates and thioureas in enzyme hydrolysates of *Tropaeolum tuberosum*, *Phytochemistry* **20**, 2687–9.

Johns, T., Z. Huamán, C. Ochoa & P. E. Schmiediche 1987. Relationships among wild, weed and cultivated potatoes in the *Solanum×ajanhuiri* complex. *Systematic Botany*, **12**, 541–52.

Johns, T., W. D. Kitts, F. Newsome & G. H. N. Towers 1982. Antireproductive and other medicinal effects of *Tropaeolum tuberosum*. *Journal of Ethnopharmacology* **5**, 149–61.

Lancaster, P. A., J. S. Ingram, M. Y. Lim & D. G. Coursey 1982. Traditional cassava-based foods: survey of processing techniques. *Economic Botany* **36**, 12–45.

Laufer, B. 1930. Geophagy. *Field Museum of Natural History, Anthropological Series* **18**, 99–198.

Leopold, A. C. & R. Ardrey 1972. Toxic substances in plants and the food habits of early man. *Science* **176**, 512–14.

Liener, I. E. 1980. *Toxic constituents of plant foodstuffs*, 2nd edn. New York: Academic Press.

MacLeod, A. J. 1976. Volatile flavour compounds in the Cruciferae. In *The biology and chemistry of the Cruciferae*, J. G. Vaughan, A. J. MacLeod & B. M. G. Jones (eds), 307–30. London: Academic Press.

McKey, D. B., J. S. Cartlan, P. G. Waterman & G. M. Choo 1981. Food selection by Black Colobus monkeys (*Colobus satanas*) in relation to plant chemistry. *Biological Journal of the Linnean Society* **16**, 115–46.

Mamani, M. 1981. El chuño: preparation, uso, almacenamiento. In *La technologia en el mundo andino*, Vol. 1, H. Lechtman & A. M. Soldi (eds), 235–46. Mexico: Universidad Nacional Autonoma de Mexico.

Oblitas Poblete, E. 1969. *Plantas medicinales de Bolivia*. Cochabamba: Editorial 'Los Amigos del Libro'.

Osman, S. F., T. Johns & K. Price 1986. Sisunine, a new glycoalkaloid found in hybrids between *Solanum×ajanhuiri*. *Phytochemistry* **25**, 967–8.

Pierpoint, W. S. 1983. Reactions of phenolic compounds with proteins, and their relevance to the production of leaf protein. In *Leaf protein concentrates*, L. Telek & H. D. Graham (eds), 235–67. Wesport, Conn.: AVI Publishing.

Rhoades, D. F. 1985. Pheromonal communication between plants. In *Chemically mediated interactions between plants and other organisms. Recent advances in phytochemistry*, Vol. 19, G. A. Cooper-Driver, T. Swain & E. E. Conn (eds), 195–218. New York: Plenum.

Rindos, D. 1980. Symbiosis, instability, and the origins and spread of agriculture: a new model. *Current Anthropology* **21**, 751–72.

Seaman, F. C., N. H. Fischer & T. F. Stuessy 1980. Systematic implications of sesquiterpene lactones in the subtribe *Melampodiinae*. *Biochemical Systematics and Ecology* **8**, 263–71.

Simmonds, N. W. 1976. Potatoes. In *Evolution of crop plants*, N. W. Simmonds (ed.), 279–83. London: Longman.

Sinden, S. L., K. L. Deahl & B. B. Aulenbach 1976. Effects of glycoalkaloids and phenolics on potato flavor. *Journal of Food Science* **41**, 520–3.

Sinden, S. L., L. L. Sanford & R. E. Webb 1984. Genetic and environmental control of potato glycoalkaloids. *American Potato Journal* **61**, 141–56.

Small, E. 1984. Hybridization in the domesticated–weed–wild complex. In *Plant biosystematics*, W. F. Grand (ed.), 139–210. Toronto: Academic Press.

Stahl, A. B. 1984. Hominid dietary selection before fire. *Current Anthropology* **25**, 151–68.

Stahl, A. B. 1989. Plant-food processing: implications for dietary quality. In *Foraging and farming: the evolution of plant exploitation*, D. R. Harris & G. C. Hillman (eds), ch. 11. London: Unwin Hyman.

Uehara, S. 1982. Seasonal changes in the techniques employed by wild chimpanzees in the Mahale Mountains, Tanzania, to feed on termites (*Pseudacanthotermes spiniger*). *Folia Primatologia* **37**, 44–76.

Weiss, P. 1953. Los comedores peruanos de tierras. *Peru Indigena* **5**, 12–21.

Werge, R. W. 1979. Potato processing in the central highlands of Peru. *Ecology of Food and Nutrition* **7**, 229–34.

Williams, W. 1984. Lupins in crop production. *Outlook on Agriculture* **13**, 69–76.

Whiting, A. F. 1939. Ethnobotany of the Hopi. *Museum of Northern Arizona, Bulletin* **15**.

Wrangham, R. W. & P. G. Waterman 1981. Feeding behavior of vervet monkeys on *Acacia tortilis* and *Acacia xanthophiloea*: with special reference to reproductive strategies and tannin production. *Journal of Animal Ecology* **50**, 715–31.

# AGRARIAN PLANT EXPLOITATION: THE EVOLUTION OF AGRICULTURAL SYSTEMS

# 33 *From foraging to food production in northeastern Venezuela and the Caribbean*

MARIO SANOJA

(translated from the Spanish by Heather Brothwell)

Study of the historical processes which led from foraging to food production in northern South America is largely related to pre-Columbian systems of production based on tropical vegeculture. Separately, or together with cereal cultivation, vegeculture can be seen as part of a process by which methods of gathering plant foods were improved before agriculture became the dominant method of tribal food production.

Unlike maize and other cereals, vegetatively reproduced plants do not require a substantial input of effort and labour for their controlled reproduction. The transition from the gathering of plants such as manioc or *yuca* (*Manihot esculenta*) to their reproduction under human control seems to have mainly involved the process of separating clones of the sweet or non-toxic varieties and the toxic ones, by means of taking cuttings. This process, by which human groups deliberately cultivated the plant in accordance with their social needs, made possible the clear separation of non-toxic varieties, which could be eaten immediately as roast or boiled vegetables, from toxic varieties which were processed into flour due to their greater starch content. For such processing, there developed a complex of baskets, wooden boards inset with microliths, artefacts made from fired clay, wooden containers, and a range of manufacturing and processing techniques which involved all the technological knowledge of the aboriginal communities in using the raw materials available to them.

So far the earliest evidence of hoe cultivation, and the consumption of manioc processed into flour and cassava, has been found in the archaeological record of ceramic groups at Monsú on the lower Magdalena River in Colombia, at around 3090 bc (Reichel-Dolmatoff 1985). Angulo's current work (pers. comm.) in this same region shows that the treatment of manioc in the way described above continued to develop among later ceramic communities, together with such methods of wild-food procurement (or 'extractive food production') as collecting shellfish, hunting, and fishing, until the beginning of the last millennium bc. From this time, vegeculture seems to have become increasingly important among the different methods of food procurement and production, in parallel with increases in the size and social complexity of the village settlements (Angulo 1981, Sanoja 1982a, 1982b, in press a).

The example of Monsú typifies the initial process by which 'controlled food production' developed in different parts of northern South America, based on ecosystems blessed with particularly rich natural subsistence resources. This, however, constitutes a condition, not the cause, of the process.

## Social conditions for controlled food production

In hunter–gatherer society, hunting is an activity carried out to obtain food by concentrating on capture of prey. Gathering is an activity which, in addition to procuring the food, transports it to a central place or base, with the aim of immediate consumption and distribution. The hunter–gatherer must familiarize himself with the environment in which he lives, and weigh up the relative importance of the different animal and vegetable resources from which he obtains food and raw materials for social reproduction. This process translates into a programme of activities which the individual and/or the community must design in order to take advantage of the opportunities which each natural resource offers. There is a point at which this programming of activities must include not only the tools needed to obtain foods for immediate consumption, but also those tools which permit more complex activities to be undertaken, such as forest clearance, tillage, the processing of fibrous plant materials, the grinding of foods, and the use of varied techniques to make more efficient tools. This technological transition appears to have been a major step in the development of the social potential for food production, i.e. a greater capacity on the part of the human group to invest more productive work in its social reproduction. When this programme of work-processes organizes itself around a central base, with activity areas, and relatively stable covered spaces in which the products of wild-food procurement are regularly processed, distributed, and consumed, we have evidence of a re-structuring of work which differs from the predatory relationship of immediate consumption. We can say that this is the basis of sedentary communal life.

The objective of human labour at this point of technological transition, as Marx says, is to achieve collective adaptation to, and use of, the soil (environment), which is only possible through the tribal community. Achieving this objective will depend, to a greater or lesser extent, on environmental and historical conditions, but in essence, we can say that sedentary living is necessary for the development of controlled food production. Experience tends to show us that the 'Garden of Eden-like' regions, i.e. those naturally favoured with abundant wild plant and animal resources, offer the conditions necessary for sedentary living to begin to develop on the basis of wild-food procurement, and thus make possible a re-structuring of the work force and the beginnings of controlled food production. An opposing view claims that it is 'stressful' environmental conditions, or precarious subsistence resources, that favour innovation and the adoption of food production. But, in accepting as a causal factor either the presence of 'Garden of Eden-like' or 'stressful' conditions, both positions favour a concept of the environment as the determining factor in a process where society, as a passive element, must respond with *ad hoc* adaptative mechanisms in order to survive.

In contrast, our position is that it is internal social causes which bring about the abandonment of the hunter–gatherer methods of wild-food procurement, and external social causes which determine the conditions under which the process occurs. Using these assumptions as a starting point, archaeological investigation should first clarify the social contexts in which changes in the uses of labour, the land, and the whole environment are produced. Otherwise, the analysis of the development of agriculture becomes little more than a history of cultivated plants, instead of a history of human labour.

Regardless of the 'Garden of Eden-like' or 'stressful' characteristics that these environments may have, the 'neolithicization' of society requires the existence of necessary social conditions to lead it towards sedentism. The fundamental change which this process brings about is the constant and collective, as opposed to the individual and intermittent, appropriation of natural resources by villages, and the controlled production of food and consumer goods. A number of general conditions must be met in order that the proces of neolithicization can run its course. They are listed below.

(a)  The human group should be able to make use of a combination of different ecosystems and ecological niches which represents alternative possibilities for extractive production (wild-food procurement).

(b)  The ecosystems and ecological niches should represent a spatially and temporally dense array of natural resources and raw materials for extractive or controlled food production, including the manufacture of tools.

(c)  The group must have the capacity to organize a strategy for extractive or controlled production in the different ecosystems and niches of their habitat, and create conditions of work which permit the continued existence and social reproduction of the group under stable conditions.

(d)  The group must have the capacity to manage the exploitation, distribution, processing, and consumption of foods and raw materials, and, in particular, it must be capable of stimulating deferred as opposed to immediate consumption.

(e)  The group must have the capacity to develop labour specialization, as indicated by the design, manufacture, and/or acquisition of specialized production tools.

(f)  The group must have the capacity to develop ways of working which can be reproduced systematically in time and space, giving rise to traditions of labour which are linked to certain kinds of social organization for production purposes.

(g)   The group must have the capacity to develop mechanisms of solidarity and affinity which permanently maintain an available work force based on co-operative practices.

(h)   The possibility must exist for dialectical conditions to develop between the size of the work force and the objective possibilities of increasing the extractive or controlled production of goods for subsistence.

(i)   The possibility must exist for certain natural components of the ecosystems and niches to be subject to controlled reproduction by means of the continuous input of human labour.

(j)   That the new methods of controlled production of food and tools, which result from the reorganization of the work force, must come to predominate over all other forms of production.

## The development of early village communities in northeastern Venezuela

Our current investigations in northeastern Venezuela have revealed the presence of gathering, hunting, and fishing populations in the Gulf of Paria, Sucre State, at about 4000 bc. Initially, these communities developed a system of food procurement which was based on the exploitation of the mangrove formations which appear to have covered a large part of what constituted the coastal region at that time. It should be pointed out that, whether due to epeirogenic activity or to the transgressive post-glacial rise of sea-level (Hurt 1974, Fairbridge 1976), the sea seems to have covered a large part of the lowlands of northeastern Venezuela, possibly giving rise to extensive mangrove formations in what today constitute the foothills of the mountain system farther east (Fig. 33.1). This is associated with the formation of habitation sites on the edges of the large inland estuaries, lagoons, and swamps where mangroves co-existed with deciduous woodland, thorn-brush, and humid tropical forest.

As is well known, the mangrove ecosystem constitutes more than a simple plant formation: it is also the habitat for numerous animal species – gastropods, bivalves, crustaceans, fish, birds, and reptiles – which help to provide protein for human sustenance, and other useful raw materials such as wood, resins, and vegetable oils, as well as forming soils rich in organic content.

The stratigraphy and the content of the cultural layers of the different archaeological sites which have been studied to date indicate that these early gatherer communities were able to exploit intensively the mollusc resources within a given mangrove formation, abandon them temporarily when their productivity declined, and open up a new niche for food procurement. This resulted in cultural deposits which can reach depths of nearly 4 m, marked by alternating hearths and sterile layers.

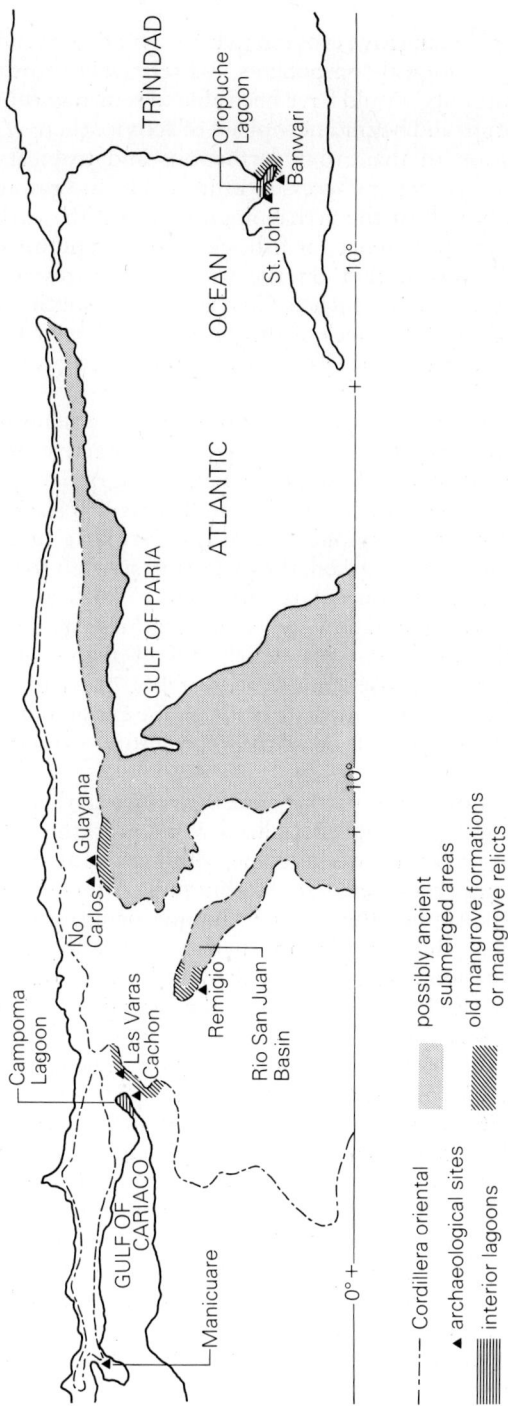

**Figure 33.1** Northeastern Venezuela and Trinidad: early hunter–gatherer sites and environments, 6000–1000 bc.

Given that the mangrove ecosystem can, provided it is not over-exploited, regenerate its biological components in a relatively short time, the original gatherer community would have been able to return within a few years to its previous location and begin a new phase of activity there. On the other hand, the juxtaposition of mangrove formations and tropical forest may have given these human groups access to other wild-food resources, both animal and plant, although in the archaeological record the earliest communities appear to show a preference for fish, gastropods, and bivalves. We have no archaeological information on the use of plant resources at this time, although in some places, such as Guayana on the southern side of the Paria Peninsula (Fig. 33.1), groves of the palm *Acrocomia sclerocarpa* occur in the foothills of the Sierra de Paria where there are also pre-ceramic shell middens.

It appears that these ancient communities of gatherer–fishers must have been able to practise what we call 'itinerant extractive production' of food and raw materials which, as with itinerant or migratory agriculture based on 'slash-and-burn' (swidden) cultivation (Harris 1971), is characterized by intensive and cyclical exploitation, in this case of a mangrove formation: when the resources diminished, the mangrove was left to lie fallow for future re-exploitation. This concept of 'harvesting' cyclically a mangrove formation and leaving it fallow when its productivity declined, may have constituted the material basis which would shape, at a later date, the rationality of the semi-sedentary way of life, particularly that related to agricultural methods intermediate between the extractive production and the controlled production of food in the vegecultural variant (Veloz-Maggiolo 1976, p. 273).

The production tools of the ancient hunter–gatherers of northeastern Venezuela seem to indicate specialized wood working. Most of these tools were made of fine-grained sandstone, although some were made of jasper and schist, using crude percussive techniques. A few show signs of flaking, abrasion, or polishing, this latter technique being used to make adzes or small hoes like those found in shell middens in Guayana. A similar contextual situation is found in the shell middens of Banwari Trace and St. John, on the coast of Trinidad opposite the Paria Peninsula, dated to 4500 bc. They differ from the Venezuelan mangrove shell middens mainly in the presence, at this date, of conical grinding *manos*, pestles, and anvils, apparently used for grinding plant foods (Harris 1973, 1976, Veloz-Maggiolo 1976, p. 47). Newly discovered sites such as Remigio, in the foothills of the mountains which form the southern border of the San Juan River Basin in Venezuela, may represent an equivalent cultural and chronological context to that of Banwari and St. Johns in Trinidad (Fig. 33.1).

It is difficult, in the light of what we know about the prehistory of northeastern South America, to evaluate the early (i.e. pre-2000 bc) presence of production tools made of polished stone and abraded stone, bearing in mind that they could have been exchange goods obtained from more advanced hunter–gatherer communities. It is more likely, however, that

they were produced by the hunter–gatherer groups of northeastern Venezuela who were already fully familiar with simple percussive techniques, such
as flaking stone. Advanced techniques for the making of production tools –
flaking, abrasion, and polishing of the stone – did not replace the simple
percussive techniques used to make the flakes and choppers used in the
processing of fibrous plant materials. This may be due to the fact that the
activities which required the most efficient production tools, such as conical
*manos*, hoes, and axes, did not occupy a prominent position, during the 4th
and 3rd millennia bc, in the kind of extractive production practised by these
hunter–gatherers.

The type of dwelling typical of that time appears to have been a simple
shelter, containing a fireplace or hearth where food was cooked. It is possible
that the inhabited sites were more-or-less temporary camps. The presence of
possible fishing-net weights and semi-circular abrasive tools made of
sandstone indicate the use of fishing nets and the manufacture of spears and
darts. In the same way, 'exotic' raw materials such as cores of haematite, iron
pyrites, and jasper show that attempts were made to obtain these materials
from beyond the Paria Peninsula (Sanoja 1979, 1980, 1982a, 1983, 1985, in
press a & b, in prep.).

Around 2600 bc the typology and stratigraphy seem to show a substantial
change in the method of hunter–gatherer food production, exemplified by
the site of Las Varas at the base of the Araya Peninsula. After that time, the
production tools made by means of simple percussive techniques – flakes,
choppers, scrapers, etc. – begin increasingly to be replaced in the archaeological record by specialized tools made by polishing and abrasion – conical
*manos*, axes, hoes, adzes, and stone plates. The same is true, to a lesser extent,
of gouges and containers made of shell, which are already present in shell
middens on Cubagua Island by *c.* 2300 bc (Cruxent & Rouse 1961, p. 56).
Similarly, bone projectile points increase, and their variety of shape reflects a
diversity of functions linked to specialized hunting and fishing, on land as
well as in estuaries and rivers.

The habitation site of Las Varas is today situated some 10 km east of the
coast of the Gulf of Cariaco on one of the low hills which surround the
ancient coastline of the Campoma Lagoon and fringed by relict mangrove
formations (Fig. 33.1). Unlike the earlier sites, Las Varas, which is dated to
*c.* 2600 bc, seems to have been a village laid out in a rectangular plan. The
concentration of production artefacts near food remains in different activity
areas shows that the work processes (food preparation, tool-making, etc.)
were carried out around a main fire or hearth. The food remains provide
evidence of intensive fishing and hunting (both terrestrial and aquatic),
together with the collection of bivalves and gastropods from mangrove
formations. The dead were buried inside the dwellings, apparently as
secondary burials in baskets, judging by the position of the bones. The soil
on the hillsides surrounding the ancient lagoon is a very compact reddish
clay. In contrast, the area near the settlement is covered by a layer of black
compact soil, covering an area of approximately 2000 m$^2$. It resembles the

so-called *terras pretas* often found in Brazil, along the Lower Orinoco, and in Columbia, which are thought to be anthropic soils (Eden *et al.* 1984).

In general, therefore, we can say that the community of Las Varas represents, within the regional prehistory of northeastern Venezuela, the presence of relatively stable villages whose inhabitants carried out their food-producing activities with agricultural tools, processed plant materials, and fished, hunted, and collected. Apart from the absence of pottery, this cultural context appears equivalent to that of the tribal groups of ceramic horticulturalists who emigrated from the Middle and Lower Orinoco towards northeastern Venezuela at the start of the Christian era, mixing with the autochthonous populations who had already been living in the region for nearly 4000 years (Sanoja 1979, 1982a, 1982b, 1985, Vargas 1979, 1981, Sanoja & Vargas 1983).

On the other hand, the presence of villages or habitation sites of hunter–gatherers has been reported by Cruxent & Rouse (1961) and Rouse & Cruxent (1963) from the coast of Anzóategui State (the Pedro García Complex) and from the lands around the lake of Valencia in Carabobo State (the Michelena Complex) where stone plates and conical *manos* similar to those from northeastern Venezuela occur. The date of 600 bc for the Pedro García Complex could be regarded as the period of decline of hunter–gatherer society in northeastern Venezuela, given that already by 900 bc tribal society, horticulture, and pottery are clearly established along the Lower and Middle Orinoco (Sanoja 1979, Vargas 1979, 1981).

Although we do not know what types of cultigen may have been gathered or cultivated by the hunter–gatherers of northeastern Venezuela, we can say that, in addition to *Manihot esculenta* (or *yuca*), native species such as *Xanthosoma sagittifolium* (or *ocumo*) and *Calathea alouia* (or *lerén*), which are eaten today by the local population, would have been available and may have been included in the hunter–gatherers' diet as sources of carbohydrate. It is certain that the processing of *yuca* into flour and cassava was introduced into northeastern Venezuela by the immigrant ceramic horticulturalists of the Middle and Lower Orinoco, from the beginning of the Christian era. Current evidence also indicates that these horticultural peoples of the Middle and Lower Orinoco had immigrated to the Orinoco Valley from other parts of northern South America (Sanoja 1979, pp. 301–4).

It is plausible that *Manihot esculenta*, as Sauer (1952, p. 46) suggested, existed as a wild plant in the Venezuelan savannas, and it is possible that it was secondarily domesticated at around 900 bc by the people of Barrancas and Ronquín in the Orinoco Valley. Both groups already practised a mixed economy of vegeculture, hunting, fishing, and river shellfish gathering. When they migrated towards the northeast coast, they would have assimilated the working methods of the hunter–gatherers, thus reinforcing their own system by incorporating into the diet protein-rich marine resources, together with the roots and rhizomes which they had already domesticated in the Orinoco Valley (Sanoja 1979, Vargas 1979, 1981, Sanoja & Vargas 1978, 1983). This would explain the ease and speed with which the ceramic horticulturalists of the Middle and Lower Orinoco established themselves on the island of Trinidad and on the coast of northeastern Venezuela, where, by AD 200, they consisted of large populations, with houses built on mounds. They had already colonized all the Lesser Antilles as far as Puerto Rico by AD 65 (Chanlatte 1983), perhaps making use of the experience of the hunter–gatherer communities of northeastern Venezuela and Trinidad who had reached the Greater Antilles by around 3000 bc (Veloz-Maggiolo & Vega 1982).

At about 2330 bc, a different variant of the hunter–gatherer way of life appeared in northeastern Venezuela, designated Manicuare Series by Rouse and Cruxent (Cruxent & Rouse 1961, Rouse & Cruxent 1963). The habitation sites of these communities were preferentially located on the ocean coastlines of the Araya Peninsula, and on the islands off the northeast coast of Venezuela. Their subsistence economy is characterized by a marked dependence also on plant resources. The tools of food production include *Strombus gigas* shell axes, gouges, and containers, stone *manos* and *metates*, and bone harpoon and arrow heads. The same range of tools occurs at various sites in Cuba, such as Guayabo Blanco, Cayo Redondo, and Cueva Funche, with radiocarbon dates from $2050 \pm 150$ bc to $120 \pm 50$ bc at Cueva Funche, and from 2000 bc to 1500 bc at Guayabo Blanco (Sanoja 1982a, in press a) revealing an apparent relationship between the Manicuare and Antillean communities who shared this variant hunter–gatherer way of life. But, in Venezuela, as appears also to be the case in Cuba, the cultural and economic characteristics of those populations remained stable, unlike those of the inhabitants of the mangrove forests living around the interior lagoons and estuaries who began to overcome their dependence on their environment by working the land and managing their plant resources. This suggests that relatively similar environments *per se* do not generate linear ecological responses in human communities but that, instead, sedentism, the reorganization of the work force, and the general development of food-production potential are all connected in one historical process.

## Hunter–gatherer communities of the Greater Antilles and the processing of plant foods

Hunter–gatherer habitation sites in the Dominican Republic represent an interesting parallel with those of the autochthonous peoples of northeastern Venezuela and the island of Trinidad regarding the complex of production tools which, in both areas, is characterized by conical *manos*, mortars, and stone plates; although butterfly-shaped axes and coral graters used to process plant foods are found only at the pre-ceramic sites of the Dominican Republic. In the same way, from the time of the first hunter–gatherer settlements such as Hoyo del Toro, Madrigales, and El Porvenir, which occur between 2000 and 1500 bc, there was a tendency towards exploitation of the mangrove ecosystem and the gathering and processing of the roots of *Zamia debilis* (or *guayiga*) and of *Clausea rosa* (or *cupey*), which have been identified by pollen analysis and from macroscopic remains at El Porvenir (dated to 1250 bc) and at Cueva de Berna (dated to 1890 bc) (Veloz-Maggiolo *et al.* 1977, Veloz-Maggiolo 1980).

The use of *Zamia* as a plant food is interesting because the process of turning the root of the plant into flour – using coral graters to turn it into pulp, leaving it to rot in order to release its poisons, and then cooking it in little loaves – is very similar to the processing of bitter manioc. From the point of view of the transference of technical knowledge, this could have facilitated the later introduction of bitter-manioc cultivation from northeastern Venezuela. As has already been mentioned, from 2000 bc groups were present in the Dominican Republic who were culturally related to northeastern Venezuela and Trinidad and who already had coral graters, stone plates or *metates*, rectangular *manos* made from igneous rock, and stone axes or hoes, oval-shaped and waisted halfway along their length (Veloz-Maggiolo 1976, p. 137, 1980, pp. 51–3). This could indicate that *Zamia* roots had been processed since very early times by hunter–gatherer communities in the Dominican Republic.

Another important element in the study of food production in the Greater Antilles is the presence of maize pollen in sites such as El Curro (1450 bc) and Puerto Alejandro (of similar antiquity) in the Dominican Republic. The tools typically used for maize processing are not present, but the authors relate this absence to the pre-Columbian custom of eating young maize raw and roasting it when mature (Ortega & Guerrero 1981, pp. 48, 86).

The life of the hunter–gatherers in the Dominican Republic seems to have been particularly hard and difficult. This comes out clearly in the research of Luna Calderón and Veloz-Maggiolo in Cueva de Berna (1890 bc) and Cueva Roja (1225 bc) (Veloz-Maggiolo *et al.* 1977, Luna Calderón 1979, pp. 43–79). Palaeopathological study of the skeletal remains buried in the domestic area at these sites has revealed serious food deficiencies among the population, as well as anaemia, infectious disease, arthritis, degeneration of the bones, and work accidents, suggesting a life expectancy of between $12\frac{1}{2}$ and 30 years of age. The precarious condition of these poulations may – despite their exploitation of starch-rich local plants such as *Zamia* – be ascribed to an excessive intake of proteins, and to their failure to develop controlled food production as a means of achieving a better balance in their diet between carbohydrates and proteins.

The final break with local dependence on the environment for food, and the step towards a new historical condition, took place with the migrations towards the Antilles of the ceramic–horticulturalist–hunter–gatherers which began in northeastern Venezuela at the start of the Christian era or in the last centuries preceding it (Sanoja 1979, 1980, in press b, Sanoja & Vargas 1978, 1983, Vargas 1979, 1981). Overall regional trends from foraging to food production in northern South America and the Caribbean are summarized schematically in Figure 33.2.

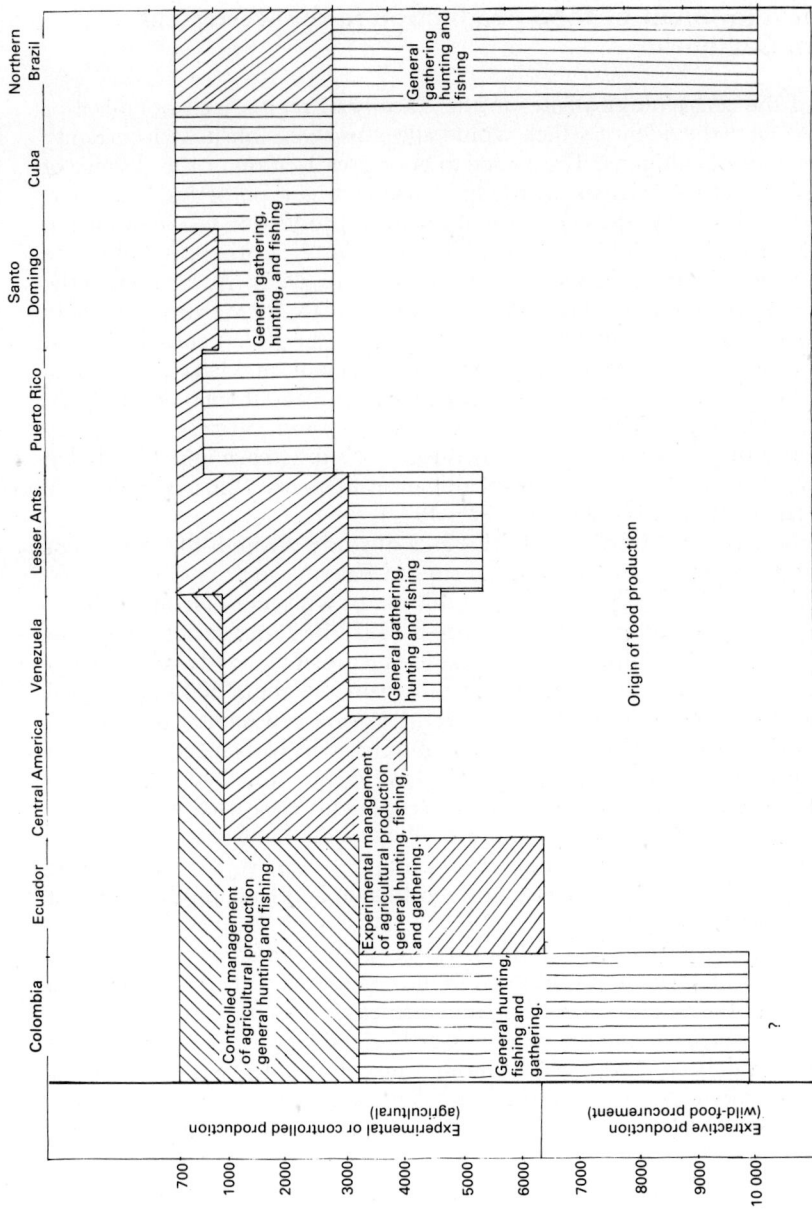

**Figure 33.2**  Schematic representation of the development of food production in northern South America and the Caribbean.

# The development of food production in the western and eastern Caribbean

Most of the archaeological sites in the Caribbean region lack botanical or other ecofactual evidence which would allow us to establish with certainty the existence of cultigens. This is due to poor preservation or the absence of archaeobotanical specialists with experience in this type of research, but, despite this difficulty, the evolution of the food-production tool complex in northeastern South America and the Greater Antilles brings to mind the sequence described by Ranere in Panama (Ranere 1976). According to the results published to date, a transformation took place there from essentially predatory forms of food procurement, such as the Talamanca Phase, to forms of food production, possibly experimental in character, in the Boquete Phase. This process appears to have begun about 5000 years ago (c. 3000 bc) and to have culminated between 940 ± 70 and 350 ± 75 bc with the appearance of pottery and a diversified form of subsistence which included not only vegeculture but also the cultivation of maize (Linares & Ranere 1971, Ranere 1972, 1976, Linares 1975, 1977).

Piperno has also contributed to this area of study through the analysis of phytoliths collected at archaeological sites in Panama such as Cueva de los Vampiros. Her work suggests the possible use of wild cereals from 6610 bc, and the almost certain presence of maize by 4910 bc at habitation sites with no trace of pottery. Similarly, she suggests the possible practice of forms of swidden or slash-and-burn agriculture in Panama by about 3000 bc, as well as a possible increase in indicators of deforestation and habitat destruction through the use of fire by the 1st millennium bc, when advanced systems of agricultural production are thought to have begun to develop (Piperno Ch. 34, this volume). Her research supports not only the earlier propositions of Ranere & Linares, but also those of Pickersgill & Heiser (1978: 137), Pickersgill (Ch. 27, this volume) and Sanoja (1982b, p. 87) on the role played by early hunter–gatherers in the diffusion and later modification of different types of maize.

In comparing *prima facie* the historical processes which characterize the development of agricultural production in the western Caribbean mainland with those of the eastern Caribbean (i.e. northeastern South America and the Antilles), it is clear that in the western Caribbean the presence of cereals – at first wild and later cultivated – among ancient peoples without pottery appears to derive from the migrations of hunter–gatherers who were the vehicle by which plants such as maize were dispersed between Mesoamerica and the Central Andes, possibly as long ago as 7000–6000 bc. In northeastern South America, far away from this main axis of population movements and cereal dispersal, the ancient hunter–gatherer communities seem to have depended, for their supply of carbohydrates, on the selection, collection, and possible cultivation of species native to the region, especially certain roots and rhizomes, as indeed appears to have been the case in the greater part of South America before the appearance of the high-yield cereal maize (Sanoja

1982b, p. 119). This raises the possibility that centres of origin may have existed for *Manihot esculenta* and *Ipomoea batatas* in northern South America, particularly in Venezuela (Hawkes, Ch. 31, this volume).

The role of roots and tubers in the subsistence economy gives a distinctive character to the processes of social transformation which developed within the hunter–gatherer population of northeastern South America. Here the possibilities of developing food production and transcending the precariousness implicit in dependence on wild-food procurement depended heavily on organizing the work force to cope in situations of both scarcity and abundance in the availability of natural subsistence resources. Conditions of environmental 'stress', such as occurred among hunter–gatherers in the Dominican Republic, whether determined by the instability of certain wild resources or, on the other hand, by gluts in times of abundance, do not constitute a causality which produces linear ecological responses in human communities, as we have said. The history of agriculture is not just the history of plants and the environment. On the contrary, it is the history of human labour, of which agriculture is a by-product.

# References

Angulo, C. 1981. *La tradición Malambo*. Bogotá: Fundación de Investigaciones Arqueológicas Nacionales, Banco de la Republica.

Chanlatte, L. 1983. *Arqueología de Vieques*. San Juan: Universidad de Puerto Rico.

Cruxent, J. M. & I. Rouse 1961. *Arqueología cronológica de Venezuela*. Washington, DC: Union Panamericana, Estudios Monográficos no. 6.

Eden, M. J., W. Bray, L. Herrera & C. McEwan 1984. *Terra Preta* soils and their archaeological context in the Caquetá Basin of southeast Colombia. *American Antiquity* **19**, 125–40.

Fairbridge, R. 1976. Shellfish-eating preceramic Indians in coastal Brazil. *Science* **191**, 353–9.

Harris, D. R. 1971. The ecology of swidden cultivation in the upper Orinoco rain forest, Venezuela. *Geographical Review* **61**, 475–95.

Harris, P. O'B. 1973. Preliminary Report on Banwari Trace. *Actas del IV Congreso Internacional para el Estudio de las Culturas Precolombinas de las Pequeñas Antillas*, St. Lucia, 115–25.

Harris, P. O'B. 1976. The Preceramic Period in Trinidad. In *Proceedings of the first Puerto Rican symposium on archaeology*, L. S. Robinson (ed.), 33–64. San Juan: Fundación Arqueológica, Antropológica, e História de Puerto Rico.

Hawkes, J. G. 1989. The domestication of roots and tubers in the American tropics. In *Foraging and farming: the evolution of plant exploitation*, D. R. Harris & G. C. Hillman (eds), ch. 31. London: Unwin Hyman.

Hurt, W. 1974. *The interrelationship between the natural environment and four sambaquis, coast of Santa Catarina, Brazil*. Occasional Papers and Monographs, no. 1, Indiana University Museum, Bloomington.

Linares, O. 1975. De la recolección a la agricultura en el Itsmo. *Revista Panameña de Antropología* **1**, 9–27.

Linares, O. 1977. *Ecology and the arts in ancient Panama*. Washington, DC: Dumbarton Oaks, Trustees for Harvard University.

Linares, O. & A. J. Ranere 1971. Human adaptation to the tropical forests of western Panama. *Archaeology* **24**, 346–55.

Luna Calderón, F. 1979. Antropología y paleopatología de Cueva Roja, Provincia de Pedernales, Republica Dominicana. In *Investigaciones Arqueologicas en la Provincia de Pedernales*, M. Veloz-Maggiolo, F. Luna Calderón & R. Rimoli (eds), 43–79. Universidad Central del Este, Serie Científica VIII, San Pedro de Marcorís, Republica Dominicana.

Ortega, E. & J. Guerrero 1981. *Cuatro nuevos sitios paleoarcaicos en las isla de Santo Domingo*. Santo Domingo: Ediciones Museo del Hombre Dominicano.

Pickersgill, B. & C. B. Heiser, Jr. 1978. Origins and distribution of plants domesticated in the New World tropics. In *Advances in Andean archaeology*, D. L. Browman (ed.), 133–65. The Hague: Mouton.

Pickersgill, B. 1989. Cytological and genetical evidence on the domestication and diffusion of crops within the Americas. In *Foraging and farming: the evolution of plant exploitation*, D. R. Harris & G. C. Hillman (eds), ch. 27. London: Unwin Hyman.

Piperno, D. R. 1989. Non-affluent foragers: resource availability, seasonal shortages, and the emergence of agriculture in Panamanian tropical forests. In *Foraging and farming: the evolution of plant exploitation*, D. R. Harris & G. C. Hillman (eds), ch. 34. London: Unwin Hyman.

Ranere, A. 1972. Ocupación Precerámica en las Tierras Altas de Chiriquí. *Actas del II Simposio Nacional de Antropología, Arqueología y Etnohistoria de Panamá*, 197–207, Universidad de Panamá.

Ranere, A. J. 1976. The Preceramic of Panama: the view from the interior. In *Proceedings of the first Puerto Rican symposium on archaeology*, L. S. Robinson (ed.), 103–38. San Juan: Fundación Arqueológica, Antropológica, e Histórica de Puerto Rico.

Reichel-Dolmatoff, G. 1985. *Monsú. Un sitio arqueológico*. Bogotá: Biblioteca del Banco Popular, Textos Universitarios.

Rouse, I. & J. M. Cruxent 1963. *Venezuelan archaeology*. New Haven: Yale University Press.

Sanoja, M. 1979. *Las Culturas Formativas del Oriente de Venezuela. La Tradición Barrancas del Bajo Orinoco*. Caracas: Ediciones de la Academia Nacional de la Historia, Colección Estudios, Monografías y Ensayos, no. 6.

Sanoja, M. 1980. Los recolectores tempranos del Golfo de Paria. *Arizona State University Anthropological Research Papers* **22**, 139–51.

Sanoja, M. 1982a. *Historia General de América*. Vol. 3: *De la recolección a la agricultura*. Caracas: Academia Nacional de la Historia.

Sanoja, M. 1982b. *Los hombres de la yuca y el maíz*. Caracas: Monte Avila Editores.

Sanoja, M. 1983. Tipología de concheros precerámicos del noreste de Venezuela. *Actas del IX Congreso Internacional para el Estudio de las Culturas Precolumbinas de las Pequeñas Antillas*, República Dominicana, 15–26. Centre de Recherches Caraibes, Université de Montréal.

Sanoja, M. 1985. La sociedad tribal del Oriente de Venezuela. *Revista Gens* (Socieded Venezolana de Arqueólogos) **3**, 41–67.

Sanoja, M. In press a. La formación de cazadores recolectores de Venezuela. In *Actas de la II reunión de Vieques*, I. Vargas (ed.). Caracas: Fundación de Arqueología del Caribe.

Sanoja, M. In press b. Orígenes de la producción de alimentos en la América Central, Colombia, Venezuela, Amazonia, Ecuador y Las Antillas. In *Historia Científica y Cultural de la Humanidad*. Vol. II: *6000–750 BC*, A. H. Dani (ed.). Paris: UNESCO.

Sanoja, M. In prep. *Investigaciones arqueológicas en el Golfo de Paria, Venezuela: los sitios de Guayana y No Carlos*.

Sanoja, M. & I. A. Vargas 1978. The Formative Cultures of the Venezuela Oriente. In *Advances in Andean archaeology*, D. L. Browman (ed.), 259–76. The Hague: Mouton.

Sanoja, M. & I. A. Vargas 1983. New light on the prehistory of eastern Venezuela. In *Advances in world archaeology*, Vol. II, F. Wendorf & A. Close (eds), 205–44. New York: Academic Press.

Sauer, C. O. 1952. *Agricultural origins and dispersals*. New York: American Geographical Society.

Vargas, I. A. 1979. *La Tradición Saladoide del Oriente de Venezuela: La Fase Cuartel*. Caracas: Academia Nacional de la Historia, Colección Estudios, Monografías y Ensayos, no. 5.

Vargas, I. A. 1981. *Investigaciones arqueológicas en Parmana: los sitios de la Gruta y Ronquín, Estado Guarico, Venezuela*. Caracas: Academia Nacional de la Historia, Colección Estudios, Monografías y Ensayos, no. 20.

Veloz-Maggiolo, M. 1976. *Medicambiente y adaptación humana en la prehistoria de Santo Domingo*, Vol. I. Santo Domingo: Editorial de la Universidad Autónoma de Santo Domingo, Colleción Historia y Sociedad, no. 24.

Veloz-Maggiolo, M. 1980. *Las sociedades Arcaicas de Santo Domingo*. Santo Domingo: Coediciones del Museo del Hombre Dominicano y la Fundación García Areval, no. 43.

Veloz-Maggiolo, M. & B. Vega 1982. The Antillean Preceramic: a new approximation. *Journal of New World Archaeology* **5**, 33–44.

Veloz-Maggiolo, M., E. Ortega, J. Nadal, F. Luna Calderón & R. Rimoli 1977. *Arqueología de Cueva de Berna*. Universidad Central del Este, Serie Científica V, San Pedro de Marcorís, Republica Dominicana.

# 34 Non-affluent foragers: resource availability, seasonal shortages, and the emergence of agriculture in Panamanian tropical forests

DOLORES R. PIPERNO

## Introduction

The concept that hunters and gatherers are affluent; i.e. that there exists a positive relationship between population and available resources enabling a considerable degree of cultural development, has become a dominant theme in studies of foraging societies, past and present. Ethnographic studies over the past 15 years have demonstrated that many foraging groups have fairly stable and secure resource bases, leading to a life that is neither nasty, brutish, nor short (Lee & DeVore 1968) to quote the original counter-argument to traditional portrayals of hunting and gathering.

Recent archaeological investigations have carried this concept even further. Economic, technological, and settlement data from Late Pleistocene and early Holocene occupations in many parts of the world have been interpreted as indicating that prehistoric hunters and gatherers were sedentary, increasing and intensifying production of resources, and developing complex social organizations (Koyama & Thomas 1981, Price & Brown 1985). The broad economic shifts immediately antecedent to the Neolithic, variously called the Archaic in the Americas or the Mesolithic in parts of Europe, are increasingly seen as parts of trends toward population growth, settlement nucleation and permanence, and social complexity. Domesticated food sources are almost viewed as by-products of the successes of early Holocene hunting and gathering (see the papers in Price & Brown 1985).

The corollary to the view that hunters and gatherers are well provisioned with high-quality, reliable resources, and spend little time in the food quest (but see Hawkes & O'Connell 1981, O'Connell & Hawkes 1981) is the argument that early farmers experienced diminishing returns to labour as they were forced to increasingly rely on lower quality, less preferred foodstuffs. Therefore, food production, though severely increasing the demands of labour, was necessitated by increasing population densities and/or declining wild resources (Binford 1968, Cohen 1977).

In reading this literature one can lose sight of the fact that hunters and gatherers are adversely affected by periodic imbalances with resources, and random, severe fluctuations in rates of mortality and fertility brought about by small group size and high mobility. Negative aspects of foraging life have been underplayed in recent evaluations of prehistoric non-food producing societies because of the view that marginal environments occupied by present-day foragers represent an inappropriate analog by which to judge the environs of archaeological hunters and gatherers. This is undoubtedly true for some, but not for all situations.

This chapter re-examines these issues with regard to data from the tropical forests of Panama. Characteristics of the natural environment as potential food sources for hunter–gatherers are described, and evidence is presented that wild resources, especially plant carbohydrates, were severely limited, unstable, and unpredictable, making life as a forager tenuous and highly mobile. It is suggested that the initial domestication of indigenous plants and acceptance of introduced cultivars represented a low-cost strategy to buffer resource variation and unpredictability. Wild resource availability in Panamanian forests is estimated by reference to plant and, to a lesser degree, animal distribution and fluctuations in mature and late secondary vegetational formations. Given the limited mammalian fauna, assessments of plant productivity and quality should lead to a reasonably accurate picture of the food supply. Archaeological settlement and botanical data are then presented for early human occupations of the forests, which were apparently numerous, stable, and, in the Darwinian sense of the word, successful, only after food producing strategies were employed 7000 years ago.

Archaic and early food producing economies in American tropical forests have seldom been considered from either an archaeological perspective or one that considers the productivity of the natural plant environment. Archaeological sequences that span long periods of the Holocene are notoriously difficult to acquire, and relevant subsistence, settlement, and demographic data are accordingly rare. Similarly, insufficient information about the highly diverse and complex tropical forest flora and fauna make estimations of food availability in natural situations difficult. In Panama, neither of these factors pose singular problems. The Proyecto Santa Maria, a large multi-disciplinary archaeological project directed by Anthony Ranere and Richard Cooke, has accumulated an impressive body of information on settlement, economy, and population over the past 9000 years in Central Pacific Panama. Phytolith, pollen, and macro-botanical data on wild and domesticated plant usage spanning this period are available.

The tropical forests of Panama are arguably among the best studied in the world. The Missouri Botanical Garden sponsored a formal effort to catalogue all the plants occurring in Panama. Published as '*The Flora of Panama*' (*Annals of the Missouri Botanical Garden* 1943–1981) it includes descriptions, ranges, and habitats for over 5000 species of plants. Collections by specialists continue in remote and inaccessible areas, and recent updates of the expanded floral inventory have been published (D'Arcy & Correa 1985). In addition, long-term ecological studies of semi-evergreen forests have been made, leading to new information on forest dynamics, seasonal rhythms, and multi-annual fluctuations of resources (Leigh *et al.* 1982). Some mature sections of these forests have been mapped and recorded, tree by tree (Hubbell & Foster 1983), providing sound quantitative data on resource density.

Intensive investigations have been carried out in the deciduous forests in Guanacaste Province, Costa Rica (Frankie *et al.* 1974, Opler *et al.* 1980). They probably form the nearest modern analogue to formations that once existed in much of the Proyecto Santa Maria study area, but which are now almost completely gone. Deciduous and semi-evergreen forests are focused on here because it is in these contexts that the earliest domesticated foodstuffs are found.

## Wild resource availability in tropical forests

### *The question of carbohydrate limitation*

In analysing the relationship between tropical-forest peoples and their environment, much attention has been paid to the role of protein scarcity as a major factor limiting population size and permanence (e.g. Gross 1975, Ross 1978, Beckerman 1979, Chagnon & Hames 1979, 1980). However, very little consideration has been given to the issues of caloric extraction and its predictability and reliability due to seasons and multi-annual fluctuations of wild-plant resources. Earle (1980, p. 3) reminds us that the 'primary objective of all procurement strategies under investigation is their caloric yield . . . in as much as energy is a most basic requirement of any population'. Recent ethnographic data from tropical forests suggest that the traditional emphasis on protein availability has indeed been misdirected.

Milton (1984) presents evidence showing that fisher-farmers in Amazonia exist at much higher population density than neighbouring hunter–gatherers primarily because they have an ample supply of carbohydrates, while experiencing seasonal shortages of protein. Hunter–gatherers were limited mainly by severe seasonal and annual shortages of carbohydrates from wild resources. Hart & Hart (1986) document a similar situation in the rain forests of Zaire, where Mbuti pygmies, though having ample meat resources all year round, experience severe seasonal shortages of starch-dense foods from wild plants.

Further, it is suggested that neither protein nor carbohydrates as such, but the relative proportions of calories derived from plant and animal foods, are important in determining population size. The demographic implications of a subsistence strategy that derives calories mainly from animal foods have received little attention from anthropologists, but they appear to be extremely important. Milton (1984) notes that, in general, populations oriented toward securing food from the first trophic level (plants) are numerically more abundant than populations relying primarily on animal resources. A primary reason for this relationship is the high metabolic costs of extracting calories from protein, which becomes necessary if meat is not high in fat.

> Typically, the higher the trophic level the fewer the organisms . . . A population meeting much of its energetic as well as protein needs from animal food will require considerable more meat each day to sustain itself than will a population meeting energy needs from plant foods and using animal foods only to meet protein requirements. Given the same amount of available protein the second population will be able to exist at a higher density, all else being equal . . . Indeed, catabolizing protein for energy is a wasteful process because of the costs involved in degradation of the individual carbon skeletons of the amino acids (Milton 1984, pp. 19–20).

It is predicted that a resource base deficient in available carbohydrates, especially from plants, should support only small populations. Such a situation appears to have existed in Panama. A complete list of forest plants with edible parts would be lengthy, as would a list of wild plants incidentally eaten at one time or another by Archaic and early food-producing populations in Panama. However, the number of edible resources turns out to be an inaccurate measure of environmental productivity, as inspection of species inventoried in dry and semi-evergreen forests shows that few are heavy producers of food calories; good starch producers are scarce (Frankie *et al.* 1974, Croat 1978, Hubbell 1979, Opler *et al.* 1980, Hubbell & Foster 1983, Foster & Piperno field observations). Wild herbaceous perennials with large roots and tubers that might serve as good energy sources, such as *Dioscorea*, *Calathea*, *Ipomoea*, *Heliconia*, and *Xanthosoma*, are scarce in undisturbed contexts. They are, however, common in secondary growth, a point that is explored further below.

In addition, useful plants tend to be too dispersed in mature forest to support sizeable, even semi-permanent human communities. That tropical forests have a great diversity of species and widely dispersed food sources are hardly new revelations. However, quantitative data on these patterns are now available from dry forests in Guanacaste Province, Costa Rica and semi-evergreen forest on Barro Colorado Island (BCI), Panama (Hubbell 1979, Hubbell & Foster 1983).

In the 400–600-year-old forest on BCI (Piperno in press a) only 33 species out of 186 (with diameter at breast height of at least 20 cm) had an average density of one or more trees per hectare (Hubbell & Foster 1983). Many forest plants bear small fruits no more than 2–3 cm in diameter which are consumed and dispersed by bats, birds, and other forest animals. Large quantities of such fruits would have to be collected and processed to provide a significant level of energy for human consumption. One must also take into account the high proportion of plants with secondary or toxic compounds (Janzen 1969, Freeland & Janzen 1974), which either would render them inedible or lead to increased processing time to achieve edible foodstuffs.

Hubbell's and Foster's studies have shown that many trees in the forest are clumped, i.e. they show significantly greater probabilities of one or more conspecifics among their nearest neighbours than would be expected statistically. However, for a number of reasons, too much significance should not be attached to this in relation to the human exploitation of resources. Clumped dispersion patterns are exhibited at very local scales and many species show a greater tendency to be clumped simply because they are among the most common. Furthermore 'clumped' species are still widely dispersed in space when compared to, say, the dense stands of wild legumes, cactuses, and grasses that fed Mesoamerican Archaic populations (Flannery 1968, 1985). For example, Flannery (1986) estimates that *mesquite* (*Prosopis* sp.) and other wild plants known to have been heavily exploited during the Pre-Ceramic period in the Oaxaca Valley achieve densities of several hundred individuals per hectare. Compare this figure with tree density in dry forests, where the degree of clumping is greatest because of decreased species diversity, and yet no more than 12 adult conspecifics can be expected to occur within 100 m of an adult of that species (Hubbell 1979). The combination of these factors – high diversity, dispersion, and the production of predominantly small fruits – makes for resources whose utilization costs in terms of search and handling (collecting, processing) time are high.

Palms are frequently cited as providing a major source of calories and perhaps high-quality protein for tropical forest groups (e.g. Levi-Strauss 1950, Beckerman 1979, Hawkes *et al.* 1982). The extensive use of wild plants today by South American indigenous populations is heavily oriented toward palm products. It is of major significance then that palms are rare or inconspicuous components of mature and late secondary dry and semi-evergreen forests in Costa Rica and Panama. Major economic taxa such as *Acrocomia vinifera* (corozo palm), *Euterpe* sp., *Manicaria* sp., and *Bactris gasipaes* (peach palm) do not appear on the extensive species lists available from these areas, nor have they been observed in these forests (author and Robin Foster, observations) or in those of the same type from other regions in Panama (Hugh Churchill & Greg DeNevers, pers. comm.). Peach palm, an important source of calories to contemporary indigenous populations, is almost certainly an introduction, and the same may be true of the corozo palm. Janzen (1983) notes that in Costa Rica it is never found in any habitat except sites disturbed by humans: pastures, old fields, roadsides, and house sites. The situation is the same in Panama and Janzen suspects, as I do, that the palm was introduced into southern Central America.

Deciduous forests, especially, are depauperate in palms. There are virtually none in extensive stretches of Santa Rosa National Park and other areas of Guanacaste Province, Costa Rica, far removed from human influences (Frankie *et al.* 1974, Opler *et al.* 1980, author's observations). Gallery forests today contain numbers of *Scheelia zonensis* and *Bactris* spp., as they no doubt did in the past, and edaphically distinctive sites like seasonal and stream-fed swamps may have contained concentrations of such species as *Elaeis oleifera* and *Bactris* sp. But it is clear that in deciduous forest the availability of palms is low, and that they could hardly have provided much in the way of food to hunting and gathering populations.

In sum, the picture that emerges is an environment seriously deficient in available carbohydrates. There are certainly many edible species, but these are dispersed in space, supply little in the way of bulk, and are likely to yield low returns per unit of foraging time because their search and handling costs are high. These are not the only negative aspects of a foraging existence, for the seasonality of wild tropical resources may have presented other serious problems to human exploitation.

## Seasonality of resources

Seasonality has long been considered an important factor influencing many aspects of hunting and gathering life. It determines changes in diet, patterns of mobility, group size, and reproductive strategy (e.g. Lee 1979, Wilmsen 1981). As Hill *et al.* (1984) have noted, the effects of seasonal variability on human behaviour are generally considered to be greater at higher latitudes and least pronounced in equatorial regions. However, recent studies of seasonal rhythms in tropical forests leave little doubt that marked seasonality of rainfall in tropical environments can have fundamental effects on biological productivity that parallel seasonal temperature changes at higher latitudes (Leigh *et al.* 1982, Harris 1978).

Many forest species show considerable seasonal variation in phenological activity. In the semi-deciduous forests of Panama there are two peaks of fruiting, occurring in September–October and March–June. The late wet and early dry seasons (November–February) are known as the 'season of scarcity', when wild plant resources, including fruits, nuts, and young leaves, are at a minimum and, in response, mammals are leaner and fewer in number (Foster 1982a). In deciduous forests there is a single peak of fruiting occurring during March–June and especially at the end of the dry season in April, so the lean season here is much longer (Frankie *et al.* 1974, Opler *et al.* 1980).

Multi-annual variation in vegetal production can also be extreme. There are years when many species do not fruit, or fruit very little, after having produced copious or moderate amounts in preceding years. Two-year lags in production have been noted for several species (Foster 1982a). These phenomena, though not widely discussed in the literature, are common to many tropical trees. After rainy dry seasons, a circumstance which happens on average about once every 5 years, near-famine conditions exist, with virtually no fruit production occurring. Animal populations during these years are under severe stress, exemplified by their leaner body weight and high mortality rates (Foster 1982b).

Tropical forests have often been depicted as benign, stable environments rich in wild plant resources resulting from the diversity and productivity of plant biomass. However, the Panamanian example makes it clear that neither the stability nor the quality of the edible resource base is positively correlated with the diversity and overall productivity of the ecosystem. Carbohydrates are in short supply. Seasonal and annual scarcities of high-quality fruit and leaf items occur, which, in turn, cause fluctuations in the availability of animals. Recent ethnographic evidence from Amazonia documents the implications of the resource base for human habitation. Milton (1984) found that the Maku, a group of interfluve hunter–gatherers, experienced serious seasonal shortages of carbohydrates from wild fruits and other forest products, during which time they gave meat or labour to neighbouring horticulturalists (who were experiencing seasonal shortages of protein) in exchange for manioc.

The natural environment of Panama would have presented serious con-straints on environmental adaptation by foraging groups. Selective pressures favoured small group sizes, high mobility, and the enforcement of appro-priate cultural reproductive measures to ensure small, highly mobile popu-lations. This portrayal of a rather tenuous existence hardly fits the concept of affluent foragers. I suggest that in these circumstances an economic strategy predicated on some degree of food production would result in a *more* predictable, secure, and synchronous resource base, in addition to a sub-stantial increase in the total recoverable yield during any single year.

I suspect that the proximal cause of the shift toward horticulture may have been a conscious, short-term goal of ensuring the society's immediate needs; i.e. getting them through the lean periods that occurred every year and avoiding the sudden and unpredictable crashes that occurred every few years. Ultimately, one of the results was a very substantial increase in population, largely made possible by the dramatically increased calorific food base from domesticated plants and also from useful wild plants whose reproductive fitness and densities were increased by the developing agroeco-logy. Evidence for the earliest domesticated plants in Panama and their ecological correlates and consequences will now be presented.

## Early plant domestication in Panama

The Proyecto Santa Maria (PSM), which is studying human adaptations in the Santa Maria watershed of Central Pacific Panama, has carried out systematic surveys from the coast to the Continental Divide and discovered over 500 archaeological sites, 250 of which are pre-ceramic, or at least 'aceramic' (Cooke & Ranere 1984, Weiland 1984, Ranere in press, Weiland in press). Archaeobotanical analysis has been carried out on stratified deposits from eight rockshelters, one early 1st millennium bc nucleated village, and one late 1st millenium bc village. Seven of the rockshelters contain both pre-ceramic and early ceramic components which are dated by radiocarbon from 6700 bc to 1000 bc. It is possible to trace over a period of 9000 years the initial and partial conversion of foraging into horticultural economies, the elaboration of these into slash-and-burn (swidden) systems, and, after a 4000-year period of relatively small-scale cultivation, the development of fully agricultural economies that supported nucleated and sedentary villages.

The PSM has accumulated an extraordinary amount of data on subsistence, settlement, and demography, and much of this is still being analysed. In broad outline, it appears that the region was very sparsely inhabited until around 7000 years ago, when the number of sites and the density of material found in them increase dramatically. Bifacial flaking as a strategy for shaping chipped stone tools disappears from Central Panama before 5000 bc (Cooke & Ranere 1984, Ranere in press). Only ten sites with bifacial work have been identified, whereas pre-ceramic occupations without bifacial work and hence dating from 5000 bc to 2500 bc number about 250 (Weiland 1984, in press). At several excavated rockshelters, occupations do not begin until 5000 bc or shortly after, and at others very small amounts of bifacial and associated material are overlain by substantially greater quantities of later pre-ceramic debris. The bifacial assemblages indicate that the natural environment supported very small, widely dispersed populations until 7000 years ago, when a dramatic increase in population number and density becomes apparent. This demographic upturn appears to be associated with the introduction of maize, and almost certainly other crops, by 5000 bc.

## Maize

We have documented an early pattern of seed cropping in Central Panama. Maize pollen and phytoliths were recovered from the pre-ceramic occupation of a rockshelter, Cueva de los Ladrones, the earliest levels of which are radio-carbon dated to 4910 bc (Piperno & Husum-Clary 1984, Piperno et al. 1985). Maize phytoliths are also present in the pre-ceramic levels of another rockshelter radiocarbon dated to 5125 bc. This evidence confirms suspicions long held by botanists (e.g. Pickersgill & Heiser 1977, Pickersgill Ch. 27, this volume) that early dispersals of primitive maize from Mexico to South America occurred. It indicates that cultivation practices coeval, or nearly coeval, with those in highland Mexico (MacNeish 1967) and Peru (Kaplan et al. 1973) were present in the humid tropical lowland forest of Panama.

Because phytolith analysis is a relatively recent development in archaeobotany, a brief digression on the technique and on the maize-identification system used is necessary. Phytoliths are the most ubiquitous type of plant material recovered from tropical archaeological sites, and they appear to be sensitive, accurate, and reliable indicators of prehistoric cropping patterns and land usage; in some cases, even more so than either pollen or macro-botanical remains. Many plants, both monocots and dicots, contribute highly diagnostic shapes that are constant within species sampled from widely different environmental regions, and phytoliths are no more prone to vertical and horizontal movement in soils after deposition than are pollen grains (Piperno 1984, 1985a, 1985b, 1985c, 1988, Piperno & Starczak 1985).

The maize-identification procedure rests on morphological and metric attributes of 'cross-shaped' phytoliths found only in maize. These attributes are short axis length, three-dimensional structure, and percentages of cross-shaped phytoliths in leaf specimens. They have been determined for 23 races of maize, six races of teosinte, and 39 wild grasses forming the native Panicoid grass cover of Panama. To provide a measure of interpopulation variability of phytoliths, four replicate samples of different plants were studied for wild species where cross- or dumbbell-shaped phytoliths were most common. For five races of maize, husks, leaves, and tassels of four replicate samples from distinct plants were studied (Piperno 1984, 1988, Piperno & Starczak 1985).

The results indicate that shapes and sizes of short-cell phytoliths are constant in, and characteristic of, species in which they occur, regardless of environmental conditions of growth. Moreover, there is clearly a correlation between the types of phytoliths and the taxonomic affinities of plants containing them. Therefore, short-cell phytolith morphology and size must be under a great deal of genetic control. Maize phytoliths were consistently larger than those of most wild grasses ($P < 0.05$) and displayed a predominance of 'Variant 1-type' (Piperno 1984) three-dimensional morphology, in contrast to many wild grasses. These variables of modern plants were used in a discriminant function analysis, which demonstrated that maize and wild grasses could be separated into two groups on a formal statistical basis (Piperno & Starczak 1985, Piperno 1988). A discriminant function analysis of archaeological cross-shaped phytoliths indicated that the pre-ceramic deposits mentioned above, dated to the late 6th and early 5th millennia bc, contained maize (Piperno 1988), confirming identifications made on a more intuitive basis (Piperno 1984, Piperno et al. 1985).

It has often been assumed, for rather tenuous reasons (see Rindos 1984), that the cultivation of root and tuber crops would have been the earliest form of food production adopted in the humid tropics. However, consideration of the ecology of maize and its probable wild ancestor teosinte, and of the early evolutionary history of maize, shows why its occurrence by 7000 years ago in Central Pacific Panama is not surprising. Recent protein evidence assembled by Doebley, Goodman, and others indicates that of six extant teosinte varieties, the Balsas populations, native to the seasonally dry Balsas watershed of western Mexico, are genetically closest to maize and may be its wild ancestor (Doebley 1983, Doebley et al. 1984, Smith et al. 1984, cf. Wilkes Ch. 28, this volume). The Tehuacan Valley, where a completely domesticated maize morphologically far removed from teosinte was present 7000 years ago, and indeed all of the Central Mexican highland region, may have been marginal at best to the earliest evolutionary history of maize, if maize, as seems possible, was domesticated considerably earlier in the wetter, low- to mid-altitudinal environments of western Mexico.

A description of the general ecology of the regions where Balsas teosinte is found applies almost equally well to Central Pacific Panama – thorn scrub and tropical deciduous forest, warm, seasonally dry, receiving an annual rainfall of 1200–2000 mm. Primitive races of maize were then pre-adapted to the environments of the study region. The similarity of ecology may have promoted a rapid spread of early maize, although an average diffusion rate of only 2 km a year is required to bring the plant from western Mexico to Central Panama by 7000 years ago, assuming that maize domestication was well underway by 8000 years ago. Rates of 1 km per year have been proposed for the spread of wheat and barley from Southwest Asia into Europe, through environments that sometimes differed drastically in rainfall, temperature, length of growing season, and photoperiod (Ammerman & Cavalli-Sforza 1984). The process by which maize may have spread is not considered here, but Ammerman & Cavalli-Sforza's model for Europe of local small-scale movements of individuals may be preferable to postulating long-distance population migrations or population replacement.

Recently, maize pollen has been discovered in geological deposits from the Calima Valley, Colombia, radiocarbon dated to 5300 bc (Monsalve 1985). Maize phytoliths are also present in the pre-ceramic late Vegas occupation of the Santa Elena Peninsula, Ecuador, dated to the late 6th millenium bc (Piperno in press). It seems that we may not as yet have placed the earliest date on maize in Central Panama and that the diffusion from North to South America was indeed a fairly rapid one through seasonally dry, warm environments.

## Other crops

No other crop plants have as yet been evidenced during the period from 7000 to 1000 bc. It is exceedingly difficult to demonstrate the presence of root crops, especially because many, including manioc, *Xanthosoma* sp., and sweet potato, have no identifiable siliceous remains. Squash (*Cucurbita*) phytoliths do not occur until about 300 bc, in contexts associated with nucleated and sedentary villages. However, because the rinds of different squash varieties appear to be somewhat capricious in terms of their production of the distinctive spherical, scalloped phytoliths, I believe their late appearance may not indicate a late introduction of *Cucurbita* itself, but perhaps of different species moving as a complex with productive races of maize from South America. Despite the paucity of crop plants recovered thus far, it is probable that maize was only one of a large number of species taken into cultivation by 7000 years ago.

There is a significant degree of variability between the phytolith records of the excavated rockshelters. On-site cultivation of maize is not indicated for several shelters during either the Pre-Ceramic or the early Ceramic period. At two sites 80 per cent of the fine-silt phytolith record is contributed by the remains of arboreal fruits and seeds such as *Chrysobalanus icaco* and *Hirtella* spp., and there is no indication of environmental disturbance near the sites in the form of grass, sedge, or *Heliconia* phytoliths. A long-term, stable orientation toward the exploration of tree products seems to be indicated, qualified, however, by the fact that we can say little about the possible contribution of root crops.

It would surely be misleading to assume that all residential groups in Central Panama from 5000 to 1000 bc were cultivating crops, the same crops, or the same crop mixtures. Considerable variation in subsistence practices probably existed, with economic reciprocity between foragers and farmers occurring that may have further raised the carrying capacity of the region. Local groups no doubt engaged to varying degrees in each economic strategy from one year to the next. Hence, the characterization of economies as either agricultural or hunting–gathering during this period probably has little meaning.

## Early land usage and the 'cost' of early food production

The nature and chronology of the archaeological settlement data from Central Panama suggest that pre-ceramic and early ceramic-phase maize (5100–1000 bc) was part of a shifting system carried out by small groups who exploited environments away from the major rivers. Settlements were often less than one hectare in size and situated on promontories overlooking streams, or on interfluvial spurs (Weiland in press). The earliest nucleated and sedentary village situated on river alluvium, La Mula-Sarigua, was not occupied until around 870 bc. Thus, for at least 4000 years, a shifting and small-scale system of cultivation appears to have been practised. At first, land was plentiful, gardens and fields small, and fallow periods optimal, and low population density prevented the competition and social conflicts created by conditions of dense settlement. Similarly, crop pests may not have been a serious problem because small, polycultural plots did not provide a dense enough host population for major outbreaks of pest infestations. Therefore, early food production may have been a relatively energetically inexpensive and reliable subsistence strategy which provided the most secure and preferred food base compared both to hunting-gathering and developed agriculture.

Pollen and phytolith data from geological sequences which would allow us to measure the environmental impact of early cultivation are not yet available from Central Panama. We can, however, look to Eastern Panama for evidence on the nature of land usage from 5000 to 1000 bc. Phytolith evidence from geological profiles here indicates that maize had expanded into the Caribbean watershed near the present-day Panama Canal by 5000 years ago (Piperno 1985c). Associated with the appearance of maize are significant increases in phytoliths from weedy plants, and in phytoliths with carbon occlusions, which are the remains of burnt plants. It appears that a slash-and-burn mode of planting involving the clearing of new spaces for fields was being carried out by 5000 years ago. It is important to emphasize that this region, although receiving an annual rainfall of 2600 mm, still has a long and marked dry season, one favourable to the niche expansions of crop plants through the cutting and burning of vegetation.

We can envisage that the drier and more burnable forests of Central Pacific Panama were also in some degree of slash-and-burn agriculture and out of a 'kitchen garden' horticultural pattern by at least 5000 years ago. The numerous small settlements that pre-date 1000 bc which have been found by the PSM survey may represent hamlet clusters of several families. Bearing in mind that the amount of land required to feed even a small family of five or six amounts to several hectares (Bort 1979), and that the number of sites identified on a 4 per cent coverage survey exceeded 500, it is reasonable to conclude that extensive areas of land would have been either in cultivation or in fallow by 1000 bc.

By 300 bc, large-scale environmental degradation is indicated. In deposits from the coastal plain rockshelter of Aguadulce, phytoliths from *Curatella americana*, a major indicator species for fire disclimax vegetation, increase markedly in strata dated to the 1st millennium bc, indicating severe deforestation and habitat destruction near the site by that time (Piperno 1985a). Scarcity of good agricultural land in the interior forests, the soil cover of which had been exhausted, may have been an important factor in the settlement shift to the alluvium of major rivers. In these locations, sedentary villages with primarily agricultural economies are numerous by shortly after the beginning of the Christian era.

## The implications of wild resource availability in regenerating plots and other regrowth vegetation

In all stages of regeneration the total yield of wild useful products appears greater than under purely natural conditions. Wild tuber-producing plants are common in abandoned plots. Many other herbaceous and woody plants valued for their leaves and fruits are more common in regrowth vegetation, and they provide important dietary supplements and utilitarian items to indigenous populations. When humans cleared the forests and planted their fields they unknowingly increased the reproductive fitness of many plants most beneficial in the diet. In fact, one major effect of early domestication may have been the increased densities of important wild resources favoured by regrowth ecology.

## Conclusions

In Panama, fixed or partly fixed settlements, population growth, and intensification of production post-dated the first appearance of domesticated plants. If, as seems likely, such trends among hunter–gatherers are a response to a secure subsistence base, then they did not develop in the Panamanian tropical forests because of the low ecological potential. As Gould (1985) has argued, we must guard against the assumption that nucleation and sedentism are inevitable in the evolution of hunter–gatherer societies. Panama was one place where such developments apparently did not take place.

In considering the factors limiting population size and permanence, it has been argued that calories, and severe seasonal and multi-annual fluctuations in their availability, were far more serious constraints than were protein shortages. Small-scale food production significantly increased the yield of available plant calories and, over the long term, this resulted in a significant increase in population and in the permanence of settlements. However, in considering proximal factors, the dietary importance of a resource should not be measured solely in terms of its calorific contribution. 'Reliability' of resources looms large as a major factor contributing to diet choice among present-day hunter–gatherers (Lee 1968, 1979, Hayden 1981). Maize may have been a more reliable carbohydrate source than indigenous plants in the prehistoric economy, and was thus accepted into tropical forest subsistence systems at an early date.

In searching for proximal causes of early farming in Panama, I take the view that food production represented a reliable and inexpensive alternative and buffer to the low productivity and periodic shortages of naturally available foodstuffs. I suggest that people with short-term goals consciously sought to improve their food supply; thus human decision-making, on this level, is seen as an essential part of the process. In Panama, population growth was a correlate, not a cause, of the adoption of agricultural practices.

This is not to dispute the current widely held view that mobile hunting and gathering is generally less laborious than settled, large-scale agriculture. However, in Panama these two extremes of socio-economic development were separated by at least 4000 years of small-scale, shifting agriculture, the advent of which was preceded by a low-density, highly mobile foraging existence. In such circumstances, the negative correlation often drawn between early agriculture, labour demands, and the quality and desirability of foods (e.g. Cohen 1977) is probably not applicable.

Although I take an essentially ecological view of events and causation, decisions made by people that altered their economic, demographic, and social situation were certainly made in the context of a social group. As Hawkes et al. (1982, p. 380) have noted, 'appeals to cultural preference or systems of meaning beg precisely the question with which we are concerned, namely the explanation of the preferences themselves'. It seems likely that economic and ecological factors were critical determinants of subsistence during the development of early food production in Panama.

## Acknowledgements

This research was supported by a post-doctoral fellowship from the Smithsonian Tropical Research Institute, Balboa, Panama, and a Scholarly Studies grant (1234S407) from the Smithsonian Institution, Washington.

# References

Ammerman, A. & L. L. Cavalli-Sforza 1984. *The Neolithic transition and the genetics of populations in Europe.* Princeton: Princeton University Press.

Beckerman, S. 1979. The abundance of protein in Amazonia: a reply to Gross. *American Anthropologist* **81**, 533–60.

Binford, L. 1968. Post-Pleistocene adaptations. In *New perspectives in archeology*, S. R. Binford & L. Binford (eds), 313–41. Chicago: Aldine.

Bort, J. 1979. Ecology and subsistence on opposite sides of the Talmancan Range. In *Adaptive radiations in prehistoric Panama*, O. Linares & A. Ranere (eds), 499–509. Peabody Museum Monographs no. 5, Cambridge, Mass.

Chagnon, N. & R. Hames 1979. Protein deficiency and tribal warfare in Amazonia: new data. *Science* **20**, 910–13.

Chagnon, N. & R. Hames 1980. La 'Hipotesis Proteica' y la adaptacion indigena a la cuenca del Amazonas: una revision critica de los datos y la teoria. *Interciencia* **5**, 346–58.

Cohen, M. 1977. *The food crisis in prehistory.* New Haven: Yale University Press.

Cooke, R. & A. Ranere 1984. The 'Proyecto Santa Maria'. A multidisciplinary analysis of prehistoric adaptations to a tropical watershed in Panama. In *Recent developments in Isthmian archaeology*, F. Lange (ed.), 3–30. Proceedings of the 44th International Congress of Americanists, Oxford: British Archaeological Reports, International Series 212.

Croat, T. 1978. *The flora of Barro Colorado Island.* Stanford: Stanford University Press.

D'Arcy M. D. & Correa A. 1985. *The botany and natural history of Panama.* St. Louis: Missouri Botanical Garden.

Doebley, J. F. 1983. The maize × teosinte male inflorescence: a numerical taxonomic study. *Annals of the Missouri Botanical Garden* **70**, 32–70.

Doebley, J. F., M. Goodman & C. Stuber 1984. Isoenzymatic variation in *Zea*. *Systematic Botany* **9**, 203–18.

Duke, J. 1975. Ethnobotanical observations on the Cuna Indians. *Economic Botany* **29**, 278–93.

Earle, T. 1980. A model of subsistence change. In *Modeling change in prehistoric subsistence economies*, T. Earle & A. Christenson (eds), 1–29. New York: Academic Press.

Flannery, K. 1968. Archeological systems theory and early Mesoamerica. In *Anthropological archeology in the Americas*, B. J. Meggers (ed.), 67–87. Washington, DC: Anthropological Society of Washington.

Flannery, K. (ed.) 1986. *Guila Naquitz: archaic foraging and early agriculture in Oaxaca, Mexico.* Orlando: Academic Press.

Foster, R. 1982a. The seasonal rhythm of fruitfall on Barro Colorado Island. In *The ecology of a tropical forest: seasonal rhythms and long-term changes*, E. Leigh, A. S. Rand & D. Windsor (eds), 151–72. Washington, DC: Smithsonian Institution Press.

Foster, R. 1982b. Famine on Barro Colorado Island. In *The ecology of a tropical forest: seasonal rhythms and long-term changes*, E. Leigh, A. S. Rand & D. Windsor (eds), 201–12. Washington, DC: Smithsonian Institution Press.

Frankie, G., H. Baker & P. Opler 1974. Comparative phenological studies of trees in tropical wet and dry forests in the lowlands of Costa Rica. *Journal of Ecology* **62**, 881–919.

Freeland, W. J. & D. H. Janzen 1974. Strategies in herbivory by mammals: the role of plant secondary compounds. *American Naturalist* **108**, 269–89.

Gould, R. 1985. 'Now Let's Invent Agriculture . . . ': a critical review of concepts of complexity among hunter–gatherers. In *Prehistoric hunter–gatherers: the emergence of cultural complexity*, T. Price & J. Brown (eds), 426–42. New York: Academic Press.

Gross, D. 1975. Protein capture and cultural development in the Amazon Basin. *American Anthropologist* **77**, 526–49.

Harris, D. R. 1978. Adaptation to a tropical rainforest environment: Aboriginal subsistence in northeastern Queensland. In *Human behaviour and adaptation*, N. Blurton-Jones & V. Reynolds (eds), 113–34. London: Taylor & Francis.

Hart, T. & J. Hart 1986. The ecological basis of hunter–gatherer subsistence in African rain forests: the Mbuti of eastern Zaire. *Human Ecology* **14**, 29–55.

Hayden, B. 1981. Subsistence and ecological adaptations of modern hunter/ gatherers. In *Omnivorous primates*, R. S. Harding & G. Teleki (eds), 344–422. New York: Columbia University Press.

Hawkes, K. & J. O'Connell 1981. Affluent hunters? Some comments in light of the Alyawara case. *American Anthropologist* **82**, 622–6.

Hawkes, K., K. Hill & J. O'Connell 1982. Why hunters gather: optimal foraging and the Ache of eastern Paraguay. *American Ethnologist* **9**, 379–91.

Hill, K., K. Hawkes, M. Murtado & H. Kaplan 1984. Seasonal variance in the diet of Ache hunter–gatherers in eastern Paraguay. *Human Ecology* **12**, 101–35.

Hubbell, S. 1979. Tree dispersion, abundance, and diversity in a tropical dry forest. *Science* **203**, 1299–1309.

Hubbell, S. & R. Foster 1983. Diversity of canopy trees in a Neotropical forest and implications for conservation. In *Tropical rain forest: ecology and management*, S. Sutton, T. Whitmore & S. Chadwick (eds), 25–41. Oxford: Blackwell Scientific Publications.

Janzen, D. 1969. Seed-eaters versus seed size, number, toxicity and dispersal. *Evolution* **23**, 1–27.

Janzen, D. 1983. 'Species accounts'. In *Costa Rican Natural History*, D. Janzen (ed.), 184–5. Chicago: University of Chicago Press.

Kaplan, L., T. Lynch & C. E. Smith 1973. Early cultivated beans (*Phaseolus vulgaris*) from an intermontane Peruvian valley. *Science* **179**, 76–7.

Koyama, S. & D. Hurst Thomas (eds) 1981. *Affluent foragers, Pacific coasts east and west*. Senri Ethnological Series 9.

Lee, R. 1968. What hunters do for a living or how to make out on scarce resources. In *Man the hunter*, R. Lee & I. DeVore (eds), 30–43. Chicago: Aldine.

Lee, R. 1979. *The Kung San*. New York: Cambridge University Press.

Lee, R. & I. Devore (eds) 1968. *Man the Hunter*. Chicago: Aldine.

Leigh, E., A. Rand & D. Windsor (eds) 1982. *The ecology of a tropical forest: seasonal rhythms and long-term changes*. Washington, DC: Smithsonian Institution Press.

Levi-Strauss, C. 1950. The use of wild plants in tropical South America. In *Handbook of South American Indians*, Vol. 6, J. Steward (ed.), 465–86. Washington, DC: Bureau of American Ethnology.

MacNeish, R. 1967. A summary of subsistence. In *The prehistory of the Tehuacan Valley*, Vol. 1, D. Byers (ed.), 290–309. Austin: University of Texas Press.

Milton, K. 1984. Protein and carbohydrate resources of the Maku Indians of northwestern Amazonia. *American Anthropologist* **86**, 7–27.

Monsalve, J. 1985. A pollen core from the Hacienda Lusitania. *Pro Calima* **4**, 40–4. Basil: Vereinigung Pro Calima.

O'Connell, J. & K. Hawkes 1981. Alyawara plant use and optimal foraging theory. In *Hunter–gatherer foraging strategies: ethnographic and archaeological analyses*, B. Winterhalder & E. Smith (eds), 788–93. Chicago: University of Chicago Press.

Opler, P., G. Frankie & H. Baker 1980. Comparative phenological studies of treelet and shrub species in tropical wet and dry forests in the lowlands of Costa Rica. *Journal of Ecology* **68**, 167–88.

Pickersgill, B. 1989. Cytological and genetical evidence on the domestication and diffusion of crops within the Americas. In *Foraging and farming: the evolution of plant exploitation*, D. R. Harris & G. C. Hillman (eds), ch. 27. London: Unwin Hyman.

Pickersgill, B. & C. Heiser 1977. Origins and distributions of plants domesticated in the New World tropics. In *The origins of agriculture*, C. Reed (ed.), 803–35. The Hague: Mouton.

Piperno, D. 1984. A comparison and differentiation of phytoliths from maize and wild grasses: use of morphological criteria. *American Antiquity* **49**, 361–83.

Piperno, D. 1985a. Phytolith taphonomy and distributions in archaeological sediments from Panama. *Journal of Archaeological Science* **12**, 247–67.

Piperno, D. 1985b. Phytolith analysis and tropical paleoecology: forms in New World plant domesticates and wild species. *Review of Paleobotany and Palynology* **45**, 185–228.

Piperno, D. 1985c. Phytolithic analysis of geological sediments from Panama. *Antiquity* **LIX**, 13–19.

Piperno, D. 1988. *Phytolith analysis: an archaeological and geological perspective.* San Diego: Academic Press.

Piperno, D. in press a. Fitalitos, arquealogia y cambias prehistoricas en la historia vegetal de una parcela di cincuenta hectores en la Isla de Barro Colorado, Panama. In *The ecology of a tropical forest: seasonal rhythms and long-term changes.* (Spanish edition), E. Leigh, A. S. Rand & D. Windsor (eds), Washington, D.C.: Smithsonian Institution Press.

Piperno, D. in press b. First report on the phytolith analysis of the Vegas Site OGSE-80, Ecuador. In *The Vegas Culture: early prehistory of the Santa Elena Peninsula*, K. Stothert (ed.). Guayaquil: Mueso Antropológico, Banco Central, Ecuador.

Piperno, D. & K. Husum-Clary 1984. Early plant use and cultivation in the Santa Maria Basin, Panama: data from phytoliths and pollen. In *Recent developments in Isthmian archaeology*, F. Lange (ed.), 85–121. Proceedings of the 44th International Congress of Americanists, Oxford: British Archaeological Reports, International Series 212.

Piperno, D. & V. Starczak 1985. Numerical analysis of maize and wild grass phytoliths using multivariate techniques. Paper read at the 2nd Phytolith Research Workshop, Duluth, Minnesota.

Piperno, D., K. Husum-Clary, R. Cooke, A. Ranere & D. Weiland 1985. Preceramic maize from Central Panama: evidence from phytoliths and pollen. *American Anthropologist* **87**, 871–8.

Price, T. & J. Brown (eds) 1985. *Prehistoric hunter–gatherers: the emergence of cultural complexity.* New York: Academic Press.

Ranere, A. in press. The manufacture and use of stone tools during the preceramic in the Santa Maria Basin of Central Panama. In *Cazadores y recolectores prehistoricas en Centro- y Suramerica*, G. Correal & R. Cooke (eds). Oxford: British Archaeological Reports, International Series.

Rindos, D. 1984. *The origins of agriculture.* Orlando: Academic Press.

Ross, E. 1978. Food taboos, diet, and hunting strategy: the adaptation to animals in Amazon cultural ecology. *Current Anthropology* **19**, 1–36.

Smith, J., M. Goodman & C. Stuber 1985. Relationships between maize and teosinte of Mexico and Guatemala: numerical analysis of allozyme data. *Economic Botany* **39**, 12–24.

Weiland, D. 1984. Prehistoric settlement patterns in the Santa Maria Drainage of Central Pacific Panama: a preliminary analysis. In *Recent developments in Isthmian archaeology*, F. Lange (ed.), 31–53. Proceedings of the 44th International Congress of Americanists, Oxford: British Archaeological Reports, International Series 212.

Weiland, D. in press. Preceramic settlement patterns in the Santa Maria Basin, Central Pacific Panama. In *Cazadores y recolectores prehistóricas en Centro- y Suramerica*, G. Correal & R. Cooke (eds). Oxford: British Archaeological Reports, International Series.

Wilkes, G. 1989. Maize: domestication, racial evolution, and spread. In *Foraging and farming: the evolution of plant exploitation*, D. R. Harris & G. C. Hillman (eds), ch. 28. London: Unwin Hyman.

Wilmsen, E. 1982. Studies in diet, nutrition, and fertility among a group of Kalahari Bushman in Botswana. *Social Science Information* **21**, 5–125.

# 35 *Early plant cultivation in the Eastern Woodlands of North America*

PATTY JO WATSON

## Introduction

Twenty-five years ago Joseph Caldwell prepared a summary of Eastern Woodlands prehistory, with emphasis on the origins of food production and subsequent developments, for a volume of comparative cultural-historical studies entitled *Courses toward urban life* (Caldwell in Braidwood & Willey 1962). In some ways, Caldwell's chapter in that volume served as a foil or counterpoise for the other chapters because in the 1950s the Eastern Woodlands seemed to have been one of the backwaters of world prehistory where no cultural climaxes worthy of international attention were known until very late in the sequence, where in fact pre-Columbian urban life may not have been present at all, or if so only under strong stimulus from centres of civilization in Mexico. Thus, this region was cast as a kind of control situation, where nothing much happened in pre-history, at any rate no dramatic transformation from hunting–gathering to agriculture to literate, state-based and urbanized civilization. The issue of food production, in particular, seemed to be a relatively trivial affair involving transfer of cultigens – maize, squash, pumpkins, gourds, and beans – from the Southwest whence they had, in turn, diffused from Mexico.

Although there were those (Linton 1924, Gilmore 1931, Jones 1936, Quimby 1946) who wrote of indigenous Eastern Woodlands horticulture, no one thought it was of much general significance, even if it had been present here and there. Then, approximately 20 years ago, empirical evidence about plant use, sought systematically by a few archaeologists and archaeobotanists (Struever 1962, 1968, Watson 1969, 1974, Yarnell 1969, 1972, 1974, Munson *et al.* 1972, Struever & Vickery 1973), began to reveal unexpected and complex patterns. Over the past ten years, the tempo of research focused on the beginnings of plant cultivation in eastern North America has quickened to the point that it is difficult just to keep abreast of the basic data, and nearly impossible to maintain up-to-date syntheses of the data.

## Eastern Woodlands prehistory: a brief summary

Detailed accounts of the culture history of the eastern United States are to be found in several sources (e.g. Willey 1966, Jennings 1974, Stoltman 1978, Griffin 1983, Muller 1983, Stoltman & Baerreis 1983, Meltzer & Smith 1986, Smith 1986).

Although the time of human entry into the Americas is a topic that inspires more or less perennial controversy (for an excellent review see Dincauze 1985), there is no question about the presence of human groups by 12 000–15 000 bp. These hunter–gatherers of the Paleoindian period are best known for their success in killing various species of now extinct animals, many of which were considerably larger than their modern descendants, hence the phrase 'Pleistocene megafauna' that is often applied to them. However, it is unlikely that such megafauna were the focus of subsistence among most Paleoindian groups, or even a particularly significant part of it (Meltzer & Smith 1986).

By approximately 10 000 bp, a closed-canopy, deciduous forest containing oak, hickory, and chestnut as dominant species covered most of the mid-latitude United States from the Mississippi River to the east coast (Delcourt & Delcourt 1981, 1983, Wright 1981, Watts 1983). Except for the very important interval known as the Hypsithermal (Wright 1976, King & Allen 1977, McMillan & Klippel 1981) – a warm, dry period between 8000 and 5000 bp when the prairie and the more xeric vegetation zones between it and the Mississippi River expanded to the east – this deciduous forest cover is the most distinctive and characteristic feature of the North American environment between the Mississippi and the Atlantic up to the present time.

The human inhabitants of this forest were hunters, gatherers, and fishers throughout the pre-Columbian millennia. Beginning approximately 4000 bp, some of them were also part-time horticulturalists, and by about 1000 bp many groups along the central Mississippi valley, the Ohio River, and their major tributaries were heavily committed to maize agriculture. Archaeologists use a complex series of local chronological frameworks to order the material remains left by these early Eastern Woodland peoples, and these have replaced the vaguer, older terminology in many places. That older terminology is ubiquitous in all but the very latest literature, however, and is still useful as a general chronological guide; hence it is summarized in narrative fashion below.

Broadly speaking, post-Paleoindian Eastern Woodlands prehistory is divided into three phases labelled, from early to late, Archaic, Woodland, and Mississippian/Fort Ancient (Fort Ancient comprises the Mississippian period societies of the Ohio River, primarily in southern Ohio and Indiana, and in West Virginia and northern Kentucky). As traditionally conceived, Archaic groups were thought to be pre-ceramic hunter–gatherer–fishers, exploiters *par excellence* of the plant and animal foods afforded by the Holocene deciduous forest. Woodland groups were pottery-makers and part-time horticulturalists, some of whom participated in elaborate mortuary ritual systems, and in trade networks by which spectacular and exotic items (e.g. obsidian, copper, mica sheets carefully worked into human and animal forms, pearl-inlaid grizzly-bear teeth) were distributed far and wide from their sources. Mississippian peoples were maize-farmers, hunters, gatherers, fishers, priests, and chieftains, most of whom lived in ranked societies in densely populated villages and towns in or near the floodplains of the Mississippi and the Ohio rivers and their major tributaries.

Older syntheses often emphasize the distinctiveness and discontinuity of these categories, but current literature stresses the remarkable degree of continuity now evident throughout the whole of Eastern Woodlands prehistory. Some aspects of this continuity are stressed in this chapter, my focus being upon the late Archaic and succeeding Woodland groups, with some attention also paid to the development of maize agriculture by later Woodland and Mississippian peoples.

## Early plant cultivation in the Eastern Woodlands

### The nature of the evidence

Primary evidence of plant use in general and of cultigens in particular derives from a variety of sources: pollen; macrobotanical remains in open sites, rockshelters, and caves; trace-element analyses of human bone. Macrobotanical remains may be charred or uncharred (the latter comprising those preserved in a desiccated but perfect state in dry caves and rockshelters), and they furnish the most abundant data, although the information provided by the other sources is always illuminating and often crucial (e.g. Bender *et al.* 1981, Delcourt *et al.* 1986, Lynott *et al.* 1986). Charred macrobotanical material is usually recovered by flotation and other water-separation processes (Struever 1968, Watson 1976, Wagner in press b), whereas uncharred plant material is obtained simply by systematic collection, sometimes supplemented by dry-screening. A category of uncharred remains that deserves special mention is that of desiccated human faecal material. Human palaeofaeces, sometimes present in considerable quantities in dry rockshelters and caves, are excellent sources of dietary and palaeoenvironmental information (they usually contain pollen, as well as macrobotanical and animal remains), and they can also be individually dated by the radiocarbon technique (e.g. Yarnell 1969, 1974, Bryant 1974, Marquardt 1974, Stewart 1974).

There are, of course, numerous problems that have not been solved, or – in some cases – even widely recognized, with respect to the analysis and interpretation of archaeological remains relevant to early plant use and cultivation (Hastorf & Popper in press). These range from uncertainties of identification to issues of meaningful quantification.

## The earliest cultigens

Asch & Asch (1985a, Conard *et al.* 1984) have identified 7000-year-old, charred cucurbit-rind fragments from the Koster and Napoleon Hollow sites in Illinois as *Cucurbita pepo*, a warm-temperate to tropical domestic species usually thought to have first been taken into cultivation somewhere south of the Mexican border, perhaps as early as the end of the 9th millennium bc (Whitaker & Cutler 1986). The species identification for the early Illinois cucurbit is resisted by some scholars (Heiser 1985, King 1985, Smith 1987), who make two kinds of counter-claims. The first is that the rind fragments, although surely of the *Cucurbita* genus, may be from the fruits of native wild species, either *C. foetidissima*, the buffalo gourd, which is now distributed from Mexico across the Southwest and Texas to southwestern Missouri, Nebraska, and Kansas, or a variety of *C. texana*, now found only in southern Texas. The *Cucurbita* remains may then simply derive from a weedy indigenous plant tolerated, occasionally used, or even completely ignored when it sprang up near a habitation site.

The second counter-claim is that the Illinois cucurbit may indeed be an early cultigen, but one derived from *C. foetidissima* or *C. texana* rather than from *C. pepo* (introduced in a domesticated form from Mexico), although this interpretation may now be modified in view of Heiser's latest hypothesis (Ch. 30, this volume) that *C. pepo* could have been domesticated in eastern North America (as well as separately in Mexico) from *C. texana* (see also Dexter 1986, and Decker & Wilson 1987) when the latter was more widely distributed during the Hypsithermal interval.

The evidence does not yet allow a decisive choice to be made among these competing interpretations, but there are an increasing number of third-millennium bc *C. pepo* occurrences reported for various parts of the midwestern and midsouthern regions of the Eastern Woodlands. It has been identified in third-millennium bc deposits at Phillips Spring in western Missouri (Kay *et al.* 1980, King 1985, Kay 1986), at the Napoleon Hollow, Lagoon, and Kuhlman sites in Illinois (Asch & Asch 1985a, p. 153), at Cloudsplitter Shelter in eastern Kentucky (Cowan 1985, Watson 1985, pp. 130–1), at the Carlston Annis shellmound in west-central Kentucky (Crawford 1982, in prep., Watson 1985, pp. 112, 133), and at Bacon Bend in Tennessee (Chapman & Shea 1981). In addition, it has recently been reported from a fourth-millennium bc context at the Hayes site in Tennessee (Crites 1987).

Bottle gourd (*Lagenaria siceraria*) is also present at Phillips Spring, and appears at other sites in the succeeding two millennia: Jernigan II and Rose Island in Tennessee (Crites 1978, Chapman & Shea 1981); Riverton, Illinois (Yarnell in press b); Salts Cave, Kentucky (Gardener 1987). Smith (1987, p. 21) refers to the identification (by Newsom & Decker) of bottle gourd dating to 7300 bp at the Windover site in Florida, but this material has not yet been published.

Although there is considerable debate about the age and precise identity of the earliest *Cucurbita* species – cf. Heiser (Ch. 30, this volume) and the results of the recent allozyme analyses by Decker (1986) and Decker & Wilson (1987) – there is general agreement that, if it were used by human groups at all, it was not primarily as food but rather – together with the bottle gourd somewhat later – as a container. Even if the remains recovered archaeologically are from *C. pepo*, which is the squash and pumpkin taxon, it was a thick-walled (averaging 2 mm or thicker if domestic), thin-fleshed, gourd-like variety of the modern *C. pepo* var. *ovifera* (ornamental gourd) type; i.e. the earliest *Cucurbita* grown in the Eastern Woodlands, whatever its derivation (*foetidissima*, *texana*, or *pepo*), had a gourd-like fruit, and is best referred to as a *Cucurbita* gourd.

The earliest evidence for a cultivated food plant is of *Iva annua* (sumpweed or marshelder, an inconspicuous weedy plant that produces small, oily seeds) from Napoleon Hollow, Illinois, radiocarbon dated by the accelerator mass spectrometric method to *c.* 2000 bc (Conard *et al.* 1984, Asch & Asch 1985a, p. 161, Yarnell in press a & b). The seeds average 4.4 mm long and are significantly larger than those from wild populations. A mean length of 4 mm or greater is usually regarded as evidence for domestication (Asch & Asch 1978, 1985a, Yarnell 1978, 1981) because seeds from wild *Iva* stands have means ranging from 2.5 to 3.2 mm.

The next oldest cultigen on the present evidence is a subspecies of grain-bearing *Chenopodium berlandieri*, a thin-testa early domesticated form (Smith 1985a, 1985b) being present in eastern Kentucky well before 1000 bc (Smith & Cowan 1987). Although it has been suggested that domesticated thin-testa *Chenopodium* was imported into the eastern United States from Mexico (where it is known as *chia* and is still grown, Wilson 1981), it is equally possible that native wild *Chenopodium berlandieri/bushianum* (cf. Pickersgill Ch. 27, this volume) was domesticated in the Eastern Woodlands to produce a cultivar, thin-testa form there (Asch & Asch 1985a, pp.181–3, Smith 1987, Watson 1988, Yarnell in press b).

The third of the early trio of domesticates is sunflower (*Helianthus annuus*), seeds of which had reached cultigen size (7 mm or longer: Yarnell 1978, in press b) by about 1000 bc, as indicated by finds at the Higgs site in Tennessee (Brewer 1973) and at the Marble Bluff shelter in Arkansas (Fritz 1986).

## Later prehistoric cultigens

The time-space pattern of cultigen emergence alters significantly after 1000 bc. Between 800 and 700 bc, several cultigens and quasi-cultigens appear in Arkansas, Kentucky, and Tennessee. By 500 bc a full-fledged horticultural complex is evident at several sites: Marble Bluff, Arkansas (Fritz 1986); Salts and Mammoth Caves in west-central Kentucky (Watson 1969, 1974, Yarnell 1969, 1974); Cloudsplitter and Cold Oak shelters in eastern Kentucky (Cowan 1985, Gremillion & Yarnell pers. comm.); Higgs (Brewer 1973, McCollough 1973), and several other sites in Tennessee (Chapman & Shea 1981, Crites 1987). This Early Woodland garden complex includes the two container species (*Cucurbita* gourd and bottle gourd), two oily seeded species (sumpweed and sunflower), and at least two starchy-seeded species (*Chenopodium* and maygrass). Although the maygrass (*Phalaris caroliniana*) found archaeologically does not differ from the wild plant, its depositional context and the frequency of its occurrence in archaeological sites with the other domesticates is strong evidence that it was cultivated (Asch & Asch 1985a, Fritz 1986, Yarnell in press b).

In the succeeding centuries other starchy-seeded plants are added as cultigens or, in some places, as propagens – knotweed (*Polygonum erectum*), little barley (*Hordeum pusillum*), and giant ragweed (*Ambrosia trifida*) (Yarnell in press a & b) – and coalesce into a variegated Middle Woodland complex. An additional species distinguishing some Middle Woodland gardens from their Late Archaic and Early Woodland predecessors is tobacco (*Nicotiana* sp., perhaps *N. rustica*: Asch & Asch 1985a, pp. 195–6), which has recently been identified in west-central Illinois (Asch & Asch 1985b), and – rarely and in small quantities – maize (*Zea mays*, presumably of the Chapalote/Tropical Flint/Midwestern 12-row variety), which appears between ad 200 and 600 in a few sites in Tennessee, Ohio, and Illinois (Crites 1978, Yarnell 1983, in press a, Johannessen 1984, Asch & Asch 1985a, pp. 169–99, Lopinot *et al.* 1986, Chapman & Crites 1987). Present evidence, although quite scanty, can be read as suggesting the subsequent development of historic Northern Flint corn (also called Eastern 8-row) somewhere in the more northerly regions of the Eastern Woodlands by about 800 (Stothers 1976, Blake 1986, Doebley *et al.* 1986, Watson 1988; and, for an alternative view, Lathrap 1987). Eastern 8-row/Northern Flint is the maize variety central to the economic foundation of the eastern Mississippian cultural climax known as Fort Ancient, but the Mississippian societies farther west, along the Mississippi River itself, simply added maize (primarily varieties of Midwestern 12-row) to the older starchy-seed complex of Woodland times. At least by these late prehistoric times, a panoply of tolerated, encouraged, or quasi-cultivated plants was also present. Yarnell (in press a & b) refers to some 20 species altogether, including – besides those already referred to – amaranth (*Amaranthus* sp.), maypops (*Passiflora incarnata*), wild beans (*Strophostyles helvola* and *Phaseolus polystachios*), purslane (*Portulaca oleracea*), pokeweed (*Phytolocca americana*), Jerusalem artichoke (*Helianthus tuberosus*), spurge (*Euphorbia maculata*), carpetweed (*Mollugo verticillata*), black nightshade (*Solanum americanum*), and ground nut (*Apios americana*). In addition, there are ethnohistorical accounts describing the semi-cultivation of *Ilex vomitoria* (*yapon* or *yaupon*, source of the Black Drink, which was of great ceremonial importance in the Southeast) and of a salt plant (perhaps a species of *Atriplex*) as well as fibre-yielding plants (Swanton 1948, pp. 176, 270). These historically recorded plants were probably also in use by late prehistoric times if not before.

# Aboriginal subsistence in the eastern forests

## The role of wild food resources

Wild food resources – plant and animal, terrestrial and aquatic – were extremely important everywhere at all time periods from at least 8000 bp, a generalization that is confirmed by both archaeological and ethnographic documentation (already referred to and, for the ethnographic information, Swanton 1948, Yarnell 1964, in press b, Parker 1968, and Hudson 1976).

Although domestic dogs were eaten occasionally, the bulk of animal food comprised deer, turkey, raccoon, possum, squirrel, rabbit and other small mammals, as well as a wide variety of aquatic fauna. These animals were taken by various means: spears, atlatl-and-dart (in the Archaic to Early Woodland), bow-and-arrow (later prehistoric periods), snares, traps, harpoons, hooks, gorges, and nets. Many species of wild herbaceous plants, trees, and bushes were resorted to for food, medicine, dyes, cordage, and textiles, or were employed in constructing houses, boats, containers and other domestic equipment, tools, and weapons, as well as ceremonial objects and structures. On the average and through the millennia, the role played by plant domesticates seems to have been relatively modest. Only in the very latest prehistoric periods, and then only in those few locales where Fort Ancient and Middle Mississippian societies reached high population densities and high levels of socio-political elaboration, do domesticated plants (Northern Flint/Eastern 8-row maize and Midwestern 12-row maize, *Cucurbita pepo*, and – after ad 1000 – beans, *Phaseolus vulgaris*) become critically important. From Middle Archaic to Late Woodland times, nuts (especially hickory and acorn, but also walnut, hazel, chestnut, and beechnut) and nut products (flour and oil) are the most important staple plant foods rather than any of the cultigens discussed earlier in this chapter.

A series of related points follows from this basic one, in combination with the new archaeological evidence about early cultigens. First, semi-sedentary societies following well-established seasonal rounds and based on a diverse subsistence economy persisted in the Eastern Woodlands for very long periods of time (several millennia) in the absence of cultigens of any sort, but making considerable use of storage and preservation techniques for a variety of wild plant and animal foods (e.g. drying and smoking fish and other meat, perhaps including the flesh of freshwater or marine shellfish; drying soft fruits such as persimmons; accumulating large quantities of nuts in pits or above-ground cribs and containers, as well as processing them, and other plant seeds, to produce oil and flour).

Secondly, this same forest-food pattern, with only a modest augmentation of garden plants yielding starchy or oily seeds (sumpweed, sunflower, *Chenopodium*, knotweed, maygrass), provided the economic basis for year-around settlement (Smith 1986, p. 41) and, somewhat later, for the first widely recognized cultural climax in the Eastern Woodlands, that called Adena (known to us primarily as a mortuary complex). For all practical purposes this same subsistence system was also the basis for the subsequent Hopewellian florescence and related developments in the Midwest, Mid-south, and Southeast. This last statement is debatable until much more is known about the archaeobotany and human-bone chemistry of the large, classic Hopewell sites, but I do not think it likely that maize will be found to have played a critical role. Certainly the present evidence does not indicate significant levels of maize consumption prior to Fort Ancient/Mississippian times (Vogel & van der Merwe 1977, van der Merwe & Vogel 1978, Bender *et al.* 1981, Broida 1983, Lynott *et al.* 1986, Wagner 1987, in press a). In other words, it appears that a case can be made for the indigenous development of a middle-range society (i.e. one with marked high- and low-status positions), certainly of the Big Man type (Sahlins 1963) if not some form of chiefdom (i.e. a society in which status is inherited: Service 1962), based upon essentially non-maize horticulture. (For differing opinions about Hopewellian social organization see Braun 1979, Seeman 1979, Smith 1986.)

### Possible Mesoamerican influence on the origins of food production

There has long been a spectrum of informed opinion about Mesoamerican influences upon cultural developments in the Eastern Woodlands in general, and upon the origins of food production there in particular. With respect to horticultural origins, the evidence is still inconclusive, as indicated above, because the identification of the oldest (7000–5000 bp) finds of *Cucurbita* is not unequivocal. Nevertheless, one can argue convincingly that even if these ancient remains of *Cucurbita* turn out to be of *C. pepo* derived from Mexico, the unfolding of early horticulture in the Eastern Woodlands is an independent and autonomous development because the earliest food plants are native to the United States (Smith 1987). Certainly the archaeological and botanical evidence is now sufficiently abundant to show that, regardless of the question of the possible priority of some limited Mesoamerican influence, the evolution of horticulture and of social complexity in the aboriginal eastern United States are intricate indigenous phenomena with trajectories that can be traced over very long periods (at least from Middle Archaic through Woodland to the beginning of Mississippian and Fort Ancient times) without significant perturbation from outside.

### Late Archaic/Early Woodland horticulture vs. Mississippian/Fort Ancient agriculture

As already made clear, at least in a summary manner, the earliest food-producing economy in the Eastern Woodlands comprised hoe and/or digging-stick cultivation of garden plots often – probably rather casual – in which some six or fewer plant species were raised. The produce of these gardens was supplementary to a considerable diversity of wild plant and animal foods, the most important of which (generally more important than the cultivated seeds) were nuts, especially hickory, acorn, and walnut. Although a moderate amount of horticultural intensification is apparent in the Little Tennessee River sequence for this time period (Chapman & Shea 1981, Delcourt *et al*. 1986), whole-hearted commitment to plant cultivation and thoroughgoing agriculture is not evidenced before Fort Ancient/ Mississippian times (*c*. 1000 bp) when Eastern 8-row (Northern Flint) and Midwestern 12-row maize was intensively grown along the Ohio River, the central Mississippi River, and the valleys of various tributaries. Inference based on ethnographic, ethnohistorical, and archaeological evidence leads to a number of tentative conclusions about late prehistoric agriculture that contrast it with the earlier (Late Archaic to Middle Woodland) horticulture.

The Mississippian and Fort Ancient peoples are thought to have grown maize, squash, gourds, and beans in fields rather than, or as well as, in gardens, and to have reaped harvests sufficiently abundant to last until the succeeding autumn, at least when supplemented by wild plant and animal food (especially nuts, deer, turkey, and aquatic fauna and flora). The centre of gravity with respect to subsistence as a whole had by then shifted from dependence on wild species with supplementary use of the cultigens to dependence on the cultigens with supplementary use of wild foods. Yet the Mississippians (but apparently not the Fort Ancient branch, Wagner 1987) continued to grow the older Woodland crops (sumpweed, sunflower, *Chenopodium*, maygrass, knotweed, little barley, tobacco), perhaps in household gardens rather than fields (for recent summaries of Mississippian plant use, see Watson 1988, Yarnell in press a). Mississippian field systems are believed to have been extensive as well as rather formally planned, laid out, and maintained, although still, of course, worked by hand with hoes and digging sticks (Fowler 1969, p. 374, Riley *et al*. 1980–81, Sears 1982, Riley 1986, Watson 1988). By early historic times at least, intercropping and multiple cropping were commonly practised in the Southeast, whereas farther north maize planting was staggered to produce a series of small harvests two to three weeks apart, thus spreading the risk of crop failure (Hudson 1976, p. 298).

## Interpretations of the evidence and the processes

Regarding the antecedents and origins of plant cultivation and domestication, there seems now to be a consensus that some version of the 'dump-heap theory' is most plausible in seeking to explain the initial appearance of cultigens (Anderson 1952, Fowler 1957, Harlan *et al*. 1973, de Wet and Harlan 1975, Smith 1987). The hypothesis is that the Archaic foragers who lived in the Eastern Woodlands from the earliest establishment of the deciduous forest created fertile disturbed patches in and around their settlements where many of the weedy early domesticates would have thrived after colonizing such openings on their own, or being accidentally or deliberately introduced by humans. In one of the most recent formulations of this type of explanatory model, Smith (1987) refers to climatic change (the

Hypsithermal) as resulting in a greater degree of sedentism, with more regular and more prolonged use of optimal floodplain locales. This is seen as a co-evolutionary trajectory between human settlements and various plant species, especially those that were the first domesticates (pre-3000 bp *Cucurbita* gourd [which he believes to be a native species not derived from Mexican *C. pepo*], sumpweed, and *Chenopodium*). This construction is persuasive in many respects, although alternative variants are available (see Neusius 1986) emphasizing some form of social imperative (Braun 1977, Bender 1985, Brown 1985), or even the older favourite of demographic pressure, which was adopted by many anthropologists and archaeologists from Boserup (1965) during the 1960s and 1970s. This is not to say that such interpretations are mutually exclusive, far from it as all these factors (climatic fluctuations, trends in social organization and sedentism, demographic variation) are related. However, the interpretations most favoured at present seem to be those that de-emphasize stress while focusing upon long-term congruence between the behaviour of skilfully foraging human populations and the ecology of certain plant communities cohabiting with them along the streams and in the uplands of the Eastern Woodlands.

As to the consequences of early horticulture in the Eastern Woodlands, there are several relevant points to be made. First, it is very difficult to decide where to draw the line and to say that certain groups are significantly horticultural and others are not. All human communities whose economies have been investigated archaeologically appear to have been very skilful at exploiting their environments, expertly deploying a wide array of forest resources, season by season and generation by generation. Even after cultigens are undeniably in evidence, the situation is not one of presence or absence, but rather a kaleidoscopic mosaic where a small array of fully morphologically domestic plants are used in varying combinations with a much larger variety of quasi-cultigens, encouraged, and tolerated species, and a wider variety still of wild herbaceous plants, shrubs, and trees. The total combination varied seasonally, geographically, and doubtless according to local cultural preferences as well. There must also have been occasional major shifts in subsistence pattern in response to short-term climatic fluctuations (extraordinarily dry, wet, or cold years, for example, or an extraordinarily long winter with a correspondingly more severe famine period in late winter/early spring). The function of plant-food species at the time of their initial cultivation was surely most often as a buffer, an additional resource for those periods when wild foods were scarce or temporarily inaccessible.

Secondly, the span of 'early horticulture' is very long, extending minimally from 3500 bp to 2000 bp, and maximally (pending more details on Hopewellian subsistence) to 1000 bp.

Thirdly, a great many pre-Columbian groups never made the change in emphasis from harvesting of wild plants and foraging among the other resources of the forests and streams to primary dependence upon cultivated species, but relied upon some combination of the two universes or – especially in floodplains of large rivers – subsisted wholly off wild foods.

These characteristics of plant use in the Eastern Woodlands are probably widely generalizable. One thinks immediately of close parallels in several parts of Europe (Dennell in press), also in Southwest Asia (Hillman *et al.* Ch. 14, this volume, Miller in press) and in Middle and South America (Flannery 1986, McClung de Tapia in press, Pearsall in press). In this respect the counterpoise role played by the Eastern Woodlands in comparative studies in the past, as in the Braidwood and Willey (1962) symposium referred to at the start of this chapter, is no longer appropriate. The Eastern Woodlands cannot now be regarded as a region important only in a negative sense as one where nothing much happened, or where the course of cultural history was essentially idiosyncratic and thus irrelevant to comparative studies of long-term cultural-ecological processes.

## Acknowledgements

I am grateful to David Harris and Gordon Hillman for inviting me to contribute to this book. I am also indebted to Richard A. Yarnell and to Gayle Fritz for providing copies of their unpublished works and for alerting me to references I would otherwise have missed.

## References

Anderson, E. 1952. *Plants, man and life*. Berkeley: University of California Press.

Asch, D. L. & N. B. Asch 1978. The economic potential of *Iva annua* and its prehistoric importance in the lower Illinois valley. In *The nature and status of ethnobotany*, R. Ford (ed.), 301–14. University of Michigan, Museum of Anthropology Anthropological Papers 67, Ann Arbor.

Asch, D. L. & N. B. Asch 1985a. Prehistoric plant cultivation in west-central Illinois. In *Prehistoric food production in North America*, R. Ford (ed.), 149–204. University of Michigan, Museum of Anthropology Anthropological Papers 75, Ann Arbor.

Asch, D. L. & N. B. Asch 1985b. Archeobotany. In *Smiling Dan: structure and function at a Middle Woodland settlement in the lower Illinois River Valley*, B. Stafford & M. Sant (eds), 327–401. Center for American Archaeology, Research Series 2, Kampsville.

Bender, B. 1985. Emergent tribal formations in the American midcontinent. *American Antiquity* **50**, 52–62.

Bender, M., D. Baerreis & R. Steventon 1981. Further light on carbon isotopes and Hopewell agriculture. *American Antiquity* **46**, 346–53.

Blake, L. 1986. Corn and other plants from prehistory into history in the eastern United States. In *The Protohistoric Period in the Mid-South: 1500–1700*, D. Dye & R. Brister (eds) 3–13. Mississippi Department of Archives and History, Archaeological Report 18.

Boserup, E. 1965. *The conditions of agricultural growth*. Chicago: Aldine.

Braidwood, R. J. & G. R. Willey (eds) 1962. *Courses toward urban life: archeological considerations of some cultural alternates*. Viking Fund Publications in Anthropology No. 32. Chicago: Aldine.

Braun, D. P. 1977. Middle woodland – (Early) Late Woodland social change in the prehistoric central midwestern U.S. Unpublished PhD dissertation, University of Michigan, Ann Arbor. Ann Arbor: University Microfilms 77–26,210.

Braun, D. P. 1979. In Illinois Hopewell burial practices and social organization: a re-examination of the Klunk–Gibson round group *Hopewell archaeology*, D. Braun & N. Greber (eds), 66–79. Kent, Ohio: Kent State University Press.

Brewer, A. J. 1973. Analysis of floral remains from the Higgs site (40Lo45). In *Excavation of the Higgs and Doughty sites: I–75 salvage archaeology*, M. McCollough & C. Faulkner (eds), 141–4. Tennessee Archaeological Society Miscellaneous Papers 12, Knoxville.

Broida, M. 1983. Maize in Kentucky Fort Ancient diets: an analysis of carbon isotope ratios in human bone. Unpublished MA thesis, Department of Anthropology, University of Kentucky, Lexington.

Brown, J. A. 1985. Long term trends to sedentism and the emergence of complexity in the American midwest. In *Prehistoric hunter–gatherers: the emergence of cultural complexity*, T. D. Price & J. A. Brown (eds), 201–34. Orlando: Academic Press.

Bryant, V. 1974. Pollen analysis of prehistoric human feces from Mammoth Cave. In *Archaeology of the Mammoth Cave area*, P. J. Watson (ed.), 203–9. New York: Academic Press.

Caldwell, J. R. 1962. Eastern North America. In *Courses toward urban life*, R. Braidwood & G. Willey (eds), 288–308. Chicago: Aldine.

Chapman, J. & G. Crites 1987. Evidence for early maize (*Zea mays*) from the Icehouse Bottom site, Tennessee. *American Antiquity* **52**, 352–4.

Chapman, J. & A. B. Shea 1981. The archaeobotanical record: Early Archaic to Contact in the lower Little Tennessee River valley. *Tennessee Anthropologist* **6**, 64–84.

Conard, N., D. Asch, N. Asch, D. Elmore, H. Gove, M. Rubin, J. Brown, M. Wiant, K. Farnsworth & T. Cook 1984. Accelerator radiocarbon dating of evidence of prehistoric horticulture in Illinois. *Nature* **308**, 443–6.

Cowan, C. W. 1985. Understanding the evolution of plant husbandry in eastern North America: lessons from botany, ethnography, and archaeology. In *Prehistoric food production in North America*, R. Ford (ed.), 205–44. University of Michigan, Museum of Anthropology Anthropological Papers 75, Ann Arbor.

Crawford, G. 1982. Late Archaic plant remains from west-central Kentucky: a summary. *Midcontinental Journal of Archaeology* **7**, 205–24.

Crawford, G. Identification and interpretation of macrobotanical remains from Carlston Annis, the Bowles Site, and Peter Cave. In *Archaeology of the Middle Green River, Kentucky*, W. Marquardt, P. J. Watson & M. C. Kennedy (eds). Kent, Ohio: Kent State University Press. In preparation.

Crites, G. 1978. *Paleoethnobotany of the Normandy Reservoir in the upper Duck River valley, Tennessee*. Unpublished MA Thesis, Department of Anthropology, University of Tennessee, Knoxville.

Crites, G. 1987. Middle and Late Holocene ethnobotany of the Hayes site (40ML139): evidence from unit 990N918E. *Midcontinental Journal of Archaeology* **12**, 3–32.

de Wet, J. M. J. & J. R. Harlan 1975. Weeds and domesticates: evolution in the man-made habitat. *Economic Botany* **29**, 99–107.

Decker, D. S. 1986. *A biosystematic study of Cucurbita pepo*. Unpublished PhD dissertation, Department of Biology, Texas A & M University, College Station, Texas.

Decker, D. S. & H. D. Wilson 1987. Allozyme variation in the *Cucurbita pepo* complex: *C. pepo* var. *ovifera* vs. *C. texana*. *Systematic Botany* **12**, 263–73.

Delcourt, P. A. & H. R. Delcourt 1981. Vegetation maps for eastern North America. In *Geobotany II*, R. Romans (ed.), 123–65. New York: Plenum.

Delcourt, P. A. & H. R. Delcourt 1983. Late Quaternary vegetational dynamics and community stability reconsidered. *Quaternary Research* **19**, 265–71.

Delcourt, P. A., H. R. Delcourt, P. Cridlebaugh & J. Chapman 1986. Holocene ethnobotanical and paleoecological record of human impact on vegetation in the Little Tennessee River valley, Tennessee. *Quaternary Research* **25**, 330–49.

Dennell, R. in press. The origins and early development of European agriculture: a summary and discussion of the current evidence. In *Agricultural origins in world perspective*, P. J. Watson & C. W. Cowan (eds). Washington, DC: Smithsonian Institution Publications in Anthropology.

Dincauze, D. F. 1985. An archaeo-logical evaluation of the case for pre-Clovis occupations. *Advances in World Archaeology* **3**, 275–323. San Diego: Academic Press.

Doebley, J., M. Goodman & C. W. Stuber 1986. Exceptional genetic divergence of Northern Flint corn. *American Journal of Botany* **73**, 64–9.

Flannery, K. V. 1986. *Guilá Naquitz: archaic foraging and early agriculture in Oaxaca, Mexico*. Orlando: Academic Press.

Fowler, M. 1957. The origin of plant cultivation in the central Mississippi Valley: a hypothesis. Paper presented at the annual meeting of the American Anthropological Association.

Fowler, M. 1969. Middle Mississippian agricultural fields. *American Antiquity* **34**, 365–75.

Fritz, G. 1986. *Prehistoric Ozark agriculture: the University of Arkansas rockshelter collections*. Unpublished PhD dissertation, Department of Anthropology, University of North Carolina-Chapel Hill.

Gardner, P. S. 1987. New evidence concerning the chronology and paleoethnobotany of Salts Cave, Kentucky. *American Antiquity* **52**, 358–67.

Gilmore, M. 1931. Vegetal remains of the Ozark Bluff-Dweller culture. *Papers of the Michigan Academy of Sciences, Arts and Letters* **14**, 83–106.

Griffin, J. B. 1983. The Midlands. In *Ancient North Americans*, J. Jennings (ed.), 243–301. San Francisco: W. H. Freeman.

Harlan, J. R., J. M. J. de Wet & E. G. Price 1973. Comparative evolution of cereals. *Evolution* **27**, 311–25.

Hastorf, C. & V. Popper (eds) in press. *Current paleoethnobotany: analytical methods and cultural interpretations of archaeological plant remains*. Chicago: University of Chicago Press.

Heiser, C. B. 1985. Some botanical considerations of the early domesticated plants north of Mexico. In *Prehistoric food production in North America*, R. Ford (ed.), 57–72. University of Michigan, Museum of Anthropology Anthropological Papers 75, Ann Arbor.

Heiser, C. B. 1989. Domestication of Cucurbitaceae: *Cucurbita* and *Lagenaria*. In *Foraging and farming: the evolution of plant exploitation*, D. R. Harris & G. C. Hillman (eds), ch. 30. London: Unwin Hyman.

Hillman, G. C., S. M. Colledge & D. R. Harris. 1989. Plant-food economy during the Epipalaeolithic at Tell Abu Hureyra, Syria: dietary diversity, seasonality, and modes of exploitation. In *Foraging and farming: the evolution of plant exploitation*, D. R. Harris & G. C. Hillman (eds), ch. 13. London: Unwin Hyman.

Hudson, C. 1976. *The Southeastern Indians*. Knoxville: University of Tennessee Press.

Jennings, J. 1974. *Prehistory of North America*. New York: McGraw-Hill.

Johannessen, S. 1984. Paleoethnobotany. In *American Bottom Archaeology*, C. Bareis & J. Porter (eds), 197–214. Urbana and Chicago: University of Illinois Press.

Jones, V. 1936. The vegetal remains of Newt Kash Hollow Shelter. In *rock shelters in Menifee County, Kentucky*, W. Webb & W. Funkhouser (eds), 147–65. University of Kentucky, Reports in Archaeology and Anthropology 3, Lexington.

Kay, M. 1986. Phillips Spring: a synopsis of Sedalia Phase settlement and subsistence. In *Foraging, collecting, and harvesting: Archaic Period subsistence and settlement in the Eastern Woodlands*, S. Neusius (ed.), 275–88. Southern Illinois University, Center for Archaeological Investigations, Occasional Paper no. 6, Carbondale.

Kay, M., F. King & C. Robinson 1980. Cucurbits from Phillips Spring: new evidence and interpretations. *American Antiquity* **45**, 806–22.

King, F. 1985. Early cultivated cucurbits in eastern North America. In *Prehistoric food production in North America*, R. Ford (ed.) 73–97. University of Michigan, Museum of Anthropology, Anthropological Papers 75, Ann Arbor.

King, J. & W. H. Allen 1977. A Holocene vegetation record from the Mississippi River valley, southeastern Missouri. *Quaternary Research* **8**, 307–23.

Lathrap, D. W. 1987. The introduction of maize in prehistoric eastern North America: the view from Amazonia and the Santa Elena peninsula. In *Emergent horticultural economies in the Eastern Woodlands*, W. Keegan (ed.), 345–71. Southern Illinois University, Center for Archaeological Investigations, Occasional Paper no. 7, Carbondale.

Linton, R. 1924. The significance of certain traits in North American maize culture. *American Anthropologist* **26**, 345–9.

Lopinot, N., J. Harl, P. Wright & J. Nixon 1986. *Cultural resource testing and assessments: the 1985 season at Lake Shelbyville, Shelby and Moultrie Counties, Illinois*. US Army Corps of Engineers, St. Louis District, Cultural Resource Management Report 30.

Lynott, M. J., T. Boutton, J. Price & D. Nelson 1986. Stable carbon isotopic evidence for maize agriculture in southeastern Missouri and northeastern Arkansas. *American Antiquity* **51**, 15–65.

McClung de Tapia, E. M. in press. Mesoamerica and Central America. In *Agricultural origins in world perspective*, P. J. Watson & C. W. Cowan (eds). Washington, DC: Smithsonian Institution Publications in Anthropology.

McCollough, M. C. R. 1973. Supplemental chronology for the Higgs Site (40Lo45), with an assessment of Terminal Archaic living and structure floors. *Tennessee Archaeologist* **29**, 63–8.

McMillan, B. & W. Klippel 1981. Post-glacial environmental change and hunting–gathering societies of the southern Prairie Peninsula. *Journal of Archaeological Science* **8**, 215–45.

Marquardt, W. H. 1974. A statistical analysis of constituents in paleofecal specimens from Mammoth Cave. In *Archaeology of the Mammoth Cave area*, P. J. Watson (ed.), 193–202. New York: Academic Press.

Meltzer, D. & B. Smith 1986. Paleoindian and Early Archaic subsistence strategies in eastern North America. In *Foraging, collecting, and harvesting: Archaic Period subsistence and settlement in the Eastern Woodlands*, S. Neusius (ed.), 3–31. Southern Illinois University, Center for Archaeological Investigations, Occasional Paper no. 6, Carbondale.

Miller, N. in press. The origins of plant cultivation in the Near East. In *Agricultural origins in world perspective*, P. J. Watson & C. W. Cowan (eds). Washington, DC: Smithsonian Institution Publications in Anthropology.

Muller, J. 1983. The Southeast. *Ancient North Americans*, J. Jennings (ed.), 373–419. San Francisco: W. H. Freeman.

Munson, P. J., P. Parmalee & R. Yarnell 1972. Subsistence ecology of Scovill, a Terminal Middle Woodland village. *American Antiquity* **36**, 410–31.

Neusius, S. W. 1986. Generalized and specialized resource ultilization during the Archaic Period: implications of the Koster site faunal record. In *Foraging, collecting, and harvesting; Archaic Period subsistence and settlement in the Eastern Woodlands*, S. Neusius (ed.), 117–43. Southern Illinois University, Center for Archaeological Investigations, Occasional Paper no. 6, Carbondale.

Parker, A. C. 1968. Iroquois uses of maize and other plant foods. In *Parker on the Iroquois*, W. Fenton (ed.), 1–119. Syracuse: Syracuse University Press.

Pearsall, D. in press. The origins of plant cultivation in South America. In *Agricultural origins in world perspective*, P. J. Watson & C. W. Cowan (eds). Washington, DC: Smithsonian Institution Publications in Anthropology.

Pickersgill, B. 1989. Cytological and genetical evidence on the domestication and diffusion of crops within the Americas. In *Foraging and farming: the evolution of plant exploitation*, D. R. Harris & G. C. Hillman (eds), ch. 27. London: Unwin Hyman.

Quimby, G. 1946. The possibility of an independent agricultural complex in the southeastern United States. *Human origins: an introductory course in anthropology; selected readings Series* **31**, 206–10. Chicago: Department of Anthropology, University of Chicago.

Riley, T. 1986. Ridged fields and the Mississippian economic pattern. Paper presented at the Conference on Emergent Horticultural Economies of the Eastern Woodlands, Southern Illinois University, Carbondale, March 28–29, 1986.

Riley, T., C. Moffat & G. Freimuth 1980–81. Prehistoric raised fields in the upper midwestern United States: an innovation in response to marginal growing conditions. *North American Archaeologist* **2**, 101–16.

Sahlins, M. 1963. Poor man, rich man, big-man, chief: political types in Melanesia and Polynesia. *Comparative Studies in Society and History* **5**, 285–303.

Sears, W. H. 1982. *Fort Center: an archaeological site in the Lake Okeechobee basin.* Gainesville: University Presses of Florida.

Seeman, M. 1979. Feasting with the dead: Ohio Hopewell charnel house ritual as a context for redistribution. In *Hopewell archaeology*, D. Brase & N. Greber (eds), 39–46. Kent, Ohio: Kent State University Press.

Service, E. 1962. *Primitive social organization.* New York: Random House.

Smith, B. 1985a. The role of *Chenopodium* as a domesticate in pre-maize garden systems of the eastern United States. *Southeastern Archaeology* **4**, 51–72.

Smith, B. 1985b. *Chenopodium berlandieri* ssp. *jonesianum*: evidence for a Hopewellian domesticate from Ash Cave, Ohio. *Southeastern Archaeology* **4**, 107–33.

Smith, B. 1986. The archaeology of the southeastern United States: from Dalton to de Soto, 10 500 B.P.–500 B.P. In *Advances in World Archaeology*, Vol. 5, F. Wendorf & A. Close (eds), 1–92. Orlando: Academic Press.

Smith, B. 1987. The independent domestication of indigenous seed-bearing plants in eastern North America. In *Emergent horticultural economies of the Eastern Woodlands*, W. Keegan (ed.), 3–47. Occasional Paper no. 7, Center for Archaeological Investigations, Southern Illinois University, Carbondale.

Smith, B. & C. W. Cowan 1987. The age of domesticated *Chenopodium* in prehistoric North America: new accelerator dates from eastern Kentucky. *American Antiquity* **52**: 355–7.

Stewart, R. B. 1974. Identification and quantification of components in Salts Cave paleofeces, 1970–72. In *Archaeology of the Mammoth Cave Area*, P. J. Watson (ed.), 41–8. New York: Academic Press.

Stoltman, J. 1978. Temporal models in prehistory: an example from eastern North America. *Current Anthropology* **19**, 703–28.

Stoltman, J. & D. Baerreis 1983. The evolution of human ecosystems in the eastern United States. In *Late-Quarternary environments of the United States*. Vol. 2: *The Holocene*, H. E. Wright, Jr. (ed.), 252–68. Minneapolis: University of Minnesota Press.

Stothers, D. M. 1976. The Princess Point complex: a regional representative of the Early Late Woodland horizon in the Great Lakes area. In *The late prehistory of the Lake Erie drainage basin*, D. Broze (ed.), 137–61. Cleveland: Cleveland Museum of Natural History.

Struever, S. 1962. Implications of vegetal remains from an Illinois Hopewell site. *American Antiquity* **27**, 564–87.

Struever, S. 1968. Flotation techniques for the recovery of small-scale archaeological remains. *American Antiquity* **33**, 353–62.

Struever, S. & K. Vickery 1973. The beginnings of cultivation in the Midwest-riverine area of the United States. *American Anthropologist* **75**, 1197–220.

Swanton, J. R. 1948. *The Indians of the southeastern United States*. Bureau of American Ethnology Bulletin 137. (Reprinted 1979 by the Smithsonian Institution Press.)

van der Merwe, N. J. & J. C. Vogel 1978. $^{13}$C content of human collagen as a measure of prehistoric diet in Woodland North America. *Nature* **276**, 815–16.

Vogel, J. C. & N. van der Merwe 1977. Isotopic evidence for early maize cultivation in New York State. *American Antiquity* **42**, 238–42.

Wagner, G. E. 1987. *Uses of plants by the Fort Ancient Indians*. Unpublished PhD dissertation, Department of Anthropology, Washington University, St. Louis.

Wagner, G. E. in press a. The corn and cultivated beans of the Fort Ancient Indians. *The Missouri Archaeologist* **47**.

Wagner, G. E. in press b. Comparability among recovery techniques. In *Current paleoethnobotany: analytical methods and cultural interpretations of archaeological plant remains*, C. Hastorf & V. Popper (eds). Chicago: University of Chicago Press.

Watson, P. J. (ed.) 1969. *The prehistory of Salts Cave, Kentucky*. Illinois State Museum Reports of Investigations no. 16, Springfield.

Watson, P. J. 1974. *Archaeology of the Mammoth Cave area*. New York: Academic Press.

Watson, P. J. 1976. In pursuit of prehistoric subsistence: a comparative analysis of some contemporary flotation techniques. *Midcontinental Journal of Archaeology* **1**, 77–100.

Watson, P. J. 1985. The impact of early horticulture in the upland drainages of the Midwest and Midsouth. In *Prehistoric food production in North America*, R. Ford (ed.), 73–98. University of Michigan, Museum of Anthropology, Anthropological Papers 75, Ann Arbor.

Watson, P. J. 1988. Prehistoric gardening and agriculture in the Midwest and Midsouth. In *Interpretations of culture change in the Eastern Woodlands during the Late Woodland period*, R. Yerkes (ed.), 39–67. Department of Anthropology, Ohio State University, Occasional Papers in Anthropology no. 3, Columbus, Ohio.

Watts, W. A. 1983. Vegetational history of the eastern United States 25 000 to 10 000 years ago. In *Late-Quaternary environments of the United States*. Vol. 1: *The Late Pleistocene*, H. Wright & S. Porter (eds), 294–310. Minneapolis: University of Minnesota Press.

Whitaker, T. & H. Cutler 1986. Cucurbits from preceramic levels at Guilá Naquitz. In *Guilá Naquitz*, K. Flannery (ed.), 275–9. Orlando: Academic Press.

Willey, G. R. 1966. *An introduction to American archaeology*. Vol. 1: *North and Middle America*. Englewood Cliffs, NJ: Prentice-Hall.

Wilson, H. 1981. Domesticated *Chenopodium* of the Ozark Bluff Dwellers. *Economic Botany* **35**, 233–9.

Wright, H. E., Jr. 1976. The dynamic nature of Holocene vegetation: a problem in paleoclimatology, biogeography, and stratigraphic nomenclature. *Quaternary Research* **6**, 581–96.

Wright, H. E., Jr. 1981. Vegetation east of the Rocky Mountains 18 000 years ago. *Quaternary Research* **15**, 113–25.

Yarnell, R. A. 1964. *Aboriginal relationships between culture and plant life in the Upper Great Lakes region.* University of Michigan, Museum of Anthropology, Anthropological Papers no. 23, Ann Arbor.

Yarnell, R. A. 1969. Contents of human paleofeces. In *The prehistory of Salts Cave, Kentucky*, P. J. Watson (ed.), 41–54. Illinois State Museum, Reports of Investigations no. 16, Springfield.

Yarnell, R. A. 1972. *Iva annua* var. *macrocarpa*: extinct American cultigen? *American Anthropologist* **74**, 335–41.

Yarnell, R. A. 1974. Plant food and cultivation of the Salts Cavern. In *Archaeology of the Mammoth Cave Area*, P. J. Watson (ed.), 113–22. New York: Academic Press.

Yarnell, R. A. 1981. Inferred dating of the Ozark Bluff Dweller occupations based on the achene size of sunflower and sumpweed. *Journal of Ethnobiology* **1**, 55–60.

Yarnell, R. A. 1983. Prehistory of plant foods and husbandry in North America. Paper presented at the 48th Annual Meeting of the Society for American Archaeology, Pittsburgh.

Yarnell, R. A. in press a. A survey of prehistoric crop plants in eastern North America. *The Missouri Archaeologist* **47**.

Yarnell, R. A. in press b. Sunflower, sumpweed, small grains and crops of lesser status. In *Handbook of North American Indians*, Vol. 3, *Environment, origins, and population*, R. L. Ford (ed.).

# 36 *Agricultural intensification and ridged-field cultivation in the prehistoric upper Midwest of North America*

JAMES P. GALLAGHER

## Introduction

In late prehistoric times (*c.* ad 1300–1600), various native populations in the upper Midwestern area of the United States developed techniques of agricultural intensification. This intensification and its effects were of lesser magnitude than major food-production patterns in Mesoamerica, or even in other parts of continental North America; nevertheless, the transformation had a significant impact on regional cultural patterns.

Following the lead of Barker and Gamble (1985), this chapter examines systems of production and strategies of intensification, focusing not on the origins or impacts of these developments, but rather on understanding of the process by which agriculture was practised in the upper Midwest, in a climate only marginally suited for growing food crops of tropical origin. In addition, the chapter includes some comparative discussion of similar processes of intensification in the British Isles. The use of the term intensification refers to increases in both productivity and production, as used by Lourandos (1985, p. 389) and others.

The upper Midwest is part of the 'humid cool temperate' zone (Thorne & Thorne 1979, p. 24). It includes the upper Mississippi River and Great Lakes drainage systems and encompasses the present states of Wisconsin, eastern Minnesota, eastern Iowa, northern Illinois, and western Michigan. The area includes the Central Lowland and Laurentian Upland physiographic provinces of North America and has relatively long cold winters and humid, warm to hot summers (Martin 1965, p. 23).

It is clear that no single factor was responsible for a shift to intensive agriculture in the late prehistoric Midwest. In fact, many of the basic ingredients were present in earlier periods. However, new developments following *c.* ad 900–1300, added to antecedent patterns, resulted in considerable cultural change. These earlier patterns were characterized by maximum resource exploitation without agriculture, including the exploitation of selected high-yield riverine resources such as shellfish, migratory waterfowl, fish, deer, nuts, and seeds (see also Bender 1985, Brown 1985). Horticulture is thought to have had only limited economic importance. Cultivation involved the growing of *Iva* (sumpweed or marsh elder), *Polygonum* sp. (smartweed), *Chenopodium* sp. (goosefoot or lamb-quarters), *Cucurbita pepo* (squash), and other plants (for further discussion see Asch & Asch 1985, Ford 1985, Smith 1987, Watson Ch. 35, this volume).

Starting perhaps as early as ad 900 and well developed by ad 1300, a shift away from intensive foraging and horticulture occurred in the upper Midwest. This shift toward intensive farming (with foraging) was accompanied by more densely settled populations and increased cultural complexity, as described by Fowler (1969), Gibbon (1972), Ford (1977), Hall (1980), Dobbs (1982), and others (for an opposing view see Overstreet 1985). Significant factors that were involved in this process in the upper Midwest included the development of superior strains of crops, the careful selection of soils suitable for agriculture, and, most importantly, the construction of ridged fields, which enabled Native Americans to practise efficient tillage techniques and to control microclimatic variables related to air and soil temperature and soil moisture.

## The development of superior plant varieties

Harlan (1972) pointed out the role of the introduction of new plant varieties to agricultural systems in expanding the range of agricultural settlement. The late prehistoric cultural patterns in the upper Midwest were directly related, in part, to the development of new plant varieties, specifically, hardier strains of maize and the introduction of beans.

Although maize was introduced to the upper Midwest by at least ad 600 (Asch & Asch 1985, pp. 196–9) the early varieties, referred to by Cutler & Blake (1976) as 'North American Pop', were poorly adapted to the upper Midwest. This maize produced limited yields primarily because it was ill-adapted to the shorter frost-free growing season and the shorter night photoperiod of northern latitudes (Hall 1980, p. 414).

After ad 1100, a superior strain, Northern Flint Corn, was developed (Wagner 1986, pp. 11–12). This variety, also referred to as *Harinoso de Ocho* by Galinat (1985) and Eastern Eight-Row by Cutler & Blake (1973), had a number of qualities that resulted in its rapid adoption by prehistoric farmers in the upper Midwest. The qualities of this eight-row variety, summarized by Hall (1980, pp. 421–42; see also Galinat (1985) include:

(a)  a photoperiodic response that favoured the short summer months of northern latitudes;
(b)  greater resistance to insect damage both on the ear and in storage;
(c)  extremely high yield;

(d)    loose husks that allowed drying of mature ears during the cool rainy fall;
(e)    a growth pattern that slowed the production of foliage prior to flowering, causing earlier maturation and reduced risk of exposure to fall frosts.

Scullin (1985) discusses the importance of tillering (the production of auxiliary stalks or 'suckers') which was developed as an adaptation to cooler climate. Tillering produces higher yields because the tillers produce full-sized ears and promote early flowering. Tillering also protects the plants from cold temperatures by concentrating the leaves at the base of the plant, thus reducing heat loss from radiation cooling (see also Galinat 1967, p. 6).

Perhaps the most beneficial aspect of this new variety of maize was its ability to withstand a wide range of cooler climatic conditions. The endurance and hardiness of Northern Flint is summarized by Will & Hyde (1964, p. 73):

It is extremely hardy, not only adapting itself to varying amounts of moisture and producing some crop under drought conditions, but resistant also to the unseasonable frosts which are apt to occur in the home region. It will sprout in spring weather that would rot most varieties of (maize), and once sprouted it grows very rapidly. Its period from planting to maturity is about 60 days in a favorable year and rarely is more than 70 days required (see also Will 1924, p. 204).

The hardiness of Northern Flint is demonstrated by its spread in historic times into extremely cold environments, as far as 50° N, near Lake Winnepeg, Manitoba (Moodie & Kaye 1969).

According to Hall (1980, p. 452), the appearance of this new eight-row maize and the appearance of beans after ad 1000 directly contributed to the expansion and rapid growth of more complex upper Midwestern prehistoric cultures. Maize and beans are complementary crops in that while maize removes nitrogen from the soil, beans replace it, thus delaying soil exhaustion (Grigg 1982, p. 76, Hudson 1976, pp. 293–4). More importantly, beans contain the amino acids lysine and tryptophan, which are absent in maize. The combined vegetable proteins of maize and beans are adequate for all the normal protein needs of a community, with the possible exception of nursing mothers (Kaplan 1965), and they formed an important link in the development of an intensive agricultural system.

Squash, one of the earliest North American domesticates (see Asch & Asch 1985, Ford 1985, Smith 1987, Heiser Ch. 30, Watson Ch. 35, this volume) has similar soil-moisture and temperature requirements as those of beans and maize, and the three crops are unusually well suited to being grown together. Beans can be grown up the maize stalks, while squash, planted between the maize plants, needs little hoeing, and its broad leaves provide shade that reduces evaporation from the soil and inhibits weed growth.

## Site location

Upper Midwest populations also increased agricultural production through careful selection of planting sites, taking into account growing season, temperature, and soil characteristics. Yarnell (1964, p. 131) points out that the most important factor for aboriginal agriculture in northern latitudes was the length of the growing season. Yarnell's study of the distribution of agricultural sites shows that virtually all of them were within the modern zone of greater than 130 consecutive frost-free days (120 days is considered the minimum number of frost-free days for reliable maize production). Sites were also located south of the isotherm of 19° C (66° F) average July temperature.

As an indication of how careful the site-selection process was, Yarnell (1964) notes that agricultural sites in northern North America were consistently situated in locations where the growing season was longer than the average for that latitude. Frequently, they were located in pockets or extensions of areas with relatively long growing seasons. In the La Crosse, Wisconsin, locality studied by the present author there are numerous agricultural sites concentrated in a zone of 160 frost-free days, a growing season 20–40 days longer than that in nearby counties at the same latitude.

In addition to the length of growing season and temperature, sites were also carefully chosen for optimal soil quality and adequate moisture. In the upper Midwest, with its wide range of productive soils, preferred locations included bottomlands, sandy or silty ridges in bottomlands, wooded slopes, and loessial uplands (Hall 1980). Hall notes that in Illinois there was a clear preference for bottomland soils because they have a high organic content, are easy to work, and have a high water table. Woods (1987) also notes the close association of agricultural sites and floodplains throughout the eastern United States. Studies in the Mississippi Valley (Gallagher & Stevenson 1982) also show a strong preference for rich bottomland soils in the area around La Crosse, Wisconsin.

## Ridged fields

In the upper Midwest, Native Americans constructed ridged agricultural fields in late prehistoric times. This technique is found in many different parts of the world but is particularly useful in temperate climates. Ridged fields are widespread throughout the American upper Midwest (Fox 1959, Moffat 1979) and they also occur in Great Britain and Ireland where they are called 'ridge and furrow', 'rig (or rigg) and furrow' and 'lazy beds' (Bowen 1961, pp. 3–4, 47, Fowler 1983, pp. 154–6). The Irish and British fields range in age from the Neolithic to the 19th century ad. They are dug by spade or produced by plough and may range in size from 1 to 9 m in width and up to 1 m or more in height. Today they appear with greatest frequency in agriculturally marginal upland ares of relatively high rainfall and low temperatures (for examples see Baker & Butlin 1973, pp. 565–6, 576, Jones 1975, p. 100, Parry 1976, 1978, pp. 113–16, Halliday et al. 1981, pp. 55–6).

The ridges of the upper Midwest are relatively low (10–40 cm), generally less than 2 m wide, and were constructed with hoes made of large mammal scapulas (Gallagher et al. 1985). Recent studies in the La Crosse, Wisconsin, area have suggested that these ridges had two major functions: for tillage, and as devices to extend the growing season (Sasso et al. 1985, Gallagher & Sasso 1987, Gallagher et al. 1987).

A primary requirement for the production of any domesticated plant is to provide what has traditionally been called tilth: the physical qualities of the soil that will be favourable for plant growth. The production of tilth usually involves some form of tillage. In general, the function of ridging can best be seen in terms of the purposes of tillage, which include:

(a)  Aeration. Working the soil maintains pore spaces which are filled with air and water for use by the plant. Good tilth requires extensive aeration for high water-holding capacity and plant respiration. Poor aeration affects the growth of plants by lowering nutrient and water absorption, accelerating the formation of toxic inorganic compounds (allelopaths), and curtailing root gas exchange (Wang 1963, p. 173, Janick et al. 1969, p. 205).

(b)  Change in soil structure. Tilling reduces soil compaction and crusting, making it easier to plant seeds, providing a good bed for the germination of seeds and for optimal root development, and improving the intake, storage, and transmission of moisture. Ridging further reduces compaction by restricting walking to paths between the ridges. Wang (1963, p. 177) reports studies that show that the danger of frost to young seedlings is increased by soil compaction.

Well-loosened soil permits closer plantings and, thus, higher yield, and reduces loss of plant moisture by transpiration. In addition, plants are less susceptible to wind damage. Dense crops, in turn, provide less space and light for weed growth.

Tillage breaks capillary connections with the subsoil. thus, while tilled layers dry out quickly by evaporation, they also serve as a natural mulch conserving subsoil moisture (Wilkin 1972, p. 553, Chang 1968, p. 95). Improved soil structure nearly doubles the yield of maize in experimental plots (Wang 1963, p. 173).

(c)  Weed control. Weed control in maize fields is essential if maximum yields are to be obtained, especially because maize is a poor competitor with weeds (Pearson 1967, pp. 317–18). Weeds rob the plants of nutrients, water, and sunlight. When worked into the soil they provide a good source of nutrients through decomposition. As a form of tillage, ridging also aids in weed control by providing pathways between the crops and easy access to the plants. Weeding is done primarily by hoeing or hand (Wedel 1961, p. 566). Loosened weeds and earth are added to the ridges and provide nutrients and physical support to the plants. Scullin (1986, pp. 16–17), using his own experimental data and ethnohistorical records, argues that the main function of maize hills and ridges is to provide physical support for unsteady plants.

(d)    The incorporation of crop residues into the soil. 'Crop residues are the most important source of organic materials for soils . . . ' (Thorne & Thorne 1979, p. 86). In addition, if ridging techniques are used, this residue and any fertilizer that may be added to the soil are concentrated near the plants, rather than spread out all over the field (Seamus Caulfield, pers. comm.).

(e)    Other benefits. Tillage also helps to destroy soil–dwelling insects and to aid in erosion control (Pearson 1967, pp. 142, Starna et al. 1984).

The technique of ridging had special adaptive advantages in temperate climates, in addition to those related to tillage. Specifically, the technique of ridging extends and alters the growing season by helping to control three critical variables: frost, soil moisture, and soil temperatures.

Radiation frosts tend to be caused by temperature inversions – when cool dense air sinks or subsides into areas of low topographic relief (Geiger 1965, pp. 396–403, 412). When such inversions occur, the length of the growing season is shortened (Peterson & Clay 1985, pp. 3–4).

Radiation frost is generally formed during a clear, calm, and fairly dry night. Usually, lowland soils with poor thermal conductivity (wet soil) and little or no vegetative coverage, are most susceptable . . . The process of frost prevention consists essentially of raising the temperature a few degrees higher than the critical temperature during the critical period, which may range from a few hours to several hours (Wang 1963, p. 547).

Riley & Freimuth (1979) provide impressive and convincing experimental, distributional, and ethnographic data to suggest that ridged fields do serve to reduce the risk of frost. Ridge and furrow systems 'retard the development of frosts simply by creating drainage conditions in which the dense cold air . . . is drained by gravity to the lower furrows. Frost, then, settles to the bottom of the plots and does little or no damage to the crops at the top of the ridge' (1979, p. 275). Their experiments showed that ridge-top temperatures were frequently above freezing while furrow temperatures were below freezing, thus potentially sparing crops from a killing frost. Because maize was probably the single most important aboriginal crop in the upper Midwest, and because it is very susceptible to frost (Pearson 1967, p. 317), the frost-control function of ridging may have been critical to the intensification of agriculture in that region.

In addition to frost control, the location and physical setting of the ridged–field sites in the upper Midwest area suggest other specific functions related to extending the growing season: soil moisture and soil temperature control. A primary function of the ridged fields may have been to raise the crops' root systems above water during periods of temporary flooding and to provide drainage of the root system when soil moisture was high, a chronic problem for floodplain agriculture.

Studies by Wang (1963, p. 164) indicate that under the prolonged retention of excessive moisture, soil aeration is severely reduced which, in turn, restricts root growth, microbial activity, nutrient availability, and nutrient absorption. Maize, in particular, is severely affected by wet conditions. Experiments reported by Brower (1977, p. 242) document that poor aeration due to excess water can cause the death of maize within four days.

One of the most important variables for agriculture in temperate climates is soil temperature, which is directly related to soil moisture:

> Wet soils are slow to warm in spring . . . Five times the amount of heat energy is required to raise the temperature of water one degree than is required to raise the temperature of an equivalent weight of dry mineral soil by the same amount. In one study it was found that the heat required to evaporate water from a saturated soil would raise the temperature of soil with optimal moisture control more than 5° C. (Janick et al. 1969, pp. 204–5)

Solar heat is also lost as water holding the heat seeps to layers below the growth zone (Thorne & Thorne 1979, pp. 74–5).

The effects of low soil temperatures include:

(a) Delayed planting. Early planting of maize generally results in slightly higher yields, shorter plants that do not uproot as easily, and rapid growth which shades weeds better (Janick et al. 1969, p. 362, Shaw 1983, p. 52). Delayed planting also increases the risk of frost damage in the fall (Dale 1983, p. 25).

(b) Slow germination. 'Germination of seeds or growth of plant roots may be affected more by soil temperature than any other physical factor except moisture' (Thorne & Thorne 1979, p. 75). Low temperatures delay the start of germination or slow the germination process; at worst, they may cause the seed to decay or rot. Slow germination results in low plant vigour which in turn leads to susceptibility to disease and insects.

(c) Decreased growth. The growth of maize plants during their early stages increases lineally with increasing soil temperature from 16° to 24° C (Willis 1956). Larson et al. (1960) reported that only a 2° F lowering of soil temperature decreased early growth of maize by about 50 per cent in northern latitudes.

(d) Reduced yields. According to Chang (1968, pp. 96–7), maize yields increase in direct proportion to increases in soil temperatures up to 81.3° F (see also Willis 1956, Shaw 1983, p. 54).

The construction of ridges not only mounds up the soil above the saturation level, keeping it dry, it also increases the active ground surface by 20–25 per cent, and creates an artificial slope that boosts the absorption of radiation from the sun. According to experiments conducted by Seeman *et al.* (1979, p. 138), the soil temperature of agricultural ridges on test plots was an average of 2°–3° C higher than soil temperatures on level plots. Burrows (1963) reported similar test results and noted that the greatest increases in temperature occur in the spring, when optimal soil temperatures are most crucial (see also Chang 1968, pp. 94–5, Duckham & Masefield 1970, p. 32, Wilken 1972, pp. 549–50, Seeman *et al.* 1979, p. 136). In addition, warm, well-drained soil cools less rapidly at night and is, in turn, more resistant to frost (Barlett 1909, pp. 48–9).

The British and Irish ridged fields seen to have greater variation in form and function than their North American counterparts. The larger ridges, measuring 1–9 m wide, are apparently medieval and later. The functions of these fields seem to be primarily water drainage. Many fields, including examples seen by this author in Co. Mayo on and adjacent to Achill Island, have ridges running straight down the slopes, apparently for drainage. These ridges were probably constructed for growing potatoes in the 18th and 19th centuries ad, and a few fields are still in cultivation today. A second function of the construction of the larger ridges seems to be to break waste land for cultivation (O'Danachair 1970, pp. 51–5, Parry 1976, Hall 1982, p. 6, Bell 1984). Ridged-field construction was particularly suitable for the small-scale, labour-intensive methods available to poor 18th-century farmers, who used them to reclaim land. Productivity of these fields, reported to be very high, was due to the increased drainage provided by the furrows and the superior seed bed found in the ridges, made up of loosened soil, manure, decayed plant material, and sometimes lime (Bell 1974, p. 90).

These larger, fairly recent ridge systems seem to differ significantly from some prehistoric ridged fields, such as those in Ireland (Herity 1971, 1981, Caulfield 1978, 1983). These ridges are much smaller than the wide ridges of the Middle Ages and the 18th and 19th centuries; indeed they are the same size or smaller than the ridges from the upper Midwest of North America. The prehistoric varieties, examples of which in Co. Mayo were kindly shown to me by Seamus Caulfield, were for the production of wheat and barley and seem to have been constructed for a broader range of functions, like their Midwestern American counterparts. For example, the prehistoric Irish ridges in Co. Mayo are not oriented in regard to the natural contours of the land. Instead, they form blocks of ridges that run perpendicular to each other.

The construction of earthen ridges gave prehistoric native agriculturalists in both western Europe and North America all of the necessary benefits of tillage, and enabled them to expand the growing season by controlling factors of air and soil temperature and soil moisture. In North America, the process of ridging allowed the late prehistoric inhabitants of the upper Midwest to take advantage of highly productive, organic-rich floodplain soils that would ordinarily have been more susceptible to low temperature and high moisture during critical stages in the germination and growth of the crops.

## Field burning

Archaeological evidence from one ridged-field site (Gallagher & Sasso 1987) as well as ethnographic data (Wedel 1961, p. 564) indicates that field clearance may have involved burning. The process of burning would have complemented and enhanced many of the functions described for ridged fields. Burning kills surface insects and removes dead crop residue, weeds, and litter from the previous season. The removal of this litter plays an important role in warming the soil by removing the layer of materials which block both solar radiation and the evaporation of moisture (and hence retard soil warming).

Burning also blackens the surface of the fields, increasing the ability of the fields to absorb solar radiation. Darkening a soil during clear weather decreases the albedo by as much as 5 per cent and increases the absorption of radiation by as much as 15 per cent (Seeman et al. 1979, p. 137). Surface temperatures in areas that have been burned may be several degrees higher than in unburned areas (Janick et al. 1969, p. 170; see also Wilken 1972, p. 549).

Working ash into the soil in the process of ridging will, of course, add nutrients such as phosphorus and potash. Burrows (1963, p. 350) reports that fertilizer, especially phosphorous, can also overcome to some extent the deleterious effects of low soil temperature.

## Summary

In the upper Midwest of North America techniques indicative of agricultural intensification appear in late prehistoric times. These techniques enabled native farmers to obtain potentially high yields by the development of superior varieties of domesticates, the careful selection of agricultural sites, and the development of ridged-field technology. Ridging provided the basic functions of tillage, and it maintained critical levels of moisture and temperature necessary for the growth of light- and heat-sensitive cultigens. Further research is now needed to quantify increases in productivity and production resulting from the developments described here, and to explore their ramifications.

## Acknowledgements

The author is indebted to the following individuals whose assistance made this study possible: Robert Sasso, James Knox, Robert Boszhardt, Katherine Stevenson, Amy

Berezinski, James Theler, Cindi Stiles-Hanson, Dale Agger, Seamus Caulfield, Peter Reynolds, and William Green. Support for investigations into ridged fields was provided by the National Science Foundation grant #BNS-8406863, support from the Gelatt Foundation, and a sabbatical leave granted by the University of Wisconsin-La Crosse.

# References

Asch, D. L. & N. B. Asch 1985. Prehistoric plant cultivation in west-central Illinois. In *Prehistoric food production in North America*, R. I. Ford (ed.), 149–203. Anthropological Papers no. 75, Museum of Anthropology, University of Michigan, Ann Arbor.

Baker, A. R. H. & R. A. Butlin (eds) 1973. *Studies of field systems in the British Isles.* Cambridge: Cambridge University Press.

Barker, G. & C. Gamble 1985. Beyond domestication: a strategy for investigating the process and consequences of social complexity. In *Beyond domestication in prehistoric Europe*, G. Barker & C. Gamble (eds), 1–32. New York: Academic Press.

Bartlett, J. L. 1909. Frosts in Wisconsin: occurrence, prediction, methods of prevention. *Bulletin of the University of Wisconsin Extension* **1**, 40–81.

Bell, J. 1984. A contribution to the study of cultivation ridges in Ireland. *Journal of the Royal Society of Antiquaries of Ireland* **114**, 80–97.

Bender, B. 1985. Prehistoric developments in the American midcontinent and in Brittany, northwest France. In *Prehistoric hunter–gatherers, the emergence of cultural complexity*, T. D. Price & J. A. Brown (eds), 21–58. New York: Academic Press.

Bowen, H. C. 1961. *Ancient fields: a tentative analysis of vanishing earthworks and landscapes*, British Association for the Advancement of Science, London.

Brower, R. 1977. Root functioning. In *Environmental effects of crop physiology*, J. J. Landsberg & C. V. Cutting (eds), 229–46. New York: Academic Press.

Brown, J. A. 1985. Long-term trends to sedentism and the emergence of complexity in the American Midwest. In *Prehistoric hunter–gatherers, the emergence of cultural complexity*, T. D. Price & J. A. Brown (eds), 201–31. New York: Academic Press.

Burrows, W. C. 1963. Characterization of soil temperature distribution from various tillage-induced microreliefs. *Soil Science Society Proceedings* **27**, 350–3.

Caulfield, S. 1978. Neolithic fields: the Irish evidence. In *Early land allotment in the British Isles*, H. C. Bowen & P. J. Fowler (eds), 137–43. British Archaeological Reports no. 48.

Caulfield, S. 1983. The Neolithic settlement of North Connaught. In *Landscape archaeology in Ireland*, T. Reeves-Smith & F. Homand (eds), 195–215. British Archaeological Reports no. 116.

Chang, Jen-Hu 1968. *Climate and agriculture, an ecological study.* Chicago: Aldine.

Cutler, H. C. & L. W. Blake 1973. *Plants from archaeological sites east of the Rockies.* Missouri Botanical Gardens, St. Louis.

Cutler, H. C. & L. W. Blake 1976. Plants from archaeological sites east of the Rockies. *American Archaeology Reports* no. 1, Microfiche, American Archaeology Division, University of Missouri-Columbia.

Dale, R. F. 1983. Temperature perturbations in the midwestern and southeastern United States important for corn production. In *Crop reactions to water and temperature stresses in humid temperate climates*, D. Raper, Jr. & P. Kramer (eds), 21–31. Boulder, Colorado: Westview Press.

Dobbs, C. A. 1982. Oneota origins and development: the radiocarbon evidence. In *Oneota studies*, G. Gibbon (ed.), 91–106. University of Minnesota, Publications in Anthropology no. 1.

Duckham, A. N. & G. B. Masefield 1970. *Farming systems of the world*. London: Chatto and Windus.

Ford, R. I. 1977. Evolutionary ecology and the evolution of human ecosystems: a case study from the midwestern U.S.A. In *Explanation of prehistoric change*, J. N. Hill (ed.), 153–84. Albuquerque: University of New Mexico Press.

Ford, R. I. 1985. Patterns of prehistoric food production in North America. In *Prehistoric food production in North America*, R. I. Ford (ed.), 341–64. Anthropological Papers no. 75, Museum of Anthropology, University of Michigan, Ann Arbor.

Fowler, M. L. 1969. Middle Mississippian agricultural fields. *American Antiquity* **34**, 365–75.

Fowler, P. J. 1983. *The farming of prehistoric Britain*. Cambridge: Cambridge University Press.

Fox, G. R. 1959. The prehistoric garden beds of Wisconsin and Michigan and the Fox Indians. *The Wisconsin Archeologist* **40**, 1–19.

Galinat, W. C. 1967. *Plant habitat and the adaptation of corn*. Massachusetts Agricultural Experiment Station Bulletin no. 565.

Galinat, W. C. 1985. Domestication and diffusion of maize. In *Prehistoric food production in North America*, R. I. Ford (ed.), 245–307. Anthropological Papers no. 75, Museum of Anthropology, University of Michigan, Ann Arbor.

Gallagher, J. P. & R. Sasso 1987. Investigations into Oneota ridged field agriculture on the northern margin of the Prairie Penninsula. *Plains Anthropologist* **32**, 141–51.

Gallagher, J. P. & K. Stevenson 1982. Oneota subsistence and settlement in southwestern Wisconsin. In *Oneota studies*, G. Gibbon (ed.), 15–28. University of Minnesota, Publications in Anthropology no. 1.

Gallagher, J. P., F. R. Boszhardt, R. F. Sasso & K. Stevenson 1985. Oneota ridged field agriculture in southwestern Wisconsin, *American Antiquity* **50** 605–12.

Gallagher, J. P., R. F. Boszhardt, R. F. Sasso & K. Stevenson 1987. Floodplain agriculture in the driftless area: a reply to Overstreet. *American Antiquity* **52**, 398–404.

Geiger, R. 1965. *The climate near the ground*. Cambridge, Mass.: Harvard University Press.

Gibbon, G. 1972. Cultural dynamics and the development of the Oneota life-way in Wisconsin. *American Antiquity* **37**, 166–85.

Grigg, D. 1982. *The dynamics of agricultural change*. New York: St. Martins Press.

Hall, D. 1982. *Medieval fields*. Aylesbury, Buckinghamshire: Shire Publications.

Hall, R. L. 1980. An interpretation of the two-climax model of Illinois prehistory. In *Early native Americans: prehistoric demography, economy, and technology*, D. Browman (ed.), 401–65. The Hague: Mouton.

Halliday, S. P., P. J. Hill and J. B. Stevenson 1981. Early agriculture in Scotland. In *Farming practice in British prehistory*, R. Mercer (ed.), 55–65. Edinburgh: Edinburgh University Press.

Harlan, J. R. 1972. Crops that extend the range of agricultural settlement. In *Man, settlement and urbanism*, P. J. Ucko, R. Tringham & G. W. Dimbleby (eds), 239–43. London: Duckworth.

Herity, M. 1971. Prehistoric fields in Ireland. *Irish University Review*, Spring, 258–65.

Herity, M. 1981. A Bronze Age farmstead at Glenree, County Mayo. *Popular Archaeology* **2**, 36–7.

Hudson, C. 1976. *The southeastern Indians*. Knoxville: University of Tennessee Press.

Janick, J., R. Scherz, F. Woods & V. Ruttan 1969. *Plant science*. San Francisco: W. H. Freeman.

Jones, B. 1975. The north-western interface. In *Recent work in rural archaeology*, P. J. Fowler (ed.), 93–106. Totowa, N.J.: Rowman and Littlefield.

Kaplan, L. 1965. Archaeology and domestication in American *Phaseolus* (Beans). *Economic Botany* **19**, 358–68.

Larson, W. E., W. C. Burrows & W. O. Willis 1960. Soil temperature, soil moisture and corn growth as influenced by mulches of crop residues. *Transactions of the International Congress of Soil Sciences Seventh Congress* **1**, 629–37.

Lourandos, H. 1985. Intensification and Australian prehistory. In *Prehistoric hunter–gatherers, the emergence of cultural complexity*, T. D. Price & J. A. Brown (eds), 385–423. New York: Academic Press.

Martin, L. 1965. *The physical geography of Wisconsin*, 3rd edn. Madison: University of Wisconsin Press.

Moffat, C. H. 1979. Some observations of the distribution and significance of the garden beds of Wisconsin. *The Wisconsin Archeologist* **60**, 222–50.

Moodie, D. W. & B. Kaye 1969. The northern limit of Indian agriculture in North America. *Geographical Review* **59**, 513–29.

O'Danachair, C. 1970. The use of the spade in Ireland. In *The spade in northern and Atlantic Europe*, A. Gailey & A. Fenton (eds), 49–56. Illustrated Folk Museum, Institute of Irish Studies, Queens University, Belfast.

Overstreet, D. F. 1985. Corn and community congregation – the view from Lake Winnebago. Paper presented at the 84th Annual Meeting of the American Anthropological Association, December 1985, Washington, DC.

Parry, M. L. 1976. A typology of cultivation ridges in southern Scotland. *Tools and Tillage,* **3**, 3–19.

Parry, M. L. 1978. *Climatic change, agriculture and settlement*. Folkestone, and Hamden, Conn.: Dawson & Anchor Books.

Pearson, L. C. 1967. *Principles of agronomy*. New York: Reinhold.

Peterson, K. L. & V. L. Clay 1985. *Characteristics and archaeological implication of cold air drainage in the Dolores Project area, south-western Colorado*. Dolores Archaeological Program Technical Reports, no. DAP-206, National Technical Information Service, Springfield, Virginia.

Riley, T. J. & G. Freimuth 1979. Field systems and frost drainage in the prehistoric agriculture of the upper Great Lakes. *American Antiquity* **44**, 271–84.

Sasso, T. J., R. F. Boszhardt, J. C. Knox, J. L. Theler, K. Stevenson, J. P. Gallagher & C. Stiles-Hanson 1985. *Prehistoric ridged field agriculture in the Upper Mississippi Valley*. Reports of Investigations no. 8. Mississippi Valley Archaeology Center at the University of Wisconsin-La Crosse, La Crosse, Wisconsin.

Scullin, M. 1985. *The adaptive features of tillering in Northern Flint corn*. Unpublished manuscript on file, Department of Anthropology, Mankato State University, Mankato, Minnesota.

Scullin, M. 1986. *Corn cobs and tree-rings II: climate, crops, and culture in the Middle Missouri region*. Unpublished manuscript on file, Department of Anthropology, Mankato State University, Mankato, Minnesota.

Seeman, J., Y. I. Chirko, J. Lomas & B. Primault 1979. *Agrometeorology*. Berlin: Springer-Verlag.

Shaw, R. H. 1983. Estimate of yield reductions in corn caused by water and temperature stress. In *Crop reactions by water and temperature stresses in humid temperate climates*, D. Raper & P. Kramer (eds), 49–66. Boulder, Colorado: Westview Press.

Smith, B. D. 1987. The independent domestication of indigenous seed-bearing plants in eastern North America. In *Emergent horticultural economies of the Eastern Woodlands*, W. F. Keegan (ed.), 3–48. Occasional Paper no. 7, Center for Archaeological Investigations, Southern Illinois University, Carbondale.

Starna, W. A., G. R. Hamell & W. C. Butts 1984. Northern Iroquoian horticulture and insect infestation: a cause for village removal. *Ethnohistory* **31**, 197–207.

Thorne, D. W. & M. D. Thorne 1979. *Soil, water and crop production*. Westport, Connecticut: AVI Publishing Co.

Wagner, G. E. in press. The corn and cultivated beans of the Fort Ancient Indians. *The Missouri Archaeologist* **47**.

Wang, Jen-Yu 1963. *Agricultural meteorology*. Milwaukee: Pacemaker Prss.

Watson, P. J. 1989. Early plant cultivation in the Eastern Woodlands of North America. In *Foraging and farming: the evolution of plant exploitation*, D. R. Harris & G. C. Hillman (eds), ch. 35. London: Unwin Hyman.

Wedel, M. M. 1961. Indian villages of the Upper Iowa River. *Palimpsest* **42**, 561–92. Iowa City.

Wilken, G. C. 1972. Microclimatic management by traditional farmers, *Geographical Review* **62**, 544–60.

Will, G. F. 1924. Indian agriculture at the northern limits in the Great Plains region of North America. *Annals of the International Congress of Americanists 1922* **1**, 203–5.

Will, G. F. & G. Hyde 1964. *Corn among the Indians of the Upper Missouri*, Lincoln: University of Nebraska.

Willis, W. O. 1956. *Soil temperature, mulches and corn growth*. Unpublished PhD dissertation, Iowa State University, Ames.

Woods, W. I. 1987. Maize agriculture and the late prehistoric: a characterization of settlement location strategies. In *Emergent horticultural economies of the Eastern Woodlands*, W. F. Keegan (ed.), 275–94. Occasional Paper no. 7, Center for Archaeological Investigations, Southern Illinois University, Carbondale.

Yarnell, R. A. 1964. *Aboriginal relationships between culture and plant life in the upper Great Lakes region*, University of Michigan, Museum of Anthropology, Anthropological Paper no. 23, Ann Arbor.

# 37 The spread of agriculture in western Europe: Indo-European and (non-) pre-Indo-European linguistic evidence

T. L. MARKEY

## Introduction

The thesis of an aggressive east-to-west incursion of Indo-Europeans, supposedly in chronologically distinct strata, into Atlantic Europe is a framework that has long been generally accepted by historical linguists; see, for example, the recent summaries by Schlerath (1973), Tovar (1982), and Adrados (1982), and for the three supposedly distinct waves of Kurgan (= Indo-European) penetrations see Gimbutas (1982, particularly pp. 18–19).

Initially, linguistic comparatists received archaeological support for this conventional interpretation from the works of V. Gordon Childe (during the 1920s and 1930s) and then from the early works of Gimbutas (e.g. 1956, but particularly 1965). However, such studies could not take full advantage of radiocarbon dating, nor of the many improved techniques of excavation that are now employed. Simplistically, on the part of some, an artefactually identifiable western Bell Beaker complex was thought to have been displaced by an eastern Corded Ware/Battle Axe group. In a prefatory summary of what is to follow, Gimbutas (1965, pp. 21–3) tells us that a new Kurgan people may have arrived 'no later than 2300–2200 BC in the eastern Balkans, the Aegean area, western Anatolia, central Europe, all of the western and eastern Baltic area, and central Russia.' These Kurgan peoples are supposed to have domesticated the horse, perfected vehicles, had a knowledge of metallurgy, and evolved certain socio-economic structures (presumably à la Georges Dumézil). Their central European successors are said to have expanded south to Italy, Greece, and Anatolia in the 13th century BC and to have brought about the destruction of the Mycenaean civilization and the Hittite Empire (Gimbutas 1965, p. 23).

In politically slanted accounts from the 1930s and 1940s, as well as in a recently highly biased sketch (Haudry 1981), the Indo-Europeans are portrayed as having been ethnically and culturally superior to any indigenous groups. These exaggerated portraits are portrayals of colonization on a par with the Victorian conquest of Africa, or the white man's arrival in the Western Hemisphere. Waves of nomadic pastoralists from the East are thought to have effected a wholesale displacement of indigenous agrarian groups – by virtue of technical superiority, chariot warfare, and better hierarchical organization, etc. The supposed superiority of the putatively culturally homogenous Indo-Europeans (presumed to share poetic formulae, literary topoi, culinary habitats, etc.) is also seen in their virtually complete displacements of the language(s) of the West. Indeed, the evidence for non- or pre-Indo-European in the West is at best fragmentary, but certainly illusive. Etruscan, which we can read but barely comprehend; the fictive (?) Pelasgian advocated by Georgiev (e.g. 1981); Iberian, the forefather of Basque (?), with which Jürgen Untermann has wrestled largely unsuccessfully for decades; Pictish (?); perhaps Rhetic (see Risch 1970). The silence of the pre-/non-Indo-European West is overwhelming. Were the builders of Stonehenge (final phase *c.* 1680 bc) catatonic? If they spoke, then how could the natives have been so typologically disadvantaged as to have lost nearly everything except those forms we inconveniently gloss, as '*bisher unerklärt, vielleicht nicht indogermanisch, dunkel*'. Was there, perhaps, massive relexification along the lines we now find in creoles? Do the western Indo-European languages represent some kind of restructuring on indigenous semantactic scaffolding? May not the gradual erosion, as one moves from east to west across the presumed Indo-European speech community, of the assumed parent's participial morphology be an indication of this? Is not, perhaps, the advanced suppletion of Celtic an indication of a language-contact battle? Are not those supposedly unsifted forms in Hans Kuhn's Northwest Block the phonological detritus of a native population?

Then, too, just how reliable is that now traditional archaeological scenario, a staging that is supposedly based on a far more probative empirical foundation than a linguistic comparatist could ever hope to conjure? Scepticism mounts when, for example, one finds bits of information studded throughout Gimbutas (1965), say, that smack of personal interviews, e.g. 'In all Indo-European groups the axe was a life-stimulating symbol and was protection against evil powers. Like the snake, it was inseparable from fertility cults' (p. 497).

We may label the east–west incursion theory 'the (Kurgan) displacement hypothesis'. It was certainly designed as an interpretive model, but it obviously works toward dependent conventional interpretations, inherent biases, persistent stereotypes, and once prevalent ideologies, e.g. the claimed linguistic/cultural superiority and eventual victory of the Indo-Europeans. As David Clarke ([1976] 1978, p. 5) said critically of the fictive 'Neolithic Revolution' in an analogous context, it yields 'a satisfactory evolutionary picture of the displacement of lower cultures and economies by higher ones, what one might call Social Darwinism in action'. Compare, similarly,

Grahame Clark's (1980) critique of Childe's 'gap', and consider that explanatory models which incorporate discontinuities (in the form of gaps or jumps) as fundamental epistemic explicators are equally untenable. Social Darwinism is a theology of colonization, and a colonization of Bronze-Age Europe may well have borne little if any resemblance to the colonizations witnessed by the Victorians.

The displacement hypothesis remains a model of expectation, rather than the interpretive absolute it is held out to be, unless and until it is properly evaluated on ecological, ethnographic, economic, and far firmer theoretical grounds. Forced fits of philological and artefactual expectations alone, invariably lead to misinformation. Correlation of archaeologically traced Corded Ware with an invasion of ethnographically 'different' nomadic pastoralists from the East may not have been decisive (or even correct!), though an increased recognition of the importance of domesticated animals, particularly the horse *Equus caballus*, and the subsequent evolution of chariot warfare, must have been highly significant (see Piggott 1968, Drower 1969, Champion *et al.* 1984, pp. 163–9). (*E. caballus* was present on the Pontic steppes north and east of the Black Sea at least by *c.* 2800–2700 bc. By 2000 bc it was distributed from Greece to Scotland (Clutton-Brock 1981, p. 84), and the earliest European depiction of it is found in the fifth shaft-grave at Mycenae.) Caucasian metallurgical advances, such as the presumably imported single-edged shaft-hole axe, were also significant, but evidence for extensive steppe connections is actually extremely limited and doubtful (see Ecsedy 1979, Häusler 1981). Moreover, Barker (1985), who judiciously questions the evidence for Gimbutas' 'Kurgan displacement hypothesis', suggests that changes in Europe reflect a far more complex process than could ever be predicted (or anticipated) by the colonization model. Realistically, there must have been subtle combinations of local and intrusive developments.

The closely spaced social and political regionalism of modern Europe is rooted in closely knit agricultural regionalism (recall that it is the agricultural details, not the industrial exigencies, that has long delayed finalization of the 'unification' of Europe by the European Economic Commission). The subsistence geography of modern Europe is, indeed, highly localized, a fact that is readily apparent to any dialect geographer who has observed the amazingly – especially to an American – varied pattern of local adaptation of agrarian techniques and tools: hay-drying styles that shift in detail every few kilometres, fertilization procedures, cheese processing, denominations of particular instruments, and so on. From the archaeological evidence, particularly as summarized by Barker (1985) and others recently in updating Grahame Clark's classic, *Prehistoric Europe – the economic basis* (1952), there is no compelling reason to assume that Europe has ever *not* been regionally particularistic agriculturally. This is the working assumption that underlies what follows. In comparison, note that the agriculture of Polynesia is, despite vast (oceanic) distances, much more uniform. Europe's agricultural regionalism is, moreover, not just restricted to the land. It also applies to the sea. The *fiskimid* methods of Scandinavia are not replicated elsewhere in Atlantic Europe, and, within Scandinavia itself, they reveal considerable local variation in technique.

Another dialectological truism that is significant for the present context is the fact that regionally restricted labels in Europe's regionally restricted agricultural patterns are highly stable: they are seldom replaced or restructured. The more local, the more conservative. Indeed, they not only offer secure proof of relationship (in *Sprachinselforschung*), but often reflect freezes. Regional subsistence agriculture is a source for lingual cryogenics. This suggests that agricultural lexicon, particularly the vocabulary of plants and animals, would be a productive device for plumbing the depths of a pre-/non-Indo-European substrate in western Europe.

By the end of the 5th millennium bc, a farming economy based on cereal cultivation, limited horticulture, and animal husbandry (sheep, goats, cattle, pigs, but not the horse) was well in place in western Europe. The following scenario of subsequent developments in agricultural production is based on recent general archaeological accounts (e.g. Champion *et al.* 1984), but it must be stressed that not all the postulated components of the developing agricultural economy are demonstrable in the bioarchaeological record. During the 4th millennium there is thought to have been an intensification of agriculture involving the development of mixed farming with an integration of ploughing, wheeled transport (oxen), and animal harvests (milk, wool). The earliest varieties of sheep did not bear wool. Cattle were raised for transport and fertilizer, not consumption. The drinking of milk and the eating of beef were rare, as they were in medieval times. The pig, a prolific breeder and versatile eater, with its easily processed and cured meat, was the preferred domestic animal. Intensified agriculture afforded increased production, and settlement expanded, but, in general, social patterns appear to have been relatively egalitarian, a typology that was broken by the prestige-oriented hierarchical stratification of the early Bronze Age (*c.* 2300–1800 bc). This, in brief, is one of the current interpretations of western European socio-economic development at the presumed point of entry and subsequent expansion of the Indo-European intruders. In view of the importance of cereal cultivation, particularly barley, etymological scrutiny of grain labels would appear to be a promising initial lever to uncover early agricultural and settlement/socio-economic patterns.

Most models for the adoption of cereal cultivation typically show it following an increase in population, and the eco-husbandry of the adoption process is sequentially staged: manipulation (wild species tended/ gathered) → exploitation (wild species under – even marginal – pre-agricultural cultivation) → domestication (varietal selection and agriculture) → controlled plant breeding and specialized agriculture (cf. Harris (Ch. 1, this volume) for a somewhat similar sequence, but without the presumption of population increase as a causal factor).

# The case of barley

The precise area of origin of barley, one of the oldest cereal crops, is unknown (Renfrew 1969, pp. 164–5, 1973, pp. 69–81, 205–8, Harlan 1979). [All the most recent archaeological evidence suggests that wild barley (*Hordeum spontaneum*) was first taken into cultivation somewhere in Southwest Asia, probably in the Levant; see, for example, Bar-Yosef & Kislev Ch. 40, this volume, and Zohary Ch. 22, this volume, eds.] In contrast to Sauer's (1952) specific loci and diffusionist views, Harlan (1979) argues for diffuse (in time and space) origins and dispersals of barley, with a Southwest Asian two-rowed variety as progenitor (monophyletic origin based on *Hordeum spontaneum*), selection of a tough-rachis type in initial phases of domestication, and the later derivation of six-rowed barley. Barley was presumbly cultivated in Central Europe by 4000 bc and in most of northern Europe by 3000 bc. As a hardy, early maturing, saline-tolerant grain, barley (like oats and rye) extended the range of agriculture (Harlan 1972). Naked barley does not occur in the wild, although the archaeobotanical evidence suggests that naked six-rowed barley made quite an early appearance in the domestic crop assemblage. In some areas where barley was a dietary mainstay, the naked variety was apparently preferred, although the archaeological evidence indicates that both hulled and naked six-rowed barley were widely cultivated in early northern Europe, and that, in early southern Europe, both these six-rowed forms were cultivated alongside the hulled two-rowed variety. Bronze-Age finds of two-rowed barley in Central Europe are rare, although there are too few large assemblages of crop remains from Bronze-Age sites for this negative evidence to be given much weight.

The early dialectical evidence appears to reflect the same north/south repartitioning that is suggested by the archaeological evidence. Southern dialects (Lat. *hordeum*, dial. *fordeum*, also the bulk of Romance successors, but Sp. *cebada*, orig. 'fodder'; Gk. *krīthé*; Alb. *drith/drithë*; Alemannian-Bavarian (Alpine Germanic), OHG *gersta*) form a cohesive regional block with reflexes of $*\hat{g}herzd(h)$-$/*\hat{g}hṛzd(h)$- 'prickly, spiked, bearded (grain)' adj., as first proposed by Hoops (1905, pp. 364–70), cf. correctively, Pokorny (1959, p. 446). This block is surely archaic; note Homeric *krī* sg., *krīthé* pl. only. (Georgian *ger* may have supplied Armenian *gari*.) Gk. *-th-* < $*-dh-$, while Germanic may have had *-t-* or *-d-* (Pre-Gmc. $*\hat{g}hérzdā$- f.), but Lat. *-d-* is ambiguous, and Ernout & Meillet (1967, p. 299a) tentatively posit $*\hat{g}hr^{o}zdh$- for Gk. *krīthé*. In illustrating a well-known principle of derivational repartition, Benveniste (1935, p. 76) astutely shows that *hordeum* (nominalized adjective) < $*\hat{g}hṛzdéy\text{-}om$ issued from a neuter $*horde$ ($*\hat{g}hṛzdy$-), which was, in turn, built on a basic $*hor$ ($*\hat{g}hṛzd$-).

Operating with Benveniste's theory of the root, we see the southern 'barley' term built on State I, whose alternative (State II) could then have supplied Goth. *gras* 'grass, plant' (etc.) and, with suffixal comparability to *hordeum*, OCS *grozdŭ* (besides *grezdŭ*, *groznŭ* with successors in all dialects) 'vine (branch)':

| State I | State II |
|---------|----------|
| *$\hat{g}h^e$/ór-s-d(h)- | *$\hat{g}hr$-$^e$/ós-d(h)- |
| (Gerste) | (grozdŭ) |

This pattern of systemic *Schwebeablaut* sets mirrors a customary Indo-European procedure for deriving botanical nomenclature, and the pattern itself has heuristic value. Benveniste obviously considered his thesis a model that corresponded, however approximately, to a pre-existing reality for reconstructing forward, as Watkins (1962, p. 5) has so succinctly put it, rather than backward in time. Note, further, Hamp's (1982–83) effective use of predictive models in accounting for substantives in *-mo- and *-má- and his (1976) programmatic account of some Celtic verbal nouns.

Hamp (1986) has now convincingly accounted for the ever-problematic source of affiliated Goth. *bagms*, OHG *boum*, ON *baðmr*, ON -*barmr* by designing a nomen actionis *bargmaz '(high) growth', later concretized, from *bhorĝh-mó-s to a basic *bherĝh-. In line with our comments about predictive models and botanical nomenclature, a search for reflexes of an alternative (State II), *bhr-éĝh- (bhrĝh-, bhruĝh-, etc.), is in order. As *bhruĝh-, this shape underlies OE *brogne* 'branch, bush', a Nordic loan, cf. Nw. dial. *brogn(e)* 'tree branch, (raspberry) bush', W *brwyn-en* 'rush', etc. Verner variants (cf. OS *rokko* ~ *roggo*, OHG *rokko*, Germ. *Roggen* 'rye') of this shape may have supplied ME *braken* 'bracken (fern)', a Nordic loan, cf. OSw. *brækne*, OIc. *burkn*, and note EFr. *brāk* 'branch, bush', MLG *brake* 'branch'. If from a *brēgmaz, rather than the traditionally and tentatively posited *brēmaz, then Engl. *broom*, also in *broom grass*, *broomcorn* 'millet', OHG *bramo* 'bramble', etc. may also belong here. Is there a possibility of contrasting semanticizations of contrasted shapes: *bherĝh- '(high) growth' vs. *bhreĝh- '(low) growth'?

Returning to 'barley', W *haidd*, Br. *heiz* = Skt. *sasya-*, Av. *hahya-* 'grain' and OCS (etc.) *ječĭnŭ* 'prickly, bearded', ultimately from *ank- 'bent, curved', need not detain us.

The Baltic 'barley' terms present a crux: Lith. *miežiai* (pl.), Latv. *mieži* (pl.), OPr. *moasis* are considered etymologically opaque. The Latvian connection between 'barley' and 'bread' (*maize* f.) is paralleled by Celtic, good evidence for the centrality of this cereal in both localities, see below.

Connection of ON *bygg* 'barley, grain' and congeners (Sw. *bjugg*, Shetl. *bigg(in)*, north. Engl. dial. *bigg*, OE *beo*, *bēow*, and *beowod* 'harvest, grain', reiterated by OS *beō*, *bewō* gen. pl. 'seed, crop, yield', *bewod* 'harvest' in the *Heliand* – a loan from Anglo-Saxon?) with ON *búa* 'to dwell, till' is implausible. A Gmc. *bewwu-/-a- would provide an acceptable progenitor, also for ON *bjórr* 'beer', if from *beuza-/*beura-, sometimes compared with OHG *biost* (etc.) 'first milk of the mother cow'. West Gmc. 'beer' (OHG *bior*, OE *bēor*, etc.) is traditionally and correctly seen as a late borrowing from VLat. *biber* to denote the introduced, malted variety vs. an indigenous 'ale' (< *alu-, ON *ǫl*, OS *alu*, etc.). Association *à la* Pokorny (1959, p. 149) and others of an underlying *bhe-u-wo- (or the like) as the source for *bygg/bjórr* with *\*bheu-/\*bhū-* is improbable. The suggested semantics (*\*bewwa-/\*bwweu-* as 'cultivated grain') appear contrived and hence weak. Then, as we have seen, this etymology has now been deprived of the support lent to it by associating it with *bagms* (etc.) derived from a *\*bhou̯(ð)-mó-*, so, tentatively, Pokorny (ibid.). A *\*bhe-u-* is not only uncanonical, but is also dialectally isolated: Northwest Germanic alone. It does, however, fit an emerging pattern for North European substrate forms, particularly, but far from exclusively, those with ecological connections: *\*ɔbl-u-* 'apple', *\*sɔl-u->*ON *sǫl* 'seaweed, algae', *\*ɔl-u-* 'ale', *\*ket-u->*ON *kjǫt* 'meat, usually a prepared variety, by drying or smoking', *\*mɔ́g(h)-u-* 'servant' > Goth. *magus/mawi* (etc.) vs. *\*mðk-ú-* 'kinship term' > Celtic *\*makʷos/ \*makʷkʷos*, see Hamp (1975, 1979, 1983, forthcoming), Markey (forthcoming a, b). Extraction of *-u-* appears well motivated, and this element may well have been an animate/inanimate marker (*à la* Algonquian), or a suffixed noun class marker, or derive from a combination of the two strategies (as in the ancestors of the northeastern Caucasian languages). Compare fossilized traces of a noun class systems posited for Proto-Semitic, e.g. *-b* as the sign for the class of wild/harmful animals, so *\*di'-ib-* 'wolf'. The truly interesting typological fact is that the basic strategies that are either attested by or retrievable for the non-Indo-European languages of Europe (exclusive of Uralic) are the very strategies that are *commonly* scrapped/ ousted upon contact, e.g. ergativity (Basque). Noun class grammaticalization usually gives way to gender. It is possible that a pre-/non-Indo-European *\*b(h)e-u-* denoted 'barley, harvestable grain' in a North European substate prior to Indo-European settlement and that an adopted *\*be-u-* was areally integrated as *\*beuwiza* (cf. Gmc. *\*bariza-* 'bearded (grain), barley', an *es*-stem) to yield *bjórr*.

It is clear that Alpine Germanic was not alone in generalizing *gersta*, as this etymon is also typical for Frankish, Saxon, and Dutch (*gerst*): it is the only form in the *Freckenhorster Heberolle* (MS K = 10th century?, M = late 11th century, but reveals Frisian influence, not altogether unexpected for this Frisian foundation). In opposition to what may be considered a southern *gersta*, Gothic, Nordic, and the core of the so-called 'Ingwaeonic' dialects all reflect derivations of an *es*-stem *\*bariza-*: Goth. *barizeins* adj., cf. *baira-bagma* 'mulberry tree' (1 ×, L 17.6); OE *bere, baer-lic*>*barley*; OFr. *ber-*, particularly in *ber-ielda* 'grain tax/payment', cf. Germ. *Bargeld*, NFr. *ber(e), bar, bär* (insular dialects and therefore archaic). Note, further, OIr. *bairgen*< *\*bharigenā* 'bread', lit. 'that bread made from barley', W *bara* id., cf. Lat. *farrāgō*.

Germanic dialects with dual 'barley' labels (*\*bariza-*: *\*gersta-*) are paralleled by the Italic situation with *far* (*\*bhars*): *hordeum* (*\*ĝhṛzdh-*) resp.: Lat. *fār* (gen. *farris*<*fars-es*) 'grain', earlier 'spelt', cf. Umbr. *far, farsio*, OSc. *far* id. In Italic, *\*bhars* became the unmarked generic term ('grain, corn'), while *\*ĝhṛzd-* was generated for a specific, marked taxum ('barley').

The further distribution of *\*bhar-* is indicated by Slavic with, for example, OCS *brašĭno* 'food', Russ. *bor* 'millet', *bórošno* 'rye', SCr. *brašno* 'flour' and Albanian with *bar* 'grass'. Recall the Celtic 'bread' terms with *\*bhar-* and note replacement in Old and Modern Irish by *eorna* < *es-orniā*, which contains the originally heteroclitic 'harvest' word, *$\star^e$/os-ōr/-en-*, e.g. Goth. *asans*, so Pokorny (1928, p. 306), see now Schindler (1975).

An apparent early absence of *$\star$bhar-* as a grain term in Greek is belied by the Hesychius gloss *fēron* (< *$\star$ferson* ?): *è tōn àrchaiōn theōn trofē*, as well as, significantly, its onomasticization in *Persephone* lit. 'the grain killeress', corresponding to the fertility goddess *Feronia/Faronia*, who was celebrated on Mount Soracte near the Tiber and elsewhere in Etruria with an annual grain tribute.

The grain tribute, in both secular and non-secular contexts with emphasis on an identification of certain grains and measures with certain social classes and men vs. gods, as well as the importance of well-defined measures (large measure = low tariff), is certainly archaic. Binchy (1966) has given us an admirably detailed account of this institution's manifestations in early Irish. The association of grain tributes with fertility cults is also well known. The Carinthian *Vierbergelauf*, situated in a perfect Celtic substratum of Noricum, is surely a modern continuation of this socio-economic and religious practice. This ritual was formerly held on *Dreinagelfreitag* (= the third Friday after Easter), but now takes place on the Sunday after Easter. At dawn that day, a procession sets out from Magdalensberg, site of one of the largest Celto-Roman *oppida* in Noricum and close to ancient Virunum (Zollfeld- = *solium*), the capital of Noricum, and moves to Ulrichsberg and thence to St. Veitsberg and ends in Lorenziberg, that is, the procession makes a clockwise circle (east–south–west–north) of mountain-top churches, a graphic representation of the daily course of the sun, and must be completed in one day (sunrise to sunset). At each church the runners offer a fistful of grain and recieve a fistful of earth in return. Each of the saints after whom the churches are named had firm associations with fire/light. In the centre of this circle of churches lies Hohenstein with its archaeologically well-identified Celtic temple site, an area known to have been consecrated to Noreia (= Isis), the Celtic fertility deity of the region. The *Vierbergelauf* is the Carinthian equivalent of the Rhenish *Matronenkult*.

Grain tributes/payments were expressed in set phrases with fixed measures, a legal codification. For example, in the *Freckenhorster Heberolle*, referenced above, we repeatedly find *muddi (gerston/hauoron)* and *malt (gerston/hauoron)*, terms that are specifically reserved for grain measures. Similarly, in Irish we have *míach* o.n. and f., primarily for grain, e.g. *míach eorna (Laws* v. 82.17), and note 'the feast of the bushel', 'hosting of the measure', and 'Meath of the corn-measures', where *míach* < *$\star$meig(h)-*, the required and appropriate source for Baltic *mież-* 'barley', which was left behind after deletion of its head-noun, the same syntactically promoted morphologization that, as Hamp (1980) has proposed, yielded the Germanic neuter *$\star$blōd-* 'blood'. If so, then we have further evidence of the early significance of barley among the Indo-European intruders.

In summary, *$\star$bhar-* and *$\star$ĝhŗzdh-* were primary sources for 'barley' terms in western/Atlantic Europe, with the former predominant in the north and the latter predominant in the south. In the south, *bhar- became a generic, and, as Berlin (1971) points out in his impressive analysis of folk biotaxonomies, unmarked, inclusive generic labels usually represent an older class derived from what were formerly specific, intermediate taxa. It may be that *bhar- originally referred to the northern hulled six-rowed variety, the form with longer awns, while *ĝhr̥zdh- was later designed to refer to the specifically southern hulled two-rowed variety. The old term then became a generic in parts of the south, but its antiquity is reflected by its socioreligious extensions (Feronia/Faronia, Persephone). A suggested north European substrate term, *b(h)e-u-, apparently co-existed with *bhar-, originally, as we shall see in greater detail below, a purely descriptive epithet, i.e. 'the bearded, prickly (grain)'. Further support for the indigenous, non-pre-Indo-European status of *b(h)e-u- may be inferred from the Eddic distinction, surely ancient: Bygg heitir með mǫnnum, en barr með goðom (Alvíssmál 32). This is congruent with the theophoric onomasticizations cited above.

The primordial term for 'beard' in Indo-European appears to have been *(s)m^e/ok(r)-, see Pokorny (1959, pp. 968–9) for an inventory. The original term was then replaced in a western dialectal group by *bhar-dhā-. The problem is, then, to account for the distinction, if any, between *smek- and *bhar-dhā- and the introduction of the latter; see Markey (1984a), from which the following discussion was abstracted. We assume that the formal distinction reflected a deeper semantic repartition. As a term for both 'beard' and 'chin', it seems obvious that *smek- referred to the general locus of facial hair. The value 'chin' was primary for *smek-, while 'beard' was secondary. In contrast, it seems likely that *bhar-dhā-, ultimately related to Engl. bristle (etc.), originally referred to the quality, as opposed to the locus, of facial hair. The innovation signalled by *bhar-dhā- was triggered by requirements of greater semantic specificity, as was the later Indic dichotomization between 'beard' and 'moustache' (Marathi dādhī 'beard' vs. miśā pl. 'moustache', etc.). At the outset, 'beard' was referenced by general facial location, and then, secondarily in the West, by the quality of that facial hair as being prickly, spinous, reminiscent of awns. Indeed, it is precisely in those dialects of Indo-European in which we find 'barley' characterized by *bhar- that we also find *bhar-dhā- most firmly entrenched, as well as its further semantic extention as 'man/male, husband' and ethnographic (Langobardi) use.

## Rye and oats

As cereal cultivars, oats and rye appear to be chronologically secondary to barley, although, in reviewing the state of knowledge a decade ago, Hillman (1978) showed that rye, at least, was already present in fully domesticated form (if only as a domesticated weed of other crops) by the 7th millennium bc in Turkey and, as a crop in its own right, by the time of the Hittites, at least. He also noted that it was under cultivation in Czechoslovakia by the Bronze Age (1500–1800 bc) and that it was present as a weed (and perhaps as a crop) long before that in parts of Poland. In northwestern Europe, however, it emerged substantially later. The chronology of the domestication and spread of oats is far less clear. As winter-hardy cereals, most varieties of rye and oats, would have been pre-adapted to the suggested climatic deterioration of the Late Bronze Age.

Italic, Slavic, Baltic etyma for 'oats', as well as OHG *evina*, are uniformly retraceable to something like Łat. *avēna* (*avīna* ?), but the precise design of their relational chain is impossible, and we may be looking at a complex series of areal borrowings and reborrowings. The situation is analogous to that for non-Indo-European *silver* (OCS *srebro*, Goth. *silubr*, etc.) in the northeast vs. the IE *argent* word elsewhere. The source is surely non-Indo-European, and the *na*-suffix cannot be assumed for the Baltic and Slavic shapes (Etruscan ?, cf. Lat. *persōna* and Etr. *φersu* 'mask' + Etr. suffix *-nV*, e.g. Etr. *pumpu* vs. *pumpuni*, *aisuna/aisna* adj. 'divine'). The Celtic 'oats' word has also been presumed to be non-Indo-European: Ir. *coirce*, W *ceirch*, Br. *kerc'h*, but this is best seen as a dissimilation product of *korkryo-* to OIr. (etc.) *corc* 'hair' (Met. Gl. Eg. 27) as 'the hairy grain'. For the Romans, oats were a leading grain crop, not only as a consumable cereal, but also, militarily, as fodder: as a non-nutrient, wheat straw is never used for feeding livestock, and barley and rye only very occasionally. Lat. *avēna* penetrated southern Germany (OHG *evina*), the Rhenish settlements around Trier and Cologne (*even*), and the Netherlands (dial. *even*). Ingwaeonic *āt- (OE *āte* 'weed', ME *ote(s)*, Du. dial. *ate*, Fr. *et-* in compounds) probably derives from *oid- (Pokorny 1959, p. 774) and originally referred to the grain, the kernel itself, cf. ON *eitill* 'nodule'. Norse *hafri*, Germ. *Hafer*, Du. *haver*, Engl. dial (north.) *haver* (from Scandinavian) are traditionally derived from *hab(e)r- = Lat. *caper* 'goat' with the semantic motivation that oats were the principal fodder/feed for goats, which is contrived and unsatisfactory, as is, similarly, a connection of *avēna* with *owi- 'sheep'. Where *hafer/haver* and *even* co-exist dialectically in West Germanic, they refer to different varieties, autumn-sown and spring-sown respectively: *avēna* (and successors) is clearly southern, while *hafer* (besides the regional innovation *āt-) is clearly northern, where it is firmly ensconced. This geographical repartition prompts us to recall OGut. *hagri*, Md.Gut. *hāgra*, Nw. and Sw. dial. *hagre* 'oats', a form that is lacking in insular Nordic but one that is necessarily very archaic given the set of necessarily early Finno-Ugric loans, e.g. Finn. *kakra*, *kaura*. We see *habr- and *hagr- as alternants (*-b-* ~ *-g-*), comparable to OFr. *si(u)gun*, ONw. *siug* vs. OS (etc.) *sebun* '7', that is, as another instance of the Germanic *samprasāraṇa*-like alternation, see Markey (1984b). It is phonologically reasonable to assume that *-g-* could have developed as a dissimilation product [-round] in [+ coronal] sequences, and it is a well known fact that backness in vowels/glides is paralleled by velarness in consonants. Compare Finn. *kaura*: *kakra*, Karel. *kagra*, Weps. *kagr*, Est. *kaer*, and recall that Finnish lacks *b*, but has *v* only initially and medially. Having related *habr- and *hagr-, we suggest that *hagr- was the more original shape, which we then connect with NW. dial. (etc.) *harg* nt. 'coarse hair on the tail or mane of a horse', Skt. *saca*,

OPr. *sexti* (etc.), that is, *kaĝh-/*koĝh-* 'hair'. We then project the same semanticization as that proposed for Celtic 'oats'. It is possible that *habr-/*hagr-* and the Celtic terms originally referred to *Avena strigosa*, the bristle-pointed oat, while *avēna* (and the other members of this group) refer to *Avena brevis*, a less bristled, short-stemmed variety. Gk. *brómos* (Md.Gk. *brómē*) remains opaque, unless it is somehow a derivation of *bhregh-*, see above.

Exclusively High Germ. (OHG *dinchel*) *Dinkel*, variously glossed as 'emmer', spelt, rye' and the generic term 'corn, grain' in Swabia, the area in which it is predominant, also as a toponym (e.g. *Dinkelsbühl*), is totally opaque except for its obvious diminutive final. Operating with a *teng-* gets us nowhere, and this term may well derive from some substrate source. This is a highly regional term, probably archaic, and may have referred to some intermediate taxon, perhaps originally a semi-domesticated fodder grass. [However, *Dinkel* is generally applied specifically to spelt wheat, *Triticum spelta*, which, in German-speaking areas, survives as a field crop only in Schwabia. Eds.]

The western/Atlantic words for 'rye' display less variation than those for 'oats'. Other than the bread wheats, rye is the only cereal with qualities necessary for making a fully leavened (risen) bread, but it is slightly inferior to wheat for that purpose, lacking the elasticity of the best 'hard' wheats.

Lat. *secale*, which supplied the bulk of the Romance forms, as well as Ir. *secul*, Br. *segal*, is probably non-Indo-European. Roman (Christian) influence is again obvious in OHG *sihhila*, OE *sicol* (via Irish in the monastic foundations). A pre-Gmc. *rughi-*, for which there is no corresponding form in eastern Indo-European, is evidenced by Lith. *rugŷs*, pl. *rugiai*, OCS *ružĭ* (Pol. *reż*, Russ. *rož*, SCr. *raž*). A Gmc. *rugi-* bifurcated as *rug-n- > *ruggn-*, the source of the Saxon, High German, Dutch, and Frisian forms, and *rug-iz* (with and without umlaut due to alternative occurrence in compounds, i.e. *rug-*), which supplied the English and Nordic forms. It appears that the early onomastic derivations also belong here: *Roga-land*, *Rugii*, *Rygir*, *Rügen* 'the rye eaters'(?). Gk. *briza*, quoted by Galen (*de alim. facult.* I, 13.6), a native of Mysia (b. 131 – d. *c.* 201 AD), as the name of 'rye' raised in Thrace and Macedonia, is a Thracian word. Bulg. *brica* 'a sort of summer grain' is a continuation. This word has been unsatisfactorily equated with *rugi-* on the basis of a reconstructed *urugiā < *rughyō-*, or Skt. *vrīhí-* 'rice', Afgan *vriže* id., or Lith. *brŷzas* 'bacon slice' as 'that which is cut off, harvested', see Duridanov (1969, pp. 9, 85, 1976, p. 21), Georgiev (1977, pp. 22, 103, 168). Given other, exclusively Thracian–Baltic botanical parallels (e.g. Thr. *sinupyla* = Lith. *šŭn-obuolos* lit. 'dog apple'), it is tempting to see a Baltic congener, but none of the etymologies proposed to date is fully convincing, least of all equation with *rughi-*. In view of the extensive Finno-Ugric parallels and phonological difficulties, it is likely that this *Wanderwort* is non-Germanic, probably also non-Indo-European. As for *briza*, it might somehow be related to the mysterious Gk. *brómos* 'oats'. Recall that the Romans had originally considered *avēna* a bad weed (as opposed to barley), and it is frequently collocated with *lolium*, and thus regarded as a darnel. Here, the 4th-century commentator, Servius, is enlightening. On *avēna*, he says: *steriles . . . secundum situm Italiae, nam in Thracia fructuosae sunt.* (B. 5.37). As inferior (to wheat and barley) grasses, oats and rye might well have been grouped together and shared the same original base, but detailed and satisfactory pedigrees for *briza* and *brómos* elude us.

Terms for 'wheat', 'emmer', and 'spelt', as well as 'millet', have been excluded, as has einkorn wheat. Analysis of the terms for barley, oats, and rye, the early winter-hardy grains for the emerging agriculture of western Europe, is sufficient for the present descriptive frame of early socio-economic conditions.

## The plough (and the pig)

The development of more extensive grain cultivation and mixed farming well may have required an improved plough. There is now good evidence that plough agriculture was established throughout Europe from *c.* 2000 bc, or even earlier in some parts of the continent (Gilman 1981, pp. 5–6), although some authors argue that it was present from the beginning of European agriculture, having spread with the crops from Southwest Asia. The lynchets of prehistoric Europe are the fossil remains of property boundaries newly erected in a system of intensive plough agriculture. The earliest plough finds (e.g. at Lavagnone, Walle/East Friesland, *c.* 1500 bc) are all crude ards, and the well-known etymological evidence for 'plough, to plough' indicates that the ard was also known to the Indo-Europeans. The heavier, metal-tipped ard, even those with more developed mould-boards that could tackle heavier soils, did not come into existence until the late 1st millennium bc. Recall the advanced ard of the Etruscan bronze ploughman of Arezzo (6th century BC), Villa Giulia Museum, Rome). Extensive grain agriculture is unlikely to have developed early, and oats and rye are apparently more recent cultigens in most areas. The evolution of plough agriculture must have had subtle, but highly significant, socio-economic consequences, factors that have seemingly been overlooked by comparatists. Extensive ploughing initially requires labour-intensive clearance, an investment in land that is not readily abandoned. It also requires animal traction: the heavier the plough, the more traction needed. Ploughing with wider, deeper furrows allowed by advanced mould-board ploughs also permitted more evaporation from the soil and increased the likelihood of wind erosion, whereas shallow ard ploughing that merely pulverized loose soils retained moisture. Heavier ploughs required larger teams, with all that that entailed: pasture, fodder/feed, barns, carts. The cycle of ploughing–fodder/fertilizer was a precarious one in a subsistence system. If the animals were fed, then the family might starve, or vice versa, and even Roman agronomists period-ically suggested that the farmer feed his oxen on 'whatever leaves are available' from March to September. Legumes, pulses, and fallowing could renew soil fertility, but many of the terms for these crops are probably non-Indo-European (e.g. Gk. *fásēlos, pisos, kriós*, Lat. *pisum*), and the same holds for garden crops (e.g. Lat. *cēpa, cēpulla* > Germ. *Zwiebel*). The pre-historic and medieval cow was about half (or even less in some cases) the size of the modern version, and, correspondingly, produced about half the animal fertilizer. Per capita, oxen are not nearly as good suppliers of nitrogen fertilizer as sheep, and the advantages of mixed farming and plough agriculture over a pastoral system supplemented by hunting, fishing, and gathering must not always have been obvious. Indeed, the ploughing–fodder/fertilizer cycle was still seen as precarious well within living memory in Scandinavia, where even the previous generation often had to resort to feeding moss to cattle to carry them through a winter. A new, prehistoric agricultural technology (heavier ploughs, bronze instead of flint sickles, etc.) had many hidden costs and only became widespread well after the arrival of the Indo-Europeans.

In short, the advantages of the new agricultural technologies must have been carefully weighed against their disadvantages in the context of a subsistence system that simply could not afford more than limited experi-mentation. On this basis, Barker (1985) suggests that these new technologies spread very, very slowly and that, upon the arrival of the presumed largely pastoral Indo-Europeans, Europe must have been faced with a sort of technologically triggered farm crisis. He suggests (others would disagree) that the supposedly new technology had not yet been debugged. In contrast, pastoralists could engage in limited swidden agriculture and readily sup-plement their food supply by fishing, hunting, and gathering. Here it is worth noting that the vast majority of what is generally considered the earliest tier of Germanic settlement names on the Continent refer to clearing and swidden agriculture, e.g. *hurst/horst, thwaite, rode/rade* (etc.). Then, too, Classical reporters repeatedly tell us that the *Germanii* legally restricted themselves from remaining more than one year in one place for cultivation, further evidence of swidden farming as a deeply embedded practice. Moreover, an originally swidden toponym provided the base for a plough term: the connection between *rode/rade/riet/rud* (etc.) 'clearing (by burning)' and OS *rioster*, OE *rēost* 'share-beam' is obvious (Markey 1972, 1978). Germanic agriculture had its roots in swidden farming, but, as Harris (1972) and others have shown, swidden ecological factors conspire to maintain dispersed patterns of settlement, low population densities, and few cultural or material advancements. Indication of dispersed settlement patterns and low population densities in northern/Atlantic Europe may well be indicated by loss of *$w^e$/oik-* (*vīcus*) in Celtic, as well as replacement of the *domus-* term in both Celtic and Germanic by a term (or terms) for *house* that had only physical, and no institutional, significance, that is, house as enclosure, as dwelling place, cottage, hut, and the like (Markey 1986).

There is no indication that this late prehistoric–early historic continental pattern of Germanic swidden agriculture (*c.* 500 bc–ad 200) represents a reversion (due to climatic deterioration, social unrest, over-population, or some vague need to be on the move) after an earlier accomplishment of more advanced and better organized mixed farming. The *Völkerwanderungen* are best seen as small-group movements in quest of better subsistence, even by pillaging (another form of gathering), a migration southward in search of more affluent and advanced ways of life. The arresting fact is that highly prized agricultural products typically have southern labels, and these southern labels are frequently non-Indo-European in origin, e.g. *līno-* 'flax, linen', the earliest form of prehistoric textiles in the absence of wool; Lat. (and successors) *cannabis*, and the grain terms cited above.

Early Celtic agrarian patterns were probably no better than those of the *Germanii*. While the textual evidence Jackson (1964) has marshalled may offer inferential glimpses of an earlier, undocumented culture, one must proceed with caution (Megaw 1985). In the absence of firm evidence for well-articulated Megalithic farming, some archaeologists have proposed that the major source of food during this period was the sea, the pursuit of fish, as well as crustaceans, presumably in skin boats by sailors with a keen knowledge of navigation (Case 1969, Johnstone 1972, Clark 1980, pp. 98–100). In their dependence on the sea and achievement of collective art forms, the North Atlantic Megalithic peoples were akin to the Amerindians of the Pacific Northwest of North America. (Indo-European is notably poor in navigational and maritime terminology.) Donnchadh Ó Corráin (pers. comm.) points out that much of the Irish crustacean terminology is clearly non-Irish and suggests that this lexicon somehow managed to survive among non-Goidelic groups until it was integrated. Apparently, North Atlantic Celtic (and Germanic) settlers adopted (portions of) a sea-harvesting system that was already in place – a possibility that invites further investigation.

For the northern Indo-European peoples, intensified swine husbandry already embryonically in place upon their arrival, may have been crucial for survival. The prominent role of the pig, as well as its ritualized apportionment, among the Celtic peoples are both well known. Obviously, the pig was known to the Indo-Europeans (Benveniste 1949). The particular ecology of northern Europe may have given it a different contextualization, even culturally. Recently, Hamp (1985) has succeeded in relating the *kul-* contained in *Culhwch*, a tautology, to the Lithuanian pig word, *kiaŭlė*, cf. Lith. *kuilỹs* 'boar', reminiscent of *Cilydd*, the name of Culhwch's father. He posits an underlying *\*keul-* from a North European substrate, yet another non-Indo-European agrarian term. Compare, further, Latv. *kuilis* 'boar' and OIr. *cullach* (*coillte* pl.). The Baltic and Celtic distribution of a *\*keul-* (or the like) as a pig term seems assured.

This particular datum is extraordinarily valuable if brought into the context of the plough and its evolution. Pigs that are penned intensively will naturally churn the soil very thoroughly, destroy every weed, and also manure the churned plot. As rooters, they are natural ploughs. The metaphorical transfer of natural terms to mechanical devices is probably universal: (bird) wing→(airplane) wing. The anticipation is that swine terms would readily transfer to cover plough parts, particularly as the plough evolved (from the hoe or ard). Then, too, there are well-documented associations of female fertility deities with pigs: the boar is the representative of Freyja/Frigg, an hypostasis of Gefjun, well known for her ploughing (*Gylfaginning*), and Diana–Artemis (*Odyssey*, 6.104). The pig, in addition to the sheep and the steer, was a usual sacrificial animal in Rome. Ritually, Lat. *amburvāre* signified 'a furrow drawn around the city as a sacral border' (Ennius, *Andromeda* 117), cf., perhaps, Osc. *uruvú* (1×, *Cippus Abellanus* B.30). These fragments suggest an archaic constellation: *pig–fertility–plough*.

W *swch* signifies both 'pig snout' and 'plough-share' < *\*sukko-* (details of a borrowing/reborrowing criss-cross that gave rise to Engl. *sow*: *hog(g)* need not detain us here), as does OIr. *soc(c)*, Corn. *soch*, Br. *souc'h*, which entered dialectal French as *souche* (*soc*), cf. MLat. *soccus*, perhaps OSp. *segur*, if not from Lat. *secum/seca* to *secāre*, which also entered Alpine Germanic. Traditionally, it is assumed that Lat. *culter* (Fr. *coutre*, It. *coltro*) supplied OE *culter* 'colter', Rhenish and Low German *kolter*, Du. *kouter* (vs. ON *skalm*) as a *Wanderwort*, but the further etymology of Lat. *culter* is highly speculative, so Ernout & Meillet (1967, pp. 155–6). In light of the semantic bivalence of OIr. (etc.) *soc(c)* as 'pig/boar snout' and 'plough-share', we would prefer to see a reflex here of the substrate pig word (*\*keul-/\*kul-*) contained in *culter*. This suggestion is supported by the set: Germ. *Furche* 'furrow': *Ferkel* 'farrow':: Lat. *porca*: *porcus*.

The central Germanic set of 'plough' words (Germ. *Pflug*, etc. < *\*plōgh-*, Langb. *plovum*, a term cited in a well-known passage by Pliny as being a wheeled plough type stemming from the Rhaetii) are certainly substratal, despite a lengthy research history of (often enough, highly contrived) attempts to render them Indo-European (Trier 1945). OE *sulh* = Lat. *sulcus* was replaced by ON *plōgr c.* 1000. This is probably a southern (Alpine ?, straddling the convergence of Roman/Germanic contact) substrate word that referred to some more advanced form of plough which had evolved in a regional agriculture. The term appears to have been picked up in Latin and to have then spread northward to Germanic and eastward to Slavic and Baltic.

## Indo-Europeans in western Europe: the evidence of the apple

A major problem in any discussion of non-Indo-European/Indo-European contact is that of relative chronology: when did the Indo-Europeans first confront the early agricultures of western Europe?

As Hamp (1979) has shown, Engl. *apple* and its cognates in all the languages of northern Europe (Germanic, Slavic, Baltic, Celtic) point to an underlying *\*ɔbl-u-*, clearly a substrate form. Similarly, the southern word for 'apple' (Lat. *mālum* and its Greek and Anatolian congeners, etc.) is non-Indo-European; Markey forthcoming a). The line between *\*ɔbl-u-* and *mālum* (or the like) establishes a border between basic non-Indo-European speech (and agrarian) communities. This isogloss is virtually coincidental with that for the non-Indo-European terms for 'stone': *mal- in 'Old Europe' vs. *kar-/*karant- elsewhere. The non-Indo-European origin of 'apple' and its later Indo-European adoption have echoes in myth and legend. The dramatic focus of all of the earliest adoption legends is a contest by members of one (= Indo-European) pantheon to steal the apples from members of another (= non-Indo-European) pantheon: the apples of the Hesperides were dutifully procured by Hercules; in Norse legend, the goddess Iduna was kidnapped and her apples stolen; the mythical Celtic Tuirenn stole the apples that formed part of the treasure of the Tuatha Dé Danann.

The relevant botanical details may be summarized as follows, see Schery (1952, pp. 453–6), Berger (1956), Burkill (1962), Hyams (1971, pp. 119–28), Simmonds (1976, pp. 248–50).

The cultivated apple, traditionally classified as *Malus pumila* (which includes *domestica* and *sylvestris* = the wild crab apple), of which there are 25 infertile species (mostly 2 × and s−i), is a relatively recent temperate-zone fruit tree domesticate. It is self-incompatible and can be hybridized (or grafted) readily with most *Malus* or *Pyrus* species. In fact, horticultural hybridization was necessary to have palatable fruit of any size from the wild state. Its domestication (and value) therefore required some horticultural attention, but it would have been favoured by more or less primitive agrarians. This is suggested by the fact that pre-harvest drop (still occurring today, on unsprayed trees) would have permitted collection with little effort, and such fruit are in fact preferable for winter storage: the overripe fruit will not keep so well. The apple's native habitat and primary centre of origin, also as a cultivar, was Asia Minor and the Caucasus, where native wild forms are still found today; most European and Southwest Asian species have contributed to today's cultivars. In Europe, and this is the salient fact that comparatists have overlooked, it may only be as old as the Middle Neolithic or Early Bronze Age, that is, between c. 3000 and 2000 bc.

The archaeobotanical evidence, etymological details, and mythological evidence may be plausibly orchestrated to yield the following scenario. A domesticated apple did not become part of an established horticultural inventory in northern Europe before c. 2500–2000 bc. It is entirely possible, though not very likely, that its North European label, *ɔbl-u- (in opposition to *mālum* or the like in southern Europe) antedates its acceptance and integration as a cultivar in that region, but certainly not its introduction. We may, therefore, infer a reasonable terminus *post quem* for *ɔbl-u- of c. 3000–2500 bc and, simultaneously, a plausible terminus *ante quem non* for that term's adoption by northern Indo-Europeans: presumably, Indo-European did not enter the *ɔbl-u- sector before c. 3000–2500 bc, but probably a more realistic date is c 2000 bc.

# Conclusion

As a categorial summary of the linguistic evidence, we note that early basic agrarian vocabulary is either (a) transparently Indo-European (e.g. Lat. *hordeum*), or (b) it is not, and is then either (i) traceable to some areally defined source (e.g. 'apple' as *ɔbl-u-*), or (ii) not so traceable (e.g. *līno-*). There is an immediate opposition between native and non-native. Significantly, however, we do not find oppositions between (putative) loans and native syntagms, the situation reflected by Sp. *cacahuate* vs. Germ. *Erd + nuss* 'peanut', a state of affairs that points to recent acculturation. Then, too, tautologies with glossarial reciprocity (e.g. Engl. onomastic *Cheetwood-* < British *cēt* + OE *wudu*, Rhenish *öllich* (or the like) < Lat. *unio* + OS *lōk*) are rare, and Hamp's *Culhwch* is a distinct exception. Such fusions reflect one-on-one (cultural) diglossia and are largely unknown (synchronically) from any true creole. Finally, there is the total novelty that indicates confrontation with an unknown, e.g. no Indo-European term for *apple* is demonstrably Indo-European. Compare, incidentally, *tobacco* (regionally from Algonquian, e.g. Fox *tatabagi* 'leaf'), Engl. *jerky* (meat) < Sp. *charqui* < Quechua *ch'arki* 'dried meat'. The paucity of fusion formations that imply concession and accommodation, immediate non-native vs. native dichotomizations without intermediate syntagmatic glossing, the outright adoption of terms to cover phenomena that were presumably unknown previously, rather than attempt translations, all plausibly mirror social cleavage: native vs. non-native, and, with a social gloss, agrarian vs. non-agrarian. The *Wanderwort* character and frequent regional distribution of distinctly non-Indo-European agrarian terms (e.g. the *avēna* group, *plōg-*, *b(h)e-u-*) may well reveal an initial localized confrontation with regionally adapted subsistence systems. For example, the evolution of heavier plough-types is suggested by some archaeologists to have spread from some central (Alpine ?) location, and this may be correlatable with the diffusion of *plōg-*; earlier in Alpine Romance than Germanic, earlier in Alpine Germanic than Slavic, and so on.

The Europe into which a 3rd-millennium intruder entered may have been in the midst of an agricultural revolution and, simultaneously, a subsistence crisis, particularly so north of the Alps. To adapt and survive, intruders were at the mercy of the regionally specific farming and sea-harvesting knowledge long accumulated by indigenous peoples. Those indigenous peoples were tied to precariously fragile seasonal eco-cycles. Failures were probably commonplace, and catastrophic. But to read massive invasions into shifts in a particular stratigraphy (e.g. 'the (Kurgan) displacement hypothesis') is unjustified. What may well have been at work was the displacement of one subsistence system by another in the hands of successive generations of one and the same ethnic group, not conquest. Pastoralism could perhaps have been a response to soil exhaustion. New crops such as oats and rye could have been a response to cooler and wetter conditions. These new crops entailed modified technologies and, concomitantly, they presented new problems; e.g. heavier ploughing is claimed to be particularly important for the root system of some races of rye, but heavier ploughing requires more traction, and more traction inevitably requires more fodder.

A dichotomy between (superior) nomadic pastoralists and (inferior) sedentary farmers, groups that can and do in fact co-exist (e.g. Hausa and Fulani), even to their mutual benefit, has been highly over-emphasized by comparatists in their depiction of Indo-European intrusion. What is significant is the archaeologically attested emergence of social stratification in Bronze-Age Europe in the wake of a linguistically evidenced Indo-European intrusion. Prior to this period, all indicators seem to point to widespread egalitarianism and orientation toward a matriarchy (typical, incidentally, for hoe agriculturalists), as well as the distinct lack of feudalized land-tenure control practices. The massive defences, hillforts, discrepancies in wealth in burials, and so on of the Bronze Age indicate social stratification and the presence of an elite, and a patrilineal elite at that, with agricultural produce as a major prize. We are then faced with the problem, as Harris (1972, p. 258) has so succinctly said, of discovering 'how mechanisms of centralized controls were generated to convert a population of autonomous cultivators into a dependent peasantry'. A very productive way of resolving this problem has, we believe, been suggested by Gilman (1981). First, we note that the linguistic evidence assembled above – indicative of much more comparable evidence – is readily and convincingly open to a social gloss: an agrarian vs. a non-agrarian class. The central point of Gilman's view is that, in the emergence of Bronze-Age elites, '"protectors" established and consolidated their power over the capital-intensive food producers under them' (p. 8). He (ibid.) concludes with the fruitful suggestion that: 'A focus on exploitation, rather than management, as the central "function" of the ruling class constitutes a more uniformitarian view of social process in stratified societies.' This suggestion is in full harmony with the linguistic and palaeoagricultural/archaeological evidence. Utilizing it opens a remarkable possibility for integrating various, otherwise disparate and problematic, modalities of evidence. Fragile subsistence systems might well have welcomed protectionism, however elitist. A culturally homogeneous, hierarchically attuned group would have been the most likely candidate for that role. The Dumézilian patterns display the requisite appreciation of hierarchies, including a fluid, open slot for peasants (with a covert promise of later advancement up the class ladder). The discovery of uniform articulations, not just etyma, despite vast distances of time and space, beginning with Adalbert Kuhn's equation in 1853 of *kléos áphthiton* and *śráva(s)* . . . *ákṣitam* in Homeric Greek and Vedic Sanskrit, respectively, and admirably continued today by Calvert Watkins and others, is secure proof of cultural homogeneity, at least in the basics. The archaism, also underscored here, of agrarian tributes (grain taxes/payments/offerings) evidences a pay-off situation on the part of agriculturalists. The need for and desirability of a less populous class of elite protectors in a more fragile or marginal subsistence system and, conversely, a larger number of protectors in less fragile subsistence environments, is obvious. This correlation is matched by the linguistic evidence: the peripheral, more fragile swidden system retrievable for the early Germanic world is also demonstrably less Indo-European-like in its lexicon, see Polomé (forthcoming) and, provocatively, Vennemann (1984), and note such etymologically opaque everyday words as *folk*. A requirement of elite protectors does not call for massive invasions, and they are nowhere evidenced in the properly interpreted archaeological record. The colonization model in its traditional format is superfluous. Language 'tip' is generally in the direction of prestige/elitism: Indo-European survived and expanded, while non-Indo-European is barely recoverable, and then largely from the agrarian sphere alone. The non-Indo-European elements of agrarian vocabulary bespeak regionalism, but also the diffusion of successful regionalisms (e.g. the spread of *plōg*-), presumably at the hands of a more mobile elite rather than a sedentary peasantry. Elitist allowances for a dependent peasantry are firmly evidenced by the theophoric onomastics of Europe. Relationship to the people is clearly shown by Lat. *Quirinus*, segmented as *co-uir-ino-*, thus containing *vir-* 'man' (cf. Umbr. *ueiro*), and its Umbrian analogue, *Vofionus* < *leudhyon-*, which contains the same root as that reflected in Germ. *Leute*. The deities of the cultivators are potentially distinct from those belonging to other social classes. The integrational nature of Indo-European is well known: recall the definite eclecticism of the pantheons of Imperial Rome and Anatolia.

To date, then, the retrievable impact of non-Indo-European on Indo-European in western/Atlantic Europe remains largely lexical, but those lexical fragments are precious, for, when coupled with an assessment of the archaeological record (armed with anthropological insights), they afford a clearer than heretofore perspective of the roots of Western culture. The fabric of a clefted European feudalism with its tradition of *weregild* and deeply embedded gift/exchange processes is apparently far, far older than we ever assumed previously. The *figura etymologica* of *móitmos gho-móinis* > *maiþmaz gamainiz* '(dutifully, communally) given gift/exchange' that is specifically reconstructible for Pre-Germanic may now be given a meaningful socio-economic context, and the enactment of this *figura*, despite the masking in which it has been wrapped by successive cultural exigencies, is reflected yet today in the Carinthian *Vierbergelauf*.

News, time, and weather were the same for some (e.g. Sl. *vrijeme*, and note the etymological opacity of Lat. *tempus*), but were different for others less immediately concerned with the land and its products.

# References

Adrados, F. R. 1982. *Die räumliche und zeitliche Differenzierung des Indoeuropäischen im Lichte der Vor- und Frühgeschichte.* (Innsbrucker Beiträge, Vorträge u. kleinere Schriften, 27.) Innsbruck: Institut für Sprachwissenschaft.
Bar-Yosef, O. & M. Kislev. This volume. Early farming communities in the Jordan Valley. In *Foraging and farming: the evolution of plant exploitation,* D. R. Harris & G. C. Hillman (eds), ch. 40. London: Unwin Hyman.

Barker, G. 1985. *Prehistoric farming in Europe.* Cambridge: Cambridge University Press.

Benveniste, E. 1935. *Origines de la formation des noms en indo-européen.* Paris: Maisonneuve.

Benveniste, E. 1949. Noms d'animaux en indo-européen. *BSL* **45**, 74–103.

Berger, H. 1956. Mittelmeerische Kulturpflanzen aus dem Burushaski. *Münchener Studien zur Sprachwissenschaft* **9**, 4–34.

Berlin, B. 1971. *Speculations on the growth of ethnobotanical nomenclature.* Working Paper no. 39, Language Behavior Research Library, University of California, Berkeley.

Binchy, D. A. 1966. *Bretha Déin Chécht. Ériu* **20**, 1–66.

Burkill, I. H. 1962 (1951–52). Habits of man and the origins of the cultivated plants of the Old World. In *Readings in cultural geography*, P. L. Wagner & M. W. Mikesell (eds), 248–81. Chicago: The University of Chicago Press.

Case, H. 1969. Neolithic explanations. *Antiquity* **43**, 176–86.

Champion, T., C. Gamble, S. Shennan & A. Whittle 1984. *Prehistoric Europe.* London: Academic Press.

Clark, G. 1952. *Prehistoric Europe – the economic base.* London: Methuen.

Clark, G. 1980. *Mesolithic prelude. The Palaeolithic–Neolithic transition in Old World prehistory.* Edinburgh: Edinburgh University Press.

Clarke, D. (1976), 1978. *Mesolithic Europe: the economic basis.* London: Duckworth.

Clutton-Brock, J. 1981. *Domesticated animals from early times.* London: Heinemann & British Museum (Natural History).

Drower, M. S. 1969. The domestication of the horse. *The domestication and exploitation of plants and animals*, P. J. Ucko & G. W. Dimbleby (eds), 471–8. London: Duckworth.

Duridanov, I. 1969. *Thrakisch-Dakische Studien. 1. Die thrakisch- und dakisch-baltischen Sprachbeziehungen.* (Linguistique balkanique, 13.2.). Sofia: Bulgarian Academy of Sciences.

Duridanov, I. 1976. *Exikut na trakite.* Sofia: Bulgarian Academy of Sciences.

Ecsedy, J. 1979. *The people of the pit-grave Kurgans in eastern Hungary.* Budapest: Akadémiai Kiadó.

Ernout, A. & A. Meillet 1967. *Dictionnaire étymologique de la langue latine. Histoire des mots*, 4th edn. Paris: Klincsieck.

Georgiev, V. I. 1977. *Trakite i texnijat ezik.* Sofia: Bulgarian Academy of Sciences.

Georgiev, V. I. 1981. *Introduction to the history of the Indo-European languages*, 3rd edn. Sofia: Bulgarian Academy of Sciences.

Gilman, A. 1981. The development of social stratification in Bronze Age Europe. *Current Anthropology* **22**, 1–23.

Gimbutas, M. 1956. *The prehistory of Eastern Europe.* Harvard University Bulletin, no. 20. Cambridge, Mass.: American School of Prehistoric Research, Peabody Museum.

Gimbutas, M. 1965. *Bronze Age cultures in central and eastern Europe.* The Hague: Mouton.

Gimbutas, M. 1982. Old Europe in the fifth millennium B.C.: the European situation on the arrival of Indo-Europeans. In *The Indo-Europeans in the fourth and third millennia*, E. C. Polomé (ed.), 1–60. Ann Arbor: Karoma Publishers.

Hamp, E. P. 1975. 'cut' and 'meat' in Germanic. *Acta Philologica Scandinavica* **30**, 49–51.

Hamp, E. P. 1976. On some Gaulish names in *-ant-* and Celtic verbal nouns. *Ériu* **27**, 1–20.

Hamp, E. P. 1979. The North European word for 'apple'. *Zeitschrift für celtische Philologie* **37**, 158–66.

Hamp, E. P. 1980. Germanic *blood/Blut*. *Folia Linguistica Historica* **1**, 389–92.

Hamp, E. P. 1982–83. Indo-European substantives in *-mó-* and *-mã̊-. *KZ* **96**, 171–7.

Hamp, E. P. 1983. Three pseudo-problems. *IF* **88**, 93–5.

Hamp, E. P. 1985. *Culhwch*, the Swine. *Zeitschrift für celtische Philologie* **41**, 257–8.

Hamp, E. P. 1986. German *Baum*, English *beam*. In *Linguistics across historical and geographical boundaries*. Vol. I: *Linguistic theory and historical linguistics*. D. Kastowsky & A. Szwedek (eds), 344–6. Berlin: Mouton de Gruyter.

Hamp, E. P. in press. *magu-/mak^w-*. *Filipović Festschrift*.

Harlan, J. R. 1972. Crops that extend the range of agricultural settlement. In *Man, settlement and urbanism*, P. J. Ucko, R. Tringham & G. W. Dimbleby (eds), 239–43. London: Duckworth.

Harlan, J. R. 1979. On the origin of barley. In *Barley: origin, botany, culture, winter hardiness, genetics, utilization, pests*, 10–36. Agriculture Handbook no. 338, Science and Education Administration, United States Department of Agriculture, Washington, DC.

Harris, D. R. 1972. Swidden systems and settlement. In *Man, settlement and urbanism*, P. J. Ucko, R. Tringham & G. W. Dimbleby (eds), 252–62. London: Duckworth.

Harris, D. R. 1989. An evolutionary continuum of people–plant interaction. In *Foraging and farming: the evolution of plant exploitation*, D. R. Harris & G. C. Hillman (eds), ch. 1. London: Unwin Hyman.

Haudry, J. 1981. *Les indo-européens*. Que sais-je? no. 1965. Paris: Presses Universitaires de France.

Häusler, A. 1981. Zur Frage der Beziehungen zwischen dem nordpontischen Raum und den neolithischen Kulturen Mitteleuropas. *Jahresschrift für mitteldeutsche Vorgeschichte* **64**, 229–36.

Hillman, G. C. 1978. On the origins of domestic rye – *Secale cereale*. *Anatolian Studies* **28**, 157–74.

Hoops, J. 1905. *Waldbäume und Kulturpflanzen im germanischen Altertum*. Strassburg: Karl J. Trübner.

Hyams, E. 1971. *Plants in the service of man*. Philadelphia: J. B. Lippincott.

Jackson, K. H. 1964. *The oldest Irish tradition: a window on the Iron Age*. Cambridge: Cambridge University Press.

Johnstone, P. 1972. Bronze Age sea trial. *Antiquity* **46**, 269–74.

Markey, T. L. 1972. The place-name element *-hurst* (*-horst*). *Naamkunde* **4**, 26–35.

Markey, T. L. 1978. Nordic *tveit/-tved-* names and settlement history. *Onoma (Kongressberichte Bern, 1975)* **22**, 47–83.

Markey, T. L. 1984a. IE 'beard' and related matters. *Linguistique balkanique* **27**, 71–3.

Markey, T. L. 1984b. IE *-w->Gmc. -g-* and OFr. *si(u)gun* '7' and *ni(u)gun* '9'. In *Miscellanea Frisica*, N. R. Århammar, *et al.* (eds), 67–77. Assen: Van Gorcum.

Markey, T. L. 1986. Social spheres and national groups in Germania. In *Der Germanenbegriff in heutiger Sicht*, H. Beck (ed.), 248–66. Berlin: Mouton de Gruyter.

Markey, T. L. in press a. Eurasian 'apple' as arboreal unit and item of culture. In *Festschrift for Edgar C. Polomé*, M. A. Jazayery & W. Winter (eds). Berlin: Mouton de Gruyter.

Markey, T. L. in press b. The lexical semantics of western Indo-European 'girl'. In *Festschrift for Mario Alinei*. Vol. 2: *Lexical semantics and related disciplines*.

Megaw, J. V. S. 1985. Meditations on a Celtic hobby-horse: notes toward a social archaeology of Iron Age art. In *Settlement and society. Aspects of West European prehistory in the first millennium B.C.*, T. C. Champion & J. V. S. Megaw (eds), 161–91. Leicester: Leicester University Press.

Piggott, S. 1968. The earliest wheeled vehicles and the Caucasian evidence. *Proceedings of the Prehistoric Society* **34**, 266–318.

Pokorny, J. 1928. Miszellen. *Zeitschrift für celtische Philologie* **17**, (*Festschrift Thürneysen*) 304–6.

Pokorny, J. 1959. *Indogermanisches Etymologisches Wörterbuch*. Bern: Francke Verlag.

Polomé, E. C. in press. The non-Indo-European component of the Germanic lexicon. *Festschrift Ernst Risch*.

Renfrew, J. M. 1969. The archaeological evidence for the domestication of plants: methods and problems. In *The domestication and exploitation of plants and animals*, P. J. Ucko & G. W. Dimbleby (eds), 149–72. London: Duckworth.

Renfrew, J. M. 1973. *Palaeoethnobotany. The prehistoric food plants of the Near East and Europe*. London: Methuen.

Risch, E. 1970. Die Räter als sprachliches Problem. *Jahrbuch der Schweizerischen Gesellschaft für Ur- und Frühgeschichte* **55**, 127–34.

Sauer, C. O. 1952. *Agricultural origins and dispersals*. New York: American Geographical Society.

Schery, R. W. 1952. *Plants for man* Englewood Cliffs, NJ: Prentice-Hall.

Schindler, J. 1975. l'Apophonie des thèmes indo-européennes en -*r/n-*. *BSL* **70**, 1–20.

Schlerath, B. 1973. *Die Indogermanen. Das Problem der Expansion eines Volkes im Lichte seiner sozialen Struktur*. Innsbrucker Beiträge, Vorträge u. kleinere Schriften, 8, Institut für Sprachwissenschaft, Innsbruck.

Simmonds, N. W. (ed.) 1976. *Evolution of crop plants*. London: Longman.

Tovar, A. 1982. *Die Indoeuropäisierung Westeuropas*. Innsbrucker Beiträge, Vorträge u. kleinere Schriften, 28, Institut für Sprachwissenschaft, Innsbruck.

Trier, J. 1945. Pflug. *PBB* **67**, 110–50.

Vennemann, T. 1984. Bemerkung zum frühgermanischen Wortschatz. In *Studia Linguistica et Philologica. Festschrift für Klaus Matzel*, H.-W. Eroms, B. Gajek & H. Kolb (eds), 105–19. Heidelberg: Carl Winter Universitäts Verlag.

Watkins, C. 1962. *Indo-European origins of the Celtic verb. I. The sigmatic aorist*. Dublin: Institute for Advanced Studies.

Zohary, D. 1989. Domestication of the Southwest Asian Neolithic crop assemblage of cereals, pulses, and flax: the evidence from the living plants. In *Foraging and farming: the evolution of plant exploitation*, D. R. Harris & G. C. Hillman (eds), ch. 22. London: Unwin Hyman.

# 38 *Agricultural evolution north of the Black Sea from the Neolithic to the Iron Age*

## ZOYA V. YANUSHEVICH

(translated from the Russian by Katharine Judelson)[*]

The data presented here concern plant remains recovered from sites in the steppe and forest-steppe of Moldavia, the Ukraine, and the Crimea (Fig. 38.1). The plant remains discussed survived in charred form and as impressions in pottery and the mud daub of dwellings.

## The Neolithic

The earliest traces of cultivation throughout this region are linked with the Neolithic phase of the Bug-Dniester Culture which appeared in the extreme southwest of the area during the 6th millennium bc (Markevich 1974). In the same territory are found sites of later cultivators of the Linearbandkeramik Culture which dates from the later 5th millennium bc (Passek & Chernysh 1963) and which extended across much of central and western Europe. Initially, it appears that both of these cultures used only cut wild grasses when tempering pottery or adobe. Later, however, we find impressions of cultivated cereals and occasionally also legumes and the stones of soft fruits. The species identified in remains from this period are listed in Tables 38.1 and 38.2.

### (a) Bug-Dniester Culture (Early Neolithic)

The most commonly represented plant imprints found in adobe from the Bug-Dniester Culture are three glume wheats: einkorn, emmer, and spelt. At the site of Sakharovka I, two of these wheats were also accompanied by naked barley (*Hordeum vulgare* var. *coeleste*), the pea, and a range of fruits (Table 38.1). The chaff imprints in clay from this site included the diagnostic spikelet forks of glume wheats which were present in sufficient quantities to allow quantitative analyses to be undertaken. These analyses suggest that

[*]Modern Languages Department, Totton Sixth Form College, Hampshire.

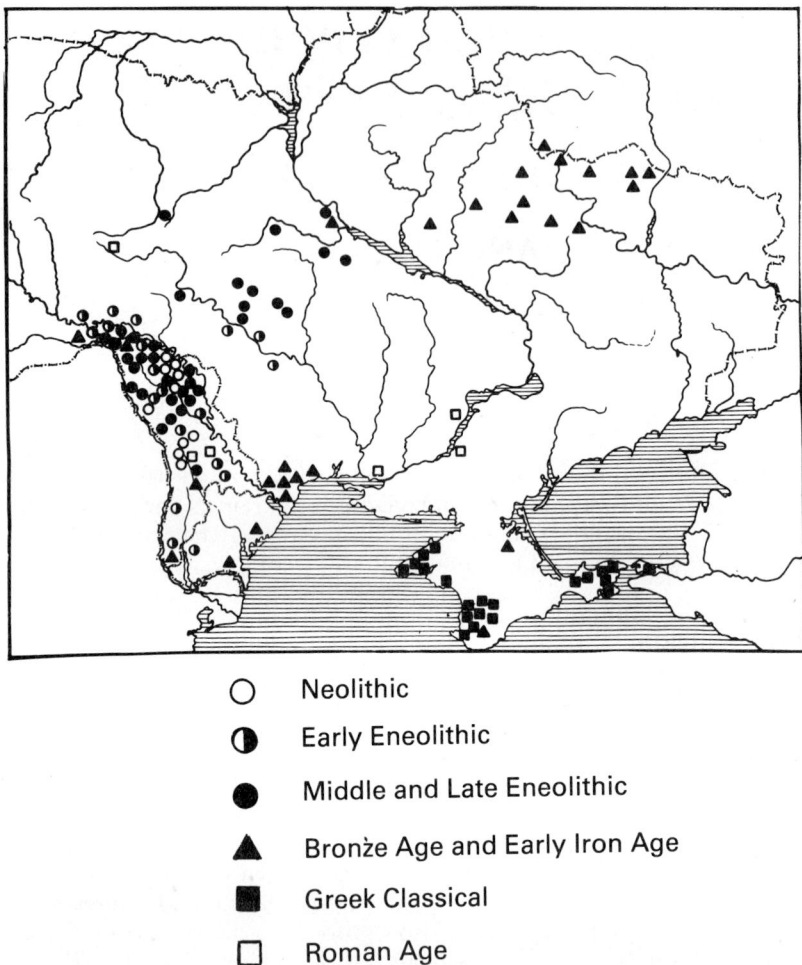

| ○ | Neolithic |
| ◑ | Early Eneolithic |
| ● | Middle and Late Eneolithic |
| ▲ | Bronze Age and Early Iron Age |
| ■ | Greek Classical |
| □ | Roman Age |

**Figure 38.1**   Map of regions north of the Black Sea, showing sites from which plant remains have been identified in significant quantities.

emmer wheat (*Triticum dicoccum*) was perhaps the most widely sown of the crop plants during this period.

Fruit foods are also represented, but for them it is difficult to draw a clear line dividing cultivation from gathering. *Prunus spinosa*, the sloe, would have been found growing in the local woods, whereas *Prunus cerasifera* (syn. *P. divaricata*), the cherry plum, must have been brought in at an early stage from Asia Minor, perhaps as a cultigen. *Prunus insititia*, the bullace, is a spontaneous hybrid of these two species. It might originally have grown spontaneously in surrounding woods and have been gathered from the wild,

**Table 38.1**  Imprints of food plants in sherds from Neolithic sites of the Bug-Dniester Culture.

| Sites (with dates bc) | Triticum monococcum | T. dicoccum | T. spelta | Hordem vulgare | H. vulgare var. coeleste | Avena sp. | Panicum sp. | Pisum sp. | Prunus insititia | Prunus spinosa | Malus sp. | Cornus mas |
|---|---|---|---|---|---|---|---|---|---|---|---|---|
| Soroki II (4880 ± 150 bc) | × | × | — | — | — | — | — | — | — | — | — | × |
| Soroki III (4800 ± 100 bc) | × | × | × | — | — | — | — | — | — | — | — | × |
| Soroki V (4545 ± 100 bc) | × | × | × | — | — | — | — | — | — | — | — | — |
| Ruptura (4880 ± 100 bc) | × | × | × | — | — | — | ×? | — | — | — | — | ×× |
| Sakharovka I (4700 ± 50 bc) | — | ××× | × | ×? | ××× | × | — | × | × | × | × | × |

××× = abundant; ×× = frequent to occasional; × = rare; ×? = doubtful.

**Table 38.2** Identifications of food plants from Linearbandkeramik settlements of the Dniester-Prut region. (The first of each pair of figures represents the number of sherd fragments bearing imprints; the second figure represents the total number of imprints.)

| Sites (all 5th millennium bc) | Number of sherd fragments | Triticum monococcum | T. dicoccum | T. spelta | T. aestivo-compactum | Triticum sp. | Hordeum vulgare | H. vulgare var. coeleste | Hordeum sp. | Panicum miliaceum | Pisum sp. | Lathyrus sp. | Prunus cerasifera | Cornus mas | Cannabis sativa |
|---|---|---|---|---|---|---|---|---|---|---|---|---|---|---|---|
| Dantcheny I | 643 | 22/58 | 17/43 | 1/1 | 8/9 | 23/45 | 5/5 | — | 1/1 | 44/59 | 12/13 | 2/2 | 1/1 | 1/1 | 6/9 |
| Floreshty I, V | 15 | 4/4 | — | — | — | 2/2 | — | — | — | — | — | — | 1/1 | — | — |
| Novy Ruseshty I, II | 30 | 2/5 | 4/5 | 2/2 | — | — | — | — | — | — | — | — | — | — | — |
| Braneshty I | 13 | — | 2/4 | 2/4 | — | — | — | — | — | 1/1 | — | — | — | — | — |
| Gura-Kamenka | 12 | — | 2/2 | — | — | — | — | — | — | — | — | — | — | — | — |

but it could also have been cultivated around dwellings as, indeed, could *Prunus cerasifera*.

## (b) Linearbandkeramik Culture of the Dniester-Prut region (Middle Neolithic)

The range of species of cultivated plants found in remains from the ensuing Linearbandkeramik Culture so far appears to be somewhat different. As before, they include cultivated glume wheats with, in contrast to Sakharovka, einkorn wheat, (*Triticum monococcum*) apparently playing a prominent role. Dwarf bread wheat (*Triticum aestivo-compactum*) also appears early. Traces of barley are insignificant and naked barley is entirely absent. Common millet (*Panicum mileaceum*) was found in large quantities, preserved not only as grain but also as chaff winnowed free of the grain and used as temper. For the first time in Neolithic remains there are imprints not only of peas (*Pisum sativum*) but also of a vetchling (*Lathyrus* sp.) and of the seeds of hemp (*Cannabis sativa*), a plant of supposedly central Asian or even Chinese origin. Occasional stones (endocarps) of cherry plum and cornel (*Cornus mas*) were also found.

## The Eneolithic

The range of species of cultivated plants identified from Eneolithic settlements is listed in Table 38.3. Most of the source sites belong to the Tripolye Culture. They are situated between the Prut and Dnieper rivers, but the greatest concentration is in Moldavia, between the Prut and Dniester rivers (Fig. 38.1). In all settlements and all phases (early, middle, and late Eneolithic) glume wheats and naked barley appear to have predominated. Among the glume wheats, emmer was apparently pre-eminent, with naked (free threshing) wheat and oats (*Avena* spp.) as minor admixtures. Two types of leguminous plant are clearly distinguishable, namely bitter vetch (*Vicia ervilia*) and peas. Charred cherry plum, apricot, and primitive plum stones have also been found, and in two instances so have imprints of seeds from grape vines of a cultivated type (*Vitis vinifera*). In the case of the people of the Tripolye Culture therefore, it appears that food production included the cultivation of fruit plants. However, regular finds of cornel and wild cherry stones, acorns, and apple and pear seeds, testify to the continuation of foraging for wild fruits in the local woods. No traces of rye (*Secale cereale*) have yet been found in remains from Eneolithic settlements, and millet has been identified only rarely and never in bulk caches. In the settlement of the ensuing Gumelnitsa Culture the range of species of cultivated plants is similar to that of the Tripolye Culture.

**Table 38.3** Charred remains and imprints of food plants from Eneolithic and Bronze-Age settlements of Moldavia and the Ukraine.

| Epoch, culture, and date bc | Number of sites | Triticum monococcum | T. dicoccum | T. spelta | T. aestivo-compactum | Hordeum vulgare | H. vulgare var. coeleste | Panicum miliaceum | Avena sp. | Secale sp. | Pisum sp. | Vicia ervilia | Lens culinaris | Lathyrus sp. | Prunus cerasifera | Prunus institita | Armeniaca vulgaris | Vitis sp. | Cornus mas | Cerasus sp. |
|---|---|---|---|---|---|---|---|---|---|---|---|---|---|---|---|---|---|---|---|---|
| **Eneolithic** | | | | | | | | | | | | | | | | | | | | |
| Early Tripolye (3850–3645 bc) | 17 | XXX | XXXX | XX | X | X | XXX | X | X | — | X | XXX | — | X? | XXXX | XX | X | — | X | X? |
| Middle Tripolye (3520 ± 100 bc) | 26 | X | XXXX | X | X | X | XXXX | X | — | — | X | XX | X? | X? | — | — | — | X | X | — |
| Late Tripolye | 8 | XXXX | XXXX | XX | X | X | XXXX | XX | X | — | XX | — | X? | X? | XX | X | — | X | XXX | X |
| Gumelnitsa | 2 | X | XXX | X | — | X | XXXX | X | X | — | — | — | — | — | — | — | — | — | — | — |
| **Bronze Age** | | | | | | | | | | | | | | | | | | | | |
| End of the 3rd millennium | 15 | XXX | XXX | XX | XX | XXX | X | XXX | X | X | — | — | — | — | — | — | — | X | X | — |

XXX = abundant; XX = frequent to occasional; X = rare; X? = doubtful.

## Bronze Age

In the Bronze Age, hulled glume wheats continue to predominate, but they are now accompanied by increased percentages of the dwarf form of naked bread wheat (*Triticum aestivo-compactum*). At the same time, naked barley is replaced by a hulled form, and finds of millet become much more common, primarily as masses of imprints on the bottom surfaces of pots. We also now encounter admixtures of rye grains among the wheat and barley. Traces of fruit plants include seeds from the wild forest vine (*Vitis sylvestris*) which would probably have grown in abundance in valley-bottom forest in these areas to the north of the Black Sea.

The dramatic increase in the abundance of millet in the Bronze Age may indicate changes in tillage techniques. Certainly its sensitivity to weed infestation is well known, as is the fact that it produces the best yields when it is sown on virgin land.

## Iron Age

In this period, Scythian sites on the banks of the Dnieper, and in the basin of its western tributary the Vorskla (Fig. 38.1), especially deserve attention. In the agrarian settlements we find a preponderance of emmer wheat and hulled barley, with an admixture of a special form of barley which was separated by Bakhteyev (1956) as an independent species: *Hordeum lagunculiforme*. Millet still occupies a significant place among the crops, but for the first time we find pure caches of rye (e.g. at the site of Malaya Rublyovka) indicating its cultivation as a crop in its own right. Peas are the only leguminous crop found so far, and at the city site of Trachtemirov traces of hemp have also been identified. Einkorn wheat and spelt (*Triticum spelta*) admixtures are found among the emmer-wheat harvests, but significant quantities of naked wheat have yet to be identified. All these cultigens were apparently supplemented by wild fruits gathered in the local woods (Table 38.4).

## Summary of records for the steppe and wooded-steppe zones

From the Neolithic through to the Scythian period, crops grown in the steppe and wooded steppe were apparently dominated by emmer wheat. However, some caution is needed here because the processing of hulled wheats such as emmer makes it likely that they are over-represented in charred remains relative to barley and naked wheats. There is little, if any, evidence of mixed sowing, judging by the pure caches of charred grain which testify to the frequency of sowing individual species as relatively pure crops and not as mixtures.

Earlier this century the agricultural botanist Vavilov proposed that the whole of the ancient southwest of the USSR would have provided an ideal

**Table 38.4** Charred remains and imprints of food plants from Bronze-Age and Early Iron-Age settlements of the forest-steppe region of the Ukraine.

| Epoch, culture, and date bc | Number of sites | Triticum monococcum | T. dicoccum | T. spelta | T. aestivo-compactum | Hordeum vulgare | H. vulgare var. coeleste | H. lagunculiforme | Panicum miliaceum | Panicum italicum | Secale cereale | Pisum sp. | Cannabis sativa | Vicia sp. | Prunus/Cerasus sp. | Malus/Pyrus sp. | Quercus sp. |
|---|---|---|---|---|---|---|---|---|---|---|---|---|---|---|---|---|---|
| Bronze Age Srubnaja (1500–900) | 4 | — | × | — | — | × | — | — | ×× | — | — | — | — | — | — | — | — |
| Late Bronze Age to Early Iron Age Bondarichinskaja, XII–VII | 6 | — | × | — | × | ××× | — | — | ××× | — | — | × | — | — | — | — | — |
| Iron Age Scythian, VII–III | 10 | × | ××× | × | × | ××× | × | × | ××× | — | ×× | ×× | — | × | × | × | × |
| Scythian, VI, Trachtemirov | 1 | — | × | — | × | × | × | — | ××× | × | — | × | × | — | — | — | — |

××× = abundant; ×× = frequent to occasional; × = rare.

unbroken habitat for the cultivation of emmer wheat. Present archaeobotanical evidence reinforces his proposition. The predominance of emmer in the lands north of the Black Sea has also been shown to have characterized the ensuing Hellenistic, Roman, and early medieval periods. Only in the later medieval period was it finally replaced by naked wheat, in this case the dwarf form of bread wheat. This presents a marked contrast to the crop chronologies of central and western Europe where emmer largely disappeared by Roman times or shortly thereafter.

## The Crimea

The Crimean territories present an exception. Material from 20 sites so far investigated, which date from the 10th to the 2nd millennia bc, has shown that the range of species of cultivated plants was quite different from that described above (Table 38.5). By the Bronze and Early Iron Ages naked wheat is already widespread in the remains recovered from agrarian sites. Particularly abundant are finds of small round grains which we have identified as dwarf bread wheat. The small settlements concerned were astonishingly uniform archaeobotanically, and at all sites rye was consistently found mixed with the caches of bread wheat grain. This pattern of rye infestation of naked wheats accords with the present-day ecology of weed ryes as observed in areas such as Anatolia on the opposite shore of the Black Sea (Hillman 1978).

In the coastal area of the northwestern Crimea at two settlements dating from the 4th century bc, the amount of rye among the wheat finds suddenly increases to as much as 80 per cent. This phenomenon may possibly indicate a switch to the winter sowing of naked wheats, if this was not already standard practice. Rye is more resistant to cold than most varieties of wheat and would therefore have better tolerated the cold winters. Once transferred from warmer areas, therefore, the weed rye would in any case have gradually ousted the main crop. This accords with the suggested pattern of emergence of rye as a crop in its own right, as first proposed by Vavilov (1967).

Barley (*Hordeum sativum* agg.) in the Crimean sites is represented primarily by hulled varieties which are morphologically similar in all settlements. However, among the barley grains is a constant admixture of the archaic form separated by Bachteyev (1956) as *Hordeum lagunculiforme*). A similar admixture is also encountered in the Scythian settlements on the east bank of the Dnieper.

Legumious plants are represented in the Crimea by a range of species: peas, chick peas (*Cicer arietinum*), lentils (*Lens culinaris*), vetch (*Vicia sativa*), and bitter vetch (*V. ervilia*). At most sites it is the latter which predominates. A particularly large quantity of bitter vetch was found during excavations of ancient farmsteads in the area immediately adjacent to Chersoneos, dating from the 4th century bc (Nikolayenko 1980). Finds of charred seeds of vetch and of grape seeds have so far always been found to coincide. This has led us

**Table 38.5** Charred remains and imprints of food plants from Late Bronze-Age and Early Iron-Age settlements of the Crimea.

| Epoch, culture, and date | Number of settlements N | Triticum monococcum | T. dicoccum | T. spelta | T. durum | T. aestivo-compactum | Hordeum vulgare | H. vulgare var. coeleste | H. lagunculiforme | Secale sp. | Panicum miliaceum | Vicia ervilia | Pisum sp. | Cicer arietinum | Lens culinaris | Lathyrus sp. | Vitis sp. | Juglans regia | Purus/Malus sp. |
|---|---|---|---|---|---|---|---|---|---|---|---|---|---|---|---|---|---|---|---|
| **Bronze Age** | | | | | | | | | | | | | | | | | | | |
| Bolotnoye (11th millennium bc) | 1 | ××× | ××× | — | — | — | — | — | — | — | — | — | — | — | — | — | — | — | — |
| Uch-Bash (10th–9th century BC) | 1 | × | × | × | ××× | ××× | ××× | × | × | — | — | — | × | — | — | — | × | — | — |
| **Iron Age** | | | | | | | | | | | | | | | | | | | |
| Greek Classical (4th–2nd century BC) | 8 | × | × | × | × | ××× | ××× | × | × | ××× | × | ××× | × | × | × | × | ××× | — | — |
| Scythian (3rd century BC to 3rd century AD) | 10 | × | × | × | ×× | ××× | ××× | × | × | ××× | ××× | × | × | — | × | — | ××× | × | × |

××× = abundant; ×× = frequent to occasional; × = rare.

to suggest provisionally that the vetch was sown between the rows of vines in order to enrich the stony soils of that area, and, in addition, to provide seed-based fodder for draught animals. Certainly, there is mention of such a practice in the writings of Pliny the Elder (*Historia Naturalis* XVIII).

There have been numerous finds of grape seeds in the Crimea dating from the Classical period, and they are uniform in their morphology throughout the Chersonesos area. A characteristic feature of these seeds is their small size, close to that of the seeds of the wild Crimean forest grapes. Despite their small size, however, each assemblage includes a small quantity of seeds of a cultivated type. There are no clear dividing lines between the wild and cultivated seeds, but a range of transitional forms has been observed and it is these which predominate. Such a pattern suggests that the selection of strains for cultivation involved the use of primitive local clones, a practice which has already been suggested for Greek settlements in this same Crimean area.

## General conclusions

The data summarized here suggest that within the region to the north of the Black Sea crop assemblages developed differently, area by area, despite the fact that the crops appear to have originated from a common source, namely Anatolia. The mosaic reflects not only the pattern of relationships between the different cultural groups, but, more importantly, differences in local edaphic, biotic, and climatic conditions, and the economic constraints which these differences engendered.

The finds also indicate that, within this broad area, domesticated crops and their cultivation appeared first in the extreme southwest of the USSR and, therefore, that they arrived via the Balkans rather than via the Caucasus or around the northern end of the Caspian Sea. This is borne out by the uniformity in the species found in both areas, and also by the chronology of their earliest records, first in the Neolithic settlements of Bulgaria and thereafter in the territory between the Dniester and Prut rivers (Yanushevich 1983).

As described above, the first major cereal crops to become established north of the Black Sea appear to have been glume wheats and naked barley. The long period during which glume wheats, especially emmer, continued to be grown in almost all parts of the region, particularly in the grassy and wooded steppes, can perhaps be explained by emmer's edaphic and climatic preferences. Wheats such as emmer are well known for their hardiness in drought conditions, and, as in the Balkans, their cultivation would not have required irrigation even though the climate was fairly dry. They would also have offered the advantage of being able to grow on a wide range of soil types and of being relatively resistant to lodging and disease. Although yields are not high, they are consistent. Above all, the grain is protected from bird damage by the tough glumes (hulls). This last feature would have been particularly important in the early phases of agricultural spread when there were still relatively few fields in an otherwise uncultivated landscape and when the crops were therefore particularly vulnerable to predation by non-territorial birds such as sparrows. The grain of glume wheats has a protein content which is somewhat higher than most naked wheats, and it also has a pleasant taste, a fact that would not have gone unnoticed by the cultivators of ancient times.

Naked barleys were attractive because the grains were easy to process and also because they are agronomically undemanding. Like the glume wheats, they were clearly a food crop for humans and not intended for animal feed. The relative uniformity of the barley populations in terms of grain morphology shows that most of the major stages of selection were completed during the earliest phases of agricultural evolution, presumably south of the Black Sea in the ancient Near East.

The areas to the east of the Black Sea have a damper climate than the territory to the west, and here naked wheats – both bread wheat (*Triticum aestivum*) and its dwarf form (*T. aestivo-compactum*) – appear to have been the two most widespread crops. These bread wheats are generally less resistant to drought than the hulled wheats. The earliest finds of ordinary bread wheat and dwarf wheat in Transcaucasia to the southeast have been dated to the 6th millennium bc (Yanushevich & Rusishvili 1984).

From Hellenistic and Roman deposits at sites in the northern Caucasus it has also been found that samples of naked wheat (both bread and dwarf) are invariably infested to varying degrees with seeds of segetal rye (Flyaksberger 1940, Gaydukevich 1949). Despite the early establishment of agriculture in the Caucasus, cultivated plants appear to have reached the territories to the north of the Black Sea far later via the Caucasian route than they did via the Balkan peninsula. According to existing archaeological data, agriculture reached the territories of the Crimea at the end of the Bronze Age or the beginning of the Iron Age. Despite the drier climate of the Crimea in comparison with Transcaucasia, crops of naked bread and dwarf wheats became universally established soon after their introduction. This replacement of the glume wheats by naked bread wheats appears to have been stimulated primarily by demands for export. Certainly, the export of small, round-grained wheat (i.e. *Triticum aestivo-compactum*) from the Euxine (Pontus) coast is mentioned by Theophrastus and Pliny the Elder.

In the Crimean steppes unconscious, or perhaps conscious, selection produced varieties of naked wheat which were well adapted to local conditions. Thereafter, these same advanced forms of wheat began to spread to areas farther to the north of the Black Sea so that, by the end of the 1st century AD, they had reached the Golden Cape (Zolotoi Mys) settlement in the estuary of the River Dnieper and a number of other settlements along its banks (Pashkevich 1984).

It should finally be noted that many finds of the remains of cultivated plants, both from early (Neolithic, Eneolithic) and from later periods (Bronze and Early Iron Ages), were represented by material consisting of only one species, which bears witness to the practice of sowing unmixed crops. Emmer, bread wheat and dwarf wheat, naked and hulled barleys, bitter vetch, peas, vines, and plums were all exposed to selective pressures arising from local conditions and this process would inevitably have produced well-adapted local varieties.

Within each area we also find a remarkable measure of continuity. This is presumably the product of traditional agrarian techniques having been applied consistently over successive generations, as opposed to a constant striving for alternatives to established and well-proven practice. It must be stressed that this agrarian conservatism will inevitably have applied not only to the crop varieties selected for sowing, but also to the methods applied in their husbandry and processing. Whatever the mechanism of agricultural spread, it is unlikely to have resulted in new crops being disseminated separately from the knowledge necessary for their cultivation.

# References

Bakhteyev, F. Kh. 1956. Barley cultivation in the USSR [in Russian]. In *Materialy po istorii zemledeliya SSSR*, Vol. 2, 204–57. Moscow & Leningrad: USSR Academy of Sciences.

Flyaksberger, K. A. 1940. Archaeological finds of bread-grain plants in areas adjoining the Black Sea [in Russian]. *Kratkiye soovshcheniya Instituta istorii material-noy kultury* **8**, 117–20.

Gaydukevich, B. F. 1949. The kingdom of Bosphor [in Russian], 95–6. Moscow & Leningrad: USSR Academy of Sciencies.

Hillman, G. C. 1978. On the origins of domestic rye *Secale cereale* Linn.: the finds from aceramic Can Hasan III in Turkey. *Anatolian Studies* **28**, 157–74.

Markevich, V. I. 1974. The Bug-Dniester culture in Moldavia [in Russian]. Kishinev: Shtiintsa.

Nikolayenko, G. M. 1980. The agrarian system of Hellenistic Chersonesos [in Russian]. In *Problemy antichnoy istorii i klassicheskoy filologii*, 125–7. Kharkov: Kharkov University.

Pashkevich, G. A. 1984. Palaeothenobotanical examination of archaeological sites in the Lower Dnieper region, dated to the last centuries BC and the first centuries AD. In *Plants and ancient man: studies in palaeoethnobotany*, W. van Zeist & W. C. Casparie (eds), 277–83. Rotterdam: Balkema.

Passek, T. S. & Ye. K. Chernysh 1963. Relics of linear bandceramics in the USSR [in Russian]. In *Svod arkheologicheshkikh istochnikov*, Series B, Vol. 2, 1–70. Moscow: USSR Academy of Sciences.

Pliny. *Historia Naturalis* XVIII. (In the Russian translation: *Yestestvennaya istoriya*, Chapter as published in the journal *Vestnik drevney istorii* **2**, 271–317).

Vavilov, N. I. 1967 (posthumous). Centres of origin of cultivated plants [in Russian]. In *Izbrannyye proizvedeniya v dvukh tomakh* (Leningrad) **1**, 88–202.

Yanushevich, Z. V. 1983. Finds of cultivated plants in late Neolithic layers in Ovcharovo [in Russian]. In *Razkopki i Prouchvaniya*, Vol. 9, Kh. Todorova & V. Vasilev (eds), 1–127. Sofia: Bulgarian Academy of Sciences.

Yanushevich, Z. V. & N. Sh. Rusishvili 1984. New palaeoethnobotanical finds at the Eneolithic site of Arukhlo 1 [in Russian]. In *Chelovek i okruzhayushchaya yego sreda*, Vol. 9, 21–33. Tbilisi: Metsniyereba.

# 39   *The transition from foraging to farming in Southwest Asia: present problems and future directions*

A. M. T. MOORE

## Significance of the development of agriculture

The purpose of this chapter is to review the development of a farming way of life in Southwest Asia from an archaeological perspective. I shall indicate why our current thinking concerning the genesis of this mode of existence remains so superficial and point out some of the deficiencies in our knowledge that hinder deeper understanding of the question. I shall go on to suggest several approaches that might usefully be followed in future research.

The Southwest Asian version of an agricultural economy was based first on the domestication of wheat, barley, pulses, and caprines, with cattle and swine seemingly added later on. These domesticates remain basic to many agricultural systems today and their continued development is a central concern of present-day agronomists. It seems that in many parts of Southwest Asia agriculture was practised from the beginning by people who lived in permanently inhabited villages. The adoption of farming was accompanied by the emergence of more complex patterns of social organization, population growth, and an array of cultural innovations, among them new forms of settlements, types of dwellings, and crafts. The development of agriculture and sedentary life were also essential prerequisites for the formation of civilized societies in Southwest Asia and the Nile valley, while the spread of this way of life to the rest of Africa and Europe made possible remarkable economic and cultural changes in those continents.

These consequences are well known, but the processes of change that gave rise to them are not. It seems most probable that the circumstances that encouraged the initial development of an agricultural way of life were different from those in which the longer-term consequences became manifest. Thus, understanding the dynamics of the world of settled farming villages and subsequent complex societies may provide little insight into the genesis of agriculture precisely because the transformation was so complete.

Archaeologists, botanists, zoologists, and others seek fuller understanding of the processes of agricultural development in Southwest Asia because the consequences are of such significance. Yet we continue to make only slow progress towards achieving this aim. This is in part because few scientists are actively engaged in the necessary field and laboratory research: no more than half a dozen archaeologists, with about the same number of zooarchaeologists and archaeobotanists. There is a sharp contrast here between the generally-accepted significance of the problem – it is taught, after all, in every university introductory course on human cultural development – and the remarkably few people who are seeking new insights in the field. This has become a matter of great concern because archaeological sites in many of the most significant areas are rapidly being destroyed in the huge agricultural and construction projects undertaken by several Southwest Asian countries in the past 20 years.

Archaeologists who seek to elucidate the development of agriculture have, until recently, concentrated on excavating villages that flourished during the 7th and 8th millennia bc, mistakenly believing that it was during this period, the early Neolithic, that the key processes of the adoption of cultivation, domestication, and a shift towards a more sedentary existence occurred. One result of this research has been greatly to increase our understanding of the relationships between agricultural productivity, population growth, modifications in the patterns of settlement, and greater cultural complexity in the early Holocene, after the adoption of food production. A second result has been the realization that fully domesticated cereals and pulses were already being cultivated and caprines herded in some Southwest Asian villages by about 8000 bc, that is at the beginning of the Neolithic (Moore 1982, p. 230). Thus, the agricultural way of life characteristic of the earliest Neolithic developed in the preceding stage, the Epipalaeolithic (c. 18 000–8000 bc), as a result of changes that, in turn, had their roots in the way of life of Upper Palaeolithic groups (c. 35 000–18 000 bc).

The Epipalaeolithic and Upper Palaeolithic have been studied more intensively in the Levant than anywhere else in Southwest Asia in recent years (Cauvin & Sanlaville 1981), but the focus of enquiry has been almost exclusively on the definition of successive cultural patterns rather than questions of adaptation. The Epipalaeolithic–Neolithic transition represents a conceptual divide in the thinking of archaeologists working in the Levant who have failed to recognize that the agricultural way of life typical of the earlier Neolithic developed because of changes in adaptation that had occurred in the stage before. Elsewhere in Southwest Asia, the Epipalaeolithic is so little known that hardly anything useful can be said about the changes in resource use that may have taken place. Traditional archaeological preoccupations have thus prevented broad programmes of research on the question of initial agricultural development and very few recent studies have examined changes in human adaptation across the Pleistocene–Holocene boundary. Garrard's research in the Azraq basin (Jordan) (Garrard et al. 1985) is one of the rare exceptions.

Nonetheless, a considerable amount of data has accumulated in the past decade that pertains to the foraging–farming transition, even if much of it has been obtained with other concerns in mind. This information has made it clear that none of the traditional models adequately explains what actually happened (Moore 1985, p. 48) because they were conceived at too general a level to account for those local factors of environment, resource availability, and culture that strongly affected the changes in economy. The new data partially fill some gaps in our knowledge but also raise issues that require attention if further progress is to be made.

## The environmental background to the development of agriculture

The wild ancestors of domesticated cereals and pulses are found growing today on the fringes of the Fertile Crescent. It is in this relatively restricted geographical zone that botanists think these plants were first domesticated (Harlan & Zohary 1966, Zohary Ch. 22, this volume, Ladizinsky Ch. 23, this volume). The caprines, however, were probably domesticated in one or more locations from Anatolia and the Zagros eastward to Baluchistan (Mason 1984, p. 89, Ryder 1984, p. 66). The agricultural way of life characteristic of Southwest Asian villages of the 7th millennium bc and later developed when these two sets of domesticates were combined in a single farming system (Hole 1984, p. 57). This could only take place after the plants and animals had spread far from their loci of domestication. We need to distinguish between two processes: the domestication of the key plant and animal species in specific loci, and their subsequent rapid dispersal by man over a wide area of Southwest Asia. Domesticated wheat, barley, cattle, and caprines have recently been discovered at Mehrgarh (Pakistan), far to the east of the traditional area of concern, in levels dating to perhaps the 7th millennium bc (Jarrige & Meadow 1980, p. 122, Meadow 1984, p. 327), and fresh information is becoming available about the economy of the 6th millennium bc villages of the Jeitun culture in Turkmenia (Islamov 1981). These data suggest that we still have much to learn about both processes.

Zohary (Ch. 22, this volume) has concluded from the genetic evidence that several cereals and pulses were each probably domesticated once only, or at most a few times. The archaeological evidence suggests that the cultivated forms were adopted by many human groups across Southwest Asia soon after they were domesticated, with far-reaching consequences. This makes it exceedingly important to understand the cultural mechanisms that underlay this massive spread, and the reasons why so many groups adopted the domesticates so readily.

The initial phases of agricultural development took place at the time of the Pleistocene–Holocene transition so we need to ask what was the prevailing environment in each area of interest and how did it condition changing human resource use. The climate, vegetation, and size of lakes were all significantly different late in the Pleistocene and they varied considerably from one region to another (Brice 1978). Our understanding of climatic and vegetational change in Southwest Asia is derived mainly from a series of pollen cores from Lake Huleh (Tsukada, discussed in Bottema & van Zeist 1981, pp. 114–16), the Ghab, Lake Van and other sites in Anatolia, and Lake Zeribar in the Zagros (Bottema & van Zeist 1981). These cores are spaced far apart and there are considerable regional gaps in coverage, most conspicuously in Mesopotamia. What the cores do suggest, however, is that the pleniglacial was cool and dry in much of Southwest Asia but that there was an increase in temperature and humidity, beginning towards the end of the Pleistocene in the Levant and later in Anatolia and the Zagros (Bottema & van Zeist 1981, p. 131). The vegetation zones differed in their composition from region to region and their extent changed markedly as the climate improved.

Most of the plants and animals of importance to early farmers were taken into cultivation and domesticated during this period of environmental change. The distribution of the wild progenitors at *c*. 10 000 bc would have been significantly different from today, and it is these patterns that would have determined where they were first brought under human control. Unfortunately, we cannot yet state what the precise distributions of these wild plants and animals were during the millennia of greatest interest because we do not know what the impact of the climatic and vegetational changes was in a given locality, nor can we date the relevant changes at all precisely. Thus, we cannot yet tie changes in human resource use to detailed local environmental sequences.

## The location of sites

Early Neolithic farming villages flourished in three regions of Southwest Asia, the Levant, Anatolia, and the Mesopotamian borderlands with the Zagros. It is assumed that all three were centres of domestication, but the lack of evidence for an Epipalaeolithic stage on the Anatolian plateau makes it impossible to assess how agriculture developed there.

A number of surveys of Late Pleistocene and early Holocene sites have been carried out in recent years and further information has come from the salvage projects conducted in the Euphrates and Tigris valleys. In the Levant the core forest zone was occupied throughout, while occupation extended eastward and southward into the steppe. Much of Sinai and the Negev was inhabited at intervals from the Upper Palaeolithic through the Neolithic (Marks 1976, Bar-Yosef & Phillips 1977). On the desert fringe, the Azraq basin with its oasis was a centre of occupation in all phases (Garrard & Stanley Price 1975–77) while the Transjordan plateau was occupied from the Epipalaeolithic into the Neolithic (Betts 1983, Henry *et al.* 1983). Likewise, there is evidence that the Palmyra district and the El Kum basin (Syria) were occupied in certain phases of the Epipalaeolithic and Neolithic (Hanihara &

Akazawa 1979, J. Cauvin 1981, M.-C. Cauvin 1981). The salvage project in the Middle Euphrates valley above Tabqa (Syria) has revealed that this stretch of the river was an important focus of occupation in the Epipalaeolithic and earlier Neolithic. Farther up-river, traces of early occupation have been found in the hills between Adiyaman and Urfa (Turkey) but nothing in the valley itself near Samsat. Similarly, no occupation has been found prior to the 7th millennium bc east of Malatya and in the Keban.

The evidence from the Mesopotamian fringes and the Zagros mountains is equivocal. We have long known that the mountains were occupied during the Epipalaeolithic but there is no positive indication that the plains were inhabited then, even though this zone was probably more advantageous during the winter months. It is only with the early Neolithic that sites are found on the lowlands, most notably in Deh Luran (Iran), as well as in the mountains. Recent work in the Eski Mosul area and in the Jebel Hamrin (Iraq) has not altered this distribution pattern. Were the plains really uninhabited at the time of the Pleistocene–Holocene transition, have all the sites disappeared, or have they simply been overlooked? Whatever the answer, it looks as though any occupation would have been intermittent and modest in scale, otherwise sites comparable to those in the Middle Euphrates would have been found.

A reconnaissance in 1984 by Moore and Hole of the Jezireh near Hasseke (Syria), down the Euphrates from Raqqa to Zenobiye, and south of Aleppo to the desert edge, has confirmed that there was remarkably little use of the steppe zone during the periods in question. Traces of late Epipalaeolithic and early Neolithic occupation were found in shelters on the north scarp of the Jebel Abd el Aziz but nothing in the Khabur basin itself. Likewise, no significant traces of settlement were found in the other areas examined. Earlier surveys along the Euphrates north of Lake Assad (Sanlaville 1985) failed to detect either Epipalaeolithic or early Neolithic occupation, in spite of ample evidence for such settlement in the segment from Meskene to Tabqa.

It seems that occupation during the critical phases before and immediately after the adoption of agriculture was confined to the Levant and the Zagros with its western foothills. There appears to have been little penetration of Anatolia and remarkably sparse use of the northern Jezireh eastward to the Zagros. Within the inhabited areas there were certain locations that were highly favoured for settlement, presumably because they offered a particular set of desired resources. These were the Jordan valley, the Damascus basin, and the Middle Euphrates in the west, the Deh Luran plain and certain valleys of the Zagros from Rowanduz to Kermanshah in the east. Present evidence suggests, therefore, that the initial transition to agriculture took place in these few locations, although once certain plants and animals were domesticated, farming spread widely.

Over 500 Epipalaeolithic and Neolithic sites have been found in the Levant, far more than in any other region of Southwest Asia. The changing patterns of size and distribution of sites during these periods have been studied and compared with other sources of evidence in order to document population growth and alterations in society and economy (Moore 1983). The size and density of sites increased in the Epipalaeolithic, beginning about 12 000 bc although more conspicuously after 10 000 bc. This suggests that the population was growing, a trend that coincided with an improvement in the environment in this region. Some groups began to live in villages all the year round and this would have required new forms of social organization. It was during this time of change that the major cereals and pulses were probably first taken into cultivation and – in some cases – domesticated.

The pattern of settlement altered in the first stage of the Neolithic, Neolithic 1, beginning before 8000 bc. The sites were permanently occupied, substantial villages of mudbrick houses located on or beside cultivable land in the mediterranean forest zone and better-watered steppe. From the outset their inhabitants depended on domesticated plants for food. This is confirmed by finds of domesticated cereals and pulses at several sites, and is reflected in their form and situation. The pattern of settlement suggests that the cultivation of plants had spread widely in Southwest Asia and was the basis of the economy almost everywhere, although it appears that wild foods may still have been important. In other words, the Neolithic Revolution had already taken place. The longer-term consequences of this emerged in Neolithic 2, after 7600 bc. Sites increased in size and number while settlement extended far out into the steppe. It appears that the population grew substantially during this stage, a delayed result of the development of agriculture. These changes coincided with the adoption of caprine herding in the Levant.

After 6000 bc, in Neolithic 3, there was a radical shift in settlement as the steppe was seemingly abandoned and new villages were founded in the mediterranean zone. Humans had apparently degraded the steppe, partly through overgrazing and removal of vegetation, and this was exacerbated by the onset of more arid conditions. A decision appears to have been taken to rely entirely on agriculture for food, with the addition now of domesticated cattle and pigs, and to pursue it in the zone with higher rainfall. This was followed by further population growth after 5000 bc in Neolithic 4.

## Interpretations

I have recently reviewed many of the best-known models for the development of agriculture in Southwest Asia (Moore 1985, pp. 43–9) so desire only to make some further observations arising from that discussion. Many of the models that have been proposed so far have been concerned with defining a series of economic and cultural stages that document the transition from foraging to farming (for example Braidwood & Howe 1960, Ch. 10, Hole & Flannery 1967). Those who thought that domestication occurred relatively late, during the earlier Neolithic, were inclined to discount the significance of environmental change for this process (Braidwood & Howe

1960, p. 181, Flannery 1969, p. 75, Cauvin 1977, p.42). It seems, on the evidence outlined above, that cultivation and perhaps domestication began before the inception of the Neolithic as currently defined. However, more is now known about climatic and vegetational change in the late Pleistocene and early Holocene. Consequently, the changes in environment have come to be recognized as important conditioning factors in the development of agriculture and sedentary life, even if their precise impact remains uncertain.

Most of the explanatory models for agricultural development are based on consideration of the evidence for entire regions, usually the Levant or Mesopotamia with the Zagros. They have tended to invoke changes in one or two major aspects of human society as causative factors. Thus Binford (1968), Smith & Young (1983), and others have emphasized the importance of increases in population, Cauvin (1978, p. 140) has invoked cultural dynamics, and Bender (1978) social imperatives. Several of these models are helpful because they illuminate certain general aspects of the transition to a farming way of life, but they all share one important weakness. None of them can be applied to the genesis of agriculture as it may have occurred in key localities within each of the major regions. I happen to favour a model (Moore 1985, pp. 46–7) in which several related factors seem to have been significant at various moments in the transition: environmental change, increases in population, and alterations to the economy; but I am well aware that this scheme does not take into account the varying densities of population across Southwest Asia, nor does it tell us very much about what actually happened in, for example, the Jordan valley or the Kermanshah district. This is in part because our samples of sites in such localities are so modest, but also because we lack a close understanding of how late foraging societies were using their environs immediately prior to the adoption of cultivation, and the ways in which these patterns of use subsequently changed.

There are two current views on how Epipalaeolithic subsistence patterns in the Levant should be interpreted. According to the first, the economy depended entirely upon mobile hunting and gathering, especially hunting (Perrot 1968, col. 383, Bar-Yosef 1980, pp. 121–4). A wide range of wild foods was exploited in an unspecialized manner and the choice was determined entirely by what was available in the immediate vicinity of the site (Bar-Yosef 1981, pp. 403–6). Henry has argued (1981, p. 429) that the productivity of this system was increased after 10 000 bc as wild cereals were gathered for the first time, thus permitting the establishment of sedentary settlements. According to this model, a rather general pattern of unintensive hunting and gathering was pursued until the advent of agriculture. In these circumstances it is difficult to understand why people began to cultivate plants and to rear animals, unless one relies exclusively on cultural or social mechanisms.

A second view has it that the Epipalaeolithic economy was based on hunting and gathering, probably with about equal emphasis on each, but the patterns of exploitation of these wild foods grew more intensive and specialized through time (Moore 1982, p. 227). Domestication followed this long period of progressively more concentrated use of selected wild species.

Both interpretations are derived from the same body of evidence which indicates that throughout the Epipalaeolithic large percentages of usually a single species, often gazelle but sometimes fallow deer or goats, were killed for food by the inhabitants of individual sites, even though many other species were eaten on occasion. These species were abundant in the local environment but several other ungulates that would have been present in fair numbers were largely ignored. For example, onagers were probably a major constituent of the local wild fauna around Abu Hureyra (Syria), yet the inhabitants of the Epipalaeolithic settlement there chose to concentrate on gazelle. These constituted 80 per cent of the mammal bones from the site (Legge & Rowley-Conwy 1987, p. 76). A similar pattern can be seen at Nahal Oren (Israel) where the percentage of gazelle taken increased from 74 per cent in the Kebaran to 82 per cent in the Natufian (Noy et al. 1973, Table 3), with few fallow deer, caprines, or cattle being killed, even though they were present in the neighbourhood. Numerous pigs lived near many excavated Epipalaeolithic sites but are poorly represented among the animal bones found. This evidence strongly supports the view that the inhabitants of Epipalaeolithic sites chose a few animals to exploit intensively and that this trend became more marked through time. The Epipalaeolithic groups that began to rear animals and to cultivate plants were such specialized hunters, at least, that they were already managing their environment to a significant degree.

## Fresh insights and future directions

Plant and animal scientists today study the genetic and phenotypic character-istics of the main domesticates in order to breed more productive varieties tolerant of a wide range of environmental conditions. They have used their data to model the evolutionary history of these species yet their insights have rarely been co-ordinated with the evidence recovered by archaeologists for what actually happened. There is still great scope for integrating the evolutionary scenarios of the botanists and zoologists with those for human behaviour generated by archaeologists.

Recent archaeological research suggests that, in the transition from hunting and gathering to farming in Southwest Asia, the economic adjust-ments and related cultural changes appear to have occurred abruptly. Once plants and animals were subjected to sufficiently close human control for domestication to take place, radical changes in both subsistence and settle-ment patterns followed almost immediately. Thus in the Jordan valley and the Damascus basin the earliest sites at which morphologically domesticated cereals and other plants have been recovered – Pre-Pottery Neolithic A Jericho, Netiv Hagdud and Tell Aswad (van Zeist & Bakker-Heeres 1979, Hopf 1983, pp. 607–8, Bar-Yosef & Kislev Ch. 40, this volume) – were already substantial villages. These sites postdate by no more than a few centuries smaller Epipalaeolithic settlements at which only morphologically wild plants have been found.

The same is true at Abu Hureyra. The Epipalaeolithic settlement here yielded a wide range of morphologically wild food-plants and animals while the economy of the overlying Neolithic village was based on the cultivation of seven species of fully domesticated cereals and pulses (Hillman *et al.* Ch.14, this volume). These two settlements were different in form and had different assemblages of artefacts. The AMS and conventional radiocarbon dates for Abu Hureyra (Moore *et al.* 1986) indicate that less than half a millennium separated the end of the Epipalaeolithic settlement (just before 8000 bc) and the founding of the Neolithic village (about 7700 bc). So far as the exploitation of animals was concerned, Legge & Rowley-Conwy (1987) have demonstrated that gazelle were hunted in a remarkably regular and intensive manner by the inhabitants of both the Epipalaeolithic and early Neolithic settlements. Then within the space of only a generation or two around 7000 bc they made an abrupt switch to herding domesticated sheep and goats. A similar rapid adoption of caprine herding has been noted at Çayönü in southeastern Turkey (Lawrence 1982, pp. 175–6).

Present evidence suggests that the initial transition to cultivation and herding in Southwest Asia took place in only a few localities from the Mediterranean to the Zagros, and perhaps farther east. Immediately after plants and animals were domesticated, farming was adopted widely, accompanied by dramatic cultural change and population growth. Nonetheless, there seem to have been variations in the patterns of subsistence both before and immediately after the inception of agriculture. This was so, not only in the localities in which agriculture developed, but also in adjacent inhabited regions. In the Zagros and nearby plains there was an early emphasis on herded caprines. Contemporary with this, the inhabitants of the steppic hinterland of the Levant developed highly specialized modes of gazelle hunting. Later, in the 7th millennium bc, when agriculture and sedentary life were firmly in place in the more fertile and better-watered areas, the people of Sinai, while perhaps engaging in modest cultivation, continued to follow a more mobile way of life that depended heavily on the exploitation of animals (Bar-Yosef 1984).

Plants and animals, whether wild or domesticated, need to be exploited in significantly different ways. Herds of domesticated caprines, in particular, are raised most effectively in Southwest Asia by mobile herdsmen who can take the animals to fresh pasture in a seasonal cycle. Cereal crops, on the other hand, can best be sown, protected, and harvested if the farmer stays close by, at least during the growing season. There is a tension here that was present in modified form in pre-agricultural times and that had to be resolved in order that the sedentary life, seemingly characteristic of early agricultural villages throughout Southwest Asia, could take hold. If sedentism was such a distinctive feature of the first villages, then, until we understand how it came about, we shall not comprehend why an agricultural economy developed in the way it did.

In seeking to understand how the changes we observe took place, we need to consider very carefully the question of constraints on human choices. On the evidence from Abu Hureyra, both Epipalaeolithic foragers and early Neolithic farmers along the Middle Euphrates caught remarkably few fish. The inhabitants of this site and Mureybit (Ducos 1978, Fig. 3), as elsewhere, also showed little interest in pork. In the face of such evidence it is obviously inappropriate to invoke severe dietary pressure or marked scarcity of resources as agents of change in the local economies.

A fresh examination of the problem of agricultural development in Southwest Asia must take account of the fact that the adoption of food production was not inevitable. The approach should extend beyond the investigation of a single site to include a variety of sites within well-defined localities. We require a much firmer grasp of the presures to which human groups were subject, from environmental limitations to competition with other mammals (Garrard 1984, p. 271). We need to know what resources were available to late Epipalaeolithic foragers in each area and which of these they chose to consume. We must investigate in greater detail how the climate and vegetation changed in each significant locality and what effect this had on human use of wild resources. That will bring us much closer to understanding how humans came to cultivate the plants and rear the animals on which they have since depended for food.

# References

Bar-Yosef, O. 1980. Prehistory of the Levant. *Annual Review of Anthropology* **9**, 101–33.

Bar-Yosef, O. 1981. The Epi-Palaeolithic complexes of the southern Levant. In *Préhistoire du Levant*. J. Cauvin & P. Sanlaville (eds), 389–408. Actes du Colloque International CNRS 598. Paris: CNRS.

Bar-Yosef, O. 1984. Seasonality among Neolithic hunter–gatherers in southern Sinai. In *Animals and archaeology*, Vol. 3, J. Clutton-Brock & C. Grigson (eds), 145–60. Oxford: British Archaeological Reports International Series 202.

Bar-Yosef, O. & M. Kislev. 1989. Early farming communities in the Jordan Valley. In *Foraging and farming: the evolution of plant exploitation*, D. R. Harris & G. C. Hillman (eds), ch. 40. London: Unwin Hyman.

Bar-Yosef, O. & J. L. Phillips (eds) 1977. *Prehistoric investigations in Gebel Maghara, Northern Sinai*. Qedem 7. Jerusalem: Hebrew University.

Bender, B. 1978. Gatherer–hunter to farmer: a social perspective. *World Archaeology* **10**, 204–22.

Betts, A. 1983. Black Desert Survey, Jordan: first preliminary report. *Levant* **15**, 1–10.

Binford, L. R. 1968. Post-Pleistocene adaptations. In *New perspectives in archeology*, S. R. Binford & L. R. Binford (eds), 313–41. Chicago: Aldine.

Bottema, S. & W. van Zeist 1981. Palynological evidence for the climatic history of the Near East, 50,000–6,000 BP. In *Préhistoire du Levant*, J. Cauvin & P. Sanlaville (eds), 111–32. Actes du Colloque International CNRS 598. Paris: CNRS.

Braidwood, R. J. & B. Howe 1960. *Prehistoric investigations in Iraqi Kurdistan*.

Studies in Ancient Oriental Civilization 31. Chicago: University of Chicago Press.

Brice, W. C. (ed.) 1978. *The environmental history of the Near and Middle East since the last Ice Age.* London: Academic Press.

Cauvin, J. 1977. Les fouilles de Mureybet (1971–1974) et leur signification pour les origines de la sédentarisation au Proche-Orient. *Annual of the American Schools of Oriental Research* **44**, 19–48.

Cauvin, J. 1978. *Les premiers villages de Syrie-Palestine du IXème au VIIème millénaire avant J.C.* Lyon: Maison de l'Orient.

Cauvin, J. 1981. L'occupation néolithique de la région d'el Kowm: résultats 1978–1979. In *Préhistoire du Levant*, J. Cauvin & P. Sanlaville (eds), 471–83. Actes du Colloque International CNRS 598. Paris: CNRS.

Cauvin, J. & P. Sanlaville (eds) 1981. *Préhistoire du Levant.* Actes du Colloque International CNRS 598. Paris: CNRS.

Cauvin, M.-C. 1981. L'Epipaléolithique de Syrie d'après les premières recherches dans la cuvette d'el Kowm (1978–1979). In *Préhistoire du Levant*, J. Cauvin & P. Sanlaville (eds), 375–88. Actes du Colloque International CNRS 598. Paris: CNRS.

Ducos, P. 1978. *Tell-Mureybet étude archéozoologique et problèmes d'écologie humaine 1.* Paris: CNRS.

Flannery, K. V. 1969. Origins and ecological effects of early domestication in Iran and the Near East. In *The domestication and exploitation of plants and animals*, P. J. Ucko & G. W. Dimbleby (eds), 73–100. London: Duckworth.

Garrard, A. N. 1984. Community ecology and Pleistocene extinctions in the Levant. In *Hominid evolution and community ecology*, R. Foley (ed.), 261–77. London: Academic Press.

Garrard, A. N. & N. P. Stanley Price 1975–1977. A survey of prehistoric sites in the Azraq basin, eastern Jordan. *Paléorient* **3**, 109–26.

Garrard, A. N., B. Byrd, P. Harvey & F. Hivernel 1985. Prehistoric environment and settlement in the Azraq basin. A report on the 1982 survey season. *Levant* **17**, 1–28.

Harlan, J. R. & D. Zohary 1966. Distribution of wild wheats and barley. *Science* **153**, 1074–80.

Hanihara, K. & T. Akazawa (eds) 1979. Paleolithic site of Douara Cave and Paleogeography of Palmyra basin in Syria part II. Prehistoric occurrences and chronology in Palmyra basin. *Bulletin of the University Museum. University of Tokyo* 16.

Henry, D. O. 1981. An analysis of settlement patterns and adaptive strategies of the Natufians. In *Préhistoire du Levant* J. Cauvin & P. Sanlaville (eds), 421–31. Actes du Colloque International CNRS 598. Paris: CNRS.

Henry, D. O., F. A. Hassan, K. C. Henry & M. Jones 1983. An investigation of the prehistory of southern Jordan. *Palestine Exploration Quarterly* (1983), 1–24.

Hillman, G. C., S. M. Colledge & D. R. Harris. 1989. Plant-food economy during the Epipalaeolithic period at Tell Abu Hureyra, Syria: dietary diversity, seasonality, and modes of exploitation. In *Foraging and farming: the evolution of plant exploitation*, D. R. Harris & G. C. Hillman (eds), ch. 13. London: Unwin Hyman.

Hole, F. 1984. A reassessment of the Neolithic revolution. *Paléorient* **10**, 49–60.

Hole, F. & K. V. Flannery 1967. The prehistory of southwestern Iran: a preliminary report. *Proceedings of the Prehistoric Society* **33**, 147–206.

Hopf, M. 1983. Jericho plant remains. In *Excavations at Jericho*, Vol. V. K. M. Kenyon & T. A. Holland, 576–621. London: British School of Archaeology in Jerusalem.

Islamov, U. I. 1981. Neolithic sources of ancient civilizations in central Asia. Paper given at first USA–USSR Archaeological Symposium, Harvard University.

Jarrige, J.-F. & R. H. Meadow 1980. The antecedents of civilization in the Indus valley. *Scientific American* **243**, 122–33.

Ladizinsky, G. 1989. Origin and domestication of the Southwest Asian grain legumes. In *Foraging and farming: the evolution of plant exploitation*, D. R. Harris & G. C. Hillman (eds), ch. 23. London: Unwin Hyman.

Lawrence, B. 1982. Prehistoric food animals at Çayönü. In *Prehistoric village archaeology in south-eastern Turkey*, L. S. Braidwood & R. J. Braidwood (eds), 175–99. Oxford: British Archaeological Reports International Series 138.

Legge, A. J. & P. A. Rowley-Conwy 1987. Gazelle killing in Stone Age Syria. *Scientific American* **257**, 76–83.

Marks, A. E. (ed.) 1976. *Prehistory and paleoenvironments in the central Negev, Israel*, Vol. 1. Dallas: Southern Methodist University Press.

Mason, I. L. 1984. Goat. In *Evolution of domesticated animals*, I. L. Mason (ed.), 85–99. London: Longman.

Meadow, R. H. 1984. Animal domestication in the Middle East: a view from the eastern margin. In *Animals and archaeology*, Vol. 3, J. Clutton-Brock & C. Grigson (eds), 309–37. Oxford: British Archaeological Reports International Series 202.

Moore, A. M. T. 1982. Agricultural origins in the Near East: a model for the 1980s. *World Archaeology* **14**, 224–36.

Moore, A. M. T. 1983. The first farmers in the Levant. In *The hilly flanks and beyond: essays on the prehistory of southwestern Asia*, T. C. Young, Jr, P. E. L. Smith & P. Mortensen (eds), 91–111. Studies in Ancient Oriental Civilization 36. Chicago: University of Chicago Press.

Moore, A. M. T. 1985. The development of Neolithic societies in the Near East. *Advances in World Archaeology*, Vol. 4, F. Wendorf & A. E. Close (eds), 1–69. New York: Academic Press.

Moore, A. M. T., J. A. J. Gowlett, R. E. M. Hedges, G. C. Hillman, A. J. Legge & P. A. Rowley-Conwy 1986. Radiocarbon accelerator (AMS) dates for the Epipalaeolithic settlement at Abu Hureyra. *Radiocarbon* **28**, 1068–76.

Noy, T., A. J. Legge & E. S. Higgs 1973. Recent excavations at Nahal Oren, Israel. *Proceedings of the Prehistoric Society* **39**, 75–99.

Perrot, J. 1968. La préhistoire palestinienne. In *Supplément au dictionnaire de la Bible*, Vol. 8, Letouzey & Ané (eds), cols 286–446.

Ryder, M. L. 1984. Sheep. In *Evolution of domesticated animals*, I. L. Mason (ed.), 63–85. London: Longman.

Sanlaville, P. (ed.) 1985. *Holocene settlement in north Syria*. Oxford: British Archaeological Reports International Series 238.

Smith, P. E. L. & T. C. Young, Jr. 1983. The force of numbers: population pressure in the central western Zagros 12,000–4500 B.C. In *The hilly flanks and beyond: essays on the prehistory of southwestern Asia*, T. C. Young, Jr, P. E. L. Smith & P. Mortensen (eds), 141–62. Studies in Ancient Oriental Civilization 36. Chicago: University of Chicago Press.

van Zeist, W. & J. A. H. Bakker-Heeres 1979. Some economic and ecological aspects of the plant husbandry of Tell Aswad. *Paléorient* **5**, 161–9.

Zohary, D. 1989. Domestication of the Southwest Asian Neolithic crop assemblage of cereals, pulses, and flax: the evidence from the living plants. In *Foraging and farming: the evolution of plant exploitation*, D. R. Harris & G. C. Hillman (eds), ch. 22. London: Unwin Hyman.

# 40 Early farming communities in the Jordan Valley

OFER BAR-YOSEF and
MORDECHAI E. KISLEV

The origins of farming in Southwest Asia as a revolutionary subsistence strategy can be traced to a particular geographical belt. When the sites in which the earliest remains of domesticated plants (dated to 10 300–9300 bp) are plotted on a map, one is struck by their strip-like distribution. The strip or corridor stretches from the Middle Euphrates Valley (Mureybit and Abu Hureyra) through the Damascus Basin (Tel Aswad and Tel Ghoraife) into the Jordan Valley between Lake Kinneret and the Dead Sea. It largely coincides with the ecotone between the Mediterranean and Irano-Tunanian vegetational zones and, prior to the beginnings of cultivation, this same ecotone probably supported dense concentrations of wild cereals. This apparent correlation may reflect historical reality or be no more than coincidence. Either way, the local climatic conditions in this ecotone certainly provided these earliest Neolithic sites with excellent conditions for preservation of charred remains of food plants.

Additional contemporary sites of this earliest Neolithic period (known in the southern Levant as Pre-Pottery Neolithic A (PPNA)) are located on the western side of the corridor and in most cases on terra rossa soils or clayey colluvium where plant preservation is very poor (e.g. at Nahal Oren, Hatoula). However, when site size is taken into account, the impression of a north–south strip-like distribution is enhanced. This pattern is further reinforced by evidence from the ensuing period dating from about 9300 to 8000 bp and known in the southern Levant as Pre-Pottery Neolithic B (PPNB).

The zone of earliest farming sites includes the entire Jordan Valley and the Mediterranean vegetational zone along the Trans-Jordanian plateau. The Jordan Valley therefore forms an important segment of the area where systematic plant cultivation as a new subsistence strategy was adopted, probably sometime during the 11th millennium bp. The aim of this chapter is to examine the archaeological and archaeobotanical evidence from the Jordan Valley itself.

## Changes preceding the Neolithic

A model explaining why early farming communities were established in the Levantine corridor is summarized elsewhere (Bar-Yosef 1987), and an expanded version with full details of the archaeological evidence is currently in press (Bar-Yosef & Belfer-Cohen in press). We therefore include only a brief outline here.

From our interpretation of the available data we suggest that the principal steps preceding the emergence of the earliest Neolithic were as follows. (All dates are uncalibrated radiocarbon dates bp.)

(a)   From *c.* 19 000 or 18 000 bp until 14 500 bp small bands of Kebaran hunter–gatherers occupied the Mediterranean coastal ranges and the western sector of the Trans-Jordanian plateau. Cold, dry conditions limited the exploitation of the desertic regions farther inland. The spatial and seasonal distribution of food resources (gazelle, fallow deer, and possibly wild cereals, pulses, acorns, and fruits) dictated a relatively mobile way of life.

(b)   Between *c.* 14 500 and 12 500 bp, increasing annual rainfall allowed a much wider area to be exploited than hitherto. The number of sites increased, but the small-band organization was maintained and this is attributable both to the fission of bands following population growth among the Geometric Kebaran cultures, and to the penetration of groups of the Mushabian and related cultures from the Nile delta and the Red Sea hills.

(c)   Abrupt climatic change towards drier conditions around 12 500 bp caused the retraction of the hunter–gatherers back into the Mediter- ranean coastal territories from which they originated. They were forced to adopt a 'broad-spectrum' subsistence strategy and to operate from large aggregated sites in the new ecotones, Thus, the previously semi-sedentary mobility pattern of hunter–gatherers in the Mediter- ranean vegetational belt, with equipment such as pounding tools pre-adapted to more intensive food procurement, was transformed into a settlement pattern of small Early Natufian sedentary villages.

In these first three steps of the model the prime movers are seen as a combination of climatic and vegetational changes, increase in population densities, and the existence of a subsistence strategy which was pre-adapted to low mibility (see Hassan 1981, Hole 1984, Smith & Young 1983, Cohen 1985, Henry 1985, Moore 1985, Bar-Yosef 1987). Once residential mobility was given up in the Levant, the ensuing socio-economic developments were unavoidable.

(d)   During the 11th millennium bp the Natufian economy – now based in sedentary villages – appears to have expanded from the Mediterranean vegetational belt into neighbouring areas within the drier Irano- Turanian belt. It is quite possible that, under the Late Pleistocene climatic regime, these Irano-Turanian areas (such as the Middle Euph- rates and the Negev Highlands) had a higher annual precipitation than today, and were perhaps included within the marginal Mediterranean steppe or park-steppe zone. This Late Natufian expansion can be interpreted as partially due to population growth within the original Natufian homeland.

(e)   The abrupt climatic changes of the terminal Pleistocene around 10 500–10 000 bp from wetter to drier conditions, coupled with the development of large communities in which social complexity required organizational changes, forced the Late Natufians to adopt systematic cultivation of cereals and pulses. Hunting, some fishing, and the gathering of wild fruits, seeds, and green plants supplemented a diet based on the products of cultivation. This phase is especially well represented in the archaeological record of the Jordan Valley. Late Natufian desertic adaptations (such as the Negev Harifian Culture) disappeared by the end of this dry phase.

## The early Neolithic (*c.* 10 500–9300 bp) in the Jordan Valley

The available radiocarbon dates, if interpreted correctly, suggest that the transition from the Natufian culture to a variety of Neolithic archaeological entities was a rapid one in the Jordan Valley and neighbouring regions. An ill-defined entity, the 'Khiamian', is considered as either a continuation of the Natufian or the earliest Neolithic culture. Its assemblages are characterized by arrowheads ('Khiam' points), a proliferation of perforators, a decrease in the frequencies of microliths, and the presence of bitumen-hafted sickle blades (Bar-Yosef 1980, Crowfoot-Payne 1983, Lechevallier & Ronen 1985). This entity was seemingly of short duration and, so far, information comes only from two small soundings in Nahal Ein Gev II east of Lake Kinneret and Salibiya IX between Netiv Hagdud and Gilgal, from El-Khiam Terrace in the Judean Desert, and from Hatoula on the western flanks of the Judean Hills. A similar transition was observed by Cauvin (1977) at Mureybit on the Middle Euphrates where this type of lithic industry is named 'Epi-Natufian' (= Mureybit IB).

The early Neolithic (PPNA) farming communities in the Jordan Valley from north to south are: Gesher, Netiv Hagdud, Gilgal, and Jericho (Bar-Yosef *et al.* 1980, Noy *et al.* 1980, Kenyon & Holland 1981, 1982, 1983, Garfinkel pers. comm.). It is not surprising that, given the depth of alluvium and colluvium which accumulated during the early Holocene, the Hula Valley produced no evidence for the presence of equivalent sites.

The sites in the Lower Jordan Valley are larger than the preceding Natufian ones. PPNA Jericho has a surface area of about 2.5 ha, Netiv Hagdud about 1.5 ha, and Gilgal about 1.0 ha. All are located within a radius of 15 km. Netiv Hagdud and Gilgal, which are only 2 km apart, raise the question of whether they were contemporary or sequential settlements. The first radiocarbon dates from Gilgal support our view that it is older than Netiv Hagdud and might have been contemporary with the earliest PPNA levels of Jericho (Bar-Yosef in press). Site-catchment analyses and the preliminary analysis of the bio-remains support this contention. Cereal cultivation was practised at all three sites (Hopf 1983, Kislev *et al.* 1986), together with the gathering of wild seeds, fruits, and plants for basketry, building materials, firewood, etc. The diet also included hunted animals such as gazelle, wild boar, foxes, and numerous bird species, especially ducks.

Both Netiv Hagdud and Jericho have a similar site location on the apex or edges of alluvial fans. This situation, coupled with settlements on alluvial terraces, is also typical of later Neolithic sites dated to the Pre-Pottery Neolithic B Period (9300–8000 bp), such as Beisamoun, Tell 'Eli, Munhata, Yiftah'el, 'Ain Ghazal, and Beidha (e.g. Garfinkel 1987, Rollefson & Simmons 1986). It is assumed that cultivation was based on sowing on alluvial fans and terraces as well as on the edges of freshwater swamps where the water table was always high and the soil was fertilized by silt deposited by periodic floods. As yet, there is no evidence for irrigation. Indeed, the exploitation of naturally wetted soils (without evidence of irrigation) is also evidenced at other early agricultural sites in Southwest Asia such as Tell Aswad and Ghoraife in the Damascus Basin (van Zeist & Bakker-Heeres 1982) and the Neolithic site at Tell Abu Hureyra dating from *c.* 9500 bp (Hillman *et al.* Ch. 14, this volume). Thus the optimal situation for sedentary farming communities was in the proximity of the fields where water for daily use and for the building of mud bricks was available within a short distance.

However, settlement locations on alluvial fans and terraces often resulted in the burying and disappearance of sites which can now only be found accidentally as a result of erosion or modern construction work. In the case of Jericho, the need for protection against run-off and, more specifically, against floodwater and silt from a nearby wadi is suggested as the main reason for building the walls (Bar-Yosef 1986). A similar solution was reached by the inhabitants of Beidha who erected a terrace wall along the wadi course in order to protect their site against erosion. One might expect comparable discoveries at the mound of Netiv Hagdud which is buried beneath the alluvial fan of Wadi Bakar, and at PPNB sites such as Tell'Eli, Munhata, and Beisamoun.

The domestic architecture of PPNA sites in the Jordan Valley includes round and oval houses built from loaf-shaped mud bricks on stone-lined semi-subterranean foundations. The energy investment in building these huts was much higher than in the Natufian dwellings where the super-structures were probably constructed from organic materials (branches, hides, etc.). This suggestion explains the observations of high artefact densities in Natufian sites relative to PPNA sites where the considerable volumes of fill from decomposed mud brick has a 'diluting' effect. It also implies that the allocation of time and energy during the latter period was different in the PPNA and possibly benefited from the built-in security of the new subsistence strategy.

Fireplaces are found inside and outside the roofed rooms. Storage facilities included small bins built of stone slabs and large granaries (about 1 m in diameter) built of mud bricks. Stone slabs with cupholes are the common pounding utensil, but large rounded grinding bowls occur as well. Hand stones (*manos*) and pestles, often made of basalt, are found in large numbers.

The chipped stone industry, generally made on blades, includes the Khiam arrowheads, perforators, sickle blades, burins, end-scrapers and bifacial axes. All are made of various kinds of flint, the sources of which are as yet unidentified. The presence of heat-treated artefacts is also suspected in Jericho and Netiv Hagdud (Crowfoot-Payne 1983) but this still requires experimental confirmation. Well-polished celts of limestone and basalt are also quite common.

The bone industry exhibits a marked proliferation of burnishers, together with various awls and points. This is interpreted as reflecting the continued importance of hide working relative to basketry (Marshall 1982). On the other hand, the excavation of Netiv Hagdud revealed the remains of a basket made by a very fine close twining technique, and fragments of strings made of unspun plant fibres (T. Schick pers. comm.).

Burials under floors and in empty spaces are common for individuals but rare for groups. Skulls were removed from adults but their final place of disposal remains unknown. Clay and stone figurines of females (including the 'seated woman') are interpreted as representing an unknown belief system.

Trade or barter is indicated by finds of Anatolian obsidian, marine shells from both the Mediterranean and the Black Sea, amulets and greenstone beads. Procurement of raw materials such as flint involved distances greater than the suggested optimum of 5 km radius. This raises the possibility that mutual exchange between the farmer–hunters and groups of hunter–gatherers who occupied the semi-arid regions or the higher hilly areas could account for the observed variation in non-locally produced articles found in these early farming communities. Of all the sites of the Lower Jordan Valley, Jericho stands out by virtue of its size and the evidence for its complex social organization and relative wealth (the walls, the tower, the larger quantities of Anatolian obsidian), all of which is taken as indicating its importance within the region.

## Botanical rationale for barley being the first crop in the Jordan Valley

An explanation is· required for barley and emmer wheat being the only domesticated cereals so far identified from the early PPNA settlements of Jericho and Netiv Hagdud in the Jordan Valley and Aswad in the Damascus Basin (van Zeist & Bakker-Heeres 1979, 1982, Hopf 1983, Kislev *et al.* 1986). If we assume that the origins of Southwest Asian cereal agriculture are to be traced to the Levant, then this enables us to produce a detailed model of the advantages of wild barley (*Hordeum spontaneum*) and wild emmer *Triticum dicoccoides*) over other grasses as species for early cultivation.

There are at least seven characteristics which are likely to have determined which species of the diverse Jordan Valley grass flora might have been selected as crops by the first farmers in this area. These primary determinants are grain size and weight, local abundance of each species, generation length, seed dormancy, ploidy level, harvesting efficiency, and the ease of dehusking the grains ready for their preparation as food. The first two of these factors may also have played a central role in determining patterns of preference among pre-agrarian foragers as well. Twenty-three of the most palatable large-grained grasses from the two sides of the present-day Jordan Valley are listed in Table 40.1 together with indices of the state of the seven determining factors observable in each species. The 23 grasses belong mainly to the tribes Triticeae (17 species), Bromeae (three species), Aveneae (two species), and Poeae (one specie) (Feinbrun-Dothan 1986). New, adventive species such as *Bromus catharticus* are not included. Also, the possible presence of the rare perennial *Hordeum secalinum* was not checked because reference material was not available. The grains of all these species are assumed to be edible and may have been consumed by humans.

In Table 40.1, the 23 species are arranged in order of decreasing grain volumes. The measurements are averages generally based on 3–6 modern grains from samples in the reference collection established in the Laboratory of Archaeobotany at Bar-Ilan University. The measurements clearly cannot be expected to embrace the full range of variation to be encountered within each of the species concerned, but they do offer a basis for comparing the principal features of the different species in the list. Length, width, and thickness are based on the largest measurement, and when comparing grains of different shapes there is inevitably a lack of correlation between these measurements and grain weight. For example, grains of *T. dicoccoides* with their sharp edges have somewhat larger dimensions but weigh less than grains of *H. spontaneum*. Similarly, the weight of the long, broad grains of *Bromus lanceolatus* is less than half the weight of other grains of similar length and breadth because of their flat, concave form. (The discrepancy is even greater with the measurements of grain volume as these were based on simple multiplication of the linear measurements.) As for the abundance indices, they are strictly relative: 1 = very rare, 2 = rare, 3 = rather common or locally common, 4 = common, 5 = very common (M. Zohary, 1976). The ploidy levels are taken from Feinbrun-Dothan (1986). All are wild plants except *Lolium temulentum* which is today an obligate weed, though its grain was smaller in ancient times (Kislev 1980), a fact which may reflect earlier non-segetal habitat preferences.

We will now consider in turn each of the seven factors which are likely to have determined whether they would have been perceived as suitable for sowing as crops by the earliest cultivators.

**Table 40.1**   Large-seeded grasses of the Jordan Valley area: characteristics which are likely to have determined their attractiveness as potential crops. The grasses are arranged in order of decreasing grain volumes. Each measurement represents the mean for 3–6 grains from modern plants.

| Species | A | L | B | T | V | W | P |
|---------|---|-----|-----|-----|----|----|------|
| Triticum dicoccoides | 3 | 8.3 | 2.2 | 2.1 | 37 | 20 | 4 |
| Hordeum spontaneum | 5 | 8.1 | 2.6 | 1.6 | 33 | 24 | 2 |
| Aegilops peregrina | 5 | 7.2 | 2.6 | 1.8 | 32 | 20 | 4 |
| A. geniculata | 3 | 6.2 | 2.7 | 1.7 | 28 | 14 | 4 |
| A. triuncialis | 2 | 7.9 | 2.3 | 1.5 | 28 | 12 | 4 |
| Taeniatherum crinitum | 2 | 11.4 | 1.7 | 1.2 | 23 | 13 | — |
| Bromus lanceolatus | 4 | 12.0 | 2.2 | 0.8 | 22 | 4 | 4 |
| Aegilops biuncialis | 3 | 7.1 | 2.2 | 1.5 | 22 | 9 | 4 |
| Lolium temulentum | 3 | 4.8 | 2.4 | 1.7 | 20 | 17 | 2 |
| Aegilops kotschyi | 3 | 6.9 | 2.0 | 1.4 | 20 | 11 | 4 |
| Avena sterilis | 5 | 7.5 | 1.8 | 1.4 | 19 | 11 | 6 |
| Secale montanum | 3 | 6.7 | 1.4 | 2.0 | 19 | 7 | 2 |
| Avena longiglumis | 1 | 7.8 | 1.6 | 1.4 | 17 | 13 | 2 |
| Hordeum bulbosum | 5 | 7.8 | 2.0 | 1.0 | 16 | 10 | 2, 4 |
| Aegilops crassa | 1 | 6.3 | 2.2 | 1.1 | 16 | 14 | 4, 6 |
| Bromus diandrus | 3 | 14.3 | 1.9 | 0.6 | 15 | 8 | 8 |
| Hetheranthelium piliferum | 2 | 5.6 | 2.0 | 1.3 | 14 | 8 | — |
| Aegilops longissima | 2 | 7.1 | 1.9 | 1.0 | 14 | 11 | 2 |
| A. sharonensis | 4 | 6.3 | 1.8 | 1.1 | 13 | 10 | 2 |
| A. searsii | 2 | 7.2 | 1.7 | 0.9 | 12 | 5 | 2 |
| Bromus sterilis | 4 | 15.4 | 1.0 | 0.7 | 11 | 6 | 4 |
| Elymus panormitanus | 2 | 7.7 | 1.6 | 0.9 | 11 | 7 | — |
| Aegilops speltoides | 2 | 6.0 | 1.6 | 1.0 | 10 | 5 | 2 |

A = relative abundance in local vegetation ranging from 5 (very common) to 1 (rare); L = grain length (mm); B = grain breadth (mm); T = grain thickness (mm); V = grain volume (mm$^3$); W = grain weight (mg); P = ploidy level.

## Grain size and weight

It is assumed that the early farmers of this region preferred large heavy-grained grasses to sow as their first crops. However, the number of such candidates from both sides of the Jordan Valley exceeds 20 (Table 40.1). *Bromus lanceolatus, B. sterilis, Aegilops searsii, A. speltoides,* and some others, including even *A. sharonensis,* are probably to be excluded because their grains are too light.

## Local abundance

After grain size and weight, the next most important factor affecting the probable attractiveness of the grass as a potential crop is its local abundance. A common plant can generally survive in a range of different habitats and on a variety of soil types. It can also grow densely and may dominate some areas, forming field-like vegetation. This characteristic is likely to have made such grasses attractive to both hunter–gatherers and their agrarian successors.

## Generation length

Perennial species such as *H. bulbosum* and *Secale montanum* cannot be serious candidates for a fast evolutionary process, such as cereal domestication, because of their long generation length. However, the point at which this was perceived as a disadvantage by the first farmers must remain unknown.

These first three determinants eliminate all but four species which meet the requirements for man's first domesticated cereals, namely, *H. spontaneum* and *Aegilops peregrina* (both are very common species with large, heavy grains), *T. dicoccoides* (locally common and with large, heavy grains), and *Avena sterilis* (very common but with rather smaller grains). Each of these four remaining species offers its own advantages and disadvantages.

## Complete first-year germination

First, *H. spontaneum* has the advantage of being the only species of the four which has only one grain in each of its dispersal units. In the other three grasses (as well as in most of the others listed in Table 40.1) there are 2–3 grains in each spikelet, and at least one of the grains does not germinate immediately due to the presence of germination inhibitors (D. Zohary 1969, Lavie *et al.* 1974, Ladizinsky pers. comm.). The number of seeds required for sowing such grasses, especially in new fields, is therefore twice that required when sowing the one-seeded dispersal units of barley, although the total number of sown spikelets (dispersal units) remains the same in either case.

## Diploidy

Another advantage of wild barley is its ploidy level. It is almost the only abundant, annual, large-grained grass that has the basic diploid number of chromosomes, $2n = 14$ (Table 40.1). Though not yet tested experimentally, it is assumed that higher ploidy levels, as in *T. dicoccoides*, reduce the chance of – or lengthen the time needed for – domestication. In contrast to the one gene which controls rachis fragility in wild barley (Nilan 1964), it is likely that each of the genomes of a polyploid grass has its own gene controlling disarticulation of the rachis and enabling effective natural dispersal of its seeds. The hexaploid wild oat, *Avena sterilis*, which has only one such gene (G. Ladizinsky pers. comm.) may be regarded as an exception, as may the disarticulation of intact ears in the goat-face grasses *Aegilops peregrina* and *A. geniculata* where a single gene is again involved.

*Adherence of grain to husks*

The only obvious disadvantage of wild barley is the adherence of its grains to the husks, a feature which is common to most grasses but is not found in the wild wheat (Table 40.1).

*Harvesting efficiency*

Finally, collecting wild wheat has been found to be more efficient than wild barley, probably because the former produces two grains in each spikelet (Ladizinsky 1975).

Despite these last two disadvantages, we consider that, for the first farmers in the Jordan Valley, barley would have been the most attractive of the local large-grained grasses and the first to be domesticated because it is a very common annual throughout the area, has no germination inhibitors, and has only one gene controlling disarticulation. Indeed, we suggest that the domestication of wild emmer wheat *T. dicoccoides* occurred as a result of having grown as a weed in fields of barley which was already either domesticated or pre-domesticated. The morphological and ecological similarity of the two species would have enabled the wild wheat to survive in the barley fields for many generations until the mutations for tough rachis occurred and achieved fixation. Only then, perhaps, would farmers have separated them as independent crops.

## Conclusions

The studies at early sites in the Jordan Valley and adjacent areas allow the identification of a series of steps leading to the adoption of crop husbandry. So far, the plant remains recovered from early Neolithic sites such as Aswad, Jericho, Netiv Hagdud, and Gilgal suggest that barley and wheat were the earliest domesticated cereals. The location of these pioneering settlements in the Jordan Valley and its adjacent hilly and plateau areas is most readily explained by the natural distribution of the wild ancestors of these cereals, especially wild barley. Although not the only grass with attractive seeds, wild barley has a variety of features which are likely to have made it the best candidate for initial cultivation and domestication; these include grain size, ploidy level, local abundance, and tolerance of a very wide range of soil types, altitudes, and temperatures.

## References

Bar-Yosef, O. 1980. A figurine from a Khiamian site in the lower Jordan Valley. *Paléorient* **6**, 193–200.

Bar-Yosef, O. 1986. The walls of Jericho: an alternative interpretation. *Current Anthropology* **27**, 157–62.

Bar-Yosef, O. 1987. Late Pleistocene adaptations in the Levant. In *The Pleistocene Old Word: regional perspectives*, O. Soffer (ed.), 219–36. Plenum Press.

Bar-Yosef, O. In press. PPNA sites in the Jordan Valley. *Paléorient*.

Bar-Yosef, O. & A. Belfer-Cohen In press. The origins of sedentison and farming communities in the Levant. *Journal of World Prehistory*.

Cauvin, J. 1977. Les fouilles de Mureybit (1971–1974) et leur signification pour les origines de la sédentarisation au Proche Orient. *Annual of the American Schools of Oriental Research* **44**, 19–48.

Cohen, M. N. 1985. Prehistoric hunter–gatherers: the meaning of social complexity. In *Prehistoric hunter–gatherers: the emergence of social complexity*, T. D. Price & J. A. Brown (eds), 99–119. New York: Academic Press.

Crowfoot-Payne, J. 1983. The flint industries of Jericho. In *Excavations at Jericho*, Vol. 5, K. M. Kenyon & T. A. Holland (eds), 622–59. London: British School of Archaeology in Jerusalem.

Feinbrun-Dothan, N. 1986. *Flora Palestina*, Vol. 4 . Jerusalem: Israel Academy of Sciences and Humanities.

Garfinkel, Y. 1987. Yiftahel: a Neolithic village from the seventh millennium BC in lower Galilee, Israel. *Journal of Field Archaeology* **14**, 199–212.

Hassan, F. A. 1981. *Demographic archaeology*. New York: Academic Press.

Henry, D. O. 1985. Preagricultural sedentism: the Natufian example. In *Prehistoric hunter–gatherers: the emergence of cultural complexity*, T. D. Price & J. A. Brown (eds), 365–84. New York: Academic Press.

Hillman, G. C., S. M. Colledge & D. R. Harris. 1989. Plant-foot economy during the Epipalaeolithic period at Tell Abu Hureyra, Syria: dietary diversity, seasonality, and modes of exploitation. In *Foraging and farming: the evolution of plant exploitation*, D. R. Harris & G. C. Hillman (eds), ch. 13. London: Unwin Hyman.

Hole, F. 1984. 1984. A reassessment of the Neolithic Revolution. *Paléorient* **10**, 49–60.

Hopf, M. 1983. Jericho plant remains. In *Excavations at Jericho*, Vol. 5, K. M. Kenyon & T. A. Holland (eds), 576–621. London: British School of Archaeology in Jerusalem.

Kenyon, K. M. & T. A. Holland 1981. *Excavations at Jericho*. Vol. 3: *The architecture and stratigraphy of the Tell*. London: British School of Archaeology in Jerusalem.

Kenyon, K. M. & T. A. Holland 1982. *Excavations at Jericho*. Vol. 4: *The pottery type series and other finds*. London: British School of Archaeology in Jerusalem.

Kenyon, K. M. & T. A. Holland 1983. *Excavations at Jericho*. Vol. 5: *The pottery phases of the Tell and other finds*. London: British School of Archaeology in Jerusalem.

Kislev, M. 1980. Contenu d'un silo à blé de l'époque du fer ancien. In *Tell Keisan*, J. Briend & J. B. Humbert (eds), 361–79. Fribourg: Editions Universitaires; Gottingen: Vandenhoeck & Ruprecht; Paris: Gabalda.

Kislev, M. E., O. Bar-Yosef & A. Gopher 1986. Early Neolithic domesticated and wild barley from the Netiv Hagdud region of the Jordan Valley. *Israel Journal of Botany* **35**, 197–201.

Ladizinsky, G. 1975. Collection of wild cereals in the Upper Jordan Valley. *Economic Botany* **29**, 264–7.

Lavie, D., E. C. Levy, A. Cohen, M. Evanari & Y. Guttermann 1974. New germination inhibitor from *Aegilops ovata*. *Nature* **249**, 388.

Lechevallier, M. & A. Ronen 1985. *Le site Natoufien-Khiamien de Hatoula*. Cahiers du Centre de Recherche Français, Vol. 1. Jerusalem.

Marshall, D. N. 1982. Jericho bone tools and objects. In *Excavations at Jericho*, Vol. 4, K. M. Kenyon & T. A. Holland (eds), 570–622. London: British School of Archaeology in Jerusalem.

Moore, A. 1985. The development in Neolithic societies in the Near East. In *Advances in world archaeology*, Vol. 4, F. Wendorf & A. E. Close (eds), 1–69. New York: Academic Press.

Nilan, R. A. 1964. *The cytology and genetics of barley*. Research Studies, Monthly supplement 3, Washington State University, Washington.

Noy, T., J. Schuldenrein & E. Tchernov 1980. Gilgal, a Pre-Pottery Neolithic A site in the Lower Jordan Valley. *Israel Exploration Journal* **30**, 63–82.

Rollefson, G. O. & A. H. Simmons 1986. The Neolithic village of 'Ain Ghazal, Jordan: preliminary report on the 1984 season. *Bulletin of the American Schools of Oriental Research*, supplement 24, 145–64.

Smith, P. E. L. & T. C. Young, Jr. 1983. The force of numbers: population pressure in the central western Zagros 12,000–4500 bc. In *The hilly flanks and beyond: essays on the prehistory of southwestern Asia*, T. C. Young, Jr., P. E. L. Smith & P. Mortensen (eds), 141–62. Studies in Ancient Oriental Civilization 36. Chicago: University of Chicago Press.

van Zeist, W. & J. A. H. Bakker-Heeres 1979. Some economic and ecological aspects of the plant husbandry of Tell Aswad. *Paléorient* **5**, 161–9.

van Zeist, W. & J. A. H. Bakker-Heeres 1982. Archaeobotanical studies of the Levant I: Neolithic sites in the Damascus Basin: Aswad, Ghoraife, Ramad. *Paleohistoria* **24**, 165–256.

Zohary, D. 1969. The progenitors of wheat and barley in relation to domestication and agricultural dispersal in the Old World. In *The domestication and exploitation of plants and animals*, P. J. Ucko & G. W. Dimbleby (eds), 47–66. London: Duckworth.

Zohary, M. 1976. *A new analytical flora of Israel* [in Hebrew]. Tel Aviv: Am Oved.

# 41 *Prehistoric agriculture in China*

## AN ZHIMIN

In the past three decades, archaeology in New China has made unprecedented strides, with large-scale archaeological reconnaissance and excavations conducted throughout the country (CASS 1984). The discovery of over 7000 Neolithic sites, and the systematic excavation of hundreds of them, has eliminated most regional and chronological gaps, and the distribution and interrelationships of different types of cultural complexes have been progressively investigated. Meanwhile, the application to archaeology of the methods and techniques of the natural sciences has achieved great success, especially in radiocarbon dating (CASS 1983). Laboratories have now produced over a thousand radiocarbon dates on which to build an absolute chronology of Neolithic China.

## The Neolithic cultural sequence

The general outline of the Chinese Neolithic is now clear, with the earlier interpretations now corrected and supplemented on a large scale (An 1982). Most of the Neolithic cultures so far investigated by means of excavation focus on the Yellow River Valley and the middle and lower reaches of the Yangtze River, and they have the closest relationship with the origin and development of agriculture in prehistoric China. In the Yellow River Valley as a whole, the earliest Neolithic complexes are represented by the Peiligang, Cishan, and Dadiwan cultures. They are followed by the Yangshao culture and its successor, the Longshan culture, which in turn leads to the historical Shang period. A degree of regional variation is displayed in the Yellow River Valley by the Beixin, Dawenkou, Majiayao, and several other cultures. In the lower reaches of the Yangtze River, the cardinal sequence of development consists of the Hemudu, Majiabang, Songze, and Liangzhu cultures, and in the middle reaches of the river there are the Daxi and Qujialing cultures. All these cultures are based on an agricultural economy. Their correlation and absolute chronology is shown in Figure 41.1.

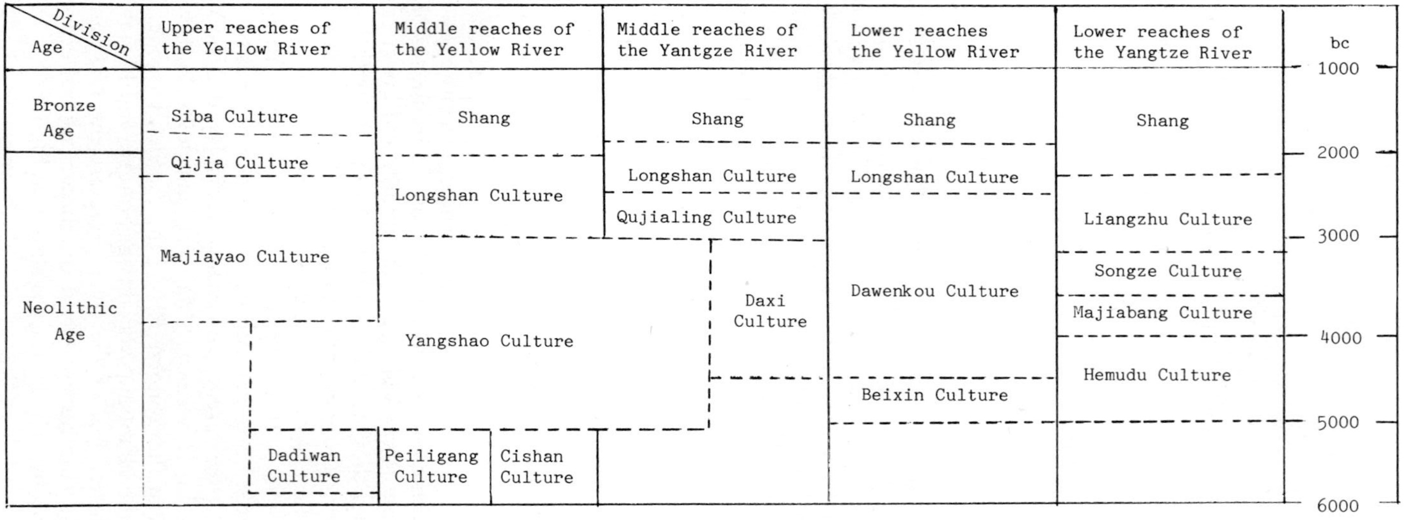

| Division | Upper reaches of the Yellow River | Middle reaches of the Yellow River | Middle reaches of the Yangtze River | Lower reaches of the Yellow River | Lower reaches of the Yangtze River | bc |
|---|---|---|---|---|---|---|
| Bronze Age | Siba Culture | Shang | Shang | Shang | Shang | 1000 |
| | Qijia Culture | | | | | |
| Neolithic Age | | Longshan Culture | Longshan Culture | Longshan Culture | | 2000 |
| | Majiayao Culture | | Qujialing Culture | | Liangzhu Culture | |
| | | | | Dawenkou Culture | Songze Culture | 3000 |
| | | Yangshao Culture | Daxi Culture | | Majiabang Culture | |
| | | | | | Hemudu Culture | 4000 |
| | Dadiwan Culture | Peiligang Culture / Cishan Culture | | Beixin Culture | | |
| | | | | | | 5000 |
| | | | | | | 6000 |

**Figure 41.1** Chronological table of Neolithic cultures in the Yellow River and Yangtze River valleys.

# The development of agriculture

The farming cultures in prehistoric China were based on a distinctive association of settlement, productive activities, farm tools, crops, and domestic animals which directly influenced the development of agriculture in the historical period.

Prehistoric agriculture developed early in both the Yellow River Valley and the middle and lower reaches of the Yangtze River. Abundant remains of farming cultures, dating to at least 7000–8000 years ago, have been found, and the origin of Chinese agriculture can be traced back to a still earlier period. With the appearance and development of agriculture, settlements became more permanent and larger communities came into being. As a defence against floods, the sites in North China were generally located on river terraces, whereas those in South China, in lower, flatter regions with a more humid climate, are found mainly on mounds. The farmland was located near the village settlements. Because of the exhaustion of soil fertility which occurred after a period of farming, settlements had to move from place to place frequently to sustain production and therefore groups of sites can be found along the same river.

Various farming systems developed in response to different environments. For example, the vegetation in the Yellow River Valley consisted of extensive grassland with scattered woodland, so a system of crop rotation and fallow was adopted, i.e. after a period of cultivation, fields were fallowed for some time to recover their soil fertility. In the Yangtze Valley and in southern areas, where the vegetation consisted of dense forest and bush, the so-called 'slash-and-burn' method was adopted, i.e. trees and shrubs were cut down and burned in order to create fields for cultivation. These two farming systems persisted into historical times. The antiquity of irrigation is uncertain. No archaeological evidence of it has been found so far in a Neolithic context and it may have developed later.

# Crops

Large quantities of cereal remains have been discovered archaeologically, most of which consist of foxtail millet, broomcorn millet, and rice. The prehistoric distributions of these cereal crops can be divided geographically by the Qinling Mountains and Huaihe River. The crops planted to the north (Huang 1982–83) were different from those to the south, which implies that prehistoric agriculture was limited by environmental conditions.

Foxtail millet (*Setaria italica*) is generally found in the Yellow River Valley (Gansu 1984). It has been found at more than 20 sites, often stored in pits or pottery vessels, its grains having been charred or reduced to ashes. It can be identified to genus and species by morphological observation (Fig. 41.2) and by spodogram analysis (Fig. 41.3) (Huang 1982). The results of $^{13}$C analysis of human skeletal remains from some sites in this region also suggest that

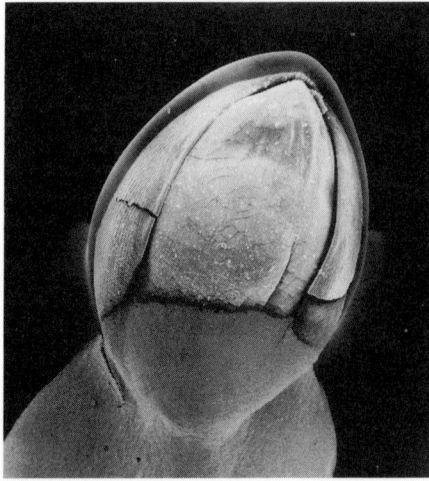

**Figure 41.2**   Floret of a *Setaria* species, probably *Sitalica* (foxtail millet), from the Majiayao culture. The photograph shows the palea and the edges of the indurated lemma which together enclose the small grain. From the site of Linjia in Dingxiang Autonomous County, Gansu  Province. (Approximate magnification: × 30.)

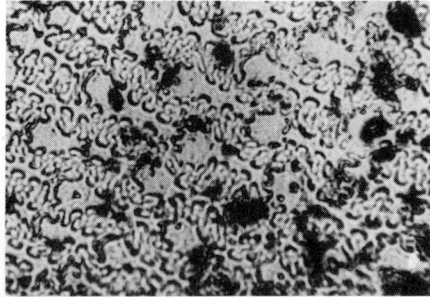

**Figure 41.3**   Spodogram (presumably from the lemma or palea) of a *Setaria* sp., probably *S. italica* (foxtail millet), from the Majiayao culture. From the site of Liuwan in Ledu County, Qinghai Province. (Approximate magnification: × 600.)

foxtail millet was the main cereal food (Cai & Qiu 1984). Beyond the Yellow River Valley, foxtail millet, which is adapted to aridity and high elevations, is today grown in the northeastern and southwestern regions of the country and in Taiwan. It is believed to have been domesticated from green bristlegrass (*Setaria viridis*), and may have originated in the Yellow River Valley. By at latest 8000 years ago, it began to be widely cultivated in the Peiligang and Cishan cultures and it was the main crop in North China from prehistoric times to the historical period.

Broomcorn millet (*Panicum miliaceum*), as charred or ashy remains, can be

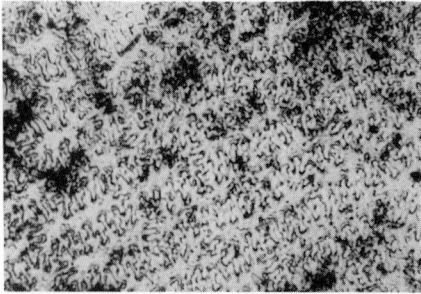

**Figure 41.4** Spodogram of *Panicum miliaceum* (broomcorn millet) from the Yangshao culture. From the site of Jiangzhai in Lintong County, Shaanxi Province. (Approximate magnification: × 600.)

mistaken for foxtail millet. But on the basis of morphological examination and spodogram analysis (Fig. 41.4) broomcorn millet has been recorded from two sites belonging to the Dadiwan and Yangshao cultures respectively. Its first appearance and geographical distribution corresponds to that of foxtail millet, and it was cultivated in parallel with the latter.

Rice (*Oryza sativa*), in the form of charred grains and husks in burnt clay, including those of long-grained non-glutinous rice (*indica* type) and round-grained non-glutinous rice (*japonica* type = *sinica*, cf. Chang Ch. 25, this volume), has been recovered from more than 30 sites in the Yangtze Valley and along the southeast coast (Yan 1982). Most of the finds are of the *indica* type, but the proportion of *japonica* rice increased as time went on. Rice-farming agriculture first appeared in the Hemudu culture 7000 years ago. In view of the wide distribution of wild rice in southern China, the middle and lower reaches of the Yangtze River must have been one of the centres of origin of cultivated rice. In North China, however, rice cultivation was deterred by natural conditions. It only became established there in the early historical period and was never practised on a large scale.

Other crops, such as wheat and kaoliang sorghum, have also been found archaeologically. But the former first appeared only in historical times, namely in the Shang-Zhou period, and the latter cannot be securely identified morphologically or by spodogram analysis. Peanut, broad bean, and sesame are also reported from a few sites, but it is uncertain whether they date from the prehistoric times. Finally, seeds of rape (*Brassica* sp.) and hemp (*Cannabis sativa*) (Gansu 1984) have been found in several Neolithic sites, which implies that these plants also have a long history of cultivation.

## Agricultural implements

The farm tools found in prehistoric sites are made of stone, bone, shell, or wood. They can be divided into three types in accordance with their functions.

Tilling tools consist of the spade, fork, and hoe, and all of them are digging implements with wooden handles. The stone spades from the Peiligang culture are long, narrow, flat, and thin, with rounded edges at their two ends, in contrast to those from the Yangshao culture which are broad, heavy, and thick. Both kinds of spades were used to cultivate loess soil. The bone spade, which is characteristic of the Hemudu culture, is made of buffalo shoulder-blades by retouching and perforating, and it has a very sharp edge. There are some wooden spades of a similar shape. These implements were used in rice fields. Traces of a fork with two prongs have been observed in the Miaodigou II culture, and a fork of the same type was still used in historical times. The hoe, a tool with a stone or shell adze fixed to a handle in the shape of a carpenter's square, was used for digging soil and uprooting weeds. Use of the plough in prehistoric times cannot be demonstrated; it may only have appeared later.

Harvesting tools include the knife and sickle. The knife varies in form and is made of different materials. The chipped knife is made of oval pebble flakes, notched on both sides. The pottery knife made of potsherds has the same form. The ground stone knife has a lunate or rectangular shape, with one or two perforations. There are some knives of the same form made of shells or pottery fragments. These knife-shaped tools, which were fixed to the handle with string through perforations, may have been used to cut the ears of cereals. Such knives, though made of iron, were still used in historical times. The stone sickle, a harvesting implement with a wooden handle, made its first appearance in the Peiligang culture, but it was very rare in the Yangshao culture, and then reappeared and became widespread in the Longshan culture, which had shell as well as stone sickles. Their form is the same as that of today's iron sickles.

Grain-processing tools, represented by stone querns and rollers, made their first appearance in the Peiligang and Cishan cultures, and declined in the Yangshao period. Pestles and mortars are seldom found, perhaps owing to the fact that wood was used as the main material for making such implements.

## Domestic animals

With the development of agriculture, animal husbandry flourished. Bones of pigs, dogs, and poultry, as well as a few ox bones, have been recovered from the earlier Neolithic cultures in North China; and later, in the Longshan culture, sheep, goats, and horses appeared. The domestic goat may have originated from western Asia; but the horse of Neolithic China may not have been a domesticated species. Pigs and dogs are frequently found in the Neolithic cultures of South China, and buffaloes have also been discovered occasionally. By the Shang period all these animals were regularly raised.

## Conclusion

The archaeological evidence as a whole indicates that, by 7000–8000 years ago, sedentary life had developed throughout much of China on the basis of an agricultural economy. At the same time, the crops, farm tools, and domestic animals displayed distinctive regional characteristics. The progressive development of the agricultural economy of the Yellow River Valley led directly to the emergence of a class state and fostered the Shang and Zhou Civilizations. There is thus no doubt that China is one of the centres of origin of agriculture in the world, and that the development of prehistoric agriculture, in East Asia at least, is indissolubly linked to the contributions of China (Chang 1970, Ho 1975, An 1984).

## References

An Zhimin 1982. *Essays on the Neolithic of China* [in Chinese]. Beijing: Wenwu Press.
An Zhimin 1984. Effect of the prehistoric cultures in the lower reaches of the Yangtze River on ancient Japan [in Chinese]. *Kaogu* 1984 **5**, 439–48.
Cai Lianzhen & Qiu Shihua 1984. Carbon 13 evidence for ancient diets in China. 1984 *Kaogu* [in Chinese] **10**, 949–55.
CASS (Chinese Academy of Social Sciences, Institute of Archaeology) 1983. *Radiocarbon dating in Chinese archaeology* [in Chinese]. Beijing: Wenwu Press.
CASS (Chinese Academy of Social Sciences, Institute of Archaeology) 1984. *Archaeological excavations and researches in New China* [in Chinese]. Beijing: Wenwu Press.
Chang Kwang-chi 1970. The beginnings of agriculture in the Far East. *Antiquity* **44**, 175–85.
Chang, T. W. 1989. Domestication and spread of the cultivated rices. In *Foraging and farming: the evolution of plant exploitation*, D. R. Harris & G. C. Hillman (eds), ch. 25. London: Unwin Hyman.
Gansu Provincial Museum and the Teachers College of Northwest China 1984. Studies on remains of millet and hemp unearthed from a Majiayao Culture site at Linjia, Dongxiang, Gansu [in Chinese]. *Kaogu* 1984 **7**, 654–5.
Ho Ping-ti 1975. *The cradle of the east*. Hong Kong: The Chinese University of Hong Kong.
Huang Qixu 1982. Application of spodogram analysis to archaeology [in Chinese]. *Kaogu* 1982 **4**, 418–20.
Huang Qixu 1982–83. Neolithic crops in the Huanghe River Valley [in Chinese]. *Nongye Kaogu* 1982 **2**, 55–61; 1983 **1**, 39–50; 1983 **2**, 86–90.
Yan Wenming 1982. Origin of rice growing in China [in Chinese]. *Nongye Kaogu* 1982 **1**, 19–31; 1982 **2**, 50–4.

# 42 *Coastal adaptation, sedentism, and domestication: a model for socio-economic intensification in prehistoric Southeast Asia*

CHARLES HIGHAM and BERNARD MALONEY

## Introduction

As archaeological research in the valleys of the Red, Chao Phraya, and Mekong rivers proceeds, so evidence is accumulating for a major cultural change probably during the 3rd millennium bc. This change involves the occupation of the tributary valleys of these major river systems by groups who lived in relatively small (0.5–5 ha) settlements, and who, to judge from the build-up of occupation layers, occupied their settlements permanently. In the Middle Country above the Red River delta, the earliest settlements of this expansionary phenomenon are called after the site of Phung Nguyen (Hoang Xuan Chinh & Nguyen Ngoc Bich 1978). This eponymous site has been intensively excavated and has yielded a material culture devoid of any evidence for bronze, but rich in the remains of polished stone axes and bracelets. Vietnamese archaeologists have no hesitation in describing it as a fully 'Neolithic' culture (Ha Van Tan 1980). In Northeast Thailand, the sites of Non Nok Tha, Ban Chiang, Ban Phak Top, and Non Kao Noi best document this initial, expansionary phase of human settlement onto the Khorat plateau. The preferred location was on slightly elevated ground near naturally flooded marshland. There are numerous sites in the lower valley of the Mekong, perhaps the best known being Samrong Sen, the subject of archaeological enquiry for well over a century. Finally, recent research in the Chao Phraya catchment has disclosed at Ban Tha Kae, as well as at Khok Charoen and Ban Kao, widespread early village settlements (Fig. 42.1; Sørensen & Hatting 1967, Ho 1984, Natapintu 1985).

According to the analysis of the biological remains from these settlements, the occupants were wide-ranging in their subsistence activities. One finds substantial evidence for fishing, the collection of shellfish, the trapping and hunting of small mammals, the hunting of large mammals such as the

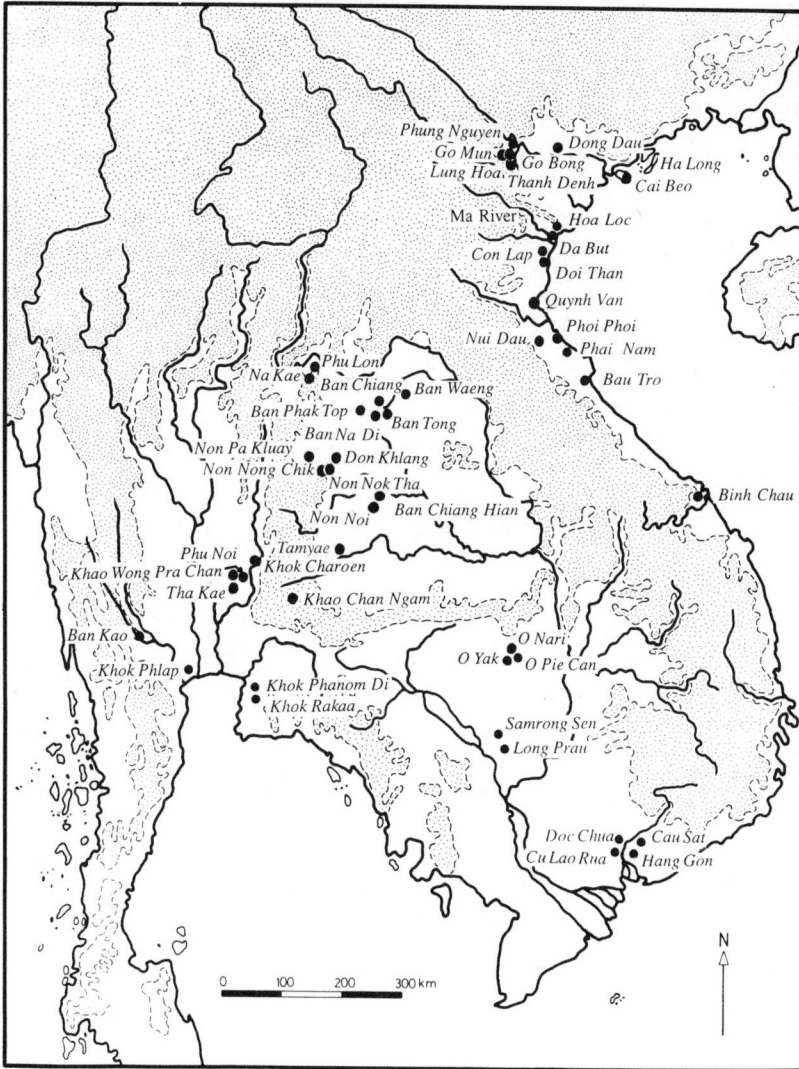

**Figure 42.1**  The location of the principal prehistoric village settlements in Southeast Asia.

Sambar deer and wild cattle, and the raising of domestic pigs and cattle. There is little doubt that plant foods, too, were widely exploited, although archaeological plant remains are scarce because recovery techniques to date have been crude. The remains of rice, however, are frequently recovered, either as grains (Chang & Loresto 1984) or as tempering in pottery. Opinion

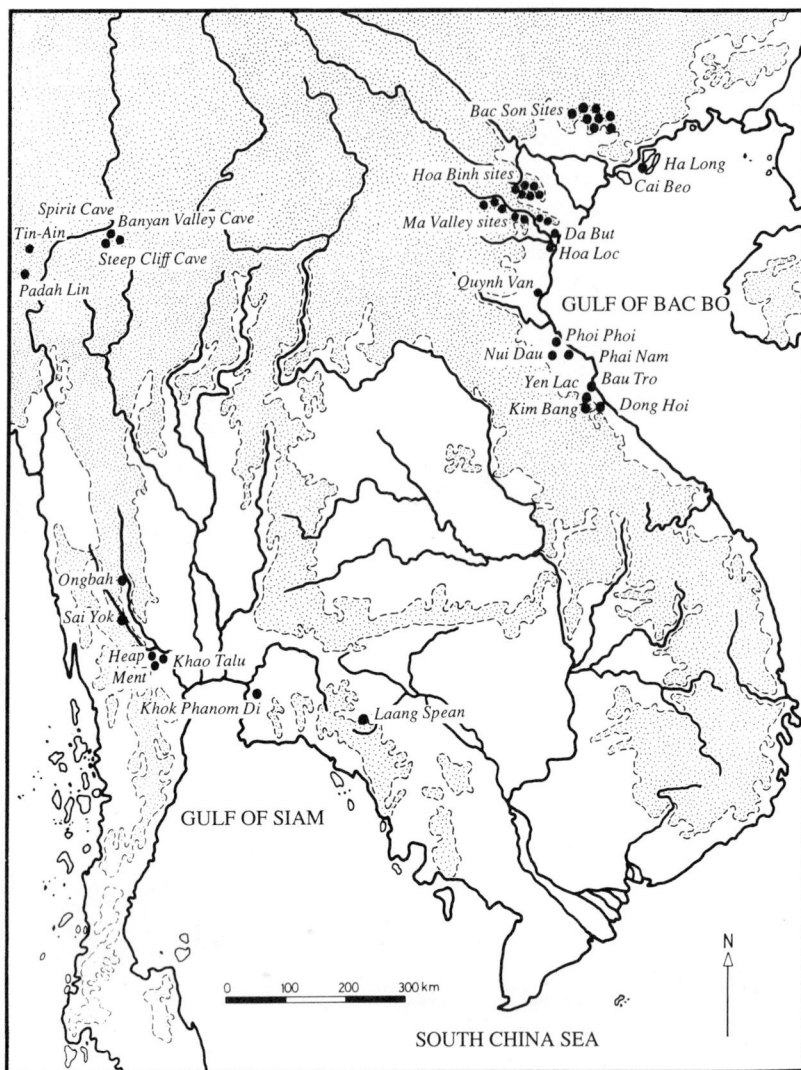

**Figure 42.2**   The location of the principal prehistoric hunter–gatherer sites in Southeast Asia.

on the status of this rice is divided (Yen 1982), but the harvesting of rice in one form or another is attested and it still grows wild along stream and swamp margins in the area (cf. White Ch. 9, this volume).

Tracing the origins of this expansionary phenomenon has been made difficult by two factors. It is clear that there was a long-term tradition of broad-spectrum foraging in the upland terrain of Southeast Asia, where, in

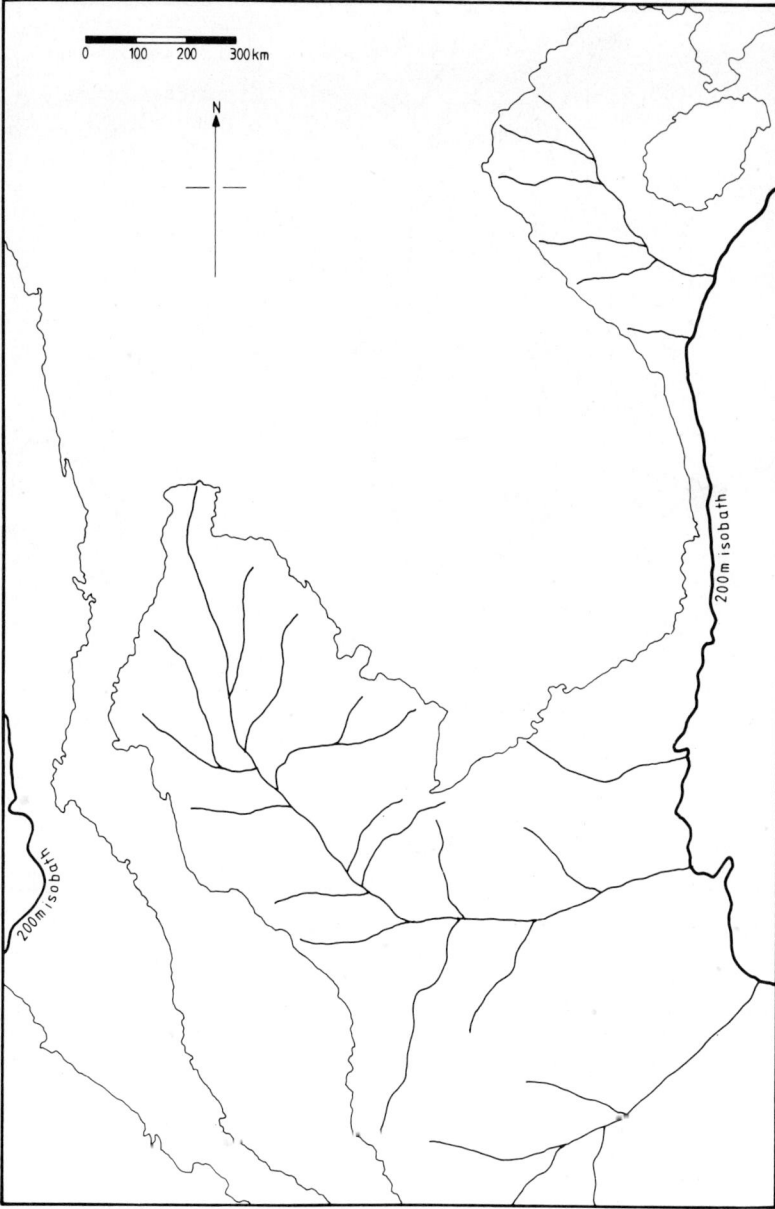

**Figure 42.3** The likely sea-level in Southeast Asia towards the end of the Pleistocene period.

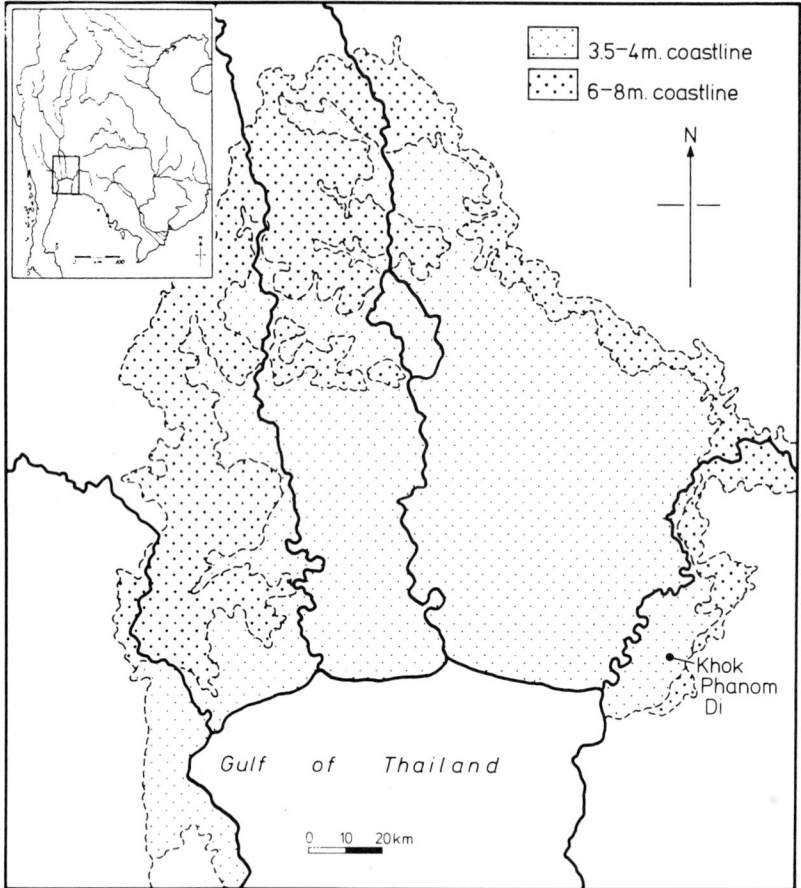

**Figure 42.4**  The location of Khok Phanom Di relative to raised shore lines of the period 4000–1000 bc.

contrast to the sub-tropical deciduous forest cover of the river-valley systems, a canopied evergreen forest dominated. This so-called Hoabinhian tradition incorporates the transitory settlement of small rockshelters (Fig. 42.2). According to the radiocarbon dates from a number of sites, this adaptive pattern lasted in the uplands of northern Thailand, central Cambodia, and doubtless elsewhere, into the Christian era. The second obstacle is the rapid post-Pleistocene rise of sea-level. The particularly flat nature of the terrain led to a rapid and very great loss of land (Fig. 42.3). It is a reasonable hypothesis that the former coasts and river valleys of this drowned landscape were formerly settled, but evidence for coastal settlement between about 8000 and 4000 bc is now beyond normal means of archaeological investigation.

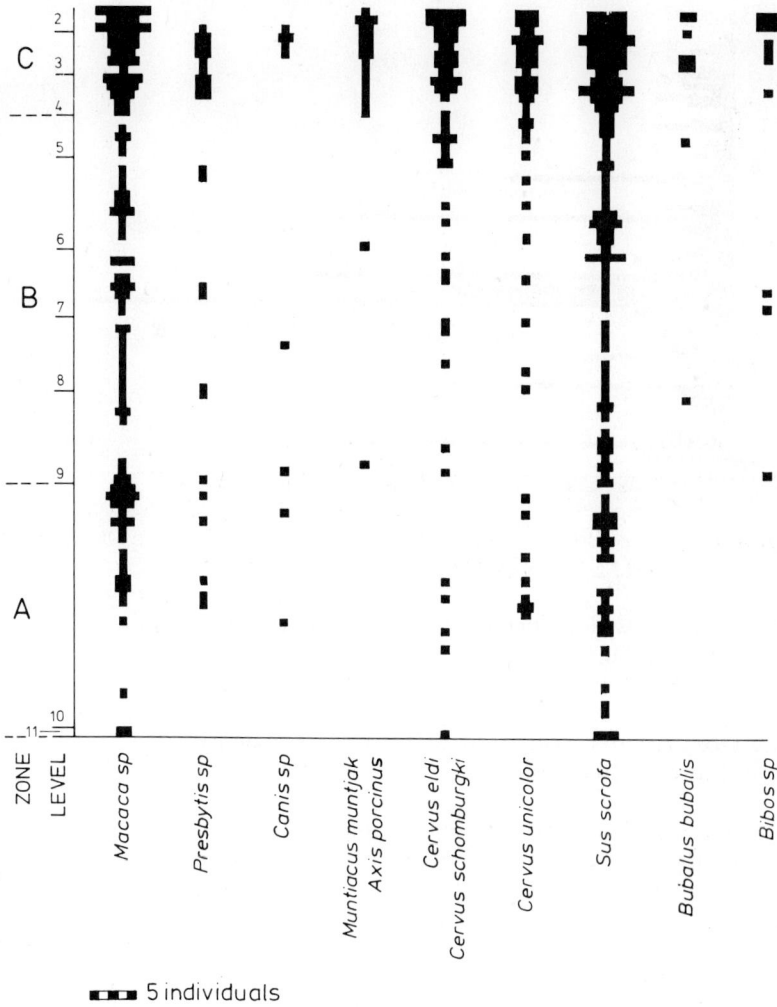

**Figure 42.5** The distribution of large mammalian fauna expressed as the minimum number of individuals represented per stratigraphic unit (courtesy Alan Grant).

Nevertheless, some insights can be gained because from about 6000 to 1500 bc – the actual dates have not been settled and will vary regionally – the sea-level fluctuated within a few metres of its present position. Marine and brackish-water clays were deposited and raised beaches were formed. These can be recognized, and archaeological site surveys have disclosed prehistoric settlements which are now some distance from the shore, but which were formerly coastal. It is the aim of this chapter to explore the nature of this coastal adaptation, and to suggest its wider place in later prehistoric

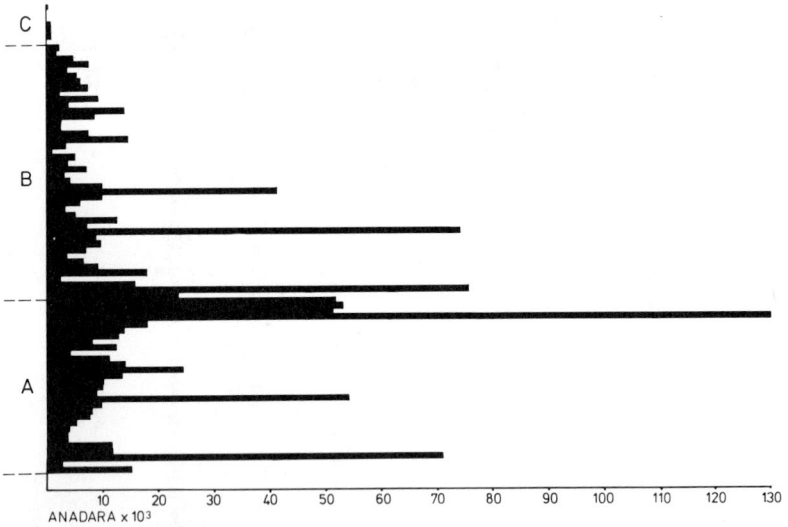

**Figure 42.6**    The distribution of *Anadara* shellfish at Khok Phanom Di expressed as the number of individuals found.

developments, with particular reference to the 1985 excavation of the site of Khok Phanom Di.

## The site and environment of Khok Phanom Di: faunal and pollen evidence

Khok Phanom Di is a 5-ha site now located 22 km from the shore of the Gulf of Siam (Fig. 42.4). It stands on marine clays which were laid down during a series of high sea-levels, probably between 5000 and 2000 bc. Excavations revealed a 7-m stratigraphy divided into three major occupation zones. The lowest, zone A, furnished a huge sample of biological material as well as 104 inhumation graves disposed in what we believe are lineage clusters. Zone B contained 51 graves, a few being extremely rich in terms of grave goods, associated with a raised mortuary platform with 43 successive floors. Zone C was only a metre deep, and was devoid of burials. Like its predecessors, it contained much biological material.

At present, we have 18 conventional radiocarbon dates from the cultural deposits and eight accelerator mass spectrometer (AMS) radiocarbon dates from the pollen cores taken from the surrounding area. (Table 42.1). The former series indicates that the deposits ascribed to zones A and B built up between *c.* 2000 and 1500 bc. The dates so far received from the pollen cores allow a tentative correlation to be made with the cultural occupation of Khok Phanom Di.

Grant and Higham's analysis of the larger mammalian fauna (Fig. 42.5)

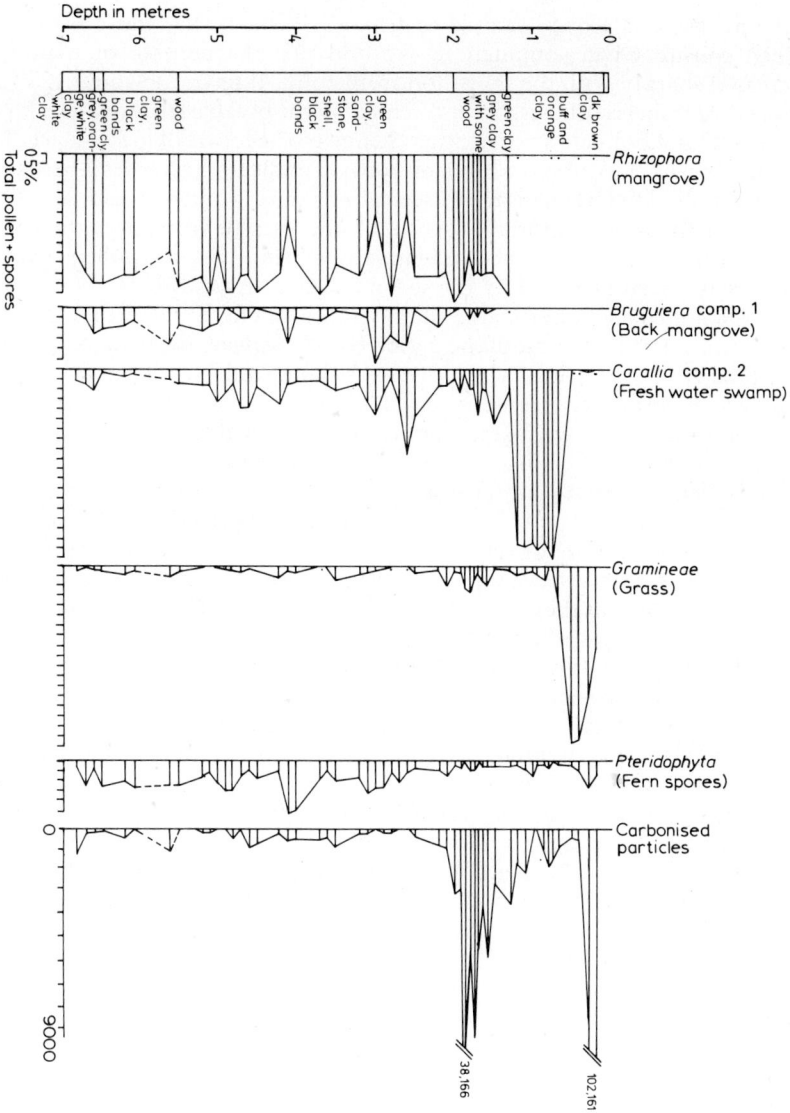

**Figure 42.7** A pollen diagram from BMR2, Khok Phanom Di, showing selected taxa only.

reveals a limited range of species and relatively few individuals during zones A and B. We have found no grounds for inferring domestication. West's analysis of the microfauna is proceeding, and she has identified the remains of essentially aquatic species. This situation is amply confirmed by other remains: there is a huge sample of fish, shellfish, turtle, and crustaceans. When considered in conjunction, we find that the number of mammals increased sharply with the transition from zones B to C, i.e. about 1250 bc, while the marine resources, as represented by the bivalve *Anadara*, fell almost to zero (Fig. 42.6). We attribute this change to the local fall in sea-level. The coastal species identified are unanimous in indicating a coastal–estuarine habitat dominated by mangrove associations during zones A and B.

One of the most important aspects of our current research is the correlation of the cultural sequence and faunal spectrum with the pollen analyses which have been prepared by the second author. As may be seen in Figure 42.7, the pollen diagram for core site BMR2, located 200 m northwest of the site, is dominated for most of the period by *Rhizophora*, the mangrove of the intertidal zone. *Bruguiera*, which occupies the inland side of the *Rhizophora* belt, was probably also present. *Bruguiera* and *Ceriops* cannot be separated palynologically, but two discrete pollen types labelled *Bruguiera* comp. 1 and *Bruguiera* comp. 2 (*Carallia* = *Bruguiera* comp. 2) have been distinguished. Grass pollen is present almost throughout the pollen record, but in restricted amounts until about 1 m below datum, when it came to dominate. Some, at least, of the grasses are of rice type, others are of *Paspalum, Eragrostis*, and, very rarely, possibly *Coix* type. *Paspalum, Eragrostis*, and *Coix* are typical rice-field weeds, but they also occur in other habitats. The weed flora of rice fields in the environs of Khok Phanom Di during the dry season, when the second author was at the site, consisted mainly of grasses and sedges. The sedges included species of *Scirpus, Cyperus*, and *Fimbristylis* which, again, occur in many habitats. They can be distinguished from each other palynologically, but this does not tell us very much. Other rice-field weeds included the fern *Ceratopteris thalictroides, Monochoria vaginalis* (used locally as a vegetable), *Neptunia oleracea, Ludwigia octovalis*, and *Nymphoides indicum*. When the normally fragile outer wall, the perine, of *Ceratopteris thalictroides* is present, the spore can be identified to the species. It is unfortunate, therefore, that it cannot be used on its own as a rice-field indicator, because it is characteristic of mangrove, a frequent contributor to the Khok Phanom Di palynological record, but one which has clearly adapted to changed ecological conditions over time. *Neptunia* does not contribute to the pollen record at all and *Monochoria* occurs very rarely, but, where grass is the dominant, two *Ludwigia* species, *Nymphoides*, and *Ceratopteris thalictroides* all occur. In view of the large size of the *Ceratopteris* spores, and their probable poor spatial dispersal, when they occur in combination with the grass, sedge, and other pollen taxa mentioned above, the almost inescapable conclusion is that they represent not a herbaceous swamp flora but rice-field weeds. Perhaps the most important inference from the grass pollen itself, however, is that which can be made in conjunction with the values for the charcoal particles. There was a huge increase in charcoal within the sample column at a depth of about 2 m, associated with three small rises in the grass pollen percentages, which should date to *c*. 4000 bc.

Core BMR2 should be considered in conjunction with core KL2 (Fig.

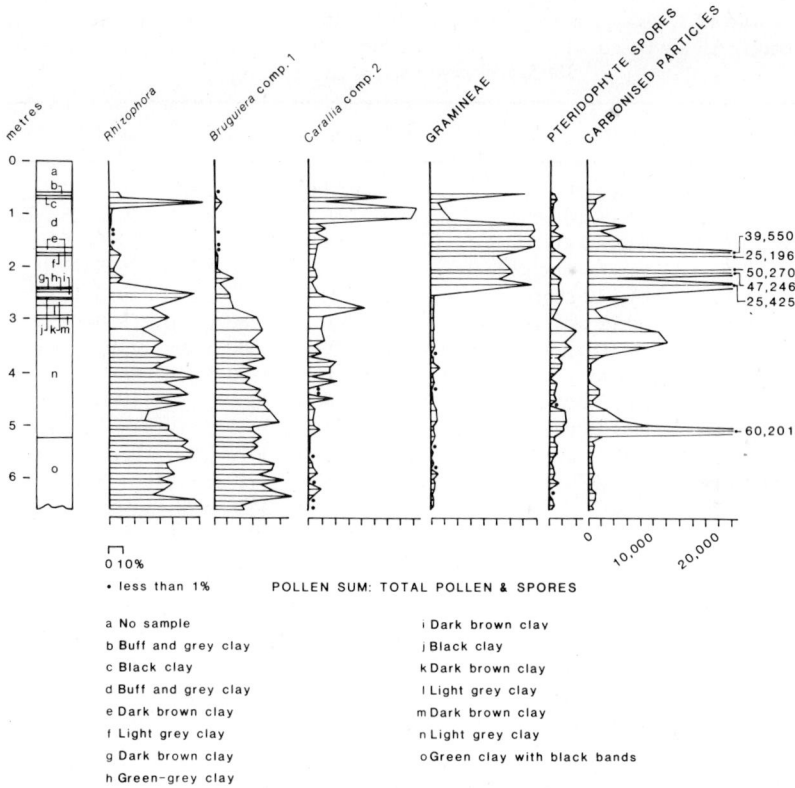

**Figure 42.8**  A pollen diagram from KL2, Khok Phanom Di, showing selected taxa only.

42.8). While they have a number of features in common, KL2 provides some important additional data: there was a massive influx of charcoal at a low level which is not represented in BMR2. There then follows a similar pattern between the two cores, including some minor rises in grass pollen in association with charcoal peaks. Again, there was a sudden reduction in the mangrove association but in this core there is evidence for a later and brief rise in sea-level (the upper *Rhizophora* peak) which dates to 2000 bc.

A detailed consideration of the preservation status of the pollen and spores in both cores adds further to the story. The BMR2 core shows little variation in the percentage of extremely corroded and probably re-deposited grains until 2 m below datum, but peaks occur associated with the troughs in the minor grass pollen risen above this level and to a lesser extent when the grass becomes dominant as *Bruguiera* comp. 2 declines. The KL2 core is radically different in places, and, because re-deposition and associated minor grass pollen peaks may correlate with local erosion consequent upon disturbance

**Table 42.1**  Radiocarbon dates from Khok Phanom Di and associated pollen cores. All are based on a 5570-year half-life, calibrated according to Klein *et al.* (1982) and expressed at the 2σ range.

| Context | Source | Lab. no. | yrs BP | yrs BC |
|---|---|---|---|---|
| Layer 6:6 | charcoal | ANU 5482 | 3310 ± 128 | 1875–1400 |
| Layer 8:2 | lens 4 ash lens | NZ7020 | 1840 ± 310 | 405–625 AD |
| Layer 8:2 | lens 4 ash lens | ANU 5483 | 3430 ± 80 | 1990–1560 |
| Layer 8:3 | lens 6 ash charcoal | NZ7021 | 3670 ± 140 | 2525–1710 |
| Layer 8:7 | lens 10 charcoal | NZ6973 | 3272 ± 200 | 1975–1120 |
| Layer 9:1 | white ash lens | NZ7033 | 3280 ± 110 | 1860–1390 |
| Layer 9:6 | charcoal under lens 9 | NZ7060 | 3680 ± 90 | 2395–1785 |
| Layer 9:7 | hearth | NZ7063 | 4310 ± 310 | 3650–2310 |
| Layer 10:6 | lens 3 hearth | ANU 5484 | 3280 ± 140 | 1900–1325 |
| Layer 10:13 | lens 10 charcoal lens | ANU 5485 | 3410 ± 110 | 1975–1545 |
| Layer 10:15 | lens 11 ash lens | ANU 5486 | 3610 ± 90 | 2305–1720 |
| Layer 10:19 | hearth 7 | ANU 5487 | 3420 ± 110 | 2135–1655 |
| Layer 10:21 | hearth 15 | ANU 5489 | 3420 ± 90 | 1980–1555 |
| Layer 10:22 | hearth 19 | ANU 5488 | 3580 ± 100 | 2290–1695 |
| Layer 10:24 | charcoal in ash lens | ANU 5491 | 3530 ± 80 | 2165–1675 |
| Layer 10:25 | hearth 27 | ANU 5492 | 3480 ± 110 | 2125–1650 |
| Layer 10:25 | charcoal | ANU 5490 | 3730 ± 100 | 2525–1885 |
| Layer 11: | hearth 1 | ANU 5493 | 3560 ± 80 | 2185–1685 |
| KL2 | 0.87–0.91 m | OxA 1354 | 3360 ± 120 | 1910–1435 |
| KL2 | 1.46–1.50 m | OxA 1355 | 560 ± 150 | 1235–1595 AD |
| KL2 | 2.25–2.29 m | OxA 1356 | 5560 ± 160 | 4710–3960 |
| KL2 | 3.50–3.54 m | OxA 1357 | 6060 ± 200 | 5330–4555 |
| KL2 | 4.82–4.86 m | OxA 1358 | 6280 ± 130 | 5530–4935 |
| KL2 | 4.91–4.95 m | OxA 1359 | 6400 ± 300 | 5800–4755 |
| BMR2 | 3.96–4.00 m | OxA 1360 | 6560 ± 100 | 5767–5230 |
| BMR2 | 6.60–6.64 m | OxA 1361 | 6610 ± 140 | 5855–5230 |

of the vegetation on the site itself, the briefly summarized results which follow suggest that pollen and chemical analyses of a new core, which it is hoped to obtain from as near the north side of the site as possible, may add further valuable information.

Below 5.1 m depth re-deposited pollen predominates. This may be indicative of longshore drift before the Khok Phanom Di mound formed, but it is impossible to be certain without a geomorphologist's opinion on the nature of the mound. From 5.1 to 4.8 m there was a period of stability. However, four large peaks of re-deposited material occurred between 4.8 and 3.5 m, possibly related to overtopping of the mound by ocean waves or to erosion of the mound itself as a result of minor vegetation clearances (but the charcoal peaks are below and above these changes). Stability was regained until the major rise in grass pollen, and between 1.54 and 1.0 m when grass remained dominant, but the final peak occurred before the large increase in *Bruguiera* comp. 2. This core was taken from an irrigation canal and the upper 62 cm of deposit is missing, so more precise correlation with the BMR2 sequence is hindered. Additionally, the possibility of non-sequences in both cores must not be ignored. Sediments from open-basin depositional environments are far from ideal for the pollen analyst to investigate, but use of volume magnetic susceptibility on all the cores collected may help unravel many of the problems.

The results of the AMS (OxA) radiocarbon dates (Table 42.1) indicate that there was a long period of human interference with the environment in the vicinity of the coring locations before Khok Phanom Di was itself occupied. From core KL2, there are two burning episodes dated to 4755–5800 BC and 4555–5300 BC. These are not associated with any marked rise in grass pollen or weeds of rice fields, and may reflect a number of causes, such as natural conflagrations and hunter–gatherer induced burnoffs. The third major rise in charcoal at a depth of 2.3 m in this core, however, is associated with a major increase in the pollen of Gramineae and significant increases in a suite of plants which flourish in rice fields. This episode is dated to 3960–4710 BC.

We await the results of two further accelerator determinations from core BMR2, but the rise in charcoal there at a depth of just under 2 m may reflect the initial occupation of Khok Phanom Di. Alternatively, the late rise in sea-level seen at a depth of 1 m in KL2 may be the occasion when the site was occupied. There is a date of 1435–1910 BC for this horizon in the core, which provides a good fit with the culturally derived dates, but the situation is obscured by an anomalous date of 1235–1595 AD from a slightly lower context.

In summary, there are grounds for suspecting that rice was propagated in the area by the 4th millennium BC, but the archaeological context for this activity is presumably blanketed by the deposition of marine clays during a period of high sea-level. The establishment of Khok Phanom Di itself *c.* 2000 BC involved forest clearance and rice consumption along with a diet dominated by marine species. While the data are not yet analysed in full, we increasingly incline to the view that some of this rice was deliberately cultivated.

## Coastal adaptation and sedentism

There are several reasons why we believe that Khok Phanom Di was permanently occupied. First, inhumation burials were found within a stratigraphical build up of 5.5 m. From first to last, the same grave ritual was followed. The dead were buried with heads pointing to the rising sun. They were disposed in clear clusters, which comprised adults of both sexes, children, and infants. The style of the shell jewellery was similar, as was the habit of covering the corpse with red ochre and wrapping it in a shroud made of unwoven, bast-like material. Perhaps the most compelling point, however, is the finding that the clusters themselves were positioned over each other, in the same part of the site, over such a lengthy time span. Of course, this could indicate that the site was no more than a central cemetery visited only for mortuary rites. This, however, would not accommodate the abundant evidence of occupation in the form of middens and the ash spreads interpreted as areas for firing pottery vessels. Without marshalling every available piece of evidence, it is noted here that there are reasonable grounds for asserting that Khok Phanom Di was occupied permanently for about six centuries, following at least two millennia of human coastal occupation in the general area.

Inasmuch as the diet was reliant on the harvesting of marine species in addition to the propagation of rice, the situation is in direct contrast to the more traditional view of Southeast Asian hunter–gatherer–foragers, which is centred on the temporary occupation of upland rockshelters. Nor is Khok Phanom Di in fact alone in documenting a rich coastal settlement. For many decades, deeply stratified and large sites on raised fossil beaches have been known in Vietnam. Such coastal situations, particularly where they incorporate estuaries, are particularly advantageous in fostering enhanced territoriality. The architectural features found at Khok Phanom Di suggest the construction of houses and ritual structures. Living together permanently in one place, occupying houses, regarding the settlement environs as the group's preserve, and sharing the living place with the ancestors – all these represent a radical contrast with the mobile upland groups.

The contrast can be summarized in the word domestication. Sedentism at its simplest level permits people to accumulate possessions, to make a new range of artefacts, and to be predictably present in one place for exchange. But it is far more than that. It opens up a new conception of the place of the individual in the community, and indeed in the very ordering of it. Where food resources are predictable, sufficient, and storable, human behaviour in burgeoning sedentary communities can expand their horizons, develop complex ranking behaviour, and accumulate status and obligations. New demands are made on the creation of goods to signal such status. At Khok Phanom Di, we have turtle-shell breastplates, superb pottery vessels, and a woman buried with 120 000 shell beads. Again, ranking invokes ritual. The raised platform structure of Khok Phanom Di remains unique in Southeast Asia.

The evidence from the 1985 excavation at Khok Phanom Di, then, indicates, through its structures and burials, domestication not necessarily of plants and animals, but rather of people; and the radiocarbon dates from the pollen cores suggest that human modification of the vegetation of the area occurred from ʼc. 6000 BC. The sedentary nature of the settlement, it is argued, also fostered population growth and the expansion of new communities. In this context, it is immaterial whether the plants found there were cultivated or not, or whether animal behaviour was yet modified by people to the point of herd maintenance.

Sedentary communities such as Khok Phanom Di, set in rich habitats, permit population growth, though given the high incidence of infant mortality in zone A, this may have taken time to manifest itself. Now high co-residential populations invoke the problems recently addressed by Johnson (1982) and described as scalar stress. This involves a series of population thresholds which, when approached, invite new responses. One option is fission, whereby a segment of the community moves elsewhere. This is straightforward in the absence of social circumscription, and was doubtless commonly taken. When alternative coastal enclaves are already taken up, however, and the more marginal hinterland also suffers a packing of communities, options narrow and may invoke conflict or new forms of social organization, such as ranking and the increased use of ritual to resolve conflict. Ranking is a means of reducing stress through vesting leadership and status in one or a few individuals. It hardly needs emphasis that it is also a convenient mechanism for the ordering of exchange relationships and the storage and distribution of foodstuffs. In turn, it accentuates a demand for prestige goods which act as emblems of the highly ranked.

The issue of food storage brings us to rice, a plant which was harvested at Khok Phanom Di, and, to judge from the context of the rice remains, was locally husked. Processing rice is not as arduous as wheat or barley because it can be cooked as whole grains. Once the husks are removed, rice can be stored and consumed without further processing. Indeed, brown rice is more nutritious than the white polished grain. Rice was present from the basal layers as an inclusion in potting clay, and then became more abundant as chaff found in occupation layers.

Data from zone A may be seen as a microcosm of similar events which may well have preceded it at other sites in this rich, coastal tract. They reflect a sedentary population, which, as it grew in numbers, expanded its resource base and encountered scalar stress. Let us assume that, initially at least, the last problem was resolved by fission. Similar coastal enclaves would soon be taken up if they were not already occupied. The next best option for settlement was probably along the river valleys and particularly the tributary streams which provided routes, water, and aquatic resources, and which suffered minimal flood risk. In Northeast Thailand, it is just these positions which witnessed early occupation at, for example, Ban Chiang, Non Kao Noi, and Non Nok Tha. The earliest biological remains from Ban Chiang reveal a broadly based gathering, fishing, and collecting pattern allied with the maintenance of domestic cattle, pig, and dog, and the harvesting of rice. This form of adaptation appears to have been successful biologically, as there are numerous such sites and their inhabitants were robust, well fed, and healthy. They are held to represent a successful adaptation to the inland stream valleys by sedentary, partially agricultural village communities. Being removed from the coast meant that such inland areas were more affected by the long dry season, and, in this respect, they can be termed 'marginal'.

This habitat, however, is marginal only in relation to the concentrated biomass characteristic of the coastal estuarine enclaves where the impact of the long dry season was lessened by proximity to the sea. It is not hard to imagine that the tracts just behind the optimal coastal zone filled fairly rapidly, if the sedentary coastal settlements are seen as the original donors. The point is that for sites like Khok Phanom Di, fission is an option only until social circumscription takes effect. The converse is continuing population growth and the possibility that more intense social ranking systems and attendant ritual developed to cope with scalar stress.

## Intensification

Evidence for such intensification could take the form of growing disparity in the wealth of grave goods among individuals buried at about the same time, differential energy expended in burying the higher ranked individuals, evidence for population growth, more restricted distribution of valuables, and, perhaps, modification of the environment to encourage certain food resources. Such intensification could, for example, take the form of expanding, through clearance of the natural freshwater swamp vegetation, the area within which rice flourished. The local intensification of rice production need not have involved any conceptual break with the preceding system of harvesting, but rather increased interference with competitors to enlarge suitable habitats. Such improvement of the natural habitat for rice would, however, have increased territoriality.

The above model sees sedentism, population growth, and fissioning to more marginal habitats, followed by crowding in the optimal zone and increased social ranking, as factors involved in trends towards the intensified exploitation of rice. How do the data from Khok Phanom Di fit the model, and how might it be tested in the future? Initial settlement is seen as reflecting the pull of predictable and concentrated marine food resources to hunter–gatherers already probably logistically mobile and accustomed to a marine habitat. They secured food through exploiting optimum resources, a strategy greatly assisted by marine transport. As settlement developed through zone B, population grew and the co-residing group underwent a process of fissioning whereby certain emigrant groups occupied more marginal inland locations, including tributary stream valleys. Marsh clearance there expanded or opened up areas suitable for the proliferation of rice, but this plant was one, possibly minor, component in a very flexible and wide-ranging subsistence strategy. Domestic cattle, which were not suited to the coastal swamps, and domestic pigs, were maintained in the marginal zones. The relatively large co-residential group at Khok Phanom Di encouraged ranking behaviour, as did participation in exchange networks to supply interior communities with desirable marine products, particularly shell jewellery and ceramics. This is reflected in some disparity in individual wealth among the zone A burials of adults and children.

This phase of fissioning may well have fluctuated within and between sites, depending on their length of occupation. In the case of Khok Phanom

Di, six centuries of permanent occupation may well have been long enough to trigger fissioning tendencies. During a long standstill in sea-level, the process could have been repeated at earlier sites now lost to the sea. By the time of the sharp change seen at the start of zone B at Khok Phanom Di, increased circumscription and the developing exchange networks, as well as the growing population, entailed investing more energy in ritual and ascriptive ranking. Burials display an increased dichotomy between rich and poor, and there is some evidence that those skilled in primary production of quality ceramics were among the most highly ranked echelon. Indeed, a child too young to have been skilled in pottery making was buried with much shell jewellery together with a miniature potter's anvil. Increased ritual and attention to burial rites is indicated by the transition of the part of the site excavated from an occupation area with burials to a specific cemetery complete with a raised platform structure. It is considered likely that rice was by now at least encouraged by the expansion of its preferred habitat.

## Conclusion

The model we favour visualizes rice harvesting in both the marginal and optimal zones as a component part of a flexible multi-faceted subsistence strategy. During the period under review, rice was significant more for its potential for intensification than the realization of more extensive or productive cultivation. Indeed, the first major intensification in agricultural methods probably came with the formation of centralized chiefdoms between 500 and 0 BC. The crucial issue is not the cultivation of rice, nor any other food resource, but rather the increasing domestication of human beings through the conditions of sedentism, territoriality, and the re-working of their personal relations. It was this change, now perceived through the excavation of Khok Phanom Di, which, it is argued, stimulated the rich cultural expression of social ranking and leadership expressed in the material panoply of status. It also illustrates one way in which the great expansion of human settlement which occurred from the 3rd millennium BC may have begun.

## Acknowledgements

We wish to thank the Director General of the Fine Arts Department and Pisit Charoenwongsa for their constant and friendly assistance while we were working in Thailand. The Ford Foundation; Shell Company of Thailand; Universities of Cambridge, Belfast, and Otago; British Academy; Wenner Gren Foundation; and the Centre for Field Research made the research possible through their generous financial assistance. To our many co-workers on the Khok Phanom Di project, we offer our thanks. We are particularly indebted to Rachanie Bannanurag, co-director of the project, for her many efforts on our behalf.

# References

Chang, T. T. & E. Loresto, 1984. The rice remains. In *Prehistoric investigations in Northeast Thailand*, C. F. W. Higham & A. Kijngam (eds), 384–5. Oxford: British Archaeological Reports, International Series 231.

Ha Van Tan 1980. Nouvelles recherches préhistoriques et protohistoriques au Viet Nam. *Bulletin de l'École Française de l'Extrême-Orient* **LXVIII**, 113–54.

Ho, C. M. 1984. *The pottery of Khok Charoen in its wider context.* Unpublished PhD dissertation, University of London (External).

Hoang Xuan Chinh & Nguyen Ngic Bich 1978. *Di Chi Khao Co Hoc Phung Nguyen.* Ha Noi: Nha Xuat Ban Khoa Hox Xa Hoi.

Johnson, G. A. 1982. Organisational structure and scalar stress. In *Theory and explanation in archaeology*, A. C. Renfrew, M. J. Rowlands & B. A. Segraves (eds) New York: Academic Press.

Klein, J., J. C. Leiman, P. E. Damen & E. K. Ralph 1982. Calibration of radiocarbon dates. *Radiocarbon* **24**, 103–50.

Maloney, B. K., C. F. W. Higham & R. Bannanurag. In press. Vegetation disturbance and early rice in Thailand: the archaeological and palynological evidence from Khok Phanom Di. *Nature.*

Natapintu, S. 1985. *Prehistoric investigations in the lower Chao Phraya Valley 1983–5.* Bangkok: Fine Arts Department.

Sørensen, P. & T. Hatting. 1967. *Archaeological investigations in Thailand.* Vol. II. *Ban Kao.* Part 1: *The archaeological materials from the burials.* Copenhagen: Munskgard.

Yen, D. E. 1982. Ban Chiang pottery and rice. *Expedition* **24**, 51–64.

White, J. C. 1989 Ethnoecological observations on wild and cultivated rice and yams in northeastern Thailand. In *Foraging and farming: the evolution of plant exploitation*, D. R. Harris & G. C. Hillman (eds), ch. 9. London: Unwin Hyman.

# 43 *The transition from stone to steel in the prehistoric swidden agricultural technology of the Kantu' of Kalimantan, Indonesia*

MICHAEL R. DOVE

## Introduction

Hand-forged iron tools are an important component of the swidden (shifting cultivation) technology of the contemporary Kantu' of West Kalimantan, Indonesia.[1] As among other tribal swidden groups in Kalimantan (Borneo), however, there is relatively little archaeological, documentary-historical, or oral-historical evidence regarding the origins of this metallurgy. As a result, the role of metallurgy in the evolution of the sophisticated Dayak system of swidden agriculture remains obscure. The aim of this chapter is to illuminate this role using a heretofore unutilized source of evidence, namely contemporary myth and ritual.

## Iron among the contemporary Kantu'

The Kantu' forge by hand all of the iron tools used in their daily life. While not every man knows how to forge the more difficult tools (e.g. war swords or shotguns), there are few adult males who do not know how to forge the simpler ones. They obtain scrap iron (often old automobile springs) for this purpose through trade. The *besi* or 'iron' is worked in a fire, which is stoked with charcoal from the ironwood tree (*Eusideroxylon zwageri*), and fanned with typical Malayic piston bellows made of bamboo.

The most common products of the Kantu' forges, and the most important tools for swidden cultivation, are the *duko'* or 'brush sword' and the *beliong* or 'adze'. The former comprises a heavy, slightly convex, single-edged blade, at least 50 cm in length, which is hafted to a wooden hilt with natural resins; the latter is an equally heavy (1.5 kg) iron blade, with a small, convex cutting edge, which is fixed at an oblique angle to a wooden shaft by means of a rattan seating that tightens with every stroke of the adze. The brush sword is used for the initial clearing of brush, vines, and saplings on prospective swidden sites; while the adze is used for the subsequent felling of the larger trees. In contempoary swiddens, the dividing line between trees that are slashed with the brush sword and trees that are left to be felled with the adze is a trunk diameter of approximately 8 cm (Dove 1985).

The Kantu' make their brush-sword cuts at waist level or below, and they make their adze cuts at chest level. On occasion, however, especially when clearing older forest containing many large trees, they make a higher adze cut, 3 or 4 m from the ground. They achieve this by standing atop either a *tanga'*, a log with steps cut into it that is leaned against the tree trunk, or a *tunai*, two or more poles that are lashed against the trunk to form a crude platform.

The Kantu' say that there are several reasons why this high cut is desirable when felling large trees. First, they say that the wood lower down on the trunk is the hardest – and hence the most difficult to cut – wood on the tree. This difference is of little importance when felling small trees, but it is associated with significantly different expenditures of labour when felling large trees (i.e. those up to 1 m or more in diameter). The second reason that the Kantu' give for making high cuts on large trees is to get above the buttresses, which are found on many of the species growing in the older forest in their territory. By cutting above the buttresses, the total amount of wood that the feller needs to cut is significantly reduced (I measured reductions in total cutting area of over one-third that were achieved by cutting above the buttresses). The third reason for making high cuts in primary forest is *adat*, i.e. 'tradition' or 'customary law'. The Kantu' say that according to their *adat*, they have to make high cuts on at least one or two trees in every primary forest swidden, so that the rice plants that are eventually planted there will 'see' the tall tree stumps that are left by this cutting and will try to grow as tall themselves.

Knowledge of when, where, and how the Kantu' first acquired either iron tools or their ability to forge iron tools is not present in either the memory or the oral history of the contemporary Kantu'. This is the norm for the interior tribal groups of Borneo. In her comments on the iron technology of the Lun Dayeh (who live in the highland region where the borders of Kalimantan, Sarawak, and Sabah meet), Padoch (1983, p. 36) simply remarks that they 'have traded for iron as long as is remembered in their oral histories'. In his analysis of the Iban of Sarawak, Freeman (1970, p. 174) notes '... nor is there any mention in their traditions of stone tools'. He attributes this to the antiquity of iron use among the Iban, saying (ibid, p. 175) 'it may well be that the Iban were in possession of iron before their arrival in Borneo'. Hose & McDougal (1912 I, p. 193) proposed an identical thesis with regard to the Kayan: 'The origin of their knowledge of iron and the processes of smelting and forging remains hidden in mystery; but there can be little doubt that the Kayans were familiar with these processes before they entered Borneo.' Speaking of the Kelabit, on the other hand, Harrisson (1965, p. 139) suggested that they still possessed a lithic technology when they settled their homeland in the uplands of central Borneo, and that their transition to a metal technology took place there.

## Stone among the Kantu'

The principal stone tool in common use among the Kantu' today is the *batu ansah* or 'whetstone'. These are used daily to sharpen the edges of adzes, brush swords, and other cutting tools. Most whetstones are just common rocks from river beds, selected for their density and the presence of a flat side against which a blade can be easily stroked. Some whetstones, however, are believed to have been given by spirits to the ancestors of the Kantu', and these have been passed down as heirlooms to the contemporary generations. These stones, called *batu umai* or 'swidden stones', are used only during the clearing of forest for swiddens and are the object of great respect and frequent rituals. Their prominent role in the swidden cycle can be inferred from the fact that the major ceremony of the entire cycle, which is held after the rice crop has been harvested, is called the *gawa' batu* or '(whet)stone feast' (cf. Sandin 1962). This veneration extends to certain other stones as well, in particular the curing stones used by shamans (cf. King 1975).

Blades from archaic stone tools were discovered (either in the ground or in the possession of tribesmen) by early European travellers at many different locales in Borneo, but never in quantity (Hose & McDougall 1912 II, p. 11n, Bartlett 1957, p. 128). In the course of my own research in several different parts of Kalimantan, carried out at intervals over the years 1974–84, I encountered only one or two (see below). This paucity of stone-tool relics was noted over one century ago by the Italian naturalist Beccari, who attempted to explain it by suggesting that the people who first settled the island were a 'civilized' race, already in the possession of an iron technology (Bartlett 1957, p. 127) – a suggestion that has been made by other Bornean scholars as well, as noted earlier. While some of the latter-day immigrants to Borneo may indeed have brought an Iron-Age technology with them, this could not have been the case with the first inhabitants of the island – because human habitation has been documented as early as 40 000 years ago (Majid 1982, p. 1).

The few stone relics that remain are usually found in the possession of shamans, who regard them as having supernatural curative power (cf. King 1985, p. 145). One Kantu' shaman, for example, possessed a curing stone shaped like an arrowhead, which he called *batu melaban* or 'fighting stone'. In his Iban dictionary, Richards (1981, p. 29) similarly notes that *batu beliong* or 'adze stone' and *batu kapak* or 'axe stone' are terms for charms used by shaman. In what appears to be a majority of cases, however, these celts-cum-charms – especially adze blades – are given names that associate them with thunder and lightning. Thus, the Kelabit call them *batu prahit* or 'thunder-bolts' (Harrisson 1965, p. 133); the Kenyah call them 'teeth ... of the thunder-god' (Hose & McDougall 1912 II, p. 11n); and the Iban call them *batu nitar* or 'lightning stones' (Richards 1981, p. 29), as do the Maloh (King 1984, p. 145).[2]

The Dayak, indeed, believe that lightning, or the spirit of lightning, is the source of these stones. While they identify these stone relics – from their distinctive shape – as adze blades (etc.) and name them accordingly, they do not identify them as *human* adze blades. That is, they do not identify them as the remains of tools that they – or their ancestors – might have used. Neither the Kantu', nor any other Dayak group apparently, make any reference in their oral history or mythology to the former use of stone tools by themselves or their ancestors, as noted earlier.

## The evolution from stone to iron

Although the Neolithic past of the Kantu', and the evolution of their technology, are not recorded directly or explicitly in their oral history, they are recorded – albeit indirectly – in the contemporary practices surrounding the felling of the forest. Felling places greater demands upon the contemporary steel technology of the Kantu' than does any other activity. Indeed, on occasion this technology is inadequate to meet these demands and the felling techniques must be modified accordingly. One example of such modification is the already discussed use of felling stands in primary forest, which permits the feller to make his cut above the buttresses and dense wood at the base of the tree. A second example is the practice of simply by-passing the largest trees with the hardest wood, when clearing primary forest. (As long as no more than a few trees are left standing, they will usually die when the trees that have been felled around them are later burned.) There is a third example of modification of felling techniques, which is due not to the inadequacies of the contemporary steel technology, but rather – as is suggested below – to the inadequacies of the prehistoric lithic technology. This involves the practice of *nyarau* or 'pollarding', which is carried out on a limited scale in every contemporary Kantu' swidden cut from secondary forest.

Pollarding is carried out during the swidden stage in which the forest is felled, as opposed to the preceding stage in which the forest is slashed. Unlike most other felling operations, however, pollarding is carried out with the brush sword, not the adze. There are two distinct pollarding techniques: one consists in climbing the trunk of a tree and lopping off its main branches where they join the trunk; and the other consists in climbing out onto these branches and lopping off the secondary and tertiary branches instead. The latter technique involves more climbing and cutting and it accordingly consumes several times as much labour per tree as the first technique. However, even the first technique consumes several times as much labour as the standard felling technique of simply cutting the tree through at its base, with an adze. (The Kantu' fell secondary forest at an average rate of 102 cm$^2$ of wood per minute – based on measurements of the area of the cross-sections of trees at chest level – whereas even the fastest pollarding technique achieves a rate – again referring to the areas of the cross sections, at chest level, of the trees pollarded – of only 31 cm$^2$ per minute.) Because the added labour that the Kantu' must devote to pollarding does not accomplish any more thoroughly the normal goals of felling – removing the forest canopy so that the sun's rays can penetrate to the surface of the swidden, and transforming the forest into a layer of nutrient-rich ash on which food crops will grow – the question arises as to why the Kantu' pollard some of the trees in their swiddens, as opposed to just felling them all.

Some Kantu' say that the reason they pollard trees is to provide vertical supports – from the still standing trunks of pollarded trees – for the climbing legumes that they will later plant in the swidden (i.e. after the completion of felling and burning). However, the small number of trees pollarded (the average is two per swidden), and the large size of the swiddens (the average swidden cut from secondary forest averages 2.3 ha in area), indicates that pollarding does not significantly contribute to the support of climbing legumes and that this cannot, consequently, be the main reason for its practice. A second explanation for its practice, which is more commonly cited by the Kantu', is *adat* or 'custom'. In the earlier discussion of the reasons given by the Kantu' for their use of felling stands in primary forest, it was noted that in addition to the desirability of cutting above the buttresses and dense wood at the base of the tree, the Kantu' say that the resultant tall stumps will provide a model for the subsequent growth of the rice plants. This latter explanation is also cited for the practice of pollarding in secondary forest: i.e. the Kantu' say that the tall standing trunks that are left after this operation will provide a visual stimulus to the rice plants to grow tall. More generally, the Kantu' say that the tall trunks that result from pollarding in secondary forest are necessary because they are *klai'* or 'symbol' of a swidden. (Note that pollarding is confined to secondary forest, and that the use of felling stands is confined to primary forest: the trees in the latter are too large to permit climbing and pollarding, and the trees in the former are too small to require the use of felling stands.)

The role of pollarding in symbolizing a swidden, combined with its ritual role in stimulating the all-important growth of the rice plants, is not in keeping with the very minor role that this technique occupies in the contemporary swidden technology of the Kantu'. The most likely explanation of this anomaly is that pollarding once played a much more important role in their swidden technology. Because pollarding is more time-consuming than felling, and is also more dangerous, the Kantu' would have made greater use of it in the past only if felling were a less viable alternative than it is today – which is very likely to have once been the case. Because tree trunks are thicker than tree branches, they are harder to cut through and require a proportionately more sophisticated cutting tool. Accordingly, during the course of development of the Kantu' forest-clearing technology, there would have been a stage at which their ancestors possessed tools with which they could sever tree branches, but could not yet easily cut through entire tree trunks. This stage probably occurred during the late Neolithic, when their foremost cutting tool was the stone adze. During this stage in their technological development, I suggest that the Kantu' customarily cleared forest – specifically secondary forest – by pollarding with the stone adze. This interpretation is supported by observations of contemporary groups in New Guinea, who were using stone adzes to pollard trees until their recent acquisition of steel axes and brush swords, when they began to fell them instead (Bartlett 1957, p. 470). I further suggest that this central role of pollarding in Kantu' historic swidden-making is reflected today in the cultural identification of pollarded trees as the 'sign' of a swidden.

This suggestion is supported by the fact that the contemporary Kantu' do not regard the stumps left by the use of felling stands as the sign of a swidden. That is, although they ascribe ritual value to these stumps (vis-à-vis the growth of the rice plants), they do not call them the klai' or 'sign' of a swidden, as they do pollarded trees. I suggest that this is primarily due to the fact that these stands still have utilitarian value (as noted earlier). Practical considerations require their presence in all contemporary primary forest swiddens. In contrast, the presence of pollarded trees in contemporary secondary forest swiddens is not required. On the basis of practical considerations alone, they could be absent. It is this possibility of their absence, in fact, that makes their presence a 'sign' – a sign that although there may be no contemporary need for them, there was such a need historically.

The practice of pollarding is restricted to secondary forest, as noted previously. The Kantu' simply say that the trees in primary forest are too tall to climb and lop. In addition, they say, the practice is pantang or 'tabooed' in primary forest. The converse is not the case, however: the use of felling stands is not pantang or 'tabooed' in secondary forest. These data suggest that the historic use of pollarding was also restricted to secondary forest. It remains to ask how, at that stage of development, when the Kantu' did not yet possess a technology capable of felling even secondary forest trees, they were able to fell the much more difficult primary forest trees. (The suggestion that the Kantu' were clearing secondary forest at that point in their history – with the aid of pollarding techniques – of course implies that they were clearing primary forest as well: without clearing primary forest, there would have been no secondary forest to pollard.) There are no contemporary data from the Kantu' that throw any light on this question. However, data on contemporary Stone-Age peoples in New Guinea suggest two possibilities. First, the Neolithic ancestors of the Kantu' may have used fire to burn through the trunks of primary forest trees at the base (cf. Bartlett 1957, pp. 153, 189). Secondly, they may have used the stone adze (the same one that they used for pollarding) to ring the bark at the base of the trees (cf. Bartlett 1957, pp. 129, 189). There is some evidence that favours this second possibility: ringing would leave tall standing trunks in the swidden, which is conceivably reflected in the ritual valuation of tall standing stumps in contemporary primary forest swiddens.

Ringing or barking has the advantage of being relatively fast, but it has the disadvantage of producing relatively little biomass (i.e. only fallen leaves) for the swidden burn, and hence relatively little ash to nourish the subsequent swidden crops. Burning through the trunk (until the tree topples) has the advantage of making the entire biomass of the tree available for the subsequent swidden burn, but it has the disadvantage of being a very time-consuming technique. The technique of pollarding is also a time-consuming one, as noted earlier, and in addition it is relatively dangerous. All of these archaic techniques of forest clearing, therefore, possessed serious drawbacks – compared with simply cutting through the tree at its base. Consequently, as soon as the latter was made possible by the development of metallurgical skills, the former techniques were abandoned.

The thesis that the ancestors of the Kantu' possessed a less adequate technology for clearing the forest than contemporary Kantu' is also supported by mythological evidence that the former cultivated root crops, whereas the latter cultivate mostly rice (Dove 1983). Root crops would have been better adapted to a swidden environment in which more trees (or more parts of them) were left standing and in which there was consequently less ash and also less sunlight available for crops planted on the swidden's surface. The cultivation of rice, which demands both more nutrients and more sunlight, might, indeed, not have been possible until the tree-felling technology was improved to the point where all (or most) of the trees in a swidden could be cut down and burned.

## Supporting evidence

The Kantu', like other groups in Borneo and indeed throughout Southeast Asia, have many myths regarding human petrification. For example, there are three stones on the banks of the Empanang River (where it courses through the Kantu' territory) that the Kantu' call *batu nyadi* or 'become stones'. The Kantu' say that a man, a woman, and a child once were fishing at that spot, when they happened to laugh at the fish that they had caught, whereupon they were turned to stone. The Kantu' tell a similar story of the petrification of an entire longhouse in the Ketunggau River Valley, which lies to the southeast of their territory. According to this story, during a feast in the longhouse a man and his grandson started to throw a cat back-and-forth between them. The guests who were attending the feast laughed at the sight of this, whereupon they – along with the longhouse itself, and a boat that was moored in the river in front of the longhouse – were turned to stone.

The common element in these and similar stories is that humans are petrified when they mock animals or, more generally, when they engage in unusual relations (i.e. relations outside those dictated by subsistence needs) with animals (cf. Needham 1967, King 1975). There may be many reasons for a society to proscribe the mockery of animals; but why should a society select petrification – in its mythology – as the sanction for violations of this proscription? Petrification was selected, I suggest, because it was stone that first gave men power over animals, i.e. it was stone weapons that first gave men the power of life or death over the major game animals of the Southeast Asian forests; animals that in Palaeolithic times included such formidable beasts as elephant, two-horned rhinoceros, wild buffalo, wild ox, and giant pig, as evidenced by the excavations of the Niah Caves in western Borneo (Harrisson 1959, p. 2). This power was probably accompanied by a sense of responsibility for its proper exercise, as is the case in contemporary hunting societies in Southeast Asia (and, indeed, in hunting societies throughout the world). Among the Neolithic Mentawei of Siberut island (off the southern coast of Sumatra), for example, hunting is governed by a wide variety of proscriptions, the strict observance of which is believed to be essential to the continued health of both people and game (Schefold 1988). Indeed, the relationship between the hunters and their game is viewed as a sort of pact, involving mutual give and take, and governed by mutual obligations. Mockery of the game, whether among contemporary or historic hunting societies – or the latter's agricultural descendants – is a clear violation of this pact, and it is punished, I suggest, in a very telling manner. For violating the responsibility that must be assumed along with the power (over animals) of stone weapons, man himself is turned to stone. If man abuses the power of stone, it is turned against him.

This interpretation of the myths regarding petrification as punishment for mockery of animals, is supported by the existence of other beliefs regarding death by lightning, as punishment for the same offence. In Blust's review (1981) of this complex of Southeast Asian beliefs, the most common form of supernatural punishment (for a variety of offences, including, but not limited to, the mockery of animals) is petrification, and the second most common is death by lightning (1981, Table II). Among the Kantu', as among other peoples in the area, it is believed that the destructive power of lightning is delivered by means of a stone bolt – which is their perception (as discussed earlier) of the Neolithic adzes that they occasionally unearth – and the striking of a man by one of these bolts is likened to the striking of a tree, their more usual target. As put by Scharer (quoted in Needham 1967, p. 282), men who mock animals are killed 'like a tall tree in the forest cracked by the storm'. According to these beliefs, therefore, man stands in relation to the lightning god – with respect to vulnerability to stone weapons – just as animals stand in relation to him; and if he abuses the power that stone weapons give him over animals then these weapons are turned against him.

This belief in stone lightning bolts supports the analysis in this chapter in a more direct way as well. When forest trees are split or felled by lightning, this – just as in the case of a man struck by lightning – is attributed to the stone bolts of an angered lightning god (cf. Blust 1981, Table II, Needham 1967, pp. 275, 281). In other words, the lightning god is believed to fell trees with the prehistoric adze blades that the Kantu' and other peoples call 'lightning stones'. In these beliefs the true function of the stone adzes – namely, as instruments with which to fell trees – is present or, more accurately, is preserved. I suggest that the contemporary perception of stone adzes as the tool with which the god of lightning fells trees, represents the cultural memory of the prehistoric role of stone adzes as the tool with which men felled trees. I suggest that it is because the stone adze was a tree-cutting tool in prehistoric fact, that it became a tree-cutting tool in contemporary myth.

This suggestion is supported by the wide distribution of the belief in lightning gods that fell trees with stone adzes. For example, Skeat reported (1900, p. 27) that on the nearby Malay peninsula, stone adzes are also called *batu halilantar* or 'lightning stones'. More impressive yet, 8000 miles away in West Africa, the Azande call prehistoric stone adzes or *mangua n'gamba* 'axes of the lightning'. Their beliefs were reported as follows by Alexander (cited in Bartlett 1957, p. 18):

> They say that these axes may often be discovered by turning up the soil after a tree has been struck by lightning; a little later it would be no good, because the stone would have gone back to the clouds in order to strike again.

The similarity in belief between Borneo and the Malay peninsula might be attributable to common cultural heritage (but see Needham 1967, pp. 280–3), but this is wholly improbable in the case of the similarity between Borneo and West Africa. While there are great differences between the cultures of the latter two areas, however, there would have been relatively little difference in their Neolithic stone technologies. Therefore, if both the Dayak and the Azande believe that stone adzes are the bolts with which the lightning god fells trees, it cannot be because they both believe in the same god(s), which they do not; it can only be because the ancestors of both used similar tools to fell trees.

## Conclusion

I began this chapter with a discussion of the contemporary technology and known history of iron and stone (respectively) among the Kantu'. I then analysed the practice of ritual pollarding in contemporary swiddens and suggested that it represents the cultural memory of a time when forest clearing in swidden agriculture was carried out using Neolithic tools. In support of this thesis, I next analysed two contemporary Kantu' myths, one regarding human punishment by petrification or lightning, which represents cultural recognition of the power over nature that stone tools give to man, and a second regarding stone lightning bolts, which represents similar recognition of the historic use of stone adzes to cut down trees.

This analysis is relevant to the debate as to whether the swidden system of the Kantu' and like groups could have been carried out before an iron technology was available. Freeman (1970, p. 174) suggested that it could not, saying:

> it may be noted that the Iban system of agriculture, involving as it does, the felling of large areas of virgin forest, is dependent on the use of iron tools. Such methods could not be followed by a neolithic people.

Padoch (1983, p. 36) has more recently drawn a similar conclusion, in her explanation of the system of wet-rice cultivation found among the Lun Dayeh in the interior of Borneo. However, the evidence presented in this chapter regarding the Neolithic origins of the technology that the Kantu' use to clear the forest, strongly suggests that the ancestors of the Dayak were in fact clearing forest (primary as well as secondary) for swiddens long before they possessed metal tools.

More generally, the evidence in this chapter suggests that man's transformation and exploitation of the tropical rain forest was already underway during Neolithic times and was not, therefore, initiated by the development of metal tools. Some scholars have suggested, to the contrary, that man's entry into the tropical forest (as a cultivator, not as a hunter) would not have been possible without metal tools. In the absence of these, they suggest, early agriculture would necessarily have been confined to environments such as swampy or seasonally inundated land, where – it is presumed – non-metallic tools could have been more readily employed (e.g. Bartlett 1962, p. 272). The evidence presented in this chapter shows that, while it may have been more difficult to cultivate forest than swampland with Neolithic tools, it was not impossible – and was, indeed, routinely practised by the ancestors of the Kantu'.

## Notes

1   Fieldwork among the Kantu' was carried out during 1974–76 under the sponsorship of the Indonesian Institute of Science and Knowledge (LIPI), with the support of a training grant from the National Institute of General Medical Sciences, and with research funds from Stanford University (CRIS) and the National Science Foundation (grant # GS–42605).
2   Richards (1981, p. 29) erroneously translates *batu nitar* as 'thunderbolt', not 'lightning bolt'. This error appears to be a common one, e.g. Skeat (1900, p. 276) similarly mistranslated *batu halilantar* as 'thunderbolt', whereas its literal meaning is clearly 'lightning stone' or 'bolt'. This error is perhaps due to the fact that 'thunder bolt' is a more common term in English than 'lightning bolt'; which in turn is due to the fact that, regardless of what gods the Iban and Malay believe in, the Anglo-Saxon ancestors of many English speakers believed in a god of thunder (i.e. Thor) rather than a god of lightning.

   Blust (1981, p. 300) noted the same problem in the literature on this topic, and wrote that descriptions of thunder gods among Malay and Philippine Negritos 'sound suspiciously like a personification of lightning'. However, he appears to attribute this not to translator's error (which it clearly is in the cases that I cited), but to a historical substitution of an original thunder god by a later lightning god.

# References

Bartlett, H. H. 1957. *Fire in relation to primitive agriculture and grazing in the tropics*, Vol. II. Ann Arbor: University of Michigan Department of Botany.

Bartlett, H. H. 1962. Possible separate origin and evolution of the Ladang and Sawah types of tropical agriculture. *Proceedings of the 9th Pacific Science Congress* **4**, 270–3.

Blust, R. 1981. Linguistic evidence for some early Austronesian taboos. *American Anthropologist* **83**, 285–319.

Dove, M. R. 1983. Evidence from contemporary myth and ritual regarding the origins of agriculture in Southeast Asia. Paper read at the 82nd annual meeting of the American Anthropological Association, 16–20 November, Chicago.

Dove, M. R. 1985. *Swidden agriculture in Indonesia: the subsistence strategies of the Kalimantan Kantu'*. Berlin: Mouton.

Freeman, D. 1970. *Report on the Iban*. L.S.E. Monographs on Social Anthropology, no. 4. London: Athlone Press.

Harrisson, T. 1959. New archaeological and ethnological results from Niah Caves, Sarawak. *Man* **59**, 1–8.

Harrisson, T. 1965. Six specialized stone tools from upland and south-west Borneo. *Sarawak Museum Journal* **XII**, 25–6, 133–42.

Hose, C. & W. McDougall 1912. *The pagan tribes of Borneo*, 2 vols. London: Macmillan.

King. V. T. 1975. Stones and the Maloh. *Journal of the Malysian Branch of the Royal Asiatic Society* **XLVIII**, 104–19.

King, V. 1985. Symbolism and material culture: some footnotes for Penny van Esterich. *Bijdragen* **141**, 142–7.

Majid, Z. 1982. The west mouth, Niah, in the prehistory of Southeast Asia. *Sarawak Museum Journal* **XXXI**, 52 (Special Monograph no. 3).

Needham, R. 1967. Blood, thunder and mockery of animals. In *Myth and cosmos*, J. Middleton (ed.), 271–85. Garden City, N.Y.: American Museum of Natural History.

Padoch, C. 1983. Agricultural practices of the Kerayan Lun Dayeh. *Borneo Research Bulletin* **15**, 33–8.

Richards, A. 1981. *An Iban–English dictionary*. Oxford: Oxford University Press.

Sandin, B. 1962. Gawai Batu: the Iban whetstone feast. *Sarawak Museum Journal* **XI**, 19–20, 329–408.

Schefold, R. 1988. The Mentawei equilibrium and the modern world. In *The real and imagined role of culture in development: case studies from Indonesia*, M. R. Dove (ed.), Honolulu: University of Hawaii Press.

Skeat, W. W. 1900. *Malay magic: an introduction to the folklore and popular religion of the Malay peninsula*. London: Macmillan.

# 44  *The origins and development of New Guinea agriculture*

JACK GOLSON

Discussions of agricultural origins and relationships in the South Pacific have traditionally been carried out within a framework of assumptions to which many eminent botanists and geographers over the years have more-or-less explicitly subscribed (cf. Yen 1980, pp. 140–2, Golson 1985, pp. 307–8 and references cited). The basic notion was that the tuberous plants, and fruit and nut trees, which, together with their often vegetative reproduction, are characteristic of New Guinea and the Pacific Islands, formed the basis of an original agriculture in Southeast Asia, which was subsequently replaced by systems based on the cereal rice. It was only a short step from this to suggest that the agriculture found in New Guinea and the Pacific Islands was actually derived from Southeast Asia, the people who carried it eastward doing so before rice became dominant in the homeland. This chapter is concerned with the processes by which thinking about Pacific agricultural origins has slowly freed itself from these inherited concepts.

## Agricultural origins

In 1976 I gave a paper at the Nice Congress of the UISPP (Golson & Hughes 1980) proposing an antiquity for plant and animal husbandry on the island of New Guinea greater than 9000 years. This proposition was based on the results of multi-disciplinary research being carried on in the Western Highlands of Papua New Guinea and focused on swampland at Kuk Agricultural Research Station near Mount Hagen in the upper Wahgi Valley, at an altitude of 1550 m.

The Kuk swamp proved to have a long history as an agricultural site, up to 100 or so years ago, which was characterized by episodes of large-scale drainage for cultivation separated by often substantial periods of abandonment. The evidence for agriculture consisted of a stratified sequence of features cut into the swamp deposits and representing, on the one hand, the drainage channels by which water was removed from the site and, on the other, the ditches, basins, and other diggings belonging to the associated agricultural systems then established there. These structures – channels, ditches, basins – formed virtually the totality of the archaeological evidence with which we had to work: there was no evidence of habitation until the very end of the sequence, no recognizable evidence for cultivated plants until the same period, and then always in association with houses, and no evidence for agricultural tools (almost exclusively of wood) before about 500 years ago, older ones presumably having rotted because of fluctuating water levels in the swamp caused by its periodic drainage (Golson & Steensberg 1985, pp. 348–9). We interpreted the restricted range of archaeological evidence available in the close light of concurrent studies of the geomorphology of the swamp and its margins and palynological investigations into local and regional vegetation history, with attention to the literature on New Guinea cultivated plants and agricultural systems and the very sketchy archaeological record for the region.

In the light of this wider array of evidence, claims for agriculture in the Kuk swamp back to about 6000 years ago were fully acceptable. Pig, an animal not native to New Guinea, was well attested in the archaeological record about this date or slightly later, and throughout the Pacific, in general, pigs and agriculture go hand in hand. In addition, the pollen record showed that substantial inroads had been made into Highlands forests, a circumstance interpreted as the result of clearance for agriculture. Beyond 6000 years, however, the general archaeological record became exiguous indeed, and that for vegetation history in the zone of agricultural settlement was missing altogether until well back into the Late Pleistocene (cf. Groube Ch. 17, this volume). Much of the Nice paper was therefore devoted to arguing from geomorphological evidence that features in the Kuk swamp 9000 years ago were best interpreted as an early form of the agricultural management manifest in later times.

I cannot claim that the past ten years have added much to the record on this score: the evidence I must use to argue a 9000-year antiquity for agriculture at Kuk is essentially the same now as then, though there is more of it. What there is to report for that ten-year period on the matter of agricultural origins concerns new thinking and new data relevant to the question of the independence or otherwise of those origins. In large part, this question has been formulated in terms of the plants that might have been cultivated in New Guinea 9000 years ago.

The 1976 paper was also exercised on this matter. Given the absence of botanical remains, the approach was perforce to inspect the range of traditional crops cultivated in New Guinea gardens and make some sort of intelligent choice. The American sweet potato (*Ipomoea batatas*), which is today dominant in Highlands agriculture, could be dismissed as an introduction of the late prehistoric period, less than 500 years ago. As regards other important plants, taro (*Colocasia esculenta*) and certain species of yam (*Dioscorea alata, D. esculenta*) and of banana (*Musa* of the Eumusa section) appeared to be of Southeast Asian origin. Indeed, the Nice paper was written in the light of the accepted view that New Guinea agriculture, and that of the Pacific as a whole, was basically derived from Southeast Asia. The discussion nonetheless paid attention to Yen's early indication (1971, 1973) and Powell's later detailed documentation (1976) of the richness of New Guinea in plants of economic importance, including minor species of yam and banana. Some of these, including a number of apparent endemics, were accepted as having been domesticated in New Guinea, and early enough for plants such as Australimusa bananas and sugar cane to be included in the cultural equipment of the people who colonized the islands of the Pacific from perhaps 4000 years ago. All this, as Yen (1971, pp. 6–7, 1973, pp. 73–5, cf. 1980, p. 144) and Powell (1976, pp. 175–6) pointed out, suggested the potential for independent origins of plant domestication in New Guinea. A possible solution to the problem seemed to be offered by the pig, an exotic item in the New Guinea fauna for whose presence the most satisfactory explanation was seen to be its introduction by human agency from Southeast Asia as a husbanded animal. There were, and still are, claims for the presence of pig in two Highlands rockshelters around 10 000 years ago (Bulmer 1975, p. 18; 1982, p. 188). If a Southeast Asian animal had indeed been introduced into New Guinea around the end of the Pleistocene, it was possible to think that Southeast Asian plants might be incorporated in, indeed responsible for, the agriculture claimed for Kuk at 9000 years ago.

A few years later, in a paper revised for the proceedings of a conference in Poona held in 1978 (Golson 1985), I attempted to address this question in the only way I felt was possible, given the dearth of information about early agriculture in island Southeast Asia and the failure of archaeological research on the Southeast Asian mainland to throw light on the antiquity, indeed the presence, of root-crop, tree-fruit agriculture. This was to inspect the records of vegetation history becoming available for the region as a result of pollen-analytical research, in order to see whether the impact of human interference by way of agriculture was visible in them and, if so, from what date. The exercise was prompted by the clear evidence for such interference in the pollen diagrams for the Papua New Guinea Highlands, which have been described (Flenley 1979, p. 122) as providing the most striking pollen evidence of recent years for early clearance, speaking on a pan-tropical or even world scale. The pollen diagrams from Southeast Asia provided no such clear evidence until far too late a date to support the hypothesis of New Guinea agricultural origins there – around 4000 bp and probably associated with rice – though the absence of evidence was not *decisive* in rejecting the hypothesis, since it might be due to the failure of less ecologically harmful forms of forest clearance under shifting cultivation to be registered (Flenley 1985, p. 304). The result in any case was to emphasize the need to look for explanations in evidence from New Guinea itself.

Over the past few years there have been two practical exercises of this kind, one in the laboratory, the other in the field.

The laboratory project, undertaken by S. M. Wilson while a student at the Australian National University, concerned phytoliths (Wilson 1985). Of the cultivated plants in terms of which discussions about early agriculture at Kuk had taken place, taro and yam do not produce phytoliths, but bananas do. Fortunately, banana is an important plant from the point of view of the independent or derivative nature of New Guinea agricultural origins, as already indicated. While the Eumusa section of the genus is considered to be of Southeast Asian origin, the Australimusa section is thought to belong to the New Guinea region and to have been domesticated there. Wilson (1985, p. 94) found 'consistent, although not dramatic, differences in phytolith size and morphology' between the two sections of the genus, but phytoliths from *Musa ingens*, the wild New Guinea banana which is the only member of the third, Ingentimusa, section of the genus as recognized by Argent (1975), are indistinguishable from those of Eumusa. Twenty-three banana phytoliths were found in a core through the Kuk deposits, only two of which were of the probable Australimusa type, neither of them in informative chronological position from the present point of view (Wilson 1985, Fig. 4). The others were found in levels contemporary with agricultural activity, back to 9000 years ago, and not in earlier deposits. In view of the impossibility of discriminating between phytoliths of the Eumusa and Ingentimusa sections, however, the conclusions remain equivocal as to whether we are dealing with bananas of early Indo-Malayan origin in the early agricultural phases at Kuk (Wilson 1985, p. 97) or a wild New Guinea plant able to colonize areas disturbed in the course of agricultural activities (Wilson 1985, p. 93). Work on phytolith discrimination between different New Guinea banana species, both wild and cultivated, is proceeding in the laboratory of H. Fujiwara, Miyazaki University, Japan.

The field investigation to which reference was made earlier was part of a larger project initiated by P. P. Gorecki of the Australian National University in the archaeologically unknown (and ethnographically little better served) region of the lower Jimi and upper Yuat valleys in the mid-montane zone (*c.* 500 m. altitude) north of Mount Hagen. The attention devoted to agricultural history was prompted by a conclusion and a challenge of the 1976 Nice paper (Golson & Hughes 1980, p. 301). The conclusion was that the agriculture seen at Kuk at 9000 years ago did not originate at that altitude, which today is towards the upper limit for the cultivation of virtually all the relevant cultigens, and at the time must only just have been achieving the present temperature regime during the climatic amelioration which ended the Pleistocene. The challenge was to extend the search into lowland areas. In the event Gorecki's exploratory work has not established the presence of agriculture earlier than 5000 years ago (Gillieson *et al.* 1985 and subsequent unpublished revisions, Gorecki pers. comm.), though the type of activity revealed bears a satisfactory resemblance to gardening systems at Kuk of a broadly similar date.

The new thinking that has been mentioned has been the insistence by Yen (1982 in particular) that serious consideration of the hypothesis of an independent evolution of agriculture in New Guinea is warranted by an assessment of the origins of the plants incorporated in traditional Melanesian systems overall, not simply in the Highlands, and an appreciation of the Kuk drainage record as revealing an evolutionary sequence of intensification in the sphere of production (1982, p. 292). As regards the plants, two points emerge (1982, p. 288): the central role of New Guinea in the plant-domestication process, independent of ultimate origins; and the fact that these domesticates as a whole cover virtually the range of environmental conditions in Melanesia, swamp, coral island, coast, interior, and mountain. As regards the agricultural systems, Yen (1982, p. 292) considers a logical sequence of events to be plant domestication earlier than environmental management through drainage, and suggests that such domestication might have begun in the 'variable ecologies of mid-altitude regions', with the development of 'simpler regimes of swidden modes of agriculture' following 'the long hunter–gatherer "phase"'. It is, of course, precisely to one such region that Gorecki's attention has been directed, as described.

The hypothesis which Yen (1982, p. 291) puts forward is one of the independent origins and development of agriculture in New Guinea, based on the domestication of a suite of plants that included basic staples, vegetables, and fruits able to sustain populations in various environments. At a later stage these indigenous developments were interrupted by the arrival of colonists out of Asia, who introduced domesticated plants 'which were to dominate, in many cases, the earlier evolved cultivation of indigenous domesticates'.

In these discussions Yen (1982, pp. 254, 292–3) is exercised by the question of taro, invoked in a number of my own publications as an appropriate crop for the drained swamp systems of Kuk. Taro is a plant for which an Indian origin has been proposed, and whose carriage into New Guinea and the Pacific by human agency is taken for granted. Yen (1982, p. 284) refers, however, to the 'uncertain status of the origin of feral types found in New Guinea, and more recently by R. Jones and B. Meehan (pers. comm.) in inland Arnhem Land, Australia' (see Jones & Meehan Ch. 7, this volume, and cf. Lawrence 1968, p. 205 for eastern Cape York, under *Colocasia antiquorum*), commenting that they may not be garden escapees, which explanation in the Arnhem Land case would require a very complex hypothesis indeed.

Yen has taken up this matter in the context of a wider project on Australia as bystander in Pacific agricultural development, in which one focus of interest is the occurrence amongst Australian Aboriginal food plants of genera familiar as cultivated foods in Asia and Oceania (Yen 1985a, pp. 317–18, 1985b, p. 494, cf. Golson 1971). Yam, as well as taro, is relevant in this connection. As early as the Nice Congress of 1976, Yen (1980, p. 45) made reference to the parallelism in the distributions of the genus *Dioscorea* (yams) and the genus *Oryza* (rices), for which latter one hypothesis exists for its origin in Gondwanaland (see Chang Ch. 25, this volume). At the time, Yen could only comment on the impossibility of applying the evidence of plate tectonics for the origins of *Dioscorea*, particularly in view of the lack of basic study of the genus in New Guinea and Australia, a deficiency which one aspect of his current project begins to address (see Yen Ch. 4, this volume). The concept of a Gondwanaland inheritance as basic to the question of agricultural origins in New Guinea now arises, however, in a different and more concrete form. This results from the continued discovery in remote areas of tropical Australia of taro traditionally used by Aborigines as food (Jones & Meehan Ch. 7, this volume for Arnhem Land, Crawford 1984, pp. 40–1 for the Kimberleys, as *Colocasia antiquorum*). Detailed genetic work relevant to this matter is currently under way by P. Matthews, one of Yen's students at the Australian National University, who is investigating the relationship between wild and cultivated taro from Papua New Guinea, and between wild taro from Papua New Guinea and Australia, by means of electrophoretic analysis. The aim is to clarify phylogenetic issues raised in recent research by the more 'traditional' approach of cytology and perhaps produce biological definitions for domestication in the species.

## Agricultural development

If the discussion of agricultural origins in New Guinea just concluded has addressed itself to narrower questions than those of ultimate causes, it is because the data, biological, environmental, and archaeological, necessary for framing the relevant hypotheses are insufficient. Perhaps issues raised by research on the subsequent history of New Guinea Highlands agriculture make a more immediate contribution at a general level. The issues involved are relevant to the concept of agricultural intensification which has been much discussed in the literature of a number of disciplines since the publication of Boserup's *The conditions of agricultural growth* in 1965.

This is a vast subject, which I shall address here from a highly particular standpoint. Contemporary New Guinea Highlands agriculture, based on the sweet potato, which is grown in large, orderly plantations in an environment characterized by large areas of grassland and shrubby regrowth, is described (Brookfield with Hart 1971, p. 111) as exhibiting 'a fairly high modal level of intensity', defining intensity as 'the degree to which technology is applied to land so as to economize in its use, while gaining roughly equal or greater output per hectare' (Brookfield with Hart 1971, p. 92). The technology applied in the Highlands (e.g. Brookfield with Hart 1971, pp. 111–13) consists of a distinctive set of procedures designed to allow frequent or continuous agricultural use of grassland soils.

Now it is clear from pollen-analytical research that the open landscapes which form the agricultural setting are the product of millennia of history and it is generally agreed that the major agency in their creation out of an originally forested environment was sustained clearance for cultivation (e.g. Powell 1982, pp. 28–30). In so far, therefore, as the technical features of traditional Highlands agriculture were designed to ensure the productivity of agriculture in conditions of grassland and degraded regrowth, they were responses to circumstances of increasing and irreversible deforestation brought about by the practice of agriculture itself. It is in the light of this proposition that the long prehistoric sequence of ever more complex drainage and gardening has been interpreted at Kuk (e.g. Golson 1982).

The details need not detain us here, but there is a general point to make. If the interpretation of developments at Kuk is correct, that they were geared to an ecological transformation, from forest to grassland, which was common to the Highlands as a whole, there ought to be evidence in other areas for corresponding responses in the realm of agricultural technology (cf. Golson 1982, pp. 135–6). Up until very recently, however, Kuk and the swamplands of the upper Wahgi stood alone.

The discovery which has supplied the confirmatory evidence has come in an unexpected way, through the reinterpretation as agricultural terracing of an extensive set of landscape features in a tolerably well-known part of the country, which, when mentioned in the literature at all, have been interpreted as purely natural phenomena (Sullivan *et al.* 1986). Only preliminary investigations have been carried out so far, but as the area is shortly to be impacted by the second stage of a major hydroelectricity scheme, it is likely that further information will become available from salvage work ahead of development. There are some general observations that can already be made, however, relevant to the issue of developments in agricultural technology in the face of environmental change.

The terraced landscapes in question occupy in discontinuous fashion some 16 km$^2$ of the 40 km$^2$ of the Arona Basin on the upper Ramu River about 1300 m above sea-level in the Eastern Highlands of Papua New Guinea. They are situated on hillslopes developed in a sedimentary formation comprising poorly consolidated gravelly sands and clays and rich in reworked volcanic ash. Other occurrences of this formation in the region appear, from aerial photographs and some ground reconnaissance, to be terraced also. The region in question is characterized by a comparatively low rainfall for the New Guinea Highlands (less than 2000 mm per year), with not only pronounced seasonality of precipitation but its occurrence as heavy downpours separated by long dry periods. In response to this character of the rainfall, the staple sweet potato is grown in beds of rectangular shape running up and down the slopes and often provided with bordering drains. The landscape in which this gardening takes place is one of extensive, short, stabilized grassland devoid of natural woodland over large areas, this extreme degree of ecological transformation being the result of the proneness of the region to drought exacerbated by firing (Brookfield 1964, pp. 32–3).

There is no vegetation history for the Eastern Highlands of Papua New Guinea, so that we do not know over what period deforestation took place. It can be argued, however, that the hillslope terracing was an appropriate response to it in an area of low, seasonal, and heavy episodic rain, since it would have served to counter rapid runoff on steep grassed slopes and to retain moisture in the soil on top of terrace platforms. It can be further argued that such a role would have been appropriate for the cultivation of taro, which has been regularly proposed as a staple of Highlands agriculture before the arrival of the sweet potato within the last few hundred years. Certainly, it appears that the terraces are earlier than the sweet potato, because not only do local inhabitants not recognize them as other than natural features of the landscape but their sweet potato gardens are aligned quite differently and pay no regard to the presence of the terraces where they are superimposed on them.

## Concluding remarks

It is, I think, obvious from the avove that the study of agricultural origins and developments in New Guinea is still at an early stage, where the basic parameters for discussion are still in flux as new and often unexpected data are gathered. Enough is known, however, to suggest that the ancient continent of which, with its larger neighbour, Australia, New Guinea forms a part holds promise of producing evidence in the long run for an independent and distinctive history in that field of socio-economic development with which this book is concerned.

## Acknowledgements

My debt to co-workers in fieldwork and to present and past colleagues at the Australian National University is abundantly clear from citations in the text above and in the reference list which follows. The prominence of the name D. E. Yen in both is a measure of his influence on my own thinking and his contribution to the field in general.

## References

Argent, H. 1975. The wild bananas of Papua New Guinea. *Bulletin of the Royal Botanical Gardens, Edinburgh* **30**, 77–114.

Boserup, E. 1965. *The conditions of agricultural growth: the economics of agrarian change under population pressure.* London: Allen & Unwin.

Brookfield, H. C. 1964. The ecology of highland settlement: some suggestions. In *New Guinea: the Central Highlands,* J. B. Watson (ed.), 20–38. *American Anthropologist* **66**, Special Publication.

Brookfield, H. C. with D. Hart 1971. *Melanesia: a geographical interpretation of an island world.* London: Methuen.

Bulmer, S. 1975. Settlement and economy in prehistoric Papua New Guinea: a review of the archaeological evidence. *Journal de la Société des Oceanisters* **31**, 7–75.

Bulmer, S. 1982. Human ecology and cultural variation in prehistoric Papua New Guinea. *Monographicae Biologicae* **42**, 169–206.

Chang, T. T. 1989. Domestication and spread of the cultivated rices. In *Foraging and farming: the evolution of plant exploitation,* D. R. Harris & G. C. Hillman (eds), ch. 25. London: Unwin Hyman.

Crawford, I. M. 1984. *Traditional Aboriginal plant resources in the Kalumburu area: aspects in ethno-economics.* Perth: Records of the Western Australian Museum, Supplement no. 15.

Flenley, J. R. 1979. *The equatorial rain forest: a geological history.* London: Butterworth.

Flenley, J. R. 1985. Man's impact on the vegetation of Southeast Asia: the pollen evidence. In *Recent advances in Indo-Pacific prehistory*, V. N. Misra & P. Bellwood (eds), 297–305. Proceedings of the international symposium, Poona, 19–21 December 1978. New Delhi: Oxford and IBH.

Gillieson, D., P. Gorecki & G. Hope 1985. Prehistoric agricultural systems in a lowland swamp, Papua New Guinea. *Archaeology in Oceania* **20**, 32–7.

Golson, J. 1971. Australian Aboriginal food plants: some ecological and culture-historical implications. In *Aboriginal man and environment in Australia*, D. J. Mulvaney & J. Golson (eds), 196–238. Canberra: Australian National University Press.

Golson, J. 1982. The Ipomoean revolution revisited: society and the sweet potato in the Upper Wahgi Valley. In *Inequality in New Guinea Highlands societies*, A. Strathern (ed.), 109–36. Cambridge: Cambridge University Press, Cambridge Papers in Social Anthropology 11.

Golson, J. 1985. Agricultural origins in Southeast Asia: a view from the east. In *Recent advances in Indo-Pacific prehistory*, V. N. Misra & P. Bellwood (eds), 307–14. Proceedings of the international symposium, Poona, 19–21 December 1978. New Delhi: Oxford and IBH.

Golson, J. & P. J. Hughes 1980. The appearance of plant and animal domestication in New Guinea. *Journal de la Société des Océanistes* **36**, 294–303.

Golson, J. & A. Steensberg 1985. The tools of agricultural intensification in the New Guinea Highlands. In *Prehistoric intensive agriculture in the tropics*, Part i, I. S. Farrington (ed.), 347–84. Oxford: British Archaeological Reports International Series 232.

Groube, L. 1989. The taming of the rain forests: a model for Late Pleistocene forest exploitation in New Guinea. In *Foraging and farming: the evolution of plant exploitation*, D. R. Harris & G. C. Hillman (eds), ch. 17. London: Unwin Hyman.

Jones, R. & B. Meehan. 1989. Plant foods of the Gidjingali: ethnographic and archaeological perspectives from northern Australia on tuber and seed exploitation. In *Foraging and farming: the evolution of plant exploitation*, D. R. Harris & G. C. Hillman (eds), ch. 7. London: Unwin Hyman.

Lawrence, R. 1968. *Aboriginal habitat and economy*. Occasional Papers no. 6, Department of Geography, School of General Studies, Australian National University, Canberra.

Powell, J. M. 1976. Ethnobotany. In *New Guinea vegetation*, K. Paijmans (ed.), 106–83. Canberra: Australian National University Press.

Powell, J. M. 1982. Plant resources and palaeobotanical evidence for plant use in the Papua New Guinea Highlands. *Archaeology in Oceania* **17**, 28–37.

Sullivan, M. E., P. Hughes & J. Golson 1986. Prehistoric engineers of the Arona valley. *Science in New Guinea* **12**, 27–41.

Wilson, S. M. 1985. Phytolith evidence from Kuk, an early agricultural site in Papua New Guinea. *Archaeology in Oceania* **20**, 90–7.

Yen, D. E. 1971. The development of agriculture in Oceania. In *Studies in Oceanic culture history*, Vol. 2, R. C. Green & M. Kelly (eds), 1–12 Pacific Anthropological Records no. 12, Department of Anthropology, Bernice P. Bishop Museum, Honolulu, Hawaii.

Yen, D. E. 1973. The origins of Oceanic agriculture. *Archaeology and Physical Anthropology in Oceania* **8**, 68–85.

Yen, D. E. 1980. The Southeast Asian foundations of Oceanic agriculture: a reassessment. *Journal de la Société des Océanistes* **36**, 140–7.

Yen, D. E. 1982. The history of cultivated plants. In *Melanesia: beyond diversity*, Vol. 1, R. J. May & H. Nelson (eds), 281–95. Canberra: Australian National University, Research School of Pacific Studies.

Yen, D. E. 1985a. Wild plants and domestication in Pacific islands. In *Recent advances in Indo-Pacific prehistory*, V. N. Misra & P. Bellwood (eds), 315–26. Proceedings of the international symposium, Poona, 19–21 December 1978. New Delhi: Oxford and IBH.

Yen, D. E. 1985b. The genetic effects of agricultural intensification. In *Prehistoric intensive agriculture in the tropics*, Part ii, I. S. Farrington (ed.), 491–9. Oxford: British Archaeological Reports International Series 232.

Yen, D. E. 1989. The domestication of environment. In *Foraging and farming: the evolution of plant exploitation*, D. R. Harris & G. C. Hillman (eds), ch. 4. London: Unwin Hyman.

# 45 *Gardens in the south: diversity and change in prehistoric Maaori agriculture*

SUSAN BULMER

## Introduction

New Zealand (Aotearoa) was the last large island environment to be settled by humans. It contains the archaeological record of perhaps 1500 years of interaction between plants, animals, and humans in the adaptation of a tropical people and their culture to a non-tropical environment (Kirch 1982). This has an interesting parallel in the Papua New Guinea Highlands, where people with a coastal tropical way of life moved into a temperate mountain environment, many thousands of years earlier (cf. Golson Ch. 44, Groube Ch. 17, this volume).

After their voyages of more than 2000 km from the islands of the eastern Pacific, the Maaori settlers found parts of Aotearoa (New Zealand) less than inviting. Its climate is subtropical (at best) in the north and subarctic (at worst) in the south, and it is generally much colder and drier and has a greater variety of landforms and soils, some of which are unsuited to the kind of agriculture practised in the tropical Pacific.

However, the history of the Maaori people in Aotearoa is a success story. Maaori traditions recount the complex histories of the 50 or so tribes that were encountered by the first European visitors of the late 18th and early 19th centuries. The Maaori people, numbered in the hundreds of thousands, had fortified settlements, some of which were unusually large by world standards, and were heavily dependent on agriculture.

This chapter reviews the archaeological record of the development of agriculture in Aotearoa. Although this subject has been recently reviewed (Leach 1984), new archaeological evidence considerably changes the picture of the past and calls into question some previous assumptions about Maaori agriculture. In particular, the new evidence does not support the idea that Maaori agriculture was not possible until specialization in sweet-potato (*kuumara, Ipomoea batatas*) cultivation, and its winter storage in pits, was practised. There is now substantial evidence for the presence of 'broad-spectrum' unspecialized cultivation, of a variety of crops using a variety of garden forms, in the Auckland area until relatively recent times, possibly into the 18th century. The main food cultigens of the Maaori (Best 1925) were *tii*, the cabbage tree (*Cordyline* spp.), the fruit of the gourd, *kotawa* (*Lagenaria siceraria*), taro (*Colocasia esculenta*), yam, *uuwhi* (*Dioscorea* sp.), and *aruhe*, bracken-fern root (*Pteridium esculentum*).

Archaeological investigation of garden cultivation has seldom been attempted, in New Zealand or elsewhere. Prehistoric agriculture is more often studied from the evidence of plant remains rather than from that of garden sites. There has so far been very little archaeobotanical evidence of cultigens found in New Zealand, but considerable attention has been paid to the extent of suitable garden soils (*e.g.* Jones & Law 1987) and to 'made' soils, where materials such as gravel, sand, and shells have been added to gardens (Law 1968, Walton 1982), as well as to evidence in soil profiles of 'mixing' and digging. This chapter reviews these kinds of edaphic evidence, as indicative of garden systems, but focuses on the gardens themselves and their landscape context.

## Reconstructing the prehistoric landscape

Garden sites can only be properly understood if they are set in the context of the landscape in which they functioned. The landscape is partly human-made and is amenable to empirical description and analysis. Also, the processes of landscape change need to be understood, in order to cope with the 'warps' and 'white holes', i.e. biases in the survival of field evidence, and the difficulty of obtaining empirical evidence for the processes of past change (Moseley 1983).

The empirical study of gardens and their landscapes has been recently developed and expanded in New Zealand, especially in the volcanic fields and other sites with stone constructions discussed in this chapter. This kind of study was begun by Sullivan (1972) and Leach (1979a & b). Sullivan's investigations of Matukurua (Wiri) gardens, in a zone of most favourable climate, have been augmented by a relatively large volume of more recent studies (Bulmer 1987a). In contrast, the gardens at Palliser Bay studied by Leach are in a much less favourable climatic zone.

The empirical analysis of the form, content, and spatial relationships of garden sites has been made possible, indeed necessary, by the complexity and high visibility of the constructed landscape, the diversity of its features, and the capacity to delimit the boundaries of the 'system', i.e. the land utilized by a specific community. Individual structural and natural components, such as mounds, terraces, and walls, can be studied in their own right, or combined according to whether they are connected (compound features) or spatially arranged in a meaningful way (feature complexes). Where garden plots or groups of plots still exist, they are investigated as such, but the method of analysis permits the consideration of only partially preserved systems. This kind of analysis has also been used in Hawaii (Weisler & Kirch 1985) and Easter Island (McCoy 1976) where similarly complex field evidence has been found. These studies were carried out earlier than much of the New Zealand research, and they provide a wealth of comparative information and insight.

The Maaori landscape can be classed into four categories, based on the suitability of the soils and climate for agriculture and the size of the suitable area of land (Best 1925, p. 27).

(a)    Prime land. There were a few large areas of good quality soil and favourable climate, such as the Taamaki volcanic zone, that supported large numbers of people.

(b)    Other garden land. There were many small areas of good soil with favourable climate that supported small numbers of people, or were used by larger groups in combination with other small garden areas.

(c)    In a large proportion of the country the climate and/or soils made traditional Maaori gardening difficult, cultivated foods were a luxury, and a small population depended mainly on collected wild foods.

(d)    Areas where cultivation was impossible supported sparse populations, living on collecting and hunting, who obtained garden produce only by trade.

Within these land categories, garden landscapes can be divided according to the landforms they utilized and/or created, and according to the specific forms of gardens included. The landforms vary in size and complexity and include volcanic stonefields, major and minor river valleys, natural swamps, natural and human-made terraces, stream beds, slopes, and coastal shelves. Specific garden forms include walled and ditched slopes, walls and ditches on coastal shelves and on river and stream flats, stone-edged dry and wet terraces, stone-and-earth mounds and walls, sinkholes, and natural scarps and gullies.

The majority of Maaori gardens were on coastal land in the northern half of the North Island, in the most favourable climatic zone (Fig. 45.1), although there were also major inland agricultural areas, such as the Waikato, in second-priority climatic areas. A few parts of the South Island had suitable conditions for traditional gardens, including the northern coast (Fig. 45.1) and parts of the West Coast, Kaikoura, and Banks Peninsula (not illustrated). Within the best climatic zone, there were a few very large areas of prime garden land [(a) above]: two major volcanic zones (Taamaki and the Bay of Islands), a few major river valleys (such as Oruru, Victoria, Wairoa), and three extensive natural swamps (Kaitaia, north of Whangarei, and Wairoa River). In contrast to these few large prime areas, there were many small areas [(b) above].

## Archaeological evidence of Maaori garden systems

The archaeological evidence for ten examples of prehistoric Maaori garden system is next reviewed (Table 45.1). These are the most detailed studies of

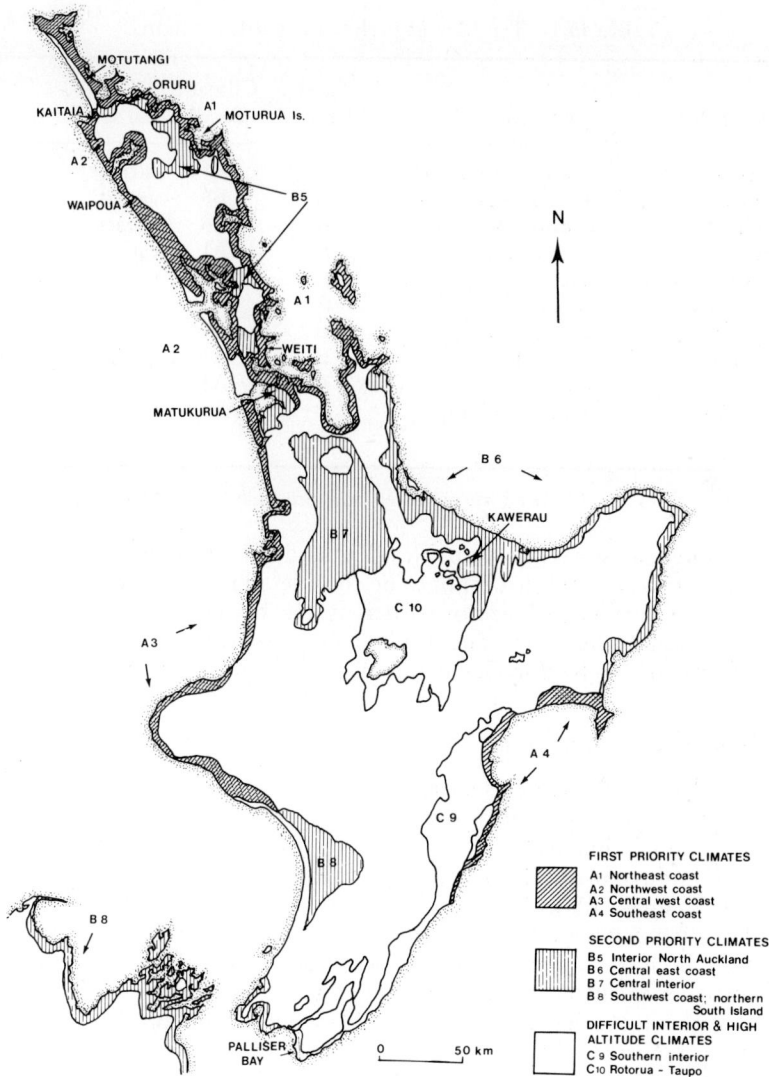

**Figure 45.1** Agricultural climatic zones of North Island, New Zealand.

garden systems and illustrate the known range of garden forms and landscapes. Most are in first-priority climatic zones and half are in prime garden-land areas. They can be classified into eight kinds of system according to their landform and the variety of types of gardens they include. Two of the garden forms discussed – ditched swamps and cross-terraced

**Table 45.1**     Ten Maaori prehistoric garden systems.

| Name of system | Landform | Land category | Climatic zone* | Garden forms |
|---|---|---|---|---|
| 1  Matukurua | volcanic stonefields | A | A1 | varied** |
| 2  Palliser | coastal slope, flats | B | B8 | varied |
| 3  Kawerau | stream valleys, hills | A | B6 | terraced, flats |
| 4a Oruru | river valley | A | A1 | varied |
| 4b Waipoua | river valley | B | A2 | varied |
| 5  Kaitaia | swamps, hills | A | A1 | varied |
| 6  Weiti | terraces, swamps | B | A1 | terraced, ditched |
| 7a Moturua | slopes, flats | B | A1 | ditched |
| 7b Motutangi | slopes, flats | A | A1 | ditched |
| 8  Various | streams, swamps | B | A1, 2 | terraced, streams, mounds |

*See Figure 45.1;    **varied means three or more forms of garden.

stream plots – are so far known in New Zealand only from unexcavated field evidence. However, this list is not to be considered representative of the full range of complexity and size of garden systems. There are relatively few archaeological studies so far, and it is likely that a greater diversity of garden systems remains to be discovered and excavated.

## Volcanic fields of Matukurua

Volcanic basaltic stone fields surrounding scoria cones were prime garden land and were used by Maaori cultivators everywhere that they were present in a favourable climatic zone. Garden sites of this kind have so far been recorded in three places in the relatively favourable northeast coast climatic zone; in Taamaki (Auckland), the Taiamai Plains (include Bay of Islands) (Phillips 1980, Sutton 1984), and west of Waitangi (Bay of Islands). The first two have been studied archaeologically but detailed evidence is available so far only from Auckland. There are also rocky volcanic areas in valleys and on offshore islands that have comparable field evidence, but none has so far been studied or reported in detail.

Prehistoric gardens and associated settlements were present throughout the basaltic land surrounding the volcanic cones in the Taamaki volcanic zone (Sullivan 1972, 1974, Rickard *et al.* 1983, Veart 1986, Bulmer 1987b, 1987c). The scoria cones were the terraced sites of *paa* (fortified settlements), with their surrounding fields spread over an area of about 50 km². Altogether there was a total of about 8000 ha of red and brown loam soils, with an equivalent area of tuff soils. The fields of individual cones were generally separated from each other by land with heavy clay soils, much less inviting for agricultural use. The 24 individual fields within the volcanic zone (Bulmer 1987b) ranged in size from a few hundred square metres to four large fields of more than 1000 ha each. The volcanic soils of Taamaki supported a large Maaori population, and the fields that still survive the development of the city contain a wide variety of garden and settlement features.

Matukurua (Wiri-McLaughlins), together with East Taamaki and South-west Maangere, is one of the three surviving Taamaki field systems currently being investigated in detail (Bulmer 1987b). The Matukurua field contained two volcanic-cone *paa* with a combined field of about 500 ha in extent, with its western side next to the Manukau harbour. Five archaeological projects have been or are being carried out in this field as it has been quarried and otherwise developed. These are: on Wiri Mount and some nearby features (Sullivan 1974, 1975a, 1975b), Puhinui (Lawlor 1981), and the Wiri Oil Terminal Site (Bulmer 1983, Bulmer in press); the Wiri Railway Site (Coates 1985); and the remaining northern lower slope of Wiri mountain (Foster 1987).

Matukurua had a garden system based on major linear land divisions radiating from the cone to the perimeter of the volcanic fields. The land between the two cones had interconnecting land units, showing that it was a single overall system. The cones were sites of fortified settlements, but there were also unfortified residential clusters in the fields surrounding the cones, in among the gardens. The radiating land units were marked by large stone and stone-and-earth walls, some over 1 km long and generally 25–50 m apart. The linear land units were subdivided by internal linear and cross walls and alignments. The main boundary walls appear to have been in use over a long period, indicating that the plots in between were re-used. Each major land unit contained a variety of forms of garden related to topography and soils. Radiocarbon dates (calibrated) indicate that the gardens were in existence at least as early as AD 905–1425 and were probably used until the 18th century (Bulmer 1987c).

The Matukurua gardens contained many thousands of constructed stone and earth features. More than 1200 structural components were mapped on the 20 ha of the Wiri Oil Terminal Site. This portion of Matukurua included 17 kinds of garden structure (Bulmer in press). These provide evidence of a wide variety of agronomic conditions, which can be attributed to the growing of a variety of crops, not specialized *kuumara* gardens. The gardens probably contained *tii*, taro, *kuumara*, *uuwhi*, *hue*, *kotawa*, and a variety of greens. The identification of charcoal from hearths, ovens, garden soils, and house floors shows that there was lowland forest near the volcanic field during its occupation, probably on the heavy clay lands surrounding it. The forest would have had stands of semi-cultivated fruit trees and other edible and useful plants, as well as protecting the cultivated land from winds off the harbour.

The stone constructions and other features at Matukurua show that careful attention was paid to the microenvironment of the gardens; they appear to provide for fertile soils, warmer temperatures, moisture control, adequate nutrient suppiy, and protection from wind and frost. Constructed stone-edged terraces, earth and rock walls, and mounds created cultivable spaces, even in the rockiest areas where cultivation might not otherwise have been possible. In the context of a rainfall too low to support taro (Spriggs 1982), use was made of swamp-edge terrace gardens and mounds for moisture-loving crops.

## Walled gardens at Palliser Bay

The stone-walled systems of the eastern Palliser Bay area provide an example of a very different kind of land use (Leach 1979a & b). Other walled systems have also been investigated (e.g. McFadgen 1980). These gardens on coastal shelves and slopes are the kind of agricultural system that is thought to have been the earliest form in New Zealand. However, Palliser Bay may have been settled later than other areas of milder climate. The Palliser Bay stone-walled gardens are similar to stone-walled complexes found along the Wairarapa and Wellington coasts. There are also similar garden systems in parts of the South Island with relatively favourable climate for agriculture, such as Kaikoura, Nelson, Marlborough, D'Urville Island, Blenheim, and the southernmost at Banks Peninsula (Leach 1984).

The walled-garden systems at Palliser Bay occur intermittently along the coast, focused on stream mouths. There were nine such wall complexes along the 70 km of coast on the eastern side of the Bay, covering a total of about 80 ha of land. There were two main forms of garden: walled gardens on the erosion fans on the slopes behind the coastal shelf, and walled plots on the level shelf behind the beach. The gardens contained some constructed features, such as mounds and terraces, but in general they were open plots. The Washpool complex (Leach 1979a, p. 140) is a typical example. It covered nearly 10 ha and included a variety of garden and habitation features. The complex was 900 m long and stretched inland for 100–200 m, limited on the inland side by the steep contours of the slopes. The seaward perimeters of the gardens were marked by cross-walls at right angles to the walls that ran downslope in roughly parallel lines toward the beach. Gardens and habitations were also found up to 4 km inland in the valleys of the streams they were centred on, but the greatest concentration of archaeological features was around the stream mouths. This garden system is thought to have been used primarily for the cultivation of kuumara and gourds, the only crops that could have matured in a single season in the climate of Palliser Bay. Crops such as taro, which matured over more than one season, could not be, or were not, grown at Palliser Bay. The gardens began as early as the 11th century AD and were characteristic of a basically Polynesian system of agriculture, in an area that is not a prime settlement zone. The gardens were abandoned in the 16th century, possibly due to deterioration of climate and/or soils. The Palliser Bay gardens can be seen as a kind of specialized garden, derived from early extensive 'broad-spectrum' generalized agriculture, such as that of the Auckland volcanic sites, selecting for the few crops that would succeed in a situation of marginal climate.

## Inland hills and valleys of Kawerau

Archaeological investigations at Kawerau in the Bay of Plenty (Lawlor 1983) were concerned with gardens and settlements in back-swamp lowlands, some 20 km from the coast. This exemplifies another but different kind of specialized Maaori garden system. In a zone of relatively favourable climate for Maaori agriculture, the Kawerau soils were possibly particularly suitable for specialized agriculture They were based on a thick layer of wind-borne tuffaceous ash, deposited sometime between AD 1200 and 1400 (Lawlor 1983, pp. 223–8). No evidence of gardening or other features has been found underneath this ash, but the ash itself was extensively gardened, on the slopes and on terraces on the slopes, and in the floors of the valleys in between the gently rolling hills. The valley floors were extensively ditched, to remove excess moisture in order for *kuumara* to be grown on the rich but naturally swampy soils of the valleys. This is traditionally considered to be prime *kuumara* growing land, and there are an estimated 10 000 store pits on the ridges and terraces. These pits were used for winter storage of seed tubers and food supplies.

The Kawerau people may also have grown other crops in addition to *kuumara*. However, the gardens attributed to *kuumara* cover hundreds of hectares at Kawerau and other equivalent inland areas in the Bay of Plenty, a specialized system that would have supported a substantial population. The gardens are likely to have belonged to the Maaori people who were associated with nearby fortified *paa* between the 15th and 18th centuries AD.

## Valleys in the north: Waipoua and Oruru

Valleys offer a variety of land forms and contrasting soils within a coherent land unit defined by the valley itself. This is a common type of agricultural system in the Pacific Islands. There are also a large number of valley systems in New Zealand, but few have seen excavations of garden sites. Two in Northland have recently been studied, the Waipoua Valley, in the northwest coast climatic zone (Smith 1985) and the Oruru Valley, in the northeast coast climatic zone (Johnson 1986). Both valleys contain a variety of archaeo-logical features of settlement and gardens, including ditched swamps, slope gardens, terraces, and mounds and walls. However, they contrast in size, density of settlement, and the specific archaeological features present.

The Waipoua Valley has sites of dispersed hamlets and gardens in a deep valley, up to 11 km inland. There is relatively little evidence of settlement at the mouth of the river, a coastal strip of sand dunes and uninviting soils. Settlements focused on a few fortified *paa* on prominent ridges above both sides of the valley, to which the residents retired in times of danger. The hamlet residences and gardens were situated along the ridges on the lower slopes of the valley. The archaeological field evidence indicates gardens on these slopes and on the middle valley floor near the hamlets. There are few stone walls and alignments that look like land boundaries, and no sign of an overall permanent land-division system comparable to the volcanic field systems. The slope gardens may have been small plots used with bush fallow, involving repeated shifts around the valley.

Habitation deposits have been found deeply buried under the sedimentary soils of the lower floor of the valley, suggesting an earlier occupation next to the river prior to a period of heavy erosion of the slopes above, possibly due to forest clearance or increased rainfall. Stream-valley sedimentation has been found to be episodic throughout New Zealand (Grant 1985) and may indicate long-term fluctuations in rainfall. Deposition of eroded soils formed, or extended, flat land on the valley floor, and thus created a new niche for cultivation. Such erosion has been correlated with changes in the agricultural patterns of valley systems in other parts of the Pacific Islands (Brookfield 1984, p. 22, Golson & Steensberg 1985, Spriggs 1985). This kind of environmental change was widespread in Polynesia and has been attributed to a general degradation of soils in the uplands, during the 1st millennium AD. It is not possible, of course, to assume that such erosion would have occurred in the same period in Northland, but the dating of the formation of the Waipoua and other valley swamplands will be of considerable interest.

There are some signs of ditched gardens in the Waipoua Valley floor (I. Smith, pers. comm.) and it seems likely that such gardens may have been fairly extensive. As well, a small ditched swamp garden has been found in a side valley, high above the main valley, showing that this garden form was known to the prehistoric residents.

The settlements and garden systems of the Oruru Valley in the far north have been extensively mapped (Johnson 1986), although only test excavations have so far been carried out. This is a larger valley than Waipoua (20 km long) and has a greater concentration of much larger settlements, including dense settlement on the coast at the river mouth, and fortified *paa* on its side ridges, probably indicating a much larger population than that of the Waipoua Valley. The Oruru Valley has ditched swamp gardens (Barber 1984, pp. 160–2, Johnson 1986) and a variety of dryland gardens as well, including two ditched slope gardens of 2 and 70 ha in extent.

## Ditched swamps at Kaitaia

Extensive ditched gardens and canals have been recorded in at least nine natural swampy areas in Northland (Barber 1982, pp. 143–65), the largest of which is near Kaitaia (Wilson 1921). Ditched areas in very large natural swamps may have constituted garden systems in their own right, as they did in the Highlands of Papua New Guinea (Golson Ch. 44, this volume, Golson & Steensberg 1985). As has already been pointed out, they were also components of valley and coastal systems. The smaller ditched swamps, such as the one at Waipoua, occur in combination with other kinds of garden, as already discussed. Unfortunately, ditched swamps have not yet been investigated by means of archaeological excavation.

The Kaitaia ditch systems were studied by Barber (1984, pp. 153–60) and by Johnson (1986). Their former extent can be seen on early maps and aerial photographs over an area of about 15 km², from south of Kaitaia to Awanui and westward for 10 km along the southern side of former Lake Tangonge toward the coast. The largest portion so far mapped is at Pukepoto (Barber 1984, pp. 153–60) and covers about 125 ha.

The ditched swamp systems are comparable to the ditched swamp gardens of the Wahgi Valley in Highland Papua New Guinea (Golson Ch. 44, this volume, Golson & Steensberg 1985). There they are believed to have supported mixed gardens, accommodating both wet crops in and on the sides of the ditches and dry crops that required well-drained conditions on the plots in-between. On the other hand, both Barber (1984) and Johnson (1986) are of the opinion that the ditched swamps in New Zealand were devoted to specialized taro cultivation.

There is field evidence of other ditched swamp sites in nine other areas of Northland (Barber 1982, 1984). Most are relatively small; only two other large areas of swamp are present in Northland that may have supported extensive systems comparable to those of the Kaitaia swamps, i.e. the Wairoa River, North Kaipara, and the valleys north of Hikurangi, between Whangarei and the Bay of Islands.

## Terrace gardens at Weiti

The use of natural or artificial terraces for gardening occurs both as a part of complex garden systems, as in the stonefields and valley systems, and as a type of garden in its own right. The field evidence of garden terraces is often ambiguous, and most terraces are assumed to be house sites, but they occur in dry situations as well as on the margins of swamps and streams. Their general functions are to retain soil, provide level plots for cultivation, and conserve moisture.

A relatively small number of garden terraces in complex systems have been archaeologically studied, including examples at Kawerau, Palliser Bay, and the Auckland stonefields. Only one specialized garden terrace system has been archaeologically studied so far, at Weiti, north of Auckland. It has been briefly excavated (Coates & Richard 1985) and more extensive excavations are pending, following detailed mapping (Robinson 1987). A large number of presumably natural slump terraces, up to 1 km inland and up to about 25 m above sea-level, have evidence on them of gardens and habitation, in the form of patches of modified garden soils made of mixed shell and topsoil. The terraces occur along a series of small inland valleys in a zone of heavy clay soils. They resemble the large probably artificial garden terraces recently recognized in the Eastern Highlands of Papua New Guinea which were formerly thought to be natural slump terraces (Golson Ch. 44, this volume & pers. comm.). Fortified *paa* on nearby coastal headlands may be the settlements responsible for the gardens. There is no indication of slope gardens nearby, but there appear to be ditched plots in a large swamp on the coastal side of the terraces.

*Ditched slopes at Motutangi and Moturua*

There are a large number of recorded sites of prehistoric ditching on slopes (Barber 1982), only two of which have been excavated. This archaeological evidence indicates two contrasting functions for ditched-slope sites. The Moturua site, in the Bay of Islands (Peters 1975), was a garden where the ditches served for boundaries, and possibly to drain rainfall and retard erosion as similar ditches do in the Papua New Guinea Highlands. In an attempt to distinguish between the two functions, Barber (1982) subdivided the recorded sites in Northland according to their angle: 45 sites had slopes of less than 15°, some of which could be further examples of irrigated gardens, while 48 had a slope of more than 15° and are thought to be drained slope gardens.

The Moturua garden excavation carried out in 1966 and 1968 (Peters 1975) showed two superimposed garden soils, the more recent of which was associated with the ditches. The site was on poor-quality greywacke clay, and the garden soils were made by mixing beach shell, pebbles, and charcoal with the topsoil, both on the slope and on the flats below. Excavations showed that the earlier garden covered 100 m$^2$ and the later soil was present over an area of 500 m$^2$. The flat land at the base of the slope was also gardened, but no features other than one possible ditch were found associated with the garden soil on the flats. The earlier soil was dated by radiocarbon to AD 780–1210 and AD 1180–1400 (calibrated date ranges based on Klein *et al.* 1982) and the later soil to AD 1275–1500 and 1295–1505 (Peters 1975, pp. 178–9).

The ditched gardens at Tupou Bay (Nicholls 1965), illustrate a much larger and more complicated ditch system than Moturua, including ditched slope plots and ditched and banked gardens on the flat land behind the beach below, covering in all about 15 ha.

The ditched slope at Motutangi in the Far North, was found to be an irrigated garden, in use between about AD 1500 and 1650 (Barber 1984; p. 123), and possibly earlier. Natural springs on the uphill perimeter of the garden were used as a source of water, which was channelled into a network of ditches, using overspill to gently irrigate the gardens. Water was guided by blocking the junctions of cross and downhill ditches with vegetation. These gardens were situated on land just above the Motutangi swamp, which contained garden ditches as well. These two ditch systems together covered about 50 ha, the largest of a small number of such systems in the vicinity.

Ditched-slope garden sites also occur widely in other parts of the country, but they are not yet properly understood in archaeological terms. For example, there is no evidence yet for whether there is a variety of kinds of soils used or created in the slope gardens, and little analysis of their form. They are easily destroyed by farming and other development, and their investigation is a matter of priority because of the threat to their preservation.

## Terraced streams and valleys

This type of garden feature is known so far in New Zealand from the recording of surface features and traditional practice, rather than through archaeological excavation. However, terraced streams and valleys were probably a common component of complex systems, such as the volcanic field systems, as well as occurring in isolation. Such features are a simple form of water-reticulation terracing, used widely in the Pacific islands. They are difficult to recognize in field survey and it can therefore be assumed that there may be many others that have not been recorded.

An example of three terraces in a running stream, found at Woodhill, north of Auckland, with taro still growing in it, had been missed·by site recorders in an earlier survey. Other examples have been recorded in small valleys on Browns Island, a volcanic island lacking surface water, where the terraces would have trapped soil wash and taken advantage of surface water during rain. Another stream-terrace site, at Pukepoto, west of Kaitaia, is fed with water which drains from a nearby swamp, and it is still used for taro cultivation.

## Agricultural diversity and change in Aotearoa

The archaeological evidence for diversity in Maaori garden systems is of considerable interest, especially because it does not fit comfortably with the stereotype of a Maaori agriculture based primarily on *kuumara* cultivation. The diversity relates not only to environmental variation in soils, land form, and climate, but also to the different forms of gardening that Maaori people applied to the landscape. Maaori agriculture is characterized by the utilization and creation of a diversity of microenvironmental conditions, and this can only be seen as a deliberate strategy.

There was, of course, also specialization in Maaori garden systems; some of those described above apparently focused on only one or two garden forms. However, further information is needed for specialized systems to be understood. It may be that some apparently specialized systems are only surviving segments of former larger and more varied systems. It is also possible that specialized agriculture, particularly a dependence on *kuumara* in some districts, was a relatively recent development in New Zealand, as it was in Papua New Guinea (Golson Ch. 44, this volume, Golson & Steensberg 1985). *Kuumara*, sweet potato, is of South American origin (Hawkes Ch. 31, this volume) and is thought to have reached New Zealand and New Guinea by different routes, the earliest indications of it so far in New Zealand being dated to the 11th century AD.

Too few detailed data are so far available for most of the prehistoric Maaori garden systems to allow the number of crops grown to be established, but it is unlikely that there was a simple equivalance of crops to garden forms. In late 18th-century Maaori agriculture, as in tropical Polyne-

**Table 45.2**  Radiocarbon chronology of the Maaori garden systems discussed, according to their climatic zone and land category.

| | Settlement AD ?–800 | Archaic AD 800–1200 | Expansion and change AD 1200–1500 | Traditional AD 1500–1769 |
|---|---|---|---|---|
| *First-priority climate* | | | | |
| prime land | ?Bay of Islands | ?Matukurua | Matukurua | Matukurua Motutangi (Kaitaia) (Oruru) |
| other areas | — | ?Moturua | Moturua | (Waipoua) |
| *Second-priority climate* | | | | |
| prime land | — | — | — | (Kawerau) |
| other areas | — | Palliser Bay | Palliser Bay | (Weiti) |

Names in parentheses indicate systems not dated yet by radiocarbon, but their use in recent times is known through traditional histories.

sia, it was common for a variety of crops to be intermixed in the same plot. Ditched swamp gardens in New Zealand have not yet been investigated, but similar (ethnographically known) garden systems in the Papua New Guinea Highlands supported a variety of cultigens. This is a subject that needs to be pursued further, particularly through the evidence of both pollen, and plant opals or phytoliths (cf. Piperno Ch. 34, this volume).

In order to consider whether differences in Maaori agriculture reflect change and not just variation, the chronology of the different garden systems discussed in this chapter, has been compared (Table 45.2). The three periods of cultural change proposed by Davidson (1984, pp. 223–4) are used, with the addition of an earlier settlement period. An earlier period is needed because there are now a number of indications that New Zealand may originally have been settled long before the date of AD 800 which is generally accepted (Davidson 1984). For example, recent pollen evidence from the Bay of Islands suggests forest clearance as early as about AD 600, and extensive by about AD 1300 (Chester 1986). Even though there is, as yet, no habitation or garden evidence to confirm the earlier date, such evidence is likely to be found in due course; and even earlier evidence has been obtained recently for settlement in Hawaii (Kirch 1985), a land harder to reach by sea from east Polynesia than New Zealand (Kirch 1985). The early date for possible forest clearance at the Bay of Islands is plausible because it comes from an area of first-priority climate and prime garden land, and it is consistent with pollen evidence for later forest clearance elsewhere. In second- and third-priority climatic zones, forest clearance began by about AD 900, and there was widespread forest clearance throughout the country by about AD 400 (McGlone 1984). There is also widespread evidence in soils for the disturbance of vegetation between about 550 BC and AD 450, which may indicate even earlier original settlement of New Zealand (Sutton 1987).

None of the Maaori garden systems studied has yet provided evidence of the proposed early settlement period. Matukurua is the earliest known garden system on prime land in a first-priority climatic zone, and there cultivation had begun by about 760 ± 200 bp, i.e. between approximately AD 1000 and AD 1400 (Sullivan 1975b). However, Matukurua and other similar sites do not represent the earliest evidence of cultivation because there is evidence for earlier gardens not on prime land in a second-priority climatic zone at Palliser Bay (Table 45.2). There is also evidence of pit storage, presumed to relate to agriculture, on medium-quality land in a first-priority climatic zone in the Coromandel Peninsula (Davidson 1984, p. 123).

Where should we look for the earliest garden systems? The Taamaki volcanic fields, the Northland valley systems, and the Kaitaia swamp gardens can be expected to contain very early evidence of gardening. Further research needs to be carried out with a view to finding such early evidence.

In spite of the fact that some span more than one cultural period, none of the prehistoric garden sites so far studied has been found to have undergone substantial change. The systems appear to be consistent throughout and were relatively long-lived, each lasting for centuries. The exception is the Moturua ditched-slope garden, which had two discrete stages of use, with similar forms of garden in both stages, except for the addition of ditching in the more recent stage.

The lack of archaeological evidence so far for evolution within Maaori garden systems is likely to be due to bias in the survival of evidence, the 'warps' and 'white holes' inherent in landscape archaeology (Moseley 1983), referred to earlier. Particularly in garden sites on prime land, the same soils were re-used, restored, and added to, erasing indications of earlier systems. Only in special circumstances is evidence of earlier gardens likely to remain, such as in terraces, where soil has accumulated, leaving earlier garden soils underneath the more recent soils, or 'trapped' under structures, such as stone walls placed on top of earlier layers. A search for such fragmentary early evidence should be a part of any archaeological investigation of garden systems.

Garden sites are also particularly vulnerable to both accidental and deliberate destruction, another significant source of bias in the survival of their field evidence. They are seldom obvious in terms of surface evidence, and, even if recognized, they are apt to be judged not 'important' for protection from development. This means that a system can seldom be studied in its totality; it normally must be reconstructed from only fragmentary evidence and from its topographic position. A corollary of this is that it is generally garden sites on non-prime land that have survived best, because they have been less attractive for subsequent gardening and farming.

There are, however, some sites that are likely to yield long sequences of stratified garden deposits and soils. The most likely are the large natural swamps. Similar sites in the Highlands of Papua New Guinea have deep and complex stratified deposits. Such sites should be excavated in New Zealand, even where their surface evidence has been damaged or destroyed through subsequent land use.

In view of the present lack of good evidence for any internal evolution of Maaori garden systems, are the differences between systems an indication of change, with one kind of system being replaced by another kind at a different location? This has been argued in respect to the Palliser Bay system (Leach 1979b), where the restricted number of cultigens was thought to indicate secondary adaptation to an area of relatively poor climate. Four stages of agricultural change were suggested for the country as a whole, largely on the basis of the Palliser Bay sites (Leach 1979b, and summarized by Davidson 1984, p. 117): introduction, experiment, regional consolidation, and retrenchment. This sequence assumes that earlier agriculture than that found at Palliser Bay had been previously established in areas of better climate, and that the end of the system was due to climatic change and soil deterioration. This is an argument based on first principles (Brookfield 1984), which lacks direct archaeological evidence in the crucial area, i.e. that of first agricultural settlement. Until such evidence is found, the argument cannot be tested.

Another argument about agricultural change in New Zealand based on first principles relates to the processes of landscape change resulting from agriculture. The formation and extension of valley-floor sediments through human-induced erosion of the hill slopes has been found to have been significant in agricultural change elsewhere in eastern Polynesia (Spriggs 1985). This subject has not yet been investigated in New Zealand, although widespread periodic changes in sedimentation in river valleys have been identified (Grant 1985). However, this was thought to have resulted from changes in rainfall, rather than from forest clearance. The geomorphology of valleys that were gardened by Maaori people needs to be investigated in combination with the archaeological study of the garden systems themselves.

This chapter thus ends with the identification of many tasks that remain to be done in order to understand Maaori garden systems properly. There is much that needs to be learned about the history of Maaori agriculture from the archaeological study of garden sites. In a country so large and diverse, ten examples of eight kinds of garden system are clearly inadequate to properly document variety and change. However, what is known so far shows the high degree of Maaori skill and knowledge that enabled their gardens to succeed so well in the southern latitudes, a story that has interest and significance far beyond the shores of Aotearoa.

# References

Barber, I. G. 1982. *Archaeological ditch systems in Taitokerau (Northland). A site survey and comparative analysis.* Auckland: New Zealand Historic Places Trust.

Barber, I. G. 1984. *Prehistoric wetland cultivation in far northern Aotearoa; an archaeological investigation*. Unpublished MA thesis, Anthropology Department, University of Auckland.

Best, E. 1925. *Maori agriculture*. Dominion Museum Bulletin no. 9. Wellington: Government Printer.

Brookfield, H. C. 1984. Intensification revisited. *Pacific Viewpoint* **25**, 15–44.

Bulmer, S. 1983. *Preliminary report on archaeological investigations at the Wiri Oil Terminal Site (N42/1224)*. Auckland: New Zealand Historic Places Trust.

Bulmer, S. 1987a. *Archaeological investigations of the stonefields sites of Taamaki Makaurau*. Auckland: New Zealand Historic Places Trust.

Bulmer, S. 1987b. Space and settlement size on the volcanic cone *paa* of Taamaki. Seminar paper, Anthropology Department University of Auckland.

Bulmer, S. 1987c. Settlement patterns in the volcanic stonefields of Taamaki. Paper read to the Indo–Pacific Prehistory Association Congress, Tokyo.

Bulmer, S. (ed.) in press. *Archaeological investigations at the Wiri Oil Terminal Site*. Auckland: New Zealand Historic Places Trust.

Chester, P. I. 1986. *Forest clearance in the Bay of Islands*. Unpublished MA thesis, Anthropology Department, University of Auckland.

Coates, J. 1985. *Preliminary report, Wiri excavation. Environmental and experimental section*. Auckland: New Zealand Historic Places Trust.

Coates, J. & V. Rickard 1985. *Archaeological investigations at a garden terrace site, Weiti Station*. Auckland: New Zealand Historic Places Trust.

Davidson, J. M. 1984. *The prehistory of New Zealand*. Auckland: Longman Paul.

Foster, R. 1987. Archaeological mapping on the northern slopes of Wiri mountain. Mimeo, 19 pp.

Golson, J. 1989. The origins and development of New Guinea agriculture. In *Foraging and farming: the evolution of plant exploitation*, D. R. Harris & G. C. Hillman (eds), ch. 44. London: Unwin Hyman.

Golson, J. & A. Steensberg 1985. The tools of agricultural intensification in the New Guinea Highlands. In *Prehistoric intensive agriculture in the tropics*, Part i, I. S. Farrington (ed.), 347–84. Oxford: British Archaeological Reports International Series 232.

Grant, P. J. 1985. Major periods of erosion and alluvial sedimentation in New Zealand during the Late Holocene. *Journal of the Royal Society of New Zealand* **15**, 67–121.

Groube, L. 1989. The taming of the rain forests: a model for Late Pleistocene forest exploitation in New Guinea. In *Foraging and farming: the evolution of plant exploitation*, D. R. Harris & G. C. Hillman (eds), ch. 17. London: Unwin Hyman.

Hawkes, J. G. 1989. The domestication of roots and tubers in the American tropics. In *Foraging and farming: the evolution of plant exploitation*, D. R. Harris & G. C. Hillman (eds), ch. 31. London: Unwin Hyman.

Johnson, L. 1986. *Aspects of the prehistory of the Far Northern valley systems*. Unpublished MA thesis, Anthropology Department, University of Auckland.

Jones, K. L. & R. G. Law 1987. Prehistoric population estimates for the Tolaga Bay vicinity, East Coast, North Island, New Zealand. *New Zealand Journal of Archaeology* **9**, 81–114.

Kirch, P. V. 1982. Ecology and the adaptation of Polynesian agricultural systems. *Archaeology in Oceania* **17**, 1–6.

Kirch, P. V. 1985. *Feathered gods and fishhooks. An introduction to Hawaiian archaeology and prehistory*. Honolulu: University of Hawaii Press.

Klein, J., J. C. Lerman, P. E. Damon & E. K. Ralph 1982. Calibration of radiocarbon dates. *Radiocarbon* **24**, 103–50.

Law, R. G. 1968. Maori soils in the lower Waikato. *New Zealand Archaeological Association Newsletter* **11**, 67–75.

Lawlor, I. G. 1981. *Puhinui excavation report.* Department of Anthropology, University of Auckland.

Lawlor, I. G. 1983. Rua kuumara o Kawerau. In *A lot of spadework to be done*, S. Bulmer, R. Law & D. S. Sutton (eds), 213–48. New Zealand Archaeological Association Monograph no. 14, Auckland.

Leach, H. 1979a. Evidence of prehistoric gardens in Palliser Bay. In *Prehistoric man in Palliser Bay*, B. F. Leach & H. Leach (eds), 137–61. Bulletin of the National Museum. Wellington.

Leach, H. 1979b. The significance of early horticulture in Palliser Bay for New Zealand prehistory. In *Prehistoric man in Palliser Bay*, B. F. Leach & H. Leach (eds), 241–9. Bulletin of the National Museum, Wellington.

Leach, H. 1984. *1000 years of gardening in New Zealand.* Wellington: Reed.

McCoy, P. C. 1976. *Easter Island settlement patterns in the late prehistoric and protohistoric periods.* Bulletin 5, Easter Island Committee of the International Fund for Monuments, New York.

McFadgen, B. G. 1980. A stone row system at Okoropunga on the southeast Wairarapa coast and inferences about stone rows elsewhere in New Zealand. *New Zealand Journal of Science* **23**, 189–97.

McGlone, M. S. 1984. Polynesian deforestation of New Zealand; a preliminary synthesis. *Archaeology in Oceania* **18**, 11–25.

Moseley, M. E. 1983. Patterns of settlement and preservation in the Viru and Moche Valleys. In *Prehistoric settlement patterns: essays in honor of Gordon R. Willey*. E. Z. Vogt & R. M. Lewenthal (eds), 423–42. Albuquerque: University of New Mexico Press.

Nicholls, M. P. 1965. Some probable pre-European agricultural evidence in Northland. *New Zealand Archaeological Association Newsletter* **8**, 148–9.

Peters, K. M. 1975. Agricultural gardens on Moturua Island in the Bay of Islands. *New Zealand Archaeological Association Newsletter* **18**, 171–80.

Phillips, C. 1980. Site recording at Pouerua, Bay of Islands. *New Zealand Archaeological Association Newsletter* **23**, 148–60.

Piperno, D. R. 1989. Non-affluent foragers: resource availability, seasonal shortages, and the emergence of agriculture in Panamanian tropical forests. In *Foraging and farming: the evolution of plant exploitation*, D. R. Harris & G. C. Hillman (eds), ch. 34. London: Unwin Hyman.

Rickard, V., D. Veart & S. Bulmer 1983. *A review of the archaeological stone structures of South Auckland.* Auckland: New Zealand Historic Places Trust.

Robinson, J. 1987. *An intensive survey of the proposed Dacre Crest Residential development.* Auckland: New Zealand Historic Places Trust.

Smith, I. 1985. *Waipoua archaeology: research objectives, priorities and proposals.* Auckland: New Zealand Historic Places Trust.

Spriggs, M. 1982. Taro cropping systems in the Southeast Asian–Pacific region: archaeological evidence. *Archaeology in Oceania* **17**, 7–15.

Spriggs, M. 1985. Prehistoric man-induced landscape enhancement in the Pacific: examples and limitations. In *Prehistoric intensive agriculture in the tropics*, Part i, I. S. Farrington (ed.), 409–37. Oxford: British Archaeological Reports International Series 232.

Sullivan, A. 1972. Stone walled complexes of central Auckland. *New Zealand Archaeological Association Newsletter* **15**, 148–60.

Sullivan, A. 1974. Scoria mounds at Wiri. *New Zealand Archaeological Association Newsletter* **17**, 128–44.

Sullivan, A. 1975a. *Slope gardens at Wiri Mountain*. Working Papers in Anthropology, Anthropology Department, University of Auckland.

Sullivan, A. 1975b. Radiocarbon ages from Wiri. *New Zealand Archaeological Association Newsletter* **18**, 206–7.

Sutton, D. S. 1984. The Pouerua project: Phase II, an interim report. *New Zealand Archaeological Association Newsletter* **27**, 30–8.

Sutton, D. S. 1987. A paradigmatic shift in Polynesian prehistory: implications for New Zealand. *New Zealand Journal of Archaeology* **9**, 135–56.

Veart, D. 1986. *Stone structures and land use at three South Auckland volcanic sites.* Unpublished MA thesis, Anthropology Department, University of Auckland.

Walton, T. 1982. Rethinking made soils. *New Zealand Archaeological Association Newsletter* **25**, 16–29.

Weisler, M. & P. V. Kirch 1985. The structure of settlement space in a Polynesian chiefdom: Kawela, Moloka'i, Hawaiian Islands. *New Zealand Journal of Archaeology* **7**, 129–58.

Wilson, D. M. 1921. Ancient drains at Kaitaia swamp. *Journal of the Polynesian Society* **30**, 185–8.

# Index*

*Abelmoschus* 300

aboriginal peoples of Australia: agronomy 61–2, 129; antiquity of land use 145–7; hunter-gatherer systems, stability of 133; plant classsification 42; proto-horticulture 64; *see also* proto-cultivation; planting by hunter-gatherers; response to colonial agricultural development 52; seed-gathering 305–14; view of agriculture 129

Abu Hureyra 208, 214, 221–2, 229, 240–68, 380, 386, 628, 629, 632, 635; AMS dates 241, 628; dietary diversity at 240–68

*Acacia* 176, 220, 226; Australian species 61, 99–104, 109, 112, 313; distribution, effect of fires 103; edible seeds 100, 107–9, 219–21, 231; seed collection/storage 107; seed grinding 109; seed processing time 313; seed toxicity 109; spiny 336; *A. ligulata*, wood ash for *pituri* 61; *A. nilotica* 219, 221, 231

accelerator mass spectrometry 1, 214–15, 241, 245, 499, 559, 628, 656, 661

*Acer* 258–9

*achira* 484, 486, 491–2

*achis* 327

acorns 20, 160, 163, 176–8, 185, 199, 225, 256, 561, 563, 611, 633; flour of 163; planting of 163; remains of 256; transplanting of 20

*Acrocomia* 102–4, 109, 528, 542

adaptation, coastal 650–66

*Adonis* 253–4

*Aegilops* 638–9

*Aellenia* 262

*afeso* 84

*afezu* 84

*Agave* 164; Kumeyaay fire management and planting of 164

agricultural conservatism, Black Sea region 619

agricultural implements, in Chinese Neolithic 647–8

agricultural systems, evolution 5, 28–39

agricultural origins; cultural selection model 28; ecosystem management vs. replacement 482; equilibrium model 37; evolutionary model 65; population-pressure model 37; social causes 523–5; social constraints against 49; *see also* resistance to agriculture; domestication of environment; proto-cultivation; food production

agriculture, as a concept 4, 11–23, 43; behaviourist definition 50; definition 159, 299; differences between initial and developed system 620; diffusion *vs.* developed vs. poly-agrogenesis 456; field 16; incipient: *see* proto-cultivation; origins *vs.* effects xi, 7; proto-: *see* proto-cultivation; static modelling, problem of xiv; *see also* cultivation

agronomy, as a concept 15–16, 55–72; amongst hunter-gatherers 55–72

Aguadulce (Panama) 549

*aibica* 300

'Ain Ghazal (Jordan) 635

'Ain Mallaha (Eynan, Israel) 214, 240

*Aizoon* 248, 254

*ajawiri* 509–10

*ajipa* 484, 493

alcohol 93; as fuel, from *Bourgou* grasses 93

alder seeds 430

Ali Kosh (Iran) 240

*Alisma* corms 260

alkaloids, in potato domestication 508, 512–13

allozyme analysis; in *Cucurbita* 472, 559; in *Lens* spp. 370–1

*alluia* 484, 490

almonds 198, 201, 203

*Alocasia* 293

*Alyssum* 247

Amaranthaceae 461

amaranths 164, 456, 560

*Amaranthus* 319–26, 560; *A. caudatus* 327

*Ambrosia trifida* 560

American Bottom, maize introduction 30–4

amino acids; from fermentation 179; increase in seed sprouts 181

AMS: *see* accelerator mass spectrometry

*Anabasis* 246

anatomy of pulse testas 390–405

*Note that place names (barring archaeological sites) and names of authors and other persons referred to in the text are excluded from this index.

Ño Carlos (Venezuela) 527
*Noaea* 246, 262
Nochixtlan 489
Non Kao Noi (Thailand) 650, 663
Non Nok Tha (Thailand) 650, 663
Novy Ruseshty (USSR) 610
null alleles, in *Chenopodium* 434
nut groves, incidental domestication 32; *see also* acorn planting
nut-grass, wild tubers 207, 212–16, 220, 224, 226, 231–2, 260; incidental cultivation of 20, 227; *see also* proto-cultivation; productivity of 225–6; *see also Cyperus*
nutlets; of *Scirpus*, as Palaeolithic food 219–20, 231, 260; silicified, of Boraginaceae 249
nutrient analyses; of Australian small-seed foods (range of taxa) 111; of *Chenopodium* 110; of coca 516; of *Cyperus rotundus* tubers 224; of *Panaulauca* spp. 325–6; of *Pandanus* nuts 126; of yams 348
nutrient losses; from milling 174; from soaking 177
nutrient status; effect of processing 3, 5, 171–186; effects of heating 182; wild *vs* domestic grain 80
nutrition, tropical forests, protein scarcity *vs.* calories 540
nutritional impact of fermentation 178–9
nuts; cycad 125; hazel 561; hickory 561; mongongo 225; *Pandanus* 124; tree 30–6; zamia 140; *see also* acorns
*nyanmi* 102
Nyctaginaceae 494, 507
Nymphaceae 209, 211, 219–21; consumption of roots/seeds 125, 219–21; pollen/flower buds as Palaeolithic food 220
*Nymphaea* 122, 125, 129, 231; *N. gigantea* 312
*Nymphoides* pollen 658; as weed of rice 658

oaks 160, 163, 199, 211, 245, 256–8, 363, 365, 367, 369, 446, 556; groves planted by Kumeyaay 160; holm 199; wood charcoal 256; *see also* acorns
oats 92, 181, 342, 611; Abyssinian, incidental domestication 342; Ethiopian 92–3; European wild 162; green 342; wild 639
Oaxaca (Mexico) 475
*oca* 327, 484, 492, 496–7, 506; wild 496
Ocampo Caves (Mexico), appearance of domesticated *Cucurbita* 472
occupation, of sites: *see* seasons of site occupation; sedentism
*ocumo* 530
oil seeds 30–3
oil, from *Croton* seeds 288

*Olea* 199–200, 202–3
olive, wild 198–9, 201–3
onager 259, 261
*Onobrychis* 248, 254
*Opimoea* 541
opium poppies, marking for high yield 443
optimal foraging theory, limitations 184
*Opuntia* 164, 320–1, 325; *O. floccosa* 319, 326
orange, wild 103, 289
orchids, wild 226
*Ornithogalum* 254
Oruru Valley garden sites (New Zealand) 696
*Oryza* 120, 127, 129, 408–9, 416, 682; evolutionary pathway 408–9; *O. barthii* 79, 88, 90–1; *O. barthii*, marketing of wild grain in N. Africa 88; *O. fatua* 312; *O. glaberrima* 341, 408, 415; *O. glumaepatula* 409; *O. granulata* 409; *O. indica* 413–14; *O. japonica* 414; *O. javanica* 403, 415; *O. longistaminata* 92; *O. meridionalis* 409; *O. meyeriana* 409; *O. minuta* 409; *O. officinalis* 409; *O. punctata* 88–90; *O. ridleyi* 409; *O. rufipogon* 122, 127, 289; *O. sativa* 89, 289, 408, 414–15, 646; *O. sativa* forma spontanea 411; *O. sinica* 403, 414, 647; *see also* rice
ownership, by foragers 163; *see also* hunter-gatherers' usage rights; territories
oxalic acid, in *Oxalis* 506
Oxalidaceae 506
*Oxalis* 464, 492, 496; *O. tuberosa* 327, 464, 484, 496–7, 506; *O. tuberosa*, oxalic acid in 506

Pachacamac (Peru) 492, 495
Pachamachay Cave (Peru) 330
*Pachyrhizus* 484, 493–4; *P. ajipa* 493–4; *P. ajipa*, in burial 494; *P. erosus* 483–4, 493–4; *P. tuberosus* 464, 483–4, 493–4; *P. tuberosus*, in mummy bundle 494
Pacific cultigens, chemical markers 421
palaeoeconomy, Higgs "school" of 14
palaeoeconomic classification of people-plant interactions 14
palaeofaeces 306, 429, 457–8, 557; charred, from Epipalaeolithic infants 241; charred, from Late Palaeolithic infants 214, 217, 228–30, 233; identification of food processing methods from 186; *see also* coprolites
Palaeolithic; gardening 130, 301–2, 678–83; plant foods 207–33; proto-cultivation 226–7
palaeopathological analysis 532
palatability, perception of xiv; *see also* taste